AMMO & BALLISTICS 3

AMM◎ & BALLISTICS 3

Ballistic Data out to 1,000 Yards for over 160 Calibers and over 2,000 Different Factory Loads. Includes Data on all Factory Centerfire and Rimfire Cartridges for Rifles & Handguns.

by
Bob Forker

SAFARI PRESS INC

The trademark Safari Press ® is registered with the U.S. Patent and Trademark Office and in other countries.

Forker, Robert

Third edition

Safari Press Inc.

2006, Long Beach, California

ISBN 1-57157-244-9

Library of Congress Catalog Card Number: 99071025

10 9 8 7 6 5 4 3 2

Readers wishing to receive the Safari Press catalog, featuring many fine books on big-game hunting, wingshooting, and sporting firearms, should write to Safari Press Inc., P.O. Box 3095, Long Beach, CA 90803, U.S.A. Tel: (714) 894-9080 or visit our Web site at www.safaripress.com.

Table of Contents

Data for Small and Medium Rifle Cartridges

Data for Small and Medium Centerfire Rifle Cartridges (continued)

Data for Cartridges Suitable for Dangerous Game

Data for Pistol and Revolver Cartridges

Data for Rimfire Ammunition

Foreword
by
Craig T. Boddington

In the course of the past quarter century or so, I have written a dozen books and hundreds of magazine articles that directly or indirectly have something to do with shooting. This is my life as much as my hobby, and I've been fortunate to have turned it into a profession. Mind you, I enjoy sitting down and doing the writing almost as much as the "research"—the shooting and hunting—it requires. Most of my work is designed, as Bob Petersen always says, to "entertain and instruct," probably in that order. I am not of a technical bent, and I have no background in any scientific discipline; however, it is possible that some of my writings have been of some help to my readers in making sound choices in firearms and ammunition for various purposes.

If that is so, it is largely because I have received similar help from others who do have technical knowledge and expertise. As shooters, we all need help. The world of cartridges, calibers, bullets, ballistics, and trajectories is growing ever more diverse, and although the basic theories don't change, the myriad choices available today make choosing the right tool ever more complex. I also need help as a writer for shooters and about shooting. Like most writers, I have a fairly extensive reference library. Some books I refer to once in a while, others fairly frequently. A very few are referred to almost daily and are literally coming apart from use.

Those hard-used volumes include the reloading manuals from the major bullet makers, along with two more prized references: Frank Barnes's *Cartridges of the World* and Bill Matthews's *Shoot Better II*. This book by Bob Forker is going to be one of those books that will be used regularly, and it will soon become dog-eared. In fact, I intend to buy two of them—one for my bookcase, and one for my travel kit!

I will not say that Bob Forker's book replaces, supplants, or renders obsolete my other favorite resources. This book deals with current factory-loaded cartridges, but the various excellent reloading manuals must remain a primary source for loading recipes. Frank Barnes's timeless work remains *the* reference for thumbnail sketches of cartridges of all ages, especially the obsolete and obscure. Bill Matthews's landmark work provides excellent and detailed ballistics and trajectory data on cartridges from the major manufacturers, and it essentially popularized the concept of sighting in for "Maximum Point-Blank Range." These works remain invaluable.

However, Bob Forker has compiled a mountain of data and information into one volume, data that have *never* been available in one place. Yes, this book is about factory ammunition, but that's a lot like saying *The Old Man and the Sea* is about fishing. There is much more here. In addition to data from the major ammunition manufacturers, he has included data from literally every manufacturer, large or small, that currently markets "ready-made" ammunition in the United States.

Naturally you will find ballistics figures and trajectory curves, but you will also find detailed cartridge diagrams; pressure and ballistic coefficients; standard rifling twists; recoil indexes; and even Taylor's "Knock-Out" (KO) values. These are the kinds of things that we shooters love to argue about around a campfire, and in the past I have spent countless hours running from one reference to another looking for these priceless crumbs of information. Now I will have them all in one place. Be forewarned: If you and I engage in a campfire argument, I'll have Forker's book in my duffel bag to back me up!

Of course, you will find much more than raw data in this volume. You will also find clear and concise writing that clarifies the complexities of ballistics coefficients, energy versus momentum, and so much more. Over the years a number of readers have suggested that I compile a volume similar to this one. I never would for two good reasons. First, I am not qualified to do so. Second, it would entail *TOO MUCH WORK!*

I don't want to delay you much longer in getting past the traditional necessity of a foreword so you can delve into the meat of this book, but let me just elaborate on these two considerations.

Unlike myself and most other gunwriters of this and every other generation, Bob Forker is truly a "technical gunwriter." He has contributed to *Guns & Ammo* magazine for over thirty-five years, and more importantly, he has a genuine engineering background. During his career in the aerospace industry, Bob's specialty was gun and ammunition development and weapons-system installation in fixed and rotary-wing aircraft. He designed the underground ballistics laboratory at Bob Petersen's ranch that has contributed so much to *G&A* and other

Petersen publications. During my own long tenure at Petersen Publishing, the rules were very simple: If you had a really knotty problem dealing with ballistics, you called Bob Forker! He usually had the answer, but if he didn't, he would find it. Quickly.

I've known Bob Forker some twenty years. We've shot together, hunted together, done shows together, and commiserated over the vagaries of editors and publishers. His is the finest "gun mind" I know, the kind required to distill a mountain of raw data from innumerable sources into a cohesive whole. I couldn't have done it, and, moreover, I wouldn't have wanted to.

You are holding in your hands a work unequaled by anything Hercules had to tackle. I am awed by the scope and breadth of this work, and, above all, I am most grateful to Bob Forker for having done this for all of us. This is not a "read and enjoy" book. Rather, it is a "read, study, and revisit" book. You will revisit it often, as will I.

Note to the Third Edition

I can't believe it's already time for a third edition of Bob Forker's milestone work. Well, I can believe it. During the past few years we've seen an unprecedented number of new cartridge introductions, and yet loyalty remains strong for a large number of "oldies but goodies" ranging from small and medium on up to extra large. The reality is that, in a comprehensive reference book such as this, the work is never done. There will always be new cartridges and, thank goodness, there will always be new loads for old favorites.

So, regrettably, even this third edition, the most complete and most comprehensive yet, will undoubtedly have gaps before the ink is dry, and when the passing months and year—and the new developments they bring—have created too many gaps to ignore, my esteemed colleague and old friend Mr. Bob Forker will have to go back to work once more. Actually, as you probably know, there was much literary license in the preceding sentence. Forker will go back to work collecting data for updates long before the ink is dry on this, the most current edition.

And God bless him for it. As I said in my foreword to the first edition, a book like this entails *TOO MUCH WORK*. I'd love to have a book in my body of work that sells like this one, but I'm a guy who can barely change a tire. Maybe I can write a good hunting story and even the occasional decent gun article, but I lack the patience, the attention to detail, and the sheer love of all things technical required to compile a volume like this—especially since, as we now see after three editions, such a work becomes a lifelong task of continual upgrading and updating. Fortunately, Forker is up to the task: He has the technical expertise, the interest, the patience, and the dedication that this ongoing project demands.

Some of you will be enjoying and using this work for the first time. Many of you, like me, have beaten up your first and second editions. Mine have been all over the world as an integral part of the very small library that forms my "emergency story writing kit" during lengthy hunts or military deployments. Where else can you find a thumbnail sketch of commonly available loads for a given factory cartridge? Where else can you compare velocity, foot-pounds, and Taylor Knock-out values? Where else but in the text preceding the tables can you find good, solid technical advice to help you choose cartridges, loads, and bullets for your next outing? Or just something to dream about and argue over with your buddies? Of course, most (but not all) of this information can be found in multiple places—but in a single volume? I don't think so.

So I expect the third edition to be as much thumbed through, and to become as dog-eared, as the ones that preceded it. And now I believe that this may not be the last time I append a note to an upcoming edition of Bob Forker's work. As this was the first time, it's an honor—and I'm anxious for these lines to see the light of day. My second edition is nearly worn out, and it's missing some new cartridges that I constantly need info on! So I will enjoy this book every bit as much as you will.

Craig Boddington

Acknowledgments

We wish to thank all the people who have contributed to this database. The list is long, but without the cooperation of each and every one of these contributors the book would be less useful.

A-Square Company, Inc.
•
Aguila
•
ATK
•
Black Hills Ammunition, Inc.
•
CCI / Speer
•
Cor-Bon Bullet Co.
•
Dakota Arms, Inc.
•
Eley Ltd.
•
Federal Cartridge Company
•
Fiocchi
•
Hirtenberger Aktiengesellschaft
•
Hornady Manufacturing Company
•
Patria Lapua Oy
•
Lazzeroni Arms Company
•
Kynoch (Kynamco Limited)
•
MagTech
•
Norma Precision AB
•
PMC (Eldorado Cartridge Corp.)
•
Remington Arms
•
Dynamit Nobel-RWS Inc.
•
Sellier & Bellot, USA
•
Ultramax Ammunition
•
Weatherby
•
Winchester Ammunition

A very special thank you goes to Bob Nosler of Nosler Bullets who has so generously allowed us to use their cartridge drawings in this book. Many of the drawings used were furnished by Nosler.

The ballistic calculations included in this book were done using Dr. Ken Oehler's (Oehler Research, Inc.) Ballistic Explorer program.

Mr. Ken Green, Director of Technical Affairs for SAAMI has been most generous with his assistance in establishing the performance specifications for new cartridges. Without his help the book would be less complete.

Martin Tulp furnished the metric designations for American cartridges.

Introduction

There was a time when someone who needed ammunition went to his local hardware store and said he wanted a box of, let's say, .30-30 ammunition. That was it, he was lucky to find any ammo in the right caliber, let alone to have any choice of different bullets, brands, performance levels, etc. He took his box of cartridges and went hunting. Life was simple.

Today we "suffer" from just the opposite problem, we have far more variations than anyone can remember. For just the .30-30 Winchester there are at least 75 different combinations of bullet weight, brand, etc., available for retail sale in the U.S. That may be a problem, but it's a good class of problem. This book provides a way to see just what factory ammunition is available, in what caliber, in what bullet styles, and with enough detailed performance data so that you are able to make some meaningful comparisons between the selection choices.

As we started to collect this data we immediately ran into the question of how much to include, and where to cut off. That's not an easy decision, and the decisions we ultimately made are certain to not please everyone. We started with the fundamental decision to include only factory made ammunition. That excludes custom reloaders and wildcat calibers. Since there is more than a little bit of factory ammunition sold in the U.S. that is not actually made here (Lapua, MagTech, and Norma come quickly to mind) we did decide to include foreign manufacturers who have a distribution system in place in this country. To keep the size of this book within reasonable bounds, we have limited the listings to calibers that are well known in the U.S.

As soon as you begin to get past the calibers that are standardized in the U.S. by the Small Arms and Ammunition Manufacturers' Institute (SAAMI) you get into a large gray area. Weatherby's cartridges provide an excellent example of this category. When the Weatherby line of cartridges was first introduced, you either bought your ammunition from the Weatherby factory or loaded your own. The concept of proprietary cartridges furnished by custom gun makers is not at all new. Just after about 1900 in England, that practice was more the rule than the exception. The .375 Holland & Holland Magnum was once a proprietary number. Like the .375 H&H, over time, several of the Weatherby calibers have received SAAMI standardization. Ammunition for these calibers is now produced by independent ammunition makers. That certainly takes those calibers out of the "proprietary" designation. For other Weatherby calibers, the only factory ammunition that gets to the dealer's shelves still comes exclusively through Weatherby. That isn't bad, it is just the way things are. As of this writing, I believe that all Weatherby calibers that are not covered by SAAMI standards are controlled by CIP, the agency that oversees ammunition producers in Western Europe.

There are several U.S. companies who, relatively recently, have each developed their own lines of proprietary calibers. In general, these companies provide a source of factory loaded ammunition for their own calibers. While most of these cartridges have not received formal standardization in the U.S. or elsewhere, these folks are building their products under their own closely controlled conditions, which quite often include outside testing by independent laboratories. Deciding which of these calibers to include in the listings wasn't easy. We did our best to make the book as inclusive as possible.

Having a comprehensive listing of what's offered is only the start of the ammunition selection process. The performance data allows you to compare velocity, energy, Taylor KO Index, bullet path, and wind drift for various ranges. With that information you can quickly see the trade-offs between light and fast bullets and the heavier and slower offerings.

In compiling this comparison data we have, whenever possible, used the manufacturer's own data. When the manufacturer was unable to supply specific data, we have used our best efforts to construct the missing items, using the best supporting information we could find.

Author's Notes

How to Select Ammunition

When you set out to buy ammunition you usually know at least two things right at the start. You know what caliber you want and generally know what the ammunition will be used for, for instance, target or hunting. If the use is target, the selection process is relatively easy because once the caliber has been selected, your primary concern is accuracy. All you need to do is to test all the possible candidates in your caliber (and there won't be many) to see which performs better in your gun.

The hunting problem is considerably more complicated. The ultimate goal in the hunt is to obtain a reliable, clean kill. The first step in this is to get a hit. While a hit is certainly a necessary condition for a kill, after you get that hit the bullet has to finish the job. Up until about fifty years ago there was little done to design bullets specifically for the hunting application. Most of the attention that was paid to bullet performance was in the African calibers. Of course, the direct consequences (to the shooter) of poor bullet performance on an African hunt are much easier to visualize.

In the U.S., John Nosler developed the partition bullet and brought it into general usage. But Nosler's bullets were only available to reloaders, and as late as the mid-'60s they weren't being used by the major manufacturers to produce factory ammunition.

I can remember getting letters in that time period that asked if there were any bullets that got Nosler performance that didn't cost so much. After all, Nosler partition bullets cost about a dime each at that time. That seemed like a lot to folks who were used to paying no more than a nickel for the same weight bullet. What these folks didn't seem to realize was that it's the worst sort of economy to accept poor terminal performance to save a few cents per bullet. Thirty years ago it amazed me to see how many hunters couldn't understand that.

The results obtained with the Nosler and other premium performance hunting bullets that followed gradually convinced more and more hunters that these "expensive" bullets were a bargain when they produced good kills. But the benefits of these bullets were still limited to the hunters who were loading their own ammo. As time went on the benefits of good bullets became clearer to an increasing proportion of hunters. Once they could see that there was a market established, it wasn't long before the custom reloaders began offering ammunition loaded with premium bullets.

When the ammo factories saw the custom reloaders cutting into their sales they began to get the picture. Maybe there really was a market for ammunition loaded with premium bullets. From a tentative start with one premium loading, the main line factories are offering more and more choices of premium bullets. Today these choices include not only specialty bullets furnished by individual makers but also improved performance bullet designs produced by the ammo factories themselves. It is this increased offering of premium bullets that's mostly responsible for the quantum jump in the number of ammunition variations offered today.

As to the question of which premium bullet to use, that question goes beyond the scope of this book. There are now so many specialized forms of high-performance bullet incorporated in factory ammunition that giving meaningful advice about which bullet might work best for your requirement just isn't possible without testing in your specific hunting conditions. It could very well be that several brands will give nearly identical performance in your application. That's a good class of problem. If you can't tell the difference between two or three brands it really comes down to which is the easiest to locate.

The value of this book is that it can help to narrow the selection process down to a few promising candidates. With the list narrowed down to a manageable number you can check with either the manufacturers or with gun shops in your area for more information with which to make your decision. My own recommendation is that when you find a bullet that works well for you, just stick with it. Unless you particularly enjoy trying new things there's no point switching around if you are getting good results.

Within this book the listings are first divided into four sections; Centerfire rifle cartridges, African cartridges, pistol cartridges, and rimfire cartridges. Within the separate parts, the listings are next divided by caliber and specific cartridge listings. Within a cartridge listing, the entries run in increasing order of bullet weight. Within a bullet weight the listings are by bullet style, then velocity.

Find the cartridge you want, go to the desired bullet weight range, and then look through the listings to see just who makes what. Check the bullet description and the performance numbers to see if this is what you need.

If you aren't quite satisfied, you might want to check listings for higher or lower bullet weights. If the performance you want isn't listed here it probably isn't available as a factory product.

Standardization

It's only about 150 years since the breechloading guns firing ammunition contained in metal cartridge cases began to come into common use. The first of these cartridges in popular usage were rimfire rounds with about .50 caliber projectiles. Soon after, the centerfire primer system took over and continues today. All the early centerfire cartridges were loaded with black powder, but after about 1890 the nitro (smokeless) powders made their appearance and soon became the product of choice.

Smokeless powder brought the potential for greatly increased performance and a less critical cleaning requirement. This improved performance came at the price of significantly increased working pressures. As the government became more and more intrusive into our lives the U.S. ammunition makers of the early 1900s recognized that sooner or later they were going to have to get together to adopt industry standards or be subject to some government type of regulation that was already beginning in Europe.

Ultimately, the Small Arms and Ammunition Manufacturers' Institute was formed in the U.S. SAAMI, as the group is called, is a voluntary organization. You don't have to be a member of SAAMI to manufacture ammunition in the U.S. Neither do members have to conform to SAAMI standards with their ammunition. For liability reasons, if for no other, a manufacturer would be foolish in the extreme to make a product that, at least in terms of chamber pressure, didn't follow the collective experience lead of SAAMI.

In addition to the velocity and chamber pressure standardization that SAAMI provides, they also distribute dimensional standards for both cartridges and chambers. It's easy to see the value of the dimensional standards. When you go out to buy ammunition for your gun you want it to fit in that gun's chamber. This is an important function. Imagine the chaos that would result if every gun and every ammunition manufacturer worked to their own idea of the correct dimensions. Proprietary cartridges don't have this level of formal control (nor

do they need it) until they cease to be exclusively proprietary and there is more than one maker of guns and ammunition for the caliber.

In Europe, most ammunition is controlled by an organization called Commission Internationale Permanente (CIP). CIP's approach to ammunition performance standardization seems to be that they will mandate maximum average chamber pressures but will allow individual manufacturers to load any bullet weight to any velocity desired so long as the maximum average pressure limits are observed. From the pure "blow up the gun" standpoint, controlling maximum pressures is all that matters. For European manufacturers, conforming to CIP standards is often a matter of law; it's not voluntary in many countries.

Unlike CIP, SAAMI specifications do control velocities and in doing so, specify the bullet weights that are associated with each of these standard velocities. The tolerance on the velocities called out in the specifications is a wopping 90 feet per second. That means that if a particular cartridge and bullet weight have a nominal velocity of 2700 fps, the ammunition conforms to the standard if the average velocity for the lot is between 2610 fps and 2790 fps. No ammunition that I know of has shot to shot variations of 180 fps. That would be pretty awful stuff. But if a manufacturer makes up a run of ammunition that turns out to have an average velocity of, let's say, 2615 fps when the nominal is 2700 fps, and other characteristics (especially pressure) are nominal, the ammunition still conforms to the SAAMI standards.

Several ammunition companies have developed new high-energy propellants or highly specialized loading techniques that allow loading of some calibers to as much as 200 fps faster than the commonly advertised loading velocity levels without exceeding the allowable pressures. This high-performance ammunition offers a way to get near magnum performance from a "standard" rifle.

Energy vs. Momentum—The "Great" Debate

It started with hunters. There was and is a genuine difference of opinion between those folks who believe that high velocity is "everything" and the higher the striking velocity the better. They are opposed by another group who feel as strongly that as long as the striking velocity meets some minimum standard, the best measure of effectiveness is bullet weight and perhaps the size of the hole the bullet makes. It's pretty obvious that neither position, as simplified above, is a perfect measure of effectiveness. Within the last 15 years or so, this debate has expanded from the hunting fields into the city streets and has become an important consideration in selection of ammunition for the self-defense application.

Because, for almost every specific factory cartridge, the user has a choice of bullet weight, this debate has become a problem for everyone who buys ammunition. You can characterize the debate as light and fast vs: heavy and slow. In physics terms, the debate comes down to whether effectiveness is more nearly comparable to energy than it is to momentum. Let's look at these terms a little more deeply. Energy is defined as one-half of Mass times the square of Velocity. As long as we confine our discussion to the Earth (and I understand there's not much to hunt on the moon), we can think of Mass as being the same as weight. Momentum is defined as Mass times Velocity. When you look at these two definitions, you see that since Energy is proportional to velocity squared and Momentum is proportional to velocity to the first power, Energy puts a premium in velocity. That means that if you are on the side of light and fast, you are saying that Energy is the better measure of effectiveness.

As near as I can determine, the heavy and slow school was dominated in the early days by the professional British African hunters. This school of thought was responsible for pushing the African guns into some impressively large calibers. John "Pondoro" Taylor wanted a measure effectiveness that he believed reflected his real world. He finally settled on a measure that is Bullet Weight (pounds) times Velocity (fps) times the Bullet Diameter (inches), and which was called the Taylor Knock Out Index. Taylor's KO Index needs some explanation. Taylor didn't think of the index as a measure of killing power but rather in the boxing sense of actually producing a short term knock out of the animal. Because of this he restricted the bullets to solids. His theory was that if the bullet didn't penetrate the skull on a brain shot it still had the capability of stunning out the animal for a few seconds so that the hunter could get off a second, more lethal shot.

Since the Taylor KO index represents a momentum value (times bullet diameter) it can be used as an alternate to the energy value. We have included it for all bullet styles for this purpose, although some bullets, especially varmint styles, will clearly not come close to meeting the original intent.

If you take either measure to extremes you find that these measures both fall apart. The particles (electrons or some such little things) fired into patients to break up kidney stones are more energetic than bullets because they are traveling tens or even hundreds of thousands of feet per second. These highly energetic, but very light, particles break up the stones but don't kill the patient, clearly demonstrating that energy isn't a perfect measure of killing power. At the same time, a professional football quarterback can put more momentum (or Taylor Index for that matter) on a thrown football than many guns can put onto their bullets. Since we don't lose a dozen or so wide receivers each weekend, momentum isn't a perfect measure of killing power either. Part of the explanation of this is because neither measure (energy or momentum) by itself, takes bullet construction into account. The terminal performance of the bullet on the target is at least (and possibly more) important than which measure you prefer to use. Generally the more effective cartridges have not only more energy but also more momentum so it is not easy to find a clean demonstration of which measure is best.

When the military is looking at the effectiveness of weapon systems, one factor that gets into the effectiveness calculation is the probability of a kill for each shot. But the probability of a kill depends on two factors, the probability of a hit and the probability of a kill *given* a hit. The probability of a hit depends on many things, the accuracy of the shooter and his equipment and of course the accuracy of the bullet. Velocity probably plays a part in probability of a hit because higher velocity leads to flatter trajectory and lower wind drift.

The probability of a kill *given* a hit depends heavily on the bullet construction. It also depends on striking velocity. It is generally accepted that for a bullet to be effective it must penetrate deeply enough to reach a vital organ. It must also leave a large enough bullet path to provide a conduit for blood to "drain". This definition of how the bullet should perform leads us our current crop of high-performance hollowpoint and controlled expansion bullets.

There are at least two applications that seem to contradict this conventional wisdom. The first comes along with light varmint hunting. In this application, the ability to get a hit isn't a foregone conclusion. A two inch target at three hundred yards isn't all that easy to hit and it takes an accurate bullet to even get a hit. At the same time, almost any hit with almost any bullet will produce a kill. Generally speaking, target bullets work well on light varmints.

In this example, bullet performance after the hit isn't nearly as important as getting a hit in the first place. When we go through the probability of a kill equation, we find that in this application the hit probability is the controlling factor.

There is a class of heavy, and by implication, dangerous, game which is so tough skinned that conventional expanding bullets can't achieve the required penetration. Getting a hit is not the hard part but penetrating into a vital organ isn't easy (see the comments on Taylor's KO Index). For this application, hunters have concluded that solid bullets or bullets with very, very thick jackets, possibly with a core of compressed powdered tungsten, give the best performance. Within broad limits, accuracy doesn't matter.

Just as it isn't possible to generalize about the "best" bullet for every application, neither is it possible to come up with a single "best" caliber. In the final analysis, the shooter has to do his homework. He should look at the printed data and talk to other shooters to see what they are using. Then the final decision point has to come when he tries his selection under his own field conditions. After all, performance in the field is the only thing that really matters.

Ballistics—Trajectory and All That Good Stuff

If you never take a shot beyond 100 yards or so you can skip this section. But anyone, either hunter or target shooter, who is even thinking about firing at longer ranges should have at least a basic idea of why a bullet flys the way it does. Let's begin with the concept of a bullet that is fired in a more or less horizontal direction, the way 99.99% of all bullets are fired. After the bullet leaves the gun it encounters two major external forces: One is gravity, and the other is the resistance of the air to the passage of the bullet. As you can no doubt guess, the air resistance acts to slow the bullet and gravity pulls it down. The big question is how much of each.

If we start with the gravity business, the classic comparison is that if a bullet were fired horizontally and another bullet were dropped from the height of the gun at the same time the gun was fired they would both reach the ground at the same time. That's true only in an over-simplified sense. In the real world, the fired bullet ends up getting some "lift" from the air in a fashion similar to a modern ski-jumper who gets some "lift" by laying out his body over the tips of the skis. This lift actually reduces the amount of bullet drop from what would be obtained in a place with no atmosphere (and therefore no air resistance), somewhere like the surface of the moon. But air resistance plays a much more important role than simply reducing the amount of bullet drop. Air resistance starts slowing the bullet soon after it leaves the muzzle. The amount of slowing at any time during the flight depends on speed of the bullet at that time. Near the muzzle the amount of slowing is relatively large and as the bullet goes on down range the rate of slowing goes down. If you get out near the maximum range of the gun, or for bullets fired in a near-vertical direction, the bullet slows until reaching the top of the trajectory and then, as it starts down, starts speeding up again. As the bullet continues downward it encounters a more dense atmosphere and may actually start slowing again, even as it continues to fall. All that happens at ranges a long way beyond any range that is useful for either hunting or target work and we don't need to concern ourselves with those very long trajectories.

Along about 1890, when smokeless powder was beginning to come into general military usage, the performance of military rifles and cannon took a quantum jump. The world's military powers all began a scientific study of the flight of projectiles. There was some data, mostly empirical, that existed but all of a sudden the ranges and times of flight to be considered were much larger than in the black powder days. It is interesting that at roughly the same time aviation began to develop for heavier-than-air machines, first with gliders and then with powered aircraft. Since both ballistics and aerodynamics involve things flying through the air, you might wonder why the two sciences proceeded down very separate paths for the best part of 70 years. There's no explanation that satisfies me (and I've worked both sides of that street), but I suppose it boils down to the fact that the two groups didn't talk to each other. And to be fair, the velocity ranges of concern to each group were very different indeed. Today, at the professional level, the speed of aeronautical things moving through the air has caught up with bullet speeds and the science of ballistics is slowly moving closer to the aerodynamic approach.

For the average shooter, the older ballistics work is still valid and probably easier to use. Let's take a little look at how some of this science evolved and what it means to you today. The first big breakthrough came when the various countries began to conduct firing programs with "standard" projectiles. These programs were undoubtedly carried out separately and each country jealously protected its own data. The concept of a "standard" projectile was a big breakthrough. The problems resulting from trying to draw meaningful comparisons of data from numerous shots is hard enough if all the projectiles are alike. It isn't hard to understand that it becomes impossible if all the data is for different projectiles. In the United States the work was led by a Captain James M. Ingalls. Working with his own data and from earlier work by a Russian, Col. Mayevski, Ingalls produced a table that showed what happened to the speed of a bullet as it proceeded downrange. This data started with the highest velocity Ingalls could obtain from his test gun and documented the projectile's speed as a function of time. The tables also showed how far the bullet had traveled in the previous time increments. Ingalls's second breakthrough came when he recognized that if the standard projectile was moving at, let's say, 2000 feet per second, it didn't matter what the original launch speed was, the standard bullet was always going to slow down from 2000 fps to 1900 fps in the same elapsed time, and cover the same distance while it did so.

Those two insights allowed the use of Ingalls' tables to predict trajectory data for any gun firing the standard projectile, no matter what the muzzle velocity. Ingalls's standard projectile was one inch in diameter and weighed one pound. It was pretty clear that something more was needed if the concept was to be useful for more than just the standard projectile. Ingalls's third breakthrough came when he saw that he could "adjust" his tables by a factor that compensated for changes in the size, shape and weight of the bullet. This factor became known as Ingalls' Ballistic Coefficient (C_I). If you knew the Ballistic Coefficient and muzzle velocity of a bullet you could do a pretty fair job of predicting downrange performance. It wasn't long before some other bright lad found a way to predict the bullet drop when the downrange time, distance, and velocity factors were known.

Shortly after the turn of the century, a group called the Gavre Commission combined the ballistic work of Ingalls with that from other countries and produced some new, and slightly improved, tables. These new tables recognized that the velocity decay for a flat-based projectile was different from a boattail projectile. The different projectile shapes were assigned to tables known as G1, G2, G3, etc. (the "G" being for Gavre). With these new tables the precision of the performance predictions was improved by a small amount. The multiple forms of ballistic coefficient generated a new class of problem. The ballistic coefficient for a projectile that used the G1 table could not be compared with the coefficient for a projectile that used the G2 table. That wasn't too much of a problem if you were working with only one or two different bullets, but became a nightmare as the number of different bullet shapes increased.

Within about the last 10 or 15 years, the various ammunition and bullet manufacturers have agreed that since any ballistic prediction is by its nature, never absolutely perfect, they would standardize on using the equivalent of G1 coefficients for all bullets. The error that this approach introduces is quite small for all realistic ranges. As they say in aerospace, the results are "close enough for government work." By using one type of coefficient you can look at the coefficients for a variety of bullets and know that a coefficient of 0.400 is always "better" than a coefficient of 0.300. All the performance tables in this book are based on the G1 coefficients.

Maximum Effective and Point Blank Ranges

There are two ballistic concepts that are much more important to hunters than to target shooters. These are Maximum Effective Range (MER) and Maximum Point-Blank Range (MPBR). These two ranges are not the same thing at all. MPBR is defined as the maximum range for which a gun will keep the bullets within a given distance of the aim point (without changing the sights or "holding off"). In its pure form it really doesn't depend on the ability of the shooter, only on his equipment.

MER, on the other hand, depends heavily on the shooter. By my definition, MER is the longest range at which a shooter can keep his bullets within a given size circle. To do this he can adjust sights, hold off, or use any other means at his disposal to get his hit. Any given shooter has a variety of MER's depending on the equipment he is using, the type of rest he has available, and what the weather, especially the wind, is doing.

Maximum Effective Range

Let's look at MER in more detail. I've done this test myself and with a variety of other shooters of different skill levels. Take a paper plate of any convenient size (6 or 8 inches diameter will do for a start) and staple the plate to a stick. We can start with a simple situation. Using any gun with iron sights from a free standing position, how far out can you keep 9 out of 10 shots on the plate. If you are an "average" shot you may have trouble keeping 9 out of 10 on the plate at 50 yards. Some people think that 4 out of 5 is a good enough hit percentage. What we are after here is to demonstrate a high probability that you can hit the vital zone with your first shot. This test is most valid if done using simulated hunting conditions, starting with a cold gun and without any shooting prior to your first shot. If 50 yards is too easy for you then start increasing the range until you start to see misses. If you use a gun with a scope instead of the iron sights you might move the plate out a bit farther still.

Now, let's take another step. If you fire from a good rest with a flat shooting gun using a scope, you might be able to do the 9 out of 10 thing out to 200 or even 300 yards. If you aren't a practiced long-range shooter it's unlikely you are going to be able to get out much beyond 300 yards. These tests are only for a stationary target. Could you do better on a moving target? Few of us can! If the target is presented at ranges other than the even 50- or 100-yard increments, the problem gets a lot harder, especially when the range starts to get to be much beyond 200 yards, and nearly impossible beyond 300 yards.

What does this test represent? The size of the plate represents the lethal area of deer-size game. If you can't reliably put your shots into the lethal area beyond any given range then you shouldn't be taking a shot at game under those conditions. It is bad enough to miss completely but it is far worse to gut shoot a buck and

have it run off too fast and too far to track, only to die somewhere in the brush and be wasted. Maximum Effective Range depends far more on the shooter, his equipment, and the conditions under which the shot was taken, than on the detail ballistics of the cartridge.

Maximum Point-Blank Range

The concept of MPBR is that for any given lethal zone diameter, and for any gun, there exists one sighting distance at which the gun can be "zeroed" that will cause the trajectory between the 1st crossing of the sight line (for practical purposes, starting at the muzzle) and the zero range to be above the sight line by no more than the radius of the lethal area. Furthermore, from the zero range on out to MPBR the bullet's trajectory will be below the sight line. At MPBR the impact point will be one lethal zone radius BELOW the sight line. The idea is that out

Maximum Point-Blank Range
Scope Sight
Use This Table for 2-Inch-Diameter Lethal Zone
(Varmint Shooting)

Ballistic Coefficient	Muzzle Velocity fps	First LOS Crossing yards	High Point yards	"Zero" Range yards	Max. Point Blank Range yards
0.200	2000	25	70	110	125
	2500	35	85	135	155
	3000	40	105	160	185
	3500	45	120	185	210
	4000	50	135	210	235
0.300	2000	25	75	115	130
	2500	35	85	140	160
	3000	40	105	165	190
	3500	45	120	195	220
	4000	50	140	220	250
0.400	2000	25	75	115	135
	2500	35	85	145	170
	3000	40	110	170	200
	3500	45	125	200	230
	4000	55	140	225	260
0.500	2000	25	75	120	135
	2500	35	90	145	170
	3000	40	110	175	230
	3500	45	125	200	230
	4000	55	145	230	265

to the MPBR, the bullet will always be within the lethal radius from the sight line and the shooter shouldn't have to hold high (or low), but instead to always hold dead on.

Using a .22-250 for an example, in a varmint application with a 2-inch diameter lethal circle, the bullet will be one inch high at about 125 yards if you have the gun zeroed for 200 yards. The MPBR for this example is 230 yards. If you had a lethal circle that was 8 inches in diameter the 4-inch high point would be reached at about 170 yards with a 275-yard zero and a MPBR of 370 yards. You can see that the MPBR depends heavily on the size of the lethal circle.

The concept of MPBR is not without controversy. The controversy isn't about the concept itself or even the actual MPBR numbers, it is about what happens in the field. I know two professional guides who are 180 degrees apart on this subject. One loves the idea. He says that he has the client demonstrate where the client's gun is zeroed before the hunt. The guide judges the range to the target and instructs the client to hold dead on if he (the guide) decides the range is within MPBR. The idea of Maximum Effective Range also gets into his decision to tell the client to shoot. For most shooters with modern guns, their Maximum Effective Range is shorter than the MPBR, sometimes very much shorter.

The second professional guide says that in his experience the MPBR idea may be technically correct but is terrible in practice. No matter where he tells the client to hold the client makes his own adjustment for range. Furthermore, the client almost always overestimates the range. The combination of holding high for a real range that is shorter (often much shorter) than the estimated range and shooting at a range shorter than the zero range (where the trajectory is above the sight line) results far too often in shooting over the back of the game.

What these two positions clearly say to me is that if the shooter can determine the range accurately, either by lots of practice estimating, by using a rangefinder, or by listening to his guide, AND if he knows where his gun will shoot at that range, AND if he can hold well enough, he will get good hits. If you don't start holding off, the MPBR concept puts an upper limit on the range at which you should attempt a shot. If you want to start holding off, you need to know both the range to the target and how high you must hold to get hits at that range. That knowledge doesn't come without lots and lots of practice. Finally, given a good hit, the rest depends on the quality of the bullet. If the bullet doesn't perform, everything else is wasted.

The tables below list MPBR's for bullets with assorted ballistic coefficients at different muzzle velocities, and for both 2-inch and 6-inch lethal areas. You may wonder why bullet weight isn't included in the tabulated data. The fact is that any bullet with a ballistic coefficient of, let's say 0.350, that launched at a given muzzle velocity (for instance 3000 fps) will fly along the same trajectory path. Bullet weight does get into the ballistic coefficient number because ballistic coefficient equals sectional density divided by the

Maximum Point-Blank Range Scope Sight Use This Table for 6-Inch-Diameter Lethal Zone (Large Game Shooting)					
Ballistic Coefficient	Muzzle Velocity fps	First LOS Crossing yards	High Point yards	"Zero" Range yards	Max. Point Blank Range yards
0.200	2000	20	90	155	180
	2500	20	110	190	220
	3000	25	130	225	260
	3500	30	150	260	300
	4000	35	165	290	335
0.300	2000	20	95	165	195
	2500	20	115	205	235
	3000	25	140	240	280
	3500	30	160	275	320
	4000	35	180	310	360
0.400	2000	20	95	170	200
	2500	20	115	210	245
	3000	25	140	250	290
	3500	30	160	285	335
	4000	35	185	325	375
0.500	2000	20	100	175	205
	2500	25	120	215	250
	3000	25	140	255	300
	3500	30	165	295	345
	4000	35	190	330	390

bullet's form (shape) factor. Sectional density is bullet weight divided by the bullet diameter squared. The caliber of the gun doesn't matter in the table but is also indirectly involved in two ways. Small calibers have lighter bullets which need better form factors to have the same ballistic coefficient as a heavier bullet. The smaller caliber guns generally produce higher velocities than the larger calibers. These tables are calculated using a sight height above the bore line of 1.5 inches which is pretty standard for most scope-sighted rifles. A third table shows what happens if the gun has iron sights (0.9 inches above the bore line).

To use these tables, start with the table for the correct lethal zone diameter (2 inch or 6 inch). Once you find the approximate ballistic coefficient of your bullet and pick the line nearest to your muzzle velocity, you can read across the table to see the following data: the range at which the bullet first crosses the line of sight

Maximum Point-Blank Range Iron Sights Use This Table for 6-Inch-Diameter Lethal Zone (Large Game Shooting)					
Ballistic Coefficient	Muzzle Velocity fps	First LOS Crossing yards	High Point yards	"Zero" Range yards	Max. Point Blank Range yards
0.200	2000	10	85	150	175
	2500	15	105	185	220
	3000	15	125	220	255
	3500	20	140	250	290
	4000	20	160	280	325
0.300	2000	10	85	160	185
	2500	15	110	195	230
	3000	15	130	235	275
	3500	20	150	270	315
	4000	20	170	300	355
0.400	2000	10	90	165	195
	2500	15	110	200	240
	3000	15	130	240	285
	3500	20	150	275	325
	4000	20	175	310	370
0.500	2000	10	90	165	200
	2500	15	115	205	245
	3000	15	130	245	290
	3500	20	155	285	335
	4000	25	175	320	380

(going up), the distance to the high point of the trajectory, the range that the gun should be zeroed (where the bullet comes down to cross the line of sight for the second time, and finally the Maximum Point Blank Range.

For example, let's look at MPBR for a .300 Winchester firing 180-grain Hornady ammunition. The Ballistic coefficient of the ammunition is 0.436 and the nominal muzzle velocity is 2960 fps. We will use the chart for scope sights and a 6-inch lethal zone. In the 6-inch table, use a Ballistic Coefficient of 0.400. If you look at the listing for a BC of 0.500 you will find that large changes in the BC

number don't make a huge difference in the MPBR data. Likewise, use the line for 3000 fps. Again that's close enough to 2960. You can then read that the first crossing is at 25 yards (all this data is rounded to the nearest 5 yards), the high point is at 140 yards, the zero range is 250 yards, and the MPBR is 290 yards.

If the gun had iron sights the numbers would be as follows: first crossing - 15 yards, high point - 130 yards, zero range - 240 yards, and MPBR - 285 yards. You can see here that the sight height above the bore line does change the numbers a little. I wonder how many people can keep 9 out of 10 (or even 4 out of 5) in 6 inches at 285 yards using a gun with open iron sights. I'll wager there aren't many. I sure can't.

There Is Always A Trade Off

When we select ammunition for a specific application there's always a trade off. If we can have the luxury of selecting the very "best" gun for the application, the trade offs are lessened. But few of us are fortunate to have guns for every possible situation. For certain applications, like varmint shooting or target work, we can trade a hunting bullet effectiveness for accuracy. For general hunting, the last little bit of accuracy, or for that matter the last little bit of ballistic coefficient, doesn't justify trading away any bullet performance.

You can begin to get the idea here. In the final analysis you, and only you, can decide which way to lean on each of these trades. You can get help from various sources, friends, gun shop employees, and especially from professional guides. You have to then evaluate just what the advice from each source is worth. The guide probably has the most to lose if he gives you bad advise. If your hunt isn't successful you won't be back.

This book provides the technical information on cartridge performance you need to help you decide on what trades are best from the purely technical standpoint. We don't even attempt to take a stand on light and fast vs. heavy and slow. That's a fundamental choice you must make for yourself. After that, good luck and good shooting!

CAUTION and WARNING!

Common sense needs to be used when handling and discharging a firearm. **Always keep the following in mind:** Always point a firearm in a safe direction, and never point a firearm at another person. Treat all firearms as though they are loaded. Wear eye and hearing protection at all times when handling firearms. Only adults competent in handling firearms and ammunition should ever attempt to load or discharge a firearm.

Do not attempt to use this book to handload your own ammunition up to the bullet velocities listed on these pages. Your firearm may not be able to withstand the pressures generated by the loads listed in this book. If you aren't sure about your gun, consult a competent gunsmith. The handloading of ammunition and the discharging of a firearm should never be attempted without the supervision of an adult experienced in both handloading and firearms. Do not attempt to handload ammunition without knowing how to read signs of (excessive) pressure in both guns and ammunition. Keep these principles of safety in mind so as to provide a safe environment for everyone.

How to Use This Book

The listings in this book are divided into four sections: Small and Medium Cartridges, Dangerous Game Cartridges, Pistol and Revolver Cartridges, and Rimfire Cartridges. Within these four sections the listings begin with the smallest and end with the largest caliber. If you refer to the sample listing on page *xxi*, you will see that there is a ❶ description (with short historical notes) and a ❷ drawing of each caliber.

For each caliber we list a ❸ Relative Recoil Factor to give you some idea of the recoil the caliber will generate. Most shooters can handle the recoil of a .30-06 reasonably well with some practice; it has a relative recoil factor of 2.19. Should you carry a .700 Nitro Express, you will note that its relative recoil factor is 9.00, more than four times what a .30-06 generates! Relative recoil factor is based on the muzzle momentum of the bullet and the expelled powder gas for a typical loading. Below the relative recoil factor, you will find the **controlling agency for standardization of this ammunition.** In the Author's Notes there is a discussion of standardization and what it means to the shooter.

Item ❹ gives the standard performance numbers that have been established for this caliber. We list the Maximum Average Pressures obtained by both the Copper Crusher and the Transducer methods. Number ❺ gives two figures. The first is the standard barrel length the factories use to create their velocity figures. If you shoot a .300 Weatherby Magnum with a 22-inch barrel, do not be surprised if your chronograph shows velocities significantly below the factory figures provided here; the reason for this is that this caliber is tested in the factory with a 26-inch barrel. The second number is the twist rate of the rifling the factories use in the factory test barrels.

Next come the listings of all the factory loads currently available in this caliber. The listings start with the lightest bullet and progress **down** to the heaviest bullet available in factory loadings. Within each bullet weight there are listings for the bullet styles available. Within each bullet style, the listings run from the highest muzzle velocity to the lowest.

Under each specific loading you will find ❻ manufacturer, ❼ bullet weight, ❽ the manufacturer's name for his loading, and ❾ the factory stock number (in parentheses) that can be used to order that particular cartridge and load. The individual cartridge listings also provide ❿ velocity, ⓫ energy, and ⓬ Taylor's Knock-Out Index. (See "The 'Great' Debate" in "How to Select Ammunition" for a discussion of the significance of these factors.) ⓭ The figures for the category of "path • inches" show the bullet's position relative to the line of sight at ranges up to 1,000 yards (depending on the listings section). For small and medium centerfire listings, the figures assume a scope-sighted rifle that is set at a 200-yard "zero." For the dangerous-game calibers, the figures are based on iron sights and a 150-yard "zero." The rimfire listings are based on scope sights with a 100-yard "zero." Note that for handgun cartridges the "path • inches" listing is replaced by figures for mid-range trajectory height in inches.

⓮ The category of "wind • drift inches" shows how much the bullet is pushed off-course by a direct crosswind of 10 mph at ranges out to 1,000 yards. The G1 Ballistic Coefficient value ⓯ is useful for those shooters who want to calculate their own ballistic data.

Find the cartridge you want and locate the desired bullet weight; then look through the entries to see who makes what. Check the performance numbers to see whether a particular load is what you need. If you aren't quite satisfied, you can check the listings for the next higher or lower bullet weight in this caliber. If you are just playing "What if," you can also try other calibers to see if you can find a load that would do your job. If you cannot find a load with the performance you want, it probably isn't available as a factory product. Please note that some listings in this book are followed by a legend, such as "(Discontinued in 2004)." These listings have dropped out of the manufacturer's catalog but may still be available at your local supplier.

.223 Remington

When the .223 Remington cartridge was adopted by the U.S. Army as M193 5.56mm Ball ammunition in 1964, that action ensured that the .223 would become the most popular .22 centerfire on the list. Every cartridge that becomes a U.S. Army standard, with the possible exception of the .30 Carbine, has gone on to a long and useful commercial life. Just look the .45-70, the .45 Colt, the .30-06, and the .45 ACP. The .223 case has been "necked" to every possible size, the TCU series of cartridges and the .30 Whisper being examples.

Even without the military application, the .223 Remington had plenty of potential to become popular. Based on the .222 and the .222 Remington Magnum, the .223 provides an excellent balance of accuracy and performance with good case and barrel life. It has become the standard by which all other .22s are judged.

Most of guns chambered for the .223 have a barrel twist of 1 turn in 14 inches. That twist provides enough stability for bullets up to 55 grains but begins to be marginal above that level. Today there are bullets available in loaded ammunition weighing as much as 77 grains (80-grain bullets for the handloader). It takes a faster twist to stabilize those heavier bullets, and some gunmakers offer barrel twists as fast as 1 turn in 7 inches in .223 caliber. If you have one of the fast-twist barrels, you may have problems with the very light varmint loads. The high velocities attained with the quick twist combine to produce a bullet spin rate that can literally rip thin-jacketed bullets apart. Guns equipped with quick- twist barrels will usually do better with 55-grain and heavier bullets.

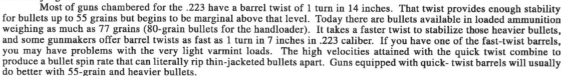

Relative Recoil Factor = 0.80

Specifications

Controlling Agency for Standardization of this Ammunition: SAAMI

Bullet Weight Grains	Velocity fps	Maximum Average Pressure Copper Crusher	Transducer
53	3,305	52,000 cup	55,000 psi
55	3,215	52,000 cup	55,000 psi
60	3,200	52,000 cup	55,000 psi
64	3,000	52,000 cup	55,000 psi

Standard barrel for velocity testing: 24 inches long - 1 turn in 12-inch twist

Availability

Cor-Bon 40-grain BlitzKing (22340BK/20)
G1 Ballistic Coefficient = 0.200

Distance • Yards	Muzzle	100	200	300	400	500	600	800	1000
Velocity • fps	3800	3248	2761	2323	1927	1577	1291	976	831
Energy • Ft-lbs	1283	937	677	479	330	221	148	85	61
Taylor KO Index	4.9	4.2	3.5	3.0	2.5	2.0	1.7	1.2	1.1
Path • Inches	-1.5	+0.9	0.0	-5.5	-17.6	-39.4	-76.1	-223.5	-505.8
Wind Drift • Inches	0.0	1.2	4.9	11.8	22.9	39.3	62.5	130.8	220.8

Hornady 40-grain V-Max (8326) - Moly VX (83253)
G1 Ballistic Coefficient = 0.218

Distance • Yards	Muzzle	100	200	300	400	500	600	800	1000
Velocity • fps	3800	3305	2845	2424	2044	1715	1421	1045	882
Energy • Ft-lbs	1282	970	719	502	371	261	179	97	69
Taylor KO Index	4.9	4.2	3.6	3.1	2.6	2.2	1.8	1.3	1.1
Path • Inches	-1.5	+0.9	0.0	-5.2	-16.4	-36.0	-68.3	-195.5	-445.2
Wind Drift • Inches	0.0	1.0	4.4	10.7	20.4	34.7	54.8	115.2	198.2

Cor-Bon 40-grain JHP (22340/20) (While supply lasts)
G1 Ballistic Coefficient = 0.180

Distance • Yards	Muzzle	100	200	300	400	500	600	800	1000
Velocity • fps	3800	3191	2660	2186	1765	1409	1148	903	771
Energy • Ft-lbs	1283	905	629	425	277	176	117	72	53
Taylor KO Index	4.9	4.1	3.4	2.8	2.3	1.8	1.5	1.2	1.0
Path • Inches	-1.5	+1.0	0.0	-6.0	-19.4	-44.6	-88.7	-264.1	-591.3
Wind Drift • Inches	0.0	1.3	5.5	13.5	26.5	46.2	74.0	151.6	250.8

25

Conversion Charts

After the first edition of *Ammo & Ballistics* reached the readers, we were surprised to discover how many readers wanted to use data in the metric system. In this edition we are providing conversion charts to aid these users. Most of the conversions are straightforward, but there is one point that should be born in mind. It is easy to convert the velocities shown to meters per second. But when you do that you must remember that those metric velocities are correct at the ranges shown in YARDS. You can also convert the yardages into metric distances, and the results will be correct but the increments will be 91.44 meters (not 100 meters). If you want metric velocity data for even 100-meter increments, the easiest way is to use the ballistic coefficient and the metric muzzle velocity with an external ballistics program (like Ken Oehler's Ballistic Explorer) to compute a new, all-metric table.

To accomplish these conversions, you have two choices. The charts give conversion values for even increments. If you want to find the metric equivalent of 2,750 fps, you add the numbers for 2,000 fps (609.57), 700 fps (213.35), and 50 fps (15.24). The result is 838.16 meters per second.

As an alternative, you can simply multiply the number to be converted by the conversion factor given. In the above example, this would be: 2,750 fps times .3048 equals 838.2 meters per second. In all conversions, you can expect small differences in the last digit due to round-off effects.

Medium Length Conversions
Foot/Meter Length Conversions
Feet times .3048 equals Meters
Meters times 3.281 equals Feet

Feet ..... Meters	Meters ..... Feet
1,000 ...... 304.8	1,000 ...... 3,281.0
900 ...... 274.3	900 ...... 2,952.9
800 ...... 243.8	800 ...... 2,624.8
700 ...... 213.4	700 ...... 2,296.7
600 ...... 182.9	600 ...... 1,968.6
500 ...... 152.4	500 ...... 1,640.5
400 ...... 121.9	400 ...... 1,312.4
300 ...... 91.4	300 ...... 984.3
200 ...... 61.0	200 ...... 656.2
100 ...... 30.5	100 ...... 328.1
90 ...... 27.4	90 ...... 295.3
80 ...... 24.4	80 ...... 262.5
70 ...... 21.3	70 ...... 229.7
60 ...... 18.3	60 ...... 196.9
50 ...... 15.2	50 ...... 164.1
40 ...... 12.2	40 ...... 131.2
30 ...... 9.1	30 ...... 98.4
20 ...... 6.1	20 ...... 65.6
10 ...... 3.0	10 ...... 32.8
9 ...... 2.7	9 ...... 29.5
8 ...... 2.4	8 ...... 26.2
7 ...... 2.1	7 ...... 23.0
6 ...... 1.8	6 ...... 19.7
5 ...... 1.5	5 ...... 16.4
4 ...... 1.2	4 ...... 13.1
3 ...... 0.9	3 ...... 9.8
2 ...... 0.6	2 ...... 6.6
1 ...... 0.3	1 ...... 3.3

Large Length Conversions
Yard/Meter Length Conversions
Yards times .9144 equals Meters
Meters times 1.094 equals Yards

Yards .... Meters	Meters ... Yards
1,000 ..... 914.4	1,000 .... 1,094.0
900 ..... 823.0	900 .... 984.6
800 ..... 731.5	800 .... 875.2
700 ..... 640.1	700 .... 765.8
600 ..... 548.6	600 .... 656.4
500 ..... 457.2	500 .... 547.0
400 ..... 365.8	400 .... 437.6
300 ..... 274.3	300 .... 328.2
200 ..... 182.9	200 .... 218.8
100 ..... 91.4	100 .... 109.4
90 ..... 82.3	90 .... 98.5
80 ..... 73.2	80 .... 87.5
70 ..... 64.0	70 .... 76.6
60 ..... 54.9	60 .... 65.6
50 ..... 45.7	50 .... 54.7
40 ..... 36.6	40 .... 43.8
30 ..... 27.4	30 .... 32.8
20 ..... 18.3	20 .... 21.9
10 ..... 9.1	10 .... 10.9
9 ..... 8.2	9 .... 9.8
8 ..... 7.3	8 .... 8.8
7 ..... 6.4	7 .... 7.7
6 ..... 5.5	6 .... 6.6
5 ..... 4.6	5 .... 5.5
4 ..... 3.7	4 .... 4.4
3 ..... 2.7	3 .... 3.3
2 ..... 1.8	2 .... 2.2
1 ..... 0.9	1 .... 1.1

Velocity Conversions
FPS/Meters Per Sec. Conversions
FPS times .3048 equals MPS
MPS times 3.281 equals FPS

FPS ..... MPS	MPS ... FPS
4000 ...... 1,219.20	2000 .... 6,562.0
3000 ...... 914.40	1000 .... 3,281.0
2000 ...... 609.60	900 .... 2,952.9
1000 ...... 304.80	800 .... 2,624.8
900 ...... 274.32	700 .... 2,296.7
800 ...... 243.84	600 .... 1,968.6
700 ...... 213.36	500 .... 1,640.5
600 ...... 182.88	400 .... 1,312.4
500 ...... 152.40	300 .... 984.3
400 ...... 121.92	200 .... 656.2
300 ...... 91.44	100 .... 328.1
200 ...... 60.96	90 .... 295.3
100 ...... 30.48	80 .... 262.5
90 ...... 27.43	70 .... 229.7
80 ...... 24.38	60 .... 196.9
70 ...... 21.34	50 .... 164.1
60 ...... 18.29	40 .... 131.2
50 ...... 15.24	30 .... 98.4
40 ...... 12.19	20 .... 65.6
30 ...... 9.14	10 .... 32.8
20 ...... 6.10	9 .... 29.5
10 ...... 3.05	8 .... 26.2
9 ...... 2.74	7 .... 23.0
8 ...... 2.44	6 .... 19.7
7 ...... 2.13	5 .... 16.4
6 ...... 1.83	4 .... 13.1
5 ...... 1.52	3 .... 9.8
4 ...... 1.22	2 .... 6.6
3 ...... 0.91	1 .... 3.3
2 ...... 0.61	
1 ...... 0.30	

Energy Conversions

Ft-Lbs times 1.356 equals Joules
Joules times .7376 equals Ft-Lbs

Ft-Lbs ... Joules	Joules ... Ft-Lbs
10,000 13,560	10,000 7,376
9,000 12,204	9,000 6,638
8,000 10,848	8,000 5,901
7,000 9,492	7,000 5,163
6,000 8,136	6,000 4,426
5,000 6,780	5,000 3,688
4,000 5,424	4,000 2,950
3,000 4,068	3,000 2,213
2,000 2,712	2,000 1,475
1,000 1,356	1,000 738
900 1,220	900 664
800 1,085	800 590
700 949	700 516
600 814	600 443
500 678	500 369
400 542	400 295
300 407	300 221
200 271	200 148
100 136	100 74
90 122	90 66
80 108	80 59
70 95	70 52
60 81	60 44
50 68	50 37
40 54	40 30
30 41	30 22
20 27	20 15
10 14	10 7

Weight Conversions

Grains times 0.06481 equals Grams
Grams times 15.43 equals Grains

Grains ... Grams	Grams .. Grains
1,000 ... 64.81	100 .... 1,543.0
900 ... 58.33	90 ... 1,388.7
800 ... 51.85	80 ... 1,234.4
700 ... 45.37	70 ... 1,080.1
600 ... 38.89	60 ... 925.8
500 ... 32.41	50 ... 771.5
400 ... 25.92	40 ... 617.2
300 ... 19.44	30 ... 462.9
200 ... 12.96	20 ... 308.6
100 ... 6.48	10 ... 154.3
90 ... 5.83	9 ... 138.9
80 ... 5.18	8 ... 123.4
70 ... 4.54	7 ... 108.0
60 ... 3.89	6 ... 92.6
50 ... 3.24	5 ... 77.2
40 ... 2.59	4 ... 61.7
30 ... 1.94	3 ... 46.3
20 ... 1.30	2 ... 30.9
10 ... 0.65	1 ... 15.4
9 ... 0.58	0.9 ... 13.9
8 ... 0.52	0.8 ... 12.3
7 ... 0.45	0.7 ... 10.8
6 ... 0.39	0.6 ... 9.3
5 ... 0.32	0.5 ... 7.7
4 ... 0.26	0.4 ... 6.2
3 ... 0.19	0.3 ... 4.6
2 ... 0.13	0.2 ... 3.1
1 ... 0.06	0.1 ... 1.5
0.9 ... 0.06	
0.8 ... 0.05	
0.7 ... 0.05	
0.6 ... 0.04	
0.5 ... 0.03	
0.4 ... 0.03	
0.3 ... 0.02	
0.2 ... 0.01	
0.1 ... 0.01	

Inch-millimeter Conversions

Inches times 25.40 equals millimeters
Millimeters times .03937 equals inches

in ... mm	mm .. in
1,000 25,400	10,000 ... 393.70
900 22,860	9,000 ... 354.33
800 20,320	8,000 ... 314.96
700 17,780	7,000 ... 275.59
600 15,240	6,000 ... 236.22
500 12,700	5,000 ... 196.85
400 10,160	4,000 ... 157.48
300 7,620	3,000 ... 118.11
200 5,080	2,000 ... 78.74
100 2,540	1,000 ... 39.37
90 2,286	900 ... 35.43
80 2,032	800 ... 31.50
70 1,778	700 ... 27.56
60 1,524	600 ... 23.62
50 1,270	500 ... 19.69
40 1,016	400 ... 15.75
30 762	300 ... 11.81
20 508	200 ... 7.87
10 254	100 ... 3.94
9 229	90 ... 3.54
8 203	80 ... 3.15
7 178	70 ... 2.76
6 152	60 ... 2.36
5 127	50 ... 1.97
4 102	40 ... 1.57
3 76	30 ... 1.18
2 51	20 ... 0.79
1 25	10 ... 0.39
0.9 23	9 ... 0.35
0.8 20	8 ... 0.31
0.7 18	7 ... 0.28
0.6 15	6 ... 0.24
0.5 13	5 ... 0.20
0.4 10	4 ... 0.16
0.3 8	3 ... 0.12
0.2 5	2 ... 0.08
0.1 3	1 ... 0.04

DISCLAIMER

The reader may notice certain discrepancies in spellings in this book. Unlike most books where consistency is paramount, the author and the publisher decided to reproduce the actual word usage for the cartridges exactly as they appear in the manufacturers' catalogs. This is where the discrepancies arise. One manufacturer may use *Soft Nose* as part of its description for the ammunition in its catalog, while another might use *Softnose, soft nose, or softnose.* (Safari Press's style is to combine the two words and lowercase it—softnose.) Furthermore, when you go to your local shop to buy any ammunition, you may find the word usage on the box differs slightly from what you will find in this book. This further discrepancy is the result of a manufacturer failing to replicate exactly the wording in its catalog to that found on its cartridge boxes. For the purpose of this book, we have used only those names supplied from the manufacturer's catalog, which may differ slightly from what is printed on the cartridge box or seen elsewhere.

Figuring the Angles and Other Problems

Craig T. Boddington

It was from this exact spot that I missed the biggest bull elk I've ever seen. The range was about 500 yards, very far but quite practical with the equipment I had—except I failed to take into account a deceptively steep uphill angle, and I shot right over his back.

The buck was at the bottom of a big, open slide, and I was at the top. He was the biggest mule deer I'd ever seen—and he hasn't grown any smaller in my mind's eye as the years have passed. He was very far away, but I couldn't get any closer on the open mountainside. And yet I had lots of time. I examined the distance over and over again and balanced that against the trajectory of the .264 Winchester Magnum I was carrying. It was a makable shot, very much so; all I had to do was hold a slight bit of daylight between the horizontal crosswire and the buck's backline, and I'd have him.

At the shot he turned his head as if to look around for the buzzing insect; then he took four slow steps and vanished forever into a deep canyon. I went down to look for blood and didn't find any. But I did confirm that the distance was everything I thought it was.

That buck bothered me a lot and could well have become one of those "mystery misses"—except that the answer was all too obvious. I'd held on the buck as though I was shooting on level ground, but I wasn't. That mountainside fell away at a 45-degree angle, and at that distance it was altogether a different shot than it would have been on the flat.

There are a number of ways to explain the effects of uphill/downhill shooting, but I've never been particularly happy with any of them. It's simple enough, yet it's one of those mystifying phenomena that almost defy words. But I'll give it a shot. First off, it doesn't matter whether you're shooting uphill or downhill; the effect is exactly the same either way. No, shooting on the slant does not cause the bullet to "rise" more, and it doesn't go faster when fired downhill.

Laser rangefinders like this Leupold binocular/rangefinder are wonderful tools—but they can only tell you the actual straight-line difference to your target. At longer range they're almost essential, but once you read the actual or "slant range," you'd better take a hard look at the angle—you may need to hold a bit lower than you think.

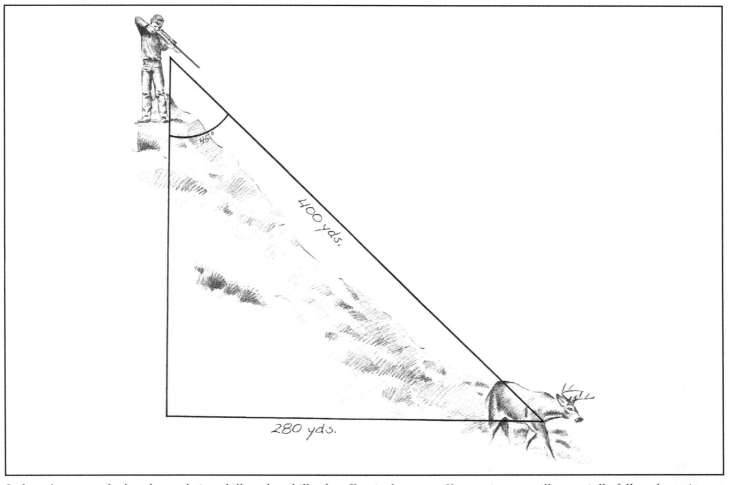

It doesn't matter whether the angle is uphill or downhill—the effect is the same. Your trajectory will essentially follow the trajectory curve of a bullet fired at the horizontal distance to your target.

All bullets start to lose velocity and "fall" the instant they leave the muzzle. Two factors cause this: wind resistance and gravity. The aerodynamics of a bullet has a lot to do with its ability to retain velocity against air resistance, but nothing can alter the effects of gravity. If the rifle barrel were pointed exactly parallel to the earth's surface, the bullet would never reach the line of sight; it would start to drop immediately. When we sight-in a rifle, we "cheat the act" by tilting the muzzle upward slightly in relation to the line of sight. By so doing, we haven't altered the workings of gravity in any way, but we have put the bullet's path to good use. Now, with the barrel tilted upward, the bullet will cross the line of sight at a relatively short range and then continue to climb above the line of sight. Gravity is working on it all the time, and its path is curved from the instant it leaves the muzzle. Eventually that curve turns downward strongly enough that the bullet will cross the line of sight a second and last time. By then

the bullet has slowed markedly. Gravity is really working, and the trajectory arcs downward faster and faster until the bullet finally impacts the ground.

That's what trajectory is all about, and it doesn't depend on whether you're shooting uphill or downhill. Gravity acts in a straight vertical line from the earth's surface; it doesn't take into account the fact that the surface is far from flat. Regardless of the angle at which your shot is fired, all that matters, as far as Old Man Gravity is concerned, is the *horizontal* distance between you and your target.

Let's say my mule deer buck was exactly 400 yards downhill from me at a 45-degree angle. Think of a triangle, with the long leg running from the buck to me. The two short legs run vertical and horizontal—the vertical pull of gravity and the horizontal distance the bullet traveled. These two legs meet in a right angle directly underneath me, somewhere down in the mountain. As far as gravity

TRAJECTORY DIFFERENCES AT VARIOUS ANGLES

Trajectory
(200-yard zero, drop in inches)

Cartridge	Bullet Wt. (grains)	Muzzle Velocity (fps)	Horizontal 100 yd	Horizontal 300 yd	Horizontal 400 yd	15° 100 yd	15° 300 yd	15° 400 yd	30° 100 yd	30° 300 yd	30° 400 yd	45° 100 yd	45° 300 yd	45° 400 yd
.270 Win.	130	3060	+1.5	-6.8	-20.0	+1.6	-6.6	-19.3	+1.7	-5.9	-17.3	+1.9	-4.8	-14.1
.30-06	165	2800	+2.0	-8.7	-25.7	+2.1	-8.4	-24.8	+2.3	-7.5	-22.3	+2.6	-6.2	-18.2
7mm Rem. Mag.	150	3110	+1.4	-6.7	-19.9	+1.4	-6.5	-19.2	+1.4	-5.8	-17.2	+1.8	-4.7	-14.1

is concerned, forget the actual distance. All that matters is the horizontal distance. In this case, if the long leg of the triangle is 400 yards, then the short legs are slightly under 300 yards.

To be exact without giving a mathematics lesson (not my strong suit anyway!), you multiply the cosine of the angle, which is .707 for a 45-degree angle, by the length of the hypotenuse, which is the long leg. The exact horizontal distance is 282.8 yards. And if I wanted to hit the buck, I should have held as though he were 282.8 yards away, not 400. On the level, sighted about 2½ inches

high at 100 yards, that 140-grain .264 bullet would have dropped something like 16 or 17 inches at 400 level yards. At 282.8 yards the bullet would have dropped about four inches. In other words, my bullet skinned right over him.

Now, it should be obvious that the distance must be long and the angle very steep before any correction needs to be made. When these conditions occur, the trajectory is stretched out. In theory, if you were shooting at a buck from a vertical cliff and if he were directly below you, the distance wouldn't matter: Your bullet would travel in a straight line. But wait—remember that the path of your

The uphill/downhill factor is always present, but with a centerfire rifle it isn't significant enough to worry about it until you have a long shot, a very steep angle, or a combination of both. Then it becomes just one more factor that you must consider.

Mountains are steep and mountain game is often taken at some range, a combination of factors that get you in trouble with uphill/downhill angles. I figured it right on this Marco Polo argali.

bullet and your line of sight aren't exactly parallel; we've tilted the barrel slightly upward to force the bullet's path to cross the line of sight.

So if you have the misfortune to shoot at an animal almost directly above or below you, keep in mind that your bullet will cross the line of sight at short range, as usual—but it may never cross it again because of the stretching out of the vertical trajectory. Even at a modest distance like 200 yards, on a near-vertical shot I would hold a couple of inches below where I wanted to hit.

How do you figure the angles in the mountains? Well, you really can't. Few of us carry surveyor's equipment with us. And it's not necessary to be able to figure an angle exactly or know its exact effect. You do need to remember that it makes a difference, and when the distance starts getting long and the angle becomes steep, aim a bit lower than you normally would. If your rifle is accurate and your position steady, the size of an animal's vital area should be sufficient to ensure a solid hit at

sensible shooting distances if you give this angle question a passing bit of attention.

Most of the areas we have discussed in this chapter and the previous one are quite critical to the ability to hit game. Range estimation is the most important, but if you consistently ignore wind drift and steep angles, you will surely come to grief eventually.

Now let's talk about a couple of worrisome subjects that are most assuredly not critical. Hunters come in all shapes and sizes. Some are just natural-born worriers, and over the years I've received quite a few letters asking about the effects of altitude and temperature on trajectory.

Perhaps I shouldn't make light of these concerns, for the letter writers are dead right: Altitude above sea level and air temperature do influence the ballistics of your hunting cartridge. But the horror stories circulated about these effects are just that, and I suspect they've been used as excuses for missing often enough that a lot of folks believe them.

With outfitter Kirk Kelso behind me on the big binocular, I took this position to shoot my desert sheep. The distance on the rangefinder was 334 yards, but look at the angle. The actual drop was somewhat less, and I held accordingly and made the shot.

Air is "thinner" at high altitude. That's a fact. Thus it follows that air resistance to the path of a bullet is less. That's also a fact. Tremendous increases in elevation will have the effect of stretching out your trajectory slightly. If you travel from sea level to Nepal to hunt blue sheep at 18,000 feet, your rifle will indeed shoot a bit flatter than you're used to. But if you travel from sea level to, say, elk country at 4,000 to 7,000 feet elevation, the difference might be there—but it's unlikely you'll notice it.

Incidentally, the reverse would be true as well. If you live on top of Pike's Peak and travel to Oregon to hunt blacktails on the coast, chances are your rifle won't shoot quite as flat as it did at home. There are so many more significant factors, however, that a change in elevation isn't one to worry about.

Far more important is the necessity of checking the zero on any hunting rifle after traveling a great distance—whether you have changed elevation or

not—especially if you use commercial transportation of any kind. Your ability to hit game is in much more danger from the airline baggage-smashers than from any change in elevation!

Temperature is less significant than altitude. Extremely low (and extremely high) temperatures do indeed have an effect on the combustion speed of propellant powders. In extreme cold the burning rate is a bit slower, and the bullet will travel a bit slower; the reverse is true at very high temperatures. The surface of the earth gets neither cold enough nor hot enough, however, to make a noticeable difference in the field under any but the most unusual circumstances.

One warning, though: Ammunition should not be left out in direct, hot sunlight. Air temperature won't make a noticeable difference, but metal-cased cartridges roasted in hot sunshine can become very hot indeed, in more ways than one. It would be most unusual for an unsafe situation

My desert bighorn was taken with a .300 H&H firing a 150-grain bullet pushed very fast. The distance was 334 yards, not excessive for the rifle or load, but the uphill angle was severe, so I cut down the holdover and hit the ram perfectly. I haven't always remembered to do this.

to develop—but it's possible, especially if you start out with handloads a bit on the warm side pressure-wise.

How much difference does air temperature make? Well, if you sight your rifle in at about 70 degrees Fahrenheit and then travel to the Arctic to hunt muskox at minus 30 degrees, you can count on losing about 100 feet per second. For a normal mid- to high-velocity load, that equates to something like three to four percent—nothing to worry about. Moving from a temperate or cool climate to a very hot area is a greater consideration, not from the standpoint of trajectory but from that of firearm functioning.

My load development for an African hunt is usually done in 50 to 60 degrees weather, and I know that I could

have 90 to 100 degrees middays over there. The last thing you need is sticky extraction caused by a bit of unexpected pressure, so I don't handload to the top of the charts for African hunting; I make sure there's a bit of room for unexpected pressure just in case. With factory loads there's absolutely no worry; plenty of safety margin is built in.

Check your rifle's zero when you change location, climate, and altitude as a matter of routine. This ritual is a good basic check and will alert you to genuine problems such as a scope getting knocked out of alignment—which will shift things much more than any climatic change anywhere on earth possibly can.

Data for Small and Medium Centerfire Rifle Cartridges

.17 Remington

The .17 Remington was introduced in 1971. While it is based on the .222 Remington case, this design isn't just a .222 necked to .17 caliber. The case body was lengthened and the neck shortened to provide just a little more case volume than a simple necking down of the .222 would have created. The .17 Remington has never become as popular as some of its larger cousins, the .222 and .223 for instance, and as a result there are only two factory loadings available for this caliber.

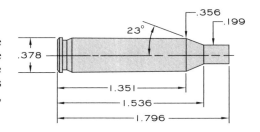

Relative Recoil Factor = 0.45

Specifications

Controlling Agency for Standardization of this Ammunition: SAAMI

Bullet Weight Grains	Velocity fps	Maximum Average Pressure	
		Copper Crusher	Transducer
25	4,000	52,000 cup	N/S

Standard barrel for velocity testing: 24 inches long—1 turn in 9-inch twist

Availability

Remington 20-grain Accutip BT (PRA17RA)

G1 Ballistic Coefficient = 0.185

Distance • Yards	Muzzle	100	200	300	400	500	600	800	1000
Velocity • fps	4250	3594	3028	2529	2081	1684	1352	983	826
Energy • Ft-lbs	802	574	407	284	192	126	81	43	30
Taylor KO Index	2.1	1.8	1.5	1.2	1.0	0.8	0.7	0.5	0.4
Path • Inches	-1.5	+0.6	0.0	-4.4	-14.4	-32.8	-64.3	-197.3	-463.4
Wind Drift • Inches	0.0	1.1	4.7	11.4	22.0	37.8	60.5	129.5	222.5

Remington 25-grain Hornady Hollow Point (R17R2)

G1 Ballistic Coefficient = 0.151

Distance • Yards	Muzzle	100	200	300	400	500	600	800	1000
Velocity • fps	4040	3284	2644	2086	1606	1235	1020	818	688
Energy • Ft-lbs	906	599	388	242	143	85	58	37	26
Taylor KO Index	2.5	2.0	1.6	1.3	1.0	0.8	0.6	0.5	0.4
Path • Inches	-1.5	+0.9	0.0	-6.0	-20.3	-49.2	-102.4	-310.2	-699.4
Wind Drift • Inches	0.0	1.4	6.3	15.7	31.5	56.2	90.6	181.2	296.2

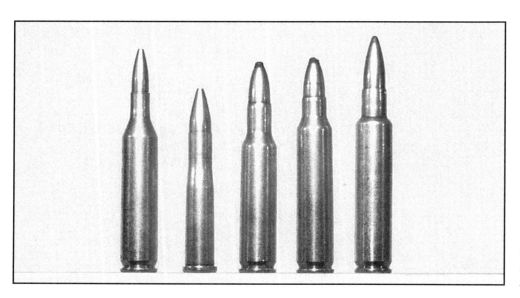

(Left to right) .17 Remington, .22 Hornet, .222 Remington, .223 Remington, .222 Remington Magnum.

.204 Ruger

Though the .17 centerfires have been around for quite a while, there have not been any factory 5mm's until 2004. There have been .20 caliber and 5mm (pretty much the same thing) for 50 years or so, but no factory wanted to go to the trouble. Ruger induced Hornady to design and develop this round, which has already been chambered in two Ruger rifle styles. The cartridge designer started with the .222 Remington Magnum length rather than the .223 length, and that resulted in a case with enough volume to give this cartridge the second highest advertised muzzle velocity on the market today.

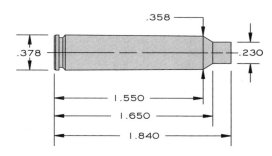

Relative Recoil Factor = 0.60

Specifications:

Controlling Agency for Standardization of this Ammunition: SAAMI

Bullet Weight Grains	Velocity fps	Maximum Average Pressure	
		Copper Crusher	Transducer
32 grain	4075	N/S	57,500 psi

Standard barrel for velocity testing: 24 inches long—1 turn in 12-inch twist

Availability

Hornady 32-grain V-MAX (83204)   G1 Ballistic Coefficient = 0.203

Distance • Yards	Muzzle	100	200	300	400	500	600	800	1000
Velocity • fps	4225	3632	3114	2652	2234	1856	1505	1064	883
Energy • Ft-lbs	1268	937	689	500	355	245	161	80	55
Taylor KO Index	3.9	3.4	2.9	2.1	1.5	1.7	1.4	1.0	0.8
Path • Inches	-1.5	+0.6	0.0	-4.2	-13.5	-30.0	-56.9	-164.1	-393.7
Wind Drift • Inches	0.0	1.0	4.3	10.2	19.6	33.3	52.6	112.6	197.6

Remington 32-grain AccuTip-V (PRA204A)   G1 Ballistic Coefficient = 0.207

Distance • Yards	Muzzle	100	200	300	400	500	600	800	1000
Velocity • fps	4225	3632	3114	2652	2234	1856	1529	1077	890
Energy • Ft-lbs	1268	937	689	500	355	245	166	82	56
Taylor KO Index	3.9	3.4	2.9	2.1	1.5	1.7	1.4	1.0	0.8
Path • Inches	-1.5	+0.6	0.0	-4.1	-13.1	-28.9	-56.6	-166.3	-393.7
Wind Drift • Inches	0.0	1.0	4.2	10.1	19.2	32.6	51.5	110.2	194.2

Winchester 34-grain Hollow Point (X204R)   G1 Ballistic Coefficient = 0.168

Distance • Yards	Muzzle	100	200	300	400	500	600	800	1000
Velocity • fps	4025	3339	2751	2232	1775	1393	1119	878	743
Energy • Ft-lbs	1223	842	571	376	238	146	95	58	42
Taylor KO Index	4.0	3.3	2.7	2.2	1.8	1.4	1.1	0.9	0.7
Path • Inches	-1.5	+0.8	0.0	-5.5	-18.1	-42.0	-86.8	-265.6	-603.9
Wind Drift • Inches	0.0	1.3	5.6	13.8	27.3	47.9	77.4	159.5	264.5

Hornady 40-grain V-MAX (83206)   G1 Ballistic Coefficient = 0.255

Distance • Yards	Muzzle	100	200	300	400	500	600	800	1000
Velocity • fps	3900	3451	3046	2677	2336	2021	1731	1264	1007
Energy • Ft-lbs	1351	1058	824	636	485	363	266	142	90
Taylor KO Index	4.6	4.0	3.6	3.1	2.7	2.4	2.0	1.5	1.2
Path • Inches	-1.5	+0.7	0.0	-4.5	-13.9	-29.7	-54.1	-142.4	-318.6
Wind Drift • Inches	0.0	0.9	3.6	8.6	16.2	27.0	41.7	86.4	154.2

Remington 40-grain AccuTip (PRA204B)   G1 Ballistic Coefficient = 0.257

Distance • Yards	Muzzle	100	200	300	400	500	600	800	1000
Velocity • fps	3900	3451	3046	2677	2336	2021	1731	1264	1007
Energy • Ft-lbs	1351	1058	824	636	485	363	266	142	90
Taylor KO Index	4.5	4.0	3.6	3.1	2.7	2.4	2.0	1.5	1.2
Path • Inches	-1.5	+0.7	0.0	-4.3	-13.2	-28.1	-54.2	-144.7	-327.9
Wind Drift • Inches	0.0	0.9	3.6	8.6	16.2	26.9	41.6	86.2	154.0

.22 Hornet

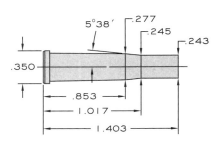

The oldest of the centerfire .22s in use today is the .22 Hornet. The Hornet was developed from an old black-powder number called the .22 WCF (Winchester Center Fire). Winchester introduced the Hornet as a factory cartridge in the early 1930s. The initial success of the .22 Hornet probably came because there wasn't any competition. Hornets have a very mixed reputation for accuracy. Some guns do very well while others are terrible. Part of this seems to be the result of some strange chambering practices in factory guns produced in the U.S. Unlike the .218 Bee, the Hornet appears to be showing some new life. It's still an excellent little varmint cartridge when fired from a "good" gun, as long as the range is limited to about 200 yards.

Relative Recoil Factor = 0.54

Specifications

Controlling Agency for Standardization of this Ammunition: SAAMI

Bullet Weight Grains	Velocity fps	Maximum Average Pressure	
		Copper Crusher	Transducer
45	2,655	43,000 cup	N/S
46	2,655	43,000 cup	N/S

Standard barrel for velocity testing: 24 inches long—1 turn in 16-inch twist

Availability

Winchester 34-grain Jacketed Hollow Point (S22H1)
G1 Ballistic Coefficient = 0.097

Distance • Yards	Muzzle	100	200	300	400	500	600	800	1000
Velocity • fps	3050	2132	1415	1017	852	741	650	502	384
Energy • Ft-lbs	700	343	151	78	55	41	32	19	11
Taylor KO Index	3.3	2.3	1.5	1.1	0.9	0.8	0.7	0.5	0.4
Path • Inches	-1.5	+3.3	0.0	-21.2	-75.8	-178.2	-323.7	-873.3	-1956
Wind Drift • Inches	0.0	3.4	16.5	44.1	83.9	113.2	192.2	343.0	549.4

Hornady 35-grain V-MAX (8302)
G1 Ballistic Coefficient = 0.110

Distance • Yards	Muzzle	100	200	300	400	500	600	800	1000
Velocity • fps	3100	2278	1601	1135	929	811	717	571	453
Energy • Ft-lbs	747	403	199	100	67	51	40	25	16
Taylor KO Index	3.5	2.6	1.8	1.3	1.0	0.9	0.8	0.6	0.5
Path • Inches	-1.5	+2.8	0.0	-16.9	-60.4	-144.7	-271.0	-722.6	-1572
Wind Drift • Inches	0.0	2.9	13.5	36.2	71.3	115.5	168.0	299.4	473.2

Remington 35-grain Pointed Soft Point (PRA22HNA)
G1 Ballistic Coefficient = 0.109

Distance • Yards	Muzzle	100	200	300	400	500	600	800	1000
Velocity • fps	3100	2271	1591	1127	924	806	712	566	447
Energy • Ft-lbs	747	401	197	99	66	51	39	25	16
Taylor KO Index	3.5	2.5	1.8	1.3	1.0	0.9	0.8	0.6	0.5
Path • Inches	-1.5	+3.0	0.00	-17.6	-62.5	-144.4	-273.8	-730.9	-1592
Wind Drift • Inches	0.0	2.9	13.7	36.6	72.0	116.6	169.4	302.0	477.7

Remington 45-grain Pointed Soft Point (R22HN1)
G1 Ballistic Coefficient = 0.130

Distance • Yards	Muzzle	100	200	300	400	500	600	800	1000
Velocity • fps	2690	2042	1502	1128	948	840	756	622	513
Energy • Ft-lbs	723	417	225	127	90	70	57	39	26
Taylor KO Index	3.9	2.9	2.2	1.6	1.4	1.2	1.1	0.9	0.7
Path • Inches	-1.5	+3.6	0.0	20.0	-66.9	-148.6	-275.7	-702.5	-1458
Wind Drift • Inches	0.0	2.9	13.5	34.8	66.7	106.4	153.3	268.4	416.3

Winchester 45-grain Soft Point (X22H1)
G1 Ballistic Coefficient = 0.130

Distance • Yards	Muzzle	100	200	300	400	500	600	800	1000
Velocity • fps	2690	2042	1502	1128	948	840	756	622	513
Energy • Ft-lbs	723	417	225	127	90	70	57	39	26
Taylor KO Index	3.9	2.9	2.2	1.6	1.4	1.2	1.1	0.9	0.7
Path • Inches	-1.5	+3.6	0.0	-20.0	-66.9	-148.6	-275.7	-702.5	-1458
Wind Drift • Inches	0.0	2.9	13.5	34.8	66.7	106.4	153.3	268.4	416.3

Hirtenberger 45-grain Sierra Soft Point
G1 Ballistic Coefficient = 0.166

Distance • Yards	Muzzle	100	200	300	400	500	600	800	1000
Velocity • fps	2526	2029	1597	1256	1044	927	845	719	618
Energy • Ft-lbs	639	412	256	158	109	86	71	52	38
Taylor KO Index	3.6	2.9	2.3	1.8	1.5	1.3	1.2	1.0	0.9
Path • Inches	-1.5	+3.6	0.0	-17.6	-57.8	-128.9	-236.8	-590.6	-1186
Wind Drift • Inches	0.0	2.2	9.8	24.7	47.7	77.4	112.3	218.9	335.8

Sellier & Bellot 45-grain Soft Point (SBA22002)
G1 Ballistic Coefficient = 0.102

Distance • Yards	Muzzle	100	200	300	400	500	600	800	1000
Velocity • fps	2346	1707	1242	904	782	688	608	474	366
Energy • Ft-lbs	547	289	153	81	61	47	37	22	13
Taylor KO Index	3.4	2.5	1.8	1.3	1.1	1.0	0.9	0.7	0.5
Path • Inches	-1.5	+6.4	0.0	-34.2	-107.3	-231.3	-421.5	-1087	-2357
Wind Drift • Inches	0.0	4.8	22.5	53.5	94.0	143.6	202.8	354.7	563.5

Remington 45-grain Hollow Point (R22HN2)
G1 Ballistic Coefficient = 0.130

Distance • Yards	Muzzle	100	200	300	400	500	600	800	1000
Velocity • fps	2690	2042	1502	1128	948	840	756	622	513
Energy • Ft-lbs	723	417	225	127	90	70	57	39	26
Taylor KO Index	3.9	2.9	2.2	1.6	1.4	1.2	1.1	0.9	0.7
Path • Inches	-1.5	+3.6	0.0	20.0	-66.9	-148.6	-275.7	-702.5	-1458
Wind Drift • Inches	0.0	2.9	13.5	34.8	66.7	106.4	153.3	268.4	416.3

Sellier & Bellot 45-grain FMJ (SBA22001)
G1 Ballistic Coefficient = 0.102

Distance • Yards	Muzzle	100	200	300	400	500	600	800	1000
Velocity • fps	2346	1707	1242	904	782	688	608	474	366
Energy • Ft-lbs	547	289	153	81	61	47	37	22	13
Taylor KO Index	3.4	2.5	1.8	1.3	1.1	1.0	0.9	0.7	0.5
Path • Inches	-1.5	+6.4	0.0	-34.2	-107.3	-231.3	-421.5	-1087	-2357
Wind Drift • Inches	0.0	4.8	22.5	53.5	94.0	143.6	202.8	354.7	563.5

Winchester 46-grain Hollow Point (X22H2)
G1 Ballistic Coefficient = 0.130

Distance • Yards	Muzzle	100	200	300	400	500	600	800	1000
Velocity • fps	2690	2042	1502	1128	948	840	756	622	513
Energy • Ft-lbs	723	417	225	127	90	70	57	39	26
Taylor KO Index	3.9	2.9	2.2	1.6	1.4	1.2	1.1	0.9	0.7
Path • Inches	-1.5	+3.6	0.0	20.0	-66.9	-148.6	-275.7	-702.5	-1458
Wind Drift • Inches	0.0	2.9	13.5	34.8	66.7	106.4	153.3	268.4	416.3

.218 Bee

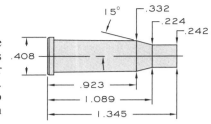

The .218 Bee can be thought of as a slight improvement over the .22 Hornet. Don't be fooled by the .218 designation. This cartridge uses standard 0.224-inch bullets, the same as all other centerfire .22s. Introduced in 1938, the Bee was created from the .25-20 Winchester case (.32-20s can also be used) especially for the Model 65 Winchester (a lever-action rifle). It does have about 30 percent more case capacity than the Hornet, which allows the Bee to get about 50 fps more velocity from its 46-grain bullet. While the Bee could have been an excellent little cartridge in an accurate gun, and has found a following in single-shot guns, the factory loading has just about run out its lifetime, as evidenced by the fact that only Winchester makes a factory loading and only loads a single bullet choice. Today, there are just too many good centerfire .22s to spend very much time, money, or effort to build up a new rifle chambered for this cartridge, although TC barrels are available.

Relative Recoil Factor = 0.56

Specifications

Controlling Agency for Standardization of this Ammunition: SAAMI

Bullet Weight Grains	Velocity fps	Maximum Average Pressure	
		Copper Crusher	Transducer
46	2,725	40,000 cup	N/S

Standard barrel for velocity testing: 24 inches long—1 turn in 16-inch twist

Availability

Winchester 46-grain Hollow Point (X218B)
G1 Ballistic Coefficient = 0.130

Distance • Yards	Muzzle	100	200	300	400	500	600	800	1000
Velocity • fps	2760	2102	1550	1156	961	850	763	628	518
Energy • Ft-lbs	778	451	245	136	94	74	60	40	27
Taylor KO Index	4.1	3.1	2.3	1.7	1.4	1.3	1.1	0.9	0.8
Path • Inches	-1.5	+3.4	0.0	-18.8	-63.6	-142.5	-265.4	-680.2	-1417
Wind Drift • Inches	0.0	2.8	13.0	33.6	65.4	104.4	151.3	265.9	413.0

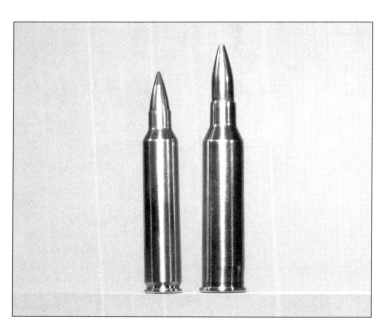

(Left to right) .204 Ruger and the .225 Winchester.

.221 Remington Fireball

When Remington introduced the XP-100 bolt-action pistol in 1962, they wanted a new cartridge to complete the package. The .221 Remington Fireball is that cartridge. It is noticeably shorter than the .222 Remington (0.3 inches to be exact) and, when compared with the .222, has the reduced performance you might expect from its smaller volume. The combination of the XP-100 pistol and the .221 Remington Fireball cartridge developed a reputation for fine accuracy. This cartridge dropped out of Remington's catalog a number of years ago, but in 2004, Remington decided to reopen the production line. If you have a .221 and are nearly out of ammo, you might seriously consider stocking up before production is stopped again.

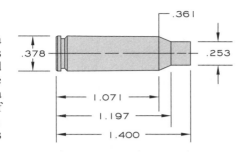

Relative Recoil Factor = 0.67

Specifications:

Controlling Agency for Standardization of this Ammunition: SAAMI

Bullet Weight Grains	Velocity fps	Maximum Average Pressure	
		Copper Crusher	Transducer
50	2520	52,000 cup	N/S

Standard barrel for velocity testing: 10.5 inches long—1 turn in 12-inch twist*

*The ballistic data shown here were taken in a 24-inch barrel.

Availability

Remington 50-grain AccuTip BT (PRA221FB)

G1 Ballistic Coefficient = 0.238

Distance • Yards	Muzzle	100	200	300	400	500	600	800	1000
Velocity • fps	2995	2605	2247	1918	1622	1368	1170	9554	837
Energy • Ft-lbs	996	753	560	408	292	208	152	101	78
Taylor KO Index	4.8	4.2	3.6	3.1	2.6	2.2	1.9	1.5	1.3
Path • Inches	-1.5	+1.8	0.0	-8.8	-27.1	-59.0	-110.2	-295.4	-619.5
Wind Drift • Inches	0.0	1.3	5.4	13.2	25.4	43.2	67.2	132.5	215.2

Although small, .22 centerfire cartridges have taken deer. The editors of this book, however, strongly advise against it. (Photo from Ask the Whitetail Guides by J. Y. Jones, Safari Press, 2006)

.222 Remington

The .222 Remington, when introduced in 1950, was a whole new cartridge design. This new cartridge, which was an instant hit, would drive a 50-grain bullet in excess of 3,100 fps. The design combined a rimless 0.378-inch head diameter with a bottlenecked case, a conservative 23-degree shoulder, and a 0.3127-inch neck length to produce a cartridge that had all the elements needed to be superbly accurate. The .222 soon caught on as a varmint rifle and for many years was the caliber of choice in benchrest competitions. Today, its popularity has been somewhat diluted by the .223 Remington (5.56 NATO), which is the U.S. standard infantry cartridge, but the .222 remains an excellent little cartridge. Most of the ammunition manufacturers load for this caliber. There is a wide range of ammunition choices available.

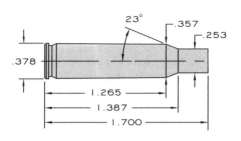

Relative Recoil Factor = 0.74

Specifications

Controlling Agency for Standardization of this Ammunition: SAAMI

Bullet Weight Grains	Velocity fps	Maximum Average Pressure	
		Copper Crusher	Transducer
50–52	3,110	46,000 cup	50,000 psi
55	3,000	46,000 cup	50,000 psi

Standard barrel for velocity testing: 24 inches long—1 turn in 14-inch twist

Availability

Hornady 40-grain V-MAX Moly VX (83113) (Discontinued in 2005)
G1 Ballistic Coefficient = 0.218

Distance • Yards	Muzzle	100	200	300	400	500	600	800	1000
Velocity • fps	3600	3117	2673	2269	1911	1596	1326	1005	859
Energy • Ft-lbs	1151	863	634	457	324	226	156	90	66
Taylor KO Index	4.6	4.0	3.4	2.9	2.4	2.0	1.7	1.3	1.1
Path • Inches	-1.5	+1.1	0.0	-6.1	-18.9	-41.2	-78.1	-222.1	-495.6
Wind Drift • Inches	0.0	1.1	4.7	11.4	22.0	37.5	59.3	123.1	208.0

Federal 40-grain Nosler Ballistic Tip (P222C)
G1 Ballistic Coefficient = 0.218

Distance • Yards	Muzzle	100	200	300	400	500	600	800	1000
Velocity • fps	3450	3000	2570	2190	1840	1530	1279	969	851
Energy • Ft-lbs	1055	790	585	425	300	210	145	87	64
Taylor KO Index	5.5	4.8	4.1	3.5	2.9	2.4	2.0	1.6	1.4
Path • Inches	-1.5	+1.2	0.0	-6.5	-20.4	-44.7	-85.2	-239.6	-526.5
Wind Drift • Inches	0.0	1.2	4.9	11.9	23.0	39.1	61.6	126.6	211.6

Winchester 40-grain Ballistic Silvertip (SBST222)
G1 Ballistic Coefficient = 0.221

Distance • Yards	Muzzle	100	200	300	400	500	600	800	1000
Velocity • fps	3370	2915	2503	2127	1786	1487	1248	976	843
Energy • Ft-lbs	1009	755	556	402	283	196	138	85	63
Taylor KO Index	4.3	3.7	3.2	2.7	2.3	1.9	1.6	1.2	1.1
Path • Inches	-1.5	+1.3	0.0	-6.9	-21.5	-47.2	-90.0	-251.7	-546.5
Wind Drift • Inches	0.0	1.2	5.1	12.3	23.8	40.6	63.5	129.5	215.0

Hirtenberger 50-grain Sierra SP (82200428)
G1 Ballistic Coefficient = 0.230

Distance • Yards	Muzzle	100	200	300	400	500	600	800	1000
Velocity • fps	3231	2806	2418	2063	1740	1458	1231	975	846
Energy • Ft-lbs	1160	875	649	472	336	236	168	106	80
Taylor KO Index	5.2	4.5	3.9	3.3	2.8	2.3	2.0	1.6	1.4
Path • Inches	-1.5	+1.5	0.0	-7.5	-23.2	-50.9	-95.7	-263.6	-566.9
Wind Drift • Inches	0.0	1.1	4.6	11.2	21.6	36.8	57.6	129.3	213.3

Norma 50-grain Soft Point (15711)
G1 Ballistic Coefficient = 0.185

Distance • Yards	Muzzle	100	200	300	400	500	600	800	1000
Velocity • fps	3199	2679	2215	1800	1439	1171	1010	840	726
Energy • Ft-lbs	1136	797	545	360	230	152	113	78	59
Taylor KO Index	5.1	4.3	3.5	2.9	2.3	1.9	1.6	1.3	1.2
Path • Inches	-1.5	+1.7	0.0	-9.0	-29.1	-67.0	-113.0	-361.3	-765.4
Wind Drift • Inches	0.0	1.6	6.8	16.8	33.2	57.6	89.9	172.4	274.9

Sellier & Bellot 50-grain SP (SBA22202)
G1 Ballistic Coefficient = 0.185

Distance • Yards	Muzzle	100	200	300	400	500	600	800	1000
Velocity • fps	3215	2655	2193	1811	1457	1186	1021	849	734
Energy • Ft-lbs	1147	782	534	364	236	156	116	80	60
Taylor KO Index	5.1	4.2	3.5	2.9	2.3	1.9	1.6	1.4	1.2
Path • Inches	-1.5	+1.7	0.0	-8.8	-28.5	-65.5	-128.2	-353.8	-750.0
Wind Drift • Inches	0.0	1.5	6.6	16.5	32.6	56.6	88.4	126.6	271.2

Federal 50-grain HI-Shok Soft Point (222A)
G1 Ballistic Coefficient = 0.176

Distance • Yards	Muzzle	100	200	300	400	500	600	800	1000
Velocity • fps	3140	2600	2120	1700	1350	1110	971	813	700
Energy • Ft-lbs	1095	750	500	320	200	135	105	73	54
Taylor KO Index	5.0	4.2	3.4	2.7	2.2	1.8	1.6	1.3	1.1
Path • Inches	-1.5	+1.9	0.0	-9.7	-31.6	-71.3	-145.1	-394.4	-829.3
Wind Drift • Inches	0.0	1.7	7.3	18.3	36.3	62.9	97.4	183.4	290.0

Remington 50-grain Pointed Soft Point (R222R1)
G1 Ballistic Coefficient = 0.176

Distance • Yards	Muzzle	100	200	300	400	500	600	800	1000
Velocity • fps	3140	2600	2120	1700	1350	1110	971	813	700
Energy • Ft-lbs	1095	750	500	320	200	135	105	73	54
Taylor KO Index	5.0	4.2	3.4	2.7	2.2	1.8	1.6	1.3	1.1
Path • Inches	-1.5	+1.9	0.0	-9.7	-31.6	-71.3	-145.1	-394.4	-829.3
Wind Drift • Inches	0.0	1.7	7.3	18.3	36.3	62.9	97.4	183.4	290.0

Winchester 50-grain Pointed Soft Point (X222R)
G1 Ballistic Coefficient = 0.176

Distance • Yards	Muzzle	100	200	300	400	500	600	800	1000
Velocity • fps	3140	2600	2120	1700	1350	1110	971	813	700
Energy • Ft-lbs	1095	750	500	320	200	135	105	73	54
Taylor KO Index	5.0	4.2	3.4	2.7	2.2	1.8	1.6	1.3	1.1
Path • Inches	-1.5	+1.9	0.0	-9.7	-31.6	-71.3	-145.1	-394.4	-829.3
Wind Drift • Inches	0.0	1.7	7.3	18.3	36.3	62.9	97.4	183.4	290.0

PMC 50-grain Soft Point (222B)
G1 Ballistic Coefficient = 0.221

Distance • Yards	Muzzle	100	200	300	400	500	600	800	1000
Velocity • fps	3050	2617	2226	1873	1565	1312	1121	922	806
Energy • Ft-lbs	1033	761	550	389	272	191	139	94	72
Taylor KO Index	4.9	4.2	3.6	3.0	2.5	2.1	1.8	1.5	1.3
Path • Inches	-1.5	+1.8	0.0	-8.8	-27.6	-61.0	-115.6	-313.5	-659.1
Wind Drift • Inches	0.0	1.4	5.8	14.2	27.6	47.1	73.6	144.0	232.2

Remington 50-grain Hollow Point Power-Lokt (R222R3)
G1 Ballistic Coefficient = 0.188

Distance • Yards	Muzzle	100	200	300	400	500	600	800	1000
Velocity • fps	3140	2635	2182	1777	1432	1172	1015	847	733
Energy • Ft-lbs	1094	771	529	351	228	152	114	80	60
Taylor KO Index	5.0	4.2	3.5	2.8	2.3	1.9	1.6	1.4	1.2
Path • Inches	-1.5	+1.8	0.0	-9.2	-29.8	-67.1	-132.8	-363.1	-764.9
Wind Drift • Inches	0.0	1.6	6.8	16.8	33.1	57.2	89.2	170.3	271.0

Hornady 50-grain V-MAX Moly (83153)
G1 Ballistic Coefficient = 0.238

Distance • Yards	Muzzle	100	200	300	400	500	600	800	1000
Velocity • fps	3140	2743	2380	2045	1740	1471	1251	991	861
Energy • Ft-lbs	1094	835	529	464	336	240	174	109	82
Taylor KO Index	5.0	4.4	3.8	3.3	2.8	2.4	2.0	1.6	1.4
Path • Inches	-1.5	+1.6	0.0	-7.8	-23.9	-51.9	-96.7	-262.2	-560.4
Wind Drift • Inches	0.0	1.2	5.0	12.1	23.3	39.5	61.7	124.4	205.5

Remington 50-grain AccuTip Boat Tail (PRV222RB) G1 Ballistic Coefficient = 0.242

Distance • Yards	Muzzle	100	200	300	400	500	600	800	1000
Velocity • fps	3140	2744	2380	2045	1740	1471	1253	994	864
Energy • Ft-lbs	1094	836	629	464	336	240	174	110	83
Taylor KO Index	5.0	4.4	3.8	3.3	2.8	2.4	2.0	1.6	1.4
Path • Inches	-1.5	+1.5	0.0	-7.8	-23.9	-51.7	-96.6	-261.6	-558.4
Wind Drift • Inches	0.0	1.2	5.0	12.2	23.4	39.6	61.6	124.0	204.8

Remington 50-grain V-Max, Boat Tail (PRV222RA) (Discontinued in 2004) G1 Ballistic Coefficient = 0.242

Distance • Yards	Muzzle	100	200	300	400	500	600	800	1000
Velocity • fps	3140	2744	2380	2045	1740	1471	1253	994	864
Energy • Ft-lbs	1094	836	629	464	336	240	174	110	83
Taylor KO Index	5.0	4.4	3.8	3.3	2.8	2.4	2.0	1.6	1.4
Path • Inches	-1.5	+1.5	0.0	-7.8	-23.9	-51.7	-96.6	-261.6	-558.4
Wind Drift • Inches	0.0	1.2	5.0	12.2	23.4	39.6	61.6	124.0	204.8

Norma 50-grain Full Metal Jacket (15715) G1 Ballistic Coefficient = 0.192

Distance • Yards	Muzzle	100	200	300	400	500	600	800	1000
Velocity • fps	3199	2693	2240	1833	1481	1208	1036	859	744
Energy • Ft-lbs	1136	805	557	373	244	167	119	82	62
Taylor KO Index	5.1	4.3	3.6	2.9	2.4	1.9	1.7	1.4	1.2
Path • Inches	-1.5	+1.6	0.0	-8.7	-28.0	-63.2	-125.4	-345.9	-733.2
Wind Drift • Inches	0.0	1.5	6.5	16.0	31.7	54.8	85.9	165.7	265.1

Sellier & Bellot 50-grain FMJ (SBA22201) G1 Ballistic Coefficient = 0.231

Distance • Yards	Muzzle	100	200	300	400	500	600	800	1000
Velocity • fps	3169	2761	2406	2097	1796	1528	1302	1021	885
Energy • Ft-lbs	1115	847	643	488	358	259	188	116	87
Taylor KO Index	5.1	4.4	3.8	3.4	2.9	2.4	2.1	1.6	1.4
Path • Inches	-1.5	+1.5	0.0	-7.5	-22.9	-49.4	-91.4	-246.4	-528.2
Wind Drift • Inches	0.0	1.1	4.8	11.5	22.1	37.3	58.2	117.7	196.1

Norma 50-grain Full Metal Jacket (15713) G1 Ballistic Coefficient = 0.198

Distance • Yards	Muzzle	100	200	300	400	500	600	800	1000
Velocity • fps	2790	2344	1942	1587	1296	1094	975	830	727
Energy • Ft-lbs	864	610	419	280	187	133	106	77	59
Taylor KO Index	4.5	3.8	3.1	2.5	2.1	1.8	1.6	1.3	1.2
Path • Inches	-1.5	+2.4	0.0	-11.8	37.6	-84.2	-159.8	-427.4	-897.8
Wind Drift • Inches	0.0	1.6	6.8	16.8	33.0	56.2	85.3	157.5	246.2

Hirtenberger 55-grain Nosler SP (82200314) G1 Ballistic Coefficient = 0.250

Distance • Yards	Muzzle	100	200	300	400	500	600	800	1000
Velocity • fps	3068	2687	2340	2018	1724	1465	1252	998	870
Energy • Ft-lbs	1160	883	669	497	363	262	191	122	92
Taylor KO Index	5.4	4.7	4.1	3.6	3.0	2.6	2.2	1.8	1.5
Path • Inches	-1.5	+1.7	0.0	-8.1	-24.8	-53.5	-99.2	-265.9	-563.8
Wind Drift • Inches	0.0	1.2	5.0	12.1	23.2	39.3	61.2	122.5	202.0

PMC 55-grain PSP (222C) G1 Ballistic Coefficient = 0.264

Distance • Yards	Muzzle	100	200	300	400	500	600	800	1000
Velocity • fps	2950	2594	2266	1966	1693	1459	1256	1009	883
Energy • Ft-lbs	1063	822	627	472	350	260	193	124	952
Taylor KO Index	5.2	4.6	4.0	3.5	3.0	2.6	2.2	1.8	1.5
Path • Inches	-1.5	+1.8	0.0	-8.6	-26.2	-56.1	-103.0	-271.4	-568.8
Wind Drift • Inches	0.0	1.2	5.0	12.0	22.9	38.6	59.8	119.0	195.5

Lapua 55-grain Soft Point (4315030) G1 Ballistic Coefficient = 0.184

Distance • Yards	Muzzle	100	200	300	400	500	600	800	1000
Velocity • fps	2890	2402	1968	1581	1273	1070	952	806	699
Energy • Ft-lbs	1020	705	471	305	198	140	111	79	60
Taylor KO Index	5.1	4.2	3.5	2.8	2.2	1.9	1.7	1.4	1.2
Path • Inches	-1.5	+2.3	0.0	-11.5	-37.1	-84.2	-164.2	-431.7	-888.5
Wind Drift • Inches	0.0	1.8	7.8	19.6	38.7	66.0	100.3	184.9	289.2

Hirtenberger 55-grain Nosler Ballistic Tip (82200470)

G1 Ballistic Coefficient = 0.274

Distance • Yards	Muzzle	100	200	300	400	500	600	800	1000
Velocity • fps	3068	2721	2399	2100	1823	1574	1357	1063	919
Energy • Ft-lbs	1150	904	703	538	406	302	225	138	103
Taylor KO Index	5.4	4.8	4.2	3.7	3.2	2.8	2.4	1.9	1.6
Path • Inches	-1.5	+1.6	0.0	-7.7	-23.3	-49.6	-90.5	-237.4	-504.4
Wind Drift • Inches	0.0	1.1	4.5	10.8	20.6	34.6	53.6	108.1	181.2

Federal 55-grain Full Metal Jacket Boat Tail (222B)

G1 Ballistic Coefficient = 0.340

Distance • Yards	Muzzle	100	200	300	400	500	600	800	1000
Velocity • fps	3020	2740	2480	2230	1990	1780	1581	1251	1045
Energy • Ft-lbs	1115	915	750	610	485	385	305	191	133
Taylor KO Index	5.3	4.8	4.4	3.9	3.5	3.1	2.8	2.2	1.6
Path • Inches	-1.5	+1.6	0.0	-7.7	-22.7	-45.3	-78.7	-194.2	-402.3
Wind Drift • Inches	0.0	0.9	3.7	8.7	16.2	26.8	40.7	81.1	139.3

Lapua 55-grain Full Metal Jacket (4315020)

G1 Ballistic Coefficient = 0.218

Distance • Yards	Muzzle	100	200	300	400	500	600	800	1000
Velocity • fps	2890	2475	2096	1752	1455	1218	1058	889	780
Energy • Ft-lbs	1020	748	536	375	259	181	137	97	74
Taylor KO Index	5.1	4.4	3.7	3.1	2.6	2.1	1.9	1.6	1.4
Path • Inches	-1.5	+2.1	0.0	-10.1	-31.7	-69.9	-133.9	-355.6	-734.8
Wind Drift • Inches	0.0	1.5	6.4	15.7	30.6	52.1	80.6	153.8	244.3

Norma 62-grain Soft Point (15716)

G1 Ballistic Coefficient = 0.214

Distance • Yards	Muzzle	100	200	300	400	500	600	800	1000
Velocity • fps	2887	2464	2078	1731	1426	1191	1039	875	767
Energy • Ft-lbs	1148	836	595	413	280	195	149	105	81
Taylor KO Index	5.7	4.9	4.1	3.4	2.8	2.4	2.1	1.7	1.5
Path • Inches	-1.5	+2.1	0.0	-10.3	-32.6	-72.7	-138.2	-367.0	-758.0
Wind Drift • Inches	0.0	1.5	6.6	16.2	31.6	54.0	83.4	158.4	251.1

Well-known booking agent Jack Atcheson Jr. with a large Montana elk. (Photo from *Ask the Elk Guides* by J. Y. Jones, Safari Press, 2005)

.222 Remington Magnum

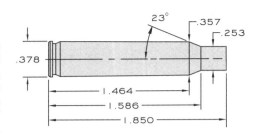

Remington's .222 Magnum is a cartridge that never really had a good chance to become popular. The .222 RM started life as an experimental military cartridge based on the .222 Remington case. Remington began to load for this "improved" .222 in 1958, but the .223 Remington, which was adopted as a military cartridge, signed its death warrant in 1964. There's nothing wrong with the .222 Remington Magnum as a cartridge; in fact, the slightly greater volume and longer neck make it a bit "better" than the .223 on a technical basis. But historically, a cartridge that's almost identical to a standard military cartridge is going nowhere. While Hirtenberger is still making three loads (using American bullets) for this cartridge, the last catalog listing by Remington for its .222 Magnum was in 1997.

Relative Recoil Factor = 0.79

Specifications

Controlling Agency for Standardization of this Ammunition: SAAMI

Bullet Weight Grains	Velocity fps	Maximum Average Pressure	
		Copper Crusher	Transducer
55	3,215	50,000 cup	N/S

Standard barrel for velocity testing: 24 inches long—1 turn in 14-inch twist

Availability

Hirtenberger 55-grain Nosler SP (82200317)
G1 Ballistic Coefficient = 0.235

Distance • Yards	Muzzle	100	200	300	400	500	600	800	1000
Velocity • fps	3281	2859	2475	2122	1800	1514	1278	999	864
Energy • Ft-lbs	1315	999	748	550	396	280	200	122	91
Taylor KO Index	5.8	5.0	4.4	3.7	3.2	2.7	2.2	1.8	1.6
Path • Inches	-1.5	+1.4	0	-7.1	-22.1	-48.0	-90.0	-247.4	-535.6
Wind Drift • Inches	0.0	1.2	4.9	11.7	22.8	38.7	60.7	123.4	205.5

Hirtenberger 55-grain Sierra SP (82200447)
G1 Ballistic Coefficient = 0.209

Distance • Yards	Muzzle	100	200	300	400	500	600	800	1000
Velocity • fps	3133	2677	2263	1889	1558	1286	1096	902	786
Energy • Ft-lbs	1199	875	626	436	296	202	147	99	75
Taylor KO Index	5.5	4.7	4.0	3.3	2.7	2.3	1.9	1.6	1.4
Path • Inches	-1.5	+1.7	0	-8.6	-27.1	-60.6	-116.2	-319.0	-674.8
Wind Drift • Inches	0.0	1.4	6.0	14.7	28.6	49.2	77.0	150.1	242.7

Hirtenberger 55-grain Nosler Ballistic Tip (82200471)
G1 Ballistic Coefficient = 0.264

Distance • Yards	Muzzle	100	200	300	400	500	600	800	1000
Velocity • fps	3281	2904	2557	2235	1937	1666	1428	1092	930
Energy • Ft-lbs	1315	1030	798	610	458	339	249	146	106
Taylor KO Index	5.8	5.1	4.5	4.1	3.4	2.9	2.5	1.9	1.6
Path • Inches	-1.5	+1.3	0	-6.7	-20.4	-43.5	-79.6	-211.8	-459.6
Wind Drift • Inches	0.0	1.0	4.3	10.3	19.6	32.9	51.1	104.5	177.9

.223 Remington

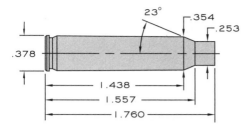

When the .223 Remington cartridge was adopted by the U.S. Army as M193 5.56mm Ball ammunition in 1964, that action ensured that the .223 would become the most popular .22 centerfire on the list. Every cartridge that becomes a U.S. Army standard, with the possible exception of the .30 Carbine, has gone on to a long and useful commercial life. Just look at the .45-70, the .45 Colt, the .30-06, and the .45 ACP. The .223 case has been "necked" to every possible size, the TCU series of cartridges and the .30 Whisper being examples.

Even without the military application, the .223 Remington had plenty of potential to become popular. Based on the .222 and the .222 Remington Magnum, the .223 provides an excellent balance of accuracy and performance with good case and barrel life. It has become the standard by which all other .22s are judged.

Most of the guns chambered for the .223 have a barrel twist of 1 turn in 14 inches. That twist provides enough stability for bullets up to 55 grains but begins to be marginal above that level. Today there are bullets available in loaded ammunition weighing as much as 77 grains (80-grain bullets for the handloader). It takes a faster twist to stabilize those heavier bullets, and some gunmakers offer barrel twists as fast as 1 turn in 7 inches in .223 caliber. If you have one of the fast-twist barrels, you may have problems with the very light varmint loads. The high velocities attained with the quick twist combine to produce a bullet spin rate that can literally rip thin-jacketed bullets apart. Guns equipped with quick-twist barrels will usually do better with 55-grain and heavier bullets.

Relative Recoil Factor = 0.80

Specifications

Controlling Agency for Standardization of this Ammunition: SAAMI

Bullet Weight Grains	Velocity fps	Maximum Average Pressure Copper Crusher	Transducer
53	3,305	52,000 cup	55,000 psi
55	3,215	52,000 cup	55,000 psi
60	3,200	52,000 cup	55,000 psi
64	3,000	52,000 cup	55,000 psi

Standard barrel for velocity testing: 24 inches long—1 turn in 12-inch twist

Availability

PMC 40-grain Non-Toxic Frangible (223HRA)
G1 Ballistic Coefficient = 0.112

Distance • Yards	Muzzle	100	200	300	400	500	600	800	1000
Velocity • fps	3500	2606	1871	1315	1009	865	764	610	488
Energy • Ft-lbs	1088	603	311	154	90	66	52	32	21
Taylor KO Index	4.5	3.3	2.4	1.7	1.3	1.1	1.0	0.8	0.6
Path • Inches	-1.5	+1.9	0.0	-12.3	-45.9	-111.7	-218.5	-602.0	-1328
Wind Drift • Inches	0.0	2.4	11.0	29.6	61.0	102.8	152.8	277.7	441.5

Cor-Bon 40-grain BlitzKing (22340BK/20)
G1 Ballistic Coefficient = 0.200

Distance • Yards	Muzzle	100	200	300	400	500	600	800	1000
Velocity • fps	3800	3248	2761	2323	1927	1577	1291	976	831
Energy • Ft-lbs	1283	937	677	479	330	221	148	85	61
Taylor KO Index	4.9	4.2	3.5	3.0	2.5	2.0	1.7	1.2	1.1
Path • Inches	-1.5	+0.9	0.0	-5.5	-17.6	-39.4	-76.1	-223.5	-505.8
Wind Drift • Inches	0.0	1.2	4.9	11.8	22.9	39.3	62.5	130.8	220.8

Hornady 40-grain V-Max (8325)—Moly VX (83253)
G1 Ballistic Coefficient = 0.218

Distance • Yards	Muzzle	100	200	300	400	500	600	800	1000
Velocity • fps	3800	3305	2845	2424	2044	1715	1421	1045	882
Energy • Ft-lbs	1282	970	719	502	371	261	179	97	69
Taylor KO Index	4.9	4.2	3.6	3.1	2.6	2.2	1.8	1.3	1.1
Path • Inches	-1.5	+0.9	0.0	-5.2	-16.4	-36.0	-68.3	-195.5	-445.2
Wind Drift • Inches	0.0	1.0	4.4	10.7	20.4	34.7	54.8	115.2	198.2

Cor-Bon 40-grain JHP (22340/20)

G1 Ballistic Coefficient = 0.180

Distance • Yards	Muzzle	100	200	300	400	500	600	800	1000
Velocity • fps	3800	3191	2660	2186	1765	1409	1148	903	771
Energy • Ft-lbs	1283	905	629	425	277	176	117	72	53
Taylor KO Index	4.9	4.1	3.4	2.8	2.3	1.8	1.5	1.2	1.0
Path • Inches	-1.5	+1.0	0.0	-6.0	-19.4	-44.6	-88.7	-264.1	-591.3
Wind Drift • Inches	0.0	1.3	5.5	13.5	26.5	46.2	74.0	151.6	250.8

Federal 40-grain Nosler Ballistic Tip (P223P)

G1 Ballistic Coefficient = 0.221

Distance • Yards	Muzzle	100	200	300	400	500	600	800	1000
Velocity • fps	3700	3210	2770	2370	2010	1680	1396	1038	880
Energy • Ft-lbs	1215	915	680	500	360	250	173	96	69
Taylor KO Index	4.7	4.1	3.5	3.0	2.6	2.2	1.8	1.3	1.1
Path • Inches	-1.5	+1.0	0.0	-8.0	-17.3	-37.8	-71.6	-203.4	-458.9
Wind Drift • Inches	0.0	1.1	4.5	10.8	20.8	35.3	55.6	116.3	199.0

Winchester 40-grain Ballistic Silvertip (SBST223A)

G1 Ballistic Coefficient = 0.202

Distance • Yards	Muzzle	100	200	300	400	500	600	800	1000
Velocity • fps	3700	3166	2693	2245	1879	1540	1262	966	826
Energy • Ft-lbs	1216	891	644	456	314	211	141	83	61
Taylor KO Index	4.7	4.1	3.5	2.9	2.4	2.0	1.6	1.2	1.1
Path • Inches	-1.5	+1.0	0.0	-5.8	-18.4	-40.9	-80.4	-234.4	-525.3
Wind Drift • Inches	0.0	1.2	5.0	12.1	23.5	40.3	64.1	133.2	223.4

Black Hills 40-grain Nosler Ballistic Tip (M223N11)

G1 Ballistic Coefficient = 0.221

Distance • Yards	Muzzle	100	200	300	400	500	600	800	1000
Velocity • fps	3600	3120	2689	2297	1939	1619	1348	1018	869
Energy • Ft-lbs	1150	865	643	469	334	233	162	92	67
Taylor KO Index	4.6	4.0	3.4	2.9	2.5	2.1	1.7	1.3	1.1
Path • Inches	-1.5	+1.0	0.0	-5.9	-18.5	-40.6	-76.6	-217.1	-484.7
Wind Drift • Inches	0.0	1.1	4.7	11.2	21.6	36.8	57.9	120.3	204.0

Ultramax 40-grain Nosler Ballistic Tip (223R5)

G1 Ballistic Coefficient = 0.221

Distance • Yards	Muzzle	100	200	300	400	500	600	800	1000
Velocity • fps	3200	2762	2363	1999	1672	1391	1175	946	823
Energy • Ft-lbs	910	678	496	355	248	172	123	80	60
Taylor KO Index	4.1	3.5	3.0	2.6	2.1	1.8	1.5	1.2	1.1
Path • Inches	-1.5	+1.6	0.0	-7.8	-24.5	-54.2	-102.7	-283.2	-605.4
Wind Drift • Inches	0.0	1.3	5.4	13.2	25.6	43.8	68.8	133.3	224.4

Ultramax 42-grain Frangible (223RF1)

G1 Ballistic Coefficient = 0.200

Distance • Yards	Muzzle	100	200	300	400	500	600	800	1000
Velocity • fps	3000	2538	2121	1747	1426	1180	1028	862	752
Energy • Ft-lbs	840	601	420	285	190	130	99	69	53
Taylor KO Index	4.0	3.4	2.9	2.3	1.9	1.6	1.4	1.2	1.0
Path • Inches	-1.5	+2.0	0.0	-9.8	-31.4	-70.8	-136.0	-365.6	-761.4
Wind Drift • Inches	0.0	1.5	6.7	16.5	32.4	55.7	86.3	164.1	260.4

UMC (Remington) 45-grain Jacketed Hollow Point (L223R7A)

G1 Ballistic Coefficient = 0.175

Distance • Yards	Muzzle	100	200	300	400	500	600	800	1000
Velocity • fps	3550	2953	2430	1968	1564	1245	1044	850	728
Energy • Ft-lbs	1259	871	590	387	245	155	109	72	53
Taylor KO Index	5.2	4.4	3.6	3.0	2.4	2.0	1.6	1.3	1.1
Path • Inches	-1.5	+1.3	0.0	-7.2	-23.8	-55.4	-110.8	-319.8	-698.3
Wind Drift • Inches	0.0	1.4	6.3	15.5	30.8	53.9	85.7	169.2	274.0

USA (Winchester) 45-grain Jacketed Hollow Point (USA2232)

G1 Ballistic Coefficient = 0.173

Distance • Yards	Muzzle	100	200	300	400	500	600	800	1000
Velocity • fps	3600	3033	2533	2085	1687	1356	1119	896	769
Energy • Ft-lbs	1295	919	641	434	284	184	125	80	59
Taylor KO Index	5.2	4.4	3.6	3.0	2.4	2.0	1.6	1.3	1.1
Path • Inches	-1.5	+1.2	0.0	-6.7	-21.4	-48.7	-97.4	-283.3	-623.5
Wind Drift • Inches	0.0	1.3	5.7	14.0	27.6	47.9	76.4	154.0	252.4

UMC (Remington) 45-grain Jacketed Hollow Point (L223R7A)

G1 Ballistic Coefficient = 0.173

Distance • Yards	Muzzle	100	200	300	400	500	600	800	1000
Velocity • fps	3550	2953	2430	1962	1557	1239	1042	850	729
Energy • Ft-lbs	1259	871	590	385	242	153	108	72	53
Taylor KO Index	5.1	4.3	3.5	2.8	2.2	1.8	1.5	1.2	1.0
Path • Inches	-1.5	+1.3	0.0	-7.3	-23.7	-54.8	-108.6	-320.3	-725.2
Wind Drift • Inches	0.0	1.4	6.3	15.6	31.0	54.3	86.3	169.9	274.9

UMC (Remington) 50-grain Jacketed Hollow Point (L223R7B)

G1 Ballistic Coefficient = 0.194

Distance • Yards	Muzzle	100	200	300	400	500	600	800	1000
Velocity • fps	3425	2899	2430	2010	1637	1327	1108	895	772
Energy • Ft-lbs	1302	933	655	449	298	196	136	89	66
Taylor KO Index	5.5	4.6	3.9	3.2	2.6	2.1	1.8	1.4	1.2
Path • Inches	-1.5	+1.3	0.0	-7.3	-23.4	-53.2	-104.0	-296.6	-644.1
Wind Drift • Inches	0.0	1.4	5.8	14.3	28.0	48.5	76.9	153.5	250.2

Winchester 50-grain Ballistic Silvertip (SBST223)

G1 Ballistic Coefficient = 0.239

Distance • Yards	Muzzle	100	200	300	400	500	600	800	1000
Velocity • fps	3410	2982	2593	2235	1907	1613	1363	1039	890
Energy • Ft-lbs	1291	987	746	555	404	289	206	120	88
Taylor KO Index	5.5	4.8	4.1	3.6	3.1	2.6	2.2	1.7	1.4
Path • Inches	-1.5	+1.2	0.0	-6.4	-19.8	-42.8	-80.2	-220.8	-485.1
Wind Drift • Inches	0.0	1.1	4.6	11.1	21.2	35.8	55.8	115.0	194.5

American Eagle (Federal) 50-grain Jacketed Hollow Point (AE223G)

G1 Ballistic Coefficient = 0.204

Distance • Yards	Muzzle	100	200	300	400	500	600	800	1000
Velocity • fps	3400	2910	2460	2060	1700	1390	1160	927	801
Energy • Ft-lbs	1285	940	875	470	320	215	149	95	71
Taylor KO Index	5.4	4.7	3.9	3.3	2.7	2.2	1.9	1.5	1.3
Path • Inches	-1.5	+1.3	0.0	-7.1	-22.6	-50.2	-98.0	-278.0	-604.1
Wind Drift • Inches	0.0	1.3	5.5	13.4	26.2	45.3	71.3	143.6	235.6

Black Hills 50-grain V-Max (M223N7)

G1 Ballistic Coefficient = 0.242

Distance • Yards	Muzzle	100	200	300	400	500	600	800	1000
Velocity • fps	3300	2909	2626	2173	1850	1562	1324	1024	882
Energy • Ft-lbs	1231	940	708	524	380	271	195	116	86
Taylor KO Index	5.3	4.7	4.2	3.5	3.0	2.5	2.1	1.6	1.4
Path • Inches	-1.5	+1.3	0.0	-6.8	-21.1	-45.6	-85.8	-234.6	-5.9.6
Wind Drift • Inches	0.0	1.1	4.7	11.4	21.9	37.1	57.6	117.6	197.3

Federal 50-grain Speer TNT HP (P223V1) (Discontinued in 2004)

G1 Ballistic Coefficient = 0.223

Distance • Yards	Muzzle	100	200	300	400	500	600	800	1000
Velocity • fps	3300	2860	2450	2080	1750	1460	1225	968	839
Energy • Ft-lbs	1210	905	670	480	340	235	167	104	78
Taylor KO Index	5.3	4.6	3.9	3.3	2.8	2.3	2.1	1.6	1.4
Path • Inches	-1.5	+1.4	0.0	-7.3	-22.6	-49.7	-92.8	-256.4	-567.9
Wind Drift • Inches	0.0	1.2	5.2	12.5	24.2	41.3	65.0	131.5	217.2

PMC 50-grain BlitzKing (223BKA)

G1 Ballistic Coefficient = 0.236

Distance • Yards	Muzzle	100	200	300	400	500	600	800	1000
Velocity • fps	3300	2874	2484	2130	1809	1530	1295	1007	870
Energy • Ft-lbs	1209	917	685	504	363	260	186	113	84
Taylor KO Index	5.3	4.6	4.0	3.4	2.9	2.4	2.1	1.6	1.4
Path • Inches	-1.5	+1.4	0.0	-7.0	-21.8	-47.0	-88.1	-242.2	-525.4
Wind Drift • Inches	0.0	1.1	4.8	11.7	22.4	38.1	59.6	121.6	203.0

Remington 50-grain AccuTip Boat Tail (PRV223RB)

G1 Ballistic Coefficient = 0.242

Distance • Yards	Muzzle	100	200	300	400	500	600	800	1000
Velocity • fps	3300	2889	2514	2168	1851	1586	1346	1037	892
Energy • Ft-lbs	1209	927	701	522	380	273	201	119	88
Taylor KO Index	5.3	4.6	4.0	3.5	3.0	2.5	2.2	1.7	1.4
Path • Inches	-1.5	+1.6	0.0	-7.8	-22.9	-45.5	-84.3	-229.4	-498.6
Wind Drift • Inches	0.0	1.1	4.7	11.4	21.8	36.9	56.2	114.9	193.4

Remington 50-grain V-Max (PRV223RA) (Discontinued in 2004)   G1 Ballistic Coefficient = 0.239

Distance • Yards	Muzzle	100	200	300	400	500	600	800	1000
Velocity • fps	3300	2889	2514	2168	1851	1586	1346	1037	892
Energy • Ft-lbs	1209	927	701	522	380	273	201	119	88
Taylor KO Index	5.3	4.6	4.0	3.5	3.0	2.5	2.2	1.7	1.4
Path • Inches	-1.5	+1.6	0.0	-7.8	-22.9	-45.5	-84.3	-229.4	-498.6
Wind Drift • Inches	0.0	1.1	4.7	11.4	21.8	36.9	56.2	114.9	193.4

Ultramax 50-grain TNT (223R9)   G1 Ballistic Coefficient = 0.223

Distance • Yards	Muzzle	100	200	300	400	500	600	800	1000
Velocity • fps	3100	2672	2282	1926	1608	1338	1138	928	810
Energy • Ft-lbs	1067	793	578	412	287	199	144	96	73
Taylor KO Index	5.0	4.3	3.7	3.1	2.6	2.1	1.8	1.5	1.3
Path • Inches	-1.5	+1.7	0.0	-8.4	-26.5	-58.4	-110.8	-302.7	-641.0
Wind Drift • Inches	0.0	1.3	5.7	13.8	26.8	45.8	71.8	141.7	229.8

Ultramax 50-grain Nosler Ballistic Tip (223R4)   G1 Ballistic Coefficient = 0.238

Distance • Yards	Muzzle	100	200	300	400	500	600	800	1000
Velocity • fps	3100	2700	2334	1997	1692	1426	1214	974	850
Energy • Ft-lbs	1067	810	605	443	318	226	164	105	80
Taylor KO Index	5.0	4.3	3.7	3.2	2.7	2.3	1.9	1.6	1.4
Path • Inches	-1.5	+1.6	0.0	-8.1	-25.0	-54.5	-101.8	-275.9	-585.6
Wind Drift • Inches	0.0	1.2	5.2	12.6	24.4	41.4	64.6	129.0	211.4

Federal 52-grain Sierra MatchKing BTHP (P223K) (Discontinued in 2004)   G1 Ballistic Coefficient = 0.225

Distance • Yards	Muzzle	100	200	300	400	500	600	800	1000
Velocity • fps	3300	2860	2460	2090	1790	1470	1235	974	844
Energy • Ft-lbs	1255	945	700	505	360	250	176	110	82
Taylor KO Index	5.5	4.8	4.1	3.5	2.9	2.4	2.1	1.6	1.4
Path • Inches	-1.5	+1.4	0.0	-7.2	-22.4	-49.2	-91.8	-253.2	-560.7
Wind Drift • Inches	0.0	1.2	5.1	12.4	23.9	40.8	64.1	129.9	215.0

Black Hills 52-grain Match HP (M223N3)   G1 Ballistic Coefficient = 0.223

Distance • Yards	Muzzle	100	200	300	400	500	600	800	1000
Velocity • fps	3250	2810	2411	2046	1716	1430	1205	960	833
Energy • Ft-lbs	1220	912	671	483	340	236	163	106	80
Taylor KO Index	5.4	4.7	4.0	3.4	2.9	2.4	2.0	1.6	1.4
Path • Inches	-1.5	+1.5	0.0	-7.5	-23.5	-51.6	-97.7	-270.6	-581.9
Wind Drift • Inches	0.0	1.2	5.3	12.8	24.8	42.2	66.4	133.5	219.6

PMC 52-grain BTHP Match (223SMA)   G1 Ballistic Coefficient = 0.251

Distance • Yards	Muzzle	100	200	300	400	500	600	800	1000
Velocity • fps	3200	2808	2447	2117	1817	1553	1322	1021	891
Energy • Ft-lbs	1182	910	691	517	381	278	202	123	92
Taylor KO Index	5.6	4.9	4.3	3.7	3.2	2.6	2.2	1.7	1.5
Path • Inches	-1.5	+1.5	0.0	-7.3	-22.4	-47.9	-88.9	-239.6	-515.4
Wind Drift • Inches	0.0	1.1	4.7	11.3	21.7	36.6	57.0	115.7	193.5

Ultramax 52-grain HP (223R1)   G1 Ballistic Coefficient = 0.224

Distance • Yards	Muzzle	100	200	300	400	500	600	800	1000
Velocity • fps	3000	2586	2207	1862	1556	1301	1116	922	807
Energy • Ft-lbs	1039	772	563	400	280	195	144	98	75
Taylor KO Index	5.0	4.3	3.7	3.1	2.6	2.2	1.9	1.5	1.3
Path • Inches	-1.5	+1.9	0.0	-9.1	-28.4	-62.6	-118.4	-319.0	-667.5
Wind Drift • Inches	0.0	1.4	5.9	14.3	27.8	47.4	73.8	143.8	231.4

Hornady 53-grain Hollow Point Match (8023)   G1 Ballistic Coefficient = 0.223

Distance • Yards	Muzzle	100	200	300	400	500	600	800	1000
Velocity • fps	3330	2882	2477	2106	1710	1475	1236	972	841
Energy • Ft-lbs	1306	978	722	522	369	256	180	111	83
Taylor KO Index	5.6	4.9	4.2	3.6	3.0	2.5	2.1	1.6	1.4
Path • Inches	-1.5	+1.7	0.0	-7.4	-22.7	-49.1	-92.2	-257.0	-557.6
Wind Drift • Inches	0.0	1.2	5.1	12.4	23.9	40.8	64.2	130.4	215.9

Winchester 53-grain Hollow Point (X223RH)

G1 Ballistic Coefficient = 0.223

Distance • Yards	Muzzle	100	200	300	400	500	600	800	1000
Velocity • fps	3330	2882	2477	2106	1710	1475	1236	972	841
Energy • Ft-lbs	1306	978	722	522	369	256	180	111	83
Taylor KO Index	5.6	4.9	4.2	3.6	3.0	2.5	2.1	1.6	1.4
Path • Inches	-1.5	+1.7	0.0	-7.4	-22.7	-49.1	-92.2	-257.0	-557.6
Wind Drift • Inches	0.0	1.2	5.1	12.4	23.9	40.8	64.2	130.4	215.9

Cor-Bon 53-grain Deep Penetrating X Bullet

G1 Ballistic Coefficient = 0.256

Distance • Yards	Muzzle	100	200	300	400	500	600	800	1000
Velocity • fps	3300	2910	2553	2222	1917	1640	1400	1071	916
Energy • Ft-lbs	1282	997	767	581	433	317	231	135	99
Taylor KO Index	5.6	4.9	4.3	3.8	3.3	2.8	2.4	1.8	1.6
Path • Inches	-1.5	+1.3	0.0	-6.7	-20.5	-43.9	-80.8	-217.0	-471.8
Wind Drift • Inches	0.0	1.0	4.4	10.6	20.2	34.0	52.8	108.2	183.5

PMC 53-grain XLC-HP (223XLA) (Discontinued in 2005)

G1 Ballistic Coefficient = 0.256

Distance n Yards	Muzzle	100	200	300	400	500	600	800	1000
Velocity • fps	3200	2815	2461	2136	1840	1578	1347	1046	902
Energy • Ft-lbs	1205	933	713	537	398	293	214	129	96
Taylor KO Index	5.4	4.8	4.2	3.6	3.1	2.7	2.3	1.8	1.5
Path • Inches	-1.5	+1.5	0.0	-7.2	-22.2	-47.2	-87.1	-233.6	-502.6
Wind Drift • Inches	0.0	1.1	4.6	11.1	21.1	35.6	55.4	112.5	188.9

Sellier & Bellot 55-grain Soft Point (SBA22302)

G1 Ballistic Coefficient = 0.238

Distance • Yards	Muzzle	100	200	300	400	500	600	800	1000
Velocity • fps	3301	2854	2487	2152	1830	1545	1305	1013	875
Energy • Ft-lbs	1352	1011	767	575	409	291	208	125	93
Taylor KO Index	5.8	5.0	4.4	3.8	3.2	2.7	2.3	1.8	1.5
Path • Inches	-1.5	+1.4	0.0	-7.0	-21.5	-46.5	-86.3	-234.0	-516.5
Wind Drift • Inches	0.0	1.1	4.8	11.6	22.2	37.6	58.9	120.2	201.0

Hirtenberger 55-grain Nosler SP (82200320)

G1 Ballistic Coefficient = 0.235

Distance • Yards	Muzzle	100	200	300	400	500	600	800	1000
Velocity • fps	3281	2860	2476	2123	1801	1516	1280	1000	865
Energy • Ft-lbs	1315	999	749	550	396	281	200	122	91
Taylor KO Index	5.8	5.0	4.4	3.7	3.2	2.7	2.3	1.8	1.5
Path • Inches	-1.5	+1.4	0.0	-7.0	-22.0	-47.8	-88.8	-241.6	-532.8
Wind Drift • Inches	0.0	1.0	4.4	10.7	20.5	34.8	54.5	110.9	184.7

Federal 55-grain Hi-Shok Soft Point (223A)

G1 Ballistic Coefficient = 0.198

Distance • Yards	Muzzle	100	200	300	400	500	600	800	1000
Velocity • fps	3240	2750	2300	1910	1550	1270	1081	888	771
Energy • Ft-lbs	1280	920	650	445	295	195	143	96	73
Taylor KO Index	5.7	4.8	4.0	3.4	2.7	2.2	1.9	1.6	1.4
Path • Inches	-1.5	+1.6	0.0	-8.2	-26.1	-58.3	-112.4	-316.6	-697.4
Wind Drift • Inches	0.0	1.4	6.1	15.0	29.3	50.6	79.6	155.9	251.4

Hornady 55-grain TAP-FPD (83278)

G1 Ballistic Coefficient = 0.257

Distance • Yards	Muzzle	100	200	300	400	500	600	800	1000
Velocity • fps	3240	2854	2500	2172	1871	1598	1364	1051	903
Energy • Ft-lbs	1282	995	763	576	427	312	227	135	100
Taylor KO Index	5.7	5.0	4.4	3.8	3.3	2.8	2.4	1.8	1.6
Path • Inches	-1.5	+1.4	0.0	-7.0	-21.4	-45.9	-84.8	-227.8	-492.9
Wind Drift • Inches	0.0	1.1	4.5	10.9	20.8	35.1	54.6	111.4	187.9

Remington 55-grain Pointed Soft Point (R223R1)

G1 Ballistic Coefficient = 0.198

Distance • Yards	Muzzle	100	200	300	400	500	600	800	1000
Velocity • fps	3240	2750	2300	1910	1550	1270	1081	888	771
Energy • Ft-lbs	1280	920	650	445	295	195	143	96	73
Taylor KO Index	5.7	4.8	4.0	3.4	2.7	2.2	1.9	1.6	1.4
Path • Inches	-1.5	+1.6	0.0	-8.2	-26.1	-58.3	-112.4	-316.6	-697.4
Wind Drift • Inches	0.0	1.4	6.1	15.0	29.3	50.6	79.6	155.9	251.4

Winchester 55-grain Pointed Soft Point (X223R)

G1 Ballistic Coefficient = 0.198

Distance • Yards	Muzzle	100	200	300	400	500	600	800	1000
Velocity • fps	3240	2750	2300	1910	1550	1270	1081	888	771
Energy • Ft-lbs	1280	920	650	445	295	195	143	96	73
Taylor KO Index	5.7	4.8	4.0	3.4	2.7	2.2	1.9	1.6	1.4
Path • Inches	-1.5	+1.6	0.0	-8.2	-26.1	-58.3	-112.4	-316.6	-697.4
Wind Drift • Inches	0.0	1.4	6.1	15.0	29.3	50.6	79.6	155.9	251.4

USA (Winchester) 55-grain Pointed Soft Point (USA223RF)

G1 Ballistic Coefficient = 0.197

Distance • Yards	Muzzle	100	200	300	400	500	600	800	1000
Velocity • fps	3240	2747	2304	1904	1554	1270	1077	886	768
Energy • Ft-lbs	1282	921	648	443	295	197	142	96	72
Taylor KO Index	5.7	4.8	4.1	3.4	2.7	2.2	1.9	1.6	1.4
Path • Inches	-1.5	+1.6	0.0	-8.2	-26.2	-58.7	-115.5	-321.2	-684.6
Wind Drift • Inches	0.0	1.4	6.1	15.0	29.5	50.9	80.1	156.7	252.5

Norma 55-grain Soft Point (15717)

G1 Ballistic Coefficient = 0.235

Distance • Yards	Muzzle	100	200	300	400	500	600	800	1000
Velocity • fps	3215	2800	2420	2072	1748	1468	1241	980	851
Energy • Ft-lbs	1263	957	716	524	373	263	188	117	88
Taylor KO Index	5.7	4.9	4.3	3.6	3.1	2.6	2.2	1.7	1.5
Path • Inches	-1.5	+1.5	0.0	-7.5	-23.3	-50.8	-95.2	-261.2	-561.8
Wind Drift • Inches	0.0	1.2	5.1	12.3	23.7	40.2	63.0	127.4	210.7

Black Hills 55-grain Soft Point (M223N2)

G1 Ballistic Coefficient = 0.245

Distance • Yards	Muzzle	100	200	300	400	500	600	800	1000
Velocity • fps	3200	2803	2438	2102	1795	1522	1293	1013	878
Energy • Ft-lbs	1251	959	726	540	394	283	204	125	94
Taylor KO Index	5.6	4.9	4.3	3.7	3.2	2.7	2.3	1.8	1.5
Path • Inches	-1.5	+1.5	0.0	-7.4	-22.7	-49.1	-91.2	-247.3	-531.6
Wind Drift • Inches	0.0	1.1	4.8	11.7	22.4	37.8	59.0	119.7	199.2

Hirtenberger 55-grain Sierra SMP (82200440)

G1 Ballistic Coefficient = 0.208

Distance • Yards	Muzzle	100	200	300	400	500	600	800	1000
Velocity • fps	3133	2675	2260	1885	1553	1282	1093	901	785
Energy • Ft-lbs	1199	874	624	434	295	201	146	99	75
Taylor KO Index	5.5	4.7	4.0	3.3	2.7	2.3	1.9	1.6	1.4
Path • Inches	-1.5	+1.7	0.0	-8.6	-27.1	-60.2	-114.5	-317.5	-692.0
Wind Drift • Inches	0.0	1.2	5.4	13.3	25.9	44.5	69.7	136.2	219.3

Lapua 55-grain Soft Point (4315050)

G1 Ballistic Coefficient = 0.225

Distance • Yards	Muzzle	100	200	300	400	500	600	800	1000
Velocity • fps	3133	2708	2321	1966	1648	1376	1167	946	825
Energy • Ft-lbs	1199	896	658	472	332	231	167	109	83
Taylor KO Index	5.5	4.8	4.1	3.5	2.9	2.4	2.1	1.7	1.5
Path • Inches	-1.5	+0.9	0.0	-8.2	-25.4	-55.6	-104.3	-285.2	-621.4
Wind Drift • Inches	0.0	1.3	5.5	13.4	25.9	44.1	69.1	137.3	223.7

Aguila 55-grain Soft Point (Discontinued in 2004)

G1 Ballistic Coefficient = 0.281

Distance • Yards	Muzzle	100	200	300	400	500	600	800	1000
Velocity • fps	3100	2759	2443	2148	1875	1626	1407	1227	1095
Energy • Ft-lbs	1174	930	729	564	429	323	242	184	146
Taylor KO Index	5.5	4.9	4.3	3.8	3.3	2.9	2.5	2.2	1.9
Path • Inches	-1.5	+1.5	0.0	-7.4	-22.4	-47.4	-86.1	-143.1	-224.3
Wind Drift • Inches	0.0	1.0	4.3	10.4	19.6	32.9	50.8	102.7	173.4

PMC 55-grain Pointed Soft Point (223B)

G1 Ballistic Coefficient = 0.236

Distance • Yards	Muzzle	100	200	300	400	500	600	800	1000
Velocity • fps	3100	2689	2314	1974	1670	1414	1205	969	845
Energy • Ft-lbs	1174	883	654	476	341	244	177	115	87
Taylor KO Index	5.5	4.7	4.1	3.5	2.9	2.5	2.1	1.7	1.5
Path • Inches	-1.5	+2.0	0.0	-9.0	-26.7	-55.3	-102.8	-278.8	-591.6
Wind Drift • Inches	0.0	1.2	5.3	12.8	24.6	41.8	65.4	130.4	213.5

Ultramax 55-grain Soft Point (223R3)
G1 Ballistic Coefficient = 0.230

Distance • Yards	Muzzle	100	200	300	400	500	600	800	1000
Velocity • fps	3000	2596	2226	1888	1586	1331	1140	936	820
Energy • Ft-lbs	1099	823	605	435	307	216	159	107	82
Taylor KO Index	5.3	4.6	3.9	3.3	2.8	2.3	2.0	1.6	1.4
Path • Inches	-1.5	+1.8	0.0	-8.9	-27.8	-61.0	-114.7	-308.9	-647.2
Wind Drift • Inches	0.0	1.3	5.7	13.8	26.8	45.6	71.1	139.3	224.9

Hirtenberger 55-grain Nosler Ballistic Tip (82200472)
G1 Ballistic Coefficient = 0.264

Distance • Yards	Muzzle	100	200	300	400	500	600	800	1000
Velocity • fps	3281	2904	2557	2236	1938	1667	1429	1093	931
Energy • Ft-lbs	1315	1030	799	611	459	340	250	146	106
Taylor KO Index	5.8	5.1	4.5	3.9	3.4	2.9	2.5	1.9	1.6
Path • Inches	-1.5	+1.3	0.0	-6.7	-20.4	-43.4	-79.0	-207.3	-451.5
Wind Drift • Inches	0.0	0.9	3.9	9.3	17.6	29.6	45.9	93.9	163.1

Federal 55-grain Nosler Ballistic Tip (P223F)
G1 Ballistic Coefficient = 0.268

Distance • Yards	Muzzle	100	200	300	400	500	600	800	1000
Velocity • fps	3240	2870	2530	2220	1920	1660	1426	1095	934
Energy • Ft-lbs	1280	1005	780	600	450	336	248	146	107
Taylor KO Index	5.7	5.1	4.5	3.9	3.4	2.9	2.5	1.9	1.6
Path • Inches	-1.5	+1.4	0.0	-6.8	-20.8	-44.2	-80.3	-209.8	-454.7
Wind Drift • Inches	0.0	1.0	4.3	10.3	19.6	32.8	50.9	103.8	176.4

Federal 55-grain Sierra BlitzKing (P223J) (Discontinued in 2004)
G1 Ballistic Coefficient = 0.264

Distance • Yards	Muzzle	100	200	300	400	500	600	800	1000
Velocity • fps	3240	2870	2520	2200	1910	1640	1407	1081	925
Energy • Ft-lbs	1280	1005	775	590	445	330	242	143	105
Taylor KO Index	5.7	5.1	4.4	3.9	3.4	2.9	2.5	1.9	1.6
Path • Inches	-1.5	+1.4	0.0	-6.9	-20.9	-45.0	-81.4	-213.7	-464.3
Wind Drift • Inches	0.0	1.0	4.4	10.5	19.9	33.5	52.0	106.1	179.9

Federal 55-grain Sierra Gameking Boat-Tail Hollow Point (P223E)
G1 Ballistic Coefficient = 0.207

Distance—Yards	Muzzle	100	200	300	400	500	600	800	1000
Velocity • fps	3240	2770	2340	1950	1610	1330	1122	913	794
Energy • Ft-lbs	1280	935	670	465	315	215	154	102	77
Taylor KO Index	5.7	4.9	4.1	3.4	2.8	2.3	2.0	1.6	1.4
Path • Inches	-1.5	+1.4	0.0	-8.0	-25.3	-56.6	-106.2	-297.1	-654.8
Wind Drift • Inches	0.0	1.3	5.8	14.1	27.3	47.4	74.5	147.6	239.5

Hornady 55-grain V-Max (8327)—Moly (83273)
G1 Ballistic Coefficient = 0.258

Distance • Yards	Muzzle	100	200	300	400	500	600	800	1000
Velocity • fps	3240	2859	2507	2181	1891	1628	1392	1071	919
Energy • Ft-lbs	1282	998	767	581	437	324	237	140	103
Taylor KO Index	5.7	5.0	4.4	3.8	3.3	2.9	2.4	1.9	1.6
Path • Inches	-1.5	+1.4	0.0	-7.1	-21.4	-45.2	-82.3	-216.8	-471.8
Wind Drift • Inches	0.0	1.0	4.4	10.6	20.2	34.0	52.9	107.8	182.5

PMC 55-grain Hollow Point Boat-Tail (223VB)
G1 Ballistic Coefficient = 0.185

Distance • Yards	Muzzle	100	200	300	400	500	600	800	1000
Velocity • fps	3240	2717	2250	1832	1473	1196	1027	852	736
Energy • Ft-lbs	1282	901	618	410	265	175	129	89	66
Taylor KO Index	5.7	4.8	4.0	3.2	2.6	2.1	1.8	1.5	1.3
Path • Inches	-1.5	+0.9	0.0	-8.6	-27.7	-62.2	-125.9	-348.7	-740.9
Wind Drift • Inches	0.0	1.5	6.6	16.3	32.3	56.0	87.6	168.8	270.0

Remington 55-grain AccuTip Boat Tail (PRA223RC)
G1 Ballistic Coefficient = 0.255

Distance • Yards	Muzzle	100	200	300	400	500	600	800	1000
Velocity • fps	3240	2854	2500	2172	1871	1598	1363	1053	905
Energy • Ft-lbs	1282	995	763	576	427	312	227	135	100
Taylor KO Index	5.7	5.0	4.4	3.8	3.3	2.8	2.4	1.9	1.6
Path • Inches	-1.5	+1.4	0.0	-7.1	-21.7	-46.3	-84.8	-227.9	-492.5
Wind Drift • Inches	0.0	1.1	4.6	10.9	20.8	35.1	54.6	111.4	187.7

Remington 55-grain Hollow Point Power-Lokt (R223R2)   G1 Ballistic Coefficient = 0.209

Distance • Yards	Muzzle	100	200	300	400	500	600	800	1000
Velocity • fps	3240	2773	2352	1969	1627	1341	1131	919	799
Energy • Ft-lbs	1282	939	675	473	323	220	156	103	78
Taylor KO Index	5.7	4.9	4.1	3.5	2.9	2.4	2.0	1.6	1.4
Path • Inches	-1.5	+1.5	0.0	-7.9	-24.8	-55.1	-104.9	-293.0	-645.9
Wind Drift • Inches	0.0	1.3	5.7	14.0	27.2	46.7	73.5	145.8	237.0

Winchester 55-grain Ballistic Silvertip (SBST223B)   G1 Ballistic Coefficient = 0.267

Distance • Yards	Muzzle	100	200	300	400	500	600	800	1000
Velocity • fps	3240	2871	2531	2215	1923	1657	1422	1092	932
Energy • Ft-lbs	1282	1006	782	599	451	335	247	146	106
Taylor KO Index	5.7	5.1	4.5	3.9	3.4	2.9	2.5	1.9	1.6
Path • Inches	-1.5	+1.4	0.0	-6.8	-20.8	-44.3	-81.1	-214.8	-463.8
Wind Drift • Inches	0.0	1.0	4.3	10.3	19.6	33.0	51.1	104.2	177.1

Cor-Bon 55-grain BlitzKing (22355BK/20)   G1 Ballistic Coefficient = 0.200

Distance • Yards	Muzzle	100	200	300	400	500	600	800	1000
Velocity • fps	3200	2718	2284	1891	1547	1268	1079	889	772
Energy • Ft-lbs	1251	902	637	437	292	196	142	96	73
Taylor KO Index	5.6	4.8	4.0	3.3	2.7	2.2	1.9	1.6	1.4
Path • Inches	-1.5	+1.6	0.0	-8.4	-26.8	-60.3	-116.7	-522.8	-685.8
Wind Drift • Inches	0.0	1.4	6.1	15.0	29.4	50.7	79.6	115.6	250.4

Cor-Bon 55-grain JHP (22355/20)   G1 Ballistic Coefficient = 0.210

Distance • Yards	Muzzle	100	200	300	400	500	600	800	1000
Velocity • fps	3200	2740	2323	1945	1608	1327	1123	916	797
Energy • Ft-lbs	1251	917	659	462	316	215	154	103	78
Taylor KO Index	5.6	4.8	4.1	3.4	2.8	2.3	2.0	1.6	1.4
Path • Inches	-1.5	+1.6	0.0	-8.1	-25.6	-57.1	109.5	302.9	645.4
Wind Drift • Inches	0.0	1.3	5.8	14.1	27.5	47.2	74.2	146.5	237.5

Federal 55-grain Trophy Bonded Bear Claw (P223T2)   G1 Ballistic Coefficient = 0.203

Distance • Yards	Muzzle	100	200	300	400	500	600	800	1000
Velocity • fps	3100	2630	2210	1830	1500	1240	1064	883	770
Energy • Ft-lbs	1175	845	595	410	275	185	138	95	72
Taylor KO Index	5.5	4.6	3.9	3.2	2.6	2.2	1.9	1.6	1.4
Path • Inches	-1.5	+1.8	0.0	-8.9	-28.7	-64.5	-121.2	-335.7	-729.1
Wind Drift • Inches	0.0	1.4	6.3	15.5	30.3	52.0	81.3	157.2	251.8

Ultramax 55-grain Nosler Ballistic Tip (223R7)   G1 Ballistic Coefficient = 0.267

Distance • Yards	Muzzle	100	200	300	400	500	600	800	1000
Velocity • fps	3000	2650	2325	2024	1748	1501	1293	1029	896
Energy • Ft-lbs	1099	858	661	501	373	275	204	129	98
Taylor KO Index	5.3	4.7	4.1	3.6	3.1	2.6	2.3	1.8	1.6
Path • Inches	-1.5	+1.4	0.0	-8.2	-25.0	-53.4	-97.8	-257.7	-543.2
Wind Drift • Inches	0.0	1.1	4.8	11.5	22.0	37.0	57.4	150.7	190.2

Hirtenberger 55-grain Full Jacketed Pointed (82200411)   G1 Ballistic Coefficient = 0.258

Distance • Yards	Muzzle	100	200	300	400	500	600	800	1000
Velocity • fps	3313	2925	2569	2239	1935	1658	1416	1081	923
Energy • Ft-lbs	1341	1045	806	612	457	336	245	143	104
Taylor KO Index	5.8	5.1	4.5	3.9	3.4	2.9	2.5	1.9	1.6
Path • Inches	-1.5	+1.3	0.0	-6.6	-20.2	-43.1	-78.8	-208.5	-456.4
Wind Drift • Inches	0.0	0.9	3.9	9.4	17.9	30.1	46.8	95.9	163.1

Sellier & Bellot 55-grain FMJ (SBA22301)   G1 Ballistic Coefficient = 0.238

Distance • Yards	Muzzle	100	200	300	400	500	600	800	1000
Velocity • fps	3301	2854	2487	2152	1830	1545	1305	1013	875
Energy • Ft-lbs	1352	1011	767	575	409	291	208	125	93
Taylor KO Index	5.8	5.0	4.4	3.8	3.2	2.7	2.3	1.8	1.5
Path • Inches	-1.5	+1.4	0.0	-7.0	-21.5	-46.5	-86.3	-234.0	-516.5
Wind Drift • Inches	0.0	1.1	4.8	11.6	22.2	37.6	58.9	120.2	201.0

American Eagle (Federal) 55-grain FMJ Boat-Tail (AE223)
G1 Ballistic Coefficient = 0.340

Distance • Yards	Muzzle	100	200	300	400	500	600	800	1000
Velocity • fps	3240	2950	2670	2410	2170	1940	1725	1359	1106
Energy • Ft-lbs	1280	1060	875	710	575	460	364	225	149
Taylor KO Index	5.7	5.2	4.6	4.2	3.8	3.4	3.0	2.4	1.9
Path • Inches	-1.5	+0.9	0.0	-6.1	-18.3	-37.8	-66.7	-162.8	-335.2
Wind Drift • Inches	0.0	0.8	3.3	7.8	14.6	24.0	36.7	73.2	127.5

Federal 55-grain FMJ Boat-Tail (223B)
G1 Ballistic Coefficient = 0.340

Distance • Yards	Muzzle	100	200	300	400	500	600	800	1000
Velocity • fps	3240	2950	2670	2410	2170	1940	1725	1359	1106
Energy • Ft-lbs	1280	1060	875	710	575	460	364	225	149
Taylor KO Index	5.7	5.2	4.6	4.2	3.8	3.4	3.0	2.4	1.9
Path • Inches	-1.5	+0.9	0.0	-6.1	-18.3	-37.8	-66.7	-162.8	-335.2
Wind Drift • Inches	0.0	0.8	3.3	7.8	14.6	24.0	36.7	73.2	127.5

Remington 55-grain Metal Case (R223R3)
G1 Ballistic Coefficient = 0.202

Distance • Yards	Muzzle	100	200	300	400	500	600	800	1000
Velocity • fps	3240	2759	2326	1933	1587	1301	1099	899	781
Energy • Ft-lbs	1282	929	660	456	307	207	148	99	75
Taylor KO Index	5.7	4.9	4.1	3.4	2.8	2.3	1.9	1.6	1.4
Path • Inches	-1.5	+1.6	0.0	-8.1	-25.5	-57.0	-109.5	-307.6	-677.9
Wind Drift • Inches	0.0	1.4	5.9	14.6	28.5	49.1	77.3	152.1	246.0

UMC (Remington) 55-grain Metal Case (L223R3)
G1 Ballistic Coefficient = 0.202

Distance • Yards	Muzzle	100	200	300	400	500	600	800	1000
Velocity • fps	3240	2759	2326	1933	1587	1301	1099	899	781
Energy • Ft-lbs	1282	929	660	456	307	207	148	99	75
Taylor KO Index	5.7	4.9	4.1	3.4	2.8	2.3	1.9	1.6	1.4
Path • Inches	-1.5	+1.6	0.0	-8.1	-25.5	-57.0	-109.5	-307.6	-677.9
Wind Drift • Inches	0.0	1.4	5.9	14.6	28.5	49.1	77.3	152.1	246.0

USA (Winchester) 55-grain Full Metal Jacket (USA223R1)
G1 Ballistic Coefficient = 0.255

Distance • Yards	Muzzle	100	200	300	400	500	600	800	1000
Velocity • fps	3240	2854	2499	2172	1869	1597	1363	1053	905
Energy • Ft-lbs	1282	995	763	576	427	311	227	135	100
Taylor KO Index	5.7	5.0	4.4	3.8	3.3	2.8	2.4	1.9	1.6
Path • Inches	-1.5	+1.4	0.0	-7.0	-21.4	-45.9	-84.8	-227.9	-492.5
Wind Drift • Inches	0.0	1.1	4.6	10.9	20.8	35.1	54.6	111.4	187.7

PMC 55-grain FMJ-Boat Tail (223A)
G1 Ballistic Coefficient = 0.256

Distance • Yards	Muzzle	100	200	300	400	500	600	800	1000
Velocity • fps	3200	2833	2493	2180	1893	1635	1404	1083	928
Energy • Ft-lbs	1250	980	759	580	438	326	241	143	105
Taylor KO Index	5.6	5.0	4.4	3.8	3.3	2.9	2.5	1.9	1.6
Path • Inches	-1.5	+1.4	0.0	-7.1	-21.5	-45.5	-83.3	-220.3	-474.0
Wind Drift • Inches	0.0	1.0	4.4	10.5	19.9	33.4	51.8	105.4	178.5

Lapua 55-grain FMJ (4315040)
G1 Ballistic Coefficient = 0.247

Distance • Yards	Muzzle	100	200	300	400	500	600	800	1000
Velocity • fps	3133	2742	2383	2052	1750	1482	1262	998	867
Energy • Ft-lbs	1199	918	694	514	374	268	194	122	92
Taylor KO Index	5.5	4.8	4.2	3.6	3.1	2.6	2.2	1.8	1.5
Path • Inches	-1.5	+1.6	0.0	-7.8	-23.9	-51.6	-96.0	-259.4	-554.3
Wind Drift • Inches	0.0	1.2	5.0	12.0	23.0	39.0	60.8	122.6	203.0

Ultramax 55-grain FMJ (223R2)
G1 Ballistic Coefficient = 0.240

Distance • Yards	Muzzle	100	200	300	400	500	600	800	1000
Velocity • fps	3000	2612	2256	1928	1633	1379	1180	961	842
Energy • Ft-lbs	1099	834	622	454	326	232	170	113	87
Taylor KO Index	5.3	4.6	4.0	3.4	2.9	2.4	2.1	1.7	1.5
Path • Inches	-1.5	+1.8	0.0	-8.7	-26.9	-58.6	-109.3	-293.2	-615.8
Wind Drift • Inches	0.0	1.3	5.4	13.1	25.3	43.0	66.9	132.1	214.7

Federal 60-grain Nosler Partition (P223Q)

G1 Ballistic Coefficient = 0.228

Distance • Yards	Muzzle	100	200	300	400	500	600	800	1000
Velocity • fps	3160	2740	2350	2000	1680	1410	1192	958	835
Energy • Ft-lbs	1330	1000	740	535	380	265	189	122	93
Taylor KO Index	6.1	5.3	4.5	3.8	3.2	2.7	2.3	1.8	1.6
Path • Inches	-1.5	+1.6	0.0	-7.9	-24.7	-54.2	-102.0	-279.5	-596.0
Wind Drift • Inches	0.0	1.2	5.3	13.0	25.1	42.7	66.9	133.6	218.8

Hornady 60-grain TAP-FPD (83288)

G1 Ballistic Coefficient = 0.267

Distance • Yards	Muzzle	100	200	300	400	500	600	800	1000
Velocity • fps	3100	2684	2303	1955	1642	1375	1169	948	828
Energy • Ft-lbs	1293	1010	780	593	443	327	241	147	109
Taylor KO Index	6.0	5.3	4.6	4.1	3.5	3.0	2.6	2.0	1.7
Path • Inches	-1.5	+1.6	0.0	-7.5	-22.9	-48.9	-89.8	-238.2	-508.9
Wind Drift • Inches	0.0	1.1	4.6	11.0	21.0	35.3	54.8	110.9	185.9

Black Hills 60-grain Nosler Partition (M223N14)

G1 Ballistic Coefficient = 0.228

Distance • Yards	Muzzle	100	200	300	400	500	600	800	1000
Velocity • fps	3100	2684	2303	1955	1642	1375	1169	948	828
Energy • Ft-lbs	1281	960	707	509	359	252	182	120	91
Taylor KO Index	6.0	5.2	4.4	3.8	3.2	2.6	2.2	1.8	1.6
Path • Inches	-1.5	+1.7	0.0	-8.3	-25.9	-56.8	-107.0	-291.3	-617.0
Wind Drift • Inches	0.0	1.3	5.5	13.3	25.8	44.0	68.7	136.3	221.9

Black Hills 60-grain Soft Point (M223N4)

G1 Ballistic Coefficient = 0.265

Distance • Yards	Muzzle	100	200	300	400	500	600	800	1000
Velocity • fps	3100	2735	2399	2087	1800	1542	1323	1039	900
Energy • Ft-lbs	1281	997	767	580	432	317	233	144	108
Taylor KO Index	6.0	5.3	4.6	4.0	3.5	3.0	2.5	2.0	1.7
Path • Inches	-1.5	+1.6	0.0	-7.7	-23.4	-50.1	-92.0	-244.4	-520.6
Wind Drift • Inches	0.0	1.1	4.7	11.3	21.5	36.2	56.2	113.5	189.0

Black Hills 60-grain V-Max (M223N10)

G1 Ballistic Coefficient = 0.260

Distance • Yards	Muzzle	100	200	300	400	500	600	800	1000
Velocity • fps	3100	2733	2394	2080	1791	1533	1314	1033	896
Energy • Ft-lbs	1281	995	764	576	428	313	230	142	107
Taylor KO Index	6.0	5.2	4.6	4.0	3.4	2.9	2.5	2.0	1.7
Path • Inches	-1.5	+1.6	0.0	-7.7	-23.5	-50.4	-92.7	-246.8	-525.6
Wind Drift • Inches	0.0	1.1	4.6	10.9	20.8	34.9	54.2	110.0	184.8

Ultramax 60-grain Nosler Partition (223R11)

G1 Ballistic Coefficient = 0.228

Distance • Yards	Muzzle	100	200	300	400	500	600	800	1000
Velocity • fps	3100	2684	2303	1955	1642	1375	1169	948	828
Energy • Ft-lbs	1281	960	707	509	359	252	182	120	91
Taylor KO Index	6.0	5.2	4.4	3.8	3.2	2.6	2.2	1.8	1.6
Path • Inches	-1.5	+1.7	0.0	-8.3	-25.6	-56.8	-107.0	-291.3	-617.0
Wind Drift • Inches	0.0	1.3	5.5	13.3	25.8	44.0	68.7	136.3	221.9

Remington 62-grain Hollow Point Match (R223R6)

G1 Ballistic Coefficient = 0.205

Distance • Yards	Muzzle	100	200	300	400	500	600	800	1000
Velocity • fps	3025	2572	2162	1792	1471	1217	1051	878	767
Energy • Ft-lbs	1260	911	643	442	298	204	152	106	81
Taylor KO Index	6.0	5.2	4.3	3.6	2.9	2.4	2.1	1.7	1.5
Path • Inches	-1.5	+1.9	0.0	-9.4	-29.9	-66.4	-126.9	-348.7	-751.3
Wind Drift • Inches	0.0	1.5	6.4	15.8	31.0	53.2	82.7	158.7	253.0

USA (Winchester) 62-grain Full Metal Jacket (USA223R3)

G1 Ballistic Coefficient = 0.284

Distance • Yards	Muzzle	100	200	300	400	500	600	800	1000
Velocity • fps	3100	2762	2448	2155	1884	1636	1420	1104	946
Energy • Ft-lbs	1323	1050	825	640	488	368	277	168	123
Taylor KO Index	6.2	5.5	4.9	4.3	3.7	3.2	2.8	2.2	1.9
Path • Inches	-1.5	+1.5	0.0	-7.4	-22.3	-47.1	-85.3	-221.4	-471.2
Wind Drift • Inches	0.0	1.0	4.3	10.2	19.4	32.4	50.0	101.1	171.1

American Eagle (Federal) 62-grain FMJ (AE223N) G1 Ballistic Coefficient = 0.255

Distance • Yards	Muzzle	100	200	300	400	500	600	800	1000
Velocity • fps	3020	2650	2310	2000	1718	1460	1252	1002	875
Energy • Ft-lbs	1225	970	735	550	405	290	216	138	105
Taylor KO Index	6.0	5.3	4.6	4.0	3.4	2.9	2.5	2.0	1.7
Path • Inches	-1.5	+1.7	0.0	-8.4	-25.5	-54.7	-99.8	-263.7	-565.6
Wind Drift • Inches	0.0	1.2	5.0	12.1	23.2	39.1	60.7	121.3	199.7

Black Hills 62-grain "Heavy" Full Metal Jacket (M223N8) (Discontinued in 2004) G1 Ballistic Coefficient = 0.260

Distance • Yards	Muzzle	100	200	300	400	500	600	800	1000
Velocity • fps	2950	2595	2266	1961	1684	1440	1240	999	876
Energy • Ft-lbs	1198	927	707	530	391	286	212	138	106
Taylor KO Index	5.9	5.1	4.5	3.9	3.3	2.9	2.5	2.0	1.7
Path • Inches	-1.5	+1.5	0.0	-8.7	-26.5	-56.6	-103.6	-271.9	-578.9
Wind Drift • Inches	0.0	1.2	5.1	12.2	23.4	39.4	61.1	121.4	199.1

Ultramax 62-grain FMJ (223R10) G1 Ballistic Coefficient = 0.260

Distance • Yards	Muzzle	100	200	300	400	500	600	800	1000
Velocity • fps	2925	2572	2244	1942	1667	1425	1229	994	872
Energy • Ft-lbs	1178	911	694	519	383	280	208	136	105
Taylor KO Index	5.8	5.1	4.5	3.9	3.3	2.8	2.4	2.0	1.7
Path • Inches	-1.5	+1.9	0.0	-8.8	-27.0	-58.0	-106.8	-281.6	-588.3
Wind Drift • Inches	0.0	1.2	5.1	12.4	23.7	39.9	61.9	122.5	200.3

Federal 64-grain Soft Point (223L) G1 Ballistic Coefficient = 0.238

Distance • Yards	Muzzle	100	200	300	400	500	600	800	1000
Velocity • fps	3090	2690	2325	1990	1680	1420	1209	972	848
Energy • Ft-lbs	1360	1030	770	560	400	285	208	134	102
Taylor KO Index	6.3	5.5	4.8	4.1	3.4	2.9	2.5	2.0	1.7
Path • Inches	-1.5	+1.5	0.0	-8.2	-25.2	-54.7	-102.6	-277.8	-589.1
Wind Drift • Inches	0.0	1.2	5.2	12.7	24.5	41.6	64.9	129.4	212.0

Winchester 64-grain Power Point Plus (SHV223R2) G1 Ballistic Coefficient = 0.234

Distance • Yards	Muzzle	100	200	300	400	500	600	800	1000
Velocity • fps	3090	2684	2312	1971	1664	1398	1191	962	840
Energy • Ft-lbs	1357	1024	760	552	393	278	202	131	100
Taylor KO Index	6.3	5.5	4.7	4.0	3.4	2.8	2.4	2.0	1.7
Path • Inches	-1.5	+1.5	0.0	-8.2	-25.4	-55.1	-126.9	-279.2	-605.3
Wind Drift • Inches	0.0	1.2	5.4	13.0	25.0	42.6	66.5	132.4	216.3

Winchester 64-grain Power Point (X223R2) G1 Ballistic Coefficient = 0.258

Distance • Yards	Muzzle	100	200	300	400	500	600	800	1000
Velocity • fps	3020	2656	2320	2009	1724	1473	1265	1010	881
Energy • Ft-lbs	1296	1003	765	574	423	308	227	145	110
Taylor KO Index	6.2	5.4	4.8	4.1	3.5	3.0	2.6	2.1	1.8
Path • Inches	-1.5	+1.7	0.0	-8.2	-25.1	-53.6	-98.6	-260.0	-557.1
Wind Drift • Inches	0.0	1.2	5.0	11.9	22.8	38.5	59.7	119.5	197.1

PMC 64-grain Pointed Soft Point (223C) G1 Ballistic Coefficient = 0.341

Distance • Yards	Muzzle	100	200	300	400	500	600	800	1000
Velocity • fps	2800	2503	2241	2009	1803	1619	1436	1151	990
Energy • Ft-lbs	1114	891	714	573	462	373	293	188	139
Taylor KO Index	5.7	5.1	4.6	4.1	3.7	3.3	2.9	2.4	2.0
Path • Inches	-1.5	+2.0	0.0	-9.0	-26.7	-55.3	-94.3	-233.3	-478.9
Wind Drift • Inches	0.0	1.0	4.1	9.6	18.1	30.0	45.8	90.7	152.6

Ultramax 68-grain HP (223R6) G1 Ballistic Coefficient = 0.338

Distance • Yards	Muzzle	100	200	300	400	500	600	800	1000
Velocity • fps	2900	2627	2370	2128	1900	1689	1498	1192	1014
Energy • Ft-lbs	1270	1042	848	684	545	431	339	215	155
Taylor KO Index	6.3	5.7	5.2	4.6	4.1	3.7	3.3	2.6	2.2
Path • Inches	-1.5	+1.8	0.0	-8.0	-23.7	-49.1	-86.9	-215.0	-443.6
Wind Drift • Inches	0.0	0.9	3.9	9.2	17.2	28.5	43.5	86.6	146.9

Black Hills 68-grain "Heavy" Match Hollow Point (M223N5)
G1 Ballistic Coefficient = 0.339

Distance • Yards	Muzzle	100	200	300	400	500	600	800	1000
Velocity • fps	2850	2581	2327	2088	1863	1656	1469	1174	1004
Energy • Ft-lbs	1227	1006	818	658	524	414	326	208	152
Taylor KO Index	6.2	5.6	5.1	4.5	4.1	3.6	3.2	2.6	2.2
Path • Inches	-1.5	+1.9	0.0	-8.3	-24.6	-51.0	-90.2	-221.2	-453.2
Wind Drift • Inches	0.0	0.9	4.0	9.4	17.6	29.2	44.5	88.4	149.4

Lapua 69-grain Scenar (4315510)
G1 Ballistic Coefficient = 0.317

Distance • Yards	Muzzle	100	200	300	400	500	600	800	1000
Velocity • fps	3035	2736	2456	2193	1946	1718	1511	1185	1002
Energy • Ft-lbs	1412	1147	924	737	580	452	350	215	154
Taylor KO Index	6.7	6.0	5.4	4.8	4.3	3.8	3.3	2.6	2.2
Path • Inches	-1.5	+1.6	0.0	-7.4	-22.0	-45.9	-81.9	-205.8	-431.6
Wind Drift • Inches	0.0	0.9	3.9	9.3	17.4	28.9	44.3	88.9	151.8

Cor-Bon 69-grain BTHP (PM22369/20)
G1 Ballistic Coefficient = 0.338

Distance • Yards	Muzzle	100	200	300	400	500	600	800	1000
Velocity • fps	3000	2721	2459	2211	1978	1761	1562	1297	1037
Energy • Ft-lbs	1379	1135	927	749	600	475	374	234	165
Taylor KO Index	6.6	6.0	5.4	4.9	4.4	3.9	3.4	2.9	2.3
Path • Inches	-1.5	+1.6	0.0	-7.4	-21.9	-45.4	-80.2	-198.2	-410.6
Wind Drift • Inches	0.0	0.9	3.7	8.7	16.4	27.1	41.3	82.4	141.2

Federal 69-grain Sierra MatchKing HPBT (GM223M)
G1 Ballistic Coefficient = 0.338

Distance • Yards	Muzzle	100	200	300	400	500	600	800	1000
Velocity • fps	3000	2720	2460	2210	1980	1760	1562	1237	1037
Energy • Ft-lbs	1379	1135	926	749	600	475	374	234	165
Taylor KO Index	6.6	6.0	5.4	4.9	4.4	3.9	3.4	2.7	2.3
Path • Inches	-1.5	+1.6	0.0	-7.4	-21.9	-45.4	-80.1	-196.3	-403.9
Wind Drift • Inches	0.0	0.9	3.7	8.8	16.4	27.1	41.3	82.5	141.3

Remington 69-grain Hollow Point Boat-Tail (Match) (RM223R1)
G1 Ballistic Coefficient = 0.336

Distance • Yards	Muzzle	100	200	300	400	500	600	800	1000
Velocity • fps	3000	2920	2457	2209	1975	1758	1556	1231	1033
Energy • Ft-lbs	1379	1133	925	747	598	473	371	232	164
Taylor KO Index	6.6	6.0	5.4	4.9	4.4	3.9	3.4	2.7	2.3
Path • Inches	-1.5	+1.6	0.0	-7.4	-21.9	-45.4	-80.6	-199.3	-413.5
Wind Drift • Inches	0.0	0.9	3.7	8.8	16.5	27.3	41.6	83.1	142.3

PMC 69-grain Hollow Point Boat-Tail Match (223SBM)
G1 Ballistic Coefficient = 0.390

Distance • Yards	Muzzle	100	200	300	400	500	600	800	1000
Velocity • fps	2900	2591	2304	2038	1791	1572	1375	1092	947
Energy • Ft-lbs	1288	1029	813	636	492	379	290	183	137
Taylor KO Index	6.4	5.7	5.1	4.5	4.0	3.5	3.0	2.4	2.1
Path • Inches	-1.5	+1.8	0.0	-8.4	-25.3	-52.8	-95.0	-242.0	-504.3
Wind Drift • Inches	0.0	1.0	4.4	10.5	19.8	33.0	50.8	101.3	169.4

Black Hills 69-grain Sierra BTHP MatchKing (M223N12)
G1 Ballistic Coefficient = 0.338

Distance • Yards	Muzzle	100	200	300	400	500	600	800	1000
Velocity • fps	2850	2580	2326	2086	1861	1653	1466	1171	1002
Energy • Ft-lbs	1245	1020	829	667	531	419	329	210	154
Taylor KO Index	6.3	5.7	5.1	4.6	4.1	3.6	3.2	2.6	2.2
Path • Inches	-1.5	+1.9	0.0	-8.3	-24.7	-51.2	-90.6	-224.1	-461.1
Wind Drift • Inches	0.0	1.0	4.0	9.4	17.7	29.3	44.7	88.7	149.8

Black Hills 73-grain Berger BTHP (M223N12) (Discontinued in 2005)
G1 Ballistic Coefficient = 0.338

Distance • Yards	Muzzle	100	200	300	400	500	600	800	1000
Velocity • fps	2750	2520	2302	2095	1898	1715	1545	1261	1071
Energy • Ft-lbs	1226	1030	859	711	584	477	387	258	186
Taylor KO Index	6.4	5.9	5.4	4.9	4.4	4.0	3.6	2.9	2.5
Path • Inches	-1.5	+2.0	0.0	-8.6	-25.1	-51.3	-89.5	-214.1	-429.3
Wind Drift • Inches	0.0	0.9	3.6	8.4	15.7	25.8	39.0	76.5	129.6

Ultramax 75-grain Boat-Tail Hollow Point Match (223R8)

G1 Ballistic Coefficient = 0.390

Distance • Yards	Muzzle	100	200	300	400	500	600	800	1000
Velocity • fps	2800	2568	2347	2137	1939	1752	1579	1286	1086
Energy • Ft-lbs	1306	1098	918	761	626	511	416	276	197
Taylor KO Index	6.7	6.2	5.6	5.1	4.7	4.2	3.8	3.1	2.6
Path • Inches	-1.5	+1.9	0.0	-8.2	-24.1	-49.2	-85.8	-205.2	-411.8
Wind Drift • Inches	0.0	0.8	3.5	8.2	15.3	25.1	38.0	74.6	126.7

Hornady 75-grain TAP-FPD (80268)

G1 Ballistic Coefficient = 0.438

Distance • Yards	Muzzle	100	200	300	400	500	600	800	1000
Velocity • fps	2790	2582	2383	2193	2012	1840	1678	1392	1172
Energy • Ft-lbs	1296	1110	946	801	674	564	469	323	229
Taylor KO Index	6.7	6.2	5.7	5.3	4.8	4.4	4.0	3.3	2.8
Path • Inches	-1.5	+1.9	0.0	-8.0	-23.2	-47.1	-81.3	-190.0	-373.2
Wind Drift • Inches	0.0	0.8	3.1	7.3	13.5	22.0	33.2	64.5	109.7

Hornady 75-grain Boat-Tail Hollow Point Match (8026)

G1 Ballistic Coefficient = 0.390

Distance • Yards	Muzzle	100	200	300	400	500	600	800	1000
Velocity • fps	2790	2554	2330	2119	1926	1744	1572	1281	1083
Energy • Ft-lbs	1296	1086	904	747	617	506	412	273	195
Taylor KO Index	6.7	6.1	5.6	5.1	4.6	4.2	3.8	3.1	2.6
Path • Inches	-1.5	+2.4	0.0	-8.8	-25.1	-50.8	-86.4	-205.7	-410.2
Wind Drift • Inches	0.0	0.8	3.5	8.2	15.4	25.2	38.2	75.0	127.4

Black Hills 75-grain "Heavy" Match Hollow Point (M223N6)

G1 Ballistic Coefficient = 0.390

Distance • Yards	Muzzle	100	200	300	400	500	600	800	1000
Velocity • fps	2750	2520	2302	2094	1898	1714	1545	1260	1071
Energy • Ft-lbs	1259	1058	883	731	600	489	397	265	191
Taylor KO Index	6.6	6.0	5.5	5.0	4.6	4.1	3.7	3.0	2.6
Path • Inches	-1.5	+2.0	0.0	-8.6	-25.1	-51.3	-89.4	-212.8	-424.2
Wind Drift • Inches	0.0	0.9	3.6	8.4	15.7	25.8	39.0	76.6	129.7

Federal 77-grain (GM223M3)

G1 Ballistic Coefficient = 0.390

Distance • Yards	Muzzle	100	200	300	400	500	600	800	1000
Velocity • fps	2750	2500	2270	2050	1840	1650	1470	1190	1020
Energy • Ft-lbs	1285	1070	880	715	580	465	370	240	180
Taylor KO Index	6.8	6.2	5.6	5.1	4.5	4.1	3.6	2.9	2.5
Path • Inches	-1.5	+1.6	0.0	-7.4	-21.9	-45.5	-80.5	-198.9	-411.9
Wind Drift • Inches	0.0	0.9	3.8	9.0	16.8	27.9	42.6	85.3	146.0

Black Hills 77-grain Sierra MatchKing HP (M223N9)

G1 Ballistic Coefficient = 0.390

Distance • Yards	Muzzle	100	200	300	400	500	600	800	1000
Velocity • fps	2750	2520	2302	2094	1898	1714	1545	1260	1071
Energy • Ft-lbs	1259	1086	906	750	616	503	408	272	196
Taylor KO Index	6.9	6.2	5.8	5.2	4.7	4.2	3.8	3.1	2.6
Path • Inches	-1.5	+2.0	0.0	-8.6	-25.1	-51.3	-89.4	-212.8	-424.2
Wind Drift • Inches	0.0	0.9	3.6	8.4	15.7	25.8	39.0	76.6	129.7

.22-250 Remington

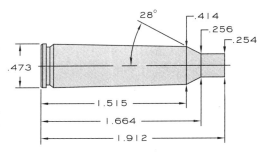

The .22-250, which became a standardized factory cartridge in 1965, has a history that starts about 1915 when Charles Newton designed the .250 Savage. In the late 1920s and early 1930s a number of people began experimenting with the .250 Savage necked to .22 caliber. One early number was the .220 Wotkyns Original Swift. J. E. Gebby and J. Bushnell Smith called their version the .22 Varminter and copyrighted the name. Most gunsmiths, when chambering guns for the .22 caliber version of the .250 Savage, simply called the cartridge the .22-250 to avoid any copyright troubles.

Remington's introduction of the .22-250 finally brought this fine cartridge its deserved recognition as a standardized factory caliber. In the fastest loading today, the .22-250 is only 50 fps slower than the .220 Swift. Some of the wildcat loadings from the 1950s produced velocities about 200 fps higher than today's factory standards. They also produced pressures to match, and that fact explains why the factories are sometimes slow to adopt wildcat designs and why they seldom achieve the velocity claims of the wildcat inventors.

Relative Recoil Factor = 0.90

Specifications

Controlling Agency for Standardization of this Ammunition: SAAMI

Bullet Weight Grains	Velocity fps	Maximum Average Pressure	
		Copper Crusher	Transducer
40	3,975	53,000 cup	65,000 psi
52	3,740	53,000 cup	65,000 psi
53–55	3,650	53,000 cup	65,000 psi
60	3,600	53,000 cup	65,000 psi

Standard barrel for velocity testing: 24 inches long—1 turn in 14-inch twist

Availability

Federal 40-grain Nosler BT (P22250H)

G1 Ballistic Coefficient = 0.222

Distance • Yards	Muzzle	100	200	300	400	500	600	800	1000
Velocity • fps	4150	3610	3130	2700	2300	1940	1618	1143	930
Energy • Ft-lbs	1530	1155	870	645	470	335	233	116	77
Taylor KO Index	5.3	4.6	4.0	3.5	2.9	2.5	2.1	1.5	1.2
Path • Inches	-1.5	+0.6	0.0	-4.2	-13.2	-28.8	-54.4	-154.5	-363.1
Wind Drift • Inches	0.0	0.9	4.0	9.5	18.0	30.3	47.4	100.5	178.8

Federal 40-grain Sierra Varminter Hollow Point (P22250V) (Discontinued in 2005)

G1 Ballistic Coefficient = 0.166

Distance • Yards	Muzzle	100	200	300	400	500	600	800	1000
Velocity • fps	4000	3320	2720	2200	1740	1360	1108	874	741
Energy • Ft-lbs	1420	980	680	430	265	164	109	68	49
Taylor KO Index	5.1	4.2	3.5	2.8	2.2	1.7	1.4	1.1	0.9
Path • Inches	-1.5	+0.8	0.0	-5.6	-18.4	-42.8	-86.4	-266.6	-629.5
Wind Drift • Inches	0.0	1.3	5.7	14.1	27.8	48.9	78.8	161.4	266.8

Hornady 40-grain V-Max (8335) (Moly VX—83353)

G1 Ballistic Coefficient = 0.220

Distance • Yards	Muzzle	100	200	300	400	500	600	800	1000
Velocity • fps	4150	3631	3147	2699	2293	1932	1613	1141	930
Energy • Ft-lbs	1529	1171	879	647	467	331	231	116	77
Taylor KO Index	5.3	4.6	4.0	3.5	3.0	2.5	2.1	1.5	1.2
Path • Inches	-1.5	+0.5	0.0	-4.2	-13.3	-28.9	-54.1	-150.8	-354.1
Wind Drift • Inches	0.0	0.9	4.0	9.5	18.0	30.4	47.6	100.9	179.3

Winchester 40-grain Ballistic Silvertip (SBST22250A)

G1 Ballistic Coefficient = 0.215

Distance • Yards	Muzzle	100	200	300	400	500	600	800	1000
Velocity • fps	4150	3591	3099	2658	2257	1893	1572	1112	914
Energy • Ft-lbs	1530	1146	853	628	453	318	220	110	74
Taylor KO Index	5.3	4.6	4.0	3.4	2.9	2.4	2.0	1.4	1.2
Path • Inches	-1.5	+0.6	0.0	-4.2	-13.4	-29.5	-55.5	-156.4	-369.0
Wind Drift • Inches	0.0	1.0	4.1	9.8	18.6	31.4	49.3	104.9	185.4

USA (Winchester) 45-grain Jacketed Hollow Point (USA222502)
G1 Ballistic Coefficient = 0.175

Distance • Yards	Muzzle	100	200	300	400	500	600	800	1000
Velocity • fps	4000	3346	2781	2281	1837	1458	1175	909	772
Energy • Ft-lbs	1598	1118	773	520	337	212	138	83	60
Taylor KO Index	5.8	4.8	4.0	3.3	2.6	2.1	1.7	1.3	1.1
Path • Inches	-1.5	+0.8	0.0	-5.4	-17.5	-40.2	-81.5	-248.1	-564.8
Wind Drift • Inches	0.0	1.2	5.4	13.1	25.7	44.8	72.2	149.9	250.1

Winchester 50-grain Ballistic Silvertip (SBST22250)
G1 Ballistic Coefficient = 0.238

Distance • Yards	Muzzle	100	200	300	400	500	600	800	1000
Velocity • fps	3810	3341	2919	2536	2182	1859	1568	1140	941
Energy • Ft-lbs	1611	1239	946	714	529	384	273	144	98
Taylor KO Index	6.1	5.4	4.7	4.1	3.5	3.0	2.5	1.8	1.5
Path • Inches	-1.5	+0.8	0.0	-4.9	-15.2	-32.9	-61.0	-165.4	-376.4
Wind Drift • Inches	0.0	1.0	4.0	9.6	18.2	30.6	47.7	99.8	175.2

Hornady 50-grain V-Max (8336) (Moly VX—83363)
G1 Ballistic Coefficient = 0.240

Distance • Yards	Muzzle	100	200	300	400	500	600	800	1000
Velocity • fps	3800	3349	2925	2535	2178	1862	1576	1147	946
Energy • Ft-lbs	1603	1245	950	713	527	385	276	146	99
Taylor KO Index	6.1	5.4	4.7	4.1	3.5	3.0	2.5	1.8	1.5
Path • Inches	-1.5	+0.8	0.0	-5.0	-15.6	-33.3	-60.9	-164.5	-373.5
Wind Drift • Inches	0.0	1.0	4.0	9.5	18.0	30.3	47.3	98.8	173.6

Remington 50-grain AccuTip (PRA2250RB)
G1 Ballistic Coefficient = 0.242

Distance • Yards	Muzzle	100	200	300	400	500	600	800	1000
Velocity • fps	3800	3339	2925	2546	2198	1878	1592	1158	950
Energy • Ft-lbs	1603	1238	949	720	536	392	282	149	100
Taylor KO Index	6.1	5.3	4.7	4.1	3.5	3.0	2.5	1.9	1.5
Path • Inches	-1.5	+0.8	0.0	-4.9	-15.2	-32.8	-60.7	-166.0	-377.7
Wind Drift • Inches	0.0	0.9	3.9	9.4	17.8	29.9	46.6	97.3	171.3

PMC 50-grain XLC-HP (22-250XLA) (Discontinued in 2005)
G1 Ballistic Coefficient = 0.244

Distance • Yards	Muzzle	100	200	300	400	500	600	800	1000
Velocity • fps	3725	3280	2871	2495	2152	1840	1562	1145	947
Energy • Ft-lbs	1540	1195	915	691	514	376	271	146	100
Taylor KO Index	6.0	5.2	4.6	4.0	3.4	2.9	2.5	2.0	1.6
Path • Inches	-1.5	+0.9	0.0	-5.1	-15.9	-34.2	-63.2	-172.6	-389.8
Wind Drift • Inches	0.0	1.0	4.0	9.6	18.1	30.4	47.4	98.8	173.0

PMC 50-grain BlitzKing (22-250BKA)
G1 Ballistic Coefficient = 0.235

Distance • Yards	Muzzle	100	200	300	400	500	600	800	1000
Velocity • fps	3725	3264	2641	2455	2103	1785	1504	1103	922
Energy • Ft-lbs	1540	1183	896	669	491	354	251	135	94
Taylor KO Index	6.0	5.2	4.2	3.9	3.4	2.9	2.4	1.8	1.5
Path • Inches	-1.5	+0.8	0.0	-5.0	-15.5	-33.6	-65.7	-182.4	-412.8
Wind Drift • Inches	0.0	1.0	4.2	10.0	19.0	32.1	50.2	104.9	182.3

Remington 50-grain V-Max Boat-Tail (PRV2250A) (Discontinued in 2004)
Use EtronX (EL2250A) for Remington Electronic Rifle
G1 Ballistic Coefficient = 0.242

Distance • Yards	Muzzle	100	200	300	400	500	600	800	1000
Velocity • fps	3725	3272	2864	2491	2147	1832	1549	1134	941
Energy • Ft-lbs	1540	1188	910	689	512	372	266	143	98
Taylor KO Index	6.0	5.2	4.6	4.0	3.4	2.9	2.5	1.8	1.5
Path • Inches	-1.5	+0.8	0.0	-5.0	-15.5	-33.6	-63.3	-170.7	-385.8
Wind Drift • Inches	0.0	1.0	4.1	9.8	18.6	31.3	48.0	100.3	175.2

Black Hills 50-grain Nosler Ballistic Tip (2C22250BHGN1)
G1 Ballistic Coefficient = 0.238

Distance • Yards	Muzzle	100	200	300	400	500	600	800	1000
Velocity • fps	3700	3242	2830	2453	2106	1790	1510	1109	927
Energy • Ft-lbs	1520	1167	896	668	493	356	253	137	95
Taylor KO Index	5.9	5.2	4.5	3.9	3.4	2.9	2.4	1.8	1.5
Path • Inches	-1.5	+0.9	0.0	-5.3	-16.4	-35.5	-65.9	-181.9	-410.8
Wind Drift • Inches	0.0	1.1	4.6	11.0	21.0	35.6	56.2	116.2	197.5

Norma 53-grain Soft Point (15733)
G1 Ballistic Coefficient = 0.237

Distance • Yards	Muzzle	100	200	300	400	500	600	800	1000
Velocity • fps	3707	3246	2830	2451	2106	1788	1507	1107	925
Energy • Ft-lbs	1618	1240	943	707	522	376	267	191	144
Taylor KO Index	6.3	5.5	4.8	4.2	3.6	3.0	2.6	1.9	1.6
Path • Inches	-1.5	+0.9	0.0	-5.3	-16.4	-35.5	-65.9	-182.2	-411.7
Wind Drift • Inches	0.0	1.0	4.2	10.0	18.9	31.9	49.9	104.2	181.0

Federal 55-grain Sierra BlitzKing (P22250C) (Discontinued in 2004)
G1 Ballistic Coefficient = 0.263

Distance • Yards	Muzzle	100	200	300	400	500	600	800	1000
Velocity • fps	3680	3270	2890	2540	2220	1920	1652	1223	994
Energy • Ft-lbs	1655	1300	1020	790	605	450	333	183	121
Taylor KO Index	6.5	5.8	5.1	4.5	3.9	3.4	2.9	2.2	1.7
Path • Inches	-1.5	+0.9	0.0	-5.1	-15.6	-33.1	-60.3	-157.6	-348.4
Wind Drift • Inches	0.0	0.9	3.7	8.9	16.8	28.0	43.3	89.4	157.7

Federal 55-grain Hi-Shok Soft Point (22250A)
G1 Ballistic Coefficient = 0.198

Distance • Yards	Muzzle	100	200	300	400	500	600	800	1000
Velocity • fps	3680	3140	2660	2220	1830	1490	1221	946	811
Energy • Ft-lbs	1655	1200	860	605	410	270	182	109	80
Taylor KO Index	6.5	5.5	4.7	3.9	3.2	2.6	2.1	1.7	1.4
Path • Inches	-1.5	+1.0	0.0	-6.0	-19.1	-42.8	-82.7	-240.2	-552.7
Wind Drift • Inches	0.0	1.2	5.2	12.5	24.3	41.9	67.2	138.6	231.1

Remington 55-grain Pointed Soft Point (R22501)
G1 Ballistic Coefficient = 0.198

Distance • Yards	Muzzle	100	200	300	400	500	600	800	1000
Velocity • fps	3680	3137	2656	2222	1832	1493	1228	950	814
Energy • Ft-lbs	1654	1201	861	603	410	272	184	110	81
Taylor KO Index	6.5	5.5	4.7	3.9	3.2	2.6	2.2	1.7	1.4
Path • Inches	-1.5	+1.0	0.0	-6.0	-19.1	-42.8	-82.1	-238.2	-548.2
Wind Drift • Inches	0.0	1.2	5.2	12.5	24.3	41.8	66.6	137.6	229.7

Winchester 55-grain Pointed Soft Point (X222501)
G1 Ballistic Coefficient = 0.198

Distance • Yards	Muzzle	100	200	300	400	500	600	800	1000
Velocity • fps	3680	3137	2656	2222	1832	1493	1228	950	814
Energy • Ft-lbs	1654	1201	861	603	410	272	184	110	81
Taylor KO Index	6.5	5.5	4.7	3.9	3.2	2.6	2.2	1.7	1.4
Path • Inches	-1.5	+1.0	0.0	-6.0	-19.1	-42.8	-82.1	-238.2	-548.2
Wind Drift • Inches	0.0	1.2	5.2	12.5	24.3	41.8	66.6	137.6	229.7

Federal 55-grain Trophy Bonded Bear Claw (P22250T1)
G1 Ballistic Coefficient = 0.203

Distance • Yards	Muzzle	100	200	300	400	500	600	800	1000
Velocity • fps	3600	3080	2610	2190	1810	1490	1230	955	820
Energy • Ft-lbs	1585	1155	835	590	400	270	185	111	82
Taylor KO Index	6.3	5.4	4.6	3.9	3.2	2.6	2.2	1.7	1.4
Path • Inches	-1.5	+1.1	0.0	-6.2	-19.8	-44.5	-83.9	-241.0	-550.2
Wind Drift • Inches	0.0	1.2	5.2	12.4	24.3	41.8	66.1	136.1	226.7

PMC 55-grain Pointed Soft Point (22-250B)
G1 Ballistic Coefficient = 0.234

Distance • Yards	Muzzle	100	200	300	400	500	600	800	1000
Velocity • fps	3580	3129	2716	2339	1996	1689	1422	1062	900
Energy • Ft-lbs	1565	1196	901	668	487	348	247	138	99
Taylor KO Index	6.3	5.5	4.8	4.1	3.5	3.0	2.5	1.9	1.6
Path • Inches	-1.5	+1.0	0.0	-5.8	-18.0	-38.8	-72.8	-202.1	-451.4
Wind Drift • Inches	0.0	1.0	4.4	10.6	20.2	34.2	53.5	111.3	190.6

Federal 55-grain Sierra GameKing BTHP (P22250B)
G1 Ballistic Coefficient = 0.276

Distance • Yards	Muzzle	100	200	300	400	500	600	800	1000
Velocity • fps	3680	3280	2929	2590	2280	1990	1725	1289	1032
Energy • Ft-lbs	1655	1315	1040	815	630	480	364	203	130
Taylor KO Index	6.5	5.8	5.1	4.6	4.0	3.5	3.0	2.3	1.8
Path • Inches	-1.5	+0.9	0.0	-5.0	-15.1	-32.0	-57.8	-148.6	-324.1
Wind Drift • Inches	0.0	0.8	3.6	8.4	15.8	26.3	40.4	82.8	146.8

Federal 55-grain Nosler Ballistic Tip (P22250F)

G1 Ballistic Coefficient = 0.266

Distance • Yards	Muzzle	100	200	300	400	500	600	800	1000
Velocity • fps	3680	3270	2900	2560	2240	1940	1670	1239	1003
Energy • Ft-lbs	1655	1305	1025	800	615	460	341	187	123
Taylor KO Index	6.5	5.8	5.1	4.5	3.9	3.4	2.9	2.2	1.8
Path • Inches	-1.5	+0.9	0.0	-5.0	-15.4	-32.8	-59.9	-158.0	-351.6
Wind Drift • Inches	0.0	0.9	3.8	9.1	17.3	28.9	44.5	92.1	162.2

Hornady 55-grain V-Max (8337) (Moly VX—83373)

G1 Ballistic Coefficient = 0.258

Distance • Yards	Muzzle	100	200	300	400	500	600	800	1000
Velocity • fps	3680	3265	2876	2517	2183	1887	1623	1198	979
Energy • Ft-lbs	1654	1302	1010	772	582	433	322	175	117
Taylor KO Index	6.5	5.7	5.1	4.4	3.8	3.3	2.9	2.1	1.7
Path • Inches	-1.5	+0.9	0.0	-5.3	-16.1	-34.1	-61.3	-161.5	-358.8
Wind Drift • Inches	0.0	0.9	3.8	9.1	17.3	28.9	44.5	92.1	162.2

PMC 55-grain Hollow Point Boat-Tail (22-250VB)

G1 Ballistic Coefficient = 0.190

Distance • Yards	Muzzle	100	200	300	400	500	600	800	1000
Velocity • fps	3680	3104	2596	2141	1737	1395	1143	906	776
Energy • Ft-lbs	1654	1176	823	560	368	238	160	100	74
Taylor KO Index	6.5	5.5	4.6	3.8	3.1	2.5	2.0	1.6	1.4
Path • Inches	-1.5	+1.1	0.0	-6.3	-20.2	-45.8	-92.2	-270.7	-600.5
Wind Drift • Inches	0.0	1.3	5.6	13.6	26.6	46.0	74.1	150.8	248.5

Remington 55-grain Hollow Point Power-Lokt (R22502)

G1 Ballistic Coefficient = 0.230

Distance • Yards	Muzzle	100	200	300	400	500	600	800	1000
Velocity • fps	3680	3209	2785	2400	2046	1725	1446	1069	902
Energy • Ft-lbs	1654	1257	947	703	511	363	255	140	99
Taylor KO Index	6.5	5.6	4.9	4.2	3.6	3.0	2.5	1.9	1.6
Path • Inches	-1.5	+1.0	0.0	-5.5	-17.0	-37.0	-68.7	-189.1	-430.2
Wind Drift • Inches	0.0	1.0	4.3	10.4	19.9	33.7	52.8	110.3	190.1

Winchester 55-grain Ballistic Silvertip (SBST22250B)

G1 Ballistic Coefficient = 0.267

Distance • Yards	Muzzle	100	200	300	400	500	600	800	1000
Velocity • fps	3680	3272	2900	2559	2240	1946	1676	1244	1006
Energy • Ft-lbs	1654	1307	1027	799	613	462	343	189	124
Taylor KO Index	6.5	5.8	5.1	4.5	3.9	3.4	2.9	2.2	1.8
Path • Inches	-1.5	+0.9	0.0	-5.0	-15.4	-32.8	-59.6	-156.9	-349.0
Wind Drift • Inches	0.0	0.9	3.7	8.7	16.4	27.4	42.3	87.2	154.1

Remington 60-grain Nosler Partition (PRP2250RA)

G1 Ballistic Coefficient = 0.228

Distance • Yards	Muzzle	100	200	300	400	500	600	800	1000
Velocity • fps	3500	3045	2634	2258	1914	1607	1345	1022	875
Energy • Ft-lbs	1632	1235	924	679	488	344	241	139	102
Taylor KO Index	6.7	5.8	5.1	4.3	3.7	3.1	2.6	2.0	1.7
Path • Inches	-1.5	+1.1	0.0	-6.2	-19.3	-42.2	-79.2	-221.6	-490.3
Wind Drift • Inches	0.0	1.1	4.7	11.2	21.6	36.6	57.5	119.0	201.1

Hornady 60-grain Soft Point (8039)

G1 Ballistic Coefficient = 0.264

Distance • Yards	Muzzle	100	200	300	400	500	600	800	1000
Velocity • fps	3600	3195	2826	2485	2169	1878	1611	1198	983
Energy • Ft-lbs	1727	1360	1064	823	627	470	346	191	129
Taylor KO Index	6.9	6.1	5.4	4.8	4.2	3.6	3.1	2.3	1.9
Path • Inches	-1.5	+1.0	0.0	-5.4	-16.3	-34.8	-63.3	-165.5	-364.8
Wind Drift • Inches	0.0	0.9	3.8	9.1	17.2	28.7	44.4	91.7	160.9

Black Hills 60-grain Nosler Partition (2C22250BHGN2)

G1 Ballistic Coefficient = 0.229

Distance • Yards	Muzzle	100	200	300	400	500	600	800	1000
Velocity • fps	3550	3091	2677	2299	1953	1642	1375	1036	884
Energy • Ft-lbs	1679	1273	955	704	508	359	252	143	104
Taylor KO Index	6.8	5.9	5.1	4.4	3.7	3.2	2.6	2.0	1.7
Path • Inches	-1.5	+1.1	0.0	-6.0	-18.6	-40.6	-76.1	-212.9	-473.7
Wind Drift • Inches	0.0	1.1	4.6	11.0	21.0	35.6	56.0	116.2	197.5

Federal 60-grain Nosler Partition (P22250G)

G1 Ballistic Coefficient = 0.229

Distance • Yards	Muzzle	100	200	300	400	500	600	800	1000
Velocity • fps	3500	3050	2630	2260	1910	1610	1351	1026	877
Energy • Ft-lbs	1630	1235	925	680	490	345	243	140	103
Taylor KO Index	6.7	5.9	5.0	4.3	3.7	3.1	2.6	2.0	1.7
Path • Inches	-1.5	+1.1	0.0	-6.2	-19.3	-41.9	-78.8	-220.2	-487.3
Wind Drift • Inches	0.0	1.1	4.6	11.2	21.4	36.4	57.2	118.2	200.0

Remington 60-grain Nosler Partition (PRP2250RA) (Discontinued in 2004)

G1 Ballistic Coefficient = 0.228

Distance • Yards	Muzzle	100	200	300	400	500	600	800	1000
Velocity • fps	3500	3045	2634	2258	1914	1607	1345	1022	875
Energy • Ft-lbs	1632	1235	924	679	488	344	241	139	102
Taylor KO Index	6.7	5.8	5.1	4.3	3.7	3.1	2.6	2.0	1.7
Path • Inches	-1.5	+1.1	0.0	-6.2	-19.3	-42.2	-79.2	-221.6	-490.3
Wind Drift • Inches	0.0	1.1	4.7	11.2	21.6	36.6	57.5	119.0	201.1

Winchester 64-grain Power Point (X222502)

G1 Ballistic Coefficient = 0.253

Distance • Yards	Muzzle	100	200	300	400	500	600	800	1000
Velocity • fps	3500	3086	2708	2360	2033	1744	1482	1107	931
Energy • Ft-lbs	1741	1353	1042	791	590	432	312	174	123
Taylor KO Index	7.2	6.3	5.5	4.8	4.2	3.6	3.0	2.3	1.9
Path • Inches	-1.5	+1.1	0.0	-5.9	-18.0	-38.6	-71.3	-193.1	-428.2
Wind Drift • Inches	0.0	1.0	4.2	10.0	19.0	32.0	49.8	103.0	177.7

José A. Martínez de Hoz traveled from Argentina to Botswana to shoot sitatunga antelope, which mainly occur in swamps. (Photo from *A Sporting Life* by José A. Martínez de Hoz, 2005, Safari Press)

.225 Winchester (Relisted in 2004)

The .225 Winchester was introduced in 1964 as a replacement for the .220 Swift. It is classified as semi-rimless rather than rimmed, and while it can be used in Model 70s and other box-magazine guns, it seems to have found the most favor in various single-shot actions. Remington's standardization of the .22-250 in 1965 may have dealt the .225 a severe, and nearly fatal, blow. Winchester dropped this cartridge from their catalog but relisted it in 2004.

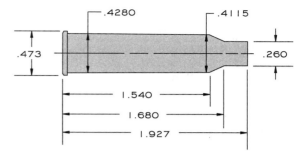

Relative Recoil Factor = 0.90

Specifications

Controlling Agency for Standardization of this Ammunition: SAAMI

Bullet Weight Grains	Velocity fps	Maximum Average Pressure	
		Copper Crusher	Transducer
55	3,650	N/A	60,000 psi

Standard barrel for velocity testing: 24 inches long—1 turn in 14-inch twist

Availability

Winchester 55-grain Pointed Soft Point (X2251)

G1 Ballistic Coefficient = 0.208

Distance • Yards	Muzzle	100	200	300	400	500	600	800	1000
Velocity • fps	3570	3066	2616	2208	1838	1514	1255	969	832
Energy • Ft-lbs	1556	1148	836	595	412	280	192	115	85
Taylor KO Index	6.2	5.4	4.6	3.9	3.2	2.7	2.2	1.7	1.5
Path • Inches	-1.5	+1.1	0.0	-6.3	-19.8	-43.7	-84.1	-241.2	-534.8
Wind Drift • Inches	0.0	1.2	5.0	12.2	23.7	40.7	64.0	132.0	220.6

(Left to right) .225 Winchester, .224 Weatherby, .22-250 Remington, .220 Swift.

.224 Weatherby Magnum

Weatherby's .224 Magnum, introduced in 1963, is a miniaturized version of the .300 Weatherby, belt, venturi shoulder, and all. This nifty little cartridge provides just a shade less performance than the current king of the centerfire .22s, the .22-250. At one time Norma loaded a 53-grain bullet in this case, but that loading was dropped a couple years ago. While Weatherby no longer list new rifles in this caliber, they continue to provide this one loading.

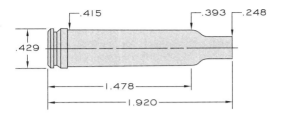

Relative Recoil Factor = 0.90

Specifications

Controlling Agency for Standardization of this Ammunition: CIP

Bullet Weight Grains	Velocity fps	Maximum Average Pressure	
		Copper Crusher	Transducer
N/S	N/S	3,800 bar	4,370 bar

Standard barrel for velocity testing: 26 inches long—1 turn in 14-inch twist

Availability

Weatherby 55-grain Pointed—Expanding (H 224 55 SP)

G1 Ballistic Coefficient = 0.235

Distance • Yards	Muzzle	100	200	300	400	500	600	800	1000
Velocity • fps	3650	3192	2780	2403	2056	1741	1462	1081	910
Energy • Ft-lbs	1627	1244	944	705	516	370	261	143	101
Taylor KO Index	6.4	5.6	4.9	4.2	3.6	3.1	2.6	1.9	1.6
Path • Inches	-1.5	+1.0	0.0	-5.5	-17.1	-37.0	-69.2	-192.1	-432.0
Wind Drift • Inches	0.0	1.0	4.3	10.2	19.6	33.0	51.8	108.0	186.4

PH Joe Coogan (right) with a client and a good Botswana leopard. (Photo from African Hunter II *by Craig Boddington and Peter Flack, 2004, Safari Press)*

.220 Swift

When it was introduced in 1935, the .220 Swift was the "swiftest" cartridge in the factory inventory. Today, the Swift still claims the "record" for .22's (4250 fps with a 40-grain bullet). Much of what has been written about the Swift is a direct steal from the stories about King Arthur's sword, mostly myth. The .220 Swift doesn't need any fiction. It's a very high velocity .22, one suitable for all varmint applications. Part of the Swift's bad press has resulted from shooters using thin-jacketed varmint bullets on deer-size game. The results are seldom satisfactory, but it is unfair to blame the cartridge for the foolishness of a few uninformed people.

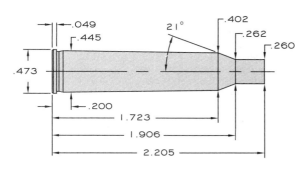

Relative Recoil Factor = 0.90

Specifications

Controlling Agency for Ammunition Standardization: CIP

Bullet Weight Grains	Velocity fps	Maximum Average Pressure Copper Crusher	Transducer
55	3,650	54,000 cup	N/A
60	3,600	54,000 cup	N/A

Standard barrel for velocity testing: 24 inches long—1 turn in 14-inch twist

Availability

Federal 40-grain Nosler Ballistic Tip (P220B)

G1 Ballistic Coefficient = 0.221

Distance • Yards	Muzzle	100	200	300	400	500	600	800	1000
Velocity • fps	4250	3690	3200	2770	2370	2000	1674	1177	947
Energy • Ft-lbs	1605	1210	910	680	500	355	249	123	80
Taylor KO Index	5.4	4.7	4.1	3.5	3.0	2.6	2.1	1.5	1.2
Path • Inches	-1.5	+0.5	0.0	-3.9	-12.5	-27.3	-51.2	-145.0	-342.6
Wind Drift • Inches	0.0	0.9	3.8	9.2	17.4	29.2	45.7	96.8	173.4

Hornady 40-grain V-Max Moly VX (83203)

G1 Ballistic Coefficient = 0.220

Distance • Yards	Muzzle	100	200	300	400	500	600	800	1000
Velocity • fps	4200	3678	3190	2739	2329	1962	1637	1153	936
Energy • Ft-lbs	1566	1201	904	666	482	342	238	118	78
Taylor KO Index	5.4	4.7	4.1	3.5	3.0	2.5	2.1	1.5	1.2
Path • Inches	-1.5	+0.5	0.0	-4.0	-12.9	-27.4	-53.0	-150.8	-355.4
Wind Drift • Inches	0.0	0.9	3.9	9.4	17.8	29.9	46.8	99.4	177.3

Winchester 40-grain Ballistic Silvertip (SBST220)

G1 Ballistic Coefficient = 0.221

Distance • Yards	Muzzle	100	200	300	400	500	600	800	1000
Velocity • fps	4050	3518	3048	2624	2238	1885	1569	1118	920
Energy • Ft-lbs	1457	1099	825	611	445	316	219	111	75
Taylor KO Index	5.2	4.5	3.9	3.4	2.9	2.4	2.0	1.4	1.2
Path • Inches	-1.5	+0.7	0.0	-4.4	-13.9	-30.4	-57.6	-163.7	-381.5
Wind Drift • Inches	0.0	1.0	4.1	9.7	18.5	31.2	48.9	103.7	182.9

Norma 50-grain Soft Point (15701)

G1 Ballistic Coefficient = 0.185

Distance • Yards	Muzzle	100	200	300	400	500	600	800	1000
Velocity • fps	4019	3395	2853	2371	1939	1562	1260	949	806
Energy • Ft-lbs	1794	1280	904	624	418	271	176	100	72
Taylor KO Index	6.4	5.4	4.6	3.8	3.1	2.5	2.0	1.5	1.3
Path • Inches	-1.5	+0.8	0.0	-5.1	-16.5	-37.2	-72.5	-217.6	-516.6
Wind Drift • Inches	0.0	1.0	4.5	11.0	21.3	36.8	59.0	124.2	209.8

Winchester 50-grain Pointed Soft Point (X220S)

G1 Ballistic Coefficient = 0.200

Distance • Yards	Muzzle	100	200	300	400	500	600	800	1000
Velocity • fps	3870	3310	2816	2373	1972	1616	1318	985	837
Energy • Ft-lbs	1663	1226	881	625	432	290	193	108	78
Taylor KO Index	6.2	5.3	4.5	3.8	3.2	2.6	2.1	1.6	1.3
Path • Inches	-1.5	+0.8	0.0	-5.2	-16.7	-37.1	-72.9	-215.0	-490.0
Wind Drift • Inches	0.0	1.1	4.8	11.6	22.4	38.4	61.1	128.4	218.1

Remington 50-grain Pointed Soft Point (R220S1)

G1 Ballistic Coefficient = 0.175

Distance • Yards	Muzzle	100	200	300	400	500	600	800	1000
Velocity • fps	3780	3158	2617	2135	1710	1357	1108	882	752
Energy • Ft-lbs	1586	1107	760	506	325	204	136	86	63
Taylor KO Index	6.0	5.1	4.2	3.4	2.7	2.2	1.8	1.4	1.2
Path • Inches	-1.5	+1.0	0.0	-6.2	-20.1	-46.2	-94.2	-279.7	-623.6
Wind Drift • Inches	0.0	1.3	5.7	14.1	27.8	48.6	78.2	158.6	260.8

Hornady 50-grain V-Max Moly VX (83213)

G1 Ballistic Coefficient = 0.233

Distance • Yards	Muzzle	100	200	300	400	500	600	800	1000
Velocity • fps	3850	3396	2970	2576	2215	1894	1602	1162	952
Energy • Ft-lbs	1645	1280	979	736	545	398	285	150	101
Taylor KO Index	6.2	5.4	4.8	4.1	3.5	3.0	2.6	1.9	1.5
Path • Inches	-1.5	+0.7	0.0	-4.8	-15.1	-32.2	-59.5	-163.3	-372.9
Wind Drift • Inches	0.0	0.9	3.9	9.4	17.7	29.8	46.4	97.2	171.4

Remington 50-grain V-Max Boat-Tail (PRV220SA) (Discontinued in 2004)

Use EtronX (EL220SA) for Remington Electronic Rifle

G1 Ballistic Coefficient = 0.239

Distance • Yards	Muzzle	100	200	300	400	500	600	800	1000
Velocity • fps	3780	3321	2908	2532	2185	1866	1577	1150	948
Energy • Ft-lbs	1586	1224	939	711	530	387	276	147	100
Taylor KO Index	6.0	5.3	4.7	4.1	3.5	3.0	2.5	1.8	1.5
Path • Inches	-1.5	+0.8	0.0	-5.0	-15.4	-33.2	-61.6	-168.8	-383.3
Wind Drift • Inches	0.0	0.9	4.0	9.5	18.0	30.2	47.1	98.4	172.8

Federal 52-grain Nosler Ballistic Tip (P220V)

G1 Ballistic Coefficient = 0.246

Distance • Yards	Muzzle	100	200	300	400	500	600	800	1000
Velocity • fps	3830	3370	2960	2600	2230	1910	1622	1180	964
Energy • Ft-lbs	1695	1310	1010	765	575	420	304	160	107
Taylor KO Index	6.4	5.6	4.9	4.3	3.7	3.2	2.7	2.0	1.6
Path • Inches	-1.5	+0.8	0.0	-4.8	-14.9	-31.9	-59.1	-160.9	-366.4
Wind Drift • Inches	0.0	0.9	3.9	9.2	17.5	29.3	45.5	95.0	167.9

Federal 55-grain Trophy Bonded Bear Claw (P220T1) (Discontinued in 2004)

G1 Ballistic Coefficient = 0.202

Distance • Yards	Muzzle	100	200	300	400	500	600	800	1000
Velocity • fps	3700	3170	2690	2270	1880	1540	1262	966	826
Energy • Ft-lbs	1670	1225	885	625	430	290	195	114	83
Taylor KO Index	6.5	5.8	4.7	4.0	3.3	2.7	2.2	1.7	1.5
Path • Inches	-1.5	+1.0	0.0	-5.8	-18.5	-40.3	-80.4	-234.4	-525.3
Wind Drift • Inches	0.0	1.2	5.0	12.1	23.5	40.3	64.1	133.2	223.4

Hornady 55-grain V-Max Moly VX (83243)

G1 Ballistic Coefficient = 0.258

Distance • Yards	Muzzle	100	200	300	400	500	600	800	1000
Velocity • fps	3680	3215	2876	2517	2183	1887	1615	1191	975
Energy • Ft-lbs	1654	1302	1010	772	582	435	319	173	116
Taylor KO Index	6.5	5.7	5.1	4.4	3.8	3.3	2.8	2.1	1.7
Path • Inches	-1.5	+0.9	0.0	-5.3	-16.1	-34.1	-61.9	-165.7	-371.2
Wind Drift • Inches	0.0	0.9	3.8	9.1	17.2	28.8	44.8	92.8	163.3

Hornady 60-grain Hollow Point (8122)

G1 Ballistic Coefficient = 0.264

Distance • Yards	Muzzle	100	200	300	400	500	600	800	1000
Velocity • fps	3600	3199	2824	2475	2156	1868	1604	1191	978
Energy • Ft-lbs	1727	1364	1063	816	619	465	343	189	128
Taylor KO Index	6.9	6.1	5.4	4.8	4.1	3.6	2.8	2.1	1.7
Path • Inches	-1.5	+1.0	0.0	-5.4	-16.3	-34.8	-63.8	-169.6	-376.9
Wind Drift • Inches	0.0	0.9	3.9	9.2	17.3	29.0	44.7	92.3	162.0

.223 Winchester Super Short Magnum (WSSM)

Winchester's success with their Short Magnum cartridges led them to introduce a new series of Super Short Magnum cartridges beginning in 2003. The .223 WSSM is the .22-caliber version of that new series. The .223 WSSM has factory performance numbers that are slightly better than the .220 Swift but not up to what can be done with the wildcat .22-.284. It is a potent cartridge that lends itself to use in very short actions.

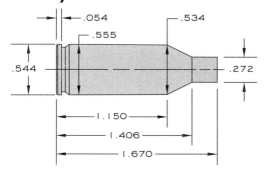

Relative Recoil Factor = 0.95

Specifications:

Controlling Agency for Standardization of this Ammunition: SAAMI

Bullet Weight Grains	Velocity fps	Maximum Average Pressure	
		Copper Crusher	Transducer
55	6850	N/S	65,000 psi

Standard barrel for velocity testing: 24 inches long—1 turn in 12-inch twist

Availability

Winchester 55-grain Ballistic Silvertip (SBST223SS)
G1 Ballistic Coefficient = 0.276

Distance • Yards	Muzzle	100	200	300	400	500	600	800	1000
Velocity • fps	3850	3438	2780	2403	2056	1741	1462	1081	910
Energy • Ft-lbs	1627	1244	944	705	516	370	261	143	101
Taylor KO Index	6.4	5.6	4.9	4.2	3.6	3.1	2.6	1.9	1.6
Path • nches	-1.5	+1.0	0.0	-5.5	-17.1	-37.0	-69.2	-192.1	-432.0
Wind Drift • Inches	0.0	1.0	4.3	10.2	19.6	33.0	51.8	108.0	186.4

Winchester 55-grain Pointed Soft Point (X223WSS)
G1 Ballistic Coefficient = 0.233

Distance • Yards	Muzzle	100	200	300	400	500	600	800	1000
Velocity • fps	3850	3192	2780	2403	2056	1741	1462	1081	910
Energy • Ft-lbs	1627	1244	944	705	516	370	261	143	101
Taylor KO Index	6.4	5.6	4.9	4.2	3.6	3.1	2.6	1.9	1.6
Path • Inches	-1.5	+1.0	0.0	-5.5	-17.1	-37.0	-69.2	-192.1	-432.0
Wind Drift • Inches	0.0	1.0	4.3	10.2	19.6	33.0	51.8	108.0	186.4

Winchester 64-grain Power Point (X223WSS1)
G1 Ballistic Coefficient = 0.235

Distance • Yards	Muzzle	100	200	300	400	500	600	800	1000
Velocity • fps	3600	3144	2732	2356	2011	1698	1428	1062	898
Energy • Ft-lbs	1841	1404	1061	786	574	410	290	160	115
Taylor KO Index	7.4	6.4	5.6	4.8	4.1	3.5	2.9	2.2	1.8
Path • Inches	-1.5	+1.0	0.0	-5.7	-17.7	-38.5	-72.0	-200.3	-448.9
Wind Drift • Inches	0.0	1.0	4.4	10.5	20.1	34.0	53.3	111.0	190.6

.243 Winchester

The .243 Winchester (1955) was the first of the spin-offs of the .308 cartridge after the .308's military adoption in 1954. There were few other 6mm cartridges to compete against. Except for the 6mm Navy, which was very much unloved and effectively obsolete, the 6mm size didn't go anywhere in the United States until after the announcement of the .243 Winchester. Today the 6mm calibers have taken over the middle ground between the .22s and the 7mms. Except for the .25-06, the .25-caliber guns are not doing well at all. The .243 is a truly versatile cartridge, one that's an excellent varmint caliber with the lighter bullets while retaining a very good capability against deer-size game, with bullets in the 100-grain weight class.

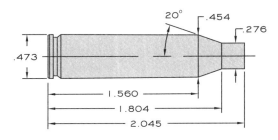

Relative Recoil Factor = 1.25

Specifications

Controlling Agency for Standardization of this Ammunition: SAAMI

Bullet Weight Grains	Velocity fps	Maximum Average Pressure	
		Copper Crusher	Transducer
75	3,325	52,000 cup	60,000 psi
80	3,325	52,000 cup	60,000 psi
85-87	3,300	52,000 cup	60,000 psi
100	2,950	52,000 cup	60,000 psi

Standard barrel for velocity testing: 24 inches long—1 turn in 10-inch twist

Availability

Winchester 55-grain Ballistic Silvertip (SBST243)
G1 Ballistic Coefficient = 0.276

Distance • Yards	Muzzle	100	200	300	400	500	600	800	1000
Velocity • fps	3910	3493	3114	2766	2444	2144	1865	1393	1084
Energy • Ft-lbs	1867	1489	1184	934	729	562	425	237	144
Taylor KO Index	7.4	6.5	5.8	5.1	4.5	3.9	3.4	2.5	2.0
Path • Inches	-1.5	+0.6	0.0	-4.3	-13.1	-27.8	-50.2	-128.4	-279.8
Wind Drift • Inches	0.0	0.8	3.5	8.2	15.4	25.6	39.5	81.2	144.9

Federal 55-grain Nosler Ballistic Tip (P243H)
G1 Ballistic Coefficient = 0.268

Distance • Yards	Muzzle	100	200	300	400	500	600	800	1000
Velocity • fps	3850	3430	3040	2690	2360	2060	1783	1320	1042
Energy • Ft-lbs	1810	1435	1130	880	680	515	388	213	133
Taylor KO Index	7.5	6.7	5.9	5.3	4.7	4.1	3.6	2.7	2.1
Path • Inches	-1.5	+0.7	0.0	-4.5	-13.9	-29.5	-53.5	-140.0	-312.5
Wind Drift • Inches	0.0	0.8	3.3	7.8	14.6	24.2	37.1	75.8	135.7

Black Hills 55-grain Nosler Ballistic Tip
G1 Ballistic Coefficient = 0.276

Distance • Yards	Muzzle	100	200	300	400	500	600	800	1000
Velocity • fps	3800	3393	3022	2682	2365	2071	1799	1343	1058
Energy • Ft-lbs	1763	1406	1116	878	683	524	395	220	137
Taylor KO Index	7.3	6.5	5.8	5.1	4.5	4.0	3.4	2.6	2.0
Path • Inches	-1.5	+0.8	0.0	-4.6	-14.0	-29.7	-53.7	-139.4	-308.2
Wind Drift • Inches	0.0	0.8	3.4	8.1	15.1	25.1	38.6	79.0	140.8

Hornady 58-grain V-MAX Moly VX (83423)
G1 Ballistic Coefficient = 0.252

Distance • Yards	Muzzle	100	200	300	400	500	600	800	1000
Velocity • fps	3750	3308	2905	2544	2206	1895	1616	1193	966
Energy • Ft-lbs	1811	1409	1090	833	627	463	336	180	120
Taylor KO Index	7.6	6.7	5.8	5.1	4.4	3.8	3.3	2.4	1.9
Path • Inches	-1.5	+0.8	0.0	-5.0	-15.4	-33.0	-60.6	-163.8	-370.0
Wind Drift • Inches	0.0	0.9	3.9	9.2	17.4	29.2	45.2	94.1	166.0

Federal 70-grain Nosler Ballistic Tip (P243F)

G1 Ballistic Coefficient = 0.310

Distance • Yards	Muzzle	100	200	300	400	500	600	800	1000
Velocity • fps	3400	3070	2760	2470	2200	1950	1717	1323	1070
Energy • Ft-lbs	1785	1465	1185	950	755	590	458	272	178
Taylor KO Index	8.3	7.5	6.7	6.0	5.3	4.7	4.2	3.2	2.6
Path • Inches	-1.5	+1.1	0.0	-5.7	-17.1	-35.7	-63.5	-158.2	-333.3
Wind Drift • Inches	0.0	0.8	3.4	8.1	15.2	25.2	38.5	77.8	136.3

Federal 70-grain Speer TNT HP (P243V1) (Discontinued in 2004)

G1 Ballistic Coefficient = 0.282

Distance • Yards	Muzzle	100	200	300	400	500	600	800	1000
Velocity • fps	3400	3040	2700	2390	2100	1830	1588	1203	995
Energy • Ft-lbs	1795	1435	1135	890	685	520	392	225	154
Taylor KO Index	8.4	7.4	6.6	5.8	5.1	4.4	3.9	2.9	2.4
Path • Inches	-1.5	+1.1	0.0	-5.9	-18.0	-37.9	-68.4	-175.5	-378.9
Wind Drift • Inches	0.0	0.9	3.8	9.1	17.1	28.5	44.0	89.8	156.3

Remington 75-grain V-Max Boat Tail (PRV243WC) (Discontinued in 2004)

G1 Ballistic Coefficient = 0.331

Distance • Yards	Muzzle	100	200	300	400	500	600	800	1000
Velocity • fps	3375	3065	2775	2504	2248	2008	1786	1399	1125
Energy • Ft-lbs	1897	1564	1282	1044	842	671	532	326	211
Taylor KO Index	8.8	8.0	7.2	6.5	5.9	5.2	4.6	3.6	2.9
Path • Inches	-1.5	+1.1	0.0	-5.6	-16.8	-34.9	-61.6	-151.0	-312.4
Wind Drift • Inches	0.0	0.0	3.2	7.6	14.2	23.4	35.6	71.3	124.8

Remington 75-grain AccuTip Boat Tail (PRA243WB)

G1 Ballistic Coefficient = 0.330

Distance • Yards	Muzzle	100	200	300	400	500	600	800	1000
Velocity • fps	3375	3065	2775	2504	2248	2008	1782	1395	1122
Energy • Ft-lbs	1897	1564	1282	1044	842	671	529	324	210
Taylor KO Index	8.8	8.0	7.2	6.5	5.9	5.2	4.6	3.6	2.9
Path • Inches	-1.5	+1.1	0.0	-5.6	-16.8	-35.0	-61.8	-156.2	-319.6
Wind Drift • Inches	0.0	0.8	3.2	7.6	14.2	23.5	35.8	71.6	125.4

Hornady 75-grain HP (8040)

G1 Ballistic Coefficient = 0.296

Distance • Yards	Muzzle	100	200	300	400	500	600	800	1000
Velocity • fps	3400	3051	2729	2428	2147	1885	1645	1253	1023
Energy • Ft-lbs	1925	1550	1240	982	768	592	451	262	174
Taylor KO Index	8.9	7.9	7.1	6.3	5.6	4.9	4.3	3.3	2.7
Path • Inches	-1.5	+1.1	0.0	-5.8	-17.6	-36.9	-66.3	-169.7	-366.5
Wind Drift • Inches	0.0	0.9	3.6	8.6	16.2	27.0	41.4	84.3	147.5

Federal 80-grain Speer Hot-Cor (243AS)

G1 Ballistic Coefficient = 0.256

Distance • Yards	Muzzle	100	200	300	400	500	600	800	1000
Velocity • fps	3350	2960	2590	2260	1950	1670	1427	1085	924
Energy • Ft-lbs	1995	1550	1195	905	675	495	362	209	152
Taylor KO Index	9.3	8.2	7.2	6.3	5.4	4.6	4.0	3.0	2.6
Path • Inches	-1.5	+1.3	0.0	-6.4	-19.7	-42.2	-77.3	-204.9	-450.0
Wind Drift • Inches	0.0	1.0	4.3	10.4	19.8	33.2	51.7	106.1	180.9

Remington 80-grain Pointed Soft Point (R243W1)

G1 Ballistic Coefficient = 0.256

Distance • Yards	Muzzle	100	200	300	400	500	600	800	1000
Velocity • fps	3350	2955	2593	2259	1951	1670	1427	1085	924
Energy • Ft-lbs	1993	1551	1194	906	676	495	362	209	152
Taylor KO Index	9.3	8.2	7.2	6.3	5.4	4.6	4.0	3.0	2.6
Path • Inches	-1.5	+1.2	0.0	-6.5	-19.8	-42.4	-77.3	-204.9	-449.9
Wind Drift • Inches	0.0	1.0	4.4	10.4	19.9	33.4	51.7	106.1	180.9

Winchester 80-grain Pointed Soft Point (X2431)

G1 Ballistic Coefficient = 0.256

Distance • Yards	Muzzle	100	200	300	400	500	600	800	1000
Velocity • fps	3350	2955	2593	2259	1951	1670	1427	1085	924
Energy • Ft-lbs	1993	1551	1194	906	676	495	362	209	152
Taylor KO Index	9.3	8.2	7.2	6.3	5.4	4.6	4.0	3.0	2.6
Path • Inches	-1.5	+1.2	0.0	-6.5	-19.8	-42.4	-77.3	-204.9	-449.9
Wind Drift • Inches	0.0	1.0	4.4	10.4	19.9	33.4	51.7	106.1	180.9

PMC 80-grain Pointed Soft Point (243A)

G1 Ballistic Coefficient = 0.315

Distance • Yards	Muzzle	100	200	300	400	500	600	800	1000
Velocity • fps	3200	2885	2590	2315	2059	1827	1608	1250	1034
Energy • Ft-lbs	1819	1478	1192	952	753	590	460	277	190
Taylor KO Index	8.9	8.0	7.2	6.4	5.7	5.1	4.5	3.5	2.9
Path • Inches	-1.5	+1.4	0.0	-6.6	-19.6	-40.9	-72.5	-182.2	-385.1
Wind Drift • Inches	0.0	0.9	3.7	8.7	16.2	26.9	41.2	83.1	143.8

Remington 80-grain Hollow Point Power-Lokt (R243W2)

G1 Ballistic Coefficient = 0.256

Distance • Yards	Muzzle	100	200	300	400	500	600	800	1000
Velocity • fps	3350	2955	2593	2259	1951	1670	1427	1085	924
Energy • Ft-lbs	1993	1551	1194	906	676	495	362	209	152
Taylor KO Index	9.3	8.2	7.2	6.3	5.4	4.6	4.0	3.0	2.6
Path • Inches	-1.5	+1.2	0.0	-6.5	-19.8	-42.4	-77.3	-204.9	-449.9
Wind Drift • Inches	0.0	1.0	4.4	10.4	19.9	33.4	51.7	106.1	180.9

Norma 80-grain Full Metal Jacket (16007) (Discontinued in 2004)

G1 Ballistic Coefficient = 0.262

Distance • Yards	Muzzle	100	200	300	400	500	600	800	1000
Velocity • fps	3117	2750	2412	2098	1812	1553	1332	1043	903
Energy • Ft-lbs	1736	1344	1034	782	583	429	315	193	145
Taylor KO Index	8.7	7.6	6.7	5.8	5.0	4.3	3.7	2.9	2.5
Path • Inches	-1.5	+1.6	0.0	-7.6	-23.1	-49.5	-90.8	-241.3	-514.9
Wind Drift • Inches	0.0	1.1	4.6	11.2	21.3	35.7	55.7	112.6	188.1

Federal 85-grain Sierra GameKing BTHP (P243D)

G1 Ballistic Coefficient = 0.402

Distance • Yards	Muzzle	100	200	300	400	500	600	800	1000
Velocity • fps	3320	3070	2830	2600	2380	2180	1984	1629	1333
Energy • Ft-lbs	2080	1770	1510	1280	1070	890	743	501	335
Taylor KO Index	9.8	9.1	8.4	7.7	7.0	6.4	5.9	4.8	3.9
Path • Inches	-1.5	+1.1	0.0	-5.5	-16.1	-32.8	-56.9	-133.6	-263.4
Wind Drift • Inches	0.0	0.6	2.7	6.2	11.6	18.8	28.3	55.3	95.3

PMC 85-grain Hollow Point Boat Tail (243VA)

G1 Ballistic Coefficient = 0.282

Distance • Yards	Muzzle	100	200	300	400	500	600	800	1000
Velocity • fps	3275	2922	2596	2292	2009	1748	1513	1156	972
Energy • Ft-lbs	2024	1611	1272	991	761	577	432	252	178
Taylor KO Index	9.7	8.6	7.7	6.8	5.9	5.2	4.5	3.4	2.9
Path • Inches	-1.5	+1.3	0.0	-6.5	-19.7	-41.4	-75.2	-195.4	-421.9
Wind Drift • Inches	0.0	1.0	4.0	9.6	18.0	30.1	46.5	94.7	163.0

Remington 90-grain Swift Scirocco Bonded (PRSC243WA)

G1 Ballistic Coefficient = 0.390

Distance • Yards	Muzzle	100	200	300	400	500	600	800	1000
Velocity • fps	3120	2871	2636	2411	2199	1997	1806	1467	1204
Energy • Ft-lbs	1946	1647	1388	1162	966	797	652	430	290
Taylor KO Index	9.7	9.0	8.2	7.5	6.9	6.2	5.6	4.6	3.8
Path • Inches	-1.5	+1.4	0.0	-6.4	-18.8	-38.3	-66.8	-158.7	-318.5
Wind Drift • Inches	0.0	0.7	3.0	7.0	13.0	21.3	32.2	63.3	109.3

Remington 90-grain Pointed Soft Point, Ballistic Tip (PRT243WC) (Discontinued in 2004)
Use EtronX (EL243WC) for Remington Electronic Rifle

G1 Ballistic Coefficient = 0.390

Distance • Yards	Muzzle	100	200	300	400	500	600	800	1000
Velocity • fps	3120	2871	2636	2411	2199	1997	1806	1467	1204
Energy • Ft-lbs	1946	1647	1388	1162	966	797	652	430	290
Taylor KO Index	9.7	9.0	8.2	7.5	6.9	6.2	5.6	4.6	3.8
Path • Inches	-1.5	+1.4	0.0	-6.4	-18.8	-38.3	-66.8	-158.7	-318.5
Wind Drift • Inches	0.0	0.7	3.0	7.0	13.0	21.3	32.2	63.3	109.3

Lapua 90-grain FMJ (4316052)

G1 Ballistic Coefficient = 0.378

Distance • Yards	Muzzle	100	200	300	400	500	600	800	1000
Velocity • fps	2904	2659	2427	2206	1998	1801	1620	1309	1096
Energy • Ft-lbs	1686	1413	1117	973	798	649	524	343	240
Taylor KO Index	9.1	8.3	7.6	6.9	6.2	5.6	5.1	4.1	3.4
Path • Inches	-1.5	+1.7	0.0	-7.6	-22.4	-46.0	-80.3	-191.9	-385.3
Wind Drift • Inches	0.0	0.8	3.4	8.1	15.0	24.7	37.4	73.8	126.2

Hirtenberger 95-grain Nosler SP (82200323)

G1 Ballistic Coefficient = 0.284

Distance • Yards	Muzzle	100	200	300	400	500	600	800	1000
Velocity • fps	3084	2748	2436	2144	1874	1628	1411	1100	944
Energy • Ft-lbs	2022	1605	1261	977	746	563	423	257	189
Taylor KO Index	10.2	9.1	8.0	7.1	6.2	5.4	4.7	3.6	3.1
Path • Inches	-1.5	+1.6	0.0	-7.5	-22.5	-47.6	-85.8	-220.4	-469.4
Wind Drift • Inches	0.0	1.0	4.3	10.3	19.5	32.6	50.4	101.8	172.0

Hornady 95-grain SST-LM (85464)

G1 Ballistic Coefficient = 0.355

Distance • Yards	Muzzle	100	200	300	400	500	600	800	1000
Velocity • fps	3100	2828	2572	2331	2102	1887	1685	1342	1104
Energy • Ft-lbs	2027	1687	1396	1146	932	751	599	360	257
Taylor KO Index	10.2	9.3	8.5	7.7	6.9	6.2	5.6	4.4	3.6
Path • Inches	-1.5	+1.4	0.0	-6.7	-19.8	-40.8	-71.8	-174.7	-358.9
Wind Drift • Inches	0.0	0.6	3.2	7.7	14.6	24.1	36.6	73.0	126.3

Remington 95-grain AccuTip Boat Tail (PRA243WA)

G1 Ballistic Coefficient = 0.355

Distance • Yards	Muzzle	100	200	300	400	500	600	800	1000
Velocity • fps	3120	2847	2590	2347	2118	1902	1699	1353	1111
Energy • Ft-lbs	2053	1710	1415	1162	946	763	609	386	260
Taylor KO Index	10.3	9.4	8.5	7.7	7.0	6.3	5.6	4.5	3.7
Path • Inches	-1.5	+1.3	0.0	-6.6	-19.5	-40.2	-70.7	-172.1	-353.5
Wind Drift • Inches	0.0	0.8	3.3	7.8	14.6	24.0	36.4	72.4	125.3

Hirtenberger 95-grain Nosler Ballistic Tip (82200475)

G1 Ballistic Coefficient = 0.349

Distance • Yards	Muzzle	100	200	300	400	500	600	800	1000
Velocity • fps	3117	2839	2578	2332	2099	1881	1677	1331	1095
Energy • Ft-lbs	2050	1701	1403	1148	930	746	594	374	253
Taylor KO Index	10.3	9.4	8.5	7.7	6.9	6.2	5.5	4.4	3.6
Path • Inches	-1.5	+1.4	0.0	-6.7	-19.7	-40.7	-71.6	-173.8	-355.3
Wind Drift • Inches	0.0	0.8	3.4	8.0	14.9	24.5	37.3	74.3	128.6

Winchester 95-grain Ballistic Silvertip (SBST243A)

G1 Ballistic Coefficient = 0.400

Distance • Yards	Muzzle	100	200	300	400	500	600	800	1000
Velocity • fps	3100	2854	2626	2410	2203	2007	1819	1486	1223
Energy • Ft-lbs	2021	1719	1455	1225	1024	850	698	466	316
Taylor KO Index	10.2	9.4	8.7	7.9	7.3	6.6	6.0	4.9	4.0
Path • Inches	-1.5	+1.4	0.0	-6.4	-18.9	-38.4	-66.8	-157.3	-311.6
Wind Drift • Inches	0.0	0.7	3.0	6.9	12.9	20.9	31.5	61.7	106.3

Federal 95-grain Nosler Ballistic Tip (P243J)

G1 Ballistic Coefficient = 0.375

Distance • Yards	Muzzle	100	200	300	400	500	600	800	1000
Velocity • fps	3030	2770	2540	2310	2100	1900	1700	1369	1130
Energy • Ft-lbs	1930	1625	1360	1125	930	750	609	395	270
Taylor KO Index	10.0	9.1	8.4	7.6	6.9	6.3	5.6	4.5	3.7
Path • Inches	-1.5	+1.5	0.0	-6.9	-20.4	-41.8	-73.1	-175.8	-356.4
Wind Drift • Inches	0.0	0.8	3.3	7.6	14.2	23.4	35.4	70.0	120.5

Black Hills 95-grain Nosler Ballistic Tip (2C243BHGN1)

G1 Ballistic Coefficient = 0.379

Distance • Yards	Muzzle	100	200	300	400	500	600	800	1000
Velocity • fps	2950	2703	2469	2248	2037	1839	1654	1337	1112
Energy • Ft-lbs	1836	1542	1287	1066	876	714	577	377	261
Taylor KO Index	9.7	8.9	8.1	7.4	6.7	6.1	5.5	4.4	3.7
Path • Inches	-1.5	+1.6	0.0	-7.4	-21.6	-44.3	-77.3	-185.7	-375.5
Wind Drift • Inches	0.0	0.8	3.3	7.8	14.6	24.0	36.4	71.8	123.1

Hornady 95-grain SST (80464)

G1 Ballistic Coefficient = 0.355

Distance • Yards	Muzzle	100	200	300	400	500	600	800	1000
Velocity • fps	2950	2687	2439	2205	1983	1776	1584	1265	1060
Energy • Ft-lbs	1835	1523	1255	1025	829	665	529	338	237
Taylor KO Index	9.7	8.9	8.0	7.3	6.5	5.9	5.2	4.2	3.5
Path • Inches	-1.5	+1.7	0.0	-7.5	-22.2	-45.8	-80.6	-196.8	-403.4
Wind Drift • Inches	0.0	0.6	3.3	8.2	15.6	25.8	39.4	78.5	134.6

RWS 100-grain Cone Point (211 6812) (Discontinued in 2004)

G1 Ballistic Coefficient = 0.300

Distance • Yards	Muzzle	100	200	300	400	500	600	800	1000
Velocity • fps	3130	2852	2591	2345	2112	1893	1689	1341	1101
Energy • Ft-lbs	2089	1735	1432	1172	951	764	609	384	258
Taylor KO Index	10.1	9.5	8.6	7.8	7.0	6.3	5.6	4.5	3.7
Path • Inches	-1.5	+1.4	0.0	-6.6	-19.5	-40.3	-70.9	-173.0	-356.7
Wind Drift • Inches	0.0	0.8	3.4	7.9	14.8	24.3	37.0	73.6	127.4

Hirtenberger 100-grain Nosler SP (82200324)

G1 Ballistic Coefficient = 0.314

Distance • Yards	Muzzle	100	200	300	400	500	600	800	1000
Velocity • fps	3018	2717	2436	2171	1924	1696	1490	1169	993
Energy • Ft-lbs	2023	1640	1318	1047	822	639	493	304	219
Taylor KO Index	10.5	9.4	8.5	7.5	6.7	5.9	5.2	4.1	3.4
Path • Inches	-1.5	+1.6	0.0	-7.5	-22.4	-46.8	-83.3	-208.0	-434.5
Wind Drift • Inches	0.0	1.0	4.0	9.4	17.8	29.5	45.3	90.8	154.7

RWS 100-grain SP (231 4430) (Discontinued in 2005)

G1 Ballistic Coefficient = 0.350

Distance • Yards	Muzzle	100	200	300	400	500	600	800	1000
Velocity • fps	3018	2747	2492	2251	2024	1811	1614	1284	1068
Energy • Ft-lbs	2023	1678	1380	1126	910	728	578	366	253
Taylor KO Index	10.5	9.5	8.7	7.8	7.0	6.3	5.6	4.5	3.7
Path • Inches	-1.5	+1.6	0.0	-7.2	-21.2	-43.8	-77.2	-188.9	-388.9
Wind Drift • Inches	0.0	0.8	3.5	8.3	15.6	25.7	39.1	77.7	133.6

Hornady 100-grain BTSP—Light Magnum (8546)

G1 Ballistic Coefficient = 0.408

Distance • Yards	Muzzle	100	200	300	400	500	600	800	1000
Velocity • fps	3100	2861	2634	2419	2213	2018	1833	1501	1236
Energy • Ft-lbs	2133	1817	1541	1299	1087	904	746	501	339
Taylor KO Index	10.8	9.9	9.1	8.4	7.7	7.0	6.4	5.2	4.3
Path • Inches	-1.5	+1.4	0.0	-6.4	-18.8	-38.2	-66.3	-156.3	-311.0
Wind Drift • Inches	0.0	0.7	2.9	6.8	12.6	20.5	31.0	60.6	104.3

Winchester 100-grain Power Point Plus (SHV2432)

G1 Ballistic Coefficient = 0.355

Distance • Yards	Muzzle	100	200	300	400	500	600	800	1000
Velocity • fps	3090	2818	2562	2321	2092	1877	1679	1337	1102
Energy • Ft-lbs	2121	1764	1458	1196	972	782	626	397	269
Taylor KO Index	10.7	9.8	8.9	8.1	7.3	6.5	5.8	4.6	3.8
Path • Inches	-1.5	1.3	0.0	-6.7	-20.0	-41.1	-72.3	-174.8	-355.9
Wind Drift • Inches	0.0	0.8	3.4	7.9	14.8	24.4	37.0	73.5	127.0

Speer 100-grain Grand Slam (24500) (Discontinued in 2004)

G1 Ballistic Coefficient = 0.351

Distance • Yards	Muzzle	100	200	300	400	500	600	800	1000
Velocity • fps	3025	2754	2500	2259	2033	1820	1623	1292	1073
Energy • Ft-lbs	2032	1684	1387	1133	918	736	585	371	256
Taylor KO Index	10.5	9.6	8.7	7.8	7.1	6.3	5.6	4.5	3.7
Path • Inches	-1.5	+1.6	0.0	-7.1	-21.1	-43.9	-76.4	-185.5	-378.6
Wind Drift • Inches	0.0	0.8	3.5	8.3	15.4	25.4	38.7	77.0	132.5

Norma 100-grain Oryx (16008)

G1 Ballistic Coefficient = 0.257

Distance • Yards	Muzzle	100	200	300	400	500	600	800	1000
Velocity • fps	3018	2653	2316	2004	1713	1460	1252	1000	872
Energy • Ft-lbs	2023	1563	1191	892	652	474	348	222	169
Taylor KO Index	10.5	9.2	8.0	7.0	5.9	5.1	4.3	3.5	3.0
Path • Inches	-1.5	+1.7	0.0	-8.3	-25.4	-54.6	-100.9	-268.8	-567.7
Wind Drift • Inches	0.0	1.2	5.0	12.1	23.1	39.0	60.7	121.4	200.0

Lapua 100-grain Soft Point (4316056)

G1 Ballistic Coefficient = 0.479

Distance • Yards	Muzzle	100	200	300	400	500	600	800	1000
Velocity • fps	2986	2788	2598	2417	2242	2075	1916	1621	1369
Energy • Ft-lbs	1980	1726	1499	1297	1117	956	815	584	416
Taylor KO Index	10.4	9.7	9.0	8.4	7.8	7.2	6.7	5.6	4.8
Path • Inches	-1.5	+1.5	0.0	-696	-19.3	-38.8	-66.4	-152.0	-292.2
Wind Drift • Inches	0.0	0.6	2.6	5.9	11.0	17.7	26.3	51.1	86.7

Federal 100-grain Nosler Solid Base BT (P243S1)

G1 Ballistic Coefficient = 0.367

Distance • Yards	Muzzle	100	200	300	400	500	600	800	1000
Velocity • fps	2970	2720	2490	2280	2070	1870	1675	1344	1111
Energy • Ft-lbs	1950	1645	1380	1150	950	780	623	401	274
Taylor KO Index	10.3	9.4	8.6	7.9	7.2	6.5	5.8	4.7	3.9
Path • Inches	-1.5	+1.5	0.0	-7.2	-21.1	-43.2	-74.1	-179.1	-364.9
Wind Drift • Inches	0.0	0.6	3.1	7.6	14.4	23.8	36.3	72.0	124.1

Federal 100-grain Sierra GameKing BTSP (P243C)

G1 Ballistic Coefficient = 0.471

Distance • Yards	Muzzle	100	200	300	400	500	600	800	1000
Velocity • fps	2960	2760	2570	2380	2210	2040	1880	1585	1336
Energy • Ft-lbs	1950	1690	1460	1260	1080	925	785	558	396
Taylor KO Index	10.3	9.6	8.9	8.3	7.7	7.1	6.5	5.5	4.6
Path • Inches	-1.5	+1.5	0.0	-6.8	-19.8	-39.9	-68.3	-156.6	-300.7
Wind Drift • Inches	0.0	0.6	2.6	6.1	11.3	18.3	27.4	53.0	90.0

Federal 100-grain Nosler Partition (P243E)

G1 Ballistic Coefficient = 0.406

Distance • Yards	Muzzle	100	200	300	400	500	600	800	1000
Velocity • fps	2960	2730	2510	2300	2100	1910	1734	1420	1179
Energy • Ft-lbs	1945	1650	1395	1170	975	805	667	448	309
Taylor KO Index	10.3	9.5	8.7	8.0	7.3	6.6	6.0	4.9	4.1
Path • Inches	-1.5	+1.6	0.0	-7.1	-20.8	-42.5	-73.6	-173.4	-342.8
Wind Drift • Inches	0.0	0.7	3.1	7.2	13.4	22.0	33.1	64.9	111.2

Federal 100-grain Hi-Shok Soft Point (243B)

G1 Ballistic Coefficient = 0.358

Distance • Yards	Muzzle	100	200	300	400	500	600	800	1000
Velocity • fps	2960	2700	2450	2220	1990	1790	1600	1280	1070
Energy • Ft-lbs	1945	1615	1330	1090	880	710	569	364	254
Taylor KO Index	10.3	9.4	8.5	7.7	6.9	6.2	5.6	4.4	3.7
Path • Inches	-1.5	+1.6	0.0	-7.9	-22.0	-45.4	-79.4	-192.2	-390.4
Wind Drift • Inches	0.0	0.8	3.5	8.4	15.6	25.7	39.0	77.4	132.7

Hornady 100-grain BTSP (8046)

G1 Ballistic Coefficient = 0.406

Distance • Yards	Muzzle	100	200	300	400	500	600	800	1000
Velocity • fps	2960	2728	2508	2299	2099	1910	1734	1420	1179
Energy • Ft-lbs	1945	1653	1397	1174	979	810	667	448	309
Taylor KO Index	10.3	9.5	8.7	8.0	7.3	6.6	6.0	4.9	4.1
Path • Inches	-1.5	+1.6	0.0	-7.2	-21.0	-42.8	-73.6	-173.4	-342.8
Wind Drift • Inches	0.0	0.7	3.1	7.2	13.4	22.0	33.1	64.9	111.2

PMC 100-grain Soft Point Boat Tail (243HB)

G1 Ballistic Coefficient = 0.431

Distance • Yards	Muzzle	100	200	300	400	500	600	800	1000
Velocity • fps	2960	2742	2534	2335	2144	1964	1794	1487	1240
Energy • Ft-lbs	1945	1669	1426	1211	1021	856	715	491	341
Taylor KO Index	10.3	9.5	8.8	8.1	7.4	6.8	6.2	5.2	4.3
Path • Inches	-1.5	+1.6	0.0	-7.0	-20.5	-41.4	-71.3	-166.5	-327.2
Wind Drift • Inches	0.0	0.7	2.9	6.8	12.5	20.4	30.7	59.7	102.1

Remington 100-grain Pointed Soft Point, Boat Tail (PRB243WA) (Discontinued in 2004)

G1 Ballistic Coefficient = 0.391

Distance • Yards	Muzzle	100	200	300	400	500	600	800	1000
Velocity • fps	2960	2720	2492	2275	2069	1875	1694	1377	1144
Energy • Ft-lbs	1945	1642	1378	1149	950	780	638	421	291
Taylor KO Index	10.3	9.4	8.7	7.9	7.2	6.5	5.9	4.8	4.0
Path • Inches	-1.5	+1.6	0.0	-7.2	-21.2	-43.3	-75.2	-178.5	-355.8
Wind Drift • Inches	0.0	0.8	3.2	7.6	14.0	23.0	34.8	68.4	117.3

Remington 100-grain Core-Lokt Ultra Bonded (PRC243WC)

G1 Ballistic Coefficient = 0.373

Distance • Yards	Muzzle	100	200	300	400	500	600	800	1000
Velocity • fps	2960	2709	2471	2246	2033	1832	1644	1324	1102
Energy • Ft-lbs	1945	1629	1356	1120	917	745	600	390	270
Taylor KO Index	10.3	9.4	8.6	7.8	7.1	6.4	5.7	4.6	3.8
Path • Inches	-1.5	+1.5	0.0	-7.3	-21.6	-44.3	-77.5	-186.7	-379.0
Wind Drift • Inches	0.0	0.8	3.4	8.0	14.8	24.5	36.8	73.3	125.2

Remington 100-grain Core-Lokt Pointed Soft Point (R243W3)

G1 Ballistic Coefficient = 0.356

Distance • Yards	Muzzle	100	200	300	400	500	600	800	1000
Velocity • fps	2960	2697	2449	2215	1993	1786	1594	1274	1065
Energy • Ft-lbs	1945	1615	1332	1089	882	708	564	360	252
Taylor KO Index	10.3	9.4	8.5	7.7	6.9	6.2	5.5	4.4	3.7
Path • Inches	-1.5	+1.6	0.0	-7.5	-22.0	-45.4	-79.8	-193.1	-392.8
Wind Drift • Inches	0.0	0.8	3.6	8.4	15.7	25.9	39.3	78.0	133.7

Winchester 100-grain Power-Point (X2432)

G1 Ballistic Coefficient = 0.356

Distance • Yards	Muzzle	100	200	300	400	500	600	800	1000
Velocity • fps	2960	2697	2449	2215	1993	1786	1594	1274	1065
Energy • Ft-lbs	1945	1615	1332	1089	882	708	564	360	252
Taylor KO Index	10.3	9.4	8.5	7.7	6.9	6.2	5.5	4.4	3.7
Path • Inches	-1.5	+1.6	0.0	-7.5	-22.0	-45.4	-79.8	-193.1	-392.8
Wind Drift • Inches	0.0	0.8	3.6	8.4	15.7	25.9	39.3	78.0	133.7

Sellier & Bellot 100-grain Soft Point (SBA24301)

G1 Ballistic Coefficient = 0.249

Distance • Yards	Muzzle	100	200	300	400	500	600	800	1000
Velocity • fps	2904	2505	2161	1865	1581	1339	1154	951	836
Energy • Ft-lbs	1877	1398	1040	774	555	398	296	201	155
Taylor KO Index	10.1	8.7	7.5	6.5	5.5	4.6	4.0	3.3	2.9
Path • Inches	-1.5	+2.0	0.0	-9.4	-28.9	-62.7	-116.7	-309.8	-643.8
Wind Drift • Inches	0.0	1.3	5.6	13.6	26.1	44.3	68.8	134.4	216.9

Estate 100-grain PSP (E243-1) (Discontinued in 2004)

G1 Ballistic Coefficient = 0.300

Distance • Yards	Muzzle	100	200	300	400	500	600	800	1000
Velocity • fps	2900	2594	2307	2039	1791	1565	1368	1087	943
Energy • Ft-lbs	1867	1494	1182	924	712	544	415	263	197
Taylor KO Index	10.1	9.0	8.0	7.1	6.2	5.4	4.7	3.8	3.3
Path • Inches	-1.5	+1.8	0.0	-8.4	-25.2	-53.1	-95.5	-243.8	-508.2
Wind Drift • Inches	0.0	1.0	4.4	10.6	20.0	33.3	51.2	102.3	170.8

PMC 100-grain Pointed Soft Point (243B)

G1 Ballistic Coefficient = 0.378

Distance • Yards	Muzzle	100	200	300	400	500	600	800	1000
Velocity • fps	2800	2566	2354	2161	1985	1825	1661	1372	1154
Energy • Ft-lbs	1741	1462	1230	1037	875	739	613	418	296
Taylor KO Index	9.7	8.9	8.2	7.5	6.9	6.3	5.8	4.8	4.0
Path • Inches	-1.5	+1.9	0.0	-8.2	-23.8	-48.4	-81.8	-192.0	-379.1
Wind Drift • Inches	0.0	0.8	3.2	7.5	13.8	22.6	34.1	66.5	113.0

Hirtenberger 100-grain Sierra SMT (82200450)

G1 Ballistic Coefficient = 0.345

Distance • Yards	Muzzle	100	200	300	400	500	600	800	1000
Velocity • fps	2887	2620	2369	2131	1908	1700	1512	1207	1024
Energy • Ft-lbs	1851	1525	1246	1009	809	642	507	323	233
Taylor KO Index	10.0	9.1	8.2	7.4	6.6	5.9	5.2	4.2	3.7
Path • Inches	-1.5	+1.8	0.0	-8.0	-23.7	-49.0	-86.4	-211.0	-431.2
Wind Drift • Inches	0.0	0.9	3.8	9.0	16.9	28.0	42.6	84.7	143.8

6mm Remington

Remington's 6mm was introduced in 1963 as a replacement for a basically identical 1955 cartridge called the .244 Remington. Remington expected that cartridge (the .244) to be a formidable competitor for Winchester's .243, but their guns were built with a 1 turn in 12-inch twist (vs. the .243's 1 turn in 10 inches). This left the .244 unable to stabilize 100- and 105-grain bullets reliably. In 1963 the caliber was renamed the 6mm Remington, and the rifles were manufactured with a twist rate of 1 turn in 9 inches. The popularity of this cartridge now approaches that of the .243.

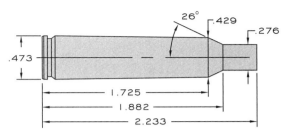

Relative Recoil Factor = 1.40

Specifications

Controlling Agency for Standardization of this Ammunition: SAAMI

Bullet Weight Grains	Velocity fps	Maximum Average Pressure	
		Copper Crusher	Transducer
80	3,400	52,000 cup	65,000 psi
90	3,175	52,000 cup	65,000 psi
100	3,090	52,000 cup	65,000 psi

Standard barrel for velocity testing: 24 inches long—1 turn in 9-inch twist

Availability

Remington 75-grain V-Max Boat Tail (PRV6MMRC) (Discontinued in 2004) G1 Ballistic Coefficient = 0.331

Distance • Yards	Muzzle	100	200	300	400	500	600	800	1000
Velocity • fps	3400	3088	2795	2524	2267	2026	1803	1412	1133
Energy • Ft-lbs	1925	1587	1303	1061	856	683	542	332	214
Taylor KO Index	8.8	8.0	7.3	6.6	5.9	5.3	4.7	3.7	2.9
Path • Inches	-1.5	+1.1	0.0	-5.5	-16.5	-34.3	-60.6	-148.4	-306.9
Wind Drift • Inches	0.0	0.8	3.2	7.5	14.1	23.2	35.2	70.5	123.6

Federal 80-grain Speer Hot-Cor SP (6AS) G1 Ballistic Coefficient = 0.256

Distance • Yards	Muzzle	100	200	300	400	500	600	800	1000
Velocity • fps	3470	3060	2690	2350	2040	1750	1493	1120	941
Energy • Ft-lbs	2140	1665	1290	980	735	540	396	223	157
Taylor KO Index	9.6	8.5	7.5	6.5	5.7	4.9	4.1	3.1	2.6
Path • Inches	-1.5	+1.1	0.0	-5.9	-18.2	-38.4	-71.0	-188.1	-415.6
Wind Drift • Inches	0.0	1.0	4.1	9.9	18.8	31.6	49.0	101.2	174.6

Hornady 95-grain SST (81664) G1 Ballistic Coefficient = 0.355

Distance • Yards	Muzzle	100	200	300	400	500	600	800	1000
Velocity • fps	3100	2828	2572	2331	2102	1887	1685	1342	1104
Energy • Ft-lbs	2027	1687	1396	1146	932	751	599	360	257
Taylor KO Index	10.2	9.3	8.5	7.7	6.9	6.2	5.6	4.4	3.6
Path • Inches	-1.5	+1.4	0.0	-6.7	-19.8	-40.8	-71.8	-174.7	-358.9
Wind Drift • Inches	0.0	0.6	3.2	7.7	14.6	24.1	36.6	73.0	126.3

Hornady 100-grain BTSP—LM Interlock (8566) G1 Ballistic Coefficient = 0.408

Distance • Yards	Muzzle	100	200	300	400	500	600	800	1000
Velocity • fps	3250	3003	2769	2547	2335	2134	1942	1595	1307
Energy • Ft-lbs	2345	2001	1702	1440	1211	1011	838	565	380
Taylor KO Index	11.3	10.4	9.6	8.8	8.1	7.4	6.7	5.5	4.5
Path • Inches	-1.5	+1.2	0.0	-5.7	-16.8	-34.3	-59.5	-139.9	-277.6
Wind Drift • Inches	0.0	0.7	2.7	6.4	11.8	19.2	28.9	56.4	97.3

Federal 100-grain Nosler Partition (P6C)
G1 Ballistic Coefficient = 0.406

Distance • Yards	Muzzle	100	200	300	400	500	600	800	1000
Velocity • fps	3100	2860	2640	2420	2220	2020	1835	1504	1240
Energy • Ft-lbs	2135	1820	1545	1300	1090	910	748	502	341
Taylor KO Index	10.8	9.9	9.2	8.4	7.7	7.0	6.4	5.2	4.3
Path • Inches	-1.5	+1.4	0.0	-6.4	-18.8	-38.2	-66.2	-155.6	-307.1
Wind Drift • Inches	0.0	0.7	2.9	6.8	12.6	20.5	30.9	60.5	104.0

Federal 100-grain Hi-Shok Soft Point (6B)
G1 Ballistic Coefficient = 0.357

Distance • Yards	Muzzle	100	200	300	400	500	600	800	1000
Velocity • fps	3100	2830	2570	2330	2100	1890	1692	1349	1110
Energy • Ft-lbs	2135	1775	1470	1205	985	790	636	404	273
Taylor KO Index	10.8	9.8	8.9	8.1	7.3	6.6	5.9	4.7	3.9
Path • Inches	-1.5	+1.4	0.0	-6.7	-19.8	-40.8	-71.5	-172.6	-350.9
Wind Drift • Inches	0.0	0.8	3.3	7.8	14.6	24.1	36.5	72.5	125.4

Hornady 100-grain BTSP (8166)
G1 Ballistic Coefficient = 0.405

Distance • Yards	Muzzle	100	200	300	400	500	600	800	1000
Velocity • fps	3100	2861	2634	2419	2231	2018	1832	1501	1237
Energy • Ft-lbs	2134	1818	1541	1300	1068	904	746	500	340
Taylor KO Index	10.8	9.9	9.1	8.4	7.7	7.0	6.4	5.2	4.3
Path • Inches	-1.5	+1.4	0.0	-6.4	-18.8	-38.3	-66.3	-155.8	-307.9
Wind Drift • Inches	0.0	0.7	2.9	6.8	12.6	20.6	31.0	60.7	104.4

Remington 100-grain Pointed Soft Point, Boat Tail (PRB6MMRA) (Discontinued in 2004)
G1 Ballistic Coefficient = 0.390

Distance • Yards	Muzzle	100	200	300	400	500	600	800	1000
Velocity • fps	3100	2852	2617	2394	2183	1982	1791	1456	1196
Energy • Ft-lbs	2134	1806	1621	1273	1058	872	713	471	318
Taylor KO Index	10.8	9.9	9.1	8.3	7.5	6.8	6.2	5.1	4.2
Path • Inches	-1.5	+1.4	0.0	-6.5	-19.1	-38.5	-67.7	-160.4	-319.5
Wind Drift • Inches	0.0	0.7	3.1	7.2	13.4	22.0	32.5	64.0	110.3

Remington 100-grain Core-Lokt Pointed Soft Point (R6MM4)
G1 Ballistic Coefficient = 0.356

Distance • Yards	Muzzle	100	200	300	400	500	600	800	1000
Velocity • fps	3100	2829	2573	2332	2104	1889	1689	1346	1107
Energy • Ft-lbs	2133	1777	1470	1207	983	792	633	402	272
Taylor KO Index	10.8	9.8	8.9	8.1	7.3	6.6	5.9	4.7	3.8
Path • Inches	-1.5	+1.4	0.0	-6.7	-19.8	-40.8	-71.6	-173.0	-352.0
Wind Drift • Inches	0.0	0.8	3.3	7.9	14.7	24.1	36.7	72.8	125.9

Winchester 100-grain Power Point (X6MMR2)
G1 Ballistic Coefficient = 0.356

Distance • Yards	Muzzle	100	200	300	400	500	600	800	1000
Velocity • fps	3100	2829	2573	2332	2104	1889	1689	1346	1107
Energy • Ft-lbs	2133	1777	1470	1207	983	792	633	402	272
Taylor KO Index	10.8	9.8	8.9	8.1	7.3	6.6	5.9	4.7	3.8
Path • Inches	-1.5	+1.4	0.0	-6.7	-19.8	-40.8	-71.6	-173.0	-352.0
Wind Drift • Inches	0.0	0.8	3.3	7.9	14.7	24.1	36.7	72.8	125.9

.243 Winchester Super Short Magnum (WSSM)

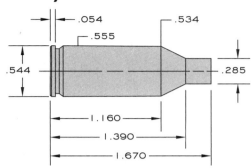

In the flurry of new cartridges in 2003, Winchester added a 6mm version of their WSSM, the .243. The .243 WSSM is interesting at least partly because the internal case volume is nearly identical to the "standard" .243 Winchester. That would suggest that the performance of the two cartridges should be essentially identical. But bullet-for-bullet the .243 WSSM outperforms its older cousin. Some experts have suggested that this is entirely due to the cartridge shape, but they overlook the fact that the SSM uses a significantly higher working pressure level. Since there are no "old" guns chambered for .243 WSSM that have to be accommodated, Winchester can set the working pressure level at any number they think is appropriate.

Relative Recoil Factor = 1.37

Specifications

Controlling Agency for Standardization of this Ammunition: SAAMI

Bullet Weight Grains	Velocity fps	Maximum Average Pressure	
		Copper Crusher	Transducer
55	4000	N/S	65,000 psi
95	3250	N/S	65,000 psi

Standard barrel for velocity testing: 24 inches long—1 turn in 9-inch twist

Availability

Winchester 55-grain Ballistic Silvertip (SBST243SS)
G1 Ballistic Coefficient = 0.276

Distance • Yards	Muzzle	100	200	300	400	500	600	800	1000
Velocity • fps	4060	3628	3237	2880	2550	2243	1956	1463	1122
Energy • Ft-lbs	2013	1607	1280	1013	794	614	468	261	154
Taylor KO Index	7.8	6.9	6.2	5.5	4.9	4.3	3.7	2.8	1.9
Path • Inches	-1.5	+0.6	0.0	-3.9	-12.0	-25.5	-46.1	-118.7	-262.5
Wind Drift • Inches	0.0	0.8	3.2	7.5	14.0	23.0	35.2	71.8	129.0

Winchester 95-grain Ballistic Silvertip (SBST243SSA)
G1 Ballistic Coefficient = 0.400

Distance • Yards	Muzzle	100	200	300	400	500	600	800	1000
Velocity • fps	3250	3000	2763	2538	2325	2121	1928	1578	1292
Energy • Ft-lbs	2258	1898	1610	1359	1140	949	784	526	352
Taylor KOc Index	10.7	9.9	9.1	8.4	7.7	7.0	6.4	5.2	4.3
Path • Inches	-1.5	+1.2	0.0	-5.7	-16.9	-34.5	-59.9	-141.3	-281.2
Wind Drift • Inches	0.0	0.7	2.8	6.5	12.0	19.5	29.4	57.5	99.1

Winchester 100-grain Power-Point (X2423WSS)
G1 Ballistic Coefficient = 0.356

Distance • Yards	Muzzle	100	200	300	400	500	600	800	1000
Velocity • fps	3110	2838	2583	2341	2112	1897	1696	1351	1110
Energy • Ft-lbs	2147	1789	1481	1217	991	799	639	405	274
Taylor KO Index	10.8	9.9	9.0	8.1	7.3	6.6	5.9	4.7	3.9
Path • Inches	-1.5	+1.4	0.0	-6.6	-19.7	-40.5	-71.2	-173.0	-355.1
Wind Drift • Inches	0.0	0.8	3.3	7.8	14.6	24.0	36.5	72.5	125.4

6.17mm (.243) Lazzeroni Spitfire

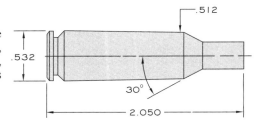

Lazzeroni has two lines of high-performance cartridges. The smallest of these is the 6.17mm Spitfire. This is factory production ammunition, not a wildcat caliber, although like many cartridges it started as one. The Spitfire is a "short" magnum, suitable for adaptation to all actions designed for the .308 case. Performance levels of this and other Lazzeroni calibers are impressive.

Relative Recoil Factor = 1.37

Specifications

Controlling Agency for Standardization of this Ammunition: Factory

Availability

Lazzeroni 85-grain Nosler Partition (617SF085P)

G1 Ballistic Coefficient = 0.404

Distance • Yards	Muzzle	100	200	300	400	500	600	800	1000
Velocity • fps	3618	3316	3036	2772	2523	2287	2064	1660	1328
Energy • Ft-lbs	2471	2077	1704	1450	1202	987	805	520	333
Taylor KO Index	10.7	9.8	9.0	8.2	7.4	6.7	6.1	4.9	3.9
Path • Inches	-1.5	+0.8	0.0	-4.6	-13.8	-28.4	-49.7	-118.9	-239.3
Wind Drift • Inches	0.0	0.6	2.7	6.3	11.7	19.1	28.8	56.7	98.8

Hubert Thummler with a pasang or Persian ibex fron Iran, which is once again open to hunting. (Photo from Wind in My Face *by Hubert Thummler, 2006, Safari Press)*

.240 Weatherby Magnum

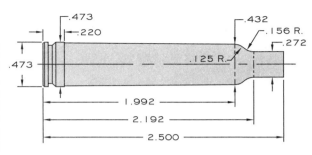

Weatherby's .240 Magnum fills the 6mm place in their extended family of cartridges. The .240 is a belted case (many people think that's what makes it a "magnum") with Weatherby's trademark venturi shoulder. If you look closely at the dimensions, you will see that this cartridge comes very, very close to duplicating the .30-06's dimensions, for all intents and purposes making it a 6mm-06. That's plenty of cartridge to give the .240 Weatherby the best performance on the 6mm list (with the exception of the Lazzeroni Spitfire's latest numbers). The .240 drives a 100-grain bullet about 300 fps faster than the 6mm Remington and 450 fps faster than the .243 Winchester with the same bullet. Rifles chambered for the .240 Weatherby have dropped off the current Weatherby inventory.

Relative Recoil Factor = 1.46

Specifications

Controlling Agency for Standardization of this Ammunition: CIP

Bullet Weight Grains	Velocity fps	Maximum Average Pressure Copper Crusher	Transducer
N/S	N/S	3,800 bar	4,370 bar

Standard barrel for velocity testing: 26 inches long—1 turn in 10-inch twist

Availability

Weatherby 87-grain Pointed-Expanding (H 240 87 SP) G1 Ballistic Coefficient = 0.328

Distance • Yards	Muzzle	100	200	300	400	500	600	800	1000
Velocity • fps	3523	3199	2898	2617	2352	2103	1873	1465	1164
Energy • Ft-lbs	2399	1977	1622	1323	1069	855	678	415	262
Taylor KO Index	10.6	9.7	8.8	7.9	7.1	6.4	5.7	4.4	3.5
Path • Inches	-1.5	+0.7	0.0	-4.7	-15.3	-31.8	-56.2	-137.5	-284.8
Wind Drift • Inches	0.0	0.7	3.1	7.3	13.6	22.3	33.9	67.8	119.2

Weatherby 90-grain Barnes X-Bullet (B 240 90 XS) G1 Ballistic Coefficient = 0.382

Distance • Yards	Muzzle	100	200	300	400	500	600	800	1000
Velocity • fps	3500	3222	2962	2717	2484	2264	2053	1671	1352
Energy • Ft-lbs	2448	2075	1753	1475	1233	1024	843	558	365
Taylor KO Index	10.9	10.1	9.3	8.5	7.8	7.1	6.4	5.2	4.2
Path • Inches	-1.5	+0.9	0.0	-5.0	-14.5	-29.8	-51.9	-122.8	-244.2
Wind Drift • Inches	0.0	0.6	2.6	6.2	11.4	18.6	28.0	54.9	95.2

Weatherby 95-grain Nosler Ballistic Tip (N 240 95 BST) G1 Ballistic Coefficient = 0.379

Distance • Yards	Muzzle	100	200	300	400	500	600	800	1000
Velocity • fps	3420	3146	2888	2645	2414	2195	1987	1611	1303
Energy • Ft-lbs	2467	2087	1759	1475	1229	1017	833	548	358
Taylor KO Index	11.3	10.4	9.5	8.7	8.0	7.2	6.6	5.3	4.5
Path • Inches	-1.5	+1.2	0.0	-5.6	-15.4	-31.5	-54.9	-130.3	-260.1
Wind Drift • Inches	0.0	0.7	2.8	6.4	11.9	19.4	29.2	57.4	99.7

Weatherby 100-grain Pointed-Expanding (H 240 100 SP) G1 Ballistic Coefficient = 0.381

Distance • Yards	Muzzle	100	200	300	400	500	600	800	1000
Velocity • fps	3406	3134	2878	2637	2408	2190	1983	1610	1304
Energy • Ft-lbs	2576	2180	1839	1544	1287	1065	874	576	379
Taylor KO Index	11.8	10.9	10.0	9.2	8.4	7.6	6.9	5.6	4.5
Path • Inches	-1.5	+0.8	0.0	-5.1	-15.5	-31.8	-55.3	-131.0	-261.2
Wind Drift • Inches	0.0	0.7	2.8	6.4	11.9	19.4	29.2	57.4	99.5

Weatherby 100-grain Nosler Partition (N 240 100 PT)

G1 Ballistic Coefficient = 0.385

Distance • Yards	Muzzle	100	200	300	400	500	600	800	1000
Velocity • fps	3406	3136	2882	2642	2415	2199	1996	1624	1318
Energy • Ft-lbs	2576	2183	1844	1550	1294	1073	885	586	386
Taylor KO Index	11.8	10.9	10.0	9.2	8.4	7.6	6.9	5.6	4.6
Path • Inches	-1.5	+0.8	0.0	-5.0	-15.4	-31.6	-55.0	-130.0	-258.5
Wind Drift • Inches	0.0	0.7	2.7	6.4	11.7	19.1	28.8	56.5	97.9

Dr. J. Y. Jones with a giant Roosevelt elk from Vancouver Island. (Photo from *Ask the Elk Guides* by J. Y. Jones, 2005, Safari Press.)

.25-20 Winchester

The .25-20 Winchester is an outgrowth of the .25-20 Single Shot. At the time of its introduction in 1893 for Winchester's Model 92 rifle, it was considered radical because of its "sharp" 16-degree shoulder. This caliber has almost reached the end of its commercial life.

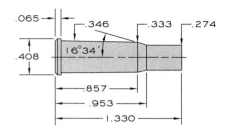

Relative Recoil Factor = 0.57

Specifications

Controlling Agency for Standardization of this Ammunition: SAAMI

Bullet Weight Grains	Velocity fps	Maximum Average Pressure Copper Crusher	Transducer
86	1,445	28,000 cup	N/S

Standard barrel for velocity testing: 24 inches long—1 turn in 14-inch twist

Availability

Remington 86-grain Soft Point (R25202)   G1 Ballistic Coefficient = 0.191

Distance • Yards	Muzzle	100	200	300	400	500	600	800	1000
Velocity • fps	1460	1194	1030	931	858	797	744	696	572
Energy • Ft-lbs	407	272	203	165	141	122	106	81	63
Taylor KO Index	4.6	3.8	3.3	3.0	2.7	2.5	2.4	2.2	1.8
Path • Inches	-1.5	+1.4	0.0	-44.1	-128.3	-259.9	-430.6	-972.6	-1824
Wind Drift • Inches	0.0	4.0	15.7	33.7	56.7	84.5	116.8	196.3	297.0

Winchester 86-grain Soft Point (X25202)   G1 Ballistic Coefficient = 0.191

Distance • Yards	Muzzle	100	200	300	400	500	600	800	1000
Velocity • fps	1460	1194	1030	931	858	798	744	696	572
Energy • Ft-lbs	407	272	203	165	141	122	106	81	63
Taylor KO Index	4.6	3.8	3.3	3.0	2.7	2.5	2.4	2.2	1.8
Path • Inches	-1.5	+1.4	0.0	-44.1	-128.3	-259.9	-430.6	-972.6	-1824
Wind Drift • Inches	0.0	4.0	15.7	33.7	56.7	84.5	116.8	196.3	297.0

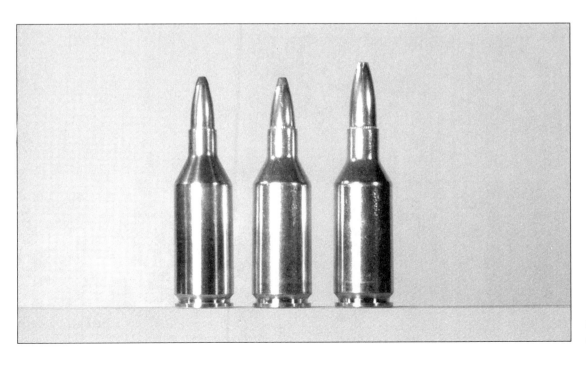

(Left to right) .223 WSSM, .243 WSSM, .25 WSSM.

.25-35 Winchester

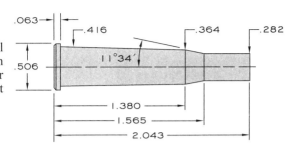

Introduced in 1895, the .25-35 Winchester has enough terminal performance at short ranges to be effective on deer-size game. The 117-grain bullet at 2,230 fps certainly isn't in the same class as a .30-30, but this caliber continues to hang on in Winchester's catalog. This cartridge is also on its last legs, with only one loading offered.

Relative Recoil Factor = 1.18

Specifications

Controlling Agency for Standardization of this Ammunition: SAAMI

Bullet Weight Grains	Velocity fps	Maximum Average Pressure	
		Copper Crusher	Transducer
117	2,210	37,000 cup	N/S

Standard barrel for velocity testing: 24 inches long—1 turn in 8-inch twist

Availability

Winchester 117-grain Soft Point (X2535)

G1 Ballistic Coefficient = 0.214

Distance • Yards	Muzzle	100	200	300	400	500	600	800	1000
Velocity • fps	2230	1866	1545	1282	1097	984	906	791	700
Energy • Ft-lbs	1292	904	620	427	313	252	213	163	127
Taylor KO Index	9.6	8.0	6.7	5.5	4.7	4.2	3.9	3.4	3.0
Path • Inches	-1.5	+4.3	0.0	-19.0	-59.2	-128.1	-231.9	-559.3	-1087
Wind Drift • Inches	0.0	2.2	9.6	23.5	44.5	71.8	104.3	182.1	276.8

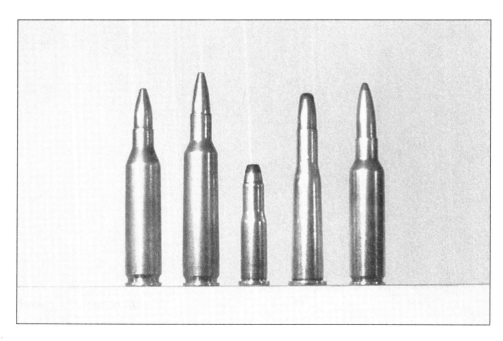

(Left to right) .243 Winchester, 6mm Remington, .25-20, .25-35, .250 Savage.

.250 Savage

The .250 Savage is another cartridge that's nearing the end of a long and useful life. Announced in 1915, it was intended for the Savage 99 lever-action rifle. Because the 87-grain bullet would reach 3,000 fps (at least in the advertising literature), the cartridge became known as the .250-3000. While the introduction of the .243 Winchester has cut deeply into the popularity of the .250 Savage, it will live for many more years in the form of the .22-250, which was based on the .250 case.

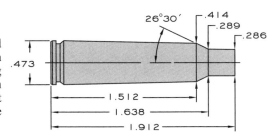

Relative Recoil Factor = 1.27

Specifications

Controlling Agency for Standardization of this Ammunition: SAAMI

Bullet Weight Grains	Velocity fps	Maximum Average Pressure Copper Crusher	Transducer
87	3,010	45,000 cup	N/S
100	2,800	45,000 cup	N/S

Standard barrel for velocity testing: 24 inches long—1 turn in 14-inch twist

Availability

Remington 100-grain Pointed Soft Point (R250SV)

G1 Ballistic Coefficient = 0.286

Distance • Yards	Muzzle	100	200	300	400	500	600	800	1000
Velocity • fps	2820	2504	2210	1936	1684	1461	1272	1029	903
Energy • Ft-lbs	1765	1392	1084	832	630	473	359	235	181
Taylor KO Index	10.4	9.2	8.1	6.7	6.2	5.4	4.7	3.8	3.3
Path • Inches	-1.5	+2.0	0.0	-9.2	-27.7	-58.6	-106.6	-274.8	-568.7
Wind Drift • Inches	0.0	1.2	4.7	11.7	22.2	37.1	57.2	113.1	185.7

Winchester 100-grain Silvertip (X2503)

G1 Ballistic Coefficient = 0.255

Distance • Yards	Muzzle	100	200	300	400	500	600	800	1000
Velocity • fps	2820	2467	2140	1839	1569	1339	1162	961	847
Energy • Ft-lbs	1765	1351	1017	751	547	398	300	205	159
Taylor KO Index	10.4	9.1	7.9	6.8	5.8	4.9	4.3	3.5	3.1
Path • Inches	-1.5	+2.1	0.0	-9.8	-29.4	-64.6	-119.2	-312.4	-644.6
Wind Drift • Inches	0.0	1.3	5.5	13.4	25.7	43.4	67.1	130.7	210.7

.257 Roberts

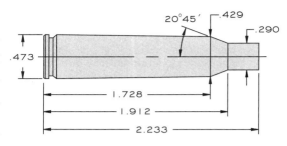

Remington adopted the .257 Roberts as a factory number in 1934, and Winchester followed a year later. The design of the .257 cartridge stemmed from work done as early as 1909 by Griffin & Howe, A. O. Niedner, and Major Ned Roberts. Their work culminated in the early 1930s with a cartridge called the .25 Roberts. The .25 Roberts was a little different from the .257 Roberts, hence the two different descriptions. Both cartridges were certainly closely related to the 7x57 Mauser (as was the .30-06). The .257 Roberts is an "oldie but goodie" and still provides a useful capability, as both a varmint rifle and a gun for deer-size game.

Relative Recoil Factor = 1.47

Specifications

Controlling Agency for Standardization of this Ammunition: SAAMI

Bullet Weight Grains	Velocity fps	Maximum Average Pressure	
		Copper Crusher	Transducer
87	3,150	45,000 cup	54,000 psi
100	2,880	45,000 cup	54,000 psi
117	2,630	45,000 cup	54,000 psi
+ P Loads			
100	2,980	50,000 cup	58,000 psi
117	2,760	50,000 cup	58,000 psi

Standard barrel for velocity testing: 24 inches long—1 turn in 10-inch twist

Availability

Hornady 117-grain BTSP—Light Magnum Interlock (85354)

G1 Ballistic Coefficient = 0.393

Distance • Yards	Muzzle	100	200	300	400	500	600	800	1000
Velocity • fps	2940	2701	2474	2258	2053	1859	1678	1363	1133
Energy • Ft-lbs	2245	1895	1589	1324	1095	898	732	483	333
Taylor KO Index	11.9	11.0	10.0	9.2	8.3	7.6	6.8	5.5	4.6
Path • Inches	-1.5	+1.6	0.0	-7.3	-21.5	-39.9	-76.6	-182.6	-366.9
Wind Drift • Inches	0.0	0.8	3.2	7.6	14.2	23.3	35.2	69.2	118.8

Hornady 117-grain BTSP Interlock (8135)

G1 Ballistic Coefficient = 0.392

Distance • Yards	Muzzle	100	200	300	400	500	600	800	1000
Velocity • fps	2780	2550	2331	2122	1925	1740	1571	1281	1084
Energy • Ft-lbs	2007	1689	1411	1170	963	787	641	427	306
Taylor KO Index	11.9	11.0	10.0	9.1	8.3	7.5	6.7	5.5	4.7
Path • Inches	-1.5	+1.9	0.0	-8.3	-24.4	-49.9	-86.9	-206.5	-411.3
Wind Drift • Inches	0.0	0.8	3.5	8.2	15.4	25.3	38.1	74.8	127.0

Remington 117-grain Soft Point Core-Lokt (R257)

G1 Ballistic Coefficient = 0.240

Distance • Yards	Muzzle	100	200	300	400	500	600	800	1000
Velocity • fps	2650	2291	1961	1663	1404	1199	1059	902	800
Energy • Ft-lbs	1824	1363	999	718	512	373	291	211	166
Taylor KO Index	11.4	9.8	8.4	7.1	6.0	5.2	4.5	3.9	3.4
Path • Inches	-1.5	+2.6	0.0	-11.7	-36.1	-78.2	-144.9	-376.8	-779.8
Wind Drift • Inches	0.0	1.5	6.5	15.9	30.6	51.5	78.6	147.7	232.6

Winchester 117-grain Power Point + P (X257P3)

G1 Ballistic Coefficient = 0.241

Distance • Yards	Muzzle	100	200	300	400	500	600	800	1000
Velocity • fps	2780	2411	2071	1761	1488	1263	1102	925	816
Energy • Ft-lbs	2009	1511	1115	806	576	415	316	222	173
Taylor KO Index	11.9	10.4	8.9	7.6	6.4	5.4	4.7	4.0	3.5
Path • Inches	-1.5	+2.6	0.0	-10.8	-33.0	-70.0	-130.8	-342.1	-701.0
Wind Drift • Inches	0.0	1.4	6.0	14.7	28.3	47.8	73.8	141.3	225.2

Federal 120-grain High Velocity + P, Nosler Partition (P257B)

G1 Ballistic Coefficient = 0.414

Distance • Yards	Muzzle	100	200	300	400	500	600	800	1000
Velocity • fps	2780	2560	2360	2160	1970	1790	1624	1336	1127
Energy • Ft-lbs	2060	1750	1480	1240	1030	855	703	476	338
Taylor KO Index	12.2	11.3	10.4	9.5	8.7	7.9	7.2	5.9	5.0
Path • Inches	-1.5	+1.9	0.0	-8.2	-24.0	-48.9	-84.2	-197.9	-390.1
Wind Drift • Inches	0.0	0.8	3.3	7.8	14.4	23.6	35.5	69.4	117.9

Western bongo from the Sudan, which in the 1980s was the best place to hunt these elusive forest-dwelling antelope. Because hunting is currently closed in Sudan, bongo hunting has shifted to the C.A.R. and Cameroon. (Photo from Wind in My Face by Hubert Thummler, 2006, Safari Press)

.25 Winchester Super Short Magnum (WSSM)

To complete their Super Short line, at least for the moment, Winchester has introduced the .25 WSSM. The .25 WSSM's ballistic data is identical to that of the .25-06. The pressure numbers haven't been announced, but it is a good bet that the pressures will be in the 65,000-psi class.

Relative Recoil Factor = 1.57

Specifications

Controlling Agency for Standardization of this Ammunition: SAAMI

Bullet Weight Grains	Velocity fps	Maximum Average Pressure	
		Copper Crusher	Transducer

Unavailable at this writing.

Availability

Winchester 85-grain Ballistic Silvertip (SBST25WSS)

G1 Ballistic Coefficient = 0.334

Distance • Yards	Muzzle	100	200	300	400	500	600	800	1000
Velocity • fps	3470	3156	2863	2589	2331	2088	1862	1462	1166
Energy • Ft-lbs	2273	1880	1548	1266	1026	823	654	404	257
Taylor KO Index	10.8	9.8	8.9	8.1	7.3	6.5	5.8	4.6	3.5
Path • Inches	-1.5	+1.0	0.0	-5.2	-15.7	-32.5	-57.5	-141.4	-294.2
Wind Drift • Inches	0.0	0.7	3.1	7.3	13.5	22.2	33.8	67.5	118.4

Winchester 110-grain AccuBond CT (S25WSCT)

G1 Ballistic Coefficient = 0.424

Distance • Yards	Muzzle	100	200	300	400	500	600	800	1000
Velocity • fps	3100	2870	2651	2442	2243	2053	1874	1548	1280
Energy • Ft-lbs	2347	2011	1716	1456	1228	1029	858	585	400
Taylor KO Index	11.8	11.0	10.1	9.3	8.6	7.8	7.2	5.9	4.9
Path • Inches	-1.5	+1.3	0.0	-6.3	-18.5	-37.6	-64.9	-151.9	-299.4
Wind Drift • Inches	0.0	0.7	2.8	6.5	12.0	19.6	29.5	57.5	98.6

Winchester 115-grain Ballistic Silvertip (SBST25WSSA)

G1 Ballistic Coefficient = 0.447

Distance • Yards	Muzzle	100	200	300	400	500	600	800	1000
Velocity • fps	3060	2844	2639	2442	2254	2074	1905	1593	1330
Energy • Ft-lbs	2392	2066	1778	1523	1298	1099	927	648	452
Taylor KO Index	12.9	12.0	11.1	10.3	9.5	8.8	8.0	6.7	5.6
Path • Inches	-1.5	+1.4	0.0	-6.4	-18.6	-37.7	-64.9	-150.2	-292.4
Wind Drift • Inches	0.0	0.6	2.7	6.2	11.4	18.6	27.9	54.0	92.2

Winchester 120-grain Positive Expanding Point (X25WSS)

G1 Ballistic Coefficient = 0.345

Distance • Yards	Muzzle	100	200	300	400	500	600	800	1000
Velocity • fps	2990	2717	2459	2216	1987	1773	1579	1254	1050
Energy • Ft-lbs	2383	1967	1612	1309	1053	838	664	419	294
Taylor KO Index	13.2	12.0	10.8	9.8	8.8	7.8	7.0	5.5	4.6
Path • Inches	-1.5	+1.6	0.0	-7.4	-21.8	-45.1	-79.7	-195.8	-404.1
Wind Drift • Inches	0.0	0.9	3.6	8.6	16.1	26.5	40.4	80.4	137.9

.25-06 Remington

The history of the conversion of wildcat cartridges to factory numbers is rather spotty. Part of this is because, until recently, wildcatters almost never had a numerical way to measure pressures and kept loading the charges (pressures) higher and higher until something looked like it was going to let go. That almost always led to factory velocities (at rational pressures) that were substantially lower than the wildcatter's claims. In 1969 Remington made the .25-06 into a factory cartridge. As a wildcat it had been around since the early 1920s. A few of today's .25-06 factory loadings list velocities for the 117-grain bullet in excess of 3000 fps. By comparison, some old wildcat data list velocities well over 3200 fps with the same bullets.

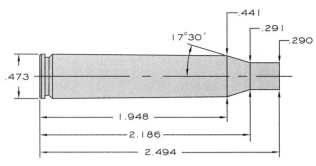

Relative Recoil Factor = 1.57

Specifications

Controlling Agency for Standardization of this Ammunition: SAAMI

Bullet Weight Grains	Velocity fps	Maximum Average Pressure	
		Copper Crusher	Transducer
87	3,420	53,000 cup	63,000 psi
90	3,420	53,000 cup	63,000 psi
100	3,210	53,000 cup	63,000 psi
117	2,975	53,000 cup	63,000 psi
120	2,975	53,000 cup	63,000 psi

Standard barrel for velocity testing: 24 inches long—1 turn in 10-inch twist

Availability

Federal 85-grain Nosler Ballistic Tip (P2506G)   G1 Ballistic Coefficient = 0.332

Distance • Yards	Muzzle	100	200	300	400	500	600	800	1000
Velocity • fps	3550	3230	2930	2640	2380	2130	1898	1487	1178
Energy • Ft-lbs	2380	1965	1615	1320	1070	855	680	417	262
Taylor KO Index	10.5	9.5	8.6	7.8	7.0	6.3	5.6	4.4	3.5
Path • Inches	-1.5	+0.9	0.0	-5.0	-15.0	-31.2	-55.0	-135.3	-283.0
Wind Drift • Inches	0.0	0.7	3.0	7.2	13.3	21.9	33.3	66.5	117.0

Winchester 85-grain Ballistic Silvertip (SBST2506A)   G1 Ballistic Coefficient = 0.334

Distance • Yards	Muzzle	100	200	300	400	500	600	800	1000
Velocity • fps	3470	3156	2864	2590	2332	2089	1862	1462	1166
Energy • Ft-lbs	2273	1880	1548	1266	1026	824	654	404	257
Taylor KO Index	10.8	9.8	8.9	8.1	7.3	6.5	5.8	4.6	3.6
Path • Inches	-1.5	+1.0	0.0	-5.2	-15.7	-32.5	-57.5	-140.2	-289.0
Wind Drift • Inches	0.0	0.7	3.1	7.3	13.5	22.2	33.8	67.5	118.4

Federal 90-grain Sierra Varminteer HP (P2506V) (Discontinued in 2004)   G1 Ballistic Coefficient = 0.260

Distance • Yards	Muzzle	100	200	300	400	500	600	800	1000
Velocity • fps	3440	3040	2680	2340	2030	1750	1498	1126	947
Energy • Ft-lbs	2364	1850	1435	1100	825	610	449	254	179
Taylor KO Index	11.4	10.0	8.9	7.7	6.7	5.8	4.9	3.7	3.1
Path • Inches	-1.5	+1.2	0.0	-5.8	-17.0	-34.8	-71.9	-192.2	-422.9
Wind Drift • Inches	0.0	1.0	4.1	9.8	18.6	31.3	48.5	100.0	172.5

Winchester 90-grain Positive Expanding Point (X25061)   G1 Ballistic Coefficient = 0.260

Distance • Yards	Muzzle	100	200	300	400	500	600	800	1000
Velocity • fps	3440	3043	2680	2344	2034	1749	1498	1126	947
Energy • Ft-lbs	2364	1850	1435	1098	827	611	449	254	179
Taylor KO Index	11.4	10.1	8.9	7.7	6.7	5.8	4.9	3.7	3.1
Path • Inches	-1.5	+1.4	0.0	-6.0	-18.4	-39.3	-71.5	-188.3	-414.3
Wind Drift • Inches	0.0	1.0	4.1	9.8	18.6	31.3	48.6	100.0	172.5

Remington 100-grain Core-Lokt Pointed Soft Point (R25062)

G1 Ballistic Coefficient = 0.293

Distance • Yards	Muzzle	100	200	300	400	500	600	800	1000
Velocity • fps	3230	2893	2580	2287	2014	1762	1536	1181	989
Energy • Ft-lbs	2316	1858	1478	1161	901	689	524	310	217
Taylor KO Index	12.0	10.6	9.5	8.4	7.4	6.5	5.6	4.3	3.6
Path • Inches	-1.5	+1.3	0.0	-6.6	-19.8	-41.7	-74.9	-190.2	-405.5
Wind Drift • Inches	0.0	0.9	3.9	9.3	17.6	29.2	45.0	91.2	157.2

Federal 100-grain Barnes Triple Shock (P2506H)

G1 Ballistic Coefficient = 0.421

Distance • Yards	Muzzle	100	200	300	400	500	600	800	1000
Velocity • fps	3210	2970	2750	2540	2330	2140	1955	1618	1336
Energy • Ft-lbs	2290	1965	1680	1430	1205	1015	849	581	396
Taylor KO Index	11.8	10.9	10.1	9.3	8.6	7.9	7.2	5.9	4.9
Path • Inches	-1.5	+1.6	0.0	-7.0	-20.8	-34.7	-60.0	-140.1	-275.5
Wind Drift • Inches	0.0	0.6	2.7	6.2	11.5	18.6	28.0	54.6	93.6

Federal 100-grain Barnes XLC Coated X-Bullet (P2506F) (Discontinued in 2004)

G1 Ballistic Coefficient = 0.421

Distance • Yards	Muzzle	100	200	300	400	500	600	800	1000
Velocity • fps	3210	2970	2750	2540	2330	2140	1955	1618	1336
Energy • Ft-lbs	2290	1965	1680	1430	1205	1015	849	581	396
Taylor KO Index	11.8	10.9	10.1	9.3	8.6	7.9	7.2	5.9	4.9
Path • Inches	-1.5	+1.2	0.0	-5.8	-17.0	-34.8	-60.0	-139.7	-273.3
Wind Drift • Inches	0.0	0.6	2.7	6.2	11.5	18.6	28.0	54.6	93.6

Black Hills 100-grain Barnes X-Bullet (2C2506BHGN2)

G1 Ballistic Coefficient = 0.420

Distance • Yards	Muzzle	100	200	300	400	500	600	800	1000
Velocity • fps	3200	2964	2740	2527	2323	2129	1945	1609	1328
Energy • Ft-lbs	2273	1951	1667	1418	1199	1007	840	575	391
Taylor KO Index	11.8	10.9	10.1	9.3	8.6	7.9	7.2	5.9	4.9
Path • Inches	-1.5	+1.2	0.0	-5.9	-17.2	-35.0	-60.4	-141.3	-278.2
Wind Drift • Inches	0.0	0.6	2.7	6.2	11.5	18.8	28.2	55.0	94.4

Black Hills 100-grain Nosler Ballistic Tip (2C2506BHGN1)

G1 Ballistic Coefficient = 0.393

Distance • Yards	Muzzle	100	200	300	400	500	600	800	1000
Velocity • fps	3200	2948	2710	2484	2269	2065	1872	1525	1247
Energy • Ft-lbs	2273	1930	1631	1370	1144	947	778	516	346
Taylor KO Index	11.7	10.8	9.9	9.1	8.3	7.6	6.9	5.6	4.6
Path • Inches	-1.5	+1.3	0.0	-6.0	-17.6	-36.0	-62.7	-148.6	-297.2
Wind Drift • Inches	0.0	0.7	2.9	6.7	12.5	20.4	30.7	60.3	104.1

PMC 100-grain SPBT Game (2506VA)

G1 Ballistic Coefficient = 0.341

Distance • Yards	Muzzle	100	200	300	400	500	600	800	1000
Velocity • fps	3200	2925	2650	2395	2145	1910	1697	1336	1091
Energy • Ft-lbs	2273	1895	1561	1268	1019	811	640	397	264
Taylor KO Index	11.1	10.2	9.2	8.3	7.4	6.6	5.9	4.6	3.8
Path • Inches	-1.5	+1.3	0.0	-6.3	-18.6	-38.4	-68.8	-169.2	-352.1
Wind Drift • Inches	0.0	0.8	3.4	8.0	14.9	24.5	37.4	74.7	129.8

Winchester 110-grain AccuBond CT (S2506CT)

G1 Ballistic Coefficient = 0.424

Distance • Yards	Muzzle	100	200	300	400	500	600	800	1000
Velocity • fps	3100	2870	2651	2442	2243	2053	1874	1548	1260
Energy • Ft-lbs	2347	2011	1716	1456	1228	1029	858	585	400
Taylor KO Index	11.8	11.0	10.1	9.3	8.6	7.8	7.2	5.9	4.8
Path • Inches	-1.5	+1.3	0.0	-6.3	-18.5	-37.6	-64.9	-151.9	-299.4
Wind Drift • Inches	0.0	0.7	2.8	6.5	12.0	19.6	29.5	57.5	98.6

Remington 115-grain Core-Lokt Ultra Bonded (PRC2506RA)

G1 Ballistic Coefficient = 0.380

Distance • Yards	Muzzle	100	200	300	400	500	600	800	1000
Velocity • fps	3000	2751	2516	2293	2081	1881	1693	1368	1131
Energy • Ft-lbs	2298	1933	1616	1342	1106	903	732	478	327
Taylor KO Index	12.0	11.0	10.0	9.2	8.3	7.5	6.8	5.5	4.5
Path • Inches	-1.5	+1.4	0.0	-7.1	-20.7	-42.5	-74.2	-177.8	-359.4
Wind Drift • Inches	0.0	0.8	3.2	7.6	14.2	23.3	35.3	69.6	118.8

Federal 115-grain Trophy Bonded Bear Claw (P2506T1)

G1 Ballistic Coefficient = 0.372

Distance • Yards	Muzzle	100	200	300	400	500	600	800	1000
Velocity • fps	2990	2740	2500	2270	2050	1850	1662	1338	1110
Energy • Ft-lbs	2285	1910	1590	1310	1075	870	706	457	314
Taylor KO Index	12.6	11.6	10.6	9.6	8.7	7.8	7.0	5.6	4.7
Path • Inches	-1.5	+1.6	0.0	-7.2	-21.1	-43.2	-75.8	-182.7	-371.1
Wind Drift • Inches	0.0	0.8	3.3	7.9	14.7	24.1	36.5	72.2	124.3

Federal 115-grain Nosler Ballistic Tip (P2506D)

G1 Ballistic Coefficient = 0.393

Distance • Yards	Muzzle	100	200	300	400	500	600	800	1000
Velocity • fps	3210	2960	2720	2490	2289	2070	1879	1531	1252
Energy • Ft-lbs	2290	1940	1640	1380	1150	1050	902	599	401
Taylor KO Index	13.6	12.5	11.5	10.5	9.7	8.7	7.9	6.5	5.3
Path • Inches	-1.5	+1.2	0.0	-6.0	-17.5	-35.8	-62.2	-146.9	-291.7
Wind Drift • Inches	0.0	0.7	2.9	6.7	12.4	20.3	30.6	60.0	103.6

Winchester 115-grain Ballistic Silvertip (SBST2506)

G1 Ballistic Coefficient = 0.449

Distance • Yards	Muzzle	100	200	300	400	500	600	800	1000
Velocity • fps	3060	2844	2639	2442	2254	2074	1903	1590	1326
Energy • Ft-lbs	2392	2066	1778	1523	1298	1099	925	646	449
Taylor KO Index	12.2	11.4	10.5	9.7	9.0	8.3	7.6	6.3	5.3
Path • Inches	-1.5	+1.3	0.0	-6.4	-18.6	-37.7	-65.0	-150.4	-293.0
Wind Drift • Inches	0.0	0.6	2.7	6.2	11.5	18.6	28.0	54.2	92.6

Federal 115-grain Nosler Partition (P2506E)

G1 Ballistic Coefficient = 0.392

Distance • Yards	Muzzle	100	200	300	400	500	600	800	1000
Velocity • fps	2990	2750	2520	2300	2100	1900	1718	1379	1157
Energy • Ft-lbs	2285	1930	1620	1350	1120	915	754	499	342
Taylor KO Index	12.6	11.6	10.6	9.7	8.9	8.0	7.3	5.9	4.9
Path • Inches	-1.5	+1.6	0.0	-7.0	-20.8	-42.2	-73.4	-173.9	-346.5
Wind Drift • Inches	0.0	0.8	3.2	7.4	13.8	22.6	34.1	67.1	115.2

Hornady 117-grain BTSP-Light Magnum (8545)

G1 Ballistic Coefficient = 0.382

Distance • Yards	Muzzle	100	200	300	400	500	600	800	1000
Velocity • fps	3110	2862	2627	2405	2193	1992	1804	1467	1205
Energy • Ft-lbs	2512	2128	1793	1502	1249	1030	846	560	378
Taylor KO Index	13.4	12.3	11.3	10.3	9.4	8.6	7.7	6.3	5.2
Path • Inches	-1.5	+1.4	0.0	-6.4	-18.9	-38.6	-67.0	-159.2	-319.2
Wind Drift • Inches	0.0	0.7	3.0	7.0	13.0	21.3	32.2	63.2	109.0

Federal 117-grain Sierra GameKing BTSP (P2506C)

G1 Ballistic Coefficient = 0.437

Distance • Yards	Muzzle	100	200	300	400	500	600	800	1000
Velocity • fps	2990	2770	2570	2370	2190	2000	1830	1521	1269
Energy • Ft-lbs	2320	2000	1715	1465	1240	1045	870	601	418
Taylor KO Index	12.8	11.9	11.0	10.2	9.4	8.6	7.9	6.5	5.5
Path • Inches	-1.5	+1.5	0.0	-6.8	-19.9	-40.4	-69.2	-160.6	-312.8
Wind Drift • Inches	0.0	0.7	2.8	6.6	12.1	19.8	29.7	57.7	98.6

Federal 117-grain Speer Hot-Cor SP (2506BS)

G1 Ballistic Coefficient = 0.363

Distance • Yards	Muzzle	100	200	300	400	500	600	800	1000
Velocity • fps	2990	2730	2480	2250	2030	1820	1628	1302	1081
Energy • Ft-lbs	2320	1935	1600	1315	1070	860	689	440	304
Taylor KO Index	12.1	11.1	10.1	9.1	8.2	7.4	6.6	5.3	4.4
Path • Inches	-1.5	+1.6	0.0	-7.2	-21.4	-43.9	-77.4	-187.9	-384.4
Wind Drift • Inches	0.0	0.8	3.5	8.2	15.2	25.1	38.1	75.5	129.8

Hornady 117-grain BTSP (8145)

G1 Ballistic Coefficient = 0.391

Distance • Yards	Muzzle	100	200	300	400	500	600	800	1000
Velocity • fps	2990	2749	2520	2302	2096	1900	1716	1394	1155
Energy • Ft-lbs	2322	1962	1649	1377	1141	938	765	505	347
Taylor KO Index	12.8	11.8	10.8	9.9	9.0	8.2	7.4	6.0	5.0
Path • Inches	-1.5	+1.6	0.0	-7.0	-20.7	-42.2	-73.5	-174.3	-347.4
Wind Drift • Inches	0.0	0.8	3.2	7.4	13.8	22.6	34.2	67.3	115.7

PMC 117-grain Pointed Soft Point (25-06B) (Discontinued in 2004)

G1 Ballistic Coefficient = 0.384

Distance • Yards	Muzzle	100	200	300	400	500	600	800	1000
Velocity • fps	2950	2706	2472	2253	2047	1852	1668	1351	1124
Energy • Ft-lbs	2261	1900	1588	1319	1088	891	723	474	328
Taylor KO Index	14.2	13.4	12.6	11.8	11.1	10.4	9.7	8.4	7.2
Path • Inches	-1.5	+1.6	0.0	-7.3	-21.5	-44.1	-76.7	-183.6	-370.2
Wind Drift • Inches	0.0	0.8	3.3	7.7	14.4	23.6	35.7	51.3	120.9

Hornady 117-grain SST Interlock (81454)

G1 Ballistic Coefficient = 0.390

Distance • Yards	Muzzle	100	200	300	400	500	600	800	1000
Velocity • fps	2990	2748	2519	2312	2093	1897	1713	1391	1152
Energy • Ft-lbs	2322	1962	1648	1375	1138	935	762	503	345
Taylor KO Index	12.8	11.8	10.8	9.9	9.0	8.1	7.4	6.0	4.9
Path • Inches	-1.5	+1.7	0.0	-7.4	-21.5	-47.8	-73.7	-175.6	-352.7
Wind Drift • Inches	0.0	0.8	3.2	7.5	13.9	22.7	34.4	67.6	116.1

Speer 120-grain Grand Slam (24514) (Discontinued in 2004)

G1 Ballistic Coefficient = 0.329

Distance • Yards	Muzzle	100	200	300	400	500	600	800	1000
Velocity • fps	3025	2736	2465	2210	1970	1747	1544	1216	1022
Energy • Ft-lbs	2439	1995	1620	1302	1034	814	635	394	279
Taylor KO Index	13.3	12.1	10.9	9.7	8.7	7.7	6.8	5.4	4.5
Path • Inches	-1.5	+1.6	0.0	-7.3	-21.8	-45.3	-80.2	-198.1	-410.3
Wind Drift • Inches	0.0	0.8	3.4	8.0	15.1	25.0	38.3	76.6	131.1

Remington 120-grain Pointed Soft Point Core-Lokt (R25063)

G1 Ballistic Coefficient = 0.363

Distance • Yards	Muzzle	100	200	300	400	500	600	800	1000
Velocity • fps	2990	2730	2484	2252	2032	1825	1635	1310	1090
Energy • Ft-lbs	2383	1995	1644	1351	1100	887	713	458	316
Taylor KO Index	13.2	12.0	10.9	9.9	9.0	8.0	7.2	5.8	4.8
Path • Inches	-1.5	+1.6	0.0	-7.2	-21.4	-44.1	-76.9	-185.4	-375.5
Wind Drift • Inches	0.0	0.8	3.4	8.1	15.1	24.9	37.7	74.8	128.5

Winchester 120-grain Positive Expanding Point (X25062)

G1 Ballistic Coefficient = 0.363

Distance • Yards	Muzzle	100	200	300	400	500	600	800	1000
Velocity • fps	2990	2717	2459	2216	1987	1773	1578	1252	1047
Energy • Ft-lbs	2382	1967	1612	1309	1053	838	663	418	292
Taylor KO Index	13.2	12.0	10.9	9.9	9.0	8.0	7.2	5.8	4.8
Path • Inches	-1.5	+1.5	0.0	-7.4	-21.8	-45.1	-76.8	-196.0	-404.8
Wind Drift • Inches	0.0	0.9	3.6	8.6	16.1	26.5	40.4	80.6	138.2

6.53mm (.257) Lazzeroni Scramjet

The 6.53mm Scramjet is the .25-caliber entry in the Lazzeroni line of high-performance cartridges. The cases in the Lazzeroni line are not based on any existing cartridge. Three different case-head sizes are used. (See the case drawings for details.) With a muzzle velocity of 3,750 fps, the 6.53 slightly exceeds the performance of the .257 Weatherby in this one specific loading.

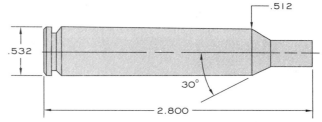

Relative Recoil Factor = 1.69

Specifications

Controlling Agency for Standardization of this Ammunition: Factory

Availability

Lazzeroni 100-grain Nosler Partition (653SJ100P)

G1 Ballistic Coefficient = 0.454

Distance • Yards	Muzzle	100	200	300	400	500	600	800	1000
Velocity • fps	3750	3501	3266	3044	2833	2631	2437	2076	1749
Energy • Ft-lbs	3123	2722	2370	2058	1782	1537	1319	957	679
Taylor KO Index	13.8	12.9	12.0	11.2	10.4	9.7	8.9	7.6	6.4
Path • Inches	-1.5	+0.7	0.0	-3.9	-11.6	-23.7	-40.7	-93.5	-178.8
Wind Drift • Inches	0.0	0.5	2.0	4.7	8.6	13.9	20.7	39.4	66.7

Kudu are about as large as a small elk. They have a reputation for being "soft" but nonetheless a caliber of 7mm on up should be considered a safe minimum for these antelope. (Photo from African Hunter II *by Craig Boddington and Peter Flack, 2004, Safari Press)*

.257 Weatherby Magnum

If you want the highest velocity from any .25-caliber gun that fires factory ammunition, the .257 Weatherby is the caliber for you. Late in the WWII time frame, Roy Weatherby shortened a .300 Magnum case and necked it to .25 caliber, thereby creating a case with significantly more volume than the .25-06. All other things being equal, a larger case volume translates directly into higher velocity. With the same bullet, the .257 Weatherby Magnum is about 200 fps faster than the .25-06 and at least 400 fps faster than the .257 Roberts. The .257 Weatherby is certainly the king of the .25-caliber hill.

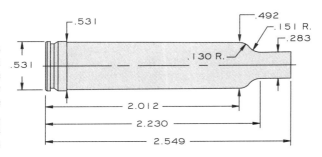

Relative Recoil Factor = 1.76

Specifications

Controlling Agency for Standardization of this Ammunition: CIP

Bullet Weight Grains	Velocity fps	Maximum Average Pressure	
		Copper Crusher	Transducer
N/S	N/S	3,800 bar	4,370 bar

Standard barrel for velocity testing: 26 inches long—1 turn in 10-inch twist

Availability

Weatherby 87-grain Pointed-Expanding (H 257 87 SP)
G1 Ballistic Coefficient = 0.323

Distance • Yards	Muzzle	100	200	300	400	500	600	800	1000
Velocity • fps	3825	3472	3147	2845	2563	2297	2051	1606	1255
Energy • Ft-lbs	2826	2328	1913	1563	1269	1019	813	498	304
Taylor KO Index	12.2	11.1	10.1	9.1	8.2	7.3	6.6	5.1	4.0
Path • Inches	-1.5	+0.7	0.0	-4.2	-12.7	-26.6	-47.0	-115.0	-238.1
Wind Drift • Inches	0.0	0.7	2.9	6.7	12.4	20.4	30.9	61.5	108.6

Weatherby 100-grain Pointed-Expanding (H 257 100 SP)
G1 Ballistic Coefficient = 0.358

Distance • Yards	Muzzle	100	200	300	400	500	600	800	1000
Velocity • fps	3602	3298	3016	2750	2500	2266	2043	1638	1309
Energy • Ft-lbs	2881	2416	2019	1515	1260	1040	927	596	380
Taylor KO Index	13.2	12.1	11.1	10.1	9.2	8.3	7.5	6.0	4.8
Path • Inches	-1.5	+0.8	0.0	-4.7	-14.0	-28.8	-50.5	-120.9	-244.1
Wind Drift • Inches	0.0	0.7	2.7	6.4	11.9	19.4	29.3	62.2	100.8

Weatherby 115-grain Nosler Ballistic Tip (N 257 115 BST)
G1 Ballistic Coefficient = 0.453

Distance • Yards	Muzzle	100	200	300	400	500	600	800	1000
Velocity • fps	3400	3170	2952	2745	2547	2357	2175	1837	1537
Energy • Ft-lbs	2952	2566	2226	1924	1656	1419	1208	862	604
Taylor KO Index	14.4	13.4	12.5	11.6	10.8	10.0	9.2	7.8	6.5
Path • Inches	-1.5	+1.0	0.0	-5.0	-14.6	-29.6	-50.8	-116.7	-224.3
Wind Drift • Inches	0.0	0.6	2.3	5.3	9.8	15.8	23.7	45.4	77.2

Federal 115-grain Nosler Partition (P257WBA) (Discontinued in 2004)
G1 Ballistic Coefficient = 0.391

Distance • Yards	Muzzle	100	200	300	400	500	600	800	1000
Velocity • fps	3150	2900	2660	2420	2220	2020	1830	1488	1220
Energy • Ft-lbs	2535	2145	1810	1515	1260	1040	855	566	380
Taylor KO Index	13.3	12.2	11.2	10.2	9.4	8.5	7.7	6.3	5.2
Path • Inches	-1.5	+1.3	0.0	-6.2	-18.4	-37.5	-65.2	-154.2	-306.8
Wind Drift • Inches	0.0	0.7	3.0	6.9	12.8	21.0	31.7	62.2	107.4

Weatherby 115-grain Barnes X-Bullet (B 257 115 XS)

G1 Ballistic Coefficient = 0.430

Distance • Yards	Muzzle	100	200	300	400	500	600	800	1000
Velocity • fps	3400	3158	2929	2711	2504	2306	2118	1769	1465
Energy • Ft-lbs	2952	2546	2190	1877	1601	1358	1146	799	548
Taylor KO Index	14.4	13.3	12.4	11.4	10.6	9.7	8.9	7.5	6.2
Path • Inches	-1.5	+1.0	0.0	-5.1	-14.8	-30.2	-52.1	120.7	-234.2
Wind Drift • Inches	0.0	0.6	2.4	5.6	10.4	16.8	25.1	48.6	83.3

Weatherby 117-grain Round Nose-Expanding (H 257 117 RN)

G1 Ballistic Coefficient = 0.256

Distance • Yards	Muzzle	100	200	300	400	500	600	800	1000
Velocity • fps	3402	2984	2595	2240	1921	1639	1389	1056	902
Energy • Ft-lbs	3007	2320	1742	1302	956	690	502	290	212
Taylor KO Index	14.6	12.8	11.1	9.6	8.3	7.0	6.0	4.5	3.9
Path • Inches	-1.5	+1.2	0.0	-6.4	-19.7	-42.4	-78.1	-210.3	-466.4
Wind Drift • Inches	0.0	1.1	4.5	10.8	20.6	34.7	54.2	111.6	189.6

Weatherby 120-grain Nosler Partition (N 257 120 PT)

G1 Ballistic Coefficient = 0.392

Distance • Yards	Muzzle	100	200	300	400	500	600	800	1000
Velocity • fps	3305	3046	2801	2570	2350	2141	1944	1586	1293
Energy • Ft-lbs	2910	2472	2091	1760	1471	1221	1088	671	446
Taylor KO Index	14.6	13.4	12.3	11.3	10.4	9.4	8.6	7.0	5.7
Path • Inches	-1.5	+1.1	0.0	-5.6	-16.4	-33.6	-58.3	-137.5	-272.8
Wind Drift • Inches	0.0	0.7	2.8	6.5	12.0	19.5	29.4	57.6	99.6

A desert mule deer shot by Hubert Thummler in Sonora, Mexico. (Photo from *Wind in My Face* by Hubert Thummler, 2006, Safari Press)

6.5x54 MS (6.5 Mannlicher-Schoenauer)

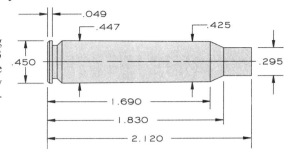

At one time this cartridge was popular enough in the U.S. that the big American ammo companies considered it profitable to load. Introduced in 1903 for Austrian-made Mannlicher rifles bought by the Greek army, this cartridge is still manufactured in Europe. Although no American riflemakers offer factory rifles in this caliber, the performance is practically identical to that of the .30-30, and the caliber is entirely adequate for deer-size game.

Relative Recoil Factor = 1.60

Specifications

Controlling Agency for Standardization of this Ammunition: CIP

Bullet Weight Grains	Velocity fps	Maximum Average Pressure	
		Copper Crusher	Transducer
	N/S		

Standard barrel for velocity testing: N/S inches long—1 turn in 7.87-inch twist

Availability

Hirtenberger 160-grain Sierra SP (82200477)

G1 Ballistic Coefficient = 0.352

Distance • Yards	Muzzle	100	200	300	400	500	600	800	1000
Velocity • fps	2198	1975	1766	1575	1403	1257	1140	991	897
Energy • Ft-lbs	1722	1390	1112	884	702	563	463	350	287
Taylor KO Index	14.0	12.5	11.2	10.0	8.9	8.0	7.2	6.3	5.7
Path • Inches	-1.5	+3.7	0.0	-14.9	-43.9	-90.6	-159.4	-381.6	-745.5
Wind Drift • Inches	0.0	1.3	5.6	13.2	24.8	40.6	60.7	112.7	177.1

Brian Marsh and Pierre Chamorel from Switzerland with a lion taken at Sijarira, Zimbabwe. (Photo from *Pioneering Hunter* by Brian Marsh, 2006, Safari Press)

6.5x57 Mauser

Even Paul Mauser couldn't resist the temptation to neck down and neck up cartridge designs. The 6.5x57 is nothing more or less than a 7x57 necked to 6.5mm. The case can be made from .257 Roberts cases and vice versa. This is another cartridge that remains reasonably popular in Europe but is seldom seen in the U.S. The cartridge appeared in the mid-1890s, but there doesn't seem to be any record of it ever being adopted as a military number. Performance-wise it is a hair more powerful than the 6.5x55 MS, but the difference isn't anything to write home about. Because of its early origins, the working pressures are held very much on the mild side.

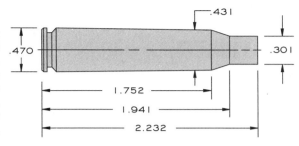

Relative Recoil Factor = 1.62

Specifications

Controlling Agency for Standardization of this Ammunition: CIP

Bullet Weight Grains	Velocity fps	Maximum Average Pressure	
		Copper Crusher	Transducer
	N/S		

Standard barrel for velocity testing: N/S inches long—1 turn in 7.87-inch twist

Availability

Hirtenberger 105-grain Nosler SP (82200330)
G1 Ballistic Coefficient = 0.264

Distance • Yards	Muzzle	100	200	300	400	500	600	800	1000
Velocity • fps	3084	2723	2390	2081	1797	1541	1324	1041	903
Energy • Ft-lbs	2218	1730	1332	1010	753	554	409	253	190
Taylor KO Index	12.9	11.4	10.0	8.7	7.5	6.4	5.5	4.3	3.8
Path • Inches	-1.5	+1.6	0.0	-7.7	-23.6	-50.2	-91.7	-240.4	-516.7
Wind Drift • Inches	0.0	1.1	4.7	11.2	21.4	36.1	56.0	112.8	188.2

Hirtenberger 120-grain Sierra SP (82200452)
G1 Ballistic Coefficient = 0.412

Distance • Yards	Muzzle	100	200	300	400	500	600	800	1000
Velocity • fps	2887	2663	2449	2245	2052	1868	1696	1393	1164
Energy • Ft-lbs	2221	1890	1599	1344	1122	930	766	517	361
Taylor KO Index	13.8	12.7	11.7	10.7	9.8	8.9	8.1	6.6	5.5
Path • Inches	-1.5	+1.7	0.0	-7.5	-22.0	-44.7	-77.3	-181.8	-358.6
Wind Drift • Inches	0.0	0.8	3.2	7.4	13.7	22.4	33.8	66.0	112.8

Hirtenberger 125-grain Nosler SP (82200328)
G1 Ballistic Coefficient = 0.434

Distance • Yards	Muzzle	100	200	300	400	500	600	800	1000
Velocity • fps	2838	2627	2426	2233	2050	1875	1711	1419	1192
Energy • Ft-lbs	2236	1916	1634	1385	1166	976	812	559	394
Taylor KO Index	14.1	13.0	12.0	11.1	10.2	9.3	8.5	7.0	5.9
Path • Inches	-1.5	+1.8	0.0	-7.7	-22.4	-45.4	-78.3	-182.2	-355.9
Wind Drift • Inches	0.0	0.7	3.0	7.1	13.2	21.5	32.4	63.1	107.4

Sellier & Bellot 131-grain Soft Point (SBA65502)
G1 Ballistic Coefficient = 0.325

Distance • Yards	Muzzle	100	200	300	400	500	600	800	1000
Velocity • fps	2543	2264	2054	1804	1594	1407	1249	1038	922
Energy • Ft-lbs	1894	1501	1235	954	740	576	454	314	248
Taylor KO Index	13.2	11.8	10.7	9.4	8.3	7.3	6.5	5.4	4.8
Path • Inches	-1.5	+2.6	0.0	-11.0	-32.8	-68.3	-121.5	-299.8	-606.6
Wind Drift • Inches	0.0	1.2	4.9	11.7	22.1	36.6	55.7	107.3	174.7

Hirtenberger 140-grain Nosler SP (82200329)

G1 Ballistic Coefficient = 0.417

Distance • Yards	Muzzle	100	200	300	400	500	600	800	1000
Velocity • fps	2657	2446	2245	2054	1872	1701	1543	1275	1090
Energy • Ft-lbs	2201	1866	1572	1315	1093	903	743	507	370
Taylor KO Index	14.0	12.9	11.9	10.8	9.9	9.0	8.1	6.7	5.8
Path • Inches	-1.5	+2.2	0.0	-9.1	-26.4	-53.7	-93.1	-218.8	-430.4
Wind Drift • Inches	0.0	0.8	3.5	8.2	15.3	25.0	37.7	73.5	123.8

Wyoming guide Ron Dube with an excellent free-range elk from his home state. (Photo from *Ask the Elk Guides* by J. Y. Jones, 2005, Safari Press)

6.5x55mm Swedish Mauser

One of the oldest cartridges in the factory inventory, the 6.5x55mm Mauser was adopted as a military cartridge over 100 years ago. The cartridge has been very popular in Europe and still ranks somewhere like 25th in the list of American reloading die sales (only a couple places behind the .30-30). Performance-wise, this cartridge is virtually identical to the .257 Roberts. Because it is used in many military surplus guns with a wide range of strength characteristics, the factory specifications have been set very much on the mild side.

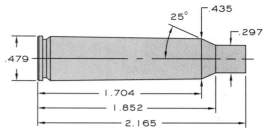

Relative Recoil Factor = 1.72

Specifications

Controlling Agency for Standardization of this Ammunition: SAAMI

Bullet Weight Grains	Velocity fps	Maximum Average Pressure Copper Crusher	Transducer
160	2,380	46,000 cup	N/S

Standard barrel for velocity testing: 24 inches long—1 turn in 7.87-inch twist

Availability

Norma 100-grain Hollow point (16527) (Discontinued in 2004)
G1 Ballistic Coefficient = 0.322

Distance • Yards	Muzzle	100	200	300	400	500	600	800	1000
Velocity • fps	2625	2354	2100	1862	1645	1449	1282	1054	931
Energy • Ft-lbs	1530	1232	980	771	601	446	365	247	192
Taylor KO Index	9.9	8.9	7.9	7.0	6.2	5.5	4.9	4.0	3.5
Path • Inches	-1.5	+2.4	0.0	-10.3	-30.7	-64.0	-113.9	-282.4	-575.6
Wind Drift • Inches	0.0	1.3	4.8	11.4	21.4	35.5	54.1	105.6	172.6

Lapua 100-grain Scenar (4316035)
G1 Ballistic Coefficient = 0.442

Distance • Yards	Muzzle	100	200	300	400	500	600	800	1000
Velocity • fps	2625	2426	2236	2054	1881	1718	1566	1304	1114
Energy • Ft-lbs	1535	1311	1114	940	788	658	547	379	276
Taylor KO Index	9.9	9.1	8.4	7.7	7.1	6.5	5.9	4.9	4.2
Path • Inches	-1.5	+2.2	0.0	-9.2	-26.6	-53.9	-93.1	-217.6	-426.6
Wind Drift • Inches	0.0	0.7	3.0	7.1	13.2	21.5	32.4	62.8	105.8

Norma 100-grain Hollow Point (16523)
G1 Ballistic Coefficient = 0.345

Distance • Yards	Muzzle	100	200	300	400	500	600	800	1000
Velocity • fps	2625	2373	2135	1912	1704	1514	1347	1102	967
Energy • Ft-lbs	1530	1251	1013	812	645	509	403	270	208
Taylor KO Index	9.9	9.0	8.1	7.2	6.5	5.7	5.1	4.2	3.7
Path • Inches	-1.5	+2.4	0.0	-10.0	-29.6	-61.2	-108.0	-263.8	-533.8
Wind Drift • Inches	0.0	0.9	4.0	9.4	17.6	29.1	44.3	86.7	143.1

Lapua 100-grain FMJ (4316033)
G1 Ballistic Coefficient = 0.416

Distance • Yards	Muzzle	100	200	300	400	500	600	800	1000
Velocity • fps	2723	2509	2304	2109	1924	1750	1588	1309	1110
Energy • Ft-lbs	1647	1398	1179	988	822	680	560	380	274
Taylor KO Index	10.3	9.5	8.7	8.0	7.3	6.6	6.0	4.9	4.2
Path • Inches	-1.5	+2.0	0.0	-8.6	-25.0	-50.8	-88.1	-208.0	-412.0
Wind Drift • Inches	0.0	0.8	3.4	7.9	14.8	24.2	36.4	71.1	120.4

Lapua 108-grain Scenar HPBT (C316031)
G1 Ballistic Coefficient = 0.400

Distance • Yards	Muzzle	100	200	300	400	500	600	800	1000
Velocity • fps	3019	2781	2556	2341	2137	1943	1761	1437	1188
Energy • Ft-lbs	2186	1855	1567	1315	1095	905	743	496	339
Taylor KO Index	12.3	11.3	10.4	9.5	8.7	7.9	7.2	5.9	4.8
Path • Inches	-1.5	+1.5	0.0	-6.8	-20.0	-40.9	-71.0	-168.1	-335.7
Wind Drift • Inches	0.0	0.7	3.0	7.2	13.3	21.7	32.8	64.3	110.4

Lapua 108-grain Scenar HPBT (4316031)

G1 Ballistic Coefficient = 0.471

Distance • Yards	Muzzle	100	200	300	400	500	600	800	1000
Velocity • fps	2953	2753	2562	2379	2203	2034	1874	1581	1332
Energy • Ft-lbs	2092	1818	1575	1357	1164	993	843	599	426
Taylor KO Index	12.0	11.2	10.4	9.7	9.0	8.3	7.7	6.5	5.4
Path • Inches	-1.5	+1.6	0.0	-6.8	-19.9	-40.0	-68.6	-157.4	-302.4
Wind Drift • Inches	0.0	0.6	2.6	6.2	11.3	18.4	27.6	53.2	90.3

Norma 120-grain Nosler BST (16522)

G1 Ballistic Coefficient = 0.430

Distance • Yards	Muzzle	100	200	300	400	500	600	800	1000
Velocity • fps	2822	2609	2407	2213	2030	1855	1690	1399	1176
Energy • Ft-lbs	2123	1815	1544	1305	1098	917	761	522	369
Taylor KO Index	12.8	11.8	10.9	10.0	9.2	8.4	7.6	6.3	5.3
Path • Inches	-1.5	+1.8	0.0	-7.8	-22.7	-46.1	-79.7	-186.6	-367.2
Wind Drift • Inches	0.0	0.8	3.1	7.3	13.5	22.0	33.1	64.4	109.7

Norma 120-grain Full Jacket (16542) (Discontinued in 2004)

G1 Ballistic Coefficient = 0.191

Distance • Yards	Muzzle	100	200	300	400	500	600	800	1000
Velocity • fps	2690	2238	1833	1482	1212	1040	937	801	699
Energy • Ft-lbs	1929	1336	897	587	391	288	234	171	130
Taylor KO Index	12.2	10.1	8.3	6.7	5.5	4.7	4.2	3.6	3.2
Path • Inches	-1.5	+2.8	0.0	-13.3	-42.9	-96.9	-181.9	-465.6	-941.7
Wind Drift • Inches	0.0	1.9	8.3	20.8	40.6	68.4	102.4	185.4	287.5

Lapua 123-grain Scenar HPBT (C316032)

G1 Ballistic Coefficient = 0.435

Distance • Yards	Muzzle	100	200	300	400	500	600	800	1000
Velocity • fps	2920	2706	2501	2306	2119	1942	1773	1472	1230
Energy • Ft-lbs	2329	2000	1709	1453	1227	1030	859	592	414
Taylor KO Index	13.5	12.6	11.6	10.7	9.8	9.0	8.2	6.8	5.7
Path • Inches	-1.5	+1.6	0.0	-7.2	-20.9	-42.4	-73.2	-170.8	-335.0
Wind Drift • Inches	0.0	0.7	2.9	6.8	12.6	20.6	31.0	60.2	102.8

Lapua 123-grain Scenar HPBT (4316032)

G1 Ballistic Coefficient = 0.535

Distance • Yards	Muzzle	100	200	300	400	500	600	800	1000
Velocity • fps	2855	2682	2516	2356	2202	2053	1911	1643	1415
Energy • Ft-lbs	2225	1965	1729	1517	1324	1152	998	741	547
Taylor KO Index	13.2	12.4	11.7	10.9	10.2	9.5	8.9	7.7	6.6
Path • Inches	-1.5	+1.7	0.0	-7.2	-20.6	-41.2	-70.1	-158.0	-297.5
Wind Drift • Inches	0.0	0.9	3.6	8.4	15.7	25.6	24.8	47.4	79.7

Hornady 129-grain SP-Light Magnum (8550) (Discontinued in 2005)

G1 Ballistic Coefficient = 0.444

Distance • Yards	Muzzle	100	200	300	400	500	600	800	1000
Velocity • fps	2750	2548	2355	2171	1995	1827	1667	1389	1175
Energy • Ft-lbs	2166	1860	1589	1350	1139	956	796	553	395
Taylor KO Index	13.4	12.4	11.5	10.6	9.7	8.9	8.1	6.8	5.7
Path • Inches	-1.5	+2.2	0.0	-8.5	-24.4	-49.6	-83.1	-193.0	-375.6
Wind Drift • Inches	0.0	0.8	3.1	7.3	13.5	22.0	33.0	64.2	108.8

Norma 130-grain Hollow Point (16530) (Discontinued in 2004)

G1 Ballistic Coefficient = 0.548

Distance • Yards	Muzzle	100	200	300	400	500	600	800	1000
Velocity • fps	2953	2781	2615	2455	2301	2152	2009	1741	1502
Energy • Ft-lbs	2518	2233	1974	1740	1529	1338	1166	875	651
Taylor KO Index	14.5	13.6	12.8	12.0	11.3	10.6	9.8	8.5	7.4
Path • Inches	-1.5	+1.5	0.0	-6.6	-19.0	-37.9	-64.4	-144.4	-270.8
Wind Drift • Inches	0.0	0.6	2.2	5.2	9.5	15.4	22.9	43.6	73.2

Norma 130-grain Hollow Point (16513) (Discontinued in 2004)

G1 Ballistic Coefficient = 0.548

Distance • Yards	Muzzle	100	200	300	400	500	600	800	1000
Velocity • fps	2723	2559	2402	2249	2104	1961	1826	1577	1360
Energy • Ft-lbs	2141	1891	1665	1461	1276	1111	963	718	534
Taylor KO Index	13.4	12.5	11.8	11.0	10.3	9.6	9.0	7.7	6.7
Path • Inches	-1.5	+1.9	0.0	-7.9	-22.8	-45.4	-77.2	-173.8	-327.6
Wind Drift • Inches	0.0	0.6	2.5	5.9	10.7	17.4	25.9	49.3	82.8

PMC 130-grain Pointed Soft Point (6.5MB)

G1 Ballistic Coefficient = 0.430

Distance • Yards	Muzzle	100	200	300	400	500	600	800	1000
Velocity • fps	2550	2348	2156	1975	1803	1645	1496	1246	1076
Energy • Ft-Lbs	2007	1701	1435	1204	1004	835	691	479	357
Taylor KO Index	13.4	12.3	11.3	10.4	9.5	8.6	7.8	6.5	5.6
Path • Inches	-1.5	+2.4	0.0	-9.9	-28.7	-58.2	-100.6	-236.3	-464.1
Wind Drift • Inches	0.0	0.9	3.6	8.4	15.7	25.6	38.6	74.8	125.0

Sellier & Bellot 131-grain SP (SBA65504)

G1 Ballistic Coefficient = 0.341

Distance • Yards	Muzzle	100	200	300	400	500	600	800	1000
Velocity • fps	2602	2336	2098	1884	1677	1488	1323	1086	956
Energy • Ft-lbs	1971	1590	1282	1034	818	645	510	343	266
Taylor KO Index	12.9	11.5	10.4	9.3	8.2	7.4	6.5	5.4	4.7
Path • Inches	-1.5	+2.4	0.0	-10.3	-30.4	-63.0	-111.6	-274.9	-554.5
Wind Drift • Inches	0.0	1.1	4.5	10.7	20.1	33.2	50.6	98.8	162.3

Lapua 139-grain Scenar HPBT (C316030)

G1 Ballistic Coefficient = 0.512

Distance • Yards	Muzzle	100	200	300	400	500	600	800	1000
Velocity • fps	2740	2564	2396	2233	2077	1927	1784	1523	1303
Energy • Ft-lbs	2318	2030	1772	1539	1332	1146	983	716	524
Taylor KO Index	14.4	13.4	12.6	11.7	10.9	10.1	9.4	8.0	6.8
Path • Inches	-1.5	+1.9	0.0	-8.0	-22.9	-45.9	-76.3	-178.1	-339.4
Wind Drift • Inches	0.0	0.6	2.7	6.2	11.5	18.6	27.8	53.4	89.9

Lapua 139-grain Scenar HPBT (4316030)

G1 Ballistic Coefficient = 0.601

Distance • Yards	Muzzle	100	200	300	400	500	600	800	1000
Velocity • fps	2625	2478	2337	2200	2068	1940	1818	1590	1389
Energy • Ft-lbs	2127	1896	1680	1494	1320	1162	1020	780	596
Taylor KO Index	13.8	13.0	12.3	11.5	10.8	10.2	9.6	8.4	7.3
Path • Inches	-1.5	+2.1	0.0	-8.4	-24.1	-47.9	-80.9	-180.1	-334.6
Wind Drift • Inches	0.0	0.6	2.4	5.6	10.2	16.5	24.5	46.4	77.3

Norma 140-grain Nosler Partition (16522)

G1 Ballistic Coefficient = 0.467

Distance • Yards	Muzzle	100	200	300	400	500	600	800	1000
Velocity • fps	2690	2500	2317	2142	1976	1817	1668	1402	1192
Energy • Ft-lbs	2250	1943	1669	1427	1214	1027	865	611	442
Taylor KO Index	14.2	13.2	12.2	11.3	10.4	9.6	8.8	7.4	6.3
Path • Inches	-1.5	+2.0	0.0	-8.5	-24.6	-49.6	-85.2	-196.9	-381.6
Wind Drift • Inches	0.0	0.7	3.1	7.1	13.1	21.4	32.1	62.0	104.7

Sellier & Bellot 140-grain SP (SBA65505)

G1 Ballistic Coefficient = 0.338

Distance • Yards	Muzzle	100	200	300	400	500	600	800	1000
Velocity • fps	2671	2399	2156	1937	1723	1528	1356	1103	965
Energy • Ft-Lbs	2199	1775	1433	1156	923	726	572	379	290
Taylor KO Index	14.1	12.7	11.4	10.2	9.1	8.1	7.2	5.8	5.1
Path • Inches	-1.5	+2.2	0.0	-9.7	-28.7	-59.6	-105.6	-261.1	-530.1
Wind Drift • Inches	0.0	1.0	4.4	10.4	19.5	32.3	49.3	96.7	160.1

Federal 140-grain Hi-Shok Soft Point (6555B)

G1 Ballistic Coefficient = 0.440

Distance • Yards	Muzzle	100	200	300	400	500	600	800	1000
Velocity • fps	2600	2400	2220	2040	1860	1700	1551	1293	1109
Energy • Ft-lbs	2100	1795	1525	1285	1080	900	748	520	382
Taylor KO Index	13.7	12.7	11.7	10.8	9.8	9.0	8.2	6.9	5.9
Path • Inches	-1.5	+2.3	0.0	-9.4	-27.2	-55.0	-95.0	-221.2	-431.0
Wind Drift • Inches	0.0	0.8	3.4	8.0	14.8	24.2	36.4	70.5	118.6

Speer 140-grain Grand Slam (24520) (Discontinued in 2004)

G1 Ballistic Coefficient = 0.386

Distance • Yards	Muzzle	100	200	300	400	500	600	800	1000
Velocity • fps	2600	2375	2161	1960	1770	1594	1435	1180	1024
Energy • Ft-lbs	2101	1753	1452	1194	975	791	640	433	326
Taylor KO Index	13.8	12.6	11.5	10.4	9.4	8.4	7.6	6.3	5.4
Path • Inches	-1.5	+2.5	0.0	-9.8	-28.7	-58.7	-102.4	-244.5	-486.5
Wind Drift • Inches	0.0	0.9	3.9	9.3	17.3	28.4	43.1	84.0	140.1

PMC 140-grain SPBT Game (6.5HB)

G1 Ballistic Coefficient = 0.495

Distance • Yards	Muzzle	100	200	300	400	500	600	800	1000
Velocity • fps	2560	2386	2218	2057	1903	1757	1619	1375	1182
Energy • Ft-lbs	2037	1769	1529	1315	1126	960	815	588	435
Taylor KO Index	13.5	12.6	11.7	10.9	10.0	9.3	8.5	7.3	6.2
Path • Inches	-1.5	+2.3	0.0	-9.4	-27.1	-54.2	-92.8	-212.5	-407.9
Wind Drift • Inches	0.0	0.7	3.1	7.2	13.2	21.5	32.2	61.8	103.6

Remington 140-grain Pointed Soft Point Core-Lokt (R65SWE1)

G1 Ballistic Coefficient = 0.436

Distance • Yards	Muzzle	100	200	300	400	500	600	800	1000
Velocity • fps	2550	2353	2164	1984	1814	1655	1508	1258	1085
Energy • Ft-lbs	2022	1720	1456	1224	1023	850	707	492	366
Taylor KO Index	13.5	12.4	11.4	10.5	9.6	8.7	8.0	6.7	5.8
Path • Inches	-1.5	+2.4	0.0	-9.8	-27.0	-57.8	-99.8	-232.8	-454.1
Wind Drift • Inches	0.0	0.8	3.5	8.3	15.4	25.2	37.2	73.4	122.9

Winchester 140-grain Soft Point (X6555)

G1 Ballistic Coefficient = 0.450

Distance • Yards	Muzzle	100	200	300	400	500	600	800	1000
Velocity • fps	2550	2359	2176	2002	1836	1680	1584	1285	1107
Energy • Ft-lbs	2022	1731	1473	1246	1048	878	732	514	381
Taylor KO Index	13.5	12.5	11.5	10.6	9.7	8.9	8.4	6.8	5.9
Path • Inches	-1.5	+2.4	0.0	-9.7	-28.1	-56.8	-98.1	-227.7	-441.9
Wind Drift • Inches	0.0	0.8	3.4	8.0	14.8	24.2	36.4	70.4	118.0

Hornady 140-grain SP Interlock (6.5SMA)

G1 Ballistic Coefficient = 0.469

Distance • Yards	Muzzle	100	200	300	400	500	600	800	1000
Velocity • fps	2525	2341	2165	1996	1836	1635	1545	1300	1120
Energy • Ft-lbs	1982	1704	1457	1239	1048	882	742	526	390
Taylor KO Index	13.3	12.4	11.4	10.5	9.7	8.9	8.2	6.9	5.9
Path • Inches	-1.5	+2.4	0.0	-5.9	-28.5	-57.4	-98.6	-228.3	-442.6
Wind Drift • Inches	0.0	0.8	3.3	7.8	14.5	23.6	35.4	68.3	114.3

PMC 140-grain Hollow Point Boat Tail Match (6.5SMA)

G1 Ballistic Coefficient = 0.536

Distance • Yards	Muzzle	100	200	300	400	500	600	800	1000
Velocity • fps	2560	2398	2243	2093	1949	1811	1681	1445	1249
Energy • Ft-lbs	2037	1788	1563	1361	1181	1020	879	649	485
Taylor KO Index	13.5	12.7	11.8	11.1	10.3	9.6	8.9	7.6	6.6
Path • Inches	-1.5	+2.3	0.0	-9.2	-26.4	-52.7	-89.5	-202.6	-383.9
Wind Drift • Inches	0.0	0.7	2.8	6.6	12.1	19.6	29.2	55.7	93.3

Sellier & Bellot 140-grain FMJ (SBA65506)

G1 Ballistic Coefficient = 0.465

Distance • Yards	Muzzle	100	200	300	400	500	600	800	1000
Velocity • fps	2582	2389	2211	2046	1883	1729	1585	1332	1143
Energy • Ft-lbs	2079	1780	1524	1305	1103	929	781	552	406
Taylor KO Index	13.6	12.6	11.7	10.8	9.9	9.1	8.4	7.0	6.0
Path • Inches	-1.5	+2.3	0.0	-9.4	-27.1	-54.6	-93.8	-217.1	-421.1
Wind Drift • Inches	0.0	0.8	3.2	7.6	14.0	22.8	34.3	66.2	111.2

PMC 140-grain FMJ (6.5MA)

G1 Ballistic Coefficient = 0.504

Distance • Yards	Muzzle	100	200	300	400	500	600	800	1000
Velocity • fps	2550	2377	2212	2055	1904	1761	1626	1384	1192
Energy • Ft-lbs	2079	1807	1565	1350	1160	992	822	596	442
Taylor KO Index	13.5	12.6	11.7	10.9	10.1	9.3	8.6	7.3	6.3
Path • Inches	-1.5	+2.3	0.0	-9.4	-27.1	-54.4	-92.8	-212.0	-405.8
Wind Drift • Inches	0.0	0.7	3.0	7.1	13.0	21.2	31.6	60.7	101.7

Lapua 155-grain Mega SP (4316021)

G1 Ballistic Coefficient = 0.630

Distance • Yards	Muzzle	100	200	300	400	500	600	800	1000
Velocity • fps	2559	2421	2288	2159	2033	1913	1797	1581	1390
Energy • Ft-lbs	2253	2017	1801	1603	1423	1259	1112	861	665
Taylor KO Index	15.0	14.2	13.4	12.6	11.9	11.2	10.5	9.3	8.2
Path • Inches	-1.5	+2.2	0.0	-8.9	-25.2	-50.0	-84.2	-186.5	344.7
Wind Drift • Inches	0.0	0.6	2.4	5.5	10.2	16.2	24.0	45.5	75.5

Norma 156-grain Oryx SP (16562)

G1 Ballistic Coefficient = 0.348

Distance • Yards	Muzzle	100	200	300	400	500	600	800	1000
Velocity • fps	2559	2313	2081	1862	1660	1477	1317	1086	958
Energy • Ft-lbs	2269	1854	1500	1202	955	756	601	409	318
Taylor KO Index	15.1	13.7	12.3	11.0	9.8	8.7	7.8	6.4	5.7
Path • Inches	-1.5	+2.5	0.0	-10.6	-31.2	-64.5	-113.8	-277.4	-558.3
Wind Drift • Inches	0.0	1.1	4.5	10.7	20.1	33.2	50.5	98.2	161.0

Norma 156-grain Alaska SP (16552)

G1 Ballistic Coefficient = 0.276

Distance • Yards	Muzzle	100	200	300	400	500	600	800	1000
Velocity • fps	2559	2250	1964	1701	1466	1269	1121	949	845
Energy • Ft-lbs	2269	1755	1336	1002	745	558	435	312	248
Taylor KO Index	15.1	13.2	11.6	10.0	8.6	7.5	6.6	5.6	5.0
Path • Inches	-1.5	+2.7	0.0	-11.7	-35.8	-76.3	-139.0	-352.3	-708.0
Wind Drift • Inches	0.0	1.4	5.9	14.1	27.0	45.1	68.9	130.9	207.8

Norma 156-grain Vulcan HP (16556)

G1 Ballistic Coefficient = 0.354

Distance • Yards	Muzzle	100	200	300	400	500	600	800	1000
Velocity • fps	2644	2395	2159	1937	1730	1540	1372	1120	979
Energy • Ft-lbs	2422	1987	1616	1301	1037	822	653	435	332
Taylor KO Index	15.6	14.1	12.7	11.4	10.2	9.1	8.1	6.6	5.8
Path • Inches	-1.5	+2.2	0.0	-9.7	-28.9	-59.6	-105.1	-256.1	-517.6
Wind Drift • Inches	0.0	1.0	4.3	10.1	19.0	31.4	47.8	93.7	155.2

Hirtenberger 160-grain Sierra SP (82200479)

G1 Ballistic Coefficient = 0.364

Distance • Yards	Muzzle	100	200	300	400	500	600	800	1000
Velocity • fps	2493	2261	2041	1835	1643	1469	1317	1093	967
Energy • Ft-lbs	2209	1816	1481	1196	959	767	616	425	332
Taylor KO Index	15.1	13.7	12.4	11.1	10.0	8.9	8.0	6.6	5.9
Path • Inches	-1.5	+2.7	0.0	-11.0	-32.4	-66.8	-117.3	-283.0	-564.7
Wind Drift • Inches	0.0	1.0	4.0	9.5	17.8	29.4	44.5	86.2	141.0

.260 Remington

Perhaps the story of the .260 Remington (introduced in 2001) should start out, "Where have you been?" That's because the .260 Remington is simply a 6.5mm-308. Since the .243 Winchester (1955) is a 6mm-08 and Remington began offering the 7mm-08 in 1980, the only logical reason the 6.5mm-08 didn't develop sooner is that the 6.5mm caliber has only recently had a good selection of bullets for the reloader. Time will tell if the .260 Remington has what it takes to become a popular "standard."

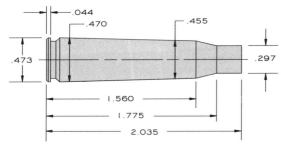

Relative Recoil Factor = 1.73

Specifications

Controlling Agency for Standardization of this Ammunition: SAAMI

Bullet Weight Grains	Velocity fps	Maximum Average Pressure	
		Copper Crusher	Transducer
140	2,725	N/A	60,000 psi

Standard barrel for velocity testing: 24 inches long—1 turn in 9-inch twist

Availability

Federal 120-grain Nosler Ballistic Tip (P260B)
G1 Ballistic Coefficient = 0.461

Distance • Yards	Muzzle	100	200	300	400	500	600	800	1000
Velocity • fps	2950	2750	2550	2360	2180	2010	1846	1547	1299
Energy • Ft-lbs	2320	2005	1730	1485	1265	1075	908	638	449
Taylor KO Index	13.4	12.4	11.5	10.7	9.9	9.1	8.4	7.0	5.9
Path • Inches	-1.5	+1.6	0.0	-6.9	-20.1	-40.5	-69.7	-161.0	-312.3
Wind Drift • Inches	0.0	0.7	2.7	6.4	11.7	19.0	28.6	55.3	94.2

Remington 120-grain AccuTip Boat Tail (PRT260RA)
G1 Ballistic Coefficient = 0.480

Distance • Yards	Muzzle	100	200	300	400	500	600	800	1000
Velocity • fps	2890	2697	2512	2334	2163	2000	1843	1558	1317
Energy • Ft-lbs	2392	2083	1807	1560	1340	1146	906	647	462
Taylor KO Index	13.1	12.2	11.4	10.6	9.8	9.1	8.3	7.1	6.0
Path • Inches	-1.5	+1.5	0.0	-7.2	-20.7	-41.7	-71.4	-163.8	-315.3
Wind Drift • Inches	0.0	0.6	2.7	6.2	11.4	18.6	27.8	53.6	90.9

Remington 125-grain Nosler Partition (PRT260RA) (Discontinued in 2005)
G1 Ballistic Coefficient = 0.450

Distance • Yards	Muzzle	100	200	300	400	500	600	800	1000
Velocity • fps	2875	2669	2473	2285	2105	1934	1773	1480	1244
Energy • Ft-lbs	2294	1977	1697	1449	1230	1037	872	608	430
Taylor KO Index	13.6	12.6	11.7	10.8	9.9	9.1	8.4	7.0	5.9
Path • Inches	-1.5	+1.7	0.0	-7.4	-21.4	-43.4	-74.6	-172.5	-334.5
Wind Drift • Inches	0.0	0.7	2.9	6.7	12.4	20.5	30.4	58.9	100.2

Federal 140-grain Sierra GameKing (P260A)
G1 Ballistic Coefficient = 0.489

Distance • Yards	Muzzle	100	200	300	400	500	600	800	1000
Velocity • fps	2750	2570	2390	2220	2060	1900	1753	1485	1264
Energy • Ft-lbs	2350	2045	1775	1535	1315	1125	956	986	497
Taylor KO Index	14.5	13.6	12.6	11.7	10.9	10.0	9.3	7.9	6.7
Path • Inches	-1.5	+1.9	0.0	-8.0	-23.1	-46.1	-79.3	-181.2	-346.8
Wind Drift • Inches	0.0	0.7	2.8	6.5	12.1	19.6	29.3	56.4	95.3

Federal 140-grain Trophy Bonded Bear Claw (P260T1) (Discontinued in 2005)
G1 Ballistic Coefficient = 0.431

Distance • Yards	Muzzle	100	200	300	400	500	600	800	1000
Velocity • fps	2750	2540	2340	2150	1970	1800	1640	1359	1149
Energy • Ft-lbs	2350	2010	1705	1440	1210	1010	836	574	410
Taylor KO Index	14.5	13.4	12.4	11.4	10.4	9.5	8.7	7.2	6.1
Path • Inches	-1.5	+1.9	0.0	-8.4	-24.1	-48.8	-84.4	-197.1	-385.6
Wind Drift • Inches	0.0	0.8	3.2	7.5	14.0	22.8	34.3	66.8	113.3

Remington 140-grain Core-Lokt Pointed Soft Point (PRC260RB)
G1 Ballistic Coefficient = 0.457

Distance • Yards	Muzzle	100	200	300	400	500	600	800	1000
Velocity • fps	2750	2554	2365	2185	2013	1849	1693	1417	1199
Energy • Ft-lbs	2351	2027	1739	1484	1260	1063	891	624	447
Taylor KO Index	14.5	13.4	12.4	11.4	10.4	9.6	8.8	7.3	6.1
Path • Inches	-1.5	+1.7	0.0	-8.1	-23.6	-47.6	-81.9	-189.8	-369.4
Wind Drift • Inches	0.0	0.7	3.0	7.0	13.0	21.2	31.9	61.7	104.6

Remington 140-grain Core-Lokt Pointed Soft Point (R260R1)
G1 Ballistic Coefficient = 0.436

Distance • Yards	Muzzle	100	200	300	400	500	600	800	1000
Velocity • fps	2750	2544	2347	2158	1979	1812	1651	1371	1159
Energy • Ft-lbs	2352	2011	1712	1488	1217	1021	847	584	417
Taylor KO Index	14.5	13.4	12.4	11.4	10.4	9.6	8.8	7.3	6.1
Path • Inches	-1.5	+1.9	0.0	-8.3	-24.0	-47.2	-83.9	-195.5	-381.6
Wind Drift • Inches	0.0	0.8	3.2	7.4	13.8	22.5	33.8	65.8	111.5

Speer 140-grain Grand Slam (24554) (Discontinued in 2004)
G1 Ballistic Coefficient = 0.386

Distance • Yards	Muzzle	100	200	300	400	500	600	800	1000
Velocity • fps	2725	2494	2274	2066	1870	1686	1518	1367	1057
Energy • Ft-lbs	2308	1933	1607	1327	1087	884	716	477	347
Taylor KO Index	14.4	13.2	12.1	10.9	9.9	8.9	8.0	7.2	5.6
Path • Inches	-1.5	+2.0	0.0	-8.8	-25.8	-52.7	-91.9	-219.2	-437.6
Wind Drift • Inches	0.0	0.8	3.3	7.8	14.5	23.8	36.1	70.8	119.6

Sherwin Scott with a red-flanked duiker from the C.A.R. (Photo from *African Hunter II* by Craig Boddington and Peter Flack, Safari Press, 2004)

6.71mm (.264) Lazzeroni Phantom

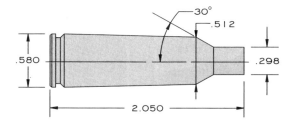

The second caliber in John Lazzeroni's short magnum series is his 6.71mm Phantom. While it is difficult to make a perfect comparison, the factory loading for this round sets its performance at a level almost identical to that of the .264 Winchester Magnum.

Relative Recoil Factor = 1.79

Specifications

Controlling Agency for Standardization of this Ammunition: Factory

Availability

Lazzeroni 120-grain SP (671)

G1 Ballistic Coefficient = 0.525

Distance • Yards	Muzzle	100	200	300	400	500	600	800	1000
Velocity • fps	3312	3117	2930	2751	2579	2414	2255	1955	1681
Energy • Ft-lbs	2923	2589	2289	2018	1773	1553	1356	1019	753
Taylor KO Index	15.0	14.1	13.3	12.5	11.7	10.9	10.2	8.8	7.6
Path • Inches	-1.5	+1.0	0.0	-5.1	-14.8	-29.7	-50.6	-113.9	-214.4
Wind Drift • Inches	0.0	0.5	2.0	4.7	8.6	13.8	20.4	38.9	65.2

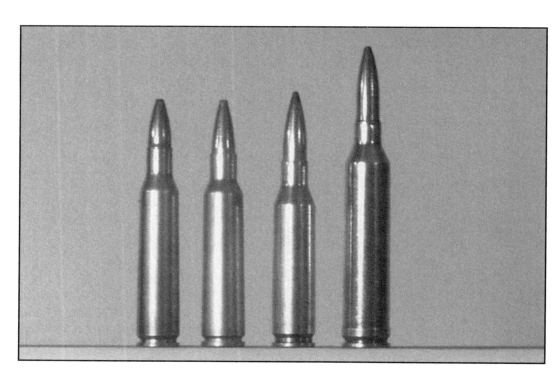

(Left to right) .257 Roberts, 6.5x55, .260 Remington, .264 Winchester Magnum.

.264 Winchester Magnum

Winchester's .264 Magnum was touted to be a world beater when it was introduced in 1958. It never quite reached the popularity that was anticipated. This generally isn't because it lacked performance. The .264 WM could reach factory velocities well in excess of 3000 fps even with the heavier bullet offerings. Nothing else in the 6.5 mm class came close. Barrel life questions and a general shortage of good 6.5 mm bullets for reloading didn't help its popularity. Winchester, who had previously dropped this caliber, reintroduced it into their catalog in 2001. Remington (who have dropped their own 6.5 mm Remington Magnum) also make factory ammo for the .264 Winchester Magnum, offering (like Winchester) only one loading, a 140-grain bullet.

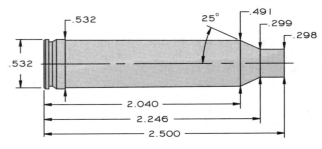

Relative Recoil Factor = 1.91

Specifications

Controlling Agency for Standardization of this Ammunition: SAAMI

Bullet Weight Grains	Velocity fps	Maximum Average Pressure	
		Copper Crusher	Transducer
100	3,300	54,000 cup	64,000 psi
140	3,015	54,000 cup	64,000 psi

Standard barrel for velocity testing: 24 inches long—1 turn in 9-inch twist

Availability

Remington 140-grain Soft Point (R264W2)

G1 Ballistic Coefficient = 0.385

Distance • Yards	Muzzle	100	200	300	400	500	600	800	1000
Velocity • fps	3030	2782	2548	2326	2114	1914	1726	1397	1153
Energy • Ft-lbs	2854	2406	2018	1682	1389	1139	926	607	414
Taylor KO Index	16.0	14.7	13.5	12.3	11.2	10.1	9.1	7.4	6.1
Path • Inches	-1.5	+1.5	0.0	-7.2	-20.8	-42.2	-72.0	-172.1	-347.0
Wind Drift • Inches	0.0	0.8	3.2	7.4	13.9	22.7	34.3	67.6	116.3

Winchester 140-grain Power Point (X2642)

G1 Ballistic Coefficient = 0.385

Distance • Yards	Muzzle	100	200	300	400	500	600	800	1000
Velocity • fps	3030	2782	2548	2326	2114	1914	1726	1397	1153
Energy • Ft-lbs	2854	2406	2018	1682	1389	1139	926	607	414
Taylor KO Index	16.0	14.7	13.5	12.3	11.2	10.1	9.1	7.4	6.1
Path • Inches	-1.5	+1.5	0.0	-7.2	-20.8	-42.2	-72.0	-172.1	-347.0
Wind Drift • Inches	0.0	0.8	3.2	7.4	13.9	22.7	34.3	67.6	116.3

6.8mm Remington SPC

This is a new cartridge, introduced in 2004, that was developed to fill the desire of various military units for a round that would allow heavier bullets to be fired in M-16-type rifles. It is obvious that, as a minimum, the gun's barrel must be changed, but the conversion looks pretty easy. Based on the .30 Remington case, the 6.8 mm Remington is considerably more potent than the .30 M1 Carbine and seems to be well suited to the assault rifle role. It is actually slightly more powerful than the 7.62x39 round. Ultimately its popularity will probably depend on what rifle selections become available.

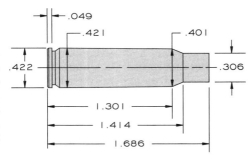

Relative Recoil Factor = 1.41

Specifications

Controlling Agency for Standardization of this Ammunition: SAAMI

Bullet Weight Grains	Velocity fps	Maximum Average Pressure Copper Crusher	Transducer
115	2780	N/S	55,000 psi

Standard barrel for velocity testing: 24 inches long—1 turn in 10-inch twist

Availability

Remington 115-grain Core-Lokt Ultra Bonded (PRC68R4)
G1 Ballistic Coefficient = 0.295

Distance • Yards	Muzzle	100	200	300	400	500	600	800	1000
Velocity • fps	2775	2472	2190	1926	1683	1467	1284	1039	912
Energy • Ft-lbs	1966	1561	1224	947	723	549	421	276	212
Taylor KO Index	12.6	11.2	10.0	8.8	7.7	6.7	5.8	4.7	4.2
Path • Inches	-1.5	+2.1	0.0	-9.4	-28.2	-59.4	-107.4	-274.2	-565.2
Wind Drift • Inches	0.0	1.0	4.3	10.3	19.6	32.7	50.2	99.1	162.9

Remington 115-grain Open Tip Match (R68R1)
G1 Ballistic Coefficient = 0.340

Distance • Yards	Muzzle	100	200	300	400	500	600	800	1000
Velocity • fps	2775	2511	2263	2028	1809	1607	1426	1146	988
Energy • Ft-lbs	1966	1610	1307	1050	835	659	520	336	249
Taylor KO Index	12.6	11.4	10.3	9.2	8.2	7.3	6.5	5.2	4.5
Path • Inches	-1.5	+2.0	0.0	-8.8	-26.4	-54.2	-95.9	-237.0	-485.3
Wind Drift • Inches	0.0	0.9	3.7	8.7	16.4	27.2	41.4	82.0	137.6

Remington 115-grain Sierra Hollow Point Boat Tail (R68R2)
G1 Ballistic Coefficient = 0.340

Distance • Yards	Muzzle	100	200	300	400	500	600	800	1000
Velocity • fps	2775	2511	2263	2028	1809	1607	1426	1146	988
Energy • Ft-lbs	1966	1610	1307	1050	835	659	520	336	249
Taylor KO Index	12.6	11.4	10.3	9.2	8.2	7.3	6.5	5.2	4.5
Path • Inches	-1.5	+2.0	0.0	-8.8	-26.4	-54.2	-95.9	-237.0	-485.3
Wind Drift • Inches	0.0	0.9	3.7	8.7	16.4	27.2	41.4	82.0	137.6

Remington 115-grain Full Metal Jacket (RM68R1)
G1 Ballistic Coefficient = 0.340

Distance • Yards	Muzzle	100	200	300	400	500	600	800	1000
Velocity • fps	2775	2511	2263	2028	1809	1607	1426	1146	988
Energy • Ft-lbs	1966	1610	1307	1050	835	659	520	336	249
Taylor KO Index	12.6	11.4	10.3	9.2	8.2	7.3	6.5	5.2	4.5
Path • Inches	-1.5	+2.0	0.0	-8.8	-26.4	-54.2	-95.9	-237.0	-485.3
Wind Drift • Inches	0.0	0.9	3.7	8.7	16.4	27.2	41.4	82.0	137.6

.270 Winchester

When Winchester took the .30-06 in 1925 and necked it to .270, I doubt if they even guessed that it would become one of the most popular nonmilitary calibers sold in the U.S. The popularity of this cartridge is demonstrated by the fact that there are about fifty factory loadings available for the .270. That's a larger number than any other cartridge that is not a military standard. This popularity isn't an accident. The .270 drives 130-grain bullets to just over 3,000 fps, providing an excellent flat-shooting capability that's bettered only by the magnums.

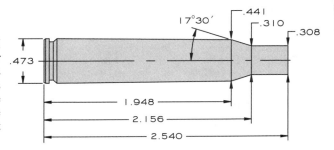

Relative Recoil Factor = 1.82

Specifications

Controlling Agency for Standardization of this Ammunition: SAAMI

Bullet Weight Grains	Velocity fps	Maximum Average Pressure	
		Copper Crusher	Transducer
100	3,300	52,000 cup	65,000 psi
130	3,050	52,000 cup	65,000 psi
140	2,950	52,000 cup	65,000 psi
150	2,830	52,000 cup	65,000 psi
160	2,650	52,000 cup	65,000 psi

Standard barrel for velocity testing: 24 inches long—1 turn in 10-inch twist

Availability

Remington 100-grain Pointed Soft Point (R270W1)

G1 Ballistic Coefficient = 0.252

Distance • Yards	Muzzle	100	200	300	400	500	600	800	1000
Velocity • fps	3320	2924	2561	2225	1916	1636	1395	1067	912
Energy • Ft-lbs	2448	1898	1456	1099	815	594	432	253	185
Taylor KO Index	13.1	11.6	10.1	8.8	7.6	6.5	5.5	4.2	3.6
Path • Inches	-1.5	+1.2	0.0	-6.2	-20.3	-43.6	-79.9	-212.6	-466.8
Wind Drift • Inches	0.0	1.0	4.4	10.7	20.3	34.2	53.3	109.2	185.3

Remington 115-grain Core-Lokt Pointed Soft Point (R270W2)

G1 Ballistic Coefficient = 0.295

Distance • Yards	Muzzle	100	200	300	400	500	600	800	1000
Velocity • fps	2710	2412	2133	1873	1636	1425	1247	1020	
Energy • Ft-lbs	1875	1485	1161	895	683	519	397	266	20
Taylor KO Index	12.3	11.0	9.7	8.5	7.4	6.5	5.7	4.6	4.1
Path • Inches	-1.5	+2.2	0.0	-10.0	-29.9	-63.1	-114.0	-290.3	-594.2
Wind Drift • Inches	0.0	1.2	5.0	11.9	22.6	37.8	58.0	113.6	185.3

Hornady 130-grain InterBond-LM (85549)

G1 Ballistic Coefficient = 0.463

Distance • Yards	Muzzle	100	200	300	400	500	600	800	1000
Velocity • fps	3215	2998	2792	2595	2406	2225	2051	1730	1450
Energy • Ft-lbs	2983	2594	2249	1943	1671	1429	1215	864	607
Taylor KO Index	16.5	15.4	14.4	13.3	12.4	11.4	10.6	8.9	7.5
Path • Inches	-1.5	+1.2	0.0	-5.7	-16.5	-33.3	-57.2	-131.5	-253.8
Wind Drift • Inches	0.0	0.6	2.4	5.6	10.3	16.7	25.0	48.3	82.2

Winchester 130-grain Power-Point Plus (SHV2705)

G1 Ballistic Coefficient = 0.363

Distance • Yards	Muzzle	100	200	300	400	500	600	800	1000
Velocity • fps	3150	2881	2628	2388	2161	1946	1745	1396	1141
Energy • Ft-lbs	2865	2396	1993	1646	1348	1094	879	563	376
Taylor KO Index	16.3	14.9	13.6	12.3	11.2	10.0	9.2	7.2	5.9
Path • Inches	-1.5	+1.3	0.0	-6.4	-18.9	-38.8	-68.2	-163.8	-331.8
Wind Drift • Inches	0.0	0.7	2.9	6.8	12.6	20.7	31.4	62.3	107.9

Norma 130-grain Soft Point (16902)

G1 Ballistic Coefficient = 0.359

Distance • Yards	Muzzle	100	200	300	400	500	600	800	1000
Velocity • fps	3140	2862	2601	2354	2122	1903	1700	1350	1107
Energy • Ft-lbs	2847	2365	1953	1600	1300	1046	834	526	354
Taylor KO Index	16.2	14.7	13.4	12.1	10.9	9.8	8.8	7.0	5.7
Path • Inches	-1.5	+1.3	0.0	-6.5	-19.4	-39.9	-70.1	-169.9	-346.9
Wind Drift • Inches	0.0	0.8	3.3	7.8	14.7	24.1	36.6	72.9	126.3

RWS 130-grain Soft Point (211 8440)

G1 Ballistic Coefficient = 0.375

Distance • Yards	Muzzle	100	200	300	400	500	600	800	1000
Velocity • fps	3140	2880	2634	2402	2181	1972	1776	1431	1171
Energy • Ft-lbs	2847	2395	2004	1665	1373	1123	911	591	396
Taylor KO Index	16.2	14.9	13.6	12.4	11.3	10.2	9.2	7.4	6.0
Path • Inches	-1.5	+1.4	0.0	-6.4	-18.8	-38.5	-67.3	-161.4	-327.2
Wind Drift • Inches	0.0	0.8	3.1	7.3	13.5	22.2	33.6	66.3	114.7

Speer 130-grain Grand Slam (24501) (Discontinued in 2004)

G1 Ballistic Coefficient = 0.346

Distance • Yards	Muzzle	100	200	300	400	500	600	800	1000
Velocity • fps	3140	2858	2593	2342	2107	1885	1679	1329	1092
Energy • Ft-lbs	2846	2357	1940	1584	1282	1026	814	510	344
Taylor KO Index	15.8	14.6	13.4	12.1	10.9	9.7	8.7	6.9	5.6
Path • Inches	-1.5	+1.8	0.0	-6.6	-19.5	-40.3	-70.9	-172.6	-353.8
Wind Drift • Inches	0.0	0.8	3.4	8.0	15.0	24.6	37.5	74.8	129.5

Estate 130-grain PSP (E270-1) (Discontinued in 2004)

G1 Ballistic Coefficient = 0.350

Distance • Yards	Muzzle	100	200	300	400	500	600	800	1000
Velocity • fps	3060	2787	2530	2286	2057	1841	1642	1305	1080
Energy • Ft-lbs	2702	2242	1847	1509	1222	979	778	492	337
Taylor KO Index	15.8	14.4	13.1	11.8	10.6	9.5	8.5	6.7	5.6
Path • Inches	-1.5	+1.5	0.0	-6.9	-20.6	-42.4	-74.7	-182.7	-376.4
Wind Drift • Inches	0.0	0.8	3.5	8.2	15.3	25.1	36.2	76.1	131.2

Federal 130-grain Sierra GameKing BTSP (P270D)

G1 Ballistic Coefficient = 0.425

Distance • Yards	Muzzle	100	200	300	400	500	600	800	1000
Velocity • fps	3060	2830	2620	2410	2220	2030	1854	1534	1272
Energy • Ft-lbs	2700	2320	1980	1680	1420	1190	992	679	467
Taylor KO Index	15.7	14.6	13.5	12.4	11.4	10.4	9.6	7.9	6.6
Path • Inches	-1.5	+1.4	0.0	-6.5	-19.0	-38.5	-66.6	-155.2	-303.5
Wind Drift • Inches	0.0	0.7	2.8	6.6	12.1	19.8	29.7	57.9	99.2

Federal 130-grain Nosler Partition (P270P)

G1 Ballistic Coefficient = 0.418

Distance • Yards	Muzzle	100	200	300	400	500	600	800	1000
Velocity • fps	3060	2830	2610	2400	2200	2010	1830	1506	1245
Energy • Ft-lbs	2705	2310	1965	1665	1400	1170	966	655	447
Taylor KO Index	15.7	14.6	13.4	12.3	11.3	10.3	9.4	7.7	6.4
Path • Inches	-1.5	+1.4	0.0	-6.5	-19.1	-38.8	-67.4	-158.3	-313.2
Wind Drift • Inches	0.0	0.7	2.9	6.7	12.5	20.3	30.6	59.8	102.6

Federal 130-grain Trophy Bonded Bear Claw (P270T2) (Discontinued in 2005)

G1 Ballistic Coefficient = 0.383

Distance • Yards	Muzzle	100	200	300	400	500	600	800	1000
Velocity • fps	3060	2810	2570	2340	2130	1930	1740	1407	1159
Energy • Ft-lbs	2785	2275	1905	1585	1310	1070	874	572	388
Taylor KO Index	15.7	14.5	13.2	12.0	11.0	9.9	9.0	7.3	6.0
Path • Inches	-1.5	+1.5	0.0	-6.7	-19.8	-40.5	-70.6	-168.1	-336.6
Wind Drift • Inches	0.0	0.8	3.2	7.4	13.8	22.5	34.0	67.2	115.8

Federal 130-grain Hi-Shok Soft Point (270A)

G1 Ballistic Coefficient = 0.371

Distance • Yards	Muzzle	100	200	300	400	500	600	800	1000
Velocity • fps	3060	2880	2560	2330	2110	1900	1708	1373	1131
Energy • Ft-lbs	2700	2265	1890	1585	1285	1043	842	544	370
Taylor KO Index	15.7	14.8	13.2	12.0	10.9	9.8	8.8	7.1	5.8
Path • Inches	-1.5	+1.5	0.0	-6.8	-20.0	-41.1	-71.9	-172.2	-347.1
Wind Drift • Inches	0.0	0.8	3.2	7.6	14.2	23.4	35.4	70.0	120.8

Hornady 130-grain SST InterLock (8054)

G1 Ballistic Coefficient = 0.463

Distance • Yards	Muzzle	100	200	300	400	500	600	800	1000
Velocity • fps	3060	2851	2651	2460	2277	2101	1933	1625	1362
Energy • Ft-lbs	2702	2345	2028	1746	1496	1275	1079	763	536
Taylor KO Index	15.7	14.7	13.6	12.7	11.7	10.8	9.9	8.4	7.0
Path • Inches	-1.5	+1.4	0.0	-6.3	-18.5	-37.3	-64.0	-147.4	-285.3
Wind Drift • Inches	0.0	0.6	2.6	6.0	11.1	18.0	26.9	52.0	88.6

Remington 130-grain Swift Scirocco (PRSC270WA)

G1 Ballistic Coefficient = 0.433

Distance • Yards	Muzzle	100	200	300	400	500	600	800	1000
Velocity • fps	3060	2838	2627	2425	2232	2048	1872	1555	1293
Energy • Ft-lbs	2702	2325	1991	1697	1438	1211	1012	698	482
Taylor KO Index	15.8	14.7	13.6	12.5	11.5	10.6	9.7	8.0	6.7
Path • Inches	-1.5	+1.4	0.0	-6.5	-18.8	-38.2	-66.0	-153.2	-298.6
Wind Drift • Inches	0.0	0.6	2.5	5.8	10.7	17.4	26.1	50.8	87.0

Remington 130-grain AccuTip Boat Tail (PRA270WA)

G1 Ballistic Coefficient = 0.447

Distance • Yards	Muzzle	100	200	300	400	500	600	800	1000
Velocity • fps	3060	2776	2510	2259	2022	1801	1599	1262	1051
Energy • Ft-lbs	2702	2225	1818	1472	1180	936	738	460	319
Taylor KO Index	15.7	14.6	13.6	12.6	11.6	10.7	9.8	8.2	6.8
Path • Inches	-1.5	+1.4	0.0	-6.4	-18.6	-37.7	-64.9	-150.2	-292.4
Wind Drift • Inches	0.0	0.6	2.7	6.2	11.4	18.6	27.9	54.0	92.3

Remington 130-grain Swift Scirocco Bonded (PRSC270WA)

G1 Ballistic Coefficient = 0.433

Distance • Yards	Muzzle	100	200	300	400	500	600	800	1000
Velocity • fps	3060	2838	2627	2425	2232	2048	1873	1555	1292
Energy • Ft-lbs	2702	2325	1991	1697	1438	1211	1013	699	482
Taylor KO Index	15.7	14.6	13.5	12.5	11.5	10.5	9.6	8.0	6.6
Path • Inches	-1.5	+1.4	0.0	-6.5	-18.8	-38.2	-65.9	-153.5	-300.9
Wind Drift • Inches	0.0	0.7	2.8	6.4	11.9	19.3	29.0	56.4	96.6

Remington 130-grain Pointed Soft Point Core-Lokt (R270W2)

G1 Ballistic Coefficient = 0.336

Distance • Yards	Muzzle	100	200	300	400	500	600	800	1000
Velocity • fps	3060	2776	2510	2259	2022	1801	1599	1262	1051
Energy • Ft-lbs	2702	2225	1818	1472	1180	936	738	460	319
Taylor KO Index	15.7	14.3	12.9	11.6	10.4	9.3	8.3	6.5	5.4
Path • Inches	-1.5	+1.5	0.0	-7.0	-20.9	-43.3	-76.6	-187.6	-386.6
Wind Drift • Inches	0.0	0.9	3.6	8.5	16.0	26.4	40.2	80.4	138.4

Winchester 130-grain Power-Point (X2705)

G1 Ballistic Coefficient = 0.372

Distance • Yards	Muzzle	100	200	300	400	500	600	800	1000
Velocity • fps	3060	2802	2559	2329	2110	1904	1711	1376	1134
Energy • Ft-lbs	2702	2267	1890	1565	1285	1046	845	547	371
Taylor KO Index	15.7	14.4	13.2	12.0	10.9	9.9	8.8	7.1	5.9
Path • Inches	-1.5	+1.8	0.0	-7.1	-20.6	-42.0	-71.8	-171.8	-346.1
Wind Drift • Inches	0.0	0.8	3.2	7.6	14.2	23.3	35.3	69.8	120.3

Winchester 130-grain Silvertip (X2703)

G1 Ballistic Coefficient = 0.337

Distance • Yards	Muzzle	100	200	300	400	500	600	800	1000
Velocity • fps	3060	2776	2510	2259	2022	1801	1599	1262	1051
Energy • Ft-lbs	2702	2225	1818	1472	1180	936	738	460	319
Taylor KO Index	15.7	14.3	12.9	11.6	10.4	9.3	8.3	6.5	5.4
Path • Inches	-1.5	+1.5	0.0	-7.0	-20.9	-43.3	-76.6	-187.6	-386.6
Wind Drift • Inches	0.0	0.9	3.6	8.5	16.0	26.4	40.2	80.4	138.4

Federal 130-grain Nosler Solid Base BT (P270S1)

G1 Ballistic Coefficient = 0.422

Distance • Yards	Muzzle	100	200	300	400	500	600	800	1000
Velocity • fps	3050	2820	2600	2400	2200	2010	1832	1511	1251
Energy • Ft-lbs	2685	2295	1955	1660	1395	1165	969	659	452
Taylor KO Index	15.7	14.5	13.4	12.3	11.3	10.3	9.4	7.8	6.4
Path • Inches	-1.5	+1.4	0.0	-6.5	-19.2	-39.0	-67.6	-158.4	-312.8
Wind Drift • Inches	0.0	0.7	2.9	6.7	12.4	20.2	30.4	59.3	101.7

PMC 130-grain SPBT Game (270HA)

G1 Ballistic Coefficient = 0.437

Distance • Yards	Muzzle	100	200	300	400	500	600	800	1000
Velocity • fps	3050	2830	2620	2421	2229	2047	1875	1560	1290
Energy • Ft-lbs	2685	2312	1982	1691	1435	1209	1015	703	487
Taylor KO Index	15.7	14.6	13.5	12.5	11.5	10.5	9.6	8.0	6.6
Path • Inches	-1.5	+1.5	0.0	-6.5	-19.0	-38.5	-66.1	-153.7	-300.7
Wind Drift • Inches	0.0	0.7	2.7	6.4	11.8	19.2	28.8	56.0	95.7

Federal 130-grain Nosler Ballistic Tip (P270F)

G1 Ballistic Coefficient = 0.435

Distance • Yards	Muzzle	100	200	300	400	500	600	800	1000
Velocity • fps	3060	2840	2630	2430	2230	2050	1878	1561	1299
Energy • Ft-lbs	2700	2325	1990	1700	1440	1210	1018	704	487
Taylor KO Index	15.7	14.6	13.5	12.5	11.5	10.5	9.7	8.1	6.7
Path • Inches	-1.5	+1.4	0.0	-6.5	-18.8	-38.2	-65.8	-152.7	-297.3
Wind Drift • Inches	0.0	0.7	2.7	6.4	11.8	19.2	28.8	56.1	95.9

Federal 130-grain Barnes XLC Coated X-Bullet (P270H)

G1 Ballistic Coefficient = 0.430

Distance • Yards	Muzzle	100	200	300	400	500	600	800	1000
Velocity • fps	3060	2840	2620	2432	2220	2040	1866	1547	1285
Energy • Ft-lbs	2705	2320	1985	1690	1425	1203	1018	704	487
Taylor KO Index	15.8	14.7	13.5	12.5	11.5	10.5	9.6	8.0	6.6
Path • Inches	-1.5	+1.4	0.0	-6.4	-18.9	-38.4	-66.2	-153.9	-300.4
Wind Drift • Inches	0.0	0.7	2.8	6.5	12.0	19.5	29.3	57.0	97.5

Federal 130-grain Barnes Triple Shock (P270L)

G1 Ballistic Coefficient = 0.427

Distance • Yards	Muzzle	100	200	300	400	500	600	800	1000
Velocity • fps	3060	2830	2620	2420	2220	2030	1852	1531	1269
Energy • Ft-lbs	2705	2320	1980	1685	1425	1195	990	677	465
Taylor KO Index	15.7	14.6	13.5	12.4	11.4	10.4	9.5	7.9	6.5
Path • Inches	-1.5	+1.4	0.0	-6.4	-18.9	-38.5	-66.6	-155.8	-306.8
Wind Drift • Inches	0.0	0.7	2.8	6.6	12.2	19.8	29.8	58.1	99.5

Winchester 130-grain Ballistic Silvertip (SBST270)

G1 Ballistic Coefficient = 0.436

Distance • Yards	Muzzle	100	200	300	400	500	600	800	1000
Velocity • fps	3050	2828	2618	2416	2224	2040	1866	1549	1287
Energy • Ft-lbs	2685	2309	1978	1685	1428	1202	1005	693	479
Taylor KO Index	15.7	14.6	13.6	12.6	11.6	10.7	9.8	8.2	6.8
Path • Inches	-1.5	+1.4	0.0	-6.5	-18.9	-38.4	-66.4	-154.7	-303.3
Wind Drift • Inches	0.0	0.7	2.8	6.4	11.9	19.4	29.2	56.7	97.0

Hirtenberger 130-grain Nosler Partition (82200342)

G1 Ballistic Coefficient = 0.750 (?)

Distance • Yards	Muzzle	100	200	300	400	500	600	800	1000
Velocity • fps	2986	2859	2735	2614	2497	2383	2272	2058	1856
Energy • Ft-lbs	2574	2359	2159	1973	1800	1639	1490	1223	995
Taylor KO Index	15.4	14.8	14.1	13.5	12.9	12.3	11.7	10.6	9.6
Path • Inches	-1.5	+1.4	0.0	-6.0	-17.1	-33.8	-56.6	-123.2	-222.7
Wind Drift • Inches	0.0	0.4	1.6	3.7	6.6	10.6	15.6	29.1	47.8

PMC 130-grain PSP (270A)

G1 Ballistic Coefficient = 0.364

Distance • Yards	Muzzle	100	200	300	400	500	600	800	1000
Velocity • fps	2950	2691	2447	2217	2001	1799	1611	1292	1079
Energy • Ft-lbs	2512	2090	1728	1419	1156	935	749	482	336
Taylor KO Index	15.2	13.9	12.6	11.4	10.3	9.3	8.3	6.7	5.6
Path • Inches	-1.5	+1.7	0.0	-7.5	-22.1	-45.4	-79.4	-192.4	-392.4
Wind Drift • Inches	0.0	0.8	3.5	8.2	15.4	25.3	38.4	76.1	130.2

Hirtenberger 130-grain Sierra SBT Bullet (82200461)

G1 Ballistic Coefficient = 0.688

Distance • Yards	Muzzle	100	200	300	400	500	600	800	1000
Velocity • fps	2920	2783	2651	2522	2397	2275	2157	1932	1722
Energy • Ft-lbs	2462	2237	2029	1837	1659	1495	1344	1077	856
Taylor KO Index	15.1	14.4	13.7	13.0	12.4	11.7	11.1	10.0	8.9
Path • Inches	-1.5	+1.5	0.0	-6.4	-18.4	-36.3	-61.0	-133.6	-243.9
Wind Drift • Inches	0.0	0.4	1.6	3.7	6.8	10.8	16.0	30.0	49.6

Remington 130-grain Bronze Point (270W3)

G1 Ballistic Coefficient = 0.372

Distance • Yards	Muzzle	100	200	300	400	500	600	800	1000
Velocity • fps	3060	2802	2559	2329	2110	1904	1711	1376	1134
Energy • Ft-lbs	2702	2267	1890	1565	1285	1046	845	547	371
Taylor KO Index	15.7	14.4	13.2	12.0	10.9	9.9	8.8	7.1	5.9
Path • Inches	-1.5	+1.8	0.0	-7.1	-20.6	-42.0	-71.8	-171.8	-346.1
Wind Drift • Inches	0.0	0.8	3.2	7.6	14.2	23.3	35.3	69.8	120.3

Black Hills 130-grain Barnes X-Bullet

G1 Ballistic Coefficient = 0.466

Distance • Yards	Muzzle	100	200	300	400	500	600	800	1000
Velocity • fps	2950	2748	2555	2371	2193	2054	1862	1567	1319
Energy • Ft-lbs	2513	2181	1885	1623	1389	1183	1001	709	502
Taylor KO Index	15.2	14.1	13.1	12.2	11.3	10.6	9.6	8.1	6.8
Path • Inches	-1.5	+1.6	0.0	-6.9	-20.0	-40.3	-69.1	-159.1	-307.7
Wind Drift • Inches	0.0	0.6	2.7	6.2	11.5	18.6	28.0	54.0	91.8

Black Hills 130-grain Nosler Ballistic Tip

G1 Ballistic Coefficient = 0.433

Distance • Yards	Muzzle	100	200	300	400	500	600	800	1000
Velocity • fps	2950	2733	2527	2329	2141	1961	1791	1486	1240
Energy • Ft-lbs	2513	2157	1843	1567	1323	1111	926	637	444
Taylor KO Index	15.2	14.1	13.0	12.0	11.0	10.1	9.2	7.6	6.4
Path • Inches	-1.5	+1.6	0.0	-7.0	-20.5	-41.6	-71.7	-167.3	-328.4
Wind Drift • Inches	0.0	0.7	2.9	6.8	12.5	20.4	30.6	59.7	101.9

PMC 130-grain Barnes-XLC-HP (270XLA) (Discontinued in 2005)

G1 Ballistic Coefficient = 0.485

Distance • Yards	Muzzle	100	200	300	400	500	600	800	1000
Velocity • fps	2910	2717	2533	2356	2186	2023	1869	1583	1341
Energy • Ft-lbs	2444	2131	1852	1602	1379	1181	1008	724	519
Taylor KO Index	15.0	14.0	13.1	12.2	11.3	10.4	9.6	8.2	6.9
Path • Inches	-1.5	+1.6	0.0	-7.1	-20.4	-41.1	-70.0	-160.1	-307.4
Wind Drift • Inches	0.0	0.6	2.6	6.1	11.2	18.1	27.2	52.3	88.6

PMC 130-grain Pointed Soft Point (270A)

G1 Ballistic Coefficient = 0.409

Distance • Yards	Muzzle	100	200	300	400	500	600	800	1000
Velocity • fps	2816	2593	2381	2179	1987	1805	1638	1344	1130
Energy • Ft-lbs	2288	1941	1636	1370	1139	941	774	521	368
Taylor KO Index	14.5	13.3	12.2	11.2	10.2	9.3	8.4	6.9	5.8
Path • Inches	-1.5	+1.8	0.0	-8.0	-23.2	-47.3	-82.4	-194.8	-387.3
Wind Drift • Inches	0.0	0.8	3.3	7.7	14.3	23.4	35.4	69.2	117.9

Federal 140-grain Trophy Bonded Bear Claw-HE (P270T3)

G1 Ballistic Coefficient = 0.398

Distance • Yards	Muzzle	100	200	300	400	500	600	800	1000
Velocity • fps	3100	2860	2620	2400	2200	2000	1814	1480	1218
Energy • Ft-lbs	2990	2535	2140	1795	1500	1240	1023	691	461
Taylor KO Index	17.2	15.8	14.5	13.3	12.2	11.1	9.4	7.6	6.3
Path • Inches	-1.5	+1.4	0.0	-6.4	-18.9	-38.7	-67.0	-157.9	-313.1
Wind Drift • Inches	0.0	0.7	3.0	6.9	12.9	21.0	31.7	62.2	107.1

Hornady 140-grain BTSP—LM InterLock (8556)

G1 Ballistic Coefficient = 0.490

Distance • Yards	Muzzle	100	200	300	400	500	600	800	1000
Velocity • fps	3100	2900	2709	2525	2349	2180	2019	1718	1453
Energy • Ft-lbs	2987	2614	2280	1982	1715	1477	1267	917	657
Taylor KO Index	17.2	16.1	15.0	14.0	13.0	12.1	11.2	9.5	8.0
Path • Inches	-1.5	+1.3	0.0	-6.1	-17.6	-35.4	-60.6	-138.1	-264.2
Wind Drift • Inches	0.0	0.6	2.4	5.5	10.2	16.5	24.6	47.3	80.3

Remington 140-grain Nosler Ballistic Tip (PRT270WB) (Discontinued in 2005)

G1 Ballistic Coefficient = 0.456

Distance • Yards	Muzzle	100	200	300	400	500	600	800	1000
Velocity • fps	2960	2754	2557	2368	2187	2014	1850	1548	1296
Energy • Ft-lbs	2724	2358	2032	1743	1487	1262	1064	745	524
Taylor KO Index	16.4	15.3	14.2	13.1	12.1	11.2	10.3	8.6	7.2
Path • Inches	-1.5	+1.6	0.0	-6.9	-20.0	-40.3	-69.1	-159.4	-308.3
Wind Drift • Inches	0.0	0.7	2.7	6.4	11.7	19.1	29.4	57.0	97.2

Remington 140-grain Pointed Soft Point, Boat Tail (PRB270WA) (Discontinued in 2005)

G1 Ballistic Coefficient = 0.446

Distance • Yards	Muzzle	100	200	300	400	500	600	800	1000
Velocity • fps	2960	2749	2548	2355	2171	1995	1828	1525	1276
Energy • Ft-lbs	2723	2349	2018	1724	1465	1237	1039	723	506
Taylor KO Index	16.4	15.2	14.1	13.0	12.0	11.0	10.2	8.5	7.1
Path • Inches	-1.5	+1.6	0.0	-6.9	-20.1	-40.7	-70.1	-162.2	-314.7
Wind Drift • Inches	0.0	0.7	2.8	6.5	12.0	19.6	29.4	57.0	97.2

Winchester 140-grain AccuBond CT (S270CT)

G1 Ballistic Coefficient = 0.475

Distance • Yards	Muzzle	100	200	300	400	500	600	800	1000
Velocity • fps	2950	2751	2560	2378	2203	2035	1874	1580	1332
Energy • Ft-lbs	2705	2352	2038	1757	1508	1287	1092	777	551
Taylor KO Index	16.3	15.2	14.2	13.2	12.2	11.3	10.4	8.8	7.4
Path • Inches	-1.5	+1.6	0.0	-6.9	-19.9	-38.4	-66.4	-154.7	-303.3
Wind Drift • Inches	0.0	0.7	2.8	6.4	11.9	19.4	29.2	56.7	97.0

Federal 140-grain Trophy Bonded Bear Claw (P270T1)

G1 Ballistic Coefficient = 0.391

Distance • Yards	Muzzle	100	200	300	400	500	600	800	1000
Velocity • fps	2940	2700	2480	2260	2060	1860	1680	1366	1136
Energy • Ft-lbs	2685	2270	1905	1590	1313	1080	878	580	402
Taylor KO Index	16.3	15.0	13.7	12.5	11.4	10.3	9.3	7.6	6.3
Path • Inches	-1.5	+1.8	0.0	-7.3	-21.5	-43.7	-76.4	-181.4	-361.6
Wind Drift • Inches	0.0	0.8	3.2	7.6	14.2	23.2	35.1	69.1	118.4

Hornady 140-grain Boat-Tail Soft Point InterLock (8056)

G1 Ballistic Coefficient = 0.490

Distance • Yards	Muzzle	100	200	300	400	500	600	800	1000
Velocity • fps	2940	2747	2562	2384	2214	2050	1895	1607	1361
Energy • Ft-lbs	2687	2345	2040	1767	1523	1307	1117	803	576
Taylor KO Index	16.3	15.2	14.2	13.2	12.3	11.4	10.5	8.9	7.5
Path • Inches	-1.5	+1.6	0.0	-6.9	-19.8	-39.9	-68.3	-156.1	-299.3
Wind Drift • Inches	0.0	0.6	2.6	6.0	11.0	17.8	26.6	51.2	86.8

Remington 140-grain Core-Lokt Ultra Bonded (PRC270WB)

G1 Ballistic Coefficient = 0.360

Distance • Yards	Muzzle	100	200	300	400	500	600	800	1000
Velocity • fps	2925	2667	2424	2193	1975	1771	1582	1268	1064
Energy • Ft-lbs	2659	2211	1826	1495	1212	975	778	500	352
Taylor KO Index	16.3	14.8	13.5	12.2	11.0	9.8	8.8	7.1	5.9
Path • Inches	-1.5	+1.7	0.0	-7.6	-22.5	-46.4	-81.6	-198.3	-405.2
Wind Drift • Inches	0.0	0.8	3.6	8.4	15.8	26.0	39.5	78.2	133.7

Remington 140-grain Swift A-Frame PSP (RS270WA)

G1 Ballistic Coefficient = 0.339

Distance • Yards	Muzzle	100	200	300	400	500	600	800	1000
Velocity • fps	2925	2652	2394	2152	1923	1711	1517	1207	1023
Energy • Ft-lbs	2659	2186	1782	1439	1150	910	716	453	325
Taylor KO Index	16.2	14.7	13.3	11.9	10.7	9.5	8.4	6.7	5.7
Path • Inches	-1.5	+1.7	0.0	-7.8	-23.2	-48.0	-84.9	208.1	426.9
Wind Drift • Inches	0.0	0.9	3.8	9.0	17.0	28.0	42.7	85.0	144.6

Hornady 140-grain SST InterLock (80564)

G1 Ballistic Coefficient = 0.499

Distance • Yards	Muzzle	100	200	300	400	500	600	800	1000
Velocity • fps	2940	2750	2569	2394	2226	2065	1965	1627	1381
Energy • Ft-lbs	2687	2351	2051	1781	1540	1325	1336	823	593
Taylor KO Index	16.3	15.2	14.2	13.3	12.3	11.4	10.6	9.0	7.7
Path • Inches	-1.5	+1.4	0.0	-6.8	-19.7	-39.7	-67.7	-154.4	-295.0
Wind Drift • Inches	0.0	0.6	2.5	5.8	10.8	17.4	26.0	50.0	84.6

Winchester 140-grain Fail Safe (S270X)

G1 Ballistic Coefficient = 0.373

Distance • Yards	Muzzle	100	200	300	400	500	600	800	1000
Velocity • fps	2920	2671	2435	2211	1999	1799	1617	1303	1090
Energy • Ft-lbs	2651	2218	1843	1519	1242	1007	813	528	369
Taylor KO Index	16.2	14.8	13.5	12.2	11.1	10.0	9.0	7.2	6.1
Path • Inches	-1.5	+1.7	0.0	-7.6	-22.3	-45.7	-79.9	-191.6	-385.7
Wind Drift • Inches	0.0	0.8	3.4	8.1	15.2	24.9	37.8	74.6	127.6

Federal 145-grain Soft Point (270LR1)

G1 Ballistic Coefficient = 0.414

Distance • Yards	Muzzle	100	200	300	400	500	600	800	1000
Velocity • fps	2200	2010	1830	1660	1500	1360	1239	1064	958
Energy • Ft-lbs	1560	1295	1070	885	725	595	494	364	296
Taylor KO Index	12.6	11.5	10.5	9.5	8.6	7.8	7.1	6.1	5.5
Path • Inches	-1.5	+3.5	0.0	-14.3	-40.8	-83.4	-144.4	-340.0	-655.9
Wind Drift • Inches	0.0	1.1	4.7	11.1	20.6	33.5	50.3	94.8	151.7

Federal 150-grain Sierra GameKing BTSP—HE (P270G) (Discontinued in 2005)

G1 Ballistic Coefficient = 0.482

Distance • Yards	Muzzle	100	200	300	400	500	600	800	1000
Velocity • fps	3000	2800	2620	2430	2260	2090	1932	1638	1384
Energy • Ft-lbs	2995	2615	2275	1975	1700	1460	1244	894	638
Taylor KO Index	17.9	16.7	15.6	14.5	13.5	12.5	11.5	9.8	8.2
Path • Inches	-1.5	+1.5	0.0	-6.5	-18.9	-38.3	-65.5	-150.0	-286.1
Wind Drift • Inches	0.0	0.6	2.5	5.9	10.8	17.5	26.2	50.4	85.4

Estate 150-grain PSP (E270-2) (Discontinued in 2004)

G1 Ballistic Coefficient = 0.380

Distance • Yards	Muzzle	100	200	300	400	500	600	800	1000
Velocity • fps	2950	2704	2471	2249	2039	1841	1657	1340	1115
Energy • Ft-lbs	2900	2436	2034	1686	1386	1130	915	598	414
Taylor KO Index	17.6	16.1	14.7	13.4	12.1	11.0	9.9	8.0	6.6
Path • Inches	-1.5	+1.6	0.0	-7.3	-21.6	-44.2	-77.2	-185.2	-374.4
Wind Drift • Inches	0.0	0.8	3.3	7.8	14.6	23.9	36.3	71.5	122.7

Winchester 150-grain Power Point Plus (SHV2704)

G1 Ballistic Coefficient = 0.345

Distance • Yards	Muzzle	100	200	300	400	500	600	800	1000
Velocity • fps	2950	2679	2425	2184	1957	1746	1553	1236	1040
Energy • Ft-lbs	2900	2391	1959	1589	1276	1016	803	509	360
Taylor KO Index	17.6	16.0	14.4	13.0	11.7	10.4	9.3	7.4	6.2
Path • Inches	-1.5	+1.7	0.0	-7.6	-22.6	-46.6	-82.1	-200.3	-410.1
Wind Drift • Inches	0.0	0.9	3.7	8.8	16.4	27.0	41.2	82.0	140.1

Winchester 150-grain Partition Gold (SPG270)

G1 Ballistic Coefficient = 0.392

Distance • Yards	Muzzle	100	200	300	400	500	600	800	1000
Velocity • fps	2930	2693	2468	2254	2051	1859	1681	1369	1140
Energy • Ft-lbs	2860	2416	2030	1693	1402	1152	942	624	433
Taylor KO Index	17.5	16.0	14.7	13.4	12.2	11.1	10.0	8.2	6.8
Path • Inches	-1.5	+1.7	0.0	-7.4	-21.6	-44.1	-76.7	-181.7	-361.7
Wind Drift • Inches	0.0	0.8	3.2	7.6	14.2	23.3	35.0	68.7	117.7

Speer 150-grain Grand Slam (24502) (Discontinued in 2005)

G1 Ballistic Coefficient = 0.384

Distance • Yards	Muzzle	100	200	300	400	500	600	800	1000
Velocity • fps	2930	2688	2458	2240	2032	1836	1654	1340	1117
Energy • Ft-lbs	2859	2406	2013	1671	1375	1123	912	599	416
Taylor KO Index	17.5	16.0	14.6	13.3	12.1	10.9	9.9	8.0	6.7
Path • Inches	-1.5	+1.7	0.0	-7.4	-21.8	-44.7	-77.9	-185.5	-371.2
Wind Drift • Inches	0.0	0.8	3.3	7.8	14.6	23.9	36.2	71.2	122.0

Norma 150-grain Oryx (16901)

G1 Ballistic Coefficient = 0.373

Distance • Yards	Muzzle	100	200	300	400	500	600	800	1000
Velocity • fps	2854	2608	2376	2155	1942	1745	1564	1261	1062
Energy • Ft-lbs	2714	2267	1880	1547	1256	1015	815	530	376
Taylor KO Index	16.9	15.5	14.1	12.8	11.5	10.4	9.3	7.5	6.3
Path • Inches	-1.5	+1.8	0.0	-8.0	-23.6	-48.4	-84.8	-204.9	-416.0
Wind Drift • Inches	0.0	0.9	3.6	8.5	15.8	26.0	39.4	77.9	132.7

Federal 150-grain Sierra GameKing BTSP (P270C)

G1 Ballistic Coefficient = 0.482

Distance • Yards	Muzzle	100	200	300	400	500	600	800	1000
Velocity • fps	2850	2660	2480	2300	2130	1970	1817	1537	1302
Energy • Ft-lbs	2705	2355	2040	1760	1510	1290	1100	787	565
Taylor KO Index	16.9	15.8	14.7	13.7	12.6	11.7	10.8	9.2	7.8
Path • Inches	-1.5	+1.7	0.0	-7.4	-21.4	-43.0	-73.6	-168.4	-322.6
Wind Drift • Inches	0.0	0.6	2.7	6.3	11.6	18.9	28.2	54.4	92.2

Federal 150-grain Nosler Partition (P270E)

G1 Ballistic Coefficient = 0.464

Distance • Yards	Muzzle	100	200	300	400	500	600	800	1000
Velocity • fps	2850	2650	2460	2280	2110	1940	1782	1497	1262
Energy • Ft-lbs	2705	2345	2020	1735	1480	1255	1058	748	531
Taylor KO Index	17.0	15.8	14.7	13.6	12.6	11.6	10.6	8.9	7.5
Path • Inches	-1.5	+1.7	0.0	-7.5	-21.6	-43.6	-74.9	-172.9	-335.0
Wind Drift • Inches	0.0	0.7	2.8	6.6	12.1	19.7	29.6	57.3	97.2

Federal 150-grain Hi-Shok Soft Point RN (270B)

G1 Ballistic Coefficient = 0.262

Distance • Yards	Muzzle	100	200	300	400	500	600	800	1000
Velocity • fps	2850	2500	2180	1890	1620	1390	1202	984	866
Energy • Ft-lbs	2705	2085	1585	1185	870	643	482	322	250
Taylor KO Index	16.9	14.8	12.9	11.2	9.6	8.3	7.2	5.9	5.2
Path • Inches	-1.5	+2.0	0.0	-9.4	-28.6	-61.0	-111.7	-291.3	-614.2
Wind Drift • Inches	0.0	1.2	5.3	12.8	24.4	41.1	63.5	124.7	202.6

PMC 150-grain SPBT Game (270HB)

G1 Ballistic Coefficient = 0.483

Distance • Yards	Muzzle	100	200	300	400	500	600	800	1000
Velocity • fps	2850	2660	2477	2302	2134	1973	1819	1539	1304
Energy • Ft-lbs	2705	2355	2043	1765	1516	1296	1102	789	566
Taylor KO Index	16.9	15.8	14.7	13.7	12.7	11.7	10.8	9.1	7.7
Path • Inches	-1.5	+1.7	0.0	-7.4	-21.4	-43.0	-73.5	-168.5	-324.0
Wind Drift • Inches	0.0	0.6	2.7	6.3	11.6	18.8	28.2	54.3	91.9

Remington 150-grain Nosler Partition (PRP270WD) (Discontinued in 2005)

G1 Ballistic Coefficient = 0.465

Distance • Yards	Muzzle	100	200	300	400	500	600	800	1000
Velocity • fps	2850	2645	2463	2282	2108	1942	1784	1499	1265
Energy • Ft-lbs	2705	2343	2021	1734	1480	1256	1061	749	533
Taylor KO Index	17.0	15.8	14.7	13.6	12.6	11.6	10.3	8.9	7.5
Path • Inches	-1.5	+1.7	0.0	-7.5	-21.6	-43.6	-74.9	-172.3	-332.1
Wind Drift • Inches	0.0	0.7	2.8	6.6	12.1	19.7	29.5	57.1	97.0

Remington 150-grain Soft Point Core-Lokt (R270W4)

G1 Ballistic Coefficient = 0.261

Distance • Yards	Muzzle	100	200	300	400	500	600	800	1000
Velocity • fps	2850	2504	2183	1886	1618	1385	1199	982	864
Energy • Ft-lbs	2705	2087	1587	1185	872	639	479	321	249
Taylor KO Index	16.9	14.9	13.0	11.2	9.6	8.2	7.1	5.8	5.1
Path • Inches	-1.5	+2.0	0.0	-9.4	-28.6	-61.2	-112.1	-292.6	-617.1
Wind Drift • Inches	0.0	1.2	5.3	12.8	24.5	41.3	63.9	125.3	203.4

Winchester 150-grain Power-Point (X2704)

G1 Ballistic Coefficient = 0.345

Distance • Yards	Muzzle	100	200	300	400	500	600	800	1000
Velocity • fps	2850	2585	2344	2108	1886	1673	1488	1191	1016
Energy • Ft-lbs	2705	2226	1817	1468	1175	932	737	472	344
Taylor KO Index	16.9	15.3	13.9	12.5	11.2	9.9	8.9	7.1	6.1
Path • Inches	-1.5	+2.2	0.0	-8.6	-25.0	-51.4	-89.0	-217.5	-444.1
Wind Drift • Inches	0.0	0.9	3.9	9.2	17.3	28.5	43.5	86.2	145.9

Hornady 150-grain Soft Point (8058)

G1 Ballistic Coefficient = 0.457

Distance • Yards	Muzzle	100	200	300	400	500	600	800	1000
Velocity • fps	2840	2641	2450	2267	2092	1926	1767	1481	1249
Energy • Ft-lbs	2686	2322	1999	1712	1458	1235	1040	781	520
Taylor KO Index	16.9	15.7	14.5	13.5	12.4	11.4	10.5	8.8	7.4
Path • Inches	-1.5	+2.0	0.0	-7.8	-22.5	-45.0	-75.9	-174.9	-337.9
Wind Drift • Inches	0.0	0.7	2.9	6.7	12.4	20.1	30.1	58.3	98.9

Hirtenberger 150-grain Nosler Partition (82200343)

G1 Ballistic Coefficient = 0.750

Distance • Yards	Muzzle	100	200	300	400	500	600	800	1000
Velocity • fps	2822	2699	2580	2463	2350	2240	2132	1926	1733
Energy • Ft-lbs	2653	2427	2217	2022	1840	1671	1514	1236	1001
Taylor KO Index	16.8	16.1	15.4	14.7	14.0	13.3	12.7	11.5	10.3
Path • Inches	-1.5	+1.6	0.0	-6.9	-19.4	-38.3	-64.2	-139.6	-252.7
Wind Drift • Inches	0.0	0.4	1.6	3.6	6.5	10.4	15.3	28.5	46.8

Norma 150-grain Soft Point (16903) (Discontinued in 2005)

G1 Ballistic Coefficient = 0.370

Distance • Yards	Muzzle	100	200	300	400	500	600	800	1000
Velocity • fps	2799	2555	2323	2104	1896	1703	1526	1234	1049
Energy • Ft-lbs	2610	2175	1798	1475	1198	966	776	508	367
Taylor KO Index	16.6	15.2	13.8	12.5	11.3	10.1	9.1	7.4	6.2
Path • Inches	-1.5	+2.0	0.0	-8.6	-24.7	-50.6	-88.6	-213.2	-429.4
Wind Drift • Inches	0.0	0.9	3.7	8.7	16.3	26.8	40.7	80.2	136.0

RWS 150-grain Cone Point (211 7282)

G1 Ballistic Coefficient = 0.365

Distance • Yards	Muzzle	100	200	300	400	500	600	800	1000
Velocity • fps	2799	2551	2317	2095	1886	1691	1512	1221	1039
Energy • Ft-lbs	2610	2169	1788	1462	1185	952	762	497	360
Taylor KO Index	16.6	15.2	13.8	12.5	11.2	10.1	9.0	7.3	6.2
Path • Inches	-1.5	+1.9	0.0	-8.4	-24.8	-51.0	-89.6	-217.5	-441.7
Wind Drift • Inches	0.0	0.9	3.8	8.8	16.6	27.3	41.4	81.8	138.4

PMC 150-grain Pointed Soft Point (270B)

G1 Ballistic Coefficient = 0.411

Distance • Yards	Muzzle	100	200	300	400	500	600	800	1000
Velocity • fps	2750	2530	2321	2123	1936	1760	1595	1812	1110
Energy • Ft-lbs	2519	2131	1794	1501	1248	1032	848	573	410
Taylor KO Index	16.4	15.1	13.8	12.6	11.5	10.5	9.5	7.8	6.6
Path • Inches	-1.5	+2.0	0.0	-8.4	-24.6	-50.0	-86.8	-205.2	-407.5
Wind Drift • Inches	0.0	0.8	3.4	7.9	14.8	24.2	36.5	71.2	120.8

Sellier & Bellot 150-grain SP (SBA27001)

G1 Ballistic Coefficient = 0.381

Distance • Yards	Muzzle	100	200	300	400	500	600	800	1000
Velocity • fps	2625	2387	2170	1973	1781	1602	1439	1180	1022
Energy • Ft-lbs	2289	1893	1565	1294	1056	855	690	464	348
Taylor KO Index	15.6	14.2	12.9	11.8	10.6	9.5	8.6	7.0	6.1
Path • Inches	-1.5	+2.3	0.0	-9.6	-28.2	-57.8	-101.2	-243.6	-487.8
Wind Drift • Inches	0.0	0.9	3.9	9.3	17.3	28.5	43.2	84.4	140.9

PMC 150-grain Barnes-XLC-HP (270XLB) (Discontinued in 2005)

G1 Ballistic Coefficient = 0.560

Distance • Yards	Muzzle	100	200	300	400	500	600	800	1000
Velocity • fps	2700	2541	2387	2238	2095	1957	1825	1580	1368
Energy • Ft-lbs	2428	2150	1897	1668	1461	1275	1110	832	623
Taylor KO Index	16.0	15.1	14.2	13.3	12.4	11.6	10.8	9.4	8.1
Path • Inches	-1.5	+2.0	0.0	-8.1	-23.1	-46.0	-78.0	-175.2	-329.2
Wind Drift • Inches	0.0	0.6	2.5	5.8	10.6	17.1	25.5	48.6	81.4

.270 Winchester Short Magnum

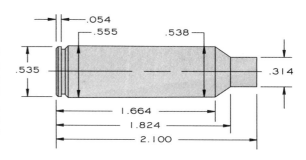

When Winchester announced the .300 WSM (2001), nearly everyone knew that a .270 WSM was sure to follow, and probably sooner rather than later. The idea behind all the Short Magnums is that they can be used in the "short" actions, the ones that were designed for .308-size cases. The .270 WSM follows the recent trend toward unbelted magnums. The case volume, and also the performance, fall right between the .270 Winchester and the .270 Weatherby. The caliber seems to be really taking off, as evidenced by the number of loadings offered today.

Relative Recoil Factor = 2.00

Specifications

Controlling Agency for Standardization of this Ammunition: SAAMI
Specifications Pending
Standard barrel for velocity testing: Pending*
*Preliminary Value: 24 inches long—1 turn in 10-inch twist

Availability

Norma 130-grain Nosler BST (16925)

G1 Ballistic Coefficient = 0.433

Distance • Yards	Muzzle	100	200	300	400	500	600	800	1000
Velocity • fps	3281	3047	2825	2614	2408	2215	2030	1691	1399
Energy • Ft-lbs	3108	2681	2305	1973	1674	1416	1190	825	566
Taylor KO Index	16.9	15.7	14.5	13.4	12.4	11.4	10.4	8.7	7.2
Path • Inches	-1.5	+1.1	0.0	-5.5	-16.1	-32.7	-56.4	-131.2	-256.4
Wind Drift • Inches	0.0	0.6	2.5	5.9	10.9	17.6	26.4	51.3	87.8

Federal 130-grain Nosler Solid Base BT (P270WSMS1)

G1 Ballistic Coefficient = 0.422

Distance • Yards	Muzzle	100	200	300	400	500	600	800	1000
Velocity • fps	3280	3040	2810	2600	2390	2190	2002	1657	1365
Energy • Ft-lbs	3105	2665	2280	1945	1645	1385	1157	793	538
Taylor KO Index	16.9	15.6	14.5	13.4	12.3	11.3	10.3	8.5	7.0
Path • Inches	-1.5	+1.1	0.0	-5.6	-16.2	-33.1	-57.2	-133.6	-262.8
Wind Drift • Inches	0.0	0.6	2.6	6.1	11.2	18.2	27.3	53.1	91.3

Federal 130-grain Nosler Partition (P270WSMF)

G1 Ballistic Coefficient = 0.418

Distance • Yards	Muzzle	100	200	300	400	500	600	800	1000
Velocity • fps	3280	3040	2810	2590	2380	2180	1991	1645	1353
Energy • Ft-lbs	3105	2665	2275	1935	1635	1375	1145	781	529
Taylor KO Index	16.9	15.6	14.5	13.3	12.2	11.2	10.2	8.5	7.0
Path • Inches	-1.5	+1.1	0.0	-5.6	-16.3	-33.2	-57.5	-134.5	-265.2
Wind Drift • Inches	0.0	0.6	2.6	6.1	11.3	18.4	27.6	53.8	92.6

Federal 130-grain Nosler Ballistic Tip (P270WSMB)

G1 Ballistic Coefficient = 0.43822

Distance • Yards	Muzzle	100	200	300	400	500	600	800	1000
Velocity • fps	3300	3070	2840	2630	2430	2240	2057	1718	1425
Energy • Ft-lbs	3145	2710	2335	2000	1705	1445	1222	852	586
Taylor KO Index	17.0	15.8	14.6	13.5	12.5	11.5	10.6	8.8	7.3
Path • Inches	-1.5	+1.1	0.0	-5.4	-15.8	-32.2	-55.4	-128.4	-250.3
Wind Drift • Inches	0.0	0.6	2.5	5.8	10.6	17.2	25.8	50.0	85.6

Winchester 130-grain Ballistic Silvertip (SBST2705)

G1 Ballistic Coefficient = 0.432

Distance • Yards	Muzzle	100	200	300	400	500	600	800	1000
Velocity • fps	3275	3041	2820	2609	2408	2215	2031	1693	1403
Energy • Ft-lbs	3096	2669	2295	1964	1673	1416	1191	827	568
Taylor KO Index	16.9	15.7	14.6	13.5	12.4	11.4	10.5	8.7	7.2
Path • Inches	-1.5	+1.1	0.0	-5.5	-16.1	-32.8	-56.5	-131.3	-256.5
Wind Drift • Inches	0.0	0.6	2.5	5.9	10.8	17.6	26.4	51.1	87.5

Federal 130-grain Barnes Triple Shock X-Bullet (P270WSMD)

G1 Ballistic Coefficient = 0.422

Distance • Yards	Muzzle	100	200	300	400	500	600	800	1000
Velocity • fps	3280	3040	2810	2600	2390	2190	2002	1657	1365
Energy • Ft-lbs	3105	2665	2280	1945	1645	1385	1157	793	538
Taylor KO Index	16.9	15.6	14.5	13.4	12.3	11.3	10.3	8.5	7.0
Path • Inches	-1.5	+1.1	0.0	-5.6	-16.2	-33.1	-57.2	-133.6	-262.8
Wind Drift • Inches	0.0	0.6	2.6	6.1	11.2	18.2	27.3	53.1	91.3

Federal 130-grain Nosler Solid Base BT (P270WSMS1)

G1 Ballistic Coefficient = 0.422

Distance • Yards	Muzzle	100	200	300	400	500	600	800	1000
Velocity • fps	3280	3040	2810	2600	2390	2190	2002	1657	1365
Energy • Ft-lbs	3105	2665	2280	1945	1645	1385	1157	793	538
Taylor KO Index	16.9	15.6	14.5	13.4	12.3	11.3	10.3	8.5	7.0
Path • Inches	-1.5	+1.1	0.0	-5.6	-16.2	-33.1	-57.2	-133.6	-262.8
Wind Drift • Inches	0.0	0.6	2.6	6.1	11.2	18.2	27.3	53.1	91.3

Federal 140-grain Trophy Bonded Bear Claw (P270WSMT1)

G1 Ballistic Coefficient = 0.390

Distance • Yards	Muzzle	100	200	300	400	500	600	800	1000
Velocity • fps	3200	2950	2700	2480	2260	2050	1855	1506	1229
Energy • Ft-lbs	3185	2695	2275	1905	1585	1310	1070	705	470
Taylor KO Index	16.9	15.6	14.5	13.4	12.3	11.3	10.3	8.5	7.0
Path • Inches	-1.5	+1.3	0.0	-6.0	-17.7	-36.3	-63.2	-150.3	-301.8
Wind Drift • Inches	0.0	0.7	2.9	6.8	12.7	20.7	31.3	61.6	106.4

Federal 140-grain Nosler AccuBond (P270WSMA1)

G1 Ballistic Coefficient = 0.502

Distance • Yards	Muzzle	100	200	300	400	500	600	800	1000
Velocity • fps	3200	3000	2810	2630	2450	2280	2119	1815	1544
Energy • Ft-lbs	3185	2795	2455	2145	1865	1615	1396	1025	741
Taylor KO Index	17.7	16.6	15.6	14.6	13.6	12.6	11.7	10.1	8.6
Path • Inches	-1.5	+1.2	0.0	-5.6	-16.2	-32.7	-55.8	-126.7	-240.8
Wind Drift • Inches	0.0	0.5	2.2	5.2	9.5	15.3	22.8	43.7	73.8

Winchester 140-grain AccuBond CT (S270WSMCT)

G1 Ballistic Coefficient = 0.476

Distance • Yards	Muzzle	100	200	300	400	500	600	800	1000
Velocity • fps	3200	2989	2789	2579	2413	2236	2067	1753	1476
Energy • Ft-lbs	3184	2779	2418	2097	1810	1555	1329	955	678
Taylor KO Index	17.7	16.6	15.5	14.3	13.4	12.4	11.5	9.7	8.2
Path • Inches	-1.5	+1.2	0.0	-5.7	-16.5	-33.3	-57.1	-130.7	-250.9
Wind Drift • Inches	0.0	0.6	2.4	5.5	10.1	16.3	24.4	46.8	79.6

Black Hills 140-grain Nosler AccuBond (1C270WSMBHGN1)

G1 Ballistic Coefficient = 0.502

Distance • Yards	Muzzle	100	200	300	400	500	600	800	1000
Velocity • fps	3100	2905	2718	2538	2366	2200	2041	1745	1482
Energy • Ft-lbs	2987	2623	2297	2004	1741	1506	1296	947	683
Taylor KO Index	17.0	16.3	15.0	13.7	12.5	11.4	10.3	8.3	6.8
Path • Inches	-1.5	+1.1	0.0	-5.6	-16.2	-33.1	-57.2	-133.6	-262.8
Wind Drift • Inches	0.0	0.6	2.6	6.1	11.2	18.2	27.3	53.1	91.3

Norma 140-grain Barnes Triple Shock (16933)

G1 Ballistic Coefficient = 0.497

Distance • Yards	Muzzle	100	200	300	400	500	600	800	1000
Velocity • fps	3150	2952	2762	2580	2401	2233	2071	1769	1501
Energy • Ft-lbs	3085	2709	2372	2070	1793	1550	1333	973	700
Taylor KO Index	17.5	16.4	15.3	14.3	13.3	12.4	11.5	9.8	8.3
Path • Inches	-1.5	+1.2	0.0	-5.8	-16.9	-34.0	-58.0	-132.1	-251.7
Wind Drift • Inches	0.0	0.6	2.3	5.3	9.8	15.8	23.6	45.3	76.7

Winchester 140-grain Fail Safe (S270WSMX)

G1 Ballistic Coefficient = 0.373

Distance • Yards	Muzzle	100	200	300	400	500	600	800	1000
Velocity • fps	3125	2865	2619	2386	2165	1956	1759	1416	1160
Energy • Ft-lbs	3025	2550	2132	1769	1457	1189	962	623	418
Taylor KO Index	17.4	15.9	14.6	13.3	12.0	10.9	9.8	7.9	6.4
Path • Inches	-1.5	+1.4	0.0	-6.5	-19.0	-39.1	-68.3	-164.0	-332.9
Wind Drift • Inches	0.0	0.8	3.1	7.4	13.7	22.5	34.1	67.3	116.4

Federal 150-grain Soft Point (270WSME)

G1 Ballistic Coefficient = 0.369

Distance • Yards	Muzzle	100	200	300	400	500	600	800	1000
Velocity • fps	3250	2980	2720	2480	2250	2030	1827	1464	1187
Energy • Ft-lbs	3519	2953	2466	2048	1684	1374	1112	715	470
Taylor KO Index	19.3	17.7	16.1	14.7	13.4	12.0	10.8	8.7	7.0
Path • Inches	-1.5	+1.2	0.0	-5.9	-17.5	-36.0	-63.0	-151.7	-308.9
Wind Drift • Inches	0.0	0.7	3.0	7.1	18.2	21.7	32.9	65.1	113.0

Norma 150-grain Oryx (16932)

G1 Ballistic Coefficient = 0.373

Distance • Yards	Muzzle	100	200	300	400	500	600	800	1000
Velocity • fps	3117	2856	2611	2378	2152	1942	1746	1402	1148
Energy • Ft-lbs	3237	2718	2271	1884	1543	1257	1016	655	439
Taylor KO Index	18.5	17.0	15.5	14.1	12.8	11.5	10.4	8.3	6.8
Path • Inches	-1.5	+1.4	0.0	-6.5	-19.2	-39.4	-69.0	-166.0	-337.6
Wind Drift • Inches	0.0	0.8	3.2	7.5	13.9	22.8	34.5	68.2	118.0

Federal 150-grain Nosler Partition (P270WSMC)

G1 Ballistic Coefficient = 0.468

Distance • Yards	Muzzle	100	200	300	400	500	600	800	1000
Velocity • fps	3160	2950	2750	2550	2370	2190	2020	1705	1432
Energy • Ft-lbs	3225	2895	2515	2175	1870	1600	1359	969	683
Taylor KO Index	18.8	17.5	16.3	15.1	14.1	13.0	12.0	10.1	8.5
Path • Inches	-1.5	+1.3	0.0	-5.9	-17.0	-34.5	-59.2	-135.9	-262.0
Wind Drift • Inches	0.0	0.6	2.4	5.7	10.4	16.9	25.3	48.8	83.1

Federal 150-grain Soft Point (270WSME)

G1 Ballistic Coefficient = 0.369

Distance • Yards	Muzzle	100	200	300	400	500	600	800	1000
Velocity • fps	3250	2867	2601	2350	2113	1890	1683	1330	1092
Energy • Ft-lbs	3304	2737	2252	1839	1487	1190	943	590	397
Taylor KO Index	18.8	17.1	15.5	14.0	12.6	11.3	10.0	7.9	6.5
Path • Inches	-1.5	+1.4	0.0	-6.5	-19.4	-40.1	-70.6	-173.2	-358.6
Wind Drift • Inches	0.0	0.8	3.4	8.0	14.9	24.6	37.5	74.7	129.5

Winchester 150-grain Power-Point (X270WSM)

G1 Ballistic Coefficient = 0.344

Distance • Yards	Muzzle	100	200	300	400	500	600	800	1000
Velocity • fps	3150	2867	2601	2350	2113	1890	1683	1330	1092
Energy • Ft-lbs	3304	2737	2252	1839	1487	1190	943	590	397
Taylor KO Index	18.8	17.1	15.5	14.0	12.6	11.3	10.0	7.9	6.5
Path • Inches	-1.5	+1.4	0.0	-6.5	-19.4	-40.1	-70.6	-173.2	-358.6
Wind Drift • Inches	0.0	0.8	3.4	8.0	14.9	24.6	37.5	74.7	129.5

Winchester 150-grain Ballistic Silvertip (SBST27005A)

G1 Ballistic Coefficient = 0.500

Distance • Yards	Muzzle	100	200	300	400	500	600	800	1000
Velocity • fps	3120	2923	2734	2554	2380	2213	2053	1754	1490
Energy • Ft-lbs	3243	2845	2490	2172	1886	1613	1405	1025	739
Taylor KO Index	18.5	17.4	16.2	15.2	14.1	13.1	12.2	10.4	8.8
Path • Inches	-1.5	+1.3	0.0	-5.9	-17.2	-34.7	-59.2	-134.5	-256.2
Wind Drift • Inches	0.0	0.6	2.3	5.4	9.9	16.0	23.8	45.6	77.1

.270 Weatherby Magnum

The .270 Weatherby fills the space between the 7mm Weatherby Magnum and the .257 Weatherby Magnum. From a performance standpoint, it isn't different enough from the 7mm Weatherby Magnum for anyone to want both, except perhaps to be able to brag that he has a Weatherby gun in every caliber. It's a screamer: Bullet for bullet, Weatherby's .270 is 250 to 300 fps faster than the .270 Winchester, and that makes the caliber a great choice for hunting on the high plains. A good selection of bullet weights and styles is available.

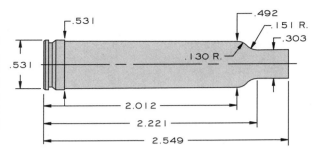

Relative Recoil Factor = 2.05

Specifications

Controlling Agency for Standardization of this Ammunition: CIP

Bullet Weight Grains	Velocity fps	Maximum Average Pressure Copper Crusher	Transducer
N/S	N/S	3,800 bar	4,370 bar

Standard barrel for velocity testing: 26 inches long—1 turn in 10-inch twist

Availability

Weatherby 100-grain Pointed-Expanding (H 270 100 SP)
G1 Ballistic Coefficient = 0.307

Distance • Yards	Muzzle	100	200	300	400	500	600	800	1000
Velocity • fps	3760	3396	3061	2751	2462	2190	1935	1490	1164
Energy • Ft-lbs	3139	2560	2081	1681	1346	1065	832	493	301
Taylor KO Index	14.9	13.4	12.1	10.9	9.7	8.7	7.7	5.9	4.6
Path • Inches	-1.5	+0.8	0.0	-4.5	-13.6	-28.5	-50.6	-125.7	-264.8
Wind Drift • Inches	0.0	0.7	3.1	7.2	13.5	22.2	33.8	68.0	120.7

Weatherby 130-grain Pointed-Expanding (H 270 130 SP)
G1 Ballistic Coefficient = 0.409

Distance • Yards	Muzzle	100	200	300	400	500	600	800	1000
Velocity • fps	3375	3123	2885	2659	2444	2240	2044	1686	1383
Energy • Ft-lbs	3288	2815	2402	2041	1724	1448	1206	821	552
Taylor KO Index	17.4	16.1	14.8	13.7	12.6	11.5	10.6	8.7	7.1
Path • Inches	-2.5	+1.0	0.0	-5.2	-15.4	-31.4	-54.3	-127.0	-249.2
Wind Drift • Inches	0.0	0.6	2.6	6.0	11.1	18.0	27.0	52.7	90.7

Weatherby 130-grain Nosler Partition (N 270 130 PT)
G1 Ballistic Coefficient = 0.417

Distance • Yards	Muzzle	100	200	300	400	500	600	800	1000
Velocity • fps	3375	3127	2892	2670	2458	2256	2066	1712	1409
Energy • Ft-lbs	3288	2822	2415	2058	1744	1470	1232	846	574
Taylor KO Index	17.4	16.1	14.9	13.7	12.6	11.6	10.7	8.8	7.3
Path • Inches	-1.5	+1.0	0.0	-5.2	-15.3	-31.1	-60.8	-141.9	-278.4
Wind Drift • Inches	0.0	0.6	2.5	5.9	10.8	17.6	26.4	51.3	88.1

Federal 130-grain Nosler Solid Base BT (P270WBS1)
G1 Ballistic Coefficient = 0.422

Distance • Yards	Muzzle	100	200	300	400	500	600	800	1000
Velocity • fps	3280	3040	2810	2600	2390	2190	2002	1657	1365
Energy • Ft-lbs	3105	2665	2280	1945	1645	1385	1157	793	538
Taylor KO Index	16.9	15.6	14.5	13.4	12.3	11.3	10.3	8.5	7.0
Path • Inches	-2.5	+1.1	0.0	-5.6	-16.2	-33.1	-57.2	-133.6	-262.8
Wind Drift • Inches	0.0	0.6	2.6	6.1	11.2	18.2	27.3	53.1	91.3

Federal 130-grain Sierra GameKing BTSP (P270WBB)
G1 Ballistic Coefficient = 0.459

Distance • Yards	Muzzle	100	200	300	400	500	600	800	1000
Velocity • fps	3200	2980	2780	2580	2400	2210	2038	1718	1439
Energy • Ft-lbs	2955	2570	2230	1925	1655	1415	1199	852	598
Taylor KO Index	16.5	15.3	14.3	13.3	12.3	11.4	10.5	8.9	7.4
Path • Inches	-1.5	+1.2	0.0	-5.7	-16.6	-33.7	-57.9	-133.0	-255.7
Wind Drift • Inches	0.0	0.6	2.4	5.7	10.4	16.9	25.3	48.7	83.0

Federal 130-grain Nosler Partition (P270WBA)

G1 Ballistic Coefficient = 0.416

Distance • Yards	Muzzle	100	200	300	400	500	600	800	1000
Velocity • fps	3200	2960	2740	2520	2320	2120	1935	1597	1316
Energy • Ft-lbs	2955	2530	2160	1835	1550	1300	1081	736	500
Taylor KO Index	16.5	15.2	14.1	13.0	11.9	10.9	10.0	8.2	6.8
Path • Inches	-1.5	+1.2	0.0	-5.9	-17.3	-35.1	-60.8	-141.9	-278.4
Wind Drift • Inches	0.0	0.6	2.7	6.3	11.7	19.0	23.6	55.7	95.8

Weatherby 140-grain Nosler Ballistic Tip (N 270 140 BST)

G1 Ballistic Coefficient = 0.456

Distance • Yards	Muzzle	100	200	300	400	500	600	800	1000
Velocity • fps	3300	3077	2865	2663	2470	2285	2107	1777	1488
Energy • Ft-lbs	3385	2943	2551	2204	1896	1622	1380	982	688
Taylor KO Index	18.3	17.0	15.9	14.8	13.7	12.7	11.7	9.9	8.3
Path • Inches	-1.5	+1.1	0.0	-5.3	-15.6	-31.5	-54.2	-124.4	-239.1
Wind Drift • Inches	0.0	0.6	2.4	5.5	10.1	16.3	24.4	47.0	80.0

Weatherby 140-grain Barnes-X (B 270 140 XS)

G1 Ballistic Coefficient = 0.463

Distance • Yards	Muzzle	100	200	300	400	500	600	800	1000
Velocity • fps	3250	3032	2825	2628	2438	2257	2084	1762	1479
Energy • Ft-lbs	3283	2858	2481	2146	1848	1583	1351	965	680
Taylor KO Index	18.0	16.8	15.7	14.6	13.5	12.5	11.6	9.8	8.2
Path • Inches	-1.5	+1.1	0.0	-5.5	-16.0	-32.4	-55.7	-127.6	-244.9
Wind Drift • Inches	0.0	0.6	2.4	5.5	10.1	16.4	24.4	47.1	80.1

Federal 140-grain Trophy Bonded Bear Claw (P270WBT1)

G1 Ballistic Coefficient = 0.378

Distance • Yards	Muzzle	100	200	300	400	500	600	800	1000
Velocity • fps	3100	2840	2600	2370	2150	1950	1757	1418	1164
Energy • Ft-lbs	2990	2510	2100	1745	1440	1175	960	625	421
Taylor KO Index	17.2	15.7	14.4	13.1	11.9	10.8	9.8	7.9	6.5
Path • Inches	-1.5	+1.4	0.0	-6.6	-19.3	-39.6	-69.0	-164.4	-329.9
Wind Drift • Inches	0.0	0.8	3.1	7.4	13.7	22.4	33.9	66.8	115.4

Weatherby 150-grain Pointed-Expanding (H 270 150 SP)

G1 Ballistic Coefficient = 0.462

Distance • Yards	Muzzle	100	200	300	400	500	600	800	1000
Velocity • fps	3245	3028	2821	2623	2434	2253	2078	1756	1473
Energy • Ft-lbs	3507	3053	2650	2292	1973	1690	1439	1027	723
Taylor KO Index	19.3	18.0	16.7	15.6	14.4	13.4	12.4	10.5	8.8
Path • Inches	-1.5	+1.2	0.0	-5.5	-16.1	-32.6	-55.9	-128.3	-246.2
Wind Drift • Inches	0.0	0.6	2.4	5.5	10.2	16.4	24.6	47.3	80.5

Weatherby 150-grain Nosler Partition (N 270 150 PT)

G1 Ballistic Coefficient = 0.466

Distance • Yards	Muzzle	100	200	300	400	500	600	800	1000
Velocity • fps	3245	3029	2823	2627	2439	2259	2087	1786	1484
Energy • Ft-lbs	3507	3055	2655	2298	1981	1699	1451	1040	734
Taylor KO Index	19.3	18.0	16.8	15.6	14.5	13.4	12.4	10.6	8.8
Path • Inches	-1.5	+1.2	0.0	-5.5	-16.1	-32.5	-55.7	-127.6	-244.5
Wind Drift • Inches	0.0	0.6	2.4	5.5	10.1	16.3	24.3	46.8	79.5

7-30 Waters

The name of the 7-30 Waters could be a bit misleading. This is not a 7x30mm cartridge, as you might get fooled into expecting from the designation. Instead it is a 7mm-(.30-30), hence 7-30. Ken Waters reportedly designed this to be a flat-shooting round that could be used in 7mm conversions of Winchester Model 94 guns. The pressure limits are, as for the .30-30, very mild by today's standards. A word of warning here: The only factory ammunition available today should definitely NOT be used in guns with tubular magazines. If you have a tubular magazine gun chambered for the 7-30 Waters, you are stuck with handloading with flat-nose bullets.

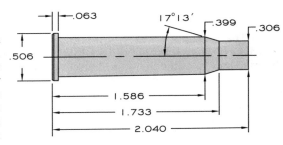

Relative Recoil Factor = 1.46

Specifications

Controlling Agency for Standardization of this Ammunition: SAAMI

Bullet Weight Grains	Velocity fps	Maximum Average Pressure	
		Copper Crusher	Transducer
120	2,700	40,000 cup	45,000 psi

Standard barrel for velocity testing: 24 inches long—1 turn in 9.5-inch twist

Availability
Federal 120-grain Sierra GameKing BTSP (P730A)

G1 Ballistic Coefficient = 0.219

Distance • Yards	Muzzle	100	200	300	400	500	600	800	1000
Velocity • fps	2700	2300	1930	1600	1330	1140	1014	866	764
Energy • Ft-lbs	1940	1405	990	685	470	345	274	200	156
Taylor KO Index	13.1	11.2	9.4	7.8	6.5	5.6	4.9	4.2	3.7
Path • Inches	-1.5	+2.4	0.0	-11.9	-37.2	-81.9	-153.2	-403.5	-839.9
Wind Drift • Inches	0.0	1.6	7.0	17.3	33.6	56.8	86.6	160.9	252.1

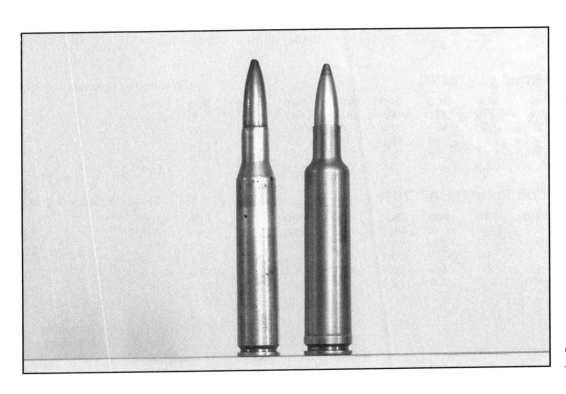

(Left to right) .270 Winchester, .270 Weatherby.

7x57mm Mauser

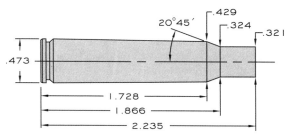

The 7x57mm Mauser is the granddaddy of all modern centerfire-rifle cartridges. It was introduced in 1892 for a bolt-action rifle that ultimately became known as the Spanish Mauser. Used in Cuba in the Spanish-American War, the rifle and cartridge so far outperformed the .30-40 Krags used by the U.S. Army at that time that it moved the War Department to expedite development of a new U.S. military rifle and cartridge. The army wanted a .30 caliber and started by simply necking the 7x57 to .30 caliber. That's the easiest kind of designing: Simply copy what works for someone else and put your own name on it. In any event, the outcome of all this was the 1903 Springfield rifle and the .30-06 cartridge, both classics. The 7x57 has been a commercial cartridge in the U.S. since the early 1900s. It has never been hugely popular, but, at an age in excess of 100 years, it is still a very functional number. Because some old guns can't stand today's working pressures, factory ammunition for the 7x57 Mauser is loaded to rather mild pressure levels.

Relative Recoil Factor = 1.68

Specifications

Controlling Agency for Standardization of this Ammunition: SAAMI

Bullet Weight Grains	Velocity fps	Maximum Average Pressure Copper Crusher	Transducer
120	2,700	40,000 cup	45,000 psi
139	2,650	46,000 cup	51,000 psi
145	2,680	46,000 cup	51,000 psi
154	2,600	46,000 cup	51,000 psi
160	2,500	46,000 cup	51,000 psi
175	2,420	46,000 cup	51,000 psi

Standard barrel for velocity testing: 24 inches long—1 turn in 8.75-inch twist

Availability

Hornady 139-grain SST-LM InterLock (85554)

G1 Ballistic Coefficient = 0.490

Distance • Yards	Muzzle	100	200	300	400	500	600	800	1000
Velocity • fps	2830	2642	2461	2287	2121	1961	1810	1533	1300
Energy • Ft-lbs	2471	2153	1869	1615	1388	1187	1012	726	522
Taylor KO Index	16.0	14.9	13.9	12.9	12.0	11.1	10.2	8.6	7.3
Path • Inches	-1.5	+1.7	0.0	-7.5	-21.6	-43.5	-74.4	-170.4	-327.4
Wind Drift • Inches	0.0	0.6	2.7	6.3	11.6	18.8	28.2	54.3	91.9

Hornady 139-grain SP-LM InterLock (8557)

G1 Ballistic Coefficient = 0.395

Distance • Yards	Muzzle	100	200	300	400	500	600	800	1000
Velocity • fps	2680	2455	2241	2038	1846	1667	1503	1230	1052
Energy • Ft-lbs	2216	1860	1550	1282	1052	858	697	467	342
Taylor KO Index	15.1	13.8	12.6	11.5	10.4	9.4	8.5	6.9	5.9
Path • Inches	-1.5	+2.1	0.0	-9.1	-26.6	-54.3	-94.7	-226.4	-452.8
Wind Drift • Inches	0.0	0.9	3.7	8.7	16.2	26.8	40.3	78.8	132.8

Sellier & Bellot 139-grain Soft Point (SBA75701)

G1 Ballistic Coefficient = 0.224

Distance • Yards	Muzzle	100	200	300	400	500	600	800	1000
Velocity • fps	2651	2330	2048	1800	1561	1355	1189	989	877
Energy • Ft-lbs	2167	1674	1293	999	752	567	436	302	238
Taylor KO Index	15.0	13.1	11.5	10.2	8.8	7.6	6.7	5.6	4.9
Path • Inches	-1.5	+2.4	0.0	-10.7	-32.2	-68.2	-123.8	-315.5	-640.3
Wind Drift • Inches	0.0	1.3	5.4	12.8	24.4	40.9	62.7	121.2	195.1

Hirtenberger 140-grain Nosler Soft Point (82200345)
G1 Ballistic Coefficient = 0.431

Distance • Yards	Muzzle	100	200	300	400	500	600	800	1000
Velocity • fps	2788	2578	2377	2186	2003	1830	1668	1382	1164
Energy • Ft-lbs	2417	2066	1757	1486	1248	1041	865	594	421
Taylor KO Index	15.8	14.6	13.5	12.4	11.4	10.4	9.5	7.8	6.6
Path • Inches	-1.5	+1.9	0.0	-8.0	-23.4	-47.4	-81.8	-190.9	-373.4
Wind Drift • Inches	0.0	0.8	3.2	7.4	13.7	22.3	33.6	65.4	111.2

Hirtenberger 140-grain Sierra SBT (82200454)
G1 Ballistic Coefficient = 0.403

Distance • Yards	Muzzle	100	200	300	400	500	600	800	1000
Velocity • fps	2788	2564	2350	2147	1954	1772	1603	1313	1108
Energy • Ft-lbs	2417	2044	1718	1433	1187	977	799	536	382
Taylor KO Index	15.8	14.6	13.3	12.2	11.1	10.1	9.1	7.5	6.3
Path • Inches	-1.5	+1.9	0.0	-8.2	-24.0	-48.9	-84.9	-200.7	-397.6
Wind Drift • Inches	0.0	0.8	3.4	8.0	14.8	24.2	36.6	71.7	121.9

Federal 140-grain Speer Hot-Cor SP (7B)
G1 Ballistic Coefficient = 0.430

Distance • Yards	Muzzle	100	200	300	400	500	600	800	1000
Velocity • fps	2660	2450	2260	2070	1890	1730	1573	1305	1113
Energy • Ft-lbs	2200	1865	1585	1330	1110	930	770	530	385
Taylor KO Index	15.1	13.9	12.8	11.8	10.7	9.8	8.9	7.4	6.3
Path • Inches	-1.5	+2.1	0.0	-9.0	-26.0	-52.8	-91.3	-214.2	-421.6
Wind Drift • Inches	0.0	0.8	3.4	7.9	14.7	24.0	36.2	70.4	118.7

Federal 140-grain Nosler Partition (P7C)
G1 Ballistic Coefficient = 0.430

Distance • Yards	Muzzle	100	200	300	400	500	600	800	1000
Velocity • fps	2660	2450	2260	2070	1890	1730	1573	1305	1113
Energy • Ft-lbs	2200	1865	1585	1330	1110	930	770	530	385
Taylor KO Index	15.1	13.9	12.8	11.8	10.7	9.8	8.9	7.4	6.3
Path • Inches	-1.5	+2.1	0.0	-9.0	-26.0	-52.8	-91.3	-214.2	-421.6
Wind Drift • Inches	0.0	0.8	3.4	7.9	14.7	24.0	36.2	70.4	118.7

PMC 140-grain Pointed Soft Point (7MA)
G1 Ballistic Coefficient = 0.431

Distance • Yards	Muzzle	100	200	300	400	500	600	800	1000
Velocity • fps	2600	2365	2145	1937	1744	1569	1406	1154	1005
Energy • Ft-lbs	2101	1739	1430	1167	945	765	615	414	314
Taylor KO Index	14.8	13.4	12.2	11.0	9.9	8.9	8.0	6.6	5.7
Path • Inches	-1.5	+2.4	0.0	-10.0	-29.2	-59.8	-104.8	-253.1	-507.1
Wind Drift • Inches	0.0	1.0	4.1	9.6	18.0	29.6	44.9	87.6	145.6

Remington 140-grain Pointed Soft Point Core-Lokt (R7MSR1)
G1 Ballistic Coefficient = 0.390

Distance • Yards	Muzzle	100	200	300	400	500	600	800	1000
Velocity • fps	2660	2435	2221	2018	1827	1648	1484	1216	1046
Energy • Ft-lbs	2199	1843	1533	1266	1037	844	685	460	340
Taylor KO Index	15.1	13.8	12.6	11.5	10.4	9.4	8.4	6.9	5.9
Path • Inches	-1.5	+2.2	0.0	-9.2	-27.4	-55.3	-96.5	-229.9	-457.5
Wind Drift • Inches	0.0	0.9	3.8	8.9	16.5	27.1	41.0	80.3	134.8

Sellier & Bellot 140-grain FMJ (SBA75707)
G1 Ballistic Coefficient = 0.382

Distance • Yards	Muzzle	100	200	300	400	500	600	800	1000
Velocity • fps	2621	2405	2206	2023	1844	1679	1520	1258	1079
Energy • Ft-lbs	2119	1783	1500	1262	1058	873	719	492	362
Taylor KO Index	14.9	13.7	12.5	11.5	10.5	9.5	8.6	7.1	6.1
Path • Inches	-1.5	+2.2	0.0	-9.4	-27.2	-55.4	-96.0	-226.6	-447.7
Wind Drift • Inches	0.0	0.8	3.6	8.4	15.6	25.4	38.4	74.7	125.5

Winchester 145-grain Power-Point (X7MM1)
G1 Ballistic Coefficient = 0.355

Distance • Yards	Muzzle	100	200	300	400	500	600	800	1000
Velocity • fps	2660	2413	2180	1959	1754	1564	1396	1137	990
Energy • Ft-lbs	2279	1875	1530	1236	990	788	628	417	318
Taylor KO Index	15.6	14.2	12.8	11.5	10.3	9.2	8.2	6.7	5.8
Path • Inches	-1.5	+2.2	0.0	-9.6	-28.3	-58.3	-102.6	-249.2	-503.1
Wind Drift • Inches	0.0	1.0	4.2	9.9	18.5	30.6	66.6	91.1	151.6

Norma 150-grain Soft Point (17002) (Discontinued in 2003)

G1 Ballistic Coefficient = 0.421

Distance • Yards	Muzzle	100	200	300	400	500	600	800	1000
Velocity • fps	2690	2480	2279	2087	1905	1734	1575	1302	1107
Energy • Ft-lbs	2411	2048	1730	1451	1209	1002	826	564	409
Taylor KO Index	16.4	15.1	13.9	12.7	11.6	10.6	9.6	7.9	6.7
Path • Inches	-1.5	+2.1	0.0	-8.8	-25.6	-52.0	-90.0	-211.2	-414.8
Wind Drift • Inches	0.0	0.7	3.1	7.2	13.4	21.8	32.9	64.2	108.4

Norma 156-grain Oryx (17001)

G1 Ballistic Coefficient = 0.332

Distance • Yards	Muzzle	100	200	300	400	500	600	800	1000
Velocity • fps	2641	2377	2128	1894	1679	1484	1314	1074	944
Energy • Ft-lbs	2417	1957	1569	1243	977	763	599	399	309
Taylor KO Index	16.7	15.0	13.5	12.0	10.6	9.4	8.3	6.8	6.0
Path • Inches	-1.5	+2.3	0.0	-10.0	-29.8	-62.1	-110.5	-274.6	-557.3
Wind Drift • Inches	0.0	1.1	4.6	10.9	20.5	33.9	51.8	101.4	166.9

Sellier & Bellot 158-grain HPC (SBA75703)

G1 Ballistic Coefficient = 0.376

Distance • Yards	Muzzle	100	200	300	400	500	600	800	1000
Velocity • fps	2484	2272	2078	1901	1728	1568	1421	1185	1034
Energy • Ft-lbs	2156	1804	1510	1263	1048	862	709	492	375
Taylor KO Index	15.9	14.6	13.3	12.2	11.1	10.1	9.1	7.6	6.6
Path • Inches	-1.5	+2.6	0.0	-10.6	-30.9	-62.8	-109.1	-258.0	-507.7
Wind Drift • Inches	0.0	0.9	3.9	9.1	17.0	27.8	42.0	81.2	134.6

Sellier & Bellot 173-grain SPCE (SBA75702)

G1 Ballistic Coefficient = 0.307

Distance • Yards	Muzzle	100	200	300	400	500	600	800	1000
Velocity • fps	2379	2109	1869	1657	1459	1288	1153	985	884
Energy • Ft-lbs	2171	1706	1341	1053	818	638	511	373	301
Taylor KO Index	16.7	14.8	13.1	11.6	10.2	9.0	8.1	6.9	6.2
Path • Inches	-1.5	+3.1	0.0	-13.0	-38.8	-81.1	-144.9	-355.9	-701.4
Wind Drift • Inches	0.0	1.3	5.6	13.3	25.0	41.4	62.6	118.1	187.1

Hirtenberger 175-grain Nosler SP (82200349)

G1 Ballistic Coefficient = 0.471

Distance • Yards	Muzzle	100	200	300	400	500	600	800	1000
Velocity • fps	2494	2314	2141	1975	1818	1669	1531	1293	1118
Energy • Ft-lbs	2418	2080	1781	1516	1284	1083	911	650	486
Taylor KO Index	17.7	16.4	15.2	14.0	12.9	11.8	10.9	9.2	7.9
Path • Inches	-1.5	+2.5	0.0	-10.1	-29.1	-58.7	-100.8	-232.3	-447.5
Wind Drift • Inches	0.0	0.8	3.4	7.9	14.6	23.7	35.6	68.5	114.4

Federal 175-grain Hi-Shok Soft Point (7A)

G1 Ballistic Coefficient = 0.272

Distance • Yards	Muzzle	100	200	300	400	500	600	800	1000
Velocity • fps	2440	2140	1860	1600	1380	1200	1074	925	828
Energy • Ft-lbs	2315	1775	1340	1000	740	585	448	332	267
Taylor KO Index	17.3	15.2	13.2	11.4	9.8	8.5	7.6	6.6	5.9
Path • Inches	-1.5	+3.1	0.0	-13.3	-40.1	-84.6	-155.0	-389.7	-787.2
Wind Drift • Inches	0.0	1.5	6.4	15.4	29.4	48.9	73.9	137.3	215.2

PMC 175-grain Soft Point (7MB)

G1 Ballistic Coefficient = 0.388

Distance • Yards	Muzzle	100	200	300	400	500	600	800	1000
Velocity • fps	2400	2183	1979	1788	1613	1457	1314	1102	978
Energy • Ft-lbs	2238	1852	1522	1242	1011	825	671	472	372
Taylor KO Index	17.0	15.5	14.1	12.7	11.5	10.3	9.3	7.8	6.9
Path • Inches	-1.5	+2.9	0.0	-11.8	-34.5	-70.5	-123.0	-294.3	-579.2
Wind Drift • Inches	0.0	1.0	4.4	10.4	19.4	31.8	48.0	92.3	150.5

7mm-08 Remington

It took quite a while for the wildcat 7mm-08 to go commercial. There were 7mm wildcat versions of the .308 as early as about 1956 or '57, soon after the .308 appeared. Remington announced the 7mm-08 in 1980. All the cartridges based on the .308 Winchester (7.62 NATO) are excellent, and the 7mm-08 is certainly no exception. With a volume about 18 percent smaller than that of the .30-06, the .308 variants work out very nicely for calibers all the way down to the .243. The 7mm-08 and the .260 Remington (6.5mm-08) are the latest to become commercial, but they may very well be the best of all.

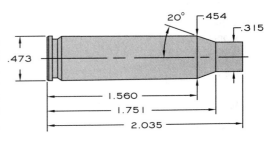

Relative Recoil Factor = 1.80

Specifications

Controlling Agency for Standardization of this Ammunition: SAAMI

Bullet Weight Grains	Velocity fps	Maximum Average Pressure	
		Copper Crusher	Transducer
120	2,990	52,000 cup	61,000 psi
140	2,845	52,000 cup	61,000 psi

Standard barrel for velocity testing: 24 inches long—1 turn in 9.5-inch twist

Availability

Remington 120-grain Hollow Point (R7M082)

G1 Ballistic Coefficient = 0.344

Distance • Yards	Muzzle	100	200	300	400	500	600	800	1000
Velocity • fps	3000	2725	2467	2223	1992	1778	1582	1256	1050
Energy • Ft-lbs	2398	1979	1621	1316	1058	842	667	420	294
Taylor KO Index	14.6	13.3	12.0	10.8	9.7	8.7	7.7	6.7	5.1
Path • Inches	-1.5	+1.9	0.0	-7.6	-21.7	-44.9	-79.1	-193.1	-395.8
Wind Drift • Inches	0.0	0.9	3.6	8.6	16.0	26.5	40.4	80.4	138.0

Hornady 139-grain SST-LM Interlock (85574)

G1 Ballistic Coefficient = 0.486

Distance • Yards	Muzzle	100	200	300	400	500	600	800	1000
Velocity • fps	3000	2804	2617	2437	2265	2099	1940	1647	1394
Energy • Ft-lbs	2777	2427	2113	1833	1583	1360	1162	837	600
Taylor KO Index	16.9	15.8	14.8	13.7	12.8	11.8	10.9	9.3	7.9
Path • Inches	-1.5	+1.5	0.0	-6.5	-19.0	-38.2	-65.3	-149.1	-287.2
Wind Drift • Inches	0.0	0.6	2.5	5.89	10.7	17.3	25.9	49.8	84.4

Hornady 139-grain SP-LM InterLock (8557)

G1 Ballistic Coefficient = 0.392

Distance • Yards	Muzzle	100	200	300	400	500	600	800	1000
Velocity • fps	3000	2759	2530	2312	2106	1910	1725	1403	1161
Energy • Ft-lbs	2777	2348	1975	1650	1368	1126	919	608	416
Taylor KO Index	16.9	15.6	14.3	13.0	11.9	10.8	9.7	7.9	6.5
Path • Inches	-1.5	+1.5	0.0	-7.0	-20.5	-41.9	-72.9	-173.4	-348.0
Wind Drift • Inches	0.0	0.8	3.2	7.4	13.7	22.4	34.0	66.8	114.7

PMC 139-grain Pointed Soft Point (7mm-08A)

G1 Ballistic Coefficient = 0.386

Distance • Yards	Muzzle	100	200	300	400	500	600	800	1000
Velocity • fps	2850	2610	2384	2170	1969	1780	1604	1302	1094
Energy • Ft-lbs	2507	2103	1754	1454	1197	978	794	524	370
Taylor KO Index	16.1	14.7	13.4	12.2	11.1	10.0	9.0	7.3	6.3
Path • Inches	-1.5	+1.8	0.0	-7.9	-23.3	-47.6	-82.9	-198.4	-399.4
Wind Drift • Inches	0.0	0.8	3.4	8.1	15.1	24.7	37.5	73.7	125.6

Federal 140-grain Nosler AccuBond (P708A2)

G1 Ballistic Coefficient = 0.486

Distance • Yards	Muzzle	100	200	300	400	500	600	800	1000
Velocity • fps	3000	2800	2620	2440	2260	2100	1940	1647	1394
Energy • Ft-lbs	2800	2445	2130	1845	1590	1370	1170	843	604
Taylor KO Index	17.0	15.9	14.9	13.9	12.8	11.9	11.0	9.4	7.2
Path • Inches	-1.5	+1.5	0.0	-6.5	-18.9	-38.2	-65.3	-149.1	-285.7
Wind Drift • Inches	0.0	0.6	2.5	5.8	10.7	17.3	25.9	49.8	84.3

Federal 140-grain Nosler Solid Base BT (P708S1)

G1 Ballistic Coefficient = 0.386

Distance • Yards	Muzzle	100	200	300	400	500	600	800	1000
Velocity • fps	2880	2680	2490	2310	2130	1960	1801	1512	1273
Energy • Ft-lbs	2580	2235	1925	1655	1410	1200	1009	711	504
Taylor KO Index	16.4	15.2	14.1	13.1	12.1	11.1	10.2	8.6	7.2
Path • Inches	-1.5	+1.7	0.0	-7.2	-21.2	-42.6	-73.3	-169.2	-328.1
Wind Drift • Inches	0.0	0.7	2.8	6.5	12.0	19.5	29.3	56.7	96.3

Winchester 140-grain Power-Point Plus (SHV708)

G1 Ballistic Coefficient = 0.330

Distance • Yards	Muzzle	100	200	300	400	500	600	800	1000
Velocity • fps	2875	2597	2336	2090	1859	1647	1456	1159	993
Energy • Ft-lbs	2570	2097	1697	1358	1075	843	659	418	307
Taylor KO Index	16.3	14.8	13.3	11.9	10.6	9.4	8.3	6.6	5.6
Path • Inches	-1.5	+1.8	0.0	-8.2	-24.4	-50.6	-90.0	-222.4	-458.0
Wind Drift • Inches	0.0	1.0	4.0	9.6	18.0	29.8	45.6	90.7	153.1

Remington 140-grain Pointed Soft Point, Boat Tail (PRB7M08RA) (Discontinued in 2004)

G1 Ballistic Coefficient = 0.450

Distance • Yards	Muzzle	100	200	300	400	500	600	800	1000
Velocity • fps	2860	2656	2460	2273	2094	1923	1761	1470	1236
Energy • Ft-lbs	2542	2192	1881	1606	1363	1150	964	672	475
Taylor KO Index	16.2	15.1	14.0	12.9	11.9	10.9	10.0	8.3	7.0
Path • Inches	-1.5	+1.7	0.0	-7.5	-21.7	-43.9	-75.5	-174.6	-338.8
Wind Drift • Inches	0.0	0.7	2.9	6.8	12.5	20.4	30.6	59.4	101.1

Remington 140-grain Nosler Partition (PRP7M08RB) (Discontinued in 2004)

G1 Ballistic Coefficient = 0.435

Distance • Yards	Muzzle	100	200	300	400	500	600	800	1000
Velocity • fps	2860	2648	2446	2253	2068	1893	1729	1434	1203
Energy • Ft-lbs	2542	2180	1860	1577	1330	1114	929	640	450
Taylor KO Index	16.2	15.0	13.9	12.8	11.7	10.8	9.8	8.1	6.8
Path • Inches	-1.5	+1.7	0.0	-7.6	-22.0	-44.6	-76.87	-178.8	-349.0
Wind Drift • Inches	0.0	0.7	3.0	7.0	13.0	21.2	32.0	62.2	106.0

Remington 140-grain Core-Lokt Pointed Soft Point (P7M081)

G1 Ballistic Coefficient = 0.390

Distance • Yards	Muzzle	100	200	300	400	500	600	800	1000
Velocity • fps	2860	2625	2402	2189	1988	1798	1621	1318	1106
Energy • Ft-lbs	2542	2142	1793	1490	1228	1005	817	540	380
Taylor KO Index	16.2	14.9	13.6	12.4	11.3	10.2	9.2	7.5	6.3
Path • Inches	-1.5	+1.8	0.0	-9.2	-22.9	-46.8	-81.6	-194.0	-387.1
Wind Drift • Inches	0.0	0.8	3.4	8.0	14.8	24.3	36.8	72.3	123.4

Federal 140-grain Nosler Partition (P708A)

G1 Ballistic Coefficient = 0.431

Distance • Yards	Muzzle	100	200	300	400	500	600	800	1000
Velocity • fps	2800	2590	2396	2200	2020	1840	1676	1388	1169
Energy • Ft-lbs	2435	2085	1775	1500	1265	1060	873	599	425
Taylor KO Index	15.9	14.7	13.6	12.5	11.5	10.5	9.5	7.9	6.6
Path • Inches	-1.5	+1.8	0.0	-8.0	-23.1	-46.6	-81.0	-189.0	-369.8
Wind Drift • Inches	0.0	0.8	3.1	7.3	13.6	22.2	33.4	65.0	110.6

Winchester 140-grain Power-Point (X708)

G1 Ballistic Coefficient = 0.360

Distance • Yards	Muzzle	100	200	300	400	500	600	800	1000
Velocity • fps	2800	2549	2312	2087	1876	1679	1499	1208	1031
Energy • Ft-lbs	2437	2020	1661	1354	1094	876	699	454	330
Taylor KO Index	15.9	14.5	13.1	11.9	10.7	9.5	8.5	6.9	5.9
Path • Inches	-1.5	+1.9	0.0	-8.5	-24.9	-51.3	-90.4	-220.1	-447.9
Wind Drift • Inches	0.0	0.9	3.8	9.0	16.8	27.7	42.2	83.3	140.9

Winchester 140-grain Fail Safe (S708)

G1 Ballistic Coefficient = 0.358

Distance • Yards	Muzzle	100	200	300	400	500	600	800	1000
Velocity • fps	2760	2506	2271	2048	1839	1645	1467	1185	1017
Energy • Ft-lbs	2360	1953	1603	1304	1051	841	669	437	322
Taylor KO Index	15.7	14.2	12.9	11.6	10.4	9.3	8.3	6.7	5.8
Path • Inches	-1.5	+2.0	0.0	-8.8	-25.9	-53.2	-93.6	-226.9	-459.4
Wind Drift • Inches	0.0	0.9	3.9	9.2	17.3	28.6	43.5	85.7	144.4

Remington 140-grain AccuTip (PRA7M08RB)

G1 Ballistic Coefficient = 0.486

Distance • Yards	Muzzle	100	200	300	400	500	600	800	1000
Velocity • fps	2860	2670	2489	2314	2146	1986	1832	1552	1316
Energy • Ft-lbs	2542	2216	1925	1664	1432	1225	1044	749	538
Taylor KO Index	16.2	15.2	14.1	13.1	12.1	11.3	10.4	8.8	7.5
Path • Inches	-1.5	+1.7	0.0	-7.3	-21.1	-42.5	-72.4	-166.5	-319.7
Wind Drift • Inches	0.0	0.6	2.7	6.2	11.4	18.6	27.8	53.6	90.7

Remington 140-grain Nosler Ballistic Tip (PRT7M08RA) (Discontinued in 2004)

G1 Ballistic Coefficient = 0.471

Distance • Yards	Muzzle	100	200	300	400	500	600	800	1000
Velocity • fps	2860	2670	2488	2313	2145	1984	1831	1551	1315
Energy • Ft-lbs	2543	2217	1925	1663	1431	1224	1043	748	538
Taylor KO Index	16.2	15.2	14.1	13.1	12.1	11.3	10.4	8.8	7.5
Path • Inches	-1.5	+1.7	0.0	-7.3	-21.2	-42.6	-72.8	-166.3	-318.1
Wind Drift • Inches	0.0	0.7	2.7	6.2	11.5	18.6	27.8	53.6	90.8

Norma 140-grain Nosler BST (P708B)

G1 Ballistic Coefficient = 0.485

Distance • Yards	Muzzle	100	200	300	400	500	600	800	1000
Velocity • fps	2822	2633	2452	2278	2112	1953	1801	1524	1293
Energy • Ft-lbs	2476	2156	1870	1614	1387	1186	1009	723	520
Taylor KO Index	16.0	15.0	13.9	12.9	12.0	11.1	10.2	8.7	7.3
Path • Inches	-1.5	+1.8	0.0	-7.6	-21.7	-43.7	-74.8	-171.4	-329.5
Wind Drift • Inches	0.0	0.7	2.7	6.4	11.7	19.0	28.4	58.4	92.8

Federal 140-grain Nosler Ballistic Tip (P708B)

G1 Ballistic Coefficient = 0.489

Distance • Yards	Muzzle	100	200	300	400	500	600	800	1000
Velocity • fps	2800	2610	2430	2260	2100	1940	1791	1518	1289
Energy • Ft-lbs	2440	2135	1840	1590	1360	1165	997	716	517
Taylor KO Index	15.9	14.8	13.8	12.8	11.9	11.0	10.2	8.6	7.3
Path • Inches	-1.5	+1.6	0.0	-8.4	-25.4	-44.5	-76.2	-173.9	-332.6
Wind Drift • Inches	0.0	0.7	2.7	6.4	11.7	19.0	28.5	54.9	92.9

Winchester 140-grain Ballistic Silvertip (SBST708)

G1 Ballistic Coefficient = 0.455

Distance • Yards	Muzzle	100	200	300	400	500	600	800	1000
Velocity • fps	2770	2572	2382	2200	2026	1860	1704	1425	1205
Energy • Ft-lbs	2386	2056	1764	1504	1276	1076	903	632	451
Taylor KO Index	15.7	14.6	13.5	12.5	11.5	10.6	9.7	8.1	6.8
Path • Inches	-1.5	+1.9	0.0	-8.0	-23.2	-46.9	-80.8	-186.7	-361.7
Wind Drift • Inches	0.0	0.7	3.0	7.0	13.0	21.1	31.7	61.4	104.2

Speer 145-grain Grand Slam (24567) (Discontinued in 2004)

G1 Ballistic Coefficient = 0.328

Distance • Yards	Muzzle	100	200	300	400	500	600	800	1000
Velocity • fps	2810	2534	2274	2030	1804	1595	1409	1129	976
Energy • Ft-lbs	2542	2067	1664	1327	1048	819	640	411	307
Taylor KO Index	16.5	14.9	13.4	11.9	10.6	9.4	8.3	6.6	5.7
Path • Inches	-1.5	+2.0	0.0	-8.7	-25.9	-53.8	-95.5	-236.1	-485.6
Wind Drift • Inches	0.0	1.0	4.2	10.0	18.8	31.1	47.6	94.3	158.0

Federal 150-grain Speer Hot-Cor SP (708CS)

G1 Ballistic Coefficient = 0.414

Distance • Yards	Muzzle	100	200	300	400	500	600	800	1000
Velocity • fps	2650	2440	2230	2040	1860	1690	1532	1265	1082
Energy • Ft-lbs	2340	1980	1660	1390	1150	950	782	533	390
Taylor KO Index	16.1	14.8	13.6	12.4	11.3	10.3	9.3	7.7	6.6
Path • Inches	-1.5	+2.2	0.0	-9.2	-26.7	-54.4	-94.0	-221.4	-436.1
Wind Drift • Inches	0.0	0.8	3.5	8.3	15.5	25.3	38.2	74.5	125.5

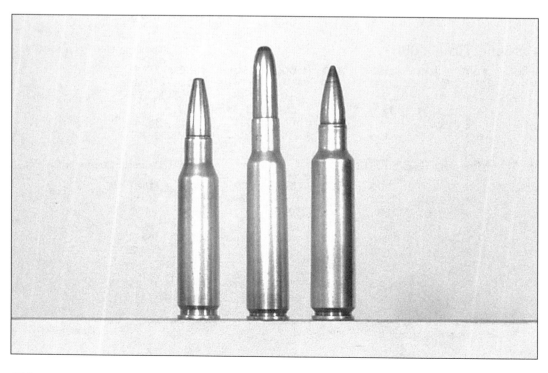

(Left to right) 7mm-08 Remington, 7mm Mauser, .284 Winchester.

7x64mm Brenneke

This cartridge has been around for a very long time. Wilhelm Brenneke designed the 7x64mm in 1917. It is for all practical purposes a 7mm-06, although Wilhelm undoubtedly used a Mauser cartridge for his development brass. In terms of muzzle velocity, the 7x64mm is very close to the .280 Remington, the .270 Winchester, and the .284 Winchester when you compare similar weight bullets, but certainly slower than the 7mm Remington Magnum and the 7mm Weatherby Magnum. It has never been very popular in the U.S., perhaps because there are too many similar performers in the ammunition catalogs.

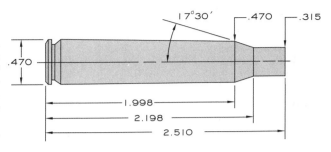

Relative Recoil Factor = 1.85

Specifications

Controlling Agency for Standardization of this Ammunition: CIP

Bullet Weight Grains	Velocity fps	Maximum Average Pressure	
		Copper Crusher	Transducer
N/A	N/A	—	60,000 psi (estimated)

Standard barrel for velocity testing: 24 inches long—1 turn in 8.66-inch twist

Availability

Sellier & Bellot 139-grain SP (SBA76401)
G1 Ballistic Coefficient = 0.229

Distance • Yards	Muzzle	100	200	300	400	500	600	800	1000
Velocity • fps	2808	2454	2144	1874	1615	1388	1205	988	871
Energy • Ft-lbs	2432	1857	1418	1082	805	595	448	301	234
Taylor KO Index	15.8	13.8	12.1	10.6	9.1	7.8	6.8	5.6	4.9
Path • Inches	-1.5	+2.1	0.0	-9.6	-29.2	-62.4	-114.4	-297.6	-614.0
Wind Drift • Inches	0.0	1.2	5.3	12.7	24.2	40.7	62.9	123.2	199.8

Norma 140-grain Nosler AccuBond (17069)
G1 Ballistic Coefficient = 0.485

Distance • Yards	Muzzle	100	200	300	400	500	600	800	1000
Velocity • fps	2953	2759	2572	2394	2223	2059	1902	1613	1365
Energy • Ft-lbs	2712	2366	2058	1782	1537	1318	1125	809	579
Taylor KO Index	16.8	15.7	14.6	13.6	12.6	11.7	10.8	9.2	7.8
Path • Inches	-1.5	+1.5	0.0	-6.8	-19.7	-39.6	-67.7	-154.8	-297.0
Wind Drift • Inches	0.0	0.6	2.6	6.0	11.0	17.8	26.6	51.1	86.7

Hirtenberger 140-grain Nosler SP (82200357)
G1 Ballistic Coefficient = 0.398

Distance • Yards	Muzzle	100	200	300	400	500	600	800	1000
Velocity • fps	2920	2686	2464	2253	2052	1862	1684	1374	1144
Energy • Ft-lbs	2651	2244	1888	1578	1309	1078	882	587	407
Taylor KO Index	16.6	15.3	14.0	12.8	11.7	10.6	9.6	7.8	6.5
Path • Inches	-1.5	+1.7	0.0	-7.4	-21.7	-44.2	-76.9	-181.8	-361.2
Wind Drift • Inches	0.0	0.7	2.9	6.8	12.6	20.7	31.2	61.3	105.0

Hirtenberger 140-grain Sierra SBT (82200442)
G1 Ballistic Coefficient = 0.367

Distance • Yards	Muzzle	100	200	300	400	500	600	800	1000
Velocity • fps	2920	2667	2428	2201	1986	1785	1599	1286	1077
Energy • Ft-lbs	2651	2212	1832	1506	1227	991	795	514	360
Taylor KO Index	16.6	15.1	13.8	12.5	11.3	10.1	9.1	7.3	6.1
Path • Inches	-1.5	+1.7	0.0	-7.6	-22.4	-46.1	-80.7	-194.3	-392.6
Wind Drift • Inches	0.0	0.8	3.2	7.4	13.9	22.9	34.7	68.7	117.3

Norma 140-grain Nosler BST (17052) (Discontinued in 2004)

G1 Ballistic Coefficient = 0.445

Distance • Yards	Muzzle	100	200	300	400	500	600	800	1000
Velocity • fps	2854	2647	2449	2260	2081	1909	1746	1455	1223
Energy • Ft-lbs	2533	2179	1865	1588	1346	1133	948	658	465
Taylor KO Index	16.2	15.0	13.9	12.8	11.8	10.8	9.9	8.3	6.9
Path • Inches	-1.5	+1.7	0.0	-7.5	-21.9	-44.3	-76.3	-177.3	-346.4
Wind Drift • Inches	0.0	0.7	2.9	6.9	12.7	20.7	31.1	60.5	102.9

Sellier & Bellot 140-grain FMJ (SBA76404)

G1 Ballistic Coefficient = 0.403

Distance • Yards	Muzzle	100	200	300	400	500	600	800	1000
Velocity • fps	2772	2540	2328	2133	1941	1760	1592	1304	1102
Energy • Ft-lbs	2370	1990	1671	1403	1171	963	788	529	378
Taylor KO Index	15.7	14.4	13.2	12.1	11.0	10.0	9.0	7.4	6.3
Path • Inches	-1.5	+1.9	0.0	-8.3	-24.3	-49.6	-86.1	-204.5	-407.8
Wind Drift • Inches	0.0	0.8	3.4	8.0	14.9	24.4	37.0	72.3	122.8

Hirtenberger 155-grain ABC Bullet (82200359)

G1 Ballistic Coefficient = 0.290

Distance • Yards	Muzzle	100	200	300	400	500	600	800	1000
Velocity • fps	2690	2388	2105	1843	1605	1395	1222	1008	892
Energy • Ft-lbs	2491	1963	1526	1170	886	670	514	350	274
Taylor KO Index	16.9	15.0	13.2	11.6	10.1	8.8	7.7	6.3	5.6
Path • Inches	-1.5	+2.3	0.0	-10.2	-30.7	-64.8	-116.9	-296.5	-612.6
Wind Drift • Inches	0.0	1.1	4.6	11.1	21.1	35.2	54.0	105.2	170.6

Norma 156-grain Oryx (17053)

G1 Ballistic Coefficient = 0.330

Distance • Yards	Muzzle	100	200	300	400	500	600	800	1000
Velocity • fps	2789	2516	2259	2017	1793	1587	1403	1127	975
Energy • Ft-lbs	2695	2193	1768	1410	1114	872	682	440	330
Taylor KO Index	17.7	15.9	14.3	12.8	11.3	10.0	8.9	7.1	6.2
Path • Inches	-1.5	+2.0	0.0	-8.8	-26.3	-54.6	-97.1	-241.6	-496.2
Wind Drift • Inches	0.0	1.0	4.2	10.0	18.8	31.2	47.7	94.4	158.0

Sellier & Bellot 158-grain HPC (SBA76403)

G1 Ballistic Coefficient = 0.408

Distance • Yards	Muzzle	100	200	300	400	500	600	800	1000
Velocity • fps	2638	2415	2211	2024	1841	1669	1510	1245	1068
Energy • Ft-lbs	2431	2038	1708	1432	1189	977	801	544	400
Taylor KO Index	16.9	15.5	14.2	13.0	11.8	10.7	9.7	8.0	6.8
Path • Inches	-1.5	+2.2	0.0	-9.3	-27.1	-55.2	-95.9	-227.5	-451.4
Wind Drift • Inches	0.0	0.9	3.6	8.5	15.8	26.0	39.2	76.4	128.5

Speer 160-grain Grand Slam (24521) (Discontinued in 2004)

G1 Ballistic Coefficient = 0.388

Distance • Yards	Muzzle	100	200	300	400	500	600	800	1000
Velocity • fps	2600	2376	2164	1962	1774	1598	1440	1184	1027
Energy • Ft-lbs	2401	2006	1663	1368	1118	908	737	498	374
Taylor KO Index	16.9	15.4	14.0	12.7	11.5	10.4	9.3	7.7	6.7
Path • Inches	-1.5	+2.3	0.0	-9.8	-28.6	-58.5	-102.1	-243.5	-484.1
Wind Drift • Inches	0.0	0.9	3.9	9.2	17.2	28.3	42.8	83.4	139.2

PMC 170-grain Soft Point (7X64B)

G1 Ballistic Coefficient = 0.393

Distance • Yards	Muzzle	100	200	300	400	500	600	800	1000
Velocity • fps	2625	2401	2189	1989	1801	1629	1468	1206	1040
Energy • Ft-lbs	2601	2175	1808	1493	1224	1001	813	549	409
Taylor KO Index	18.1	16.6	15.1	13.7	12.4	11.2	10.1	8.3	7.2
Path • Inches	-1.5	+2.3	0.0	-9.6	-27.9	-56.9	-99.2	-237.3	-473.2
Wind Drift • Inches	0.0	0.8	3.4	8.1	15.0	24.7	37.3	72.8	122.0

Norma 170-grain Plastic point (17019)

G1 Ballistic Coefficient = 0.378

Distance • Yards	Muzzle	100	200	300	400	500	600	800	1000
Velocity • fps	2756	2519	2294	2081	1879	1691	1519	1234	1052
Energy • Ft-lbs	2868	2396	1987	1635	1333	1079	871	575	418
Taylor KO Index	19.0	17.4	15.8	14.4	13.0	11.7	10.5	8.5	7.3
Path • Inches	-1.5	+2.0	0.0	-8.6	-25.3	-51.9	-90.6	-217.1	-435.3
Wind Drift • Inches	0.0	0.9	3.7	8.7	16.3	26.7	40.5	79.6	134.7

Norma 170-grain Vulcan HP (17018)

G1 Ballistic Coefficient = 0.353

Distance • Yards	Muzzle	100	200	300	400	500	600	800	1000
Velocity • fps	2756	2503	2263	2037	1824	1628	1451	1171	1008
Energy • Ft-lbs	2865	2362	1931	1564	1257	1001	795	518	383
Taylor KO Index	19.0	17.3	15.6	14.0	12.6	11.2	10.0	8.1	7.0
Path • Inches	-1.5	+2.0	0.0	-8.8	-26.1	-53.9	-95.1	-232.7	-473.8
Wind Drift • Inches	0.0	1.0	4.0	9.4	17.6	29.1	44.4	87.5	147.1

Sellier & Bellot 173-grain SPCE (SBA76402)

G1 Ballistic Coefficient = 0.333

Distance • Yards	Muzzle	100	200	300	400	500	600	800	1000
Velocity • fps	2526	2259	2020	1807	1601	1417	1260	1048	930
Energy • Ft-lbs	2449	1958	1566	1253	985	771	610	422	332
Taylor KO Index	17.7	15.9	14.2	12.7	11.2	9.9	8.8	7.4	6.5
Path • Inches	-1.5	+2.6	0.0	-11.1	-32.9	-68.5	-121.7	-300.5	-601.9
Wind Drift • Inches	0.0	1.1	4.8	11.5	21.6	35.8	54.5	105.4	171.0

Hirtenberger 175-grain Nosler SP (82200358)

G1 Ballistic Coefficient = 0.456

Distance • Yards	Muzzle	100	200	300	400	500	600	800	1000
Velocity • fps	2658	2465	2280	2102	1933	1773	1623	1359	1158
Energy • Ft-lbs	2746	2361	2020	1718	1453	1222	1024	718	521
Taylor KO Index	18.9	17.5	16.2	14.9	13.7	12.6	11.5	9.6	8.2
Path • Inches	-1.5	+2.1	0.0	-8.8	-25.5	-51.6	-86.7	-205.2	-397.5
Wind Drift • Inches	0.0	0.7	2.9	6.7	12.4	20.2	30.3	58.7	99.0

Hirtenberger 175-grain Sierra SBT (82200466)

G1 Ballistic Coefficient = 0.646

Distance • Yards	Muzzle	100	200	300	400	500	600	800	1000
Velocity • fps	2625	2489	2356	2228	2104	1984	1868	1650	1455
Energy • Ft-lbs	2678	2407	2158	1930	1721	1530	1356	1058	823
Taylor KO Index	18.6	17.7	16.7	15.8	14.9	14.1	13.3	11.7	10.3
Path • Inches	-1.5	+2.1	0.0	-8.3	-23.6	-46.8	-78.9	-174.2	-320.8
Wind Drift • Inches	0.0	0.5	2.0	4.6	8.5	13.6	20.2	38.2	63.4

Speer 175-grain Grand Slam (24522) (Discontinued in 2004)

G1 Ballistic Coefficient = 0.466

Distance • Yards	Muzzle	100	200	300	400	500	600	800	1000
Velocity • fps	2550	2365	2188	2019	1857	1705	1563	1315	1131
Energy • Ft-lbs	2527	2173	1859	1583	1341	1130	949	672	498
Taylor KO Index	18.1	16.8	15.5	14.3	13.2	12.1	11.1	9.3	8.0
Path • Inches	-1.5	+2.3	0.0	-9.6	-27.8	-56.1	-96.4	-222.5	-429.4
Wind Drift • Inches	0.0	0.8	3.3	7.7	14.3	23.2	34.9	67.3	112.8

.284 Winchester

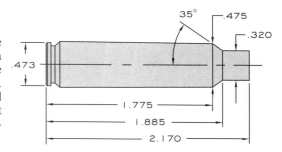

Winchester's .284 came on the scene in 1963. In a search for a cartridge case with the .30-06's volume that would work in shorter actions, Winchester went to a larger (0.5008-inch) body with the .30-06's 0.473-inch head size. This technique of a fat body and reduced head anticipated the design of the .300 WSM by 38 years. A cartridge with this form of reduced head size is known as having a "rebated head." The .284 never really set the world on fire as a 7mm, but two of its wildcat spin-offs, the 6mm-284 and the 6.5mm-284, have earned a following among long-range target shooters. Only one loading remains in the current catalogs.

Relative Recoil Factor = 1.93

Specifications

Controlling Agency for Standardization of this Ammunition: SAAMI

Bullet Weight Grains	Velocity fps	Maximum Average Pressure	
		Copper Crusher	Transducer
125	3,125	54,000 cup	56,000 psi
150	2,845	54,000 cup	56,000 psi

Standard barrel for velocity testing: 24 inches long—1 turn in 10-inch twist

Availability

Winchester 150-grain Power-Point (X2842)

G1 Ballistic Coefficient = 0.367

Distance • Yards	Muzzle	100	200	300	400	500	600	800	1000
Velocity • fps	2860	2609	2371	2145	1933	1734	1551	1248	1052
Energy • Ft-lbs	2724	2243	1830	1480	1185	940	744	476	345
Taylor KO Index	17.4	15.9	14.4	13.1	11.8	10.6	9.4	7.6	6.4
Path • Inches	-1.5	+1.8	0.0	-8.0	-23.6	-48.6	-85.2	-206.9	-421.4
Wind Drift • Inches	0.0	0.9	3.6	8.6	16.0	26.4	40.2	79.4	135.3

Gregor Woods with a blesbok from South Africa which can be effectively hunted with any decent whitetail deer caliber. (Photo from *African Hunter II* by Craig Boddington and Peter Flack, 2004, Safari Press)

.280 Remington

Remington introduced its .280 cartridge in 1957. This cartridge has been the source of numerous articles comparing it with cartridges such as the .30-06 and the .270 Winchester. There really isn't much of a story here. Both the .270 and the .280 are little more than .30-06 cartridges necked to .270 and 7mm, respectively. As a result, the performance of these cartridges is so similar that it comes down to exactly which bullet you prefer to use. Both are excellent calibers, and if you have a gun in .280 caliber, there's absolutely no reason to feel you have any more, or any less, gun than your friend's .270.

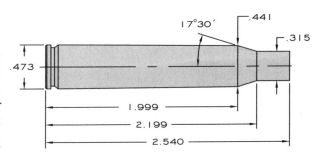

Relative Recoil Factor = 1.95

Specifications

Controlling Agency for Standardization of this Ammunition: SAAMI

Bullet Weight Grains	Velocity fps	Maximum Average Pressure	
		Copper Crusher	Transducer
120	3,135	52,000 cup	60,000 psi
140	2,985	52,000 cup	60,000 psi
150	2,875	52,000 cup	60,000 psi
165	2,800	52,000 cup	60,000 psi

Standard barrel for velocity testing: 24 inches long—1 turn in 10-inch twist

Availability

Hornady 139-grain SST Moly LM InterLock (85584)

G1 Ballistic Coefficient = 0.486

Distance • Yards	Muzzle	100	200	300	400	500	600	800	1000
Velocity • fps	3110	2910	2717	2532	2356	2187	2025	1723	1458
Energy • Ft-lbs	2985	2612	2178	1979	1713	1475	1266	916	656
Taylor KO Index	17.5	16.4	15.3	14.3	13.3	12.3	11.4	9.7	8.2
Path • Inches	-1.5	+1.3	0.0	-6.2	-18.0	-36.0	-60.1	-137.2	-262.5
Wind Drift • Inches	0.0	0.6	2.4	5.5	10.2	16.4	24.5	47.1	79.9

Hornady 139-grain BTSP—LM Moly (85583) (Discontinued in 2005)

G1 Ballistic Coefficient = 0.438

Distance • Yards	Muzzle	100	200	300	400	500	600	800	1000
Velocity • fps	3110	2888	2675	2473	2280	2096	1922	1601	1332
Energy • Ft-lbs	2985	2573	2209	1887	1604	1355	1140	792	548
Taylor KO Index	17.5	16.3	15.1	13.9	12.9	11.8	10.8	9.0	7.5
Path • Inches	-1.5	+1.4	0.0	-6.5	-18.6	-37.3	-63.2	-146.4	-284.4
Wind Drift • Inches	0.0	0.6	2.7	6.2	11.4	18.6	27.9	54.2	92.7

Federal 140-grain Nosler Solid Base BT (P280S1)

G1 Ballistic Coefficient = 0.461

Distance • Yards	Muzzle	100	200	300	400	500	600	800	1000
Velocity • fps	3030	2820	2620	2430	2250	2080	1913	1608	1350
Energy • Ft-lbs	2855	2475	2140	1840	1575	1340	1138	804	566
Taylor KO Index	17.2	16.0	14.9	13.8	12.8	11.8	10.9	9.1	7.7
Path • Inches	-1.5	+1.4	0.0	-6.4	-19.0	-38.4	-65.4	-150.6	-291.4
Wind Drift • Inches	0.0	0.6	2.6	6.1	11.2	18.2	27.2	52.6	89.6

Federal 140-grain Nosler AccuBond (P280A2)

G1 Ballistic Coefficient = 0.487

Distance • Yards	Muzzle	100	200	300	400	500	600	800	1000
Velocity • fps	3000	2800	2620	2440	2260	2100	1942	1649	1396
Energy • Ft-lbs	2800	2445	2130	1845	1590	1370	1173	846	606
Taylor KO Index	17.0	15.9	14.9	13.9	12.8	11.9	11.0	9.4	7.9
Path • Inches	-1.5	+1.5	0.0	-6.5	-18.9	-38.2	-65.2	-148.9	-285.2
Wind Drift • Inches	0.0	0.6	2.5	5.8	10.7	17.3	25.8	49.6	84.1

Remington 140-grain AccuTip (PRA280RA)

G1 Ballistic Coefficient = 0.486

Distance • Yards	Muzzle	100	200	300	400	500	600	800	1000
Velocity • fps	3000	2804	2607	2437	2265	2099	1940	1647	1394
Energy • Ft-lbs	2797	2444	2129	1846	1594	1369	1170	843	604
Taylor KO Index	17.0	15.9	14.8	13.8	12.9	11.9	11.0	9.4	7.9
Path • Inches	-1.5	+1.5	0.0	-6.6	-19.0	-38.1	-65.3	-149.1	-285.7
Wind Drift • Inches	0.0	0.6	2.5	5.8	10.7	17.3	25.9	49.8	84.4

Remington 140-grain Pointed Soft Point, Boat Tail (PRB280RA) (Discontinued in 2005)

G1 Ballistic Coefficient = 0.450

Distance • Yards	Muzzle	100	200	300	400	500	600	800	1000
Velocity • fps	3000	2789	2588	2395	2211	2035	1866	1561	1306
Energy • Ft-lbs	2797	2418	2081	1783	1519	1287	1083	758	531
Taylor KO Index	17.0	15.8	14.7	13.6	12.6	11.6	10.6	8.9	7.4
Path • Inches	-1.5	+1.5	0.0	-6.7	-19.5	-39.4	-67.7	-156.3	-302.5
Wind Drift • Inches	0.0	0.7	2.7	6.3	11.7	19.0	28.5	55.2	94.1

Remington 140-grain Core-Lokt Pointed Soft Point (R280R3)

G1 Ballistic Coefficient = 0.391

Distance • Yards	Muzzle	100	200	300	400	500	600	800	1000
Velocity • fps	3000	2758	2528	2309	2102	1905	1723	1400	1159
Energy • Ft-lbs	2797	2363	1986	1657	1373	1128	923	610	418
Taylor KO Index	17.0	15.7	14.4	13.1	11.9	10.8	9.8	8.0	6.6
Path • Inches	-1.5	+1.5	0.0	-7.0	-20.5	-42.0	-72.9	-172.9	-344.6
Wind Drift • Inches	0.0	0.8	3.2	7.4	13.8	22.5	34.1	67.0	115.1

Federal 140-grain Nosler Ballistic Tip (P280D)

G1 Ballistic Coefficient = 0.491

Distance • Yards	Muzzle	100	200	300	400	500	600	800	1000
Velocity • fps	2990	2800	2610	2430	2260	2100	1942	1651	1400
Energy • Ft-lbs	2780	2430	2120	1840	1590	1365	1172	848	609
Taylor KO Index	17.0	15.9	14.8	13.8	12.8	11.9	11.0	9.4	8.0
Path • Inches	-1.5	+1.5	0.0	-6.5	-19.0	-38.4	-65.4	-149.3	-285.6
Wind Drift • Inches	0.0	0.6	2.5	5.8	10.6	17.2	25.7	49.4	83.6

Federal 140-grain Soft Point (280CS)

G1 Ballistic Coefficient = 0.376

Distance • Yards	Muzzle	100	200	300	400	500	600	800	1000
Velocity • fps	2990	2740	2500	2270	2060	1860	1674	1350	1119
Energy • Ft-lbs	2770	2325	1940	1605	1320	1070	871	567	390
Taylor KO Index	16.9	15.6	14.2	12.9	11.7	10.6	9.5	7.7	6.4
Path • Inches	-1.5	+1.7	0.0	-7.5	-20.8	-42.6	-75.2	-179.9	-361.6
Wind Drift • Inches	0.0	0.8	3.3	7.8	14.5	23.8	36.0	71.1	122.3

Winchester 140-grain Ballistic Silvertip (SBST280)

G1 Ballistic Coefficient = 0.485

Distance • Yards	Muzzle	100	200	300	400	500	600	800	1000
Velocity • fps	3040	2842	2653	2471	2297	2130	1969	1672	1414
Energy • Ft-lbs	2872	2511	2187	1898	1640	1410	1205	869	622
Taylor KO Index	17.3	16.1	15.1	14.0	13.0	12.1	11.2	9.5	8.0
Path • Inches	-1.5	+1.4	0.0	-6.3	-18.4	-37.0	-63.4	-144.6	-276.1
Wind Drift • Inches	0.0	0.6	2.5	5.7	10.5	17.0	25.4	48.9	83.0

Winchester 140-grain Fail Safe (S280XA)

G1 Ballistic Coefficient = 0.324

Distance • Yards	Muzzle	100	200	300	400	500	600	800	1000
Velocity • fps	3050	2756	2480	2221	1977	1751	1546	1215	1020
Energy • Ft-lbs	2893	2362	1913	1533	1216	953	744	459	324
Taylor KO Index	17.3	15.7	14.1	12.6	11.2	9.9	8.8	6.9	5.8
Path • Inches	-1.5	+1.3	0.0	-6.3	-21.5	-44.7	-79.3	-16.5	-408.2
Wind Drift • Inches	0.0	0.9	3.8	9.0	16.8	27.9	42.7	85.5	146.6

Remington 140-grain Nosler Ballistic Tip (PRT280RA) (Discontinued in 2005) G1 Ballistic Coefficient = 0.485

Distance • Yards	Muzzle	100	200	300	400	500	600	800	1000
Velocity • fps	3000	2804	2616	2436	2263	2097	1938	1645	1391
Energy • Ft-lbs	2799	2445	2128	1846	1593	1368	1168	841	602
Taylor KO Index	17.0	15.9	14.9	13.8	12.9	11.9	11.0	9.3	7.9
Path • Inches	-1.5	+1.5	0.0	-6.6	-19.0	-38.2	-65.3	-149.1	-284.8
Wind Drift • Inches	0.0	0.6	2.5	5.8	10.7	17.4	26.0	49.9	84.6

Speer 145-grain Grand Slam (24553) (Discontinued in 2005) G1 Ballistic Coefficient = 0.327

Distance • Yards	Muzzle	100	200	300	400	500	600	800	1000
Velocity • fps	2860	2581	2318	2071	1840	1627	1437	1145	985
Energy • Ft-lbs	2633	2144	1729	1381	1090	852	665	422	312
Taylor KO Index	16.8	15.2	13.6	12.2	10.8	9.6	8.5	6.7	5.8
Path • Inches	-1.5	+1.9	0.0	-8.4	-24.9	-51.7	-91.8	-227.2	-468.4
Wind Drift • Inches	0.0	1.0	4.1	9.7	18.3	30.4	46.5	92.5	155.8

Federal 150-grain Nosler Partition (P280A) G1 Ballistic Coefficient = 0.458

Distance • Yards	Muzzle	100	200	300	400	500	600	800	1000
Velocity • fps	2890	2690	2490	2310	2130	1960	1800	1509	1269
Energy • Ft-lbs	2780	2405	2070	1770	1510	1275	1080	759	537
Taylor KO Index	17.6	16.4	15.2	14.1	13.0	11.9	11.0	9.2	7.7
Path • Inches	-1.5	+1.7	0.0	-7.2	-21.1	-42.5	-73.1	-168.4	-325.5
Wind Drift • Inches	0.0	0.7	2.8	6.5	12.1	19.6	29.5	57.1	97.0

Federal 150-grain Hi-Shok Soft Point (280B) G1 Ballistic Coefficient = 0.417

Distance • Yards	Muzzle	100	200	300	400	500	600	800	1000
Velocity • fps	2890	2670	2460	2260	2060	1880	1710	1408	1176
Energy • Ft-lbs	2780	2370	2015	1695	1420	1180	974	660	461
Taylor KO Index	17.6	16.2	15.0	13.8	12.5	11.4	10.4	8.6	7.2
Path • Inches	-1.5	+1.7	0.0	-7.5	-21.8	-44.3	-76.7	-179.8	-353.7
Wind Drift • Inches	0.0	0.8	3.1	7.3	13.5	22.0	33.2	64.8	110.7

Remington 150-grain Core-Lokt Pointed Soft Point (R280R1) G1 Ballistic Coefficient = 0.346

Distance • Yards	Muzzle	100	200	300	400	500	600	800	1000
Velocity • fps	2890	2624	2373	2135	1912	1705	1517	1211	1027
Energy • Ft-lbs	2781	2293	1875	1518	1217	968	766	489	351
Taylor KO Index	17.6	16.0	14.4	13.0	11.6	10.4	9.2	7.4	6.3
Path • Inches	-1.5	+1.8	0.0	-8.0	-23.6	-48.8	-86.0	-209.8	-428.7
Wind Drift • Inches	0.0	0.9	3.8	9.0	16.8	27.8	42.4	84.1	143.0

Norma 156-grain Oryx (17048) G1 Ballistic Coefficient = 0.330

Distance • Yards	Muzzle	100	200	300	400	500	600	800	1000
Velocity • fps	2789	2516	2259	2017	1793	1587	1403	1127	975
Energy • Ft-lbs	2695	2193	1768	1410	1114	872	682	440	330
Taylor KO Index	17.7	15.9	14.3	12.8	11.3	10.0	8.9	7.1	6.2
Path • Inches	-1.5	+2.0	0.0	-8.8	-26.3	-54.6	-97.1	-241.6	-496.2
Wind Drift • Inches	0.0	1.0	4.2	10.0	18.8	31.2	47.7	94.4	158.0

Speer 160-grain Grand Slam (24515) (Discontinued in 2005) G1 Ballistic Coefficient = 0.387

Distance • Yards	Muzzle	100	200	300	400	500	600	800	1000
Velocity • fps	2850	2613	2389	2175	1973	1783	1606	1305	1096
Energy • Ft-lbs	2885	2426	2026	1681	1383	1129	917	605	427
Taylor KO Index	18.5	17.0	15.5	14.1	12.8	11.6	10.4	8.5	7.1
Path • Inches	-1.5	+1.8	0.0	-7.9	-23.2	-47.4	-82.7	-196.9	-393.3
Wind Drift • Inches	0.0	0.8	3.4	8.1	15.0	24.7	37.4	73.5	125.3

Federal 160-grain Nosler AccuBond (P280A1) G1 Ballistic Coefficient = 0.530

Distance • Yards	Muzzle	100	200	300	400	500	600	800	1000
Velocity • fps	2800	2630	2460	2300	2150	2000	1860	1599	1372
Energy • Ft-lbs	2785	2455	2155	1885	1645	1425	1229	909	669
Taylor KO Index	18.2	17.1	16.0	14.9	14.0	13.0	12.1	10.4	8.9
Path • Inches	-1.5	+1.8	0.0	-7.5	-21.6	-43.1	-73.5	-166.1	-314.5
Wind Drift • Inches	0.0	0.6	2.5	5.8	10.7	17.3	25.8	49.4	83.0

Federal 160-grain Trophy Bonded Bear Claw (P280T3)

G1 Ballistic Coefficient = 0.417

Distance • Yards	Muzzle	100	200	300	400	500	600	800	1000
Velocity • fps	2800	2580	2370	2170	1980	1810	1644	1354	1140
Energy • Ft-lbs	2785	2365	2000	1675	1395	1160	961	652	462
Taylor KO Index	18.2	16.7	15.4	14.1	12.9	11.7	10.7	8.8	7.4
Path • Inches	-1.5	+1.9	0.0	-8.1	-23.5	-46.9	-82.5	-193.6	-381.2
Wind Drift • Inches	0.0	0.8	3.2	7.6	14.1	23.1	34.8	68.0	115.8

Remington 165-grain Core-Lokt Soft Point (R280R2)

G1 Ballistic Coefficient = 0.291

Distance • Yards	Muzzle	100	200	300	400	500	600	800	1000
Velocity • fps	2820	2510	2220	1950	1701	1479	1291	1042	914
Energy • Ft-lbs	2913	2308	1805	1393	1060	801	611	398	306
Taylor KO Index	18.9	16.8	14.9	13.1	11.4	9.9	8.6	7.0	6.1
Path • Inches	-1.5	+2.0	0.0	-9.1	-27.4	-57.8	-104..2	-265.2	-553.6
Wind Drift • Inches	0.0	1.1	4.8	11.4	21.7	36.2	55.8	110.4	181.7

Norma 170-grain Plastic point (17060)

G1 Ballistic Coefficient = 0.373

Distance • Yards	Muzzle	100	200	300	400	500	600	800	1000
Velocity • fps	2707	2468	2241	2026	1825	1638	1473	1199	1030
Energy • Ft-lbs	2767	2299	1896	1550	1258	1013	819	543	401
Taylor KO Index	18.7	17.0	15.5	14.0	12.6	11.3	10.2	8.3	7.1
Path • Inches	-1.5	+2.1	0.0	-9.1	-26.6	-54.6	-95.3	-229.0	-459.7
Wind Drift • Inches	0.0	0.9	3.9	9.1	17.1	28.1	42.4	83.2	139.9

Norma 170-grain Vulcan (17051)

G1 Ballistic Coefficient = 0.357

Distance • Yards	Muzzle	100	200	300	400	500	600	800	1000
Velocity • fps	2592	2346	2113	1894	1692	1507	1359	1116	978
Energy • Ft-lbs	2537	2078	1686	1354	1081	857	698	470	361
Taylor KO Index	17.9	16.2	14.6	13.1	11.7	10.4	9.4	7.7	6.7
Path • Inches	-1.5	+2.0	0.0	-9.1	-27.4	-57.8	-108.6	-263.2	-529.3
Wind Drift • Inches	0.0	1.0	4.4	10.3	19.5	32.2	47.9	93.5	154.4

Alaskan brown bear shot with a .375 H&H, an excellent caliber for these potentially dangerous animals. (Photo from Wind in My Face by Hubert Thummler, 2006, Safari Press)

7mm Remington Magnum

Since it became a standardized cartridge in 1962, the 7mm Remington Magnum has easily been the most popular 7mm cartridge in the inventory. That popularity applies to reloaders as well. The 7mm RM has been on the top ten list of reloading die sales for years. The overall length, slightly smaller than the full-length magnums, allows the 7mm RM to be used in standard-length actions, yet the cartridge case volume is large enough to give excellent ballistics. The caliber is versatile: With the lighter bullets the velocities are right around 3,200 fps, and that translates into a flat shooter right out to the longest practical hunting ranges. With the 175-grain bullets in the 2,850 fps class, you have a gun that easily outperforms the legendary .30-06.

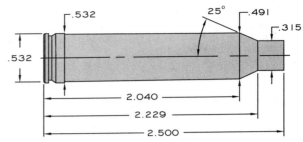

Relative Recoil Factor = 2.06

Specifications

Controlling Agency for Standardization of this Ammunition: SAAMI

Bullet Weight Grains	Velocity fps	Maximum Average Pressure	
		Copper Crusher	Transducer
125	3,290	52,000 cup	61,000 psi
139	3,150	52,000 cup	61,000 psi
150	3,100	52,000 cup	61,000 psi
154	3,035	52,000 cup	61,000 psi
160–162	2,940	52,000 cup	61,000 psi
175	2,850	52,000 cup	61,000 psi

Standard barrel for velocity testing: 24 inches long—1 turn in 9.5-inch twist

Availability

Hornady 139-grain SST Moly InterLock (85594)
G1 Ballistic Coefficient = 0.486

Distance • Yards	Muzzle	100	200	300	400	500	600	800	1000
Velocity • fps	3250	3044	2847	2657	2475	2300	2132	1820	1541
Energy • Ft-lbs	3259	2860	2501	2178	1890	1633	1404	1022	733
Taylor KO Index	18.3	17.2	16.1	15.0	14.0	13.0	12.0	10.3	8.7
Path • Inches	-1.5	+1.1	0.0	-5.5	-16.2	-32.6	-54.5	-124.1	-236.0
Wind Drift • Inches	0.0	0.5	2.0	4.7	8.6	13.9	20.8	39.8	67.3

Hornady 139-grain InterBond HM Moly (85599)
G1 Ballistic Coefficient = 0.487

Distance • Yards	Muzzle	100	200	300	400	500	600	800	1000
Velocity • fps	3250	3043	2845	2656	2475	2301	2135	1823	1544
Energy • Ft-lbs	3259	2857	2498	2177	1890	1634	1407	1026	736
Taylor KO Index	18.5	17.3	16.2	15.1	14.1	13.1	12.1	10.4	8.8
Path • Inches	-1.5	+1.1	0.0	-5.4	-15.8	-31.8	-54.4	-123.9	-236.4
Wind Drift • Inches	0.0	0.5	2.2	5.2	9.5	15.4	23.0	44.0	74.5

Hornady 139-grain Boat Tail Soft Point InterLock (8059)
G1 Ballistic Coefficient = 0.453

Distance • Yards	Muzzle	100	200	300	400	500	600	800	1000
Velocity • fps	3150	2933	2727	2530	2341	2160	1987	1668	1394
Energy • Ft-lbs	3063	2656	2296	1976	1692	1440	1218	859	600
Taylor KO Index	17.8	16.5	15.4	14.3	13.2	12.2	11.2	9.4	7.9
Path • Inches	-1.5	+1.3	0.0	-6.1	-17.7	-35.5	-60.3	-139.2	-269.8
Wind Drift • Inches	0.0	0.6	2.5	5.9	10.8	17.6	26.3	50.8	86.6

Hirtenberger 140-grain Sierra Soft Point (82200462)

G1 Ballistic Coefficient = 0.493

Distance • Yards	Muzzle	100	200	300	400	500	600	800	1000
Velocity • fps	3232	2972	2726	2494	2273	2063	1865	1511	1232
Energy • Ft-lbs	3248	2746	2311	1934	1606	1324	1082	710	472
Taylor KO Index	18.4	16.9	15.5	14.2	12.9	11.7	10.6	8.6	7.0
Path • Inches	-1.5	+1.2	0.0	-5.9	-17.4	-35.7	-62.2	-148.1	-298.2
Wind Drift • Inches	0.0	0.6	2.6	6.2	11.4	18.6	28.2	55.4	96.0

Hirtenberger 140-grain Nosler Soft Point (82200366)

G1 Ballistic Coefficient = 0.493

Distance • Yards	Muzzle	100	200	300	400	500	600	800	1000
Velocity • fps	3215	3012	2819	2633	2455	2284	2120	1813	1539
Energy • Ft-lbs	3223	2829	2477	2162	1880	1627	1402	1025	738
Taylor KO Index	18.3	17.1	16.0	15.0	13.9	13.0	12.0	10.3	8.7
Path • Inches	-1.5	+1.2	0.0	-5.6	-16.1	-32.4	-55.4	-126.1	-240.2
Wind Drift • Inches	0.0	0.5	2.0	4.7	8.6	13.9	20.7	39.6	67.0

Winchester 140-grain AccuBond CT (S7MMCTA)

G1 Ballistic Coefficient = 0.460

Distance • Yards	Muzzle	100	200	300	400	500	600	800	1000
Velocity • fps	3180	2965	2760	2565	2377	2197	2023	1707	1430
Energy • Ft-lbs	3143	2733	2368	2044	1756	1501	1275	906	636
Taylor KO Index	18.1	16.8	15.7	14.6	13.5	12.5	11.5	9.7	8.1
Path • Inches	-1.5	+1.2	0.0	-5.8	-16.9	-34.2	-58.6	-134.9	-260.4
Wind Drift • Inches	0.0	0.6	2.4	5.7	10.5	17.0	25.4	49.0	83.5

Remington 140-grain Pointed Soft Point, Boat Tail (PRB7MMRA) (Discontinued in 2005)

G1 Ballistic Coefficient = 0.450

Distance • Yards	Muzzle	100	200	300	400	500	600	800	1000
Velocity • fps	3175	2956	2747	2547	2356	2174	1999	1677	1400
Energy • Ft-lbs	3133	2715	2345	2017	1726	1469	1242	874	609
Taylor KO Index	18.0	16.8	15.6	14.5	13.4	12.3	11.4	9.5	8.0
Path • Inches	-1.5	+1.2	0.0	-5.9	-17.1	-34.6	-54.5	-137.3	-266.3
Wind Drift • Inches	0.0	0.6	2.5	5.8	10.8	17.5	26.2	50.6	86.4

Remington 140-grain Core-Lokt Pointed Soft Point, Boat Tail (R7MM4)

G1 Ballistic Coefficient = 0.390

Distance • Yards	Muzzle	100	200	300	400	500	600	800	1000
Velocity • fps	3175	2923	2684	2458	2243	2039	1845	1500	1225
Energy • Ft-lbs	3133	2655	2240	1878	1564	1292	1059	700	469
Taylor KO Index	18.0	16.6	15.2	14.0	12.7	11.6	10.5	8.5	7.0
Path • Inches	-1.5	+1.3	0.0	-6.1	-18.0	-36.8	-64.1	-152.3	-305.3
Wind Drift • Inches	0.0	0.7	2.9	6.9	12.7	20.8	31.4	61.7	106.5

Remington 140-grain Core-Lokt Ultra Bonded (PRC7MMRA)

G1 Ballistic Coefficient = 0.409

Distance • Yards	Muzzle	100	200	300	400	500	600	800	1000
Velocity • fps	3175	2934	2707	2490	2283	2086	1898	1560	1283
Energy • Ft-lbs	3133	2676	2277	1927	1620	1353	1120	756	512
Taylor KO Index	18.0	16.7	15.4	14.1	13.0	11.8	10.8	8.9	7.3
Path • Inches	-1.5	+1.3	0.0	-6.0	-17.7	-36.0	-62.4	-146.8	-290.9
Wind Drift • Inches	0.0	0.6	2.5	5.8	10.8	17.6	26.6	51.9	89.4

Black Hills 140-grain Nosler Ballistic Tip (1C7MMRMBHGN2)

G1 Ballistic Coefficient = 0.491

Distance • Yards	Muzzle	100	200	300	400	500	600	800	1000
Velocity • fps	3150	2930	2710	2510	2320	2130	1954	1630	1356
Energy • Ft-lbs	3085	2660	2290	1960	1670	1415	1188	827	572
Taylor KO Index	17.9	16.6	15.4	14.3	13.2	12.1	11.1	9.3	7.3
Path • Inches	-1.5	+1.3	0.0	-6.0	-17.5	-35.6	-61.3	-142.2	-277.3
Wind Drift • Inches	0.0	0.6	2.6	6.1	11.2	18.2	27.3	53.0	90.6

Black Hills 140-grain Nosler AccuBond (1C7MMRMBHGN3)

G1 Ballistic Coefficient = 0.485

Distance • Yards	Muzzle	100	200	300	400	500	600	800	1000
Velocity • fps	3150	2930	2710	2510	2320	2130	1954	1630	1356
Energy • Ft-lbs	3085	2660	2290	1960	1670	1415	1188	827	572
Taylor KO Index	17.9	16.6	15.4	14.3	13.2	12.1	11.1	9.3	7.3
Path • Inches	-1.5	+1.3	0.0	-6.0	-17.5	-35.6	-61.3	-142.2	-277.3
Wind Drift • Inches	0.0	0.6	2.6	6.1	11.2	18.2	27.3	53.0	90.6

Black Hills 140-grain Barnes Triple Shock (1C7MMRMBHGN1)   G1 Ballistic Coefficient = 0.471

Distance • Yards	Muzzle	100	200	300	400	500	600	800	1000
Velocity • fps	3150	2930	2710	2510	2320	2130	1954	1630	1356
Energy • Ft-lbs	3085	2660	2290	1960	1670	1415	1188	827	572
Taylor KO Index	17.9	16.6	15.4	14.3	13.2	12.1	11.1	9.3	7.3
Path • Inches	-1.5	+1.3	0.0	-6.0	-17.5	-35.6	-61.3	-142.2	-277.3
Wind Drift • Inches	0.0	0.6	2.6	6.1	11.2	18.2	27.3	53.0	90.6

Federal 140-grain Nosler Partition (P7RG)   G1 Ballistic Coefficient = 0.439

Distance • Yards	Muzzle	100	200	300	400	500	600	800	1000
Velocity • fps	3150	2930	2710	2510	2320	2130	1954	1630	1356
Energy • Ft-lbs	3085	2660	2290	1960	1670	1415	1188	827	572
Taylor KO Index	17.9	16.6	15.4	14.3	13.2	12.1	11.1	9.3	7.3
Path • Inches	-1.5	+1.3	0.0	-6.0	-17.5	-35.6	-61.3	-142.2	-277.3
Wind Drift • Inches	0.0	0.6	2.6	6.1	11.2	18.2	27.3	53.0	90.6

Norma 140-grain Nosler Partition (17061) (Discontinued in 2005)   G1 Ballistic Coefficient = 0.460

Distance • Yards	Muzzle	100	200	300	400	500	600	800	1000
Velocity • fps	3150	2936	2732	2537	2351	2173	2002	1686	1413
Energy • Ft-lbs	3085	2680	2320	2001	1719	1468	1246	884	621
Taylor KO Index	17.9	16.7	15.5	14.4	13.4	12.3	11.4	9.6	8.0
Path • Inches	-1.5	+1.2	0.0	-5.9	-17.3	-34.9	-59.9	-137.8	-266.3
Wind Drift • Inches	0.0	0.5	2.2	5.2	9.6	15.5	23.2	44.8	76.2

Winchester 140-grain Fail Safe (S7MAGXB)   G1 Ballistic Coefficient = 0.337

Distance • Yards	Muzzle	100	200	300	400	500	600	800	1000
Velocity • fps	3150	2861	2589	2333	2092	1866	1658	1306	1074
Energy • Ft-lbs	3085	2544	2085	1693	1361	1083	855	530	359
Taylor KO Index	17.9	16.3	14.7	13.3	11.9	10.6	9.4	7.4	6.1
Path • Inches	-1.5	+1.4	0.0	-6.6	-19.5	-40.5	-71.7	-176.7	-367.6
Wind Drift • Inches	0.0	0.8	3.5	8.2	15.3	25.3	38.5	77.0	133.4

PMC 140-grain Soft Point Boat Tail (7HA)   G1 Ballistic Coefficient = 0.417

Distance • Yards	Muzzle	100	200	300	400	500	600	800	1000
Velocity • fps	3125	2891	2669	2457	2255	2063	1882	1552	1282
Energy • Ft-lbs	3035	2597	2213	1877	1580	1322	1101	749	511
Taylor KO Index	17.8	16.4	15.2	14.0	12.8	11.7	10.7	8.8	7.3
Path • Inches	-1.5	+1.4	0.0	-6.3	-18.4	-37.2	-64.1	-150.2	-296.5
Wind Drift • Inches	0.0	0.7	2.8	6.5	12.0	19.6	29.5	57.6	98.8

Norma 140-grain Barnes Triple-Shock (17054)   G1 Ballistic Coefficient = 0.477

Distance • Yards	Muzzle	100	200	300	400	500	600	800	1000
Velocity • fps	3117	2912	2716	2529	2350	2178	2012	1706	1439
Energy • Ft-lbs	3021	2637	2294	1988	1717	1474	1259	905	644
Taylor KO Index	17.7	16.5	15.4	14.4	13.3	12.4	11.4	9.7	8.2
Path • Inches	-1.5	+1.3	0.0	-6.0	-17.5	-35.2	-60.3	-138.1	-265.0
Wind Drift • Inches	0.0	0.6	2.4	5.8	10.3	18.7	25.0	48.2	81.8

Federal 140-grain Nosler AccuBond (P7RA2)   G1 Ballistic Coefficient = 0.487

Distance • Yards	Muzzle	100	200	300	400	500	600	800	1000
Velocity • fps	3110	2910	2720	2530	2360	2190	2027	1725	1460
Energy • Ft-lbs	3005	2630	2295	1995	1725	1485	1278	926	663
Taylor KO Index	17.7	16.5	15.4	14.4	13.4	12.4	11.5	9.8	8.3
Path • Inches	-1.5	+1.3	0.0	-6.0	-17.4	-35.2	-60.1	-137.1	-262.1
Wind Drift • Inches	0.0	0.6	2.4	5.5	10.1	16.4	24.5	47.0	79.7

Federal 140-grain Nosler Ballistic Tip (P7RL)   G1 Ballistic Coefficient = 0.487

Distance • Yards	Muzzle	100	200	300	400	500	600	800	1000
Velocity • fps	3100	2900	2710	2530	2350	2180	2019	1718	1454
Energy • Ft-lbs	2985	2615	2280	1985	1715	1480	1268	918	658
Taylor KO Index	17.6	16.5	15.4	14.4	13.3	12.4	11.5	9.8	8.3
Path • Inches	-1.5	+1.3	0.0	-6.1	-17.5	-35.4	-60.5	-138.1	-264.1
Wind Drift • Inches	0.0	0.6	2.4	5.5	10.2	16.5	24.6	47.2	80.1

PMC 140-grain Pointed Soft Point (7A)

G1 Ballistic Coefficient = 0.370

Distance • Yards	Muzzle	100	200	300	400	500	600	800	1000
Velocity • fps	3100	2837	2589	2355	2135	1929	1733	1392	1142
Energy • Ft-lbs	2987	2503	2084	1725	1417	1156	934	602	406
Taylor KO Index	17.6	16.1	14.7	13.4	12.1	11.0	9.8	7.9	6.5
Path • Inches	-1.5	+1.4	0.0	-6.6	-19.5	-40.1	-69.9	-168.4	-342.5
Wind Drift • Inches	0.0	0.7	2.9	6.8	12.6	20.7	31.4	62.0	107.2

Winchester 140-grain Ballistic Silvertip (SBST7A)

G1 Ballistic Coefficient = 0.460

Distance • Yards	Muzzle	100	200	300	400	500	600	800	1000
Velocity • fps	3100	2889	2687	2494	2310	2133	1964	1653	1385
Energy • Ft-lbs	2988	2595	2245	1934	1659	1414	1199	849	597
Taylor KO Index	17.6	16.4	15.2	14.2	13.1	12.1	11.2	9.4	7.9
Path • Inches	-1.5	+1.3	0.0	-6.2	-17.9	-38.1	-62.1	-143.0	-276.6
Wind Drift • Inches	0.0	0.6	2.5	5.9	10.9	17.6	26.4	51.0	86.8

PMC 140-grain XLC—HP (7XLA) (Discontinued in 2005)

G1 Ballistic Coefficient = 0.497

Distance • Yards	Muzzle	100	200	300	400	500	600	800	1000
Velocity • fps	3000	2808	2624	2448	2279	2116	1961	1672	1419
Energy • Ft-lbs	2797	2451	2141	1863	1614	1391	1195	869	626
Taylor KO Index	17.0	15.9	14.9	13.9	12.9	12.0	11.1	9.5	8.1
Path • Inches	-1.5	+1.5	0.0	-6.6	-18.9	-38.0	-64.6	-147.1	-280.7
Wind Drift • Inches	0.0	0.6	2.4	5.7	10.4	16.9	25.2	48.3	81.8

Speer 145-grain Grand Slam (24552) (Discontinued in 2005)

G1 Ballistic Coefficient = 0.327

Distance • Yards	Muzzle	100	200	300	400	500	600	800	1000
Velocity • fps	3100	2805	2529	2269	2025	1798	1589	1246	1038
Energy • Ft-lbs	3094	2533	2060	1658	1321	1041	813	500	347
Taylor KO Index	18.2	16.5	14.9	13.3	11.9	10.6	9.3	7.3	6.1
Path • Inches	-1.5	+1.5	0.0	-6.9	-20.6	-42.8	-75.9	-187.4	-388.8
Wind Drift • Inches	0.0	0.8	3.3	7.8	14.6	24.2	37.0	74.2	127.9

Winchester 150-grain Power-Point Plus (SHV7MMR1)

G1 Ballistic Coefficient = 0.346

Distance • Yards	Muzzle	100	200	300	400	500	600	800	1000
Velocity • fps	3130	2849	2586	2337	2102	1881	1676	1327	1091
Energy • Ft-lbs	3264	2705	2227	1819	1472	1179	936	587	396
Taylor KO Index	19.0	17.3	15.7	14.2	12.8	11.4	10.2	8.1	6.6
Path • Inches	-1.5	+1.4	0.0	-6.6	-19.6	-40.4	-71.4	-174.9	-361.6
Wind Drift • Inches	0.0	0.8	3.4	8.0	15.0	24.7	35.5	74.8	129.5

Norma 150-grain Swift Scirocco (17062)

G1 Ballistic Coefficient = 0.536

Distance • Yards	Muzzle	100	200	300	400	500	600	800	1000
Velocity • fps	3117	2934	2758	2589	2428	2272	2121	1837	1581
Energy • Ft-lbs	3237	2869	2535	2234	1964	1719	1498	1124	833
Taylor KO Index	19.0	17.9	16.8	15.8	14.8	13.8	12.9	11.2	9.6
Path • Inches	-1.5	+1.2	0.0	-5.8	-16.9	-33.8	-57.4	-129.3	-243.1
Wind Drift • Inches	0.0	0.5	1.9	4.4	8.2	13.2	19.6	37.2	62.5

Federal 150-grain Sierra GameKing (P7RD)

G1 Ballistic Coefficient = 0.526

Distance • Yards	Muzzle	100	200	300	400	500	600	800	1000
Velocity • fps	3110	2920	2750	2580	2410	2250	2098	1811	1554
Energy • Ft-lbs	3220	2850	2510	2210	1930	1690	1467	1093	804
Taylor KO Index	18.9	17.8	16.7	15.7	14.7	13.7	12.8	11.0	9.5
Path • Inches	-1.5	+1.3	0.0	-5.9	-17.0	-34.2	-58.2	-131.2	-247.6
Wind Drift • Inches	0.0	0.5	2.2	5.1	9.3	15.0	22.3	42.5	71.6

Remington 150-grain AccuTip Boat Tail (PRA7MMRB)

G1 Ballistic Coefficient = 0.530

Distance • Yards	Muzzle	100	200	300	400	500	600	800	1000
Velocity • fps	3110	2926	2749	2579	2415	2258	2105	1820	1563
Energy • Ft-lbs	3221	2850	2516	2215	1943	1697	1476	1103	814
Taylor KO Index	18.9	17.8	16.7	15.7	14.7	13.7	12.8	11.1	9.5
Path • Inches	-1.5	+1.3	0.0	-5.9	-17.0	-34.1	-58.0	-130.7	-248.3
Wind Drift • Inches	0.0	0.5	2.2	5.0	9.2	14.8	22.1	42.1	70.8

Remington 150-grain Pointed Soft Point Core-Lokt (R7MM2)
G1 Ballistic Coefficient = 0.346

Distance • Yards	Muzzle	100	200	300	400	500	600	800	1000
Velocity • fps	3110	2830	2568	2320	2085	1866	1662	1317	1085
Energy • Ft-lbs	3221	2667	2196	1792	1448	1160	921	578	392
Taylor KO Index	18.9	17.2	15.6	14.1	12.7	11.4	10.1	8.0	6.6
Path • Inches	-1.5	+1.3	0.0	-6.6	-20.2	-43.4	-72.5	-177.6	-367.2
Wind Drift • Inches	0.0	0.8	3.4	8.1	15.1	24.9	37.9	75.5	130.6

Federal 150-grain Hi-Shok Soft Point (7RA)
G1 Ballistic Coefficient = 0.347

Distance • Yards	Muzzle	100	200	300	400	500	600	800	1000
Velocity • fps	3110	2830	2570	2320	2090	1870	1666	1320	1087
Energy • Ft-lbs	3220	2670	2200	1790	1450	1160	924	581	394
Taylor KO Index	18.9	17.2	15.6	14.1	12.7	11.4	10.1	8.0	6.6
Path • Inches	-1.5	+1.4	0.0	-6.7	-19.9	-41.0	-72.4	-177.1	-365.9
Wind Drift • Inches	0.0	0.8	3.4	8.1	15.1	24.8	24.1	46.3	78.3

Winchester 150-grain Power-Point (X7MMR1)
G1 Ballistic Coefficient = 0.373

Distance • Yards	Muzzle	100	200	300	400	500	600	800	1000
Velocity • fps	3090	2831	2587	2356	2136	1929	1735	1396	1147
Energy • Ft-lbs	3100	2670	2229	1848	1520	1239	1003	649	438
Taylor KO Index	18.8	17.2	15.7	14.3	13.0	11.7	10.6	8.5	7.0
Path • Inches	-1.5	+1.4	0.0	-6.6	-19.5	-40.1	-70.1	-168.5	-342.0
Wind Drift • Inches	0.0	0.8	3.2	7.5	13.9	22.9	34.6	68.5	118.2

Federal 150-grain Nosler Ballistic Tip (P7RH)
G1 Ballistic Coefficient = 0.493

Distance • Yards	Muzzle	100	200	300	400	500	600	800	1000
Velocity • fps	3110	2910	2720	2540	2370	2200	2039	1739	1475
Energy • Ft-lbs	3220	2825	2470	2150	1865	1610	1385	1008	725
Taylor KO Index	18.9	17.7	16.6	15.5	14.4	13.4	12.4	10.6	9.0
Path • Inches	-1.5	+1.3	0.0	-6.0	-17.4	-35.0	-59.8	-136.1	-259.6
Wind Drift • Inches	0.0	0.6	2.4	5.4	10.0	16.2	24.1	46.3	78.3

Remington 150-grain Swift Scirocco (PRSC7MMB)
G1 Ballistic Coefficient = 0.534

Distance • Yards	Muzzle	100	200	300	400	500	600	800	1000
Velocity • fps	3110	2927	2751	2582	2419	2262	2111	1827	1571
Energy • Ft-lbs	3437	3044	2689	2369	2080	1819	1584	1186	877
Taylor KO Index	20.2	19.0	17.9	16.8	15.7	14.7	13.7	11.9	10.2
Path • Inches	-1.5	+1.3	0.0	-5.9	-17.0	-34.0	-57.9	-130.2	-244.5
Wind Drift • Inches	0.0	0.5	1.9	4.5	8.2	13.3	19.7	37.6	63.1

Remington 150-grain Nosler Ballistic Tip (PRT7MMC) (Discontinued in 2005)
G1 Ballistic Coefficient = 0.493

Distance • Yards	Muzzle	100	200	300	400	500	600	800	1000
Velocity • fps	3110	2912	2723	2542	2367	2200	2039	1739	1475
Energy • Ft-lbs	3222	2825	2470	2152	1867	1612	1385	1008	725
Taylor KO Index	18.9	17.7	16.6	15.5	14.4	13.4	12.4	10.6	9.0
Path • Inches	-1.5	+1.2	0.0	-5.9	-17.3	-34.8	-59.8	-136.1	-259.6
Wind Drift • Inches	0.0	0.6	2.4	5.4	10.0	16.2	24.1	46.3	78.3

Winchester 150-grain Ballistic Silvertip (SBST7)
G1 Ballistic Coefficient = 0.489

Distance • Yards	Muzzle	100	200	300	400	500	600	800	1000
Velocity • fps	3110	2903	2714	2533	2359	2192	2031	1730	1465
Energy • Ft-lbs	3200	2806	2453	2136	1853	1600	1374	997	715
Taylor KO Index	18.9	17.7	16.5	15.4	14.4	13.3	12.4	10.5	8.9
Path • Inches	-1.5	+1.3	0.0	-6.0	-17.5	-35.1	-60.0	-136.7	-261.2
Wind Drift • Inches	0.0	0.6	2.4	5.5	10.1	16.3	24.4	46.8	79.2

Federal 150-grain Nosler Solid Base BT (P7RS1)
G1 Ballistic Coefficient = 0.459

Distance • Yards	Muzzle	100	200	300	400	500	600	800	1000
Velocity • fps	3100	2890	2690	2500	2310	2130	1962	1650	1383
Energy • Ft-lbs	3200	2780	2405	2075	1775	1515	1282	907	637
Taylor KO Index	18.9	17.6	16.4	15.2	14.1	13.0	11.9	10.0	8.4
Path • Inches	-1.5	+1.3	0.0	-6.2	-17.8	-36.2	-62.2	-143.2	-277.1
Wind Drift • Inches	0.0	0.6	2.5	5.9	10.9	17.7	26.5	51.1	87.1

Hornady 154-grain InterBond (80629)

G1 Ballistic Coefficient = 0.530

Distance • Yards	Muzzle	100	200	300	400	500	600	800	1000
Velocity • fps	3035	2854	2680	2512	2351	2196	2046	1766	1515
Energy • Ft-lbs	3149	2784	2455	2158	1890	1648	1432	1066	785
Taylor KO Index	19.0	17.8	16.7	15.7	14.7	13.7	12.8	11.0	9.5
Path • Inches	-1.5	+1.4	0.0	-6.2	-18.0	-36.0	-61.3	-138.2	-260.6
Wind Drift • Inches	0.0	0.6	2.2	5.2	9.5	15.4	22.9	43.7	73.5

Hornady 154-grain SST (8062)

G1 Ballistic Coefficient = 0.525

Distance • Yards	Muzzle	100	200	300	400	500	600	800	1000
Velocity • fps	3035	2852	2677	2508	2345	2189	2037	1755	1504
Energy • Ft-lbs	3149	2781	2449	2150	1880	1638	1420	1054	774
Taylor KO Index	19.0	17.8	16.7	15.7	14.7	13.7	12.7	11.0	9.4
Path • Inches	-1.5	+1.4	0.0	-6.2	-18.0	-36.1	-61.5	-138.9	-262.4
Wind Drift • Inches	0.0	0.6	2.3	5.2	9.6	15.5	23.2	44.2	74.4

Hornady 154-grain Soft Point (8060)

G1 Ballistic Coefficient = 0.434

Distance • Yards	Muzzle	100	200	300	400	500	600	800	1000
Velocity • fps	3035	2814	2604	2404	2212	2029	1857	1542	1283
Energy • Ft-lbs	3151	2708	2319	1977	1674	1408	1179	813	563
Taylor KO Index	19.0	17.6	16.3	15.0	13.8	12.7	11.6	9.6	8.0
Path • Inches	-1.5	+1.3	0.0	-6.7	-19.3	-39.3	-67.1	-156.3	-306.2
Wind Drift • Inches	0.0	0.7	2.8	6.5	12.0	19.5	29.3	57.0	97.4

Norma 156-grain Oryx (17047)

G1 Ballistic Coefficient = 0.330

Distance • Yards	Muzzle	100	200	300	400	500	600	800	1000
Velocity • fps	2953	2670	2404	2153	1920	1702	1505	1191	1010
Energy • Ft-lbs	3021	2470	2002	1607	1277	1004	785	492	354
Taylor KO Index	18.7	16.9	15.2	13.6	12.2	10.8	9.5	7.5	6.4
Path • Inches	-1.5	+1.7	0.0	-7.7	-23.0	-47.7	-84.7	-210.8	-437.6
Wind Drift • Inches	0.0	0.7	3.6	9.0	17.0	28.4	43.5	87.0	148.3

Federal 160-grain Nosler AccuBond (P7RA1)

G1 Ballistic Coefficient = 0.533

Distance Yards	Muzzle	100	200	300	400	500	600	800	1000
Velocity • fps	2950	2770	2600	2440	2280	2130	1983	1711	1469
Energy • Ft-lbs	3090	2730	2405	2110	1845	1610	1398	1040	766
Taylor KO Index	19.1	18.0	16.9	15.8	14.8	13.8	12.9	11.1	9.5
Path • Inches	-1.5	+1.5	0.0	-6.6	-19.1	-38.4	-65.2	-147.0	-277.3
Wind Drift • Inches	0.0	0.6	2.3	5.4	9.9	15.9	23.7	45.3	76.2

Federal 160-grain Nosler Partition (P7RF)

G1 Ballistic Coefficient = 0.507

Distance • Yards	Muzzle	100	200	300	400	500	600	800	1000
Velocity • fps	2950	2770	2590	2420	2250	2090	1939	1657	1412
Energy • Ft-lbs	3090	2715	2375	2075	1800	1555	1336	976	709
Taylor KO Index	19.1	18.0	16.8	15.7	14.6	13.6	12.6	10.8	9.2
Path • Inches	-1.5	+1.5	0.0	-6.7	-19.4	-39.0	-66.6	-151.0	-286.6
Wind Drift • Inches	0.0	0.6	2.4	5.7	10.4	16.9	25.2	48.4	81.7

Remington 160-grain Nosler Partition (PRP7MMA) (Discontinued in 2005)

G1 Ballistic Coefficient = 0.475

Distance • Yards	Muzzle	100	200	300	400	500	600	800	1000
Velocity • fps	2950	2752	2563	2381	2207	2040	1880	1587	1339
Energy • Ft-lbs	3091	2690	2333	2014	1730	1478	1255	895	637
Taylor KO Index	19.1	17.7	16.6	15.5	14.3	13.2	12.2	10.3	8.7
Path • Inches	-1.5	+1.6	0.0	-6.8	-19.8	-40.0	-68.5	-157.0	-301.2
Wind Drift • Inches	0.0	0.6	2.6	6.1	11.2	18.2	27.3	52.7	89.5

Remington 160-grain Core-Lokt Ultra Bonded (PRC7MMRC)

G1 Ballistic Coefficient = 0.415

Distance • Yards	Muzzle	100	200	300	400	500	600	800	1000
Velocity • fps	2950	2724	2510	2305	2109	1924	1749	1438	1196
Energy • Ft-lbs	3090	2730	2405	2110	1845	1610	1398	1040	766
Taylor KO Index	19.1	17.7	16.3	15.0	13.7	12.5	11.4	9.3	7.8
Path • Inches	-1.5	+1.6	0.0	-7.1	-20.8	-42.4	-73.4	-172.6	-342.0
Wind Drift • Inches	0.0	0.7	3.0	7.1	13.1	21.5	32.4	63.2	108.3

Winchester 160-grain AccuBond CT (S7MMCT)

G1 Ballistic Coefficient = 0.511

Distance • Yards	Muzzle	100	200	300	400	500	600	800	1000
Velocity • fps	2950	2766	2590	2420	2257	2099	1947	1666	1421
Energy • Ft-lbs	3091	2718	2382	2080	1809	1566	1347	987	718
Taylor KO Index	19.1	18.0	16.8	15.7	14.7	13.6	12.6	10.8	9.2
Path • Inches	-1.5	+1.5	0.0	-6.7	-19.4	-38.9	-66.3	-150.4	-285.9
Wind Drift • Inches	0.0	0.6	2.4	5.6	10.3	16.7	25.0	47.8	80.7

Winchester 160-grain Partition Gold (SPG7MAG)

G1 Ballistic Coefficient = 0.455

Distance • Yards	Muzzle	100	200	300	400	500	600	800	1000
Velocity • fps	2950	2743	2546	2357	2176	2003	1839	1540	1292
Energy • Ft-lbs	3093	2674	2303	1974	1682	1425	1202	843	593
Taylor KO Index	19.1	17.8	16.5	15.3	14.1	13.0	11.9	10.0	8.4
Path • Inches	-1.5	+1.6	0.0	-6.9	-20.1	-40.7	-70.0	-161.4	-312.0
Wind Drift • Inches	0.0	0.7	2.7	6.4	11.8	19.2	28.8	55.8	95.0

Federal 160-grain Trophy Bonded Bear Claw (P7RT2)

G1 Ballistic Coefficient = 0.408

Distance • Yards	Muzzle	100	200	300	400	500	600	800	1000
Velocity • fps	2940	2710	2500	2290	2100	1900	1724	1413	1175
Energy • Ft-lbs	3070	2615	2215	1870	1565	1300	1056	709	491
Taylor KO Index	19.1	17.6	16.2	14.9	13.6	12.3	11.2	9.2	7.6
Path • Inches	-1.5	+1.6	0.0	-7.2	-21.0	-42.8	-74.6	-175.6	-346.9
Wind Drift • Inches	0.0	0.7	2.8	6.5	12.1	19.8	29.9	58.6	100.4

Federal 160-grain Speer Hot-Cor (7RJS)

G1 Ballistic Coefficient = 0.437

Distance • Yards	Muzzle	100	200	300	400	500	600	800	1000
Velocity • fps	2940	2730	2520	2320	2140	1960	1792	1489	1244
Energy • Ft-lbs	3070	2640	2260	1920	1620	1360	1142	788	550
Taylor KO Index	19.1	17.7	16.4	15.1	13.9	12.7	11.6	9.7	8.1
Path • Inches	-1.5	+1.6	0.0	-7.1	-20.6	-42.2	-71.9	-167.1	-325.6
Wind Drift • Inches	0.0	0.7	2.9	6.7	12.4	20.3	30.5	59.3	101.2

Winchester 160-grain Fail Safe (S7MAGX)

G1 Ballistic Coefficient = 0.385

Distance • Yards	Muzzle	100	200	300	400	500	600	800	1000
Velocity • fps	2920	2678	2449	2331	2025	1830	1649	1337	1115
Energy • Ft-lbs	3030	2549	2131	1769	1457	1190	967	635	442
Taylor KO Index	19.0	17.4	15.9	15.1	13.1	11.9	10.7	8.7	7.2
Path • Inches	-1.5	+1.7	0.0	-7.5	-22.0	-44.9	-78.4	-186.7	-373.4
Wind Drift • Inches	0.0	0.8	3.3	7.8	14.6	23.9	36.2	71.4	122.2

PMC 160-grain Soft Point Boat Tail (7HB)

G1 Ballistic Coefficient = 0.456

Distance • Yards	Muzzle	100	200	300	400	500	600	800	1000
Velocity • fps	2900	2696	2501	2314	2135	1965	1803	1510	1269
Energy • Ft-lbs	2987	2582	2222	1903	1620	1371	1156	810	572
Taylor KO Index	18.8	17.5	16.2	15.0	13.9	12.8	11.7	9.8	8.2
Path • Inches	-1.5	+1.7	0.0	-7.2	-21.0	-42.3	-72.9	-167.6	-324.2
Wind Drift • Inches	0.0	0.7	2.8	6.5	12.1	19.6	29.5	57.1	97.2

PMC 160-grain Pointed Soft Point (7B)

G1 Ballistic Coefficient = 0.409

Distance • Yards	Muzzle	100	200	300	400	500	600	800	1000
Velocity • fps	2900	2671	2455	2249	2055	1871	1698	1392	1162
Energy • Ft-lbs	2988	2535	2140	1797	1500	1244	1024	68*9	480
Taylor KO Index	18.8	17.3	15.9	14.6	13.3	12.1	11.0	9.0	7.5
Path • Inches	-1.5	+1.7	0.0	-7.5	-21.6	-44.5	-76.9	-181.7	-361.3
Wind Drift • Inches	0.0	0.7	2.8	6.6	12.3	20.2	30.4	59.6	101.9

Remington 160-grain A-Frame Pointed Soft Point (RS7MMA)

G1 Ballistic Coefficient = 0.383

Distance • Yards	Muzzle	100	200	300	400	500	600	800	1000
Velocity • fps	2900	2639	2484	2212	2006	1812	1630	1321	1104
Energy • Ft-lbs	2785	2474	2192	1935	1430	1166	944	620	433
Taylor KO Index	18.8	17.1	16.1	14.4	13.0	11.8	10.6	8.6	7.2
Path • Inches	-1.5	+1.7	0.0	-7.6	-22.4	-44.7	-79.9	-190.6	-381.6
Wind Drift • Inches	0.0	0.8	3.4	8.0	14.8	24.3	36.9	72.6	124.2

Federal 160-grain Barnes Triple Shock X-Bullet (P7RN)

G1 Ballistic Coefficient = 0.463

Distance • Yards	Muzzle	100	200	300	400	500	600	800	1000
Velocity • fps	2940	2740	2540	2360	2180	2010	1849	1553	1306
Energy • Ft-lbs	3070	2660	2300	1975	1690	1435	1214	857	606
Taylor KO Index	19.6	17.8	16.5	15.3	14.2	13.0	12.0	10.1	8.5
Path • Inches	-1.5	+1.6	0.0	-6.9	-20.2	-40.7	-69.9	-161.1	-311.8
Wind Drift • Inches	0.0	0.6	2.7	6.3	11.6	18.9	28.3	54.8	93.1

Federal 160-grain XLC Coated Barnes-X (P7RK) (Discontinued in 2005)

G1 Ballistic Coefficient = 0.512

Distance • Yards	Muzzle	100	200	300	400	500	600	800	1000
Velocity • fps	2940	2760	2580	2410	2240	2090	1940	1661	1417
Energy • Ft-lbs	3070	2695	2360	2060	1785	1545	1337	980	714
Taylor KO Index	19.1	17.9	16.7	15.6	14.5	13.6	12.6	10.8	9.2
Path • Inches	-1.5	+1.5	0.0	-6.8	-19.6	-39.3	-66.8	-151.4	-286.8
Wind Drift • Inches	0.0	0.5	2.2	5.1	9.3	15.1	22.5	43.2	72.9

PMC 160-grain XLC—HP (7XLB)

G1 Ballistic Coefficient = 0.568

Distance • Yards	Muzzle	100	200	300	400	500	600	800	1000
Velocity • fps	2800	2639	2484	2334	2189	2049	1915	1665	1443
Energy • Ft-lbs	2785	2478	2192	1935	1703	1492	1304	985	740
Taylor KO Index	18.2	17.1	16.1	15.2	14.2	13.3	12.4	10.8	9.4
Path • Inches	-1.5	+1.8	0.0	-7.4	-21.2	-42.3	-71.5	-160.1	-299.1
Wind Drift • Inches	0.0	0.6	2.3	5.4	9.9	16.0	23.8	45.2	75.7

Hornady 162-grain SST (80634)

G1 Ballistic Coefficient = 0.515

Distance • Yards	Muzzle	100	200	300	400	500	600	800	1000
Velocity • fps	2940	2769	2604	2446	2292	2145	2002	1735	1497
Energy • Ft-lbs	3109	2758	2439	2151	1890	1654	1442	1084	807
Taylor KO Index	19.3	18.2	17.1	16.1	15.1	14.1	13.2	11.4	9.8
Path • Inches	-1.5	+1.5	0.0	-6.6	-19.1	-38.2	-64.9	-145.6	-273.6
Wind Drift • Inches	0.0	0.5	2.2	5.2	9.5	15.4	22.9	39.3	66.0

Hornady 162-grain Boat Tail Soft Point (8063)

G1 Ballistic Coefficient = 0.515

Distance • Yards	Muzzle	100	200	300	400	500	600	800	1000
Velocity • fps	2940	2757	2582	2413	2251	2094	1945	1667	1424
Energy • Ft-lbs	3110	2735	2399	2095	1823	1578	1361	1000	729
Taylor KO Index	19.3	18.1	17.0	15.9	14.8	13.8	12.8	11.0	9.4
Path • Inches	-1.5	+1.5	0.0	-6.7	-19.7	-39.3	-66.7	-150.9	-285.6
Wind Drift • Inches	0.0	0.6	2.4	5.6	10.3	16.7	24.9	47.6	80.3

Federal 165-grain Sierra GameKing BTSP (P7RE)

G1 Ballistic Coefficient = 0.616

Distance • Yards	Muzzle	100	200	300	400	500	600	800	1000
Velocity • fps	2950	2800	2650	2510	2370	2230	2100	1854	1627
Energy • Ft-lbs	3190	2865	2570	2300	2050	1825	1617	1259	970
Taylor KO Index	19.7	18.7	17.7	16.8	15.9	14.9	14.1	12.4	10.9
Path • Inches	-1.5	+1.5	0.0	-6.4	-18.4	-36.6	-61.8	-136.9	-252.7
Wind Drift • Inches	0.0	0.5	2.00	4.6	8.4	13.5	20.2	37.7	62.7

Norma 170-grain Oryx SP (17023) (Discontinued in 2003)

G1 Ballistic Coefficient = 0.321

Distance • Yards	Muzzle	100	200	300	400	500	600	800	1000
Velocity • fps	2887	2601	2333	2080	1844	1627	1433	1139	979
Energy • Ft-lbs	3147	2555	2055	1634	1284	999	776	490	362
Taylor KO Index	19.9	17.9	16.1	14.3	12.7	11.2	9.9	7.9	6.8
Path • Inches	-1.5	+1.8	0.0	-8.2	-24.6	-51.2	-91.0	-226.3	-468.5
Wind Drift • Inches	0.0	1.0	4.1	9.8	18.5	30.7	47.0	93.7	157.9

Norma 170-grain Plastic point (17027)

G1 Ballistic Coefficient = 0.378

Distance • Yards	Muzzle	100	200	300	400	500	600	800	1000
Velocity • fps	2953	2705	2470	2247	2037	1839	1654	1335	1111
Energy • Ft-lbs	3293	2763	2304	1907	1567	1276	1032	673	466
Taylor KO Index	20.4	18.7	17.0	15.5	14.0	12.7	11.4	9.2	7.7
Path • Inches	-1.5	+1.6	0.0	-7.3	-21.6	-44.2	-77.3	-185.6	-375.6
Wind Drift • Inches	0.0	0.7	3.0	7.1	13.2	21.6	32.8	64.8	111.1

Norma 170-grain Vulcan HP (17024)

G1 Ballistic Coefficient = 0.353

Distance • Yards	Muzzle	100	200	300	400	500	600	800	1000
Velocity • fps	2953	2688	2438	2201	1977	1769	1577	1258	1055
Energy • Ft-lbs	3293	2728	2244	1830	1476	1181	938	597	420
Taylor KO Index	20.4	18.5	16.8	15.2	13.6	12.2	10.9	8.7	7.3
Path • Inches	-1.5	+1.6	0.0	-7.5	-22.3	-46.0	-81.0	-197.9	-406.5
Wind Drift • Inches	0.0	0.8	3.2	7.7	14.4	23.7	36.1	71.6	122.6

Federal 175-grain Hi-Shok Soft Point (7RB)

G1 Ballistic Coefficient = 0.428

Distance • Yards	Muzzle	100	200	300	400	500	600	800	1000
Velocity • fps	2860	2650	2440	2240	2060	1880	1713	1417	1187
Energy • Ft-lbs	3180	2720	2310	1960	1640	1370	1141	780	548
Taylor KO Index	20.3	18.8	17.3	15.9	14.6	13.3	12.2	10.1	8.4
Path • Inches	-1.5	+1.7	0.0	-7.6	-22.1	-44.9	-77.5	-180.8	-354.1
Wind Drift • Inches	0.0	0.7	3.1	7.2	13.3	21.7	32.6	63.6	108.4

Federal 175-grain Trophy Bonded Bear Claw (P7RT1)

G1 Ballistic Coefficient = 0.418

Distance • Yards	Muzzle	100	200	300	400	500	600	800	1000
Velocity • fps	2860	2640	2430	2230	2040	1860	1690	1392	1166
Energy • Ft-lbs	3180	2710	2295	1930	1615	1340	1111	753	528
Taylor KO Index	20.3	18.7	17.3	15.8	14.5	13.2	12.0	9.9	8.3
Path • Inches	-1.5	+1.7	0.0	-7.7	-22.4	-45.2	-78.5	-184.6	-365.5
Wind Drift • Inches	0.0	0.8	3.1	7.4	13.6	22.3	33.6	65.6	112.0

Hornady 175-grain Soft Point (8065)

G1 Ballistic Coefficient = 0.428

Distance • Yards	Muzzle	100	200	300	400	500	600	800	1000
Velocity • fps	2860	2650	2440	2240	2060	1880	1713	1417	1187
Energy • Ft-lbs	3180	2720	2310	1960	1645	1374	1141	780	548
Taylor KO Index	20.3	18.8	17.3	15.9	14.6	13.3	12.2	10.1	8.4
Path • Inches	-1.5	+1.7	0.0	-7.6	-22.1	-44.8	-77.5	-180.8	-354.1
Wind Drift • Inches	0.0	0.7	3.1	7.2	13.3	21.7	32.6	63.6	108.4

PMC 175-grain Pointed Soft Point (7C)

G1 Ballistic Coefficient = 0.428

Distance • Yards	Muzzle	100	200	300	400	500	600	800	1000
Velocity • fps	2860	2645	2442	2244	2057	1879	1713	1417	1187
Energy • Ft-lbs	3178	2718	2313	1956	1644	1372	1141	780	548
Taylor KO Index	20.3	18.8	17.3	15.9	14.6	13.3	12.2	10.1	8.4
Path • Inches	-1.5	+2.0	0.0	-7.9	22.7	-45.8	-77.5	-180.8	-354.1
Wind Drift • Inches	0.0	0.7	3.1	7.2	13.3	21.7	32.6	63.6	108.4

Remington 175-grain Pointed Soft Point Core-Lokt (R7MM3)

G1 Ballistic Coefficient = 0.428

Distance • Yards	Muzzle	100	200	300	400	500	600	800	1000
Velocity • fps	2860	2645	2442	2244	2057	1879	1713	1417	1187
Energy • Ft-lbs	3178	2718	2313	1956	1644	1372	1141	780	548
Taylor KO Index	20.3	18.8	17.3	15.9	14.6	13.3	12.2	10.1	8.4
Path • Inches	-1.5	+2.0	0.0	-7.9	22.7	-45.8	-77.5	-180.8	-354.1
Wind Drift • Inches	0.0	0.7	3.1	7.2	13.3	21.7	32.6	63.6	108.4

Winchester 175-grain Power-Point (X7MMR2)

G1 Ballistic Coefficient = 0.428

Distance • Yards	Muzzle	100	200	300	400	500	600	800	1000
Velocity • fps	2860	2645	2442	2244	2057	1879	1713	1417	1187
Energy • Ft-lbs	3178	2718	2313	1956	1644	1372	1141	780	548
Taylor KO Index	20.3	18.8	17.3	15.9	14.6	13.3	12.2	10.1	8.4
Path • Inches	-1.5	+2.0	0.0	-7.9	22.7	-45.8	-77.5	-180.8	-354.1
Wind Drift • Inches	0.0	0.7	3.1	7.2	13.3	21.7	32.6	63.6	108.4

Hirtenberger Nosler Partition (82200367)

G1 Ballistic Coefficient = 0.506

Distance • Yards	Muzzle	100	200	300	400	500	600	800	1000
Velocity • fps	2854	2672	2497	2329	2167	2011	1863	1589	1355
Energy • Ft-lbs	3166	2775	2423	2108	1825	1573	1349	982	713
Taylor KO Index	20.3	19.0	17.7	16.5	15.4	14.3	13.2	11.3	9.6
Path • Inches	-1.5	+1.7	0.0	-7.3	-21.0	-42.1	-71.8	-163.3	-311.3
Wind Drift • Inches	0.0	0.6	2.3	5.4	9.9	16.0	23.9	45.8	77.4

Speer 175-grain Grand Slam (24503)

G1 Ballistic Coefficient = 0.463

Distance • Yards	Muzzle	100	200	300	400	500	600	800	1000
Velocity • fps	2850	2653	2463	2282	2105	1937	1780	1494	1260
Energy • Ft-lbs	3156	2734	2358	2023	1723	1458	1231	868	617
Taylor KO Index	20.2	18.8	17.5	16.2	14.9	13.8	12.6	10.6	8.9
Path • Inches	-1.5	+1.7	0.0	-7.5	-21.7	-43.6	-75.0	-172.8	-333.4
Wind Drift • Inches	0.0	0.7	2.8	6.6	12.3	20.0	29.7	57.5	97.6

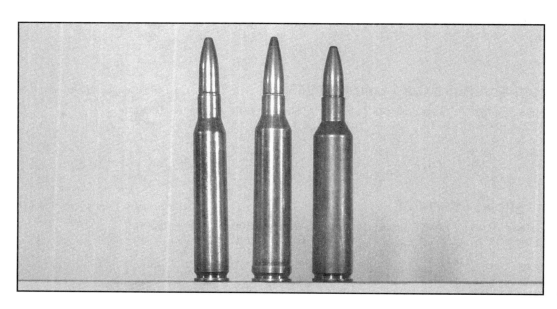

(Left to right) .280 Remington, 7mm Remington Magnum, 7mm Dakota.

7mm Winchester Short Magnum (WSM)

When Winchester introduced the .300 WSM, almost everyone present at that introduction predicted that a .270 WSM and a 7mm WSM would soon follow. *Guns & Ammo* magazine printed calculated performance figures for a series of wildcats based on the .300 WSM in June of 2001. The 7mm as a factory cartridge came into being in 2002. The short magnums as a group give improved performance when compared with cartridges based on the .308 or the .30-06 cases, but they can't quite equal the full-length magnum performances except in a few rare instances.

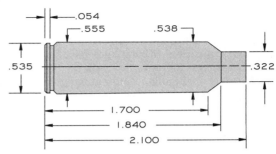

Relative Recoil Factor = 2.06

Specifications

Controlling Agency for Standardization of this Ammunition: SAAMI

Bullet Weight Grains	Velocity fps	Maximum Average Pressure	
		Copper Crusher	Transducer
N/A	N/A	—	65,000 psi

Standard barrel for velocity testing: 24 inches long—1 turn in 10-inch twist

Availability

Winchester 140-grain AccuBond CT (S7MMWSMCTA)

G1 Ballistic Coefficient = 0.461

Distance • Yards	Muzzle	100	200	300	400	500	600	800	1000
Velocity • fps	3225	3008	2801	2604	2415	2233	2061	1740	1459
Energy • Ft-lbs	3233	2812	2439	2107	1812	1550	1321	941	662
Taylor KO Index	18.3	17.1	15.9	14.8	13.7	12.7	11.7	9.9	8.3
Path • Inches	-1.5	+1.2	0.0	-5.6	-16.4	-33.1	-56.7	-130.4	-251.4
Wind Drift • Inches	0.0	0.6	2.4	5.6	10.3	16.6	24.8	47.9	81.5

Winchester 140-grain BST (SBST7MMS)

G1 Ballistic Coefficient = 0.461

Distance • Yards	Muzzle	100	200	300	400	500	600	800	1000
Velocity • fps	3225	3008	2801	2604	2415	2233	2061	1740	1459
Energy • Ft-lbs	3233	2812	2439	2107	1812	1550	1321	941	662
Taylor KO Index	18.3	17.1	15.9	14.8	13.7	12.7	11.7	9.9	8.3
Path • Inches	-1.5	+1.2	0.0	-5.6	-16.4	-33.1	-56.7	-130.4	-251.4
Wind Drift • Inches	0.0	0.6	2.4	5.6	10.3	16.6	24.8	47.9	81.5

Winchester 150-grain PowerPoint (X7MMWSM)

G1 Ballistic Coefficient = 0.346

Distance • Yards	Muzzle	100	200	300	400	500	600	800	1000
Velocity • fps	3225	2915	2648	2396	2157	1933	1723	1364	1112
Energy • Ft-lbs	3410	2830	2335	1911	1550	1245	989	620	412
Taylor KO Index	19.5	17.7	16.1	14.6	13.1	11.8	10.5	8.3	6.8
Path • Inches	-1.5	+1.3	0.0	-6.3	-18.6	-38.5	-67.8	-165.8	-342.9
Wind Drift • Inches	0.0	0.8	3.3	7.8	14.5	23.9	36.3	72.4	125.7

Winchester 160-grain AccuBond CT (S7MMWSMCT)

G1 Ballistic Coefficient = 0.229

Distance • Yards	Muzzle	100	200	300	400	500	600	800	1000
Velocity • fps	3050	2862	2682	2509	2342	2182	2029	1741	1486
Energy • Ft-lbs	3306	2911	2556	2237	1950	1692	1462	1077	785
Taylor KO Index	19.8	18.6	17.4	16.3	15.2	14.2	13.2	11.3	9.6
Path • Inches	-1.5	+1.4	0.0	-6.2	-17.9	-36.0	-61.4	-139.1	-263.7
Wind Drift • Inches	0.0	0.6	2.3	5.4	9.8	15.8	23.6	45.2	76.3

Winchester 160-grain Fail Safe (S7MMWSMX)

G1 Ballistic Coefficient = 0.385

Distance • Yards	Muzzle	100	200	300	400	500	600	800	1000
Velocity • fps	3225	2744	2512	2342	2081	1883	1699	1376	1140
Energy • Ft-lbs	3176	2675	2241	1864	1538	1259	1026	673	462
Taylor KO Index	19.4	17.8	16.3	15.2	13.5	12.2	11.0	8.9	7.4
Path • Inches	-1.5	+1.6	0.0	-7.1	-20.8	-42.6	-74.2	-177.4	-357.6
Wind Drift • Inches	0.0	0.8	3.2	7.6	14.1	23.1	34.9	68.8	118.2

7mm Remington Short Action Ultra Magnum

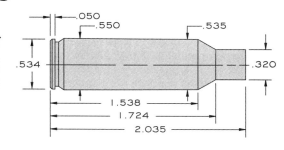

The flavor of the month at the 2002 SHOT Show was the announcement of a whole collection of cartridges based on short, fat cases. For the most part, these cartridges are designed with an overall length the same as the .308 and its necked-down versions. Remington decided that they would not be upstaged, so they introduced both this cartridge and a longer version.

Relative Recoil Factor = 2.07

Specifications

Controlling Agency for Standardization of this Ammunition: SAAMI

Bullet Weight Grains	Velocity fps	Maximum Average Pressure	
		Copper Crusher	Transducer
—	—	—	65,000 psi

Standard barrel for velocity testing: 24 inches long—1 turn in N/S inch twist

Availability

Remington 140-grain Core-Lokt Ultra Bonded (PR7SM1)
G1 Ballistic Coefficient = 0.409

Distance • Yards	Muzzle	100	200	300	400	500	600	800	1000
Velocity • fps	3175	2934	2707	2490	2283	2086	1898	1560	1283
Energy • Ft-lbs	3133	2676	2277	1927	1620	1353	1120	756	512
Taylor KO Index	18.0	16.7	15.4	14.1	13.0	11.8	10.8	8.9	7.3
Path • Inches	-1.5	+1.5	0.0	-6.8	-19.8	-40.0	-62.4	-146.8	-290.9
Wind Drift • Inches	0.0	0.6	2.5	5.8	10.8	17.6	26.6	51.9	89.4

Remington 150-grain Core-Lokt Pointed Soft Point (PR7SM2)
G1 Ballistic Coefficient = 0.346

Distance • Yards	Muzzle	100	200	300	400	500	600	800	1000
Velocity • fps	3110	2828	2583	2313	2077	1856	1652	1307	1078
Energy • Ft-lbs	3221	2663	2188	1782	1437	1147	909	569	387
Taylor KO Index	19.9	17.2	15.7	14.1	12.6	11.3	10.1	8.0	6.6
Path • Inches	-1.5	+1.4	0.0	-6.7	-20.0	-41.4	-73.0	-179.1	-371.0
Wind Drift • Inches	0.0	0.8	3.1	7.4	13.7	22.7	34.5	68.8	119.0

Remington 160-grain Nosler Partition (PR7SM3) (Discontinued in 2005)
G1 Ballistic Coefficient = 0.475

Distance • Yards	Muzzle	100	200	300	400	500	600	800	1000
Velocity • fps	2960	2762	2572	2390	2215	2048	1888	1595	1345
Energy • Ft-lbs	3112	2708	2350	2029	1743	1490	1267	904	643
Taylor KO Index	19.2	17.9	16.7	15.5	14.4	13.3	12.3	10.4	8.7
Path • Inches	-1.5	+1.5	0.0	-6.8	-19.8	-39.7	-68.0	-156.0	-300.4
Wind Drift • Inches	0.0	0.6	2.4	5.5	10.1	16.3	24.4	47.1	80.0

Remington 160-grain Core-Lokt Ultra Bonded (PR7SM4)
G1 Ballistic Coefficient = 0.414

Distance • Yards	Muzzle	100	200	300	400	500	600	800	1000
Velocity • fps	2960	2733	2518	2313	2117	1929	1753	1441	1198
Energy • Ft-lbs	3112	2654	2252	1900	1592	1322	1093	738	510
Taylor KO Index	19.2	17.7	16.3	15.0	13.7	12.5	11.4	9.4	7.8
Path • Inches	-1.5	+1.6	0.0	-7.1	-20.7	-42.9	-72.9	-171.5	-340.0
Wind Drift • Inches	0.0	0.7	3.0	7.1	13.1	21.4	32.3	68.1	108.1

7mm Remington Ultra Magnum

Remington introduced the 7mm Ultra Magnum in 2001. This cartridge should not be confused with their 7mm Short Action Ultra Magnum. As you can see from the drawings, it is a larger and more potent family member. For a given bullet weight, this larger cartridge case can produce over 200 fps more velocity. If you own one of these guns, you will have to be careful which ammo you ask for at the gun store.

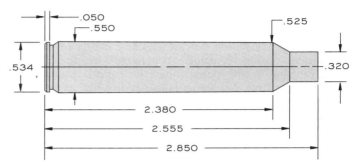

Relative Recoil Factor = 2.13

Specifications

Controlling Agency for Standardization of this Ammunition: SAAMI

Bullet Weight Grains	Velocity fps	Maximum Average Pressure	
		Copper Crusher	Transducer
N/A	N/A	—	65,000 psi

Standard barrel for velocity testing: 24 inches long—1 turn in N/S inch twist

Availability

Remington 140-grain Nosler Parttition (PR7UM2) (Discontinued in 2004)   G1 Ballistic Coefficient = 0.434

Distance • Yards	Muzzle	100	200	300	400	500	600	800	1000
Velocity • fps	3425	3184	2956	2740	2534	2336	2147	1798	1492
Energy • Ft-lbs	3646	3151	2716	2333	1995	1697	1434	1005	692
Taylor KO Index	19.5	18.1	16.8	15.6	14.4	13.3	12.2	10.2	8.5
Path • Inches	-1.5	+1.0	0.0	-5.0	-14.5	-29.6	-51.0	-118.0	-229.7
Wind Drift • Inches	0.0	0.5	2.1	5.0	9.1	14.8	22.1	42.8	73.1

Remington 140-grain Core-Lokt Ultra Bonded (PR7UM1)   G1 Ballistic Coefficient = 0.390

Distance • Yards	Muzzle	100	200	300	400	500	600	800	1000
Velocity • fps	3425	3158	2907	2669	2444	2229	2025	1653	1344
Energy • Ft-lbs	3646	3099	2626	2214	1856	1545	1275	850	562
Taylor KO Index	19.5	17.9	16.5	15.2	13.9	12.7	11.5	9.4	7.6
Path • Inches	-1.5	+1.0	0.0	-5.1	-15.1	-31.0	-53.9	-127.4	-254.3
Wind Drift • Inches	0.0	0.6	2.7	6.2	11.5	18.7	28.1	55.1	95.2

Remington 160-grain Nosler Partition (PR7UM3) (Discontinued in 2004)   G1 Ballistic Coefficient = 0.475

Distance • Yards	Muzzle	100	200	300	400	500	600	800	1000
Velocity • fps	3200	2991	2791	2600	2417	2241	2072	1759	1482
Energy • Ft-lbs	3637	3177	2767	2401	2075	1784	1526	1099	781
Taylor KO Index	20.8	19.4	18.1	16.9	15.7	14.5	13.5	11.4	9.6
Path • Inches	-1.5	+1.2	0.0	-5.7	-16.5	-33.2	-57.0	-130.3	-249.9
Wind Drift • Inches	0.0	0.5	2.1	4.9	9.0	14.6	21.8	41.9	71.1

7mm Weatherby Magnum

This cartridge was part of the early family of Weatherby magnums. The case is considerably shorter than the full-length magnums (2.549 inches vs. 2.850) but slightly longer than the 7mm Remington Magnum (2.500 inches). The 7mm Weatherby is loaded to a higher pressure than the 7mm Remington Magnum. The combination of greater volume and higher pressure gives this cartridge about another 150–200 fps velocity, but it's a push when compared with the 7mm Ultra Magnum. Using a 26-inch barrel for data collection doesn't hurt either.

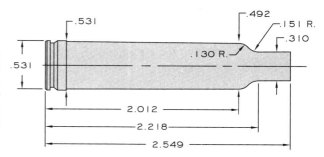

Relative Recoil Factor = 2.20

Specifications

Controlling Agency for Standardization of this Ammunition: CIP

Bullet Weight Grains	Velocity fps	Maximum Average Pressure	
		Copper Crusher	Transducer
N/S	N/S	3,800 bar	4,370 bar

Standard barrel for velocity testing: 26 inches long—1 turn in 10-inch twist

Availability

Weatherby 139-grain Soft Point (H 7mm 139 SP)
G1 Ballistic Coefficient = 0.392

Distance • Yards	Muzzle	100	200	300	400	500	600	800	1000
Velocity • fps	3340	3079	2834	2601	2380	2170	1970	1608	1310
Energy • Ft-lbs	3443	2926	2478	2088	1748	1453	1198	798	530
Taylor KO Index	18.8	17.4	16.0	14.7	13.4	12.2	11.1	9.1	7.4
Path • Inches	-1.5	+0.8	0.0	-5.1	-16.0	-32.8	-56.9	-134.2	-266.0
Wind Drift • Inches	0.0	0.7	2.7	6.4	11.8	19.2	29.0	56.7	98.1

Weatherby 140-grain Nosler Partition (N 7mm 140 PT)
G1 Ballistic Coefficient = 0.434

Distance • Yards	Muzzle	100	200	300	400	500	600	800	1000
Velocity • fps	3303	3069	2847	2636	2434	2241	2057	1717	1424
Energy • Ft-lbs	3391	2927	2519	2159	1841	1562	1315	917	631
Taylor KO Index	18.8	17.4	16.2	15.0	13.8	12.7	11.7	9.8	8.1
Path • Inches	-1.5	+0.8	0.0	-5.0	-15.8	-32.1	-55.4	-128.2	-248.7
Wind Drift • Inches	0.0	0.6	2.5	5.8	10.6	17.3	25.9	50.1	85.8

Weatherby 150-grain Nosler Ballistic Tip (N 7mm 150 BST)
G1 Ballistic Coefficient = 0.494

Distance • Yards	Muzzle	100	200	300	400	500	600	800	1000
Velocity • fps	3300	3093	2896	2708	2527	2353	2187	1875	1594
Energy • Ft-lbs	3627	3187	2793	2442	2127	1844	1594	1171	849
Taylor KO Index	20.1	18.8	17.6	16.5	15.4	14.3	13.3	11.4	9.7
Path • Inches	-1.5	+1.1	0.0	-5.2	-15.2	-30.6	-52.3	-118.7	-225.1
Wind Drift • Inches	0.0	0.5	2.2	5.0	9.2	14.8	22.1	42.3	71.4

Federal 150-grain Nosler Solid Base BT (P7WBS1)
G1 Ballistic Coefficient = 0.456

Distance • Yards	Muzzle	100	200	300	400	500	600	800	1000
Velocity • fps	3230	3010	2800	2600	2410	2230	2054	1730	1448
Energy • Ft-lbs	3475	3015	2615	2255	1935	1650	1405	997	698
Taylor KO Index	19.7	18.3	17.0	15.8	14.7	13.6	12.5	10.5	8.8
Path • Inches	-1.5	1.2	0.0	-5.6	-16.3	-33.1	-56.8	-130.8	-252.8
Wind Drift • Inches	0.0	0.6	2.4	5.6	10.4	16.8	25.1	48.5	82.6

Weatherby 150-grain Barnes-X (B 7mm 150 XS)
G1 Ballistic Coefficient = 0.488

Distance • Yards	Muzzle	100	200	300	400	500	600	800	1000
Velocity • fps	3100	2901	2710	2527	2352	2183	2021	1721	1457
Energy • Ft-lbs	3200	2802	2446	2127	1842	1588	1361	986	707
Taylor KO Index	18.9	17.7	16.5	15.4	14.3	13.3	12.3	10.5	8.9
Path • Inches	-1.5	+1.3	0.0	-6.1	-17.6	-35.4	-60.5	-137.8	-262.5
Wind Drift • Inches	0.0	0.6	2.4	5.5	10.2	16.4	24.5	47.1	79.8

Weatherby 154-grain Pointed-Expanding (H 7mm 154 SP)
G1 Ballistic Coefficient = 0.433

Distance • Yards	Muzzle	100	200	300	400	500	600	800	1000
Velocity • fps	3260	3027	2807	2597	2396	2206	2025	1689	1401
Energy • Ft-lbs	3625	3135	2694	2306	1963	1662	1402	975	671
Taylor KO Index	20.4	18.9	17.5	16.2	15.0	13.8	12.7	10.6	8.8
Path • Inches	-1.5	+1.2	0.0	-5.6	-16.3	-33.1	-57.0	-132.1	-256.5
Wind Drift • Inches	0.0	0.6	2.5	5.9	10.9	17.6	26.7	51.1	87.5

Hornady 154-grain SST (8068) (Discontinued in 2005)
G1 Ballistic Coefficient = 0.434

Distance • Yards	Muzzle	100	200	300	400	500	600	800	1000
Velocity • fps	3200	3009	2825	2648	2478	2315	2159	1863	1597
Energy • Ft-lbs	3501	3096	2729	2398	2100	1833	1594	1188	872
Taylor KO Index	20.0	18.8	17.7	16.5	15.5	14.5	13.5	11.6	10.0
Path • Inches	-1.5	+1.2	0.0	-5.7	-16.5	-33.1	-54.8	-123.8	-233.6
Wind Drift • Inches	0.0	0.5	1.9	4.4	8.1	13.1	19.5	37.2	62.6

Hornady 154-grain Soft Point (8066) (Discontinued in 2005)
G1 Ballistic Coefficient = 0.434

Distance • Yards	Muzzle	100	200	300	400	500	600	800	1000
Velocity • fps	3200	2971	2753	2546	2348	2159	1980	1649	1368
Energy • Ft-lbs	3501	3017	2592	2216	1885	1593	1341	930	641
Taylor KO Index	20.0	18.6	17.2	15.9	14.7	13.5	12.4	10.3	8.5
Path • Inches	-1.5	+1.2	0.0	-5.8	-17.0	-34.5	-59.5	-137.7	-268.0
Wind Drift • Inches	0.0	0.6	2.6	6.0	11.1	18.1	27.1	52.6	90.0

Weatherby 160-grain Nosler Partition (N 7mm 160 PT)
G1 Ballistic Coefficient = 0.475

Distance • Yards	Muzzle	100	200	300	400	500	600	800	1000
Velocity • fps	3200	2991	2791	2600	2417	2241	2072	1758	1483
Energy • Ft-lbs	3688	3177	2767	2401	2075	1781	1526	1099	781
Taylor KO Index	20.8	19.4	18.1	16.9	15.7	14.5	13.5	11.4	9.6
Path • Inches	-1.5	+1.2	0.0	-5.7	-16.5	-33.3	-57.0	-130.2	-248.9
Wind Drift • Inches	0.0	0.6	2.4	5.5	10.0	16.2	24.2	46.6	79.0

Federal 160-grain Trophy Bonded Bear Claw (P7WBT1)
G1 Ballistic Coefficient = 0.293

Distance • Yards	Muzzle	100	200	300	400	500	600	800	1000
Velocity • fps	3050	2730	2420	2140	1880	1640	1428	1116	956
Energy • Ft-lbs	3305	2640	2085	1630	1255	955	725	443	325
Taylor KO Index	19.8	17.7	15.7	13.9	12.2	10.6	9.3	7.2	6.2
Path • Inches	-1.5	+1.6	0.0	-7.6	-22.7	-47.8	-85.8	-218.5	-462.3
Wind Drift • Inches	0.0	1.0	4.2	10.1	19.1	31.9	49.1	98.8	167.2

Weatherby 175-grain Pointed-Expanding (H 7mm 175 SP)
G1 Ballistic Coefficient = 0.462

Distance • Yards	Muzzle	100	200	300	400	500	600	800	1000
Velocity • fps	3070	2861	2662	2471	2288	2113	1945	1637	1373
Energy • Ft-lbs	3662	3181	2753	2373	2034	1735	1470	1041	733
Taylor KO Index	21.8	20.3	18.9	17.5	16.2	15.0	13.8	11.6	9.7
Path • Inches	-1.5	+1.4	0.0	-6.3	-18.3	-37.0	-63.4	-145.7	-280.5
Wind Drift • Inches	0.0	0.6	2.3	5.4	9.9	16.0	24.0	46.3	78.9

Hornady 175-grain SP (8067) (Discontinued in 2005)
G1 Ballistic Coefficient = 0.463

Distance • Yards	Muzzle	100	200	300	400	500	600	800	1000
Velocity • fps	2910	2709	2516	2331	2154	1985	1826	1534	1291
Energy • Ft-lbs	3290	2850	2459	2111	1803	1531	1296	914	648
Taylor KO Index	20.7	19.2	17.9	16.6	15.3	14.1	13.0	10.9	9.2
Path • Inches	-1.5	+1.6	0.0	-7.1	-20.6	-41.7	-71.5	-164.6	-317.4
Wind Drift • Inches	0.0	0.7	2.8	6.4	11.8	19.2	28.8	55.6	94.6

7mm Dakota

The Dakota series of cartridges is (except for the .450 Dakota) based on the .404 Jeffery case. Since a good big case will outperform a good little case any day, the 7mm Dakota is no wimp. It's right up there with the other top-end 7mm performers. Ammunition is available only through Dakota Arms, Inc.

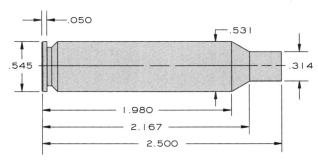

Relative Recoil Factor = 2.27

Specifications

Controlling Agency for Standardization of this Ammunition: Factory

Availability

Dakota 140-grain Swift (7MM-140FAF)

G1 Ballistic Coefficient = 0.355

Distance • Yards	Muzzle	100	200	300	400	500	600	800	1000
Velocity • fps	3400	3109	2836	2579	2337	2107	1892	1508	1211
Energy • Ft-lbs	3595	3005	2501	2069	1698	1381	1113	707	456
Taylor KO Index	19.3	17.7	16.1	14.6	13.3	12.0	10.7	8.6	6.9
Path • Inches	-1.5	+1.0	0.0	-5.4	-16.0	-33.0	-57.9	-139.4	-283.1
Wind Drift • Inches	0.0	0.6	2.7	6.3	11.6	19.1	28.9	57.3	100.0

Dakota 140-grain Nosler Partition (7MM-140NPT)

G1 Ballistic Coefficient = 0.434

Distance • Yards	Muzzle	100	200	300	400	500	600	800	1000
Velocity • fps	3400	3160	2933	2718	2512	2316	2128	1780	1477
Energy • Ft-lbs	3595	3105	2675	2296	1962	1667	1408	986	678
Taylor KO Index	19.3	17.9	16.7	15.4	14.3	13.2	12.1	10.1	8.4
Path • Inches	-1.5	+1.0	0.0	-5.0	-14.8	-30.1	-51.8	-118.0	-232.5
Wind Drift • Inches	0.0	0.5	2.2	5.0	9.2	15.0	22.4	43.3	74.0

Dakota 140-grain Nosler Ballistic Tip (7MM-140NBT)

G1 Ballistic Coefficient = 0.485

Distance • Yards	Muzzle	100	200	300	400	500	600	800	1000
Velocity • fps	3400	3185	2980	2784	2597	2418	2245	1922	1630
Energy • Ft-lbs	3595	3154	2761	2411	2098	1818	1568	1149	827
Taylor KO Index	19.3	18.1	16.9	15.8	14.8	13.7	12.8	10.9	9.3
Path • Inches	-1.5	+1.0	0.0	-4.9	-14.3	-28.8	-49.3	-112.2	-213.0
Wind Drift • Inches	0.0	0.5	1.9	4.4	8.1	13.1	19.5	27.6	63.1

Dakota 160-grain Nosler Partition (7MM-160NPT)

G1 Ballistic Coefficient = 0.475

Distance • Yards	Muzzle	100	200	300	400	500	600	800	1000
Velocity • fps	3200	2990	2791	2600	2416	2241	2072	1759	1482
Energy • Ft-lbs	3639	3178	2767	2401	2075	1784	1526	1099	781
Taylor KO Index	20.8	19.4	18.1	16.9	15.7	14.5	13.5	11.4	9.6
Path • Inches	-1.5	+1.2	0.0	-5.7	-16.5	-33.2	-57.0	-130.3	-249.9
Wind Drift • Inches	0.0	0.5	2.1	4.9	9.0	14.6	21.8	41.9	71.1

Dakota 160-grain Swift (7MM-160FAF)

G1 Ballistic Coefficient = 0.450

Distance • Yards	Muzzle	100	200	300	400	500	600	800	1000
Velocity • fps	3200	2979	2769	2568	2377	2193	2018	1694	1414
Energy • Ft-lbs	3639	3154	2754	2344	2007	1709	1447	1019	710
Taylor KO Index	20.8	19.3	18.0	16.7	15.4	14.2	13.1	11.0	9.2
Path • Inches	-1.5	+1.2	0.0	-5.8	-16.8	-34.0	-58.4	-134.8	-261.4
Wind Drift • Inches	0.0	0.5	2.2	5.2	9.6	15.6	23.3	45.0	76.8

7mm STW (Shooting Times Westerner)

The 7mm STW began when Layne Simpson decided that he wanted a high-performance 7mm. His wildcat cartridge started as a 8mm Remington Magnum case necked to 7mm. This provided a case with a little more volume than the 7mm Weatherby and, therefore, a little more performance. The idea was that rechambering 7mm Remington Magnums for the 7mm STW cartridge would provide an easy conversion. That was a completely feasible plan if the original chambers were exactly the nominal size, but the real world isn't that way. To make these conversions practical, the 7mm STW shape was "improved" by straightening out the body just a little. The 7mm STW received SAAMI standardization in late 1996.

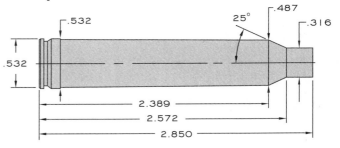

Relative Recoil Factor = 2.31

Specifications

Controlling Agency for Standardization of this Ammunition: SAAMI

Bullet Weight Grains	Velocity fps	Maximum Average Pressure Copper Crusher	Transducer
140	3,325	54,000 cup	65,000 psi
160	3,250	54,000 cup	65,000 psi

Standard barrel for velocity testing: 24 inches long—1 turn in 10-inch twist

Availability

A² 140-grain Nosler Ballistic Tip (None)

G1 Ballistic Coefficient = 0.540

Distance • Yards	Muzzle	100	200	300	400	500	600	800	1000
Velocity • fps	3450	3254	3067	2888	2715	2550	2389	2086	1808
Energy • Ft-lbs	3700	3291	2924	2592	2292	2021	1775	1354	1016
Taylor KO Index	19.6	18.5	17.4	16.4	15.4	14.5	13.6	11.8	10.3
Path • Inches	-1.5	+0.9	0.0	-4.6	-13.4	-26.8	-45.7	-102.6	-191.6
Wind Drift • Inches	0.0	0.5	1.9	4.3	7.9	12.6	18.7	35.4	59.2

Remington 140-grain Pointed Soft Point Core-Lokt (R7MSTW1)

G1 Ballistic Coefficient = 0.391

Distance • Yards	Muzzle	100	200	300	400	500	600	800	1000
Velocity • fps	3325	3064	2818	2585	2364	2153	1955	1594	1299
Energy • Ft-lbs	3436	2918	2468	2077	1737	1443	1189	790	524
Taylor KO Index	18.9	17.4	16.0	14.7	13.4	12.2	11.1	9.1	7.4
Path • Inches	-1.5	+1.1	0.0	-5.5	-16.2	-33.1	-57.6	-135.9	-269.7
Wind Drift • Inches	0.0	0.7	2.8	6.4	11.9	19.4	29.3	57.4	99.2

Remington 140-grain Swift A-Frame PSP (RS7MSTWA)

G1 Ballistic Coefficient = 0.332

Distance • Yards	Muzzle	100	200	300	400	500	600	800	1000
Velocity • fps	3325	3020	2735	2467	2215	1978	1756	1376	1112
Energy • Ft-lbs	3436	2834	2324	1892	1525	1215	959	589	384
Taylor KO Index	18.9	17.2	15.5	14.0	12.6	11.2	10.0	7.8	6.3
Path • Inches	-1.5	+1.2	0.0	-5.8	-17.4	-36.1	-63.7	-156.1	-322.9
Wind Drift • Inches	0.0	0.8	3.3	7.7	14.5	23.8	36.3	72.6	126.9

Winchester 140-grain Ballistic Silvertip (SBST7STW)

G1 Ballistic Coefficient = 0.464

Distance • Yards	Muzzle	100	200	300	400	500	600	800	1000
Velocity • fps	3300	3106	2920	2742	2570	2405	2247	1948	1675
Energy • Ft-lbs	3385	2998	2650	2336	2053	1798	1570	1180	872
Taylor KO Index	18.7	17.6	16.6	15.6	14.6	13.7	12.8	11.1	9.5
Path • Inches	-1.5	+1.0	0.0	-5.1	-14.9	-29.8	-51.0	-114.8	-215.6
Wind Drift • Inches	0.0	0.5	2.0	4.7	8.6	13.8	20.5	39.0	65.5

Speer 145-grain Grand Slam (24566) (Discontinued in 2004)

G1 Ballistic Coefficient = 0.327

Distance • Yards	Muzzle	100	200	300	400	500	600	800	1000
Velocity • fps	3250	2946	2661	2393	2142	1906	1687	1318	1076
Energy • Ft-lbs	3400	2793	2273	1844	1477	1170	917	560	373
Taylor KO Index	19.1	17.3	15.7	14.1	12.6	11.2	9.9	7.8	6.3
Path • Inches	-1.5	+1.3	0.0	-6.2	-18.5	-38.4	-68.0	-168.8	-354.2
Wind Drift • Inches	0.0	0.7	3.1	7.3	13.7	22.6	34.5	69.1	120.4

Federal 150-grain Trophy Bonded Bear Claw (P7STWT1) (Discontinued in 2004)

G1 Ballistic Coefficient = 0.413

Distance • Yards	Muzzle	100	200	300	400	500	600	800	1000
Velocity • fps	3250	3010	2770	2560	2350	2150	1963	1619	1331
Energy • Ft-lbs	3520	3012	2569	2180	1840	1540	1283	873	590
Taylor KO Index	19.8	18.3	16.9	15.6	14.3	13.1	11.9	9.9	8.1
Path • Inches	-1.5	+1.2	0.0	-5.7	-16.7	-34.2	-58.9	-137.7	-270.2
Wind Drift • Inches	0.0	0.6	2.7	6.2	11.5	18.8	28.2	55.0	94.6

Winchester 150-grain Power-Point (X7STW1)

G1 Ballistic Coefficient = 0.341

Distance • Yards	Muzzle	100	200	300	400	500	600	800	1000
Velocity • fps	3280	3018	2770	2537	2314	2103	1905	1546	1259
Taylor KO Index	3583	3032	2556	2142	1783	1473	1209	797	528
Energy • Ft-lbs	20.0	18.4	16.9	15.4	14.1	12.8	11.6	9.4	7.7
Path • Inches	-1.5	+1.2	0.0	-5.7	-16.8	-34.4	-59.9	-142.0	-283.0
Wind Drift • Inches	0.0	0.7	2.8	6.7	12.4	20.2	30.4	59.8	103.8

Federal 150-grain Nosler Solid Base BT (P7STWS1)

G1 Ballistic Coefficient = 0.457

Distance • Yards	Muzzle	100	200	300	400	500	600	800	1000
Velocity • fps	3180	2960	2760	2560	2370	2190	2018	1699	1422
Energy • Ft-lbs	3370	2925	2530	2180	1670	1595	1357	961	674
Taylor KO Index	19.4	18.0	16.8	15.6	14.4	13.3	12.3	10.3	8.7
Path • Inches	-1.5	+1.2	0.0	-5.8	-16.9	-34.3	-58.8	-135.4	-261.8
Wind Drift • Inches	0.0	0.6	2.5	5.7	10.6	17.1	25.6	49.5	84.3

A² 160-grain Nosler Partition (None)

G1 Ballistic Coefficient = 0.565

Distance • Yards	Muzzle	100	200	300	400	500	600	800	1000
Velocity • fps	3250	3071	2900	2735	2576	2422	2272	1991	1732
Energy • Ft-lbs	3752	3351	2987	2657	2357	2084	1835	1409	1066
Taylor KO Index	21.0	19.9	18.8	17.8	16.7	15.7	14.7	12.9	11.2
Path • Inches	-1.5	+1.1	0.0	-5.2	-15.1	-30.3	-51.3	-114.7	-213.3
Wind Drift • Inches	0.0	0.5	1.9	4.4	8.1	13.0	19.3	36.4	60.8

A² 160-grain Sierra Boat Tail (None)

G1 Ballistic Coefficient = 0.622

Distance • Yards	Muzzle	100	200	300	400	500	600	800	1000
Velocity • fps	3250	3087	2930	2778	2631	2490	2353	2092	1848
Energy • Ft-lbs	3752	3385	3049	2741	2460	2202	1968	1555	1213
Taylor KO Index	21.1	20.0	19.0	18.0	17.1	16.2	15.3	13.6	12.0
Path • Inches	-1.5	+1.1	0.0	-5.1	-14.8	-29.4	-49.7	-109.8	-201.9
Wind Drift • Inches	0.0	0.4	1.7	4.0	7.3	11.6	17.2	32.3	53.6

Federal 160-grain Sierra GameKing BTSP (P7STWA) (Discontinued in 2004)

G1 Ballistic Coefficient = 0.566

Distance • Yards	Muzzle	100	200	300	400	500	600	800	1000
Velocity • fps	3200	3020	2850	2677	2530	2380	2234	1956	1701
Energy • Ft-lbs	3640	3245	2890	2570	2275	2010	1773	1359	1028
Taylor KO Index	20.8	19.6	18.5	17.3	16.4	15.4	14.5	12.7	11.0
Path • Inches	-1.5	+1.1	0.0	-5.5	-15.7	-31.3	-53.1	-118.6	-220.7
Wind Drift • Inches	0.0	0.5	2.0	4.5	8.2	13.2	19.6	37.2	62.1

Federal 160-grain Nosler AccuBond (P7STWA1)

G1 Ballistic Coefficient = 0.530

Distance • Yards	Muzzle	100	200	300	400	500	600	800	1000
Velocity • fps	3100	2920	2740	2570	2410	2250	2097	1812	1556
Energy • Ft-lbs	3415	3025	2670	2350	2055	1805	1563	1167	861
Taylor KO Index	20.1	19.0	17.8	16.7	15.6	14.6	13.6	11.8	10.1
Path • Inches	-1.5	+1.3	0.0	-5.9	-17.0	-34.3	-58.4	-131.7	-248.1
Wind Drift • Inches	0.0	0.5	2.2	5.0	9.2	14.9	22.2	42.3	71.2

Winchester 160-grain Fail Safe (S7STWX)

G1 Ballistic Coefficient = 0.382

Distance • Yards	Muzzle	100	200	300	400	500	600	800	1000
Velocity • fps	3050	2767	2500	2249	2013	1792	1588	1253	1046
Energy • Ft-lbs	3304	2719	2221	1797	1439	1141	896	559	388
Taylor KO Index	19.8	18.0	16.2	14.6	13.1	11.6	10.3	8.1	6.8
Path • Inches	-1.5	+1.5	0.0	-7.1	-21.1	-43.6	-77.3	-189.8	-391.2
Wind Drift • Inches	0.0	0.9	3.6	8.6	16.1	26.6	40.6	81.2	139.6

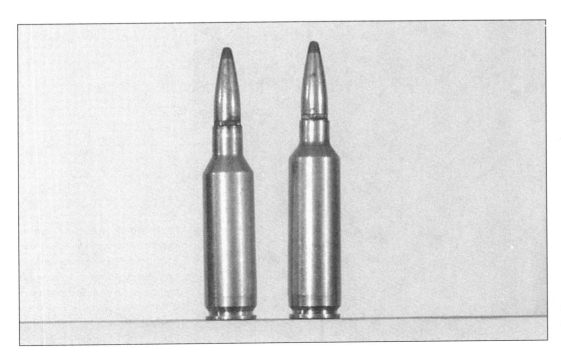

(Left to right) 7mm Remington Short Action Ultra Magnum, 7mm Winchester Short Magnum.

7.21mm (.284) Lazzeroni Firebird

Here's the 7mm Lazzeroni Magnum cartridge. This big boomer is in the same general class as the 7mm Dakota and the 7mm STW. The 140-grain bullet loading has more than a 400-fps velocity edge over the 7mm Remington Magnum.

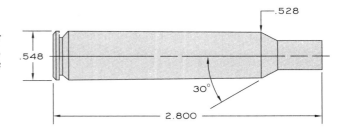

Relative Recoil Factor = 2.33

Specifications

Controlling Agency for Standardization of this Ammunition: Factory

Availability

Lazzeroni 120-grain (721FH120)

G1 Ballistic Coefficient = 0.472

Distance • Yards	Muzzle	100	200	300	400	500	600	800	1000
Velocity • fps	3950	3698	3461	3237	3024	2821	2628	2265	1931
Energy • Ft-lbs	4158	3645	3193	2792	2437	2121	1841	1367	994
Taylor KO Index	19.2	18.0	16.9	15.8	14.7	13.7	12.8	11.0	9.4
Path • Inches	-1.5	+0.5	0.0	-3.4	-10.2	-20.7	-35.6	-81.4	-154.7
Wind Drift • Inches	0.0	0.4	1.8	4.2	7.8	12.5	18.5	35.0	58.8

Lazzeroni 140-grain Nosler Partition (721FH140P)

G1 Ballistic Coefficient = 0.560

Distance • Yards	Muzzle	100	200	300	400	500	600	800	1000
Velocity • fps	3750	3522	3306	3101	2905	2718	2539	2200	1889
Energy • Ft-lbs	4372	3857	3399	2990	2625	2297	2004	1506	1110
Taylor KO Index	22.4	21.0	19.7	18.4	17.2	16.0	14.9	12.9	11.0
Path • Inches	-1.5	+0.6	0.0	-3.8	-11.3	-22.8	-39.1	-88.7	-167.5
Wind Drift • Inches	0.0	0.4	1.8	4.3	7.8	12.5	18.5	35.0	58.7

Peter Flack, who has hunted every country in Africa open to hunting, is shown here with an excellent springbuck from his home country of South Africa. (Photo from African Hunter II *by Craig Boddington and Peter Flack, 2004, Safari Press)*

.30 M1 Carbine

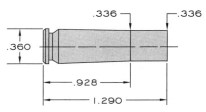

Developed shortly before WWII, the .30 M1 Carbine represented the U.S. Army's idea of what was needed in an "assault rifle" cartridge. Today's largely uninformed but, nevertheless, highly opinionated press and electronic media have succeeded in making the term "assault rifle" stand for high power, thus implying that the guns must be extremely dangerous. The fact is just the reverse. Assault rifles are (and need to be) very low-power rifles. They are designed to be controllable by the average soldier in fully automatic fire. Look at the relative recoil figure. The .30 M1 Carbine is not suitable for use on deer-size game.

Relative Recoil Factor = 0.99

Specifications

Controlling Agency for Standardization of this Ammunition: SAAMI

Bullet Weight Grains	Velocity fps	Maximum Average Pressure	
		Copper Crusher	Transducer
110	1,965	40,000 cup	40,000 psi

Standard barrel for velocity testing: 20 inches long—1 turn in 20-inch twist

Availability

Federal 110-grain Hi-Shok Soft Point RN (30CA)
G1 Ballistic Coefficient = 0.166

Distance • Yards	Muzzle	100	200	300	400	500	600	800	1000
Velocity • fps	1990	1570	1240	1040	920	840	774	665	575
Energy • Ft-lbs	965	600	375	260	210	175	146	108	81
Taylor KO Index	9.6	7.6	6.0	5.0	4.5	4.1	3.7	3.2	2.8
Path • Inches	-1.5	+6.4	0.0	-27.7	-81.8	-167.8	-346.2	-835.0	-1643
Wind Drift • Inches	0.0	3.4	15.1	35.7	63.5	97.2	136.1	230.9	349.9

Remington 110-grain Soft Point (R30CAR)
G1 Ballistic Coefficient = 0.167

Distance • Yards	Muzzle	100	200	300	400	500	600	800	1000
Velocity • fps	1990	1567	1236	1035	923	842	776	667	578
Energy • Ft-lbs	967	600	373	262	208	173	147	109	81
Taylor KO Index	9.6	7.6	6.0	5.0	4.5	4.1	3.8	3.2	2.8
Path • Inches	-1.5	+6.4	0.0	-27.7	-81.8	-167.8	-334.5	-830.7	-1634
Wind Drift • Inches	0.0	3.4	15.0	35.5	63.2	96.6	135.4	229.7	348.0

Winchester 110-grain Hollow Soft Point (X30M1)
G1 Ballistic Coefficient = 0.167

Distance • Yards	Muzzle	100	200	300	400	500	600	800	1000
Velocity • fps	1990	1567	1236	1035	923	842	776	667	578
Energy • Ft-lbs	967	600	373	262	208	173	147	109	81
Taylor KO Index	9.6	7.6	6.0	5.0	4.5	4.1	3.8	3.2	2.8
Path • Inches	-1.5	+6.4	0.0	-27.7	-81.8	-167.8	-334.5	-830.7	-1634
Wind Drift • Inches	0.0	3.4	15.0	35.5	63.2	96.6	135.4	229.7	348.0

PMC 110-grain Round Nose Soft Point (30B)
G1 Ballistic Coefficient = 0.147

Distance • Yards	Muzzle	100	200	300	400	500	600	800	1000
Velocity • fps	1930	1485	1141	970	867	788	722	611	519
Energy • Ft-lbs	910	524	316	230	184	152	127	91	66
Taylor KO Index	9.3	7.2	5.5	4.7	4.2	3.8	3.5	3.0	2.5
Path • Inches	-1.5	+7.5	0.0	-34.1	-105.1	-222.4	-395.8	-956.3	-1897
Wind Drift • Inches	0.0	4.1	17.8	41.1	71.5	108.1	150.9	256.0	390.8

Sellier & Bellot 110-grain FMJ (SBA03001) (Discontinued in 2005)
G1 Ballistic Coefficient = 0.104

Distance • Yards	Muzzle	100	200	300	400	500	600	800	1000
Velocity • fps	1991	1503	1135	856	750	664	590	466	369
Energy • Ft-lbs	971	553	315	180	137	108	85	53	33
Taylor KO Index	9.6	7.3	5.5	4.1	3.6	3.2	2.9	2.3	1.8
Path • Inches	-1.5	+9.0	0.0	-43.0	-133.6	-286.3	-518.3	-1313	-2777
Wind Drift • Inches	0.0	5.2	22.8	50.5	86.1	129.7	181.9	317.0	504.3

American Eagle (Federal) 110-grain Full Metal Jacket (AE30CB)

G1 Ballistic Coefficient = 0.166

Distance • Yards	Muzzle	100	200	300	400	500	600	800	1000
Velocity • fps	1990	1570	1240	1040	920	840	774	665	575
Energy • Ft-lbs	965	600	375	260	210	175	146	108	81
Taylor KO Index	9.6	7.6	6.0	5.0	4.5	4.1	3.7	3.2	2.8
Path • Inches	-1.5	+6.4	0.0	-27.7	-81.8	-167.8	-346.2	-835.0	-1643
Wind Drift • Inches	0.0	3.4	15.1	35.7	63.5	97.2	136.1	230.9	349.9

UMC (Remington) 110-grain Full Metal Jacket (L30CR1)

G1 Ballistic Coefficient = 0.166

Distance • Yards	Muzzle	100	200	300	400	500	600	800	1000
Velocity • fps	1990	1567	1236	1040	920	840	774	665	575
Energy • Ft-lbs	965	600	373	260	210	175	146	108	81
Taylor KO Index	9.6	7.6	6.0	5.0	4.5	4.1	3.7	3.2	2.8
Path • Inches	-1.5	+6.4	0.0	-27.7	-81.8	-167.8	-346.2	-835.0	-1643
Wind Drift • Inches	0.0	3.4	15.1	35.7	63.5	97.2	136.1	230.9	349.9

USA (Winchester) 110-grain Full Metal Jacket (Q3132)

G1 Ballistic Coefficient = 0.180

Distance • Yards	Muzzle	100	200	300	400	500	600	800	1000
Velocity • fps	1990	1596	1279	1070	952	870	804	697	610
Energy • Ft-lbs	967	622	399	280	221	185	158	119	91
Taylor KO Index	9.6	7.7	6.2	5.2	4.6	4.2	3.9	3.4	3.0
Path • Inches	-1.5	6.5	0.0	-27.9	-86.0	-181.6	-323.8	-778.3	-1522
Wind Drift • Inches	0.0	3.1	13.7	32.6	58.6	90.2	126.9	215.4	325.4

PMC 110-grain FMJ (30A)

G1 Ballistic Coefficient = 0.147

Distance • Yards	Muzzle	100	200	300	400	500	600	800	1000
Velocity • fps	1930	1485	1141	970	867	788	722	611	519
Energy • Ft-lbs	910	524	316	230	184	152	127	91	66
Taylor KO Index	9.3	7.2	5.5	4.7	4.2	3.8	3.5	3.0	2.5
Path • Inches	-1.5	+7.5	0.0	-34.1	-105.1	-222.4	-395.8	-956.3	-1897
Wind Drift • Inches	0.0	4.1	17.8	41.1	71.5	108.1	150.9	256.0	390.8

(Left to right) .30 M1 Carbine, 7.62x39, .30-30, .300 Savage, .308 Winchester.

7.62x39mm Russian

Assault rifles came into general usage during WWII when military authorities recognized that an all-up infantry rifle (the Garand, for instance) was not the best weapon for street fighting. The 7.62x39mm was the Soviet answer to this need. Introduced in 1943, it has become the standard infantry cartridge for many of the world's armies. Because some guns chambered for this cartridge use a 0.310-inch groove diameter barrel and others use 0.308 inches, it's a good idea to know the dimensions of both your gun and your ammunition before you start shooting. The SAAMI standard for this round uses bullets with a diameter tolerance of 0.309 to 0.311 inch.

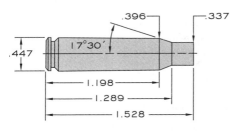

Relative Recoil Factor = 1.29

Specifications

Controlling Agency for Standardization of this Ammunition: SAAMI

Bullet Weight Grains	Velocity fps	Maximum Average Pressure	
		Copper Crusher	Transducer
123	2,350	50,000 cup	45,000 psi

Standard barrel for velocity testing: 20 inches long—1 turn in 9.45-inch twist

Availability

PMC 100-grain Non-Toxic Frangible (7.62RHRA)
G1 Ballistic Coefficient = 0.205

Distance • Yards	Muzzle	100	200	300	400	500	600	800	1000
Velocity • fps	2300	1910	1572	1298	1100	983	909	786	694
Energy • Ft-lbs	1175	810	549	374	269	215	181	137	107
Taylor KO Index	10.1	8.4	6.9	5.7	4.8	4.3	4.0	3.5	3.1
Path • Inches	-1.5	+4.0	0.0	-18.2	-57.3	-124.9	-228.5	-570.5	-1140
Wind Drift • Inches	0.0	2.2	9.7	23.7	45.2	53.3	106.5	186.5	284.2

Winchester 123-grain Soft Point (X76239)
G1 Ballistic Coefficient = 0.243

Distance • Yards	Muzzle	100	200	300	400	500	600	800	1000
Velocity • fps	2365	2030	1731	1465	1248	1093	992	864	772
Energy • Ft-lbs	1527	1129	818	586	425	327	269	204	163
Taylor KO Index	12.8	11.0	9.4	7.9	6.8	5.9	5.4	4.7	4.2
Path • Inches	-1.5	+3.8	0.0	-15.4	-46.3	-98.4	-183.9	-461.6	-926.2
Wind Drift • Inches	0.0	1.8	7.6	18.5	35.3	58.5	87.0	157.0	242.1

Sellier & Bellot 123-grain Soft Point (SBA31102) & (SBA76203)
G1 Ballistic Coefficient = 0.235

Distance • Yards	Muzzle	100	200	300	400	500	600	800	1000
Velocity • fps	2438	2069	1756	1490	1259	1095	991	859	764
Energy • Ft-lbs	1629	1173	845	609	433	328	268	202	160
Taylor KO Index	13.3	11.3	9.6	8.1	6.9	6.0	5.4	4.7	4.2
Path • Inches	-1.5	+3.3	0.0	-14.5	-45.0	-98.0	-179.8	-447.4	-884.1
Wind Drift • Inches	0.0	1.6	6.8	16.6	31.9	53.1	79.3	143.8	222.2

Federal 123-grain Hi-Shok Soft Point (76239B)
G1 Ballistic Coefficient = 0.299

Distance • Yards	Muzzle	100	200	300	400	500	600	800	1000
Velocity • fps	2300	2030	1780	1550	1350	1200	1083	941	848
Energy • Ft-lbs	1445	1125	860	655	500	395	320	242	196
Taylor KO Index	12.4	11.0	9.6	8.4	7.3	6.5	5.9	5.1	4.6
Path • Inches	-1.5	+3.5	0.0	-14.5	-43.4	-90.6	-163.0	-400.6	-795.4
Wind Drift • Inches	0.0	1.5	6.3	15.0	28.4	46.8	70.3	129.7	202.4

Sellier & Bellot 123-grain FMJ (SBA31101)
G1 Ballistic Coefficient = 0.276

Distance • Yards	Muzzle	100	200	300	400	500	600	800	1000
Velocity • fps	2412	2104	1829	1589	1372	1197	1073	926	829
Energy • Ft-lbs	1607	1214	917	692	514	392	314	234	188
Taylor KO Index	13.2	11.5	10.0	8.7	7.5	6.5	5.9	5.1	4.5
Path • Inches	-1.5	+3.2	0.0	-13.5	-41.0	-87.4	-158.4	-393.5	-777.1
Wind Drift • Inches	0.0	1.3	5.8	13.9	26.4	43.8	66.2	122.8	192.1

UMC (Remington) 123-grain MC (L762391)

G1 Ballistic Coefficient = 0.266

Distance • Yards	Muzzle	100	200	300	400	500	600	800	1000
Velocity • fps	2365	2060	1780	1528	1314	1149	1038	902	809
Energy • Ft-lbs	1527	1159	865	638	472	371	294	222	179
Taylor KO Index	12.9	11.3	9.7	8.4	7.2	6.3	5.6	4.9	4.4
Path • Inches	-1.5	+3.4	0.0	-14.4	-43.9	-93.6	-169.4	-423.3	-848.5
Wind Drift • Inches	0.0	1.6	6.9	16.6	31.6	52.4	78.5	143.6	223.1

USA (Winchester) 123-grain Soft Point (Q3174)

G1 Ballistic Coefficient = 0.245

Distance • Yards	Muzzle	100	200	300	400	500	600	800	1000
Velocity • fps	2355	2026	1726	1463	1247	1093	994	866	775
Energy • Ft-lbs	1515	1121	814	584	425	326	270	205	164
Taylor KO Index	12.7	11.0	9.3	7.9	6.7	5.9	5.4	4.7	4.2
Path • Inches	-1.5	+3.8	0.0	-15.6	-47.6	-102.0	-184.1	-461.5	-924.8
Wind Drift • Inches	0.0	1.8	7.6	18.4	35.2	58.2	87.0	156.1	240.7

PMC 123-grain Full Metal Jacket (7.62A)

G1 Ballistic Coefficient = 0.277

Distance • Yards	Muzzle	100	200	300	400	500	600	800	1000
Velocity • fps	2350	2072	1817	1583	1368	1171	1056	917	824
Energy • Ft-lbs	1495	1162	894	678	507	371	305	230	185
Taylor KO Index	12.7	11.2	9.8	8.6	7.4	6.3	5.7	5.0	4.5
Path • Inches	-1.5	+3.4	0.0	-14.3	-43.4	-91.9	-165.8	-412.3	-215.4
Wind Drift • Inches	0.0	1.6	6.6	15.9	30.3	50.2	75.3	138.4	215.4

Lapua 123-grain Full Metal Jacket (4317235)

G1 Ballistic Coefficient = 0.265

Distance • Yards	Muzzle	100	200	300	400	500	600	800	1000
Velocity • fps	2346	2041	1761	1511	1300	1139	1031	897	805
Energy • Ft-lbs	1493	1130	841	619	462	354	290	220	177
Taylor KO Index	12.7	11.0	9.5	8.2	7.0	6.2	5.6	4.9	4.4
Path • Inches	-1.5	+3.4	0.0	-14.8	-44.8	-95.6	-173.0	-431.4	-863.0
Wind Drift • Inches	0.0	1.6	7.0	16.9	32.1	53.1	79.5	144.9	224.6

American Eagle (Federal) 124-grain Full Metal Jacket (AE76239A)

G1 Ballistic Coefficient = 0.295

Distance • Yards	Muzzle	100	200	300	400	500	600	800	1000
Velocity • fps	2300	2030	1780	1560	1360	1200	1075	935	842
Energy • Ft-lbs	1455	1135	875	670	510	400	318	241	195
Taylor KO Index	12.5	11.1	9.7	8.5	7.4	6.5	5.9	5.1	4.6
Path • Inches	-1.5	+3.5	0.0	-14.6	-42.9	-90.3	-164.8	-405.5	-805.5
Wind Drift • Inches	0.0	1.5	6.3	15.1	28.5	47.1	71.4	131.5	205.0

Remington 125-grain Pointed Soft Point (R762391) (Discontinued in 2005)

G1 Ballistic Coefficient = 0.267

Distance • Yards	Muzzle	100	200	300	400	500	600	800	1000
Velocity • fps	2365	2062	1782	1533	1320	1154	1039	903	809
Energy • Ft-lbs	1552	1180	882	652	483	370	300	226	182
Taylor KO Index	13.0	11.3	9.8	8.4	7.3	6.3	5.7	5.0	4.4
Path • Inches	-1.5	+3.4	0.0	-14.4	-43.9	-93.9	-170.3	-420.4	-825.6
Wind Drift • Inches	0.0	1.6	6.8	16.5	31.4	52.1	78.2	143.1	222.3

PMC 125-grain Pointed Soft Point (7.62B)

G1 Ballistic Coefficient = 0.277

Distance • Yards	Muzzle	100	200	300	400	500	600	800	1000
Velocity • fps	2320	2046	1794	1563	1350	1156	1047	911	820
Energy • Ft-lbs	1493	1161	893	678	505	371	304	231	186
Taylor KO Index	12.8	11.3	9.9	8.6	7.4	6.4	5.8	5.0	4.5
Path • Inches	-1.5	+3.5	0.0	-14.8	-44.6	-94.6	-170.5	-422.6	-842.3
Wind Drift • Inches	0.0	1.6	6.7	16.2	30.8	51.0	76.3	139.5	216.6

Cor-Bon 125-grain Jacketed Hollow Point (SD762x39125/20)

G1 Ballistic Coefficient = 0.275

Distance • Yards	Muzzle	100	200	300	400	500	600	800	1000
Velocity • fps	2400	2102	1826	1577	1362	1189	1067	922	826
Energy • Ft-lbs	1600	1227	926	691	515	392	316	236	189
Taylor KO Index	13.3	11.7	10.1	8.8	7.6	6.6	5.9	5.1	4.6
Path • Inches	-1.5	+3.2	0.0	-13.7	-41.6	-88.6	-160.7	-398.6	-785.9
Wind Drift • Inches	0.0	1.4	5.8	14.0	26.7	44.3	66.9	123.7	193.2

Cor-Bon 150-grain Jacketed Soft Point (SD762x39150/20)

G1 Ballistic Coefficient = 0.325

Distance • Yards	Muzzle	100	200	300	400	500	600	800	1000
Velocity • fps	2300	2052	1821	1609	1420	1259	1134	978	881
Energy • Ft-lbs	1762	1403	1105	863	672	528	428	318	258
Taylor KO Index	15.3	13.7	12.1	10.7	9.5	8.4	7.6	6.5	5.9
Path • Inches	-1.5	+3.4	0.0	-13.9	-41.4	-86.3	-153.6	-373.7	-730.1
Wind Drift • Inches	0.0	1.2	5.1	12.2	23.0	38.0	57.2	106.7	168.1

Outstanding whitetail buck taken with guide Eric Albus from Montana. (Photo from *Ask the Whitetail Guides* by J. Y. Jones, 2006, Safari Press)

.30-30 Winchester

For nearly 100 years the .30-30 Winchester has been what most hunters would call your basic deer rifle. Despite the black-powder type of designation, the .30-30 was the first cartridge of its class loaded with smokeless powder. There are lots of .30-caliber cartridges with better performance, but few combine with a carbine-length lever-action rifle to offer a better combination of enough power and a super handy rifle for woods-type hunting. There is a little something to remember when looking at the performance data for the .30-30 Winchester. The velocity specifications are measured in a 24-inch barrel, and a lot of guns that are chambered for the .30-30 have 20-inch barrels. This will cost about 100–150 fps in the short barrel. Time has proved that this doesn't make much difference because .30-30s are seldom used where long shots are required.

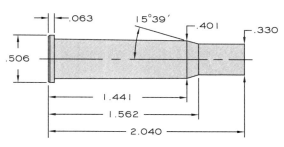

Relative Recoil Factor = 1.60

Specifications

Controlling Agency for Standardization of this Ammunition: SAAMI

Bullet Weight Grains	Velocity fps	Maximum Average Pressure	
		Copper Crusher	Transducer
55 (Saboted)	3,365	N/S	38,000 psi
125	2,550	38,000 cup	42,000 psi
150	2,370	38,000 cup	42,000 psi
170	2,180	38,000 cup	42,000 psi

Standard barrel for velocity testing: 24 inches long—1 turn in 12-inch twist

Availability

Remington Accelerator 55-grain Soft Point (R3030A)
G1 Ballistic Coefficient = 0.139

Distance • Yards	Muzzle	100	200	300	400	500	600	800	1000
Velocity • fps	3400	2693	2085	1570	1187	986	872	718	602
Energy • Ft-lbs	1412	886	521	301	172	119	93	63	44
Taylor KO Index	8.2	6.5	5.0	3.8	2.9	2.4	2.1	1.7	1.5
Path • Inches	-1.5	+1.7	0.0	-9.9	-34.3	-83.3	-168.6	-486.2	-1077
Wind Drift • Inches	0.0	1.9	8.7	22.4	45.9	79.8	121.4	224.5	354.9

Federal 125-grain Hi-Shok Hollow Point (3030C)
G1 Ballistic Coefficient = 0.174

Distance • Yards	Muzzle	100	200	300	400	500	600	800	1000
Velocity • fps	2570	2090	1660	1320	1080	960	874	747	647
Energy • Ft-lbs	1830	1210	770	480	320	260	212	155	116
Taylor KO Index	14.1	11.5	9.1	7.3	5.9	5.3	4.8	4.1	3.6
Path • Inches	-1.5	+3.3	0.0	-16.0	-50.9	-109.5	-220.2	-570.9	-117.3
Wind Drift • Inches	0.0	2.2	10.0	25.1	48.9	80.2	117.4	207.6	319.2

Winchester 150-grain Power-Point Plus (SHV30306)
G1 Ballistic Coefficient = 0.215

Distance • Yards	Muzzle	100	200	300	400	500	600	800	1000
Velocity • fps	2480	2095	1747	1446	1209	1053	957	828	733
Energy • Ft-lbs	2049	1462	1017	697	487	369	305	228	179
Taylor KO Index	16.4	13.8	11.5	9.5	8.0	6.9	6.3	5.5	4.8
Path • Inches	-1.5	+3.3	0.0	-14.7	-45.7	-98.4	-188.0	-481.3	-978.4
Wind Drift • Inches	0.0	1.9	8.2	20.1	38.9	64.6	96.0	172.6	266.2

Federal 150-grain Hi-Shok Soft Point FN (3030A)
G1 Ballistic Coefficient = 0.220

Distance • Yards	Muzzle	100	200	300	400	500	600	800	1000
Velocity • fps	2390	2020	1680	1400	1180	1040	950	826	733
Energy • Ft-lbs	1900	1355	945	650	460	355	300	227	179
Taylor KO Index	15.8	13.3	11.1	9.2	7.8	6.9	6.3	5.5	4.8
Path • Inches	-1.5	+3.6	0.0	-15.9	-49.1	-104.5	-198.2	-500.9	-1009
Wind Drift • Inches	0.0	1.9	8.4	20.6	39.6	65.3	96.4	172.1	264.2

Hornady 150-grain Round Nose InterLock (8080) G1 Ballistic Coefficient = 0.186

Distance • Yards	Muzzle	100	200	300	400	500	600	800	1000
Velocity • fps	2390	1959	1581	1276	1074	957	876	756	662
Energy • Ft-lbs	1902	1278	832	542	384	305	226	190	146
Taylor KO Index	15.8	12.9	10.4	8.4	7.1	6.3	5.8	5.0	4.4
Path • Inches	-1.5	+3.7	0.0	-18.0	-57.4	-127.0	-234.4	-592.8	-1197
Wind Drift • Inches	0.0	2.3	10.3	25.5	48.8	79.0	114.7	200.8	306.6

Remington 150-grain Core-Lokt Soft Point (R30301) G1 Ballistic Coefficient = 0.193

Distance • Yards	Muzzle	100	200	300	400	500	600	800	1000
Velocity • fps	2390	1973	1605	1303	1095	974	891	771	677
Energy • Ft-lbs	1902	1296	858	565	399	316	265	198	153
Taylor KO Index	15.8	13.0	10.6	8.6	7.2	6.4	5.9	5.1	4.5
Path • Inches	-1.5	+3.8	0.0	-17.5	-55.6	-122.5	-226.0	-571.8	-1153
Wind Drift • Inches	0.0	2.2	9.8	24.3	46.7	76.0	110.7	194.4	297.1

Winchester 150-grain Power-Point (X30306) G1 Ballistic Coefficient = 0.218

Distance • Yards	Muzzle	100	200	300	400	500	600	800	1000
Velocity • fps	2390	2018	1684	1398	1177	1036	945	822	729
Energy • Ft-lbs	1902	1356	944	651	461	357	298	225	177
Taylor KO Index	15.8	13.3	11.1	9.2	7.8	6.8	6.2	5.4	4.8
Path • Inches	-1.5	+3.6	0.0	-16.0	-49.9	-108.8	-200.0	-505.5	-1018
Wind Drift • Inches	0.0	2.0	8.5	20.9	40.1	66.1	97.4	173.6	266.4

Winchester 150-grain Silvertip (X30302) G1 Ballistic Coefficient = 0.218

Distance • Yards	Muzzle	100	200	300	400	500	600	800	1000
Velocity • fps	2390	2018	1684	1398	1177	1036	945	822	729
Energy • Ft-lbs	1902	1356	944	651	461	357	298	225	177
Taylor KO Index	15.8	13.3	11.1	9.2	7.8	6.8	6.2	5.4	4.8
Path • Inches	-1.5	+3.6	0.0	-16.0	-49.9	-108.8	-200.0	-505.5	-1018
Wind Drift • Inches	0.0	2.0	8.5	20.9	40.1	66.1	97.4	173.6	266.4

PMC 150-grain Flat Nose Soft Point (3030A) G1 Ballistic Coefficient = 0.214

Distance • Yards	Muzzle	100	200	300	400	500	600	800	1000
Velocity • fps	2300	1943	1627	1356	1152	1023	938	818	726
Energy • Ft-lbs	1762	1257	881	613	442	348	293	223	176
Taylor KO Index	15.2	12.8	10.7	8.9	7.6	6.8	6.2	5.4	4.8
Path • Inches	-1.5	+3.9	0.0	-17.2	-53.8	-116.6	-211.4	-515.0	-1005
Wind Drift • Inches	0.0	1.8	7.9	19.3	36.8	60.1	88.1	155.6	237.8

Winchester 150-grain Hollow Point (X30301) G1 Ballistic Coefficient = 0.218

Distance • Yards	Muzzle	100	200	300	400	500	600	800	1000
Velocity • fps	2390	2018	1684	1398	1177	1036	945	822	729
Energy • Ft-lbs	1902	1356	944	651	461	357	298	225	177
Taylor KO Index	15.8	13.3	11.1	9.2	7.8	6.8	6.2	5.4	4.8
Path • Inches	-1.5	+3.6	0.0	-16.0	-49.9	-108.8	-200.0	-505.5	-1018
Wind Drift • Inches	0.0	2.0	8.5	20.9	40.1	66.1	97.4	173.6	266.4

Speer 150-grain Flat Nose—UCSP (24504) (Discontinued in 2004) G1 Ballistic Coefficient = 0.268

Distance • Yards	Muzzle	100	200	300	400	500	600	800	1000
Velocity • fps	2370	2067	1788	1538	1323	1157	1044	906	813
Energy • Ft-lbs	1870	1423	1065	788	583	446	363	273	220
Taylor KO Index	15.6	13.6	11.8	10.2	8.7	7.6	6.9	6.0	5.4
Path • Inches	-1.5	+3.3	0.0	-14.4	-43.7	-92.6	-167.5	-418.6	-839.4
Wind Drift • Inches	0.0	1.6	6.8	16.4	31.2	51.7	77.6	142.3	221.3

PMC 150-grain Starfire HP (C3030SFA) G1 Ballistic Coefficient = 0.226

Distance • Yards	Muzzle	100	200	300	400	500	600	800	1000
Velocity • fps	2100	1769	1478	1242	1080	978	906	797	712
Energy • Ft-lbs	1469	1042	728	514	388	318	273	212	169
Taylor KO Index	13.9	11.7	9.8	8.2	7.1	6.5	6.0	5.3	4.7
Path • Inches	-1.5	+4.9	0.0	-20.9	-64.5	-137.7	-247.2	-600.0	-1172
Wind Drift • Inches	0.0	2.3	9.8	23.8	44.4	70.8	110.8	176.3	266.9

Federal 170-grain Nosler Partition (P3030D) (Discontinued in 2004)   G1 Ballistic Coefficient = 0.255

Distance • Yards	Muzzle	100	200	300	400	500	600	800	1000
Velocity • fps	2200	1900	1620	1380	1190	1060	975	858	771
Energy • Ft-lbs	1830	1355	990	720	535	425	359	278	225
Taylor KO Index	16.5	14.2	12.1	10.3	8.9	7.9	7.3	6.4	5.8
Path • Inches	-1.5	+4.1	0.0	-17.4	-52.4	-109.4	-204.5	-501.5	-988.1
Wind Drift • Inches	0.0	1.9	8.0	19.3	36.6	59.7	87.7	155.6	238.0

Federal 170-grain Hi-Shok Soft Point FN (3030B)   G1 Ballistic Coefficient = 0.255

Distance • Yards	Muzzle	100	200	300	400	500	600	800	1000
Velocity • fps	2200	1900	1620	1380	1190	1060	975	858	771
Energy • Ft-lbs	1830	1355	990	720	535	425	359	278	225
Taylor KO Index	16.5	14.2	12.1	10.3	8.9	7.9	7.3	6.4	5.8
Path • Inches	-1.5	+4.1	0.0	-17.4	-52.4	-109.4	-204.5	-501.5	-988.1
Wind Drift • Inches	0.0	1.9	8.0	19.3	36.6	59.7	87.7	155.6	238.0

Hornady 170-grain Flat Point InterLock (8085)   G1 Ballistic Coefficient = 0.186

Distance • Yards	Muzzle	100	200	300	400	500	600	800	1000
Velocity • fps	2200	1796	1450	1185	1022	924	850	737	645
Energy • Ft-lbs	1827	1218	793	530	395	322	273	205	157
Taylor KO Index	16.5	13.4	10.8	8.9	7.6	6.9	6.4	5.5	4.8
Path • Inches	-1.5	+4.7	0.0	-21.3	-67.4	-146.6	-266.5	-658.7	-1310
Wind Drift • Inches	0.0	2.6	11.4	28.0	52.5	83.2	119.4	205.5	312.0

Remington 170-grain Soft Point Core-Lokt (R30302)   G1 Ballistic Coefficient = 0.255

Distance • Yards	Muzzle	100	200	300	400	500	600	800	1000
Velocity • fps	2200	1895	1619	1381	1191	1061	975	858	771
Energy • Ft-lbs	1827	1355	989	720	535	425	359	278	225
Taylor KO Index	18.5	16.0	13.6	11.6	10.0	8.9	7.3	6.4	5.8
Path • Inches	-1.5	+4.1	0.0	-17.5	-53.3	-113.6	-204.5	-501.5	-988.1
Wind Drift • Inches	0.0	1.9	8.0	19.3	36.6	59.7	87.7	155.6	238.0

Winchester 170-grain Silvertip (X30304)   G1 Ballistic Coefficient = 0.278

Distance • Yards	Muzzle	100	200	300	400	500	600	800	1000
Velocity • fps	2200	1920	1665	1439	1251	1110	1015	893	806
Energy • Ft-lbs	1827	1392	1046	781	590	465	389	301	245
Taylor KO Index	16.5	14.4	12.5	10.8	9.4	8.3	7.6	6.7	6.0
Path • Inches	-1.5	+4.0	0.0	-16.6	-50.2	-106.0	-190.0	-464.2	-913.3
Wind Drift • Inches	0.0	1.7	7.2	17.4	32.9	53.8	79.7	143.2	220.1

Winchester 170-grain Power-Point (X30303)   G1 Ballistic Coefficient = 0.241

Distance • Yards	Muzzle	100	200	300	400	500	600	800	1000
Velocity • fps	2200	1879	1591	1346	1157	1034	952	837	749
Energy • Ft-lbs	1827	1332	955	783	506	405	342	264	212
Taylor KO Index	16.5	14.1	11.9	10.1	8.7	7.7	7.1	6.3	5.6
Path • Inches	-1.5	+4.2	0.0	-18.1	-55.5	-118.7	-214.5	-526.7	-1039
Wind Drift • Inches	0.0	2.0	8.5	20.7	39.1	63.6	92.9	163.7	249.6

Winchester 170-grain Silvertip (X30304)   G1 Ballistic Coefficient = 0.255

Distance • Yards	Muzzle	100	200	300	400	500	600	800	1000
Velocity • fps	2200	1895	1619	1381	1191	1061	975	858	771
Energy • Ft-lbs	1827	1355	989	720	535	425	359	278	225
Taylor KO Index	18.5	16.0	13.6	11.6	10.0	8.9	7.3	6.4	5.8
Path • Inches	-1.5	+4.1	0.0	-17.5	-53.3	-113.6	-204.5	-501.5	-988.1
Wind Drift • Inches	0.0	1.9	8.0	19.3	36.6	59.7	87.7	155.6	238.0

PMC 170-grain Flat Nose Soft Point (3030B)   G1 Ballistic Coefficient = 0.278

Distance • Yards	Muzzle	100	200	300	400	500	600	800	1000
Velocity • fps	2150	1840	1566	1333	1153	1034	954	840	753
Energy • Ft-lbs	1745	1277	926	671	502	404	343	266	214
Taylor KO Index	16.1	13.8	11.7	10.0	8.6	7.7	7.1	6.3	5.6
Path • Inches	-1.5	+5.3	0.0	-18.7	-57.3	-112.1	-218.4	-512.8	-1004
Wind Drift • Inches	0.0	2.0	8.5	20.5	38.7	62.7	91.4	160.6	244.4

Remington 170-grain Core-Lokt Hollow Point (R30303)

G1 Ballistic Coefficient = 0.255

Distance • Yards	Muzzle	100	200	300	400	500	600	800	1000
Velocity • fps	2200	1895	1619	1381	1191	1061	975	858	771
Energy • Ft-lbs	1827	1355	989	720	535	425	359	278	225
Taylor KO Index	18.5	16.0	13.6	11.6	10.0	8.9	7.3	6.4	5.8
Path • Inches	-1.5	+4.1	0.0	-17.5	-53.3	-113.6	-204.5	-501.5	-988.1
Wind Drift • Inches	0.0	1.9	8.0	19.3	36.6	59.7	87.7	155.6	238.0

Nice large-bodied whitetail buck guided by Keaton Kelso. (Photo from *Ask the Whitetail Guides* by J. Y. Jones, 2006, Safari Press)

.300 Savage

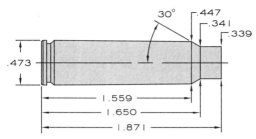

The .300 Savage cartridge was introduced in 1921 for the Savage Model 99 lever-action rifle. On the basis of case volume, it should fall just a little bit short of the .308's performance. But because the .300 Savage was to be used in guns that were not quite as strong as the current standards for bolt-action guns, the pressure specifications are about 10 percent lower than those of the .308. Even with this handicap, the .300 Savage is an entirely adequate hunting cartridge, outperforming the venerable .30-30 by about 250 fps. In spite of its performance advantage, the cartridge has never achieved the popularity of the .30-30.

Relative Recoil Factor = 1.78

Specifications

Controlling Agency for Standardization of this Ammunition: SAAMI

Bullet Weight Grains	Velocity fps	Maximum Average Pressure	
		Copper Crusher	Transducer
150	2,615	46,000 cup	47,000 psi
180	2,340	46,000 cup	47,000 psi

Standard barrel for velocity testing: 24 inches long—1 turn in 12-inch twist

Availability

Federal 150-grain Hi-Shok Soft Point (300A)

G1 Ballistic Coefficient = 0.313

Distance • Yards	Muzzle	100	200	300	400	500	600	800	1000
Velocity • fps	2630	2350	2100	1850	1630	1430	1262	1039	919
Energy • Ft-lbs	2305	1845	1460	1145	885	685	530	360	282
Taylor KO Index	17.4	15.5	13.9	12.2	10.8	9.4	8.3	6.9	6.1
Path • Inches	-1.5	+2.4	0.0	-10.4	-30.9	-64.4	-115.6	-288.2	-589.1
Wind Drift • Inches	0.0	1.2	4.9	11.6	22.0	36.6	55.8	108.8	177.2

Remington 150-grain Core-Lokt Pointed Soft Point (R30SV2)

G1 Ballistic Coefficient = 0.314

Distance • Yards	Muzzle	100	200	300	400	500	600	800	1000
Velocity • fps	2630	2354	2095	1853	1631	1432	1265	1041	921
Energy • Ft-lbs	2303	1845	1462	1143	806	685	533	361	283
Taylor KO Index	17.4	15.5	13.8	12.2	10.8	9.5	8.3	6.9	6.1
Path • Inches	-1.5	+2.4	0.0	-10.4	-30.9	-64.6	-115.3	-287.3	-587.1
Wind Drift • Inches	0.0	1.2	4.8	11.6	21.9	36.4	55.6	108.4	176.6

Winchester 150-grain Power-Point (X3001)

G1 Ballistic Coefficient = 0.271

Distance • Yards	Muzzle	100	200	300	400	500	600	800	1000
Velocity • fps	2630	2311	2015	1743	1500	1295	1139	958	852
Energy • Ft-lbs	2303	1779	1352	1012	749	558	432	306	242
Taylor KO Index	17.4	15.3	13.3	11.5	9.9	8.5	7.5	6.3	5.6
Path • Inches	-1.5	+2.8	0.0	-11.5	-34.4	-73.0	-130.9	-334.8	-690.0
Wind Drift • Inches	0.0	1.3	5.7	13.8	26.4	44.2	67.7	129.6	206.8

Federal 180-grain Hi-Shok Soft Point (300B)

G1 Ballistic Coefficient = 0.383

Distance • Yards	Muzzle	100	200	300	400	500	600	800	1000
Velocity • fps	2350	2140	1940	1750	1570	1410	1275	1077	962
Energy • Ft-lbs	2205	1825	1495	1215	985	800	650	464	370
Taylor KO Index	18.6	16.9	15.4	13.9	12.4	11.2	10.1	8.5	7.6
Path • Inches	-1.5	+3.1	0.0	-12.4	-36.1	-73.8	-129.8	-309.4	-608.5
Wind Drift • Inches	0.0	1.1	4.6	10.9	20.4	33.4	50.3	96.1	155.4

Remington 180-grain Core-Lokt Soft Point (R30SV3)

G1 Ballistic Coefficient = 0.248

Distance • Yards	Muzzle	100	200	300	400	500	600	800	1000
Velocity • fps	2350	2025	1728	1467	1252	1098	998	870	778
Energy • Ft-lbs	2207	1639	1193	860	626	482	398	302	242
Taylor KO Index	18.6	16.0	13.7	11.6	9.9	8.7	7.9	6.9	6.2
Path • Inches	-1.5	+3.5	0.0	-15.3	-46.8	-100.6	-183.1	-458.4	-918.1
Wind Drift • Inches	0.0	1.7	7.5	18.2	34.8	57.6	85.6	154.6	238.6

Crocodile shot by José A. Martínez de Hoz in Zimbabwe. (Photo from *A Sporting Life* by José A. Martínez de Hoz, 2005, Safari Press)

.308 Winchester (7.62mm NATO)

The U.S. Army was working on a potential replacement for the .30-06 cartridge during WWII. The best candidate was called the T65. By the early 1950s it was in the final stages of a serious testing process. While the T65 was not adopted as a standardized military cartridge until 1955, Winchester, who had participated in the development process, jumped the gun (no pun intended) and introduced the .308 Winchester in 1952. Any standardized U.S. military cartridge is almost certain to be "popular," and the .308 has lived up to that expectation. With just a little less recoil than the .30-06 (and a little less performance), the .308 has spawned a series of X-08 neck-downs. The number of different loadings available testifies to the popularity of this caliber.

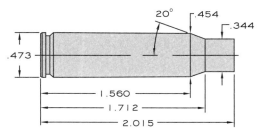

Relative Recoil Factor = 1.95

Specifications

Controlling Agency for Standardization of this Ammunition: SAAMI

Bullet Weight Grains	Velocity fps	Maximum Average Pressure	
		Copper Crusher	Transducer
55 (Saboted)	3,750	N/S	52,000 psi
110	3,150	52,000 cup	62,000 psi
125	3,030	52,000 cup	62,000 psi
150	2,800	52,000 cup	62,000 psi
165–168	2,670	52,000 cup	62,000 psi
180	2,600	52,000 cup	62,000 psi
200	2,440	52,000 cup	62,000 psi

Standard barrel for velocity testing: 24 inches long—1 turn in 12-inch twist

Availability

Ultramax 110-grain Sierra HP (308R1)
G1 Ballistic Coefficient = 0.160

Distance • Yards	Muzzle	100	200	300	400	500	600	800	1000
Velocity • fps	2875	2321	1833	1424	1133	976	879	741	635
Energy • Ft-lbs	2019	1316	821	496	314	233	189	134	98
Taylor KO Index	13.9	11.2	8.9	6.9	5.5	4.7	4.3	3.6	3.1
Path • Inches	-1.5	+2.5	0.0	-13.1	-43.7	-101.2	-195.2	-527.1	-1115
Wind Drift • Inches	0.0	2.1	9.3	23.7	47.2	74.4	118.2	213.0	331.0

PMC 120-grain NT/FR (308HRA)
G1 Ballistic Coefficient = 0.115

Distance • Yards	Muzzle	100	200	300	400	500	600	800	1000
Velocity • fps	2600	1866	1312	1020	875	775	693	560	453
Energy • Ft-lbs	1801	958	459	277	204	160	128	84	55
Taylor KO Index	13.7	9.9	6.9	5.4	4.6	4.1	3.7	3.0	2.4
Path • Inches	-1.5	+4.3	0.0	-24.3	-81.7	-184.7	-345.8	-903.8	-1918
Wind Drift • Inches	0.0	3.5	16.6	42.3	78.2	122.2	174.1	303.8	475.4

Lapua 123-grain Full Metal Jacket (4317527)
G1 Ballistic Coefficient = 0.274

Distance • Yards	Muzzle	100	200	300	400	500	600	800	1000
Velocity • fps	2936	2599	2286	1995	1728	1490	1289	1031	901
Energy • Ft-lbs	2355	1845	1428	1087	816	606	454	290	222
Taylor KO Index	15.9	14.1	12.4	10.8	9.4	8.1	7.0	5.6	4.9
Path • Inches	-1.5	+1.8	0.0	-8.5	-25.9	-54.9	-99.8	-258.4	-547.2
Wind Drift • Inches	0.0	1.1	4.8	11.6	22.0	37.0	57.2	114.0	188.2

Cor-Bon 125-grain Jacketed Hollow Point (SD308125/20)
G1 Ballistic Coefficient = 0.200

Distance • Yards	Muzzle	100	200	300	400	500	600	800	1000
Velocity • fps	3150	2673	2243	1855	1516	1245	1065	882	767
Energy • Ft-lbs	2755	1984	1397	955	638	430	315	216	163
Taylor KO Index	17.3	14.7	12.3	10.2	8.2	6.8	5.9	4.9	4.2
Path • Inches	-1.5	+1.7	0.0	-8.7	-27.8	-62.8	-121.2	-333.0	-703.9
Wind Drift • Inches	0.0	1.3	5.6	13.8	27.1	46.7	73.1	141.9	227.6

Cor-Bon 130-grain Glaser Safety (SD308125/20)
G1 Ballistic Coefficient = 0.200

Distance • Yards	Muzzle	100	200	300	400	500	600	800	1000
Velocity • fps	3000	2539	2122	1748	1427	1182	1029	863	754
Energy • Ft-lbs	2597	1861	1300	882	588	403	306	215	164
Taylor KO Index	17.2	14.5	12.1	10.0	8.2	6.8	5.9	4.9	4.3
Path • Inches	-1.5	+2.0	0.0	-9.8	-31.2	-69.8	-133.2	-365.6	-785.1
Wind Drift • Inches	0.0	1.5	6.7	16.5	32.4	55.6	86.2	163.9	260.1

Remington 125-grain Core-Lokt Pointed Soft Point (RL308W1)
G1 Ballistic Coefficient = 0.278

Distance • Yards	Muzzle	100	200	300	400	500	600	800	1000
Velocity • fps	2660	2348	2057	1788	1546	1338	1173	979	869
Energy • Ft-lbs	1964	1529	1174	837	663	497	382	266	210
Taylor KO Index	14.6	12.9	11.3	9.8	8.5	7.4	6.5	5.4	4.8
Path • Inches	-1.5	+2.4	0.0	-10.7	-32.4	-68.6	-124.4	-317.5	-655.4
Wind Drift • Inches	0.0	1.3	5.5	13.2	25.1	42.0	64.4	124.2	199.5

Hirtenberger 146-grain Full Metal Jacket (82200416)
G1 Ballistic Coefficient = 0.412

Distance • Yards	Muzzle	100	200	300	400	500	600	800	1000
Velocity • fps	2822	2601	2390	2189	1998	1817	1648	1354	1138
Energy • Ft-lbs	2582	2193	1852	1554	1294	1071	881	595	420
Taylor KO Index	18.1	16.7	15.4	14.1	12.8	11.7	10.6	8.7	7.3
Path • Inches	-1.5	+1.8	0.0	-7.9	-23.1	-47.1	-81.6	-191.9	-378.6
Wind Drift • Inches	0.0	0.7	2.9	6.9	12.8	20.8	31.5	61.5	104.8

PMC 147-grain PSP (308B)
G1 Ballistic Coefficient = 0.445

Distance • Yards	Muzzle	100	200	300	400	500	600	800	1000
Velocity • fps	2780	2575	2380	2194	2018	1859	1692	1410	1190
Energy • Ft-lbs	2522	2164	1848	1571	1329	1118	935	650	463
Taylor KO Index	18.0	16.6	15.4	14.2	13.1	12.0	10.9	9.1	7.7
Path • Inches	-1.5	+1.9	0.0	-8.0	-23.3	-47.1	-81.0	-187.8	-365.1
Wind Drift • Inches	0.0	0.7	3.0	7.1	13.2	21.5	32.4	62.8	106.7

USA (Winchester) 147-grain Full Metal Jacket (USA3081)
G1 Ballistic Coefficient = 0.417

Distance • Yards	Muzzle	100	200	300	400	500	600	800	1000
Velocity • fps	2800	2582	2374	2176	1987	1812	1646	1356	1141
Energy • Ft-lbs	2559	2176	1840	1545	1289	1072	884	600	425
Taylor KO Index	18.1	16.7	15.4	14.1	12.9	11.7	10.6	8.8	7.4
Path • Inches	-1.5	+1.9	0.0	-8.0	-23.5	-46.6	-82.4	-193.4	-380.7
Wind Drift • Inches	0.0	0.8	3.2	7.6	14.1	23.1	34.8	67.9	115.5

Sellier & Bellot 147-grain FMJ (SBA30807)
G1 Ballistic Coefficient = 0.409

Distance • Yards	Muzzle	100	200	300	400	500	600	800	1000
Velocity • fps	2808	2578	2367	2173	1982	1801	1633	1341	1128
Energy • Ft-lbs	2581	2175	1833	1545	1283	1059	870	587	416
Taylor KO Index	18.2	16.7	15.3	14.1	12.8	11.6	10.6	8.7	7.3
Path • Inches	-1.5	+1.8	0.0	-8.0	-23.4	-47.7	-82.8	-195.0	-385.2
Wind Drift • Inches	0.0	0.7	3.0	7.0	12.9	21.2	32.0	62.5	106.4

Hornady 150-grain SP-LM InterLock (8590)
G1 Ballistic Coefficient = 0.338

Distance • Yards	Muzzle	100	200	300	400	500	600	800	1000
Velocity • fps	3000	2721	2495	2212	1979	1762	1562	1237	1037
Energy • Ft-lbs	2997	2466	2014	1629	1305	1034	813	509	359
Taylor KO Index	19.8	18.0	16.5	14.6	13.1	11.6	10.3	8.2	6.8
Path • Inches	-1.5	+1.9	0.0	-7.7	-22.5	-46.2	-80.1	-196.3	-403.9
Wind Drift • Inches	0.0	0.9	3.7	8.8	16.4	27.1	41.3	82.5	141.3

Hirtenberger 150-grain Nosler Soft Point (82200384)

G1 Ballistic Coefficient = 0.343

Distance • Yards	Muzzle	100	200	300	400	500	600	800	1000
Velocity • fps	2920	2650	2395	2155	1928	1718	1526	1107	1028
Energy • Ft-lbs	2841	2339	1911	1547	1239	983	776	492	352
Taylor KO Index	19.3	17.5	15.8	14.2	12.7	11.3	10.1	7.3	6.8
Path • Inches	-1.5	+1.7	0.0	-7.8	-23.2	-47.9	-84.4	-206.5	-423.0
Wind Drift • Inches	0.0	0.8	3.4	8.0	15.1	24.8	38.0	75.6	128.8

Speer 150-grain Grand Slam (24550) (Discontinued in 2004)

G1 Ballistic Coefficient = 0.305

Distance • Yards	Muzzle	100	200	300	400	500	600	800	1000
Velocity • fps	2875	2575	2294	2032	1788	1566	1371	1092	948
Energy • Ft-lbs	2753	2208	1753	1376	1065	817	626	398	299
Taylor KO Index	19.0	17.0	15.1	13.4	11.8	10.3	9.0	7.2	6.3
Path • Inches	-1.5	+1.9	0.0	-8.5	-25.5	-53.6	-96.1	-244.3	-507.8
Wind Drift • Inches	0.0	1.0	4.4	10.5	19.8	33.0	50.87	101.1	168.8

Winchester 150-grain Partition Gold (SPG308)

G1 Ballistic Coefficient = 0.363

Distance • Yards	Muzzle	100	200	300	400	500	600	800	1000
Velocity • fps	2900	2645	2405	2177	1962	1760	1574	1264	1063
Energy • Ft-lbs	2802	2332	1927	1579	1282	1032	825	532	376
Taylor KO Index	19.1	17.5	15.9	14.4	12.9	11.6	10.4	8.3	7.0
Path • Inches	-1.5	+1.7	0.0	-7.8	-22.9	-47.0	-82.6	-199.4	-403.7
Wind Drift • Inches	0.0	0.9	3.6	8.5	15.8	26.0	39.6	78.3	133.7

Winchester 150-grain Power-Point Plus (SHV3085)

G1 Ballistic Coefficient = 0.267

Distance • Yards	Muzzle	100	200	300	400	500	600	800	1000
Velocity • fps	2900	2558	2241	1946	1678	1441	1244	1005	882
Energy • Ft-lbs	2802	2180	1672	1262	938	692	515	337	259
Taylor KO Index	19.1	16.9	14.8	12.8	11.1	9.5	8.2	6.6	5.8
Path • Inches	-1.5	+1.9	0.0	-6.3	-18.3	-37.1	-105.3	-274.0	-579.8
Wind Drift • Inches	0.0	1.2	4.9	11.7	22.3	37.3	60.4	119.6	195.9

Federal 150-grain Nosler Partition (P308S)

G1 Ballistic Coefficient = 0.384

Distance • Yards	Muzzle	100	200	300	400	500	600	800	1000
Velocity • fps	2840	2600	2380	2160	1960	1770	1593	1293	1089
Energy • Ft-lbs	2685	2255	1880	1560	1280	1040	845	557	395
Taylor KO Index	18.7	17.2	15.7	14.3	12.9	11.7	10.5	8.5	7.2
Path • Inches	-1.5	+1.8	0.0	-8.1	-23.4	-48.0	-83.7	-199.5	-399.0
Wind Drift • Inches	0.0	0.8	3.5	8.2	15.2	25.0	37.9	74.5	126.9

Federal 150-grain Hi-Shok Soft Point (308A)

G1 Ballistic Coefficient = 0.315

Distance • Yards	Muzzle	100	200	300	400	500	600	800	1000
Velocity • fps	2820	2530	2260	2010	1770	1560	1373	1100	956
Energy • Ft-lbs	2650	2140	1705	1345	1050	810	628	403	304
Taylor KO Index	18.6	16.7	14.9	13.3	11.7	10.3	9.1	7.3	6.3
Path • Inches	-1.5	+2.0	0.0	-8.8	-26.3	-54.8	-97.6	+243.8	-504.6
Wind Drift • Inches	0.0	1.0	4.4	10.4	19.6	32.6	50.0	99.2	165.5

Hornady 150-grain BTSP InterLock (8091)

G1 Ballistic Coefficient = 0.349

Distance • Yards	Muzzle	100	200	300	400	500	600	800	1000
Velocity • fps	2820	2560	2315	2084	1866	1664	1481	1190	1017
Energy • Ft-lbs	2648	2183	1785	1446	1159	992	731	471	345
Taylor KO Index	18.6	16.9	15.3	13.8	12.3	11.0	9.8	7.9	6.7
Path • Inches	-1.5	+1.9	0.0	-8.4	-24.9	-51.4	-90.5	-220.4	-448.8
Wind Drift • Inches	0.0	0.9	3.9	9.2	17.3	28.5	43.4	86.0	145.3

PMC 150-grain Soft Point Boat Tail (308HA)

G1 Ballistic Coefficient = 0.380

Distance • Yards	Muzzle	100	200	300	400	500	600	800	1000
Velocity • fps	2820	2581	2354	2139	1935	1744	1567	1271	1073
Energy • Ft-lbs	2648	2218	1846	1523	1247	1013	818	538	384
Taylor KO Index	18.6	17.0	15.5	14.1	12.8	11.5	10.3	8.4	7.1
Path • Inches	-1.5	+1.9	0.0	-8.2	-24.0	-49.0	-85.8	-206.2	-416.1
Wind Drift • Inches	0.0	0.8	3.6	8.4	15.6	25.6	38.9	76.5	130.0

Remington 150-grain Core-Lokt Ultra Bonded (PRC308WA)   G1 Ballistic Coefficient = 0.331

Distance • Yards	Muzzle	100	200	300	400	500	600	800	1000
Velocity • fps	2820	2546	2288	2048	1819	1611	1423	1140	983
Energy • Ft-lbs	2648	2159	1744	1394	1102	864	674	433	322
Taylor KO Index	18.0	16.8	15.1	13.5	12.0	10.6	9.4	7.5	6.5
Path • Inches	-1.5	+1.9	0.0	-8.6	-25.3	-53.1	-94.1	-232.4	-477.6
Wind Drift • Inches	0.0	1.0	4.1	9.8	18.5	30.6	46.8	92.9	155.9

Remington 150-grain Core-Lokt Pointed Soft Point (R308W1)   G1 Ballistic Coefficient = 0.315

Distance • Yards	Muzzle	100	200	300	400	500	600	800	1000
Velocity • fps	2820	2533	2263	2009	1774	1560	1373	1100	955
Energy • Ft-lbs	2649	2137	1705	1344	1048	810	628	403	304
Taylor KO Index	18.6	16.7	14.9	13.3	11.7	10.3	9.1	7.3	6.3
Path • Inches	-1.5	+2.0	0.0	-8.8	-26.2	-54.8	-98.1	-247.0	-510.1
Wind Drift • Inches	0.0	1.0	4.4	10.4	19.6	32.6	50.0	99.2	165.4

Winchester 150-grain Fail Safe (S308XA)   G1 Ballistic Coefficient = 0.314

Distance • Yards	Muzzle	100	200	300	400	500	600	800	1000
Velocity • fps	2820	2533	2263	2010	1775	1561	1371	1099	955
Energy • Ft-lbs	2649	2137	1706	1346	1049	812	627	402	304
Taylor KO Index	18.6	16.7	14.9	13.3	11.7	10.3	9.0	7.0	6.3
Path • Inches	-1.5	+2.0	0.0	-8.8	-26.2	-54.6	-97.8	-244.3	-505.4
Wind Drift • Inches	0.0	1.0	4.4	10.4	19.7	32.7	50.1	99.4	165.8

Winchester 150-grain Power-Point (X3085)   G1 Ballistic Coefficient = 0.271

Distance • Yards	Muzzle	100	200	300	400	500	600	800	1000
Velocity • fps	2820	2488	2179	1893	1633	1405	1221	997	878
Energy • Ft-lbs	2648	2061	1581	1193	888	657	497	313	257
Taylor KO Index	18.6	16.4	14.4	12.5	10.8	9.3	8.1	6.6	5.8
Path • Inches	-1.5	+2.4	0.0	-9.8	-29.3	-62.0	-112.0	-291.2	-601.8
Wind Drift • Inches	0.0	1.2	5.2	12.4	23.8	39.9	61.5	120.9	196.8

Federal 150-grain Nosler Solid Base BT (P308S1)   G1 Ballistic Coefficient = 0.393

Distance • Yards	Muzzle	100	200	300	400	500	600	800	1000
Velocity • fps	2800	2570	2350	2150	1950	1760	1588	1296	1094
Energy • Ft-lbs	2610	2200	1845	1535	1265	1035	840	559	398
Taylor KO Index	18.5	17.0	15.5	14.2	12.9	11.6	10.5	8.6	7.2
Path • Inches	-1.5	+1.9	0.0	-8.3	-23.9	-48.9	-85.3	-202.5	-403.1
Wind Drift • Inches	0.0	0.8	3.5	8.1	15.1	24.8	37.6	73.7	125.2

Sellier & Bellot 150-grain SPCE (SBA30801)   G1 Ballistic Coefficient = 0.326

Distance • Yards	Muzzle	100	200	300	400	500	600	800	1000
Velocity • fps	2756	2470	2213	1983	1757	1552	1371	1105	962
Energy • Ft-lbs	2524	2027	1627	1307	1029	802	626	407	308
Taylor KO Index	18.2	16.3	14.6	13.1	11.6	10.2	9.0	7.3	6.3
Path • Inches	-1.5	+2.1	0.0	-9.1	-27.2	-56.6	-100.8	-251.6	-515.6
Wind Drift • Inches	0.0	1.0	4.3	10.3	19.5	32.3	49.4	97.5	162.2

PMC 150-grain Pointed Soft Point (308A)   G1 Ballistic Coefficient = 0.333

Distance • Yards	Muzzle	100	200	300	400	500	600	800	1000
Velocity • fps	2750	2478	2224	1987	1766	1569	1388	1120	973
Energy • Ft-lbs	2519	2045	1647	1315	1036	820	642	418	315
Taylor KO Index	18.2	16.4	14.7	13.1	11.7	10.4	9.2	7.4	6.4
Path • Inches	-1.5	+2.1	0.0	-9.2	-27.1	-56.1	-99.7	-247.5	-506.4
Wind Drift • Inches	0.0	1.0	4.3	10.1	19.0	31.5	48.1	95.0	158.4

Hornady 150-grain SST-LM (8593)   G1 Ballistic Coefficient = 0.415

Distance • Yards	Muzzle	100	200	300	400	500	600	800	1000
Velocity • fps	3000	2772	2555	2348	2151	1963	1786	1470	1220
Energy • Ft-lbs	2997	2558	2173	1836	1540	1283	1063	720	496
Taylor KO Index	19.8	18.3	16.9	15.5	14.2	13.0	11.8	9.7	8.1
Path • Inches	-1.5	+1.5	0.0	-6.9	-20.0	-40.7	-70.5	-165.2	-324.9
Wind Drift • Inches	0.0	0.7	3.0	6.9	12.8	20.9	31.5	61.6	105.5

Norma 150-grain Nosler BST (17625)

G1 Ballistic Coefficient = 0.389

Distance • Yards	Muzzle	100	200	300	400	500	600	800	1000
Velocity • fps	2822	2588	2365	2154	1955	1767	1592	1296	1091
Energy • Ft-lbs	2653	2231	1864	1545	1273	1040	845	559	397
Taylor KO Index	18.6	17.1	15.6	14.2	12.9	11.7	10.5	8.6	7.2
Path • Inches	-1.5	+1.8	0.0	-8.1	-23.7	-48.4	-84.4	-201.8	-405.4
Wind Drift • Inches	0.0	0.8	3.5	8.1	15.2	24.9	37.6	74.0	125.9

Federal 150-grain Nosler Ballistic Tip (P308F)

G1 Ballistic Coefficient = 0.433

Distance • Yards	Muzzle	100	200	300	400	500	600	800	1000
Velocity • fps	2820	2610	2410	2220	2040	1860	1695	1405	1181
Energy • Ft-lbs	2650	2270	1935	1640	1380	1155	957	658	465
Taylor KO Index	18.6	17.2	15.9	14.7	13.5	12.3	11.2	9.3	7.8
Path • Inches	-1.5	+1.8	0.0	-7.8	-22.7	-46.0	-79.5	-185.3	-362.2
Wind Drift • Inches	0.0	0.7	3.1	7.2	13.4	21.8	32.8	64.0	108.8

Federal 150-grain Barnes Triple Shock X-Bullet (P308V)

G1 Ballistic Coefficient = 0.433

Distance • Yards	Muzzle	100	200	300	400	500	600	800	1000
Velocity • fps	2820	2610	2410	2220	2040	1860	1695	1405	1181
Energy • Ft-lbs	2650	2270	1935	1640	1380	1155	957	658	465
Taylor KO Index	18.6	17.2	15.9	14.7	13.5	12.3	11.2	9.3	7.8
Path • Inches	-1.5	+1.8	0.0	-7.8	-22.7	-46.0	-79.5	-185.3	-362.2
Wind Drift • Inches	0.0	0.7	3.1	7.2	13.4	21.8	32.8	64.0	108.8

Hornady 150-grain SST (8093)

G1 Ballistic Coefficient = 0.415

Distance • Yards	Muzzle	100	200	300	400	500	600	800	1000
Velocity • fps	2820	2601	2392	2192	2003	1823	1656	1362	1145
Energy • Ft-lbs	2648	2252	1905	1601	1336	1107	913	618	437
Taylor KO Index	18.6	17.2	15.8	14.5	13.2	12.0	10.9	9.0	7.6
Path • Inches	-1.5	+1.8	0.0	-7.9	-23.1	-47.1	-81.3	-190.9	-376.1
Wind Drift • Inches	0.0	0.8	3.2	7.6	14.0	22.9	34.6	67.6	115.2

Federal 150-grain Barnes XLC Coated (P308R) (Discontinued in 2005)

G1 Ballistic Coefficient = 0.429

Distance • Yards	Muzzle	100	200	300	400	500	600	800	1000
Velocity • fps	2820	2610	2400	2210	2030	1850	1686	1395	1173
Energy • Ft-lbs	2650	2265	1925	1630	1370	1140	947	649	458
Taylor KO Index	18.6	17.2	15.8	14.6	13.4	12.2	11.1	9.2	7.7
Path • Inches	-1.5	+1.8	0.0	-7.9	-22.9	-46.1	-79.9	-186.6	-365.3
Wind Drift • Inches	0.0	0.7	2.8	6.6	12.2	19.9	29.9	58.3	99.2

Hornady 150-grain SST (8093)

G1 Ballistic Coefficient = 0.342

Distance • Yards	Muzzle	100	200	300	400	500	600	800	1000
Velocity • fps	2820	2560	2315	2084	1866	1644	1459	1169	1003
Energy • Ft-lbs	2648	2183	1785	1447	1160	922	709	456	335
Taylor KO Index	18.6	16.9	15.3	13.8	12.3	10.9	9.6	7.7	6.6
Path • Inches	-1.5	+2.0	0.0	-8.5	-25.2	-51.8	-92.1	-227.2	466.0
Wind Drift • Inches	0.0	1.0	4.0	9.4	17.7	29.3	44.7	88.6	149.3

Remington 150-grain Swift Scirocco Bonded (PRSC308WA)

G1 Ballistic Coefficient = 0.422

Distance • Yards	Muzzle	100	200	300	400	500	600	800	1000
Velocity • fps	2820	2513	2333	2161	1996	1839	1672	1380	1160
Energy • Ft-lbs	2670	2313	1994	1711	1459	1239	931	634	448
Taylor KO Index	18.6	16.6	15.4	14.3	13.2	12.1	11.0	9.1	7.7
Path • Inches	-1.5	+2.0	0.0	-8.4	-24.3	-48.9	-80.6	-188.6	-370.3
Wind Drift • Inches	0.0	0.8	3.2	7.4	13.8	22.5	33.9	66.1	112.5

Winchester 150-grain Ballistic Silvertip (SBST308)

G1 Ballistic Coefficient = 0.435

Distance • Yards	Muzzle	100	200	300	400	500	600	800	1000
Velocity • fps	2810	2601	2401	2211	2028	1856	1692	1404	1181
Energy • Ft-lbs	2629	2253	1920	1627	1370	1147	954	657	465
Taylor KO Index	18.5	17.2	15.8	14.6	13.4	12.2	11.2	9.3	7.8
Path • Inches	-1.5	+1.8	0.0	-7.8	-22.8	-46.2	-80.0	-186.9	-367.0
Wind Drift • Inches	0.0	0.7	3.1	7.2	13.4	21.8	32.8	63.8	108.6

Black Hills 150-grain Nosler Ballistic Tip (SBST308)
G1 Ballistic Coefficient = 0.435

Distance • Yards	Muzzle	100	200	300	400	500	600	800	1000
Velocity • fps	2800	2591	2392	2201	2020	1847	1685	1398	1177
Energy • Ft-lbs	2612	2237	1906	1615	1359	1137	946	651	462
Taylor KO Index	18.5	17.1	15.8	14.5	13.3	12.2	11.2	9.2	7.8
Path • Inches	-1.5	+1.8	0.0	-7.9	-23.0	-46.7	-80.6	-187.6	-366.3
Wind Drift • Inches	0.0	0.8	3.1	7.2	13.4	21.9	33.0	64.1	109.0

Lapua 150-grain Mega Soft Point (4317498)
G1 Ballistic Coefficient = 0.323

Distance • Yards	Muzzle	100	200	300	400	500	600	800	1000
Velocity • fps	2789	2511	2249	2003	1774	1565	1381	1109	963
Energy • Ft-lbs	2591	2100	1685	1337	1049	816	635	410	309
Taylor KO Index	18.4	16.6	14.8	13.2	11.7	10.3	9.1	7.3	6.4
Path • Inches	-1.5	+2.0	0.0	-8.9	-26.6	-55.3	-98.7	-247.0	-507.9
Wind Drift • Inches	0.0	1.0	4.3	10.3	19.3	32.1	49.1	97.2	162.2

Lapua 150-grain Lock Base (4317538)
G1 Ballistic Coefficient = 0.488

Distance • Yards	Muzzle	100	200	300	400	500	600	800	1000
Velocity • fps	2789	2603	2424	2253	2088	1930	1781	1508	1282
Energy • Ft-lbs	2586	2253	1954	1687	1449	1239	1054	756	546
Taylor KO Index	18.4	17.2	16.0	14.9	13.8	12.7	11.8	10.0	8.5
Path • Inches	-1.5	+1.8	0.0	-7.7	-22.4	-45.0	-76.9	-175.7	-336.2
Wind Drift • Inches	0.0	0.6	2.5	5.8	10.6	17.3	25.9	49.9	84.3

PMC 150-grain Barnes XLC-HP (308XLA)
G1 Ballistic Coefficient = 0.453

Distance • Yards	Muzzle	100	200	300	400	500	600	800	1000
Velocity • fps	2700	2504	2316	2135	1964	1801	1640	1378	1170
Energy • Ft-lbs	2428	2087	1786	1518	1284	1080	905	633	456
Taylor KO Index	17.8	16.5	15.3	14.1	13.0	11.9	10.9	9.1	7.7
Path • Inches	-1.5	+2.0	0.0	-8.6	-24.7	-50.0	-85.8	-199.3	-388.5
Wind Drift • Inches	0.0	0.8	3.1	7.3	13.5	22.1	33.1	64.2	108.5

Ultramax 150-grain Nosler Ballistic Tip (308R2)
G1 Ballistic Coefficient = 0.433

Distance • Yards	Muzzle	100	200	300	400	500	600	800	1000
Velocity • fps	2700	2495	2299	2112	1934	1766	1609	1336	1134
Energy • Ft-lbs	2429	2074	1761	1486	1246	1039	862	594	429
Taylor KO Index	17.8	16.5	15.2	13.9	12.8	11.7	10.6	8.8	7.5
Path • Inches	-1.5	+2.1	0.0	-8.6	-25.1	-50.9	-87.8	-204.9	-400.4
Wind Drift • Inches	0.0	0.8	3.3	7.7	14.2	23.3	35.0	68.1	115.2

American Eagle (Federal) 150-grain Full Metal Jacket Boat-Tail (AE308D)
G1 Ballistic Coefficient = 0.455

Distance • Yards	Muzzle	100	200	300	400	500	600	800	1000
Velocity • fps	2820	2620	2430	2250	2070	1900	1742	1457	1228
Energy • Ft-lbs	2650	2285	1965	1680	1430	1205	1011	707	503
Taylor KO Index	18.6	17.3	16.0	14.9	13.7	12.5	11.5	9.1	8.1
Path • Inches	-1.5	+1.8	0.0	-7.7	-22.3	-45.1	-77.5	-179.6	-349.4
Wind Drift • Inches	0.0	0.7	2.9	6.8	12.6	20.6	30.8	59.8	101.5

UMC (Remington) 150-grain MC (L308W4)
G1 Ballistic Coefficient = 0.315

Distance • Yards	Muzzle	100	200	300	400	500	600	800	1000
Velocity • fps	2820	2533	2263	2010	1776	1561	1373	1100	955
Energy • Ft-lbs	2649	2137	1707	1347	1050	812	628	403	304
Taylor KO Index	18.6	16.7	14.9	13.3	11.7	10.3	9.1	7.3	6.3
Path • Inches	-1.5	+2.0	0.0	-8.8	-26.2	-54.8	-98.1	-247.0	-510.1
Wind Drift • Inches	0.0	1.0	4.4	10.4	19.6	32.6	50.0	99.2	165.4

Lapua 155-grain Scenar (C317073)
G1 Ballistic Coefficient = 0.510

Distance • Yards	Muzzle	100	200	300	400	500	600	800	1000
Velocity • fps	2838	2658	2458	2318	2158	2004	1857	1586	1354
Energy • Ft-lbs	2773	2432	2126	1850	1603	1383	1188	866	631
Taylor KO Index	19.4	18.1	16.9	15.8	14.7	13.7	12.7	10.8	9.2
Path • Inches	-1.5	+1.7	0.0	-7.4	-21.2	-42.5	-72.4	-164.6	-313.5
Wind Drift • Inches	0.0	0.6	2.6	6.0	11.0	17.7	26.5	50.8	85.8

Lapua 155-grain Scenar (4317073)

G1 Ballistic Coefficient = 0.254

Distance • Yards	Muzzle	100	200	300	400	500	600	800	1000
Velocity • fps	2822	2468	2141	1841	1571	1340	1161	960	847
Energy • Ft-lbs	2729	2088	1572	1161	846	615	464	317	247
Taylor KO Index	19.2	16.8	14.6	12.6	10.7	9.1	7.9	6.5	5.8
Path • Inches	-1.5	+2.1	0.0	-9.8	-29.9	-64.2	-119.3	-312.7	-645.2
Wind Drift • Inches	0.0	1.3	5.6	13.4	25.8	43.5	67.3	130.9	211.0

Federal 155-grain Sierra MatchKing BTHP (GM308M3)

G1 Ballistic Coefficient = 0.455

Distance • Yards	Muzzle	100	200	300	400	500	600	800	1000
Velocity • fps	2950	2740	2540	2350	2170	2000	1839	1541	1293
Energy • Ft-lbs	2996	2585	2225	1905	1620	1370	1165	817	575
Taylor KO Index	20.1	18.7	17.3	16.0	14.8	13.6	12.5	10.5	8.8
Path • Inches	-1.5	+1.6	0.0	-6.9	-20.2	-40.7	-69.9	-161.6	-314.0
Wind Drift • Inches	0.0	0.7	3.0	7.0	12.9	2106	31.6	61.4	104.7

Hornady 165-grain BTSP-LM InterLock (8598)

G1 Ballistic Coefficient = 0.435

Distance • Yards	Muzzle	100	200	300	400	500	600	800	1000
Velocity • fps	2880	2668	2465	2272	2087	1911	1745	1448	1214
Energy • Ft-lbs	3038	2608	2226	1890	1595	1337	1116	769	540
Taylor KO Index	20.9	19.4	17.9	16.5	15.2	13.9	12.7	10.5	8.8
Path • Inches	-1.5	+1.7	0.0	-7.4	-21.6	-43.8	-75.5	-175.7	-342.8
Wind Drift • Inches	0.0	0.7	2.8	7.4	11.8	19.3	28.8	55.8	95.0

Federal 165-grain Trophy Bonded Bear Claw—High Energy (P308T2)

G1 Ballistic Coefficient = 0.346

Distance • Yards	Muzzle	100	200	300	400	500	600	800	1000
Velocity • fps	2870	2600	2350	2120	1890	1690	1503	1202	1022
Energy • Ft-lbs	3020	2485	2030	1640	1310	1040	828	529	383
Taylor KO Index	20.8	18.9	17.1	15.4	13.7	12.3	10.9	8.7	7.4
Path • Inches	-1.5	+1.8	0.0	-8.2	-24.0	-49.9	-87.6	-215.4	-442.4
Wind Drift • Inches	0.0	0.9	3.8	9.1	17.0	28.1	42.8	85.0	144.2

Speer 165-grain Grand Slam (24505) (Discontinued in 2004)

G1 Ballistic Coefficient = 0.393

Distance • Yards	Muzzle	100	200	300	400	500	600	800	1000
Velocity • fps	2800	2569	2350	2142	1945	1759	1587	1294	1092
Energy • Ft-lbs	2872	2419	2024	1681	1386	1134	923	614	437
Taylor KO Index	20.3	18.7	17.1	15.6	14.1	12.8	11.5	9.4	7.9
Path • Inches	-1.5	+1.9	0.0	-8.2	-24.0	-49.0	-85.4	-203.8	-408.6
Wind Drift • Inches	0.0	0.8	3.5	8.1	15.1	24.8	37.6	73.8	125.4

Federal 165-grain Sierra GameKing BTSP (P308C)

G1 Ballistic Coefficient = 0.470

Distance • Yards	Muzzle	100	200	300	400	500	600	800	1000
Velocity • fps	2700	2520	2330	2160	1990	1830	1681	1414	1202
Energy • Ft-lbs	2670	2310	1990	1700	1450	1230	1035	733	530
Taylor KO Index	19.6	18.3	16.9	15.7	14.4	13.3	12.2	10.3	8.7
Path • Inches	-1.5	+2.0	0.0	-8.4	-24.3	-49.0	-84.3	-194.4	-376.3
Wind Drift • Inches	0.0	0.7	3.0	7.0	13.0	21.1	31.6	61.1	103.2

Federal 165-grain Trophy Bonded Bear Claw (P308T1)

G1 Ballistic Coefficient = 0.347

Distance • Yards	Muzzle	100	200	300	400	500	600	800	1000
Velocity • fps	2700	2440	2200	1970	1760	1570	1399	1134	985
Energy • Ft-lbs	2670	2185	1775	1425	1135	900	717	471	356
Taylor KO Index	19.6	17.7	16.0	14.3	12.8	11.3	10.2	8.2	7.2
Path • Inches	-1.5	+2.2	0.0	-9.4	-27.7	-57.5	-101.0	-248.2	-504.3
Wind Drift • Inches	0.0	1.0	4.2	9.9	18.6	30.8	46.8	92.1	154.5

Hornady 165-grain Boat Tail Soft Point (8098)

G1 Ballistic Coefficient = 0.435

Distance • Yards	Muzzle	100	200	300	400	500	600	800	1000
Velocity • fps	2700	2496	2301	2115	1937	1770	1612	1339	1137
Energy • Ft-lbs	2670	2283	1940	1639	1375	1148	953	657	473
Taylor KO Index	19.6	18.1	16.7	15.4	14.1	12.9	11.7	9.7	8.3
Path • Inches	-1.5	+2.0	0.0	-8.7	-25.2	-51.0	-87.7	-205.2	-402.9
Wind Drift • Inches	0.0	0.8	3.3	7.6	14.2	23.2	34.9	67.8	114.6

Norma 165-grain Swift A-Frame (17612)

G1 Ballistic Coefficient = 0.367

Distance • Yards	Muzzle	100	200	300	400	500	600	800	1000
Velocity • fps	2700	2459	2231	2015	1811	1623	1453	1181	1018
Energy • Ft-lbs	2672	2216	1824	1488	1202	965	774	571	380
Taylor KO Index	19.6	17.9	16.2	14.6	13.1	11.8	10.5	8.6	7.4
Path • Inches	-1.5	+2.1	0.0	-9.1	-26.9	-55.3	-97.1	-235.7	-476.0
Wind Drift • Inches	0.0	0.9	3.9	9.3	17.4	28.6	43.5	85.4	143.2

Remington 165-grain AccuTip Boat Tail (PRA308WB)

G1 Ballistic Coefficient = 0.447

Distance • Yards	Muzzle	100	200	300	400	500	600	800	1000
Velocity • fps	2700	2501	2311	2129	1956	1792	1638	1367	1160
Energy • Ft-lbs	2620	2292	1957	1661	1401	1176	983	684	493
Taylor KO Index	19.6	18.2	16.8	15.5	14.2	13.0	11.9	9.9	8.1
Path • Inches	-1.5	+2.1	0.0	-8.9	-24.8	-54.6	-97.8	-244.3	-505.4
Wind Drift • Inches	0.0	1.0	4.4	10.4	19.7	32.7	50.1	99.4	165.8

Remington 165-grain Pointed Soft Point, Boat Tail (PRB308WA) (Discontinued in 2005)

G1 Ballistic Coefficient = 0.437

Distance • Yards	Muzzle	100	200	300	400	500	600	800	1000
Velocity • fps	2700	2497	2303	2117	1941	1773	1616	1344	1140
Energy • Ft-lbs	2670	2284	1942	1642	1379	1152	958	661	477
Taylor KO Index	19.6	18.1	16.7	15.4	14.1	12.9	11.7	9.8	8.3
Path • Inches	-1.5	+2.0	0.0	-8.4	-25.0	-50.6	-87.5	-204.5	-401.2
Wind Drift • Inches	0.0	0.8	3.2	7.6	14.1	23.0	34.7	67.4	113.9

Federal 165-grain Nosler Solid Base BT (P308S2)

G1 Ballistic Coefficient = 0.426

Distance • Yards	Muzzle	100	200	300	400	500	600	800	1000
Velocity • fps	2670	2460	2270	2030	1900	1730	1573	1303	1111
Energy • Ft-lbs	2610	2225	1880	1585	1320	1100	907	623	452
Taylor KO Index	19.4	17.9	16.5	15.1	13.8	12.6	11.4	9.5	8.1
Path • Inches	-1.5	+2.1	0.0	-8.9	-25.7	-52.5	-90.9	-212.8	-417.0
Wind Drift • Inches	0.0	0.8	3.4	8.0	14.8	24.1	36.4	70.8	119.5

Black Hills 165-grain BT Soft Point (D308N4)

G1 Ballistic Coefficient = 0.440

Distance • Yards	Muzzle	100	200	300	400	500	600	800	1000
Velocity • fps	2650	2450	2259	2077	1903	1739	1586	1321	1127
Energy • Ft-lbs	2573	2200	1870	1580	1327	1108	922	640	465
Taylor KO Index	19.2	17.8	16.4	15.1	13.8	12.6	11.5	9.6	8.2
Path • Inches	-1.5	+2.2	0.0	-9.0	-26.0	-52.7	-91.0	-212.5	-416.4
Wind Drift • Inches	0.0	0.8	3.3	7.8	14.4	23.5	35.4	68.6	115.7

Lapua 165-grain Swift A-Frame (4317301)

G1 Ballistic Coefficient = 0.370

Distance • Yards	Muzzle	100	200	300	400	500	600	800	1000
Velocity • fps	2625	2390	2167	1956	1758	1576	1412	1156	1005
Energy • Ft-lbs	2525	2093	1721	1402	1133	911	731	490	370
Taylor KO Index	19.1	17.4	15.7	14.2	12.8	11.4	10.3	8.4	7.3
Path • Inches	-1.5	+2.3	0.0	-9.7	-28.6	-58.8	-103.2	-249.9	-502.0
Wind Drift • Inches	0.0	1.0	4.1	9.6	18.0	29.6	44.3	87.7	146.1

Hirtenberger 165-grain Sierra SBT (82200449)

G1 Ballistic Coefficient = 0.411

Distance • Yards	Muzzle	100	200	300	400	500	600	800	1000
Velocity • fps	2559	2350	2150	1961	1782	1615	1463	1212	1050
Energy • Ft-lbs	2400	2023	1694	1409	1164	956	784	460	404
Taylor KO Index	18.6	17.1	15.6	14.2	12.9	11.7	10.6	8.8	7.6
Path • Inches	-1.5	+2.4	0.0	-10.0	-29.0	-59.0	-102.3	-241.4	-475.3
Wind Drift • Inches	0.0	0.8	3.4	8.0	14.8	24.3	36.6	71.1	118.8

PMC 165-grain Barnes-XLC-HP (308XLB)
G1 Ballistic Coefficient = 0.497

Distance • Yards	Muzzle	100	200	300	400	500	600	800	1000
Velocity • fps	2600	2425	2256	2095	1940	1793	1653	1404	1204
Energy • Ft-lbs	2476	2154	1865	1608	1379	1177	1001	722	532
Taylor KO Index	18.9	17.6	16.4	15.2	14.1	13.0	12.0	10.2	8.7
Path • Inches	-1.5	+2.2	0.0	-9.0	-26.0	-52.4	-89.4	-204.6	-392.3
Wind Drift • Inches	0.0	0.7	3.0	7.0	12.9	20.9	31.3	60.1	100.9

Remington 165-grain Nosler Ballistic Tip (PRT308WB)
G1 Ballistic Coefficient = 0.475

Distance • Yards	Muzzle	100	200	300	400	500	600	800	1000
Velocity • fps	2700	2513	2333	2161	1996	1839	1690	1424	1212
Energy • Ft-lbs	2672	2314	1995	1711	1460	1239	1047	744	538
Taylor KO Index	19.6	18.2	16.9	15.9	14.5	13.4	12.3	10.3	8.8
Path • Inches	-1.5	+2.0	0.0	-8.4	-24.3	-48.9	-83.8	-193.0	-372.9
Wind Drift • Inches	0.0	0.7	3.0	6.9	12.8	20.8	31.2	60.2	101.7

Remington 165-grain Swift Scirocco (PRSC308WB)
G1 Ballistic Coefficient = 0.475

Distance • Yards	Muzzle	100	200	300	400	500	600	800	1000
Velocity • fps	2700	2513	2333	2161	1996	1839	1690	1424	1212
Energy • Ft-lbs	2672	2314	1995	1711	1460	1239	1047	744	538
Taylor KO Index	19.6	18.2	16.9	15.9	14.5	13.4	12.3	10.3	8.8
Path • Inches	-1.5	+2.0	0.0	-8.4	-24.3	-48.9	-83.8	-193.0	-372.9
Wind Drift • Inches	0.0	0.7	3.0	6.9	12.8	20.8	31.2	60.2	101.7

Ultramax 165-grain Nosler Ballistic Tip (308R3)
G1 Ballistic Coefficient = 0.475

Distance • Yards	Muzzle	100	200	300	400	500	600	800	1000
Velocity • fps	2680	2494	2315	2143	1979	1823	1676	1413	1204
Energy • Ft-lbs	2632	2279	1964	1684	1436	1218	1029	732	531
Taylor KO Index	19.5	18.1	16.1	15.6	14.4	13.2	12.2	10.3	8.7
Path • Inches	-1.5	+2.0	0.0	-8.6	-24.7	-49.7	-85.2	-195.8	-376.5
Wind Drift • Inches	0.0	0.7	3.0	7.0	12.9	21.0	31.5	60.9	102.7

Ultramax 165-grain Speer Boat Tail (308R4)
G1 Ballistic Coefficient = 0.471

Distance • Yards	Muzzle	100	200	300	400	500	600	800	1000
Velocity • fps	2680	2492	2312	2139	1974	1817	1669	1405	1197
Energy • Ft-lbs	2632	2279	1959	1677	1428	1210	1020	723	525
Taylor KO Index	19.5	18.1	16.8	15.5	14.3	13.2	12.1	10.2	8.7
Path • Inches	-1.5	+2.0	0.0	-8.6	-24.8	-49.9	-85.6	-196.8	-379.1
Wind Drift • Inches	0.0	0.7	3.0	7.1	13.1	21.2	31.9	61.6	103.9

Black Hills 165-grain Nosler Ballistic Tip (D308N6)
G1 Ballistic Coefficient = 0.475

Distance • Yards	Muzzle	100	200	300	400	500	600	800	1000
Velocity • fps	2650	2465	2287	2116	1953	1798	1652	1393	1189
Energy • Ft-lbs	2573	2226	1916	1641	1398	1185	1000	711	518
Taylor KO Index	19.2	17.9	16.6	15.4	14.2	13.1	12.0	10.1	8.6
Path • Inches	-1.5	+2.1	0.0	-8.8	-25.3	-51.0	-87.5	-201.1	-387.0
Wind Drift • Inches	0.0	0.7	2.8	6.4	11.9	19.3	28.9	55.8	94.1

Lapua 165-grain Scirocco (4317303) (Discontinued in 2005)
G1 Ballistic Coefficient = 0.405

Distance • Yards	Muzzle	100	200	300	400	500	600	800	1000
Velocity • fps	2625	2410	2205	2009	1825	1653	1495	1232	1060
Energy • Ft-lbs	2525	2128	1781	1480	1221	1001	819	556	411
Taylor KO Index	19.1	17.5	16.0	14.6	13.2	12.0	10.9	8.9	7.7
Path • Inches	-1.5	+2.2	0.0	-9.4	-27.5	-56.0	-97.4	-231.5	-459.7
Wind Drift • Inches	0.0	0.9	3.7	8.6	16.1	26.4	39.9	77.7	130.4

Lapua 167-grain Scenar (C317515 & 4317510)
G1 Ballistic Coefficient = 0.470

Distance • Yards	Muzzle	100	200	300	400	500	600	800	1000
Velocity • fps	2756	2564	2381	2205	2036	1875	1723	1450	1229
Energy • Ft-lbs	2817	2489	2102	1803	1537	1304	1101	758	560
Taylor KO Index	20.3	18.8	17.5	16.2	15.0	13.8	12.7	10.7	9.0
Path • Inches	-1.5	+1.9	0.0	-8.0	-23.2	-46.8	-80.4	-185.3	-358.6
Wind Drift • Inches	0.0	0.7	2.9	6.8	12.6	20.4	30.7	59.2	100.3

Lapua 167-grain Scenar (4317515)

G1 Ballistic Coefficient = 0.460

Distance • Yards	Muzzle	100	200	300	400	500	600	800	1000
Velocity • fps	2690	2497	2312	2135	1966	1805	1655	1387	1179
Energy • Ft-lbs	2684	2313	1983	1691	1433	1209	1016	714	516
Taylor KO Index	19.8	18.3	17.0	15.7	14.4	13.3	12.2	10.2	8.7
Path • Inches	-1.5	+2.0	0.0	-8.6	-24.8	-50.0	-85.9	-198.9	-386.6
Wind Drift • Inches	0.0	0.8	3.1	7.2	13.4	21.8	32.7	63.2	106.8

PMC 168-grain PSP (308E)

G1 Ballistic Coefficient = 0.443

Distance • Yards	Muzzle	100	200	300	400	500	600	800	1000
Velocity • fps	2600	2404	2216	2037	1866	1706	1557	1300	1115
Energy • Ft-lbs	2476	2064	1709	1403	1142	926	905	631	464
Taylor KO Index	19.2	17.8	16.4	15.1	13.8	12.6	11.5	9.6	8.2
Path • Inches	-1.5	+2.3	0.0	-9.8	-28.7	-58.9	-94.6	-220.0	-428.1
Wind Drift • Inches	0.0	0.8	3.4	7.9	14.7	24.0	36.0	69.8	117.4

Cor-Bon 168-grain JHP (PM308168/20)

G1 Ballistic Coefficient = 0.440

Distance • Yards	Muzzle	100	200	300	400	500	600	800	1000
Velocity • fps	2720	2517	2324	2138	1962	1795	1638	1363	1155
Energy • Ft-lbs	2719	2365	2015	1706	1436	1202	1001	693	498
Taylor KO Index	20.1	18.6	17.2	15.8	14.5	13.3	12.1	10.1	8.5
Path • Inches	-1.5	+2.0	0.0	-8.4	-24.5	-49.6	-85.6	-199.1	-388.0
Wind Drift • Inches	0.0	0.7	2.9	6.7	12.4	20.3	30.6	59.3	100.5

Hornady 168-grain A-Max Match (8096)

G1 Ballistic Coefficient = 0.475

Distance • Yards	Muzzle	100	200	300	400	500	600	800	1000
Velocity • fps	2700	2513	2333	2161	1996	1839	1691	1425	1213
Energy • Ft-lbs	2719	2355	2030	1742	1486	1261	1067	758	549
Taylor KO Index	20.0	18.6	17.2	16.0	14.8	13.6	12.5	10.5	9.0
Path • Inches	-1.5	+2.0	0.0	-8.4	-24.3	-48.9	-83.8	-192.4	-370.1
Wind Drift • Inches	0.0	0.7	3.0	6.9	12.8	20.8	31.2	60.2	101.6

Ultramax 168-grain Sierra HP Match (308R5)

G1 Ballistic Coefficient = 0.430

Distance • Yards	Muzzle	100	200	300	400	500	600	800	1000
Velocity • fps	2680	2475	2278	2091	1913	1745	1588	1318	1121
Energy • Ft-lbs	2680	2285	1937	1631	1365	1136	941	648	469
Taylor KO Index	19.8	18.3	16.8	15.5	14.1	12.9	11.7	9.7	8.3
Path • Inches	-1.5	+2.1	0.0	-8.8	-25.6	-51.9	-89.6	-209.5	-409.9
Wind Drift • Inches	0.0	0.8	3.3	7.2	14.5	23.7	35.8	69.5	117.4

Winchester 168-grain Ballistic Silvertip (SBST308A)

G1 Ballistic Coefficient = 0.476

Distance • Yards	Muzzle	100	200	300	400	500	600	800	1000
Velocity • fps	2670	2484	2306	2134	1971	1815	1669	1408	1200
Energy • Ft-lbs	2659	2301	1983	1699	1449	1229	1040	739	537
Taylor KO Index	19.7	18.4	17.0	15.8	14.6	13.4	12.3	10.4	8.9
Path • Inches	-1.5	+2.1	0.0	-8.6	-24.8	-50.0	-85.6	-197.8	-382.1
Wind Drift • Inches	0.0	0.7	3.0	7.0	13.0	21.1	31.7	61.1	103.0

Hornady 168-grain BTHP Match (8097) + Moly (80973)

G1 Ballistic Coefficient = 0.450

Distance • Yards	Muzzle	100	200	300	400	500	600	800	1000
Velocity • fps	2700	2503	2314	2133	1960	1797	1644	1373	1166
Energy • Ft-lbs	2719	2336	1997	1697	1433	1204	1008	703	507
Taylor KO Index	20.0	18.5	17.1	15.8	14.5	13.3	12.2	10.1	8.6
Path • Inches	-1.5	+2.0	0.0	-8.5	-24.7	-50.0	-86.0	-199.4	-387.1
Wind Drift • Inches	0.0	0.8	3.1	7.4	13.6	22.2	33.4	64.7	109.4

Remington 168-grain Boat Tail HP Match (R308W7)

G1 Ballistic Coefficient = 0.476

Distance • Yards	Muzzle	100	200	300	400	500	600	800	1000
Velocity • fps	2680	2496	2314	2143	1979	1823	1677	1414	1205
Energy • Ft-lbs	2678	2318	1998	1713	1460	1239	1049	746	541
Taylor KO Index	19.8	18.4	17.1	15.8	14.6	13.5	12.4	10.5	8.9
Path • Inches	-1.5	+2.1	0.0	-8.6	-24.7	-49.9	-85.2	-196.1	-378.8
Wind Drift • Inches	0.0	0.7	3.0	7.0	12.9	21.0	35.9	69.9	118.3

Winchester 168-grain Sierra MatchKing BTHP (S308M)

G1 Ballistic Coefficient = 0.453

Distance • Yards	Muzzle	100	200	300	400	500	600	800	1000
Velocity • fps	2680	2485	2297	2118	1948	1786	1635	1367	1163
Energy • Ft-lbs	2680	2303	1970	1674	1415	1190	997	698	505
Taylor KO Index	19.8	18.4	17.0	15.7	14.4	13.2	12.1	10.1	8.6
Path • Inches	-1.5	+2.1	0.0	-8.7	-25.1	-50.7	-87.2	-202.0	-391.6
Wind Drift • Inches	0.0	0.7	3.2	7.4	13.7	22.3	33.5	64.8	109.5

Black Hills 168-grain Match Hollow Point (D308N1)

G1 Ballistic Coefficient = 0.450

Distance • Yards	Muzzle	100	200	300	400	500	600	800	1000
Velocity • fps	2650	2547	2272	2095	1926	1766	1617	1354	1154
Energy • Ft-lbs	2620	2252	1926	1638	1384	1164	975	684	497
Taylor KO Index	19.6	18.8	16.8	15.5	14.2	13.1	12.0	10.0	8.5
Path • Inches	-1.5	+2.1	0.0	-8.9	-25.7	-51.9	-89.3	-206.7	-400.5
Wind Drift • Inches	0.0	0.8	3.2	7.5	13.8	22.5	33.9	65.5	110.5

Black Hills 168-grain Barnes-XLC Bullet (D308N1)

G1 Ballistic Coefficient = 0.510

Distance • Yards	Muzzle	100	200	300	400	500	600	800	1000
Velocity • fps	2650	2477	2311	2151	1998	1851	1712	1460	1252
Energy • Ft-lbs	2620	2290	1993	1727	1489	1278	1093	795	585
Taylor KO Index	19.6	18.3	17.1	15.9	14.8	13.7	12.7	10.8	9.3
Path • Inches	-1.5	+2.1	0.0	-8.6	-24.7	-49.6	-84.6	-192.7	-367.9
Wind Drift • Inches	0.0	0.6	2.5	5.9	10.9	17.7	26.5	50.8	85.4

PMC 168-grain Hollow Point Boat Tail Match (308SMB)

G1 Ballistic Coefficient = 0.463

Distance • Yards	Muzzle	100	200	300	400	500	600	800	1000
Velocity • fps	2650	2460	2278	2103	1936	1778	1631	1369	1167
Energy • Ft-lbs	2619	2257	1936	1651	1399	1179	992	699	509
Taylor KO Index	19.6	18.2	16.8	15.5	14.3	13.1	12.1	10.1	8.9
Path • Inches	-1.5	+2.1	0.0	-8.8	-25.6	-51.6	-88.6	-205.0	-398.1
Wind Drift • Inches	0.0	0.8	3.1	7.3	13.6	22.1	33.2	64.1	108.1

Sellier & Bellot 168-grain HPBT (SBA30808)

G1 Ballistic Coefficient = 0.493

Distance • Yards	Muzzle	100	200	300	400	500	600	800	1000
Velocity • fps	2628	2444	2274	2115	1958	1809	1667	1414	1211
Energy • Ft-lbs	2579	2231	1930	1670	1431	1221	1037	746	547
Taylor KO Index	19.4	18.1	16.8	15.6	14.5	13.4	12.3	10.5	9.0
Path • Inches	-1.5	+2.2	0.0	-8.8	-25.5	-51.2	-87.6	-200.6	-385.2
Wind Drift • Inches	0.0	0.7	3.0	6.9	12.8	20.7	31.1	59.7	100.5

Federal 168-grain Sierra MatchKing BTHP (GM308M)

G1 Ballistic Coefficient = 0.464

Distance • Yards	Muzzle	100	200	300	400	500	600	800	1000
Velocity • fps	2600	2410	2230	2060	1890	1740	1596	1341	1148
Energy • Ft-lbs	2522	2172	1860	1584	1342	1131	950	671	492
Taylor KO Index	19.2	17.8	17.2	15.2	14.0	12.9	11.8	9.9	8.5
Path • Inches	-1.5	+2.2	0.0	-9.2	-26.7	-53.8	-92.4	-214.0	-415.2
Wind Drift • Inches	0.0	0.8	3.2	7.5	13.9	22.7	34.1	65.7	110.5

PMC 168-grain FMJ/BT (Target) (308D)

G1 Ballistic Coefficient = 0.425

Distance • Yards	Muzzle	100	200	300	400	500	600	800	1000
Velocity • fps	2559	2354	2160	1976	1803	1642	1493	1242	1072
Energy • Ft-lbs	2443	2067	1740	1457	1212	1006	832	575	429
Taylor KO Index	18.9	17.4	16.0	14.6	13.3	12.1	11.0	9.2	7.9
Path • Inches	-1.5	+2.4	0.0	-9.9	-28.6	-58.0	-100.3	-235.1	-460.4
Wind Drift • Inches	0.0	0.9	3.6	8.5	15.8	25.8	38.9	75.4	126.2

Lapua 170-grain Lock Base (4317596)

G1 Ballistic Coefficient = 0.517

Distance • Yards	Muzzle	100	200	300	400	500	600	800	1000
Velocity • fps	2822	2645	2474	2310	2152	2001	1856	1589	1359
Energy • Ft-lbs	3007	2641	2260	2090	1749	1512	1301	954	697
Taylor KO Index	21.1	19.8	18.5	17.3	16.1	15.0	13.9	11.9	10.2
Path • Inches	-1.5	+1.7	0.0	-7.4	-21.4	-42.8	-73.0	-165.5	-314.5
Wind Drift • Inches	0.0	0.6	2.6	5.9	10.9	17.6	26.3	50.4	84.9

Lapua 170-grain FMJ—Boat Tail (4317183)
G1 Ballistic Coefficient = 0.490

Distance • Yards	Muzzle	100	200	300	400	500	600	800	1000
Velocity • fps	2560	2384	2214	2052	1897	1749	1611	1366	1174
Energy • Ft-lbs	2474	2145	1851	1590	1358	1155	980	704	521
Taylor KO Index	19.1	17.8	16.6	15.3	14.2	13.1	12.1	10.2	8.8
Path • Inches	-1.5	+2.3	0.0	-9.4	-27.1	-54.5	-93.2	-213.9	-411.2
Wind Drift • Inches	0.0	0.8	3.1	7.2	13.4	21.8	32.6	62.6	105.0

Federal 170-grain Soft Point (308LR1)
G1 Ballistic Coefficient = 0.285

Distance • Yards	Muzzle	100	200	300	400	500	600	800	1000
Velocity • fps	2000	1740	1510	1310	1160	1050	975	868	788
Energy • Ft-lbs	1510	1145	860	650	505	410	359	285	235
Taylor KO Index	15.0	13.0	11.3	9.8	8.7	7.9	7.3	6.5	5.8
Path • Inches	-1.5	+5.0	0.0	-20.5	-61.2	-128.1	-225.1	-535.3	-1030
Wind Drift • Inches	0.0	1.9	8.0	19.2	35.7	57.3	83.1	145.6	220.9

Federal 175-grain Sierra MatchKing BTHP (GM308M2)
G1 Ballistic Coefficient = 0.496

Distance • Yards	Muzzle	100	200	300	400	500	600	800	1000
Velocity • fps	2600	2420	2260	2090	1940	1790	1651	1402	1203
Energy • Ft-lbs	2627	2284	1977	1703	1460	1245	1060	764	562
Taylor KO Index	20.0	18.6	17.4	16.1	14.9	13.8	12.7	10.8	9.3
Path • Inches	-1.5	+2.2	0.0	-9.1	-26.1	-52.4	-89.5	-204.8	-393.0
Wind Drift • Inches	0.0	0.7	3.0	7.0	12.9	21.0	31.3	60.2	111.2

Black Hills 175-grain Match Hollow Point (D308N5)
G1 Ballistic Coefficient = 0.496

Distance • Yards	Muzzle	100	200	300	400	500	600	800	1000
Velocity • fps	2600	2420	2260	2090	1940	1790	1651	1402	1203
Energy • Ft-lbs	2627	2284	1977	1703	1460	1245	1060	764	562
Taylor KO Index	20.0	18.6	17.4	16.1	14.9	13.8	12.7	10.8	9.3
Path • Inches	-1.5	+2.2	0.0	-9.1	-26.1	-52.4	-89.5	-204.8	-393.0
Wind Drift • Inches	0.0	0.7	3.0	7.0	12.9	21.0	31.3	60.2	111.2

Federal 180-grain Nosler Partition—HE (P308G)
G1 Ballistic Coefficient = 0.475

Distance • Yards	Muzzle	100	200	300	400	500	600	800	1000
Velocity • fps	2740	2550	2370	2200	2030	1870	1720	1450	1231
Energy • Ft-lbs	3000	2600	2245	1925	1645	1395	1183	840	606
Taylor KO Index	21.7	20.2	18.8	17.4	16.1	14.8	13.6	11.5	9.7
Path • Inches	-1.5	+1.9	0.0	-8.2	-23.5	-47.1	-81.1	-186.6	-360.3
Wind Drift • Inches	0.0	0.7	2.9	6.8	12.5	20.4	30.5	58.9	99.6

Federal 180-grain Hi-Shok Soft Point (308B)
G1 Ballistic Coefficient = 0.382

Distance • Yards	Muzzle	100	200	300	400	500	600	800	1000
Velocity • fps	2620	2390	2180	1970	1780	1600	1438	1180	1022
Energy • Ft-lbs	2745	2290	1895	1555	1270	1030	827	556	418
Taylor KO Index	21.7	18.9	17.3	15.6	14.1	12.7	11.4	9.3	8.1
Path • Inches	-1.5	+2.3	0.0	-9.7	-28.3	-57.8	-101.5	-244.1	-483.5
Wind Drift • Inches	0.0	0.9	3.9	9.3	17.3	28.5	43.2	84.3	140.7

Federal 180-grain Nosler Partition (P308E)
G1 Ballistic Coefficient = 0.448

Distance • Yards	Muzzle	100	200	300	400	500	600	800	1000
Velocity • fps	2620	2430	2240	2060	1890	1730	1581	1321	1129
Energy • Ft-lbs	2745	2355	2005	1700	1430	1200	999	697	510
Taylor KO Index	21.7	19.2	17.7	16.3	15.0	13.7	12.5	8.9	8.1
Path • Inches	-1.5	+2.2	0.0	-9.2	-26.5	-53.6	-92.5	-215.4	-420.6
Wind Drift • Inches	0.0	0.8	3.3	7.7	14.4	23.4	35.2	68.1	114.6

PMC 180-grain Soft Point Boat Tail Game (308HC)
G1 Ballistic Coefficient = 0.502

Distance • Yards	Muzzle	100	200	300	400	500	600	800	1000
Velocity • fps	2620	2446	2278	2117	1962	1815	1676	1425	1223
Energy • Ft-lbs	2743	2391	2074	1790	1538	1316	1123	812	598
Taylor KO Index	21.7	19.4	18.0	16.8	15.5	14.4	13.3	11.3	9.7
Path • Inches	-1.5	+2.2	0.0	-9.0	-25.4	-51.3	-87.5	-199.8	-382.4
Wind Drift • Inches	0.0	0.7	2.9	6.8	12.6	20.4	30.5	58.6	98.5

Remington 180-grain Nosler Partition (PRP308WB3) (Discontinued in 2005)

G1 Ballistic Coefficient = 0.475

Distance • Yards	Muzzle	100	200	300	400	500	600	800	1000
Velocity • fps	2620	2436	2259	2089	1927	1774	1630	1374	1175
Energy • Ft-lbs	2743	2371	2039	1774	1485	1257	1062	755	552
Taylor KO Index	20.8	19.3	17.9	16.5	15.3	14.1	12.9	10.9	9.3
Path • Inches	-1.5	+2.2	0.0	-9.0	-26.0	-52.4	-89.8	-206.4	-397.2
Wind Drift • Inches	0.0	0.7	2.8	6.5	12.1	19.6	29.4	56.8	95.6

Remington 180-grain Core-Lokt Pointed Soft Point Ultra (PRC308WC)

G1 Ballistic Coefficient = 0.384

Distance • Yards	Muzzle	100	200	300	400	500	600	800	1000
Velocity • fps	2620	2404	2198	2002	1818	1644	1487	1225	1055
Energy • Ft-lbs	2743	2309	1930	1601	1320	1080	884	600	445
Taylor KO Index	20.8	19.0	17.4	15.9	14.4	13.0	11.8	9.7	8.4
Path • Inches	-1.5	+2.3	0.0	-9.5	-27.7	-56.4	-98.2	-233.4	-463.9
Wind Drift • Inches	0.0	0.9	3.7	8.7	16.2	26.6	40.2	78.4	131.6

Remington 180-grain Pointed Soft Point Core-Lokt (R308W3)

G1 Ballistic Coefficient = 0.384

Distance • Yards	Muzzle	100	200	300	400	500	600	800	1000
Velocity • fps	2620	2393	2178	1974	1782	1604	1443	1184	1025
Energy • Ft-lbs	2743	2288	1896	1557	1269	1028	833	561	420
Taylor KO Index	21.7	19.0	17.2	15.6	14.1	12.7	11.4	9.4	8.1
Path • Inches	-1.5	+2.3	0.0	-9.7	-28.3	-57.8	-101.2	-243.0	-486.1
Wind Drift • Inches	0.0	0.9	3.9	9.2	17.2	28.3	42.8	83.7	138.8

Remington 180-grain Soft Point Core-Lokt (R308W2)

G1 Ballistic Coefficient = 0.248

Distance • Yards	Muzzle	100	200	300	400	500	600	800	1000
Velocity • fps	2620	2274	1955	1666	1414	1212	1071	912	810
Energy • Ft-lbs	2743	2066	1527	1109	799	587	459	333	262
Taylor KO Index	21.7	18.0	15.5	13.2	11.2	9.6	8.5	7.2	6.4
Path • Inches	-1.5	+2.6	0.0	-11.8	-36.3	-78.2	-145.6	-372.7	-751.2
Wind Drift • Inches	0.0	1.5	6.4	15.5	29.8	50.1	76.5	143.8	226.6

Speer 180-grain Grand Slam (24506) (Discontinued in 2004)

G1 Ballistic Coefficient = 0.437

Distance • Yards	Muzzle	100	200	300	400	500	600	800	1000
Velocity • fps	2600	2391	2192	2004	1825	1658	1504	1245	1071
Energy • Ft-lbs	2702	2285	1921	1605	1332	1099	904	620	459
Taylor KO Index	20.6	18.9	17.4	15.9	14.5	13.1	11.9	9.9	8.5
Path • Inches	-1.5	+1.9	0.0	-9.5	-27.8	-56.5	-97.9	-231.3	-457.0
Wind Drift • Inches	0.0	0.9	3.6	8.5	15.8	25.8	39.0	75.8	127.1

Winchester 180-grain Silvertip (X3083)

G1 Ballistic Coefficient = 0.384

Distance • Yards	Muzzle	100	200	300	400	500	600	800	1000
Velocity • fps	2620	2393	2178	1974	1782	1604	1443	1184	1025
Energy • Ft-lbs	2743	2280	1896	1557	1269	1028	833	561	420
Taylor KO Index	21.7	19.0	17.2	15.6	14.1	12.7	11.4	9.4	8.1
Path • Inches	-1.5	+2.6	0.0	-9.9	-28.9	-58.8	-101.2	-243.0	-486.1
Wind Drift • Inches	0.0	0.9	3.9	9.2	17.2	28.3	42.8	83.7	138.8

Winchester 180-grain Power-Point (X3086)

G1 Ballistic Coefficient = 0.381

Distance • Yards	Muzzle	100	200	300	400	500	600	800	1000
Velocity • fps	2620	2392	2176	1971	1779	1600	1437	1179	1022
Energy • Ft-lbs	2743	2287	1892	1553	1264	1023	826	556	417
Taylor KO Index	20.8	18.9	17.2	15.6	14.1	12.7	11.4	9.3	8.1
Path • Inches	-1.5	+2.3	0.0	-9.7	-28.3	-58.0	-101.4	-242.6	-483.9
Wind Drift • Inches	0.0	0.9	3.9	9.3	17.4	28.5	43.2	84.5	141.0

Norma 180-grain Oryx (17675)

G1 Ballistic Coefficient = 0.288

Distance • Yards	Muzzle	100	200	300	400	500	600	800	1000
Velocity • fps	2612	2305	2019	1775	1543	1341	1180	986	876
Energy • Ft-lbs	2728	2124	1629	1232	952	719	557	389	307
Taylor KO Index	20.7	18.3	16.0	14.1	12.2	10.6	9.3	7.8	6.9
Path • Inches	-1.5	+2.5	0.0	-11.1	-33.1	-69.8	-127.0	-322.1	-651.0
Wind Drift • Inches	0.0	1.3	5.4	13.0	24.7	41.2	63.1	121.4	195.0

Norma 180-grain Alaska (17636)

G1 Ballistic Coefficient = 0.257

Distance • Yards	Muzzle	100	200	300	400	500	600	800	1000
Velocity • fps	2612	2269	1953	1687	1420	1215	1074	915	812
Energy • Ft-lbs	2728	2059	1526	1111	802	590	461	335	264
Taylor KO Index	20.7	18.0	15.5	13.2	11.2	9.6	8.5	7.2	6.4
Path • Inches	-1.5	+2.7	0.0	-11.9	-36.3	-78.3	-145.5	-371.9	-749.0
Wind Drift • Inches	0.0	1.5	6.4	15.4	29.6	49.8	76.0	142.8	225.2

Norma 180-grain Nosler Partition (17635)

G1 Ballistic Coefficient = 0.442

Distance • Yards	Muzzle	100	200	300	400	500	600	800	1000
Velocity • fps	2612	2414	2225	2044	1873	1711	1563	1304	1116
Energy • Ft-lbs	2728	2330	1979	1670	1403	1171	977	680	499
Taylor KO Index	20.7	19.1	17.6	16.2	14.8	13.6	12.4	10.3	8.8
Path • Inches	-1.5	+2.2	0.0	-9.3	-26.9	-54.4	-93.8	-219.0	-428.7
Wind Drift • Inches	0.0	0.8	3.4	7.9	14.7	24.0	35.9	69.6	117.2

Black Hills 180-grain Nosler AccuBond (2C308BHGN4)

G1 Ballistic Coefficient = 0.507

Distance • Yards	Muzzle	100	200	300	400	500	600	800	1000
Velocity • fps	2600	2428	2263	2104	1952	1807	1689	1423	1223
Energy • Ft-lbs	2701	2357	2047	1770	1523	1305	1114	809	598
Taylor KO Index	20.6	19.2	17.9	16.7	15.5	14.3	13.4	11.3	9.7
Path • Inches	-1.5	+2.2	0.0	-9.0	-25.9	-51.9	-88.6	-201.6	-383.8
Wind Drift • Inches	0.0	0.7	2.9	6.8	12.6	20.4	30.5	58.5	98.2

PMC 180-grain Pointed Soft Point (308C)

G1 Ballistic Coefficient = 0.443

Distance • Yards	Muzzle	100	200	300	400	500	600	800	1000
Velocity • fps	2550	2335	2132	1940	1760	1596	1444	1196	1038
Energy • Ft-lbs	2599	2179	1816	1504	1238	1017	834	572	431
Taylor KO Index	20.2	18.5	16.9	15.4	13.9	12.6	11.4	9.5	8.2
Path • Inches	-1.5	+2.4	0.0	-10.1	-29.5	-60.0	-104.2	-247.6	-490.3
Wind Drift • Inches	0.0	0.9	3.8	9.0	16.8	27.6	41.7	80.9	134.8

Hirtenberger 180-grain Nosler SP (82200385)

G1 Ballistic Coefficient = 0.449

Distance • Yards	Muzzle	100	200	300	400	500	600	800	1000
Velocity • fps	2526	2335	2153	1979	1814	1659	1515	1270	1096
Energy • Ft-lbs	2551	2181	1853	1566	1315	1100	918	644	480
Taylor KO Index	20.3	18.6	17.0	15.5	14.1	12.8	11.6	9.6	8.3
Path • Inches	-1.5	+2.4	0.0	-10.0	-28.8	-58.3	-100.4	-233.2	-452.6
Wind Drift • Inches	0.0	0.8	3.1	7.3	13.6	22.0	33.4	64.5	107.8

Sellier & Bellot 180-grain Soft Point (SBA30802)

G1 Ballistic Coefficient = 0.284

Distance • Yards	Muzzle	100	200	300	400	500	600	800	1000
Velocity • fps	2454	2146	1877	1642	1422	1241	1106	947	847
Energy • Ft-lbs	2414	1846	1412	1080	809	615	489	358	287
Taylor KO Index	19.4	17.0	14.9	13.0	11.3	9.8	8.8	7.5	6.7
Path • Inches	-1.5	+3.0	0.0	-12.8	-38.7	-82.1	-148.6	-370.8	-735.9
Wind Drift • Inches	0.0	1.4	6.0	14.5	27.6	45.9	69.6	130.5	205.7

Lapua 180-grain Naturalis (N317101)

G1 Ballistic Coefficient = 0.502

Distance • Yards	Muzzle	100	200	300	400	500	600	800	1000
Velocity • fps	2543	2372	2207	2049	1898	1754	1618	1378	1187
Energy • Ft-lbs	2585	2249	1947	1678	1440	1230	1047	759	564
Taylor KO Index	20.1	18.8	17.5	16.2	15.0	13.9	12.8	10.9	9.4
Path • Inches	-1.5	+2.4	0.0	-9.5	-27.3	-54.7	-93.5	-213.3	-406.9
Wind Drift • Inches	0.0	0.7	2.8	6.4	11.8	19.2	28.7	55.1	92.3

Norma 180-grain Plastic point (17628)

G1 Ballistic Coefficient = 0.358

Distance • Yards	Muzzle	100	200	300	400	500	600	800	1000
Velocity • fps	2612	2370	2141	1925	1723	1538	1374	1125	984
Energy • Ft-lbs	2737	2253	1838	1486	1187	946	755	506	387
Taylor KO Index	20.7	18.8	17.0	15.2	13.6	12.2	10.9	8.9	7.8
Path • Inches	-1.5	+2.4	0.0	-10.0	-29.4	-60.6	-106.8	-260.4	-524.2
Wind Drift • Inches	0.0	1.0	4.2	10.0	18.8	31.1	47.2	92.2	152.8

Norma 180-grain Vulcan (17660)

G1 Ballistic Coefficient = 0.305

Distance • Yards	Muzzle	100	200	300	400	500	600	800	1000
Velocity • fps	2612	2329	2064	1817	1592	1394	1229	1019	903
Energy • Ft-lbs	2737	2176	1709	1325	1014	777	604	415	326
Taylor KO Index	20.7	18.4	16.3	14.4	12.6	11.0	9.7	8.1	7.2
Path • Inches	-1.5	+2.5	0.0	-10.7	-32.0	-67.2	-120.8	-304.0	-614.9
Wind Drift • Inches	0.0	1.2	5.1	12.1	23.0	38.2	58.4	113.3	183.4

Sellier & Bellot 180-grain HPC (SBA30804)

G1 Ballistic Coefficient = 0.620

Distance • Yards	Muzzle	100	200	300	400	500	600	800	1000
Velocity • fps	2500	2359	2225	2099	1974	1854	1739	1526	1340
Energy • Ft-lbs	2205	2230	1985	1767	1558	1374	1209	930	718
Taylor KO Index	19.8	18.7	17.6	16.6	15.6	14.7	13.8	12.1	10.6
Path • Inches	-1.5	+2.4	0.0	-9.4	-26.6	-52.8	-89.2	-198.1	-367.7
Wind Drift • Inches	0.0	0.6	2.5	5.8	10.6	17.1	25.4	48.0	79.7

Sellier & Bellot 180-grain FMJ (SBA30808)

G1 Ballistic Coefficient = 0.502

Distance • Yards	Muzzle	100	200	300	400	500	600	800	1000
Velocity • fps	2411	2240	2081	1932	1787	1649	1521	1298	1131
Energy • Ft-lbs	2331	2011	1735	1497	1276	1087	985	673	511
Taylor KO Index	19.1	17.7	16.5	15.3	14.2	13.1	12.0	10.3	9.0
Path • Inches	-1.5	+2.7	0.0	-10.7	-30.8	-61.7	-105.5	-240.8	-459.0
Wind Drift • Inches	0.0	0.7	3.0	6.9	12.8	20.8	31.1	59.5	98.8

Lapua 185-grain Scenar (C317523)

G1 Ballistic Coefficient = 0.521

Distance • Yards	Muzzle	100	200	300	400	500	600	800	1000
Velocity • fps	2608	2440	2279	2124	1974	1832	1696	1451	1249
Energy • Ft-lbs	2795	2447	2134	1853	1602	1379	1183	866	641
Taylor KO Index	21.2	19.9	18.6	17.3	16.1	14.9	13.8	11.8	10.2
Path • Inches	-1.5	+2.2	0.0	-8.9	-25.5	-51.0	-86.9	-197.4	-375.6
Wind Drift • Inches	0.0	0.7	2.8	6.6	12.1	19.6	29.4	56.2	94.3

Lapua 185-grain Mega SP (4317189)

G1 Ballistic Coefficient = 0.310

Distance • Yards	Muzzle	100	200	300	400	500	600	800	1000
Velocity • fps	2510	2238	1983	1746	1532	1345	1193	1003	894
Energy • Ft-lbs	2589	2057	1615	1253	964	744	585	413	329
Taylor KO Index	20.4	18.2	16.1	14.2	12.5	10.9	9.7	8.2	7.3
Path • Inches	-1.5	+2.7	0.0	-11.6	-34.7	-72.7	-130.8	-326.0	-651.9
Wind Drift • Inches	0.0	1.2	5.3	12.6	23.9	39.7	60.4	115.7	185.5

Lapua 185-grain Scenar (4317523)

G1 Ballistic Coefficient = 0.427

Distance • Yards	Muzzle	100	200	300	400	500	600	800	1000
Velocity • fps	2477	2279	2090	1911	1742	1584	1440	1203	1049
Energy • Ft-lbs	2521	2134	1795	1500	1246	1031	852	595	452
Taylor KO Index	20.5	18.6	17.0	15.6	14.2	12.9	11.7	9.8	8.5
Path • Inches	-1.5	+2.6	0.0	-10.6	-30.7	-62.4	-108.0	-254.0	-498.0
Wind Drift • Inches	0.0	0.9	3.8	8.9	16.5	27.0	40.6	78.5	130.4

Lapua 185-grain FMJ—Boat Tail (4317590)

G1 Ballistic Coefficient = 0.490

Distance • Yards	Muzzle	100	200	300	400	500	600	800	1000
Velocity • fps	2495	2335	2181	2033	1864	1703	1570	1333	1152
Energy • Ft-lbs	2558	2240	1954	1698	1427	1192	1012	730	546
Taylor KO Index	20.3	19.0	17.8	16.5	15.2	13.9	12.8	10.9	9.4
Path • Inches	-1.5	+2.4	0.0	-9.8	-27.2	-55.1	-98.4	-225.7	-433.3
Wind Drift • Inches	0.0	0.8	3.4	7.9	14.7	24.0	33.5	64.3	107.5

Hirtenberger 190-grain Sierra HPBT Match (82200416)

G1 Ballistic Coefficient = 0.520

Distance • Yards	Muzzle	100	200	300	400	500	600	800	1000
Velocity • fps	2395	2235	2081	1933	1792	1659	1534	1315	1147
Energy • Ft-lbs	2421	2108	1827	1577	1355	1161	993	729	555
Taylor KO Index	21.4	19.6	18.0	16.4	14.9	13.5	12.2	10.1	8.8
Path • Inches	-1.5	+2.7	0.0	-10.8	-30.9	-61.8	-105.4	-239.5	-454.5
Wind Drift • Inches	0.0	0.7	2.9	6.8	12.4	20.2	30.1	57.5	95.5

Lapua 200-grain Subsonic (4317340)

G1 Ballistic Coefficient = 0.470

Distance • Yards	Muzzle	100	200	300	400	500	600	800	1000
Velocity • fps	1050	1001	961	926	894	866	839	791	748
Energy • Ft-lbs	490	445	410	381	355	333	313	278	249
Taylor KO Index	9.2	8.8	8.5	8.1	7.9	7.6	7.4	7.0	6.6
Path • Inches	-1.5	+16.6	0.0	-54.2	-148.7	-286.5	-470.4	-987.5	-1724
Wind Drift • Inches	0.0	1.2	4.8	10.5	18.3	28.0	39.7	68.7	105.4

The Spanish ibex comes in several different varieties, this being a Beceite ibex. (Photo from *Wind in My Face* by Hubert Thummler, 2006, Safari Press)

.307 Winchester

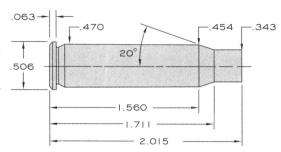

This is an interesting cartridge. If you look at the dimensions, you'll find that the .307 Winchester is externally identical to the .308 except that the .307 has a rim. Introduced in 1982, the .307 was designed to be used in U.S. Repeating Arms Company's new M94 Angle Eject lever-action rifles. Ballistics are similar to those of the .308, but the .307 has thicker case walls (smaller internal volume), and it pays a small performance penalty for that reason.

Relative Recoil Factor = 1.93

Specifications

Controlling Agency for Standardization of this Ammunition: SAAMI

Bullet Weight Grains	Velocity fps	Maximum Average Pressure	
		Copper Crusher	Transducer
150	2,705	52,000 cup	N/S
180	2,450	52,000 cup	N/S

Standard barrel for velocity testing: 24 inches long—1 turn in 12-inch twist

Availability

Winchester 180-grain Power-Point (X3076)

G1 Ballistic Coefficient = 0.253

Distance • Yards	Muzzle	100	200	300	400	500	600	800	1000
Velocity • fps	2510	2179	1874	1599	1362	1177	1051	904	306
Energy • Ft-lbs	2538	1898	1404	1022	742	554	442	327	260
Taylor KO Index	19.9	17.3	14.8	12.7	10.8	9.3	8.3	7.2	6.4
Path • Inches	-1.5	+2.9	0.0	-12.9	-39.6	-85.1	-155.6	-396.6	-808.2
Wind Drift • Inches	0.0	1.6	6.6	16.1	30.9	51.7	78.3	145.3	227.4

Peter Flack shot this western kob antelope with a .300 Winchester, his favorite caliber for African antelope. (Photo from *African Hunter II* by Craig Boddington and Peter Flack, 2004, Safari Press)

.30-06 Springfield

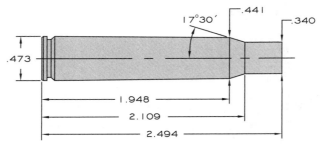

It's nearly 100 years old, but who's counting? The .30-06 is the standard by which every other U.S. cartridge is judged. Conceived in response to the embarrassment inflicted by the 7x57mm Mausers in Cuba in the Spanish-American War, this cartridge, when first developed, was little more than a 7x57 necked to .30 caliber. In its original form, the 1903 cartridge for the Model 1903 rifle used a 220-grain roundnose bullet at 2,300 fps. Three years later the 1906 version (hence the .30-06 name) adopted a 150-grain pointed bullet at 2,700 fps.

The basic design of U.S. military rifle ammunition changed very little until the 7.62 NATO cartridge (.308 Winchester) was adopted in 1952. The .30-06 remains the most popular caliber chambered in this country. There are over 100 different loadings available today. At this rate we might see .30-06s around in the year 2100.

Relative Recoil Factor = 2.19

Specifications

Controlling Agency for Standardization of this Ammunition: SAAMI

Bullet Weight Grains	Velocity fps	Maximum Average Pressure	
		Copper Crusher	Transducer
110	3,300	50,000 cup	60,000 psi
125	3,125	50,000 cup	60,000 psi
150	2,900	50,000 cup	60,000 psi
165–168	2,790	50,000 cup	60,000 psi
180	2,690	50,000 cup	60,000 psi
200	2,450	50,000 cup	60,000 psi
220	2,400	50,000 cup	60,000 psi

Standard barrel for velocity testing: 24 inches long—1 turn in 10-inch twist

Availability

Remington 55-grain Accelerator Pointed Soft Point (R30069)

G1 Ballistic Coefficient = 0.197

Distance • Yards	Muzzle	100	200	300	400	500	600	800	1000
Velocity • fps	4080	3484	2964	2499	2080	1706	1388	1009	850
Energy • Ft-lbs	2033	1482	1073	763	528	355	235	124	88
Taylor KO Index	9.9	8.4	7.2	6.0	5.0	4.1	3.4	2.4	2.1
Path • Inches	-1.5	+0.7	0.0	-4.7	-15.0	-33.6	-65.1	-194.4	-542.0
Wind Drift • Inches	0.0	1.1	4.6	11.1	21.3	36.4	57.8	123.2	212.0

PMC 100-grain NT/FR (3006HRA)

G1 Ballistic Coefficient = 0.110

Distance • Yards	Muzzle	100	200	300	400	500	600	800	1000
Velocity • fps	2700	1945	1350	1017	868	765	681	543	430
Energy • Ft-lbs	1619	840	405	230	167	130	103	65	41
Taylor KO Index	11.9	8.6	5.9	4.5	3.8	3.4	3.0	2.4	1.9
0ath • Inches	-1.5	+4.1	0.0	-24.1	-80.0	-177.2	-327.0	-846.3	-1815
Wind Drift • Inches	0.0	3.5	16.7	43.0	80.0	125.4	179.0	313.9	493.6

Lapua 123-grain Full Metal Jacket (4317577)

G1 Ballistic Coefficient = 0.274

Distance • Yards	Muzzle	100	200	300	400	500	600	800	1000
Velocity • fps	2936	2599	2286	1995	1728	1490	1289	1031	900
Energy • Ft-lbs	2364	1853	1433	1092	819	609	454	290	221
Taylor KO Index	15.9	14.1	12.4	10.8	9.4	8.1	7.0	5.6	4.9
Path • Inches	-1.5	+1.8	0.0	-8.5	-25.9	-54.9	-100.5	-262.6	-549.9
Wind Drift • Inches	0.0	1.1	4.8	11.6	22.0	37.0	57.1	113.9	188.0

Federal 125-grain Speer Hot-Cor SP (3006CS)

G1 Ballistic Coefficient = 0.269

Distance • Yards	Muzzle	100	200	300	400	500	600	800	1000
Velocity • fps	3140	2780	2450	2140	1850	1600	1376	1070	921
Energy • Ft-lbs	2735	2145	1680	1270	955	705	526	318	235
Taylor KO Index	17.3	15.3	13.5	11.8	10.2	8.8	7.6	5.9	5.1
Path • Inches	-1.5	+1.5	0.0	-7.3	-22.3	-47.5	-86.9	-229.4	-490.8
Wind Drift • Inches	0.0	1.1	4.5	10.7	20.4	34.2	53.0	107.5	180.9

Remington 125-grain Pointed Soft Point (R30061)

G1 Ballistic Coefficient = 0.268

Distance • Yards	Muzzle	100	200	300	400	500	600	800	1000
Velocity • fps	3140	2780	2447	2138	1853	1595	1371	1067	919
Energy • Ft-lbs	2736	2145	1662	1269	953	706	522	316	234
Taylor KO Index	17.3	15.3	13.5	11.8	10.2	8.8	7.5	5.9	5.1
Path • Inches	-1.5	+1.5	0.0	-7.4	-22.4	-47.6	-87.2	-230.5	-493.1
Wind Drift • Inches	0.0	1.1	4.5	10.8	20.5	34.4	53.3	108.0	181.8

Winchester 125-grain Pointed Soft Point (X30062)

G1 Ballistic Coefficient = 0.268

Distance • Yards	Muzzle	100	200	300	400	500	600	800	1000
Velocity • fps	3140	2780	2447	2138	1853	1595	1371	1067	919
Energy • Ft-lbs	2736	2145	1662	1269	953	706	522	316	234
Taylor KO Index	17.3	15.3	13.5	11.8	10.2	8.8	7.5	5.9	5.1
Path • Inches	-1.5	+1.5	0.0	-7.4	-22.4	-47.6	-87.2	-230.5	-493.1
Wind Drift • Inches	0.0	1.1	4.5	10.8	20.5	34.4	53.3	108.0	181.8

Remington 125-grain Core-Lokt Pointed Soft Point (RL30062)

G1 Ballistic Coefficient = 0.267

Distance • Yards	Muzzle	100	200	300	400	500	600	800	1000
Velocity • fps	2660	2335	2034	1757	1509	1300	1139	956	846
Energy • Ft-lbs	1964	1513	1148	856	632	469	360	254	200
Taylor KO Index	14.6	12.8	11.2	9.7	8.3	7.2	6.3	5.3	4.7
Path • Inches	-1.5	+2.5	0.0	-10.9	-33.3	-71.3	-130.6	-335.2	-680.0
Wind Drift • Inches	0.0	1.3	5.7	13.8	26.5	44.4	68.1	130.6	208.4

Cor-Bon 130-grain Glaser Safety (06000/na)

G1 Ballistic Coefficient = 0.200

Distance • Yards	Muzzle	100	200	300	400	500	600	800	1000
Velocity • fps	3100	2623	2203	1819	1436	1223	1052	815	762
Energy • Ft-lbs	2775	1995	1401	955	637	432	320	221	168
Taylor KO Index	17.7	15.0	12.6	10.4	8.5	7.0	6.0	4.7	4.4
Path • Inches	-1.5	+1.8	0.0	-9.1	-28.9	-65.3	-125.9	-343.5	-722.5
Wind Drift • Inches	0.0	1.5	6.4	15.7	30.9	53.2	82.9	159.8	255.4

USA (Winchester) 147-grain Full Metal Jacket (USA3006)

G1 Ballistic Coefficient = 0.421

Distance • Yards	Muzzle	100	200	300	400	500	600	800	1000
Velocity • fps	3020	2794	2579	2374	2178	1992	1815	1497	1243
Energy • Ft-lbs	2976	2548	2171	1839	1548	1295	1075	732	504
Taylor KO Index	19.5	18.1	16.7	15.4	14.1	12.9	11.7	9.7	8.0
Path • Inches	-1.5	+1.5	0.0	-6.7	-19.6	-39.9	-69.0	-161.6	-318.9
Wind Drift • Inches	0.0	0.7	2.9	6.8	12.5	20.4	30.7	59.8	102.5

Hornady 150-grain InterBond LM (81199)

G1 Ballistic Coefficient = 0.416

Distance • Yards	Muzzle	100	200	300	400	500	600	800	1000
Velocity • fps	3100	2867	2645	2434	2233	2041	1861	1533	1267
Energy • Ft-lbs	3200	2736	2330	1973	1660	1387	1154	783	535
Taylor KO Index	20.5	18.9	17.5	16.1	14.7	13.5	12.3	10.1	8.4
Path • Inches	-1.5	+1.4	0.0	-6.4	-18.6	-37.8	-65.4	-153.3	-303.0
Wind Drift • Inches	0.0	0.7	2.8	6.6	12.2	19.9	29.9	58.4	100.4

Hornady 150-grain SP—LM InterLock (8510)

G1 Ballistic Coefficient = 0.339

Distance • Yards	Muzzle	100	200	300	400	500	600	800	1000
Velocity • fps	3100	2815	2548	2295	2059	1835	1632	1288	1065
Energy • Ft-lbs	3200	2639	2161	1755	1410	1121	887	553	378
Taylor KO Index	20.5	18.6	16.8	15.1	13.6	12.1	10.8	8.5	7.0
Path • Inches	-1.5	+1.4	0.0	-6.8	-20.3	-42.0	-74.1	-182.6	-379.1
Wind Drift • Inches	0.0	0.8	3.5	8.4	15.6	25.8	39.2	78.2	135.0

Winchester 150-grain Power-Point Plus (SHV30061)

G1 Ballistic Coefficient = 0.262

Distance • Yards	Muzzle	100	200	300	400	500	600	800	1000
Velocity • fps	3050	2685	2352	2043	1760	1508	1293	1024	891
Energy • Ft-lbs	3089	2402	1843	1391	1032	757	561	351	266
Taylor KO Index	20.1	17.7	15.5	13.5	11.6	10.0	8.5	6.8	5.9
Path • Inches	-1.5	+1.7	0.0	-8.0	-24.3	-51.9	-95.7	-253.8	-537.8
Wind Drift • Inches	0.0	1.1	4.8	11.5	22.0	37.1	57.5	115.6	191.8

Speer 150-grain Grand Slam (24551) (Discontinued in 2004)

G1 Ballistic Coefficient = 0.305

Distance • Yards	Muzzle	100	200	300	400	500	600	800	1000
Velocity • fps	3000	2692	2404	2134	1882	1651	1445	1134	971
Energy • Ft-lbs	2997	2412	1924	1517	1180	908	695	429	314
Taylor KO Index	19.8	17.8	15.9	14.1	12.4	10.9	9.5	7.5	6.4
Path • Inches	-1.5	+1.7	0.0	-7.7	-23.1	-48.4	-86.4	-217.7	-456.7
Wind Drift • Inches	0.0	0.9	3.7	8.9	16.8	27.9	42.8	86.0	145.6

Winchester 150-grain Partition Gold (SPG3006)

G1 Ballistic Coefficient = 0.367

Distance • Yards	Muzzle	100	200	300	400	500	600	800	1000
Velocity • fps	2960	2705	2464	2235	2019	1815	1627	1306	1089
Energy • Ft-lbs	2919	2437	2022	1664	1358	1098	882	569	395
Taylor KO Index	19.5	17.9	16.3	14.8	13.3	12.0	10.7	8.6	7.2
Path • Inches	-1.5	+1.6	0.0	-7.4	-21.7	-44.6	-78.3	-189.4	-385.8
Wind Drift • Inches	0.0	0.8	3.4	8.1	15.1	24.9	37.8	74.8	128.2

Hirttenberger 150-grain Nosler Partition (82200390)

G1 Ballistic Coefficient = 0.416

Distance • Yards	Muzzle	100	200	300	400	500	600	800	1000
Velocity • fps	2936	2711	2498	2294	2099	1915	1741	1432	1193
Energy • Ft-lbs	2872	2449	2078	1753	1468	1221	1010	683	474
Taylor KO Index	19.4	17.9	16.5	15.1	13.9	12.6	11.5	9.5	7.9
Path • Inches	-1.5	+1.6	0.0	-7.2	-21.0	-42.8	-74.1	-174.2	-345.1
Wind Drift • Inches	0.0	0.7	2.7	6.4	11.9	19.4	29.2	57.2	97.8

Winchester 150-grain Fail Safe (S3006XB)

G1 Ballistic Coefficient = 0.313

Distance • Yards	Muzzle	100	200	300	400	500	600	800	1000
Velocity • fps	2920	2625	2349	2089	1848	1625	1426	1129	971
Energy • Ft-lbs	2841	2296	1838	1455	1137	880	677	425	314
Taylor KO Index	19.3	17.3	15.5	13.8	12.2	10.7	9.4	7.5	6.4
Path • Inches	-1.5	+1.8	0.0	-8.1	-24.3	-50.5	-90.7	-229.0	-477.0
Wind Drift • Inches	0.0	1.0	4.2	10.0	18.8	31.2	47.8	95.5	161.0

Winchester 150-grain Power-Point (X30061)

G1 Ballistic Coefficient = 0.270

Distance • Yards	Muzzle	100	200	300	400	500	600	800	1000
Velocity • fps	2920	2580	2265	1972	1704	1466	1265	1017	890
Energy • Ft-lbs	2839	2217	1708	1295	967	716	538	345	264
Taylor KO Index	19.3	17.0	14.9	13.0	11.2	9.7	8.3	6.7	5.9
Path • Inches	-1.5	+2.2	0.0	-9.0	-27.0	-57.1	-103.3	-270.5	-565.3
Wind Drift • Inches	0.0	1.2	4.9	11.9	22.6	38.0	58.8	117.0	192.1

Federal 150-grain Sierra GameKing BTSP (P3006G)

G1 Ballistic Coefficient = 0.410

Distance • Yards	Muzzle	100	200	300	400	500	600	800	1000
Velocity • fps	2910	2690	2480	2270	2070	1880	1707	1401	1168
Energy • Ft-lbs	2820	2420	2040	1710	1430	1180	971	654	454
Taylor KO Index	19.2	17.8	16.4	15.0	13.7	12.4	11.3	9.7	7.7
Path • Inches	-1.5	+1.7	0.0	-7.4	-21.5	-43.7	-76.2	-179.9	-357.5
Wind Drift • Inches	0.0	0.7	3.1	7.2	13.5	22.0	33.6	65.7	112.3

Federal 150-grain Hi-Shok Soft Point (3006A)

G1 Ballistic Coefficient = 0.314

Distance • Yards	Muzzle	100	200	300	400	500	600	800	1000
Velocity • fps	2910	2620	2340	2080	1840	1620	1423	1128	971
Energy • Ft-lbs	2820	2280	1825	1445	1130	875	675	424	314
Taylor KO Index	19.2	17.3	15.4	13.7	12.1	10.7	9.4	7.4	6.4
Path • Inches	-1.5	+1.8	0.0	-8.2	-24.4	-50.8	-91.2	-230.1	-478.8
Wind Drift • Inches	0.0	1.0	4.2	10.0	18.8	31.2	47.9	95.6	160.9

Hornady 150-grain InterBond (81099)

G1 Ballistic Coefficient = 0.416

Distance • Yards	Muzzle	100	200	300	400	500	600	800	1000
Velocity • fps	2910	2686	2473	2270	2077	1893	1722	1417	1182
Energy • Ft-lbs	2820	24.3	2037	1716	1436	1193	988	669	465
Taylor KO Index	19.2	17.7	16.3	15.0	13.7	12.5	11.4	9.4	7.8
Path • Inches	-1.5	+1.8	0.0	-8.2	-24.4	-50.8	-91.2	-230.1	-478.8
Wind Drift • Inches	0.0	1.0	4.2	10.0	18.8	31.2	47.9	95.6	160.9

Hornady 150-grain BTSP InterLock (8111)

G1 Ballistic Coefficient = 0.349

Distance • Yards	Muzzle	100	200	300	400	500	600	800	1000
Velocity • fps	2910	2645	2395	2159	1937	1729	1539	1228	1037
Energy • Ft-lbs	2820	2330	1911	1553	1249	996	789	503	359
Taylor KO Index	19.2	17.4	15.7	14.1	12.7	11.3	10.1	8.0	6.8
Path • Inches	-1.5	+1.7	0.0	-7.8	-23.1	-46.7	-84.3	-206.7	-424.6
Wind Drift • Inches	0.0	0.9	3.7	8.8	16.5	27.2	41.5	82.3	140.3

Hornady 150-grain SP (8110)

G1 Ballistic Coefficient = 0.338

Distance • Yards	Muzzle	100	200	300	400	500	600	800	1000
Velocity • fps	2910	2637	2380	2137	1909	1697	1504	1196	1016
Energy • Ft-lbs	2820	2315	1886	1521	1213	959	754	477	344
Taylor KO Index	19.2	17.4	15.0	14.1	12.6	11.2	9.9	7.9	6.7
Path • Inches	-1.5	+1.8	0.0	-7.9	-23.5	-48.7	-86.2	-213.2	-440.2
Wind Drift • Inches	0.0	0.9	3.9	9.1	17.2	28.4	43.3	86.1	146.4

Remington 150-grain AccuTip Boat Tail (PRA3006A)

G1 Ballistic Coefficient = 0.415

Distance • Yards	Muzzle	100	200	300	400	500	600	800	1000
Velocity • fps	2910	2686	2473	2270	2077	1893	1720	1414	1179
Energy • Ft-lbs	2820	2403	2037	1716	1436	1193	985	666	463
Taylor KO Index	19.2	17.7	15.9	16.3	15.0	13.7	12.5	11.4	9.3
Path • Inches	-1.5	+1.7	0.0	-7.4	-21.5	-43.7	-75.7	-178.2	-353.3
Wind Drift • Inches	0.0	0.7	3.1	7.2	13.4	21.9	33.0	64.6	110.4

Remington 150-grain Core-Lokt Ultra Bonded (PRC3006A)

G1 Ballistic Coefficient = 0.331

Distance • Yards	Muzzle	100	200	300	400	500	600	800	1000
Velocity • fps	2910	2631	2368	2121	1889	1674	1481	1176	1003
Energy • Ft-lbs	2820	2331	1868	1498	1188	933	731	461	335
Taylor KO Index	19.2	17.4	15.6	14.0	12.5	11.0	9.5	7.8	6.6
Path • Inches	-1.5	+1.8	0.0	-8.0	-23.8	-49.3	-87.7	-217.8	-450.8
Wind Drift • Inches	0.0	0.9	4.0	9.4	17.6	29.1	44.5	88.7	150.4

Remington 150-grain Core-Lokt Pointed Soft Point (R30062)

G1 Ballistic Coefficient = 0.315

Distance • Yards	Muzzle	100	200	300	400	500	600	800	1000
Velocity • fps	2910	2617	2342	2083	1843	1622	1427	1131	972
Energy • Ft-lbs	2820	2281	1827	1445	1131	876	678	426	315
Taylor KO Index	19.2	17.3	15.5	13.7	12.2	10.7	9.4	7.5	6.4
Path • Inches	-1.5	+1.8	0.0	-8.2	-24.4	-50.9	-91.0	-229.3	-477.1
Wind Drift • Inches	0.0	1.0	4.2	9.9	18.7	31.1	47.7	95.1	160.2

Winchester 150-grain Silvertip (X30063)

G1 Ballistic Coefficient = 0.314

Distance • Yards	Muzzle	100	200	300	400	500	600	800	1000
Velocity • fps	2910	2617	2342	2083	1843	1622	1423	1128	971
Energy • Ft-lbs	2820	2281	1827	1445	1131	876	675	424	314
Taylor KO Index	19.2	17.3	15.5	13.7	12.2	10.7	9.4	7.5	6.4
Path • Inches	-1.5	+2.1	0.0	-8.5	-25.0	-51.8	-92.1	-230.1	-478.8
Wind Drift • Inches	0.0	1.0	4.2	10.0	18.8	31.2	47.9	95.6	160.9

PMC 150-grain SPBT Game (3006HA)

G1 Ballistic Coefficient = 0.381

Distance • Yards	Muzzle	100	200	300	400	500	600	800	1000
Velocity • fps	2900	2657	2427	2208	2000	1805	1625	1315	1100
Energy • Ft-lbs	2801	2351	1961	1623	1332	1085	880	576	403
Taylor KO Index	19.1	17.5	16.0	14.6	13.2	11.9	10.7	8.7	7.3
Path • Inches	-1.5	+1.7	0.0	-7.7	-22.5	-46.0	-80.2	-192.5	-388.8
Wind Drift • Inches	0.0	0.8	3.4	8.0	14.9	24.5	37.1	73.1	125.0

Federal 150-grain Solid Base BT (P3006S1)

G1 Ballistic Coefficient = 0.395

Distance • Yards	Muzzle	100	200	300	400	500	600	800	1000
Velocity • fps	2900	2670	2440	2230	2030	1840	1662	1354	1130
Energy • Ft-lbs	2800	2365	1990	1660	1375	1130	921	611	426
Taylor KO Index	19.1	17.6	16.1	14.7	13.4	12.1	11.0	8.9	7.5
Path • Inches	-1.5	+1.7	0.0	-7.6	-22.1	-44.9	-78.3	-186.8	-374.3
Wind Drift • Inches	0.0	0.8	3.3	7.7	14.3	23.4	35.4	69.5	118.9

Sellier & Bellot 150-grain SPCE (SBA30061)

G1 Ballistic Coefficient = 0.290

Distance • Yards	Muzzle	100	200	300	400	500	600	800	1000
Velocity • fps	2887	2555	2262	2002	1749	1520	1324	1058	922
Energy • Ft-lbs	2770	2170	1700	1332	1019	770	584	373	283
Taylor KO Index	19.1	16.9	14.9	13.2	11.5	10.0	8.7	7.0	6.1
Path • Inches	-1.5	+1.9	0.0	-8.6	-26.0	-55.0	-99.4	-255.9	-533.1
Wind Drift • Inches	0.0	1.1	4.6	11.1	21.0	35.1	54.1	107.7	178.6

PMC 150-grain Pointed Soft Point (3006A)

G1 Ballistic Coefficient = 0.333

Distance • Yards	Muzzle	100	200	300	400	500	600	800	1000
Velocity • fps	2770	2497	2241	2003	1781	1582	1401	1127	977
Energy • Ft-lbs	2555	2076	1673	1336	1057	834	654	423	318
Taylor KO Index	18.3	16.5	14.8	13.2	11.8	10.4	9.2	7.4	6.4
Path • Inches	-1.5	+2.0	0.0	-9.0	-26.7	-55.2	-98.0	-243.4	-498.7
Wind Drift • Inches	0.0	1.0	4.2	10.0	18.8	31.2	47.2	94.1	157.3

Hornady 150-grain SST-LM InterLock (8519)

G1 Ballistic Coefficient = 0.415

Distance • Yards	Muzzle	100	200	300	400	500	600	800	1000
Velocity • fps	3100	2867	2545	2434	2233	2041	1856	1530	1264
Energy • Ft-lbs	3200	2736	2330	1973	1660	1387	1151	780	532
Taylor KO Index	20.5	18.9	16.8	16.1	14.7	13.5	12.2	10.1	8.3
Path • Inches	-1.5	+1.4	0.0	-6.4	-18.6	-37.8	-65.4	-153.6	-303.7
Wind Drift • Inches	0.0	0.7	2.8	6.6	12.2	20.0	30.0	58.6	100.7

Norma 150-grain Nosler Ballistic Tip (17654)

G1 Ballistic Coefficient = 0.421

Distance • Yards	Muzzle	100	200	300	400	500	600	800	1000
Velocity • fps	2936	2713	2502	2300	2108	1925	1753	1446	1205
Energy • Ft-lbs	2872	2453	2085	1762	1481	1235	1024	696	483
Taylor KO Index	19.4	17.9	16.5	15.2	13.9	12.7	11.6	9.5	8.0
Path • Inches	-1.5	+1.6	0.0	-7.1	-20.9	-42.5	-73.6	-172.7	-341.1
Wind Drift • Inches	0.0	0.7	3.0	7.0	13.0	21.2	32.0	62.5	106.8

Federal 150-grain Nosler Ballistic Tip (P3006P)

G1 Ballistic Coefficient = 0.439

Distance • Yards	Muzzle	100	200	300	400	500	600	800	1000
Velocity • fps	2910	2700	2490	2300	2110	1940	1775	1476	1235
Energy • Ft-lbs	2820	2420	2070	1760	1485	1240	1050	726	508
Taylor KO Index	19.2	17.8	16.4	15.2	13.9	12.8	11.7	9.7	8.2
Path • Inches	-1.5	+1.6	0.0	-7.3	-21.1	-42.8	-73.5	-171.0	-334.9
Wind Drift • Inches	0.0	0.7	2.9	6.8	12.6	20.5	30.8	59.8	102.0

Hornady 150-grain SST InterLock (8109)

G1 Ballistic Coefficient = 0.416

Distance • Yards	Muzzle	100	200	300	400	500	600	800	1000
Velocity • fps	2910	2686	2473	2270	2077	1893	1722	1417	1132
Energy • Ft-lbs	2820	2431	2037	1716	1436	1193	988	669	465
Taylor KO Index	19.2	17.7	16.3	15.0	13.7	12.5	11.4	9.4	7.8
Path • Inches	-1.5	+1.7	0.0	-7.4	-21.5	-43.7	-75.6	-177.9	-352.4
Wind Drift • Inches	0.0	0.7	3.1	7.2	13.4	21.8	32.9	64.4	110.0

Remington 150-grain Nosler Ballistic Tip (PRT3006A) (Discontinued in 2005)

G1 Ballistic Coefficient = 0.436

Distance • Yards	Muzzle	100	200	300	400	500	600	800	1000
Velocity • fps	2910	2696	2492	2298	2112	1934	1768	1468	1228
Energy • Ft-lbs	2821	2422	2070	1759	1485	1247	1042	718	503
Taylor KO Index	19.2	17.8	16.4	15.2	13.9	12.8	11.7	9.7	8.1
Path • Inches	-1.5	+1.6	0.0	-7.3	-21.1	-42.8	-73.7	-171.9	-337.1
Wind Drift • Inches	0.0	0.7	2.9	6.8	12.7	20.6	31.0	60.4	102.9

Remington 150-grain Swift Scirocco Bonded (PRSC3006C)
G1 Ballistic Coefficient = 0.435

Distance • Yards	Muzzle	100	200	300	400	500	600	800	1000
Velocity • fps	2910	2696	2492	2298	2111	1934	1766	1466	1226
Energy • Ft-lbs	2820	2421	2069	1758	1485	1246	1039	716	501
Taylor KO Index	19.2	17.8	16.4	15.2	13.9	12.8	11.7	9.7	8.1
Path • Inches	-1.5	+1.6	0.0	-7.3	-21.1	-42.3	-73.8	-172.2	-337.8
Wind Drift • Inches	0.0	0.7	2.9	6.9	12.7	20.7	31.1	60.5	103.3

Remington 150-grain Bronze Point (R30063)
G1 Ballistic Coefficient = 0.365

Distance • Yards	Muzzle	100	200	300	400	500	600	800	1000
Velocity • fps	2910	2656	2416	2189	1974	1773	1587	1275	1070
Energy • Ft-lbs	2820	2349	1944	1596	1298	1047	839	542	381
Taylor KO Index	19.2	17.5	15.9	14.4	13.0	11.7	10.5	8.4	7.1
Path • Inches	-1.5	+1.7	0.0	-7.7	-22.7	-46.6	-81.8	-198.3	-403.9
Wind Drift • Inches	0.0	0.8	3.6	8.4	15.6	25.7	39.1	77.3	132.0

Black Hills 150-grain Nosler Ballistic Tip (1C3006BHGN6)
G1 Ballistic Coefficient = 0.435

Distance • Yards	Muzzle	100	200	300	400	500	600	800	1000
Velocity • fps	2900	2687	2483	2289	2103	1926	1759	1459	1221
Energy • Ft-lbs	2801	2404	2054	1745	1473	1236	1030	710	497
Taylor KO Index	19.1	17.7	16.4	15.1	13.9	12.7	11.6	9.6	8.1
Path • Inches	-1.5	+1.7	0.0	-7.3	-21.2	-43.0	-74.4	-173.5	-340.6
Wind Drift • Inches	0.0	0.7	3.0	6.9	12.8	20.8	31.3	60.9	103.8

Winchester 150-grain Ballistic Silvertip (SBST3006)
G1 Ballistic Coefficient = 0.435

Distance • Yards	Muzzle	100	200	300	400	500	600	800	1000
Velocity • fps	2900	2687	2483	2289	2103	1926	1759	1459	1221
Energy • Ft-lbs	2801	2404	2054	1745	1473	1236	1030	710	497
Taylor KO Index	19.1	17.7	16.4	15.1	13.9	12.7	11.6	9.6	8.1
Path • Inches	-1.5	+1.7	0.0	-7.3	-21.2	-43.0	-74.4	-173.5	-340.6
Wind Drift • Inches	0.0	0.7	3.0	6.9	12.8	20.8	31.3	60.9	103.8

PMC 150-grain Barnes-XLC-HP (3006XLA) (Discontinued in 2005)
G1 Ballistic Coefficient = 0.453

Distance • Yards	Muzzle	100	200	300	400	500	600	800	1000
Velocity • fps	2750	2552	2361	2197	2005	1840	1686	1409	1192
Energy • Ft-lbs	2518	2168	1858	1583	1341	1129	947	661	473
Taylor KO Index	18.2	16.8	15.6	14.5	13.2	12.1	11.1	9.3	7.9
Path • Inches	-1.5	+2.0	0.0	-8.2	-23.7	-48.0	-82.3	-191.0	-372.1
Wind Drift • Inches	0.0	0.7	3.0	7.1	13.2	21.4	32.2	62.4	105.8

American Eagle (Federal) 150-grain Full Metal Jacket Boat-Tail (AE3006N)
G1 Ballistic Coefficient = 0.454

Distance • Yards	Muzzle	100	200	300	400	500	600	800	1000
Velocity • fps	2910	2710	2510	2320	2150	1970	1807	1512	1270
Energy • Ft-lbs	2820	2440	2100	1800	1535	1300	1088	762	537
Taylor KO Index	19.2	17.9	16.6	15.3	14.2	13.0	11.9	10.0	8.4
Path • Inches	-1.5	+1.6	0.0	-7.2	-20.8	-42.0	-72.2	-167.1	-325.0
Wind Drift • Inches	0.0	0.7	2.8	6.5	12.1	19.6	29.5	57.1	97.2

UMC (Remington) 150-grain MC (L30062)
G1 Ballistic Coefficient = 0.315

Distance • Yards	Muzzle	100	200	300	400	500	600	800	1000
Velocity • fps	2910	2617	2342	2085	1842	1623	1427	1131	972
Energy • Ft-lbs	2820	2281	1827	1448	1133	878	678	426	315
Taylor KO Index	19.2	17.2	15.4	13.8	12.2	10.7	9.4	7.5	6.5
Path • Inches	-1.5	+1.8	0.0	-8.2	-24.4	-50.9	-91.0	-229.3	-477.1
Wind Drift • Inches	0.0	1.0	4.2	9.9	18.7	31.1	47.7	95.1	160.2

PMC 150-grain Full Metal Jacket (3006C)
G1 Ballistic Coefficient = 0.402

Distance • Yards	Muzzle	100	200	300	400	500	600	800	1000
Velocity • fps	2770	2544	2330	2127	1936	1757	1588	1301	1100
Energy • Ft-lbs	2555	2155	1807	1507	1248	1028	840	564	403
Taylor KO Index	18.3	16.8	15.4	14.0	12.8	11.6	10.5	8.6	7.3
Path • Inches	-1.5	+1.9	0.0	-8.4	-24.4	-49.7	-86.4	-205.3	-409.5
Wind Drift • Inches	0.0	0.8	3.4	8.0	15.0	24.6	37.1	72.6	123.3

Norma 150-grain Full Jacket (17651) (Discontinued in 2005)

G1 Ballistic Coefficient = 0.423

Distance • Yards	Muzzle	100	200	300	400	500	600	800	1000
Velocity • fps	2772	2557	2353	2158	1973	1797	1636	1351	1139
Energy • Ft-lbs	2492	2121	1796	1511	1262	1048	892	608	432
Taylor KO Index	18.3	16.9	15.5	14.2	13.0	11.9	10.8	8.9	7.5
Path • Inches	-1.5	+1.9	0.0	-8.2	-23.9	-48.5	-83.9	-197.3	-389.9
Wind Drift • Inches	0.0	0.8	3.3	7.7	14.2	23.2	34.8	67.9	115.3

Federal 165-grain Sierra GameKing BTSP—HE (P3006Y) (Discontinued in 2005)

G1 Ballistic Coefficient = 0.405

Distance • Yards	Muzzle	100	200	300	400	500	600	800	1000
Velocity • fps	3000	2770	2540	2330	2130	1940	1760	1440	1193
Energy • Ft-lbs	3300	2800	2370	1990	1660	1375	1135	760	522
Taylor KO Index	21.8	20.1	18.4	16.9	15.5	14.1	12.8	10.5	8.7
Path • Inches	-1.5	+1.5	0.0	-6.9	-20.3	-41.1	-71.5	-169.0	-336.6
Wind Drift • Inches	0.0	0.7	3.0	7.1	13.2	21.6	32.6	63.8	109.4

Federal 165-grain Trophy Bonded Bear Claw—HE (P3006T4)

G1 Ballistic Coefficient = 0.344

Distance • Yards	Muzzle	100	200	300	400	500	600	800	1000
Velocity • fps	3000	2730	2470	2230	2000	1780	1582	1256	1050
Energy • Ft-lbs	3300	2720	2230	1815	1460	1160	917	578	404
Taylor KO Index	21.8	19.8	17.9	16.2	14.5	12.9	11.5	9.1	7.6
Path • Inches	-1.5	+1.4	0.0	-7.3	-21.8	-44.8	-79.2	-194.8	-402.3
Wind Drift • Inches	0.0	0.9	3.6	8.6	16.0	26.5	40.4	80.4	137.8

Hornady 165-grain InterBond LM (85159)

G1 Ballistic Coefficient = 0.447

Distance • Yards	Muzzle	100	200	300	400	500	600	800	1000
Velocity • fps	3015	2802	2599	2405	2119	2041	1871	1563	1306
Energy • Ft-lbs	3330	2876	2474	2118	1803	1526	1283	896	625
Taylor KO Index	21.9	20.3	18.9	17.5	16.1	14.8	13.6	11.3	9.5
Path • Inches	-1.5	+1.5	0.0	-6.6	-19.3	-39.0	-67.1	-155.5	-302.9
Wind Drift • Inches	0.0	0.7	2.7	6.3	11.7	19.0	28.5	55.3	94.3

Hornady 165-grain BTSP—LM InterLock (8515)

G1 Ballistic Coefficient = 0.435

Distance • Yards	Muzzle	100	200	300	400	500	600	800	1000
Velocity • fps	3015	2796	2588	2389	2199	2017	1844	1532	1276
Energy • Ft-lbs	3330	2864	2453	2090	1771	1490	1246	860	597
Taylor KO Index	21.9	20.3	18.8	17.3	16.0	14.6	13.4	11.1	9.3
Path • Inches	-1.5	+1.5	0.0	-6.7	-19.5	-39.5	-68.0	-158.4	-310.4
Wind Drift • Inches	0.0	0.7	2.8	8.5	12.0	19.6	29.5	57.4	98.0

Federal 165-grain Nosler Partition (P3006AD)

G1 Ballistic Coefficient = 0.410

Distance • Yards	Muzzle	100	200	300	400	500	600	800	1000
Velocity • fps	2830	2610	2400	2190	2000	1820	1650	1354	1137
Energy • Ft-lbs	2935	2490	2100	1760	1465	1210	998	672	474
Taylor KO Index	20.5	18.9	17.4	15.9	14.5	13.2	12.0	9.8	8.3
Path • Inches	-1.5	+1.9	0.0	-8.1	-23.4	-47.3	-81.3	-192.3	-381.9
Wind Drift • Inches	0.0	0.8	3.2	7.6	14.2	23.2	35.0	68.5	116.7

Speer 165-grain Grand Slam (24507) (Discontinued in 2005)

G1 Ballistic Coefficient = 0.425

Distance • Yards	Muzzle	100	200	300	400	500	600	800	1000
Velocity • fps	2810	2579	2359	2151	1954	1769	1596	1302	1097
Energy • Ft-lbs	2892	2436	2039	1695	1440	1146	934	621	441
Taylor KO Index	20.4	18.7	17.1	15.6	14.2	12.8	11.6	9.5	8.0
Path • Inches	-1.5	+1.9	0.0	-8.1	-23.8	-48.6	-84.5	-200.6	-399.3
Wind Drift • Inches	0.0	0.7	3.1	7.3	13.5	22.2	33.6	65.9	112.0

Federal 165-grain Sierra GameKing BTSP (P3006D)

G1 Ballistic Coefficient = 0.470

Distance • Yards	Muzzle	100	200	300	400	500	600	800	1000
Velocity • fps	2800	2610	2420	2240	2070	1910	1756	1478	1250
Energy • Ft-lbs	2870	2490	2150	1840	1580	1340	1130	800	573
Taylor KO Index	20.3	18.9	17.6	16.3	15.0	13.9	12.7	10.7	9.1
Path • Inches	-1.5	+1.8	0.0	-7.8	-22.4	-45.2	-77.6	-178.6	-345.5
Wind Drift • Inches	0.0	0.7	2.8	6.6	12.3	20.0	29.9	57.8	98.0

Federal 165-grain Sierra Pro-Hunter SP (3006TS) (Discontinued in 2005)

G1 Ballistic Coefficient = 0.381

Distance • Yards	Muzzle	100	200	300	400	500	600	800	1000
Velocity • fps	2800	2560	2340	2130	1920	1730	1556	1263	1069
Energy • Ft-lbs	2875	2410	2005	1655	1360	1100	888	585	419
Taylor KO Index	20.3	18.6	17.0	15.5	13.9	12.6	11.3	9.2	7.8
Path • Inches	-1.5	+1.9	0.0	-8.3	-24.3	-49.8	-87.1	-209.2	-421.9
Wind Drift • Inches	0.0	0.9	3.6	8.4	15.7	25.8	39.2	77.0	130.7

Federal 165-grain Soft Point (P3006TS)

G1 Ballistic Coefficient = 0.380

Distance • Yards	Muzzle	100	200	300	400	500	600	800	1000
Velocity • fps	2800	2560	2340	2120	1920	1730	1554	1260	1067
Energy • Ft-lbs	2870	2405	2000	1650	1350	1095	885	582	417
Taylor KO Index	20.3	18.6	17.0	15.4	13.9	12.6	11.3	9.2	7.7
Path • Inches	-1.5	+1.9	0.0	-8.4	-24.2	-49.9	87.2	-209.7	-423.0
Wind Drift • Inches	0.0	0.9	3.6	8.4	15.8	25.9	39.3	77.3	131.2

Federal 165-grain Trophy Bonded Bear Claw (P3006T1)

G1 Ballistic Coefficient = 0.342

Distance • Yards	Muzzle	100	200	300	400	500	600	800	1000
Velocity • fps	2800	2540	2200	2050	1830	1630	1446	1161	999
Energy • Ft-lbs	2870	2360	1915	1545	1230	972	767	494	365
Taylor KO Index	20.3	18.4	16.0	14.9	13.3	11.8	10.5	8.4	7.3
Path • Inches	-1.5	+2.0	0.0	-8.7	-25.4	-53.1	93.7	-231.1	-473.3
Wind Drift • Inches	0.0	1.0	4.0	9.5	17.9	29.6	45.2	89.4	150.5

Hornady 165-grain InterBond (81159)

G1 Ballistic Coefficient = 0.447

Distance • Yards	Muzzle	100	200	300	400	500	600	800	1000
Velocity • fps	2800	2597	2403	2217	2039	1870	1710	1426	1202
Energy • Ft-lbs	2872	2470	2115	1800	1523	1281	1072	745	530
Taylor KO Index	20.3	18.9	17.4	16.1	14.8	13.6	12.4	10.4	8.7
Path • Inches	-1.5	+1.8	0.0	-7.9	-22.8	-46.2	-79.5	-184.8	-361.0
Wind Drift • Inches	0.0	0.7	3.0	7.0	13.0	21.2	31.9	61.9	105.1

Hornady 165-grain BTSP InterLock (8115)

G1 Ballistic Coefficient = 0.435

Distance • Yards	Muzzle	100	200	300	400	500	600	800	1000
Velocity • fps	2800	2591	2392	2202	2020	1848	1685	1398	1177
Energy • Ft-lbs	2873	2460	2097	1777	1495	1252	1041	716	508
Taylor KO Index	20.3	18.8	17.4	16.0	14.7	13.4	12.2	10.1	8.5
Path • Inches	-1.5	+1.8	0.0	-8.0	-23.3	-47.0	-80.6	-188.4	-370.0
Wind Drift • Inches	0.0	0.8	3.1	7.3	13.4	21.9	33.0	64.2	109.1

Remington 165-grain AccuTip Boat Tail (PRA3006B)

G1 Ballistic Coefficient = 0.447

Distance • Yards	Muzzle	100	200	300	400	500	600	800	1000
Velocity • fps	2800	2597	2403	2217	2039	1870	1710	1426	1202
Energy • Ft-lbs	2872	2470	2115	1800	1523	1281	1072	745	530
Taylor KO Index	20.3	18.9	17.4	16.1	14.8	13.6	12.4	10.4	8.7
Path • Inches	-1.5	+1.8	0.0	-7.9	-22.8	-46.2	-79.5	-184.8	-361.0
Wind Drift • Inches	0.0	0.7	3.0	7.0	13.0	21.2	31.9	61.9	105.1

Remington 165-grain Pointed Soft Point, Boat Tail (PRB3006SA) (Discontinued in 2005)

G1 Ballistic Coefficient = 0.437

Distance • Yards	Muzzle	100	200	300	400	500	600	800	1000
Velocity • fps	2800	2592	2394	2204	2033	1852	1689	1403	1181
Energy • Ft-lbs	2872	2462	2100	1780	1500	1256	1046	721	511
Taylor KO Index	20.3	18.8	17.4	16.0	14.8	13.4	12.3	10.2	8.6
Path • Inches	-1.5	+1.8	0.0	-7.9	-23.0	-46.6	-80.4	-187.8	-368.5
Wind Drift • Inches	0.0	0.7	3.1	7.2	13.4	21.8	32.8	63.8	108.4

Remington 165-grain Core-Lokt Pointed Soft Point (R3006B)

G1 Ballistic Coefficient = 0.339

Distance • Yards	Muzzle	100	200	300	400	500	600	800	1000
Velocity • fps	2800	2534	2283	2047	1825	1621	1437	1154	993
Energy • Ft-lbs	2872	2352	1909	1534	1220	963	757	488	362
Taylor KO Index	20.3	18.4	16.6	14.9	13.2	11.8	10.4	8.4	7.2
Path • Inches	-1.5	+2.0	0.0	-8.7	-25.9	-53.2	-94.3	-233.1	-477.9
Wind Drift • Inches	0.0	1.0	4.1	9.6	18.1	30.0	45.7	90.5	152.1

Winchester 165-grain Fail Safe (S3006XA)

G1 Ballistic Coefficient = 0.348

Distance • Yards	Muzzle	100	200	300	400	500	600	800	1000
Velocity • fps	2800	2540	2295	2063	1846	1645	1464	1177	1009
Energy • Ft-lbs	2873	2365	1930	1560	1249	992	786	508	373
Taylor KO Index	20.3	18.4	16.7	15.0	13.4	11.9	10.6	8.5	7.3
Path • Inches	-1.5	+2.0	0.0	-8.6	-25.3	-52.3	-92.5	-227.2	-464.5
Wind Drift • Inches	0.0	0.9	4.0	9.4	17.6	29.0	44.1	87.3	147.2

Winchester 165-grain Pointed Soft Point (X30065)

G1 Ballistic Coefficient = 0.341

Distance • Yards	Muzzle	100	200	300	400	500	600	800	1000
Velocity • fps	2800	2536	2286	2051	1831	1627	1443	1159	997
Energy • Ft-lbs	2872	2355	1915	1541	1228	970	764	492	364
Taylor KO Index	20.3	18.4	16.6	14.9	13.3	11.8	10.5	8.4	7.2
Path • Inches	-1.5	+2.0	0.0	-8.6	-25.6	-53.0	-93.9	-231.7	-474.8
Wind Drift • Inches	0.0	1.0	4.0	9.6	18.0	29.7	45.4	89.8	151.0

Federal 165-grain Nosler Solid Base BT (P3006S2)

G1 Ballistic Coefficient = 0.430

Distance • Yards	Muzzle	100	200	300	400	500	600	800	1000
Velocity • fps	2790	2580	2380	2180	2000	1830	1667	1380	1163
Energy • Ft-lbs	2850	2435	2070	1750	1465	1220	1018	698	495
Taylor KO Index	20.3	18.7	17.3	15.8	14.5	13.3	12.1	10.0	8.4
Path • Inches	-1.5	+1.9	0.0	-8.7	-23.4	-47.3	81.8	-191.6	-377.2
Wind Drift • Inches	0.0	0.8	3.2	7.4	13.7	22.4	33.7	86.7	111.4

Hirtenberger 165-grain ABC Bullet (82200392)

G1 Ballistic Coefficient = 0.283

Distance • Yards	Muzzle	100	200	300	400	500	600	800	1000
Velocity • fps	2690	2381	2092	1825	1582	1371	1200	994	880
Energy • Ft-lbs	2652	2077	1604	1220	918	689	528	362	284
Taylor KO Index	19.5	17.3	15.2	13.2	11.5	10.0	8.7	7.2	6.4
Path • Inches	-1.5	+2.3	0.0	-10.3	-31.2	-66.3	-120.4	-308.0	-627.8
Wind Drift • Inches	0.0	1.2	5.3	12.7	24.1	40.4	62.0	120.4	194.5

Hirtenberger 165-grain Sierra SBT (82200390)

G1 Ballistic Coefficient = 0.416

Distance • Yards	Muzzle	100	200	300	400	500	600	800	1000
Velocity • fps	2575	2365	2165	1975	1795	1628	1474	1220	1054
Energy • Ft-lbs	2430	2050	1718	1429	1181	971	796	546	407
Taylor KO Index	18.7	17.2	15.7	14.3	13.0	11.8	10.7	8.9	7.7
Path • Inches	-1.5	+2.4	0.0	-9.8	-28.5	-58.1	-101.0	-239.3	-473.3
Wind Drift • Inches	0.0	0.8	3.4	7.9	14.7	24.0	36.3	70.5	117.8

Hornady 165-grain SST—LM (85154)

G1 Ballistic Coefficient = 0.448

Distance • Yards	Muzzle	100	200	300	400	500	600	800	1000
Velocity • fps	3015	2802	2599	2405	2219	2041	1873	1566	1309
Energy • Ft-lbs	3330	2876	2474	2118	1803	1526	1286	898	628
Taylor KO Index	21.9	20.3	18.9	17.5	16.1	14.8	13.6	11.4	9.5
Path • Inches	-1.5	+1.5	0.0	-6.6	-19.3	-39.0	-67.0	-155.2	-302.3
Wind Drift • Inches	0.0	0.6	2.7	6.3	11.6	18.9	28.4	55.1	94.0

Federal 165-grain Nosler Ballistic Tip (P3006Q)

G1 Ballistic Coefficient = 0.476

Distance • Yards	Muzzle	100	200	300	400	500	600	800	1000
Velocity • fps	2800	2610	2430	2250	2080	1920	1768	1491	1263
Energy • Ft-lbs	2870	2495	2155	1855	1585	1350	1145	814	584
Taylor KO Index	20.3	18.9	17.6	16.3	15.1	13.9	12.8	10.8	9.2
Path • Inches	-1.5	+1.8	0.0	-7.7	-22.3	-45.0	-77.1	-177.2	-341.8
Wind Drift • Inches	0.0	0.7	2.8	6.6	12.1	19.7	29.5	56.9	96.3

Remington 165-grain Nosler Ballistic Tip (PRT3006B) (Discontinued in 2005)

G1 Ballistic Coefficient = 0.475

Distance • Yards	Muzzle	100	200	300	400	500	600	800	1000
Velocity • fps	2800	2609	2425	2249	2080	1919	1766	1489	1261
Energy • Ft-lbs	2873	2494	2155	1854	1588	1350	1142	812	583
Taylor KO Index	20.3	18.9	17.6	16.3	15.1	13.9	12.8	10.8	9.2
Path • Inches	-1.5	+1.8	0.0	-7.7	-22.3	-45.0	-77.2	-177.4	-342.4
Wind Drift • Inches	0.0	0.7	2.8	6.6	12.1	19.7	29.5	57.0	96.6

Hornady 165-grain SST InterLock (81154)

G1 Ballistic Coefficient = 0.447

Distance • Yards	Muzzle	100	200	300	400	500	600	800	1000
Velocity • fps	2800	2597	2403	2217	2039	1870	1710	1426	1202
Energy • Ft-lbs	2872	2470	2115	1800	1523	1281	1072	745	530
Taylor KO Index	20.3	18.9	17.4	16.1	14.8	13.6	12.4	10.4	8.7
Path • Inches	-1.5	+1.8	0.0	-7.9	-22.8	-46.2	-79.5	-184.8	-361.0
Wind Drift • Inches	0.0	0.7	3.0	7.0	13.0	21.2	31.9	61.9	105.1

Black Hills 165-grain Nosler Ballistic Tip (1C3006BHGN3)

G1 Ballistic Coefficient = 0.475

Distance • Yards	Muzzle	100	200	300	400	500	600	800	1000
Velocity • fps	2750	2561	2379	2205	2038	1879	1728	1456	1236
Energy • Ft-lbs	2771	2403	2074	1781	1522	1293	1094	777	560
Taylor KO Index	20.0	18.6	17.3	16.0	14.8	13.6	12.5	10.6	9.0
Path • Inches	-1.5	+1.9	0.0	-8.1	-23.3	-46.9	-80.4	-185.0	-357.3
Wind Drift • Inches	0.0	0.7	2.9	6.8	12.5	20.2	30.4	58.6	99.1

Remington 168-grain Core-Lokt Ultra Bonded (PRC3006B)

G1 Ballistic Coefficient = 0.356

Distance • Yards	Muzzle	100	200	300	400	500	600	800	1000
Velocity • fps	2800	2546	2306	2079	1866	1668	1488	1193	1023
Energy • Ft-lbs	2924	2413	1984	1613	1299	1037	826	535	391
Taylor KO Index	20.7	18.8	17.0	15.4	13.8	12.3	11.0	8.9	7.6
Path • Inches	-1.5	+1.9	0.0	-8.5	-25.1	-51.7	-91.0	-222.4	-453.3
Wind Drift • Inches	0.0	0.9	3.8	9.1	17.1	28.1	42.8	84.6	142.9

PMC 168-grain Barnes-XLC-HP (3006XLB) (Discontinued in 2005)

G1 Ballistic Coefficient = 0.498

Distance • Yards	Muzzle	100	200	300	400	500	600	800	1000
Velocity • fps	2750	2569	2395	2228	2067	1914	1769	1503	1281
Energy • Ft-lbs	2770	2418	2101	1818	1565	1342	1146	828	602
Taylor KO Index	20.0	18.7	17.4	16.2	15.0	13.9	12.8	10.9	9.3
Path • Inches	-1.5	+1.9	0.0	-8.0	-23.0	-46.1	-78.6	-179.6	-343.8
Wind Drift • Inches	0.0	0.7	2.8	6.4	11.8	19.2	28.6	55.0	92.9

Winchester 168-grain Ballistic Silvertip (SBST3006A)

G1 Ballistic Coefficient = 0.475

Distance • Yards	Muzzle	100	200	300	400	500	600	800	1000
Velocity • fps	2790	2599	2416	2240	2072	1911	1758	1482	1256
Energy • Ft-lbs	2093	2520	2177	1872	1601	1362	1153	820	588
Taylor KO Index	20.6	19.2	17.9	16.6	15.3	14.1	13.0	11.0	9.3
Path • Inches	-1.5	+1.8	0.0	-7.8	-22.5	-45.2	-77.8	-178.9	-345.4
Wind Drift • Inches	0.0	0.7	2.8	6.6	12.2	19.8	29.7	57.3	97.1

Sellier & Bellot 168-grain HPBT (SBA30063)

G1 Ballistic Coefficient = 0.383

Distance • Yards	Muzzle	100	200	300	400	500	600	800	1000
Velocity • fps	2786	2560	2352	2161	1972	1794	1628	1339	1129
Energy • Ft-lbs	2897	2447	2066	1744	1426	1180	971	657	467
Taylor KO Index	20.6	18.9	17.4	16.0	14.6	13.3	12.0	9.9	8.3
Path • Inches	-1.5	+1.9	0.0	-8.2	-23.8	-48.4	-83.8	-197.8	-392.5
Wind Drift • Inches	0.0	0.8	3.3	7.7	14.4	23.5	35.4	69.2	117.6

Black Hills 168-grain Hornady Match BTHP (1C3006BHGN2)

G1 Ballistic Coefficient = 0.450

Distance • Yards	Muzzle	100	200	300	400	500	600	800	1000
Velocity • fps	2700	2503	2313	2133	1960	1796	1643	1372	1165
Energy • Ft-lbs	2720	2337	1997	1697	1433	1204	1077	702	506
Taylor KO Index	20.0	18.5	17.1	15.8	14.5	13.3	12.1	10.1	8.6
Path • Inches	-1.5	+2.0	0.0	-8.5	-24.7	-50.0	-86.1	-200.2	-390.8
Wind Drift • Inches	0.0	0.8	3.2	7.4	13.6	22.2	33.4	64.8	109.5

Federal 168-grain Sierra MatchKing BTHP (GM3006M)

G1 Ballistic Coefficient = 0.464

Distance • Yards	Muzzle	100	200	300	400	500	600	800	1000
Velocity • fps	2700	2510	2320	2150	1980	1820	1670	1402	1191
Energy • Ft-lbs	2720	2350	2010	1720	1460	1230	1040	733	529
Taylor KO Index	20.0	18.6	17.1	15.9	14.6	13.5	12.3	10.4	8.8
Path • Inches	-1.5	+2.0	0.0	-8.5	-24.5	-49.4	-84.8	-196.0	-380.4
Wind Drift • Inches	0.0	0.7	3.0	7.1	13.2	21.4	32.2	62.2	105.0

RWS 170-grain SH (231 4432)

G1 Ballistic Coefficient = 0.332

Distance • Yards	Muzzle	100	200	300	400	500	600	800	1000
Velocity • fps	2745	2424	2045	1985	1765	1562	1382	1116	970
Energy • Ft-lbs	2970	2453	1920	1507	1176	921	722	470	355
Taylor KO Index	20.5	18.1	15.3	14.8	13.2	11.7	10.3	8.3	7.3
Path • Inches	-1.5	+2.1	0.0	-9.2	-27.2	-56.5	-100.3	-249.3	-510.0
Wind Drift • Inches	0.0	1.0	4.3	10.2	19.2	31.7	48.5	95.6	159.3

Federal 170-grain Soft Point (3006LR1)

G1 Ballistic Coefficient = 0.286

Distance • Yards	Muzzle	100	200	300	400	500	600	800	1000
Velocity • fps	2000	1740	1510	1310	1160	1050	975	868	787
Energy • Ft-lbs	1510	1145	860	650	505	415	359	285	234
Taylor KO Index	15.0	13.0	11.3	9.8	8.7	7.9	7.3	6.5	5.9
Path • Inches	-1.5	+5.0	0.0	-20.5	-61.2	-128.1	-224.7	-526.4	-996.8
Wind Drift • Inches	0.0	1.9	8.0	19.1	35.6	57.2	83.0	145.3	220.4

Hornady 180-grain BTSP—LM InterLock (8518)

G1 Ballistic Coefficient = 0.453

Distance • Yards	Muzzle	100	200	300	400	500	600	800	1000
Velocity • fps	2900	2695	2498	2310	2131	1959	1798	1503	1263
Energy • Ft-lbs	3361	2902	2494	2133	1814	1534	1292	904	637
Taylor KO Index	23.0	21.3	19.8	18.3	16.9	15.5	14.2	11.9	10.0
Path • Inches	-1.5	+2.0	0.0	-7.5	-21.6	-43.3	-72.9	-168.7	-328.3
Wind Drift • Inches	0.0	0.7	2.8	6.6	12.2	19.8	29.7	57.6	-98.0

Federal 180-grain Nosler Partition—HE (P3006R)

G1 Ballistic Coefficient = 0.474

Distance • Yards	Muzzle	100	200	300	400	500	600	800	1000
Velocity • fps	2880	2690	2500	2320	2150	1980	1825	1539	1300
Energy • Ft-lbs	3315	2880	2495	2150	1845	1570	1331	947	676
Taylor KO Index	22.8	21.3	19.8	18.4	17.0	15.7	14.5	12.2	10.0
Path • Inches	-1.5	+1.7	0.0	-7.2	-21.0	-42.2	-72.4	-166.4	-321.0
Wind Drift • Inches	0.0	0.7	2.7	6.3	11.7	18.9	28.4	54.8	92.9

Federal 180-grain Trophy Bonded Bear Claw—HE (P3006T3)

G1 Ballistic Coefficient = 0.361

Distance • Yards	Muzzle	100	200	300	400	500	600	800	1000
Velocity • fps	2880	2630	2380	2160	1940	1740	1555	1249	1053
Energy • Ft-lbs	3315	2755	2270	1855	1505	1210	967	623	443
Taylor KO Index	22.8	20.8	18.8	17.1	15.4	13.8	12.3	9.9	8.3
Path • Inches	-1.5	+1.8	0.0	-8.0	-23.3	-48.2	-84.4	-205.3	-418.8
Wind Drift • Inches	0.0	0.9	3.6	8.6	16.1	26.5	40.3	79.7	135.8

Speer 180-grain Grand Slam (24508) (Discontinued in 2004)

G1 Ballistic Coefficient = 0.416

Distance • Yards	Muzzle	100	200	300	400	500	600	800	1000
Velocity • fps	2790	2572	2365	2167	1979	1801	1635	1346	1134
Energy • Ft-lbs	3111	2645	2235	1877	1565	1297	1069	724	514
Taylor KO Index	22.1	20.4	18.7	17.2	15.7	14.3	12.9	10.7	9.0
Path • Inches	-1.5	+1.9	0.0	-8.1	-23.6	-48.1	-83.3	-195.6	-385.3
Wind Drift • Inches	0.0	0.7	2.9	6.9	12.8	21.0	31.6	61.8	105.0

Winchester 180-grain Power-Point Plus (SHV30064)   G1 Ballistic Coefficient = 0.436

Distance • Yards	Muzzle	100	200	300	400	500	600	800	1000
Velocity • fps	2770	2563	2366	2177	1997	1826	1665	1383	1167
Energy • Ft-lbs	3068	2627	2237	1894	1594	1333	1109	764	544
Taylor KO Index	21.9	20.3	18.7	17.2	15.8	14.5	13.2	11.0	9.2
Path • Inches	-1.5	+1.9	0.0	-8.1	-23.6	-47.8	-82.6	-192.9	-378.7
Wind Drift • Inches	0.0	0.8	3.1	7.4	13.6	22.2	33.4	65.0	110.4

Winchester 180-grain AccuBond CT (S3006CT)   G1 Ballistic Coefficient = 0.509

Distance • Yards	Muzzle	100	200	300	400	500	600	800	1000
Velocity • fps	2750	2573	2403	2239	2082	1931	1788	1525	1304
Energy • Ft-lbs	3022	2646	2308	2004	1732	1491	1278	930	680
Taylor KO Index	21.8	20.4	19.0	17.7	16.5	15.3	14.2	12.1	10.3
Path • Inches	-1.5	+1.9	0.0	-7.9	-22.8	-45.6	-77.9	-176.9	-336.1
Wind Drift • Inches	0.0	0.6	2.4	5.6	10.4	16.8	25.1	48.1	81.1

Winchester 180-grain Partition Gold (SPG3006A)   G1 Ballistic Coefficient = 0.450

Distance • Yards	Muzzle	100	200	300	400	500	600	800	1000
Velocity • fps	2750	2550	2359	2176	2001	1835	1680	1402	1186
Energy • Ft-lbs	3022	2599	2223	1891	1599	1345	1128	786	562
Taylor KO Index	21.8	20.2	18.7	17.2	15.8	14.5	13.3	11.1	9.4
Path • Inches	-1.5	+1.9	0.0	-8.2	-23.7	-47.9	-82.6	-191.8	-374.3
Wind Drift • Inches	0.0	0.7	3.1	7.2	13.3	21.6	32.5	63.0	106.8

Federal 180-grain Nosler Solid Base BT (P3006S3)   G1 Ballistic Coefficient = 0.490

Distance • Yards	Muzzle	100	200	300	400	500	600	800	1000
Velocity • fps	2710	2530	2350	2180	2020	1870	1725	1462	1247
Energy • Ft-lbs	2935	2550	2210	1905	1630	1390	1190	854	621
Taylor KO Index	21.5	20.0	18.6	17.3	16.0	14.8	13.7	11.6	9.9
Path • Inches	-1.5	+2.0	0.0	-8.4	-23.9	-47.8	-81.9	-187.1	-358.0
Wind Drift • Inches	0.0	0.6	2.6	6.0	11.0	17.9	26.7	51.7	87.2

Sellier & Bellot 180-grain Soft Point (SBA30062)   G1 Ballistic Coefficient = 0.361

Distance • Yards	Muzzle	100	200	300	400	500	600	800	1000
Velocity • fps	2707	2451	2219	2009	1804	1613	1441	1170	1010
Energy • Ft-lbs	2937	2407	1973	1617	1301	1041	831	547	408
Taylor KO Index	21.4	19.4	17.6	15.9	14.3	12.8	11.4	9.3	8.0
Path • Inches	-1.5	+2.1	0.0	-9.1	-26.9	-55.5	-97.6	-237.8	-481.4
Wind Drift • Inches	0.0	1.0	4.0	9.4	17.6	29.1	44.2	87.0	145.8

A² 180-grain Mono; Dead Tough (None)   G1 Ballistic Coefficient = 0.264

Distance • Yards	Muzzle	100	200	300	400	500	600	800	1000
Velocity • fps	2700	2365	2054	1769	1524	1310	1146	958	849
Energy • Ft-lbs	2913	2235	1687	1251	928	686	525	367	288
Taylor KO Index	21.4	18.7	16.3	14.0	12.1	10.4	9.1	7.6	6.7
Path • Inches	-1.5	+2.4	0.0	-10.6	-32.4	-69.1	-127.5	-328.8	-669.9
Wind Drift • Inches	0.0	11.3	5.7	13.7	26.2	44.1	67.8	130.4	208.8

Federal 180-grain Sierra GameKing BTSP (P3006L) (Discontinued in 2005)   G1 Ballistic Coefficient = 0.539

Distance • Yards	Muzzle	100	200	300	400	500	600	800	1000
Velocity • fps	2700	2540	2380	2220	2080	1930	1795	1545	1331
Energy • Ft-lbs	2915	2570	2260	1975	1720	1495	1288	954	708
Taylor KO Index	21.4	20.1	18.8	17.6	16.5	15.3	14.2	12.2	10.5
Path • Inches	-1.5	+1.8	0.0	-7.7	-22.3	-45.0	-79.2	-178.8	-338.1
Wind Drift • Inches	0.0	0.6	2.6	6.0	11.1	17.9	26.7	51.1	85.7

Black Hills 180-grain Nosler AccuBond (1C3006BHGN5)   G1 Ballistic Coefficient = 0.458

Distance • Yards	Muzzle	100	200	300	400	500	600	800	1000
Velocity • fps	2700	2500	2320	2140	1970	1810	1658	1389	1180
Energy • Ft-lbs	2915	2510	2150	1830	1550	1310	1099	771	556
Taylor KO Index	21.4	19.8	18.4	16.9	15.6	14.3	13.1	11.0	9.3
Path • Inches	-1.5	+2.0	0.0	-8.6	-24.6	-49.6	-85.4	-197.8	-384.7
Wind Drift • Inches	0.0	0.7	3.1	7.2	13.4	21.8	32.7	63.2	106.9

Federal 180-grain Nosler AccuBond (P3006A1)

G1 Ballistic Coefficient = 0.516

Distance • Yards	Muzzle	100	200	300	400	500	600	800	1000
Velocity • fps	2700	2530	2360	2200	2060	1900	1760	1504	1289
Energy • Ft-lbs	2915	2555	2230	1940	1680	1445	1238	904	664
Taylor KO Index	21.4	20.0	18.7	17.4	16.3	15.0	13.9	11.9	10.2
Path • Inches	-1.5	+2.0	0.0	-8.3	-23.7	-47.1	-80.7	-183.4	-349.1
Wind Drift • Inches	0.0	0.7	2.7	6.3	11.6	18.9	28.2	54.0	90.9

Federal 180-grain Nosler Partition (P3006F)

G1 Ballistic Coefficient = 0.458

Distance • Yards	Muzzle	100	200	300	400	500	600	800	1000
Velocity • fps	2700	2500	2320	2140	1970	1810	1658	1389	1180
Energy • Ft-lbs	2915	2510	2150	1830	1550	1310	1099	771	556
Taylor KO Index	21.4	19.8	18.4	16.9	15.6	14.3	13.1	11.0	9.3
Path • Inches	-1.5	+2.0	0.0	-8.6	-24.6	-49.6	-85.4	-197.8	-384.7
Wind Drift • Inches	0.0	0.7	3.1	7.2	13.4	21.8	32.7	63.2	106.9

Federal 180-grain Soft Point (3006B)

G1 Ballistic Coefficient = 0.383

Distance • Yards	Muzzle	100	200	300	400	500	600	800	1000
Velocity • fps	2700	2470	2250	2040	1850	1660	1494	1219	1045
Energy • Ft-lbs	2915	2435	2025	1665	1360	1105	892	584	436
Taylor KO Index	21.4	19.6	17.8	16.2	14.7	13.1	11.8	9.7	8.3
Path • Inches	-1.5	+2.1	0.0	-9.0	-26.4	-54.0	-94.5	-227.0	-455.8
Wind Drift • Inches	0.0	0.9	3.8	8.8	16.5	27.1	41.1	80.6	135.6

Federal 180-grain Trophy Bonded Bear Claw (P3006T2)

G1 Ballistic Coefficient = 0.362

Distance • Yards	Muzzle	100	200	300	400	500	600	800	1000
Velocity • fps	2700	2460	2220	2000	1800	1610	1440	1169	1010
Energy • Ft-lbs	2915	2410	1975	1605	1290	1030	829	546	408
Taylor KO Index	21.4	19.5	17.6	15.8	14.3	12.8	11.4	9.3	8.0
Path • Inches	-1.5	+2.2	0.0	-9.2	-27.0	-56.1	-98.0	-238.6	-482.8
Wind Drift • Inches	0.0	1.0	4.0	9.4	17.7	29.1	44.3	87.0	145.7

Hornady 180-grain SP InterLock (8118)

G1 Ballistic Coefficient = 0.425

Distance • Yards	Muzzle	100	200	300	400	500	600	800	1000
Velocity • fps	2700	2491	2292	2102	1921	1751	1592	1318	1120
Energy • Ft-lbs	2913	2480	2099	1765	1475	1225	1013	694	501
Taylor KO Index	21.4	19.7	18.2	16.6	15.2	13.9	12.6	10.4	8.9
Path • Inches	-1.5	+2.1	0.0	-8.7	25.3	-51.3	-88.7	-207.6	-407.2
Wind Drift • Inches	0.0	0.7	3.0	7.1	13.1	21.4	32.3	62.9	106.3

Norma 180-grain Nosler Partition (17649)

G1 Ballistic Coefficient = 0.438

Distance • Yards	Muzzle	100	200	300	400	500	600	800	1000
Velocity • fps	2700	2497	2303	2118	1942	1775	1618	1346	1142
Energy • Ft-lbs	2914	2501	2128	1800	1507	1259	1047	724	522
Taylor KO Index	21.4	19.8	18.2	16.8	15.4	14.1	12.8	10.7	9.0
Path • Inches	-1.5	+2.0	0.0	-8.6	-25.0	-50.6	-87.4	-204.1	-400.4
Wind Drift • Inches	0.0	0.8	3.2	7.6	14.1	23.0	34.6	67.2	113.6

Norma 180-grain TXP Line, Swift (17518)

G1 Ballistic Coefficient = 0.400

Distance • Yards	Muzzle	100	200	300	400	500	600	800	1000
Velocity • fps	2700	2479	2268	2067	1877	1699	1535	1259	1074
Energy • Ft-lbs	2914	2456	2056	1708	1408	1158	942	634	461
Taylor KO Index	21.4	19.6	18.0	16.4	14.9	13.5	12.2	10.0	8.5
Path • Inches	-1.5	+2.0	0.0	-8.8	-25.9	-52.8	-92.0	-218.9	-436.5
Wind Drift • Inches	0.0	0.9	3.6	8.4	15.7	25.7	38.8	75.9	128.2

Norma 180-grain Oryx SP (17674)

G1 Ballistic Coefficient = 0.288

Distance • Yards	Muzzle	100	200	300	400	500	600	800	1000
Velocity • fps	2700	2395	2110	1846	1606	1394	1221	1006	890
Energy • Ft-lbs	2914	2301	1786	1367	1031	777	596	405	316
Taylor KO Index	21.4	19.0	16.7	14.6	12.7	11.0	9.7	8.0	7.0
Path • Inches	-1.5	+2.3	0.0	-10.1	-30.6	-64.8	-117.4	-299.9	-612.3
Wind Drift • Inches	0.0	1.2	5.1	12.3	23.5	39.2	60.2	117.4	190.3

Norma 180-grain Alaska (17648)

G1 Ballistic Coefficient = 0.257

Distance • Yards	Muzzle	100	200	300	400	500	600	800	1000
Velocity • fps	2700	2359	2044	1755	1500	1285	1124	944	836
Energy • Ft-lbs	2914	2225	1670	1231	899	660	505	356	280
Taylor KO Index	21.4	18.7	16.2	13.9	11.9	10.2	8.9	7.5	6.6
Path • Inches	-1.5	+2.4	0.0	-10.7	-33.0	-71.0	-131.0	-338.4	-688.8
Wind Drift • Inches	0.0	1.4	5.8	14.2	27.2	45.7	70.2	134.6	214.7

PMC 180-grain Sierra Soft Point Boat Tail (3006HC)

G1 Ballistic Coefficient = 0.502

Distance • Yards	Muzzle	100	200	300	400	500	600	800	1000
Velocity • fps	2700	2523	2352	2188	2030	1879	1737	1478	1263
Energy • Ft-lbs	2913	2543	2210	1913	1646	1411	1206	873	638
Taylor KO Index	21.4	20.0	18.6	17.3	16.1	14.9	13.8	11.7	10.0
Path • Inches	-1.5	+2.0	0.0	-8.3	-23.9	-47.9	-81.7	-186.4	-356.6
Wind Drift • Inches	0.0	0.7	2.8	6.5	12.0	19.5	29.2	56.0	94.4

Remington 180-grain Nosler Partition (PRP3006A) (Discontinued in 2005)

G1 Ballistic Coefficient = 0.474

Distance • Yards	Muzzle	100	200	300	400	500	600	800	1000
Velocity • fps	2700	2512	2332	2160	1995	1837	1688	1422	1210
Energy • Ft-lbs	2913	2522	2174	1864	1590	1349	1139	809	585
Taylor KO Index	21.4	19.9	18.5	17.1	15.8	14.5	13.4	11.3	9.6
Path • Inches	-1.5	+2.0	0.0	-8.4	-24.3	-48.9	-83.9	-193.3	-373.6
Wind Drift • Inches	0.0	0.7	3.0	7.0	12.8	20.9	31.3	60.4	102.0

Remington 180-grain Core-Lokt Ultra Bonded (PRC3006C)

G1 Ballistic Coefficient = 0.402

Distance • Yards	Muzzle	100	200	300	400	500	600	800	1000
Velocity • fps	2700	2480	2270	2070	1882	1704	1540	1264	1077
Energy • Ft-lbs	2913	2457	2059	1713	1415	1161	948	638	464
Taylor KO Index	21.4	19.6	18.0	16.4	14.9	13.5	12.2	10.0	8.5
Path • Inches	-1.5	+2.1	0.0	-8.9	-25.8	-52.7	-91.7	-218.0	-434.4
Wind Drift • Inches	0.0	0.8	3.6	8.4	15.6	25.5	38.6	75.4	127.3

Remington 180-grain Core-Lokt Pointed Soft Point (R30065)

G1 Ballistic Coefficient = 0.384

Distance • Yards	Muzzle	100	200	300	400	500	600	800	1000
Velocity • fps	2700	2469	2250	2042	1846	1663	1496	1221	1046
Energy • Ft-lbs	2913	2436	2023	1666	1362	1105	895	596	438
Taylor KO Index	21.4	19.6	17.8	16.2	14.6	13.2	11.8	9.7	8.3
Path • Inches	-1.5	+2.1	0.0	-9.0	26.3	-54.0	-94.3	-226.5	-454.6
Wind Drift • Inches	0.0	0.9	3.7	8.8	16.5	27.0	41.0	80.3	135.2

Remington 180-grain A-Frame Pointed Soft Point (RS3006A)

G1 Ballistic Coefficient = 0.377

Distance • Yards	Muzzle	100	200	300	400	500	600	800	1000
Velocity • fps	2700	2465	2243	2032	1833	1648	1479	1205	1034
Energy • Ft-lbs	2913	2429	2010	1650	1343	1085	874	580	428
Taylor KO Index	21.4	19.5	17.8	16.1	14.5	13.1	11.7	9.5	8.2
Path • Inches	-1.5	+2.1	0.0	-9.1	-26.6	-54.4	-95.4	-230.1	-463.2
Wind Drift • Inches	0.0	0.9	3.8	9.0	16.8	27.7	42.0	82.3	138.4

Remington 180-grain Soft Point Core-Lokt (R30064)

G1 Ballistic Coefficient = 0.248

Distance • Yards	Muzzle	100	200	300	400	500	600	800	1000
Velocity • fps	2700	2348	2023	1727	1466	1251	1097	926	820
Energy • Ft-lbs	2913	2203	1635	1192	859	625	481	343	269
Taylor KO Index	21.4	18.6	16.0	13.7	11.6	9.9	8.7	7.3	6.5
Path • Inches	-1.5	+2.4	0.0	-11.0	-33.8	-72.8	-135.9	-351.5	-714.6
Wind Drift • Inches	0.0	1.4	6.1	14.8	28.5	48.0	73.7	140.2	222.7

Winchester 180-grain Power-Point (X30064)

G1 Ballistic Coefficient = 0.381

Distance • Yards	Muzzle	100	200	300	400	500	600	800	1000
Velocity • fps	2700	2468	2247	2038	1840	1657	1490	1215	1043
Energy • Ft-lbs	2913	2433	2018	1659	1354	1097	887	591	435
Taylor KO Index	21.4	19.5	17.8	16.1	14.6	13.1	11.8	9.6	8.3
Path • Inches	-1.5	+2.1	0.0	-9.0	-26.4	-54.2	-94.6	-226.2	-452.1
Wind Drift • Inches	0.0	0.8	3.4	8.0	14.9	24.5	37.2	72.9	127.7

Winchester 180-grain Fail Safe (S3006X)

G1 Ballistic Coefficient = 0.415

Distance • Yards	Muzzle	100	200	300	400	500	600	800	1000
Velocity • fps	2700	2486	2283	2089	1904	1731	1569	1294	1100
Energy • Ft-lbs	2914	2472	2083	1744	1450	1198	984	669	484
Taylor KO Index	21.4	19.7	18.1	16.5	15.1	13.7	12.4	10.2	8.7
Path • Inches	-1.5	+2.1	0.0	-8.7	-25.5	-51.8	-90.0	-212.6	-421.2
Wind Drift • Inches	0.0	0.8	3.4	8.1	15.0	24.6	37.0	72.2	122.1

Winchester 180-grain Ballistic Silvertip (X30066)

G1 Ballistic Coefficient = 0.384

Distance • Yards	Muzzle	100	200	300	400	500	600	800	1000
Velocity • fps	2700	2469	2250	2042	1846	1663	1496	1221	1046
Energy • Ft-lbs	2913	2436	2023	1666	1362	1105	895	596	438
Taylor KO Index	21.4	19.6	17.8	16.2	14.6	13.2	11.8	9.7	8.3
Path • Inches	-1.5	+2.1	0.0	-9.0	26.3	-54.0	-94.3	-226.5	-454.6
Wind Drift • Inches	0.0	0.9	3.7	8.8	16.5	27.0	41.0	80.3	135.2

Hirtenberger 180-grain Nosler Partition (82200391)

G1 Ballistic Coefficient = 0.450

Distance • Yards	Muzzle	100	200	300	400	500	600	800	1000
Velocity • fps	2657	2461	2274	2095	1924	1763	1611	1346	1147
Energy • Ft-lbs	2822	2422	2068	1755	1480	1242	1038	725	526
Taylor KO Index	21.0	19.5	18.0	16.6	15.2	14.0	12.8	10.7	9.1
Path • Inches	-1.5	+2.1	0.0	-8.9	-25.7	-51.9	-89.4	-207.8	-405.6
Wind Drift • Inches	0.0	0.8	3.2	7.5	14.0	22.8	34.2	66.3	111.9

PMC 180-grain Pointed Soft Point (3006B)

G1 Ballistic Coefficient = 0.403

Distance • Yards	Muzzle	100	200	300	400	500	600	800	1000
Velocity • fps	2650	2450	221	2024	1839	1667	1507	1240	1064
Energy • Ft-lbs	2807	2359	1972	1638	1351	1110	909	615	452
Taylor KO Index	21.0	19.2	17.6	16.0	14.6	13.2	11.9	9.8	7.7
Path • Inches	-1.5	+2.2	0.0	-9.3	-27.0	-55.0	-95.6	-227.3	-452.2
Wind Drift • Inches	0.0	0.9	3.6	8.6	16.0	26.2	39.6	77.2	129.8

Norma 180-grain Nosler AccuBond (17563)

G1 Ballistic Coefficient = 0.506

Distance • Yards	Muzzle	100	200	300	400	500	600	800	1000
Velocity • fps	2674	2499	2331	2169	2014	1865	1724	1469	1258
Energy • Ft-lbs	2859	2497	2172	1881	1621	1391	1189	863	633
Taylor KO Index	21.2	19.8	18.5	17.2	16.0	14.8	13.7	11.6	10.0
Path • Inches	-1.5	+2.0	0.0	-8.8	-24.3	-48.7	-83.2	-189.3	-360.3
Wind Drift • Inches	0.0	0.6	2.5	5.9	10.9	17.6	26.3	50.6	85.1

PMC 180-grain HPBT Match (3006SMB)

G1 Ballistic Coefficient = 0.547

Distance • Yards	Muzzle	100	200	300	400	500	600	800	1000
Velocity • fps	2800	2622	2456	2302	2158	2024	1887	1630	1406
Energy • Ft-lbs	3133	2747	2411	2118	1861	1639	1423	1062	790
Taylor KO Index	22.2	20.8	19.5	18.2	17.1	16.0	14.9	12.9	11.1
Path • Inches	-1.5	+1.8	0.0	-7.4	-21.4	-42.7	-72.6	-163.1	-306.3
Wind Drift • Inches	0.0	0.5	2.2	5.1	9.3	15.0	22.3	42.6	71.5

Federal 180-grain Barnes XLC Coated X-Bullet (P3006Z) (Discontinued in 2004)

G1 Ballistic Coefficient = 0.509

Distance • Yards	Muzzle	100	200	300	400	500	600	800	1000
Velocity • fps	2700	2530	2360	2200	2040	1890	1745	1491	1276
Energy • Ft-lbs	2915	2550	2220	1930	1670	1430	1222	889	651
Taylor KO Index	21.4	20.0	18.7	17.4	16.2	15.0	13.8	11.8	10.1
Path • Inches	-1.5	+2.0	0.0	-8.3	-23.8	-47.3	-81.2	-184.8	-352.8
Wind Drift • Inches	0.0	0.7	2.8	6.4	11.8	19.2	28.7	55.0	92.6

Federal 180-grain Barnes Triple Shock X-Bullet (P3006AE)

G1 Ballistic Coefficient = 0.476

Distance • Yards	Muzzle	100	200	300	400	500	600	800	1000
Velocity • fps	2700	2510	2340	2160	2000	1840	1693	1427	1215
Energy • Ft-lbs	2915	2525	2180	1870	1600	1360	1145	815	590
Taylor KO Index	21.4	19.9	18.5	17.1	15.8	14.6	13.4	11.3	9.6
Path • Inches	-1.5	+2.0	0.0	-8.5	-24.2	-49.9	-83.7	-192.2	-369.4
Wind Drift • Inches	0.0	0.6	2.7	6.2	11.5	18.7	28.0	54.0	91.2

Hornady 180-grain SST InterLock (81184)

G1 Ballistic Coefficient = 0.480

Distance • Yards	Muzzle	100	200	300	400	500	600	800	1000
Velocity • fps	2700	2515	2337	2166	2003	1847	1700	1436	1223
Energy • Ft-lbs	2913	2527	2182	1875	1603	1363	1155	824	598
Taylor KO Index	19.6	19.9	18.5	17.2	15.9	14.6	13.5	11.4	9.7
Path • Inches	-1.5	+2.0	0.0	-8.4	-24.2	-48.7	-83.4	-191.2	-367.0
Wind Drift • Inches	0.0	0.6	2.6	6.2	11.4	18.5	27.7	53.4	90.2

Norma 180-grain Plastic point (17653)

G1 Ballistic Coefficient = 0.366

Distance • Yards	Muzzle	100	200	300	400	500	600	800	1000
Velocity • fps	2700	2458	2229	2013	1809	1621	1450	1179	1016
Energy • Ft-lbs	2914	2416	1987	1620	1309	1050	841	555	413
Taylor KO Index	21.4	19.5	17.7	15.9	14.3	12.8	11.5	9.3	8.0
Path • Inches	-1.5	+2.1	0.0	-9.2	-26.9	-55.4	-97.3	-236.3	477.3
Wind Drift • Inches	0.0	0.9	3.9	9.3	17.4	28.7	43.6	85.7	143.7

Norma 180-grain Vulcan HP (17659)

G1 Ballistic Coefficient = 0.315

Distance • Yards	Muzzle	100	200	300	400	500	600	800	1000
Velocity • fps	2700	2420	2158	1912	1685	1481	1305	1063	934
Energy • Ft-lbs	2914	2350	1868	1466	1135	877	681	451	349
Taylor KO Index	21.4	19.2	17.1	15.1	13.3	11.7	10.3	8.4	7.4
Path • Inches	-1.5	+2.2	0.0	-9.7	-29.0	-60.8	-108.8	-273.2	-557.7
Wind Drift • Inches	0.0	1.1	4.6	11.1	21.0	34.8	53.3	104.7	172.1

Remington 180-grain Swift Scirocco Bonded (PRSC3006B)

G1 Ballistic Coefficient = 0.500

Distance • Yards	Muzzle	100	200	300	400	500	600	800	1000
Velocity • fps	2700	2522	2351	2186	2028	1878	1734	1474	1259
Energy • Ft-lbs	2913	2542	2208	1910	1644	1409	1202	868	634
Taylor KO Index	21.4	20.0	18.6	17.3	16.1	14.9	13.7	11.7	10.0
Path • Inches	-1.5	+2.0	0.0	-8.3	-23.9	-47.9	-81.8	-186.8	-357.7
Wind Drift • Inches	0.0	0.7	2.8	6.6	12.1	19.6	29.3	56.3	94.9

Remington 180-grain Bronze Point (R30066)

G1 Ballistic Coefficient = 0.412

Distance • Yards	Muzzle	100	200	300	400	500	600	800	1000
Velocity • fps	2700	2485	2280	2084	1899	1725	1562	1287	1095
Energy • Ft-lbs	2913	2468	2077	1736	1441	1189	976	662	479
Taylor KO Index	21.4	19.7	18.1	16.5	15.0	13.7	12.4	10.2	8.7
Path • Inches	-1.5	+2.1	0.0	-8.8	25.5	-52.0	-90.4	-213.8	-424.1
Wind Drift • Inches	0.0	0.8	3.5	8.1	15.1	24.8	37.4	72.9	123.3

Sellier & Bellot 180-grain HPC (SBA30064)

G1 Ballistic Coefficient = 0.592

Distance • Yards	Muzzle	100	200	300	400	500	600	800	1000
Velocity • fps	2671	2517	2373	2236	2100	1969	1844	1610	1404
Energy • Ft-lbs	2875	2540	2256	2005	1763	1551	1359	1036	788
Taylor KO Index	21.2	19.9	18.8	17.7	16.6	15.6	14.6	12.8	11.1
Path • Inches	-1.5	+2.0	0.0	-8.2	-23.3	-46.2	-78.2	-174.5	-325.4
Wind Drift • Inches	0.0	0.6	2.4	5.5	10.1	16.3	24.3	46.0	76.8

Black Hills 180-grain Barnes—XLC Bullet (1C3006BHGN1)

G1 Ballistic Coefficient = 0.552

Distance • Yards	Muzzle	100	200	300	400	500	600	800	1000
Velocity • fps	2650	2490	2336	2187	2044	1906	1774	1532	1325
Energy • Ft-lbs	2808	2479	2181	1912	1670	1452	1259	939	702
Taylor KO Index	21.0	19.7	18.5	17.3	16.2	15.1	14.1	12.1	10.5
Path • Inches	-1.5	+2.0	0.0	-8.4	-24.1	-48.2	-81.8	-184.2	-347.1
Wind Drift • Inches	0.0	0.6	2.6	6.0	11.1	17.9	26.7	51.0	85.3

Sellier & Bellot 180-grain FMJ (SBA30066)

G1 Ballistic Coefficient = 0.552

Distance • Yards	Muzzle	100	200	300	400	500	600	800	1000
Velocity • fps	2673	2508	2353	2208	2063	1925	1792	1548	1338
Energy • Ft-lbs	2866	2522	2220	1953	1702	1481	1284	958	716
Taylor KO Index	21.2	19.9	18.6	17.5	16.3	15.2	14.2	12.3	10.6
Path • Inches	-1.5	+2.0	0.0	-8.3	-23.7	-47.3	-80.2	-180.6	-340.3
Wind Drift • Inches	0.0	0.6	2.6	6.0	10.9	17.7	26.4	50.3	84.2

Lapua 185-grain Mega SP (4317563)

G1 Ballistic Coefficient = 0.530

Distance • Yards	Muzzle	100	200	300	400	500	600	800	1000
Velocity • fps	2625	2460	2300	2147	1999	1858	1724	1479	1275
Energy • Ft-lbs	2831	2486	2174	1894	1642	1419	1221	899	668
Taylor KO Index	21.4	20.0	18.7	17.5	16.3	15.1	14.0	12.0	10.4
Path • Inches	-1.5	+2.1	0.0	-8.7	-25.0	-49.9	-85.0	-192.2	-363.4
Wind Drift • Inches	0.0	0.6	2.5	5.8	10.6	17.2	25.6	49.0	82.1

Lapua 180-grain Naturalis (N317102)

G1 Ballistic Coefficient = 0.503

Distance • Yards	Muzzle	100	200	300	400	500	600	800	1000
Velocity • fps	2657	2482	2313	2151	1996	1847	1706	1452	1244
Energy • Ft-lbs	2822	2462	2139	1850	1592	1364	843	719	619
Taylor KO Index	21.0	19.7	18.3	17.0	15.8	14.6	13.5	11.5	9.9
Path • Inches	-1.5	+2.1	0.0	-8.6	-24.7	-49.6	-84.6	-192.7	-367.2
Wind Drift • Inches	0.0	0.6	2.6	6.0	11.0	17.9	26.8	51.5	86.6

PMC 180-grain Barnes-X (3006XC) (Discontinued in 2005)

G1 Ballistic Coefficient = 0.543

Distance • Yards	Muzzle	100	200	300	400	500	600	800	1000
Velocity • fps	2650	2487	2331	2179	2034	1894	1762	1517	1309
Energy • Ft-lbs	2806	2472	2171	1898	1652	1433	1241	920	685
Taylor KO Index	21.0	19.7	18.5	17.3	16.1	15.0	14.0	12.0	10.4
Path • Inches	-1.5	+2.1	0.0	-8.5	-24.3	-48.6	-82.4	-185.9	-351.2
Wind Drift • Inches	0.0	0.6	2.6	6.2	11.3	18.3	27.2	52.0	87.2

Norma 200-grain Oryx (17677)

G1 Ballistic Coefficient = 0.338

Distance • Yards	Muzzle	100	200	300	400	500	600	800	1000
Velocity • fps	2625	2368	2125	1897	1687	1496	1329	1088	956
Energy • Ft-lbs	3061	2490	2006	1599	1265	994	784	526	406
Taylor KO Index	23.1	20.8	18.7	16.7	14.8	13.2	11.7	9.6	8.4
Path • Inches	-1.5	+2.3	0.0	-10.0	-29.9	-62.0	-110.0	-271.7	-549.4
Wind Drift • Inches	0.0	1.1	4.5	10.6	20.0	33.2	50.6	98.8	162.7

Lapua 200-grain Mega SP (4317567)

G1 Ballistic Coefficient = 0.329

Distance • Yards	Muzzle	100	200	300	400	500	600	800	1000
Velocity • fps	2543	2284	2040	1813	1604	1417	1259	1045	927
Energy • Ft-lbs	2873	2317	1849	1460	1143	892	704	485	382
Taylor KO Index	22.4	20.1	18.0	16.0	14.1	12.5	11.1	9.2	8.2
Path • Inches	-1.5	+2.6	0.0	-11.0	-32.6	-67.8	-121.0	-299.5	-601.0
Wind Drift • Inches	0.0	1.2	4.8	11.5	21.8	36.0	54.8	106.2	172.3

Federal 220-grain Soft Point (3006HS)

G1 Ballistic Coefficient = 0.296

Distance • Yards	Muzzle	100	200	300	400	500	600	800	1000
Velocity • fps	2410	2130	1870	1630	1420	1250	1117	957	859
Energy • Ft-lbs	2835	2215	1705	1300	985	760	609	448	360
Taylor KO Index	23.3	20.6	18.1	15.8	13.7	12.1	10.8	9.3	8.3
Path • Inches	-1.5	+3.1	0.0	-13.1	-39.3	-82.2	-149.3	-369.8	-730.9
Wind Drift • Inches	0.0	1.4	5.9	14.2	26.9	44.6	67.5	126.5	199.5

Remington 220-grain Core-Lokt Soft Point (R30067)

G1 Ballistic Coefficient = 0.294

Distance • Yards	Muzzle	100	200	300	400	500	600	800	1000
Velocity • fps	2410	2130	1870	1632	1422	1246	1112	954	856
Energy • Ft-lbs	2837	2216	1708	1301	988	758	604	445	358
Taylor KO Index	23.3	20.6	18.1	15.8	13.7	12.1	10.8	9.3	8.3
Path • Inches	-1.5	+3.1	0.0	-13.1	-39.4	-83.0	-150.2	-372.1	-735.3
Wind Drift • Inches	0.0	1.4	6.0	14.3	27.1	45.0	68.1	127.5	200.8

7.82mm (.308) Lazzeroni Patriot

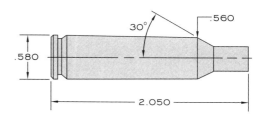

Lazzeroni has two different .30-caliber cartridges. The Patriot is the shorter of the two. A short fireplug of a case, the Patriot uses an unbelted case with a 0.580-inch head diameter to drive a 150-grain bullet to .300 Winchester Magnum velocity.

Relative Recoil Factor = 2.23

Specifications

Controlling Agency for Standardization of this Ammunition: Factory
No further data available.

Availability

Lazzeroni 130-grain Nosler

G1 Ballistic Coefficient = 0.429

Distance • Yards	Muzzle	100	200	300	400	500	600	800	1000
Velocity • fps	3571	3318	3080	2855	2640	2436	2242	1879	1558
Energy • Ft-lbs	3681	3180	2740	2354	2013	1713	1451	1019	701
Taylor KO Index	20.4	19.0	17.6	16.3	15.1	13.9	12.8	10.7	8.9
Path • Inches	-1.5	+0.8	0.0	-4.5	-13.3	-27.0	-46.6	-108.1	-210.4
Wind Drift • Inches	0.0	0.6	2.3	5.3	9.7	15.8	23.6	45.5	77.7

Lazzeroni 180-grain Nosler Partition (782PT180P)

G1 Ballistic Coefficient = 0.585

Distance • Yards	Muzzle	100	200	300	400	500	600	800	1000
Velocity • fps	3184	3000	2825	2656	2493	2336	2185	1900	1640
Energy • Ft-lbs	4052	3600	3191	2821	2485	2182	1909	1443	1075
Taylor KO Index	25.2	23.8	22.4	21.0	19.7	18.5	17.3	15.0	13.0
Path • Inches	-1.5	+1.2	0.0	-5.5	-16.0	-32.1	-54.5	-122.4	-229.5
Wind Drift • Inches	0.0	0.5	2.0	4.7	8.7	14.0	20.8	39.4	66.1

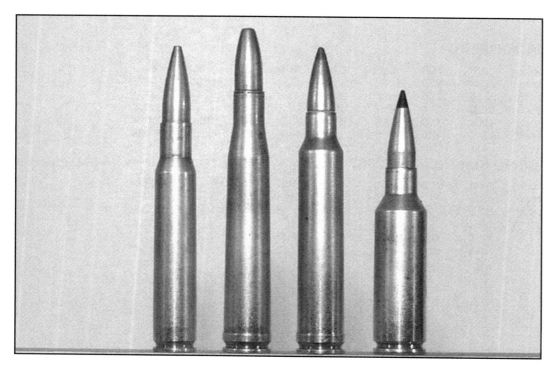

(Left to right) .30-06, .300 Holland & Holland, .300 Winchester, 7.82 Lazzeroni Patriot.

.300 H&H Magnum

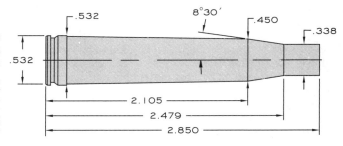

The .300 H&H Magnum (introduced about 1920) wasn't the first belted magnum; the .375 H&H actually arrived about ten years earlier. Still, the .300 H&H can be called the father of all the .300 magnums. Starting with the H&H case, wildcatters improved, reshaped, necked, and generally reformed the case into nearly every configuration they, or anyone else, could imagine. The .300 H&H has never been hugely popular in the U.S., but several of its offspring are near the top of the charts. Only two cartridge variations are factory loaded today.

Relative Recoil Factor = 2.34

Specifications

Controlling Agency for Standardization of this Ammunition: SAAMI

Bullet Weight Grains	Velocity fps	Maximum Average Pressure	
		Copper Crusher	Transducer
150	3,110	54,000 cup	N/S
180	2,780	54,000 cup	N/S
220	2,565	54,000 cup	N/S

Standard barrel for velocity testing: 24 inches long—1 turn in 10-inch twist

Availability

Federal 180-grain Nosler Partition (P300HA)

G1 Ballistic Coefficient = 0.358

Distance • Yards	Muzzle	100	200	300	400	500	600	800	1000
Velocity • fps	2880	2620	2380	2150	1930	1730	1546	1240	1047
Energy • Ft-lbs	3315	2750	2260	1840	1480	1190	956	615	439
Taylor KO Index	22.8	20.8	18.8	17.0	15.3	13.7	12.2	9.8	8.3
Path • Inches	-1.5	+1.8	0.0	-8.0	-23.4	-48.6	-84.9	-206.9	-422.6
Wind Drift • Inches	0.0	0.9	3.7	8.7	16.2	26.8	40.7	80.6	137.3

Winchester 180-grain Fail Safe (S300HX)

G1 Ballistic Coefficient = 0.366

Distance • Yards	Muzzle	100	200	300	400	500	600	800	1000
Velocity • fps	2880	2628	2390	2165	1952	1752	1569	1263	1063
Energy • Ft-lbs	3316	2762	2284	1873	1523	1227	985	637	452
Taylor KO Index	22.8	20.9	18,9	17.1	15.5	13.9	12.4	10.0	8.4
Path • Inches	-1.5	+1.8	0.0	-7.9	-23.2	-47.6	-83.6	+202.7	-412.5
Wind Drift • Inches	0.0	0.9	3.6	8.5	15.8	26.0	39.5	78.1	133.3

.300 Remington Short Action Ultra Magnum

In 2002 Remington introduced its version of a "short magnum." Like the 300 WSM, this cartridge is designed to be fired from .308-length actions. There are claims that the short, fat cases somehow provide unusual "efficiency" and that these cartridges can exceed the performance of the larger magnums. While these short magnums are useful cartridges with excellent performance, the evidence of higher efficiency is tenuous at best.

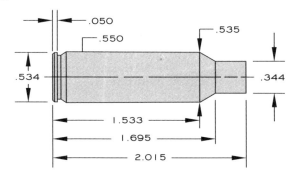

Relative Recoil Factor = 2.36

Specifications

Controlling Agency for Standardization of this Ammunition: SAAMI

Bullet Weight Grains	Velocity fps	Maximum Average Pressure Copper Crusher	Transducer
150	3,200	N/A	65,000 psi
180	2,960	N/A	65,000 psi

Standard barrel for velocity testing: 24 inches long—1 turn in 10-inch twist

Availability

Remington 150-grain Swift Scirocco (PR300SM1) (Discontinued in 2005) G1 Ballistic Coefficient = 0.330

Distance • Yards	Muzzle	100	200	300	400	500	600	800	1000
Velocity • fps	3200	2901	2622	2359	2112	1880	1666	1305	1071
Energy • Ft-lbs	3410	2803	2290	1854	1485	1177	924	567	382
Taylor KO Index	21.1	19.1	17.3	15.6	13.9	12.4	11.0	8.6	7.1
Path • Inches	-1.5	+1.3	0.0	-6.4	-19.1	-39.6	-70.1	-173.6	-363.4
Wind Drift • Inches	0.0	0.8	3.5	8.2	15.4	25.4	38.7	77.6	134.7

Remington 150-grain Core-Lokt Ultra Bonded (PR300SM1) G1 Ballistic Coefficient = 0.330

Distance • Yards	Muzzle	100	200	300	400	500	600	800	1000
Velocity • fps	3200	2901	2622	2359	2112	1880	1666	1305	1071
Energy • Ft-lbs	3410	2803	2290	1854	1485	1177	924	567	382
Taylor KO Index	21.1	19.1	17.3	15.6	13.9	12.4	11.0	8.6	7.1
Path • Inches	-1.5	+1.3	0.0	-6.4	-19.1	-39.6	-69.9	-171.8	-356.0
Wind Drift • Inches	0.0	0.8	3.1	7.4	13.8	22.8	34.8	69.7	121.0

Remington 165-grain Core-Lokt Pointed Soft Point (PR300SM2) G1 Ballistic Coefficient = 0.338

Distance • Yards	Muzzle	100	200	300	400	500	600	800	1000
Velocity • fps	3075	27921	2527	2276	2040	1819	1612	1272	1056
Energy • Ft-lbs	3464	2856	2339	1898	1525	1213	952	593	409
Taylor KO Index	22.3	20.3	18.3	16.5	14.8	13.2	11.7	9.2	7.7
Path • Inches	-1.5	+1.5	0.0	-7.0	-20.7	-42.1	-75.7	-186.7	-387.7
Wind Drift • Inches	0.0	0.8	3.6	8.4	15.8	26.1	39.8	79.5	137.0

Remington 180-grain Nosler Partition (PR300SM3) (Discontinued in 2005) G1 Ballistic Coefficient = 0.474

Distance • Yards	Muzzle	100	200	300	400	500	600	800	1000
Velocity • fps	2960	2761	2571	2389	2214	2046	1886	1592	1343
Energy • Ft-lbs	3501	3047	2642	2280	1959	1673	1422	1014	721
Taylor KO Index	23.4	21.9	20.4	18.9	17.5	16.2	14.9	12.6	10.6
Path • Inches	-1.5	+1.5	0.0	-6.8	-19.7	-39.7	-68.0	-156.2	-300.9
Wind Drift • Inches	0.0	0.6	2.6	6.1	11.2	18.2	27.2	52.6	89.2

Remington 180-grain Core-Lokt Ultra Bonded (PR300SM4)

G1 Ballistic Coefficient = 0.403

Distance • Yards	Muzzle	100	200	300	400	500	600	800	1000
Velocity • fps	2960	2727	2506	2295	2094	1904	1727	1412	1173
Energy • Ft-lbs	3501	2972	2509	2105	1753	1449	1192	797	550
Taylor KO Index	23.4	21.6	19.8	18.2	16.6	15.1	13.7	11.2	9.3
Path • Inches	-1.5	+1.6	0.0	-7.1	-20.9	-42.6	-73.9	-174.2	-345.0
Wind Drift • Inches	0.0	0.7	2.8	6.6	12.2	19.9	30.0	58.9	101.0

Remington 190-grain Boat Tail Hollow Point (Match) (RM300SM7)

G1 Ballistic Coefficient = 0.533

Distance • Yards	Muzzle	100	200	300	400	500	600	800	1000
Velocity • fps	2900	2725	2557	2395	2239	2089	1944	1676	1439
Energy • Ft-lbs	3547	3133	2758	2420	2115	1840	1595	1185	874
Taylor KO Index	24.2	22.8	21.4	20.0	18.7	17.5	16.3	14.0	12.0
Path • Inches	-1.5	+1.6	0.0	-6.9	-19.9	-39.8	-67.7	-152.6	-275.5
Wind Drift • Inches	0.0	0.5	2.1	5.0	9.1	14.7	21.9	41.8	70.3

Waterbuck are found in most of sub-Saharan Africa. This one was shot on the bank of the Zambezi River in Zimbabwe. (Photo from *A Sporting Life* by José A. Martínez de Hoz, 2005, Safari Press)

.300 Winchester Short Magnum

The first cartridge fad in the twenty-first century is the short magnum. Winchester's .30-caliber version was introduced in 2001. Like most of the other short magnums, the .300 WSM is designed for actions that will handle cartridges with an overall length of 2.810 inches, the same length as the .308 Winchester. This fat little cartridge is based on the .404 Jeffery case, much modified. As could be expected, this cartridge has already spawned a host of "necked-to" spin-offs.

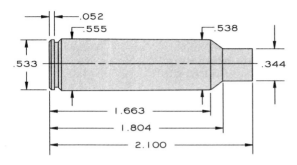

Relative Recoil Factor = 2.36

Specifications

Controlling Agency for Standardization of this Ammunition: SAAMI

Bullet Weight Grains	Velocity fps	Maximum Average Pressure	
		Copper Crusher	Transducer
150	3,300	N/A	65,000 psi
180	2,970	N/A	65,000 psi

Standard barrel for velocity testing: 24 inches long—1 turn in 10-inch twist

Availability

Winchester 150-grain Power-Point (X300WSM1)
G1 Ballistic Coefficient = 0.271

Distance • Yards	Muzzle	100	200	300	400	500	600	800	1000
Velocity • fps	3270	2903	2565	2250	1958	1692	1458	1115	946
Energy • Ft-lbs	3561	2807	2190	1686	1277	953	708	414	198
Taylor KO Index	21.6	19.2	16.9	14.9	12.9	11.2	9.6	7.4	6.2
Path • Inches	-1.5	+1.3	0.0	-6.6	-20.2	-42.9	-78.2	-206.1	-446.0
Wind Drift • Inches	0.0	1.0	4.2	10.0	19.0	31.8	49.3	100.7	172.1

Winchester 150-grain Ballistic Silvertip (SBST300S)
G1 Ballistic Coefficient = 0.425

Distance • Yards	Muzzle	100	200	300	400	500	600	800	1000
Velocity • fps	3300	3061	2834	2619	2414	2218	2032	1688	1395
Energy • Ft-lbs	3628	3121	2676	2285	1941	1638	1375	950	648
Taylor KO Index	21.8	20.2	18.7	17.3	15.9	14.6	13.4	11.1	9.2
Path • Inches	-1.5	+1.1	0.0	-5.4	-15.9	-32.4	-56.0	-130.5	-255.7
Wind Drift • Inches	0.0	0.6	2.5	5.9	10.9	17.7	26.6	51.6	88.6

Federal 150-grain Nosler Ballistic Tip (P300WSMD)
G1 Ballistic Coefficient = 0.430

Distance • Yards	Muzzle	100	200	300	400	500	600	800	1000
Velocity • fps	3200	2970	2750	2540	2340	2150	1970	1638	1357
Energy • Ft-lbs	3410	2935	2520	2155	1830	1545	1293	894	613
Taylor KO Index	21.1	19.6	18.2	16.8	15.4	14.2	13.0	10.8	9.0
Path • Inches	-1.5	+1.2	0.0	-5.8	-17.0	-34.6	-59.7	-139.0	-272.2
Wind Drift • Inches	0.0	0.6	2.6	6.1	11.2	18.2	27.4	53.2	91.2

Federal 165-grain Nosler Solid Base BT (P300WSMS1)
G1 Ballistic Coefficient = 0.431

Distance • Yards	Muzzle	100	200	300	400	500	600	800	1000
Velocity • fps	3130	2900	2690	2490	2290	2100	1920	1595	1323
Energy • Ft-lbs	3590	3090	2650	2265	1920	1620	1352	933	642
Taylor KO Index	22.7	21.1	19.5	18.1	16.6	15.2	13.9	11.6	9.6
Path • Inches	-1.5	+1.3	0.0	-6.1	-17.8	-36.3	-62.8	-146.1	-286.3
Wind Drift • Inches	0.0	0.6	2.7	6.2	11.6	18.8	28.2	54.9	94.0

Federal 165-grain Nosler Partition (P300WSME)
G1 Ballistic Coefficient = 0.413

Distance • Yards	Muzzle	100	200	300	400	500	600	800	1000
Velocity • fps	3130	2890	2670	2450	2250	2060	1875	1543	1273
Energy • Ft-lbs	3590	3065	2605	2205	1855	1545	1289	873	594
Taylor KO Index	22.7	21.0	19.4	17.8	16.3	15.0	13.6	11.2	9.2
Path • Inches	-1.5	+1.3	0.0	-6.2	-19.5	-39.3	-64.2	-150.7	-298.2
Wind Drift • Inches	0.0	0.7	2.8	6.6	12.1	19.8	29.8	58.2	100.0

Winchester 165-grain Fail Safe (S300WSMXA)
G1 Ballistic Coefficient = 0.348

Distance • Yards	Muzzle	100	200	300	400	500	600	800	1000
Velocity • fps	3125	2846	2584	2336	2102	1882	1679	1331	1094
Energy • Ft-lbs	3577	2967	2446	1999	1619	1298	1034	650	439
Taylor KO Index	22.7	20.7	18.8	17.0	15.3	13.7	12.3	9.7	7.9
Path • Inches	-1.5	+1.4	0.0	-6.6	-19.6	-40.6	-71.4	-174.6	-360.5
Wind Drift • Inches	0.0	0.8	3.4	8.0	14.9	24.5	37.3	74.4	128.7

Black Hills 175-grain Sierra MatchKing (1C300WSMBHGN2)
G1 Ballistic Coefficient = 0.496

Distance • Yards	Muzzle	100	200	300	400	500	600	800	1000
Velocity • fps	2950	2760	2578	2404	2236	2074	1920	1635	1388
Energy • Ft-lbs	3381	2961	2584	2245	1943	1672	1433	1039	749
Taylor KO Index	22.7	21.3	19.9	18.5	17.2	16.0	14.8	12.6	10.7
Path • Inches	-1.5	+1.5	0.0	-6.8	-19.6	-39.3	-67.2	-153.1	-292.5
Wind Drift • Inches	0.0	0.6	2.5	5.8	10.7	17.3	25.9	49.7	84.1

Federal 180-grain Nosler AccuBond (P300WSMA1)
G1 Ballistic Coefficient = 0.515

Distance • Yards	Muzzle	100	200	300	400	500	600	800	1000
Velocity • fps	2980	2780	2610	2440	2280	2130	1977	1696	1448
Energy • Ft-lbs	3500	3090	2715	2380	2075	1805	1563	1150	839
Taylor KO Index	23.4	22.0	20.7	19.3	18.1	16.9	15.7	13.4	11.5
Path • Inches	-1.5	+1.5	0.0	-6.6	-19.0	-38.3	-64.6	-146.3	-277.6
Wind Drift • Inches	0.0	0.6	2.4	5.5	10.1	16.3	24.3	46.6	78.5

Federal 180-grain Nosler Solid Base BT (P300WSMS2)
G1 Ballistic Coefficient = 0.490

Distance • Yards	Muzzle	100	200	300	400	500	600	800	1000
Velocity • fps	2980	2780	2600	2420	2250	2090	1932	1642	1392
Energy • Ft-lbs	3535	3095	2695	2340	2025	1740	1492	1078	774
Taylor KO Index	23.6	22.0	20.6	19.2	17.8	16.6	15.3	13.0	11.0
Path • Inches	-1.5	+1.5	0.0	-6.6	-19.2	-38.7	-66.0	-150.9	-288.3
Wind Drift • Inches	0.0	0.6	2.5	5.8	10.7	17.3	25.9	49.8	84.3

Federal 180-grain Nosler Partition (P300WSMB)
G1 Ballistic Coefficient = 0.416

Distance • Yards	Muzzle	100	200	300	400	500	600	800	1000
Velocity • fps	2980	2750	2540	2330	2140	1950	1773	1459	1212
Energy • Ft-lbs	3535	3025	2575	2175	1830	1525	1257	851	587
Taylor KO Index	23.6	21.8	20.1	18.5	16.9	15.4	14.0	11.6	9.6
Path • Inches	-1.5	+1.6	0.0	-6.9	-20.4	-41.2	-71.6	-168.2	-333.0
Wind Drift • Inches	0.0	0.7	3.0	7.0	12.9	21.1	31.8	62.1	106.3

Federal 180-grain Soft Point (300WSMC)
G1 Ballistic Coefficient = 0.204

Distance • Yards	Muzzle	100	200	300	400	500	600	800	1000
Velocity • fps	2970	2520	2110	1750	1430	1190	1034	868	758
Energy • Ft-lbs	3525	2540	1785	1220	820	565	428	301	230
Taylor KO Index	23.5	20.0	16.7	13.9	11.3	9.4	8.2	6.9	6.0
Path • Inches	-1.5	+2.0	0.0	-9.9	-31.5	-70.9	-135.8	-363.9	-756.1
Wind Drift • Inches	0.0	1.5	6.6	16.4	32.1	54.9	85.1	161.8	256.6

Black Hills 180-grain Nosler AccuBond (1C300WSMBHGN1)
G1 Ballistic Coefficient = 0.509

Distance • Yards	Muzzle	100	200	300	400	500	600	800	1000
Velocity • fps	2950	2765	2587	2417	2252	2094	1943	1662	1417
Energy • Ft-lbs	3478	3056	2676	2335	2028	1754	1510	1105	803
Taylor KO Index	23.4	21.9	20.5	19.1	17.8	16.6	15.4	13.2	11.2
Path • Inches	-1.5	+1.5	0.0	-6.7	-19.4	-38.9	-66.4	-150.8	-286.8
Wind Drift • Inches	0.0	0.6	2.5	5.8	10.7	17.3	25.9	49.7	84.1

Federal 180-grain Barnes Triple Shock X-Bullet (P300WSMF)

G1 Ballistic Coefficient = 0.467

Distance • Yards	Muzzle	100	200	300	400	500	600	800	1000
Velocity • fps	2980	2780	2580	2400	2220	2050	1887	1589	1337
Energy • Ft-lbs	3550	3085	2670	2300	1970	1680	1424	1010	715
Taylor KO Index	23.6	22.0	20.4	19.0	17.6	16.2	14.9	12.6	10.6
Path • Inches	-1.5	+1.5	0.0	-6.7	-19.5	-39.3	-67.5	-155.2	-299.8
Wind Drift • Inches	0.0	0.6	2.6	6.1	11.3	18.3	27.5	53.0	90.2

Winchester 180-grain Fail Safe (S300WSMX)

G1 Ballistic Coefficient = 0.412

Distance • Yards	Muzzle	100	200	300	400	500	600	800	1000
Velocity • fps	2970	2741	2524	2317	2120	1932	1756	1442	1198
Energy • Ft-lbs	3526	3005	2547	2147	1797	1493	1233	831	573
Taylor KO Index	23.5	21.7	20.0	18.4	16.8	15.3	13.9	11.4	9.5
Path • Inches	-1.5	+1.6	0.0	-7.0	-20.5	-41.8	-72.5	-170.8	-338.9
Wind Drift • Inches	0.0	0.7	3.0	7.1	13.1	21.4	32.3	63.2	108.3

Hubert Thummler with a maral from Kazakhstan, a species that is very closely related to the American wapiti. (Photo from *Wind in My Face* by Hubert Thummler, 2006, Safari Press)

.300 Winchester Magnum

The full-length magnums are too long to chamber in standard-length (read .30-06-length) actions. When Winchester introduced the .300 Winchester Magnum in 1963, the idea was to obtain a high-performance cartridge that could be chambered in their Model 70 actions. The effort was highly successful. The .300 Winchester Magnum sits comfortably in the top ten of reloading die sales, one place ahead of the 7mm Remington Magnum. Reloading die sales are a pretty good indication of a cartridge's popularity. The .300 Winchester Magnum's popularity is well deserved. It provides performance virtually identical to that of the .300 H&H, in a shorter action. Some factory loads drive 180-grain bullets in excess of 3,000 fps.

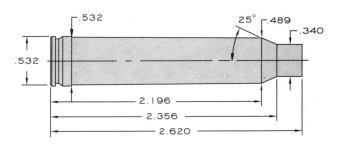

Relative Recoil Factor = 2.39

Specifications

Controlling Agency for Standardization of this Ammunition: SAAMI

Bullet Weight Grains	Velocity fps	Maximum Average Pressure Copper Crusher	Transducer
150	3,275	54,000 cup	64,000 psi
180	2,950	54,000 cup	64,000 psi
190	2,875	54,000 cup	64,000 psi
200	2,800	54,000 cup	64,000 psi
220	2,665	54,000 cup	64,000 psi

Standard barrel for velocity testing: 24 inches long—1 turn in 10-inch twist

Availability

Remington 150-grain Core-Lokt Ultra Bonded (PRC300WA)

G1 Ballistic Coefficient = 0.310

Distance • Yards	Muzzle	100	200	300	400	500	600	800	1000
Velocity • fps	3290	2967	2666	2384	2120	1873	1647	1273	1044
Energy • Ft-lbs	3605	2931	2306	1893	1496	1168	904	540	363
Taylor KO Index	21.7	19.6	17.6	15.7	14.0	12.4	10.9	8.4	6.9
Path • Inches	-1.5	+1.2	0.0	-6.1	-18.4	-38.5	-68.5	-171.1	-360.2
Wind Drift • Inches	0.0	0.8	3.2	7.6	14.3	23.7	36.3	73.4	127.8

Remington 150-grain Core-Lokt Pointed Soft Point (R300W1)

G1 Ballistic Coefficient = 0.296

Distance • Yards	Muzzle	100	200	300	400	500	600	800	1000
Velocity • fps	3290	2951	2636	2342	2068	1816	1581	1212	1005
Energy • Ft-lbs	3605	2900	2314	1827	1424	1095	833	489	337
Taylor KO Index	21.7	19.5	17.4	15.5	13.6	12.0	10.4	8.0	6.6
Path • Inches	-1.5	+1.3	0.0	-6.3	-19.0	-39.8	-71.5	-183.2	-393.3
Wind Drift • Inches	0.0	0.9	3.8	9.0	17.0	28.2	39.0	79.2	137.2

Winchester 150-grain Power-Point (X300WM1)

G1 Ballistic Coefficient = 0.295

Distance • Yards	Muzzle	100	200	300	400	500	600	800	1000
Velocity • fps	3290	2951	2636	2342	2068	1813	1581	1212	1005
Energy • Ft-lbs	3605	2900	2314	1827	1424	1095	833	489	337
Taylor KO Index	21.7	19.5	17.4	15.5	13.6	12.0	10.4	8.0	6.6
Path • Inches	-1.5	+1.3	0.0	-6.3	-19.0	-39.8	-71.5	-183.2	-393.3
Wind Drift • Inches	0.0	0.9	3.8	9.0	17.0	28.2	39.0	79.2	137.2

Federal 150-grain Speer Hot-Cor SP (300WGS)

G1 Ballistic Coefficient = 0.407

Distance • Yards	Muzzle	100	200	300	400	500	600	800	1000
Velocity • fps	3280	3030	2800	2570	2360	2160	1969	1619	1328
Energy • Ft-lbs	3570	3055	2600	2205	1860	1560	1292	874	588
Taylor KO Index	21.6	20.0	18.5	17.0	15.6	14.3	13.0	10.7	8.8
Path • Inches	-1.5	+1.1	0.0	-5.6	-16.4	-33.6	-58.1	-136.5	-270.3
Wind Drift • Inches	0.0	0.6	2.7	6.3	11.6	18.8	28.3	55.3	95.3

Federal 150-grain Trophy Bonded Bear Claw (P300WT4)

G1 Ballistic Coefficient = 0.337

Distance • Yards	Muzzle	100	200	300	400	500	600	800	1000
Velocity • fps	3280	2980	2700	2440	2190	1960	1745	1372	1112
Energy • Ft-lbs	3585	2960	2430	1980	1595	1275	1015	627	412
Taylor KO Index	21.6	19.7	17.8	16.1	14.5	12.9	11.5	9.1	7.3
Path • Inches	-1.5	+1.2	0.0	-6.0	-17.9	-37.0	-65.2	-160.2	-333.7
Wind Drift • Inches	0.0	0.8	3.3	7.7	14.5	23.8	36.3	72.5	126.4

Hornady 150-grain InterBond (82019)

G1 Ballistic Coefficient = 0.416

Distance • Yards	Muzzle	100	200	300	400	500	600	800	1000
Velocity • fps	3275	3032	2802	2584	2375	2177	1990	1645	1354
Energy • Ft-lbs	3572	3061	2615	2223	1879	1578	1319	901	611
Taylor KO Index	21.6	20.0	18.5	17.1	15.7	14.4	13.1	10.9	8.9
Path • Inches	-1.5	+1.1	0.0	-5.6	-16.4	-33.4	-57.6	-134.8	-265.6
Wind Drift • Inches	0.0	0.6	2.6	6.1	11.3	18.4	27.6	53.8	92.5

Hornady 150-grain BTSP (8201)

G1 Ballistic Coefficient = 0.350

Distance • Yards	Muzzle	100	200	300	400	500	600	800	1000
Velocity • fps	3275	2988	2718	2469	2224	1998	1789	1419	1149
Energy • Ft-lbs	3573	2974	2461	2023	1648	1330	1066	671	440
Taylor KO Index	21.6	19.7	17.9	16.3	14.7	13.2	11.8	9.4	7.6
Path • Inches	-1.5	+1.2	0.0	-6.0	-17.8	-36.5	-63.8	-155.2	-319.8
Wind Drift • Inches	0.0	0.8	3.2	7.4	13.9	22.8	34.6	68.7	119.7

Winchester 150-grain Fail Safe (S300WXB)

G1 Ballistic Coefficient = 0.314

Distance • Yards	Muzzle	100	200	300	400	500	600	800	1000
Velocity • fps	3260	2943	2647	2370	2110	1867	1643	1273	1046
Energy • Ft-lbs	3539	2884	2334	1871	1483	1161	899	540	364
Taylor KO Index	21.5	19.4	16.3	15.6	13.9	12.3	10.8	8.4	6.9
Path • Inches	-1.5	+1.3	0.0	-6.2	-18.7	-38.9	-69.6	-174.7	-370.2
Wind Drift • Inches	0.0	0.9	3.6	8.5	15.9	26.3	40.3	81.2	141.2

PMC 150-grain SPBT Game (300HA)

G1 Ballistic Coefficient = 0.380

Distance • Yards	Muzzle	100	200	300	400	500	600	800	1000
Velocity • fps	3250	2987	2739	2504	2281	2070	1869	1512	1230
Energy • Ft-lbs	3517	2970	2498	2088	1733	1426	1164	762	504
Taylor KO Index	21.4	19.7	18.1	16.5	15.1	13.7	12.3	10.0	8.1
Path • Inches	-1.5	+1.2	0.0	-6.0	-17.4	-35.6	-61.7	-147.1	-296.7
Wind Drift • Inches	0.0	0.7	2.8	6.5	12.1	19.7	31.4	61.8	107.0

Hirtenberger 150-grain Nosler Partition (82200378)

G1 Ballistic Coefficient = 0.412

Distance • Yards	Muzzle	100	200	300	400	500	600	800	1000
Velocity • fps	3199	2958	2730	2514	2307	2110	1923	1584	1303
Energy • Ft-lbs	3409	2916	2484	2105	1773	1484	1232	836	566
Taylor KO Index	21.1	19.5	18.0	16.6	15.2	13.9	12.7	10.5	8.6
Path • Inches	-1.5	+1.2	0.0	-5.9	-17.3	-35.3	-61.1	-143.4	-283.6
Wind Drift • Inches	0.0	0.6	2.5	5.8	10.6	17.3	26.0	50.8	87.4

PMC 150-grain Pointed Soft Point (300A)

G1 Ballistic Coefficient = 0.390

Distance • Yards	Muzzle	100	200	300	400	500	600	800	1000
Velocity • fps	3150	2902	2665	2438	2222	2017	1827	1485	1217
Energy • Ft-lbs	3304	2804	2364	1979	1644	1355	1112	735	493
Taylor KO Index	20.8	19.2	17.6	16.1	14.7	13.3	12.1	9.8	8.0
Path • Inches	-1.5	+1.3	0.0	-6.2	-18.3	-37.4	-65.3	-155.1	-311.2
Wind Drift • Inches	0.0	0.7	3.0	6.9	12.9	21.0	31.8	62.4	107.8

Remington 150-grain Core-Lokt Pointed Soft Point (RL3001)

G1 Ballistic Coefficient = 0.314

Distance • Yards	Muzzle	100	200	300	400	500	600	800	1000
Velocity • fps	2650	2373	2113	1870	1646	1446	1276	1048	925
Energy • Ft-lbs	2339	1875	1486	1164	902	696	543	366	285
Taylor KO Index	17.5	15.7	13.9	12.3	10.9	9.5	8.4	6.9	6.1
Path • Inches	-1.5	+2.4	0.0	-10.2	-30.4	-63.4	-113.2	-282.1	-577.3
Wind Drift • Inches	0.0	1.0	4.3	10.3	19.5	32.3	49.4	96.6	157.7

Hornady 150-grain SST (82014)

G1 Ballistic Coefficient = 0.416

Distance • Yards	Muzzle	100	200	300	400	500	600	800	1000
Velocity • fps	3275	3032	2802	2584	2375	2177	1990	1645	1354
Energy • Ft-lbs	3572	3061	2615	2223	1879	1578	1319	901	611
Taylor KO Index	21.6	20.0	18.5	17.1	15.7	14.4	13.1	10.9	8.9
Path • Inches	-1.5	+1.1	0.0	-5.6	-16.4	-33.4	-57.6	-134.8	-265.6
Wind Drift • Inches	0.0	0.6	2.6	6.1	11.3	18.4	27.6	53.8	92.5

Norma 150-grain Hornady BST (17551)

G1 Ballistic Coefficient = 0.427

Distance • Yards	Muzzle	100	200	300	400	500	600	800	1000
Velocity • fps	3250	3014	2791	2578	2377	2184	2000	1662	1374
Energy • Ft-lbs	3519	3027	2595	2215	1883	1589	1332	920	629
Taylor KO Index	21.5	19.9	18.4	17.0	15.7	14.4	13.2	11.0	9.1
Path • Inches	-1.5	+1.1	0.0	-5.6	-16.5	-33.5	-57.9	-134.7	-264.0
Wind Drift • Inches	0.0	0.6	2.6	6.0	11.1	18.0	27.0	52.5	90.0

Norma 150-grain Barnes Triple-Shock (17546)

G1 Ballistic Coefficient = 0.428

Distance • Yards	Muzzle	100	200	300	400	500	600	800	1000
Velocity • fps	3215	2982	2761	2550	2351	2160	1977	1643	1360
Energy • Ft-lbs	3444	2962	2539	2167	1842	1554	1302	1085	616
Taylor KO Index	21.2	19.7	18.2	16.8	15.5	14.3	13.0	10.8	9.0
Path • Inches	-1.5	+1.2	0.0	-5.8	-16.9	-34.3	-59.2	-137.6	-268.1
Wind Drift • Inches	0.0	0.6	2.4	5.5	10.1	16.4	24.6	47.8	82.0

PMC 150-grain Barnes XLC-HP (300XLA) (Discontinued in 2005)

G1 Ballistic Coefficient = 0.406

Distance • Yards	Muzzle	100	200	300	400	500	600	800	1000
Velocity • fps	3135	2918	2712	2515	2327	2146	1975	1658	1386
Energy • Ft-lbs	3273	2836	2449	2107	1803	1534	1300	916	640
Taylor KO Index	20.7	19.3	17.9	16.6	15.4	14.2	13.0	10.9	9.1
Path • Inches	-1.5	+1.3	0.0	-6.1	-17.7	-35.7	-61.0	-140.8	-272.9
Wind Drift • Inches	0.0	0.6	2.5	5.9	10.9	17.7	26.4	51.2	87.2

Federal 165-grain Nosler Solid Base BT (P300WT4)

G1 Ballistic Coefficient = 0.433

Distance • Yards	Muzzle	100	200	300	400	500	600	800	1000
Velocity • fps	3140	2910	2700	2500	2300	2110	1933	1607	1334
Energy • Ft-lbs	3610	3110	2670	2280	1940	1635	1369	947	652
Taylor KO Index	22.8	21.1	19.6	18.2	16.7	15.3	14.0	11.7	9.7
Path • Inches	-1.5	+1.3	0.0	-6.1	-17.7	-36.0	-62.2	-144.6	-282.9
Wind Drift • Inches	0.0	0.6	2.7	6.2	11.4	18.6	27.3	54.2	92.9

Winchester 165-grain Fail Safe (S300WXA)

G1 Ballistic Coefficient = 0.349

Distance • Yards	Muzzle	100	200	300	400	500	600	800	1000
Velocity • fps	3120	2843	2582	2336	2104	1885	1681	1334	1097
Energy • Ft-lbs	3567	2962	2444	2000	1622	1302	1035	652	441
Taylor KO Index	22.7	20.6	18.7	17.0	15.3	13.3	12.2	9.7	8.0
Path • Inches	-1.5	+1.4	0.0	-6.6	-19.6	-40.5	-71.4	-173.3	-354.1
Wind Drift • Inches	0.0	0.7	3.0	7.2	13.4	22.0	33.5	66.7	115.4

Hornady 165-grain BTSP InterLock (8202)

G1 Ballistic Coefficient = 0.435

Distance • Yards	Muzzle	100	200	300	400	500	600	800	1000
Velocity • fps	3100	2877	2665	2462	2269	2084	1908	1587	1319
Energy • Ft-lbs	3522	3033	2603	2221	1887	1592	1334	923	637
Taylor KO Index	22.5	20.9	19.3	17.8	16.5	15.1	13.9	11.5	9.6
Path • Inches	-1.5	+1.3	0.0	-6.5	-18.5	-37.3	-63.8	-148.5	-290.5
Wind Drift • Inches	0.0	0.6	2.7	6.3	11.6	18.7	28.3	55.0	94.1

Hornady 165-grain InterBond (82029)

G1 Ballistic Coefficient = 0.401

Distance • Yards	Muzzle	100	200	300	400	500	600	800	1000
Velocity • fps	3100	2883	2676	2478	2289	2108	1822	1489	1226
Energy • Ft-lbs	3520	2994	2534	2132	1781	1477	1216	813	551
Taylor KO Index	22.5	20.9	19.4	18.0	16.6	15.3	13.2	10.8	8.9
Path • Inches	-1.5	+1.3	0.0	-6.2	-18.1	-36.6	-66.7	-157.6	-314.2
Wind Drift • Inches	0.0	0.6	2.8	6.7	12.6	20.6	31.2	61.4	105.7

Federal 165-grain Nosler Partition (P300WK)

G1 Ballistic Coefficient = 0.410

Distance • Yards	Muzzle	100	200	300	400	500	600	800	1000
Velocity • fps	3050	2820	2590	2380	2180	1990	1809	1485	1228
Energy • Ft-lbs	3410	2905	2465	2080	1740	1450	1199	808	552
Taylor KO Index	22.1	20.5	18.8	17.3	15.8	14.4	13.1	10.8	8.9
Path • Inches	-1.5	+1.5	0.0	-6.6	-19.4	-39.5	-67.5	-158.2	-312.3
Wind Drift • Inches	0.0	0.7	2.9	6.7	12.4	20.2	30.3	59.2	101.5

Hirtenberger 165-grain ABC Bullet (82200380)

G1 Ballistic Coefficient = 0.278

Distance • Yards	Muzzle	100	200	300	400	500	600	800	1000
Velocity • fps	2986	2650	2338	2048	1780	1539	1331	1054	916
Energy • Ft-lbs	3268	2574	2003	1537	1161	867	649	407	307
Taylor KO Index	21.7	19.2	17.0	14.9	12.9	11.2	9.7	7.7	6.7
Path • Inches	-1.5	+1.7	0.0	-8.1	-24.6	-52.3	-95.9	-248.2	-522.7
Wind Drift • Inches	0.0	1.0	4.2	10.0	19.0	31.8	49.1	98.4	163.9

Hirtenberger 165-grain Sierra SBT (82200443)

G1 Ballistic Coefficient = 0.444

Distance • Yards	Muzzle	100	200	300	400	500	600	800	1000
Velocity • fps	2936	2725	2524	2332	2147	1972	1805	1505	1259
Energy • Ft-lbs	3159	2722	2335	1992	1690	1425	1194	830	581
Taylor KO Index	21.3	19.8	18.3	16.9	15.6	14.3	13.1	10.9	9.1
Path • Inches	-1.5	+1.6	0.0	-7.1	-20.5	-41.6	-71.6	-166.2	-324.6
Wind Drift • Inches	0.0	0.6	2.6	6.0	11.0	17.9	26.9	52.3	89.1

Norma 165-grain Swift Scirocco (17552) (Discontinued in 2005)

G1 Ballistic Coefficient = 0.500

Distance • Yards	Muzzle	100	200	300	400	500	600	800	1000
Velocity • fps	3117	2921	2734	2554	2382	2217	2057	1760	1497
Energy • Ft-lbs	3561	3127	2738	2390	2080	1801	1551	1135	821
Taylor KO Index	22.6	21.2	19.8	18.5	17.3	16.1	14.9	12.8	10.9
Path • Inches	-1.5	+1.2	0.0	-5.9	-17.2	-34.6	-59.1	-134.3	-255.5
Wind Drift • Inches	0.0	0.6	2.3	5.4	9.8	15.8	23.6	45.3	76.5

Hornady 165-grain SST (82024)

G1 Ballistic Coefficient = 0.401

Distance • Yards	Muzzle	100	200	300	400	500	600	800	1000
Velocity • fps	3100	2883	2676	2478	2289	2108	1822	1489	1226
Energy • Ft-lbs	3520	2994	2534	2132	1781	1477	1216	813	551
Taylor KO Index	22.5	20.9	19.4	18.0	16.6	15.3	13.2	10.8	8.9
Path • Inches	-1.5	+1.3	0.0	-6.2	-18.1	-36.6	-66.7	-157.6	-314.2
Wind Drift • Inches	0.0	0.6	2.8	6.7	12.6	20.6	31.2	61.4	105.7

Federal 165-grain Nosler Ballistic Tip (P300WN)

G1 Ballistic Coefficient = 0.475

Distance • Yards	Muzzle	100	200	300	400	500	600	800	1000
Velocity • fps	3050	2850	2650	2470	2290	2120	1957	1656	1396
Energy • Ft-lbs	3410	2970	2580	2230	1920	1645	1403	1005	714
Taylor KO Index	22.1	20.7	19.2	17.9	16.6	15.4	14.2	12.0	10.1
Path • Inches	-1.5	+1.4	0.0	-6.3	-18.3	-37.1	-63.5	-145.5	-279.9
Wind Drift • Inches	0.0	0.6	2.5	5.8	10.7	17.4	26.0	50.0	85.0

Sellier & Bellot 168-grain HPBT (SBA30001)

G1 Ballistic Coefficient = 0.450

Distance • Yards	Muzzle	100	200	300	400	500	600	800	1000
Velocity • fps	3064	2844	2640	2450	2264	2085	1915	1603	1340
Energy • Ft-lbs	3507	3021	2602	2242	1912	1622	1368	959	670
Taylor KO Index	22.6	21.0	19.5	18.1	16.7	15.4	14.2	11.8	9.9
Path • Inches	-1.5	+1.4	0.0	-6.4	-18.5	-37.5	-64.5	-149.1	-289.8
Wind Drift • Inches	0.0	0.6	2.6	6.1	11.3	18.4	27.6	53.4	91.2

A² 180-grain Monolithic; Dead Tough

G1 Ballistic Coefficient = 0.263

Distance • Yards	Muzzle	100	200	300	400	500	600	800	1000
Velocity • fps	3120	2756	2420	2108	1820	1559	1338	1047	905
Energy • Ft-lbs	3890	3035	2340	1776	1324	972	716	438	328
Taylor KO Index	24.7	21.8	19.2	16.7	14.4	12.3	10.6	8.3	7.2
Path • Inches	-1.5	+1.6	0.0	-7.6	-22.9	-49.0	-90.2	-239.6	-511.5
Wind Drift • Inches	0.0	1.1	4.6	11.1	21.2	35.6	55.3	111.8	187.1

Federal 180-grain Trophy Bonded Bear Claw—HE (P300WT3)

G1 Ballistic Coefficient = 0.360

Distance • Yards	Muzzle	100	200	300	400	500	600	800	1000
Velocity • fps	3100	2830	2580	2340	2110	1900	1702	1359	1117
Energy • Ft-lbs	3840	3205	2660	2190	1700	1445	1157	738	499
Taylor KO Index	24.6	22.4	20.4	18.5	16.7	15.0	13.5	10.8	8.8
Path • Inches	-1.5	+1.1	0.0	-5.4	-15.8	-32.3	-71.2	-172.5	-353.3
Wind Drift • Inches	0.0	0.8	3.3	7.8	14.5	23.8	36.1	71.7	123.9

Hornady 180-grain SP-HM InterLock (8500)

G1 Ballistic Coefficient = 0.425

Distance • Yards	Muzzle	100	200	300	400	500	600	800	1000
Velocity • fps	3100	2796	2655	2448	2251	2063	1884	1560	1293
Energy • Ft-lbs	3840	3296	2817	2396	2025	1701	1420	973	668
Taylor KO Index	24.6	22.1	21.0	19.4	17.8	16.3	14.9	12.4	10.2
Path • Inches	-1.5	+1.4	0.0	-6.3	-18.4	-37.4	-64.6	-150.4	-294.1
Wind Drift • Inches	0.0	0.6	2.5	5.8	10.7	17.4	26.0	51.0	87.4

Winchester 180-grain Partition Gold (SPG300WM)

G1 Ballistic Coefficient = 0.457

Distance • Yards	Muzzle	100	200	300	400	500	600	800	1000
Velocity • fps	3070	2859	2657	2464	2280	2103	1935	1625	1361
Energy • Ft-lbs	3768	3267	2823	2428	2978	1768	1496	1056	741
Taylor KO Index	24.3	22.6	21.0	19.5	18.1	16.7	15.3	12.9	10.8
Path • Inches	-1.5	+1.4	0.0	-6.3	-18.3	-37.1	-63.7	-146.9	-284.6
Wind Drift • Inches	0.0	0.6	2.6	6.0	11.1	18.0	27.0	52.2	88.9

Winchester 180-grain Power-Point Plus (SHV30WM2)

G1 Ballistic Coefficient = 0.431

Distance • Yards	Muzzle	100	200	300	400	500	600	800	1000
Velocity • fps	3070	2846	2633	2430	2236	2051	1876	1556	1293
Energy • Ft-lbs	3768	3239	2772	2361	1999	1681	1407	969	668
Taylor KO Index	24.3	22.5	20.9	19.2	17.7	16.2	14.9	12.3	10.2
Path • Inches	-1.5	+1.4	0.0	-6.4	-18.7	-38.0	-65.6	-152.9	-300.0
Wind Drift • Inches	0.0	0.7	2.8	6.4	11.9	19.3	29.0	56.5	96.7

Black Hills 180-grain Nosler AccuBond (1C300WMBHGN3)

G1 Ballistic Coefficient = 0.510

Distance • Yards	Muzzle	100	200	300	400	500	600	800	1000
Velocity • fps	3000	2813	2634	2462	2296	2137	1994	1699	1449
Energy • Ft-lbs	3597	3164	2774	2423	2108	1826	1574	1155	840
Taylor KO Index	23.8	22.3	20.9	19.5	18.2	16.9	15.8	13.5	11.5
Path • Inches	-1.5	+1.4	0.0	-6.5	-18.7	-37.5	-63.9	-144.9	-275.3
Wind Drift • Inches	0.0	0.6	2.4	5.5	10.1	16.4	24.4	46.7	78.9

Speer 180-grain Grand Slam (24509) (Discontinued in 2004)

G1 Ballistic Coefficient = 0.414

Distance • Yards	Muzzle	100	200	300	400	500	600	800	1000
Velocity • fps	3000	2772	2555	2348	2148	1960	1783	1466	1216
Energy • Ft-lbs	3597	3070	2609	2204	1845	1536	1270	859	591
Taylor KO Index	23.8	22.0	20.2	18.6	17.0	15.5	14.1	11.6	9.6
Path • Inches	-1.5	+1.6	0.0	-6.8	-20.0	-40.8	-70.7	-166.2	-329.3
Wind Drift • Inches	0.0	0.7	3.0	6.9	12.9	21.0	31.6	61.9	106.0

Hirtenberger 180-grain Nosler Partition (82200379)

G1 Ballistic Coefficient = 0.487

Distance • Yards	Muzzle	100	200	300	400	500	600	800	1000
Velocity • fps	2986	2791	2605	2426	2254	2089	1931	1640	1388
Energy • Ft-lbs	3565	3115	2712	2352	2031	1744	1491	1075	770
Taylor KO Index	23.6	22.1	20.6	19.2	17.9	16.5	15.3	13.0	11.0
Path • Inches	-1.5	+1.5	0.0	-6.6	-19.1	-38.5	-65.9	-150.5	-288.4
Wind Drift • Inches	0.0	0.6	2.3	5.2	9.7	15.6	23.4	45.0	76.3

Sellier & Bellot 180-grain SPCE (SBA30002)

G1 Ballistic Coefficient = 0.295

Distance • Yards	Muzzle	100	200	300	400	500	600	800	1000
Velocity • fps	2986	2654	2359	2097	1839	1605	1399	1101	949
Energy • Ft-lbs	3573	2824	2231	1763	1353	1030	782	484	360
Taylor KO Index	23.6	21.0	18.7	16.6	14.6	12.7	11.1	8.7	7.5
Path • Inches	-1.5	+1.7	0.0	-7.9	-23.8	-50.1	-90.3	-231.7	-487.2
Wind Drift • Inches	0.0	1.0	4.3	10.3	19.5	32.6	50.2	100.7	169.4

Federal 180-grain Nosler AccuBond (P300WA1)

G1 Ballistic Coefficient = 0.527

Distance • Yards	Muzzle	100	200	300	400	500	600	800	1000
Velocity • fps	2960	2780	2610	2440	2280	2130	1981	1706	1462
Energy • Ft-lbs	3500	3090	2715	2380	2075	1805	1570	1163	855
Taylor KO Index	23.4	22.0	20.7	19.3	18.1	16.9	15.7	13.5	11.6
Path • Inches	-1.5	+1.5	0.0	-6.6	-19.0	-38.3	-68.0	-146.7	-277.4
Wind Drift • Inches	0.0	0.6	2.3	5.4	9.9	16.0	23.9	45.7	76.9

Federal 180-grain Speer Hot-Cor SP (300WBS)

G1 Ballistic Coefficient = 0.438

Distance • Yards	Muzzle	100	200	300	400	500	600	800	1000
Velocity • fps	2960	2750	2540	2350	2160	1980	1810	1505	1257
Energy • Ft-lbs	3500	3015	2580	2200	1865	1570	1310	905	631
Taylor KO Index	23.4	21.8	20.1	18.6	17.1	15.7	14.3	11.9	10.0
Path • Inches	-1.5	+1.6	0.0	-6.9	-20.3	-41.0	-70.7	-164.6	-322.3
Wind Drift • Inches	0.0	0.7	2.8	6.6	12.3	20.0	30.1	58.4	99.8

Federal 180-grain Trophy Bonded Bear Claw (P300WT2)

G1 Ballistic Coefficient = 0.361

Distance • Yards	Muzzle	100	200	300	400	500	600	800	1000
Velocity • fps	2960	2700	2460	2220	2000	1800	1609	1288	1076
Energy • Ft-lbs	3500	2915	2410	1875	1605	1295	1035	644	463
Taylor KO Index	23.4	21.4	19.5	17.6	15.8	14.3	12.7	10.2	8.5
Path • Inches	-1.5	+1.6	0.0	-7.4	-21.9	-45.0	-79.2	-192.3	-392.9
Wind Drift • Inches	0.0	0.8	3.5	8.3	15.4	25.4	38.6	76.5	131.2

Federal 180-grain Nosler Partition (P300WD2)

G1 Ballistic Coefficient = 0.354

Distance • Yards	Muzzle	100	200	300	400	500	600	800	1000
Velocity • fps	2960	2700	2450	2210	1990	1780	1587	1267	1061
Energy • Ft-lbs	3500	2905	2395	1955	1585	1265	1007	642	450
Taylor KO Index	23.4	21.4	19.4	17.5	15.8	14.1	12.6	10.0	8.4
Path • Inches	-1.5	+1.6	0.0	-7.5	-22.1	-45.4	-80.2	-195.8	-401.7
Wind Drift • Inches	0.0	0.9	3.6	8.4	15.8	26.1	39.6	78.7	134.8

Hornady 180-grain SP InterLock (8200)

G1 Ballistic Coefficient = 0.425

Distance • Yards	Muzzle	100	200	300	400	500	600	800	1000
Velocity • fps	2960	2739	2528	2328	2136	1953	1780	1471	1225
Energy • Ft-lbs	3501	2998	2555	2165	1823	1525	1267	865	600
Taylor KO Index	23.4	21.7	20.0	18.4	16.9	15.5	14.1	11.7	9.7
Path • Inches	-1.5	+1.6	0.0	-7.0	-20.5	-41.6	-71.8	-168.2	-331.5
Wind Drift • Inches	0.0	0.7	2.9	6.9	12.7	20.7	31.2	60.9	104.1

Remington 180-grain AccuTip Boat Tail (PRA300WC)

G1 Ballistic Coefficient = 0.481

Distance • Yards	Muzzle	100	200	300	400	500	600	800	1000
Velocity • fps	2960	2764	2577	2397	2224	2058	1900	1609	1361
Energy • Ft-lbs	3501	3053	2653	2295	1976	1693	1444	1035	740
Taylor KO Index	23.4	21.9	20.4	19.0	17.6	16.3	15.0	12.7	10.8
Path • Inches	-1.5	1.5	0.0	-6.8	-19.6	-39.5	-67.6	-154.4	-295.5
Wind Drift • Inches	0.0	0.6	2.3	5.4	9.9	16.1	24.0	46.3	78.6

Remington 180-grain Pointed Soft Point Core-Lokt (R300W2)

G1 Ballistic Coefficient = 0.437

Distance • Yards	Muzzle	100	200	300	400	500	600	800	1000
Velocity • fps	2960	2715	2482	2262	2052	1856	1672	1354	1125
Energy • Ft-lbs	3501	2945	2463	2044	1683	1375	1118	733	506
Taylor KO Index	23.4	21.5	19.7	17.9	16.3	14.7	13.2	10.7	8.9
Path • Inches	-1.5	+1.6	0.0	-7.3	-21.3	-43.7	-76.2	-182.5	-368.3
Wind Drift • Inches	0.0	0.8	3.3	7.7	14.4	23.6	35.7	70.4	120.8

Remington 180-grain Pointed Soft Point Core-Lokt Ultra (PRC300WC)

G1 Ballistic Coefficient = 0.402

Distance • Yards	Muzzle	100	200	300	400	500	600	800	1000
Velocity • fps	2960	2727	2505	2294	2093	1903	1723	1408	1169
Energy • Ft-lbs	3501	2971	2508	2103	1751	1448	1187	793	547
Taylor KO Index	23.4	21.6	19.8	18.2	16.6	15.1	13.6	11.2	9.3
Path • Inches	-1.5	+1.6	0.0	-7.2	-20.9	-42.7	-74.1	-175.5	-350.2
Wind Drift • Inches	0.0	0.8	3.1	7.3	13.6	22.2	33.5	65.8	112.8

Remington 180-grain Nosler Partition (PRP300WA) (Discontinued in 2005)   G1 Ballistic Coefficient = 0.400

Distance • Yards	Muzzle	100	200	300	400	500	600	800	1000
Velocity • fps	2960	2725	2503	2291	2089	1898	1721	1405	1167
Energy • Ft-lbs	3501	2968	2503	2087	1744	1440	1184	790	544
Taylor KO Index	23.4	21.6	19.8	18.1	16.5	15.0	13.6	11.1	9.2
Path • Inches	-1.5	+1.6	0.0	-7.2	-20.9	-42.7	-74.2	-175.8	-351.1
Wind Drift • Inches	0.0	0.8	3.1	7.3	13.6	22.3	33.6	66.0	113.2

Winchester 180-grain Power-Point (X300WM2)   G1 Ballistic Coefficient = 0.338

Distance • Yards	Muzzle	100	200	300	400	500	600	800	1000
Velocity • fps	2960	2685	2426	2182	1952	1738	1542	1223	1030
Energy • Ft-lbs	3501	2881	2352	1902	1523	1207	951	599	424
Taylor KO Index	23.4	21.3	19.2	17.3	15.5	13.8	12.2	9.7	8.2
Path • Inches	-1.5	+1.7	0.0	-7.6	-22.5	-46.6	-82.2	-203.2	-420.6
Wind Drift • Inches	0.0	0.9	3.8	8.9	16.6	27.5	42.0	83.7	143.0

Winchester 180-grain Fail Safe (S300WX)   G1 Ballistic Coefficient = 0.411

Distance • Yards	Muzzle	100	200	300	400	500	600	800	1000
Velocity • fps	2960	2732	2514	2307	2110	1923	1746	1433	1191
Energy • Ft-lbs	3503	2983	2528	2129	1780	1478	1219	821	567
Taylor KO Index	23.4	21.6	19.9	18.3	16.7	15.2	13.8	11.3	9.4
Path • Inches	-1.5	+1.6	0.0	-7.1	-20.7	-42.1	-73.2	-172.5	-342.5
Wind Drift • Inches	0.0	0.7	3.0	7.1	13.2	21.6	32.6	63.8	109.2

Norma 180-grain Nosler AccuBond (17548)   G1 Ballistic Coefficient = 0.506

Distance • Yards	Muzzle	100	200	300	400	500	600	800	1000
Velocity • fps	2953	2767	2588	2417	2252	2093	1941	1659	1413
Energy • Ft-lbs	3486	3061	2678	2335	2027	1751	1506	1100	799
Taylor KO Index	23.4	21.9	20.5	19.1	17.8	16.6	15.4	13.1	11.2
Path • Inches	-1.5	+1.5	0.0	-6.7	-19.4	-39.0	-66.4	-150.7	-286.0
Wind Drift • Inches	0.0	0.5	2.2	5.1	9.4	15.2	22.7	43.5	73.5

Winchester 180-grain AccuBond CT (S300WMCT)   G1 Ballistic Coefficient = 0.510

Distance • Yards	Muzzle	100	200	300	400	500	600	800	1000
Velocity • fps	2950	2765	2588	2417	2253	2095	1945	1664	1419
Energy • Ft-lbs	3478	3055	2676	2334	2028	1754	1512	1107	805
Taylor KO Index	23.4	21.9	20.5	19.1	17.8	16.6	15.4	13.2	11.2
Path • Inches	-1.5	+1.5	0.0	-6.7	-19.4	-39.0	-66.4	-150.6	-286.4
Wind Drift • Inches	0.0	0.6	2.4	5.6	10.4	16.8	25.0	47.9	80.9

PMC 180-grain Pointed Soft Point (300B)   G1 Ballistic Coefficient = 0.401

Distance • Yards	Muzzle	100	200	300	400	500	600	800	1000
Velocity • fps	2850	2619	2400	2193	1998	1814	1642	1342	1125
Energy • Ft-lbs	3246	2742	2303	1923	1596	1315	1078	720	506
Taylor KO Index	22.6	20.7	19.0	17.4	15.8	14.4	13.0	10.6	8.9
Path • Inches	-1.5	+1.8	0.0	-7.8	-22.9	-46.7	-81.0	-192.3	-384.1
Wind Drift • Inches	0.0	0.8	3.3	7.7	14.4	23.6	35.6	69.9	119.2

Black Hills 180-grain Nosler Ballistic Tip (1C300WMBHGN2)   G1 Ballistic Coefficient = 0.508

Distance • Yards	Muzzle	100	200	300	400	500	600	800	1000
Velocity • fps	3000	2813	2633	2460	2294	2134	1960	1695	1445
Energy • Ft-lbs	3597	3162	2771	2419	2103	1820	1568	1149	834
Taylor KO Index	23.8	22.3	20.9	19.5	18.2	16.9	15.5	13.4	11.4
Path • Inches	-1.5	+1.4	0.0	-6.5	-18.7	-37.5	-64.0	-145.2	-276.1
Wind Drift • Inches	0.0	0.6	2.4	5.5	10.2	16.4	24.5	47.0	79.3

Norma 180-grain Plastic point (17687)   G1 Ballistic Coefficient = 0.366

Distance • Yards	Muzzle	100	200	300	400	500	600	800	1000
Velocity • fps	3018	2758	2513	2281	2063	1856	1664	1334	1105
Energy • Ft-lbs	3641	3042	2525	2080	1701	1377	1106	712	488
Taylor KO Index	23.9	21.8	19.9	18.1	16.3	14.7	13.2	10.6	8.8
Path • Inches	-1.5	+1.5	0.0	-7.0	-20.8	-42.8	-75.0	-181.3	-369.6
Wind Drift • Inches	0.0	0.8	3.4	8.0	14.8	24.2	36.8	72.9	125.4

Federal 180-grain Barnes Triple Shock X-Bullet (P300WP)
G1 Ballistic Coefficient = 0.467

Distance • Yards	Muzzle	100	200	300	400	500	600	800	1000
Velocity • fps	2960	2780	2580	2400	2220	2050	1888	1590	1338
Energy • Ft-lbs	3550	3085	2670	2300	1970	1680	1425	1011	716
Taylor KO Index	23.6	22.0	20.4	19.0	17.6	16.2	15.0	12.6	10.6
Path • Inches	-1.5	+1.5	0.0	-6.7	-19.5	-39.3	-67.5	-154.9	-297.8
Wind Drift • Inches	0.0	0.6	2.4	5.5	10.2	16.5	24.7	47.7	81.1

Hornady 180-grain SST (82194)
G1 Ballistic Coefficient = 0.481

Distance • Yards	Muzzle	100	200	300	400	500	600	800	1000
Velocity • fps	2960	2764	2575	2395	2222	2057	1900	1608	1359
Energy • Ft-lbs	3501	3052	2650	2292	1974	1691	1443	1034	739
Taylor KO Index	23.4	21.9	20.4	19.0	17.6	16.3	15.0	12.7	10.8
Path • Inches	-1.5	+1.6	0.0	-7.0	-20.1	-39.9	-67.6	-154.8	-297.3
Wind Drift • Inches	0.0	0.6	2.6	6.0	11.0	17.9	26.7	51.5	87.4

Remington 180-grain Nosler Ballistic Tip (PRT300WA) (Discontinued in 2005)
G1 Ballistic Coefficient = 0.508

Distance • Yards	Muzzle	100	200	300	400	500	600	800	1000
Velocity • fps	2960	2774	2595	2424	2259	2100	1949	1667	1421
Energy • Ft-lbs	3501	3075	2692	2348	2039	1762	1519	1111	807
Taylor KO Index	23.4	22.0	20.6	19.2	17.9	16.6	15.4	13.2	11.3
Path • Inches	-1.5	+1.5	0.0	-6.7	-19.3	-38.7	-66.0	-149.8	-284.9
Wind Drift • Inches	0.0	0.6	2.4	5.6	10.4	16.8	25.0	47.9	81.0

Remington 180-grain Swift Scirocco Bonded (PRSC300WB)
G1 Ballistic Coefficient = 0.508

Distance • Yards	Muzzle	100	200	300	400	500	600	800	1000
Velocity • fps	2960	2774	2595	2424	2259	2100	1949	1667	1421
Energy • Ft-lbs	3501	3075	2692	2348	2039	1762	1519	1111	807
Taylor KO Index	23.4	22.0	20.6	19.2	17.9	16.6	15.4	13.2	11.3
Path • Inches	-1.5	+1.5	0.0	-6.7	-19.3	-38.7	-66.0	-149.8	-284.9
Wind Drift • Inches	0.0	0.6	2.4	5.6	10.4	16.8	25.0	47.9	81.0

Black Hills 180-grain Barnes XLC-Bullet
G1 Ballistic Coefficient = 0.552

Distance • Yards	Muzzle	100	200	300	400	500	600	800	1000
Velocity • fps	2950	2779	2615	2456	2303	2155	2013	1746	1508
Energy • Ft-lbs	3479	3088	2733	2412	2120	1857	1620	1219	909
Taylor KO Index	23.4	22.0	20.7	19.5	18.2	17.1	15.9	13.8	11.9
Path • Inches	-1.5	+1.5	0.0	-6.6	-19.0	-37.9	-64.3	-144.3	-270.8
Wind Drift • Inches	0.0	0.5	2.2	5.2	9.5	15.3	22.7	43.3	72.6

PMC 180-grain HPBT Match (300SMA)
G1 Ballistic Coefficient = 0.485

Distance • Yards	Muzzle	100	200	300	400	500	600	800	1000
Velocity • fps	2950	2755	2568	2390	2219	2057	1900	1612	1364
Energy • Ft-lbs	3478	3033	2636	2283	1968	1691	1444	1038	744
Taylor KO Index	23.4	21.8	20.3	18.9	17.6	16.3	15.0	12.8	10.8
Path • Inches	-1.5	+1.5	0.0	-6.8	-19.7	-39.7	-67.8	-155.0	-296.0
Wind Drift • Inches	0.0	0.6	2.3	5.4	9.9	16.0	23.9	46.0	78.0

Winchester 180-grain Ballistic Silvertip (SBST300)
G1 Ballistic Coefficient = 0.508

Distance • Yards	Muzzle	100	200	300	400	500	600	800	1000
Velocity • fps	2950	2764	2586	2415	2250	2092	1941	1660	1415
Energy • Ft-lbs	3478	3054	2673	2333	2026	1751	1507	1102	800
Taylor KO Index	23.4	21.9	20.5	19.1	17.8	16.6	15.4	13.1	11.2
Path • Inches	-1.5	+1.5	0.0	-6.7	-19.4	-38.9	-66.5	-151.0	-287.2
Wind Drift • Inches	0.0	0.6	2.4	5.7	10.4	16.8	25.1	48.2	81.4

Norma 180-grain Swift A-Frame (17519)

G1 Ballistic Coefficient = 0.400

Distance • Yards	Muzzle	100	200	300	400	500	600	800	1000
Velocity • fps	2920	2687	2466	2256	2056	1867	1689	1379	1149
Energy • Ft-lbs	3409	2887	2432	2035	1690	1393	1141	761	528
Taylor KO Index	23.1	21.3	19.5	17.9	16.3	14.8	13.4	10.9	9.1
Path • Inches	-1.5	+1.7	0.0	-7.4	-21.6	-44.1	-76.7	-181.9	-363.1
Wind Drift • Inches	0.0	0.8	3.2	7.5	13.9	22.8	34.5	67.6	115.7

PMC 180-grain Barnes-XLC-HP (300XLC) (Discontinued in 2005)

G1 Ballistic Coefficient = 0.542

Distance • Yards	Muzzle	100	200	300	400	500	600	800	1000
Velocity • fps	2910	2738	2572	2412	2258	2109	1966	1699	1462
Energy • Ft-lbs	3384	2995	2644	2325	2037	1778	1545	1154	855
Taylor KO Index	23.0	21.7	20.4	19.1	17.9	16.7	15.6	13.5	11.6
Path • Inches	-1.5	+1.6	0.0	-6.9	-19.8	-39.4	-66.8	-150.2	-283.0
Wind Drift • Inches	0.0	0.6	2.4	5.6	10.2	15.9	23.7	45.2	76.0

Hornady 190-grain BTSP (8220) (Discontinued in 2005)

G1 Ballistic Coefficient = 0.492

Distance • Yards	Muzzle	100	200	300	400	500	600	800	1000
Velocity • fps	2900	2711	2529	2365	2187	2026	1874	1592	1351
Energy • Ft-lbs	3549	3101	2699	2340	2018	1732	1482	1069	770
Taylor KO Index	24.2	22.7	21.1	19.8	18.3	16.9	15.7	13.3	11.3
Path • Inches	-1.5	+1.6	0.0	-7.1	-20.4	-41.0	-70.1	-160.0	-306.4
Wind Drift • Inches	0.0	0.6	2.6	6.0	11.1	18.0	26.8	51.6	87.3

PMC 190-grain SBST Game (300HC)

G1 Ballistic Coefficient = 0.502

Distance • Yards	Muzzle	100	200	300	400	500	600	800	1000
Velocity • fps	2900	2714	2536	2365	2200	2042	1892	1613	1373
Energy • Ft-lbs	3549	3110	2715	2361	2044	1761	1510	1098	795
Taylor KO Index	24.2	22.7	21.2	19.8	18.4	17.1	15.8	13.5	11.5
Path • Inches	-1.5	+1.6	0.0	-7.1	-20.3	-40.8	-69.5	-158.1	-301.7
Wind Drift • Inches	0.0	0.6	2.5	5.9	10.8	17.5	26.2	50.2	84.9

Black Hills 190-grain HP Match (D300WMN1)

G1 Ballistic Coefficient = 0.560

Distance • Yards	Muzzle	100	200	300	400	500	600	800	1000
Velocity • fps	2950	2781	2619	2462	2311	2165	2025	1761	1524
Energy • Ft-lbs	3672	3265	2894	2559	2254	1978	1731	1309	980
Taylor KO Index	24.7	23.2	21.9	20.6	19.3	18.1	16.9	14.7	12.7
Path • Inches	-1.5	+1.5	0.0	-6.6	-18.9	-37.7	-63.9	-143.2	-268.2
Wind Drift • Inches	0.0	0.5	2.2	5.1	9.3	15.0	22.3	42.5	71.2

Federal 190-grain Sierra MatchKing BTHP (GM300WM)

G1 Ballistic Coefficient = 0.534

Distance • Yards	Muzzle	100	200	300	400	500	600	800	1000
Velocity • fps	2900	2730	2560	2400	2240	2090	1945	1677	1440
Energy • Ft-lbs	3550	3135	2760	2420	2115	1845	1597	1186	875
Taylor KO Index	24.2	22.8	21.4	20.1	18.7	17.5	16.3	14.0	12.0
Path • Inches	-1.5	+1.6	0.0	-6.8	-19.9	-39.8	-67.7	-152.7	-288.2
Wind Drift • Inches	0.0	0.6	2.4	5.5	10.1	16.3	24.3	46.3	78.0

Remington 190-grain Boat Tail Hollow Point (Match) (RM300W7)

G1 Ballistic Coefficient = 0.533

Distance • Yards	Muzzle	100	200	300	400	500	600	800	1000
Velocity • fps	2900	2725	2557	2395	2239	2089	1944	1676	1439
Energy • Ft-lbs	3547	3133	2758	2420	2115	1840	1595	1185	874
Taylor KO Index	24.2	22.8	21.4	20.0	18.7	17.5	16.3	14.0	12.0
Path • Inches	-1.5	+1.6	0.0	-6.9	-19.9	-39.8	-67.7	-152.6	-287.5
Wind Drift • Inches	0.0	0.5	2.1	5.0	9.1	14.7	21.9	41.8	70.3

Remington 190-grain Pointed Soft Point BT (PRB300WA) (Discontinued in 2005)

G1 Ballistic Coefficient = 0.478

Distance • Yards	Muzzle	100	200	300	400	500	600	800	1000
Velocity • fps	2885	2691	2506	2327	2156	1993	1836	1551	1311
Energy • Ft-lbs	3511	3055	2648	2285	1961	1675	1423	1015	726
Taylor KO Index	24.1	22.5	21.0	19.5	18.0	16.7	15.3	13.0	11.0
Path • Inches	-1.5	+1.6	0.0	-7.2	-20.8	-41.9	-71.9	-164.9	-317.5
Wind Drift • Inches	0.0	0.6	2.7	6.3	11.5	18.7	28.0	54.0	91.6

Speer 200-grain Grand Slam (24510) (Discontinued in 2004)

G1 Ballistic Coefficient = 0.449

Distance • Yards	Muzzle	100	200	300	400	500	600	800	1000
Velocity • fps	2800	2597	2404	2218	2041	1873	1715	1431	1206
Energy • Ft-lbs	3481	2996	2565	2185	1851	1558	1306	909	646
Taylor KO Index	24.6	22.9	21.2	19.5	18.0	16.5	15.1	12.6	10.6
Path • Inches	-1.5	+1.8	0.0	-7.9	-22.9	-46.1	-79.3	-184.2	-359.5
Wind Drift • Inches	0.0	0.7	3.0	7.0	13.0	21.1	31.7	61.5	104.4

Norma 200-grain Oryx SP (17676) (Discontinued in 2005)

G1 Ballistic Coefficient = 0.360

Distance • Yards	Muzzle	100	200	300	400	500	600	800	1000
Velocity • fps	2789	2511	2249	2003	1774	1566	1381	1109	963
Energy • Ft-lbs	3110	2520	2022	1604	1259	980	762	492	371
Taylor KO Index	24.5	22.1	19.8	17.6	15.6	13.8	12.2	9.8	8.5
Path • Inches	-1.5	+2.0	0.0	-8.9	-26.6	-55.4	-99.0	-247.0	-507.9
Wind Drift • Inches	0.0	1.0	4.3	10.3	19.3	32.1	49.1	97.2	162.2

Federal 200-grain Nosler Partition—HE (P300WE)

G1 Ballistic Coefficient = 0.412

Distance • Yards	Muzzle	100	200	300	400	500	600	800	1000
Velocity • fps	2930	2700	2480	2280	2090	1900	1727	1418	1181
Energy • Ft-lbs	3810	3247	2750	2315	1935	1608	1325	893	619
Taylor KO Index	25.8	23.8	21.8	20.1	18.4	16.7	15.2	12.5	10.4
Path • Inches	-1.5	+1.6	0.0	-7.3	-21.2	-43.2	-74.8	-176.4	-350.1
Wind Drift • Inches	0.0	07	3.1	7.2	13.4	21.9	33.0	64.6	110.4

Remington 200-grain A-Frame Pointed Soft Point (RS300WA)

G1 Ballistic Coefficient = 0.395

Distance • Yards	Muzzle	100	200	300	400	500	600	800	1000
Velocity • fps	2825	2595	2377	2169	1971	1786	1612	1315	1106
Energy • Ft-lbs	3544	2990	2508	2088	1726	1416	1154	769	544
Taylor KO Index	24.9	22.8	20.9	19.1	17.3	15.7	14.2	11.6	9.7
Path • Inches	-1.5	+1.8	0.0	-8.0	-23.4	-47.8	-83.3	-198.4	-397.1
Wind Drift • Inches	0.0	0.8	3.4	8.0	14.8	24.3	36.7	72.0	122.7

Federal 200-grain Sierra GameKing BTSP (P300WC) (Discontinued in 2005)

G1 Ballistic Coefficient = 0.598

Distance • Yards	Muzzle	100	200	300	400	500	600	800	1000
Velocity • fps	2830	2660	2530	2380	2240	2110	1980	1736	1516
Energy • Ft-lbs	3500	3180	2830	2520	2230	1870	1742	1339	1021
Taylor KO Index	24.9	23.4	22.3	20.9	19.7	18.6	17.4	15.3	13.3
Path • Inches	-1.5	+1.7	0.0	-7.1	-20.4	-40.5	-68.5	-152.3	-283.1
Wind Drift • Inches	0.0	0.5	2.2	5.0	9.2	14.8	22.0	41.6	69.4

Federal 200-grain Trophy Bonded Bear Claw (P300WT1)

G1 Ballistic Coefficient = 0.398

Distance • Yards	Muzzle	100	200	300	400	500	600	800	1000
Velocity • fps	2800	2570	2350	2150	1950	1770	1599	1307	1102
Energy • Ft-lbs	3480	2835	2460	2050	1690	1392	1136	759	539
Taylor KO Index	24.6	22.6	20.7	18.9	17.2	15.6	14.1	11.5	9.7
Path • Inches	-1.5	+1.9	0.0	-8.2	-23.9	-48.8	-84.8	-201.8	-403.4
Wind Drift • Inches	0.0	0.8	3.4	8.0	14.9	24.5	37.0	72.5	123.3

.300 Dakota

This is another of Dakota Arms's lines of proprietary cartridges based on the .404 Jeffery case. Performance-wise, it is somewhat more potent than the .300 Winchester Magnum and about equal to the .300 Weatherby Magnum, depending on which loads you use for comparison. Proprietary cartridges are not new to the ammunition business. Many of the British cartridges started life as proprietary numbers. Sometimes, as with the .375 H&H (and numerous others), they become standardized.

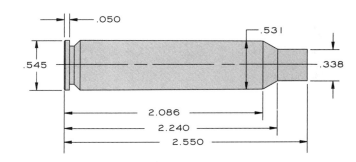

Relative Recoil Factor = 2.60

Specifications

Controlling Agency for Standardization of this Ammunition: Factory

Availability

Dakota 180-grain Nosler Partition (300-180NPT)
G1 Ballistic Coefficient = 0.474

Distance • Yards	Muzzle	100	200	300	400	500	600	800	1000
Velocity • fps	3250	3038	2835	2642	2457	2279	2108	1791	1509
Energy • Ft-lbs	4223	3689	3214	2790	2413	2076	1777	1282	911
Taylor KO Index	25.7	24.1	22.5	20.9	19.5	18.0	16.7	14.2	12.0
Path • Inches	-1.5	+1.1	0.0	-5.5	-15.9	-32.1	-55.0	-125.9	-241.4
Wind Drift • Inches	0.0	0.6	2.3	5.4	9.8	15.9	23.8	45.6	77.4

Dakota 180-grain Fail-Safe (300-180WFS)
G1 Ballistic Coefficient = 0.412

Distance • Yards	Muzzle	100	200	300	400	500	600	800	1000
Velocity • fps	3250	3006	2776	2557	2349	2150	1961	1616	1329
Energy • Ft-lbs	4223	3614	3081	2614	2205	1848	1537	1044	706
Taylor KO Index	25.7	23.8	22.0	20.3	18.6	17.0	15.5	12.8	10.5
Path • Inches	-1.5	+1.2	0.0	-5.7	-16.7	-34.0	-58.9	-138.2	-273.1
Wind Drift • Inches	0.0	0.6	2.7	6.2	11.6	18.8	28.3	55.2	94.9

Dakota 180-grain Swift A-Frame (300-180FAF)
G1 Ballistic Coefficient = 0.400

Distance • Yards	Muzzle	100	200	300	400	500	600	800	1000
Velocity • fps	3250	2999	2763	2538	2324	2121	1928	1578	1292
Energy • Ft-lbs	4223	3597	2051	2575	2160	1798	1486	996	667
Taylor KO Index	25.7	23.8	21.9	20.1	18.4	16.8	15.3	12.5	10.2
Path • Inches	-1.5	+1.2	0.0	-5.8	-16.9	-34.5	-59.9	-141.3	-281.2
Wind Drift • Inches	0.0	0.7	2.8	6.5	12.0	19.5	29.4	57.5	99.1

Dakota 180-grain Nosler Ballistic Tip (300-180NBT)
G1 Ballistic Coefficient = 0.507

Distance • Yards	Muzzle	100	200	300	400	500	600	800	1000
Velocity • fps	3250	3051	2861	2679	2504	2336	2174	1870	1596
Energy • Ft-lbs	4223	3722	3273	2869	2507	2181	1890	1398	1019
Taylor KO Index	25.7	24.2	22.7	21.2	19.8	18.5	17.2	14.8	12.6
Path • Inches	-1.5	+1.1	0.0	-5.4	-15.6	-31.4	-53.5	-121.1	-229.4
Wind Drift • Inches	0.0	0.5	2.2	5.0	9.1	14.7	21.9	41.8	70.4

Dakota 200-grain Nosler Partition (300-200NPT)
G1 Ballistic Coefficient = 0.481

Distance • Yards	Muzzle	100	200	300	400	500	600	800	1000
Velocity • fps	3050	2850	2659	2475	2299	2130	1969	1670	1410
Energy • Ft-lbs	4132	3609	3140	2722	2349	2016	1722	1239	884
Taylor KO Index	26.8	25.1	23.4	21.8	20.2	18.7	17.3	14.7	12.4
Path • Inches	-1.5	+1.4	0.0	-6.3	-18.3	-36.9	-63.2	-144.4	-277.0
Wind Drift • Inches	0.0	0.6	2.5	5.7	10.6	17.1	25.6	49.2	83.5

Dakota 200-grain Swift A-Frame (300-200FAF)

G1 Ballistic Coefficient = 0.444

Distance • Yards	Muzzle	100	200	300	400	500	600	800	1000
Velocity • fps	3050	2834	2628	2431	2242	2062	1891	1578	1317
Energy • Ft-lbs	4132	3567	3067	2624	2233	1889	1588	1107	770
Taylor KO Index	26.8	24.9	23.1	21.4	19.7	18.1	16.6	13.9	11.6
Path • Inches	-1.5	+1.4	0.0	-6.5	-18.8	-38.1	-65.6	-152.0	-296.4
Wind Drift • Inches	0.0	0.6	2.7	6.3	11.6	18.8	28.2	54.8	93.6

Buffalo come in many different varieties. This is a Central African savanna buffalo from the C.A.R. (Photo from *A Sporting Life* by José A. Martínez de Hoz, 2005, Safari Press)

.300 Weatherby Magnum

If you ask almost any group of shooters to name one caliber that exemplifies the term "high-powered rifle," chances are the answer will be the .300 Weatherby Magnum. Until it was very recently passed by the .30-378 Weatherby (and approximately equaled by the .300 RUM), Roy Weatherby's .300 Magnum was the performance leader of the .30-caliber rifles. The design has been around since the WWII years. Perhaps the most obvious identifying feature of Weatherby cartridges is the venturi shoulder. Whether or not the shoulder adds anything to velocity, the appearance is enough to ensure that most shooters will instantly recognize it as a Weatherby.

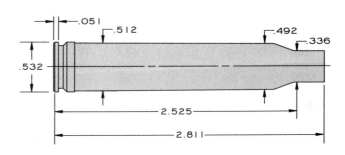

Relative Recoil Factor = 2.63

Specifications

Controlling Agency for Standardization of this Ammunition: SAAMI*

Bullet Weight Grains	Velocity fps	Maximum Average Pressure	
		Copper Crusher	Transducer
180	3,185	N/S	65,000 psi
190	3,015	N/S	65,000 psi
220	2,835	N/S	65,000 psi

Standard barrel for velocity testing: 24 inches long—1 turn in 10-inch twist

*Ammunition for the .300 Weatherby Magnum is also manufactured in Europe under CIP standards. Ammunition manufactured to CIP specifications will exhibit somewhat different performance values, but it can be safely fired in rifles in good condition.

Availability

Weatherby 150-grain Nosler Partition (N 300 150 PT)
G1 Ballistic Coefficient = 0.387

Distance • Yards	Muzzle	100	200	300	400	500	600	800	1000
Velocity • fps	3540	3263	3004	2759	2528	2307	2097	1714	1390
Energy • Ft-lbs	4173	3547	3004	2536	2128	1773	1466	979	644
Taylor KO Index	23.4	21.5	19.8	18.2	16.7	15.2	13.8	11.3	9.2
Path • Inches	-1.5	+1.0	0.0	-4.9	-14.6	-29.7	-50.2	-118.7	-236.8
Wind Drift • Inches	0.0	0.6	2.5	6.0	11.1	18.0	27.1	53.0	91.7

Weatherby 150-grain Pointed-Expanding (H 300 150 SP)
G1 Ballistic Coefficient = 0.338

Distance • Yards	Muzzle	100	200	300	400	500	600	800	1000
Velocity • fps	3540	3225	2932	2657	2399	2155	1925	1518	1206
Energy • Ft-lbs	4173	3462	2862	2351	1916	1547	1234	768	485
Taylor KO Index	23.4	21.3	19.4	17.5	15.8	14.2	12.7	10.0	8.0
Path • Inches	-1.5	+1.0	0.0	-5.2	-15.4	-31.8	-54.5	-133.1	-276.1
Wind Drift • Inches	0.0	0.7	2.9	6.8	12.6	20.6	37.3	64.4	113.0

Hornady 150-grain InterBond (82219)
G1 Ballistic Coefficient = 0.416

Distance • Yards	Muzzle	100	200	300	400	500	600	800	1000
Velocity • fps	3375	3126	2891	2669	2456	2254	2063	1709	1406
Energy • Ft-lbs	3793	3255	2784	2371	2009	1692	1418	973	659
Taylor KO Index	22.3	20.6	19.1	17.6	16.2	14.9	13.6	11.3	9.3
Path • Inches	-1.5	+1.0	0.0	-5.2	-15.3	-31.2	-53.8	-125.7	-247.2
Wind Drift • Inches	0.0	0.6	2.5	5.9	10.9	17.6	26.5	51.4	88.4

Hornady 150-grain SST (8221) (Discontinued in 2005)
G1 Ballistic Coefficient = 0.404

Distance • Yards	Muzzle	100	200	300	400	500	600	800	1000
Velocity • fps	3375	3123	2882	2652	2434	2227	2030	1670	1366
Energy • Ft-lbs	3793	3248	2766	2343	1973	1652	1373	929	622
Taylor KO Index	22.3	20.6	19.0	17.5	16.1	14.7	13.4	11.0	9.0
Path • Inches	-1.5	+1.0	0.0	-5.4	-15.8	-32.2	-54.6	-128.4	-254.3
Wind Drift • Inches	0.0	0.6	2.6	6.1	11.2	18.3	27.5	53.6	92.3

Weatherby 165-grain Hornady Pointed-Expanding (H 300 165 SP)   G1 Ballistic Coefficient = 0.387

Distance • Yards	Muzzle	100	200	300	400	500	600	800	1000
Velocity • fps	3390	3123	2872	2634	2409	2195	1990	1621	1317
Energy • Ft-lbs	4210	3573	3021	2542	2126	1765	1452	963	635
Taylor KO Index	24.6	22.7	20.9	19.1	17.5	15.9	14.4	11.8	9.6
Path • Inches	-1.5	+1.0	0.0	-5.3	-15.5	-31.8	-55.4	-131.3	-262.8
Wind Drift • Inches	0.0	0.6	2.7	6.3	11.7	19.1	28.8	56.5	97.8

Weatherby 165-grain Nosler Ballistic Tip (N 300 165 BST)   G1 Ballistic Coefficient = 0.475

Distance • Yards	Muzzle	100	200	300	400	500	600	800	1000
Velocity • fps	3350	3133	2927	2730	2542	2361	2187	1862	1572
Energy • Ft-lbs	4111	3596	3138	2730	2367	2042	1753	1271	906
Taylor KO Index	24.3	22.7	21.3	19.8	18.5	17.1	15.9	13.5	11.4
Path • Inches	-1.5	+1.0	0.0	-5.1	-14.8	-30.0	-51.4	-117.4	-224.5
Wind Drift • Inches	0.0	0.5	2.2	5.1	9.4	15.2	22.7	43.5	73.8

Weatherby 180-grain Nosler Partition (N 300 180 PT)   G1 Ballistic Coefficient = 0.474

Distance • Yards	Muzzle	100	200	300	400	500	600	800	1000
Velocity • fps	3240	3028	2826	2634	2449	2271	2102	1784	1503
Energy • Ft-lbs	4195	3665	3194	2772	2396	2062	1764	1272	904
Taylor KO Index	25.7	24.0	22.4	20.9	19.4	18.0	16.6	14.1	11.9
Path • Inches	-1.5	+1.2	0.0	-5.5	-16.0	-32.4	-55.4	-126.8	-243.2
Wind Drift • Inches	0.0	0.6	2.3	5.4	9.9	16.0	23.8	45.8	77.8

Weatherby 180-grain Hornady Pointed-Expanding (H 300 180 SP)   G1 Ballistic Coefficient = 0.425

Distance • Yards	Muzzle	100	200	300	400	500	600	800	1000
Velocity • fps	3240	3004	2781	2569	2366	2173	1987	1649	1363
Energy • Ft-lbs	4195	3607	3091	2637	2237	1886	1579	1087	743
Taylor KO Index	25.7	23.8	22.0	20.3	18.7	17.2	15.7	13.1	10.8
Path • Inches	-1.5	+1.2	0.0	-5.7	-16.6	-33.8	-58.4	-136.1	-267.1
Wind Drift • Inches	0.0	0.6	2.6	6.0	11.2	18.2	27.3	53.1	91.1

Federal 180-grain Sierra GameKing BTSP (P300WBC) (Discontinued in 2005)   G1 Ballistic Coefficient = 0.536

Distance • Yards	Muzzle	100	200	300	400	500	600	800	1000
Velocity • fps	3190	3010	2830	2660	2490	2330	2179	1890	1628
Energy • Ft-lbs	4065	3610	3195	2820	2480	2175	1897	1428	1060
Taylor KO Index	25.3	23.8	22.4	21.1	19.7	18.5	17.3	15.0	12.9
Path • Inches	-1.5	+1.2	0.0	-5.6	-16.0	-31.0	-54.5	-122.7	-230.5
Wind Drift • Inches	0.0	0.5	2.1	4.8	8.8	14.2	21.0	40.0	67.1

Federal 180-grain Nosler Partition (P300WBA)   G1 Ballistic Coefficient = 0.474

Distance • Yards	Muzzle	100	200	300	400	500	600	800	1000
Velocity • fps	3190	2980	2780	2590	2400	2230	2062	1749	1474
Energy • Ft-lbs	4055	3540	3080	2670	2305	1985	1700	1223	869
Taylor KO Index	25.3	23.6	22.0	20.5	19.0	17.7	16.3	13.9	11.7
Path • Inches	-1.5	+1.2	0.0	-5.7	-16.7	-33.6	57.4	-131.4	-252.2
Wind Drift • Inches	0.0	0.6	2.4	5.5	10.1	16.3	24.4	46.9	79.6

Speer 180-grain Grand Slam (24516) (Discontinued in 2004)   G1 Ballistic Coefficient = 0.416

Distance • Yards	Muzzle	100	200	300	400	500	600	800	1000
Velocity • fps	3125	2890	2668	2456	2254	2062	1879	1549	1279
Energy • Ft-lbs	3903	3339	2844	2411	2032	1700	1412	959	654
Taylor KO Index	24.8	22.9	21.1	19.5	17.9	16.3	14.9	12.3	10.1
Path • Inches	-1.5	+1.3	0.0	-6.2	-18.2	-37.1	-64.2	-150.4	-297.2
Wind Drift • Inches	0.0	0.7	2.8	6.5	12.1	19.7	29.6	57.7	99.2

Federal 180-grain Trophy Bonded Bear Claw (P300WBT1) G1 Ballistic Coefficient = 0.406

Distance • Yards	Muzzle	100	200	300	400	500	600	800	1000
Velocity • fps	3100	2860	2640	2430	2220	2029	1835	1504	1239
Energy • Ft-lbs	3840	3277	2785	2355	1975	1645	1346	904	614
Taylor KO Index	24.6	22.7	20.9	19.2	17.6	16.0	14.5	11.9	9.8
Path • Inches	-1.5	+1.4	0.0	-6.4	-18.7	-38.0	-66.2	-156.1	-310.4
Wind Drift • Inches	0.0	0.7	2.9	6.8	12.6	20.5	30.9	60.5	104.0

A² 180-grain Monolithic; Dead Tough (None) G1 Ballistic Coefficient = 0.264

Distance • Yards	Muzzle	100	200	300	400	500	600	800	1000
Velocity • fps	3180	2811	2471	2155	1863	1602	1375	1065	916
Energy • Ft-lbs	4041	3158	2440	1856	1387	1026	755	454	336
Taylor KO Index	25.2	22.3	19.6	17.1	14.8	12.7	10.9	8.4	7.3
Path • Inches	-1.5	+1.5	0.0	-7.2	-21.8	-46.7	-85.8	-227.9	-489.5
Wind Drift • Inches	0.0	1.1	4.5	10.8	20.5	34.4	53.4	108.6	182.9

Hornady 180-grain SP (8222) G1 Ballistic Coefficient = 0.425

Distance • Yards	Muzzle	100	200	300	400	500	600	800	1000
Velocity • fps	3120	2891	2673	2466	2268	2079	1898	1572	1301
Energy • Ft-lbs	3890	3340	2856	2430	2055	1727	1441	988	677
Taylor KO Index	24.7	22.9	21.2	19.5	18.0	16.5	15.0	12.5	10.3
Path • Inches	-1.5	+1.3	0.0	-6.2	-18.1	-36.9	-63.7	-148.7	-292.3
Wind Drift • Inches	0.0	0.7	2.7	6.4	11.8	19.2	28.9	56.2	96.4

Remington 180-grain Core-Lokt Pointed Soft Point (R300WB1) G1 Ballistic Coefficient = 0.383

Distance • Yards	Muzzle	100	200	300	400	500	600	800	1000
Velocity • fps	3120	2866	2627	2400	2184	1976	1786	1445	1185
Energy • Ft-lbs	3890	3284	2758	2301	1905	1565	1275	835	561
Taylor KO Index	24.7	22.7	20.8	19.0	17.3	15.7	14.1	11.4	9.4
Path • Inches	-1.5	+1.4	0.0	-6.4	-18.9	-38.7	-67.5	-161.0	-324.7
Wind Drift • Inches	0.0	0.7	3.1	7.2	13.3	21.8	33.0	65.0	112.2

Weatherby 180-grain BST (N 300 180 BST) G1 Ballistic Coefficient = 0.507

Distance • Yards	Muzzle	100	200	300	400	500	600	800	1000
Velocity • fps	3250	3051	2806	2676	2503	2334	2173	1869	1596
Energy • Ft-lbs	4223	3721	3271	2867	2504	2178	1888	1397	1018
Taylor KO Index	25.7	24.2	22.2	21.2	19.8	18.5	17.2	14.8	12.6
Path • Inches	-1.5	+1.1	0.0	-5.4	-15.6	-31.4	-53.5	-121.2	-223.0
Wind Drift • Inches	0.0	0.5	1.9	4.5	8.2	13.2	19.7	37.6	63.5

Weatherby 180-grain Barnes-X (B 300 180 XS) G1 Ballistic Coefficient = 0.511

Distance • Yards	Muzzle	100	200	300	400	500	600	800	1000
Velocity • fps	3190	2995	2809	2631	2459	2294	2135	1836	1569
Energy • Ft-lbs	4067	3586	3154	2766	2417	2103	1822	1348	984
Taylor KO Index	25.3	23.7	22.2	20.8	19.5	18.2	16.9	14.5	12.4
Path • Inches	-1.5	+1.2	0.0	-5.6	-16.2	-32.6	-55.6	-125.8	-238.2
Wind Drift • Inches	0.0	0.5	2.2	5.1	9.3	15.0	22.3	42.5	71.7

Hornady 180-grain SST (8223) G1 Ballistic Coefficient = 0.480

Distance • Yards	Muzzle	100	200	300	400	500	600	800	1000
Velocity • fps	3120	2916	2722	2536	2357	2186	2022	1717	1450
Energy • Ft-lbs	3890	3399	2961	2570	2220	1909	1634	1178	840
Taylor KO Index	24.7	23.1	21.6	20.1	18.7	17.3	16.0	13.6	11.5
Path • Inches	-1.5	+1.3	0.0	-6.0	-17.4	-35.1	-60.0	-137.0	-261.7
Wind Drift • Inches	0.0	0.5	2.2	5.0	9.2	14.9	22.3	42.9	72.7

Remington 190-grain Pointed Soft Point BT (PRB300WBA) (Discontinued in 2005)

G1 Ballistic Coefficient = 0.479

Distance • Yards	Muzzle	100	200	300	400	500	600	800	1000
Velocity • fps	3030	2830	2638	2455	2279	2110	1950	1651	1394
Energy • Ft-lbs	3873	3378	2936	2542	2190	1878	1604	1151	820
Taylor KO Index	25.3	23.7	22.1	20.5	19.1	17.6	16.3	13.8	11.7
Path • Inches	-1.5	+1.4	0.0	-6.4	-18.6	-37.6	-64.2	-145.0	-282.3
Wind Drift • Inches	0.0	0.6	2.5	5.8	10.7	17.4	26.0	50.0	84.8

Weatherby 200-grain Nosler Partition (N 300 200 PT)

G1 Ballistic Coefficient = 0.481

Distance • Yards	Muzzle	100	200	300	400	500	600	800	1000
Velocity • fps	3060	2860	2668	2485	2308	2139	1977	1677	1416
Energy • Ft-lbs	4158	3631	3161	2741	2366	2032	1735	1249	891
Taylor KO Index	26.9	25.2	23.5	21.9	20.3	18.8	17.4	14.8	12.5
Path • Inches	-1.5	+1.4	0.0	-6.3	-18.2	-36.6	-62.7	-143.3	-274.9
Wind Drift • Inches	0.0	0.6	2.5	5.7	10.5	17.0	25.4	49.0	83.1

Remington 200-grain Swift A-Frame PSP (RS300WBB) (Discontinued in 2004)

G1 Ballistic Coefficient = 0.396

Distance • Yards	Muzzle	100	200	300	400	500	600	800	100
Velocity • fps	2925	2690	2467	2254	2052	1861	1683	1371	1142
Energy • Ft-lbs	3799	3213	2701	2256	1870	1538	1258	835	579
Taylor KO Index	25.7	23.7	21.7	19.8	18.1	16.4	14.8	12.1	10.0
Path • Inches	-1.5	+1.7	0.0	-7.4	-21.6	-44.2	-122.0	-182.7	-365.8
Wind Drift • Inches	0.0	0.8	3.2	7.6	14.1	23.0	34.8	68.4	117.1

Weatherby 220-grain Hornady Round Nose-Expanding (H 300 220 RN)

G1 Ballistic Coefficient = 0.300

Distance • Yards	Muzzle	100	200	300	400	500	600	800	1000
Velocity • fps	2845	2543	2260	1996	1751	1530	1337	1071	933
Energy • Ft-lbs	3954	3158	2495	1946	1497	1143	873	560	426
Taylor KO Index	27.5	24.6	21.9	19.3	16.9	14.8	12.9	10.4	9.0
Path • Inches	-1.5	+2.0	0.0	-8.8	-26.4	-55.2	-100.0	-255.0	-528.7
Wind Drift • Inches	0.0	1.1	4.5	10.8	20.5	34.2	52.8	104.8	173.9

Giant eland, like this one from the C.A.R., are considered by many hunters to be the most difficult large antelope to hunt in Africa today.
(Photo from *A Sporting Life* by José A. Martínez de Hoz, 2005, Safari Press)

.300 Remington Ultra Magnum

It's clear that just plain old "magnum" isn't good enough anymore. Now we have the .300 ULTRA Magnum (introduced in 1999). This is Remington's entry into the .30-caliber class, where they have been absent for many years. The .300 RUM (now that's an unfortunate abbreviation) is something a little different from the standard belted magnum. For openers, it's beltless. It is actually based on a .404 Jeffery case necked to .308 and with a rebated head. It follows a recent trend to do away with the belt on magnum cartridges. While the data below are based on the SAAMI standard barrel length of 24 inches, you may find 26-inch data quoted by various sources. That extra two inches makes about a 50 fps of difference in muzzle velocity.

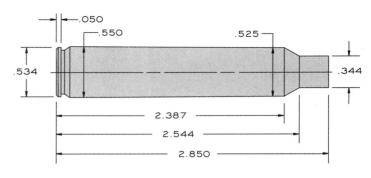

Relative Recoil Factor = 2.64

Specifications

Controlling Agency for Standardization of this Ammunition: SAAMI

Bullet Weight Grains	Velocity fps	Maximum Average Pressure	
		Copper Crusher	Transducer
180	3,250	N/A	65,000 psi

Standard barrel for velocity testing: 24 inches long—1 turn in 10-inch twist

Availability

Remington 150-grain Swift Scirocco (PR300UM5)
G1 Ballistic Coefficient = 0.436

Distance • Yards	Muzzle	100	200	300	400	500	600	800	1000
Velocity • fps	3450	3208	2980	2762	2556	2358	2170	1820	1512
Energy • Ft-lbs	3964	3427	2956	2541	2175	1852	1569	1103	761
Taylor KO Index	22.8	21.2	19.7	18.2	16.9	15.6	14.3	12.0	10.0
Path • Inches	-1.5	+0.9	0.0	-4.9	-14.3	-29.0	-50.1	-115.7	-223.8
Wind Drift • Inches	0.0	0.5	2.1	4.9	9.0	14.6	21.8	42.1	71.9

Federal 180-grain Trophy Bonded Bear Claw (P300RUMT1) (Discontinued in 2005)
G1 Ballistic Coefficient = 0.404

Distance • Yards	Muzzle	100	200	300	400	500	600	800	1000
Velocity • fps	3250	3000	2770	2550	2430	2130	1939	1591	1304
Energy • Ft-lbs	4220	3605	3065	2590	2180	1820	1503	1012	680
Taylor KO Index	25.7	23.8	21.9	20.2	19.2	16.9	15.4	12.6	10.3
Path • Inches	-1.5	+1.2	0.0	-5.7	-16.8	-34.4	-59.6	-140.2	-278.4
Wind Drift • Inches	0.0	0.7	2.7	6.4	11.8	19.3	29.0	56.7	97.7

Remington 180-grain Swift Scirocco (PR300UM3)
G1 Ballistic Coefficient = 0.501

Distance • Yards	Muzzle	100	200	300	400	500	600	800	1000
Velocity • fps	3250	3048	2856	2672	2495	2325	2163	1856	1581
Energy • Ft-lbs	4221	3714	3260	2853	2487	2160	1870	1378	999
Taylor KO Index	25.7	24.1	22.6	21.2	19.8	18.4	17.1	14.7	12.5
Path • Inches	-1.5	+1.1	0.0	-5.4	-15.6	-31.5	-53.8	-121.9	-231.4
Wind Drift • Inches	0.0	0.5	2.2	5.0	9.2	14.9	22.2	42.4	71.6

Remington 180-grain Nosler Partition (PR300UM1) (Discontinued in 2005)
G1 Ballistic Coefficient = 0.473

Distance • Yards	Muzzle	100	200	300	400	500	600	800	1000
Velocity • fps	3250	3037	2834	2640	2454	2276	2106	1788	1507
Energy • Ft-lbs	4221	3686	3201	2786	2407	2071	1773	1278	908
Taylor KO Index	25.7	24.1	22.4	20.9	19.4	18.0	16.7	14.2	11.9
Path • Inches	-1.5	+1.1	0.0	-5.5	-15.9	-32.2	-55.1	-126.1	-241.8
Wind Drift • Inches	0.0	0.6	2.3	5.4	9.9	16.0	23.8	45.8	77.6

Remington 180-grain Core-Lokt Pointed Soft Point (PR300UM4)
G1 Ballistic Coefficient = 0.389

Distance • Yards	Muzzle	100	200	300	400	500	600	800	1000
Velocity • fps	3230	2988	2742	2508	2287	2076	1881	1530	1249
Energy • Ft-lbs	4171	3535	2983	2503	2086	1725	1415	935	623
Taylor KO Index	25.6	23.7	21.7	19.9	18.1	16.4	14.9	12.1	9.9
Path • Inches	-1.5	+1.2	0.0	-5.9	-17.4	-35.5	-61.7	-146.0	-290.5
Wind Drift • Inches	0.0	0.6	2.6	6.0	11.2	18.3	27.7	54.3	93.9

Remington 200-grain Nosler Partition (PR300UM2) (Discontinued in 2005)
G1 Ballistic Coefficient = 0.482

Distance • Yards	Muzzle	100	200	300	400	500	600	800	1000
Velocity • fps	3025	2826	2636	2454	2279	2111	1952	1655	1399
Energy • Ft-lbs	4063	3547	3086	2673	2308	1978	1692	1217	869
Taylor KO Index	26.6	24.9	23.2	21.6	20.1	18.6	17.2	14.6	12.3
Path • Inches	-1.5	+1.4	0.0	-6.4	-18.6	-37.6	-64.3	-147.0	-282.0
Wind Drift • Inches	0.0	0.6	2.5	5.8	10.7	17.3	25.8	49.7	84.3

Chris Kinsey shot this Barbary sheep or aoudad in Chad, which is once more open to hunting after having been closed for over two decades. (Photo from *African Hunter II,* by Craig Boddington and Peter Flack, 2004, Safari Press)

7.82mm (.308) Lazzeroni Warbird

If the 7.82mm Patriot is Lazzeroni's "short" magnum, the Warbird is certainly a "long" magnum. This cartridge shares the lead in the .30-caliber velocity derby with the .30-378 Weatherby. It is an extremely potent cartridge and one with rather specialized applications.

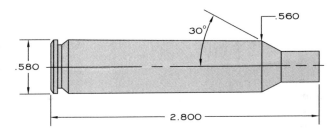

Relative Recoil Factor = 2.80

Specifications

Controlling Agency for Standardization of this Ammunition: Factory

Availability

Lazzeroni 130-grain (782WB130)

G1 Ballistic Coefficient = 0.429

Distance • Yards	Muzzle	100	200	300	400	500	600	800	1000
Velocity • fps	3975	3697	3438	3193	2962	2742	2533	2143	1791
Energy • Ft-lbs	4562	3948	3412	2944	2533	2172	1853	1327	926
Taylor KO Index	22.7	21.1	19.7	18.3	16.9	15.7	14.5	12.3	10.2
Path • Inches	-1.5	+0.5	0.0	-3.5	-10.4	-21.2	-36.7	-84.9	-164.2
Wind Drift • Inches	0.0	0.5	2.0	4.7	8.6	13.8	20.6	39.3	66.7

Lazzeroni 150-grain Nosler Partition (782WB150P)

G1 Ballistic Coefficient = 0.491

Distance • Yards	Muzzle	100	200	300	400	500	600	800	1000
Velocity • fps	3775	3542	3323	3114	2915	2724	2542	2199	1884
Energy • Ft-lbs	4747	4181	3679	3231	2831	2473	2154	1611	1182
Taylor KO Index	24.9	23.4	21.9	20.6	19.2	18.1	16.8	14.5	12.4
Path • Inches	-1.5	+0.6	0.0	-3.8	-11.2	-22.6	38.8	-88.0	-166.6
Wind Drift • Inches	0.0	0.4	1.9	4.3	7.8	12.6	18.6	35.3	59.3

Lazzeroni 180-grain Nosler Partition (782WB180P)

G1 Ballistic Coefficient = 0.549

Distance • Yards	Muzzle	100	200	300	400	500	600	800	1000
Velocity • fps	3550	3352	3163	2983	2810	2643	2483	2179	1897
Energy • Ft-lbs	5038	4493	4001	3558	3157	2794	2466	1899	1439
Taylor KO Index	29.1	26.5	25.1	23.6	22.3	20.9	19.7	17.3	15.0
Path • Inches	-1.5	+0.9	0.0	-4.3	-12.4	-25.0	-42.6	-95.4	-177.8
Wind Drift • Inches	0.0	0.4	1.8	4.1	7.4	11.9	17.7	33.3	55.5

Lazzeroni 200-grain Swift A-Frame (782WB200A)

G1 Ballistic Coefficient = 0.551

Distance • Yards	Muzzle	100	200	300	400	500	600	800	1000
Velocity • fps	3350	3162	2983	2810	2644	2484	2330	2038	1768
Energy • Ft-lbs	4985	4442	3952	3509	3106	2742	2412	1844	1389
Taylor KO Index	29.5	27.8	26.3	24.7	23.3	21.9	20.5	17.9	15.6
Path • Inches	-1.5	+1.0	0.0	-4.9	-14.2	-28.5	-48.4	-108.4	-202.3
Wind Drift • Inches	0.0	0.5	1.9	4.4	8.0	12.8	19.0	36.0	60.1

.30-378 Weatherby

Whenever a new cartridge case is introduced, the wildcat builders have a field day. The basic case is necked down, necked up, improved, and otherwise modified to conform to the whims of the wildcat "designer." The .378 Weatherby offered a tremendous opportunity. This big case was necked to both .338 and .30 calibers soon after its introduction. The wildcat versions have been around for a long time. I fired a .30-378 in 1965, and that certainly wasn't the first gun in this caliber. Recently Weatherby began offering guns and ammunition in both .30-378 and .333-378 calibers.

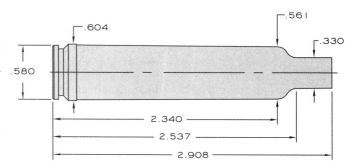

Relative Recoil Factor = 2.55

Specifications

Controlling Agency for Standardization of this Ammunition: Factory
Standard barrel for velocity testing: 26 inches long—1 turn in 10-inch twist

Availability

Weatherby 165-grain Nosler Ballistic Tip (N 303 165 BST)
G1 Ballistic Coefficient = 0.475

Distance • Yards	Muzzle	100	200	300	400	500	600	800	1000
Velocity • fps	3500	3275	3062	2859	2665	2480	2301	1966	1664
Energy • Ft-lbs	4488	3930	3435	2995	2603	2253	1940	1417	1014
Taylor KO Index	25.4	23.8	22.2	20.8	19.3	18.0	16.7	14.3	11.9
Path • Inches	-1.5	+0.9	0.0	-4.6	-13.4	-27.2	-46.6	-106.3	-202.8
Wind Drift • Inches	0.0	0.5	2.1	4.7	8.9	14.3	21.4	40.9	69.1

Weatherby 180-grain Barnes-X (B 303 180 XS)
G1 Ballistic Coefficient = 0.511

Distance • Yards	Muzzle	100	200	300	400	500	600	800	1000
Velocity • fps	3450	3243	3046	2858	2678	2504	2337	2022	1734
Energy • Ft-lbs	4757	4204	3709	3264	2865	2506	2183	1634	1202
Taylor KO Index	27.3	25.7	24.1	22.6	21.2	19.8	18.5	16.0	13.7
Path • Inches	-1.5	+0.9	0.0	-4.7	-13.6	-27.4	-46.6	-105.4	-198.8
Wind Drift • Inches	0.0	0.5	2.0	4.6	8.4	13.5	20.0	38.0	63.8

Weatherby 180-grain BST (N 303 180 BST)
G1 Ballistic Coefficient = 0.507

Distance • Yards	Muzzle	100	200	300	400	500	600	800	1000
Velocity • fps	3420	3213	3015	2826	2645	2471	2305	1990	1703
Energy • Ft-lbs	4676	4126	3634	3194	2797	2441	2124	1583	1160
Taylor KO Index	27.1	25.4	23.9	22.4	20.9	19.6	19.3	15.8	13.5
Path • Inches	-1.5	+0.9	0.0	-4.8	-13.9	-28.0	-47.8	-108.0	-203.7
Wind Drift • Inches	0.0	0.4	1.8	4.2	7.7	12.4	18.4	35.0	58.8

Weatherby 200-grain Nosler Partition (N 303 200 PT)
G1 Ballistic Coefficient = 0.481

Distance • Yards	Muzzle	100	200	300	400	500	600	800	1000
Velocity • fps	3160	2955	2759	2572	2392	2220	2054	1746	1475
Energy • Ft-lbs	4434	3877	3381	2938	2541	2188	1873	1354	966
Taylor KO Index	27.8	26.0	24.3	22.6	21.0	19.5	18.1	15.4	13.0
Path • Inches	-1.5	+1.2	0.0	-5.8	-16.9	-34.1	-58.3	-133.1	-254.9
Wind Drift • Inches	0.0	0.6	2.4	5.5	10.1	16.3	24.3	46.7	79.1

.303 British

The .303 British was Britain's service rifle cartridge from 1888 until it was replaced around 1957 by the 7.62 NATO round (.308). It started life as a lack-powder number firing a 215-grain bullet. When smokeless powder came into service use, the black powder was replaced with Cordite. Cordite is a tubular "powder" that was manufactured for this cartridge in sticks of about 0.040 inches in diameter and 1.625 inches in length, like pencil leads. Since it would have been almost impossible to load the Cordite sticks into the 0.310-inch-diameter case mouth, a flock of little old ladies in tennis shoes loaded the sticks into the cases by hand before the necks and shoulders were formed. After the propellant was inserted, the case forming was completed and the bullet seated. Talk about hard ways to do easy things.

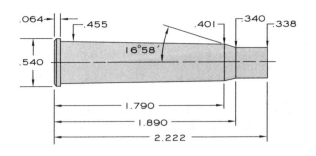

Relative Recoil Factor = 1.98

Specifications

Controlling Agency for Standardization of this Ammunition: SAAMI

Bullet Weight Grains	Velocity fps	Maximum Average Pressure	
		Copper Crusher	Transducer
150	2,685	45,000 cup	49,000 psi
180	2,450	45,000 cup	49,000 psi
215	2,155	45,000 cup	49,000 psi

Standard barrel for velocity testing: 24 inches long—1 turn in 10-inch twist

Availability

Hornady 150-grain SP-Light Magnum (8525) (Discontinued in 2005)
G1 Ballistic Coefficient = 0.356

Distance • Yards	Muzzle	100	200	300	400	500	600	800	1000
Velocity • fps	2830	2570	2325	2094	1884	1690	1507	1211	1031
Energy • Ft-lbs	2667	2199	1800	1461	1185	952	757	489	354
Taylor KO Index	19.0	17.3	15.6	14.1	12.7	11.4	10.1	8.1	6.9
Path • Inches	-1.5	+2.0	0.0	-8.4	-24.6	-50.3	-88.8	-216.8	-442.5
Wind Drift • Inches	0.0	0.9	3.8	9.0	16.8	27.7	37.9	75.0	127.1

Federal 150-grain Soft Point (303B)
G1 Ballistic Coefficient = 0.357

Distance • Yards	Muzzle	100	200	300	400	500	600	800	1000
Velocity • fps	2690	2440	2210	1980	1780	1590	1420	1153	999
Energy • Ft-lbs	2400	1980	1620	1310	1055	840	672	443	333
Taylor KO Index	18.1	16.4	14.9	13.3	12.0	10.7	9.5	7.7	6.7
Path • Inches	-1.5	+2.2	0.0	-9.4	-27.6	-56.8	-99.8	-243.8	-493.7
Wind Drift • Inches	0.0	1.0	4.1	9.6	18.1	29.8	40.8	80.2	132.9

Hornady 150-grain Soft Point (8225)
G1 Ballistic Coefficient = 0.361

Distance • Yards	Muzzle	100	200	300	400	500	600	800	1000
Velocity • fps	2685	2441	2210	1992	1767	1598	1427	1161	1004
Energy • Ft-lbs	2401	1984	1627	1321	1064	850	679	449	336
Taylor KO Index	18.1	16.4	14.9	13.4	11.9	10.8	9.6	7.8	6.7
Path • Inches	-1.5	+1.0	0.0	-9.3	-27.4	-56.5	-99.5	-242.4	-490.0
Wind Drift • Inches	0.0	1.0	4.0	9.5	17.9	29.5	40.3	79.2	132.4

Sellier & Bellot 150-grain Soft Point (SBS30304)
G1 Ballistic Coefficient = 0.276

Distance • Yards	Muzzle	100	200	300	400	500	600	800	1000
Velocity • fps	2654	2322	2032	1778	1534	1326	1163	972	863
Energy • Ft-lbs	2341	1792	1372	1050	784	586	451	315	248
Taylor KO Index	17.7	15.5	13.5	11.8	10.2	8.8	7.8	6.5	5.8
Path • Inches	-1.5	+2.4	0.0	-10.8	-32.8	-69.8	-127.2	-325.4	-660.2
Wind Drift • Inches	0.0	1.3	5.5	13.3	25.4	42.6	65.3	125.8	201.7

PMC 174-grain Hollow Point Boat Tail Match (303SMA)

G1 Ballistic Coefficient = 0.495

Distance • Yards	Muzzle	100	200	300	400	500	600	800	1000
Velocity • fps	2425	2254	2091	1936	1788	1651	1520	1294	1125
Energy • Ft-lbs	2272	1963	1690	1448	1235	1053	893	647	489
Taylor KO Index	18.8	17.5	16.2	15.0	13.9	12.8	11.8	10.1	8.7
Path • Inches	-1.5	+2.7	0.0	-10.6	-30.6	-61.3	-104.9	-240.5	-461.3
Wind Drift • Inches	0.0	0.8	3.3	7.8	14.4	23.3	31.4	60.1	100.0

UMC (Remington) 174-grain MC (L303B1)

G1 Ballistic Coefficient = 0.315

Distance • Yards	Muzzle	100	200	300	400	500	600	800	1000
Velocity • fps	2475	2209	1960	1729	1520	1337	1189	1003	896
Energy • Ft-lbs	2366	1885	1484	1155	892	691	547	389	310
Taylor KO Index	19.1	17.1	15.2	13.4	11.8	10.3	9.2	7.8	7.0
Path • Inches	-1.5	+2.8	0.0	-11.9	-35.6	-74.3	-133.4	-330.8	-659.0
Wind Drift • Inches	0.0	1.2	5.3	1.2.7	23.9	39.7	60.3	115.1	184.2

PMC 174-grain Full Metal Jacket (303A)

G1 Ballistic Coefficient = 0.459

Distance • Yards	Muzzle	100	200	300	400	500	600	800	1000
Velocity • fps	2400	2216	2042	1876	1720	1578	1445	1221	1068
Energy • Ft-lbs	2225	1898	1611	1360	1143	962	807	576	441
Taylor KO Index	18.6	17.1	15.8	14.5	13.3	12.2	11.2	9.4	8.3
Path • Inches	-1.5	+2.8	0.0	-11.2	-32.2	-64.9	-111.5	-259.0	-501.6
Wind Drift • Inches	0.0	0.9	3.7	8.6	15.9	25.9	38.9	74.6	123.5

Federal 180-grain Speer Hot-Cor SP (303AS)

G1 Ballistic Coefficient = 0.370

Distance • Yards	Muzzle	100	200	300	400	500	600	800	1000
Velocity • fps	2460	2230	2020	1820	1630	1460	1311	1093	968
Energy • Ft-lbs	2420	1985	1625	1315	1060	850	687	477	375
Taylor KO Index	19.9	18.0	16.3	14.7	13.2	11.8	10.5	8.8	7.8
Path • Inches	-1.5	+2.8	0.0	-11.3	-33.2	-68.1	-120.0	-289.9	-574.9
Wind Drift • Inches	0.0	1.1	4.5	10.6	20.0	32.6	44.4	85.7	139.9

Remington 180-grain Soft Point Core-Lokt (R303B1)

G1 Ballistic Coefficient = 0.247

Distance • Yards	Muzzle	100	200	300	400	500	600	800	1000
Velocity • fps	2460	2124	1817	1542	1311	1137	1023	884	788
Energy • Ft-lbs	2418	1803	1319	950	690	517	418	313	248
Taylor KO Index	19.9	17.1	14.7	12.5	10.6	9.2	8.2	7.1	6.3
Path • Inches	-1.5	+2.9	0.0	-13.6	-42.2	-91.0	-168.2	-420.7	833.5
Wind Drift • Inches	0.0	1.6	7.0	17.1	32.8	54.8	82.4	151.1	234.9

Winchester 180-grain Power-Point (X303B1)

G1 Ballistic Coefficient = 0.370

Distance • Yards	Muzzle	100	200	300	400	500	600	800	1000
Velocity • fps	2460	2233	2018	1816	1629	1459	1311	1093	968
Energy • Ft-lbs	2418	1993	1627	1318	1060	851	687	477	375
Taylor KO Index	19.9	18.0	16.3	14.7	13.2	11.8	10.5	8.8	7.8
Path • Inches	-1.5	+2.8	0.0	-11.3	-33.2	-68.2	-120.0	-289.9	-574.9
Wind Drift • Inches	0.0	1.1	4.5	10.6	19.8	32.6	49.3	95.2	155.4

PMC 180-grain SPBT Game (303HB)

G1 Ballistic Coefficient = 0.486

Distance • Yards	Muzzle	100	200	300	400	500	600	800	1000
Velocity • fps	2450	2276	2110	1951	1799	1656	1524	1293	1122
Energy • Ft-lbs	2399	2071	1780	1522	1295	1098	929	669	504
Taylor KO Index	19.8	18.4	17.0	15.8	14.5	13.4	12.2	10.4	9.0
Path • Inches	-1.5	+2.6	0.0	-10.4	-30.1	-60.2	-103.4	-237.8	-457.4
Wind Drift • Inches	0.0	0.8	3.3	7.8	14.4	23.5	35.1	67.4	112.3

PMC 180-grain Soft Point (303B)

G1 Ballistic Coefficient = 0.486

Distance • Yards	Muzzle	100	200	300	400	500	600	800	1000
Velocity • fps	2450	2276	2110	1951	1799	1656	1524	1293	1122
Energy • Ft-lbs	2399	2071	1780	1522	1295	1098	929	669	504
Taylor KO Index	19.8	18.4	17.0	15.8	14.5	13.4	12.2	10.4	9.0
Path • Inches	-1.5	+2.6	0.0	-10.4	-30.1	-60.2	-103.4	-237.8	-457.4
Wind Drift • Inches	0.0	0.8	3.3	7.8	14.4	23.5	35.1	67.4	112.3

Sellier & Bellot 180-grain Full Metal Jacket (SBA30303) & (SBA30301)

G1 Ballistic Coefficient = 0.564

Distance • Yards	Muzzle	100	200	300	400	500	600	800	1000
Velocity • fps	2438	2284	2140	2006	1873	1745	1625	1407	1227
Energy • Ft-lbs	2382	2092	1836	1613	1402	1218	1055	791	602
Taylor KO Index	19.5	18.3	17.1	16.0	15.0	14.0	13.0	11.3	9.8
Path • Inches	-1.5	+2.6	0.0	-10.1	-28.9	-57.6	-97.8	-220.0	-414.0
Wind Drift • Inches	0.0	0.7	2.9	6.7	12.3	19.8	29.5	56.1	93.3

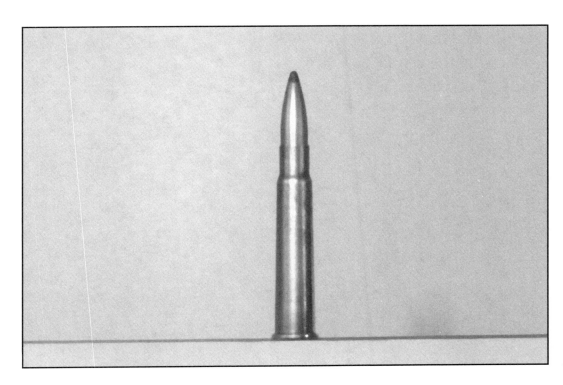

.303 British.

.32-20 Winchester

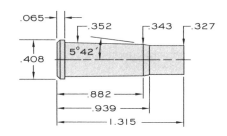

The .32-20 dates back to 1882. That's about 120 years ago. Winchester designed the .32-20 to be a midpower rifle cartridge, but it was also useful in revolvers. As is true with many of these old designations, the .32-20 isn't a .32 at all. The bore diameter is 0.305 inch. Today two companies make ammunition for this old-timer. Velocities and pressures are very low. The .32-20 isn't the caliber you would choose if you wanted a flat-shooting varmint rifle.

Relative Recoil Factor = 0.55

Specifications

Controlling Agency for Standardization of this Ammunition: SAAMI

Bullet Weight Grains	Velocity fps	Maximum Average Pressure	
		Copper Crusher	Transducer
100	1,200	16,000 cup	N/S

Standard barrel for velocity testing: 24 inches long—1 turn in 20-inch twist

Availability

Remington 100-grain Lead (R32201)

G1 Ballistic Coefficient = 0.167

Distance • Yards	Muzzle	100	200	300	400	500	600	800	1000
Velocity • fps	1210	1021	913	834	769	712	660	569	489
Energy • Ft-lbs	325	231	185	154	131	113	97	72	53
Taylor KO Index	5.4	4.5	4.1	3.7	3.4	3.2	2.9	2.5	2.1
Path • Inches	-1.5	+15.8	0.0	-57.5	-165.1	-331.5	-552.1	-1252	-2373
Wind Drift • Inches	0.0	4.2	15.5	32.4	54.8	82.6	116.0	201.2	314.4

Winchester 100-grain Lead (X32201)

G1 Ballistic Coefficient = 0.167

Distance • Yards	Muzzle	100	200	300	400	500	600	800	1000
Velocity • fps	1210	1021	913	834	769	712	660	569	489
Energy • Ft-lbs	325	231	185	154	131	113	97	72	53
Taylor KO Index	5.4	4.5	4.1	3.7	3.4	3.2	2.9	2.5	2.1
Path • Inches	-1.5	+15.8	0.0	-57.5	-165.1	-331.5	-552.1	-1252	-2373
Wind Drift • Inches	0.0	4.2	15.5	32.4	54.8	82.6	116.0	201.2	314.4

.32 Winchester Special

Winchester's .32 Winchester Special cartridge is another very old number. This cartridge is a real .32, using bullets that are 0.321 inch in diameter. It can be thought of as the .30-30 necked up to .32 caliber. Starting in 1895, Winchester's Model 94 rifles were available chambered for the .32 Winchester Special. There have not been any guns built in this caliber since about 1960, and you can expect the caliber to be dropped from the inventory in the near future.

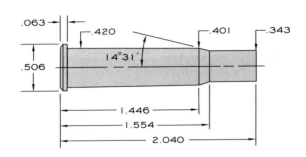

Relative Recoil Factor = 1.95

Specifications

Controlling Agency for Standardization of this Ammunition: SAAMI

Bullet Weight Grains	Velocity fps	Maximum Average Pressure	
		Copper Crusher	Transducer
170	2,235	38,000 cup	42,000 psi

Standard barrel for velocity testing: 24 inches long—1 turn in 16-inch twist

Availability

Federal 170-grain Hi-Shok Soft Point (32A)
G1 Ballistic Coefficient = 0.238

Distance • Yards	Muzzle	100	200	300	400	500	600	800	1000
Velocity • fps	2250	1920	1630	1370	1180	1040	956	837	747
Energy • Ft-lbs	1910	1395	1000	710	520	409	345	265	211
Taylor KO Index	17.5	14.9	12.7	10.6	9.2	8.1	7.5	6.5	5.8
Path • Inches	-1.5	+4.0	0.0	-17.2	-52.3	-109.8	-208.3	-504.5	-979.5
Wind Drift • Inches	0.0	1.9	8.4	20.4	38.8	63.3	92.9	164.4	251.2

Remington 170-grain Core-Lokt Soft Point (R32WS2)
G1 Ballistic Coefficient = 0.239

Distance • Yards	Muzzle	100	200	300	400	500	600	800	1000
Velocity • fps	2250	1921	1626	1372	1175	1044	957	839	749
Energy • Ft-lbs	1910	1393	998	710	521	411	346	266	212
Taylor KO Index	17.5	14.9	12.6	10.7	9.1	8.1	7.5	6.5	5.7
Path • Inches	-1.5	+4.0	0.0	-17.3	-53.2	-114.2	-207.5	-502.7	-976.0
Wind Drift • Inches	0.0	1.9	8.4	20.3	38.6	63.0	92.4	163.8	250.2

Winchester 170-grain Power-Point (X32WS2)
G1 Ballistic Coefficient = 0.205

Distance • Yards	Muzzle	100	200	300	400	500	600	800	1000
Velocity • fps	2250	1870	1537	1267	1082	971	893	777	686
Energy • Ft-lbs	1911	1320	892	606	442	356	301	228	178
Taylor KO Index	17.5	14.5	11.9	9.8	8.4	7.5	7.0	6.1	5.3
Path • Inches	-1.5	+4.3	0.0	-19.2	-60.2	-130.8	-236.4	-571.2	-1113
Wind Drift • Inches	0.0	2.3	10.0	24.5	46.4	74.7	108.0	188.1	286.1

8x57mm Mauser JS

The 8x57mm Mauser was adopted as the standard German military cartridge in 1888. It has been around for a long time, and so have some of the guns that use this caliber. Exactly because some of these old guns still exist, the SAAMI pressure specifications are very modest (see below). Interestingly, the CIP (European) specifications allow the European manufacturers to load to considerably better performance. If you have an old gun, it might be prudent to use only ammunition made in the U.S., although the European ammunition is entirely satisfactory in modern guns. You may see three versions of this cartridge: JS, JR, and JRS. The JR and JRS versions are rimmed and are used in single-shot and multi-barrel guns.

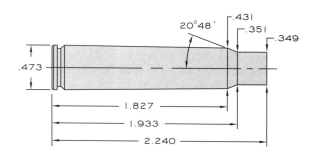

Relative Recoil Factor = 1.81

Specifications

Controlling Agency for Standardization of this Ammunition: SAAMI (see above)

Bullet Weight Grains	Velocity fps	Maximum Average Pressure	
		Copper Crusher	Transducer
170	2,340	37,000 cup	53,000 psi

Standard barrel for velocity testing: 24 inches long—1 turn in 9.5-inch twist

Availability

Federal 170-grain Hi-Shok Soft Point (8A)

G1 Ballistic Coefficient = 0.207

Distance • Yards	Muzzle	100	200	300	400	500	600	800	1000
Velocity • fps	2360	1970	1620	1330	1120	1000	916	795	701
Energy • Ft-lbs	2100	1465	995	670	475	375	317	239	186
Taylor KO Index	18.5	15.5	12.7	10.4	8.8	7.8	7.2	6.2	5.5
Path • Inches	-1.5	+3.8	0.0	-17.1	-52.9	-111.9	-215.6	-528.6	-1038
Wind Drift • Inches	0.0	2.1	9.2	22.7	43.5	71.0	103.9	183.3	280.1

PMC 170-grain Pointed Soft Point (8MA)

G1 Ballistic Coefficient = 0.341

Distance • Yards	Muzzle	100	200	300	400	500	600	800	1000
Velocity • fps	2250	2013	1793	1594	1419	1265	1143	988	892
Energy • Ft-lbs	1911	1530	1213	959	760	604	493	369	301
Taylor KO Index	17.6	15.8	14.1	12.5	11.1	9.9	9.0	7.8	7.0
Path • Inches	-1.5	+3.6	0.0	-14.4	-42.5	-88.1	-155.6	-375.1	-728.9
Wind Drift • Inches	0.0	1.3	5.6	13.3	24.9	40.9	61.4	114.5	180.3

Remington 170-grain Soft Point Core-Lokt (R8MSR)

G1 Ballistic Coefficient = 0.205

Distance • Yards	Muzzle	100	200	300	400	500	600	800	1000
Velocity • fps	2360	1969	1622	1333	1123	997	912	792	699
Energy • Ft-lbs	2102	1463	993	671	476	375	314	237	185
Taylor KO Index	18.5	15.4	12.7	10.5	8.8	7.8	7.2	6.2	5.5
Path • Inches	-1.5	+3.8	0.0	-17.2	-54.1	-118.6	-218.1	-549.3	-1103
Wind Drift • Inches	0.0	1.9	8.4	20.7	39.6	64.6	94.5	116.5	254.5

Winchester 170-grain Power-Point (X8MM)

G1 Ballistic Coefficient = 0.205

Distance • Yards	Muzzle	100	200	300	400	500	600	800	1000
Velocity • fps	2360	1969	1622	1333	1123	997	912	791	697
Energy • Ft-lbs	2102	1463	993	671	476	375	314	236	184
Taylor KO Index	18.5	15.4	12.7	10.5	8.8	7.8	7.2	6.2	5.5
Path • Inches	-1.5	+3.8	0.0	-17.2	-54.1	-118.6	-217.5	-533.2	-1048
Wind Drift • Inches	0.0	2.1	9.3	23.0	44.0	71.8	105.0	184.9	282.5

Hirtenberger 175-grain Sierra SBT (82200457)
G1 Ballistic Coefficient = 0.475

Distance • Yards	Muzzle	100	200	300	400	500	600	800	1000
Velocity • fps	2559	2377	2203	2036	1877	1726	1585	1338	1150
Energy • Ft-lbs	2545	2197	1887	1312	1370	1159	977	696	514
Taylor KO Index	20.7	19.2	17.8	16.4	15.2	13.9	12.8	10.8	9.3
Path • Inches	-1.5	+2.3	0.0	-9.5	-27.4	-55.2	-94.7	-218.5	-422.2
Wind Drift • Inches	0.0	0.7	2.9	6.8	12.5	20.3	30.5	58.7	98.5

Lapua 180-grain Naturalis (N318015)
G1 Ballistic Coefficient = 0.271

Distance • Yards	Muzzle	100	200	300	400	500	600	800	1000
Velocity • fps	2625	2307	2012	1741	1499	1295	1138	958	852
Energy • Ft-lbs	2755	2128	1619	1212	899	670	518	367	290
Taylor KO Index	21.8	19.2	16.7	14.5	12.5	10.8	9.5	8.0	7.1
Path • Inches	-1.5	+2.5	0.0	-11.2	-33.9	-72.2	-131.4	-335.8	-691.5
Wind Drift • Inches	0.0	1.2	5.2	12.5	23.8	39.8	61.0	116.7	186.0

Sellier & Bellot 196-grain SPCE (SBA85703)
G1 Ballistic Coefficient = 0.305

Distance • Yards	Muzzle	100	200	300	400	500	600	800	1000
Velocity • fps	2592	2296	2034	1802	1578	1381	1219	1014	900
Energy • Ft-lbs	2941	2294	1801	1413	1084	831	647	447	353
Taylor KO Index	23.4	20.8	18.4	16.3	14.3	12.5	11.0	9.2	8.1
Path • Inches	-1.5	+2.5	0.0	-10.9	-32.6	-68.4	-123.0	-309.1	-623.8
Wind Drift • Inches	0.0	1.2	5.1	12.3	23.2	38.6	59.0	114.0	184.4

Norma 196-grain Oryx (18004)
G1 Ballistic Coefficient = 0.331

Distance • Yards	Muzzle	100	200	300	400	500	600	800	1000
Velocity • fps	2526	2270	2028	1803	1596	1412	1255	1044	927
Energy • Ft-lbs	2778	2242	1791	1415	1109	868	686	475	374
Taylor KO Index	22.8	20.5	18.3	16.3	14.4	12.8	11.4	9.4	8.4
Path • Inches	-1.5	+2.6	0.0	-11.1	-33.0	-68.8	-122.3	-302.2	-605.3
Wind Drift • Inches	0.0	1.2	4.9	11.6	21.8	36.1	54.9	106.2	172.0

Norma 196-grain Alaska (18003)
G1 Ballistic Coefficient = 0.305

Distance • Yards	Muzzle	100	200	300	400	500	600	800	1000
Velocity • fps	2526	2248	1988	1747	1530	1341	1188	998	889
Energy • Ft-lbs	2778	2200	1720	1328	1020	783	614	433	344
Taylor KO Index	22.8	20.3	18.0	15.8	13.8	12.1	10.7	9.0	8.0
Path • Inches	-1.5	+1.6	0.0	-11.5	-34.6	-72.7	-130.6	-326.7	-654.4
Wind Drift • Inches	0.0	1.2	5.3	12.8	24.1	40.1	61.2	117.2	187.9

Sellier & Bellot 196-grain HPC (SBA85704)
G1 Ballistic Coefficient = 0.341

Distance • Yards	Muzzle	100	200	300	400	500	600	800	1000
Velocity • fps	2596	2355	2159	1979	1672	1484	1320	1084	955
Energy • Ft-lbs	2871	2413	2028	1539	1218	959	759	512	397
Taylor KO Index	23.5	21.3	19.5	17.9	15.1	13.4	11.9	9.8	8.6
Path • Inches	-1.5	+2.3	0.0	-10.3	-30.5	-63.3	-112.2	-276.4	-557.1
Wind Drift • Inches	0.0	1.1	4.5	10.7	20.2	33.4	50.8	99.0	162.7

Norma 196-grain Vulcan (18020)
G1 Ballistic Coefficient = 0.347

Distance • Yards	Muzzle	100	200	300	400	500	600	800	1000
Velocity • fps	2526	2281	2049	1832	1634	1453	1297	1075	951
Energy • Ft-lbs	2778	2264	1828	1461	1162	919	732	503	394
Taylor KO Index	22.8	20.6	18.5	16.6	14.8	13.1	11.7	9.7	8.6
Path • Inches	-1.5	+2.6	0.0	-10.9	-32.2	-66.6	-117.5	-286.2	-574.8
Wind Drift • Inches	0.0	1.1	4.2	9.8	18.5	30.5	46.4	89.9	146.8

Sellier & Bellot 196-grain Full Metal Jacket (SBA85707)
G1 Ballistic Coefficient = 0.510

Distance • Yards	Muzzle	100	200	300	400	500	600	800	1000
Velocity • fps	2589	2426	2274	2131	1989	1853	1724	1487	1287
Energy • Ft-lbs	2887	2561	2250	1976	1722	1495	1293	963	721
Taylor KO Index	23.4	21.9	20.6	19.3	18.0	16.8	15.6	13.4	11.6
Path • Inches	-1.5	+2.2	0.0	-8.9	-25.5	-50.8	-86.4	-194.6	-367.2
Wind Drift • Inches	0.0	0.6	2.7	6.3	11.5	18.6	27.8	53.0	88.7

Hirtenberger 200-grain Nosler SP (82200396)
G1 Ballistic Coefficient = 0.400

Distance • Yards	Muzzle	100	200	300	400	500	600	800	1000
Velocity • fps	2461	2251	2051	1862	1685	1522	1376	1147	1008
Energy • Ft-lbs	2690	2251	1869	1540	1261	1059	841	584	451
Taylor KO Index	22.7	20.8	18.9	17.2	15.6	14.0	12.7	10.6	9.3
Path • Inches	-1.5	+2.7	0.0	-11.0	-32.0	-65.4	-113.9	-271.3	-535.3
Wind Drift • Inches	0.0	0.9	3.7	8.7	16.2	26.6	40.1	77.6	127.8

.325 Winchester Short Magnum

This is the large end of the WSM line, introduced in late 2004. Like many other cartridges, the .325 designation is slightly inaccurate. This cartridge actually uses 8 mm bullets. That's good news because reloaders don't have to worry about a whole new caliber. Performance is very similar to the 8mm Remington Magnum, but that performance is produced with a shorter case.

Relative Recoil Factor = 2.78

Specifications

Controlling Agency for Standardization of this Ammunition: SAAMI

Bullet Weight Grains	Velocity fps	Maximum Average Pressure Copper Crusher	Transducer
200	2950	N/S	65,000 psi

Standard barrel for velocity testing: 24 inches long—1 turn in 10-inch twist

Availability

Winchester 180-grain Ballistic Silvertip (SBST325S)

G1 Ballistic Coefficient = 0.439

Distance • Yards	Muzzle	100	200	300	400	500	600	800	1000
Velocity • fps	3060	2841	2632	2432	2242	2060	1888	1573	1310
Energy • Ft-lbs	3743	3226	2769	2365	2009	1696	1425	989	686
Taylor KO Index	25.6	23.7	22.0	20.3	18.7	17.2	15.8	13.1	10.9
Path • Inches	-1.5	+1.4	0.0	-6.4	-18.7	-38.0	-65.4	-151.6	-294.7
Wind Drift • Inches	0.0	0.6	2.4	5.7	10.5	17.1	25.6	49.8	85.1

Winchester 200-grain AccuBond (S325WSMCT)

G1 Ballistic Coefficient = 0.477

Distance • Yards	Muzzle	100	200	300	400	500	600	800	1000
Velocity • fps	2950	2753	2565	2384	2210	2044	1885	1594	1346
Energy • Ft-lbs	3866	3367	2922	2524	2170	1856	1578	1128	804
Taylor KO Index	27.4	25.6	23.8	22.1	20.5	19.0	17.5	14.8	12.5
Path • Inches	-1.5	+1.5	0.0	-6.8	-19.8	-39.9	-68.4	-156.5	-299.8
Wind Drift • Inches	0.0	0.6	2.3	5.5	10.1	16.3	24.4	47.1	79.9

Winchester 220-grain Power-Point (X325WSM)

G1 Ballistic Coefficient = 0.388

Distance • Yards	Muzzle	100	200	300	400	500	600	800	1000
Velocity • fps	2840	2605	2382	2169	1968	1779	1603	1304	1097
Energy • Ft-lbs	3941	3316	2772	2300	1893	1547	1019	831	588
Taylor KO Index	29.0	26.6	24.3	22.2	20.1	18.2	16.4	13.3	11.2
Path • Inches	-1.5	+1.8	0.0	-8.0	-23.3	-47.6	-83.2	-197.8	-394.9
Wind Drift • Inches	0.0	0.7	3.1	7.3	13.5	22.2	33.6	66.1	112.6

8mm Remington Magnum

The 8mm Remington Magnum is a "full-length" magnum cartridge. That is, it is the same length as the .375 H&H, the grandfather of all belted magnums. This gives the 8mm enough case volume to produce some impressive ballistics. While the SAAMI standards list two bullet weights, the 185-grain bullet has been dropped by Remington and replaced with a 200-grain load. This makes some sense since the .300 magnums can all handle 180-grain bullets with ease. This cartridge is at least enough for all North American game.

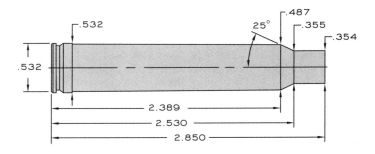

Relative Recoil Factor = 2.77

Specifications

Controlling Agency for Standardization of this Ammunition: SAAMI

Bullet Weight Grains	Velocity fps	Maximum Average Pressure	
		Copper Crusher	Transducer
185	3,065	54,000 cup	65,000 psi
220	2,815	54,000 cup	65,000 psi

Standard barrel for velocity testing: 24 inches long—1 turn in 9.5-inch twist

Availability

Remington 200-grain Swift A-Frame PSP (RS8MMRA)

G1 Ballistic Coefficient = 0.332

Distance • Yards	Muzzle	100	200	300	400	500	600	800	1000
Velocity • fps	2900	2623	2361	2115	1884	1671	1478	1175	1002
Energy • Ft-lbs	3734	3054	2476	1987	1577	1240	971	613	446
Taylor KO Index	26.8	24.2	21.8	19.5	17.4	15.4	13.6	10.8	9.2
Path • Inches	-1.5	+1.8	0.0	-8.0	-23.9	-49.6	-88.1	-218.9	-452.7
Wind Drift • Inches	0.0	0.9	4.0	9.4	17.6	29.2	44.6	88.8	150.4

California hunter Robert Laio, left, with a blue wildebeest from South Africa shot with a .30-06. (Photo from African Hunter II *by Craig Boddington and Peter Flack, 2004, Safari Press)*

.338 Winchester Magnum

The .338 Winchester Magnum and the .264 Winchester Magnum were both introduced in 1958. The .338 is still going great while the .264 is on its last legs. That may well be because the .338 Winchester Magnum filled a big void in the power spectrum of cartridges available at that time. The .338 is enough cartridge for any North American game, though possibly marginal for the largest Alaskan bears. At the same time, it can't realistically be called an "African" caliber. The .338 Winchester Magnum belongs to the family of shortened magnums designed to fit into a standard-length Model 70 action. The nearest big-factory competition comes from the 8mm Remington Magnum, which never achieved the popularity of the .338 Winchester Magnum.

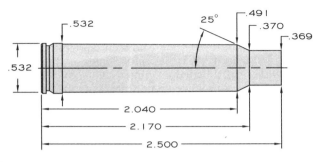

Relative Recoil Factor = 2.93

Specifications

Controlling Agency for Standardization of this Ammunition: SAAMI

Bullet Weight Grains	Velocity fps	Maximum Average Pressure	
		Copper Crusher	Transducer
200	2,940	54,000 cup	64,000 psi
210	2,855	54,000 cup	64,000 psi
225	2,770	54,000 cup	64,000 psi
250	2,645	54,000 cup	64,000 psi
300	2,415	54,000 cup	64,000 psi

Standard barrel for velocity testing: 24 inches long—1 turn in 10-inch twist

Availability

Federal 180-grain Nosler Ballistic Tip (P338J)

G1 Ballistic Coefficient = 0.372

Distance • Yards	Muzzle	100	200	300	400	500	600	800	1000
Velocity • fps	3120	2860	2610	2380	2160	1950	1754	1411	1157
Energy • Ft-lbs	3890	3270	2730	2265	1865	1525	1230	796	535
Taylor KO Index	27.1	24.9	22.7	20.7	18.8	16.9	15.2	12.3	10.1
Path • Inches	-1.5	+1.4	0.0	-6.4	-19.1	-39.1	-68.6	-164.0	-330.1
Wind Drift • Inches	0.0	0.7	2.8	6.7	12.4	20.3	30.8	60.9	105.2

Winchester 200-grain Power-Point (X3381)

G1 Ballistic Coefficient = 0.308

Distance • Yards	Muzzle	100	200	300	400	500	600	800	1000
Velocity • fps	2960	2658	2375	2110	1862	1635	1432	1129	969
Energy • Ft-lbs	3890	3137	2505	1977	1539	1187	911	566	417
Taylor KO Index	28.6	25.7	22.9	20.4	18.0	15.8	13.9	10.9	9.4
Path • Inches	-1.5	+2.0	0.0	-8.2	-24.3	-50.4	-88.9	-225.5	-471.9
Wind Drift • Inches	0.0	1.0	4.2	9.9	18.8	31.2	47.9	95.4	162.0

Remington 200-grain Nosler Ballistic Tip (PRT338WB) (Discontinued in 2005)

G1 Ballistic Coefficient = 0.415

Distance • Yards	Muzzle	100	200	300	400	500	600	800	1000
Velocity • fps	2950	2724	2509	2303	2108	1922	1749	1438	1196
Energy • Ft-lbs	3866	3295	2795	2357	1973	1641	1358	919	636
Taylor KO Index	28.5	26.3	24.2	22.2	20.4	18.6	16.9	13.9	11.6
Path • Inches	-1.5	+1.6	0.0	-7.1	-20.8	-42.4	-73.4	-172.6	-342.0
Wind Drift • Inches	0.0	0.7	3.0	7.1	13.2	21.5	32.4	63.2	108.3

Winchester 200-grain Ballistic Silvertip (SBST338)
G1 Ballistic Coefficient = 0.415

Distance • Yards	Muzzle	100	200	300	400	500	600	800	1000
Velocity • fps	2950	2724	2509	2303	2108	1922	1749	1438	1196
Energy • Ft-lbs	3866	3295	2795	2357	1973	1641	1358	919	636
Taylor KO Index	28.5	26.3	24.2	22.2	20.4	18.6	16.9	13.9	11.6
Path • Inches	-1.5	+1.6	0.0	-7.1	-20.8	-42.4	-73.4	-172.6	-342.0
Wind Drift • Inches	0.0	0.7	3.0	7.1	13.2	21.5	32.4	63.2	108.3

Federal 210-grain Nosler Partition (P338A2)
G1 Ballistic Coefficient = 0.396

Distance • Yards	Muzzle	100	200	300	400	500	600	800	1000
Velocity • fps	2830	2600	2380	2180	1980	1790	1617	1319	1110
Energy • Ft-lbs	3735	3155	2650	2210	1825	1500	1219	812	574
Taylor KO Index	28.7	26.4	24.1	22.1	20.1	18.2	16.4	13.4	11.3
Path • Inches	-1.5	+1.8	0.0	-8.0	-23.4	-47.5	-82.8	-196.3	-390.2
Wind Drift • Inches	0.0	0.7	3.0	7.1	13.3	21.8	32.9	64.6	110.0

Remington 210-grain Nosler Partition (PRP338WC) (Discontinued in 2005)
G1 Ballistic Coefficient = 0.400

Distance • Yards	Muzzle	100	200	300	400	500	600	800	1000
Velocity • fps	2830	2602	2385	2179	1983	1798	1626	1329	1116
Energy • Ft-lbs	3734	3157	2653	2214	1834	1508	1232	823	581
Taylor KO Index	28.7	26.4	24.2	22.1	20.1	18.2	16.5	13.5	11.3
Path • Inches	-1.5	+1.8	0.0	-7.9	-23.2	-47.4	-82.5	-195.9	-391.5
Wind Drift • Inches	0.0	0.8	3.3	7.8	14.6	23.9	36.2	70.9	120.7

Hornady 225-grain SP—Heavy Magnum (8505)
G1 Ballistic Coefficient = 0.398

Distance • Yards	Muzzle	100	200	300	400	500	600	800	1000
Velocity • fps	2950	2714	2491	2278	2075	1884	1706	1391	1156
Energy • Ft-lbs	4347	3680	3098	2591	2151	1772	1454	967	668
Taylor KO Index	32.0	29.5	27.1	24.7	22.5	20.5	18.6	15.2	12.6
Path • Inches	-1.5	+1.9	0.0	-7.5	-21.8	-44.1	-75.1	-178.3	-356.6
Wind Drift • Inches	0.0	0.8	3.2	7.4	13.8	22.6	34.2	67.0	114.9

Federal 225-grain Trophy Bonded Bear Claw—HE (P338T2)
G1 Ballistic Coefficient = 0.371

Distance • Yards	Muzzle	100	200	300	400	500	600	800	1000
Velocity • fps	2940	2690	2450	2230	2010	1810	1625	1308	1091
Energy • Ft-lbs	4320	3610	3000	2475	2025	1640	1319	855	595
Taylor KO Index	31.9	29.2	26.6	24.2	21.8	19.7	17.7	14.3	11.9
Path • Inches	-1.5	+1.7	0.0	-7.5	-22.0	-45.0	-79.0	-190.7	-387.4
Wind Drift • Inches	0.0	0.8	3.4	8.1	15.1	24.8	37.6	74.4	127.4

Federal 225-grain Nosler AccuBond (P338A1)
G1 Ballistic Coefficient = 0.551

Distance • Yards	Muzzle	100	200	300	400	500	600	800	1000
Velocity • fps	2800	2630	2470	2320	2170	2030	1892	1637	1413
Energy • Ft-lbs	3915	3465	3055	2685	2350	2050	1790	1339	998
Taylor KO Index	30.4	28.6	26.8	25.2	23.6	22.1	20.6	17.8	15.4
Path • Inches	-1.5	+1.7	0.0	-7.5	-22.0	-45.1	-72.6	-162.5	-304.8
Wind Drift • Inches	0.0	0.5	2.2	5.0	9.2	14.9	22.2	42.2	70.8

Federal 225-grain Trophy Bonded Bear Claw (P338T1)
G1 Ballistic Coefficient = 0.373

Distance • Yards	Muzzle	100	200	300	400	500	600	800	1000
Velocity • fps	2800	2560	2330	2110	1900	1710	1535	1242	1054
Energy • Ft-lbs	3915	3265	2700	2220	1800	1455	1177	771	555
Taylor KO Index	30.4	27.8	25.3	22.9	20.6	18.6	16.7	13.5	11.5
Path • Inches	-1.5	+1.9	0.0	-8.4	-24.5	-50.6	-88.3	-213.2	-431.3
Wind Drift • Inches	0.0	0.9	3.7	8.6	16.1	26.5	40.2	79.3	134.5

Winchester 225-grain AccuBond (S338CT)
G1 Ballistic Coefficient = 0.548

Distance • Yards	Muzzle	100	200	300	400	500	600	800	1000
Velocity • fps	2800	2634	2474	2319	2170	2026	1888	1632	1408
Energy • Ft-lbs	3918	3467	3058	2688	2353	2052	1781	1331	990
Taylor KO Index	30.4	28.6	26.9	25.2	23.6	22.0	20.5	17.7	15.3
Path • Inches	-1.5	+1.8	0.0	-7.4	-21.3	-42.6	-72.5	-162.9	-306.0
Wind Drift • Inches	0.0	0.5	2.2	5.0	9.3	15.0	22.3	42.3	71.4

Remington 225-grain A-Frame Pointed Soft Point (RS338WA)

G1 Ballistic Coefficient = 0.337

Distance • Yards	Muzzle	100	200	300	400	500	600	800	1000
Velocity • fps	2785	2517	2266	2029	1808	1605	1422	1143	987
Energy • Ft-lbs	3871	3165	2565	2057	1633	1286	1010	652	486
Taylor KO Index	30.3	27.3	24.6	22.0	19.6	17.4	15.5	12.5	10.8
Path • Inches	-1.5	+2.0	0.0	-8.8	-25.2	-54.1	-95.9	-237.4	-486.6
Wind Drift • Inches	0.0	1.0	4.1	9.8	18.4	30.5	46.5	91.9	154.1

Federal 225-grain Soft Point (338ES)

G1 Ballistic Coefficient = 0.420

Distance • Yards	Muzzle	100	200	300	400	500	600	800	1000
Velocity • fps	2780	2570	2380	2170	1980	1800	1637	1350	1138
Energy • Ft-lbs	3860	3290	2780	2340	1960	1630	1340	911	648
Taylor KO Index	30.2	27.9	25.9	23.6	21.5	19.6	17.8	14.7	12.4
Path • Inches	-1.5	+1.9	0.0	-8.2	-23.7	-48.2	-83.6	-196.7	-389.0
Wind Drift • Inches	0.0	0.8	3.2	7.6	14.2	23.1	34.9	68.0	115.6

Remington 225-grain Core-Lokt Ultra Bonded (PRC338WA)

G1 Ballistic Coefficient = 0.456

Distance • Yards	Muzzle	100	200	300	400	500	600	800	1000
Velocity • fps	2780	2582	2392	2210	2036	1871	1715	1435	1213
Energy • Ft-lbs	3860	3329	2858	2440	2071	1748	1469	1029	735
Taylor KO Index	30.2	28.1	26.0	24.0	22.1	20.3	18.6	15.6	13.2
Path • Inches	-1.5	+1.9	0.0	-7.9	-23.0	-46.5	-80.0	-184.7	-357.6
Wind Drift • Inches	0.0	0.6	2.7	6.2	11.6	18.8	28.2	54.7	92.8

Remington 225-grain Core-Lokt Pointed Soft Point (R338W1)

G1 Ballistic Coefficient = 0.435

Distance • Yards	Muzzle	100	200	300	400	500	600	800	1000
Velocity • fps	2780	2572	2374	2184	2003	1832	1670	1386	1169
Energy • Ft-lbs	3860	3305	2837	2389	1999	1663	1394	960	683
Taylor KO Index	30.2	27.9	25.8	23.7	21.8	19.9	18.2	15.1	12.7
Path • Inches	-1.5	+1.9	0.0	-8.1	-23.4	-47.5	-82.0	-191.6	-376.4
Wind Drift • Inches	0.0	0.8	3.1	7.3	13.6	22.2	33.4	64.9	110.2

Norma 225-grain TXP Bullet (18500) (Discontinued in 2005)

G1 Ballistic Coefficient = 0.384

Distance • Yards	Muzzle	100	200	300	400	500	600	800	1000
Velocity • fps	2740	2507	2286	2075	1876	1691	1521	1238	1056
Energy • Ft-lbs	3752	3141	2611	2153	1760	1423	1156	766	557
Taylor KO Index	29.8	27.2	24.8	22.5	20.4	18.4	16.5	13.4	11.5
Path • Inches	-1.5	+2.0	0.0	-8.7	-25.5	-52.2	-91.3	-219.3	-440.9
Wind Drift • Inches	0.0	0.9	3.7	8.6	16.1	26.5	40.2	78.9	133.3

Federal 225-grain Barnes XLC Coated (P338H) (Discontinued in 2005)

G1 Ballistic Coefficient = 0.427

Distance • Yards	Muzzle	100	200	300	400	500	600	800	1000
Velocity • fps	2800	2610	2430	2260	2090	1830	1667	1379	1160
Energy • Ft-lbs	3918	3345	2841	2398	2011	1676	1389	950	673
Taylor KO Index	30.4	28.4	26.4	24.6	22.7	19.9	18.1	15.0	12.6
Path • Inches	-1.5	+1.9	0.0	-7.7	-22.2	-44.7	-81.4	-190.3	-373.0
Wind Drift • Inches	0.0	0.7	2.8	6.7	12.4	20.2	30.4	59.3	100.8

PMC 225-grain Barnes-XLC (338XLA) (Discontinued in 2005)

G1 Ballistic Coefficient = 0.475

Distance • Yards	Muzzle	100	200	300	400	500	600	800	1000
Velocity • fps	2600	2415	2239	2071	1912	1760	1616	1362	1167
Energy • Ft-lbs	3377	2914	2505	2143	1826	1548	1304	928	680
Taylor KO Index	28.2	26.2	24.3	22.5	20.8	19.1	17.6	14.8	12.7
Path • Inches	-1.5	+2.2	0.0	-9.2	-26.5	-53.3	-91.4	-210.6	-407.1
Wind Drift • Inches	0.0	0.8	3.1	7.3	13.6	22.0	33.1	63.7	107.2

Winchester 230-grain Fail Safe (S338XA)

G1 Ballistic Coefficient = 0.437

Distance • Yards	Muzzle	100	200	300	400	500	600	800	1000
Velocity • fps	2780	2573	2375	2186	2005	1834	1675	1391	1173
Energy • Ft-lbs	3948	3382	1881	2441	2054	1719	1433	988	703
Taylor KO Index	30.9	28.6	26.4	24.3	22.3	20.4	18.7	15.5	13.1
Path • Inches	-1.5	+1.9	0.0	-8.1	-23.4	-47.4	-81.8	-191.0	-374.8
Wind Drift • Inches	0.0	0.8	3.1	7.3	13.5	22.1	33.2	64.5	109.5

Norma 230-grain Oryx (18511)

G1 Ballistic Coefficient = 0.370

Distance • Yards	Muzzle	100	200	300	400	500	600	800	1000
Velocity • fps	2756	2514	2284	2066	1863	1673	1499	1215	1039
Energy • Ft-lbs	3880	3228	2665	2181	1773	1429	1147	754	551
Taylor KO Index	30.6	27.6	25.4	22.9	20.7	18.6	16.6	13.5	11.5
Path • Inches	-1.5	+2.0	0.0	-8.7	-25.5	-52.4	-91.8	-220.9	-444.5
Wind Drift • Inches	0.0	0.8	3.4	8.0	15.0	24.7	37.5	73.7	124.5

Federal 250-grain Nosler Partition—HE (P338D)

G1 Ballistic Coefficient = 0.476

Distance • Yards	Muzzle	100	200	300	400	500	600	800	1000
Velocity • fps	2800	2610	2420	2250	2080	1920	1768	1491	1263
Energy • Ft-lbs	4350	3775	3260	2805	2395	2035	1735	1234	886
Taylor KO Index	33.8	31.5	29.2	27.2	25.1	23.2	21.4	18.1	15.3
Path • Inches	-1.5	+1.8	0.0	-7.8	-22.5	-44.9	-77.1	-177.2	-341.8
Wind Drift • Inches	0.0	0.7	2.8	6.6	12.1	19.7	29.5	56.9	96.3

A² 250-grain Triad (None)

G1 Ballistic Coefficient = 0.304

Distance • Yards	Muzzle	100	200	300	400	500	600	800	1000
Velocity • fps	2700	2407	2133	1877	1653	1447	1271	1039	916
Energy • Ft-lbs	4046	3216	2526	1956	1516	1162	897	600	466
Taylor KO Index	32.6	29.1	25.7	22.7	20.0	17.5	15.4	12.6	11.1
Path • Inches	-1.5	+2.3	0.0	-9.8	-29.8	-62.1	-112.0	-283.4	-578.8
Wind Drift • Inches	0.0	1.1	4.8	11.6	21.9	36.5	56.0	109.6	179.2

A² 250-grain Nosler Partition (None)

G1 Ballistic Coefficient = 0.677

Distance • Yards	Muzzle	100	200	300	400	500	600	800	1000
Velocity • fps	2700	2568	2439	2314	2193	2075	1962	1747	1550
Energy • Ft-lbs	4046	3659	3302	2972	2669	2390	2138	1694	1333
Taylor KO Index	32.6	31.0	29.4	27.9	26.5	25.0	23.8	21.2	18.8
Path • Inches	-1.5	+1.9	0.0	-7.7	-22.0	-43.4	-72.9	-160.2	-293.6
Wind Drift • Inches	0.0	0.5	2.0	4.7	8.6	13.8	20.4	38.3	63.4

Federal 250-grain Nosler Partition (P338B2)

G1 Ballistic Coefficient = 0.471

Distance • Yards	Muzzle	100	200	300	400	500	600	800	1000
Velocity • fps	2660	2470	2290	2120	1960	1800	1653	1391	1186
Energy • Ft-lbs	3925	3395	2920	2495	2120	1785	1517	1075	781
Taylor KO Index	32.1	29.8	27.6	25.6	23.7	21.7	20.0	16.8	14.4
Path • Inches	-1.5	+2.1	0.0	-8.8	-25.2	-50.7	-87.1	-200.9	-388.9
Wind Drift • Inches	0.0	0.7	3.1	7.2	13.2	21.5	32.3	62.3	105.1

Remington 250-grain Core-Lokt Pointed Soft Point (R338W2)

G1 Ballistic Coefficient = 0.432

Distance • Yards	Muzzle	100	200	300	400	500	600	800	1000
Velocity • fps	2660	2456	2261	2075	1898	1731	1575	1308	1115
Energy • Ft-lbs	3927	3348	2837	2389	1999	1663	1378	950	1115
Taylor KO Index	32.1	29.6	27.3	25.0	22.9	20.9	19.1	15.8	13.5
Path • Inches	-1.5	+2.1	0.0	-8.9	-26.0	-52.7	-91.3	-214.1	-420.9
Wind Drift • Inches	0.0	0.8	3.4	7.9	14.6	23.9	36.0	70.0	118.2

Winchester 250-grain Partition Gold (SPG338WM)

G1 Ballistic Coefficient = 0.480

Distance • Yards	Muzzle	100	200	300	400	500	600	800	1000
Velocity • fps	2650	2467	2291	2122	1960	1807	1662	1403	1198
Energy • Ft-lbs	3899	3378	2914	2500	2134	1812	1533	1093	797
Taylor KO Index	32.0	29.8	27.7	25.6	23.7	21.8	20.1	17.0	14.5
Path • Inches	-1.5	+2.1	0.0	-8.7	-25.2	-50.7	-87.0	-200.2	-386.1
Wind Drift • Inches	0.0	0.7	3.0	7.0	13.0	21.2	31.7	61.1	103.0

Speer 250-grain Grand Slam (24511) (Discontinued in 2004)

G1 Ballistic Coefficient = 0.432x

Distance • Yards	Muzzle	100	200	300	400	500	600	800	1000
Velocity • fps	2680	2475	2279	2092	1915	1748	1591	1321	1123
Energy • Ft-lbs	3987	3400	2882	2430	2037	1696	1406	968	701
Taylor KO Index	32.4	29.9	27.5	25.3	23.1	21.1	19.2	15.9	13.6
Path • Inches	-1.5	+2.1	0.0	-8.8	-25.6	-51.8	-89.5	-209.0	-408.8
Wind Drift • Inches	0.0	0.7	3.0	7.0	13.0	21.3	32.0	62.3	105.3

.330 Dakota

The .330 Dakota is a .338-caliber cartridge based on the .404 Jeffery case. As is true with several other relatively new rounds based on this same case (the original .404 Jeffery design dates to 1910), the performance is impressive. Dakota currently loads six different bullet styles for this caliber.

Relative Recoil Factor = 3.11

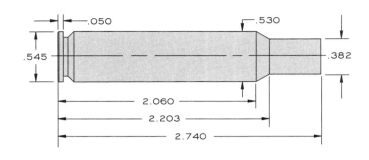

Specifications

Controlling Agency for Standardization of this Ammunition: Factory
Standard barrel for velocity testing: 24 inches long

Availability

Dakota 200-grain Nosler Ballistic Tip (330-200NBT)
G1 Ballistic Coefficient = 0.414

Distance • Yards	Muzzle	100	200	300	400	500	600	800	1000
Velocity • fps	3100	2866	2644	2432	2230	2038	1856	1528	1261
Energy • Ft-lbs	4269	3648	3104	2627	2209	1845	1530	1036	707
Taylor KO Index	30.0	27.8	25.6	23.6	21.6	19.7	18.0	14.8	12.2
Path • Inches	-1.5	+1.4	0.0	-6.4	-18.6	-37.8	-65.5	-153.8	-304.4
Wind Drift • Inches	0.0	0.7	2.8	6.6	12.3	20.0	30.1	58.8	101.1

Dakota 225-grain Nosler Partition (330-225NPT)
G1 Ballistic Coefficient = 0.454

Distance • Yards	Muzzle	100	200	300	400	500	600	800	1000
Velocity • fps	2950	2743	2545	2356	2175	2002	1837	1538	1290
Energy • Ft-lbs	4349	3760	3238	2774	2364	2003	1687	1183	832
Taylor KO Index	32.1	29.9	27.7	25.7	23.7	21.8	20.0	16.8	14.1
Path • Inches	-1.5	+1.6	0.0	-6.9	-20.1	-40.7	-70.0	-161.9	-314.6
Wind Drift • Inches	0.0	0.7	2.8	6.4	11.8	19.2	28.9	56.0	95.3

Dakota 225-grain Swift A-Frame (330-225FAF)
G1 Ballistic Coefficient = 0.384

Distance • Yards	Muzzle	100	200	300	400	500	600	800	1000
Velocity • fps	2950	2706	2475	2256	2048	1851	1668	1351	1124
Energy • Ft-lbs	4349	3660	3062	2544	2096	1713	1391	912	631
Taylor KO Index	32.1	29.5	27.0	24.6	22.3	20.2	18.2	14.7	12.2
Path • Inches	-1.5	+1.6	0.0	-7.3	-21.5	-44.0	-76.7	-183.6	-370.2
Wind Drift • Inches	0.0	0.8	3.3	7.7	14.4	23.6	35.8	70.5	120.9

Dakota 230-grain Fail-Safe (330-230WFS)
G1 Ballistic Coefficient = 0.436

Distance • Yards	Muzzle	100	200	300	400	500	600	800	1000
Velocity • fps	2950	2735	2529	2333	2146	1967	1798	1493	1247
Energy • Ft-lbs	4446	3820	3268	2781	2352	1977	1651	1139	794
Taylor KO Index	32.9	30.5	28.2	26.0	23.9	21.9	20.0	16.6	13.9
Path • Inches	-1.5	+1.6	0.0	-7.0	-20.4	-41.4	-71.4	-166.5	-326.3
Wind Drift • Inches	0.0	0.7	2.9	6.7	12.4	20.2	30.4	59.1	100.9

Dakota 250-grain Nosler Partition (330-250NPT)
G1 Ballistic Coefficient = 0.473

Distance • Yards	Muzzle	100	200	300	400	500	600	800	1000
Velocity • fps	2800	2608	2423	2247	2077	1915	1762	1484	1287
Energy • Ft-lbs	4353	3776	3261	2803	2396	2037	1724	1223	877
Taylor KO Index	33.9	31.6	29.4	27.2	25.1	23.2	21.3	18.0	15.6
Path • Inches	-1.5	+1.8	0.0	-7.7	-22.4	-45.1	-77.3	-177.9	-343.7
Wind Drift • Inches	0.0	0.7	2.8	6.6	12.2	19.8	29.7	57.3	97.1

Dakota 250-grain Swift A-Frame (330-250FAF)

G1 Ballistic Coefficient = 0.427

Distance • Yards	Muzzle	100	200	300	400	500	600	800	1000
Velocity • fps	2800	2587	2385	2191	2006	1832	1667	1379	1161
Energy • Ft-lbs	4353	3717	3158	2666	2235	1863	1544	1056	748
Taylor KO Index	33.9	31.3	28.9	26.5	24.3	22.2	20.2	16.7	14.1
Path • Inches	-1.5	+1.8	0.0	-8.0	-23.2	-47.1	-81.4	-191.0	-376.5
Wind Drift • Inches	0.0	0.8	3.2	7.4	13.7	22.4	33.8	65.8	111.9

Large Alberta whitetail shot with guides Rene and Kelly Semple. (Photo from *Ask the Whitetail Guides* by J. Y. Jones, Safari Press, 2006)

.338 A-Square

Developed in 1978, the .338 A^2 is a .338-caliber variation on the .378 Weatherby cartridge. Performance is similar to the .338-378, muzzle velocities being a little higher for two of the three bullet weights and a bit slower for the third. This cartridge was designed to fulfill the need for a flat-shooting round for long-range hunting of large game.

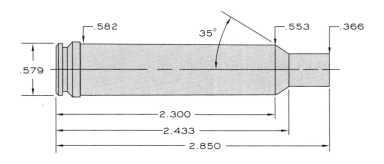

Relative Recoil Factor = 3.15

Specifications

Controlling Agency for Standardization of this Ammunition: Factory
Standard barrel for velocity testing: 26 inches long—1 turn in 10-inch twist

Availability

A^2 200-grain Nosler Ballistic Tip (None)

G1 Ballistic Coefficient = 0.457

Distance • Yards	Muzzle	100	200	300	400	500	600	800	1000
Velocity • fps	3500	3266	3045	2835	2634	2442	2260	1916	1609
Energy • Ft-lbs	5440	4737	4117	3568	3081	2648	2268	1631	1150
Taylor KO Index	33.8	31.5	29.4	27.4	25.4	23.6	21.9	18.6	15.6
Path • Inch	-1.5	+0.9	0.0	-4.6	-13.6	-27.6	-47.4	-108.7	-209.1
Wind Drift • Inches	0.0	0.5	2.2	5.1	9.3	15.0	22.4	43.0	73.0

A^2 250-grain Nosler Partition (None)

G1 Ballistic Coefficient = 0.676

Distance • Yards	Muzzle	100	200	300	400	500	600	800	1000
Velocity • fps	3120	2974	2834	2697	2565	2436	2313	2073	1849
Energy • Ft-lbs	5403	4911	4457	4038	3652	3295	2967	2386	1898
Taylor KO Index	37.7	35.9	34.2	32.6	31.0	29.4	28.0	25.1	22.4
Path • Inches	-1.5	+1.2	0.0	-5.6	-15.9	-31.5	52.9	116.1	211.9
Wind Drift • Inches	0.0	0.4	1.7	3.8	7.0	11.2	16.5	30.9	51.0

A^2 250-grain Triad (None)

G1 Ballistic Coefficient = 0.300

Distance • Yards	Muzzle	100	200	300	400	500	600	800	1000
Velocity • fps	3120	2799	2500	2220	1938	1715	1498	1163	983
Energy • Ft-lbs	5403	4348	3469	2736	2128	1634	1246	751	537
Taylor KO Index	37.7	33.8	30.2	26.8	23.6	20.7	18.1	14.1	11.9
Path • Inches	-1.5	+1.5	0.0	-7.1	-21.2	-44.6	-80.1	-204.5	-433.9
Wind Drift • Inches	0.0	1.0	4.0	9.5	17.9	29.8	45.8	92.6	158.3

.338 Remington Ultra Magnum

When the .300 Remington Ultra Magnum was introduced in 1999, it was clear that either Remington was going to follow up with a couple more calibers based on the same case or the wildcatters would do the job for them. The .338 RUM is a good, big cartridge, just slightly milder than the .338-378 Weatherby. The trend in most of the new, large magnums is to do away with the belt. The .338 RUM headspaces off the shoulder.

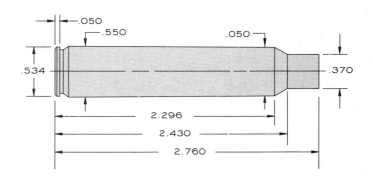

Relative Recoil Factor = 3.18

Specifications

Controlling Agency for Standardization of this Ammunition: SAAMI

Bullet Weight Grains	Velocity fps	Maximum Average Pressure	
		Copper Crusher	Transducer
25	4,000	52,000 cup	N/S

Standard barrel for velocity testing: 24 inches long—1 turn in 9-inch twist

Availability

Federal 180-grain Nosler Ballistic Tip (P338RUM8)
G1 Ballistic Coefficient = 0.507

Distance • Yards	Muzzle	100	200	300	400	500	600	800	1000
Velocity • fps	3280	3080	2890	2710	2530	2360	2198	1892	1616
Energy • Ft-lbs	4300	3790	3335	2925	2560	2225	1932	1432	1045
Taylor KO Index	28.5	26.8	25.1	23.6	22.0	20.5	19.1	16.4	14.0
Path • Inches	-1.5	+1.1	0.0	-5.3	-15.3	-30.7	-52.4	-118.6	-223.9
Wind Drift • Inches	0.0	0.5	1.9	4.4	8.1	13.1	19.4	37.1	62.5

Federal 210-grain Nosler Partition (P338RUMA)
G1 Ballistic Coefficient = 0.421

Distance • Yards	Muzzle	100	200	300	400	500	600	800	1000
Velocity • fps	3030	2800	2590	2390	2190	2000	1823	1505	1249
Energy • Ft-lbs	4280	3665	3125	2650	2235	1870	1550	1056	727
Taylor KO Index	30.7	28.4	26.3	24.2	22.2	20.3	18.5	15.3	12.7
Path • Inches	-1.5	+1.5	0.0	-6.6	-19.4	-39.4	-68.4	-159.7	-313.1
Wind Drift • Inches	0.0	0.6	2.6	6.0	11.2	18.2	27.4	53.5	91.7

Federal 225-grain Nosler AccuBond (P338RUMA1)
G1 Ballistic Coefficient = 0.549

Distance • Yards	Muzzle	100	200	300	400	500	600	800	1000
Velocity • fps	3020	2850	2680	2520	2260	2210	2065	1793	1548
Energy • Ft-lbs	4555	4045	3580	3165	2785	2440	2131	1606	1197
Taylor KO Index	32.8	31.0	29.1	27.4	25.6	24.0	22.4	19.5	16.8
Path • Inches	-1.5	+1.4	0.0	-6.2	-17.9	-36.0	-61.1	-137.1	-256.7
Wind Drift • Inches	0.0	0.5	2.0	4.5	8.3	13.4	19.9	37.8	63.4

Federal 250-grain Trophy Bonded Bear Claw (P338RUMT1)
G1 Ballistic Coefficient = 0.404

Distance • Yards	Muzzle	100	200	300	400	500	600	800	1000
Velocity • fps	2860	2630	2420	2210	2020	1830	1658	1357	1137
Energy • Ft-lbs	4540	3850	3245	2720	2265	1865	1526	1023	718
Taylor KO Index	34.5	31.7	29.2	26.7	24.4	22.1	20.0	16.4	13.7
Path • Inches	-1.5	+1.7	0.0	-7.8	-22.0	-45.8	-79.9	-181.5	-373.3
Wind Drift • Inches	0.0	0.7	2.9	6.9	12.8	20.9	31.6	61.8	105.5

Remington 250-grain Core-Lokt Pointed Soft Point (PR338UM2)

G1 Ballistic Coefficient = 0.432

Distance • Yards	Muzzle	100	200	300	400	500	600	800	1000
Velocity • fps	2860	2647	2443	2249	2064	1887	1722	1427	1196
Energy • Ft-lbs	4540	3888	3314	2807	2363	1977	1646	1130	795
Taylor KO Index	34.5	32.0	29.5	27.1	24.9	22.8	20.8	17.2	14.4
Path • Inches	-1.5	+1.7	0.0	-7.6	-22.0	-44.7	-77.1	-179.6	-351.1
Wind Drift • Inches	0.0	0.7	2.7	6.4	11.8	19.3	29.0	56.5	96.3

Remington 250-grain A-Frame Pointed Soft Point (PR338UM1)

G1 Ballistic Coefficient = 0.428

Distance • Yards	Muzzle	100	200	300	400	500	600	800	1000
Velocity • fps	2860	2645	2440	2244	2057	1879	1713	1417	1187
Energy • Ft-lbs	4540	3882	3303	2794	2347	1960	1629	1115	783
Taylor KO Index	34.5	31.9	29.5	27.1	24.8	22.7	20.7	17.1	14.3
Path • Inches	-1.5	+1.7	0.0	-7.6	-22.1	-44.9	-77.5	-180.8	-354.1
Wind Drift • Inches	0.0	0.7	2.8	6.4	12.0	20.0	29.4	57.2	97.6

Peter Flack, right, with an absolutely stunning bushbuck trophy from Zimbabwe. (Photo from *African Hunter II* by Craig Boddington and Peter Flack, Safari Press, 2004)

8.59mm (.338) Lazzeroni Titan

Lazzeroni's 8.59mm Titan is a very large capacity .338, with performance to match the case volume. This cartridge significantly outperforms the .338 Winchester Magnum. The gun is certainly adequate for any North American game, including the large bears.

Relative Recoil Factor = 3.30

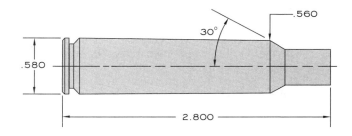

Specifications

Controlling Agency for Standardization of this Ammunition: Factory

Availability

Lazzeroni 185-grain
G1 Ballistic Coefficient = 0.501

Distance • Yards	Muzzle	100	200	300	400	500	600	800	1000
Velocity • fps	3550	3334	3129	2933	2746	2566	2394	2068	1771
Energy • Ft-lbs	5178	4568	4023	3535	3098	2706	2354	1758	1288
Taylor KO Index	31.8	29.9	28.0	26.3	24.6	23.0	21.4	18.5	15.9
Path • Inch	-1.5	+0.8	0.0	-4.4	-12.8	-25.8	-44.1	-99.9	-188.8
Wind Drift • Inches	0.0	0.5	2.0	4.5	8.2	13.3	19.7	37.4	62.9

Lazzeroni 225-grain Nosler Partition (859TN225P)
G1 Ballistic Coefficient = 0.536

Distance • Yards	Muzzle	100	200	300	400	500	600	800	1000
Velocity • fps	3300	3110	2927	2752	2584	2421	2265	1970	1700
Energy • Ft-lbs	5422	4832	4282	3785	3336	2929	2564	1939	1444
Taylor KO Index	35.9	33.8	31.8	29.9	28.1	26.3	24.2	21.5	18.5
Path • Inches	-1.5	+1.0	0.0	-5.1	-14.8	-29.7	-50.6	-113.6	-213.2
Wind Drift • Inches	0.0	0.5	2.0	4.6	8.4	13.5	20.0	38.0	63.8

Lazzeroni 250-grain Swift A-Frame (859TN250A)
G1 Ballistic Coefficient = 0.570

Distance • Yards	Muzzle	100	200	300	400	500	600	800	1000
Velocity • fps	3150	2977	2810	2649	2494	2344	2201	1927	1676
Energy • Ft-lbs	5510	4920	4384	3896	3453	3050	2689	2062	1560
Taylor KO Index	38.0	35.9	33.9	32.0	30.1	28.3	26.6	23.3	20.3
Path • Inches	-1.5	+1.2	0.0	-5.6	-16.2	-32.4	-54.8	-122.4	-228.0
Wind Drift • Inches	0.0	0.5	2.0	4.6	8.3	13.4	19.9	37.6	62.9

.340 Weatherby Magnum

The .340 Weatherby Magnum was Weatherby's 1962 entry in the .338 derby. It follows the pattern of the .300 Weatherby Magnum, being little more than the .300 necked up to .340. Until the recent introduction of the .338-378 and other high-volume cartridges, the .340 Weatherby was the king of the .338s in terms of performance. As with many other cartridge names, the .340 number has no significance. This is a .338-caliber cartridge, and a potent one, too.

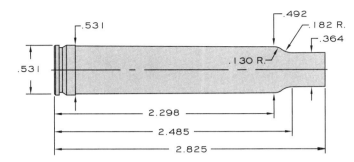

Relative Recoil Factor = 3.30

Specifications

Controlling Agency for Standardization of this Ammunition: CIP

Bullet Weight Grains	Velocity fps	Maximum Average Pressure	
		Copper Crusher	Transducer
N/S	N/S	3,800 bar	4,370 bar

Standard barrel for velocity testing: 26 inches long—1 turn in 10-inch twist

Availability

Weatherby 200-grain Nosler Ballistic Tip (N 340 200 BST)
G1 Ballistic Coefficient = 0.414

Distance • Yards	Muzzle	100	200	300	400	500	600	800	1000
Velocity • fps	3221	2980	2753	2536	2329	2133	1945	1604	1320
Energy • Ft-lbs	4607	3944	3364	2856	2409	2020	1680	1604	1320
Taylor KO Index	31.1	28.9	26.7	24.6	22.6	20.7	18.8	15.5	12.8
Path • Inches	-1.5	+1.2	0.0	-5.8	-17.0	-34.7	-60.0	-140.6	-277.7
Wind Drift • Inches	0.0	0.6	2.7	6.3	11.6	18.9	28.5	55.5	95.5

Weatherby 200-grain Hornady Soft Point (H 340 200 SP)
G1 Ballistic Coefficient = 0.361

Distance • Yards	Muzzle	100	200	300	400	500	600	800	1000
Velocity • fps	3221	2946	2688	2444	2213	1995	1789	1429	1162
Energy • Ft-lbs	4607	3854	3208	2652	2174	1767	1421	907	599
Taylor KO Index	31.1	28.4	26.0	23.6	21.4	19.3	17.3	13.8	11.3
Path • Inches	-1.5	+2.3	0.0	-6.1	-18.0	-37.0	-65.0	-157.0	-321.1
Wind Drift • Inches	0.0	0.8	3.1	7.3	13.6	22.4	34.0	67.4	117.0

Weatherby 210-grain Nosler Partition (H 340 210 PT)
G1 Ballistic Coefficient = 0.400

Distance • Yards	Muzzle	100	200	300	400	500	600	800	1000
Velocity • fps	3211	2963	2728	2505	2293	2092	1899	1554	1273
Energy • Ft-lbs	4807	4093	3470	2927	2452	2040	1683	1126	756
Taylor KO Index	32.6	30.0	27.7	25.4	23.3	21.2	19.3	15.8	12.9
Path • Inches	-1.5	+1.2	0.0	-5.9	-17.4	-35.5	-61.6	-145.4	-289.5
Wind Drift • Inches	0.0	0.7	2.8	6.6	12.1	19.8	29.9	58.5	100.9

Weatherby 225-grain Hornady Soft Point (H 340 225 SP)
G1 Ballistic Coefficient = 0.397

Distance • Yards	Muzzle	100	200	300	400	500	600	800	1000
Velocity • fps	3066	2824	2595	2377	2170	1973	1786	1456	1200
Energy • Ft-lbs	4696	3984	3364	2822	2352	1944	1595	1060	720
Taylor KO Index	33.3	30.7	28.2	25.8	23.6	21.4	19.5	15.9	13.1
Path • Inches	-1.5	+1.4	0.0	-6.6	-19.4	-39.6	-68.8	-163.1	-326.0
Wind Drift • Inches	0.0	1.4	3.0	7.0	13.1	21.4	32.3	63.4	109.2

Weatherby 225-grain Barnes X (B 340 225 XS)
G1 Ballistic Coefficient = 0.482

Distance • Yards	Muzzle	100	200	300	400	500	600	800	1000
Velocity • fps	3001	2804	2615	2434	2260	2093	1933	1639	1385
Energy • Ft-lbs	4499	3927	3416	2959	2551	2189	1867	1342	958
Taylor KO Index	32.6	30.5	28.4	26.4	24.6	22.7	21.1	17.9	15.1
Path • Inches	-1.5	+1.5	0.0	-6.6	-19.0	-38.3	-65.4	-149.7	-287.4
Wind Drift • Inches	0.0	0.6	2.5	5.9	10.8	17.5	26.1	50.3	85.3

Weatherby 250-grain Nosler Partition (N 340 250 PT)

G1 Ballistic Coefficient = 0.473

Distance • Yards	Muzzle	100	200	300	400	500	600	800	1000
Velocity • fps	2941	2743	2553	2371	2197	2029	1869	1577	1330
Energy • Ft-lbs	4801	4176	3618	3120	2678	2286	1940	1381	983
Taylor KO Index	35.5	33.1	30.8	28.6	26.5	24.5	22.6	19.1	16.1
Path • Inches	-1.5	+1.6	0.0	-6.9	-20.0	-40.4	-69.1	-158.7	-306.0
Wind Drift • Inches	0.0	0.6	2.6	6.2	11.4	18.4	27.6	53.2	90.3

Weatherby 250-grain Hornady Soft Point (H 340 250 SP)

G1 Ballistic Coefficient = 0.431

Distance • Yards	Muzzle	100	200	300	400	500	600	800	1000
Velocity • fps	2963	2745	2537	2338	2149	1968	1796	1489	1241
Energy • Ft-lbs	4873	4182	3572	3035	2563	2150	1792	1230	855
Taylor KO Index	35.8	33.1	30.6	28.2	25.9	23.8	21.7	18.0	15.0
Path • Inches	-1.5	+1.6	0.0	-7.0	-20.3	-41.2	-71.2	-166.1	-326.4
Wind Drift • Inches	0.0	0.7	2.9	6.8	12.5	20.4	30.6	59.6	101.9

A² 250-grain Nosler Partition (None)

G1 Ballistic Coefficient = 0.579

Distance • Yards	Muzzle	100	200	300	400	500	600	800	1000
Velocity • fps	2820	2684	2552	2424	2299	2179	2063	1841	1635
Energy • Ft-lbs	4414	3999	3615	3261	2935	2635	2364	1882	1485
Taylor KO Index	34.0	32.4	30.8	29.3	27.6	26.3	25.0	22.3	19.8
Path • Inches	-1.5	+1.7	0.0	-7.2	-20.7	-41.3	-66.2	-145.3	-265.8
Wind Drift • Inches	0.0	0.5	1.9	4.4	8.0	12.9	19.1	35.8	59.2

A² 250-grain Triad (None)

G1 Ballistic Coefficient = 0.303

Distance • Yards	Muzzle	100	200	300	400	500	600	800	1000
Velocity • fps	2820	2520	2238	1976	1741	1522	1333	1071	935
Energy • Ft-lbs	4414	3524	2781	2166	1683	1286	987	636	485
Taylor KO Index	34.0	30.4	27.0	23.9	21.0	18.4	16.1	13.0	11.3
Path • Inches	-1.5	+2.0	0.0	-9.0	-26.8	-56.2	-101.2	-257.4	-532.4
Wind Drift • Inches	0.0	1.1	4.6	10.9	20.6	34.3	52.7	104.5	173.2

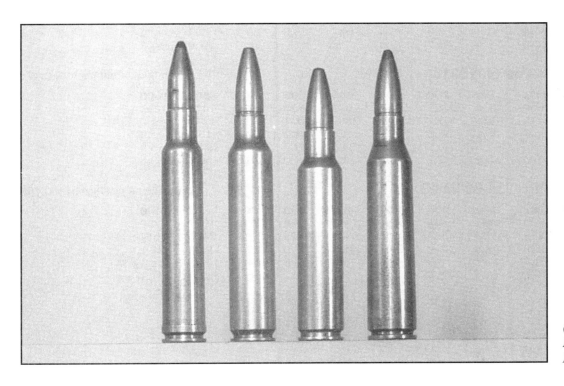

(Left to right) .340 Weatherby, .338 Remington Ultra Magnum, .330 Dakota, .338 Lapua Magnum.

.338 Lapua Magnum

This is yet another example of a big, beltless magnum case. It has found some favor with long-range shooters, especially those who use the 300-grain match bullets. The use of heavy bullets raises a small problem because the more or less standard .338 twist rate of one turn in 10 inches isn't fast enough to stabilize the long bullets. It never gets to be a serious problem since nearly all competition long-range shooting is done with custom-built guns and the barrel twist can be anything the shooter prefers. So far this caliber is a special purpose number in the U.S.

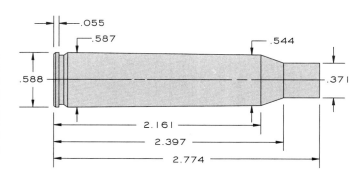

Relative Recoil Factor = 3.33

Specifications

Controlling Agency for Standardization of this Ammunition: CIP

Bullet Weight Grains	Velocity fps	Maximum Average Pressure	
		Copper Crusher	Transducer
N/A	N/A	N/A	N/A

Standard barrel for velocity testing: N/A

Availability

Lapua 250-grain Scenar (4318017) & (C318017)
G1 Ballistic Coefficient = 0.675

Distance • Yards	Muzzle	100	200	300	400	500	600	800	1000
Velocity • fps	2969	2828	2692	2559	2431	2306	2185	1953	1740
Energy • Ft-lbs	4895	4441	4023	3637	3281	2953	2650	2119	1677
Taylor KO Index	35.9	34.2	32.6	31.0	29.4	27.9	26.5	23.6	21.1
Path • Inches	-1.5	+1.4	0.0	-6.2	-17.8	-35.2	-59.1	-129.8	-237.1
Wind Drift • Inches	0.0	0.4	1.6	3.7	6.8	10.8	16.0	30.0	49.5

Lapua 250-grain Lock Base (4318033)
G1 Ballistic Coefficient = 0.661

Distance • Yards	Muzzle	100	200	300	400	500	600	800	1000
Velocity • fps	2953	2810	2671	2537	2406	2280	2157	1923	1705
Energy • Ft-lbs	4842	4384	3962	3573	3215	2886	2583	2052	1615
Taylor KO Index	35.6	33.9	32.2	30.6	29.0	27.5	26.0	23.2	20.6
Path • Inches	-1.5	+1.4	0.0	-6.3	-18.1	-35.8	-60.2	-132.4	-242.5
Wind Drift • Inches	0.0	0.4	1.7	3.8	7.0	11.2	16.5	31.0	51.3

Lapua 275-grain Swift A-Frame (4318018)
G1 Ballistic Coefficient = 0.471

Distance • Yards	Muzzle	100	200	300	400	500	600	800	1000
Velocity • fps	2690	2502	2321	2148	1982	1825	1676	1411	1201
Energy • Ft-lbs	4415	3818	3287	2815	2397	2031	1714	1215	880
Taylor KO Index	35.7	33.2	30.8	28.5	26.3	24.2	22.3	18.7	15.9
Path • Inches	-1.5	+2.0	0.0	-8.5	-24.5	-49.5	-84.8	-195.1	-375.8
Wind Drift • Inches	0.0	0.6	2.7	6.3	11.7	19.0	28.5	55.1	93.0

Dakota 300-grain MatchKing (338-300MKG)
G1 Ballistic Coefficient = 0.768

Distance • Yards	Muzzle	100	200	300	400	500	600	800	1000
Velocity • fps	2800	2681	2564	2451	2341	2233	2128	1927	1739
Energy • Ft-lbs	5224	4788	4382	4003	3651	3323	3018	2475	2014
Taylor KO Index	33.9	32.5	31.0	29.7	28.3	27.0	25.8	23.3	21.1
Path • Inches	-1.5	+1.7	0.0	-7.0	-19.7	-38.8	-64.8	-140.8	-254.4
Wind Drift • Inches	0.0	0.4	1.7	3.9	7.1	11.3	16.7	31.1	51.1

.338-378 Weatherby

As with the .30-378, Weatherby has responded to what wildcatters have been doing for years and "formalized" the .338-378. This is a very potent cartridge, one that is suitable for any African game except for the most dangerous beasties. Driving a 250-grain bullet in excess of 3,000 fps produces a recoil that certainly gets your attention. This is hardly a caliber for plinking tin cans.

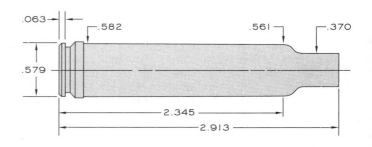

Relative Recoil Factor = 3.40

Specifications

Controlling Agency for Standardization of this Ammunition: Factory
Standard barrel for velocity testing: 26 inches long—1 turn in 10-inch twist

Availability

Weatherby 200-grain BST (N 333 200 BST)
G1 Ballistic Coefficient = 0.414

Distance • Yards	Muzzle	100	200	300	400	500	600	800	1000
Velocity • fps	3350	3102	2868	2646	2434	2232	2039	1686	1386
Energy • Ft-lbs	4983	4273	3652	3109	2631	2213	1846	1262	853
Taylor KO Index	32.4	30.0	27.7	25.6	23.5	21.6	19.7	16.3	13.4
Path • Inches	-1.5	+1.0	0.0	-5.3	-15.6	-31.7	-54.9	-128.1	-257.0
Wind Drift • Inches	0.0	0.6	2.3	5.4	9.9	16.1	24.2	47.2	81.1

Weatherby 225-grain Barnes-X (B 333 225 XS)
G1 Ballistic Coefficient = 0.482

Distance • Yards	Muzzle	100	200	300	400	500	600	800	1000
Velocity • fps	3180	2874	2778	2591	2410	2238	2071	1762	1489
Energy • Ft-lbs	5052	4420	3856	3353	2902	2501	2144	1551	1108
Taylor KO Index	34.5	31.2	30.2	28.1	26.2	24.3	22.6	19.2	16.2
Path • Inches	-1.5	+1.2	0.0	-5.7	-16.6	-33.5	-57.4	-131.0	-250.7
Wind Drift • Inches	0.0	0.6	2.3	5.4	9.9	16.0	24.0	16.1	78.1

Weatherby 250-grain Nosler Partition (N 333 250 PT)
G1 Ballistic Coefficient = 0.473

Distance • Yards	Muzzle	100	200	300	400	500	600	800	1000
Velocity • fps	3060	2856	2662	2478	2297	2125	1961	1658	1396
Energy • Ft-lbs	5197	4528	3933	3401	2927	2507	2134	1526	1082
Taylor KO Index	36.9	34.5	32.1	29.9	27.7	25.7	23.7	20.1	16.9
Path • Inches	-1.5	+1.4	0.0	-6.3	-18.3	-36.9	63.2	-144.8	-278.7
Wind Drift • Inches	0.0	0.6	2.5	5.8	10.7	17.4	26.0	50.1	85.1

.357 Magnum (Rifle Data)

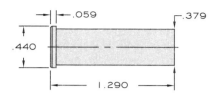

The high-performance pistol cartridges, especially the .357 Magnum and the .44 Remington Magnum, can effectively be shot from rifle-length barrels. They are especially useful in carbine-size rifles with light recoil and are effective at short ranges. The loads shown below have the same product numbers as the comparable pistol loads produced by these same companies. They represent identical loading levels. While all pistol ammunition in this caliber is suitable for use in rifles chambered for this cartridge, you can occasionally find some ammunition marked for "Rifles Only." See the .357 Magnum pistol listing for more information.

Relative Recoil Factor = 1.30

Specifications

Controlling Agency for Standardization of this Ammunition: SAAMI
See pistol data section for detailed specifications.
The data below were taken in the barrel lengths listed with each loading.

Availability

Winchester 158-grain Jacketed Soft Point (X3575P) [20-inch barrel data] G1 Ballistic Coefficient = 0.163

Distance • Yards	Muzzle	100	200	300	400	500	600	800	1000
Velocity • fps	1830	1427	1138	980	883	809	745	638	548
Energy • Ft-lbs	1175	715	454	337	274	229	195	143	105
Taylor KO Index	14.8	11.5	9.2	7.9	7.1	6.5	6.0	5.1	4.4
Path • Inches	-1.5	+7.9	0.0	-34.6	-105.4	-220.7	-372.4	-871.7	-1689
Wind Drift • Inches	0.0	3.9	16.7	38.2	66.2	100.0	139.2	234.8	355.9

Federal 180-grain Hollow Point (C357G) [18-inch barrel data] G1 Ballistic Coefficient = 0.133

Distance • Yards	Muzzle	100	200	300	400	500	600	800	1000
Velocity • fps	1550	1160	970	850	770	700	639	532	445
Energy • Ft-lbs	960	535	370	290	235	195	143	100	69
Taylor KO Index	14.2	10.6	8.9	7.8	7.1	6.4	5.9	4.9	4.1
Path • Inches	-1.5	+12.1	0.0	-49.2	-140.4	-287.9	-526.7	-1254	-2486
Wind Drift • Inches	0.0	5.0	19.6	41.4	69.2	103.2	143.7	246.4	383.7

Winchester 158-grain Jacketed Hollow Point (X3574P) [20-inch barrel data] G1 Ballistic Coefficient = 0.163

Distance • Yards	Muzzle	100	200	300	400	500	600	800	1000
Velocity • fps	1830	1427	1138	980	883	809	745	638	548
Energy • Ft-lbs	1175	715	454	337	274	229	195	143	105
Taylor KO Index	14.8	11.5	9.2	7.9	7.1	6.5	6.0	5.1	4.4
Path • Inches	-1.5	+7.9	0.0	-34.6	-105.4	-220.7	-372.4	-871.7	-1689
Wind Drift • Inches	0.0	3.9	16.7	38.2	66.2	100.0	139.2	234.8	355.9

.35 Remington

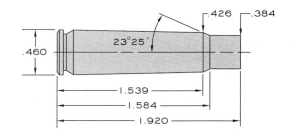

The .35 caliber, introduced by Remington in 1908, was intended as a mild round for the Model 6 semiautomatic rifle. Later it was offered in a number of slide-action and lever-action guns. Even with the pressure levels very low by modern standards, this cartridge offers more punch than the .30-30 but falls considerably short of what can be achieved by the .35 Whelen. While this cartridge is adequate for deer-size game under brush-hunting conditions, its popularity is slowly declining except for the single-shot pistol (one-hand rifle) market.

Relative Recoil Factor = 1.87

Specifications

Controlling Agency for Standardization of this Ammunition: SAAMI

Bullet Weight Grains	Velocity fps	Maximum Average Pressure	
		Copper Crusher	Transducer
150	2,275	35,000 cup	33,500 psi
200	2,055	35,000 cup	33,500 psi

Standard barrel for velocity testing: 24 inches long—1 turn in 16-inch twist

Availability

Remington 150-grain Core-Lokt Pointed Soft Point (R35R1)
G1 Ballistic Coefficient = 0.184

Distance • Yards	Muzzle	100	200	300	400	500	600	800	1000
Velocity • fps	2300	1874	1506	1218	1039	934	857	739	645
Energy • Ft-lbs	1762	1169	755	494	359	291	245	182	138
Taylor KO Index	17.7	14.4	11.6	9.4	8.0	7.2	6.6	5.7	5.0
Path • Inches	-1.5	+4.3	0.0	-19.9	-63.2	-138.7	-250.3	-608.0	-1195
Wind Drift • Inches	0.0	2.5	11.0	27.2	51.6	82.4	118.6	205.7	312.9

Federal 200-grain Soft Point RN (35A)
G1 Ballistic Coefficient = 0.193

Distance • Yards	Muzzle	100	200	300	400	500	600	800	1000
Velocity • fps	2080	1700	1380	1140	1000	910	842	733	643
Energy • Ft-lbs	1920	1280	840	575	445	368	315	238	184
Taylor KO Index	21.3	17.4	14.2	11.7	10.3	9.3	8.6	7.5	6.6
Path • Inches	-1.5	+5.4	0.0	-23.3	-70.0	-144.0	280.8	-665.4	-1285
Wind Drift • Inches	0.0	2.7	12.0	29.0	53.3	83.4	118.3	202.3	305.6

Remington 200-grain Core-Lokt Soft Point (R35R2)
G1 Ballistic Coefficient = 0.193

Distance • Yards	Muzzle	100	200	300	400	500	600	800	1000
Velocity • fps	2080	1700	1380	1140	1000	910	842	733	643
Energy • Ft-lbs	1920	1280	840	575	445	368	315	238	184
Taylor KO Index	21.3	17.4	14.2	11.7	10.3	9.3	8.6	7.5	6.6
Path • Inches	-1.5	+5.4	0.0	-23.3	-70.0	-144.0	280.8	-665.4	-1285
Wind Drift • Inches	0.0	2.7	12.0	29.0	53.3	83.4	118.3	202.3	305.6

Winchester 200-grain Power-Point (X35R1)
G1 Ballistic Coefficient = 0.193

Distance • Yards	Muzzle	100	200	300	400	500	600	800	1000
Velocity • fps	2020	1646	1335	1114	985	901	833	725	637
Energy • Ft-lbs	1812	1203	791	551	431	366	308	234	180
Taylor KO Index	20.7	16.9	13.7	11.4	10.1	9.2	8.5	7.4	6.5
Path • Inches	-1.5	+5.8	0.0	-25.4	-78.8	-168.0	-292.8	-689.6	-1327
Wind Drift • Inches	0.0	2.8	12.4	29.8	54.3	84.4	119.4	203.2	306.5

.356 Winchester

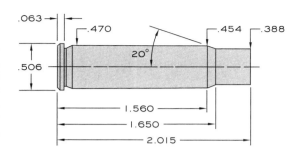

Designed as a rimmed version of the .358 Winchester for use in lever-action rifles, the .356 Winchester is a .35-caliber version of the .307 Winchester. The internal ballistics of this cartridge suffer a little because of the lower pressures allowable to be compatible with lever-action guns. The exterior ballistics also suffer from the flat-nosed bullet that is needed for use in tubular magazines. Still, the .356 is an excellent choice for deer-size game, especially in eastern-type conditions where game is nearly always taken at very modest ranges. In very light rifles, the .356's recoil gets to be a problem for recoil-sensitive shooters. Like the .307, short-barreled guns will yield lower muzzle velocities.

Relative Recoil Factor = 2.22

Specifications

Controlling Agency for Standardization of this Ammunition: SAAMI

Bullet Weight Grains	Velocity fps	Maximum Average Pressure	
		Copper Crusher	Transducer
200	2,370	52,000 cup	N/S
250	2,075	52,000 cup	N/S

Standard barrel for velocity testing: 24 inches long—1 turn in 12-inch twist

Availability

Winchester 200-grain Power-Point (X3561)

G1 Ballistic Coefficient = 0.239

Distance • Yards	Muzzle	100	200	300	400	500	600	800	1000
Velocity • fps	2460	2114	1797	1517	1284	1113	1005	870	774
Energy • Ft-lbs	2688	1985	1434	1022	732	550	449	336	266
Taylor KO Index	25.2	21.6	18.4	15.5	13.1	11.4	10.3	8.9	7.9
Path • Inches	-1.5	+3.2	0.0	-14.0	-43.3	-93.7	-173.6	-433.7	-859.0
Wind Drift • Inches	0.0	1.7	7.3	17.8	34.3	57.1	85.7	156.2	242.2

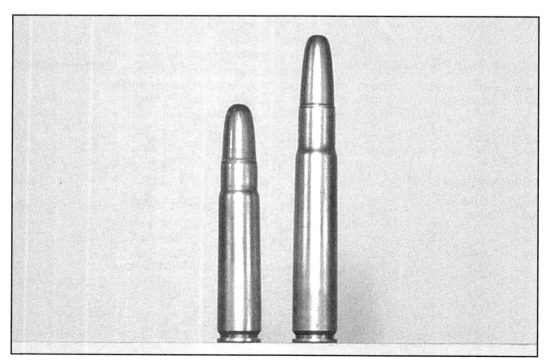

(Left to right) .35 Remington, .35 Whelen.

.35 Whelen

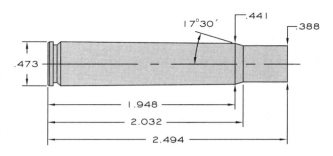

Named for Col. Townsend Whelen, this cartridge is nothing but a .30-06 necked to .35 caliber. There is some disagreement whether Col. Whelen himself or gunmaker James Howe developed the cartridge in the early 1920s, but that matters little as, in all probability, they worked together. Besides, necking an existing cartridge to another caliber is hardly the epitome of the cartridge designer's art. The .35 Whelen can handle bullets up to 250 grains, and that produces some impressive Taylor KO Index numbers, especially for a cartridge based on the .30-06 case.

Relative Recoil Factor = 2.64

Specifications

Controlling Agency for Standardization of this Ammunition: SAAMI

Bullet Weight Grains	Velocity fps	Maximum Average Pressure	
		Copper Crusher	Transducer
200	2,660	52,000 cup	N/S

Standard barrel for velocity testing: 24 inches long—1 turn in 12-inch twist

Availability

Remington 200-grain Pointed Soft Point (R35WH1)
G1 Ballistic Coefficient = 0.294

Distance • Yards	Muzzle	100	200	300	400	500	600	800	1000
Velocity • fps	2675	2378	2100	1842	1606	1399	1227	1012	896
Energy • Ft-lbs	3177	2510	1968	1506	1146	869	669	455	356
Taylor KO Index	27.3	24.3	21.4	18.8	16.4	14.3	12.6	10.4	9.2
Path • Inches	-1.5	+2.3	0.0	-10.3	-30.9	-65.0	-117.9	-299.6	-610.0
Wind Drift • Inches	0.0	1.2	5.1	12.2	23.2	38.7	59.3	115.6	187.4

Federal 225-grain Trophy Bonded Bear Claw (P35WT1)
G1 Ballistic Coefficient = 0.428

Distance • Yards	Muzzle	100	200	300	400	500	600	800	1000
Velocity • fps	2600	2400	2200	2020	1840	1680	1528	1269	1090
Energy • Ft-lbs	3375	2870	2420	2030	1690	1405	1166	805	594
Taylor KO Index	29.8	27.5	25.2	23.2	21.1	19.3	17.5	14.6	12.5
Path • Inches	-1.5	+2.3	0.0	-9.4	-27.3	-56.0	-96.4	-225.5	-441.3
Wind Drift • Inches	0.0	0.8	3.5	8.2	15.3	25.0	37.7	73.1	122.8

Remington 250-grain Pointed Soft Point (R35WH3)
G1 Ballistic Coefficient = 0.410

Distance • Yards	Muzzle	100	200	300	400	500	600	800	1000
Velocity • fps	2400	2196	2005	1823	1653	1497	1357	1139	1006
Energy • Ft-lbs	3197	2680	2230	1844	1570	1244	1023	720	562
Taylor KO Index	30.6	28.0	25.6	23.2	21.1	19.1	17.4	14.6	12.9
Path • Inches	-1.5	+2.9	0.0	-11.5	-33.6	-68.3	-118.9	-281.6	-552.0
Wind Drift • Inches	0.0	1.0	4.2	9.8	18.2	29.8	44.8	86.2	114.3

.350 Remington Magnum

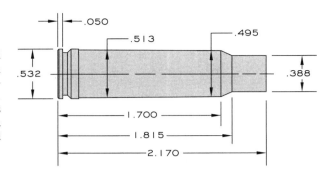

The .350 Remington Magnum was introduced in 1965. It anticipated the current craze for short magnums by nearly 40 years. At its introduction it was intended for the Model 660 Magnum carbines that sported an 18-inch barrel. I remember it as a savage kicker in those very light guns. Since the case volume was virtually identical to that of the .30-06, it has slightly better performance than the .35 Whelen (because it uses a somewhat higher working pressure.) Around 1990 the .350 RM dropped off the radar, only to reappear in 2005.

Relative Recoil Factor = 2.65

Specifications

Controlling Agency for Standardization of this Ammunition: SAAMI

Bullet Weight Grains	Velocity fps	Maximum Average Pressure	
		Copper Crusher	Transducer
200	2690	53,000 cup	N/S

Standard barrel for velocity testing: 20 inches long—1 turn in 16-inch twist

Availability

Remington 200-grain Core-Lokt Pointed Soft Point (R350M1)

G1 Ballistic Coefficient = 0.293

Distance • Yards	Muzzle	100	200	300	400	500	600	800	1000
Velocity • fps	2775	2471	2186	1921	1678	1461	1276	1037	911
Energy • Ft-lbs	3419	2711	2127	1639	1250	947	724	477	369
Taylor KO Index	28.2	25.1	22.2	19.5	17.1	14.9	13.0	10.5	9.3
Path • Inches	-1.5	+2.1	0.0	-9.4	-28.3	-59.7	-107.5	-272.7	-566.8
Wind Drift • Inches	0.0	1.1	4.8	11.6	22.0	36.7	56.4	111.2	182.4

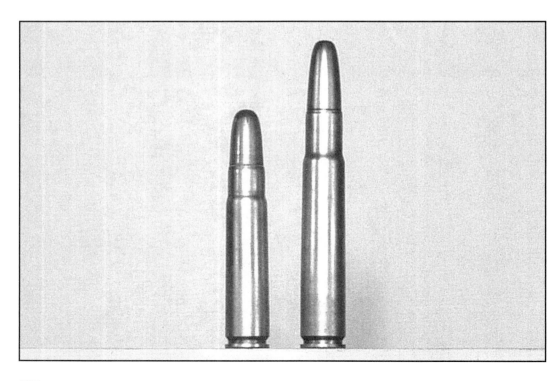

(Left to right) .35 Remington, .35 Whelen.

9.3x74R

Introduced about the same time as (or perhaps a little before) the .375 H&H, the 9.3x74R was intended primarily for the combination guns that are so popular in continental Europe. Being rimmed, it also found a good home in double rifles and single-shot guns. It is still popular in Europe but seldom seen in the United States. Reloading is limited. One reason for this is that there are very few bullets available for this caliber (0.366 inches) here, although they are available from European sources. In addition, dies are hard to find, and many of the cases utilize Berdan priming. This is an effective caliber, with very nearly the same performance as the redoubtable .375 H&H.

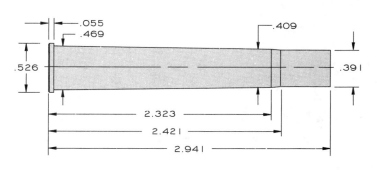

Relative Recoil Factor = 3.45

Specifications

Controlling Agency for Standardization of this Ammunition: CIP

Bullet Weight Grains	Velocity fps	Maximum Average Pressure	
		Copper Crusher	Transducer
All	N/A	43,541 cup	49,347 psi

Standard barrel for velocity testing: N/A

Availability

Norma 232-grain Vulcan (19321)
G1 Ballistic Coefficient = 0.294

Distance • Yards	Muzzle	100	200	300	400	500	600	800	1000
Velocity • fps	2559	2269	1998	1747	1523	1329	1173	986	878
Energy • Ft-lbs	3374	2652	2056	1578	1196	910	709	501	397
Taylor KO Index	31.0	27.5	24.2	21.2	18.5	16.1	14.2	12.0	10.7
Path • Inches	-1.5	+2.6	0.0	-11.4	-34.3	-72.4	-130.8	-329.5	-662.1
Wind Drift • Inches	0.0	1.3	5.4	13.1	24.8	41.3	63.1	120.9	193.5

Hirtenberger 270-grain Sierra SBT Bullet (82200406)
G1 Ballistic Coefficient = 0.398

Distance • Yards	Muzzle	100	200	300	400	500	600	800	1000
Velocity • fps	2972	2736	2511	2298	2094	1902	1721	1404	1165
Energy • Ft-lbs	5299	4489	3783	3167	2631	2170	1778	1182	814
Taylor KO Index	42.3	38.6	35.4	32.4	29.6	26.9	24.3	19.8	16.4
Path • Inches	-1.5	+1.6	0.0	-7.1	-20.8	-42.5	-73.8	-175.2	-350.4
Wind Drift • Inches	0.0	0.7	3.1	7.4	13.7	22.4	33.8	66.3	113.7

Norma 285-grain Alaska (19320)
G1 Ballistic Coefficient = 0.365

Distance • Yards	Muzzle	100	200	300	400	500	600	800	1000
Velocity • fps	2362	2137	1925	1727	1546	1384	1245	1053	942
Energy • Ft-lbs	3532	2891	2345	1887	1513	1212	901	701	561
Taylor KO Index	35.2	31.8	28.7	25.7	23.0	20.6	18.6	15.7	14.0
Path • Inches	-1.5	+3.1	0.0	-12.5	-36.7	-75.6	-132.9	-320.7	-630.3
Wind Drift • Inches	0.0	1.2	4.8	11.4	21.4	35.2	53.1	101.3	163.0

Norma 285-grain Oryx (19332)
G1 Ballistic Coefficient = 0.330

Distance • Yards	Muzzle	100	200	300	400	500	600	800	1000
Velocity • fps	2362	2114	1881	1667	1475	1308	1172	945	899
Energy • Ft-lbs	3532	2829	2241	1758	1378	1083	870	634	512
Taylor KO Index	35.2	31.5	28.0	2487	22.0	19.5	17.5	14.1	13.5
Path • Inches	-1.5	+3.1	0.0	-13.0	-38.6	-80.2	-142.1	-346.8	-690.2
Wind Drift • Inches	0.0	1.3	5.4	12.8	24.2	39.8	60.3	113.8	180.8

Sellier & Bellot 285-grain SP (SBA93741)

G1 Ballistic Coefficient = 0.327

Distance • Yards	Muzzle	100	200	300	400	500	600	800	1000
Velocity • fps	2290	2034	1806	1604	1417	1258	1133	978	882
Energy • Ft-lbs	3324	2621	2067	1630	1272	1002	813	606	492
Taylor KO Index	34.1	30.3	26.9	23.9	21.1	18.7	16.9	14.6	13.1
Path • Inches	-1.5	+3.4	0.0	-14.0	41.7	86.8	-154.4	-375.0	-731.9
Wind Drift • Inches	0.0	1.4	5.7	13.6	25.6	42.1	63.4	118.2	186.1

Norma 285-grain Plastic point (19325)

G1 Ballistic Coefficient = 0.327

Distance • Yards	Muzzle	100	200	300	400	500	600	800	1000
Velocity • fps	2362	2137	1925	1727	1546	1384	1245	1053	942
Energy • Ft-lbs	3532	2891	2345	1887	1513	1212	901	701	561
Taylor KO Index	35.2	31.8	28.7	25.7	23.0	20.6	18.6	15.7	14.0
Path • Inches	-1.5	+3.1	0.0	-12.5	-36.7	-75.6	-132.9	-320.7	-630.3
Wind Drift • Inches	0.0	1.2	4.8	11.4	21.4	35.2	53.1	101.3	163.0

Sherwin Scot with the superb giant eland trophy he won after tracking about 50 miles in 90-plus-degree heat. (Photo from *African Hunter II* by Craig Boddington and Peter Flack, 2004, Safari Press)

.375 Winchester

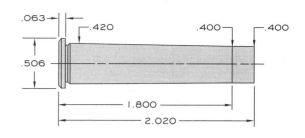

In 1978 Winchester introduced the .375 Winchester. This cartridge is certainly not a .375 Magnum. In terms of both energy and the Taylor KO Index, the .375 is inferior to the .356 Winchester. This cartridge can be thought of as a .30-30 necked to .375 caliber. The only bullet that is factory loaded is a 200-grain Power-Point. It is intended for the Model 94 Big Bore lever action that tolerates high pressures. No full-size rifles are currently being chambered for this cartridge, but it is chambered in some single-shot pistols.

Relative Recoil Factor = 1.98

Specifications

Controlling Agency for Standardization of this Ammunition: SAAMI

Bullet Weight Grains	Velocity fps	Maximum Average Pressure	
		Copper Crusher	Transducer
200	2,180	52,000 cup	N/S
250	1,885	52,000 cup	N/S

Standard barrel for velocity testing: 24 inches long—1 turn in 12-inch twist

Availability

Winchester 200-grain Power-Point (X375W)

G1 Ballistic Coefficient = 0.215

Distance • Yards	Muzzle	100	200	300	400	500	600	800	1000
Velocity • fps	2200	1841	1526	1268	1089	980	904	790	700
Energy • Ft-lbs	2150	1506	1034	714	527	427	363	277	218
Taylor KO Index	23.6	19.8	16.4	13.6	11.7	10.5	9.7	8.5	7.5
Path • Inches	-1.5	+4.4	0.0	-19.5	-60.7	-131.1	-236.0	-566.8	-1098
Wind Drift • Inches	0.0	2.2	9.8	23.8	44.9	72.2	104.4	181.7	275.9

The Marco Polo sheep of Central Asia remains one of the most difficult-to-hunt species on earth. Very long shots are required to obtain a trophy, and the altitude of 12,000 to 15,000 feet where it lives is only for the fittest of hunters. (Photo from The Dangerous Game by Walt Prothero, Safari Press, 2006)

.375 Holland & Holland Magnum

The British riflemaking firm of Holland & Holland wanted something new and different in 1912 when they introduced their .375 H&H. It was common for gunmakers in those days to have their own proprietary cartridges. Of course we don't do that any more, not much we don't. The names Weatherby, Lazzeroni, A², and Dakota all come to mind as carrying on that practice, at least to a degree. The .375 H&H is the smallest "African" cartridge allowed in many countries. It has proved its worth in over 90 years of exemplary field history. A few years after its introduction, the .375 H&H led to the .300 H&H, and that number begat nearly all the other belted magnums we use today. The .375 H&H has a well-earned place in cartridge history.

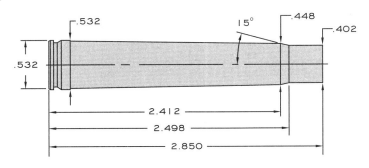

Relative Recoil Factor = 3.42

Specifications

Controlling Agency for Standardization of this Ammunition: SAAMI*

Bullet Weight Grains	Velocity fps	Maximum Average Pressure	
		Copper Crusher	Transducer
270	2,680	53,000 cup	62,000 psi
300	2,515	53,000 cup	62,000 psi

Standard barrel for velocity testing: 24 inches long—1 turn in 12-inch twist

*Some ammunition that is available in this caliber is manufactured to CIP (European) specifications.

Availability

Kynoch 235-grain Soft Nose or Solid
G1 Ballistic Coefficient = 0.340

Distance • Yards	Muzzle	100	200	300	400	500	600	800	1000
Velocity • fps	2800	2535	2284	2048	1827	1623	1440	1156	995
Energy • Ft-lbs	4090	3360	2723	2189	1742	1375	1083	698	517
Taylor KO Index	35.3	32.0	28.8	25.9	23.1	20.5	18.2	14.6	12.6
Path • Inches	-1.5	+2.0	0.0	-8.7	-25.6	-53.1	-93.8	-230.0	-470.2
Wind Drift • Inches	0.0	0.9	3.6	8.6	16.2	26.9	59.0	81.2	136.5

Federal 250-grain Trophy Bonded Bear Claw (P375T4)
G1 Ballistic Coefficient = 0.286

Distance • Yards	Muzzle	100	200	300	400	500	600	800	1000
Velocity • fps	2670	2360	2080	1820	1580	1370	1201	995	882
Energy • Ft-lbs	3955	3100	2400	1830	1380	1040	800	550	432
Taylor KO Index	35.9	31.7	27.9	24.4	21.2	18.4	16.1	13.4	11.8
Path • Inches	-1.5	+2.4	0.0	-10.4	-31.7	-67.0	-120.4	-306.0	-631.5
Wind Drift • Inches	0.0	1.1	4.7	11.4	21.7	36.2	55.6	107.9	174.2

Federal 260-grain Nosler AccuBond (P375A1)
G1 Ballistic Coefficient = 0.470

Distance • Yards	Muzzle	100	200	300	400	500	600	800	1000
Velocity • fps	2700	2510	2330	2160	1990	1830	1682	1415	1204
Energy • Ft-lbs	4210	3640	3130	2685	2235	1935	1633	1157	837
Taylor KO Index	37.6	35.0	32.5	30.1	27.7	25.5	23.4	19.7	16.8
Path • Inches	-1.5	+2.0	0.0	-8.5	-24.5	-48.9	-84.2	-193.8	-373.3
Wind Drift • Inches	0.0	0.6	2.7	6.3	11.7	19.0	28.4	54.9	92.8

Hornady 270-grain SP—Heavy Magnum InterLock (8508)
G1 Ballistic Coefficient = 0.380

Distance • Yards	Muzzle	100	200	300	400	500	600	800	1000
Velocity • fps	2870	2628	2399	2182	1976	1782	1603	1298	1090
Energy • Ft-lbs	4937	4141	3450	2853	2339	1903	1540	1010	712
Taylor KO Index	41.5	38.0	34.7	31.6	28.6	25.8	23.2	18.8	15.8
Path • Inches	-1.5	+1.8	0.0	-7.8	-23.0	-47.1	-82.2	-196.3	-393.6
Wind Drift • Inches	0.0	0.8	3.5	8.1	15.2	24.9	37.8	74.2	127.0

Federal 270-grain Hi-Shok Soft Point (375A)

G1 Ballistic Coefficient = 0.324

Distance • Yards	Muzzle	100	200	300	400	500	600	800	1000
Velocity • fps	2690	2420	2170	1920	1700	1500	1326	1079	946
Energy • Ft-lbs	4340	3510	2810	2220	1740	1351	1055	698	537
Taylor KO Index	39.0	35.1	31.5	27.8	24.7	21.8	19.2	15.6	13.7
Path • Inches	-1.5	+2.2	0.0	-9.7	-28.8	-60.2	-107.3	-267.8	-545.7
Wind Drift • Inches	0.0	1.1	4.5	10.8	20.4	33.8	51.6	101.4	167.2

Remington 270-grain Soft Point (R375M1)

G1 Ballistic Coefficient = 0.326

Distance • Yards	Muzzle	100	200	300	400	500	600	800	1000
Velocity • fps	2690	2420	2166	1928	1707	1507	1332	1083	950
Energy • Ft-lbs	4337	3510	2812	2228	1747	1361	1064	704	541
Taylor KO Index	39.0	35.1	31.4	28.0	24.8	21.9	19.3	15.7	13.8
Path • Inches	-1.5	+2.2	0.0	-9.7	-28.7	-59.8	-106.8	-266.1	-542.2
Wind Drift • Inches	0.0	1.1	4.5	10.7	20.2	33.5	51.2	100.6	166.0

Winchester 270-grain Fail Safe (S375HX)

G1 Ballistic Coefficient = 0.394

Distance • Yards	Muzzle	100	200	300	400	500	600	800	1000
Velocity • fps	2670	2447	2344	2033	1842	1664	1500	1230	1055
Energy • Ft-lbs	4275	3570	2994	2478	2035	1662	1350	907	667
Taylor KO Index	38.7	35.5	32.4	29.5	26.7	24.1	21.8	17.8	15.3
Path • Inches	-1.5	+2.0	0.0	-9.1	-28.7	-54.5	-95.3	-227.5	-454.4
Wind Drift • Inches	0.0	0.9	3.7	8.8	16.4	26.8	40.3	57.6	132.5

Kynoch 270-grain Soft Nose

G1 Ballistic Coefficient = 0.370

Distance • Yards	Muzzle	100	200	300	400	500	600	800	1000
Velocity • fps	2650	2415	2189	1977	1778	1594	1428	1166	1011
Energy • Ft-lbs	4210	3496	2874	2344	1895	1524	1223	816	612
Taylor KO Index	38.4	35.0	31.7	28.7	25.8	23.1	20.7	16.9	14.7
Path • Inches	-1.5	+2.2	0.0	-9.5	-28.0	-57.5	-100.9	-244.4	-491.8
Wind Drift • Inches	0.0	1.0	4.0	9.5	17.7	29.2	44.2	86.6	144.6

PMC 270-grain Pointed Soft Point (375HA)

G1 Ballistic Coefficient = 0.377

Distance • Yards	Muzzle	100	200	300	400	500	600	800	1000
Velocity • fps	2650	2414	2192	1984	1788	1610	1446	1182	1022
Energy • Ft-lbs	4210	3495	2882	2359	1917	1554	1254	838	626
Taylor KO Index	38.4	35.0	31.8	28.8	25.9	23.3	21.0	17.1	14.8
Path • Inches	-1.5	+2.2	0.0	-9.5	-27.8	-59.0	-99.7	-240.4	-482.7
Wind Drift • Inches	0.0	0.9	3.9	9.2	17.3	28.5	43.2	84.5	141.3

PMC 270-grain Barnes-XLC-HP (375XLA) (Discontinued in 2005)

G1 Ballistic Coefficient = 0.496

Distance • Yards	Muzzle	100	200	300	400	500	600	800	1000
Velocity • fps	2600	2423	2254	2092	1938	1791	1651	1402	1203
Energy • Ft-lbs	4053	3519	3045	2623	2251	1923	1635	1178	867
Taylor KO Index	37.7	35.1	32.7	30.3	28.1	26.0	23.9	20.3	17.4
Path • Inches	-1.5	+2.2	0.0	-9.1	-26.1	-52.4	-89.5	-204.8	-393.0
Wind Drift • Inches	0.0	0.7	3.0	7.0	12.9	20.9	31.3	60.2	101.2

Hirtenberger 272-grain ABC Bullet (82200431)

G1 Ballistic Coefficient = 0.322

Distance • Yards	Muzzle	100	200	300	400	500	600	800	1000
Velocity • fps	2644	2374	2119	1881	1662	1465	1295	1061	935
Energy • Ft-lbs	4229	3409	2718	2142	1671	1298	1014	681	529
Taylor KO Index	38.6	34.7	31.0	27.5	24.3	21.4	18.9	15.5	13.7
Path • Inches	-1.5	+2.4	0.0	-10.1	-30.1	-62.9	-112.3	-280.2	-568.6
Wind Drift • Inches	0.0	1.0	4.2	10.4	19.0	31.4	48.0	93.9	153.8

Speer 285-grain Grand Slam (24512) (Discontinued in 2004)

G1 Ballistic Coefficient = 0.354

Distance • Yards	Muzzle	100	200	300	400	500	600	800	1000
Velocity • fps	2690	2441	2205	1984	1777	1586	1414	1149	996
Energy • Ft-lbs	4579	3770	3077	2491	1999	1592	1266	835	628
Taylor KO Index	41.2	37.4	33.8	30.4	27.2	24.3	21.6	17.6	15.2
Path • Inches	-1.5	+2.2	0.0	-9.3	-27.6	-56.9	-100.2	-245.1	-496.5
Wind Drift • Inches	0.0	1.0	4.1	9.7	18.2	30.0	45.7	89.9	149.8

Federal 300-grain Soft Point (375B)

G1 Ballistic Coefficient = 0.300

Distance • Yards	Muzzle	100	200	300	400	500	600	800	1000
Velocity • fps	2630	2270	2020	1790	1580	1390	1225	1015	900
Energy • Ft-lbs	4265	3425	2720	2135	1665	1295	1000	686	540
Taylor KO Index	42.3	36.5	32.5	28.8	25.4	22.3	19.7	16.3	14.5
Path • Inches	-1.5	+2.6	0.0	-11.1	-33.5	-69.5	-119.6	-300.6	-616.1
Wind Drift • Inches	0.0	1.2	5.1	12.2	23.2	38.6	59.0	114.6	185.4

Federal 300-grain Trophy Bonded Bear Claw—HE (P375T3)

G1 Ballistic Coefficient = 0.334

Distance • Yards	Muzzle	100	200	300	400	500	600	800	1000
Velocity • fps	2600	2340	2100	1870	1660	1470	1305	1073	947
Energy • Ft-lbs	4505	3650	2835	2330	1835	1440	1135	767	597
Taylor KO Index	41.8	37.6	33.8	30.1	26.7	23.6	21.0	17.2	15.2
Path • Inches	-1.5	+2.5	0.0	-10.2	-30.8	-63.7	-112.9	-277.6	-562.5
Wind Drift • Inches	0.0	1.1	4.6	11.0	20.6	34.0	52.0	101.4	166.1

Norma 300-grain TXP Line, Swift (19503) (Discontinued in 2005)

G1 Ballistic Coefficient = 0.325

Distance • Yards	Muzzle	100	200	300	400	500	600	800	1000
Velocity • fps	2560	2296	2049	1818	1607	1418	1258	1043	925
Energy • Ft-lbs	4363	3513	2798	2203	1720	1339	1054	724	570
Taylor KO Index	41.3	37.0	33.0	29.3	25.9	22.9	20.3	16.8	14.9
Path • Inches	-1.5	+2.6	0.0	-10.9	-32.3	-67.3	-12.02	-298.5	-600.3
Wind Drift • Inches	0.0	1.2	4.9	11.6	21.9	36.3	55.2	107.0	173.7

A² 300-grain SBT (None)

G1 Ballistic Coefficient = 0.641

Distance • Yards	Muzzle	100	200	300	400	500	600	800	1000
Velocity • fps	2550	2415	2284	2157	2034	1914	1802	1589	1400
Energy • Ft-lbs	4331	3884	3474	3098	2755	2441	2163	1682	1305
Taylor KO Index	41.1	38.9	36.8	34.8	32.8	30.8	29.0	25.6	22.6
Path • Inches	-1.5	+2.2	0.0	-8.9	-25.3	-50.1	-84.3	-129.3	-344.6
Wind Drift • Inches	0.0	0.6	2.4	5.4	9.9	16.0	23.7	44.7	74.2

A² 300-grain Triad (None)

G1 Ballistic Coefficient = 0.287

Distance • Yards	Muzzle	100	200	300	400	500	600	800	1000
Velocity • fps	2550	2251	1973	1717	1496	1302	1151	971	866
Energy • Ft-lbs	4331	3375	2592	1964	1491	1130	882	629	499
Taylor KO Index	41.1	36.3	31.8	27.7	24.1	21.0	18.5	15.6	14.0
Path • Inches	-1.5	+2.7	0.0	-11.7	-35.1	-75.1	-134.8	-339.8	-682.0
Wind Drift • Inches	0.0	1.3	5.6	13.5	25.7	42.9	65.4	124.8	198.8

Federal 300-grain Nosler Partition (P375F)

G1 Ballistic Coefficient = 0.403

Distance • Yards	Muzzle	100	200	300	400	500	600	800	1000
Velocity • fps	2530	2320	2120	1930	1750	1580	1428	1184	1031
Energy • Ft-lbs	4265	3585	2990	2475	2040	1670	1359	934	709
Taylor KO Index	40.7	37.3	34.1	31.0	28.1	25.4	23.0	19.0	16.6
Path • Inches	-1.5	+2.5	0.0	-10.1	-29.8	-61.1	-106.2	-251.3	-495.8
Wind Drift • Inches	0.0	0.9	3.9	9.2	17.1	28.0	42.4	82.2	136.6

Remington 300-grain A-Frame Pointed Soft Point (RS375MA)

G1 Ballistic Coefficient = 0.297

Distance • Yards	Muzzle	100	200	300	400	500	600	800	1000
Velocity • fps	2530	2245	1979	1733	1512	1321	1060	985	878
Energy • Ft-lbs	4262	3357	2608	2001	1523	1163	910	646	514
Taylor KO Index	40.8	36.2	31.9	27.9	24.4	21.3	17.1	15.9	14.1
Path • Inches	-1.5	+2.7	0.0	-11.7	-35.0	-73.6	-133.2	-334.1	-669.3
Wind Drift • Inches	0.0	1.3	5.5	13.1	24.9	41.5	63.2	120.8	192.9

Winchester 300-grain Fail Safe (S375HXA)

G1 Ballistic Coefficient = 0.441

Distance • Yards	Muzzle	100	200	300	400	500	600	800	1000
Velocity • fps	2530	2336	2151	1974	1806	1649	1508	1257	1086
Energy • Ft-lbs	4265	3636	3081	2595	2173	1811	1506	1053	785
Taylor KO Index	40.8	37.6	34.7	31.8	29.1	26.6	24.3	20.3	17.5
Path • Inches	-1.5	+2.4	0.0	-10.0	-26.9	-58.4	-101.0	-236.2	-122.2
Wind Drift • Inches	0.0	0.8	3.5	8.3	15.4	25.2	37.8	73.1	122.2

Federal 300-grain Trophy Bonded Bear Claw (P375T1)
G1 Ballistic Coefficient = 0.338

Distance • Yards	Muzzle	100	200	300	400	500	600	800	1000
Velocity • fps	2530	2200	1970	1750	1550	1380	1232	1035	923
Energy • Ft-lbs	4000	3230	2580	2040	1605	1270	1012	714	568
Taylor KO Index	39.5	35.5	31.7	28.2	25.0	22.2	19.9	16.7	14.9
Path • Inches	-1.5	+2.9	0.0	-11.9	-35.1	-72.9	-129.2	-316.8	-629.4
Wind Drift • Inches	0.0	1.2	5.0	11.8	22.2	36.8	55.8	106.9	172.2

PMC 300-grain Barnes-XLC-HE (375XLB) (Discontinued in 2005)
G1 Ballistic Coefficient = 0.548

Distance • Yards	Muzzle	100	200	300	400	500	600	800	1000
Velocity • fps	2500	2343	2193	2048	1910	1778	1652	1424	1236
Energy • Ft-lbs	4163	3657	3202	2795	2430	2106	1818	1351	1018
Taylor KO Index	40.3	34.0	31.8	29.7	27.7	25.8	24.0	20.7	17.9
Path • Inches	-1.5	+2.4	0.0	-9.7	-27.6	-55.1	-93.6	-211.2	-398.9
Wind Drift • Inches	0.0	0.7	2.8	6.6	12.2	19.7	29.4	56.1	93.6

Hornady 300-grain FMJ RN—ENC HM (8509)
G1 Ballistic Coefficient = 0.276

Distance • Yards	Muzzle	100	200	300	400	500	600	800	1000
Velocity • fps	2705	2376	2072	1804	1560	1356	1185	983	870
Energy • Ft-lbs	4873	3760	2861	2167	1621	1222	936	644	504
Taylor KO Index	43.6	38.3	33.4	29.1	25.1	21.9	19.1	15.8	14.0
Path • Inches	-1.5	+2.7	0.0	-10.8	-32.1	-68.4	-121.6	-312.5	-637.8
Wind Drift • Inches	0.0	1.3	5.4	13.0	24.7	41.4	63.6	123.5	199.0

Speer 300-grain African Grand Slam Tungsten Solid (24517) (Discontinued in 2004)
G1 Ballistic Coefficient = 0.262

Distance • Yards	Muzzle	100	200	300	400	500	600	800	1000
Velocity • fps	2550	2227	1929	1657	1418	1224	1085	926	825
Energy • Ft-lbs	4331	3302	2479	1829	1339	998	785	572	454
Taylor KO Index	41.1	35.9	31.1	26.7	22.9	19.7	17.5	14.9	13.3
Path • Inches	-1.5	+2.8	0.0	-12.1	-37.1	-80.1	-146.8	-371.8	-744.6
Wind Drift • Inches	0.0	1.4	6.2	15.1	28.9	48.4	73.6	138.3	218.0

Federal 300-grain Trophy Bonded Sledgehammer Solid (P375T2)
G1 Ballistic Coefficient = 0.225

Distance • Yards	Muzzle	100	200	300	400	500	600	800	1000
Velocity • fps	2530	2160	1820	1520	1280	1100	990	854	756
Energy • Ft-lbs	4265	3105	2210	1550	1090	810	653	486	381
Taylor KO Index	40.8	34.8	29.3	24.5	20.6	17.7	16.0	13.8	12.2
Path • Inches	-1.5	+3.0	0.0	-13.7	-42.5	-92.9	-173.7	-437.6	-872.3
Wind Drift • Inches	0.0	1.7	7.5	18.4	35.6	59.6	89.5	163.2	253.1

Norma 300-grain Barnes Solid (19505)
G1 Ballistic Coefficient = 0.191

Distance • Yards	Muzzle	100	200	300	400	500	600	800	1000
Velocity • fps	2493	2061	1677	1356	1126	991	903	778	680
Energy • Ft-lbs	4141	2829	1873	1224	845	655	544	408	308
Taylor KO Index	40.2	33.2	27.0	21.9	18.1	16.0	14.6	12.5	11.0
Path • Inches	-1.5	+3.4	0.0	-16.0	-51.5	-114.4	-210.5	-524.3	-1043
Wind Drift • Inches	0.0	2.1	9.4	23.3	45.0	74.0	108.8	192.8	295.9

.375 Dakota

This is the .375 version of Dakota's line of proprietary cartridges. It produces 2,700 fps with a 300-grain bullet. That level of performance puts it a little ahead of the .375 H&H but also a little behind the .378 Weatherby. Dakota is currently loading four different bullets in this caliber.

Relative Recoil Factor = 3.60

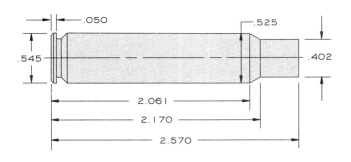

Specifications

Controlling Agency for Standardization of this Ammunition: Factory
Standard barrel for velocity testing: 26 inches long

Availability

Dakota 250-grain Swift A-Frame (375-250FAF)
G1 Ballistic Coefficient = 0.271

Distance • Yards	Muzzle	100	200	300	400	500	600	800	1000
Velocity • fps	2900	2562	2249	1958	1691	1456	1259	1015	889
Energy • Ft-lbs	4670	3645	2807	2128	1588	1177	881	572	439
Taylor KO Index	38.9	34.4	30.2	26.3	22.7	19.6	16.9	13.6	11.9
Path • Inches	-1.5	+1.9	0.0	-8.8	-26.8	-57.3	-104.7	-273.6	-570.5
Wind Drift • Inches	0.0	1.2	5.0	11.9	22.7	38.2	59.1	117.2	192.4

Dakota 300-grain Woodleigh Soft Nose (375-300WSN)
G1 Ballistic Coefficient = 0.340

Distance • Yards	Muzzle	100	200	300	400	500	600	800	1000
Velocity • fps	2700	2440	2195	1965	1750	1553	1379	1118	974
Energy • Ft-lbs	4837	3968	3211	2572	2040	1607	1267	833	632
Taylor KO Index	43.5	39.3	35.4	31.7	28.2	25.0	22.2	18.0	15.7
Path • Inches	-1.5	+2.2	0.0	-9.4	-27.9	-57.8	-102.5	-253.2	-515.1
Wind Drift • Inches	0.0	1.0	4.3	10.1	19.1	31.6	48.1	94.6	157.3

Dakota 300-grain Swift A-Frame (375-300FAF)
G1 Ballistic Coefficient = 0.325

Distance • Yards	Muzzle	100	200	300	400	500	600	800	1000
Velocity • fps	2700	2429	2173	1934	1712	1511	1335	1084	950
Energy • Ft-lbs	4857	3930	3148	2492	1953	1521	1188	784	601
Taylor KO Index	43.5	39.1	35.0	31.2	27.6	24.3	21.5	17.5	15.3
Path • Inches	-1.5	+2.2	0.0	-9.6	-28.6	-59.5	-106.1	-264.7	-539.8
Wind Drift • Inches	0.0	1.1	4.5	10.7	20.2	33.4	51.1	100.5	166.0

Dakota 300-grain Woodleigh Solid (375-300WSO)
G1 Ballistic Coefficient = 0.307

Distance • Yards	Muzzle	100	200	300	400	500	600	800	1000
Velocity • fps	2700	2413	2145	1894	1663	1456	1280	1046	921
Energy • Ft-lbs	4857	3881	3064	2389	1842	1413	1092	728	585
Taylor KO Index	43.5	38.9	34.6	30.5	26.8	23.5	20.6	16.9	14.8
Path • Inches	-1.5	+2.2	0.0	-9.8	-29.5	-61.9	-111.1	-280.5	-572.9
Wind Drift • Inches	0.0	1.1	4.8	11.4	21.6	36.0	55.2	108.3	177.3

.375 Remington Ultra Magnum

Introduced in 2002, the .375 RUM is currently the largest in the Ultra Magnum series. It continues what seems to be the recent factory preference for "unbelted" magnums. Since the belt on the classic magnums like the .375 H&H is little more than a headspace feature (no significant strength is added), the unbelted design probably simplifies manufacturing without degrading performance.

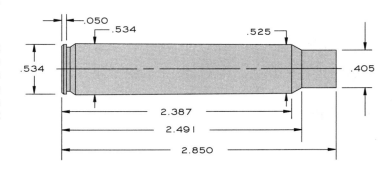

Relative Recoil Factor = 3.70

Specifications

Controlling Agency for Standardization of this Ammunition: SAAMI
Specifications pending

Availability

Remington 270-grain Soft Point (PR375UM2)

G1 Ballistic Coefficient = 0.267

Distance • Yards	Muzzle	100	200	300	400	500	600	800	1000
Velocity • fps	2900	2558	2241	1947	1678	1442	1244	1006	882
Energy • Ft-lbs	5041	3922	3010	2272	1689	1246	928	606	466
Taylor KO Index	42.1	37.1	32.5	28.2	24.3	20.9	18.0	14.6	12.8
Path • Inches	-1.5	+1.9	0.0	-8.9	-27.1	-58.0	-106.2	-278.3	-580.2
Wind Drift • Inches	0.0	1.2	5.0	12.1	23.2	39.0	60.3	119.5	195.7

Remington 300-grain A-Frame Soft Point (PR375UM3)

G1 Ballistic Coefficient = 0.350

Distance • Yards	Muzzle	100	200	300	400	500	600	800	1000
Velocity • fps	2760	2505	2263	2035	1822	1624	1445	1165	1003
Energy • Ft-lbs	5073	4178	3412	2759	2210	1757	1391	905	671
Taylor KO Index	44.5	40.4	36.5	32.8	29.4	26.2	23.3	18.8	16.2
Path • Inches	-1.5	+2.0	0.0	-8.8	-26.1	-54.0	-95.3	-233.8	-476.5
Wind Drift • Inches	0.0	1.0	4.0	9.5	17.6	29.4	44.8	88.4	148.4

.375 A-Square

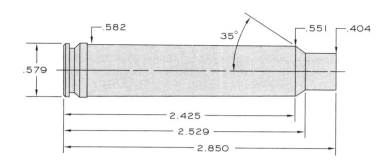

The .375 A^2 is Art Alphin's high-performance vision for this caliber. Driving a 300-grain bullet at better than 2,900 fps, the .375 A^2 stands between the .375 H&H and the .378 Weatherby. This is generally more caliber than is needed for North American hunting use, but it easily fulfills the African medium-rifle requirement.

Relative Recoil Factor = 3.94

Specifications

Controlling Agency for Standardization of this Ammunition: Factory

Availability

A^2 300-grain Triad (None)

G1 Ballistic Coefficient = 0.287

Distance • Yards	Muzzle	100	200	300	400	500	600	800	1000
Velocity • fps	2920	2598	2294	2012	1762	1531	1331	1060	922
Energy • Ft-lbs	5679	4488	3505	2698	2068	1582	1180	748	567
Taylor KO Index	47.1	41.9	37.0	32.4	28.4	24.7	21.4	17.1	14.9
Path • Inches	-1.5	+1.8	0.0	-8.4	-25.5	-53.7	-97.6	-252.1	-527.0
Wind Drift • Inches	0.0	1.1	4.6	11.0	20.9	35.0	53.9	107.7	178.9

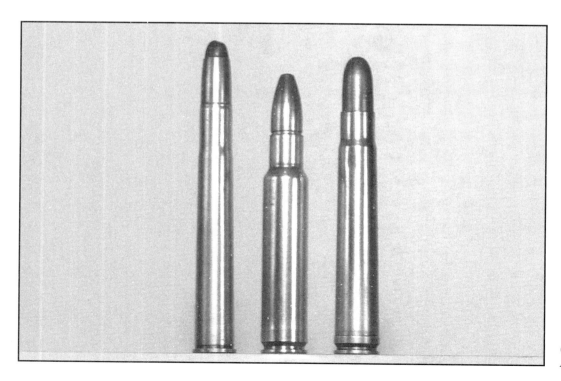

(Left to right) 9.3x74R, .375 Dakota, .375 Holland & Holland.

.375 Weatherby Magnum

This is probably the second oldest in Weatherby's line of proprietary cartridges. It was first offered in 1945. It went out of production around 1965 but has recently been reintroduced. It is nothing more than a blown out .375 H&H, but that said, its increased volume gives it a lot more punch. This cartridge has been largely superceded by the .378 Weatherby Magnum and is presently loaded in only one bullet version.

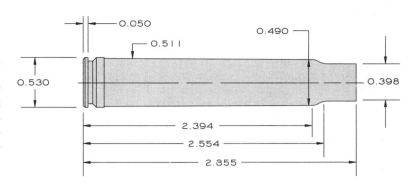

Relative Recoil Factor = 3.75

Specifications

Controlling Agency for Standardization of this Ammunition: Factory
Typical barrel for velocity testing: 26 inches long—1 turn in 12-inch twist

Availability

Weatherby 300-grain Nosler Partition (N375300PT)

G1 Ballistic Coefficient = 0.393

Distance • Yards	Muzzle	100	200	300	400	500	600	800	1000
Velocity • fps	2800	2572	2366	2140	1963	1760	1588	1296	1094
Energy • Ft-lbs	5224	4480	3696	3076	2541	2084	1680	1118	4797
Taylor KO Index	45.0	41.3	38.0	34.4	31.5	28.3	25.5	20.8	17.6
Path • Inches	-1.5	+1.9	0.0	-8.2	-24.0	-49.0	-85.3	-202.5	-403.1
Wind Drift • Inches	0.0	0.8	3.5	8.1	15.1	24.8	37.6	73.7	125.2

(Left to right) .350 Remington Magnum, .375 Weatherby Magnum.

.378 Weatherby Magnum

The .378 Weatherby Magnum goes back quite a long way. Its story starts around 1953. Roy Weatherby wanted something that was significantly more potent than the .375 H&H. His .375 Weatherby Magnum was better than the H&H but not better enough to satisfy Roy. Being very well aware that in cartridge design there's no substitute for case volume for producing velocity and bullet energy, the Weatherby company developed the .378. This cartridge takes a larger action than the standard full-length magnums like the .375. It's a big boomer and kills at both ends. If you are recoil sensitive, you would be well advised to pick a different caliber. Since its introduction, the .378 Weatherby Magnum has become the basic cartridge case for the .30-378 and the .338-378 as well as numerous wildcats.

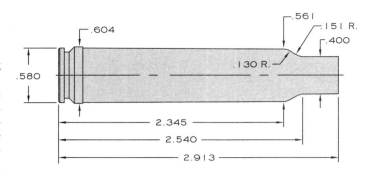

Relative Recoil Factor = 3.95

Specifications

Controlling Agency for Standardization of this Ammunition: CIP

Bullet Weight Grains	Velocity fps	Maximum Average Pressure	
		Copper Crusher	Transducer
N/S	N/S	3,800 bar	4,370 bar

Typical barrel for velocity testing: 26 inches long—1 turn in 12-inch twist

Availability

Weatherby 270-grain Pointed Expanding (H 378 270 SP)
G1 Ballistic Coefficient = 0.380

Distance • Yards	Muzzle	100	200	300	400	500	600	800	1000
Velocity • fps	3180	2921	2677	2445	2225	2017	1819	1470	1201
Energy • Ft-lbs	6062	5115	4295	3583	2968	2438	1985	1297	865
Taylor KO Index	46.4	42.6	39.0	35.6	32.4	29.4	26.4	21.3	17.4
Path • Inches	-1.5	+1.3	0.0	-6.1	-18.1	-37.1	-64.8	-154.9	-312.7
Wind Drift • Inches	0.0	0.7	3.0	7.0	13.1	21.4	32.4	63.8	110.4

Weatherby 270-grain Barnes-X (B 378 270 XS)
G1 Ballistic Coefficient = 0.503

Distance • Yards	Muzzle	100	200	300	400	500	600	800	1000
Velocity • fps	3150	2954	2767	2587	2415	2249	2089	1790	1524
Energy • Ft-lbs	2948	5238	4589	4013	3495	3031	2247	1922	1393
Taylor KO Index	45.9	43.1	40.3	37.7	35.2	32.8	30.3	26.0	22.1
Path • Inches	-1.5	+1.2	0.0	-5.8	-16.7	-33.7	-57.6	-130.6	-248.2
Wind Drift • Inches	0.0	0.6	2.3	5.2	9.6	15.5	23.1	44.2	74.7

Weatherby 300-grain Round Nose-Expanding (H 378 300 RN)
G1 Ballistic Coefficient = 0.250

Distance • Yards	Muzzle	100	200	300	400	500	600	800	1000
Velocity • fps	2925	2558	2220	1908	1627	1383	1189	971	852
Energy • Ft-lbs	5699	4360	3283	2424	1764	1274	942	628	484
Taylor KO Index	47.4	41.4	36.0	30.9	26.4	22.4	19.2	15.6	13.7
Path • Inches	-1.5	+1.9	0.0	-9.0	-27.8	-60.0	-111.3	-295.0	-615.4
Wind Drift • Inches	0.0	1.3	5.4	13.0	24.9	42.2	65.4	128.8	209.2

A² 300-grain Triad (None)
G1 Ballistic Coefficient = 0.287

Distance • Yards	Muzzle	100	200	300	400	500	600	800	1000
Velocity • fps	2900	2577	2276	1997	1747	1518	1320	1054	919
Energy • Ft-lbs	5602	4424	3452	2656	2034	1535	1161	740	563
Taylor KO Index	47.0	41.7	36.9	32.4	28.3	24.6	21.3	17.0	14.8
Path • Inches	-1.5	+1.9	0.0	-8.6	-25.9	-54.6	-99.2	-256.1	-534.4
Wind Drift • Inches	0.0	1.1	4.6	11.1	21.1	35.4	54.5	108.6	180.0

Weatherby 300-grain Full Metal Jacket (H 378 300 FJ)

G1 Ballistic Coefficient = 0.275

Distance • Yards	Muzzle	100	200	300	400	500	600	800	1000
Velocity • fps	2925	2591	2280	1991	1725	1489	1287	1031	901
Energy • Ft-lbs	5699	4470	3461	2640	1983	1476	1104	708	540
Taylor KO Index	47.4	42.0	36.9	32.3	27.9	24.1	20.7	16.6	14.5
Path • Inches	-1.5	+1.8	0.0	-8.6	-26.1	-55.4	-101.1	-263.7	-551.7
Wind Drift • Inches	0.0	1.1	4.8	11.5	21.9	36.8	57.1	113.8	187.8

Famed African PH Tony Sanchez is a fan of the .500 Jeffery cartridge. (Photo from *Elephant Hunters, Men of Legend* by Tony Sanchez-Ariño, Safari Press, 2005)

.38-40 Winchester

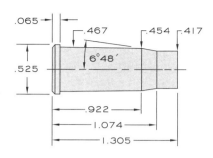

Perhaps the first thing you should know about the .38-40 is that it isn't. Isn't a .38-caliber round, that is. The .38-40 uses bullets 0.4005 inches in diameter and is really a .40 caliber. I suppose that doesn't matter too much because the .38 Special isn't a .38 either. The .38-40 goes back to the beginning of centerfire cartridges; it was introduced clear back in 1874. At the time of its introduction, the idea of using the same cartridge in both rifles and pistols had lots of support. Today, only Winchester makes ammunition in this caliber.

Relative Recoil Factor = 0.95

Specifications

Controlling Agency for Standardization of this Ammunition: SAAMI

Bullet Weight Grains	Velocity fps	Maximum Average Pressure	
		Copper Crusher	Transducer
180	1,150	14,000 cup	N/S

Standard barrel for velocity testing: 24 inches long—1 turn in 36-inch twist

Availability

Winchester 180-grain Soft Point (X3840)

G1 Ballistic Coefficient = 0.173

Distance • Yards	Muzzle	100	200	300	400	500	600	800	1000
Velocity • fps	1160	999	901	827	764	710	660	572	494
Energy • Ft-lbs	538	399	324	273	233	201	174	131	98
Taylor KO Index	11.9	10.3	9.3	8.5	7.9	7.3	6.8	5.9	5.1
Path • Inches	-1.5	+16.6	0.0	-59.4	-169.8	-339.6	-566.4	-1277	-2405
Wind Drift • Inches	0.0	3.9	14.2	29.9	50.8	77.0	108.6	189.7	297.5

The mountain nyala only occurs in Ethiopia and is considered Africa's most difficult animal to secure. (Photo from A Sporting Life *by José A. Martinez de Hoz, Safari Press, 2005)*

.38-55 Winchester

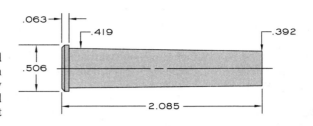

This is another example of an old, old cartridge, originally designed for use with black powder. Unlike the .38-40, this is a rifle cartridge from its introduction. The cases (not complete rounds) have been used for many years in Schutzen rifle competition, where they have established a fine record for accuracy. The cartridge is nearing the end of its useful life. After all, it has only been around since about 1884.

Relative Recoil Factor = 1.51

Specifications

Controlling Agency for Standardization of this Ammunition: SAAMI

Bullet Weight Grains	Velocity fps	Maximum Average Pressure	
		Copper Crusher	Transducer
2550	1,320	30,000 cup	N/S

Standard barrel for velocity testing: 24 inches long—1 turn in 18-inch twist

Availability

Winchester 255-grain Soft Point (X3855)

G1 Ballistic Coefficient = 0.355

Distance • Yards	Muzzle	100	200	300	400	500	600	800	1000
Velocity • fps	1320	1190	1091	1018	963	917	877	809	751
Energy • Ft-lbs	987	802	674	587	525	476	436	371	319
Taylor KO Index	18.1	16.3	15.0	14.0	13.2	12.6	12.0	11.1	10.3
Path • Inches	-1.5	+11.5	0.0	-40.7	-114.8	-226.5	-374.8	-809.7	-1448
Wind Drift • Inches	0.0	2.2	8.6	18.8	32.2	48.4	67.3	112.7	168.3

(Left to right) .38-40, .38-55, .44-40, .444 Marlin.

.405 Winchester

The .405 Winchester is an oldie that was suddenly revived. It was introduced in 1904 for Winchester's 1895 rifle. Despite its age, this cartridge was never a black-powder number. At the time of its introduction, it was the most powerful lever-action cartridge made. Hornady brought it back into production in 2002. Because the specifications have not been published at the time of this writing, potential users are advised to consult the factory before firing this ammo in any guns except brand-new models that have been factory chambered specifically for this cartridge.

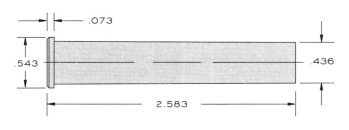

Relative Recoil Factor = 1.51

Specifications

Controlling Agency for Standardization of this Ammunition: SAAMI

Bullet Weight Grains	Velocity fps	Maximum Average Pressure	
		Copper Crusher	Transducer
300	2200	N/S	?

Standard barrel for velocity testing: N/A—1 turn in 14-inch twist

Availability

Hornady 300-grain FP InterLock (8240)

G1 Ballistic Coefficient = 0.225

Distance • Yards	Muzzle	100	200	300	400	500	600	800	1000
Velocity • fps	2200	1857	1553	1300	1117	1002	923	810	722
Energy • Ft-lbs	3224	2297	1607	1126	831	669	568	437	347
Taylor KO Index	38.8	32.7	27.4	22.9	19.7	17.6	16.3	14.3	12.7
Path • Inches	-1.5	+4.4	0.0	-18.9	-58.5	-125.8	-227.8	-560.3	-1106
Wind Drift • Inches	0.0	2.3	9.2	22.5	42.5	68.6	99.6	174.2	265.0

Hornady 300-grain SP InterLock (8241)

G1 Ballistic Coefficient = 0.250

Distance • Yards	Muzzle	100	200	300	400	500	600	800	1000
Velocity • fps	2200	1890	1610	1370	1181	1053	967	851	764
Energy • Ft-lbs	3224	2379	1727	1250	929	738	624	482	389
Taylor KO Index	38.8	33.3	28.4	24.1	20.8	18.5	17.0	15.0	13.5
Path • Inches	-1.5	+4.2	0.0	-17.7	-54.0	-115.2	-207.8	-509.8	-1005
Wind Drift • Inches	0.0	1.9	8.2	19.8	37.4	61.0	89.4	158.3	241.8

.44-40 Winchester

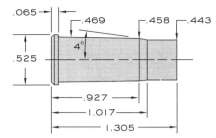

The .44-40 was developed for Winchester's Model 1873 rifle. It is yet another example of an early centerfire, black-powder cartridge that has been used in both rifles and pistols. While it is greatly outperformed by the .44 Remington Magnum, this caliber is making a comeback in Cowboy Action Shooting events. The Cowboy Action ammunition is loaded to a very much milder standard than the current SAAMI specification.

Relative Recoil Factor = 1.07

Specifications

Controlling Agency for Standardization of this Ammunition: SAAMI

Bullet Weight Grains	Velocity fps	Maximum Average Pressure	
		Copper Crusher	Transducer
200	1,175	13,000 cup	N/S

Standard barrel for velocity testing: 24 inches long—1 turn in 36-inch twist

Availability

Remington 200-grain Soft Point (R4440W)

G1 Ballistic Coefficient = 0.161

Distance • Yards	Muzzle	100	200	300	400	500	600	800	1000
Velocity • fps	1190	1006	900	822	756	699	645	553	472
Energy • Ft-lbs	629	449	360	300	254	217	185	136	99
Taylor KO Index	14.5	12.3	11.0	10.0	9.2	8.5	7.9	6.7	5.8
Path • Inches	-1.5	+16.4	0.0	-59.3	-170.3	-342.3	-571.4	-1301	-2478
Wind Drift • Inches	0.0	4.3	15.6	32.8	55.5	84.0	118.3	206.6	324.7

Winchester 200-grain Soft Point (X4440)

G1 Ballistic Coefficient = 0.161

Distance • Yards	Muzzle	100	200	300	400	500	600	800	1000
Velocity • fps	1190	1006	900	822	756	699	645	553	472
Energy • Ft-lbs	629	449	360	300	254	217	185	136	99
Taylor KO Index	14.5	12.3	11.0	10.0	9.2	8.5	7.9	6.7	5.8
Path • Inches	-1.5	+16.4	0.0	-59.3	-170.3	-342.3	-571.4	-1301	-2478
Wind Drift • Inches	0.0	4.3	15.6	32.8	55.5	84.0	118.3	206.6	324.7

.44 Remington Magnum (Rifle Data)

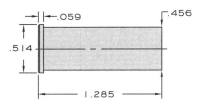

The .44 Remington Magnum defined the high-powered pistol from its introduction in 1956 until the .454 Casull came into being a few years ago. There are few shooters who can get more than a few shots out of the .44 Remington Magnum pistol before beginning to flinch. Pistol shooting is one thing, and rifle shooting is another. In carbine-style guns, the .44 Remington Magnum becomes a good choice for deer-size game. The comparison with the .30-30 is interesting. On an energy basis, the .30-30 is a little better. But when Taylor KO indexes are compared, the .44 Remington Magnum is the clear choice. It comes down to whether you believe energy (lighter bullet, higher velocity) is "everything," or whether you like heavy bullets at modest velocity. It becomes the "shooter's choice." All the cartridges listed here can be used in pistols, and any pistol cartridge in this caliber can be used in properly chambered modern rifles in good condition. (See the pistol listing for more information.)

Relative Recoil Factor = 1.90

Specifications

Controlling Agency for Standardization of this Ammunition: SAAMI

See pistol data section for detailed specifications.

All data in this section taken in 20-inch barrels.

Availability

Remington 210-grain Semi-Jacketed Hollow Point (R44MG6) (Discontinued in 2005)

G1 Ballistic Coefficient = 0.154

Distance • Yards	Muzzle	100	200	300	400	500	600	800	1000
Velocity • fps	1920	1477	1155	982	880	802	678	625	532
Energy • Ft-lbs	1719	1017	622	450	361	300	253	182	132
Taylor KO Index	24.7	19.0	14.9	12.6	11.3	10.3	8.8	8.1	6.9
Path • Inches	-1.5	+7.4	0.0	-33.3	-102.4	-216.4	-366.8	-868.2	-1700
Wind Drift • Inches	0.0	3.9	17.0	39.0	68.9	104.3	145.5	246.4	374.7

Winchester 210-grain Silvertip Hollow Point (X44MS) (Discontinued in 2005)

G1 Ballistic Coefficient = 0.142

Distance • Yards	Muzzle	100	200	300	400	500	600	800	1000
Velocity • fps	1580	1198	993	879	795	725	664	557	466
Energy • Ft-lbs	1164	670	460	361	295	245	206	145	101
Taylor KO Index	20.3	15.4	12.8	11.3	10.2	9.3	8.6	7.2	6.0
Path • Inches	-1.5	+11.4	0.0	-46.4	-137.8	-284.1	-471.6	-1108	-2174
Wind Drift • Inches	0.0	5.2	20.6	43.9	73.6	109.8	152.5	259.5	400.1

Remington 240-grain Soft Point (R44MG2)

G1 Ballistic Coefficient = 0.167

Distance • Yards	Muzzle	100	200	300	400	500	600	800	1000
Velocity • fps	1760	1380	1114	970	878	806	744	640	551
Energy • Ft-lbs	1650	1015	661	501	411	346	295	218	162
Taylor KO Index	25.9	20.3	16.4	14.3	12.9	11.9	11.0	9.5	8.2
Path • Inches	-1.5	+8.5	0.0	-36.3	-109.5	-227.8	-382.6	-889.8	-1714
Wind Drift • Inches	0.0	4.0	16.8	37.9	65.2	98.1	136.3	229.5	347.5

Federal 240-grain Hi-Shok Hollow Point (C44A)

G1 Ballistic Coefficient = 0.159

Distance • Yards	Muzzle	100	200	300	400	500	600	800	1000
Velocity • fps	1760	1380	1090	950	860	790	727	621	531
Energy • Ft-lbs	1650	1015	640	485	395	330	282	205	150
Taylor KO Index	26.1	20.4	16.1	14.1	12.7	11.7	10.8	9.2	7.9
Path • Inches	-1.5	+8.7	0.0	-37.5	-113.1	-235.5	-394.8	-922.4	-1788
Wind Drift • Inches	0.0	4.2	17.7	39.6	68.0	102.0	141.8	239.2	363.3

Remington 240-grain Semi-Jacketed Hollow Point (R44MG3)

G1 Ballistic Coefficient = 0.167

Distance • Yards	Muzzle	100	200	300	400	500	600	800	1000
Velocity • fps	1760	1380	1114	970	878	806	744	640	551
Energy • Ft-lbs	1650	1015	661	501	411	346	295	218	162
Taylor KO Index	25.9	20.3	16.4	14.3	12.9	11.9	11.0	9.5	8.2
Path • Inches	-1.5	+8.5	0.0	-36.3	-109.5	-227.8	-382.6	-889.8	-1714
Wind Drift • Inches	0.0	4.0	16.8	37.9	65.2	98.1	136.3	229.5	347.5

Winchester 240-grain Hollow Soft Point (X44MHSP2)

G1 Ballistic Coefficient = 0.159

Distance • Yards	Muzzle	100	200	300	400	500	600	800	1000
Velocity • fps	1760	1362	1094	953	861	789	727	621	531
Energy • Ft-lbs	1651	988	638	484	395	332	282	205	150
Taylor KO Index	26.1	20.4	16.1	14.1	12.7	11.7	10.8	9.2	7.9
Path • Inches	-1.5	+8.7	0.0	-37.1	-110.4	-227.0	-394.8	-922.4	-1788
Wind Drift • Inches	0.0	4.2	17.7	39.6	68.0	102.0	141.8	239.2	363.3

Winchester 250-grain Platinum Tip (S44PTHP)

G1 Ballistic Coefficient = 0.188

Distance • Yards	Muzzle	100	200	300	400	500	600	800	1000
Velocity • fps	1830	1475	1201	1032	931	857	796	695	611
Energy • Ft-lbs	1859	1208	801	591	481	408	352	268	208
Taylor KO Index	26.9	21.7	17.6	15.1	13.7	12.6	11.7	10.2	9.0
Path • Inches	-1.5	+7.3	0.0	-31.4	-95.2	-199.1	-350.2	-825.8	-1592
Wind Drift • Inches	0.0	3.3	14.3	33.1	58.2	88.5	123.6	208.4	313.8

Winchester 250-grain Partition Gold (S44MP)

G1 Ballistic Coefficient = 0.188

Distance • Yards	Muzzle	100	200	300	400	500	600	800	1000
Velocity • fps	1810	1455	1188	1025	926	853	794	693	609
Energy • Ft-lbs	1818	1175	738	583	476	404	350	267	206
Taylor KO Index	26.6	21.4	17.4	15.0	13.6	12.5	11.7	10.2	8.9
Path • Inches	-1.5	+7.5	0.0	-32.0	-96.9	-202.2	-355.1	-835.6	-1609
Wind Drift • Inches	0.0	3.3	14.4	33.3	58.4	88.6	123.7	208.3	313.6

Remington 275-grain Core-Lokt JHP (RH44MGA)

G1 Ballistic Coefficient = 0.200

Distance • Yards	Muzzle	100	200	300	400	500	600	800	1000
Velocity • fps	1580	1293	1093	976	896	832	777	683	603
Energy • Ft-lbs	1524	1020	730	582	490	422	368	285	222
Taylor KO Index	26.6	21.5	18.4	16.4	15.1	14.0	13.2	11.6	10.2
Path • Inches	-1.5	+9.7	0.0	-38.6	-113.8	-232.2	-387.6	-878.5	-1648
Wind Drift • Inches	0.0	3.6	14.8	32.7	55.9	83.8	116.1	194.4	292.2

.444 Marlin

In 1964, Marlin reopened their production line for their Model 1895 Lever Action. To make the new offering more attractive, Marlin chambered the gun for a new cartridge that had been developed by Remington, the .444. The .444 and the .45-70 are so near in physical size that you wonder, *Why bother?* The answer is that the .444 and the new Model 1895 were designed for a pressure level of 42,000 psi as opposed to the .45-70's 28,000 psi limit. While the .444 makes an excellent brush gun, the caliber never caught on with the American hunter.

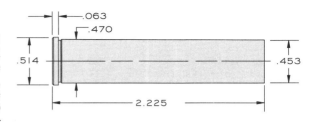

Relative Recoil Factor = 2.54

Specifications

Controlling Agency for Standardization of this Ammunition: SAAMI

Bullet Weight Grains	Velocity fps	Maximum Average Pressure	
		Copper Crusher	Transducer
240	2,320	44,000 cup	42,000 psi
265	2,100	44,000 cup	42,000 psi

Standard barrel for velocity testing: 24 inches long—1 turn in 38-inch twist

Availability

Remington 240-grain Soft Point (R444M)
G1 Ballistic Coefficient = 0.146

Distance • Yards	Muzzle	100	200	300	400	500	600	800	1000
Velocity • fps	2350	1815	1377	1087	941	846	769	646	544
Energy • Ft-lbs	2942	1755	1010	630	472	381	315	222	158
Taylor KO Index	34.6	26.8	20.3	16.0	13.9	12.5	11.4	9.5	8.0
Path • Inches	-1.5	+4.7	0.0	-23.4	-76.0	-168.1	-297.5	-730.8	-1469
Wind Drift • Inches	0.0	3.1	14.2	35.4	65.5	102.5	145.6	250.8	384.2

Cor-Bon 280-grain BondedCore SP (HT444M280BC/20)
G1 Ballistic Coefficient = 0.250

Distance • Yards	Muzzle	100	200	300	400	500	600	800	1000
Velocity • fps	2200	1890	1610	1369	1180	1051	966	850	763
Energy • Ft-lbs	3009	2200	1612	1165	865	687	581	449	362
Taylor KO Index	37.9	32.6	27.8	23.6	20.3	18.1	16.7	14.7	13.2
Path • Inches	-1.5	+4.2	0.0	-17.7	-54.0	-115.4	-208.1	-510.8	-1007
Wind Drift • Inches	0.0	1.9	8.2	19.8	37.5	61.1	89.1	158.6	242.3

Cor-Bon 305-grain FP Penetrator (HT444M305FPN/20)
G1 Ballistic Coefficient = 0.250

Distance • Yards	Muzzle	100	200	300	400	500	600	800	1000
Velocity • fps	2100	1799	1530	1303	1133	1021	945	835	751
Energy • Ft-lbs	2988	2191	1585	1151	870	707	605	472	382
Taylor KO Index	39.4	33.8	28.7	24.5	21.3	19.2	17.7	15.7	14.1
Path • Inches	-1.5	+4.7	0.0	-19.6	-59.8	-127.1	-227.6	-551.0	-1075
Wind Drift • Inches	0.0	2.0	8.8	21.1	39.5	63.6	92.4	161.5	245.1

.45-70 Government

The .45-70 Government was originally manufactured for the Model 1873 Springfield rifle. In 1866, Erskine Allin developed a way to convert 1865 Springfield muzzleloading rifles to fire a .58-caliber rimfire cartridge. By 1873, an Allin-style rifle won a competition for a new breechloading rifle. Those rifles became known as "Trapdoors" because of their breeching mechanism. Today's factory loadings are held to very mild levels because of these old guns, but handloaders have been known to push pressures up to 50,000 psi in modern guns.

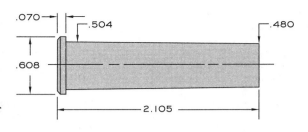

Relative Recoil Factor = 2.43

Specifications

Controlling Agency for Standardization of this Ammunition: SAAMI

Bullet Weight Grains	Velocity fps	Maximum Average Pressure	
		Copper Crusher	Transducer
300	1,830	28,000 cup	28,000 psi
405	1,320	28,000 cup	28,000 psi

Standard barrel for velocity testing: 24 inches long—1 turn in 20-inch twist

Availability

Federal 300-grain Speer Hot-Cor SP (4570AS)   G1 Ballistic Coefficient = 0.284

Distance • Yards	Muzzle	100	200	300	400	500	600	800	1000
Velocity • fps	1880	1650	1430	1240	1110	1010	945	846	768
Energy • Ft-lbs	2355	1815	1355	1015	910	680	594	476	393
Taylor KO Index	36.9	32.4	28.1	24.3	21.8	19.8	18.5	16.6	15.1
Path • Inches	-1.5	+5.8	0.0	-23.3	-69.5	-144.1	-251.4	-579.5	-1086
Wind Drift • Inches	0.0	2.1	8.8	20.7	38.0	60.1	86.1	148.4	223.4

Winchester 300-grain Jacketed Hollow Point (X4570H)   G1 Ballistic Coefficient = 0.283

Distance • Yards	Muzzle	100	200	300	400	500	600	800	1000
Velocity • fps	1880	1650	1425	1235	1105	1010	948	849	772
Energy • Ft-lbs	2355	1815	1355	1015	810	680	599	480	397
Taylor KO Index	36.9	32.4	28.0	24.2	21.7	19.8	18.6	16.7	15.2
Path • Inches	-1.5	+5.8	0.0	-23.3	-69.4	-144.1	-249.8	-575.7	-1078
Wind Drift • Inches	0.0	2.1	8.8	20.7	38.0	60.1	85.2	147.0	221.5

Winchester 300-grain Partition Gold (SPGX4570)   G1 Ballistic Coefficient = 0.215

Distance • Yards	Muzzle	100	200	300	400	500	600	800	1000
Velocity • fps	1880	1558	1292	1103	988	910	849	748	665
Energy • Ft-lbs	2355	1616	1112	811	651	551	480	373	294
Taylor KO Index	36.9	30.6	25.4	21.7	19.4	17.9	16.7	14.7	13.1
Path • Inches	-1.5	+6.5	0.0	-27.3	-83.0	-174.2	-300.6	-695.7	-1318
Wind Drift • Inches	0.0	2.8	12.0	28.2	50.8	78.4	110.5	187.1	280.8

Remington 300-grain Semi-Jacketed Hollow Point (R4570L)   G1 Ballistic Coefficient = 0.213

Distance • Yards	Muzzle	100	200	300	400	500	600	800	1000
Velocity • fps	1810	1497	1244	1073	969	895	834	735	653
Energy • Ft-lbs	2182	1492	1031	767	625	533	463	360	284
Taylor KO Index	35.5	29.4	24.4	21.1	19.0	17.6	16.4	14.4	12.8
Path • Inches	-1.5	+7.1	0.0	-29.6	-89.3	-186.0	-318.2	-731.7	-1381
Wind Drift • Inches	0.0	2.9	12.6	29.3	52.1	79.8	111.8	-188.6	-282.7

PMC 350-grain Flat Nose Soft Point +P+ (45-70HA)

G1 Ballistic Coefficient = 0.213

Distance • Yards	Muzzle	100	200	300	400	500	600	800	1000
Velocity • fps	2025	1678	1390	1168	1027	937	869	763	677
Energy • Ft-lbs	3167	2187	1502	1060	820	683	588	453	356
Taylor KO Index	46.4	38.4	31.8	26.7	23.5	21.5	19.9	17.5	15.5
Path • Inches	-1.5	+5.5	0.0	-23.7	-72.9	-153.9	-271.7	-638.8	-1222
Wind Drift • Inches	0.0	2.5	11.0	26.6	49.0	76.8	109.3	187.0	281.9

Cor-Bon 350-grain BondedCore SP (HT4570B350/20)

G1 Ballistic Coefficient = 0.213

Distance • Yards	Muzzle	100	200	300	400	500	600	800	1000
Velocity • fps	1800	1488	1238	1069	966	892	833	736	655
Energy • Ft-lbs	2519	1722	1192	889	725	619	539	421	334
Taylor KO Index	41.2	34.1	28.4	24.5	22.1	20.4	19.1	16.9	15.0
Path • Inches	-1.5	+7.2	0.0	-29.9	-90.1	-187.6	-328.7	-768.7	-1468
Wind Drift • Inches	0.0	3.0	12.6	29.4	52.2	79.9	111.9	188.7	283.0

Remington 405-grain Soft Point (R4570G)

G1 Ballistic Coefficient = 0.281

Distance • Yards	Muzzle	100	200	300	400	500	600	800	1000
Velocity • fps	1330	1168	1055	977	918	869	824	749	685
Energy • Ft-lbs	1590	1227	1001	858	758	679	611	505	421
Taylor KO Index	35.2	30.9	28.0	25.9	24.3	23.0	21.8	19.8	18.2
Path • Inches	-1.5	+12.0	0.0	-43.1	-122.7	-243.5	-402.8	-880.3	-1594
Wind Drift • Inches	0.0	2.8	10.8	23.2	39.3	58.8	81.5	136.6	204.7

Cor-Bon 450-grain FP Penetrator (HT4570405FPN/20)

G1 Ballistic Coefficient = 0.280

Distance • Yards	Muzzle	100	200	300	400	500	600	800	1000
Velocity • fps	1650	1427	1242	1105	1012	945	891	804	734
Energy • Ft-lbs	2449	1832	1389	1100	923	804	716	584	486
Taylor KO Index	43.7	37.8	32.9	29.3	26.8	25.1	23.6	21.3	19.5
Path • Inches	-1.5	+7.8	0.0	-30.4	-89.1	-181.7	-313.2	-712.4	-1327
Wind Drift • Inches	0.0	2.4	10.2	23.4	41.4	63.4	89.0	150.0	223.9

Availability

Cowboy Action Ammunition

Cor-Bon 405-grain Lead FP (US4570405BP/20)

G1 Ballistic Coefficient = 0.280

Distance • Yards	Muzzle	100	200	300	400	500	600	800	1000
Velocity • fps	1650	1427	1242	1105	1012	945	891	804	734
Energy • Ft-lbs	2449	1832	1389	1100	923	804	716	584	486
Taylor KO Index	43.7	37.8	32.9	29.3	26.8	25.1	23.6	21.3	19.5
Path • Inches	-1.5	+7.8	0.0	-30.4	-89.1	-181.7	-313.2	-712.4	-1327
Wind Drift • Inches	0.0	2.4	10.2	23.4	41.4	63.4	89.0	150.0	223.9

PMC 405-grain LFP (45-70CA)

G1 Ballistic Coefficient = 0.301

Distance • Yards	Muzzle	100	200	300	400	500	600	800	1000
Velocity • fps	1350	1193	1078	999	938	889	846	772	709
Energy • Ft-lbs	1639	1280	1046	897	792	711	643	536	452
Taylor KO Index	35.8	31.6	28.6	26.5	24.9	23.6	22.4	20.5	18.8
Path • Inches	-1.5	+11.5	0.0	-41.1	-116.5	-230.1	-386.1	-842.0	-1520
Wind Drift • Inches	0.0	2.6	10.2	22.0	37.5	56.2	78.1	130.6	195.3

.450 Marlin

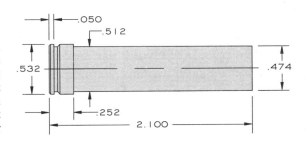

Marlin and Hornady teamed together to introduce this cartridge in 2001. Marlin wanted a high-performance cartridge to pick up in modern guns where the ancient .45-70 left off. While the cartridge volume is about the same as the .45-70, the working pressure is nearly double, producing a significant improvement in performance. Hornady's designers put an extra-wide belt on this cartridge, thereby reducing the number of possible wrong chambers that can be found. At the present time the only loading has flat-point bullets for use in tubular magazine guns.

Relative Recoil Factor = 3.27

Specifications

Controlling Agency for Standardization of this Ammunition: SAAMI

Bullet Weight Grains	Velocity fps	Maximum Average Pressure	
		Copper Crusher	Transducer
300	N/A	N/A	44,000 psi

Standard barrel for velocity testing: 18.5 inches long—1 turn in 20-inch twist (preliminary)

Availability

Hornady 300-grain FP InterLock (8250)

G1 Ballistic Coefficient = 0.195

Distance • Yards	Muzzle	100	200	300	400	500	600	800	1000
Velocity • fps	2100	1720	1397	1156	1011	920	850	741	653
Energy • Ft-lbs	3427	2298	1516	1039	795	658	562	427	332
Taylor KO Index	48.1	39.4	32.0	26.5	23.2	21.1	19.5	17.0	15.0
Path • Inches	-1.5	+5.2	0.0	-23.2	-72.4	-155.5	-279.7	-680.0	-1336
Wind Drift • Inches	0.0	2.7	11.6	28.2	52.2	82.0	116.6	199.9	302.2

Kirk Kelso with a Coues deer, the desert variety of the common whitetail. (Photo from Ask the Whitetail Guides by J. Y. Jones, 2006, Safari Press)

Rifles for Dangerous Game

Joe Coogan

We were looking over a herd of buffalo in thick cover when an irritable old bull broke from the herd and burst through the bushes without warning. He came straight for us. I had time only to throw my gun up and shoot as if at a flushing gamebird.

A 500-grain solid bullet from my .458 rifle slammed through the brute's brain, coming to rest under the thick folded skin on the back of his neck. The buffalo died on his feet, his legs buckling and his forward momentum carrying him forward for several more feet. His nose shoveled into the sand just seven paces from where I stood.

Unusual? Yes. To put the incident in perspective, that's the only time an unwounded buffalo has charged me in more than 20 years of buffalo hunting. But when an encounter such as this does happen, there's no margin for error.

This .505 Gibbs, built by Gibbs on a square-bridge Mauser Magnum action, is a good choice for game as large as elephant. However, for most dangerous game, including Cape buffalo and lion, hunters are well served with slightly smaller calibers that are more comfortable to shoot.

The best insurance against dangerous game is the rifle you carry. As such, you owe it to yourself to own the most dependable rifle you can afford. Whether you're hunting Africa's Big Five or tracking a Kodiak bear in Alaska, your rifle needs to be reliable and of sufficient caliber to stop the charge of a dangerous animal.

Calibers

Because every dangerous game hunt is different, there is no single rifle or cartridge that is perfect for every situation, but a few important guidelines apply. Most importantly, there are minimum standards for calibers that should be used for dangerous game, depending on which animal is to be hunted. Those calibers are sometimes required by law; they are always compelled by common sense.

For instance, if you're hunting thin-skinned game, such as Alaska's brown bears in open terrain or Africa's big cats, then you will want a softpoint load in a caliber that's capable of reaching out accurately for a hundred yards or more. The .375 H&H Magnum is an ideal caliber for such a job. If the terrain is brushy, thereby requiring closer shots, then you might opt for one of the .416 calibers with a low-power scope.

For larger, thick-skinned game, such as elephant, rhino, and buffalo, you will need a full-metal-jacketed (solid) load that's designed to penetrate dense muscle and thick bones—something in the .400-caliber range or larger. I can remember more than one incident when a quick shot with a solid bullet from my .458 rifle stopped things from getting messy.

The .375 H&H Magnum, classified as a medium-heavy cartridge, is perhaps the most universally accepted caliber for hunting dangerous game, but it's considered by many to be a marginal caliber for thick-skinned, heavy-boned game. The .400-caliber-class cartridges are much more suitable—and effective—for the biggest game. When hunting was still allowed in Kenya prior to the mid-1970s, an astute game department enforced a .400- or larger caliber requirement for hunting elephant, rhino, and buffalo.

Today the .400-caliber cartridges available for bolt guns begin with the British cartridges: .404 Jeffery, .416 Rigby, and .425 Westley Richards. Popular in this country

The big guns: a .416 Rigby magazine rifle; a Rigby .600 Nitro Express double rifle; and a Westley Richards .500 Nitro Express double rifle on the buffalo skull. The high cost of top-quality doubles, such as the two shown here, has caused an increase in the use of magazine rifles for dangerous game.

are the .416s in Rigby, Remington, and Weatherby flavors. The performance of these cartridges places them in a class of loads capable of generating more than 5,000 ft.-lbs. of muzzle energy, which has garnered them much respect among those who hunt dangerous game.

In 1956, Winchester introduced the .458 Winchester Magnum, the largest of Winchester's short-belted magnums and designed to function in standard-length actions. It was the first American factory cartridge designed specifically for hunting African game. The original ballistics listed a 500-grain solid and a 510-grain softpoint, both at 2,130 fps, for just above 5,000 ft.-lbs. of muzzle energy. Both bullets approximated the ballistics of the .450-class of rimmed Nitro Express cartridges used in British double rifles at the turn of the 20th century. Factory rifles chambered for the .458 Winchester Magnum are currently available from Winchester, Ruger, and Remington.

In 1958, Roy Weatherby introduced the .460 Weatherby Magnum, which fires a 500-grain bullet at 2,700 fps and generates a muzzle energy of 8,095 ft.-lbs. At the time, the .460 Weatherby replaced the .600 NE as the world's most powerful commercially made cartridge.

The next big-bore development came in 1988 with Remington's introduction of its new .416 Remington Magnum cartridge. This was based on the 8mm Remington case, necked up to .416 caliber. According to *Barnes's Cartridges of the World*, it was initially available with either a 400-grain pointed softpoint or a 400-grain solid bullet loaded to a muzzle velocity of 2,400 fps and a muzzle energy of 5,115 ft.-lbs. It was also the first American factory cartridge developed for dangerous game since the introduction of the .458 Winchester Magnum 32 years earlier.

Following quickly on the heels of Remington's .416 round came Weatherby's version of a .416 cartridge, introduced in 1989. The .416 Weatherby Magnum is based on a necked-up .378 Weatherby Magnum case, and offers 300 fps more initial velocity than the .416 Remington, with the same bullet weight. Obviously, both cartridges serve more than an adequate purpose in the field, and the choice between the two really becomes a matter of personal preference.

American gun companies that offer the .416 include Ruger, which chambers its M77 MKII Magnum rifle in .416 Rigby; Winchester, which offers its Classic Safari Express M70 in .416 Remington Magnum; and Remington, which offers a safari-grade M700 in .416 Remington Magnum. The .416 Weatherby Magnum Mark V rifles and ammunition are available only through Weatherby.

Two recent developments in big-bore cartridges are worth noting. In the USA, Ruger and Hornady both offer factory products in rifles and cartridges for the .458 Lott. In the early 1970s, gun aficionado Jack Lott began working up "ballistically improved" cartridges. When he ordered a hand-reamer ground to his specifications for rechambering existing .458 Winchester Magnum rifles to his own design, he called it the .458 Lott. His design was such that if a hunter was short on ammo, he could fire standard .458 Winchester Magnum ammo in a .458 Lott chamber with no problems. After years of proven field performance and perseverance, Lott's wildcat cartridge has finally been recognized as a significant member of the big-bore realm.

Meanwhile, the prestigious London gun company Holland & Holland has introduced two brand-new calibers for magazine rifles: a .400-caliber/400-grain (approx. 5,000 ft.-lbs.) cartridge, and a .465-caliber/480-grain (approx. 6,000 ft.-lbs.) cartridge. The .400 is ballistically similar to the .416 Remington, but the .465 is its own cartridge. Both cartridges will achieve a target velocity of 2,350 fps for moderate pressures.

These calibers will utilize bullets of standard weights and quality construction that will provide big-game

For lions, the .375 H&H Magnum is considered to be the ideal caliber when loaded with softpoint bullets.

stopping power. For practical purposes they will shoot similarly to the .375 H&H out to 150 yards. Holland & Holland is calling these new cartridges the .400 H&H Magnum Belted Rimless and the .465 H&H Magnum Belted Rimless (head-stamp .400 H&H and .465 H&H), respectively. These are H&H's first proprietary cartridges designed for magazine rifles since 1911, when the .375 H&H Magnum was introduced.

Rifles

When choosing a rifle for hunting dangerous game, look beyond cosmetics and economy to functionality, fit, and feel. Basically there are two types of rifles from which to choose a big-game stopper. The most widely used is the bolt-action magazine rifle, and the other is the reliable, but expensive, double rifle of British or European make.

Doubles were the rifles of choice for many East African professional hunters until right after World War II, when ammo began to get scarce. Most felt that a double rifle provided the advantage of two certain shots without having to cock or reload, as opposed to "maybe" three or four shots from a magazine rifle.

The double enthusiasts also noted that their guns had the advantage of shorter overall length for the same barrel length. They said this provided better balance, although some doubles tend to feel barrel-heavy. The balance and feel of a double rifle is very different from a magazine rifle, and it takes getting used to. A minimum of 100 rounds should be fired from a double rifle, or any rifle for that matter, in order to become familiar enough with it to take it hunting for dangerous game.

It is often said that doubles are more reliable because each barrel and firing mechanism works independently of the other, in effect making it two rifles in one. But the downside of a good-quality double rifle is the staggering cost. Unless you are independently wealthy, buying a double rifle is difficult to justify.

Most of us are more familiar with the magazine rifle, making it a more sensible as well as more economical choice. There are plenty of opinions about which bolt-action rifles are the best, but most savvy shooters acknowledge the Mauser Model 98 action as the finest bolt action ever designed, which is pretty amazing when you consider that it was introduced as a German military rifle back in 1898. Several quality actions have incorporated the features of the Mauser, which include controlled-round feeding, front-locking dual lugs, non-rotating external-claw extractor, and positive ejection.

When determining the merits of a particular magazine rifle, consider several factors. First and foremost, the rifle must be accurate, and the action must be smooth in order for the bolt to work quickly and reliably. Placement, position, and angle of the bolt handle determine how accessible it is, which in turn determines how quickly cartridges can be cycled. Even the position of the safety catch is important; the hunter must be completely familiar with its location and operation so he can flick it on or off without having to look away from the target.

Guns of current manufacture that incorporate features of the Mauser M98 include Winchester's Classic Model 70 rifle, Ruger's Model 77 Magnum rifle, and the Czech-made Brno ZKK 602. All of these actions are strong enough to handle the heaviest calibers.

Finally, remember that an animal is only dangerous when at close quarters, so it's crucial that a dangerous-game gun should shoot exactly to point of aim at close range. It must also function flawlessly and fit the shooter perfectly. And above all, when something tries to bite, claw, stick, or stomp you, you must have supreme confidence in your rifle and your ability to handle it under stress.

Data for Calibers Suitable for Dangerous Game

(Sometimes known as "African" Calibers)

For most hunters, the ultimate experience is an African hunt. Somehow, bagging a white-tailed deer doesn't seem to come up to the same standard as bagging a lion or a Cape buffalo. The professional hunters in Africa learned early on that if they wanted to stay in the business (read alive), they wanted guns with reliable stopping power. That led to large calibers, and generally to rather heavy rifles. Be sure to read what Joe Coogan has to say about rifles for dangerous game. The cartridges listed here represent a good selection of the cartridges that are the most suitable for someone planning (or just dreaming about) a hunt for dangerous game.

Because these guns are very seldom fired at great distances, the yardage distances listed are in 50-yard increments out to 300 yards with data for 400 yards and 500 yards included mostly for comparison purposes. The path information is based on iron sights (a 0.9-inch sight height).

.400 A-Square Dual Purpose Magnum (DPM)

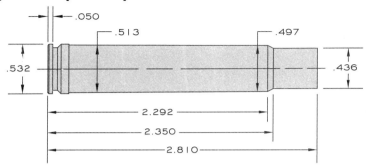

In 1992 the A-Square Company was asked to design a .40-caliber cartridge (it's actually closer to a .41) that would be legal for dangerous game in Africa and that used the basic H&H belted magnum case. The result was the .400 Pondoro. In 2005 A-Square announced the .400 DPM which is identical to the .400 Pondoro. The dual-purpose designation comes from using pistol bullets for light loads while keeping A-Square's Triad bullet loadings for major hunting applications. The light loads actually pack considerably more wallop than a .30-30 and are well suited for hunting deer-size game.

Relative Recoil Factor = 4.27

Specifications

Controlling Agency for Standardization of this Ammunition: Factory
Standard barrel for velocity testing: 26 inches long—1 turn in 10-inch twist

Availability

A² 170-grain JHC Revolver Bullet (None)

G1 Ballistic Coefficient = 0.176

Distance • Yards	Muzzle	50	100	150	200	250	300	400	500
Velocity • fps	2980	2713	2463	2224	2001	1789	1598	1272	1063
Energy • Ft-lbs	3352	2780	2289	1868	1512	1209	964	611	427
Taylor KO Index	29.7	27.0	24.5	22.1	19.9	17.8	15.9	12.7	10.6
Path • Inches	-0.9	+0.7	+1.0	0.0	-2.8	-7.8	-15.6	-42.2	-90.4
Wind Drift • Inches	0.0	0.4	1.8	4.2	7.9	13.0	19.7	39.2	67.2

A² 210-grain Revolver Bullet (None)

G1 Ballistic Coefficient = 0.208

Distance • Yards	Muzzle	50	100	150	200	250	300	400	500
Velocity • fps	2400	2201	2012	1832	1665	1509	1370	1150	1014
Energy • Ft-lbs	2686	2259	1887	1565	1292	1062	876	617	480
Taylor KO Index	29.5	27.1	24.7	22.5	20.5	18.6	16.9	14.1	12.5
Path • Inches	-0.9	+1.3	+1.7	0.0	-4.3	-11.8	-23.1	-60.6	-124.4
Wind Drift • Inches	0.0	0.5	2.0	4.8	8.9	14.6	22.0	42.2	69.4

A² 400-grain Triad (None)

G1 Ballistic Coefficient = 0.325

Distance • Yards	Muzzle	50	100	150	200	250	300	400	500
Velocity • fps	2400	2271	2146	2026	1908	1797	1689	1491	1319
Energy • Ft-lbs	5116	4584	4092	3646	3236	2869	2533	1975	1545
Taylor KO Index	56.2	53.2	50.3	47.5	44.7	42.1	39.6	34.9	30.9
Path • Inches	-0.9	+1.2	+1.5	0.0	-3.6	-9.7	-18.4	-45.4	-88.1
Wind Drift • Inches	0.0	0.3	1.3	2.9	5.4	8.6	12.8	24.0	39.7

.404 Dakota

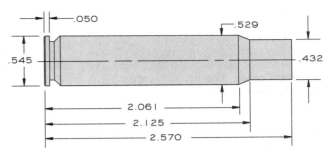

With their .404 Dakota, Dakota Arms enters into the African class of cartridges. By conservative standards the .404 is a medium African caliber—perhaps not quite enough for the toughest of the dangerous game animals in Africa, but certainly plenty for anything on the North American continent.

Relative Recoil Factor = 4.27

Specifications

Controlling Agency for Standardization of this Ammunition: Factory
Standard barrel for velocity testing: 26 inches long

Availability

Dakota 350-grain Woodleigh Soft Nose (404-350WSN)

G1 Ballistic Coefficient = 0.357

Distance • Yards	Muzzle	50	100	150	200	250	300	400	500
Velocity • fps	2550	2429	2310	2196	2084	1976	1871	1673	1493
Energy • Ft-lbs	5055	4585	4150	3747	3376	3034	2721	2175	1732
Taylor KO Index	53.9	51.4	48.9	46.4	44.1	41.8	39.6	35.4	31.6
Path • Inches	-0.9	+0.9	+1.3	0.0	-3.1	-8.2	-15.5	-37.8	-72.8
Wind Drift • Inches	0.0	0.3	1.0	2.4	4.4	7.1	10.4	19.6	32.3

Dakota 400-grain Woodleigh Soft Nose (404-400WSN)

G1 Ballistic Coefficient = 0.354

Distance • Yards	Muzzle	50	100	150	200	250	300	400	500
Velocity • fps	2400	2282	2167	2055	1947	1842	1741	1553	1385
Energy • Ft-lbs	5117	4625	4170	3751	3366	3014	2693	2142	1704
Taylor KO Index	58.0	55.2	52.4	49.7	47.1	44.5	42.1	37.5	33.5
Path • Inches	-0.9	+1.1	+1.5	0.0	-3.6	-9.4	-29.1	-43.6	-84.5
Wind Drift • Inches	0.0	0.3	1.2	2.7	4.9	7.8	11.6	21.7	35.7

Dakota 400-grain Woodleigh Solid (404-400WSO)

G1 Ballistic Coefficient = 0.358

Distance • Yards	Muzzle	50	100	150	200	250	300	400	500
Velocity • fps	2400	2283	2169	2059	1951	1848	1748	1561	1394
Energy • Ft-lbs	5117	4630	4180	3765	3383	3033	2714	2164	1725
Taylor KO Index	58.0	55.2	52.4	49.8	47.2	44.7	42.3	37.7	33.7
Path • Inches	-0.9	+1.1	+1.5	0.0	-3.5	-9.4	-29.0	-43.4	-83.4
Wind Drift • Inches	0.0	0.3	1.1	2.6	4.8	7.7	11.4	21.4	35.2

.416 Rigby

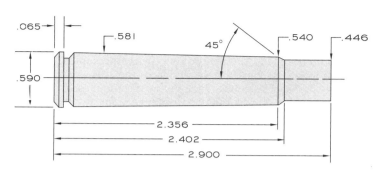

This cartridge represented what the British thought of as a minimum African cartridge when it was introduced in 1911. The .416 soon showed that it really wasn't "minimum" at all. It's a large case, roughly the same volume as the .378 and the .460 Weatherby Magnums. The .416 Rigby has always been loaded to a much more modest pressure level than the more modern cartridges of similar caliber. Today, there are other cartridges that offer similar performance in slightly smaller cases, but none of those is really a whole lot "better" in the field (where performance really counts) than the .416 Rigby.

Relative Recoil Factor = 4.27

Specifications

Controlling Agency for Standardization of this Ammunition: CIP

Bullet Weight Grains	Velocity fps	Maximum Average Pressure	
		Copper Crusher	Transducer
N/S	N/S	52,000 bar	N/A

Typical barrel for velocity testing: 26 inches long—1 turn in 16.5-inch twist

Availability

Federal 400-grain Nosler Partition (P416C)

G1 Ballistic Coefficient = 0.391

Distance • Yards	Muzzle	50	100	150	200	250	300	400	500
Velocity • fps	2440	2332	2230	2123	2020	1926	1830	1650	1490
Energy • Ft-lbs	5285	4830	4400	4005	3630	3295	2970	2420	1960
Taylor KO Index	58.0	55.4	53.0	50.5	48.0	45.8	43.5	39.2	35.4
Path • Inches	-0.9	+1.0	+1.4	0.0	-3.3	-8.8	-16.6	-40.2	-76.7
Wind Drift • Inches	0.0	0.2	1.0	2.3	4.3	6.8	10.0	18.8	30.8

A² 400-grain Dead Tough SP, Monolithic Solid, Lion Load SP (None)

G1 Ballistic Coefficient = 0.317

Distance • Yards	Muzzle	50	100	150	200	250	300	400	500
Velocity • fps	2400	2268	2140	2016	1897	1782	1673	1471	1298
Energy • Ft-lbs	5115	4570	4069	3612	3194	2823	2487	1923	1497
Taylor KO Index	57.1	53.9	50.9	47.9	45.1	42.4	39.8	35.0	30.9
Path • Inches	-0.9	+1.2	+1.5	0.0	-3.7	-9.8	-18.6	-46.0	-89.8
Wind Drift • Inches	0.0	0.3	1.3	3.0	5.5	8.6	13.2	24.8	41.1

Federal 400-grain Trophy Bonded Bear Claw (P416T1)

G1 Ballistic Coefficient = 0.375

Distance • Yards	Muzzle	50	100	150	200	250	300	400	500
Velocity • fps	2370	2259	2150	2046	1940	1845	1750	1570	1409
Energy • Ft-lbs	4990	4533	4110	3718	3350	3023	2720	2191	1765
Taylor KO Index	56.3	53.7	51.1	48.6	46.1	43.9	41.6	37.3	33.5
Path • Inches	-0.9	+1.2	+1.5	0.0	-3.6	-9.5	-18.0	-43.7	-83.7
Wind Drift • Inches	0.0	0.3	1.1	2.6	4.7	7.5	11.0	20.6	33.8

Federal 400-grain Trophy Bonded Sledgehammer Solid (P416T2)

G1 Ballistic Coefficient = 0.322

Distance • Yards	Muzzle	50	100	150	200	250	300	400	500
Velocity • fps	2370	2241	2110	1995	1880	1766	1659	1462	1293
Energy • Ft-lbs	4990	4462	3975	3535	3130	2771	2445	1899	1484
Taylor KO Index	56.3	53.3	50.2	47.4	44.7	42.0	39.4	34.8	30.7
Path • Inches	-0.9	+1.2	+1.6	0.0	-3.8	-10.0	-19.0	-47.0	-91.4
Wind Drift • Inches	0.0	0.3	1.3	3.0	5.5	8.9	13.2	24.8	41.0

Norma 400-grain Swift A-Frame (11069)

G1 Ballistic Coefficient = 0.367

Distance • Yards	Muzzle	50	100	150	200	250	300	400	500
Velocity • fps	2350	2237	2127	2021	1917	1817	1721	1541	1380
Energy • Ft-lbs	4906	4446	4021	3627	3265	2934	2631	2109	1691
Taylor KO Index	55.9	53.2	50.6	48.0	45.6	43.2	40.9	36.6	32.8
Path • Inches	-0.9	+1.2	+1.6	0.0	-3.7	-9.7	-18.4	-45.0	-86.3
Wind Drift • Inches	0.0	0.3	1.2	2.6	4.8	7.7	11.4	21.4	35.2

Federal 400-grain Speer African Grand Slam (P416A) (Discontinued in 2005)

G1 Ballistic Coefficient = 0.317

Distance • Yards	Muzzle	50	100	150	200	250	300	400	500
Velocity • fps	2370	2239	2110	1989	1870	1757	1649	1450	1281
Energy • Ft-lbs	5115	4565	4050	3603	3165	2812	2416	1869	1457
Taylor KO Index	57.7	54.6	51.4	48.5	45.6	42.8	40.2	35.3	31.2
Path • Inches	-0.9	+1.2	+1.6	0.0	-3.8	-10.0	-19.2	-47.4	-92.4
Wind Drift • Inches	0.0	0.3	1.3	3.1	5.6	9.0	13.4	25.3	41.8

Federal 400-grain Speer African Grand Slam Solid (P416B) (Discontinued in 2005)

G1 Ballistic Coefficient = 0.262

Distance • Yards	Muzzle	50	100	150	200	250	300	400	500
Velocity • fps	2370	2212	2060	1914	1780	1644	1520	1310	1140
Energy • Ft-lbs	4990	4347	3770	3255	2800	2400	2055	1515	1156
Taylor KO Index	56.3	52.6	49.0	45.5	42.3	39.1	36.1	31.1	27.1
Path • Inches	-0.9	+1.3	+1.7	0.0	-4.0	-10.8	-20.9	-53.0	-105.9
Wind Drift • Inches	0.0	0.4	1.6	3.8	6.9	11.3	16.8	32.0	53.1

Norma 400-grain Barnes Solid (11050)

G1 Ballistic Coefficient = 0.216

Distance • Yards	Muzzle	50	100	150	200	250	300	400	500
Velocity • fps	2297	2109	1930	1762	1604	1460	1330	1130	1006
Energy • Ft-lbs	4687	3953	3310	2759	2284	1895	1571	1135	899
Taylor KO Index	54.6	50.1	45.9	41.9	38.1	34.7	31.6	26.9	23.9
Path • Inches	-0.9	+1.5	+1.9	0.0	-4.7	-12.8	-25.1	-65.4	-133.0
Wind Drift • Inches	0.0	0.5	2.1	4.9	9.1	14.9	22.4	42.6	69.3

Kynoch 410-grain Solid or Soft Nose

G1 Ballistic Coefficient = 0.426

Distance • Yards	Muzzle	50	100	150	200	250	300	400	500
Velocity • fps	2300	2204	2110	2018	1929	1842	1758	1599	1453
Energy • Ft-lbs	4817	4422	4053	3708	3387	3090	2815	2328	1923
Taylor KO Index	56.0	53.7	51.4	49.2	47.0	44.9	42.8	39.0	35.4
Path • Inches	-0.9	+1.2	+1.6	0.0	-3.7	-9.8	-18.4	-44.4	-84.1
Wind Drift • Inches	0.0	0.2	1.0	2.3	4.2	6.8	10.0	18.5	30.2

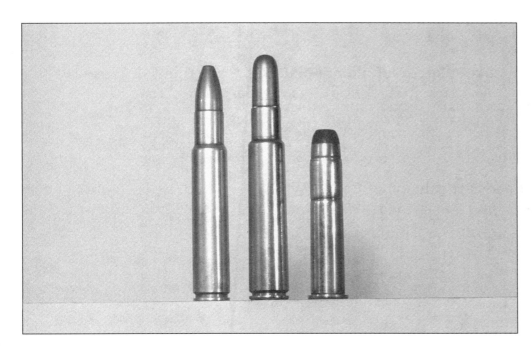

(Left to right).416 Dakota, .416 Rigby, .45-70.

.416 Remington Magnum

When Remington wanted to get onto the .416 bandwagon, they simply necked up their 8mm Magnum to make the .416 Remington Magnum (introduced in 1988). If you have to pick a single gun for your next African safari, this caliber should be on your short list. When the major factories began offering premium hunting bullets, obtained from outside suppliers, the terminal performance of factory ammo took a huge jump. All the loadings available today feature premium-style bullets. For all practical purposes, the .416 Remington Magnum offers the same performance as the legendary .416 Rigby.

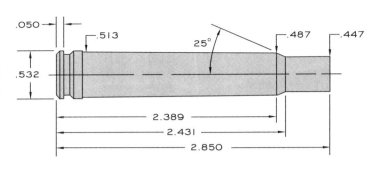

Relative Recoil Factor = 4.32

Specifications

Controlling Agency for Standardization of this Ammunition: SAAMI

Bullet Weight Grains	Velocity fps	Maximum Average Pressure	
		Copper Crusher	Transducer
350	2,525	54,000 cup	65,000 psi
400	2,400	54,000 cup	65,000 psi

Standard barrel for velocity testing: 24 inches long—1 turn in 14-inch twist

Availability

Federal 400-grain Nosler Partition (P416RT1)
G1 Ballistic Coefficient = 0.391

Distance • Yards	Muzzle	50	100	150	200	250	300	400	500
Velocity • fps	2410	2303	2200	2096	2000	1900	1810	1630	1470
Energy • Ft-lbs	5160	4710	4290	3901	3540	3206	2900	2365	1915
Taylor KO Index	57.3	54.7	52.3	49.8	47.5	45.2	43.0	38.7	34.9
Path • Inches	-0.9	+1.1	+1.4	0.0	-3.4	-9.0	-17.0	-41.4	-78.9
Wind Drift • Inches	0.0	0.3	1.0	2.4	4.3	6.9	10.4	19.1	31.4

Federal 400-grain Trophy Bonded Bear Claw (P416RT1)
G1 Ballistic Coefficient = 0.375

Distance • Yards	Muzzle	50	100	150	200	250	300	400	500
Velocity • fps	2400	2288	2180	2073	1970	1871	1770	1590	1430
Energy • Ft-lbs	5115	4652	4215	3819	3445	3110	2790	2250	1805
Taylor KO Index	57.1	54.4	51.8	49.3	46.8	44.5	42.1	37.8	34.0
Path • Inches	-0.9	+1.1	+1.5	0.0	-3.5	-9.2	-17.4	-42.5	-81.4
Wind Drift • Inches	0.0	0.3	1.1	2.5	4.6	7.3	10.8	20.2	33.2

Remington 400-grain Swift A-Frame Pointed Soft Point (R416RA)
G1 Ballistic Coefficient = 0.368

Distance • Yards	Muzzle	50	100	150	200	250	300	400	500
Velocity • fps	2400	2286	2175	2067	1962	1861	1764	1580	1415
Energy • Ft-lbs	5115	4643	4201	3797	3419	3078	2764	2218	1779
Taylor KO Index	57.1	54.3	51.7	49.1	46.6	44.2	41.9	37.6	33.6
Path • Inches	-0.9	+1.1	+1.5	0.0	-3..5	-9.3	17.6	-42.8	-82.2
Wind Drift • Inches	0.0	0.3	1.1	2.6	4.7	7.5	11.0	20.7	34.0

Federal 400-grain Trophy Bonded Sledgehammer Solid (P416T2)
G1 Ballistic Coefficient = 0.331

Distance • Yards	Muzzle	50	100	150	200	250	300	400	500
Velocity • fps	2400	2274	2150	2032	1920	1806	1700	1504	1332
Energy • Ft-lbs	5115	4592	4110	3668	3260	2899	2568	2009	1576
Taylor KO Index	57.1	54.0	51.1	48.3	45.6	42.9	40.4	35.8	31.7
Path • Inches	-0.9	+1.1	+1.5	0.0	-3..6	-9.6	-18.3	-45.0	-87.3
Wind Drift • Inches	0.0	0.3	1.2	2.9	5.2	8.4	12.5	23.5	38.9

A² 400-grain Dead Tough SP, Monolithic Solid, Lion Load SP (None)　　G1 Ballistic Coefficient = 0.317

Distance • Yards	Muzzle	50	100	150	200	250	300	400	500
Velocity • fps	2380	2249	2121	1998	1880	1766	1657	1457	1286
Energy • Ft-lbs	5031	4492	3998	3548	3139	2770	2439	1887	1470
Taylor KO Index	56.6	53.5	50.4	47.5	44.7	42.0	39.4	34.6	30.6
Path • Inches	-0.9	+1.2	+1.6	0.0	-3.7	-9.9	-18.9	-46.9	-91.5
Wind Drift • Inches	0.0	0.3	1.3	3.0	5.6	9.0	13.3	25.1	41.6

This huge-bodied bull elephant shows how big these creatures can really get. The largest elephants in Africa tend to be found on the southwestern side of the continent. (Photo from Elephant Hunters, Men of Legend *by Tony Sanchez-Ariño, Safari Press, 2005)*

.416 Dakota

The .416 Dakota is the largest round that Dakota bases on the .404 Jeffery. Power-wise, it is right in the middle of the .416s, being a bit more potent than the .416 Rigby and Remington and a slight bit milder than the .416 Weatherby and Lazzeroni offerings. I think it would take a lifetime of hunting to establish whether any practical difference is to be seen in the terminal performance of the whole collection of .416s.

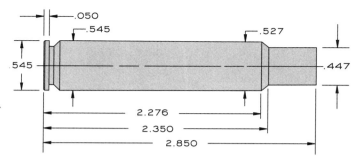

Relative Recoil Factor = 4.56

Specifications

Controlling Agency for Standardization of this Ammunition: Factory
Standard barrel for velocity testing: 24 inches long

Availability

Dakota 400-grain Swift A-Frame (416-400FAF)
G1 Ballistic Coefficient = 0.370

Distance • Yards	Muzzle	50	100	150	200	250	300	400	500
Velocity • fps	2500	2384	2271	2161	2055	1951	1851	1661	1488
Energy • Ft-lbs	5553	5050	4583	4150	3750	3381	3042	2450	1966
Taylor KO Index	60.9	58.1	55.3	52.7	50.1	47.5	45.1	40.5	36.3
Path • Inches	-0.9	+1.0	+1.3	0.0	-3.2	-8.4	-16.0	-39.0	-74.7
Wind Drift • Inches	0.0	0.2	1.0	2.4	4.4	7.0	10.3	19.3	31.8

Dakota 350-grain Woodleigh Soft Nose (416-410WSN)
G1 Ballistic Coefficient = 0.357

Distance • Yards	Muzzle	50	100	150	200	250	300	400	500
Velocity • fps	2500	2386	2274	2166	2060	1958	1858	1670	1499
Energy • Ft-lbs	5691	5183	4710	4271	3865	3490	3145	2541	2045
Taylor KO Index	60.9	58.1	55.4	52.8	50.2	47.7	45.3	40.7	36.5
Path • Inches	-0.9	+1.0	+1.3	0.0	-3.2	-8.4	-15.9	-38.8	-74.2
Wind Drift • Inches	0.0	0.2	1.0	2.4	4.3	6.9	10.2	19.0	31.3

Dakota 410-grain Woodleigh Solid (416-410WSO)
G1 Ballistic Coefficient = 0.357

Distance • Yards	Muzzle	50	100	150	200	250	300	400	500
Velocity • fps	2500	2374	2252	2134	2019	1908	1801	1600	1420
Energy • Ft-lbs	5691	5134	4620	4146	3712	3314	2953	2331	1836
Taylor KO Index	60.9	57.8	54.9	52.0	49.2	46.5	43.9	39.0	34.6
Path • Inches	-0.9	+1.0	+1.4	0.0	-3.3	-8.7	-16.4	-40.4	-78.2
Wind Drift • Inches	0.0	0.3	1.1	2.6	4.8	7.7	11.4	21.4	35.3

.416 Weatherby Magnum

The .416 Weatherby was Weatherby's answer to the popularity of the .416 caliber generally. Introduced in 1989, it is really a .416-378, that is, a .378 Weatherby case necked to .416. That puts this cartridge's performance between the .378 Weatherby and the .460 Weatherby. That's pretty awesome company. The .416 WM is a truly "African" caliber, suitable for big game anywhere.

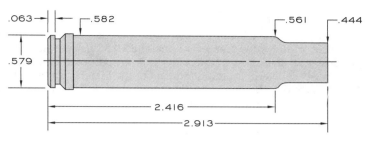

Relative Recoil Factor = 4.77

Specifications

Controlling Agency for Standardization of this Ammunition: CIP

Bullet Weight Grains	Velocity fps	Maximum Average Pressure Copper Crusher	Transducer
N/S	N/S	3,800 bar	4,370 bar

Standard barrel for velocity testing: 26 inches long—1 turn in 14-inch twist

Availability

Weatherby 350-grain Barnes-X(B 416 350 XS)　　　　G1 Ballistic Coefficient = 0.521

Distance • Yards	Muzzle	50	100	150	200	250	300	400	500
Velocity • fps	2850	2761	2673	2587	2503	2420	2399	2182	2031
Energy • Ft-lbs	6312	5924	5553	5203	4870	4553	4253	3700	3204
Taylor KO Index	59.3	57.4	55.6	53.8	52.1	50.3	49.9	45.4	42.2
Path • Inches	-0.9	+0.6	+0.9	0.0	-2.2	-5.7	-10.8	-25.8	-48.1
Wind Drift • Inches	0.0	0.2	0.6	1.4	2.5	4.0	5.8	10.6	17.2

Weatherby 400-grain Hornady Soft Point (H 416 400 RN)　　　　G1 Ballistic Coefficient = 0.311

Distance • Yards	Muzzle	50	100	150	200	250	300	400	500
Velocity • fps	2700	2556	2417	2282	2152	2025	1903	1676	1470
Energy • Ft-lbs	6474	5805	5189	4626	4113	3642	3216	2493	1918
Taylor KO Index	64.2	60.8	57.5	54.2	51.2	48.1	45.2	39.8	34.9
Path • Inches	-0.9	+0.8	+1.1	0.0	-2.8	-7.5	-14.3	-35.5	-69.2
Wind Drift • Inches	0.0	0.3	1.1	2.6	4.7	7.6	11.3	21.3	35.4

Weatherby 400-grain Swift A-Frame (W 416 400 SP) (Discontinued in 2005)　　G1 Ballistic Coefficient = 0.391

Distance • Yards	Muzzle	50	100	150	200	250	300	400	500
Velocity • fps	2650	2536	2426	2318	2213	2110	2011	1820	1644
Energy • Ft-lbs	6237	5716	5227	4773	4350	3955	3592	2941	2399
Taylor KO Index	63.0	60.3	57.7	55.1	52.6	50.1	47.8	43.3	39.1
Path • Inches	-0.9	+0.8	+1.1	0.0	-2.8	-7.3	-13.8	-33.4	-63.6
Wind Drift • Inches	0.0	0.2	0.9	2.1	3.8	6.0	8.9	16.6	27.2

A² 400-grain Dead Tough SP, Monolithic Solid, Lion Load SP (None)　　G1 Ballistic Coefficient = 0.320

Distance • Yards	Muzzle	50	100	150	200	250	300	400	500
Velocity • fps	2600	2463	2328	2202	2073	1957	1841	1624	1430
Energy • Ft-lbs	6004	5390	4813	4307	3834	3402	3011	2343	1817
Taylor KO Index	61.8	58.5	55.3	52.3	49.3	46.5	43.8	38.6	34.0
Path • Inches	-0.9	+0.9	+1.2	0.0	-3.0	-8.1	-15.4	-38.1	-74.2
Wind Drift • Inches	0.0	0.3	1.1	2.6	4.8	7.8	11.5	21.8	36.1

Weatherby 400-grain A-Square Monolithic Solid (A 416 400 SD)　　G1 Ballistic Coefficient = 0.304

Distance • Yards	Muzzle	50	100	150	200	250	300	400	500
Velocity • fps	2700	2553	2411	2273	2140	2010	1887	1656	1448
Energy • Ft-lbs	6457	5790	5162	4589	4068	3591	3161	2435	1861
Taylor KO Index	64.2	60.7	57.3	54.0	50.9	47.8	44.9	39.4	34.4
Path • Inches	-0.9	+0.8	+1.1	0.0	-2.8	-7.6	-14.4	-35.9	-70.3
Wind Drift • Inches	0.0	0.3	1.1	2.6	4.8	7.8	11.6	28.6	36.5

10.57mm (.416) Lazzeroni Meteor

The 10.57mm Meteor is the largest caliber in the Lazzeroni line. As is true of the entire Lazzeroni line, the 10.57 has considerably better performance than most of the older, more traditional cartridges in the same caliber. There's nothing mild about the Meteor. In fact, it drives a 400-grain bullet 100 fps faster than any other .416 cartridge. This is a cartridge for serious African hunters.

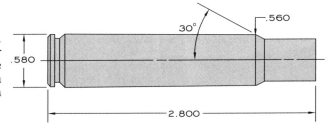

Relative Recoil Factor = 4.95

Specifications

Controlling Agency for Standardization of this Ammunition: Factory

Availability

Lazzeroni 400-grain

G1 Ballistic Coefficient = 0.550

Distance • Yards	Muzzle	50	100	150	200	250	300	400	500
Velocity • fps	2800	2716	2634	2554	2474	2396	2320	2171	2028
Energy • Ft-lbs	6965	6555	6165	5793	5440	5102	4784	4190	3656
Taylor KO Index	66.6	64.6	62.6	60.7	58.8	57.0	55.1	51.6	48.2
Path • Inches	-0.9	+0.6	+0.9	0.0	-2.3	-5.9	-11.1	-26.5	-48.2
Wind Drift • Inches	0.0	0.1	0.6	1.3	2.4	3.8	5.6	10.3	16.6

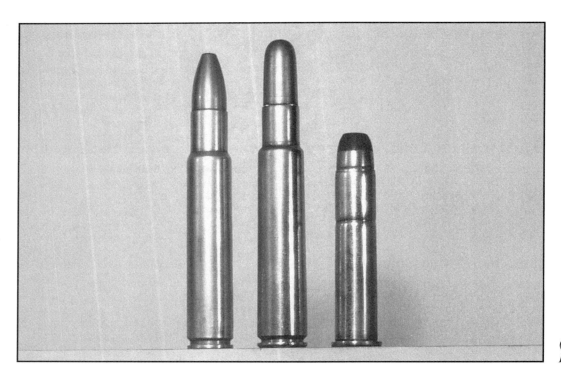

(Left to right) .416 Dakota, .416 Rigby, .45-70.

.458 Winchester Magnum

The .458 Winchester Magnum is the largest of Winchester's slightly shortened, belted magnum calibers. It was introduced in 1956, and its adaptability to standard-length actions made it popular in the United States. The difference in relative popularity between this cartridge and the British "African" cartridges is that the British cartridges are nearly always utilized in custom-made (read very expensive) rifles, while the .458 Winchester Magnum is available in the more or less over-the-counter Model 70 African. Performance-wise the .458 Winchester Magnum is, bullet for bullet, about 450 fps slower than the .460 Weatherby Magnum, which is based on the much larger volume .378 Weatherby Magnum case.

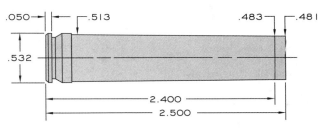

Relative Recoil Factor = 4.36

Specifications

Controlling Agency for Standardization of this Ammunition: SAAMI

Bullet Weight Grains	Velocity fps	Maximum Average Pressure	
		Copper Crusher	Transducer
500	2,025	53,000 cup	N/S
510	2,025	53,000 cup	N/S

Standard barrel for velocity testing: 24 inches long—1 turn in 14-inch twist

Availability

Federal 350-grain Soft Point (P458A) (Discontinued in 2005)

G1 Ballistic Coefficient = 0.171

Distance • Yards	Muzzle	50	100	150	200	250	300	400	500
Velocity • fps	2470	2225	1990	1778	1570	1402	1252	1060	950
Energy • Ft-lbs	4740	3847	3065	2456	1915	1529	1219	870	705
Taylor KO Index	56.6	51.0	45.6	40.7	36.0	32.1	28.7	24.0	21.3
Path • Inches	-0.9	+1.3	+1.8	0.0	-4.5	-12.5	-25.1	-68.4	-142.4
Wind Drift • Inches	0.0	0.6	2.3	5.8	10.8	17.9	27.2	52.3	84.5

Federal 400-grain Trophy Bonded Bear Claw (P458T1)

G1 Ballistic Coefficient = 0.382

Distance • Yards	Muzzle	50	100	150	200	250	300	400	500
Velocity • fps	2380	2271	2170	2061	1960	1862	1769	1591	1430
Energy • Ft-lbs	5030	4581	4185	3772	3415	3081	2778	2248	1817
Taylor KO Index	62.3	59.4	56.8	53.9	51.3	48.7	46.3	41.6	37.4
Path • Inches	-0.9	+1.1	+1.5	0.0	-3.6	-9.4	-17.7	-43.0	+82.1
Wind Drift • Inches	0.0	0.3	1.1	2.5	4.5	7.3	10.7	20.0	32.9

Remington 450-grain Swift A-Frame PSP (RS458WA) (Discontinued in 2005)

G1 Ballistic Coefficient = 0.309

Distance • Yards	Muzzle	50	100	150	200	250	300	400	500
Velocity • fps	2150	2023	1901	1784	1671	1566	1466	1290	1151
Energy • Ft-lbs	4618	4091	3609	3179	2789	2449	2148	1663	1354
Taylor KO Index	63.3	59.6	56.0	52.5	49.2	46.1	43.2	38.0	33.9
Path • Inches	-0.9	+1.6	+2.0	0.0	-4.8	-12.6	-24.0	-59.6	-116.4
Wind Drift • Inches	0.0	0.4	1.6	3.6	6.6	10.7	15.8	29.7	48.6

A² 465-grain Dead Tough SP, Monolithic Solid, Lion Load SP (None)

G1 Ballistic Coefficient = 0.358

Distance • Yards	Muzzle	50	100	150	200	250	300	400	500
Velocity • fps	2220	2108	1999	1894	1791	1694	1601	1429	1280
Energy • Ft-lbs	5088	4589	4127	3704	3312	2965	2563	2042	1639
Taylor KO Index	67.5	64.1	60.8	57.6	54.5	51.5	48.7	43.5	38.9
Path • Inches	-0.9	+1.4	+1.8	0.0	-4.2	-11.2	-21.1	-51.7	-99.4
Wind Drift • Inches	0.0	0.3	1.3	3.0	5.4	8.7	12.8	23.9	39.2

Hornady 500-grain RN InterBond (8584)

G1 Ballistic Coefficient = 0.292

Distance • Yards	Muzzle	50	100	150	200	250	300	400	500
Velocity • fps	2260	2122	1988	1860	1738	1621	1411	1318	1165
Energy • Ft-lbs	5670	4999	4390	3842	3353	2919	2539	1929	1508
Taylor KO Index	73.9	69.4	65.0	60.8	56.9	53.0	46.2	43.1	38.1
Path • Inches	-0.9	+1.4	+1.8	0.0	-4.3	-11.5	-22.1	-55.2	-108.6
Wind Drift • Inches	0.0	0.4	1.6	3.6	6.6	10.6	15.8	29.9	49.3

Norma 500-grain Swift A-Frame (11120)

G1 Ballistic Coefficient = 0.361

Distance • Yards	Muzzle	50	100	150	200	250	300	400	500
Velocity • fps	2116	2008	1903	1802	1705	1612	1523	1362	1226
Energy • Ft-lbs	4972	4477	4022	3606	3227	2885	2577	2060	1669
Taylor KO Index	69.2	65.7	62.3	59.0	55.8	52.7	49.8	44.6	40.1
Path • Inches	-0.9	+1.6	+2.0	0.0	-4.7	-12.4	-23.4	-57.2	-109.9
Wind Drift • Inches	0.0	0.3	1.4	3.1	5.7	9.2	13.6	25.3	41.2

Federal 500-grain Trophy Bonded Bear Claw (P458T2)

G1 Ballistic Coefficient = 0.342

Distance • Yards	Muzzle	50	100	150	200	250	300	400	500
Velocity • fps	2090	1977	1870	1762	1660	1565	1475	1313	1180
Energy • Ft-lbs	4850	4340	3870	3448	3065	2721	2416	1913	1546
Taylor KO Index	68.3	64.7	61.2	57.6	54.3	51.2	48.3	43.0	38.6
Path • Inches	-0.9	+1.7	+2.1	0.0	-4.9	-13.0	-24.6	-60.3	-116.5
Wind Drift • Inches	0.0	0.4	1.5	3.4	6.2	9.9	14.7	27.4	44.6

Federal 500-grain Trophy Bonded Sledgehammer Solid (P458T3)

G1 Ballistic Coefficient = 0.336

Distance • Yards	Muzzle	50	100	150	200	250	300	400	500
Velocity • fps	2090	1975	1860	1757	1650	1557	1466	1302	1170
Energy • Ft-lbs	4850	4331	3845	3427	3025	2692	2385	1883	1519
Taylor KO Index	68.4	64.6	60.2	57.5	54.0	50.9	48.0	42.6	38.3
Path • Inches	-0.9	+1.7	+2.1	0.0	-4.9	-13.0	-24.7	-60.8	-117.7
Wind Drift • Inches	0.0	0.4	1.5	3.5	6.3	10.1	15.0	28.0	45.6

Federal 500-grain Speer African Grand Slam (P458B) (Discontinued in 2005)

G1 Ballistic Coefficient = 0.285

Distance • Yards	Muzzle	50	100	150	200	250	300	400	500
Velocity • fps	2090	1955	1830	1701	1590	1475	1380	1200	1080
Energy • Ft-lbs	4850	4243	3700	3213	2790	2415	2100	1610	1300
Taylor KO Index	68.4	64.0	59.9	55.6	52.0	48.3	45.1	39.3	35.3
Path • Inches	-0.9	+1.8	+2.2	0.0	-5.2	-13.9	-26.6	-66.6	-130.8
Wind Drift • Inches	0.0	0.4	1.8	4.1	7.6	12.2	18.1	33.9	55.1

Speer 500-grain African GS Soft Point (24518) (Discontinued in 2004)

G1 Ballistic Coefficient = 0.286

Distance • Yards	Muzzle	50	100	150	200	250	300	400	500
Velocity • fps	2025	1893	1766	1646	1533	1428	1331	1172	1059
Energy • Ft-lbs	4552	3978	3463	3008	2607	2263	1969	1525	1246
Taylor KO Index	66.2	61.9	57.8	53.8	50.2	46.7	43.5	38.3	34.6
Path • Inches	-0.9	+2.0	+2.4	0.0	-5.6	-14.9	-28.4	-71.1	-139.2
Wind Drift • Inches	0.0	0.4	1.8	4.3	7.9	12.7	18.8	35.1	56.6

Hornady 500-grain FMJ RN HM InterLock (8585)

G1 Ballistic Coefficient = 0.295

Distance • Yards	Muzzle	50	100	150	200	250	300	400	500
Velocity • fps	2260	2123	1991	1864	1743	1627	1519	1326	1172
Energy • Ft-lbs	5670	5005	4401	3858	3372	2940	2562	1952	1525
Taylor KO Index	73.9	69.5	65.1	61.0	57.0	53.2	49.7	43.4	38.3
Path • Inches	-0.9	+1.4	+1.8	0.0	-4.3	-11.5	-22.0	-54.8	-107.9
Wind Drift • Inches	0.0	0.4	1.5	3.6	6.5	10.5	15.6	29.6	48.7

Federal 500-grain Speer African Grand Slam Solid (P458C) (Discontinued in 2005)

G1 Ballistic Coefficient = 0.348

Distance • Yards	Muzzle	50	100	150	200	250	300	400	500
Velocity • fps	2090	1979	1870	1768	1670	1574	1480	1320	1190
Energy • Ft-lbs	4850	4348	3880	3469	3085	2750	2440	1945	1585
Taylor KO Index	68.4	64.7	61.2	57.8	54.6	51.5	48.4	43.2	38.9
Path • Inches	-0.9	+1.7	+2.1	0.0	-4.9	-12.9	-24.4	-59.8	-115.3
Wind Drift • Inches	0.0	0.4	1.4	3.3	6.1	9.7	14.4	26.8	43.7

Norma 500-grain Barnes Solid (11110)

G1 Ballistic Coefficient = 0.235

Distance • Yards	Muzzle	50	100	150	200	250	300	400	500
Velocity • fps	2067	1905	1750	1606	1472	1352	1245	1087	986
Energy • Ft-lbs	4745	4028	3401	2865	2405	2030	1721	1312	1079
Taylor KO Index	67.6	62.3	57.3	52.5	48.2	44.2	40.7	35.6	32.3
Path • Inches	-0.9	+2.0	+2.4	0.0	-5.8	-15.6	-30.2	-77.2	-153.2
Wind Drift • Inches	0.0	0.5	2.2	5.2	9.6	15.5	23.2	43.1	68.8

Speer 500-grain African GS Tungsten Solid (24519) (Discontinued in 2004)

G1 Ballistic Coefficient = 0.278

Distance • Yards	Muzzle	50	100	150	200	250	300	400	500
Velocity • fps	2050	1913	1782	1657	1540	1432	1333	1169	1055
Energy • Ft-lbs	4665	4064	3525	3050	2633	2276	1972	1517	1235
Taylor KO Index	67.1	62.6	58.3	54.2	50.4	46.8	43.6	38.2	34.5
Path • Inches	-0.9	+1.9	+2.3	0.0	-5.5	-14.6	-28.1	-70.4	-138.4
Wind Drift • Inches	0.0	0.4	1.9	4.4	8.0	12.9	19.2	35.8	57.8

Winchester 510-grain Soft Point (X4581)

G1 Ballistic Coefficient = 0.275

Distance • Yards	Muzzle	50	100	150	200	250	300	400	500
Velocity • fps	2040	1902	1770	1645	1527	1419	1320	1158	1046
Energy • Ft-lbs	4714	4097	3548	3064	2642	2280	1973	1519	1240
Taylor KO Index	68.1	63.5	59.1	54.9	51.0	47.4	44.0	38.6	34.9
Path • Inches	-0.9	+1.9	+2.4	0.0	-5.6	-14.9	-28.5	-71.6	-140.8
Wind Drift • Inches	0.0	0.5	1.9	4.4	8.2	13.2	19.5	36.5	58.7

James Sutherland, who hunted into the 1930s, was the last legal professional ivory hunter with an unlimited license. (Photo from *Elephant Hunters, Men of Legend* by Tony Sanchez-Ariño, Safari Press, 2005)

.458 Lott

The late Jack Lott decided in the late 1960s that the .458 Winchester needed "improvement." The .458 Lott, his answer, was introduced in 1971 as a wildcat. A Square, the company, picked up on the caliber and for a number of years has furnished brass and loaded ammunition to its specifications. In 2002, Hornady took the lead to obtain SAAMI standardization for this caliber. The .458 Lott uses a case that's 0.300 inches longer than the .458 Winchester (it can be thought of as a full-length magnum), increasing both the case volume and the ballistic performance.

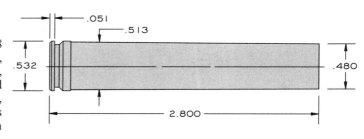

Relative Recoil Factor = 5.05

Specifications

Controlling Agency for Standardization of this Ammunition: SAAMI

Bullet Weight Grains	Velocity fps	Maximum Average Pressure	
		Copper Crusher	Transducer
500	Details pending		

Standard barrel for velocity testing: 24 inches long—1 turn in 10-inch twist

Availability

A² 465-grain Triad
G1 Ballistic Coefficient = 0.357

Distance • Yards	Muzzle	50	100	150	200	250	300	400	500
Velocity • fps	2380	2263	2150	2039	1932	1829	1730	1551	1378
Energy • Ft-lbs	5848	5290	4773	4295	3855	3455	3091	2485	1962
Taylor KO Index	72.4	68.9	65.4	62.0	58.8	55.6	52.6	47.2	41.9
Path • Inches	-0.9	+1.2	+1.9	0.0	-3.6	-9.6	-18.1	-44.2	-85.2
Wind Drift • Inches	0.0	0.3	1.2	2.7	4.9	7.8	11.6	21.7	35.8

Hornady 500-grain RN InterBond (8260)
G1 Ballistic Coefficient = 0.295

Distance • Yards	Muzzle	50	100	150	200	250	300	400	500
Velocity • fps	2300	2162	2028	1900	1777	1659	1549	1351	1191
Energy • Ft-lbs	5872	5189	4567	4008	3506	3058	2665	2026	1574
Taylor KO Index	75.2	70.7	66.3	62.2	58.1	54.3	50.7	44.2	39.0
Path • Inches	-0.9	+1.4	+1.7	0.0	-4.1	-11.0	-21.0	-52.7	-103.7
Wind Drift • Inches	0.0	0.4	1.5	3.5	6.4	10.3	15.2	28.8	47.6

Hornady 500-grain FMJ-RN (8262)
G1 Ballistic Coefficient = 0.288

Distance • Yards	Muzzle	50	100	150	200	250	300	400	500
Velocity • fps	2300	2158	2022	1890	1776	1645	1551	1333	1174
Energy • Ft-lbs	5872	5173	4537	3969	3502	3007	2671	1974	1531
Taylor KO Index	75.2	70.6	66.1	61.8	58.1	53.8	50.7	43.6	38.4
Path • Inches	-0.9	+1.4	+1.7	0.0	-4.2	-11.2	-21.3	-53.5	-105.5
Wind Drift • Inches	0.0	0.4	1.5	3.6	6.5	10.6	15.7	29.7	49.1

.450 Dakota

To complete their line of large-volume cartridges, Dakota changed to an even larger case than the .404 Jeffery. The basic case for the .450 Dakota is the .416 Rigby, but for comparison it is very much like a .378 (or .460) Weatherby without the belt. No matter what its origin, the actual case is huge and develops the performance you would expect from such a big boomer. I don't think you are going to see many of these guns in benchrest matches.

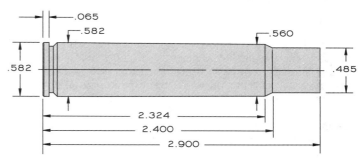

Relative Recoil Factor = 5.80

Specifications

Controlling Agency for Standardization of this Ammunition: Factory
Standard barrel for velocity testing: 24 inches long

Availability

Dakota 400-grain Swift A-Frame (450-400FAF)

G1 Ballistic Coefficient = 0.320

Distance • Yards	Muzzle	50	100	150	200	250	300	400	500
Velocity • fps	2700	2560	2425	2293	2166	2042	1923	1699	1496
Energy • Ft-lbs	6477	5823	5223	4672	4167	3706	3266	2564	1988
Taylor KO Index	70.7	67.0	63.5	60.0	56.7	53.4	50.3	44.5	39.2
Path • Inches	-0.9	+0.8	+1.1	0.0	-2.8	-7.4	-14.1	-35.0	-68.0
Wind Drift • Inches	0.0	0.3	1.1	2.5	4.6	7.3	10.9	20.6	34.1

Dakota 500-grain Swift A-Frame (450-500FAF)

G1 Ballistic Coefficient = 0.361

Distance • Yards	Muzzle	50	100	150	200	250	300	400	500
Velocity • fps	2550	2430	2313	2199	2089	1982	1878	1681	1502
Energy • Ft-lbs	7221	6577	5942	5372	4845	4360	3915	3139	2505
Taylor KO Index	83.4	79.5	75.7	71.9	68.3	64.8	61.4	55.0	49.1
Path • Inches	-0.9	+0.9	+1.3	0.0	-3.1	-8.1	-15.4	-37.7	-72.3
Wind Drift • Inches	0.0	0.2	1.0	2.4	4.4	7.0	10.3	19.3	31.9

Dakota 550-grain Woodleigh Soft Nose (450-550WSN)

G1 Ballistic Coefficient = 0.480

Distance • Yards	Muzzle	50	100	150	200	250	300	400	500
Velocity • fps	2450	2361	2275	2190	2106	2025	1946	1793	1649
Energy • Ft-lbs	7332	6812	6321	5857	5420	5010	4624	3926	3320
Taylor KO Index	88.2	85.0	81.9	78.8	75.8	66.2	63.7	58.7	53.9
Path • Inches	-0.9	+1.0	+1.3	0.0	-3.2	-8.3	-15.5	-37.0	-69.4
Wind Drift • Inches	0.0	0.2	0.8	1.9	3.4	5.4	7.9	14.6	23.8

Dakota 550-grain Woodleigh Solid (450-550WSO)

G1 Ballistic Coefficient = 0.426

Distance • Yards	Muzzle	50	100	150	200	250	300	400	500
Velocity • fps	2450	2350	2253	2158	2065	1974	1886	1718	1562
Energy • Ft-lbs	7332	6748	6200	5688	5209	4762	4347	3607	2981
Taylor KO Index	88.2	84.6	81.1	77.7	74.3	71.0	67.9	61.8	56.2
Path • Inches	-0.9	+1.0	+1.4	0.0	-3.2	-8.5	-16.0	-38.5	-73.0
Wind Drift • Inches	0.0	0.2	0.9	2.1	3.8	6.2	9.1	16.8	27.5

Dakota 600-grain Barnes Solid (450-600BSO)

G1 Ballistic Coefficient = 0.454

Distance • Yards	Muzzle	50	100	150	200	250	300	400	500
Velocity • fps	2350	2259	2169	2082	1996	1913	1832	1677	1534
Energy • Ft-lbs	7359	6798	6270	5774	5311	4877	4473	3749	3134
Taylor KO Index	92.3	88.7	85.1	81.7	78.4	75.1	71.9	65.8	60.2
Path • Inches	-0.9	+1.2	+1.5	0.0	-3.5	-9.2	-17.2	-41.4	-77.9
Wind Drift • Inches	0.0	0.2	0.9	2.1	3.8	6.1	9.0	16.6	27.1

.460 Weatherby Magnum

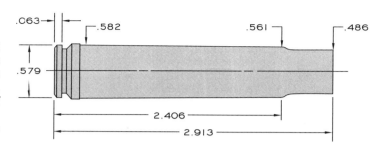

In terms of muzzle energy, the .460 Weatherby until recently was the most "powerful" cartridge available to the serious hunter. Weatherby introduced the .460 in 1958. The cartridge case is from the same basic head size as the .378. With factory loadings that produce in excess of 7,500 ft-lbs of muzzle energy, this is enough caliber for any game, anywhere. The .460 Weatherby Magnum is a caliber that very few people shoot for "fun." The recoil is fearsome even with a heavy gun.

Relative Recoil Factor = 5.86

Specifications

Controlling Agency for Standardization of this Ammunition: CIP

Bullet Weight Grains	Velocity fps	Maximum Average Pressure	
		Copper Crusher	Transducer
N/S	N/S	3,800 bar	4,370 bar

Typical barrel for velocity testing: 26 inches long—1 turn in 16-inch twist

Availability

Weatherby 450-grain Barnes-X (B 460 450 XS)

G1 Ballistic Coefficient = 0.488

Distance • Yards	Muzzle	50	100	150	200	250	300	400	500
Velocity • fps	2700	2608	2518	2429	2343	2257	2175	2013	1859
Energy • Ft-lbs	7284	6797	6333	5897	5482	5092	4725	4050	3452
Taylor KO Index	79.5	76.8	74.1	71.5	69.0	66.5	64.0	59.3	54.7
Path • Inches	-0.9	+0.7	+1.0	0.0	-2.5	-6.6	-12.4	-29.7	-55.5
Wind Drift • Inches	0.0	0.2	0.7	1.6	2.9	4.6	6.7	12.4	20.2

Weatherby 500-grain Round Nose–Expanding (H 460 500 RN)

G1 Ballistic Coefficient = 0.287

Distance • Yards	Muzzle	50	100	150	200	250	300	400	500
Velocity • fps	2600	2448	2301	2158	2022	1890	1764	1533	1333
Energy • Ft-lbs	7504	6654	5877	5174	4539	3965	3456	2608	1972
Taylor KO Index	85.1	80.1	75.3	70.6	66.1	61.8	57.7	50.2	43.6
Path • Inches	-0.9	+0.9	+1.3	0.0	-3.2	-8.4	-16.1	-40.4	-79.3
Wind Drift • Inches	0.0	0.3	1.3	3.0	5.4	8.8	13.1	25.0	41.7

A² 500-grain Dead Tough SP, Monolithic Solid, Lion Load SP (None)

G1 Ballistic Coefficient = 0.377

Distance • Yards	Muzzle	50	100	150	200	250	300	400	500
Velocity • fps	2580	2464	2349	2241	2131	2030	1929	1737	1560
Energy • Ft-lbs	7389	6743	6126	5578	5040	4576	4133	3351	2702
Taylor KO Index	84.4	80.6	76.8	73.3	69.7	66.4	63.1	56.8	51.0
Path • Inches	-0.9	+0.9	+1.2	0.0	-3.0	-7.8	-14.8	-36.0	-68.8
Wind Drift • Inches	0.0	0.2	1.0	2.2	4.1	6.5	9.6	18.0	29.6

Weatherby 500-grain Full Metal Jacket (B 460 500 FJ)

G1 Ballistic Coefficient = 0.295

Distance • Yards	Muzzle	50	100	150	200	250	300	400	500
Velocity • fps	2600	2452	2309	2170	2037	1907	1784	1557	1357
Energy • Ft-lbs	7504	6676	5917	5229	4605	4039	3534	2690	2046
Taylor KO Index	85.1	80.2	75.5	71.0	66.6	62.4	58.4	50.9	44.4
Path • Inches	0.9	+0.9	+1.3	0.0	-3.1	-8.3	-15.9	-39.8	-78.3
Wind Drift • Inches	0.0	0.3	1.2	2.9	5.3	8.5	12.7	24.1	40.2

.500-465 Nitro Express

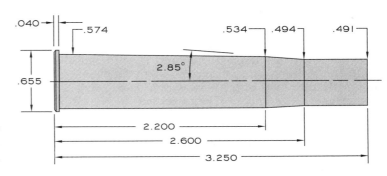

The most common practice in the U.S. when naming "necked-to" cartridges is to put the caliber first and the cartridge of origin second. An example would be the .30-378 WM, which is a .378 WM case necked to .30 caliber. The Brits seem to do just the opposite. The .500-465 Nitro Express is basically a .500 Nitro Express (it's actually closer to a .470 NE case) necked to .465 caliber. This cartridge was introduced in 1906 or 1907 by Holland & Holland when the British government outlawed .450-caliber guns in India.

Relative Recoil Factor = 4.59

Specifications

Controlling Agency for Standardization of this Ammunition: CIP

Bullet Weight Grains	Velocity fps	Maximum Average Pressure	
		Copper Crusher	Transducer
N/S	N/S	2,200 bar	2,450 bar

Standard barrel for velocity testing: 26 inches long—1 turn in 30-inch twist

Availability

A² 480-grain Dead Tough SP, Monolithic Solid, Lion Load SP (None)

G1 Ballistic Coefficient = 0.350

Distance • Yards	Muzzle	50	100	150	200	250	300	400	500
Velocity • fps	2150	2038	1926	1823	1722	1626	1534	1366	1226
Energy • Ft-lbs	4926	4426	3960	3545	3160	2817	2507	1990	1601
Taylor KO Index	69.7	66.1	62.5	59.1	55.9	52.7	49.8	44.3	39.8
Path • Inches	-0.9	+1.6	+2.0	0.0	-4.6	-12.1	-22.8	-56.1	-108.1
Wind Drift • Inches	0.0	0.3	1.4	3.2	5.8	9.3	13.7	25.7	42.0

Kynoch 480-grain Soft Point

G1 Ballistic Coefficient = 0.414

Distance • Yards	Muzzle	50	100	150	200	250	300	400	500
Velocity • fps	2150	2054	1962	1872	1784	1700	1619	1467	1332
Energy • Ft-lbs	4930	4490	4100	3735	3394	3091	2793	2295	1891
Taylor KO Index	69.7	66.6	63.6	60.7	57.9	55.1	52.5	47.6	43.2
Path • Inches	-0.9	+1.5	+1.9	0.0	-4.4	-11.5	-21.6	-52.1	-98.9
Wind Drift • Inches	0.0	0.3	1.2	2.6	4.8	7.7	11.3	21.0	34.3

Robert E. Petersen (left) took this buffalo with PH Joe Coogan in Botswana. (Photo from African Hunter II by Craig Boddington and Peter Flack, Safari Press, 2004)

.470 Nitro Express

The .470 Nitro Express is a large, rimmed cartridge in the British tradition. It is intended primarily for double rifles. Most of the traditional British African cartridges have one thing in common: They drive a large-caliber, heavy bullet at velocities in the 2,000 to 2,300 fps range. When you have a 500-grain bullet humping along at 2,150 fps, you have tremendous stopping power, and the double rifle provides the shooter with a reserve shot without any manipulation of the gun. While the recoil of these cartridges is formidable, the weight of double rifles tames down the worst of the jolt. Besides, who feels recoil in the face of a charging buffalo?

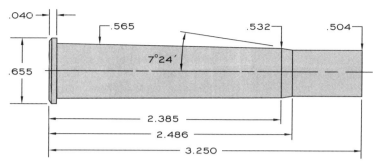

Relative Recoil Factor = 4.84

Specifications

Controlling Agency for Standardization of this Ammunition: CIP

Bullet Weight Grains	Velocity fps	Maximum Average Pressure	
		Copper Crusher	Transducer
N/S	N/S	2,400 bar	2,700 bar

Standard barrel for velocity testing: 26 inches long—1 turn in 21-inch twist

Availability

Norma 500-grain Woodleigh Soft Point (11202)
G1 Ballistic Coefficient = 0.411

Distance • Yards	Muzzle	50	100	150	200	250	300	400	500
Velocity • fps	2165	2069	1975	1884	1795	1710	1627	1474	1337
Energy • Ft-lbs	5205	4752	4330	3940	3577	3246	2940	2413	1986
Taylor KO Index	73.3	70.1	66.9	63.8	60.8	57.9	55.1	49.9	45.3
Path • Inches	-0.9	+1.5	+1.9	0.0	-4.3	-11.3	-21.3	51.5	-97.8
Wind Drift • Inches	0.0	0.3	1.2	2.6	4.8	7.7	11.3	21.0	34.3

A² 500-grain Dead Tough SP, Monolithic Solid, Lion Load SP (None)
G1 Ballistic Coefficient = 0.325

Distance • Yards	Muzzle	50	100	150	200	250	300	400	500
Velocity • fps	2150	2029	1912	1800	1693	1590	1493	1320	1180
Energy • Ft-lbs	5132	4572	4058	3597	3182	2806	2475	1935	1545
Taylor KO Index	72.9	68.8	64.8	61.0	57.4	53.9	50.6	44.7	40.0
Path • Inches	-0.9	+1.6	+2.0	0.0	-4.7	-12.4	-23.6	58.2	-113.0
Wind Drift • Inches	0.0	0.4	1.5	3.4	6.3	10.1	15.0	28.1	38.3

Federal 500-grain Trophy Bonded Bear Claw (P470T1)
G1 Ballistic Coefficient = 0.370

Distance • Yards	Muzzle	50	100	150	200	250	300	400	500
Velocity • fps	2150	2043	1940	1838	1740	1649	1563	1401	1261
Energy • Ft-lbs	5130	4635	4175	3753	3368	3018	2712	2178	1765
Taylor KO Index	72.8	69.2	65.7	62.2	58.9	55.8	53.0	47.5	42.7
Path • Inches	-0.9	+1.6	+1.9	0.0	-4.5	-11.9	-22.4	-54.6	-104.8
Wind Drift • Inches	0.0	0.3	1.3	3.0	5.5	8.8	12.9	24.0	39.3

Federal 500-grain Trophy Bonded Sledgehammer Solid (P470T2)
G1 Ballistic Coefficient = 0.370

Distance • Yards	Muzzle	50	100	150	200	250	300	400	500
Velocity • fps	2150	2043	1940	1838	1740	1649	1563	1401	1261
Energy • Ft-lbs	5130	4635	4175	3753	3368	3018	2712	2178	1765
Taylor KO Index	72.8	69.2	65.7	62.2	58.9	55.8	53.0	47.5	42.7
Path • Inches	-0.9	+1.6	+1.9	0.0	-4.5	-11.9	-22.4	-54.6	-104.8
Wind Drift • Inches	0.0	0.3	1.3	3.0	5.5	8.8	12.9	24.0	39.3

Federal 500-grain Woodleigh Weldcore SP (P470A)

G1 Ballistic Coefficient = 0.304

Distance • Yards	Muzzle	50	100	150	200	250	300	400	500
Velocity • fps	2150	2021	1890	1777	1650	1555	1440	1270	1140
Energy • Ft-lbs	5130	4535	3993	3506	3040	2687	2310	1790	1435
Taylor KO Index	70.3	66.1	61.8	58.1	54.0	50.9	47.1	41.5	37.3
Path • Inches	-0.9	+1.6	+2.0	0.0	-4.8	-12.7	-24.2	-60.3	-117.9
Wind Drift • Inches	0.0	0.4	1.6	3.7	7.0	10.9	16.6	31.1	50.6

Kynoch 500-grain Solid or Soft Nose

G1 Ballistic Coefficient = 0.382

Distance • Yards	Muzzle	50	100	150	200	250	300	400	500
Velocity • fps	2125	2023	1923	1827	1734	1644	1559	1402	1266
Energy • Ft-lbs	5015	4543	4107	3706	3338	3003	2699	2183	1780
Taylor KO Index	72.0	68.6	65.2	61.9	58.8	55.7	52.8	47.5	42.9
Path • Inches	-0.9	+1.6	+2.0	0.0	-4.6	-12.0	-22.8	-55.3	-105.6
Wind Drift • Inches	0.0	0.3	1.3	2.9	5.4	8.6	12.6	23.5	38.3

Norma 500-grain Woodleigh Full Jacket (11201)

G1 Ballistic Coefficient = 0.410

Distance • Yards	Muzzle	50	100	150	200	250	300	400	500
Velocity • fps	2165	2068	1974	1883	1794	1709	1626	1473	1336
Energy • Ft-lbs	5205	4751	4328	3937	3574	3242	2936	2408	1981
Taylor KO Index	73.3	70.0	66.8	63.8	60.8	57.9	55.1	49.9	45.3
Path • Inches	-0.9	+1.5	+1.9	0.0	-4.3	-11.3	-21.3	-51.5	-97.9
Wind Drift • Inches	0.0	0.3	1.2	2.6	4.8	7.7	11.4	21.1	34.4

Federal 500-grain Woodleigh Solid (P470B)

G1 Ballistic Coefficient = 0.304

Distance • Yards	Muzzle	50	100	150	200	250	300	400	500
Velocity • fps	2150	2021	1890	1777	1650	1555	1440	1270	1140
Energy • Ft-lbs	5130	4535	3993	3506	3040	2687	2310	1790	1435
Taylor KO Index	70.3	66.1	61.8	58.1	54.0	50.9	47.1	41.5	37.3
Path • Inches	-0.9	+1.6	+2.0	0.0	-4.8	-12.7	-24.2	-60.3	-117.9
Wind Drift • Inches	0.0	0.4	1.6	3.7	7.0	10.9	16.6	31.1	50.6

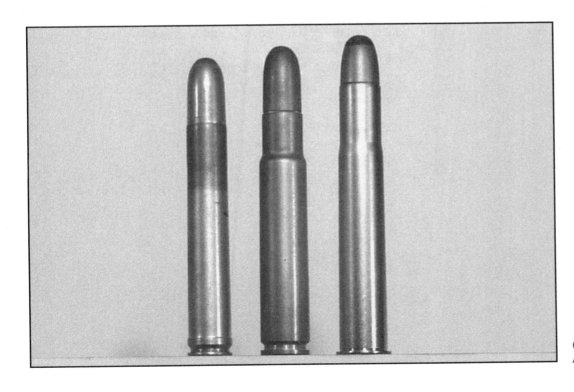

(Left to right) .458 Lott, .450 Dakota, .470 Nitro Express.

.475 Nitro Express Number 2

The .475 Nitro Express Number 2 was, like many other British cartridges, introduced in 1907. This cartridge has a case head somewhat larger than the .470 and .500 NE cartridges and has a case length of 3.500 inches. It's a big one. Over the years there have been a variety of loadings (some very mild and some pretty hot) for this cartridge—so care must be used when selecting ammunition for an old gun.

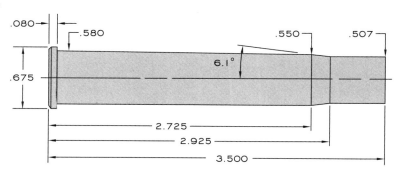

Relative Recoil Factor = 4.95

Specifications

Controlling Agency for Standardization of this Ammunition: CIP

Bullet Weight Grains	Velocity fps	Maximum Average Pressure Copper Crusher	Transducer
N/S	N/S	2,450 bar	2,750 bar

Standard barrel for velocity testing: 26 inches long—1 turn in 18-inch twist

Availability

Kynoch 480-grain Solid or Soft Nose
G1 Ballistic Coefficient = 0.348

Distance • Yards	Muzzle	50	100	150	200	250	300	400	500
Velocity • fps	2200	2084	1974	1867	1763	1664	1570	1397	1250
Energy • Ft-lbs	5160	4636	4155	3716	3315	2953	2627	2081	1665
Taylor KO Index	71.8	68.0	64.0	60.9	57.4	54.3	51.2	45.6	40.8
Path • Inches	-0.9	+1.5	+1.8	0.0	-4.4	-11.5	-21.8	-53.4	-103.1
Wind Drift • Inches	0.0	0.3	1.3	3.1	5.6	9.0	13.4	25.1	41.0

A² 500-grain Dead Tough SP, Monolithic Solid, Lion Load SP (None)
G1 Ballistic Coefficient = 0.332

Distance • Yards	Muzzle	50	100	150	200	250	300	400	500
Velocity • fps	2200	2080	1964	1852	1744	1641	1548	1366	1219
Energy • Ft-lbs	5375	4804	4283	3808	3378	2991	2645	2073	1650
Taylor KO Index	74.8	70.7	66.8	63.0	59.3	55.8	52.6	46.4	41.4
Path • Inches	-0.9	+1.5	+1.9	0.0	-4.4	-11.7	-22.2	-54.7	-106.0
Wind Drift • Inches	0.0	0.3	1.4	3.2	5.9	9.6	14.1	26.5	43.5

.495 A-Square

Art Alphin's .495 A² cartridge is basically a slightly shortened .460 Weatherby case necked to hold a 0.510-diameter bullet. When it was designed in 1977, it was intended to provide a cartridge firing .50-caliber bullets that could be adapted to existing bolt actions. Performance-wise, this cartridge is more powerful than either the .500 Nitro Express or the .505 Gibbs.

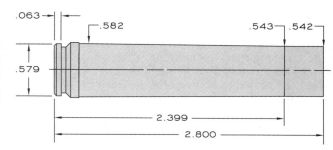

Relative Recoil Factor = 6.03

Specifications

Controlling Agency for Standardization of this Ammunition: Factory
Standard barrel for velocity testing: 26 inches long—1 turn in 10-inch twist

Availability

A² 570-grain Dead Tough SP, Monolithic Solid, Lion Load SP (None)

G1 Ballistic Coefficient = 0.348

Distance • Yards	Muzzle	50	100	150	200	250	300	400	500
Velocity • fps	2350	2231	2117	2003	1896	1790	1690	1504	1340
Energy • Ft-lbs	6989	6302	5671	5081	4552	4058	3616	2863	2272
Taylor KO Index	97.6	92.7	87.9	83.2	78.7	74.3	70.2	6+2.5	55.6
Path • Inches	-0.9	+1.2	+1.6	0.0	-3.8	-9.9	-18.8	-46.1	-88.9
Wind Drift • Inches	0.0	0.3	1.2	2.8	5.1	8.2	12.2	22.8	37.6

Elephants require big guns! Bill Feldstein (left) with a bull elephant taken with the .700 Nitro Express. (Photo from A Pioneering Hunter by Brian Marsh, 2006, Safari Press)

.500 Nitro Express 3-Inch

This cartridge was first introduced as a black-powder version (the .500 Express) about 1880. The smokeless-powder version came along about 1890. While it is an excellent cartridge and was highly respected by some of the professional hunters, the .500 NE never reached the popularity of the .470 NE.

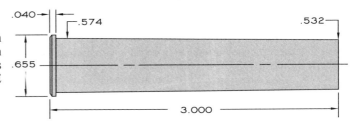

Relative Recoil Factor = 5.52

Specifications

Controlling Agency for Standardization of this Ammunition: CIP

Bullet Weight Grains	Velocity fps	Maximum Average Pressure	
		Copper Crusher	Transducer
N/S	N/S	2,500 bar	2,800 bar

Standard barrel for velocity testing: 26 inches long—1 turn in 15-inch twist

Availability

A² 570-grain Dead Tough SP, Monolithic Solid, Lion Load SP (None)   G1 Ballistic Coefficient = 0.350

Distance • Yards	Muzzle	50	100	150	200	250	300	400	500
Velocity • fps	2150	2038	1928	1823	1722	1626	1534	1366	1226
Energy • Ft-lbs	5850	5256	4703	4209	3752	3345	2977	2364	1901
Taylor KO Index	89.3	84.6	80.1	75.7	71.5	67.5	63.7	56.7	50.9
Path • Inches	-0.9	+1.6	+2.0	0.0	-4.6	-12.1	-22.9	-56.0	-108.1
Wind Drift • Inches	0.0	0.3	1.4	3.2	5.8	9.3	13.7	25.7	42.0

Kynoch 570-grain Solid or Soft Nose   G1 Ballistic Coefficient = 0.384

Distance • Yards	Muzzle	50	100	150	200	250	300	400	500
Velocity • fps	2150	2048	1948	1851	1758	1688	1532	1423	1284
Energy • Ft-lbs	5850	5300	4800	4337	3911	3521	3168	2563	2088
Taylor KO Index	89.3	85.0	80.9	76.9	73.0	70.1	65.7	59.1	53.3
Path • Inches	-0.9	+1.6	+1.9	0.0	-4.5	-11.7	-22.1	-53.8	-102.7
Wind Drift • Inches	0.0	0.3	1.2	2.9	5.2	8.4	12.4	23.0	37.5

.500 Jeffery

While the British hunters tended to prefer the big double rifles that used rimmed cartridges, German hunters preferred bolt-action rifles. This cartridge originated as the 12.7x70mm Schuler. Jeffery picked it up and offered it in his line. For many years it was the most powerful cartridge available for bolt-action rifles.

Relative Recoil Factor = 5.78

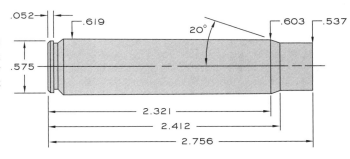

Specifications

Controlling Agency for Standardization of this Ammunition: CIP

Bullet Weight Grains	Velocity fps	Maximum Average Pressure	
		Copper Crusher	Transducer
N/S	N/S	2,850 bar	3,250 bar

Standard barrel for velocity testing: 26 inches long—1 turn in 10-inch twist

Availability

Kynoch 535-grain Solid or Soft Nose
G1 Ballistic Coefficient = 0.350

Distance • Yards	Muzzle	50	100	150	200	250	300	400	500
Velocity • fps	2400	2280	2164	2051	1942	1836	1734	1545	1376
Energy • Ft-lbs	6844	6179	5565	4999	4480	4006	3574	2835	2250
Taylor KO Index	93.5	88.9	84.3	79.9	75.7	71.6	67.6	60.2	53.6
Path • Inches	-0.9	+1.1	+1.5	0.0	-3.6	-9.4	-17.9	-43.8	-84.5
Wind Drift • Inches	0.0	0.3	1.2	2.7	4.9	7.9	11.7	22.0	36.2

This lion severely mauled PH Soren Lindstrom. In the middle and on the right are famed PHs Brian Marsh and Harry Selby. (Photo from A Pioneering Hunter *by Brian Marsh, 2006, Safari Press)*

.500 A-Square

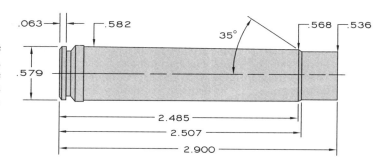

Companion cartridge to the .495 A², the .500 can be thought of as an "improved" .495. The case is 0.1-inch longer, and the body is blown out to 0.568 just at the shoulder. These changes allow the .500 A² to produce with well over 100 ft-lbs more muzzle energy than the .495. It is a potent round for bolt-action rifles.

Relative Recoil Factor = 6.68

Specifications

Controlling Agency for Standardization of this Ammunition: Factory
Standard barrel for velocity testing: 26 inches long—1 turn in 10-inch twist

Availability

A² 600-grain Dead Tough SP, Monolithic Solid, Lion Load SP (None)

G1 Ballistic Coefficient = 0.357

Distance • Yards	Muzzle	50	100	150	200	250	300	400	500
Velocity • fps	2470	2351	2235	2122	2031	1907	1804	1612	1438
Energy • Ft-lbs	8127	7364	6654	6001	5397	4844	4337	3461	2755
Taylor KO Index	108.0	102.8	97.7	92.8	88.0	83.4	78.9	70.5	62.9
Path • Inches	-0.9	+1.0	+1.4	0.0	-3.3	-8.8	-16.6	-40.7	-78.3
Wind Drift • Inches	0.0	0.3	1.1	2.5	4.6	7.4	11.0	20.6	33.9

Adrian Carr and Padro Camps Salvat with a pair of 160-pound tusks from the Southern Sudan. (Photo from *Hunting for Trouble* by Geoff Wainwright, 2006, Safari Press)

.505 Rimless Magnum (Gibbs)

Introduced about 1913, the .505 Gibbs was a proprietary cartridge designed for use in bolt-action rifles. Ammunition is a little hard to get for this caliber, but it is available from the two sources listed below. The ballistics of this cartridge are such that it's doubtful that anyone would chamber a new rifle for it today, but the cartridge was certainly well respected in the pre-WWII period.

Relative Recoil Factor = 5.44

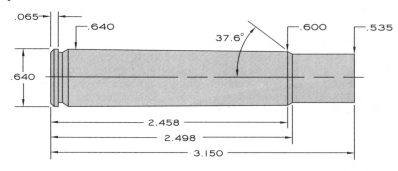

Specifications

Controlling Agency for Standardization of this Ammunition: CIP

Bullet Weight Grains	Velocity fps	Maximum Average Pressure	
		Copper Crusher	Transducer
N/S	N/S	2,400 bar	2,700 bar

Standard barrel for velocity testing: 26 inches long—1 turn in 16-inch twist

Availability

A² 525-grain Dead Tough SP, Monolithic Solid, Lion Load SP (None)
G1 Ballistic Coefficient = 0.339

Distance • Yards	Muzzle	50	100	150	200	250	300	400	500
Velocity • fps	2300	2179	2063	1949	1840	1735	1634	1449	1290
Energy • Ft-lbs	6166	5539	4962	4430	3948	3510	3115	2450	1940
Taylor KO Index	87.1	82.5	78.1	73.8	69.7	65.7	61.9	54.9	48.9
Path • Inches	-0.9	+1.3	+1.7	0.0	-4.0	-10.5	-19.9	-49.0	-94.8
Wind Drift • Inches	0.0	0.3	1.3	3.0	5.4	8.7	12.9	24.3	40.0

Kynoch 525-grain Solid or Soft Nose
G1 Ballistic Coefficient = 0.350

Distance • Yards	Muzzle	50	100	150	200	250	300	400	500
Velocity • fps	2300	2183	2070	1960	1853	1751	1653	1471	1313
Energy • Ft-lbs	6168	5558	4995	4478	4005	3575	3186	2525	2010
Taylor KO Index	87.1	82.7	78.4	74.2	70.2	66.3	62.6	55.7	49.7
Path • Inches	-0.9	+1.3	+1.7	0.0	-3.9	-10.4	-19.7	-48.2	-93.0
Wind Drift • Inches	0.0	0.3	1.2	2.9	5.2	8.4	12.5	23.4	38.5

.577 Nitro Express 3-Inch

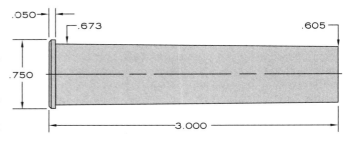

The .577 Nitro Express started life about 1880 as a black-powder cartridge (obviously not called "Nitro" then). Even before 1900, in the very dawning of the smokeless powder era, the .577 was introduced as a Nitro version. There was also a 2¾-inch version. With all these variations, any owner of a .577-caliber gun would be well advised to be very sure he knows exactly which cartridges are suitable for use in his gun. The consequences of getting the wrong ammo are just too severe.

Relative Recoil Factor = 6.93

Specifications

Controlling Agency for Standardization of this Ammunition: CIP

Bullet Weight Grains	Velocity fps	Maximum Average Pressure	
		Copper Crusher	Transducer
N/S	N/S	2,200 bar	2,450 bar

Standard barrel for velocity testing: 26 inches long—1 turn in 30-inch twist

Availability

A² 750-grain Dead Tough SP, Monolithic Solid, Lion Load SP (None)

G1 Ballistic Coefficient = 0.315

Distance • Yards	Muzzle	50	100	150	200	250	300	400	500
Velocity • fps	2050	1929	1811	1701	1595	1495	1401	1240	1116
Energy • Ft-lbs	6998	6197	5463	4817	4234	3721	3272	2560	2075
Taylor KO Index	128.5	120.8	113.5	106.6	100.0	93.7	87.8	77.7	69.9
Path • Inches	-0.9	+1.8	+2.2	0.0	-5.2	-13.9	-26.5	-65.6	-127.6
Wind Drift • Inches	0.0	0.4	1.6	3.8	7.0	11.2	16.6	30.9	50.2

Kynoch 750-grain Solid or Soft Nose

G1 Ballistic Coefficient = 0.430

Distance • Yards	Muzzle	50	100	150	200	250	300	400	500
Velocity • fps	2050	1960	1874	1790	1708	1630	1554	1414	1291
Energy • Ft-lbs	7010	6400	5860	5335	4860	4424	4024	3332	2774
Taylor KO Index	128.5	122.8	117.5	112.2	107.1	102.2	97.4	86.6	80.9
Path • Inches	-0.9	+1.7	+2.1	0.0	-4.8	-12.6	-23.7	-57.0	-107.8
Wind Drift • Inches	0.0	0.3	1.2	2.7	5.0	7.9	11.6	21.5	34.8

.577 Tyrannosaur

The .577 Tyrannosaur is an A² development, designed (about 1993) to produce a "big stopper" cartridge for a bolt-action rifle. The cartridge certainly achieves that goal, falling only about one Taylor KO index point (154 to 155) short of the legendary .600 NE. The case has a huge volume and holds something on the order of 150 grains of propellant. I think Art Alphin wins the naming award for this cartridge.

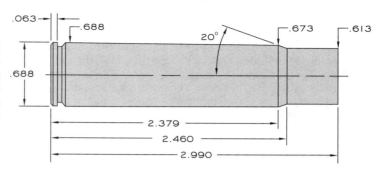

Relative Recoil Factor = 8.31

Specifications

Controlling Agency for Standardization of this Ammunition: Factory

Bullet Weight Grains	Velocity fps	Maximum Average Pressure	
		Copper Crusher	Transducer
N/S	N/S	53,000 cup	65,000 psi

Standard barrel for velocity testing: 26 inches long—1 turn in 12-inch twist

Availability

A² 750-grain Dead Tough SP, Monolithic Solid, Lion Load SP (None)   G1 Ballistic Coefficient = 0.318

Distance • Yards	Muzzle	50	100	150	200	250	300	400	500
Velocity • fps	2460	2327	2197	2072	1950	1835	1617	1576	1336
Energy • Ft-lbs	10,077	9018	8039	7153	6335	5609	4906	3831	2975
Taylor KO Index	154.2	145.9	137.7	129.9	122.2	115.0	101.4	98.8	83.7
Path • Inches	-0.9	+1.1	+1.4	0.0	-3.5	-9.2	-17.5	-43.4	-84.6
Wind Drift • Inches	0.0	0.3	1.2	2.9	5.2	8.5	12.6	23.8	39.5

Rashid Jamsheed is known as a sheep hunter, but even he could not resist the lure of Africa, where he took this good lion. (Photo from Hunting for Trouble by Geoff Wainwright, Safari Press, 2006)

.600 Nitro Express

Developed by Jeffery in 1903, the .600 Nitro Express has long held the position of the ultimate "elephant gun." If John "Pondoro" Taylor's KO index has any meaning, the .600 Nitro is more potent as a stopper than the .50 BMG. That comparison puts us right into the center of the energy vs. momentum argument, and the .600 NE is one of the foremost examples for the momentum advocates. Guns are still being built for this cartridge. Expensive guns.

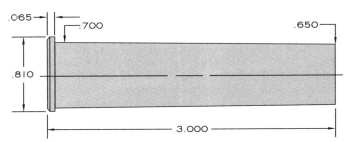

Relative Recoil Factor = 7.91

Specifications

Controlling Agency for Standardization of this Ammunition: CIP

Bullet Weight Grains	Velocity fps	Maximum Average Pressure	
		Copper Crusher	Transducer
N/S	N/S	2,200 bar	2,450 bar

Standard barrel for velocity testing: 26 inches long—1 turn in 30-inch twist

Availability

A² 900-grain Dead Tough SP, Monolithic Solid, Lion Load SP (None)
G1 Ballistic Coefficient = 0.272

Distance • Yards	Muzzle	50	100	150	200	250	300	400	500
Velocity • fps	1950	1814	1680	1564	1452	1349	1256	1111	1014
Energy • Ft-lbs	7596	6581	5634	4891	4212	3635	3155	2470	2056
Taylor KO Index	155.9	145.1	134.4	125.1	116.1	107.9	100.4	88.8	81.1
Path • Inches	-0.9	+2.2	+2.6	0.0	-6.2	-16.5	-31.6	-79.3	-154.9
Wind Drift • Inches	0.0	0.5	2.1	4.8	8.8	14.1	20.9	38.6	61.4

Kynoch 900-grain Solid or Soft Nose
G1 Ballistic Coefficient = 0.262

Distance • Yards	Muzzle	50	100	150	200	250	300	400	500
Velocity • fps	1950	1807	1676	1551	1435	1330	1237	1094	999
Energy • Ft-lbs	7600	6330	5620	4808	4117	3534	3059	2392	1996
Taylor KO Index	155.9	144.5	134.0	124.0	114.8	106.4	98.9	87.5	79.9
Path • Inches	-0.9	+2.2	+2.6	0.0	-6.3	-16.8	-32.2	-81.1	-158.6
Wind Drift • Inches	0.0	0.5	2.1	5.0	9.1	14.7	21.8	40.3	63.8

.700 Nitro Express

The .700 Nitro Express first appeared about 1988. As nearly as I can tell, the main reason for a .700 Nitro Express is that there already was a .600 Nitro Express. The .700 NE gives its owner a great "My gun is bigger than your gun" position. One wonders if it is really all that much "better." Because there are very few rifles chambered for this caliber, they are all custom made and very, very expensive.

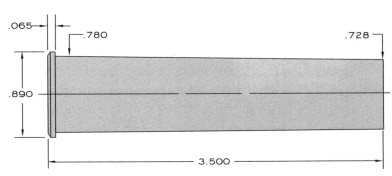

Relative Recoil Factor = 9.00

Specifications

Controlling Agency for Standardization of this Ammunition: CIP

Bullet Weight Grains	Velocity fps	Maximum Average Pressure	
		Copper Crusher	Transducer
N/S	N/S	2,200 bar*	2,450 bar*

Standard barrel for velocity testing: 26 inches long*

*Estimated

Availability

Kynoch 1000-grain Solid

G1 Ballistic Coefficient = 0.310

Distance • Yards	Muzzle	50	100	150	200	250	300	400	500
Velocity • fps	2000	1879	1762	1651	1547	1448	1357	1203	1088
Energy • Ft-lbs	8900	7842	6902	6061	5316	4663	4096	3216	2632
Taylor KO Index	206.3	193.8	181.7	170.3	159.6	149.4	140.0	124.1	112.2
Path • Inches	-0.9	+2.0	+2.4	0.0	-5.6	-14.8	28.2	-69.8	-135.6
Wind Drift • Inches	0.0	0.4	1.7	4.0	7.3	11.8	24.3	32.4	52.3

A² 1000-grain Monolithic (None)

G1 Ballistic Coefficient = 0.307

Distance • Yards	Muzzle	50	100	150	200	250	300	400	500
Velocity • fps	1900	1782	1669	1562	1461	1369	1285	1146	1048
Energy • Ft-lbs	8015	7950	6188	5419	4740	4166	3665	2917	2438
Taylor KO Index	196.0	183.8	172.1	161.1	150.7	141.1	132.5	118.2	108.1
Path • Inches	-0.9	+2.3	+2.7	0.0	-6.3	-16.6	-31.6	-78.1	-151.4
Wind Drift • Inches	0.0	0.5	1.9	4.3	7.9	12.7	18.7	34.6	55.1

Defensive Guns: Big Bore Handgun Cartridges

Jan Libourel

A guide to the best choices in the .40 group

In this article, I shall be covering the big-bore cartridges commencing at the .40 calibers. I should again like to acknowledge my indebtedness to the work on handgun stopping power conducted by Evan Marshall and Ed Sanow, which is most readily available in the three books they have published on this topic: *Handgun Stopping Power* (1992), *Street Stoppers* (1996), and *Stopping Power* (2001).

The 10mm Auto derives from a wildcat called the .40 G&A developed by a long-ago senior staff editor of *Guns & Ammo*. It was supposed to combine the virtues of the 9mm Parabellum and the .45 ACP in a custom converted Browning Hi-Power. The concept was taken up by the fledgling gunmaking firm of Dornaus & Dixon. These entrepreneurs persuaded Norma to load ammo for it. Rather than a moderate defensive load, the Norma creation was a near-magnum driving a 200-grain bullet at 1,200 fps, if memory serves. Dornaus & Dixon finally brought out the "Bren Ten," a DA autoloader styled after the CZ-75, but soon folded. Colt gave the 10mm new life by chambering a Government Model variant for it. In the wake of the 1986 Miami Shootout, the FBI settled on the

The author has been a big booster of the .45 Super cartridge, a sort of "+P+" .45 ACP, although ammo is offered by only two small firms. The top pistol is a Kimber that was customized and converted to .45 Super by Ace Custom .45's, "Home of the .45 Super." The lower pistol was assembled by Nowlin on an Entreprise frame kit and subsequently further modified and converted to .45 Super by Ace Custom.

10mm in a reduced loading, and Smith & Wesson made a couple of large pistols for it. However, the FBI's 10mm project soon foundered. The coming of the .40 S&W really put paid to the 10mm's career. These days, only two firms that I am aware of make 10mm pistols, Glock and Tanfoglio, the latter being imported by European American Armory as the "Witness." On paper, the hotter 10mm loadings surpass their .40 S&W counterparts by a modest but appreciable margin. On the street, there appears to be no difference, with one-shot stop percentages running between 86 percent and 90 percent for the 10mm. The mild loadings of the 10mm deliver stopping percentages in the low- to mid-80s. Recoil is vigorous but not intolerable with the hotter loads. Briefly, while I cannot enthusiastically endorse the acquisition of a 10mm, if you already have one, you are well armed.

The .40 S&W was introduced jointly by Smith & Wesson and Winchester at the 1990 SHOT Show. This offered the same ballistics as the mild loading of the 10mm in a cartridge small enough that most existing 9mm pistol designs could readily be adapted to it. Initial ballistics duplicated the ancient .38-40 revolver cartridge—a 180-grain JHP at 980 fps. This has proved to be a very decent stopper, with percentages in the mid-80s. A large segment of American handgunners, including many police professionals, had never entirely trusted the 9mm Parabellum, and this had only been augmented by the supposed failure of the 9mm in the FBI's Miami Shootout of 1986. Police—at that time right in the midst of making the transition from revolvers to auto pistols—flocked to the new cartridge, and it quickly established itself as one of our top combat cartridges. Today there exists a spectrum of loads. Some are quite hot; they are hard on the heels of the full-power 10mm ballistically and deliver one-shot stops almost as well as the legendary 125-grain .357 Magnum. According to Evan Marshall's data, the top stopper, at 94 percent, is the Remington 165-grain Gold Dot load at 1,150/485. Right behind at 93 percent are the Federal 155-grain Hydra-Shok (1,140/445) and the CCI 155-grain Gold Dot (1,200/496). These are among the most potent, hard-kicking loads in this caliber. There have been "light" loadings of the .40 S&W, typically featuring 165-grain bullets at moderate velocity. Marshall and Sanow counsel against use of the latter, as much from their tendency to compromise cycling reliability as from reduced stopping power. If you are looking for a serious defensive cartridge, the .40 S&W is one of your very best bets. Drawbacks are few: Gun life in some models is reputed to be a good deal shorter than in equivalent 9mm pistols. (However, the California Highway Patrol, perhaps the first major agency to adopt a .40 sidearm, reported that many of their Smith & Wesson 4006 pistols had digested 30,000 rounds of duty ammo without problems.) Accuracy is often reported to be inferior to other calibers, on the average. However, this is of little moment in a defensive pistol except for specialized uses like hostage rescue, and I personally have shot some very nice groups with pistols in this caliber.

There have been several other offerings in the .40/ .41 caliber auto pistol line. The .41 Action Express came out around the beginning of 1987. Its salient feature was a rebated case head that made it compatible with 9mm Parabellum breech faces. In theory, it was possible to convert any 9mm pistol to .41 AE by swapping barrels and magazines. In practice, the rebated case head often contributed to less than stellar reliability, and the coming of the .40 S&W largely killed it off. I don't believe anyone is making a pistol in this caliber, and I am unsure about ammo availability. Cor-Bon has a proprietary bottle-necked cartridge called the .400 Cor-Bon based on the .45 ACP necked down to .40 caliber. It is quite similar to an earlier wildcat called the .41 Avenger developed by prolific designer and experimenter J.D. Jones. Ballistics of the .400 Cor-Bon are quite fierce: Published muzzle energies for most loads are in excess of 600 foot-pounds. A simple barrel swap is supposed to suffice to convert any suitably strong .45 auto to .400 Cor-Bon. I had King's Gun Works fit a very reliable 1911 they had custom-built for me with a Bar-Sto .400 Cor-Bon barrel. It was not a harmonious mating. The pistol jammed like mad! Presumably, other people have enjoyed better success since Cor-Bon offers no fewer than five different loadings at this writing. Triton Cartridge came out with a somewhat similar cartridge called the .40 Super. It uses a slightly longer bottlenecked case based on cut-down .45 Winchester Magnum brass. Published energies for this item go as high as 971 foot-pounds, which impresses me as an awful lot to be launching from a service-sized auto pistol.

It is often said that a shiny big-bore revolver stoked with hollowpoints has a maximum intimidation value. Loaded with Cor-Bon 165-grain defensive loads, this Taurus .44 Magnum would make a potent stopper as well.

Triton Cartridge has had a somewhat checkered history and at the moment is being merged with another firm, so I am not sure about future availability of this one.

The .41 Magnum was introduced in 1964 as a result of a joint effort from Smith & Wesson, Ruger, and Remington. It was unusual in having been loaded to two power levels. One was supposed to be an ideal urban police load—a 210-grain lead semi-wadcutter at 950 fps from a 4-inch barrel. The other was a 210-grain jacketed softpoint at 1,350 fps. It was targeted to handgun hunters who wanted a powerhouse revolver but found the .44 Magnum a bit too much, highway patrolmen who needed penetration against car bodies, and rural officers who might need to put down large animals. The .41 Magnum was not a great success. The lead-bullet duty load kicked heavily, leaded barrels badly, and was not very accurate, and the full-power load was far too violent for effective defense use. The revolvers were big and heavy. A few departments adopted it or made its use optional.

Improvements in .38 Special and .357 Magnum ammo soon made a new caliber less desirable, and the widespread use of women for line police duties starting in the 1970s spelled the demise of the large-frame revolver as a duty sidearm. Ironically, in its day, the .41 "Police" load was probably the best handgun defense load offered. It delivered about 75 percent one-shot stops, which is nothing special by today's standards but certainly outclassed most, if not all, factory ammo of the mid-1960s. I always felt that the manufacturers should have made this bullet a hollowpoint. The best stopper among contemporary loads is the Winchester 175-grain Silvertip. It delivers about 90 percent stops. At 1,250 fps, it is not a full-power load, but it still kicks fairly hard. Cor-Bon offers a load with very similar ballistics. Smith & Wesson makes only one revolver in this caliber, a long-barreled hunting gun, at this time. Taurus now offers several five-shot, medium-frame revolvers in .41 Magnum, including a 2-inch "Total Titanium" snub that weighs less than 21 ounces and whose recoil with the more potent .41 Magnum loads is not something I would care to sample!

The .44 Special was introduced around 1908. For its entire history, its standard factory ballistics have been a 246-grain lead roundnose bullet at 755 fps. This is no real improvement over its predecessor, the .44 S&W Russian that dates back to 1870. The factory load is

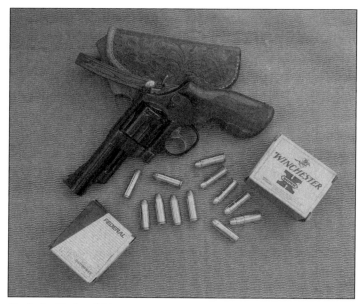

Both the Federal 225-grain lead hollowpoints and the Winchester 225-grain Silvertips in .45 Colt would make the author's Hogue-stocked Smith & Wesson Model 25 in this caliber into quite an effective defense gun. It is shown with a floral-carved Tom Threepersons holster from El Paso Saddlery.

about a 65 percent stopper in Marshall's statistics. Handloaders soon found that the factory ballistics could be much improved on, and their experiments led to the development of the .44 Magnum (a lengthened, supercharged .44 Special) in 1955. The much-loved gunwriter Elmer Keith was, of course, the foremost proponent of this practice. For many years, savvy cops often favored a .44 Special stoked with heavy handloads. The large-frame, six-shot .44 Special has been rendered largely obsolete by the coming of the .44 Magnum, but the .44 Special has had a revival in smaller five-shot revolvers. Charter 2000 is again making the very small Bulldog; Smith & Wesson is offering a 3-inch five-shooter weighing but 18 ounces in the "AirLite Ti" series, and Taurus offers an assortment of .44 Special five-shot snubs. Good factory loads in this caliber are few. For the past couple of decades Winchester has offered a 200-grain Silvertip hollowpoint and a Federal 200-grain lead hollowpoint. These are 76 percent and 73 percent stoppers, respectively, according to Marshall. This is a big improvement over the feeble standard load but no better than really good .38 Special performance. Some of the smaller firms have attractive offerings. Cor-Bon has a 165-grain JHP at 1,150 fps that looks promising, and Glaser and MagSafe loads are available.

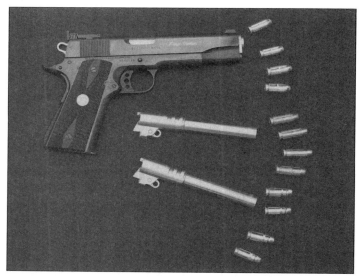

Much of the editor's shooting experience with the (from top) .40 S&W, 10mm Auto and .357 SIG has been with this Colt Delta Elite that King's Gun Works customized and fitted with interchangeable barrels in these calibers. From the 5-inch barrel, the .357 SIG really sizzles.

Any .44 Special load can be used as a subload in a .44 Magnum revolver.

As just noted, the .44 Magnum arose out of experimenters' hot loading the .44 Special. Because of its violent ballistics, it has of necessity been limited to large-frame revolvers. Full-power .44 Magnum loads are impractical for defense because of their blast and recoil. They are decent enough stoppers but no better than many lesser loads that are much easier to handle. The best factory load for which Marshall has a database is the Winchester 210-grain Silvertip that travels at 1,250 fps. These have a 92 percent OSS record. Most revolvers in this caliber are configured as hunting handguns, but some individuals have favored the 4-inch Smith & Wesson Model 29 and 629 revolvers for defensive use. The light-barreled "Mountain" versions of these revolvers might be better suited for defensive carry, at least with moderate loads. With full-power loads, recoil is positively vicious, or so I found. Smith & Wesson is currently offering a 27-ounce titanium-scandium .44 Magnum, the Model 329PD. Recoil with that one, I have been told, is enough to make a strong man weep! Smith & Wesson made several runs of 29s and 629s in a 3-inch, round-butt "belly gun" configuration, and Taurus briefly made a fixed-sight, 3-inch variant of the M44. Notwithstanding its use by "Dirty Harry" Callahan of cinematic make, the .44 Magnum revolver is not a very practical defense gun, but if you don't mind the size and weight, a .44 Magnum suitably loaded can certainly protect you well. Some authorities have recommended the 4-inch .44 Magnum as the best compromise side arm for situations calling for defense against both human attack and dangerous wild animals such as bears, big cats, or hyenas. Few of us, however, are likely to be adventurous enough to find ourselves in such a situation.

The .45 ACP is an American institution and is popular in many other parts of the world. Introduced by Colt's in 1905 and standardized as the U.S. service pistol cartridge in 1911, it has seen extensive combat use in both handguns and submachine guns. Many authorities regard it as the king of handgun defensive cartridges and with very good reason. Ironically, much of its reputation for awesome stopping power was built on the performance of military ball ammunition. Far from being the 90 percent stopper claimed by early proponents of the .45, military-style "hardball" actually has proven to be a mediocre 62

The original home of the .44 Special was in large-frame revolvers like the Hogue-stocked Smith & Wesson Model 24 at top. Today it is more commonly encountered in compact five-shooters like the Taurus Model 445 below. The Cor-Bon 165 grain JHP at 1,150 fps should be a great defensive choice in this caliber.

percent stopper in hundreds of shootings documented by Evan Marshall. This is actually inferior to 9mm Parabellum ball in Marshall's latest statistics. In the old days it was widely believed that the .45 ACP offered twice the stopping power of the 9mm with ball loads. It was also widely believed that the .45 ACP was too heavy and kicked too hard for good practical accuracy. These myths

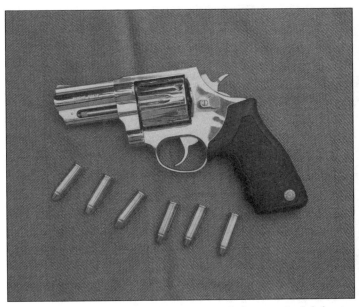

Full-power .44 Magnum loads are too much for practical defensive use, but the Cor-Bon 165-grain JHPs at 1,300 fps should be outstanding in a gun like this fixed-sight Taurus M44.

largely arose from the experience of military recruits who were utterly lacking in any kind of handgunning experience or skill at the time of their brief exposure to training with the Government Model .45 auto.

In reality, from a pistol of decent weight, the .45 ACP is a delight to shoot, and even from some of the very small compact pistols in this caliber it is far from punishing. Although hardball has been highly overrated, the better hollowpoints in this caliber are outstanding stoppers. In *Stopping Power*, Marshall lists no fewer than 11 loads that are 88 percent stoppers or better, and most of them are no more difficult to shoot than hardball. The top performers are Federal 230-grain Hydra-Shoks and Remington 185-grain Golden Sabers, both of which are tied with the best of the .357s at 96 percent. They are followed by Speer 230-grain Gold Dots at 93 percent. The .45 ACP has other virtues. It is capable of excellent inherent accuracy. It is very tolerant and easy to handload. It is a low-pressure cartridge and easy on guns. My oldest .45 has digested, by a close count, 18,400 rounds at this writing. It has had a few minor repairs over the years and the bluing is worn in spots, but it is otherwise in perfect order, and this is by no means remarkable. High-pressure +P loadings of the .45 ACP are available for those who want extra power, but they are a good deal rougher on pistols, and they

Miniaturized .45s like this Kimbler Ultra Carry have grown in popularity in the past few years. The MagSafe and Glaser loads would help compensate for a loss of power from the short barrel.

can compromise functional reliability. For those who want still more power from their .45s, there is the .45 Super conversion, pioneered by Ace Custom .45's. This uses a specially designed recoil spring and guide assembly, and requires a few other minor modifications, but it lets a .45 auto hit nearly as hard as a .41 Magnum. Unlike some similar concepts (e.g., .451 Detonics, .460 Rowland), a pistol converted to .45 Super can handle all full-power .45 ACP ammo with excellent reliability. The biggest drawback to the .45 Super is that ammo is available from only a couple of small firms, namely Texas Ammunition and Buffalo Bore Bullet Co.

Another recently announced .45 auto cartridge is the .45 Glock, which is a shortened .45 ACP for those who wish to shoot a .45-caliber bullet from a 9mm-sized Glock pistol. (I should have thought the .40 S&W filled that niche rather well for those who wanted something more than the Nine!) How similar this cartridge is to an earlier shortened .45 ACP that came out of Austria, the .45 HP (Hirtenberger Patrone), the people at Glock could not tell me. The .45 HP was designed for sale in countries like Italy, where ownership of military calibers is forbidden. Standard .45 ACPs would not fit all the way in the shorter chambers.

Over the years, from World War I onward, quite a few revolvers have been made for the .45 ACP. At this date Smith & Wesson and Taurus are producing such revolvers. Customarily, the rimless .45 ACP cartridges

Unlike some makers, Taurus beefed up the slide of their 9mm design when they introduced the PT-100 in .40 W&W. The frangible loads from MagSafe and Glaser make an already potent caliber even more formidable and may well be the best choices for some scenarios. The sharkskin flap holster is from Kramer.

are loaded into "moon clips" that provide headspacing and ease of loading. For many years, special .45 Auto Rim cartridges were loaded for use in these revolvers for those who didn't care to bother with the moon clips. As a handloader, I was very partial to the Auto Rim cartridge and did a lot of shooting with it in the 1980s, but it is no longer loaded, at least by any of the majors.

Finally, we come to the old .45 Colt that dates all the way back to 1873. In the days of the Old West, it was common to joke, "When I shoot a man with a .45 and he doesn't fall, I want to go around behind him to see what's holding him up!" The traditional 255- and 250-grain lead roundnose bullets (actually with a small flat point) from Winchester and Remington are 71 percent and 70 percent stoppers, which isn't bad. The black-powder loads of the Old West were in all probability more powerful, hence even better stoppers than their modern smokeless-powder counterparts. A number of modern loadings are offered. Marshall has databases for two: The Federal 225-grain lead semi-wadcutter hollowpoints are 81 percent stoppers, and the Winchester 225-grain Silvertips are 80 percent stoppers. Other promising loads are the CCI-Blazer, which drives a 200-grain JHP at an advertised 1,000 fps, and a Cor-Bon load also using a 200-grain JHP at 1,100 fps. The latter is a trifle more potent than the same firm's 200-grain +P .45 ACP. Cor-Bon also offers a Glaser Safety Slug load for the .45 Colt. Once upon a time, duty-style,

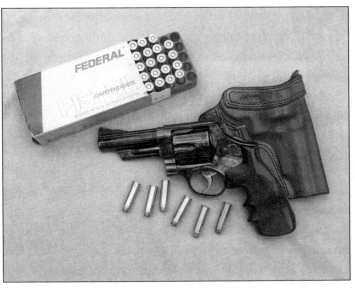

At the time of its introduction, the .41 Magnum was touted by authorities such as Elmer Keith and Bill Jordan as the ultimate gunfighter's handgun. Under their influence, the editor bought this Smith & Wesson Model 57 to celebrate finishing his doctoral dissertation 35 years ago. It now wears a Hogue Monogrip and is shown with a Kramer belt scabbard.

large-frame, six-shot revolvers in this caliber were readily available. This no longer seems to be the case. Peacemaker replicas and other cowboy-style revolvers abound, but the only company offering defense-worthy, double-action revolvers in this caliber nowadays is Taurus. These are medium-frame five-shooters, and they are offered in a fixed-sight snub configuration or as adjustable-sighted Trackers. In suitably strong revolvers, the .45 Colt can be handloaded to equal or surpass the .44 Magnum. The .45 Colt can also serve as a reduced load from a .454 Casull Magnum revolver. However, both of these facts are of little moment in a disquisition on defensive cartridges. If you like a revolver, the .45 Colt makes an excellent choice. An objection sometimes voiced to the .45 Colt in a DA revolver is that the rather narrow rims on this case can permit the case to slip under the extractor star. I think this may have been true of older ammo, but I have never experienced it with my cherished Smith & Wesson Model 25, nor did I experience it with two Taurus Tracker revolvers in this caliber that I recently reviewed for this publication.

Before wrapping this up, I should mention in passing that there are quite a few other vintage big-bore revolver cartridges available that, in the right guns and with the right loads, would make more-than-passing-fair defense cartridges.

The editor had King's Gun Works fit an interchangeable barrel for the powerful, bottlenecked .400 Cor-Bon to his Norinco 1911A1 they had previously customized.

The .38-40 and .44-40 were both developed for the Winchester Model 1873 rifle, and they were subsequently chambered by Colt and other revolver makers. For the benefit of the uninitiated, the .38-40 is actually a .40 caliber, in contrast to most other ".38" caliber handgun cartridges that take bullets ranging between .355 and .358 inches. These two cartridges have enjoyed a great revival of popularity thanks to the neo-cowboys, and quite a few Peacemaker replicas have been chambered for them. However, the last service-worthy double actions in these calibers were made before I was born, except for a 1986 run of Smith & Wesson "Texas Wagon Train Commemorative" revolvers in .44-40. With peppy hollowpoint loads, either cartridge would make a formidable stopper. I would conjecture that the available factory loads would deliver stopping percentages in the high 60s.

Another old-timer in the same class would be the .455 Webley, the best known of a number of big-bore British revolver cartridges. This cartridge has always enjoyed a good reputation as a "stopper," at least by the standards of its day. It is indigenous to the top-break Webley service revolvers, and large quantities of Colt and Smith & Wesson revolvers were made in this caliber for the British and Canadian forces during World War I. All three were very common on the surplus market in the days of my youth. I can recall Webleys selling for as little as $14.95 (probably $60 in today's dollars). A great many of these revolvers were modified to .45 ACP or .45 Colt to make them more

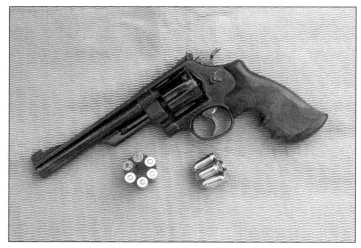

For many years, revolvers have been manufactured for the .45 ACP for use with moon clips. "Full moon" clips like these from Ranch Products have largely displaced the earlier half-moon clips. For many years a .45 Auto Rim cartridge was made for use in revolvers like this Hogue-stocked Smith & Wesson 25-2, through which the editor put about 8,000 rounds back in the 1980s.

A good .45 auto is hard, if not impossible, to beat as a defensive sidearm. Over the past decade, the editor has become a great fan of the high-capacity .45s from Para-Ordinance. Shown are two of Para's "Limited" series, a P14 with an extra-high-capacity magazine and a P12 that has been slightly modified by King's Gun Works.

salable to Americans. At this time, Fiocchi offers factory loads similar to the old British service load. At one time the British had a cup-point "Manstopper" load for use against savage tribesmen, to whom the conventions of civilized warfare did not apply. Most revolvers in this caliber are about ninety years old. For defense in the 21st century, they would be an eccentric but serviceable choice. However, most prudent individuals would prefer something more up to date.

In bringing this to a close, even though I have expended somewhat more than 8,000 words on this topic, I am still left with a feeling that I have only scratched the surface. For instance, there are quite a few small specialty ammunition makers to whom I have probably not done justice. A good example would be the ultra-high-velocity lightweight Performance Plus bullets offered in many calibers by RBCD Corporation. As regular readers may know, Jim Cirillo is a big advocate of these loads, and Jim has had a lot more firsthand experience in these matters than most of us. If I have passed over other progressive ammunition companies' offerings, I may have done so in part from lack of familiarity with their offerings and also because they do not have a track record in actual shootings, as recorded by Marshall.

At heart I am pretty conservative about these matters. If you stick to popular, readily available calibers like the .38 Special and .357 Magnum in revolvers and the 9mm Parabellum, .40 S&W and .45 ACP in auto pistols, and loads that have a proven track record, you won't go far wrong.

Data for Pistol and Revolver Cartridges

The data in this edition have been extended from 100 yards out to 200 yards. This increased distance may be useful for some of the high-powered large-caliber cartridges but is a totally impractical range for the small-caliber numbers. Nevertheless, we have included the data for all calibers so that the reader can make comparisons if and when he wishes. Some rifle manufacturers have chambered guns for several pistol calibers, such as the .44 Remington Magnum and the .357 Magnum. Where the velocity data from longer barrels are available, these calibers have also been shown in the rifle section.

.25 Auto (ACP)

The smallest of the current factory production centerfire pistol rounds, the great virtue of the .25 Auto is that it fits very small pistols. The power is so low, much lower than a .22 WMR, that its use for self-defense is limited to the deterrent effect that the mere showing of any gun provides. This cartridge has been around since 1908. That's a long time and there are still many different loadings available, so someone must be buying this ammunition.

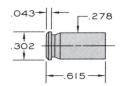

Relative Recoil Factor = 0.17

Specifications

Controlling Agency for Standardization of this Ammunition: SAAMI

Bullet Weight Grains	Velocity fps	Maximum Average Pressure	
		Copper Crusher	Transducer
35 XTP-HP	900	18,000 cup	25,000 psi
45 XP	805	18,000 cup	25,000 psi
50 MC-FMC	755	18,000 cup	25,000 psi

Standard barrel for velocity testing: 2 inches long—1 turn in 16-inch twist

Availability

Cor-Bon 35-grain Glaser Safety Slug (00200/na)
G1 Ballistic Coefficient = 0.075

Distance • Yards	Muzzle	25	50	75	100	125	150	175	200
Velocity • fps	1150	1049	977	921	874	832	795	761	729
Energy • Ft-lbs	103	86	74	66	59	54	49	45	41
Taylor KO Index	1.5	1.3	1.2	1.2	1.1	1.1	1.0	1.0	0.9
Mid-Range Trajectory Height • Inches	0.0	0.2	1.0	2.4	4.5	7.5	11.6	16.6	22.8
Drop • Inches	0.0	-0.9	-3.7	-8.8	-16.5	-27.1	-40.7	-57.8	-78.7

Magtech 35-grain JHP (25A) (Discontinued in 2004)
G1 Ballistic Coefficient = 0.073

Distance • Yards	Muzzle	25	50	75	100	125	150	175	200
Velocity • fps	930	881	827	800	764	732	701	672	644
Energy • Ft-lbs	63	60	53	50	45	42	38	35	32
Taylor KO Index	1.2	1.1	1.0	1.0	1.0	0.9	0.9	0.8	0.8
Mid-Range Trajectory Height • Inches	0.0	0.3	1.4	3.3	6.2	10.1	15.3	21.8	23.2
Drop • Inches	0.0	-1.3	-5.4	-12.6	-23.2	-37.4	-55.8	-78.5	-105.9

Hornady 35-grain JHP/XTP (90012)
G1 Ballistic Coefficient = 0.073

Distance • Yards	Muzzle	25	50	75	100	125	150	175	200
Velocity • fps	900	854	813	777	742	711	681	653	625
Energy • Ft-lbs	63	57	51	47	43	39	36	33	30
Taylor KO Index	1.1	1.1	1.0	1.0	0.9	0.9	0.9	0.8	0.8
Mid-Range Trajectory Height • Inches	0.0	0.3	1.5	3.5	6.6	10.5	16.2	23.0	31.6
Drop • Inches	0.0	-1.4	-5.8	-13.4	-24.6	-39.8	-59.2	-83.3	-112.4

Speer 35-grain Gold Dot Hollow Point (23602)
G1 Ballistic Coefficient = 0.091

Distance • Yards	Muzzle	25	50	75	100	125	150	175	200
Velocity • fps	900	863	830	799	770	743	717	693	669
Energy • Ft-lbs	63	58	53	50	46	43	40	37	35
Taylor KO Index	1.1	1.1	1.1	1.0	1.0	0.9	0.9	0.9	0.8
Mid-Range Trajectory Height • Inches	0.0	0.3	1.5	3.4	6.3	10.2	15.4	21.8	29.4
Drop • Inches	0.0	-1.4	-5.7	-13.1	-24.0	-38.5	-57.0	-79.6	-106.9

Winchester 45-grain Expanding Point (X25AXP)
G1 Ballistic Coefficient = 0.059

Distance • Yards	Muzzle	25	50	75	100	125	150	175	200
Velocity • fps	815	770	729	690	655	621	589	559	530
Energy • Ft-lbs	66	59	53	48	42	39	35	31	28
Taylor KO Index	1.3	1.2	1.2	1.1	1.1	1.0	1.0	0.9	0.9
Mid-Range Trajectory Height • Inches	0.0	0.4	1.8	4.4	8.2	13.6	20.6	29.3	41.0
Drop • Inches	0.0	-1.7	-7.1	-16.5	-30.6	-49.6	-74.3	-105.2	-143.0

Hirtenberger 49-grain FM-RN (82300015)

G1 Ballistic Coefficient = 0.071

Distance • Yards	Muzzle	25	50	75	100	125	150	175	200
Velocity • fps	722	690	661	632	605	579	554	530	507
Energy • Ft-lbs	57	52	48	44	40	37	33	31	28
Taylor KO Index	1.3	1.2	1.2	1.1	1.1	1.0	1.0	0.9	0.9
Mid-Range Trajectory Height • Inches	0.0	0.5	2.3	5.4	10.0	16.2	24.6	35.1	47.9
Drop • Inches	0.0	-2.2	-8.8	-20.5	-37.6	-60.7	-90.2	-126.8	-171.0

Sellier & Bellot 50-grain FMJ (SBA02501)

G1 Ballistic Coefficient = 0.084

Distance • Yards	Muzzle	25	50	75	100	125	150	175	200
Velocity • fps	781	751	723	696	671	646	623	600	579
Energy • Ft-lbs	69	64	59	54	50	46	43	40	37
Taylor KO Index	1.4	1.4	1.3	1.3	1.2	1.2	1.1	1.1	1.1
Mid-Range Trajectory Height • Inches	0.0	0.4	1.9	4.5	8.3	13.5	20.3	28.7	38.9
Drop • Inches	0.0	-1.8	-7.5	-17.3	-31.7	-50.8	-75.2	-105.1	-141.1

Speer 50-grain TMJ Lawman (53607)

G1 Ballistic Coefficient = 0.111

Distance • Yards	Muzzle	25	50	75	100	125	150	175	200
Velocity • fps	755	733	712	692	673	654	636	619	602
Energy • Ft-lbs	63	60	56	53	50	48	45	42	40
Taylor KO Index	1.4	1.3	1.3	1.3	1.2	1.2	1.2	1.1	1.1
Mid-Range Trajectory Height • Inches	0.0	0.5	2.0	4.7	8.6	13.7	20.4	28.6	38.5
Drop • Inches	0.0	-1.9	-7.9	-18.2	-33.0	-52.6	-77.2	-107.2	-142.9

CCI 50-grain TMJ Blazer (3501)

G1 Ballistic Coefficient = 0.111

Distance • Yards	Muzzle	25	50	75	100	125	150	175	200
Velocity • fps	755	733	712	692	673	654	636	619	602
Energy • Ft-lbs	63	60	56	53	50	48	45	42	40
Taylor KO Index	1.4	1.3	1.3	1.3	1.2	1.2	1.2	1.1	1.1
Mid-Range Trajectory Height • Inches	0.0	0.5	2.0	4.7	8.6	13.7	20.4	28.6	38.5
Drop • Inches	0.0	-1.9	-7.9	-18.2	-33.0	-52.6	-77.2	-107.2	-142.9

American Eagle (Federal) 50-grain Full Metal Jacket (AE25AP)

G1 Ballistic Coefficient = 0.155

Distance • Yards	Muzzle	25	50	75	100	125	150	175	200
Velocity • fps	760	750	730	720	700	686	672	658	645
Energy • Ft-lbs	65	60	60	55	55	52	50	48	46
Taylor KO Index	1.4	1.3	1.3	1.3	1.3	1.2	1.2	1.2	1.2
Mid-Range Trajectory Height • Inches	0.0	0.5	1.9	4.5	8.1	13.0	19.2	26.5	35.6
Drop • Inches	0.0	-1.9	-7.7	-17.6	-31.8	-50.4	-73.6	-101.7	-134.7

Federal 50-grain Full Metal Jacket (B25AP) (Discontinued in 2004)

G1 Ballistic Coefficient = 0.155

Distance • Yards	Muzzle	25	50	75	100	125	150	175	200
Velocity • fps	760	750	730	720	700	686	672	658	645
Energy • Ft-lbs	65	60	60	55	55	52	50	48	46
Taylor KO Index	1.4	1.3	1.3	1.3	1.3	1.2	1.2	1.2	1.2
Mid-Range Trajectory Height • Inches	0.0	0.5	1.9	4.5	8.1	13.0	19.2	26.5	35.6
Drop • Inches	0.0	-1.9	-7.7	-17.6	-31.8	-50.4	-73.6	-101.7	-134.7

Fiocchi 50-grain Metal Case (25AP)

G1 Ballistic Coefficient = 0.155

Distance • Yards	Muzzle	25	50	75	100	125	150	175	200
Velocity • fps	760	750	730	720	700	686	672	658	645
Energy • Ft-lbs	65	60	60	55	55	52	50	48	46
Taylor KO Index	1.4	1.3	1.3	1.3	1.3	1.2	1.2	1.2	1.2
Mid-Range Trajectory Height • Inches	0.0	0.5	1.9	4.5	8.1	13.0	19.2	26.5	35.6
Drop • Inches	0.0	-1.9	-7.7	-17.6	-31.8	-50.4	-73.6	-101.7	-134.7

Magtech 50-grain FMC (25A)

G1 Ballistic Coefficient = 0.089

Distance • Yards	Muzzle	25	50	75	100	125	150	175	200
Velocity • fps	760	733	707	682	659	636	614	593	573
Energy • Ft-lbs	64	60	56	52	48	45	42	39	36
Taylor KO Index	1.4	1.3	1.3	1.2	1.2	1.1	1.1	1.1	1.0
Mid-Range Trajectory Height • Inches	0.0	0.5	2.0	4.7	8.7	14.0	21.0	29.7	40.2
Drop • Inches	0.0	-1.9	-7.9	-18.2	-33.2	-53.2	-78.5	-109.6	-146.8

Remington 50-grain Metal Case (R25AP)

G1 Ballistic Coefficient = 0.089

Distance • Yards	Muzzle	25	50	75	100	125	150	175	200
Velocity • fps	760	733	707	682	659	636	614	593	573
Energy • Ft-lbs	64	60	56	52	48	45	42	39	36
Taylor KO Index	1.4	1.3	1.3	1.2	1.2	1.1	1.1	1.1	1.0
Mid-Range Trajectory Height • Inches	0.0	0.5	2.0	4.7	8.7	14.0	21.0	29.7	40.2
Drop • Inches	0.0	-1.9	-7.9	-18.2	-33.2	-53.2	-78.5	-109.6	-146.8

UMC (Remington) 50-grain Metal Case (L25AP)

G1 Ballistic Coefficient = 0.089

Distance • Yards	Muzzle	25	50	75	100	125	150	175	200
Velocity • fps	760	733	707	682	659	636	614	593	573
Energy • Ft-lbs	64	60	56	52	48	45	42	39	36
Taylor KO Index	1.4	1.3	1.3	1.2	1.2	1.1	1.1	1.1	1.0
Mid-Range Trajectory Height • Inches	0.0	0.5	2.0	4.7	8.7	14.0	21.0	29.7	40.2
Drop • Inches	0.0	-1.9	-7.9	-18.2	-33.2	-53.2	-78.5	-109.6	-146.8

USA (Winchester) 50-grain Full Metal Jacket (Q4203)

G1 Ballistic Coefficient = 0.100

Distance • Yards	Muzzle	25	50	75	100	125	150	175	200
Velocity • fps	760	736	707	690	669	649	629	609	591
Energy • Ft-lbs	64	60	56	53	50	47	44	41	39
Taylor KO Index	1.4	1.3	1.3	1.2	1.2	1.2	1.1	1.1	1.1
Mid-Range Trajectory Height • Inches	0.0	0.5	2.0	4.6	8.6	13.8	20.5	28.9	39.0
Drop • Inches	0.0	-1.9	-7.9	-18.1	-32.8	-52.4	-77.2	-107.5	-143.6

Aguila 50-grain FMJ

G1 Ballistic Coefficient = 0.090

Distance • Yards	Muzzle	25	50	75	100	125	150	175	200
Velocity • fps	755	728	703	679	656	633	612	591	571
Energy • Ft-lbs	63	59	55	51	48	45	42	39	36
Taylor KO Index	1.4	1.3	1.3	1.2	1.2	1.1	1.1	1.1	1.0
Mid-Range Trajectory Height • Inches	0.0	0.3	1.6	4.3	8.4	13.8	20.8	29.6	40.3
Drop • Inches	0.0	-1.9	-8.0	-18.4	-33.6	-53.8	-79.4	-110.8	-148.4

PMC 50-grain Full Metal Jacket (25A)

G1 Ballistic Coefficient = 0.084

Distance • Yards	Muzzle	25	50	75	100	125	150	175	200
Velocity • fps	750	722	695	670	645	622	599	578	557
Energy • Ft-lbs	63	58	54	50	46	43	40	37	34
Taylor KO Index	1.4	1.3	1.3	1.2	1.2	1.1	1.1	1.0	1.0
Mid-Range Trajectory Height • Inches	0.0	0.5	2.1	4.9	9.0	14.6	21.9	31.0	42.0
Drop • Inches	0.0	-2.0	-8.1	-18.8	-34.3	-55.0	-81.3	-113.7	-152.6

.30 Luger (7.65mm)

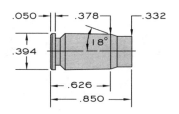

The .30 Luger actually predates the 9mm Luger, having been introduced in 1900. It is very similar to the .30 Mauser but is not interchangeable. The design is a rimless bottlenecked case that anticipated the .357 SIG design by nearly 100 years. Winchester has recently started making this ammunition. The company must think that they can sell enough to pay for tooling up the line, or they wouldn't bother.

Relative Recoil Factor = 0.52

Specifications

Controlling Agency for Standardization of this Ammunition: SAAMI

Bullet Weight Grains	Velocity fps	Maximum Average Pressure	
		Copper Crusher	Transducer
93	1,190	28,000 cup	N/S

Standard barrel for velocity testing: 4.5 inches long—1 turn in 11-inch twist

Availability

Fiocchi 93-grain Jacketed Soft Point (765A)

G1 Ballistic Coefficient = 0.184

Distance • Yards	Muzzle	25	50	75	100	125	150	175	200
Velocity • fps	1200	1147	1102	1063	1029	999	973	949	927
Energy • Ft-lbs	297	272	251	233	219	206	195	186	177
Taylor KO Index	4.9	4.7	4.5	4.4	4.2	4.1	4.0	3.9	3.8
Mid-Range Trajectory Height • Inches	0.0	0.2	0.8	1.9	3.6	5.8	8.6	12.1	16.3
Drop • Inches	0.0	-0.8	-3.2	-7.4	-13.6	-21.7	-32.1	-44.7	-59.7

Winchester 93-grain Full Metal Jacket (X30LP)

G1 Ballistic Coefficient = 0.184

Distance • Yards	Muzzle	25	50	75	100	125	150	175	200
Velocity • fps	1220	1165	1110	1075	1040	1009	982	957	934
Energy • Ft-lbs	305	280	255	239	225	210	199	189	180
Taylor KO Index	5.0	4.8	4.6	4.4	4.3	4.1	4.0	3.9	3.8
Mid-Range Trajectory Height • Inches	0.0	0.1	0.9	2.0	3.5	5.6	8.4	11.8	15.9
Drop • Inches	0.0	-0.8	-3.1	-7.2	-13.2	-21.1	-31.2	-43.5	-58.2

Fiocchi 93-grain Metal Case (765B)

G1 Ballistic Coefficient = 0.184

Distance • Yards	Muzzle	25	50	75	100	125	150	175	200
Velocity • fps	1190	1138	1094	1056	1023	994	968	945	923
Energy • Ft-lbs	293	268	247	230	216	204	194	184	176
Taylor KO Index	4.9	4.7	4.5	4.3	4.2	4.1	4.0	3.9	3.8
Mid-Range Trajectory Height • Inches	0.0	0.2	0.8	1.9	3.6	5.7	8.7	12.2	16.5
Drop • Inches	0.0	-0.8	-3.3	-7.5	-13.8	-22.0	-32.5	-45.3	-60.4

.32 Short Colt

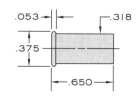

Here's another oldie (vintage of about 1875) that has been recently reintroduced into manufacturing. As with the .30 Luger, it's hard to see where the sales potential comes from, but since I know practically nothing about that part of the business, I hope the factory folks are smarter than I am.

Relative Recoil Factor = 0.27

Specifications

Controlling Agency for Standardization of this Ammunition: SAAMI

Bullet Weight Grains	Velocity fps	Maximum Average Pressure	
		Copper Crusher	Transducer
80 L	700	13,000 cup	N/S

Standard barrel for velocity testing: 4 inches long, vented—1 turn in 16-inch twist

Availability

Winchester 80-grain Lead-Round Nose (X32SCP)

G1 Ballistic Coefficient = 0.054

Distance • Yards	Muzzle	25	50	75	100	125	150	175	200
Velocity • fps	745	702	665	625	590	557	526	496	467
Energy • Ft-lbs	100	88	79	69	62	55	49	44	39
Taylor KO Index	2.6	2.5	2.4	2.2	2.1	2.0	1.9	1.8	1.7
Mid-Range Trajectory Height • Inches	0.0	0.5	2.2	5.0	9.9	16.4	25.2	36.6	50.7
Drop • Inches	0.0	-2.0	-8.5	-19.9	-36.8	-60.0	-90.2	-128.2	-175.0

Peter Hankin with a 53-inch buffalo. (Photo from *Hunting for Trouble* by Geoff Wainwright, 2006, Safari Press)

.32 Smith & Wesson

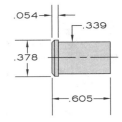

The little .32 Smith & Wesson cartridge dates clear back to 1878. It was designed when "pocket" pistols were all the rage. This is a meek and mild cartridge and can't be considered for any serious self-defense role. Both the muzzle energy and the Taylor KO indexes are far too low to be effective.

Relative Recoil Factor = 0.27

Specifications

Controlling Agency for Standardization of this Ammunition: SAAMI

Bullet Weight Grains	Velocity fps	Maximum Average Pressure	
		Copper Crusher	Transducer
85–88 L	700	12,000 cup	N/S

Standard barrel for velocity testing: 4 inches long (vented)—1 turn in 18.75-inch twist

Availability

Magtech 85-grain LRN (32SWA)

G1 Ballistic Coefficient = 0.115

Distance • Yards	Muzzle	25	50	75	100	125	150	175	200
Velocity • fps	680	662	645	627	610	594	578	562	547
Energy • Ft-lbs	87	83	78	74	70	67	63	60	57
Taylor KO Index	2.6	2.5	2.5	2.4	2.3	2.3	2.2	2.1	2.1
Mid-Range Trajectory Height • Inches	0.0	0.2	2.1	5.3	10.1	16.8	24.9	34.9	46.8
Drop • Inches	0.0	-2.4	-9.8	-22.3	-40.5	-64.4	-94.5	-131.1	-174.6

Winchester 85-grain Lead-Round Nose (X32SWP)

G1 Ballistic Coefficient = 0.115

Distance • Yards	Muzzle	25	50	75	100	125	150	175	200
Velocity • fps	680	662	645	627	610	594	578	562	547
Energy • Ft-lbs	87	83	78	74	70	67	63	60	57
Taylor KO Index	2.6	2.5	2.5	2.4	2.3	2.3	2.2	2.1	2.1
Mid-Range Trajectory Height • Inches	0.0	0.2	2.1	5.3	10.1	16.8	24.9	34.9	46.8
Drop • Inches	0.0	-2.4	-9.8	-22.3	-40.5	-64.4	-94.5	-131.1	-174.6

Remington 88-grain Lead (R32SW)

G1 Ballistic Coefficient = 0.115

Distance • Yards	Muzzle	25	50	75	100	125	150	175	200
Velocity • fps	680	662	645	627	610	594	578	562	547
Energy • Ft-lbs	87	83	78	74	70	67	63	60	57
Taylor KO Index	2.6	2.5	2.5	2.4	2.3	2.3	2.2	2.1	2.1
Mid-Range Trajectory Height • Inches	0.0	0.2	2.1	5.3	10.1	16.8	24.9	34.9	46.8
Drop • Inches	0.0	-2.4	-9.8	-22.3	-40.5	-64.4	-94.5	-131.1	-174.6

.32 Smith & Wesson Long

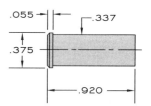

This is a very old cartridge (introduced in 1896). While it originally was considered a self-defense round for pocket pistols, today's use of this caliber is almost exclusively for target pistols. In some competitions, .32-caliber pistols meet the rules and have the virtue of very light recoil and fine accuracy. The use of this caliber in competition seems more common in Europe than in the United States.

Relative Recoil Factor = 0.35

Specifications

Controlling Agency for Standardization of this Ammunition: SAAMI

Bullet Weight Grains	Velocity fps	Maximum Average Pressure	
		Copper Crusher	Transducer
98 L	775	12,000 cup	15,000 psi

Standard barrel for velocity testing: 4 inches long—1 turn in 18.75-inch twist

Availability

Lapua 83-grain LWC (4318023)
G1 Ballistic Coefficient = 0.029

Distance • Yards	Muzzle	25	50	75	100	125	150	175	200
Velocity • fps	787	704	632	567	509	456	408	363	323
Energy • Ft-lbs	114	91	74	59	48	38	31	24	19
Taylor KO Index	2.9	2.6	2.4	2.1	1.9	1.7	1.5	1.4	1.2
Mid-Range Trajectory Height • Inches	0.0	0.5	2.2	5.6	11.0	19.5	31.4	49.2	71.9
Drop • Inches	0.0	-1.9	-8.2	-19.9	-38.4	-65.3	-102.7	-153.3	-220.7

Lapua 98-grain LWC (4318026)
G1 Ballistic Coefficient = 0.061

Distance • Yards	Muzzle	25	50	75	100	125	150	175	200
Velocity • fps	787	727	673	623	578	535	496	459	424
Energy • Ft-lbs	135	115	98	85	73	62	53	46	39
Taylor KO Index	3.4	3.2	2.9	2.7	2.5	2.4	2.2	2.0	1.9
Mid-Range Trajectory Height • Inches	0.0	0.5	2.1	5.0	9.7	16.3	25.5	37.9	53.6
Drop • Inches	0.0	-1.8	-7.8	-18.6	-35.0	-57.8	-88.2	-127.4	-177.0

Norma 98-grain Lead Wadcutter (17810)
G1 Ballistic Coefficient = 0.091

Distance • Yards	Muzzle	25	50	75	100	125	150	175	200
Velocity • fps	787	759	732	707	683	660	638	616	596
Energy • Ft-lbs	136	126	118	109	102	95	89	83	77
Taylor KO Index	3.4	3.3	3.2	3.1	3.0	2.9	2.8	2.7	2.6
Mid-Range Trajectory Height • Inches	0.0	0.4	1.9	4.4	8.1	13.1	19.6	27.7	37.4
Drop • Inches	0.0	-1.8	-7.4	-17.0	-31.0	-49.6	-73.1	-102.0	-136.7

Federal 98-grain Lead Wadcutter (C32LA)
G1 Ballistic Coefficient = 0.028

Distance • Yards	Muzzle	25	50	75	100	125	150	175	200
Velocity • fps	780	700	630	560	500	443	394	350	310
Energy • Ft-lbs	130	105	85	70	55	43	34	27	21
Taylor KO Index	3.4	3.0	2.7	2.4	2.2	2.0	1.7	1.5	1.4
Mid-Range Trajectory Height • Inches	0.0	0.5	2.2	5.8	11.1	20.2	32.8	51.2	77.0
Drop • Inches	0.0	-1.9	-8.4	-20.5	-39.6	-67.4	-106.5	-159.7	-231.1

Magtech 98-grain LWC (32SWLB)
G1 Ballistic Coefficient = 0.038

Distance • Yards	Muzzle	25	50	75	100	125	150	175	200
Velocity • fps	682	628	578	533	491	451	414	379	347
Energy • Ft-lbs	102	86	73	62	52	44	37	31	26
Taylor KO Index	3.0	2.8	2.5	2.3	2.2	2.0	1.8	1.7	1.5
Mid-Range Trajectory Height • Inches	0.0	0.6	2.3	6.7	12.6	22.3	35.1	52.8	75.2
Drop • Inches	0.0	-2.5	-10.4	-24.9	-47.1	-78.2	-120.1	-174.7	-244.6

PMC 98-grain Lead Round Nose (32SWLA)

G1 Ballistic Coefficient = 0.115

Distance • Yards	Muzzle	25	50	75	100	125	150	175	200
Velocity • fps	780	758	737	717	697	679	660	643	626
Energy • Ft-lbs	132	125	118	112	106	100	95	90	85
Taylor KO Index	3.4	3.3	3.2	3.1	3.0	3.0	2.9	2.8	2.7
Mid-Range Trajectory Height • Inches	0.0	0.4	1.8	4.4	8.0	12.8	19.1	26.7	35.9
Drop • Inches	0.0	-1.8	-7.4	-17.0	-30.8	-49.1	-72.2	-100.2	-133.4

Federal 98-grain Lead Round Nose (C32LB)

G1 Ballistic Coefficient = 0.120

Distance • Yards	Muzzle	25	50	75	100	125	150	175	200
Velocity • fps	710	690	670	650	640	623	607	592	577
Energy • Ft-lbs	115	105	100	95	90	85	80	76	72
Taylor KO Index	3.1	3.0	3.0	2.9	2.8	2.7	2.7	2.6	2.5
Mid-Range Trajectory Height • Inches	0.0	0.6	2.3	5.3	9.6	15.3	22.7	31.8	42.6
Drop • Inches	0.0	-2.2	-8.9	-20.4	-37.0	-58.9	-86.3	-119.7	-159.2

Aguila 98-grain Lead Round Nose

G1 Ballistic Coefficient = 0.122

Distance • Yards	Muzzle	25	50	75	100	125	150	175	200
Velocity • fps	705	687	667	653	636	620	604	589	575
Energy • Ft-lbs	108	103	98	93	88	84	80	76	72
Taylor KO Index	3.1	3.0	2.9	2.9	2.8	2.7	2.6	2.6	2.5
Mid-Range Trajectory Height • Inches	0.0	0.5	2.2	5.3	9.7	15.5	23.0	32.2	43.1
Drop • Inches	0.0	-2.2	-9.0	-20.7	-37.5	-59.6	-87.4	-121.2	-161.2

Magtech 98-grain LRN (32SWLA)

G1 Ballistic Coefficient = 0.119

Distance • Yards	Muzzle	25	50	75	100	125	150	175	200
Velocity • fps	705	687	670	651	635	618	602	587	572
Energy • Ft-lbs	108	103	98	92	88	83	79	75	71
Taylor KO Index	3.1	3.0	2.9	2.8	2.8	2.7	2.7	2.6	2.5
Mid-Range Trajectory Height • Inches	0.0	0.5	2.3	5.3	10.5	15.6	23.1	32.3	43.3
Drop • Inches	0.0	-2.2	-9.1	-20.8	-37.6	-59.8	-87.6	-121.5	-161.7

Remington 98-grain LRN (R32SWL)

G1 Ballistic Coefficient = 0.119

Distance • Yards	Muzzle	25	50	75	100	125	150	175	200
Velocity • fps	705	687	670	651	635	618	602	587	572
Energy • Ft-lbs	108	103	98	92	88	83	79	75	71
Taylor KO Index	3.1	3.0	2.9	2.8	2.8	2.7	2.7	2.6	2.5
Mid-Range Trajectory Height • Inches	0.0	0.5	2.3	5.3	10.5	15.6	23.1	32.3	43.3
Drop • Inches	0.0	-2.2	-9.1	-20.8	-37.6	-59.8	-87.6	-121.5	-161.7

Winchester 98-grain Lead-Round Nose (X32SWLP)

G1 Ballistic Coefficient = 0.119

Distance • Yards	Muzzle	25	50	75	100	125	150	175	200
Velocity • fps	705	687	670	651	635	618	602	587	572
Energy • Ft-lbs	108	103	98	92	88	83	79	75	71
Taylor KO Index	3.1	3.0	2.9	2.8	2.8	2.7	2.7	2.6	2.5
Mid-Range Trajectory Height • Inches	0.0	0.5	2.3	5.3	10.5	15.6	23.1	32.3	43.3
Drop • Inches	0.0	-2.2	-9.1	-20.8	-37.6	-59.8	-87.6	-121.5	-161.7

Magtech 98-grain SJHP (32SWLC)

G1 Ballistic Coefficient = 0.140

Distance • Yards	Muzzle	25	50	75	100	125	150	175	200
Velocity • fps	778	760	742	726	709	694	678	663	649
Energy • Ft-lbs	132	126	120	115	109	105	100	96	92
Taylor KO Index	3.4	3.3	3.2	3.2	3.1	3.0	3.0	2.9	2.8
Mid-Range Trajectory Height • Inches	0.0	0.5	2.2	5.2	9.6	15.3	22.5	31.4	41.9
Drop • Inches	0.0	-1.8	-7.4	-16.9	-30.6	-48.6	-71.0	-98.2	-130.4

Hirtenberger 99-grain LRN (8240002)

G1 Ballistic Coefficient = 0.090

Distance • Yards	Muzzle	25	50	75	100	125	150	175	200
Velocity • fps	837	805	776	748	722	697	673	650	628
Energy • Ft-lbs	154	142	132	123	114	107	99	93	86
Taylor KO Index	3.7	3.6	3.5	3.3	3.2	3.1	3.0	2.9	2.8
Mid-Range Trajectory Height • Inches	0.0	0.4	1.7	3.9	7.2	11.7	17.5	24.8	33.5
Drop • Inches	0.0	-1.6	-6.5	-15.1	-27.5	-44.1	-65.2	-91.0	-122.0

Sellier & Bellot 100-grain Lead Wadcutter (SBA03202)

G1 Ballistic Coefficient = 0.038

Distance • Yards	Muzzle	25	50	75	100	125	150	175	200
Velocity • fps	735	677	623	574	528	486	447	410	376
Energy • Ft-lbs	120	102	86	73	62	53	44	37	31
Taylor KO Index	3.3	3.0	2.8	2.6	2.4	2.2	2.0	1.8	1.7
Mid-Range Trajectory Height • Inches	0.0	0.5	2.3	5.8	11.3	19.3	30.5	45.5	65.5
Drop • Inches	0.0	-2.1	-9.0	-21.5	-40.6	-67.5	-103.6	-150.7	-210.6

Fiocchi 100-grain Lead Wadcutter (32LA)

G1 Ballistic Coefficient = 0.043

Distance • Yards	Muzzle	25	50	75	100	125	150	175	200
Velocity • fps	730	678	631	587	545	507	471	437	405
Energy • Ft-lbs	118	102	88	76	66	57	49	42	36
Taylor KO Index	3.3	3.0	2.8	2.6	2.5	2.3	2.1	2.0	1.8
Mid-Range Trajectory Height • Inches	0.0	0.5	2.4	5.9	11.0	18.5	28.8	42.6	60.1
Drop • Inches	0.0	-2.1	-9.0	-21.4	-40.0	-65.9	-100.3	-144.5	-200.1

Hirtenberger 100-grain WC (8240003)

G1 Ballistic Coefficient = 0.070

Distance • Yards	Muzzle	25	50	75	100	125	150	175	200
Velocity • fps	722	690	660	631	604	577	552	528	505
Energy • Ft-lbs	116	106	97	88	81	74	68	62	57
Taylor KO Index	3.2	3.1	3.0	2.8	2.7	2.6	2.5	2.4	2.3
Mid-Range Trajectory Height • Inches	0.0	0.5	2.3	5.4	10.0	16.3	24.7	35.2	48.1
Drop • Inches	0.0	-2.2	-8.9	-20.6	-37.7	-60.8	-90.4	-127.2	-171.7

PMC 100-grain Lead Wadcutter (32SWLB)

G1 Ballistic Coefficient = 0.078

Distance • Yards	Muzzle	25	50	75	100	125	150	175	200
Velocity • fps	680	655	630	607	584	562	541	520	500
Energy • Ft-lbs	103	95	88	82	76	70	65	60	56
Taylor KO Index	3.1	2.9	2.8	2.7	2.6	2.5	2.4	2.3	2.2
Mid-Range Trajectory Height • Inches	0.0	0.6	2.5	5.9	10.9	17.7	26.6	37.8	51.3
Drop • Inches	0.0	-2.4	-9.9	-22.8	-41.7	-66.9	-99.1	-138.6	-186.2

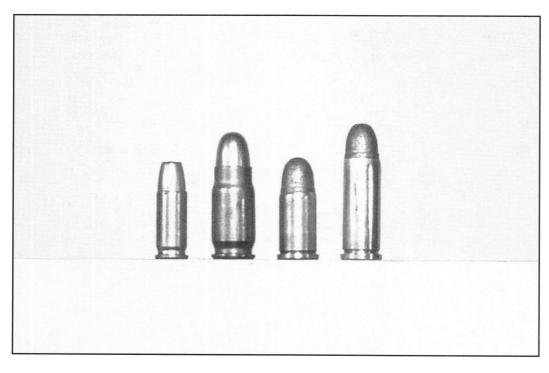

(Left to right) .25 Auto, .30 Luger, .32 Smith & Wesson, .32 Smith & Wesson Long.

.32 H&R Magnum

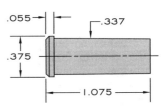

Designed in 1983, the .32 H&R (Harrington and Richardson) Magnum brings modern technology and high velocity to the .32-caliber pistol market. This cartridge is sometimes touted for hunting use but can't be taken seriously for that purpose. The .32-caliber guns have long been more popular in Europe as target pistols. This is still a new cartridge, and it will take more time for its true worth to be established by active shooters. The velocity data for this pistol round may be misleading since the standard velocity test barrel has a rifle length of 24 inches.

Relative Recoil Factor = 0.42

Specifications

Controlling Agency for Standardization of this Ammunition: SAAMI

Bullet Weight Grains	Velocity fps	Maximum Average Pressure	
		Copper Crusher	Transducer
85 JHP	1,120	21,000 cup	N/S
95 LSWC	1,020	21,000 cup	N/S

Standard barrel for velocity testing: 24 inches long—1 turn in 12-inch twist

Availability

Black Hills 85-grain JHP (D32H&RN1)
G1 Ballistic Coefficient = 0.127

Distance • Yards	Muzzle	25	50	75	100	125	150	175	200
Velocity • fps	1100	1050	1020	970	930	901	874	849	825
Energy • Ft-lbs	230	210	195	175	165	153	144	136	129
Taylor KO Index	4.2	4.0	3.8	3.7	3.5	3.4	3.3	3.2	3.2
Mid-Range Trajectory Height • Inches	0.0	0.2	1.0	2.3	4.3	7.0	10.5	14.8	19.9
Drop • Inches	0.0	-0.9	-3.8	-8.9	-16.4	-26.2	-38.8	-54.2	-72.5

Federal 85-grain Hi-Shok JHP (C32HRB)
G1 Ballistic Coefficient = 0.127

Distance • Yards	Muzzle	25	50	75	100	125	150	175	200
Velocity • fps	1100	1050	1020	970	930	901	874	849	825
Energy • Ft-lbs	230	210	195	175	165	153	144	136	129
Taylor KO Index	4.2	4.0	3.8	3.7	3.5	3.4	3.3	3.2	3.2
Mid-Range Trajectory Height • Inches	0.0	0.2	1.0	2.3	4.3	7.0	10.5	14.8	19.9
Drop • Inches	0.0	-0.9	-3.8	-8.9	-16.4	-26.2	-38.8	-54.2	-72.5

Federal 95-grain Lead Semi-Wadcutter (C32HRA)
G1 Ballistic Coefficient = 0.138

Distance • Yards	Muzzle	25	50	75	100	125	150	175	200
Velocity • fps	1030	1000	940	930	900	876	852	831	810
Energy • Ft-lbs	225	210	195	185	170	162	153	146	138
Taylor KO Index	4.4	4.2	4.1	3.9	3.8	3.7	3.6	3.6	3.5
Mid-Range Trajectory Height • Inches	0.0	0.3	1.1	2.5	4.7	7.6	11.3	15.9	21.4
Drop • Inches	0.0	-1.0	-4.3	-10.0	-18.1	-28.9	-42.5	-59.2	-78.9

Cowboy Action Loads

Black Hills 90-grain FPL (DCB32H&RN2)
G1 Ballistic Coefficient = 0.140

Distance • Yards	Muzzle	25	50	75	100	125	150	175	200
Velocity • fps	750	733	716	700	685	670	655	640	626
Energy • Ft-lbs	112	107	103	98	94	90	86	82	78
Taylor KO Index	3.0	3.0	2.9	2.8	2.8	2.7	2.7	2.6	2.5
Mid-Range Trajectory Height • Inches	0.0	0.5	2.0	4.6	8.5	13.5	20.0	27.8	37.1
Drop • Inches	0.0	-2.0	-8.0	-18.2	-32.9	-52.2	-76.3	-105.5	-140.0

.32 Auto (7.65mm Browning)

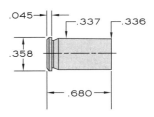

John Browning designed this little cartridge in 1899. The fact that it is still around proves that some shooters find it useful. There is some good news and some bad news about the .32 Auto. The good news is that the cartridge design yields very lightweight and compact guns. Since carrying concealed weapons has been legalized in many states, the .32 Auto finds many advocates. The bad news is that the .32 Auto isn't really enough cartridge to provide much serious self-defense. It's a difficult trade-off, one that's made only slightly easier by the availability of high-performance bullets.

Relative Recoil Factor = 0.29

Specifications

Controlling Agency for Standardization of this Ammunition: SAAMI

Bullet Weight Grains	Velocity fps	Maximum Average Pressure	
		Copper Crusher	Transducer
60 STHP	960	15,000 cup	20,500 psi
71 MC	900	15,000 cup	20,500 psi

Standard barrel for velocity testing: 4 inches long—1 turn in 16-inch twist

Availability

Cor-Bon 55-grain Glaser Safety Slug (00400/na)
G1 Ballistic Coefficient = 0.100

Distance • Yards	Muzzle	25	50	75	100	125	150	175	200
Velocity • fps	1200	1109	1039	985	941	903	869	838	809
Energy • Ft-lbs	176	150	132	119	108	100	92	86	80
Taylor KO Index	2.9	2.7	2.5	2.4	2.3	2.2	2.1	2.1	2.0
Mid-Range Trajectory Height • Inches	0.0	0.2	0.9	2.1	4.0	6.6	10.1	14.4	19.6
Drop • Inches	0.0	-0.8	-3.4	-7.9	-14.7	-24.0	-35.9	-50.7	-68.6

Fiocchi 60-grain Jacketed Hollowpoint (32APHP)
G1 Ballistic Coefficient = 0.120

Distance • Yards	Muzzle	25	50	75	100	125	150	175	200
Velocity • fps	1200	1122	1060	1011	970	934	903	874	800
Energy • Ft-lbs	200	168	150	136	125	116	109	102	96
Taylor KO Index	2.8	2.8	2.7	2.6	2.5	2.4	2.4	2.3	2.2
Mid-Range Trajectory Height • Inches	0.0	0.2	0.8	2.1	3.9	6.3	9.6	13.6	18.4
Drop • Inches	0.0	-0.8	-3.3	-7.8	-14.3	-23.2	-34.6	-48.6	-65.5

Cor-Bon 60-grain JHP (SD3260/20)
G1 Ballistic Coefficient = 0.100

Distance • Yards	Muzzle	25	50	75	100	125	150	175	200
Velocity • fps	1050	978	934	897	863	833	804	778	753
Energy • Ft-lbs	141	127	116	107	99	92	86	81	75
Taylor KO Index	2.8	2.6	2.5	2.4	2.3	2.2	2.2	2.1	2.0
Mid-Range Trajectory Height • Inches	0.0	0.3	1.1	2.7	5.0	8.1	12.1	17.2	23.2
Drop • Inches	0.0	-1.1	-4.4	-10.2	-18.7	-30.1	-44.6	-62.5	-83.8

Hornady 60-grain JHP/XTP (90062)
G1 Ballistic Coefficient = 0.091

Distance • Yards	Muzzle	25	50	75	100	125	150	175	200
Velocity • fps	1000	949	906	868	834	803	774	747	721
Energy • Ft-lbs	133	120	109	100	93	86	80	74	69
Taylor KO Index	2.7	2.5	2.4	2.3	2.2	2.1	2.1	2.0	1.9
Mid-Range Trajectory Height • Inches	0.0	0.3	1.2	2.8	5.3	8.6	13.0	18.4	25.0
Drop • Inches	0.0	-1.1	-4.7	-10.8	-19.9	-32.1	-47.6	-66.8	-89.9

PMC 60-grain Jacketed Hollow Point (32B)
G1 Ballistic Coefficient = 0.060

Distance • Yards	Muzzle	25	50	75	100	125	150	175	200
Velocity • fps	980	849	820	791	763	722	685	650	617
Energy • Ft-lbs	117	111	98	87	78	69	63	56	51
Taylor KO Index	2.6	2.3	2.2	2.1	2.1	1.9	1.8	1.8	1.7
Mid-Range Trajectory Height • Inches	0.0	0.2	0.9	2.7	5.5	9.6	14.9	21.5	29.9
Drop • Inches	0.0	-1.2	-5.0	-11.8	-21.9	-35.7	-53.6	-76.2	-103.8

Winchester 60-grain Silvertip Hollow Point (X32ASHP)
G1 Ballistic Coefficient = 0.107

Distance • Yards	Muzzle	25	50	75	100	125	150	175	200
Velocity • fps	970	930	895	864	835	809	784	760	737
Energy • Ft-lbs	125	115	107	99	93	87	82	77	72
Taylor KO Index	2.6	2.5	2.4	2.3	2.2	2.2	2.1	2.1	2.0
Mid-Range Trajectory Height • Inches	0.0	0.3	1.3	2.9	5.4	8.7	13.0	18.4	24.6
Drop • Inches	0.0	-1.2	-4.9	-11.3	-20.6	-33.0	-48.7	-67.9	-90.9

Speer 60-grain Gold Dot (23604)
G1 Ballistic Coefficient = 0.119

Distance • Yards	Muzzle	25	50	75	100	125	150	175	200
Velocity • fps	960	925	894	866	840	816	793	771	750
Energy • Ft-lbs	123	114	107	100	94	89	84	79	75
Taylor KO Index	2.6	2.5	2.4	2.3	2.2	2.2	2.1	2.1	2.0
Mid-Range Trajectory Height • Inches	0.0	0.2	1.2	3.0	5.4	8.7	13.0	18.3	24.7
Drop • Inches	0.0	-1.2	-5.0	-11.4	-20.8	-33.2	-48.9	-68.0	-90.8

Federal 65-grain Hydra-Shok JHP (P32HS1)
G1 Ballistic Coefficient = 0.116

Distance • Yards	Muzzle	25	50	75	100	125	150	175	200
Velocity • fps	950	920	890	860	830	806	783	761	740
Energy • Ft-lbs	130	120	115	105	100	94	89	84	79
Taylor KO Index	2.8	2.7	2.6	2.5	2.4	2.4	2.3	2.2	2.2
Mid-Range Trajectory Height • Inches	0.0	0.3	1.3	3.0	5.6	8.9	13.3	18.7	25.1
Drop • Inches	0.0	-1.2	-5.1	-11.7	-21.2	-33.9	-49.9	-69.5	-92.8

American Eagle (Federal) 65-grain Full Metal Jacket (AE32BP) (Discontinued in 2004)
G1 Ballistic Coefficient = 0.123

Distance • Yards	Muzzle	25	50	75	100	125	150	175	200
Velocity • fps	1000	960	930	900	870	844	820	798	776
Energy • Ft-lbs	145	135	125	115	110	103	97	92	87
Taylor KO Index	2.9	2.8	2.7	2.6	2.5	2.5	2.4	2.3	2.3
Mid-Range Trajectory Height • Inches	0.0	0.3	1.2	2.8	5.1	8.1	12.1	17.0	22.9
Drop • Inches	0.0	-1.1	-4.6	-10.6	-19.3	-30.8	-45.4	-63.2	-84.3

Magtech 71-grain JHP (32B)
G1 Ballistic Coefficient = 0.132

Distance • Yards	Muzzle	25	50	75	100	125	150	175	200
Velocity • fps	905	879	855	831	810	789	770	751	733
Energy • Ft-lbs	129	122	115	109	103	98	93	89	85
Taylor KO Index	2.9	2.8	2.7	2.6	2.6	2.5	2.5	2.4	2.3
Mid-Range Trajectory Height • Inches	0.0	0.3	1.4	3.2	5.8	9.5	14.1	19.8	26.5
Drop • Inches	0.0	-1.4	-5.5	-12.7	-23.0	-36.5	-53.6	-74.3	-98.9

Hirtenberger 71-grain FMJ-RN (82300017)
G1 Ballistic Coefficient = 0.132

Distance • Yards	Muzzle	25	50	75	100	125	150	175	200
Velocity • fps	984	952	923	896	872	849	828	808	789
Energy • Ft-lbs	153	143	134	127	120	114	108	103	98
Taylor KO Index	3.1	3.0	2.9	2.9	2.8	2.7	2.6	2.6	2.5
Mid-Range Trajectory Height • Inches	0.0	0.2	1.2	2.7	5.1	8.1	12.1	17.0	22.8
Drop • Inches	0.0	-1.2	-4.7	-10.8	-19.6	-31.2	-45.9	-63.7	-84.8

CCI 71-grain TMJ Lawman (53632)
G1 Ballistic Coefficient = 0.112

Distance • Yards	Muzzle	25	50	75	100	125	150	175	200
Velocity • fps	950	915	883	854	827	802	778	756	734
Energy • Ft-lbs	142	132	123	115	108	101	96	90	85
Taylor KO Index	3.0	2.9	2.8	2.7	2.6	2.5	2.5	2.4	2.3
Mid-Range Trajectory Height • Inches	0.0	0.3	1.2	3.0	5.6	9.0	13.4	18.9	25.5
Drop • Inches	0.0	-1.2	-5.1	-11.7	-21.3	-34.0	-50.2	-69.9	-93.5

American Eagle (Federal) 71-grain Full Metal Jacket (AE32AP)
G1 Ballistic Coefficient = 0.127

Distance • Yards	Muzzle	25	50	75	100	125	150	175	200
Velocity • fps	910	880	860	830	810	789	769	749	730
Energy • Ft-lbs	130	120	115	110	105	98	93	88	84
Taylor KO Index	2.9	2.8	2.7	2.6	2.6	2.5	2.5	2.4	2.3
Mid-Range Trajectory Height • Inches	0.0	0.3	1.4	3.2	5.9	9.5	14.1	19.7	26.4
Drop • Inches	0.0	-1.3	-5.5	-12.6	-22.8	-36.3	-53.3	-74.0	-98.5

Federal 71-grain Full Metal Jacket (32AP) (Discontinued in 2004)

G1 Ballistic Coefficient = 0.127

Distance • Yards	Muzzle	25	50	75	100	125	150	175	200
Velocity • fps	910	880	860	830	810	789	769	749	730
Energy • Ft-lbs	130	120	115	110	105	98	93	88	84
Taylor KO Index	2.9	2.8	2.7	2.6	2.6	2.5	2.5	2.4	2.3
Mid-Range Trajectory Height • Inches	0.0	0.3	1.4	3.2	5.9	9.5	14.1	19.7	26.4
Drop • Inches	0.0	-1.3	-5.5	-12.6	-22.8	-36.3	-53.3	-74.0	-98.5

Aguila 71-grain FMJ

G1 Ballistic Coefficient = 0.132

Distance • Yards	Muzzle	25	50	75	100	125	150	175	200
Velocity • fps	905	879	854	831	810	789	770	751	733
Energy • Ft-lbs	129	122	115	109	103	98	93	89	85
Taylor KO Index	2.9	2.8	2.7	2.6	2.6	2.5	2.5	2.4	2.3
Mid-Range Trajectory Height • Inches	0.0	0.3	1.4	3.2	5.8	9.5	14.1	19.8	26.5
Drop • Inches	0.0	-1.4	-5.5	-12.7	-23.0	-36.5	-53.6	-74.3	-98.9

Magtech 71-grain FMC (32A)

G1 Ballistic Coefficient = 0.132

Distance • Yards	Muzzle	25	50	75	100	125	150	175	200
Velocity • fps	905	879	855	831	810	789	770	751	733
Energy • Ft-lbs	129	122	115	109	103	98	93	89	85
Taylor KO Index	2.9	2.8	2.7	2.6	2.6	2.5	2.5	2.4	2.3
Mid-Range Trajectory Height • Inches	0.0	0.3	1.4	3.2	5.8	9.5	14.1	19.8	26.5
Drop • Inches	0.0	-1.4	-5.5	-12.7	-23.0	-36.5	-53.6	-74.3	-98.9

Remington 71-grain Metal Case (R32AP)

G1 Ballistic Coefficient = 0.132

Distance • Yards	Muzzle	25	50	75	100	125	150	175	200
Velocity • fps	905	879	855	831	810	789	770	751	733
Energy • Ft-lbs	129	122	115	109	103	98	93	89	85
Taylor KO Index	2.9	2.8	2.7	2.6	2.6	2.5	2.5	2.4	2.3
Mid-Range Trajectory Height • Inches	0.0	0.3	1.4	3.2	5.8	9.5	14.1	19.8	26.5
Drop • Inches	0.0	-1.4	-5.5	-12.7	-23.0	-36.5	-53.6	-74.3	-98.9

UMC (Remington) 71-grain Metal Case (L32AP)

G1 Ballistic Coefficient = 0.132

Distance • Yards	Muzzle	25	50	75	100	125	150	175	200
Velocity • fps	905	879	855	831	810	789	770	751	733
Energy • Ft-lbs	129	122	115	109	103	98	93	89	85
Taylor KO Index	2.9	2.8	2.7	2.6	2.6	2.5	2.5	2.4	2.3
Mid-Range Trajectory Height • Inches	0.0	0.3	1.4	3.2	5.8	9.5	14.1	19.8	26.5
Drop • Inches	0.0	-1.4	-5.5	-12.7	-23.0	-36.5	-53.6	-74.3	-98.9

USA (Winchester) 71-grain Full Metal Jacket (Q4255)

G1 Ballistic Coefficient = 0.132

Distance • Yards	Muzzle	25	50	75	100	125	150	175	200
Velocity • fps	905	879	855	831	810	789	770	751	733
Energy • Ft-lbs	129	122	115	109	103	98	93	89	85
Taylor KO Index	2.9	2.8	2.7	2.6	2.6	2.5	2.5	2.4	2.3
Mid-Range Trajectory Height • Inches	0.0	0.3	1.4	3.2	5.8	9.5	14.1	19.8	26.5
Drop • Inches	0.0	-1.4	-5.5	-12.7	-23.0	-36.5	-53.6	-74.3	-98.9

CCI 71-grain FMJ Blazer TMJ (3503)

G1 Ballistic Coefficient = 0.112

Distance • Yards	Muzzle	25	50	75	100	125	150	175	200
Velocity • fps	900	870	843	816	791	768	746	725	705
Energy • Ft-lbs	128	119	112	105	99	93	88	83	78
Taylor KO Index	2.8	2.8	2.7	2.6	2.5	2.4	2.4	2.3	2.2
Mid-Range Trajectory Height • Inches	0.0	0.3	1.4	3.3	6.1	9.9	14.7	20.7	27.8
Drop • Inches	0.0	-1.4	-5.6	-12.9	-23.5	-37.6	-55.3	-76.9	-102.6

Hornady 71-grain FMJ-RN (9007c) (Discontinued in 2004)

G1 Ballistic Coefficient = 0.119

Distance • Yards	Muzzle	25	50	75	100	125	150	175	200
Velocity • fps	900	871	845	820	797	775	754	734	714
Energy • Ft-lbs	128	120	112	106	100	95	90	85	80
Taylor KO Index	2.8	2.8	2.7	2.6	2.5	2.5	2.4	2.3	2.3
Mid-Range Trajectory Height • Inches	0.0	0.3	1.4	3.3	6.1	9.8	14.5	20.3	27.3
Drop • Inches	0.0	-1.4	-5.6	-12.9	-23.4	-37.3	-54.8	-76.2	-101.5

PMC 71-grain Full Metal Jacket (32A)

G1 Ballistic Coefficient = 0.101

Distance • Yards	Muzzle	25	50	75	100	125	150	175	200
Velocity • fps	900	869	838	809	781	756	732	710	688
Energy • Ft-lbs	128	118	110	103	96	90	85	79	75
Taylor KO Index	2.8	2.8	2.7	2.6	2.5	2.4	2.3	2.2	2.2
Mid-Range Trajectory Height • Inches	0.0	0.3	1.5	3.4	6.2	10.0	15.0	20.9	28.6
Drop • Inches	0.0	-1.4	-5.6	-13.0	-23.7	-38.0	-56.1	-78.2	-104.6

Sellier & Bellot 73-grain FMJ (SBA03201)

G1 Ballistic Coefficient = 0.116

Distance • Yards	Muzzle	25	50	75	100	125	150	175	200
Velocity • fps	1043	998	955	920	889	861	834	810	786
Energy • Ft-lbs	177	162	148	137	128	120	113	106	100
Taylor KO Index	3.4	3.2	3.1	3.0	2.9	2.8	2.7	2.6	2.6
Mid-Range Trajectory Height • Inches	0.0	0.3	1.1	2.6	4.8	7.7	11.5	16.3	22.0
Drop • Inches	0.0	-1.0	-4.3	-9.9	-18.0	-29.0	-42.8	-59.8	-80.0

Fiocchi 73-grain Metal Case (32AP)

G1 Ballistic Coefficient = 0.110

Distance • Yards	Muzzle	25	50	75	100	125	150	175	200
Velocity • fps	880	851	824	798	775	752	730	710	690
Energy • Ft-lbs	125	117	110	103	97	92	86	82	77
Taylor KO Index	2.9	2.8	2.7	2.6	2.5	2.4	2.4	2.3	2.2
Mid-Range Trajectory Height • Inches	0.0	0.4	1.5	3.5	6.4	10.3	15.4	21.6	29.1
Drop • Inches	0.0	-1.4	-5.9	-13.5	-24.6	-39.2	-57.7	-80.3	-107.2

Norma 77-grain Full Jacket, Round Nose (17614) (Discontinued in 2005)

G1 Ballistic Coefficient = 0.241

Distance • Yards	Muzzle	25	50	75	100	125	150	175	200
Velocity • fps	899	884	871	857	845	832	820	809	797
Energy • Ft-lbs	138	134	130	126	122	118	115	112	109
Taylor KO Index	3.1	3.0	3.0	2.9	2.9	2.9	2.8	2.8	2.8
Mid-Range Trajectory Height • Inches	0.0	0.3	1.4	3.2	5.7	9.0	13.2	18.3	24.0
Drop • Inches	0.0	-1.4	-5.5	-12.5	-22.4	-35.4	-51.6	-70.9	-93.6

When hunting polar bear, your gun must be completely grease and oil free or it will freeze shut. (Photo from *The Dangerous Game* by Walt Prothero, 2006, Safari Press)

.357 Magnum

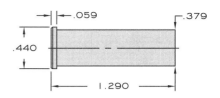

At the time of its introduction in 1935, the .357 Magnum (sometimes called the .357 Smith & Wesson Magnum) was the world's most powerful revolver cartridge. Credit for its development is usually given to Col. D. B. Wesson of Smith & Wesson and to Phil Sharpe. The .357 design is essentially a lengthened .38 Special, but the working pressure level has been pushed up to 35,000 psi, which more than doubles the .38 Special's 17,000 psi level, producing much better performance. Before the .357 was introduced, the .38 Special was the standard police sidearm in the U.S., almost the universal choice. It wasn't very long until the increased effectiveness of the .357 Magnum became known. Today, factories offer over fifty different loadings in this caliber. In the law enforcement application today, revolvers are gradually being replaced by semiautomatic pistols, not necessarily resulting in an improvement in reliability.

Relative Recoil Factor = 0.89

Specifications

Controlling Agency for Standardization of this Ammunition: SAAMI

Bullet Weight Grains	Velocity fps	Maximum Average Pressure	
		Copper Crusher	Transducer
110 JHP	1,270	45,000 cup	35,000 psi
125 SJHP	1,500*	45,000 cup	35,000 psi
125 JSP	1,400	45,000 cup	35,000 psi
140 SJHP	1,330	45,000 cup	35,000 psi
145 STHP	1,270	45,000 cup	35,000 psi
158 MP-L	1,220	45,000 cup	35,000 psi
158 SWC	1,220	45,000 cup	35,000 psi
158 SJHP	1,220	45,000 cup	35,000 psi
180 STHP	1,400*	45,000 cup	35,000 psi

Standard barrel for velocity testing: 4 inches long (vented);

(*12.493-inch alternate one-piece barrel)—1 turn in 18.75-inch twist

Availability

Cor-Bon 80-grain Glaser Safety Slug (02600/02800)

G1 Ballistic Coefficient = 0.080

Distance • Yards	Muzzle	25	50	75	100	125	150	175	200
Velocity • fps	1800	1587	1398	1240	1118	1031	967	916	872
Energy • Ft-lbs	575	447	347	273	222	189	166	149	135
Taylor KO Index	7.3	6.5	5.7	5.1	4.6	4.2	3.9	3.7	3.6
Mid-Range Trajectory Height • Inches	0.0	0.1	0.4	1.1	2.3	4.0	6.4	9.8	13.8
Drop • Inches	0.0	-0.4	-1.6	-3.9	-7.7	-13.2	-20.7	-30.6	-43.0

PMC 90-grain NT/FR (357MHRA)

G1 Ballistic Coefficient = 0.120

Distance • Yards	Muzzle	25	50	75	100	125	150	175	200
Velocity • fps	1325	1219	1139	1076	1025	981	944	911	882
Energy • Ft-lbs	351	300	261	232	210	192	178	166	156
Taylor KO Index	6.1	5.6	5.2	4.9	4.7	4.5	4.3	4.2	4.0
Mid-Range Trajectory Height • Inches	0.0	0.2	0.7	1.8	3.3	5.5	8.4	12.1	16.5
Drop • Inches	0.0	-0.6	-2.8	-6.5	-12.2	-19.9	-29.8	-42.2	-57.2

Cor-Bon 100-grain PowRBall

G1 Ballistic Coefficient = 0.090

Distance • Yards	Muzzle	25	50	75	100	125	150	175	200
Velocity • fps	1600	1429	1282	1162	1072	1005	953	909	870
Energy • Ft-lbs	569	454	365	300	255	224	202	183	168
Taylor KO Index	8.2	7.3	6.5	5.9	5.5	5.1	4.9	4.6	4.4
Mid-Range Trajectory Height • Inches	0.0	0.1	0.5	1.4	2.7	4.6	7.2	10.7	15.0
Drop • Inches	0.0	-0.5	-2.0	-4.8	-9.3	-15.6	-24.1	-35.0	-48.5

CCI 109-grain Shotshell (3709)

Muzzle Velocity = 1000 fps—Loaded with #9 Shot

Winchester 110-grain Jacketed Flat Point (SC357NT)

G1 Ballistic Coefficient = 0.118

Distance • Yards	Muzzle	25	50	75	100	125	150	175	200
Velocity • fps	1275	1182	1105	1047	998	959	924	893	865
Energy • Ft-lbs	397	341	298	268	243	225	209	195	183
Taylor KO Index	7.2	6.6	6.2	5.9	5.6	5.4	5.2	5.0	4.9
Mid-Range Trajectory Height • Inches	0.0	0.1	0.8	1.8	3.5	5.8	8.8	12.5	17.0
Drop • Inches	0.0	-0.7	-3.0	-7.0	-13.0	-21.1	-31.6	-44.6	-60.2

Cor-Bon 110-grain Jacketed Hollow Point (SD357110/20)

G1 Ballistic Coefficient = 0.100

Distance • Yards	Muzzle	25	50	75	100	125	150	175	200
Velocity • fps	1500	1356	1233	1134	1058	1000	953	914	878
Energy • Ft-lbs	550	449	372	314	274	245	222	204	188
Taylor KO Index	8.4	7.6	6.9	6.4	5.9	5.6	5.3	5.1	4.9
Mid-Range Trajectory Height • Inches	0.0	0.1	0.5	1.4	2.8	4.8	7.5	10.9	15.0
Drop • Inches	0.0	-0.5	-2.2	-5.4	-10.2	-16.9	-25.7	-36.9	-50.5

Remington 110-grain Semi-Jacketed Hollow Point (R357M7)

G1 Ballistic Coefficient = 0.099

Distance • Yards	Muzzle	25	50	75	100	125	150	175	200
Velocity • fps	1295	1182	1094	1027	975	932	894	861	830
Energy • Ft-lbs	410	341	292	258	232	212	195	181	168
Taylor KO Index	7.2	6.6	6.1	5.7	5.5	5.2	5.0	4.8	4.7
Mid-Range Trajectory Height • Inches	0.0	0.2	0.8	1.9	3.5	5.9	9.1	13.0	17.8
Drop • Inches	0.0	-0.7	-2.9	-7.0	-13.1	-21.4	-32.2	-45.6	-61.8

USA (Winchester) 110-grain Jacketed Hollow Point (Q4204)

G1 Ballistic Coefficient = 0.100

Distance • Yards	Muzzle	25	50	75	100	125	150	175	200
Velocity • fps	1295	1183	1095	1029	977	934	896	863	832
Energy • Ft-lbs	410	342	292	259	233	213	196	182	169
Taylor KO Index	7.2	6.6	6.1	5.7	5.5	5.2	5.0	4.8	4.7
Mid-Range Trajectory Height • Inches	0.0	0.2	0.8	1.9	3.5	5.9	9.0	13.0	17.7
Drop • Inches	0.0	-0.7	-2.9	-7.0	-13.1	-21.4	-32.1	-45.5	-61.6

Hornady 125-grain JFP/XTP (9053) (Discontinued in 2004)

G1 Ballistic Coefficient = 0.148

Distance • Yards	Muzzle	25	50	75	100	125	150	175	200
Velocity • fps	1500	1401	1311	1230	1161	1103	1055	1015	980
Energy • Ft-lbs	624	545	477	420	374	338	309	286	267
Taylor KO Index	9.5	8.9	8.3	7.8	7.4	7.0	6.7	6.5	6.2
Mid-Range Trajectory Height • Inches	0.0	0.1	0.6	1.3	2.5	4.2	6.4	9.3	12.8
Drop • Inches	0.0	-0.5	-2.1	-5.0	-9.3	-15.2	-22.9	-32.6	-44.2

UMC (Remington) 125-grain JSP (L357M12)

G1 Ballistic Coefficient = 0.125

Distance • Yards	Muzzle	25	50	75	100	125	150	175	200
Velocity • fps	1450	1339	1240	1158	1090	1037	994	956	924
Energy • Ft-lbs	584	497	427	372	330	299	274	254	237
Taylor KO Index	9.2	8.5	7.9	7.4	6.9	6.6	6.3	6.1	5.9
Mid-Range Trajectory Height • Inches	0.0	0.1	0.2	1.1	2.8	4.7	7.2	10.4	14.3
Drop • Inches	0.0	-0.6	-2.3	-5.5	-10.3	-16.9	-25.5	-36.2	-49.2

UMC (Remington) 125-grain Leadless (LL357M1)

G1 Ballistic Coefficient = 0.124

Distance • Yards	Muzzle	25	50	75	100	125	150	175	200
Velocity • fps	1450	1338	1240	1157	1090	1036	992	955	922
Energy • Ft-lbs	583	497	427	371	380	298	273	253	236
Taylor KO Index	9.2	8.5	7.9	7.4	6.9	6.6	6.3	6.1	5.9
Mid-Range Trajectory Height • Inches	0.0	0.1	0.6	1.5	2.8	4.7	7.3	10.6	14.5
Drop • Inches	0.0	-0.6	-2.3	-5.5	-10.3	-16.9	-25.6	-36.4	-49.6

Federal 125-grain Close Quarters Training (BC357NT3) (Discontinued in 2005)

G1 Ballistic Coefficient = 0.120

Distance • Yards	Muzzle	25	50	75	100	125	150	175	200
Velocity • fps	1350	1240	1160	1090	1035	990	951	918	888
Energy • Ft-lbs	505	425	370	330	297	272	251	234	219
Taylor KO Index	8.6	7.9	7.4	6.9	6.6	6.3	6.1	5.9	5.7
Mid-Range Trajectory Height • Inches	0.0	0.1	0.6	1.6	3.2	5.3	8.1	11.6	15.9
Drop • Inches	0.0	-0.6	-2.7	-6.3	-11.8	-19.2	-28.9	-40.9	-55.3

Winchester 125-grain Jacketed Flat Point (WC3571)

G1 Ballistic Coefficient = 0.127

Distance • Yards	Muzzle	25	50	75	100	125	150	175	200
Velocity • fps	1370	1269	1183	1112	1055	1009	970	936	906
Energy • Ft-lbs	521	447	389	343	309	283	261	243	228
Taylor KO Index	8.7	8.1	7.5	7.1	6.7	6.4	6.2	6.0	5.8
Mid-Range Trajectory Height • Inches	0.0	0.1	0.6	1.6	3.0	5.1	7.8	11.2	15.3
Drop • Inches	0.0	-0.6	-2.6	-6.1	-11.3	-18.5	-27.8	-39.4	-53.3

Black Hills 125-grain Jacketed Hollow Point-Gold Dot (M357N2)

G1 Ballistic Coefficient = 0.150

Distance • Yards	Muzzle	25	50	75	100	125	150	175	200
Velocity • fps	1500	1402	1313	1233	1164	1106	1058	1018	984
Energy • Ft-lbs	625	546	478	422	376	340	311	288	269
Taylor KO Index	9.5	8.9	8.3	7.8	7.4	7.1	6.7	6.5	6.3
Mid-Range Trajectory Height • Inches	0.0	0.1	0.6	1.3	2.5	4.2	6.4	9.3	12.7
Drop • Inches	0.0	-0.5	-2.1	-5.0	-9.3	-15.2	-22.9	-32.4	-44.0

Hornady 125-grain JHP/XTP (90502)

G1 Ballistic Coefficient = 0.151

Distance • Yards	Muzzle	25	50	75	100	125	150	175	200
Velocity • fps	1500	1403	1314	1234	1166	1108	1060	1020	985
Energy • Ft-lbs	625	546	476	423	377	341	312	289	270
Taylor KO Index	9.5	8.9	8.4	7.8	7.4	7.1	6.7	6.5	6.3
Mid-Range Trajectory Height • Inches	0.0	0.1	0.6	1.3	2.5	4.2	6.4	9.3	12.7
Drop • Inches	0.0	-0.5	-2.1	-5.0	-9.3	-15.2	-22.8	-32.4	-44.0

Cor-Bon 125-grain Jacketed Hollow Point

G1 Ballistic Coefficient = 0.150

Distance • Yards	Muzzle	25	50	75	100	125	150	175	200
Velocity • fps	1450	1356	1272	1197	1134	1081	1037	1000	968
Energy • Ft-lbs	584	511	449	398	357	324	299	278	260
Taylor KO Index	9.2	8.6	8.1	7.6	7.2	6.9	6.6	6.4	6.2
Mid-Range Trajectory Height • Inches	0.0	0.1	0.5	1.4	2.6	4.4	6.8	9.8	13.3
Drop • Inches	0.0	-0.5	-2.3	-5.3	-9.9	-16.2	-24.3	-34.4	-46.6

Federal 125-grain Hi-Shok JHP (C357B)

G1 Ballistic Coefficient = 0.130

Distance • Yards	Muzzle	25	50	75	100	125	150	175	200
Velocity • fps	1450	1350	1240	1160	1100	1047	1003	966	933
Energy • Ft-lbs	580	495	430	370	335	304	279	259	242
Taylor KO Index	9.2	8.6	7.9	7.4	7.0	6.7	6.4	6.2	5.9
Mid-Range Trajectory Height • Inches	0.0	0.1	0.6	1.5	2.8	4.6	7.1	10.3	14.1
Drop • Inches	0.0	-0.5	-2.3	-5.4	-10.2	-16.7	-25.2	-35.8	-48.6

PMC 125-grain Jacketed Hollow Point (357B)

G1 Ballistic Coefficient = 0.126

Distance • Yards	Muzzle	25	50	75	100	125	150	175	200
Velocity • fps	1450	1337	1235	1155	1093	1039	995	958	926
Energy • Ft-lbs	584	498	428	373	332	300	275	255	238
Taylor KO Index	9.2	8.5	7.9	7.4	7.0	6.6	6.3	6.1	5.9
Mid-Range Trajectory Height • Inches	0.0	0.1	0.6	1.4	2.8	4.7	7.2	10.4	14.2
Drop • Inches	0.0	-0.6	-2.3	-5.5	-10.2	-16.8	-25.4	-36.1	-49.1

Remington 125-grain Semi-Jacketed Hollow Point (R357M1)

G1 Ballistic Coefficient = 0.125

Distance • Yards	Muzzle	25	50	75	100	125	150	175	200
Velocity • fps	1450	1339	1240	1158	1090	1037	994	956	924
Energy • Ft-lbs	583	497	427	372	330	299	274	254	237
Taylor KO Index	9.2	8.5	7.9	7.4	6.9	6.6	6.3	6.1	5.9
Mid-Range Trajectory Height • Inches	0.0	0.1	0.6	1.5	2.8	4.6	7.2	10.4	14.3
Drop • Inches	0.0	-0.6	-2.3	-5.5	-10.3	-16.9	-25.5	-36.2	-49.2

Speer 125-grain Gold Dot Hollow Point (23920)

G1 Ballistic Coefficient = 0.140

Distance • Yards	Muzzle	25	50	75	100	125	150	175	200
Velocity • fps	1450	1350	1261	1183	1118	1065	1021	984	952
Energy • Ft-lbs	583	506	441	389	347	315	290	269	252
Taylor KO Index	9.2	8.6	8.0	7.5	7.1	6.8	6.5	6.3	6.1
Mid-Range Trajectory Height • Inches	0.0	0.1	0.6	1.4	2.7	4.6	7.0	10.1	13.8
Drop • Inches	0.0	-0.5	-2.3	-5.4	-10.0	-16.4	-24.7	-35.1	-47.7

Winchester 125-grain Jacketed HP (X3576P)

G1 Ballistic Coefficient = 0.124

Distance • Yards	Muzzle	25	50	75	100	125	150	175	200
Velocity • fps	1450	1338	1240	1157	1090	1036	992	955	922
Energy • Ft-lbs	583	497	427	371	380	298	273	253	236
Taylor KO Index	9.2	8.5	7.9	7.4	6.9	6.6	6.3	6.1	5.9
Mid-Range Trajectory Height • Inches	0.0	0.1	0.6	1.5	2.8	4.7	7.3	10.6	14.5
Drop • Inches	0.0	-0.6	-2.3	-5.5	-10.3	-16.9	-25.6	-36.4	-49.6

Remington 125-grain Golden Saber (GS357MA)

G1 Ballistic Coefficient = 0.148

Distance • Yards	Muzzle	25	50	75	100	125	150	175	200
Velocity • fps	1220	1152	1095	1049	1009	976	946	919	895
Energy • Ft-lbs	413	369	333	305	283	264	249	235	222
Taylor KO Index	7.8	7.3	7.0	6.7	6.4	6.2	6.0	5.9	5.7
Mid-Range Trajectory Height • Inches	0.0	0.2	0.8	1.9	3.5	5.8	8.8	12.4	16.8
Drop • Inches	0.0	-0.8	-3.2	-7.4	-13.5	-21.8	-32.3	-45.3	-60.7

Federal 130-grain Hydra-Shok JHP (PD357HS2)

G1 Ballistic Coefficient = 0.125

Distance • Yards	Muzzle	25	50	75	100	125	150	175	200
Velocity • fps	1300	1210	1130	1070	1020	979	944	912	884
Energy • Ft-lbs	490	420	370	330	300	277	257	240	226
Taylor KO Index	8.6	8.0	7.5	7.1	6.7	6.5	6.3	6.0	5.9
Mid-Range Trajectory Height • Inches	0.0	0.2	0.7	1.8	3.4	5.5	8.5	12.1	16.6
Drop • Inches	0.0	-0.7	-2.8	-6.7	-12.5	-20.3	-30.4	-43.0	-58.2

Hornady 140-grain JHP/XTP (90552)

G1 Ballistic Coefficient = 0.169

Distance • Yards	Muzzle	25	50	75	100	125	150	175	200
Velocity • fps	1350	1275	1208	1150	1106	1058	1023	991	964
Energy • Ft-lbs	566	506	454	411	376	348	325	306	289
Taylor KO Index	9.6	9.1	8.6	8.2	7.9	7.6	7.3	7.1	6.9
Mid-Range Trajectory Height • Inches	0.0	0.2	0.7	1.6	3.0	4.9	7.4	10.5	14.3
Drop • Inches	0.0	-0.6	-2.6	-6.0	-11.1	-18.0	-26.8	-37.7	-50.8

Cor-Bon 140-grain Jacketed Hollow Point

G1 Ballistic Coefficient = 0.160

Distance • Yards	Muzzle	25	50	75	100	125	150	175	200
Velocity • fps	1325	1249	1182	1124	1076	1036	1001	971	943
Energy • Ft-lbs	546	485	434	393	360	334	312	293	277
Taylor KO Index	9.5	8.9	8.4	8.0	7.7	7.4	7.1	6.9	6.7
Mid-Range Trajectory Height • Inches	0.0	0.1	0.6	1.6	3.1	5.1	7.7	10.9	14.8
Drop • Inches	0.0	-0.6	-2.7	-6.3	-11.6	-18.8	-27.9	-39.2	-52.8

Fiocchi 142-grain Truncated Cone Point (357F)

G1 Ballistic Coefficient = 0.150

Distance • Yards	Muzzle	25	50	75	100	125	150	175	200
Velocity • fps	1420	1329	1247	1176	1116	1067	1025	990	959
Energy • Ft-lbs	650	557	491	436	393	359	332	309	290
Taylor KO Index	10.3	9.6	9.0	8.5	8.1	7.7	7.4	7.2	6.9
Mid-Range Trajectory Height • Inches	0.0	0.1	0.6	1.5	2.8	4.6	7.0	10.1	13.8
Drop • Inches	0.0	-0.6	-2.4	-5.6	-10.3	-16.8	-25.2	-35.7	-48.4

Winchester 145-grain Silvertip Hollow Point (X357SHP)

G1 Ballistic Coefficient = 0.163

Distance • Yards	Muzzle	25	50	75	100	125	150	175	200
Velocity • fps	1290	1219	1155	1104	1060	1023	990	962	936
Energy • Ft-lbs	535	478	428	393	361	337	316	298	282
Taylor KO Index	9.5	9.0	8.5	8.1	7.8	7.6	7.3	7.1	6.9
Mid-Range Trajectory Height • Inches	0.0	0.2	0.8	1.7	3.5	5.2	7.9	11.3	15.3
Drop • Inches	0.0	-0.7	-2.8	-6.6	-12.1	-19.6	-29.1	-40.9	-55.0

Fiocchi 148-grain Jacketed Hollowpoint (357E)

G1 Ballistic Coefficient = 0.165

Distance • Yards	Muzzle	25	50	75	100	125	150	175	200
Velocity • fps	1500	1411	1328	1254	1188	1131	1083	1043	1008
Energy • Ft-lbs	720	654	580	517	464	421	386	358	334
Taylor KO Index	11.3	10.6	10.0	9.5	9.0	8.5	8.2	7.9	7.6
Mid-Range Trajectory Height • Inches	0.0	0.2	0.8	1.7	2.4	4.0	6.2	9.0	12.3
Drop • Inches	0.0	-0.5	-2.1	-4.9	-9.1	-14.9	-22.3	-31.6	-42.9

PMC 150-grain Jacketed Hollow Point (357C)

G1 Ballistic Coefficient = 0.145

Distance • Yards	Muzzle	25	50	75	100	125	150	175	200
Velocity • fps	1230	1158	1100	1053	1012	977	946	919	894
Energy • Ft-lbs	504	448	403	369	341	318	298	281	266
Taylor KO Index	9.4	8.9	8.4	8.1	7.7	7.5	7.2	7.0	6.8
Mid-Range Trajectory Height • Inches	0.0	0.1	0.8	1.9	3.5	5.8	8.7	12.4	16.7
Drop • Inches	0.0	-0.8	-3.1	-7.3	-13.4	-21.6	-32.0	-44.9	-60.3

Lapua 150-grain CEPP SUPER (4319213) (Discontinued in 2004)

G1 Ballistic Coefficient = 0.162

Distance • Yards	Muzzle	25	50	75	100	125	150	175	200
Velocity • fps	1214	1152	1100	1056	1019	987	959	933	909
Energy • Ft-lbs	491	442	403	372	346	325	306	290	275
Taylor KO Index	9.3	8.8	8.4	8.1	7.8	7.6	7.3	7.1	7.0
Mid-Range Trajectory Height • Inches	0.0	0.2	0.8	1.9	3.6	5.8	8.7	12.3	16.6
Drop • Inches	0.0	-0.8	-3.2	-7.4	-13.5	-21.7	-32.2	-45.0	-60.3

PMC 150-grain Starfire Hollow Point (357SFA)

G1 Ballistic Coefficient = 0.141

Distance • Yards	Muzzle	25	50	75	100	125	150	175	200
Velocity • fps	1200	1131	1076	1031	992	960	930	904	879
Energy • Ft-lbs	480	427	386	354	329	307	288	272	257
Taylor KO Index	9.2	8.7	8.2	7.9	7.6	7.3	7.1	6.9	6.7
Mid-Range Trajectory Height • Inches	0.0	0.1	0.8	2.0	3.7	6.0	9.1	12.8	17.4
Drop • Inches	0.0	-0.8	-3.3	-7.6	-14.0	-22.6	-33.4	-46.8	-62.8

Aguila 158-grain Semi Jacketed Soft Point

G1 Ballistic Coefficient = 0.079

Distance • Yards	Muzzle	25	50	75	100	125	150	175	200
Velocity • fps	1545	1360	1207	1093	1014	952	903	860	822
Energy • Ft-lbs	835	649	512	420	361	318	286	260	237
Taylor KO Index	12.4	11.0	9.7	8.8	8.2	7.7	7.3	6.9	6.6
Mid-Range Trajectory Height • Inches	0.0	0.1	0.6	1.5	3.0	5.2	8.1	12.0	16.8
Drop • Inches	0.0	-0.5	-2.2	-5.3	-10.3	-17.4	-26.9	-39.0	-54.1

Lapua 150-grain Semi-Jacketed Flat Nose (4319214) (Discontinued in 2005)

G1 Ballistic Coefficient = 0.162

Distance • Yards	Muzzle	25	50	75	100	125	150	175	200
Velocity • fps	1542	1448	1361	1282	1211	1150	1099	1055	1018
Energy • Ft-lbs	792	699	617	548	489	441	402	371	345
Taylor KO Index	11.8	11.1	10.4	9.8	9.3	8.8	8.4	8.1	7.8
Mid-Range Trajectory Height • Inches	0.0	0.1	0.5	1.2	2.4	3.9	5.9	8.6	11.8
Drop • Inches	0.0	-0.5	-2.0	-4.7	-8.7	-14.2	-21.3	-30.2	-41.1

Sellier & Bellot 158-grain SP (SBA03572)

G1 Ballistic Coefficient = 0.192

Distance • Yards	Muzzle	25	50	75	100	125	150	175	200
Velocity • fps	1394	1325	1260	1202	1151	1107	1068	1035	1006
Energy • Ft-lbs	683	617	557	507	465	430	401	376	355
Taylor KO Index	11.2	10.7	10.2	9.7	9.3	8.9	8.6	8.3	8.1
Mid-Range Trajectory Height • Inches	0.0	0.1	0.6	1.4	2.7	4.4	6.7	9.6	13.0
Drop • Inches	0.0	-0.6	-2.4	-5.6	-10.3	-16.6	-24.7	-34.7	-46.7

Ultramax 158-grain SWC (357R1)

G1 Ballistic Coefficient = 0.145

Distance • Yards	Muzzle	25	50	75	100	125	150	175	200
Velocity • fps	1300	1219	1150	1093	1046	1006	972	942	915
Energy • Ft-lbs	593	522	464	419	384	355	332	311	294
Taylor KO Index	10.5	9.8	9.3	8.8	8.4	8.1	7.8	7.6	7.4
Mid-Range Trajectory Height • Inches	0.0	0.1	0.7	1.7	3.2	5.3	8.1	11.6	15.8
Drop • Inches	0.0	-0.7	-2.8	-6.6	-12.2	-19.7	-29.5	-41.5	-56.0

Hornady 158-grain JFP/XTP (90582) (Discontinued in 2005)

G1 Ballistic Coefficient = 0.200

Distance • Yards	Muzzle	25	50	75	100	125	150	175	200
Velocity • fps	1250	1195	1147	1105	1068	1036	1008	983	960
Energy • Ft-lbs	548	501	461	428	400	377	357	339	323
Taylor KO Index	10.0	9.6	9.2	8.9	8.6	8.3	8.1	7.9	7.7
Mid-Range Trajectory Height • Inches	0.0	0.2	0.8	1.8	3.3	5.3	7.9	11.2	15.1
Drop • Inches	0.0	-0.7	-3.0	-6.8	-12.5	-20.1	-29.6	-41.3	-55.2

American Eagle (Federal) 158-grain Jacketed Soft Point (AE357A)

G1 Ballistic Coefficient = 0.149

Distance • Yards	Muzzle	25	50	75	100	125	150	175	200
Velocity • fps	1240	1160	1100	1060	1020	986	955	927	902
Energy • Ft-lbs	535	475	430	395	365	341	320	302	286
Taylor KO Index	10.0	9.3	8.8	8.5	8.2	7.9	7.7	7.5	7.3
Mid-Range Trajectory Height • Inches	0.0	0.2	0.8	1.9	3.5	5.7	8.6	12.2	16.4
Drop • Inches	0.0	-0.7	-3.1	-7.1	-13.2	-21.2	-31.5	-44.1	-59.2

Federal 158-grain Nyclad SWC-HP (P357E) (Discontinued in 2004)

G1 Ballistic Coefficient = 0.149

Distance • Yards	Muzzle	25	50	75	100	125	150	175	200
Velocity • fps	1240	1160	1100	1060	1020	986	955	927	902
Energy • Ft-lbs	535	475	430	395	365	341	320	302	286
Taylor KO Index	10.0	9.3	8.8	8.5	8.2	7.9	7.7	7.5	7.3
Mid-Range Trajectory Height • Inches	0.0	0.2	0.8	1.9	3.5	5.7	8.6	12.2	16.4
Drop • Inches	0.0	-0.7	-3.1	-7.1	-13.2	-21.2	-31.5	-44.1	-59.2

Magtech 158-grain LSWC (357C)

G1 Ballistic Coefficient = 0.146

Distance • Yards	Muzzle	25	50	75	100	125	150	175	200
Velocity • fps	1235	1164	1104	1056	1015	980	949	922	897
Energy • Ft-lbs	535	475	428	391	361	337	316	298	282
Taylor KO Index	9.9	9.4	8.9	8.5	8.2	7.9	7.6	7.4	7.2
Mid-Range Trajectory Height • Inches	0.0	0.2	0.8	1.9	3.5	5.8	8.7	12.3	16.6
Drop • Inches	0.0	-0.7	-3.1	-7.2	-13.3	-21.4	-31.8	-44.6	-59.8

Remington 158-grain LSW (R357M5)

G1 Ballistic Coefficient = 0.146

Distance • Yards	Muzzle	25	50	75	100	125	150	175	200
Velocity • fps	1235	1164	1104	1056	1015	980	949	922	897
Energy • Ft-lbs	535	475	428	391	361	337	316	298	282
Taylor KO Index	9.9	9.4	8.9	8.5	8.2	7.9	7.6	7.4	7.2
Mid-Range Trajectory Height • Inches	0.0	0.2	0.8	1.9	3.5	5.8	8.7	12.3	16.6
Drop • Inches	0.0	-0.7	-3.1	-7.2	-13.3	-21.4	-31.8	-44.6	-59.8

Speer 158-grain Gold Dot Hollow Point (23960)

G1 Ballistic Coefficient = 0.168

Distance • Yards	Muzzle	25	50	75	100	125	150	175	200
Velocity • fps	1235	1173	1119	1074	1036	1003	974	948	924
Energy • Ft-lbs	535	483	439	405	376	353	333	315	299
Taylor KO Index	10.0	9.5	9.0	8.7	8.3	8.1	7.8	7.6	7.4
Mid-Range Trajectory Height • Inches	0.0	0.2	0.8	1.9	3.5	5.6	8.4	12.0	16.1
Drop • Inches	0.0	-0.7	-3.1	-7.1	-13.0	-21.0	-31.1	-43.5	-58.3

Norma 158-grain Full Jacket Semi WC (19106) (Discontinued in 2004)

G1 Ballistic Coefficient = 0.170

Distance • Yards	Muzzle	25	50	75	100	125	150	175	200
Velocity • fps	1214	1155	1105	1062	1026	995	966	941	918
Energy • Ft-lbs	515	466	427	396	368	347	328	311	296
Taylor KO Index	9.8	9.3	8.9	8.5	8.2	8.0	7.8	7.6	7.4
Mid-Range Trajectory Height • Inches	0.0	0.4	0.8	1.9	3.6	5.7	8.6	12.1	16.3
Drop • Inches	0.0	-0.8	-3.2	-7.3	-13.4	-21.5	-31.9	-44.5	-59.5

Magtech 158-grain SJSP (357A) (357E)

G1 Ballistic Coefficient = 0.146

Distance • Yards	Muzzle	25	50	75	100	125	150	175	200
Velocity • fps	1235	1164	1104	1056	1015	980	949	922	897
Energy • Ft-lbs	535	475	428	391	361	337	316	298	282
Taylor KO Index	9.9	9.4	8.9	8.5	8.2	7.9	7.6	7.4	7.2
Mid-Range Trajectory Height • Inches	0.0	0.2	0.8	1.9	3.5	5.8	8.7	12.3	16.6
Drop • Inches	0.0	-0.7	-3.1	-7.2	-13.3	-21.4	-31.8	-44.6	-59.8

Remington 158-grain Soft Point (R357M3)

G1 Ballistic Coefficient = 0.146

Distance • Yards	Muzzle	25	50	75	100	125	150	175	200
Velocity • fps	1235	1164	1104	1056	1015	980	949	922	897
Energy • Ft-lbs	535	475	428	391	361	337	316	298	282
Taylor KO Index	9.9	9.4	8.9	8.5	8.2	7.9	7.6	7.4	7.2
Mid-Range Trajectory Height • Inches	0.0	0.2	0.8	1.9	3.5	5.8	8.7	12.3	16.6
Drop • Inches	0.0	-0.7	-3.1	-7.2	-13.3	-21.4	-31.8	-44.6	-59.8

Winchester 158-grain Jacketed Soft Point (X3575P)

G1 Ballistic Coefficient = 0.146

Distance • Yards	Muzzle	25	50	75	100	125	150	175	200
Velocity • fps	1235	1164	1104	1056	1015	980	949	922	897
Energy • Ft-lbs	535	475	428	391	361	337	316	298	282
Taylor KO Index	9.9	9.4	8.9	8.5	8.2	7.9	7.6	7.4	7.2
Mid-Range Trajectory Height • Inches	0.0	0.2	0.8	1.9	3.5	5.8	8.7	12.3	16.6
Drop • Inches	0.0	-0.7	-3.1	-7.2	-13.3	-21.4	-31.8	-44.6	-59.8

Norma 158-grain Soft Point Flat Nose (19107) (Discontinued in 2004)

G1 Ballistic Coefficient = 0.181

Distance • Yards	Muzzle	25	50	75	100	125	150	175	200
Velocity • fps	1214	1158	1110	1069	1034	1004	976	952	929
Energy • Ft-lbs	515	469	431	401	374	354	335	318	303
Taylor KO Index	9.8	9.3	8.9	8.6	8.3	8.1	7.9	7.7	7.5
Mid-Range Trajectory Height • Inches	0.0	0.4	0.8	1.9	3.5	5.6	8.5	11.9	16.1
Drop • Inches	0.0	-0.8	-3.1	-7.3	-13.3	-21.4	-31.6	-44.0	-58.8

PMC 158-grain Jacketed Soft Point (357A)

G1 Ballistic Coefficient = 0.142

Distance • Yards	Muzzle	25	50	75	100	125	150	175	200
Velocity • fps	1200	1132	1078	1033	994	961	931	905	880
Energy • Ft-lbs	505	450	408	374	347	324	304	287	272
Taylor KO Index	9.7	9.1	8.7	8.3	8.0	7.7	7.5	7.3	7.1
Mid-Range Trajectory Height • Inches	0.0	0.1	0.8	2.0	3.7	6.0	9.0	12.8	17.3
Drop • Inches	0.0	-0.8	-3.3	-7.6	-14.0	-22.5	-33.4	-46.8	-62.7

Black Hills 158-grain Semi-Wadcutter (M357N1)

G1 Ballistic Coefficient = 0.150

Distance • Yards	Muzzle	25	50	75	100	125	150	175	200
Velocity • fps	1050	1011	977	948	921	897	874	853	833
Energy • Ft-lbs	387	359	335	315	298	282	268	255	243
Taylor KO Index	8.4	8.1	7.9	7.6	7.4	7.2	7.0	6.9	6.7
Mid-Range Trajectory Height • Inches	0.0	0.3	1.1	2.5	4.5	7.2	10.8	15.2	20.3
Drop • Inches	0.0	-1.0	-4.2	-9.6	-17.4	-27.7	-40.8	-56.7	-75.5

Aguila 158-grain Semi Jacketed Hollow Point

G1 Ballistic Coefficient = 0.079

Distance • Yards	Muzzle	25	50	75	100	125	150	175	200
Velocity • fps	1545	1360	1207	1093	1014	952	903	860	822
Energy • Ft-lbs	835	649	512	420	361	318	286	260	237
Taylor KO Index	12.4	11.0	9.7	8.8	8.2	7.7	7.3	6.9	6.6
Mid-Range Trajectory Height • Inches	0.0	0.1	0.6	1.5	3.0	5.2	8.1	12.0	16.8
Drop • Inches	0.0	-0.5	-2.2	-5.3	-10.3	-17.4	-26.9	-39.0	-54.1

Lapua 158-grain Semi-Jacketed Hollow Point (4319218) (Discontinued in 2004)

G1 Ballistic Coefficient = 0.160

Distance • Yards	Muzzle	25	50	75	100	125	150	175	200
Velocity • fps	1542	1447	1359	1279	1208	1147	1095	1052	1015
Energy • Ft-lbs	834	735	648	574	512	462	421	388	361
Taylor KO Index	12.4	11.6	10.9	10.3	9.7	9.2	8.8	8.5	8.2
Mid-Range Trajectory Height • Inches	0.0	0.1	0.5	1.2	2.4	3.9	6.0	8.6	11.9
Drop • Inches	0.0	-0.5	-2.0	-4.7	-8.7	-14.2	-21.4	-30.3	-41.2

Ultramax 158-grain JHP (357R2)

G1 Ballistic Coefficient = 0.145

Distance • Yards	Muzzle	25	50	75	100	125	150	175	200
Velocity • fps	1300	1219	1150	1093	1046	1006	972	942	915
Energy • Ft-lbs	593	522	464	419	384	355	332	311	294
Taylor KO Index	10.5	9.8	9.3	8.8	8.4	8.1	7.8	7.6	7.4
Mid-Range Trajectory Height • Inches	0.0	0.1	0.7	1.7	3.2	5.3	8.1	11.6	15.8
Drop • Inches	0.0	-0.7	-2.8	-6.6	-12.2	-19.7	-29.5	-41.5	-56.0

Black Hills 158-grain Jacketed Hollow Point-Gold Dot (M357N3)

G1 Ballistic Coefficient = 0.175

Distance • Yards	Muzzle	25	50	75	100	125	150	175	200
Velocity • fps	1250	1188	1134	1088	1049	1016	986	960	936
Energy • Ft-lbs	548	495	451	416	386	362	341	323	307
Taylor KO Index	10.0	9.5	9.1	8.7	8.4	8.2	7.9	7.7	7.5
Mid-Range Trajectory Height • Inches	0.0	0.2	0.8	1.8	3.4	5.4	8.2	11.6	14.3
Drop • Inches	0.0	-0.7	-3.0	-6.9	-12.7	-20.4	-30.2	-42.3	-56.6

Hornady 158-grain JHP/XTP (90562)

G1 Ballistic Coefficient = 0.207

Distance • Yards	Muzzle	25	50	75	100	125	150	175	200
Velocity • fps	1250	1197	1150	1109	1073	1042	1014	989	966
Energy • Ft-lbs	548	503	464	431	404	381	361	343	327
Taylor KO Index	10.0	9.6	9.2	8.9	8.6	8.4	8.2	8.0	7.8
Mid-Range Trajectory Height • Inches	0.0	0.2	0.8	1.8	3.3	5.2	7.9	11.1	14.9
Drop • Inches	0.0	-0.7	-3.0	-6.8	-12.5	-20.0	-29.5	-41.1	-54.9

Federal 158-grain Hydra-Shok JHP (P357HS1)

G1 Ballistic Coefficient = 0.149

Distance • Yards	Muzzle	25	50	75	100	125	150	175	200
Velocity • fps	1240	1160	1100	1060	1020	986	955	927	902
Energy • Ft-lbs	535	475	430	395	365	341	320	302	286
Taylor KO Index	10.0	9.3	8.8	8.5	8.2	7.9	7.7	7.5	7.3
Mid-Range Trajectory Height • Inches	0.0	0.2	0.8	1.9	3.5	5.7	8.6	12.2	16.4
Drop • Inches	0.0	-0.7	-3.1	-7.1	-13.2	-21.2	-31.5	-44.1	-59.2

Federal 158-grain Hi-Shok JHP (C357E)

G1 Ballistic Coefficient = 0.149

Distance • Yards	Muzzle	25	50	75	100	125	150	175	200
Velocity • fps	1240	1160	1100	1060	1020	986	955	927	902
Energy • Ft-lbs	535	475	430	395	365	341	320	302	286
Taylor KO Index	10.0	9.3	8.8	8.5	8.2	7.9	7.7	7.5	7.3
Mid-Range Trajectory Height • Inches	0.0	0.2	0.8	1.9	3.5	5.7	8.6	12.2	16.4
Drop • Inches	0.0	-0.7	-3.1	-7.1	-13.2	-21.2	-31.5	-44.1	-59.2

Magtech 158-grain SJHP (357B)

G1 Ballistic Coefficient = 0.146

Distance • Yards	Muzzle	25	50	75	100	125	150	175	200
Velocity • fps	1235	1164	1104	1056	1015	980	949	922	897
Energy • Ft-lbs	535	475	428	391	361	337	316	298	282
Taylor KO Index	9.9	9.4	8.9	8.5	8.2	7.9	7.6	7.4	7.2
Mid-Range Trajectory Height • Inches	0.0	0.2	0.8	1.9	3.5	5.8	8.7	12.3	16.6
Drop • Inches	0.0	-0.7	-3.1	-7.2	-13.3	-21.4	-31.8	-44.6	-59.8

Remington 158-grain Semi-Jacket Hollow Point (R357M2)

G1 Ballistic Coefficient = 0.146

Distance • Yards	Muzzle	25	50	75	100	125	150	175	200
Velocity • fps	1235	1164	1104	1056	1015	980	949	922	897
Energy • Ft-lbs	535	475	428	391	361	337	316	298	282
Taylor KO Index	9.9	9.4	8.9	8.5	8.2	7.9	7.6	7.4	7.2
Mid-Range Trajectory Height • Inches	0.0	0.2	0.8	1.9	3.5	5.8	8.7	12.3	16.6
Drop • Inches	0.0	-0.7	-3.1	-7.2	-13.3	-21.4	-31.8	-44.6	-59.8

Speer 158-grain Gold Dot (23960)

G1 Ballistic Coefficient = 0.146

Distance • Yards	Muzzle	25	50	75	100	125	150	175	200
Velocity • fps	1235	1164	1104	1056	1015	980	949	922	897
Energy • Ft-lbs	535	475	428	391	361	337	316	298	282
Taylor KO Index	9.9	9.4	8.9	8.5	8.2	7.9	7.6	7.4	7.2
Mid-Range Trajectory Height • Inches	0.0	0.2	0.8	1.9	3.5	5.8	8.7	12.3	16.6
Drop • Inches	0.0	-0.7	-3.1	-7.2	-13.3	-21.4	-31.8	-44.6	-59.8

Winchester 158-grain Jacketed Hollow Point (X3574P)

G1 Ballistic Coefficient = 0.146

Distance • Yards	Muzzle	25	50	75	100	125	150	175	200
Velocity • fps	1235	1164	1104	1056	1015	980	949	922	897
Energy • Ft-lbs	535	475	428	391	361	337	316	298	282
Taylor KO Index	9.9	9.4	8.9	8.5	8.2	7.9	7.6	7.4	7.2
Mid-Range Trajectory Height • Inches	0.0	0.2	0.8	1.9	3.5	5.8	8.7	12.3	16.6
Drop • Inches	0.0	-0.7	-3.1	-7.2	-13.3	-21.4	-31.8	-44.6	-59.8

CCI 158-grain JHP (3542)

G1 Ballistic Coefficient = 0.137

Distance • Yards	Muzzle	25	50	75	100	125	150	175	200
Velocity • fps	1150	1090	1049	1000	965	934	907	881	857
Energy • Ft-lbs	475	417	378	351	320	306	288	272	258
Taylor KO Index	9.3	8.8	8.5	8.1	7.8	7.5	7.3	7.1	6.9
Mid-Range Trajectory Height • Inches	0.0	0.2	0.9	2.2	4.0	6.5	9.8	13.8	18.6
Drop • Inches	0.0	-0.8	-3.5	-8.2	-15.1	-24.2	-35.9	-50.2	-67.4

Aguila 158-grain Metal Point

G1 Ballistic Coefficient = 0.079

Distance • Yards	Muzzle	25	50	75	100	125	150	175	200
Velocity • fps	1545	1360	1207	1093	1014	952	903	860	822
Energy • Ft-lbs	835	649	512	420	361	318	286	260	237
Taylor KO Index	12.4	11.0	9.7	8.8	8.2	7.7	7.3	6.9	6.6
Mid-Range Trajectory Height • Inches	0.0	0.1	0.6	1.5	3.0	5.2	8.1	12.0	16.8
Drop • Inches	0.0	-0.5	-2.2	-5.3	-10.3	-17.4	-26.9	-39.0	-54.1

Sellier & Bellot 158-grain FMJ (SBA03571)

G1 Ballistic Coefficient = 0.192

Distance • Yards	Muzzle	25	50	75	100	125	150	175	200
Velocity • fps	1394	1325	1260	1202	1151	1107	1068	1035	1006
Energy • Ft-lbs	683	617	557	507	465	430	401	376	355
Taylor KO Index	11.2	10.7	10.2	9.7	9.3	8.9	8.6	8.3	8.1
Mid-Range Trajectory Height • Inches	0.0	0.1	0.6	1.4	2.7	4.4	6.7	9.6	13.0
Drop • Inches	0.0	-0.6	-2.4	-5.6	-10.3	-16.6	-24.7	-34.7	-46.7

Magtech 158-grain FMC-Flat (357D)

G1 Ballistic Coefficient = 0.180

Distance • Yards	Muzzle	25	50	75	100	125	150	175	200
Velocity • fps	1235	1177	1125	1082	1045	1013	985	959	936
Energy • Ft-lbs	535	468	444	411	383	360	340	323	307
Taylor KO Index	10.0	9.5	9.1	8.7	8.4	8.2	7.9	7.7	7.5
Mid-Range Trajectory Height • Inches	0.0	0.1	0.7	1.8	3.4	5.5	8.2	11.6	15.7
Drop • Inches	0.0	-0.7	-3.0	-7.1	-12.9	-20.8	-30.7	-42.9	-57.4

Remington 165-grain JHP Core-Lokt (RH357MA)

G1 Ballistic Coefficient = 0.223

Distance • Yards	Muzzle	25	50	75	100	125	150	175	200
Velocity • fps	1290	1237	1189	1146	1108	1075	1045	1019	995
Energy • Ft-lbs	610	561	518	481	450	423	400	381	363
Taylor KO Index	10.9	10.4	10.0	9.6	9.3	9.0	8.8	8.6	8.4
Mid-Range Trajectory Height • Inches	0.0	0.2	0.7	1.7	3.1	4.9	7.4	10.4	14.0
Drop • Inches	0.0	-0.7	-2.8	-6.4	-11.7	-18.7	-27.6	-38.5	-51.5

Speer 170-grain Gold Dot Soft Point (23959)

G1 Ballistic Coefficient = 0.185

Distance • Yards	Muzzle	25	50	75	100	125	150	175	200
Velocity • fps	1180	1130	1087	1051	1019	990	965	942	920
Energy • Ft-lbs	526	482	446	417	392	370	352	335	320
Taylor KO Index	10.2	9.8	9.4	9.1	8.8	8.6	8.4	8.2	8.0
Mid-Range Trajectory Height • Inches	0.0	0.2	0.9	2.0	3.7	5.9	8.8	12.4	16.7
Drop • Inches	0.0	-0.8	-3.3	-7.6	-14.0	-22.4	-33.0	-45.9	-61.3

Cor-Bon 180-grain Bonded-Core SP (HT357180BC/20)

G1 Ballistic Coefficient = 0.188

Distance • Yards	Muzzle	25	50	75	100	125	150	175	200
Velocity • fps	1265	1205	1153	1107	1068	1035	1005	978	954
Energy • Ft-lbs	640	581	531	490	456	428	404	383	364
Taylor KO Index	11.6	11.1	10.6	10.2	9.8	9.5	9.2	9.0	8.8
Mid-Range Trajectory Height • Inches	0.0	0.1	0.7	1.7	3.2	5.2	8.0	11.2	15.0
Drop • Inches	0.0	-0.7	-2.9	-6.7	-12.3	-19.8	-29.3	-41.0	-54.8

Federal 180-grain Cast Core (P357J)

G1 Ballistic Coefficient = 0.189

Distance • Yards	Muzzle	25	50	75	100	125	150	175	200
Velocity • fps	1250	1200	1160	1120	1060	1028	999	973	950
Energy • Ft-lbs	675	575	535	495	465	422	399	379	361
Taylor KO Index	11.4	11.0	10.6	10.3	9.7	9.4	9.2	8.9	8.7
Mid-Range Trajectory Height • Inches	0.0	0.2	0.8	1.8	3.3	5.3	8.0	11.3	15.3
Drop • Inches	0.0	-0.7	-3.0	-6.9	-12.6	-20.2	-29.9	-41.7	-55.8

Winchester 180-grain Partition Gold (S357P)

G1 Ballistic Coefficient = 0.188

Distance • Yards	Muzzle	25	50	75	100	125	150	175	200
Velocity • fps	1180	1131	1088	1052	1020	992	967	944	923
Energy • Ft-lbs	557	511	473	442	416	394	374	356	340
Taylor KO Index	10.8	10.4	10.0	9.6	9.3	9.1	8.9	8.7	8.5
Mid-Range Trajectory Height • Inches	0.0	0.2	0.8	2.0	3.6	5.9	8.7	12.3	16.5
Drop • Inches	0.0	-0.8	-3.3	-7.6	-13.9	-22.3	-32.9	-45.7	-61.0

Remington 180-grain Semi-Jacketed Hollow Point (R357M10)

G1 Ballistic Coefficient = 0.165

Distance • Yards	Muzzle	25	50	75	100	125	150	175	200
Velocity • fps	1145	1095	1053	1017	985	958	932	909	888
Energy • Ft-lbs	524	479	443	413	388	367	348	330	315
Taylor KO Index	10.5	10.0	9.6	9.3	9.0	8.8	8.6	8.3	8.2
Mid-Range Trajectory Height • Inches	0.0	0.2	0.9	2.1	3.9	6.3	9.4	13.2	17.7
Drop • Inches	0.0	-0.8	-3.5	-8.1	-14.9	-23.8	-35.1	-48.9	-65.2

Federal 180-grain Hi-Shok JHP (C357G)

G1 Ballistic Coefficient = 0.098

Distance • Yards	Muzzle	25	50	75	100	125	150	175	200
Velocity • fps	1090	1030	980	930	890	857	827	798	771
Energy • Ft-lbs	475	425	385	350	320	294	273	255	238
Taylor KO Index	10.0	9.4	9.0	8.5	8.1	7.9	7.6	7.3	7.1
Mid-Range Trajectory Height • Inches	0.0	0.2	1.0	2.4	4.5	7.4	11.2	16.0	21.7
Drop • Inches	0.0	-1.0	-4.0	-9.3	-17.2	-27.7	-41.1	-57.7	-77.6

Cor-Bon 200-grain Hard Cast (HT357200HC/20)

G1 Ballistic Coefficient = 0.150

Distance • Yards	Muzzle	25	50	75	100	125	150	175	200
Velocity • fps	1200	1150	1106	1069	1036	1007	981	958	937
Energy • Ft-lbs	640	587	544	507	477	451	428	408	390
Taylor KO Index	12.2	11.7	11.3	10.9	10.6	10.3	10.0	9.8	9.6
Mid-Range Trajectory Height • Inches	0.0	0.2	0.8	1.9	3.5	5.7	8.5	11.9	16.0
Drop • Inches	0.0	-0.8	-3.2	-7.4	-13.5	-21.6	-31.8	-44.3	-59.1

Cowboy Action Loads

Hornady-Frontier 140-grain L (90542) (Discontinued in 2005)

G1 Ballistic Coefficient = 0.150

Distance • Yards	Muzzle	25	50	75	100	125	150	175	200
Velocity • fps	800	783	767	750	735	718	703	688	674
Energy • Ft-lbs	199	191	183	175	168	160	154	147	141
Taylor KO Index	5.7	5.6	5.5	5.4	5.2	5.1	5.0	4.9	4.8
Mid-Range Trajectory Height • Inches	0.0	0.1	1.4	3.6	7.0	11.4	17.0	23.8	31.9
Drop • Inches	0.0	-1.7	-7.0	-16.0	-28.8	-45.7	-66.8	-92.3	-122.3

Black Hills 158-grain CNL (DCB357N1)

G1 Ballistic Coefficient = 0.150

Distance • Yards	Muzzle	25	50	75	100	125	150	175	200
Velocity • fps	800	782	765	749	733	717	702	688	674
Energy • Ft-lbs	225	215	205	197	188	181	173	166	159
Taylor KO Index	6.4	6.3	6.1	6.0	5.9	5.8	5.7	5.5	5.4
Mid-Range Trajectory Height • Inches	0.0	0.4	1.8	4.1	7.4	11.8	17.4	24.2	32.4
Drop • Inches	0.0	-1.7	-7.0	-16.0	-28.8	-45.2	-66.8	-92.3	-124.4

PMC 158-grain Lead Flat Point (357CA)

G1 Ballistic Coefficient = 0.134

Distance • Yards	Muzzle	25	50	75	100	125	150	175	200
Velocity • fps	800	780	761	743	725	708	692	676	660
Energy • Ft-lbs	225	214	203	194	185	176	168	160	153
Taylor KO Index	6.4	6.3	6.1	6.0	5.8	5.7	5.6	5.4	5.3
Mid-Range Trajectory Height • Inches	0.0	0.4	1.8	4.1	7.5	11.9	7.7	24.7	33.0
Drop • Inches	0.0	-1.7	-7.0	-16.1	-29.0	-46.3	-67.6	-93.5	-124.2

3-D (Hornady) 158-grain L (9528) (Discontinued in 2005)

G1 Ballistic Coefficient = 0.150

Distance • Yards	Muzzle	25	50	75	100	125	150	175	200
Velocity • fps	750	735	720	706	693	679	666	653	640
Energy • Ft-lbs	197	190	182	175	168	162	156	150	144
Taylor KO Index	6.0	5.9	5.8	5.7	5.6	5.5	5.4	5.3	5.2
Mid-Range Trajectory Height • Inches	0.0	0.1	1.6	4.2	7.9	12.9	19.2	26.8	35.8
Drop • Inches	0.0	-2.0	-7.9	-18.1	-32.6	-51.6	-75.4	-104.0	-176.8

Johnny Chilton with a sable from Tanzania. (Photo from *A Bullet Well Placed* by Johnny Chilton, 2005, Safari Press)

.357 SIG

This cartridge was developed in 1994 especially for the Sig P229 pistol. Design-wise, the .357 SIG comes pretty close to being a 10mm Auto cartridge necked to .357 caliber. The design follows the concept of the .30 Luger and the wildcat .38-.45 cartridge that received some interest in the early 1960s. The case volume gives the .357 SIG performance approaching that of the .357 Magnum.

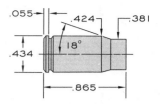

Relative Recoil Factor = 0.76

Specifications

Controlling Agency for Standardization of this Ammunition: SAAMI

Bullet Weight Grains	Velocity fps	Maximum Average Pressure	
		Copper Crusher	Transducer
125 FMJ	1,350	N/S	40,000 psi

Standard barrel for velocity testing: 4 inches long—1 turn in 16-inch twist

Availability

Cor-Bon 80-grain Glaser Safety Slug (02500/-2700)   G1 Ballistic Coefficient = 0.080

Distance • Yards	Muzzle	25	50	75	100	125	150	175	200
Velocity • fps	1650	1453	1285	1151	1055	985	931	885	845
Energy • Ft-lbs	484	375	293	235	198	173	154	139	127
Taylor KO Index	6.7	5.9	5.2	4.7	4.3	4.0	3.8	3.6	3.4
Mid-Range Trajectory Height • Inches	0.0	0.1	0.5	1.3	2.7	4.7	7.4	11.0	15.5
Drop • Inches	0.0	-0.4	-1.9	-4.7	-9.1	-15.5	-24.1	-35.2	-49.1

PMC 90-grain NT/FR (357SHRA)   G1 Ballistic Coefficient = 0.118

Distance • Yards	Muzzle	25	50	75	100	125	150	175	200
Velocity • fps	1480	1356	1245	1158	1092	1036	990	951	917
Energy • Ft-lbs	438	369	314	271	239	214	196	181	168
Taylor KO Index	6.8	6.2	5.7	5.3	5.0	4.8	4.5	4.4	4.2
Mid-Range Trajectory Height • Inches	0.0	0.1	0.6	1.5	2.8	4.7	7.2	10.5	14.5
Drop • Inches	0.0	-0.5	-2.2	-5.3	-10.0	-16.5	-25.0	-35.8	-48.9

Cor-Bon 100-grain PowRBall   G1 Ballistic Coefficient = 0.100

Distance • Yards	Muzzle	25	50	75	100	125	150	175	200
Velocity • fps	1600	1445	1309	1194	1104	1036	983	939	901
Energy • Ft-lbs	569	464	381	317	217	238	215	196	180
Taylor KO Index	8.2	7.4	6.7	6.1	5.6	5.3	5.0	4.8	4.6
Mid-Range Trajectory Height • Inches	0.0	0.1	0.5	1.3	2.6	4.4	6.9	10.1	14.2
Drop • Inches	0.0	-0.5	-2.0	-4.7	-9.0	-15.1	-23.2	-33.5	-46.3

Remington 104-grain Lead-Free Frangible (LF357SA) (Discontinued in 2004)   G1 Ballistic Coefficient = 0.143

Distance • Yards	Muzzle	25	50	75	100	125	150	175	200
Velocity • fps	1400	1307	1223	1154	1094	1047	1007	972	942
Energy • Ft-lbs	453	394	345	307	276	253	234	218	205
Taylor KO Index	7.4	6.9	6.5	6.1	5.8	5.6	5.3	5.2	5.0
Mid-Range Trajectory Height • Inches	0.0	0.1	0.6	1.5	2.9	4.8	7.3	10.5	14.3
Drop • Inches	0.0	-0.6	-2.4	-5.7	-10.7	-17.4	-26.1	-36.9	-49.9

Winchester 105-grain Jacketed Flat Point NT (SC357SNT)   G1 Ballistic Coefficient = 0.124

Distance • Yards	Muzzle	25	50	75	100	125	150	175	200
Velocity • fps	1370	1267	1179	1108	1050	1004	965	932	901
Energy • Ft-lbs	438	375	324	286	257	235	217	202	189
Taylor KO Index	7.3	6.8	6.3	5.9	5.6	5.4	5.2	5.0	4.8
Mid-Range Trajectory Height • Inches	0.0	0.2	0.7	1.7	3.1	5.2	8.0	11.4	15.7
Drop • Inches	0.0	-0.6	-2.6	-6.1	-11.4	-18.7	-28.1	-39.8	-54.0

Cor-Bon 115-grain JHP (SSD357115/20)

G1 Ballistic Coefficient = 0.140

Distance • Yards	Muzzle	25	50	75	100	125	150	175	200
Velocity • fps	1500	1395	1301	1217	1146	1088	1040	1000	966
Energy • Ft-lbs	575	497	432	378	336	302	276	255	211
Taylor KO Index	8.8	8.2	7.6	7.1	6.7	6.4	6.1	5.8	5.6
Mid-Range Trajectory Height • Inches	0.0	0.1	0.5	1.3	2.5	4.3	6.6	9.5	13.1
Drop • Inches	0.0	-0.5	-2.1	-5.0	-9.4	-15.4	-23.3	-33.2	-45.2

Hornady 124-grain JHP/XTP (9130)

G1 Ballistic Coefficient = 0.177

Distance • Yards	Muzzle	25	50	75	100	125	150	175	200
Velocity • fps	1350	1278	1208	1157	1108	1067	1031	1000	973
Energy • Ft-lbs	502	450	405	369	338	313	293	276	261
Taylor KO Index	8.4	7.9	7.5	7.2	6.9	6.6	6.3	6.1	6.0
Mid-Range Trajectory Height • Inches	0.0	0.1	0.5	1.4	2.8	4.8	7.2	10.3	14.0
Drop • Inches	0.0	-0.6	-2.6	-6.2	-11.5	-17.8	-26.5	-37.3	-50.1

PMC 124-grain Starfire Hollow Point (357Sig-SFB)

G1 Ballistic Coefficient = 0.154

Distance • Yards	Muzzle	25	50	75	100	125	150	175	200
Velocity • fps	1350	1263	1190	1132	1083	1040	1003	972	943
Energy • Ft-lbs	502	443	394	354	323	298	277	260	245
Taylor KO Index	8.5	8.0	7.5	7.2	6.8	6.6	6.3	6.1	6.0
Mid-Range Trajectory Height • Inches	0.0	0.2	0.7	1.6	3.0	5.0	7.6	10.7	14.6
Drop • Inches	0.0	-0.6	-2.6	-6.1	-11.3	-18.3	-27.3	-38.4	-51.8

PMC 124-grain Full Metal Jacket/FP (357Sig-A)

G1 Ballistic Coefficient = 0.124

Distance • Yards	Muzzle	25	50	75	100	125	150	175	200
Velocity • fps	1350	1242	1158	1093	1040	996	958	925	895
Energy • Ft-lbs	502	430	374	331	298	273	253	236	221
Taylor KO Index	8.5	7.9	7.3	6.9	6.6	6.3	6.1	5.8	5.7
Mid-Range Trajectory Height • Inches	0.0	0.2	0.7	1.7	3.2	5.3	8.1	11.5	15.7
Drop • Inches	0.0	-0.6	-2.6	-6.3	-11.7	-19.1	-28.6	-40.5	-54.8

Cor-Bon 125-grain JHP (SD357125/20)

G1 Ballistic Coefficient = 0.150

Distance • Yards	Muzzle	25	50	75	100	125	150	175	200
Velocity • fps	1425	1333	1251	1180	1119	1069	1027	991	960
Energy • Ft-lbs	564	494	435	386	348	317	293	273	256
Taylor KO Index	9.1	8.5	8.0	7.5	7.1	6.8	6.5	6.3	6.1
Mid-Range Trajectory Height • Inches	0.0	0.1	0.6	1.4	2.7	4.6	7.0	10.1	13.8
Drop • Inches	0.0	-0.6	-2.3	-5.5	-10.2	-16.7	-25.1	-35.5	-48.1

Speer 125-grain Gold Dot (23918)

G1 Ballistic Coefficient = 0.141

Distance • Yards	Muzzle	25	50	75	100	125	150	175	200
Velocity • fps	1350	1261	1184	1119	1066	1023	986	953	925
Energy • Ft-lbs	506	442	389	348	316	290	270	252	237
Taylor KO Index	8.6	8.0	7.5	7.1	6.8	6.5	6.3	6.1	5.9
Mid-Range Trajectory Height • Inches	0.0	0.2	0.7	1.7	3.1	5.1	7.8	11.2	15.2
Drop • Inches	0.0	-0.6	-2.6	-6.2	-11.4	-18.6	-27.9	-39.4	-53.2

American Eagle (Federal) 125-grain Jacketed Hollow Point (AE357S2)

G1 Ballistic Coefficient = 0.153

Distance • Yards	Muzzle	25	50	75	100	125	150	175	200
Velocity • fps	1350	1270	1190	1130	1080	1039	1002	970	942
Energy • Ft-lbs	510	445	395	355	325	299	279	261	246
Taylor KO Index	8.6	8.1	7.6	7.2	6.9	6.6	6.4	6.2	6.0
Mid-Range Trajectory Height • Inches	0.0	0.1	0.5	1.4	2.9	5.0	7.5	10.3	14.6
Drop • Inches	0.0	-0.6	-2.6	-6.1	-11.3	-18.3	-27.3	-38.5	-51.9

Black Hills 125-grain Jacketed Hollow Point (D357SIGN2) (Discontinued in 2004)

G1 Ballistic Coefficient = 0.145

Distance • Yards	Muzzle	25	50	75	100	125	150	175	200
Velocity • fps	1350	1263	1188	1124	1071	1028	991	959	930
Energy • Ft-lbs	506	443	392	351	319	293	273	255	240
Taylor KO Index	8.6	8.1	7.6	7.2	6.8	6.6	6.3	6.1	5.9
Mid-Range Trajectory Height • Inches	0.0	0.2	0.7	1.6	3.1	5.0	7.7	10.9	14.9
Drop • Inches	0.0	-0.6	-2.6	-6.1	-11.4	-18.5	-27.6	-39.0	-52.6

Federal 125-grain Jacketed Hollow Point (P357S1)

G1 Ballistic Coefficient = 0.153

Distance • Yards	Muzzle	25	50	75	100	125	150	175	200
Velocity • fps	1350	1270	1190	1130	1080	1039	1002	970	942
Energy • Ft-lbs	510	445	395	355	325	299	279	261	246
Taylor KO Index	8.6	8.1	7.6	7.2	6.9	6.6	6.4	6.2	6.0
Mid-Range Trajectory Height • Inches	0.0	0.1	0.5	1.4	2.9	5.0	7.5	10.3	14.6
Drop • Inches	0.0	-0.6	-2.6	-6.1	-11.3	-18.3	-27.3	-38.5	-51.9

Remington 125-grain Jacketed Hollow Point (R357S1)

G1 Ballistic Coefficient = 0.119

Distance • Yards	Muzzle	25	50	75	100	125	150	175	200
Velocity • fps	1350	1246	1157	1088	1032	988	950	916	886
Energy • Ft-lbs	506	431	372	329	296	271	250	233	218
Taylor KO Index	8.6	7.9	7.4	6.9	6.6	6.3	6.1	5.8	5.6
Mid-Range Trajectory Height • Inches	0.0	0.2	0.5	1.6	2.9	5.3	8.1	11.7	15.9
Drop • Inches	0.0	-0.6	-2.7	-6.3	-11.8	-19.3	-28.9	-40.9	-55.5

USA (Winchester) 125-grain Jacketed Hollow Point (USA357SJHP)

G1 Ballistic Coefficient = 0.142

Distance • Yards	Muzzle	25	50	75	100	125	150	175	200
Velocity • fps	1350	1262	1185	1120	1067	1024	987	954	926
Energy • Ft-lbs	506	442	390	348	316	291	270	253	238
Taylor KO Index	8.6	8.0	7.6	7.1	6.8	6.5	6.3	6.1	5.9
Mid-Range Trajectory Height • Inches	0.0	0.1	0.5	1.5	2.9	5.0	7.7	11.0	15.0
Drop • Inches	0.0	-0.6	-2.6	-6.2	-11.4	-18.6	-27.8	-39.2	-52.9

CCI 125-grain TMJ Lawman (53919)

G1 Ballistic Coefficient = 0.147

Distance • Yards	Muzzle	25	50	75	100	125	150	175	200
Velocity • fps	1350	1265	1190	1127	1074	1031	994	962	934
Energy • Ft-lbs	506	444	393	352	320	295	274	257	242
Taylor KO Index	8.6	8.1	7.6	7.2	6.8	6.6	6.3	6.1	6.0
Mid-Range Trajectory Height • Inches	0.0	0.2	0.7	1.7	3.1	5.1	7.7	11.0	15.0
Drop • Inches	0.0	-0.6	-2.6	-6.1	-11.4	-18.5	-27.6	-39.0	-52.6

CCI 125-grain TMJ-CF Lawman (54232)

G1 Ballistic Coefficient = 0.147

Distance • Yards	Muzzle	25	50	75	100	125	150	175	200
Velocity • fps	1350	1265	1190	1127	1074	1031	994	962	934
Energy • Ft-lbs	506	444	393	352	320	295	274	257	242
Taylor KO Index	8.6	8.1	7.6	7.2	6.8	6.6	6.3	6.1	6.0
Mid-Range Trajectory Height • Inches	0.0	0.2	0.7	1.7	3.1	5.1	7.7	11.0	15.0
Drop • Inches	0.0	-0.6	-2.6	-6.1	-11.4	-18.5	-27.6	-39.0	-52.6

CCI 125-grain TMJ (3580) (Discontinued in 2004)

G1 Ballistic Coefficient = 0.135

Distance • Yards	Muzzle	25	50	75	100	125	150	175	200
Velocity • fps	1350	1257	1177	1111	1057	1013	976	944	914
Energy • Ft-lbs	502	439	381	343	307	285	265	247	232
Taylor KO Index	8.6	8.0	7.5	7.0	6.7	6.5	6.2	6.0	5.8
Mid-Range Trajectory Height • Inches	0.0	0.2	0.5	1.6	2.9	5.1	7.8	11.2	15.2
Drop • Inches	0.0	-0.6	-2.6	-6.2	-11.5	-18.8	-28.1	-39.6	-53.6

Federal 125-grain Full Metal Jacket (C357S2) (Discontinued in 2005)

G1 Ballistic Coefficient = 0.153

Distance • Yards	Muzzle	25	50	75	100	125	150	175	200
Velocity • fps	1350	1270	1190	1130	1080	1039	1002	970	942
Energy • Ft-lbs	510	445	395	355	325	299	279	261	246
Taylor KO Index	8.6	8.1	7.6	7.2	6.9	6.6	6.4	6.2	6.0
Mid-Range Trajectory Height • Inches	0.0	0.1	0.5	1.4	2.9	5.0	7.5	10.3	14.6
Drop • Inches	0.0	-0.6	-2.6	-6.1	-11.3	-18.3	-27.3	-38.5	-51.9

Speer 125-grain TMJ (53919)

G1 Ballistic Coefficient = 0.135

Distance • Yards	Muzzle	25	50	75	100	125	150	175	200
Velocity • fps	1350	1257	1177	1111	1057	1013	976	944	914
Energy • Ft-lbs	502	439	381	343	307	285	265	247	232
Taylor KO Index	8.6	8.0	7.5	7.0	6.7	6.5	6.2	6.0	5.8
Mid-Range Trajectory Height • Inches	0.0	0.2	0.5	1.6	2.9	5.1	7.8	11.2	15.2
Drop • Inches	0.0	-0.6	-2.6	-6.2	-11.5	-18.8	-28.1	-39.6	-53.6

UMC (Remington) 125-grain MC (L357S2)

G1 Ballistic Coefficient = 0.118

Distance • Yards	Muzzle	25	50	75	100	125	150	175	200
Velocity • fps	1350	1245	1157	1087	1032	987	948	915	885
Energy • Ft-lbs	506	430	372	328	296	270	250	232	217
Taylor KO Index	8.6	7.9	7.4	6.9	6.6	6.3	6.0	5.8	5.6
Mid-Range Trajectory Height • Inches	0.0	0.2	0.7	1.7	3.2	5.4	8.2	11.9	16.2
Drop • Inches	0.0	-0.6	-2.7	-6.3	-11.8	-19.3	-29.1	-41.3	-56.0

USA (Winchester) 125-grain Full Metal Jacket-Flat Nose (Q4209)

G1 Ballistic Coefficient = 0.142

Distance • Yards	Muzzle	25	50	75	100	125	150	175	200
Velocity • fps	1350	1262	1185	1120	1067	1024	987	954	926
Energy • Ft-lbs	506	442	390	348	316	291	270	253	238
Taylor KO Index	8.6	8.0	7.6	7.1	6.8	6.5	6.3	6.1	5.9
Mid-Range Trajectory Height • Inches	0.0	0.1	0.5	1.5	2.9	5.0	7.7	11.0	15.0
Drop • Inches	0.0	-0.6	-2.6	-6.2	-11.4	-18.6	-27.8	-39.2	-52.9

Ultramax 125-grain FMJ (357SR2)

G1 Ballistic Coefficient = 0.120

Distance • Yards	Muzzle	25	50	75	100	125	150	175	200
Velocity • fps	1225	1142	1076	1024	981	944	911	882	855
Energy • Ft-lbs	417	362	322	291	267	247	231	216	203
Taylor KO Index	7.8	7.3	6.9	6.5	6.3	6.0	5.8	5.6	5.5
Mid-Range Trajectory Height • Inches	0.0	0.2	0.8	2.0	3.8	6.1	9.3	13.3	18.0
Drop • Inches	0.0	-0.8	-3.2	-7.5	-13.9	-22.5	-33.5	-47.2	-63.7

Sellier & Bellot 140-grain FMJ (SBA03573)

G1 Ballistic Coefficient = 0.112

Distance • Yards	Muzzle	25	50	75	100	125	150	175	200
Velocity • fps	1352	1247	1150	1078	1022	976	938	904	873
Energy • Ft-lbs	563	479	408	362	325	296	273	254	237
Taylor KO Index	9.7	8.9	8.2	7.7	7.3	7.0	6.7	6.5	6.2
Mid-Range Trajectory Height • Inches	0.0	0.2	0.7	1.7	3.3	5.5	8.4	12.1	16.5
Drop • Inches	0.0	-0.6	-2.7	-6.4	-11.9	-19.5	-29.4	-41.8	-56.8

Hornady 147-grain JHP/XTP (9131)

G1 Ballistic Coefficient = 0.233

Distance • Yards	Muzzle	25	50	75	100	125	150	175	200
Velocity • fps	1225	1180	1138	1104	1072	1045	1019	997	976
Energy • Ft-lbs	490	455	422	398	375	356	339	324	311
Taylor KO Index	9.2	8.8	8.5	8.3	8.0	7.8	7.6	7.5	7.3
Mid-Range Trajectory Height • Inches	0.0	0.2	0.6	1.6	3.1	5.3	8.0	11.2	15.0
Drop • Inches	0.0	-0.7	-3.0	-7.0	-12.8	-20.4	-30.0	-41.7	-55.6

Federal 150-grain Jacketed Hollow Point (P357S3) (Discontinued in 2004)

G1 Ballistic Coefficient = 0.155

Distance • Yards	Muzzle	25	50	75	100	125	150	175	200
Velocity • fps	1130	1080	1030	1000	970	942	917	893	871
Energy • Ft-lbs	420	385	355	330	313	296	280	266	253
Taylor KO Index	8.6	8.3	7.9	7.7	7.4	7.1	7.0	6.8	6.7
Mid-Range Trajectory Height • Inches	0.0	0.2	0.9	2.1	4.0	6.5	9.6	13.6	18.3
Drop • Inches	0.0	-0.9	-3.6	-8.4	-15.3	-24.5	-36.1	-50.3	-67.2

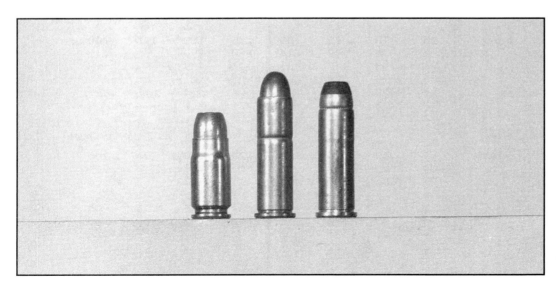

(Left to right) .357 SIG, .357 Remington Magnum, .38 Smith & Wesson.

.380 Auto (9mm Browning Short)

Another of the John Browning designs, the .380 Auto was first introduced as the 9mm Browning Short in 1908. Most decisions involving ballistics involve trade-offs. The .380 Auto makes an interesting example. The cartridge is far better than the .32 Auto in terms of energy and stopping power but still falls considerably short of either the 9mm Luger or the .38 Special. At the same time, the modest power lends itself to simple and very compact guns that are easier to carry than the more powerful calibers. The trade does not have an obvious "perfect" choice. The .380 Auto is generally accepted as "enough" gun by persons wanting a gun that's comfortable to carry (for occasional use, and perhaps never), but not "enough" gun by the law enforcement types who want all the power they can handle.

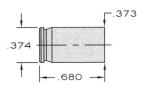

Relative Recoil Factor = 0.41

Specifications

Controlling Agency for Standardization of this Ammunition: SAAMI

Bullet Weight Grains	Velocity fps	Maximum Average Pressure	
		Copper Crusher	Transducer
85 STHP	990	17,000 cup	21,500 psi
88-90 JHP	980	17,000 cup	21,500 psi
95 MC	945	17,000 cup	21,500 psi
100 FMJ	910	17,000 cup	21,500 psi

Standard barrel for velocity testing: 3.75 inches long—1 turn in 16-inch twist

Availability

Cor-Bon 70-grain Glaser Safety Slug (00600/00800)
G1 Ballistic Coefficient = 0.070

Distance • Yards	Muzzle	25	50	75	100	125	150	175	200
Velocity • fps	1350	1183	1065	984	923	872	828	789	753
Energy • Ft-lbs	283	218	176	151	132	118	107	97	88
Taylor KO Index	4.8	4.2	3.8	3.5	3.3	3.1	2.9	2.8	2.7
Mid-Range Trajectory Height • Inches	0.0	0.2	0.8	2.0	3.8	6.5	10.0	14.7	20.3
Drop • Inches	0.0	-0.6	-2.9	-7.0	-13.3	-22.2	-34.0	-48.9	-67.3

Cor-Bon 70-grain PowRBall
G1 Ballistic Coefficient = 0.070

Distance • Yards	Muzzle	25	50	75	100	125	150	175	200
Velocity • fps	1250	1111	1016	948	894	847	806	768	733
Energy • Ft-lbs	243	192	161	140	124	112	101	92	84
Taylor KO Index	4.5	4.0	3.6	3.4	3.2	3.0	2.9	2.7	2.6
Mid-Range Trajectory Height • Inches	0.0	0.2	0.9	2.2	4.2	7.0	10.8	15.8	21.8
Drop • Inches	0.0	-0.8	-3.3	-7.9	-14.9	-24.7	-37.4	-53.6	-73.4

PMC 77-grain NT/FR (380HRA)
G1 Ballistic Coefficient = 0.069

Distance • Yards	Muzzle	25	50	75	100	125	150	175	200
Velocity • fps	1200	1095	1012	932	874	830	790	753	719
Energy • Ft-lbs	246	198	168	147	131	118	107	97	88
Taylor KO Index	4.7	4.3	4.0	3.6	3.4	3.3	3.1	2.9	2.8
Mid-Range Trajectory Height • Inches	0.0	0.2	0.9	2.3	4.4	7.4	11.4	16.5	22.7
Drop • Inches	0.0	-0.8	-3.5	-8.4	-15.8	-26.1	-39.5	-56.4	-77.2

Magtech 77-grain SCHP (FD380A)
G1 Ballistic Coefficient = 0.071

Distance • Yards	Muzzle	25	50	75	100	125	150	175	200
Velocity • fps	1099	1009	943	890	845	804	767	733	701
Energy • Ft-lbs	207	174	152	136	122	111	101	92	84
Taylor KO Index	4.3	4.0	3.7	3.5	3.3	3.1	3.0	2.9	2.7
Mid-Range Trajectory Height • Inches	0.0	0.2	1.1	2.6	4.9	8.1	12.3	17.8	24.5
Drop • Inches	0.0	-1.0	-4.0	-9.6	-17.8	-29.2	-43.8	-62.2	-84.6

Winchester 85-grain Silvertip Hollow Point (X380ASHP)

G1 Ballistic Coefficient = 0.113

Distance • Yards	Muzzle	25	50	75	100	125	150	175	200
Velocity • fps	1000	958	921	890	860	833	808	784	762
Energy • Ft-lbs	189	173	160	149	140	131	123	116	110
Taylor KO Index	4.3	4.1	4.0	3.8	3.7	3.6	3.5	3.4	3.3
Mid-Range Trajectory Height • Inches	0.0	0.3	1.2	2.8	5.1	8.2	12.3	17.3	23.4
Drop • Inches	0.0	-1.1	-4.6	-10.6	-19.4	-31.1	-45.9	-64.0	-85.6

Remington 88-grain Jacketed Hollow Point (R380A1)

G1 Ballistic Coefficient = 0.129

Distance • Yards	Muzzle	25	50	75	100	125	150	175	200
Velocity • fps	990	954	920	894	868	844	821	800	779
Energy • Ft-lbs	191	178	165	156	146	139	132	125	119
Taylor KO Index	4.4	4.2	4.1	4.0	3.9	3.8	3.7	3.6	3.5
Mid-Range Trajectory Height • Inches	0.0	0.3	1.2	2.8	5.1	8.2	12.2	17.1	23.0
Drop • Inches	0.0	-1.1	-4.7	-10.7	-19.5	-31.2	-45.8	-63.8	-85.0

Cor-Bon 90-grain JHP (SD38090/20)

G1 Ballistic Coefficient = 0.100

Distance • Yards	Muzzle	25	50	75	100	125	150	175	200
Velocity • fps	1050	994	948	908	874	842	813	786	760
Energy • Ft-lbs	220	197	180	165	153	142	132	123	116
Taylor KO Index	4.8	4.5	4.3	4.2	4.0	3.9	3.7	3.6	3.5
Mid-Range Trajectory Height • Inches	0.0	0.2	1.1	2.6	4.8	7.8	11.8	16.8	22.7
Drop • Inches	0.0	-1.0	-4.3	-9.9	-18.2	-29.3	-43.5	-60.9	-81.9

Black Hills 90-grain JHP (M380M1)

G1 Ballistic Coefficient = 0.100

Distance • Yards	Muzzle	25	50	75	100	125	150	175	200
Velocity • fps	1000	953	913	878	846	817	789	764	739
Energy • Ft-lbs	200	182	167	154	143	133	125	117	109
Taylor KO Index	4.6	4.3	4.2	4.0	3.9	3.7	3.6	3.5	3.4
Mid-Range Trajectory Height • Inches	0.0	0.3	1.2	2.8	5.2	8.4	12.6	17.9	24.2
Drop • Inches	0.0	-1.1	-4.6	-10.8	-19.7	-31.6	-46.8	-65.4	-87.8

Fiocchi 90-grain JHP (380APHP)

G1 Ballistic Coefficient = 0.100

Distance • Yards	Muzzle	25	50	75	100	125	150	175	200
Velocity • fps	1000	953	913	878	846	817	789	764	739
Energy • Ft-lbs	200	182	167	154	143	133	125	117	109
Taylor KO Index	4.6	4.3	4.2	4.0	3.9	3.7	3.6	3.5	3.4
Mid-Range Trajectory Height • Inches	0.0	0.3	1.2	2.8	5.2	8.4	12.6	17.9	24.2
Drop • Inches	0.0	-1.1	-4.6	-10.8	-19.7	-31.6	-46.8	-65.4	-87.8

Hornady 90-grain JHP/XTP (90102)

G1 Ballistic Coefficient = 0.100

Distance • Yards	Muzzle	25	50	75	100	125	150	175	200
Velocity • fps	1000	953	913	878	846	817	790	764	740
Energy • Ft-lbs	200	182	167	154	143	133	125	117	109
Taylor KO Index	4.6	4.4	4.2	4.0	3.9	3.7	3.6	3.5	3.4
Mid-Range Trajectory Height • Inches	0.0	0.3	1.2	2.8	5.2	8.4	12.7	18.0	24.3
Drop • Inches	0.0	-1.1	-4.6	-10.8	-19.7	-31.6	-46.9	-65.6	-88.0

Federal 90-grain Hydra-Shok JHP (PD380HS1)

G1 Ballistic Coefficient = 0.072

Distance • Yards	Muzzle	25	50	75	100	125	150	175	200
Velocity • fps	1000	940	890	840	800	765	731	700	670
Energy • Ft-lbs	200	175	160	140	130	117	107	98	90
Taylor KO Index	4.6	4.3	4.1	3.8	3.6	3.5	3.3	3.2	3.1
Mid-Range Trajectory Height • Inches	0.0	0.3	1.2	2.9	5.5	9.0	13.7	19.7	27.0
Drop • Inches	0.0	-1.1	-4.8	-11.1	-20.6	-33.3	-49.8	-70.3	-95.1

Federal 90-grain Hi-Shok JHP (C380BP)

G1 Ballistic Coefficient = 0.072

Distance • Yards	Muzzle	25	50	75	100	125	150	175	200
Velocity • fps	1000	940	890	840	800	765	731	700	670
Energy • Ft-lbs	200	175	160	140	130	117	107	98	90
Taylor KO Index	4.6	4.3	4.1	3.8	3.6	3.5	3.3	3.2	3.1
Mid-Range Trajectory Height • Inches	0.0	0.3	1.2	2.9	5.5	9.0	13.7	19.7	27.0
Drop • Inches	0.0	-1.1	-4.8	-11.1	-20.6	-33.3	-49.8	-70.3	-95.1

Speer 90-grain Gold Dot Hollow Point (236606)

G1 Ballistic Coefficient = 0.119

Distance • Yards	Muzzle	25	50	75	100	125	150	175	200
Velocity • fps	990	952	918	888	860	834	810	788	766
Energy • Ft-lbs	196	181	168	158	148	139	131	124	117
Taylor KO Index	4.5	4.4	4.2	4.1	3.9	3.8	3.7	3.6	3.5
Mid-Range Trajectory Height • Inches	0.0	0.3	1.2	2.8	5.2	8.3	12.4	17.5	23.5
Drop • Inches	0.0	-1.1	-4.7	-10.8	-19.7	-31.5	-46.4	-64.6	-86.4

CCI 90-grain JHP Blazer (3504)

G1 Ballistic Coefficient = 0.101

Distance • Yards	Muzzle	25	50	75	100	125	150	175	200
Velocity • fps	950	911	877	845	816	789	764	739	716
Energy • Ft-lbs	180	166	154	143	133	124	117	109	103
Taylor KO Index	4.3	4.2	4.0	3.9	3.7	3.6	3.5	3.4	3.3
Mid-Range Trajectory Height • Inches	0.0	0.3	1.3	3.1	5.7	9.2	13.7	19.4	26.2
Drop • Inches	0.0	-1.2	-5.1	-11.8	-21.5	-34.5	-51.0	-71.2	-95.4

PMC 90-grain Jacketed Hollow Point (380B)

G1 Ballistic Coefficient = 0.097

Distance • Yards	Muzzle	25	50	75	100	125	150	175	200
Velocity • fps	920	896	853	822	791	764	739	715	693
Energy • Ft-lbs	169	156	144	134	125	117	109	102	96
Taylor KO Index	4.2	4.1	3.9	3.8	3.6	3.5	3.4	3.3	3.2
Mid-Range Trajectory Height • Inches	0.0	0.3	1.4	3.3	6.0	9.7	14.6	20.6	27.9
Drop • Inches	0.0	-1.3	-5.4	-12.5	-22.9	-36.7	-54.2	-75.8	-101.5

PMC 90-grain Full Metal Jacket (380A)

G1 Ballistic Coefficient = 0.097

Distance • Yards	Muzzle	25	50	75	100	125	150	175	200
Velocity • fps	920	896	853	822	791	764	739	715	693
Energy • Ft-lbs	169	156	144	134	125	117	109	102	96
Taylor KO Index	4.2	4.1	3.9	3.8	3.6	3.5	3.4	3.3	3.2
Mid-Range Trajectory Height • Inches	0.0	0.3	1.4	3.3	6.0	9.7	14.6	20.6	27.9
Drop • Inches	0.0	-1.3	-5.4	-12.5	-22.9	-36.7	-54.2	-75.8	-101.5

Sellier & Bellot 92-grain FMJ (SBA00381)

G1 Ballistic Coefficient = 0.107

Distance • Yards	Muzzle	25	50	75	100	125	150	175	200
Velocity • fps	955	919	884	854	826	800	775	752	729
Energy • Ft-lbs	187	173	161	149	139	131	123	115	109
Taylor KO Index	4.5	4.3	4.1	4.0	3.9	3.7	3.6	3.5	3.4
Mid-Range Trajectory Height • Inches	0.0	0.3	1.3	3.0	5.6	9.0	13.4	18.9	25.6
Drop • Inches	0.0	-1.2	-5.0	-11.6	-21.2	-33.9	-50.1	-69.8	-93.4

Magtech 95-grain LRN (380A)

G1 Ballistic Coefficient = 0.078

Distance • Yards	Muzzle	25	50	75	100	125	150	175	200
Velocity • fps	951	900	861	817	781	752	722	693	666
Energy • Ft-lbs	190	171	156	141	128	119	110	101	94
Taylor KO Index	4.6	4.3	4.1	3.9	3.7	3.6	3.5	3.3	3.2
Mid-Range Trajectory Height • Inches	0.0	0.3	1.4	3.2	5.9	9.6	14.5	20.7	28.2
Drop • Inches	0.0	-1.2	-5.2	-12.1	-22.2	-35.7	-53.2	-74.7	-100.7

Winchester 95-grain SXT (S380)

G1 Ballistic Coefficient = 0.117

Distance • Yards	Muzzle	25	50	75	100	125	150	175	200
Velocity • fps	955	920	889	861	835	810	787	765	744
Energy • Ft-lbs	192	179	167	156	147	139	131	124	117
Taylor KO Index	4.6	4.4	4.3	4.1	4.0	3.9	3.8	3.7	3.6
Mid-Range Trajectory Height • Inches	0.0	0.3	1.3	3.0	5.5	8.8	13.1	18.5	24.9
Drop • Inches	0.0	-1.2	-5.0	-11.5	-21.0	-33.6	-49.4	-68.8	-91.8

Magtech 95-grain JHP (380B)

G1 Ballistic Coefficient = 0.076

Distance • Yards	Muzzle	25	50	75	100	125	150	175	200
Velocity • fps	951	900	861	817	781	748	717	688	660
Energy • Ft-lbs	190	171	156	141	128	118	109	100	92
Taylor KO Index	4.6	4.3	4.1	3.9	3.8	3.6	3.5	3.3	3.2
Mid-Range Trajectory Height • Inches	0.0	0.3	1.4	3.2	5.9	9.6	14.6	20.8	28.4
Drop • Inches	0.0	-1.2	-5.2	-12.1	-22.2	-35.9	-53.4	-75.1	-101.4

PMC 95-grain Starfire Hollow Point (380SFA)

G1 Ballistic Coefficient = 0.088

Distance • Yards	Muzzle	25	50	75	100	125	150	175	200
Velocity • fps	925	884	847	813	783	755	727	702	677
Energy • Ft-lbs	180	165	151	140	129	120	112	104	97
Taylor KO Index	4.4	4.2	4.1	3.9	3.8	3.6	3.5	3.4	3.3
Mid-Range Trajectory Height • Inches	0.0	0.3	1.4	3.3	6.1	9.8	14.7	20.9	28.3
Drop • Inches	0.0	-1.3	-5.4	-12.5	-22.9	-36.8	-54.5	-76.3	-102.5

Fiocchi 95-grain Metal Case (380AP)

G1 Ballistic Coefficient = 0.080

Distance • Yards	Muzzle	25	50	75	100	125	150	175	200
Velocity • fps	1000	943	885	854	817	783	751	722	694
Energy • Ft-lbs	211	187	169	154	141	129	119	110	102
Taylor KO Index	4.8	4.6	4.3	4.1	3.9	3.8	3.6	3.5	3.4
Mid-Range Trajectory Height • Inches	0.0	0.2	1.0	2.7	5.2	8.8	13.3	19.0	25.9
Drop • Inches	0.0	-1.1	-4.7	-11.0	-20.3	-32.7	-48.7	-68.5	-92.4

American Eagle (Federal) 95-grain Full Metal Jacket (AE380AP)

G1 Ballistic Coefficient = 0.078

Distance • Yards	Muzzle	25	50	75	100	125	150	175	200
Velocity • fps	960	910	870	830	790	758	727	698	670
Energy • Ft-lbs	190	175	160	145	130	121	111	103	95
Taylor KO Index	4.6	4.4	4.2	4.0	3.8	3.7	3.5	3.4	3.2
Mid-Range Trajectory Height • Inches	0.0	0.3	1.3	3.1	5.8	9.4	14.3	20.4	27.8
Drop • Inches	0.0	-1.2	-5.1	-11.8	-21.8	-35.2	-52.3	-73.5	-99.2

Federal 95-grain Full Metal Jacket (C80AP)

G1 Ballistic Coefficient = 0.078

Distance • Yards	Muzzle	25	50	75	100	125	150	175	200
Velocity • fps	960	910	870	830	790	758	727	698	670
Energy • Ft-lbs	190	175	160	145	130	121	111	103	95
Taylor KO Index	4.6	4.4	4.2	4.0	3.8	3.7	3.5	3.4	3.2
Mid-Range Trajectory Height • Inches	0.0	0.3	1.3	3.1	5.8	9.4	14.3	20.4	27.8
Drop • Inches	0.0	-1.2	-5.1	-11.8	-21.8	-35.2	-52.3	-73.5	-99.2

Remington 95-grain Metal Case (R380AP)

G1 Ballistic Coefficient = 0.077

Distance • Yards	Muzzle	25	50	75	100	125	150	175	200
Velocity • fps	955	904	865	821	785	753	722	693	665
Energy • Ft-lbs	190	172	160	142	130	120	110	101	93
Taylor KO Index	4.6	4.4	4.2	4.0	3.8	3.6	3.5	3.3	3.2
Mid-Range Trajectory Height • Inches	0.0	0.3	1.4	3.1	5.9	9.5	14.4	20.6	28.1
Drop • Inches	0.0	-1.2	-5.1	-12.0	-22.0	-35.5	-52.9	-74.4	-100.4

UMC (Remington) 95-grain Metal Case (L380AP)

G1 Ballistic Coefficient = 0.077

Distance • Yards	Muzzle	25	50	75	100	125	150	175	200
Velocity • fps	955	904	865	821	785	753	722	693	665
Energy • Ft-lbs	190	172	160	142	130	120	110	101	93
Taylor KO Index	4.6	4.4	4.2	4.0	3.8	3.6	3.5	3.3	3.2
Mid-Range Trajectory Height • Inches	0.0	0.3	1.4	3.1	5.9	9.5	14.4	20.6	28.1
Drop • Inches	0.0	-1.2	-5.1	-12.0	-22.0	-35.5	-52.9	-74.4	-100.4

USA (Winchester) 95-grain Full Metal Jacket (Q4206)

G1 Ballistic Coefficient = 0.082

Distance • Yards	Muzzle	25	50	75	100	125	150	175	200
Velocity • fps	955	907	865	828	794	762	733	705	678
Energy • Ft-lbs	190	173	160	145	133	123	113	105	97
Taylor KO Index	4.6	4.4	4.2	4.0	3.8	3.5	3.4	3.3	3.2
Mid-Range Trajectory Height • Inches	0.0	0.3	1.3	3.1	5.8	9.4	14.2	20.2	27.5
Drop • Inches	0.0	-1.2	-5.1	-11.9	-21.8	-35.2	-52.3	-73.4	-98.8

Winchester 95-grain Win Clean Brass Enclosed Base (WC3801)

G1 Ballistic Coefficient = 0.051

Distance • Yards	Muzzle	25	50	75	100	125	150	175	200
Velocity • fps	955	881	820	768	721	677	637	599	564
Energy • Ft-lbs	192	164	142	124	110	97	86	76	67
Taylor KO Index	4.6	4.3	4.0	3.7	3.5	3.3	3.1	2.9	2.7
Mid-Range Trajectory Height • Inches	0.0	0.3	1.4	3.3	6.4	10.7	16.6	24.2	33.7
Drop • Inches	0.0	-1.3	-5.3	-12.6	-23.5	-38.6	-58.4	-83.5	-114.6

Magtech 95-grain FMJ (380A)

G1 Ballistic Coefficient = 0.078

Distance • Yards	Muzzle	25	50	75	100	125	150	175	200
Velocity • fps	951	900	861	817	781	752	722	693	666
Energy • Ft-lbs	190	171	156	141	128	119	110	101	94
Taylor KO Index	4.6	4.3	4.1	3.9	3.7	3.6	3.5	3.3	3.2
Mid-Range Trajectory Height • Inches	0.0	0.3	1.4	3.2	5.9	9.6	14.5	20.7	28.2
Drop • Inches	0.0	-1.2	-5.2	-12.1	-22.2	-35.7	-53.2	-74.7	-100.7

Black Hills 95-grain FMJ (M380N2)

G1 Ballistic Coefficient = 0.080

Distance • Yards	Muzzle	25	50	75	100	125	150	175	200
Velocity • fps	950	901	859	822	787	756	726	698	671
Energy • Ft-lbs	190	171	156	142	131	120	111	103	95
Taylor KO Index	4.6	4.3	4.1	3.9	3.8	3.7	3.5	3.4	3.2
Mid-Range Trajectory Height • Inches	0.0	0.3	1.4	3.2	5.9	9.5	14.4	20.6	28.0
Drop • Inches	0.0	-1.2	-5.2	-12.0	-22.1	-35.6	-53.0	-74.4	-100.2

Aguila 95-grain Jacketed

G1 Ballistic Coefficient = 0.080

Distance • Yards	Muzzle	25	50	75	100	125	150	175	200
Velocity • fps	945	897	856	819	784	753	723	695	669
Energy • Ft-lbs	188	170	155	141	130	120	110	102	94
Taylor KO Index	4.6	4.3	4.1	4.0	3.8	3.6	3.5	3.4	3.2
Mid-Range Trajectory Height • Inches	0.0	0.3	1.4	3.2	5.9	9.7	14.6	20.8	28.4
Drop • Inches	0.0	-1.3	-5.2	-12.2	-22.3	-36.1	-53.5	-75.2	-101.4

CCI 95-grain TMJ Lawman (53608)

G1 Ballistic Coefficient = 0.131

Distance • Yards	Muzzle	25	50	75	100	125	150	175	200
Velocity • fps	945	915	888	862	839	817	796	776	757
Energy • Ft-lbs	188	177	166	157	149	141	134	127	121
Taylor KO Index	4.6	4.4	4.3	4.2	4.1	3.9	3.8	3.7	3.7
Mid-Range Trajectory Height • Inches	0.0	0.3	1.3	3.0	5.5	8.4	13.2	18.4	24.7
Drop • Inches	0.0	-1.2	-5.1	-11.7	-21.2	-33.8	-49.6	-68.9	-91.8

CCI 95-grain TMJ Blazer (3505)

G1 Ballistic Coefficient = 0.131

Distance • Yards	Muzzle	25	50	75	100	125	150	175	200
Velocity • fps	945	915	888	862	839	817	796	776	757
Energy • Ft-lbs	188	177	166	157	149	141	134	127	121
Taylor KO Index	4.6	4.4	4.3	4.2	4.1	3.9	3.8	3.7	3.7
Mid-Range Trajectory Height • Inches	0.0	0.3	1.3	3.0	5.5	8.4	13.2	18.4	24.7
Drop • Inches	0.0	-1.2	-5.1	-11.7	-21.2	-33.8	-49.6	-68.9	-91.8

Remington 102-grain Brass Jacketed Hollow Point (GS380B)

G1 Ballistic Coefficient = 0.195

Distance • Yards	Muzzle	25	50	75	100	125	150	175	200
Velocity • fps	940	920	901	883	866	850	835	820	805
Energy • Ft-lbs	200	192	184	177	170	164	158	152	147
Taylor KO Index	4.8	4.7	4.6	4.6	4.5	4.4	4.3	4.3	4.2
Mid-Range Trajectory Height • Inches	0.0	0.3	1.2	2.9	5.1	8.5	12.5	17.4	23.1
Drop • Inches	0.0	-1.2	-5.1	-11.6	-20.8	-33.0	-48.2	-66.4	-88.0

9mm Makarov (9x18mm)

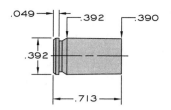

During the Cold War days, the 9mm Makarov cartridge was the standard military and police cartridge for the USSR and several Eastern Bloc countries. Since the collapse of the USSR, Makarov pistols have begun to appear in the United States, both new and surplus. Power-wise, this cartridge falls in the gap between the .380 Auto and the 9mm Luger. The dimensions are such that these rounds won't fit Luger chambers, and it isn't a good idea to try to use either .380 or 9mm cartridges in the Makarov.

Relative Recoil Factor = 0.41

Specifications

Controlling Agency for Standardization of this Ammunition: Factory
Barrel for velocity testing: 3.75 inches long—1 turn in 9.45-inch twist

Availability

Fiocchi 90-grain Jacketed Hollowpoint (9MAKHP) (Discontinued in 2004)
G1 Ballistic Coefficient = 0.107

Distance • Yards	Muzzle	25	50	75	100	125	150	175	200
Velocity • fps	1100	1037	986	944	908	875	846	818	793
Energy • Ft-lbs	242	215	194	178	165	153	143	134	126
Taylor KO Index	5.0	4.7	4.5	4.3	4.2	4.0	3.9	3.7	3.6
Mid-Range Trajectory Height • Inches	0.0	0.2	1.0	2.4	4.4	7.2	10.9	15.4	20.2
Drop • Inches	0.0	-0.9	-3.9	-9.1	-16.7	-26.9	-39.9	-55.9	-75.1

Federal 90-grain Hi-Shok JHP (C9MKB) (Discontinued in 2004)
G1 Ballistic Coefficient = 0.109

Distance • Yards	Muzzle	25	50	75	100	125	150	175	200
Velocity • fps	990	950	910	880	850	823	797	773	750
Energy • Ft-lbs	195	180	165	155	145	135	127	120	113
Taylor KO Index	4.5	4.3	4.2	4.0	3.9	3.8	3.6	3.5	3.4
Mid-Range Trajectory Height • Inches	0.0	0.3	1.2	2.9	5.3	8.4	12.6	17.7	23.9
Drop • Inches	0.0	-1.1	-4.7	-10.9	-19.8	-31.8	-46.9	-65.5	-87.6

Hornady 95-grain JHP/XTP (91002)
G1 Ballistic Coefficient = 0.128

Distance • Yards	Muzzle	25	50	75	100	125	150	175	200
Velocity • fps	1000	963	930	901	874	849	826	804	783
Energy • Ft-lbs	211	196	182	171	161	152	144	136	129
Taylor KO Index	4.8	4.7	4.5	4.3	4.2	4.1	4.0	3.9	3.8
Mid-Range Trajectory Height • Inches	0.0	0.3	1.2	2.7	5.0	8.0	12.0	16.9	22.7
Drop • Inches	0.0	-1.1	-4.6	-10.5	-19.2	-30.6	-45.1	-62.8	-83.7

Fiocchi 95-grain Metal Case (9MAK)
G1 Ballistic Coefficient = 0.130

Distance • Yards	Muzzle	25	50	75	100	125	150	175	200
Velocity • fps	1100	1047	1003	966	933	904	877	853	829
Energy • Ft-lbs	255	231	212	197	184	172	162	153	145
Taylor KO Index	5.3	5.1	4.8	4.7	4.5	4.4	4.2	4.1	4.0
Mid-Range Trajectory Height • Inches	0.0	0.2	1.0	2.3	4.3	6.9	10.4	14.7	19.8
Drop • Inches	0.0	-0.9	-3.8	-8.9	-16.3	-26.2	-38.7	-54.0	-72.2

CCI 95-grain TMJ Blazer (3506)
G1 Ballistic Coefficient = 0.131

Distance • Yards	Muzzle	25	50	75	100	125	150	175	200
Velocity • fps	1050	1006	969	936	907	880	856	833	811
Energy • Ft-lbs	220	214	188	185	174	164	154	146	139
Taylor KO Index	5.1	4.9	4.7	4.5	4.4	4.3	4.1	4.0	3.9
Mid-Range Trajectory Height • Inches	0.0	0.3	1.1	2.5	4.6	7.5	11.1	15.7	21.1
Drop • Inches	0.0	-1.0	-4.2	-9.6	-17.6	-28.2	-41.6	-58.0	-77.4

Winchester 95-grain FMJ (MC918M)

G1 Ballistic Coefficient = 0.112

Distance • Yards	Muzzle	25	50	75	100	125	150	175	200
Velocity • fps	1015	970	933	899	869	841	815	791	768
Energy • Ft-lbs	216	199	182	171	159	149	140	132	124
Taylor KO Index	4.9	4.7	4.5	4.3	4.2	4.1	3.9	3.8	3.7
Mid-Range Trajectory Height • Inches	0.0	0.3	1.2	2.7	5.0	8.1	12.1	17.1	23.1
Drop • Inches	0.0	-1.1	-4.5	-10.4	-19.0	-30.4	-44.9	-62.7	-84.0

American Eagle (Federal) 95-grain Full Metal Jacket (AE9MK)

G1 Ballistic Coefficient = 0.131

Distance • Yards	Muzzle	25	50	75	100	125	150	175	200
Velocity • fps	990	960	920	900	870	846	823	802	782
Energy • Ft-lbs	205	190	180	170	160	151	143	136	129
Taylor KO Index	4.8	4.7	4.5	4.4	4.2	4.1	4.0	3.9	3.8
Mid-Range Trajectory Height • Inches	0.0	0.3	1.2	2.8	5.1	8.1	12.1	17.0	22.9
Drop • Inches	0.0	-1.1	-4.6	-10.7	-19.5	-31.1	-45.8	-63.6	-84.8

Geoff Wainwright, a longtime African professional hunter, or "PH," with a sitatunga from Zambia. (Photo from *Hunting for Trouble* by Geoff Wainwright, 2006, Safari Press)

9mm Luger (9mm Parabellum) (9x19mm)

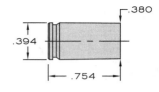

When he first introduced his 9mm pistol cartridge in 1902, Georgi Luger couldn't have even imagined what was going to happen to his brainchild. The German Navy adopted the cartridge in 1904 and the German Army in 1908. That in itself would be a pretty glowing résumé for any cartridge design, but its history was just starting. By WWII the 9mm Luger had gone on to become the standard military and police pistol cartridge in most of Western Europe. Metric cartridges weren't very popular in the United States before WWII, and the cartridge didn't get a lot of use here. With the increased popularity of semiautomatic pistols in the USA, the 9mm caliber ended up on more and more shooters' ammo shelves. Then in 1985, the U.S. Army adopted the M-9 Beretta pistol as a "replacement" for the 1911A1 .45 Auto and guaranteed the 9mm Luger at least another 50 years of useful life. Performance-wise, the 9mm Luger packs a little more punch than the .38 Special but falls well short of the .357 Magnum.

Relative Recoil Factor = 0.65

Specifications

Controlling Agency for Standardization of this Ammunition: SAAMI

Bullet Weight Grains	Velocity fps	Maximum Average Pressure	
		Copper Crusher	Transducer
88 JHP	1,500	33,000 cup	35,000 psi
95 JSP	1,330	33,000 cup	35,000 psi
100 JHP	1,210	33,000 cup	35,000 psi
115 MC	1,125	33,000 cup	35,000 psi
115 JHP	1,145	33,000 cup	35,000 psi
115 STHP	1,210	33,000 cup	35,000 psi
124 NC	1,090	33,000 cup	35,000 psi
147 MC	985	33,000 cup	35,000 psi

Standard barrel for velocity testing: 4 inches long—1 turn in 10-inch twist

Availability

CCI 64-grain Shotshell (3706)

Shot cartridge using #11 shot at 1450 fps muzzle velocity.

PMC 77-grain NT/FR (9HRA)

G1 Ballistic Coefficient = 0.120

Distance • Yards	Muzzle	25	50	75	100	125	150	175	200
Velocity • fps	1350	1240	1154	1088	1035	990	952	919	889
Energy • Ft-lbs	312	266	230	203	183	168	155	144	135
Taylor KO Index	5.3	4.9	4.5	4.3	4.1	3.9	3.7	3.6	3.5
Mid-Range Trajectory Height • Inches	0.0	0.2	0.7	1.7	3.2	5.4	8.2	11.8	16.1
Drop • Inches	0.0	-0.6	-2.7	-6.3	-11.7	-19.3	-29.0	-41.1	-55.8

Cor-Bon 80-grain Glaser Safety Slug +P (01000/01200)

G1 Ballistic Coefficient = 0.080

Distance • Yards	Muzzle	25	50	75	100	125	150	175	200
Velocity • fps	1650	1453	1285	1151	1055	985	931	885	845
Energy • Ft-lbs	484	375	293	235	198	173	154	139	127
Taylor KO Index	6.7	5.9	5.2	4.7	4.3	4.0	3.8	3.6	3.4
Mid-Range Trajectory Height • Inches	0.0	0.1	0.5	1.3	2.7	4.7	7.4	11.0	15.4
Drop • Inches	0.0	-0.4	-1.9	-4.7	-9.1	-15.5	-24.1	-35.2	-49.1

Cor-Bon 90-grain JHP +P (SD0990/20)

G1 Ballistic Coefficient = 0.085

Distance • Yards	Muzzle	25	50	75	100	125	150	175	200
Velocity • fps	1500	1333	1195	1091	1016	958	911	870	834
Energy • Ft-lbs	450	355	285	238	206	184	166	151	139
Taylor KO Index	6.9	6.1	5.5	5.0	4.7	4.4	4.2	4.0	3.8
Mid-Range Trajectory Height • Inches	0.0	0.1	0.6	1.5	3.0	5.2	8.1	11.9	16.6
Drop • Inches	0.0	-0.5	-2.3	-5.5	-10.6	-17.8	-27.4	-39.6	-54.6

Hornady 90-grain Jacketed Hollow Point/XTP (90202) (Discontinued in 2004)

G1 Ballistic Coefficient = 0.099

Distance • Yards	Muzzle	25	50	75	100	125	150	175	200
Velocity • fps	1360	1235	1134	1058	999	952	912	877	845
Energy • Ft-lbs	370	305	257	224	200	181	166	154	143
Taylor KO Index	6.2	5.6	5.2	4.8	4.6	4.4	4.2	4.0	3.9
Mid-Range Trajectory Height • Inches	0.0	0.2	0.7	1.7	3.4	5.6	8.5	12.3	16.9
Drop • Inches	0.0	-0.6	-2.7	-6.4	-12.1	-19.9	-30.0	-42.6	-58.0

Speer 90-grain Gold Dot (23606) (Discontinued in 2004)

G1 Ballistic Coefficient = 0.093

Distance • Yards	Muzzle	25	50	75	100	125	150	175	200
Velocity • fps	990	945	907	872	842	813	786	760	736
Energy • Ft-lbs	196	179	164	152	142	132	123	116	108
Taylor KO Index	4.5	4.3	4.2	4.0	3.9	3.7	3.6	3.5	3.4
Mid-Range Trajectory Height • Inches	0.0	0.3	1.2	2.8	5.2	8.5	12.8	18.1	24.4
Drop • Inches	0.0	-1.1	-4.7	-10.9	-20.0	-32.1	-47.4	-66.3	-88.9

Magtech 95-grain JSP—FLAT (9D)

G1 Ballistic Coefficient = 0.135

Distance • Yards	Muzzle	25	50	75	100	125	150	175	200
Velocity • fps	1345	1253	1174	1108	1055	1011	974	942	913
Energy • Ft-lbs	380	331	291	259	235	216	200	187	176
Taylor KO Index	6.5	6.0	5.7	5.3	5.1	4.9	4.7	4.6	4.4
Mid-Range Trajectory Height • Inches	0.0	0.2	0.8	1.7	3.4	5.1	7.8	11.2	15.3
Drop • Inches	0.0	-0.6	-2.6	-6.2	-11.6	-18.9	-28.2	-39.9	-53.9

PMC 95-grain Starfire Hollow Point (9SFL)

G1 Ballistic Coefficient = 0.200

Distance • Yards	Muzzle	25	50	75	100	125	150	175	200
Velocity • fps	1250	1195	1147	1105	1068	1036	1008	983	960
Energy • Ft-lbs	330	302	278	258	241	227	214	204	194
Taylor KO Index	6.0	5.8	5.5	5.3	5.2	5.0	4.9	4.7	4.6
Mid-Range Trajectory Height • Inches	0.0	0.1	0.7	1.7	3.3	5.3	7.9	11.2	15.1
Drop • Inches	0.0	-0.7	-3.0	-6.8	-12.5	-20.1	-29.6	-41.3	-55.2

Cor-Bon 100-grain PowRBall

Ballistic Coefficient = 0.100

Distance • Yards	Muzzle	25	50	75	100	125	150	175	200
Velocity • fps	1475	1335	1215	1120	1048	993	947	908	873
Energy • Ft-lbs	483	396	328	279	244	219	199	183	169
Taylor KO Index	7.5	6.8	6.2	5.7	5.3	5.1	4.8	4.6	4.4
Mid-Range Trajectory Height • Inches	0.0	0.1	0.6	1.5	3.0	5.0	7.8	11.3	15.7
Drop • Inches	0.0	-0.5	-2.3	-5.5	-10.5	-17.4	-26.5	-38.1	-52.3

Fiocchi 100-grain Truncated Cone Encapsulated Base (9TCEB)

G1 Ballistic Coefficient = 0.125

Distance • Yards	Muzzle	25	50	75	100	125	150	175	200
Velocity • fps	1400	1294	1203	1127	1067	1018	977	942	911
Energy • Ft-lbs	435	372	321	282	253	230	212	197	184
Taylor KO Index	7.1	6.6	6.1	5.7	5.4	5.2	5.0	4.8	4.6
Mid-Range Trajectory Height • Inches	0.0	0.1	0.7	1.6	3.0	5.0	7.7	11.1	15.2
Drop • Inches	0.0	-0.6	-2.5	-5.8	-10.4	-17.9	-27.0	-38.4	-52.2

Federal 100-grain Close Quarter Training (BC9NT3) (Discontinued in 2004)

G1 Ballistic Coefficient = 0.159

Distance • Yards	Muzzle	25	50	75	100	125	150	175	200
Velocity • fps	1230	1160	1110	1064	1025	992	962	936	911
Energy • Ft-lbs	335	300	275	251	233	218	206	194	184
Taylor KO Index	6.3	5.9	5.6	5.4	5.2	5.0	4.9	4.8	4.6
Mid-Range Trajectory Height • Inches	0.0	0.2	0.8	1.8	3.5	5.7	8.5	12.1	16.3
Drop • Inches	0.0	-0.7	-3.1	-7.2	-13.2	-21.3	-31.5	-44.1	-59.1

Remington 101-grain Disintegrator Plated Frangible (LF9MMA) (Discontinued in 2004)

G1 Ballistic Coefficient = 0.142

Distance • Yards	Muzzle	25	50	75	100	125	150	175	200
Velocity • fps	1220	1150	1092	1044	1004	969	939	912	887
Energy • Ft-lbs	334	296	267	244	226	211	198	186	176
Taylor KO Index	6.3	5.9	5.6	5.4	5.2	5.0	4.8	4.7	4.6
Mid-Range Trajectory Height • Inches	0.0	0.2	0.8	1.9	3.6	5.9	8.9	12.6	17.0
Drop • Inches	0.0	-0.8	-3.2	-7.4	-13.6	-21.9	-32.6	-45.6	-61.2

Winchester 105-grain Jacketed Soft Point NT (SC9NT)

G1 Ballistic Coefficient = 0.137

Distance • Yards	Muzzle	25	50	75	100	125	150	175	200
Velocity • fps	1200	1131	1074	1028	989	955	925	898	873
Energy • Ft-lbs	336	298	269	246	228	213	200	188	178
Taylor KO Index	6.4	6.0	5.7	5.5	5.3	5.1	4.9	4.8	4.7
Mid-Range Trajectory Height • Inches	0.0	0.2	0.8	2.0	3.7	6.1	9.1	13.0	17.5
Drop • Inches	0.0	-0.8	-3.3	-7.6	-14.1	-22.6	-33.6	-47.1	-63.2

Cor-Bon 115-grain JHP +P (SD09115/20)

G1 Ballistic Coefficient = 0.130

Distance • Yards	Muzzle	25	50	75	100	125	150	175	200
Velocity • fps	1350	1254	1172	1104	1050	1006	968	935	906
Energy • Ft-lbs	460	402	351	312	282	258	239	223	210
Taylor KO Index	7.9	7.3	6.9	6.5	6.1	5.9	5.7	5.5	5.3
Mid-Range Trajectory Height • Inches	0.0	0.1	0.6	1.6	3.1	5.2	7.9	11.4	15.6
Drop • Inches	0.0	-0.6	-2.6	-6.2	-11.6	-18.9	-28.4	-40.2	-54.5

Black Hills 115-grain Jacketed Hollow Point +P (M9N8)

G1 Ballistic Coefficient = 0.150

Distance • Yards	Muzzle	25	50	75	100	125	150	175	200
Velocity • fps	1300	1222	1155	1098	1052	1013	979	949	922
Energy • Ft-lbs	431	381	340	308	282	262	245	230	217
Taylor KO Index	7.6	7.1	6.7	6.4	6.2	5.9	5.7	5.6	5.4
Mid-Range Trajectory Height • Inches	0.0	0.2	0.7	1.7	3.3	5.3	8.0	11.4	15.4
Drop • Inches	0.0	-0.7	-2.8	-6.6	-12.1	-19.6	-29.2	-41.0	-55.2

Black Hills 115-grain (Ex-tra Power) JHP (M9N6)

G1 Ballistic Coefficient = 0.150

Distance • Yards	Muzzle	25	50	75	100	125	150	175	200
Velocity • fps	1250	1179	1118	1068	1026	991	960	932	907
Energy • Ft-lbs	400	355	319	291	269	251	235	222	210
Taylor KO Index	7.3	6.9	6.5	6.2	6.0	5.8	5.6	5.5	5.3
Mid-Range Trajectory Height • Inches	0.0	0.2	0.8	1.8	3.5	6.0	8.5	12.0	16.2
Drop • Inches	0.0	-0.7	-3.0	-7.0	-13.0	-20.9	-31.1	-43.5	-58.4

Fiocchi 115-grain Jacketed Hollowpoint (9APHP)

G1 Ballistic Coefficient = 0.145

Distance • Yards	Muzzle	25	50	75	100	125	150	175	200
Velocity • fps	1250	1176	1114	1063	1021	985	954	926	900
Energy • Ft-lbs	400	353	317	289	266	248	232	219	207
Taylor KO Index	7.3	6.9	6.5	6.2	6.0	5.8	5.6	5.4	5.3
Mid-Range Trajectory Height • Inches	0.0	0.2	0.8	1.8	3.5	5.6	8.5	12.1	16.4
Drop • Inches	0.0	-0.7	-3.0	-7.1	-13.0	-21.0	-31.3	-43.8	-58.9

Remington 115-grain Jacketed Hollow Point +P (R9MM6)

G1 Ballistic Coefficient = 0.143

Distance • Yards	Muzzle	25	50	75	100	125	150	175	200
Velocity • fps	1250	1175	1113	1061	1019	983	951	923	897
Energy • Ft-lbs	399	353	315	288	265	247	231	218	206
Taylor KO Index	7.3	6.9	6.5	6.2	6.0	5.7	5.6	5.4	5.2
Mid-Range Trajectory Height • Inches	0.0	0.2	0.8	1.9	3.5	5.6	8.5	12.1	16.4
Drop • Inches	0.0	-0.7	-3.0	-7.1	-13.0	-21.1	-31.3	-44.0	-59.1

Magtech 115-grain JHP +P + (9H)

G1 Ballistic Coefficient = 0.165

Distance • Yards	Muzzle	25	50	75	100	125	150	175	200
Velocity • fps	1328	1254	1187	1131	1084	1043	1009	978	951
Energy • Ft-lbs	451	401	360	327	300	278	260	244	231
Taylor KO Index	7.8	7.3	6.9	6.6	6.3	6.1	5.9	5.7	5.6
Mid-Range Trajectory Height • Inches	0.0	0.2	0.7	1.6	3.1	5.0	7.6	10.9	14.7
Drop • Inches	0.0	-0.6	-2.7	-6.2	-11.5	-18.6	-27.7	-38.9	-52.4

Magtech 115-grain JHP +P (GG9A)

G1 Ballistic Coefficient = 0.185

Distance • Yards	Muzzle	25	50	75	100	125	150	175	200
Velocity • fps	1246	1188	1137	1093	1056	1023	994	968	945
Energy • Ft-lbs	397	360	330	305	285	267	252	240	228
Taylor KO Index	7.3	6.9	6.6	6.4	6.2	6.0	5.8	5.7	5.5
Mid-Range Trajectory Height • Inches	0.0	0.2	0.8	1.8	3.4	5.5	8.2	11.5	15.5
Drop • Inches	0.0	-0.7	-3.0	-6.9	-12.7	-20.4	-30.2	-42.2	-56.4

Sellier & Bellot 115-grain JHP (SBA00904)

G1 Ballistic Coefficient = 0.079

Distance • Yards	Muzzle	25	50	75	100	125	150	175	200
Velocity • fps	1237	1129	1027	964	912	869	930	794	962
Energy • Ft-lbs	395	329	272	237	213	193	176	161	148
Taylor KO Index	7.2	6.6	6.0	5.6	5.3	5.1	4.9	4.6	4.5
Mid-Range Trajectory Height • Inches	0.0	0.2	0.8	2.1	4.0	6.7	10.3	14.8	20.3
Drop • Inches	0.0	-0.8	-3.3	-7.8	-14.7	-24.1	-36.3	-51.6	-70.1

Speer 115-grain Gold Dot (23614)

G1 Ballistic Coefficient = 0.125

Distance • Yards	Muzzle	25	50	75	100	125	150	175	200
Velocity • fps	1225	1145	1081	1030	987	951	919	890	863
Energy • Ft-lbs	383	335	298	271	249	231	216	202	190
Taylor KO Index	7.2	6.7	6.3	6.0	5.8	5.6	5.4	5.2	5.0
Mid-Range Trajectory Height • Inches	0.0	0.2	0.8	2.0	3.7	6.1	9.2	13.1	17.8
Drop • Inches	0.0	-0.8	-3.2	-7.4	-13.8	-22.3	-33.3	-46.8	-63.0

Winchester 115-grain Silvertip Hollow Point (X9MMSHP)

G1 Ballistic Coefficient = 0.143

Distance • Yards	Muzzle	25	50	75	100	125	150	175	200
Velocity • fps	1225	1154	1095	1047	1007	973	942	915	890
Energy • Ft-lbs	383	340	306	280	259	242	227	214	202
Taylor KO Index	7.1	6.7	6.4	6.1	5.9	5.7	5.5	5.4	5.2
Mid-Range Trajectory Height • Inches	0.0	0.2	0.8	1.9	3.6	5.8	8.8	12.5	16.9
Drop • Inches	0.0	-0.8	-3.1	-7.3	-13.5	-21.8	-32.3	-45.3	-60.8

USA (Winchester) 115-grain Jacketed Hollow Point (USA9JHP)

G1 Ballistic Coefficient = 0.142

Distance • Yards	Muzzle	25	50	75	100	125	150	175	200
Velocity • fps	1225	1154	1095	1047	1006	972	941	914	865
Energy • Ft-lbs	383	340	306	280	259	241	226	213	202
Taylor KO Index	7.2	6.7	6.4	6.1	5.9	5.7	5.5	5.3	5.1
Mid-Range Trajectory Height • Inches	0.0	0.2	0.8	1.9	3.6	5.9	8.9	12.6	17.1
Drop • Inches	0.0	-0.8	-3.1	-7.3	-13.5	-21.8	-32.5	-45.5	-61.2

PMC 115-grain Jacketed Hollow Point (9B)

G1 Ballistic Coefficient = 0.138

Distance • Yards	Muzzle	25	50	75	100	125	150	175	200
Velocity • fps	1160	1099	1049	1007	971	940	912	886	862
Energy • Ft-lbs	344	308	281	259	241	226	212	201	190
Taylor KO Index	6.8	6.4	6.1	5.9	5.7	5.5	5.3	5.2	5.0
Mid-Range Trajectory Height • Inches	0.0	0.2	0.9	2.1	4.0	6.4	9.6	13.6	18.4
Drop • Inches	0.0	-0.8	-3.5	-8.1	-14.8	-23.9	-35.4	-49.6	-66.4

Norma 115-grain Hollow point (19021) (Discontinued in 2004)

G1 Ballistic Coefficient = 0.131

Distance • Yards	Muzzle	25	50	75	100	125	150	175	200
Velocity • fps	1165	1099	1046	1003	966	934	905	878	854
Energy • Ft-lbs	344	306	277	257	236	223	209	197	186
Taylor KO Index	6.8	6.4	6.1	5.8	5.6	5.5	5.3	5.1	5.0
Mid-Range Trajectory Height • Inches	0.0	0.2	0.9	2.1	4.0	6.4	9.6	13.6	18.4
Drop • Inches	0.0	-0.8	-3.5	-8.1	-14.8	-23.9	-35.4	-49.6	-66.5

Federal 115-grain Hi-Shok JHP (C9BP)

G1 Ballistic Coefficient = 0.161

Distance • Yards	Muzzle	25	50	75	100	125	150	175	200
Velocity • fps	1160	1100	1060	1020	990	961	935	911	889
Energy • Ft-lbs	345	310	285	270	250	236	223	212	202
Taylor KO Index	6.8	6.4	6.2	5.9	5.8	5.6	5.5	5.3	5.2
Mid-Range Trajectory Height • Inches	0.0	0.2	0.9	2.1	3.8	6.2	9.2	13.0	17.5
Drop • Inches	0.0	-0.8	-3.4	-8.0	-14.6	-23.4	-34.5	-48.1	-64.3

Hornady 115-grain JHP/XTP (90252)

G1 Ballistic Coefficient = 0.141

Distance • Yards	Muzzle	25	50	75	100	125	150	175	200
Velocity • fps	1155	1095	1047	1006	971	940	913	887	864
Energy • Ft-lbs	341	306	280	258	241	226	213	201	191
Taylor KO Index	6.7	6.4	6.1	5.9	5.7	5.5	5.3	5.2	5.1
Mid-Range Trajectory Height • Inches	0.0	0.2	0.9	2.1	4.0	6.3	9.5	13.5	18.2
Drop • Inches	0.0	-0.8	-3.5	-8.1	-14.9	-24.0	-35.4	-49.5	-66.3

Magtech 115-grain JHP (9C)

G1 Ballistic Coefficient = 0.141

Distance • Yards	Muzzle	25	50	75	100	125	150	175	200
Velocity • fps	1155	1095	1047	1006	971	940	913	887	864
Energy • Ft-lbs	341	306	280	258	241	226	213	201	191
Taylor KO Index	6.7	6.4	6.1	5.9	5.7	5.5	5.3	5.2	5.1
Mid-Range Trajectory Height • Inches	0.0	0.2	0.9	2.1	4.0	6.3	9.5	13.5	18.2
Drop • Inches	0.0	-0.8	-3.5	-8.1	-14.9	-24.0	-35.4	-49.5	-66.3

Remington 115-grain Jacketed Hollow Point (R9MM1)

G1 Ballistic Coefficient = 0.141

Distance • Yards	Muzzle	25	50	75	100	125	150	175	200
Velocity • fps	1155	1095	1047	1006	971	940	913	887	864
Energy • Ft-lbs	341	306	280	258	241	226	213	201	191
Taylor KO Index	6.7	6.4	6.1	5.9	5.7	5.5	5.3	5.2	5.1
Mid-Range Trajectory Height • Inches	0.0	0.2	0.9	2.1	4.0	6.3	9.5	13.5	18.2
Drop • Inches	0.0	-0.8	-3.5	-8.1	-14.9	-24.0	-35.4	-49.5	-66.3

UMC (Remington) 115-grain Jacketed Hollow Point (L9MM1)

G1 Ballistic Coefficient = 0.141

Distance • Yards	Muzzle	25	50	75	100	125	150	175	200
Velocity • fps	1155	1095	1047	1006	971	940	913	887	864
Energy • Ft-lbs	341	306	280	258	241	226	213	201	191
Taylor KO Index	6.7	6.4	6.1	5.9	5.7	5.5	5.3	5.2	5.1
Mid-Range Trajectory Height • Inches	0.0	0.2	0.9	2.1	4.0	6.3	9.5	13.5	18.2
Drop • Inches	0.0	-0.8	-3.5	-8.1	-14.9	-24.0	-35.4	-49.5	-66.3

CCI 115-grain Jacketed Hollow Point (3508)

G1 Ballistic Coefficient = 0.119

Distance • Yards	Muzzle	25	50	75	100	125	150	175	200
Velocity • fps	1145	1078	1024	981	943	911	881	854	829
Energy • Ft-lbs	335	297	268	246	227	212	198	186	175
Taylor KO Index	6.7	6.3	6.0	5.7	5.5	5.3	5.2	5.0	4.8
Mid-Range Trajectory Height • Inches	0.0	0.2	1.0	2.2	4.1	6.6	10.0	14.2	19.2
Drop • Inches	0.0	-0.9	3.6	-8.4	-15.5	-24.9	-36.9	-51.7	-69.5

Sellier & Bellot 115-grain FMJ (SBA00902)

G1 Ballistic Coefficient = 0.102

Distance • Yards	Muzzle	25	50	75	100	125	150	175	200
Velocity • fps	1280	1180	1089	1026	975	933	897	864	834
Energy • Ft-lbs	421	358	304	269	243	222	205	191	178
Taylor KO Index	7.5	6.9	6.4	6.0	5.7	5.5	5.2	5.1	4.9
Mid-Range Trajectory Height • Inches	0.0	0.2	0.8	1.9	3.7	6.1	9.2	13.3	18.2
Drop • Inches	0.0	-0.7	-3.0	-7.1	-13.3	-21.7	-32.7	-46.3	-62.9

Aguila 115-grain Jacketed

G1 Ballistic Coefficient = 0.143

Distance • Yards	Muzzle	25	50	75	100	125	150	175	200
Velocity • fps	1250	1176	1113	1062	1020	983	952	924	898
Energy • Ft-lbs	399	353	317	288	266	247	231	218	206
Taylor KO Index	7.3	6.9	6.5	6.2	6.0	5.7	5.6	5.4	5.3
Mid-Range Trajectory Height • Inches	0.0	0.2	0.8	1.9	3.5	5.7	8.6	12.3	16.6
Drop • Inches	0.0	-0.7	-3.0	-7.1	-13.0	-21.1	-31.4	-44.1	-59.4

Fiocchi 115-grain Metal Case (9AP)

G1 Ballistic Coefficient = 0.150

Distance • Yards	Muzzle	25	50	75	100	125	150	175	200
Velocity • fps	1250	1179	1118	1068	1026	991	960	932	907
Energy • Ft-lbs	400	355	319	291	269	251	235	222	210
Taylor KO Index	7.3	6.9	6.5	6.2	6.0	5.8	5.6	5.5	5.3
Mid-Range Trajectory Height • Inches	0.0	0.2	0.8	1.8	3.5	5.6	8.4	12.0	16.2
Drop • Inches	0.0	-0.7	-3.0	-7.0	-13.0	-20.9	-31.1	-43.5	-58.4

CCI 115-grain FMJ Lawman (53615)

G1 Ballistic Coefficient = 0.151

Distance • Yards	Muzzle	25	50	75	100	125	150	175	200
Velocity • fps	1200	1137	1084	1040	1003	971	942	916	892
Energy • Ft-lbs	368	330	300	276	257	241	227	214	203
Taylor KO Index	7.0	6.6	6.3	6.1	5.9	5.7	5.5	5.4	5.2
Mid-Range Trajectory Height • Inches	0.0	0.2	0.8	2.0	3.7	6.0	9.0	12.8	17.2
Drop • Inches	0.0	-0.8	-3.3	-7.6	-13.9	-22.4	-33.1	-46.4	-62.2

USA (Winchester) 115-grain Brass Enclosed Base (WC91)

G1 Ballistic Coefficient = 0.171

Distance • Yards	Muzzle	25	50	75	100	125	150	175	200
Velocity • fps	1190	1135	1088	1048	1014	984	957	933	910
Energy • Ft-lbs	362	329	302	281	262	247	234	222	212
Taylor KO Index	6.9	6.6	6.3	6.1	5.9	5.8	5.6	5.5	5.3
Mid-Range Trajectory Height • Inches	0.0	0.2	0.9	2.1	3.7	5.9	8.8	12.4	16.7
Drop • Inches	0.0	-0.8	-3.3	-7.6	-13.9	-22.2	-32.8	-45.8	-61.2

Winchester 115-grain Full Metal Jacket (Q4172)

G1 Ballistic Coefficient = 0.143

Distance • Yards	Muzzle	25	50	75	100	125	150	175	200
Velocity • fps	1190	1125	1071	1027	990	958	929	903	878
Energy • Ft-lbs	362	323	293	270	250	234	220	208	197
Taylor KO Index	6.9	6.6	6.2	6.0	5.8	5.6	5.4	5.3	5.1
Mid-Range Trajectory Height • Inches	0.0	0.2	0.9	2.0	3.8	6.1	9.1	12.9	17.5
Drop • Inches	0.0	-0.8	-3.3	-7.7	-14.2	-22.8	-33.8	-47.3	-63.4

American Eagle (Federal) 115-grain Full Metal Jacket (AE9DP)

G1 Ballistic Coefficient = 0.161

Distance • Yards	Muzzle	25	50	75	100	125	150	175	200
Velocity • fps	1160	1100	1060	1020	990	961	935	911	889
Energy • Ft-lbs	344	313	288	267	250	236	223	212	202
Taylor KO Index	6.8	6.4	6.2	5.9	5.8	5.6	5.5	5.3	5.2
Mid-Range Trajectory Height • Inches	0.0	0.2	0.9	2.1	3.9	6.2	9.2	13.1	17.5
Drop • Inches	0.0	-0.8	-3.4	-8.0	-14.6	-23.4	-34.5	-48.1	-64.3

Black Hills 115-grain Full Metal Jacket (M9N1)

G1 Ballistic Coefficient = 0.140

Distance • Yards	Muzzle	25	50	75	100	125	150	175	200
Velocity • fps	1150	1091	1042	1002	967	937	910	884	861
Energy • Ft-lbs	336	304	278	256	239	224	211	200	189
Taylor KO Index	6.7	6.4	6.1	5.8	5.7	5.5	5.3	5.2	5.0
Mid-Range Trajectory Height • Inches	0.0	0.2	0.9	2.1	4.0	6.4	9.6	13.6	18.3
Drop • Inches	0.0	-0.8	-3.5	-8.2	-15.0	-24.1	-35.7	-49.9	-66.8

PMC 115-grain Full Metal Jacket (9A)

G1 Ballistic Coefficient = 0.165

Distance • Yards	Muzzle	25	50	75	100	125	150	175	200
Velocity • fps	1150	1099	1057	1020	988	960	935	912	890
Energy • Ft-lbs	338	309	285	266	250	236	223	212	202
Taylor KO Index	6.7	6.4	6.2	6.0	5.8	5.6	5.5	5.3	5.2
Mid-Range Trajectory Height • Inches	0.0	0.2	0.9	2.1	3.9	6.3	9.4	13.2	17.7
Drop • Inches	0.0	-0.9	-3.5	-8.1	-14.8	-23.6	-34.9	-48.6	-65.0

CCI 115-grain Totally Metal Jacket (3509)

G1 Ballistic Coefficient = 0.147

Distance • Yards	Muzzle	25	50	75	100	125	150	175	200
Velocity • fps	1145	1089	1047	1005	971	942	915	891	868
Energy • Ft-lbs	341	303	280	258	241	227	214	203	192
Taylor KO Index	6.7	6.4	6.1	5.9	5.7	5.5	5.4	5.2	5.1
Mid-Range Trajectory Height • Inches	0.0	0.2	0.9	2.1	3.9	6.4	9.6	13.5	18.2
Drop • Inches	0.0	-0.9	-3.5	-8.2	-15.1	-24.2	-35.7	-49.8	-66.6

Magtech 115-grain FMJ (9A)

G1 Ballistic Coefficient = 0.141

Distance • Yards	Muzzle	25	50	75	100	125	150	175	200
Velocity • fps	1135	1079	1027	994	961	931	905	880	857
Energy • Ft-lbs	330	297	270	253	235	222	209	198	188
Taylor KO Index	6.6	6.3	6.0	5.8	5.6	5.4	5.3	5.1	5.0
Mid-Range Trajectory Height • Inches	0.0	0.2	0.9	2.1	4.0	6.5	9.8	13.8	18.6
Drop • Inches	0.0	-0.9	-3.6	-8.4	-15.4	-24.6	-36.4	-50.8	-68.0

Remington 115-grain Metal Case (R9MM3)

G1 Ballistic Coefficient = 0.156

Distance • Yards	Muzzle	25	50	75	100	125	150	175	200
Velocity • fps	1135	1084	1041	1005	973	945	920	896	874
Energy • Ft-lbs	329	300	277	258	242	228	216	205	195
Taylor KO Index	6.6	6.3	6.1	5.9	5.7	5.5	5.4	5.2	5.1
Mid-Range Trajectory Height • Inches	0.0	0.2	0.9	2.1	4.0	6.4	9.6	13.5	17.4
Drop • Inches	0.0	-0.9	-3.6	-8.3	-15.2	-24.3	-35.9	-50.0	-66.7

UMC (Remington) 115-grain Metal Case (L9MM3)

G1 Ballistic Coefficient = 0.156

Distance • Yards	Muzzle	25	50	75	100	125	150	175	200
Velocity • fps	1135	1084	1041	1005	973	945	920	896	874
Energy • Ft-lbs	329	300	277	258	242	228	216	205	195
Taylor KO Index	6.6	6.3	6.1	5.9	5.7	5.5	5.4	5.2	5.1
Mid-Range Trajectory Height • Inches	0.0	0.2	0.9	2.1	4.0	6.4	9.6	13.5	17.4
Drop • Inches	0.0	-0.9	-3.6	-8.3	-15.2	-24.3	-35.9	-50.0	-66.7

UMC Remington 115-grain Flat Nose Enclosed Base (Leadless) Metal Case (LL9MM11)

G1 Ballistic Coefficient = 0.155

Distance • Yards	Muzzle	25	50	75	100	125	150	175	200
Velocity • fps	1135	1084	1041	1004	973	944	919	895	873
Energy • Ft-lbs	329	300	277	258	242	228	216	205	195
Taylor KO Index	6.6	6.3	6.1	5.9	5.7	5.5	5.4	5.2	5.1
Mid-Range Trajectory Height • Inches	0.0	0.2	0.9	2.1	4.0	6.4	9.6	13.5	18.2
Drop • Inches	0.0	-0.9	-3.6	-8.3	-15.2	-24.3	-35.9	-50.0	-66.8

Norma 116-grain Soft point flat nose (19026) (Discontinued in 2004)

G1 Ballistic Coefficient = 0.120

Distance • Yards	Muzzle	25	50	75	100	125	150	175	200
Velocity • fps	1165	1094	1038	992	954	920	890	862	837
Energy • Ft-lbs	349	308	278	254	235	218	204	192	180
Taylor KO Index	6.9	6.4	6.1	5.8	5.6	5.4	5.3	5.1	4.9
Mid-Range Trajectory Height • Inches	0.0	0.2	0.9	2.1	4.0	6.5	9.8	13.9	18.8
Drop • Inches	0.0	-0.8	-3.5	-8.2	-15.0	-24.2	-36.0	-50.4	-67.7

Lapua 116-grain FMJ (4319200)

G1 Ballistic Coefficient = 0.117

Distance • Yards	Muzzle	25	50	75	100	125	150	175	200
Velocity • fps	1198	1118	1056	1006	964	929	897	868	841
Energy • Ft-lbs	300	322	287	261	240	222	207	194	182
Taylor KO Index	7.0	6.6	6.2	5.9	5.7	5.5	5.3	5.1	5.0
Mid-Range Trajectory Height • Inches	0.0	0.2	0.9	2.1	3.8	6.3	9.5	13.5	18.3
Drop • Inches	0.0	-0.8	-3.3	-7.8	-14.4	-23.3	-34.7	-48.7	-65.6

Lapua 120-grain CEPP SUPER (4319175)

G1 Ballistic Coefficient = 0.129

Distance • Yards	Muzzle	25	50	75	100	125	150	175	200
Velocity • fps	1181	1111	1055	1010	971	938	909	881	856
Energy • Ft-lbs	372	329	297	272	251	234	220	207	195
Taylor KO Index	7.2	6.8	6.4	6.1	5.9	5.7	5.5	5.4	5.2
Mid-Range Trajectory Height • Inches	0.0	0.2	0.9	2.1	3.9	6.3	9.5	13.4	18.1
Drop • Inches	0.0	-0.8	-3.4	-7.9	-14.6	-23.4	-34.7	-48.7	-65.4

Lapua 120-grain CEPP EXTRA Lead Free (4319178)

G1 Ballistic Coefficient = 0.129

Distance • Yards	Muzzle	25	50	75	100	125	150	175	200
Velocity • fps	1181	1111	1055	1010	971	938	909	881	856
Energy • Ft-lbs	372	329	297	272	251	234	220	207	195
Taylor KO Index	7.2	6.8	6.4	6.1	5.9	5.7	5.5	5.4	5.2
Mid-Range Trajectory Height • Inches	0.0	0.2	0.9	2.1	3.9	6.3	9.5	13.4	18.1
Drop • Inches	0.0	-0.8	-3.4	-7.9	-14.6	-23.4	-34.7	-48.7	-65.4

Lapua 123-grain HP Megashock (4319185)

G1 Ballistic Coefficient = 0.125

Distance • Yards	Muzzle	25	50	75	100	125	150	175	200
Velocity • fps	1165	1097	1042	997	959	926	897	870	845
Energy • Ft-lbs	371	328	297	272	251	235	220	207	195
Taylor KO Index	7.3	6.8	6.5	6.2	6.0	5.8	5.6	5.4	5.3
Mid-Range Trajectory Height • Inches	0.0	0.2	0.9	2.1	4.0	6.4	9.7	13.8	18.6
Drop • Inches	0.0	-0.8	-3.5	-8.1	-14.9	-24.1	-35.7	-50.0	-67.1

Lapua 123-grain FMJ (4319230)

G1 Ballistic Coefficient = 0.136

Distance • Yards	Muzzle	25	50	75	100	125	150	175	200
Velocity • fps	1312	1225	1151	1090	1040	999	964	933	905
Energy • Ft-lbs	470	410	362	324	296	278	254	238	224
Taylor KO Index	8.2	7.6	7.2	6.8	6.5	6.2	6.0	5.8	5.7
Mid-Range Trajectory Height • Inches	0.0	0.2	0.7	1.7	3.3	5.3	8.1	11.6	15.7
Drop • Inches	0.0	-0.7	-2.8	-6.5	-12.1	-19.6	-29.4	-41.3	-55.8

Fiocchi 123-grain FMJ Truncated (9APC)

G1 Ballistic Coefficient = 0.160

Distance • Yards	Muzzle	25	50	75	100	125	150	175	200
Velocity • fps	1250	1183	1125	1077	1036	1002	971	944	919
Energy • Ft-lbs	425	388	351	322	298	274	258	243	231
Taylor KO Index	7.8	7.4	7.1	6.7	6.5	6.3	6.1	5.9	5.7
Mid-Range Trajectory Height • Inches	0.0	0.2	0.8	1.8	3.4	5.5	8.3	11.87	15.9
Drop • Inches	0.0	-0.7	-3.0	-7.0	-12.8	-20.7	-30.7	-43.0	-57.7

Fiocchi 123-grain Metal Case (9APB)

G1 Ballistic Coefficient = 0.140

Distance • Yards	Muzzle	25	50	75	100	125	150	175	200
Velocity • fps	1250	1174	1110	1059	1016	979	948	919	893
Energy • Ft-lbs	425	376	337	306	282	262	245	231	218
Taylor KO Index	7.8	7.3	6.9	6.6	6.3	6.0	5.9	5.7	5.6
Mid-Range Trajectory Height • Inches	0.0	0.2	0.8	1.9	3.5	5.7	9.3	12.0	16.6
Drop • Inches	0.0	-0.7	-3.0	-7.1	-13.1	-21.2	-31.5	-44.2	-59.4

Lapua 123-grain FMJ Combat (4319163)

G1 Ballistic Coefficient = 0.136

Distance • Yards	Muzzle	25	50	75	100	125	150	175	200
Velocity • fps	1165	1102	1050	1007	971	939	911	885	861
Energy • Ft-lbs	371	331	301	277	258	241	227	214	202
Taylor KO Index	7.3	6.9	6.5	6.3	6.1	5.9	5.7	5.5	5.4
Mid-Range Trajectory Height • Inches	0.0	0.2	0.9	2.1	3.9	6.3	9.5	13.5	18.2
Drop • Inches	0.0	-0.8	-3.4	-8.0	-14.8	-23.8	-35.2	-49.2	-66.0

Norma 123-grain Security Cartridge (19027) (Discontinued in 2004)

G1 Ballistic Coefficient = 0.091

Distance • Yards	Muzzle	25	50	75	100	125	150	175	200
Velocity • fps	1165	1074	1007	955	910	873	839	807	778
Energy • Ft-lbs	372	315	278	249	227	208	192	178	165
Taylor KO Index	7.3	6.7	6.3	6.0	5.7	5.5	5.2	5.0	4.9
Mid-Range Trajectory Height • Inches	0.0	0.2	0.9	2.2	4.3	6.9	10.5	15.1	20.5
Drop • Inches	0.0	-0.8	-3.6	-8.4	-15.7	-25.4	-38.0	-53.6	-72.4

Norma 123-grain Full Jacket (19035)

G1 Ballistic Coefficient = 0.102

Distance • Yards	Muzzle	25	50	75	100	125	150	175	200
Velocity • fps	1099	1032	980	938	899	868	837	809	783
Energy • Ft-lbs	331	292	263	241	221	206	192	179	167
Taylor KO Index	6.9	6.5	6.1	5.9	5.6	5.4	5.2	5.1	4.9
Mid-Range Trajectory Height • Inches	0.0	0.2	1.0	2.4	4.5	7.4	11.1	15.8	21.4
Drop • Inches	0.0	-0.9	-3.9	-9.1	-16.8	-27.2	-45.4	-56.8	-76.5

Lapua 123-grain FMJ (4319177)

G1 Ballistic Coefficient = 0.134

Distance • Yards	Muzzle	25	50	75	100	125	150	175	200
Velocity • fps	1050	1007	970	938	909	883	859	836	814
Energy • Ft-lbs	301	277	257	240	226	213	201	191	181
Taylor KO Index	6.5	6.3	6.1	5.9	5.7	5.5	5.4	5.2	5.1
Mid-Range Trajectory Height • Inches	0.0	0.2	1.1	2.5	4.6	7.4	11.0	15.5	20.9
Drop • Inches	0.0	-1.0	-4.2	-9.6	-17.6	-28.1	-41.4	-57.6	-76.9

Sellier & Bellot 124-grain SP (SBA00906)

G1 Ballistic Coefficient = 0.079

Distance • Yards	Muzzle	25	50	75	100	125	150	175	200
Velocity • fps	1165	1074	991	935	888	847	810	777	745
Energy • Ft-lbs	372	316	269	241	217	198	181	166	153
Taylor KO Index	7.3	6.8	6.2	5.9	5.6	5.3	5.1	4.9	4.7
Mid-Range Trajectory Height • Inches	0.0	0.2	1.0	2.3	4.4	7.3	11.2	16.1	22.1
Drop • Inches	0.0	-0.9	-3.6	-8.6	-16.1	-26.3	-39.5	-56.1	-76.3

Sellier & Bellot 124-grain LRN (SBA00903)

G1 Ballistic Coefficient = 0.086

Distance • Yards	Muzzle	25	50	75	100	125	150	175	200
Velocity • fps	1148	1067	992	940	896	857	823	791	761
Energy • Ft-lbs	361	312	269	243	221	202	186	172	159
Taylor KO Index	7.2	6.7	6.3	5.9	5.7	5.4	5.2	5.0	4.8
Mid-Range Trajectory Height • Inches	0.0	0.2	1.0	2.3	4.4	7.3	11.1	15.9	21.7
Drop • Inches	0.0	-0.9	-3.7	-8.7	-16.2	-26.4	-39.5	-55.8	-75.6

Magtech 124-grain JSP (9S)

G1 Ballistic Coefficient = 0.173

Distance • Yards	Muzzle	25	50	75	100	125	150	175	200
Velocity • fps	1109	1067	1030	999	971	946	923	901	881
Energy • Ft-lbs	339	313	292	275	259	246	234	224	214
Taylor KO Index	7.0	6.7	6.5	6.3	6.1	6.0	5.8	5.7	5.6
Mid-Range Trajectory Height • Inches	0.0	0.2	1.0	2.2	4.1	6.6	9.8	13.7	18.4
Drop • Inches	0.0	-0.9	-3.7	-8.6	-15.6	-25.0	-36.7	-51.0	-68.0

Magtech 124-grain LRN (9E)

G1 Ballistic Coefficient = 0.188

Distance • Yards	Muzzle	25	50	75	100	125	150	175	200
Velocity • fps	1095	1058	1030	997	971	948	926	906	888
Energy • Ft-lbs	339	308	292	274	259	247	236	226	217
Taylor KO Index	6.9	6.7	6.5	6.3	6.1	6.0	5.8	5.7	5.6
Mid-Range Trajectory Height • Inches	0.0	0.2	1.0	2.3	4.1	6.6	9.8	13.8	18.4
Drop • Inches	0.0	-0.9	-3.8	-8.7	-15.8	-25.3	-37.1	-51.5	-68.5

PMC 124-grain LRN (9E)

G1 Ballistic Coefficient = 0.132

Distance • Yards	Muzzle	25	50	75	100	125	150	175	200
Velocity • fps	1050	1006	969	937	908	881	857	834	812
Energy • Ft-lbs	304	279	259	242	227	214	202	191	182
Taylor KO Index	6.6	6.3	6.1	5.9	5.7	5.6	5.4	5.3	5.1
Mid-Range Trajectory Height • Inches	0.0	0.3	1.1	2.5	4.6	7.5	11.1	15.7	21.1
Drop • Inches	0.0	-1.0	-4.2	-9.6	-17.6	-28.2	-41.5	-57.9	-77.3

Black Hills 124-grain Jacketed Hollow Point +P (M9N9)

G1 Ballistic Coefficient = 0.180

Distance • Yards	Muzzle	25	50	75	100	125	150	175	200
Velocity • fps	1250	1190	1137	1092	1054	1020	991	965	941
Energy • Ft-lbs	430	390	356	328	306	287	271	256	244
Taylor KO Index	7.9	7.5	7.2	6.9	6.6	6.4	6.2	6.1	5.9
Mid-Range Trajectory Height • Inches	0.0	0.2	0.8	1.8	3.4	5.4	8.2	11.5	15.5
Drop • Inches	0.0	-0.7	-3.0	-6.9	-12.6	-20.4	-30.1	-42.1	-56.3

Speer 124-grain Gold Dot +P (23619)

G1 Ballistic Coefficient = 0.135

Distance • Yards	Muzzle	25	50	75	100	125	150	175	200
Velocity • fps	1220	1146	1085	1037	996	962	931	903	877
Energy • Ft-lbs	410	362	324	296	273	255	239	224	212
Taylor KO Index	7.7	7.2	6.8	6.5	6.3	6.1	5.9	5.7	5.5
Mid-Range Trajectory Height • Inches	0.0	0.2	0.8	2.0	3.7	6.0	9.1	12.9	17.4
Drop • Inches	0.0	-0.8	-3.2	-7.4	-13.7	-22.2	-33.0	-46.3	-62.3

Remington 124-grain Brass Jacketed Hollow Point +P (GS9MMD)

G1 Ballistic Coefficient = 0.190

Distance • Yards	Muzzle	25	50	75	100	125	150	175	200
Velocity • fps	1180	1131	1089	1053	1021	994	968	946	924
Energy • Ft-lbs	384	352	327	305	287	272	258	246	235
Taylor KO Index	7.4	7.1	6.8	6.6	6.4	6.3	6.1	6.0	5.8
Mid-Range Trajectory Height • Inches	0.0	0.2	0.8	2.0	3.8	5.8	8.7	12.3	16.5
Drop • Inches	0.0	-0.8	-3.3	-7.6	-13.9	-22.3	-32.8	-45.6	-60.9

Black Hills 124-grain Jacketed Hollow Point (M9N3)

G1 Ballistic Coefficient = 0.180

Distance • Yards	Muzzle	25	50	75	100	125	150	175	200
Velocity • fps	1150	1103	1063	1028	998	971	947	925	904
Energy • Ft-lbs	363	335	311	291	274	260	247	235	225
Taylor KO Index	7.2	6.9	6.7	6.5	6.3	6.1	5.9	5.8	5.7
Mid-Range Trajectory Height • Inches	0.0	0.2	0.9	2.1	3.8	6.1	9.2	12.9	17.3
Drop • Inches	0.0	-0.8	-3.5	-8.0	-14.6	-23.4	-34.4	-47.9	-63.9

Speer 124-grain Gold Dot (23618)

G1 Ballistic Coefficient = 0.135

Distance • Yards	Muzzle	25	50	75	100	125	150	175	200
Velocity • fps	1150	1089	1039	999	963	932	904	879	855
Energy • Ft-lbs	364	327	297	275	255	239	225	213	201
Taylor KO Index	7.3	6.9	6.6	6.3	6.1	5.9	5.7	5.5	5.4
Mid-Range Trajectory Height • Inches	0.0	0.2	0.9	2.2	4.0	6.5	9.8	13.8	18.7
Drop • Inches	0.0	-0.8	-3.5	-8.2	-15.1	-24.3	-36.0	-50.4	-67.6

Remington 124-grain Brass Jacketed Hollow Point (GS9MMB)

G1 Ballistic Coefficient = 0.150

Distance • Yards	Muzzle	25	50	75	100	125	150	175	200
Velocity • fps	1125	1074	1031	995	963	935	910	886	864
Energy • Ft-lbs	349	318	293	273	255	241	228	216	206
Taylor KO Index	7.1	6.8	6.5	6.3	6.1	5.9	5.7	5.6	5.4
Mid-Range Trajectory Height • Inches	0.0	0.2	1.0	2.2	4.0	6.5	9.8	13.8	18.5
Drop • Inches	0.0	-0.9	-3.7	-8.5	-15.5	-24.8	-36.6	-50.9	-68.0

Federal 124-grain Hydra-Shok JHP (P9HS1)

G1 Ballistic Coefficient = 0.149

Distance • Yards	Muzzle	25	50	75	100	125	150	175	200
Velocity • fps	1120	1070	1030	990	960	932	906	883	961
Energy • Ft-lbs	345	315	290	270	255	239	226	215	204
Taylor KO Index	7.0	6.7	6.5	6.2	6.0	5.9	5.7	5.6	5.4
Mid-Range Trajectory Height • Inches	0.0	0.2	0.9	2.2	4.1	6.6	9.8	13.9	18.7
Drop • Inches	0.0	-0.9	-3.7	-8.5	-15.6	-25.0	-36.8	-51.3	-68.6

Federal 124-grain Nyclad Hollow Point (P9BP) (Discontinued in 2004)

G1 Ballistic Coefficient = 0.149

Distance • Yards	Muzzle	25	50	75	100	125	150	175	200
Velocity • fps	1120	1070	1030	990	960	932	906	883	961
Energy • Ft-lbs	345	315	290	270	255	239	226	215	204
Taylor KO Index	7.0	6.7	6.5	6.2	6.0	5.9	5.7	5.6	5.4
Mid-Range Trajectory Height • Inches	0.0	0.2	0.9	2.2	4.1	6.6	9.8	13.9	18.7
Drop • Inches	0.0	-0.9	-3.7	-8.5	-15.6	-25.0	-36.8	-51.3	-68.6

Remington 124-grain Jacketed Hollow Point (R9MM10) (Discontinued in 2004)

G1 Ballistic Coefficient = 0.149

Distance • Yards	Muzzle	25	50	75	100	125	150	175	200
Velocity • fps	1120	1070	1030	990	960	932	906	883	961
Energy • Ft-lbs	345	315	290	270	255	239	226	215	204
Taylor KO Index	7.0	6.7	6.5	6.2	6.0	5.9	5.7	5.6	5.4
Mid-Range Trajectory Height • Inches	0.0	0.2	0.9	2.2	4.1	6.6	9.8	13.9	18.7
Drop • Inches	0.0	-0.9	-3.7	-8.5	-15.6	-25.0	-36.8	-51.3	-68.6

Hornady 124-grain JHP/XTP (90242)

G1 Ballistic Coefficient = 0.173

Distance • Yards	Muzzle	25	50	75	100	125	150	175	200
Velocity • fps	1110	1067	1030	999	971	946	923	901	881
Energy • Ft-lbs	339	314	292	275	260	246	235	224	214
Taylor KO Index	7.0	6.7	6.5	6.3	6.1	6.0	5.8	5.7	5.6
Mid-Range Trajectory Height • Inches	0.0	0.2	1.0	2.2	4.1	6.5	9.7	13.6	18.3
Drop • Inches	0.0	-0.9	-3.7	-8.6	-15.6	-24.9	-36.6	-50.9	-67.8

Magtech 124-grain JHP (GG9B)

G1 Ballistic Coefficient = 0.165

Distance • Yards	Muzzle	25	50	75	100	125	150	175	200
Velocity • fps	1096	1054	1017	986	958	933	910	888	868
Energy • Ft-lbs	331	306	285	268	253	240	228	217	208
Taylor KO Index	6.9	6.6	6.4	6.2	6.0	5.9	5.7	5.6	5.5
Mid-Range Trajectory Height • Inches	0.0	0.2	1.0	2.3	4.2	6.8	10.0	14.1	18.9
Drop • Inches	0.0	-0.9	-3.9	-8.8	-16.0	-25.6	-37.7	-52.4	-69.8

PMC 124-grain Starfire Hollow Point (9SFB)
G1 Ballistic Coefficient = 0.143

Distance • Yards	Muzzle	25	50	75	100	125	150	175	200
Velocity • fps	1090	1043	1003	969	939	912	887	864	842
Energy • Ft-lbs	327	299	277	259	243	229	217	206	195
Taylor KO Index	6.9	6.6	6.3	6.1	5.9	5.8	5.6	5.4	5.3
Mid-Range Trajectory Height • Inches	0.0	0.2	1.0	2.3	4.3	6.9	10.3	14.5	19.5
Drop • Inches	0.0	-0.9	-3.9	-9.0	-16.4	-26.2	-38.7	-53.8	-71.9

Sellier & Bellot 124-grain FMJ (SBA00905)
G1 Ballistic Coefficient = 0.080

Distance • Yards	Muzzle	25	50	75	100	125	150	175	200
Velocity • fps	1181	1087	1001	944	896	855	818	784	752
Energy • Ft-lbs	382	324	275	245	221	201	184	169	156
Taylor KO Index	7.4	6.9	6.3	6.0	5.7	5.4	5.2	4.9	4.7
Mid-Range Trajectory Height • Inches	0.0	0.2	0.9	2.3	4.3	7.2	11.0	15.8	21.7
Drop • Inches	0.0	-0.8	-3.5	-8.4	-15.7	-25.7	-38.7	-55.0	-74.7

USA (Winchester) 124-grain FMJ (USA9MM)
G1 Ballistic Coefficient = 0.167

Distance • Yards	Muzzle	25	50	75	100	125	150	175	200
Velocity • fps	1140	1091	1050	1015	984	957	932	821	802
Energy • Ft-lbs	311	291	275	258	244	232	220	210	200
Taylor KO Index	7.2	6.9	6.6	6.4	6.2	6.0	5.9	5.7	5.6
Mid-Range Trajectory Height • Inches	0.0	0.2	0.9	2.1	3.9	6.3	9.4	13.2	17.8
Drop • Inches	0.0	-0.9	-3.5	-8.2	-15.0	-23.9	-35.3	-49.1	-65.5

USA (Winchester) 124-grain Brass Enclosed Base (WC92)
G1 Ballistic Coefficient = 0.182

Distance • Yards	Muzzle	25	50	75	100	125	150	175	200
Velocity • fps	1130	1087	1049	1017	988	963	939	918	898
Energy • Ft-lbs	352	325	303	285	269	255	243	232	222
Taylor KO Index	7.1	6.9	6.6	6.4	6.2	6.1	5.9	5.8	5.7
Mid-Range Trajectory Height • Inches	0.0	0.2	0.9	2.1	3.9	6.4	9.4	13.3	17.8
Drop • Inches	0.0	-0.9	-3.6	-8.3	-15.1	-24.1	-35.4	-49.2	-65.6

Federal 124-grain Full Metal Jacket (C9AP) (Discontinued in 2004)
G1 Ballistic Coefficient = 0.149

Distance • Yards	Muzzle	25	50	75	100	125	150	175	200
Velocity • fps	1120	1070	1030	990	960	932	906	883	861
Energy • Ft-lbs	345	315	290	270	255	239	226	215	204
Taylor KO Index	7.0	6.7	6.5	6.2	6.0	5.9	5.7	5.6	5.4
Mid-Range Trajectory Height • Inches	0.0	0.2	0.9	2.2	4.1	6.6	9.8	13.9	18.7
Drop • Inches	0.0	-0.9	-3.7	-8.5	-15.6	-25.0	-36.8	-51.3	-68.6

Federal 124-grain Full Metal Jacket (P9CSP1) (Discontinued in 2004)
G1 Ballistic Coefficient = 0.149

Distance • Yards	Muzzle	25	50	75	100	125	150	175	200
Velocity • fps	1120	1070	1030	990	960	932	906	883	861
Energy • Ft-lbs	345	315	290	270	255	239	226	215	204
Taylor KO Index	7.0	6.7	6.5	6.2	6.0	5.9	5.7	5.6	5.4
Mid-Range Trajectory Height • Inches	0.0	0.2	0.9	2.2	4.1	6.6	9.8	13.9	18.7
Drop • Inches	0.0	-0.9	-3.7	-8.5	-15.6	-25.0	-36.8	-51.3	-68.6

Federal 124-grain Truncated FMJ Match (GM9MP) (Discontinued in 2004)
G1 Ballistic Coefficient = 0.149

Distance • Yards	Muzzle	25	50	75	100	125	150	175	200
Velocity • fps	1120	1070	1030	990	960	932	906	883	961
Energy • Ft-lbs	345	315	290	270	255	239	226	215	204
Taylor KO Index	7.0	6.7	6.5	6.2	6.0	5.9	5.7	5.6	5.4
Mid-Range Trajectory Height • Inches	0.0	0.2	0.9	2.2	4.1	6.6	9.8	13.9	18.7
Drop • Inches	0.0	-0.9	-3.7	-8.5	-15.6	-25.0	-36.8	-51.3	-68.6

American Eagle (Federal) 124-grain Full Metal Jacket (AE9AP & AE9N1)
G1 Ballistic Coefficient = 0.149

Distance • Yards	Muzzle	25	50	75	100	125	150	175	200
Velocity • fps	1120	1070	1030	990	960	932	906	883	961
Energy • Ft-lbs	345	315	290	270	255	239	226	215	204
Taylor KO Index	7.0	6.7	6.5	6.2	6.0	5.9	5.7	5.6	5.4
Mid-Range Trajectory Height • Inches	0.0	0.2	0.9	2.2	4.1	6.6	9.8	13.9	18.7
Drop • Inches	0.0	-0.9	-3.7	-8.5	-15.6	-25.0	-36.8	-51.3	-68.6

Aguila 124-grain Jacketed

G1 Ballistic Coefficient = 0.168

Distance • Yards	Muzzle	25	50	75	100	125	150	175	200
Velocity • fps	1115	1071	1033	1000	971	945	922	900	879
Energy • Ft-lbs	342	316	294	275	260	246	234	223	213
Taylor KO Index	7.0	6.8	6.5	6.3	6.1	6.0	5.8	5.7	5.5
Mid-Range Trajectory Height • Inches	0.0	0.2	1.0	2.2	4.1	6.6	9.8	13.7	18.4
Drop • Inches	0.0	-0.9	-3.7	-8.5	-15.5	-24.8	-36.6	-50.8	-67.8

PMC 124-grain Full Metal Jacket (9G)

G1 Ballistic Coefficient = 0.142

Distance • Yards	Muzzle	25	50	75	100	125	150	175	200
Velocity • fps	1110	1059	1017	980	949	921	895	871	849
Energy • Ft-lbs	339	309	285	265	248	234	221	209	199
Taylor KO Index	7.0	6.7	6.4	6.2	6.0	5.8	5.6	5.5	5.4
Mid-Range Trajectory Height • Inches	0.0	0.2	1.0	2.3	4.2	6.8	10.1	14.3	19.3
Drop • Inches	0.0	-0.9	-3.8	-8.7	-15.9	-25.5	-37.7	-52.6	-70.3

Remington 124-grain Metal Case (R9MM2)

G1 Ballistic Coefficient = 0.173

Distance • Yards	Muzzle	25	50	75	100	125	150	175	200
Velocity • fps	1110	1067	1030	999	971	946	923	901	881
Energy • Ft-lbs	339	314	292	275	260	246	235	224	214
Taylor KO Index	7.0	6.7	6.5	6.3	6.1	6.0	5.8	5.7	5.6
Mid-Range Trajectory Height • Inches	0.0	0.2	1.0	2.2	4.1	6.5	9.7	13.6	18.3
Drop • Inches	0.0	-0.9	-3.7	-8.6	-15.6	-24.9	-36.6	-50.9	-67.8

Magtech 124-grain TMJ Clean-Range (9J) (Discontinued in 2004)

G1 Ballistic Coefficient = 0.174

Distance • Yards	Muzzle	25	50	75	100	125	150	175	200
Velocity • fps	1109	1067	1030	999	971	946	923	901	881
Energy • Ft-lbs	339	314	292	275	260	246	235	224	214
Taylor KO Index	7.0	6.7	6.5	6.3	6.1	6.0	5.8	5.7	5.6
Mid-Range Trajectory Height • Inches	0.0	0.2	1.0	2.2	4.1	6.5	9.7	13.6	18.3
Drop • Inches	0.0	-0.9	-3.7	-8.6	-15.6	-24.9	-36.6	-50.9	-67.8

Magtech 124-grain FMC (9B)

G1 Ballistic Coefficient = 0.174

Distance • Yards	Muzzle	25	50	75	100	125	150	175	200
Velocity • fps	1109	1067	1030	999	971	946	923	901	881
Energy • Ft-lbs	339	314	292	275	260	246	235	224	214
Taylor KO Index	7.0	6.7	6.5	6.3	6.1	6.0	5.8	5.7	5.6
Mid-Range Trajectory Height • Inches	0.0	0.2	1.0	2.2	4.1	6.5	9.7	13.6	18.3
Drop • Inches	0.0	-0.9	-3.7	-8.6	-15.6	-24.9	-36.6	-50.9	-67.8

UMC (Remington) 124-grain Metal Case (L9MM2)

G1 Ballistic Coefficient = 0.183

Distance • Yards	Muzzle	25	50	75	100	125	150	175	200
Velocity • fps	1100	1061	1030	998	971	947	925	905	886
Energy • Ft-lbs	339	310	292	274	259	247	236	225	216
Taylor KO Index	6.9	6.7	6.5	6.3	6.1	6.0	5.8	5.7	5.6
Mid-Range Trajectory Height • Inches	0.0	0.2	1.0	2.2	4.1	6.6	9.7	13.7	18.3
Drop • Inches	0.0	-0.9	-3.8	-8.7	-15.8	25.1	36.9	-51.2	-68.2

UMC (Remington) 124-grain Flat Nose Enclosed Base (Leadless) Metal Case (LL9MM2)

G1 Ballistic Coefficient = 0.183

Distance • Yards	Muzzle	25	50	75	100	125	150	175	200
Velocity • fps	1109	1061	1030	998	971	947	925	905	886
Energy • Ft-lbs	339	310	292	274	252	247	236	226	216
Taylor KO Index	6.9	6.7	6.5	6.3	6.1	6.0	5.8	5.7	5.6
Mid-Range Trajectory Height • Inches	0.0	0.2	1.0	2.3	4.1	6.6	9.8	13.7	18.4
Drop • Inches	0.0	-0.9	-3.8	-8.7	-15.8	-25.2	-37.0	-51.3	-68.3

CCI 124-grain Clean-Fire—TMJ Blazer (3460)

G1 Ballistic Coefficient = 0.165

Distance • Yards	Muzzle	25	50	75	100	125	150	175	200
Velocity • fps	1090	1049	1014	982	955	930	907	886	866
Energy • Ft-lbs	327	303	283	266	251	238	227	216	206
Taylor KO Index	6.9	6.6	6.4	6.2	6.0	5.9	5.7	5.6	5.5
Mid-Range Trajectory Height • Inches	0.0	0.2	1.0	2.3	4.2	6.8	10.1	14.2	19.0
Drop • Inches	0.0	-0.9	-3.8	-8.9	-16.2	-25.8	-38.0	-52.8	-70.4

CCI 124-grain FMJ Blazer (3578)

G1 Ballistic Coefficient = 0.165

Distance • Yards	Muzzle	25	50	75	100	125	150	175	200
Velocity • fps	1090	1049	1014	982	955	930	907	886	866
Energy • Ft-lbs	327	303	283	266	251	238	227	216	206
Taylor KO Index	6.9	6.6	6.4	6.2	6.0	5.9	5.7	5.6	5.5
Mid-Range Trajectory Height • Inches	0.0	0.2	1.0	2.3	4.2	6.8	10.1	14.2	19.0
Drop • Inches	0.0	-0.9	-3.8	-8.9	-16.2	-25.8	-38.0	-52.8	-70.4

CCI 124-grain Clean-Fire—Totally Metal Jacket (53824)

G1 Ballistic Coefficient = 0.165

Distance • Yards	Muzzle	25	50	75	100	125	150	175	200
Velocity • fps	1090	1049	1014	982	955	930	907	886	866
Energy • Ft-lbs	327	303	283	266	251	238	227	216	206
Taylor KO Index	6.9	6.6	6.4	6.2	6.0	5.9	5.7	5.6	5.5
Mid-Range Trajectory Height • Inches	0.0	0.2	1.0	2.3	4.2	6.8	10.1	14.2	19.0
Drop • Inches	0.0	-0.9	-3.8	-8.9	-16.2	-25.8	-38.0	-52.8	-70.4

CCI 124-grain FMJ Lawman (53616)

G1 Ballistic Coefficient = 0.165

Distance • Yards	Muzzle	25	50	75	100	125	150	175	200
Velocity • fps	1090	1049	1014	982	955	930	907	886	866
Energy • Ft-lbs	327	303	283	266	251	238	227	216	206
Taylor KO Index	6.9	6.6	6.4	6.2	6.0	5.9	5.7	5.6	5.5
Mid-Range Trajectory Height • Inches	0.0	0.2	1.0	2.3	4.2	6.8	10.1	14.2	19.0
Drop • Inches	0.0	-0.9	-3.8	-8.9	-16.2	-25.8	-38.0	-52.8	-70.4

Cor-Bon 125-grain JHP +P (SD09125/20)

G1 Ballistic Coefficient = 0.140

Distance • Yards	Muzzle	25	50	75	100	125	150	175	200
Velocity • fps	1250	1174	1110	1058	1016	979	947	919	893
Energy • Ft-lbs	434	383	342	311	286	266	249	234	221
Taylor KO Index	7.9	7.5	7.1	6.7	6.5	6.2	6.0	5.8	5.7
Mid-Range Trajectory Height • Inches	0.0	0.1	0.7	1.8	3.5	5.7	8.6	12.3	16.7
Drop • Inches	0.0	-0.7	-3.0	-7.1	-13.1	-21.2	-31.6	-44.4	-59.7

Federal 135-grain Hydra-Shok JHP (PD9HS5)

G1 Ballistic Coefficient = 0.268

Distance • Yards	Muzzle	25	50	75	100	125	150	175	200
Velocity • fps	1050	1030	1010	980	970	954	938	923	909
Energy • Ft-lbs	330	315	300	290	280	273	264	256	248
Taylor KO Index	7.2	7.1	6.9	6.7	6.6	6.5	6.4	6.3	6.2
Mid-Range Trajectory Height • Inches	0.0	0.4	1.2	2.4	4.3	6.8	10.0	13.8	18.4
Drop • Inches	0.0	-1.0	-4.1	-9.3	-16.7	-26.4	-38.5	-53.1	-70.2

Sellier & Bellot 140-grain FMJ—Subsonic (SBA00907) (Discontinued in 2005)

G1 Ballistic Coefficient = 0.144

Distance • Yards	Muzzle	25	50	75	100	125	150	175	200
Velocity • fps	1001	968	938	911	886	863	842	821	802
Energy • Ft-lbs	311	291	275	258	244	232	220	210	200
Taylor KO Index	7.1	6.9	6.7	6.5	6.3	6.1	6.0	5.8	5.7
Mid-Range Trajectory Height • Inches	0.0	0.2	1.1	2.6	4.9	7.9	11.7	16.4	22.0
Drop • Inches	0.0	-1.1	-4.5	-10.4	-18.9	-30.2	-44.4	-61.6	-82.0

Winchester 147-grain Silvertip Hollow Point (X9MMST147)

G1 Ballistic Coefficient = 0.201

Distance • Yards	Muzzle	25	50	75	100	125	150	175	200
Velocity • fps	1010	985	962	940	921	902	885	869	853
Energy • Ft-lbs	333	317	302	289	277	266	256	246	237
Taylor KO Index	7.5	7.3	7.2	7.0	6.9	6.7	6.6	6.5	6.4
Mid-Range Trajectory Height • Inches	0.0	0.3	1.1	2.6	4.7	7.4	11.0	15.3	20.4
Drop • Inches	0.0	-1.1	-4.4	-10.1	-18.2	-28.9	-42.2	-58.3	-77.3

Federal 147-grain Hydra-Shok JHP (P9HS2)

G1 Ballistic Coefficient = 0.113

Distance • Yards	Muzzle	25	50	75	100	125	150	175	200
Velocity • fps	1000	960	920	890	860	833	808	784	762
Energy • Ft-lbs	325	300	275	260	240	227	213	201	189
Taylor KO Index	7.5	7.2	6.9	6.6	6.4	6.2	6.0	5.9	5.7
Mid-Range Trajectory Height • Inches	0.0	0.3	1.2	2.8	5.1	8.2	12.3	17.3	23.4
Drop • Inches	0.0	-1.1	-4.6	-10.6	-19.4	-31.1	-45.9	-64.0	-85.6

Magtech 147-grain JHP Subsonic (9K)

G1 Ballistic Coefficient = 0.204

Distance • Yards	Muzzle	25	50	75	100	125	150	175	200
Velocity • fps	990	967	945	926	907	890	873	858	843
Energy • Ft-lbs	320	305	292	280	268	259	249	240	232
Taylor KO Index	7.4	7.2	7.0	6.9	6.8	6.7	6.5	6.4	6.3
Mid-Range Trajectory Height • Inches	0.0	0.3	1.2	2.7	4.8	7.7	11.3	15.8	21.0
Drop • Inches	0.0	-1.1	-4.6	-10.5	-18.9	-29.9	-43.7	-60.3	-79.9

Remington 147-grain Jacketed Hollow Point (Subsonic) (R9MM8)

G1 Ballistic Coefficient = 0.184

Distance • Yards	Muzzle	25	50	75	100	125	150	175	200
Velocity • fps	990	964	941	920	900	881	863	846	830
Energy • Ft-lbs	320	304	289	276	264	253	243	234	225
Taylor KO Index	7.4	7.2	7.0	6.9	6.7	6.6	6.5	6.3	6.2
Mid-Range Trajectory Height • Inches	0.0	0.3	1.1	2.7	4.9	7.8	11.5	16.0	21.9
Drop • Inches	0.0	-1.1	-4.6	-10.5	-19.0	-30.1	-44.1	-61.0	-80.8

Remington 147-grain Brass Jacketed Hollow Point (GS9MMC)

G1 Ballistic Coefficient = 0.184

Distance • Yards	Muzzle	25	50	75	100	125	150	175	200
Velocity • fps	990	964	941	920	900	881	863	846	830
Energy • Ft-lbs	320	304	289	276	264	253	243	234	225
Taylor KO Index	7.4	7.2	7.0	6.9	6.7	6.6	6.5	6.3	6.2
Mid-Range Trajectory Height • Inches	0.0	0.3	1.1	2.7	4.9	7.8	11.5	16.0	21.9
Drop • Inches	0.0	-1.1	-4.6	-10.5	-19.0	-30.1	-44.1	-61.0	-80.8

Winchester 147-grain SXT (S9)

G1 Ballistic Coefficient = 0.210

Distance • Yards	Muzzle	25	50	75	100	125	150	175	200
Velocity • fps	990	967	947	927	909	892	876	861	846
Energy • Ft-lbs	320	306	293	281	270	260	251	242	234
Taylor KO Index	7.4	7.2	7.1	6.9	6.8	6.7	6.5	6.4	6.3
Mid-Range Trajectory Height • Inches	0.0	0.3	1.2	2.7	4.8	7.7	11.3	15.7	20.9
Drop • Inches	0.0	-1.1	-4.6	-10.4	-18.8	-29.8	-43.6	-60.1	-79.6

USA (Winchester) 147-grain Jacketed Hollow Point (USA9JHP2)

G1 Ballistic Coefficient = 0.200

Distance • Yards	Muzzle	25	50	75	100	125	150	175	200
Velocity • fps	990	966	945	925	906	888	872	856	840
Energy • Ft-lbs	320	305	291	279	268	258	248	239	231
Taylor KO Index	7.4	7.2	7.1	6.9	6.8	6.6	6.5	6.4	6.3
Mid-Range Trajectory Height • Inches	0.0	0.3	1.2	2.7	4.9	7.8	11.4	15.9	21.2
Drop • Inches	0.0	-1.1	-4.6	-10.5	-18.9	-30.0	-43.8	-60.5	-80.1

USA (Winchester) 147-grain Jacketed Hollow Point (WC93)

G1 Ballistic Coefficient = 0.200

Distance • Yards	Muzzle	25	50	75	100	125	150	175	200
Velocity • fps	990	966	945	925	906	888	872	856	840
Energy • Ft-lbs	320	305	291	279	268	258	248	239	231
Taylor KO Index	7.4	7.2	7.1	6.9	6.8	6.6	6.5	6.4	6.3
Mid-Range Trajectory Height • Inches	0.0	0.3	1.2	2.7	4.9	7.8	11.4	15.9	21.2
Drop • Inches	0.0	-1.1	-4.6	-10.5	-18.9	-30.0	-43.8	-60.5	-80.1

Speer 147-grain Gold Dot (23619)

G1 Ballistic Coefficient = 0.165

Distance • Yards	Muzzle	25	50	75	100	125	150	175	200
Velocity • fps	985	957	932	909	887	867	848	830	813
Energy • Ft-lbs	317	299	283	270	257	246	235	225	216
Taylor KO Index	7.4	7.2	7.0	6.8	6.6	6.5	6.3	6.2	6.1
Mid-Range Trajectory Height • Inches	0.0	0.3	1.2	2.7	5.0	8.0	11.8	16.5	22.1
Drop • Inches	0.0	-1.1	-4.6	-10.7	-19.3	-30.7	-45.0	-62.3	-82.7

Federal 147-grain Hydra-Shok JHP (C9MS)

G1 Ballistic Coefficient = 0.158

Distance • Yards	Muzzle	25	50	75	100	125	150	175	200
Velocity • fps	980	950	930	900	880	860	840	822	804
Energy • Ft-lbs	310	295	285	265	255	241	230	220	211
Taylor KO Index	7.3	7.1	6.9	6.7	6.6	6.4	6.3	6.1	6.0
Mid-Range Trajectory Height • Inches	0.0	0.3	1.2	2.8	5.1	8.1	12.0	16.7	22.3
Drop • Inches	0.0	-1.2	-4.7	-10.8	-19.6	-31.1	-45.6	-63.1	-83.9

Black Hills 147-grain Jacketed Hollow Point Subsonic (M9N5)

G1 Ballistic Coefficient = 0.275

Distance • Yards	Muzzle	25	50	75	100	125	150	175	200
Velocity • fps	975	959	943	928	914	901	889	876	864
Energy • Ft-lbs	309	300	290	281	273	265	258	251	244
Taylor KO Index	7.3	7.1	7.0	6.9	6.8	6.7	6.6	6.5	6.4
Mid-Range Trajectory Height • Inches	0.0	0.3	1.2	2.7	4.9	7.7	11.3	15.6	20.7
Drop • Inches	0.0	-1.2	-4.7	-10.6	-19.1	-30.2	-43.9	-60.4	-79.7

Fiocchi 147-grain Jacketed Hollowpoint (9APDHP)

G1 Ballistic Coefficient = 0.200

Distance • Yards	Muzzle	25	50	75	100	125	150	175	200
Velocity • fps	975	953	932	913	895	878	861	846	831
Energy • Ft-lbs	310	296	284	272	261	252	242	234	225
Taylor KO Index	7.3	7.1	6.9	6.8	6.7	6.6	6.4	6.3	6.2
Mid-Range Trajectory Height • Inches	0.0	0.3	1.2	2.7	5.0	7.9	11.7	16.2	21.6
Drop • Inches	0.0	-1.2	-4.7	-10.8	-19.4	-30.8	-45.0	-62.1	-82.2

Hornady 147-grain JHP/XTP (90282)

G1 Ballistic Coefficient = 0.214

Distance • Yards	Muzzle	25	50	75	100	125	150	175	200
Velocity • fps	975	954	935	916	899	883	868	853	839
Energy • Ft-lbs	310	297	285	274	264	255	246	238	230
Taylor KO Index	7.3	7.1	6.9	6.8	6.7	6.6	6.5	6.4	6.3
Mid-Range Trajectory Height • Inches	0.0	0.3	1.2	2.7	5.0	7.9	11.6	16.1	21.4
Drop • Inches	0.0	-1.2	-4.7	-10.7	-19.4	-30.6	-44.7	-61.7	-81.6

Fiocchi 147-grain Metal Case (9APD)

G1 Ballistic Coefficient = 0.200

Distance • Yards	Muzzle	25	50	75	100	125	150	175	200
Velocity • fps	1050	976	953	933	913	895	878	862	846
Energy • Ft-lbs	326	311	297	284	272	262	252	243	234
Taylor KO Index	7.8	7.3	7.1	7.0	6.8	6.7	6.6	6.4	6.3
Mid-Range Trajectory Height • Inches	0.0	0.3	1.1	2.6	4.8	7.6	11.2	15.6	20.8
Drop • Inches	0.0	-1.1	-4.5	-10.3	-18.5	-29.4	-43.0	-59.4	-78.7

Magtech 147-grain FMC-FLAT (Subsonic) (9G)

G1 Ballistic Coefficient = 0.204

Distance • Yards	Muzzle	25	50	75	100	125	150	175	200
Velocity • fps	990	967	945	926	907	890	873	858	843
Energy • Ft-lbs	320	305	292	280	268	259	249	240	232
Taylor KO Index	7.4	7.2	7.0	6.9	6.8	6.7	6.5	6.4	6.3
Mid-Range Trajectory Height • Inches	0.0	0.3	1.2	2.7	4.8	7.7	11.3	15.8	21.0
Drop • Inches	0.0	-1.1	-4.6	-10.5	-18.9	-29.9	-43.7	-60.3	-79.9

UMC (Remington) 147-grain Metal Case (Match) (L9MM9)

G1 Ballistic Coefficient = 0.184

Distance • Yards	Muzzle	25	50	75	100	125	150	175	200
Velocity • fps	990	964	941	920	900	881	863	846	830
Energy • Ft-lbs	320	304	289	276	264	253	243	234	225
Taylor KO Index	7.4	7.2	7.0	6.9	6.7	6.6	6.5	6.3	6.2
Mid-Range Trajectory Height • Inches	0.0	0.3	1.1	2.7	4.9	7.8	11.5	16.0	21.4
Drop • Inches	0.0	-1.1	-4.6	-10.5	-19.0	-30.1	-44.1	-61.0	-80.8

USA (Winchester) 147-grain Full Metal Jacket—Flat Nose (USA9mm1)

G1 Ballistic Coefficient = 0.199

Distance • Yards	Muzzle	25	50	75	100	125	150	175	200
Velocity • fps	990	966	945	924	906	888	871	855	840
Energy • Ft-lbs	320	305	292	279	268	257	248	239	230
Taylor KO Index	7.4	7.2	7.1	6.9	6.8	6.6	6.5	6.4	6.3
Mid-Range Trajectory Height • Inches	0.0	0.2	1.1	2.6	4.8	7.7	11.4	15.8	21.1
Drop • Inches	0.0	-1.1	-4.6	-10.5	-18.9	-30.0	-43.8	-60.4	-80.1

CCI 147-grain Clean-Fire—Totally Metal Jacket (3462)

G1 Ballistic Coefficient = 0.285

Distance • Yards	Muzzle	25	50	75	100	125	150	175	200
Velocity • fps	985	968	953	938	924	911	899	886	875
Energy • Ft-lbs	326	306	300	287	279	271	264	257	250
Taylor KO Index	7.3	7.2	7.1	7.0	6.9	6.8	6.7	6.6	6.5
Mid-Range Trajectory Height • Inches	0.0	0.3	0.5	2.6	4.7	7.5	11.0	15.3	20.3
Drop • Inches	0.0	-1.1	-4.6	-10.4	-18.7	-29.6	-43.0	-59.2	-78.0

CCI 147-grain Clean-Fire—TMJ Lawman (53826)

G1 Ballistic Coefficient = 0.188

Distance • Yards	Muzzle	25	50	75	100	125	150	175	200
Velocity • fps	985	960	938	917	898	879	862	846	830
Energy • Ft-lbs	317	301	287	275	263	253	243	233	225
Taylor KO Index	7.4	7.2	7.0	6.9	6.7	6.6	6.4	6.3	6.2
Mid-Range Trajectory Height • Inches	0.0	0.3	1.2	2.7	4.9	7.9	11.6	16.2	21.6
Drop • Inches	0.0	-1.1	-4.6	-10.6	-19.1	-30.4	-44.4	-61.4	-81.4

CCI 147-grain TMJ Lawman (53620)

G1 Ballistic Coefficient = 0.188

Distance • Yards	Muzzle	25	50	75	100	125	150	175	200
Velocity • fps	985	960	938	917	898	879	862	846	830
Energy • Ft-lbs	317	301	287	275	263	253	243	233	225
Taylor KO Index	7.4	7.2	7.0	6.9	6.7	6.6	6.4	6.3	6.2
Mid-Range Trajectory Height • Inches	0.0	0.3	1.2	2.7	4.9	7.9	11.6	16.2	21.6
Drop • Inches	0.0	-1.1	-4.6	-10.6	-19.1	-30.4	-44.4	-61.4	-81.4

PMC 147-grain Full Metal Jacket (9F)

G1 Ballistic Coefficient = 0.204

Distance • Yards	Muzzle	25	50	75	100	125	150	175	200
Velocity • fps	980	965	941	919	900	883	867	851	837
Energy • Ft-lbs	314	299	287	275	264	255	245	237	229
Taylor KO Index	7.3	7.2	7.0	6.9	6.7	6.6	6.5	6.4	6.3
Mid-Range Trajectory Height • Inches	0.0	0.3	1.2	2.7	5.0	7.9	11.6	16.1	21.5
Drop • Inches	0.0	-1.2	-4.7	-10.7	-19.2	-30.5	-44.5	-61.4	-81.3

Black Hills 147-grain Full Metal Jacket Subsonic (M9N4)

G1 Ballistic Coefficient = 0.214

Distance • Yards	Muzzle	25	50	75	100	125	150	175	200
Velocity • fps	975	954	935	916	899	883	868	853	839
Energy • Ft-lbs	310	297	285	274	264	255	246	238	230
Taylor KO Index	7.3	7.1	6.9	6.8	6.7	6.6	6.5	6.4	6.3
Mid-Range Trajectory Height • Inches	0.0	0.3	1.2	2.7	5.0	7.8	11.6	16.1	21.4
Drop • Inches	0.0	-1.2	-4.7	-10.7	-19.4	-30.6	-44.7	-61.7	-81.6

American Eagle (Federal) 147-grain Full Metal Jacket Flat Point (AE9FP)

G1 Ballistic Coefficient = 0.167

Distance • Yards	Muzzle	25	50	75	100	125	150	175	200
Velocity • fps	960	930	910	890	870	851	833	816	799
Energy • Ft-lbs	295	280	270	260	250	237	227	217	209
Taylor KO Index	7.2	6.9	6.8	6.6	6.5	6.4	6.2	6.1	6.0
Mid-Range Trajectory Height • Inches	0.0	0.3	1.3	2.9	5.3	8.3	12.3	17.1	22.9
Drop • Inches	0.0	-1.2	-4.9	-11.2	-20.2	-32.1	-47.0	-65.0	-86.3

American Eagle (Federal) 147-grain TMJ (AE9N2)

G1 Ballistic Coefficient = 0.167

Distance • Yards	Muzzle	25	50	75	100	125	150	175	200
Velocity • fps	960	930	910	890	870	851	833	816	799
Energy • Ft-lbs	295	280	270	260	250	237	227	217	209
Taylor KO Index	7.2	6.9	6.8	6.6	6.5	6.4	6.2	6.1	6.0
Mid-Range Trajectory Height • Inches	0.0	0.3	1.3	2.9	5.3	8.3	12.3	17.1	22.9
Drop • Inches	0.0	-1.2	-4.9	-11.2	-20.2	-32.1	-47.0	-65.0	-86.3

CCI 147-grain TMJ Blazer (3582)

G1 Ballistic Coefficient = 0.189

Distance • Yards	Muzzle	25	50	75	100	125	150	175	200
Velocity • fps	950	928	908	890	872	855	839	823	808
Energy • Ft-lbs	295	281	269	258	248	239	230	221	213
Taylor KO Index	7.1	6.9	6.8	6.7	6.5	6.4	6.3	6.2	6.0
Mid-Range Trajectory Height • Inches	0.0	0.3	1.3	2.9	5.3	8.4	12.4	17.2	22.9
Drop • Inches	0.0	-1.2	-5.0	-11.3	-20.4	-32.4	-47.4	-65.4	-86.6

CCI 147-grain Clean-Fire—TMJ Blazer (3562)

G1 Ballistic Coefficient = 0.189

Distance • Yards	Muzzle	25	50	75	100	125	150	175	200
Velocity • fps	950	928	908	890	872	855	839	823	808
Energy • Ft-lbs	295	281	269	258	248	239	230	221	213
Taylor KO Index	7.1	6.9	6.8	6.7	6.5	6.4	6.3	6.2	6.0
Mid-Range Trajectory Height • Inches	0.0	0.3	1.3	2.9	5.3	8.4	12.4	17.2	22.9
Drop • Inches	0.0	-1.2	-5.0	-11.3	-20.4	-32.4	-47.4	-65.4	-86.6

9mm Largo (9x23mm)*

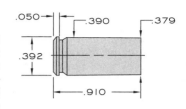

The 9mm Largo is a lengthened version of the 9mm Luger. It originated in Spain about 1913 as a variation on the earlier Bergmann-Bayard. The CCI ammunition loaded for this caliber was originally manufactured to support surplus Spanish military pistols. This cartridge has a potential for mixing with the Winchester 9x23mm.

Multiple cautions apply here. While several European 9mms are sometimes called 9x23mm, they are loaded to a much lower pressure specification than the current Winchester 9x23mm loadings. The Winchester ammunition should never be used in any 9mm Largo guns. The Largo is very similar to the .380 Super Auto, but again, the two are not interchangeable.

Relative Recoil Factor = 0.82

Specifications

Controlling Agency for Standardization of this Ammunition: Factory

Barrel used for velocity testing: 4 inches long—1 turn in 10-inch twist

Availability

CCI 124-grain HP (3513) (Until Supply Exhausted)

G1 Ballistic Coefficient = 0.121

Distance • Yards	Muzzle	25	50	75	100	125	150	175	200
Velocity • fps	1190	1114	1055	1006	966	931	900	872	846
Energy • Ft-lbs	390	342	306	279	257	239	223	209	197
Taylor KO Index	7.5	7.0	6.6	6.3	6.1	5.9	5.7	5.5	5.3
Mid-Range Trajectory Height • Inches	0.0	0.2	0.7	2.1	3.7	6.3	9.5	13.5	18.3
Drop • Inches	0.0	-0.8	-3.4	-7.9	-14.5	-23.4	-34.7	-48.8	-65.7

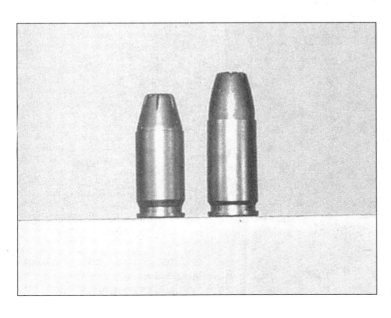

(Left to right) .380 Auto, 9mm Luger.

Winchester 9x23mm

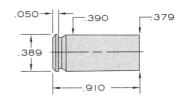

Please review the comments for the 9mm Largo. This is high-pressure ammunition that meets the performance specifications of the USPSA/IPSC competition rules. It should NOT be used in pistols that might also be marked 9x23mm but were not designed for the high pressures. If your 9x23mm gun is not a competition gun, it probably was not designed for this ammunition. CAUTION! There is a real potential for a mixup here!

Relative Recoil Factor = 0.82

Specifications

Controlling Agency for Standardization of this Ammunition: Factory
Barrel used for velocity testing: 5 inches long—The twist rate is not available

Availability

USA (Winchester) 124-grain Jacketed Flat Point (Q4304)
G1 Ballistic Coefficient = 0.181

Distance • Yards	Muzzle	25	50	75	100	125	150	175	200
Velocity • fps	1460	1381	1308	1242	1183	1131	1087	1050	1017
Energy • Ft-lbs	587	525	471	425	385	353	326	304	285
Taylor KO Index	9.2	8.7	8.2	7.8	7.4	7.1	6.9	6.6	6.4
Mid-Range Trajectory Height • Inches	0.0	0.1	0.6	1.3	2.5	4.2	6.3	9.1	12.3
Drop • Inches	0.0	-0.5	-2.2	-5.1	-9.5	-15.4	-23.0	-32.4	-43.8

Winchester 125-grain Silvertip Hollow Point (X923W)
G1 Ballistic Coefficient = 0.132

Distance • Yards	Muzzle	25	50	75	100	125	150	175	200
Velocity • fps	1450	1344	1249	1170	1103	1051	1007	970	937
Energy • Ft-lbs	583	502	433	380	338	306	281	261	244
Taylor KO Index	9.2	8.5	7.9	7.4	7.0	6.7	6.4	6.2	6.0
Mid-Range Trajectory Height • Inches	0.0	0.1	0.6	1.5	2.8	4.6	7.1	10.2	14.0
Drop • Inches	0.0	-0.5	-2.3	-5.4	-10.2	-16.6	-25.1	-35.6	-48.4

This large buck was taken in Mexico. (Photo from *Ask the Elk Guides* by J. Y. Jones, Safari Press, 2005)

.38 Short Colt

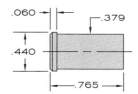

The history of the .38 Short Colt is rather cloudy. This cartridge seems to have appeared on the scene sometime in the 1880s. It has the same dimensions as the .38 Long Colt except for the case length and the overall length. Why it is still in the inventory is a mystery. Perhaps the best excuse for this cartridge is that if there hadn't been a .38 SHORT Colt there couldn't have been a .38 LONG Colt.

Relative Recoil Factor = 0.17

Specifications

Controlling Agency for Standardization of this Ammunition: SAAMI

Bullet Weight Grains	Velocity fps	Maximum Average Pressure	
		Copper Crusher	Transducer
125 L	775	12,000 cup	N/S

Standard barrel for velocity testing: 4 inches long (vented)—1 turn in 16-inch twist

Availability

Remington 125-grain Lead (R38SC)

G1 Ballistic Coefficient = 0.102

Distance • Yards	Muzzle	25	50	75	100	125	150	175	200
Velocity • fps	730	707	685	665	645	626	607	589	571
Energy • Ft-lbs	150	140	130	123	115	109	102	96	91
Taylor KO Index	4.7	4.5	4.4	4.2	4.1	4.0	3.9	3.8	3.6
Mid-Range Trajectory Height • Inches	0.0	0.5	2.1	5.0	9.2	14.8	22.1	31.1	41.9
Drop • Inches	0.0	-2.1	-8.5	-19.5	-35.5	-56.6	-83.3	-115.9	-154.8

This good gemsbok was shot in Botswana. (Photo from *A Pioneering Hunter* by Brian Marsh, Safari Press, 2006)

.38 Smith & Wesson

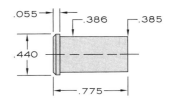

The .38 Smith & Wesson might be thought of as a forerunner of the .38 Special. Designed in 1877, it was once very popular as a police cartridge. The very modest performance (145–146 grains at 685 fps) is about like the mildest wadcutter target loads for the .38 Special.

Relative Recoil Factor = 0.45

Specifications

Controlling Agency for Standardization of this Ammunition: SAAMI

Bullet Weight Grains	Velocity fps	Maximum Average Pressure	
		Copper Crusher	Transducer
145–146	680	13,000 cup	14,500 psi

Standard barrel for velocity testing: 4 inches long—1 turn in 18.75-inch twist

Availability

Winchester 145-grain Lead (X38SWP)

G1 Ballistic Coefficient = 0.125

Distance • Yards	Muzzle	25	50	75	100	125	150	175	200
Velocity • fps	685	668	650	635	620	605	590	575	561
Energy • Ft-lbs	150	145	138	131	125	119	113	107	102
Taylor KO Index	5.1	5.0	4.9	4.8	4.6	4.5	4.4	4.3	4.2
Mid-Range Trajectory Height • Inches	0.0	0.6	2.4	5.6	10.2	16.3	24.2	33.8	45.3
Drop • Inches	0.0	-2.4	-9.6	-21.9	-39.6	-63.0	-92.3	-127.8	-169.9

Magtech 46-grain Lead (38SWA)

G1 Ballistic Coefficient = 0.135

Distance • Yards	Muzzle	25	50	75	100	125	150	175	200
Velocity • fps	686	670	655	640	625	611	597	584	570
Energy • Ft-lbs	153	146	139	133	127	121	116	110	105
Taylor KO Index	5.1	5.0	4.9	4.8	4.7	4.6	4.5	4.4	4.3
Mid-Range Trajectory Height • Inches	0.0	0.6	2.4	5.6	10.2	16.2	23.9	33.4	44.6
Drop • Inches	0.0	-2.3	-9.5	-21.8	-39.3	-62.4	-91.4	-126.4	-167.8

Remington 146-grain Lead (R38SW)

G1 Ballistic Coefficient = 0.125

Distance • Yards	Muzzle	25	50	75	100	125	150	175	200
Velocity • fps	685	668	650	635	620	605	590	575	561
Energy • Ft-lbs	150	145	138	131	125	119	113	107	102
Taylor KO Index	5.1	5.0	4.9	4.8	4.6	4.5	4.4	4.3	4.2
Mid-Range Trajectory Height • Inches	0.0	0.6	2.4	5.6	10.2	16.3	24.2	33.8	45.3
Drop • Inches	0.0	-2.4	-9.6	-21.9	-39.6	-63.0	-92.3	-127.8	-169.9

.38 Super Auto Colt

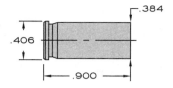

The .38 Super Auto Colt was introduced clear back in 1929 as an improved version of the even older (1900) .38 Auto. The very minimal rim feeds much better from automatic pistol magazines than ammunition with a more standard rim size, like the .38 Special. This cartridge should NOT be used in pistols chambered for .38 ACP. Performance is good, better than the .38 Special, but nowhere near the .357 Magnum with the same bullet weights. The performance of the .38 Super Auto Colt is approximately equal to the 9mm, which may explain why its popularity seems to be in decline.

Relative Recoil Factor = 0.71

Specifications

Controlling Agency for Standardization of this Ammunition: SAAMI

Bullet Weight Grains	Velocity fps	Maximum Average Pressure	
		Copper Crusher	Transducer
115 JHP	1,280	33,000 cup	36,500 psi
125 JHP	1,230	33,000 cup	36,500 psi
130 FMC	1,200	33,000 cup	36,500 psi

Standard barrel for velocity testing: 5 inches long—1 turn in 16-inch twist

Availability

PMC 115-grain Jacketed Hollow Point (38SB)

G1 Ballistic Coefficient = 0.124

Distance • Yards	Muzzle	25	50	75	100	125	150	175	200
Velocity • fps	1120	1061	1013	972	937	907	879	853	828
Energy • Ft-lbs	320	287	262	241	224	210	197	186	175
Taylor KO Index	6.6	6.2	5.9	5.7	5.5	5.3	5.2	5.0	4.9
Mid-Range Trajectory Height • Inches	0.0	0.2	1.0	2.3	4.2	6.9	10.3	14.6	19.8
Drop • Inches	0.0	-0.9	-3.7	-8.7	-15.9	-25.6	-38.0	-53.2	-71.3

Winchester 125-grain Silvertip Hollow Point [+P Load] (X38ASHP)

G1 Ballistic Coefficient = 0.183

Distance • Yards	Muzzle	25	50	75	100	125	150	175	200
Velocity • fps	1240	1182	1130	1087	1050	1018	989	964	941
Energy • Ft-lbs	427	388	354	328	306	288	272	258	246
Taylor KO Index	7.9	7.5	7.2	6.9	6.7	6.5	6.3	6.1	6.0
Mid-Range Trajectory Height • Inches	0.0	0.2	0.8	1.8	3.4	5.5	8.2	11.6	15.6
Drop • Inches	0.0	-0.7	-3.0	-7.0	-12.8	-20.6	-30.4	-42.5	-56.8

Aguila 130-grain Jacketed +P

G1 Ballistic Coefficient = 0.087

Distance • Yards	Muzzle	25	50	75	100	125	150	175	200
Velocity • fps	1220	1112	1033	973	925	883	846	813	782
Energy • Ft-lbs	426	357	308	273	248	225	207	191	177
Taylor KO Index	8.1	7.4	6.8	6.5	6.1	5.9	5.6	5.4	5.2
Mid-Range Trajectory Height • Inches	0.0	0.2	0.9	2.1	4.1	6.8	10.3	14.8	20.3
Drop • Inches	0.0	-0.8	-3.3	-7.9	-14.8	-24.2	-36.3	-51.6	-70.1

PMC 130-grain Full Metal Jacket (38SA)

G1 Ballistic Coefficient = 0.137

Distance • Yards	Muzzle	25	50	75	100	125	150	175	200
Velocity • fps	1090	1041	1000	965	934	907	881	857	835
Energy • Ft-lbs	343	331	289	269	252	237	224	212	201
Taylor KO Index	7.2	6.9	6.6	6.4	6.2	6.0	5.8	5.7	5.5
Mid-Range Trajectory Height • Inches	0.0	0.2	1.0	2.4	4.3	7.0	10.5	14.8	19.9
Drop • Inches	0.0	-0.9	-3.9	-9.0	-16.5	-26.4	-39.0	-54.4	-72.7

.38 Special (.38 Smith & Wesson Special)

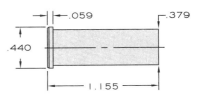

Like the .30-06 cartridge in rifles, the .38 Special is the standard to which pistol cartridges are compared. The .38 Special was introduced by Smith & Wesson in 1902, and at that time it was loaded with black powder. For many years this cartridge was the one used by most police officers. That began to change in the 1950s as other, more potent, cartridges came into general use. The +P loads were introduced in an attempt to "soup-up" the .38 Special, but even the +Ps fall well short of the performance obtainable with the .357 Magnum. Just a glance at the SAAMI pressure levels shows why this is true. Still, with a 148-grain wadcutter bullet, the .38 Special continues to be the most popular caliber for target revolvers. There are more factory loadings offered for this cartridge than for any other pistol ammunition.

Relative Recoil Factor = 0.53

Specifications

Controlling Agency for Standardization of this Ammunition: SAAMI

Bullet Weight Grains	Velocity fps	Maximum Average Pressure	
		Copper Crusher	Transducer
110 STHP	945	17,000 cup	17,000 psi
158 LSWC	750	17,000 cup	17,000 psi
200 L	630	17,000 cup	17,000 psi
+P Loads			
95 STHP	1,080	20,000 cup	18,500 psi
110 JHP	980	20,000 cup	18,500 psi
125 JHP	940	20,000 cup	18,500 psi
147 JHP	855	20,000 cup	18,500 psi
150 L	840	20,000 cup	18,500 psi
158 LSWC	880	20,000 cup	18,500 psi

Standard barrel for velocity testing: 4 inches long (vented)—1 turn in 18.75-inch twist.

Alternate one-piece barrel—7.710 inches.

Availability

Cor-Bon 80-grain Glaser Safety Slug +P (02200/02400)
G1 Ballistic Coefficient = 0.080

Distance • Yards	Muzzle	25	50	75	100	125	150	175	200
Velocity • fps	1600	1409	1249	1125	1036	971	919	875	836
Energy • Ft-lbs	455	353	277	225	191	168	150	136	124
Taylor KO Index	6.5	5.8	5.1	4.6	4.2	4.0	3.8	3.6	3.4
Mid-Range Trajectory Height • Inches	0.0	0.1	0.6	1.4	2.8	4.9	7.7	11.4	16.0
Drop • Inches	0.0	-0.5	-2.0	-5.0	-9.6	-13.3	-25.3	-36.9	-51.3

Cor-Bon 80-grain Glaser Safety Slug (01800/02000)
G1 Ballistic Coefficient = 0.080

Distance • Yards	Muzzle	25	50	75	100	125	150	175	200
Velocity • fps	1500	1324	1181	1076	1001	944	896	855	818
Energy • Ft-lbs	400	311	248	206	178	158	143	130	119
Taylor KO Index	6.1	5.4	4.8	4.4	4.1	3.9	3.7	3.5	3.3
Mid-Range Trajectory Height • Inches	0.0	0.1	0.6	1.6	3.1	5.4	8.4	12.4	17.2
Drop • Inches	0.0	-0.5	-2.3	-5.6	-10.8	-18.2	-28.0	-40.5	-56.0

PMC 90-grain NT/FR (38HRA)
G1 Ballistic Coefficient = 0.123

Distance • Yards	Muzzle	25	50	75	100	125	150	175	200
Velocity • fps	1275	1181	1109	1052	1006	967	933	902	874
Energy • Ft-lbs	325	281	247	222	202	187	174	163	153
Taylor KO Index	5.9	5.4	5.1	4.8	4.6	4.5	4.3	4.2	4.0
Mid-Range Trajectory Height • Inches	0.0	0.2	0.8	1.9	3.5	5.8	8.8	12.6	17.1
Drop • Inches	0.0	-0.7	-3.0	-7.0	-12.9	-21.0	-31.4	-44.4	-60.0

Magtech 90-grain SCHP +P (FD38A)
G1 Ballistic Coefficient = 0.095

Distance • Yards	Muzzle	25	50	75	100	125	150	175	200
Velocity • fps	1083	1017	965	921	884	850	819	790	763
Energy • Ft-lbs	247	218	197	179	165	152	141	132	123
Taylor KO Index	5.3	4.9	4.7	4.5	4.3	4.1	4.0	3.8	3.7
Mid-Range Trajectory Height • Inches	0.0	0.2	1.1	2.5	4.7	7.6	11.5	16.4	22.3
Drop • Inches	0.0	-1.0	-4.0	-9.4	-17.4	-28.1	-41.9	-58.9	-79.4

Cor-Bon 100-grain PowRBall +P
G1 Ballistic Coefficient = 0.100

Distance • Yards	Muzzle	25	50	75	100	125	150	175	200
Velocity • fps	1400	1270	1163	1081	1018	968	926	890	857
Energy • Ft-lbs	435	358	300	259	230	208	191	176	163
Taylor KO Index	7.2	6.5	5.9	5.5	5.2	5.0	4.7	4.6	4.4
Mid-Range Trajectory Height • Inches	0.0	0.2	0.7	1.7	3.2	5.4	8.3	12.1	16.7
Drop • Inches	0.0	-0.6	-2.5	-6.1	-11.5	-19.0	-28.8	-41.1	-56.2

CCI 109-grain—Shotshell (3709)
Number 9 Shot at 1000 fps

Cor-Bon 110-grain DPX
G1 Ballistic Coefficient = 0.135

Distance • Yards	Muzzle	25	50	75	100	125	150	175	200
Velocity • fps	1200	1130	1073	1026	987	953	923	896	871
Energy • Ft-lbs	352	312	281	257	238	222	208	196	185
Taylor KO Index	6.8	6.4	6.0	5.8	5.6	5.4	5.2	5.0	4.9
Mid-Range Trajectory Height • Inches	0.0	0.2	0.9	2.0	3.8	6.2	9.3	13.1	17.8
Drop • Inches	0.0	-0.8	-3.3	-7.7	-14.1	-22.7	-33.8	-47.4	-63.7

Remington 101-grain Lead-Free Frangible +P (LF38SA) (Discontinued in 2004)
G1 Ballistic Coefficient = 0.143

Distance • Yards	Muzzle	25	50	75	100	125	150	175	200
Velocity • fps	950	922	896	872	850	829	809	790	772
Energy • Ft-lbs	202	191	180	171	162	154	147	140	134
Taylor KO Index	4.9	4.7	4.6	4.5	4.4	4.3	4.2	4.1	4.0
Mid-Range Trajectory Height • Inches	0.0	0.3	1.2	2.9	5.4	8.6	12.8	17.9	24.0
Drop • Inches	0.0	-1.2	-5.0	-11.5	-20.8	-33.2	-48.7	-67.5	-89.8

Winchester 110-grain Jacketed Flat Point (SC38NT)
G1 Ballistic Coefficient = 0.118

Distance • Yards	Muzzle	25	50	75	100	125	150	175	200
Velocity • fps	975	938	906	876	849	824	800	778	756
Energy • Ft-lbs	232	215	200	188	176	166	156	148	140
Taylor KO Index	5.5	5.3	5.1	4.9	4.8	4.6	4.5	4.4	4.2
Mid-Range Trajectory Height • Inches	0.0	0.3	1.2	2.9	5.3	8.5	12.7	17.9	24.1
Drop • Inches	0.0	-1.2	-4.8	-11.1	-20.2	-32.4	-47.7	-66.4	-88.7

Cor-Bon 110-grain JHP +P (SD38110/20)
G1 Ballistic Coefficient = 0.135

Distance • Yards	Muzzle	25	50	75	100	125	150	175	200
Velocity • fps	1250	1171	1106	1053	1010	973	941	912	885
Energy • Ft-lbs	382	335	299	271	249	231	216	203	192
Taylor KO Index	7.0	6.6	6.2	5.9	5.7	5.5	5.3	5.1	5.0
Mid-Range Trajectory Height • Inches	0.0	0.1	0.7	1.8	3.5	5.8	8.7	12.5	16.9
Drop • Inches	0.0	-0.7	-3.0	-7.1	-13.2	-21.3	-31.8	-44.7	-60.2

Federal 110-grain Hydra-Shok JHP (PD38HS3H)
G1 Ballistic Coefficient = 0.136

Distance • Yards	Muzzle	25	50	75	100	125	150	175	200
Velocity • fps	1000	970	930	910	880	856	834	813	793
Energy • Ft-lbs	245	225	215	200	190	179	170	161	153
Taylor KO Index	5.6	5.4	5.2	5.1	4.9	4.8	4.7	4.6	4.4
Mid-Range Trajectory Height • Inches	0.0	0.3	1.2	2.7	5.0	8.0	11.9	16.7	22.4
Drop • Inches	0.0	-1.1	-4.6	-10.5	-19.1	-30.5	-44.8	-62.3	-83.1

Federal 110-grain Hi-Shok JHP +P (C38E) (Discontinued in 2004)
G1 Ballistic Coefficient = 0.136

Distance • Yards	Muzzle	25	50	75	100	125	150	175	200
Velocity • fps	1000	960	930	900	870	844	920	798	776
Energy • Ft-lbs	240	225	210	195	185	174	164	155	147
Taylor KO Index	5.6	5.4	5.2	5.0	4.9	4.7	4.6	4.5	4.4
Mid-Range Trajectory Height • Inches	0.0	0.2	1.1	2.7	5.0	8.1	12.1	17.0	23.0
Drop • Inches	0.0	-1.1	-4.6	-10.6	-19.3	-30.8	-45.4	-63.3	-84.5

Remington 110-grain Semi-Jacketed Hollow Point +P (R38S10)
G1 Ballistic Coefficient = 0.129

Distance • Yards	Muzzle	25	50	75	100	125	150	175	200
Velocity • fps	995	959	926	898	871	847	824	802	782
Energy • Ft-lbs	242	224	210	197	185	175	166	157	149
Taylor KO Index	5.6	5.4	5.2	5.0	4.9	4.8	4.6	4.5	4.4
Mid-Range Trajectory Height • Inches	0.0	0.3	1.2	2.7	5.1	8.1	12.1	17.0	22.8
Drop • Inches	0.0	-1.1	-4.6	-10.6	-19.4	-30.9	-45.5	-63.3	-84.5

Remington 110-grain Semi-Jacketed Hollow Point (R38S16)
G1 Ballistic Coefficient = 0.128

Distance • Yards	Muzzle	25	50	75	100	125	150	175	200
Velocity • fps	950	919	890	864	840	817	796	775	756
Energy • Ft-lbs	220	206	194	182	172	163	155	147	140
Taylor KO Index	5.3	5.2	5.0	4.8	4.7	4.6	4.5	4.3	4.2
Mid-Range Trajectory Height • Inches	0.0	0.3	1.4	3.0	5.4	8.8	13.0	18.3	24.6
Drop • Inches	0.0	-1.2	-5.0	-11.6	-21.0	-33.6	-49.3	-68.6	-91.4

Winchester 110-grain Silvertip Hollow Point (X38S9HP)
G1 Ballistic Coefficient = 0.149

Distance • Yards	Muzzle	25	50	75	100	125	150	175	200
Velocity • fps	945	918	894	871	850	830	811	792	775
Energy • Ft-lbs	218	206	195	185	176	168	161	153	147
Taylor KO Index	5.3	5.1	5.0	4.9	4.8	4.7	4.5	4.4	4.3
Mid-Range Trajectory Height • Inches	0.0	0.3	1.3	3.0	5.4	8.7	12.8	18.0	24.0
Drop • Inches	0.0	-1.2	-5.1	-11.6	-21.0	-33.4	-48.9	-67.8	-90.1

Lapua 123-grain HP Megashock (4319187) (Discontinued in 2004)
G1 Ballistic Coefficient = 0.125

Distance • Yards	Muzzle	25	50	75	100	125	150	175	200
Velocity • fps	1165	1097	1042	997	959	926	897	870	845
Energy • Ft-lbs	371	328	297	272	251	234	220	207	195
Taylor KO Index	7.3	6.9	6.5	6.3	6.0	5.8	5.6	5.5	5.3
Mid-Range Trajectory Height • Inches	0.0	0.2	0.9	2.1	4.0	6.5	9.8	13.9	18.8
Drop • Inches	0.0	-0.8	-3.5	-8.1	-14.9	-24.1	-35.8	-50.2	-67.5

Federal 125-grain Hi-Shok JSP +P (C38J) (Discontinued in 2005)
G1 Ballistic Coefficient = 0.162

Distance • Yards	Muzzle	25	50	75	100	125	150	175	200
Velocity • fps	950	920	900	880	860	841	823	806	789
Energy • Ft-lbs	250	235	225	215	205	196	188	180	173
Taylor KO Index	6.1	5.9	5.7	5.6	5.5	5.4	5.2	5.1	5.0
Mid-Range Trajectory Height • Inches	0.0	0.3	1.3	2.9	5.4	8.5	12.6	17.5	23.4
Drop • Inches	0.0	-1.2	-5.0	-11.4	-20.7	-32.8	-48.1	-66.5	-88.9

Magtech 125-grain SJSP +P (38D)
G1 Ballistic Coefficient = 0.161

Distance • Yards	Muzzle	25	50	75	100	125	150	175	200
Velocity • fps	938	914	891	870	851	832	814	797	781
Energy • Ft-lbs	245	232	220	210	200	192	184	176	169
Taylor KO Index	6.0	5.8	5.7	5.5	5.4	5.3	5.2	5.1	5.0
Mid-Range Trajectory Height • Inches	0.0	0.3	1.3	3.0	5.4	8.7	12.8	17.9	24.0
Drop • Inches	0.0	-1.3	-5.1	-11.7	-21.2	-33.6	-49.2	-68.1	-90.4

Federal 125-grain Close Quarter Training (BC38NT3) (Discontinued in 2004)
G1 Ballistic Coefficient = 0.085

Distance • Yards	Muzzle	25	50	75	100	125	150	175	200
Velocity • fps	800	770	740	713	687	662	638	615	593
Energy • Ft-lbs	175	165	150	141	131	122	113	105	98
Taylor KO Index	5.1	4.9	4.7	4.5	4.4	4.2	4.1	3.9	3.8
Mid-Range Trajectory Height • Inches	0.0	0.4	1.8	4.2	8.0	12.8	19.3	27.3	37.0
Drop • Inches	0.0	-1.7	-7.2	-16.5	-30.2	-48.5	-71.7	-100.2	-134.5

Winchester 125-grain Jacketed Soft Point (WC381)

G1 Ballistic Coefficient = 0.152

Distance • Yards	Muzzle	25	50	75	100	125	150	175	200
Velocity • fps	775	758	742	727	712	697	683	669	655
Energy • Ft-lbs	167	160	153	147	141	135	129	124	119
Taylor KO Index	4.9	4.8	4.7	4.6	4.5	4.4	4.4	4.3	4.2
Mid-Range Trajectory Height • Inches	0.0	0.5	1.5	5.3	7.8	12.5	18.5	25.7	34.3
Drop • Inches	0.0	-1.8	-7.4	-17.0	-30.7	-48.6	-71.0	-98.1	-130.1

Magtech 125-grain LRN (38G)

G1 Ballistic Coefficient = 0.142

Distance • Yards	Muzzle	25	50	75	100	125	150	175	200
Velocity • fps	686	671	659	642	628	614	601	588	575
Energy • Ft-lbs	130	125	120	114	109	105	100	96	92
Taylor KO Index	4.4	4.3	4.2	4.1	4.0	3.9	3.8	3.7	3.7
Mid-Range Trajectory Height • Inches	0.0	0.6	2.0	5.5	9.7	16.0	23.7	33.0	44.1
Drop • Inches	0.0	-2.3	-9.5	-21.7	-39.2	-62.2	-90.9	-125.7	-166.7

Cor-Bon 125-grain JHP +P (SD38125/20)

1 Ballistic Coefficient = 0.165

Distance • Yards	Muzzle	25	50	75	100	125	150	175	200
Velocity • fps	1125	1078	1038	1004	974	947	923	901	880
Energy • Ft-lbs	351	323	299	280	264	249	237	225	215
Taylor KO Index	7.2	6.9	6.6	6.4	6.2	6.0	5.9	5.7	5.6
Mid-Range Trajectory Height • Inches	0.0	0.2	0.9	2.1	4.0	6.4	9.6	13.6	18.2
Drop • Inches	0.0	-0.9	-3.6	-8.4	-15.3	-24.5	-36.2	-50.3	-67.2

Black Hills 125-grain Jacketed Hollow Point—Gold Dot +P (M38N2)

G1 Ballistic Coefficient = 0.140

Distance • Yards	Muzzle	25	50	75	100	125	150	175	200
Velocity • fps	1050	1008	973	942	914	888	865	842	821
Energy • Ft-lbs	306	282	263	246	232	219	208	197	187
Taylor KO Index	6.7	6.4	6.2	6.0	5.8	5.7	5.5	5.4	5.2
Mid-Range Trajectory Height • Inches	0.0	0.2	1.1	2.5	4.6	7.3	11.0	15.4	20.8
Drop • Inches	0.0	-1.0	-4.2	-9.6	-17.5	-28.0	-41.2	-57.4	-76.6

Magtech 125-grain JHP (GG38A)

G1 Ballistic Coefficient = 0.230

Distance • Yards	Muzzle	25	50	75	100	125	150	175	200
Velocity • fps	1017	993	971	950	931	913	896	880	865
Energy • Ft-lbs	287	274	262	250	241	231	223	215	208
Taylor KO Index	6.5	6.3	6.2	6.1	5.9	5.8	5.7	5.6	5.5
Mid-Range Trajectory Height • Inches	0.0	0.2	1.1	2.5	4.6	7.3	10.8	15.0	20.0
Drop • Inches	0.0	-1.1	-4.3	-9.9	-17.9	-28.4	-41.5	-57.3	-75.9

Remington 125-grain Brass Jacketed Hollow Point +P (GS38SB)

G1 Ballistic Coefficient = 0.175

Distance • Yards	Muzzle	25	50	75	100	125	150	175	200
Velocity • fps	975	950	929	905	885	886	848	831	814
Energy • Ft-lbs	264	250	238	227	218	208	200	192	184
Taylor KO Index	6.2	6.0	5.9	5.8	5.6	5.5	5.4	5.3	5.2
Mid-Range Trajectory Height • Inches	0.0	0.3	1.0	2.8	5.2	8.0	11.9	16.6	22.2
Drop • Inches	0.0	-1.2	-4.7	-10.8	-19.6	-31.1	-45.5	-63.0	-83.6

PMC 125-grain Jacketed Hollow Point +P (38D)

G1 Ballistic Coefficient = 0.124

Distance • Yards	Muzzle	25	50	75	100	125	150	175	200
Velocity • fps	950	920	892	864	837	814	792	771	751
Energy • Ft-lbs	251	234	219	206	195	184	174	165	157
Taylor KO Index	6.1	5.9	5.7	5.5	5.4	5.2	5.1	4.9	4.8
Mid-Range Trajectory Height • Inches	0.0	0.3	1.3	3.0	5.5	8.9	13.2	18.5	24.8
Drop • Inches	0.0	-1.2	-5.0	-11.6	-21.1	-33.7	-49.5	-68.9	-91.8

Federal 125-grain Hi-Shok JHP +P (38E)

G1 Ballistic Coefficient = 0.162

Distance • Yards	Muzzle	25	50	75	100	125	150	175	200
Velocity • fps	950	920	900	880	860	841	823	806	789
Energy • Ft-lbs	250	235	225	215	205	196	188	180	173
Taylor KO Index	6.1	5.9	5.7	5.6	5.5	5.4	5.2	5.1	5.0
Mid-Range Trajectory Height • Inches	0.0	0.3	1.3	2.9	5.4	8.5	12.6	17.5	23.4
Drop • Inches	0.0	-1.2	-5.0	-11.4	-20.7	-32.8	-48.1	-66.5	-88.9

Federal 125-grain Nyclad Hollow Point +P (P38N) (Discontinued in 2004) G1 Ballistic Coefficient = 0.162

Distance • Yards	Muzzle	25	50	75	100	125	150	175	200
Velocity • fps	950	920	900	880	860	841	823	806	789
Energy • Ft-lbs	250	235	225	215	205	196	188	180	173
Taylor KO Index	6.1	5.9	5.7	5.6	5.5	5.4	5.2	5.1	5.0
Mid-Range Trajectory Height • Inches	0.0	0.3	1.3	2.9	5.4	8.5	12.6	17.5	23.4
Drop • Inches	0.0	-1.2	-5.0	-11.4	-20.7	-32.8	-48.1	-66.5	-88.9

PMC 125-grain Starfire Hollow Point +P (38SFA) G1 Ballistic Coefficient = 0.125

Distance • Yards	Muzzle	25	50	75	100	125	150	175	200
Velocity • fps	950	918	889	863	838	815	793	772	752
Energy • Ft-lbs	251	234	219	206	195	184	174	165	157
Taylor KO Index	6.1	5.9	5.7	5.5	5.3	5.2	5.1	4.9	4.8
Mid-Range Trajectory Height • Inches	0.0	0.3	1.3	3.0	5.5	8.8	13.1	18.4	24.7
Drop • Inches	0.0	-1.2	-5.0	-11.6	-21.1	-33.6	-49.5	-68.8	-91.7

CCI 125-grain Jacketed Hollow +P Blazer (3514) G1 Ballistic Coefficient = 0.130

Distance • Yards	Muzzle	25	50	75	100	125	150	175	200
Velocity • fps	945	915	887	862	838	816	795	775	755
Energy • Ft-lbs	248	232	218	206	195	185	175	167	158
Taylor KO Index	6.0	5.8	5.7	5.5	5.4	5.2	5.1	5.0	4.8
Mid-Range Trajectory Height • Inches	0.0	0.3	1.3	3.0	5.5	8.9	13.2	18.5	24.8
Drop • Inches	0.0	-1.2	-5.1	-11.7	-21.2	-33.8	-49.7	-69.0	-92.0

Speer 125-grain Gold Dot +P (23720) G1 Ballistic Coefficient = 0.140

Distance • Yards	Muzzle	25	50	75	100	125	150	175	200
Velocity • fps	945	917	891	867	845	824	804	785	766
Energy • Ft-lbs	248	233	220	209	198	188	179	171	163
Taylor KO Index	6.0	5.9	5.7	5.5	5.4	5.3	5.1	5.0	4.9
Mid-Range Trajectory Height • Inches	0.0	0.3	1.3	3.0	5.5	8.8	13.0	18.2	24.4
Drop • Inches	0.0	-1.2	-5.1	-11.8	-21.1	-33.6	-49.3	-68.3	-90.9

Remington 125-grain Semi-Jacketed Hollow Point +P (R38S2) G1 Ballistic Coefficient = 0.165

Distance • Yards	Muzzle	25	50	75	100	125	150	175	200
Velocity • fps	945	921	898	878	858	839	822	805	788
Energy • Ft-lbs	248	235	224	214	204	196	187	180	173
Taylor KO Index	6.0	5.9	5.7	5.6	5.5	5.3	5.2	5.1	5.0
Mid-Range Trajectory Height • Inches	0.0	0.3	1.3	3.0	5.4	8.5	12.6	17.6	23.6
Drop • Inches	0.0	-1.2	-5.0	-11.5	-20.8	-33.1	-18.4	-67.0	-88.9

UMC (Remington) 125-grain Jacketed Hollow Point +P (L38S2) G1 Ballistic Coefficient = 0.164

Distance • Yards	Muzzle	25	50	75	100	125	150	175	200
Velocity • fps	945	921	898	878	858	839	822	805	788
Energy • Ft-lbs	248	235	224	214	204	196	187	180	173
Taylor KO Index	6.0	5.9	5.7	5.6	5.5	5.3	5.2	5.1	5.0
Mid-Range Trajectory Height • Inches	0.0	0.3	1.3	3.0	5.4	8.5	12.6	17.6	23.6
Drop • Inches	0.0	-1.2	-5.0	-11.5	-20.8	-33.1	-48.5	-67.0	-89.0

Winchester 125-grain Jacketed Hollow Point +P (X38S7PH) G1 Ballistic Coefficient = 0.165

Distance • Yards	Muzzle	25	50	75	100	125	150	175	200
Velocity • fps	945	921	898	878	858	839	822	805	788
Energy • Ft-lbs	248	235	224	214	204	196	187	180	173
Taylor KO Index	6.0	5.9	5.7	5.6	5.5	5.3	5.2	5.1	5.0
Mid-Range Trajectory Height • Inches	0.0	0.3	1.3	3.0	5.4	8.5	12.6	17.6	23.6
Drop • Inches	0.0	-1.2	-5.0	-11.5	-20.8	-33.1	-18.4	-67.0	-88.9

Winchester 125-grain Silvertip Hollow Point +P (X38S8HP) G1 Ballistic Coefficient = 0.165

Distance • Yards	Muzzle	25	50	75	100	125	150	175	200
Velocity • fps	945	921	898	878	858	839	822	805	788
Energy • Ft-lbs	248	235	224	214	204	196	187	180	173
Taylor KO Index	6.0	5.9	5.7	5.6	5.5	5.3	5.2	5.1	5.0
Mid-Range Trajectory Height • Inches	0.0	0.3	1.3	3.0	5.4	8.5	12.6	17.6	23.6
Drop • Inches	0.0	-1.2	-5.0	-11.5	-20.8	-33.1	-18.4	-67.0	-88.9

USA (Winchester) 125-grain Jacketed Hollow Point (USA38JHP)　　G1 Ballistic Coefficient = 0.163

Distance • Yards	Muzzle	25	50	75	100	125	150	175	200
Velocity • fps	945	920	898	877	857	838	820	803	787
Energy • Ft-lbs	248	235	224	214	204	195	187	179	172
Taylor KO Index	6.0	5.9	5.7	5.6	5.5	5.3	5.2	5.1	5.0
Mid-Range Trajectory Height • Inches	0.0	0.3	1.2	2.9	5.3	8.6	12.7	17.7	23.6
Drop • Inches	0.0	-1.2	-5.0	-11.5	-20.8	-33.1	-48.5	-67.1	-89.0

Magtech 125-grain SJHP +P (38F)　　G1 Ballistic Coefficient = 0.161

Distance • Yards	Muzzle	25	50	75	100	125	150	175	200
Velocity • fps	938	914	891	870	851	832	814	797	781
Energy • Ft-lbs	245	232	220	210	200	192	184	176	169
Taylor KO Index	6.0	5.8	5.7	5.5	5.4	5.3	5.2	5.1	5.0
Mid-Range Trajectory Height • Inches	0.0	0.3	1.3	3.0	5.4	8.7	12.9	17.9	24.0
Drop • Inches	0.0	-1.3	-5.1	-11.7	-21.2	-33.6	-49.2	-68.1	-90.4

Hornady 125-grain JHP/XTP (90322)　　G1 Ballistic Coefficient = 0.153

Distance • Yards	Muzzle	25	50	75	100	125	150	175	200
Velocity • fps	900	877	856	836	817	799	782	765	749
Energy • Ft-lbs	225	214	203	194	185	177	170	163	156
Taylor KO Index	5.7	5.6	5.5	5.3	5.2	5.1	5.0	4.9	4.8
Mid-Range Trajectory Height • Inches	0.0	0.3	1.4	3.2	5.9	9.4	13.9	19.5	26.0
Drop • Inches	0.0	-1.4	-5.6	-12.7	-23.0	-36.4	53.4	73.8	98.0

Federal 125-grain Nyclad Hollow Point (P38M) (Discontinued in 2004)　　G1 Ballistic Coefficient = 0.053

Distance • Yards	Muzzle	25	50	75	100	125	150	175	200
Velocity • fps	830	780	730	690	650	613	578	545	513
Energy • Ft-lbs	190	170	150	130	115	104	93	82	73
Taylor KO Index	5.3	5.0	4.7	4.4	4.1	3.9	3.7	3.5	3.3
Mid-Range Trajectory Height • Inches	0.0	0.4	1.8	4.3	8.1	13.5	20.7	30.2	41.9
Drop • Inches	0.0	-1.6	-6.9	-16.2	-30.1	-49.1	-73.9	-105.2	-143.9

USA (Winchester) 125-grain Jacketed Flat Point (USA38SP)　　G1 Ballistic Coefficient = 0.127

Distance • Yards	Muzzle	25	50	75	100	125	150	175	200
Velocity • fps	850	826	804	783	763	744	725	707	690
Energy • Ft-lbs	201	190	179	170	162	154	146	139	132
Taylor KO Index	5.4	5.3	5.1	5.0	4.9	4.7	4.6	4.5	4.4
Mid-Range Trajectory Height • Inches	0.0	0.3	1.5	3.6	6.7	10.7	15.9	22.3	29.9
Drop • Inches	0.0	-1.5	-6.2	-14.3	-25.9	-41.3	-60.5	-83.9	-111.7

Federal 129-grain Hydra-Shok JHP +P (P38HS1)　　G1 Ballistic Coefficient = 0.184

Distance • Yards	Muzzle	25	50	75	100	125	150	175	200
Velocity • fps	950	930	910	890	870	852	836	820	805
Energy • Ft-lbs	255	245	235	225	215	202	194	187	180
Taylor KO Index	6.3	6.1	6.0	5.9	5.7	5.6	5.5	5.4	5.3
Mid-Range Trajectory Height • Inches	0.0	0.3	1.3	2.9	5.3	8.4	12.4	17.2	22.9
Drop • Inches	0.0	-1.2	-5.0	-11.4	-20.5	-32.5	-47.5	-65.6	-86.9

Winchester 130-grain SXT (S38SP)　　G1 Ballistic Coefficient = 0.190

Distance • Yards	Muzzle	25	50	75	100	125	150	175	200
Velocity • fps	925	905	887	869	852	837	821	806	792
Energy • Ft-lbs	247	237	227	218	210	202	195	188	181
Taylor KO Index	6.1	6.0	5.9	5.8	5.6	5.5	5.4	5.3	5.3
Mid-Range Trajectory Height • Inches	0.0	0.3	1.3	3.0	5.5	8.7	12.9	17.9	23.9
Drop • Inches	0.0	-1.3	-5.2	-11.9	-21.5	-34.0	-49.7	-68.6	-90.8

American Eagle (Federal) 130-grain Full Metal Jacket (AE38K)　　G1 Ballistic Coefficient = 0.128

Distance • Yards	Muzzle	25	50	75	100	125	150	175	200
Velocity • fps	950	920	890	870	840	817	796	775	756
Energy • Ft-lbs	260	245	230	215	205	193	183	174	165
Taylor KO Index	6.3	6.1	5.9	5.8	5.6	5.4	5.3	5.1	5.0
Mid-Range Trajectory Height • Inches	0.0	0.3	1.3	3.0	5.5	8.7	13.0	18.3	24.6
Drop • Inches	0.0	-1.2	-5.0	-11.6	-21.0	-33.5	-49.3	-68.5	-91.2

UMC (Remington) 130-grain Metal Case (L38S11)

G1 Ballistic Coefficient = 0.211

Distance • Yards	Muzzle	25	50	75	100	125	150	175	200
Velocity • fps	950	931	913	895	879	864	849	835	821
Energy • Ft-lbs	261	250	240	231	223	215	208	201	195
Taylor KO Index	6.3	6.2	6.1	5.9	5.8	5.7	5.6	5.5	5.4
Mid-Range Trajectory Height • Inches	0.0	0.3	1.2	2.9	4.8	8.2	12.1	16.9	22.4
Drop • Inches	0.0	-1.2	-5.0	-11.3	-20.3	-32.2	-46.9	-64.7	-85.6

Magtech 130-grain FMJ (38T)

G1 Ballistic Coefficient = 0.190

Distance • Yards	Muzzle	25	50	75	100	125	150	175	200
Velocity • fps	800	786	773	759	746	734	721	709	698
Energy • Ft-lbs	185	178	172	166	161	155	150	145	141
Taylor KO Index	5.3	5.2	5.1	5.0	5.0	4.9	4.8	4.7	4.6
Mid-Range Trajectory Height • Inches	0.0	0.4	1.8	4.0	7.3	11.6	17.0	23.5	31.2
Drop • Inches	0.0	-1.7	-7.0	-15.8	-28.5	-45.0	-65.6	-90.4	-119.4

USA (Winchester) 130-grain Full Metal Jacket (Q4171)

G1 Ballistic Coefficient = 0.150

Distance • Yards	Muzzle	25	50	75	100	125	150	175	200
Velocity • fps	800	782	765	749	733	717	702	688	673
Energy • Ft-lbs	185	177	169	162	155	149	142	137	131
Taylor KO Index	5.3	5.2	5.1	5.0	4.9	4.8	4.7	4.6	4.5
Mid-Range Trajectory Height • Inches	0.0	0.4	1.8	4.1	7.4	11.8	17.4	24.3	32.4
Drop • Inches	0.0	-1.7	-7.0	-16.0	-28.8	-45.7	-66.9	-92.4	-121.5

UMC (Remington) 130-grain Metal Case (L38S11)

G1 Ballistic Coefficient = 0.217

Distance • Yards	Muzzle	25	50	75	100	125	150	175	200
Velocity • fps	790	778	766	755	743	733	722	711	701
Energy • Ft-lbs	180	175	169	164	160	155	150	146	142
Taylor KO Index	5.3	5.2	5.1	5.0	4.9	4.9	4.8	4.7	4.7
Mid-Range Trajectory Height • Inches	0.0	0.4	1.8	4.1	7.4	11.7	17.2	23.8	31.5
Drop • Inches	0.0	-1.8	-7.1	-16.2	-29.0	-45.8	-66.6	-91.6	-120.9

PMC 132-grain Full Metal Jacket (38G)

G1 Ballistic Coefficient = 0.123

Distance • Yards	Muzzle	25	50	75	100	125	150	175	200
Velocity • fps	841	817	795	773	752	733	714	696	679
Energy • Ft-lbs	207	195	185	175	166	158	150	142	135
Taylor KO Index	5.7	5.5	5.4	5.2	5.1	4.9	4.8	4.7	4.6
Mid-Range Trajectory Height • Inches	0.0	0.4	1.6	3.8	6.9	11.1	16.4	23.0	30.8
Drop • Inches	0.0	-1.6	-6.4	-14.7	-26.6	-42.3	-62.1	-86.2	-114.7

Hornady 140-grain Jacketed Hollow Point/XTP (90352)

G1 Ballistic Coefficient = 0.165

Distance • Yards	Muzzle	25	50	75	100	125	150	175	200
Velocity • fps	825	807	790	774	757	741	726	712	698
Energy • Ft-lbs	212	202	194	186	178	171	164	157	151
Taylor KO Index	5.9	5.8	5.6	5.5	5.4	5.3	5.2	5.1	5.0
Mid-Range Trajectory Height • Inches	0.0	0.3	1.6	3.8	6.9	11.1	16.3	22.7	30.3
Drop • Inches	0.0	-1.6	-6.6	-15.0	-27.1	-43.0	-62.8	-86.7	-115.0

Hornady 148-grain HBWC (Match) (90432) (Discontinued in 2004)

G1 Ballistic Coefficient = 0.047

Distance • Yards	Muzzle	25	50	75	100	125	150	175	200
Velocity • fps	800	746	697	652	610	570	534	499	467
Energy • Ft-lbs	210	183	160	140	122	107	94	82	72
Taylor KO Index	6.0	5.6	5.3	4.9	4.6	4.3	4.0	3.8	3.5
Mid-Range Trajectory Height • Inches	0.0	0.4	2.0	4.7	9.0	15.1	23.3	34.2	47.9
Drop • Inches	0.0	-1.8	-7.5	-17.6	-32.9	-54.2	-82.1	-117.6	-161.8

Lapua 148-grain Lead Wadcutter (4319025)

G1 Ballistic Coefficient = 0.055

Distance • Yards	Muzzle	25	50	75	100	125	150	175	200
Velocity • fps	755	712	672	635	600	566	535	505	477
Energy • Ft-lbs	187	167	149	133	118	105	94	84	75
Taylor KO Index	5.7	5.4	5.1	4.8	4.5	4.3	4.0	3.8	3.6
Mid-Range Trajectory Height • Inches	0.0	0.5	2.1	5.1	9.6	15.9	24.5	35.5	49.2
Drop • Inches	0.0	-2.0	-8.2	-19.3	-35.8	-58.4	-87.8	-124.7	-170.2

PMC 148-grain Lead Wadcutter (38C)   G1 Ballistic Coefficient = 0.084

Distance • Yards	Muzzle	25	50	75	100	125	150	175	200
Velocity • fps	730	703	677	652	628	606	584	562	542
Energy • Ft-lbs	175	162	151	140	130	121	112	104	97
Taylor KO Index	5.5	5.3	5.1	4.9	4.8	4.6	4.4	4.3	4.1
Mid-Range Trajectory Height • Inches	0.0	0.5	2.2	5.1	9.5	15.4	23.1	32.7	44.3
Drop • Inches	0.0	-2.1	-8.6	-19.8	-36.2	-58.0	-85.8	-119.9	-160.9

Federal 148-grain Lead Wadcutter Match (GM38A)   G1 Ballistic Coefficient = 0.053

Distance • Yards	Muzzle	25	50	75	100	125	150	175	200
Velocity • fps	710	670	630	600	560	528	497	468	441
Energy • Ft-lbs	165	150	130	115	105	92	81	72	64
Taylor KO Index	5.4	5.1	4.8	4.5	4.2	4.0	3.8	3.5	3.2
Mid-Range Trajectory Height • Inches	0.0	0.6	2.4	5.7	10.8	18.2	27.9	40.6	56.4
Drop • Inches	0.0	-2.2	-9.3	-21.9	-40.6	-66.3	-99.8	-142.1	-194.2

Magtech 148-grain LWC (38B)   G1 Ballistic Coefficient = 0.055

Distance • Yards	Muzzle	25	50	75	100	125	150	175	200
Velocity • fps	710	670	634	599	566	536	507	479	452
Energy • Ft-lbs	166	148	132	118	105	94	84	75	67
Taylor KO Index	5.4	5.1	4.8	4.5	4.3	4.0	3.8	3.6	3.4
Mid-Range Trajectory Height • Inches	0.0	0.6	2.4	5.7	10.8	17.9	27.4	39.7	54.9
Drop • Inches	0.0	-2.2	-9.3	-21.8	-40.4	-65.6	-98.4	-139.8	-190.6

Remington 148-grain Targetmaster Lead WC Match (R38S3)   G1 Ballistic Coefficient = 0.055

Distance • Yards	Muzzle	25	50	75	100	125	150	175	200
Velocity • fps	710	670	634	599	566	536	507	479	452
Energy • Ft-lbs	166	148	132	118	105	94	84	75	67
Taylor KO Index	5.4	5.1	4.8	4.5	4.3	4.0	3.8	3.6	3.4
Mid-Range Trajectory Height • Inches	0.0	0.6	2.4	5.7	10.8	17.9	27.4	39.7	54.9
Drop • Inches	0.0	-2.2	-9.3	-21.8	-40.4	-65.6	-98.4	-139.8	-190.6

Winchester 148-grain Lead-Wad Cutter (X38SMRP)   G1 Ballistic Coefficient = 0.055

Distance • Yards	Muzzle	25	50	75	100	125	150	175	200
Velocity • fps	710	670	634	599	566	536	507	479	452
Energy • Ft-lbs	166	148	132	118	105	94	84	75	67
Taylor KO Index	5.4	5.1	4.8	4.5	4.3	4.0	3.8	3.6	3.4
Mid-Range Trajectory Height • Inches	0.0	0.6	2.4	5.7	10.8	17.9	27.4	39.7	54.9
Drop • Inches	0.0	-2.2	-9.3	-21.8	-40.4	-65.6	-98.4	-139.8	-190.6

Sellier & Bellot 148-grain WC (SBA03801)   G1 Ballistic Coefficient = 0.125

Distance • Yards	Muzzle	25	50	75	100	125	150	175	200
Velocity • fps	699	679	663	646	629	613	598	583	568
Energy • Ft-lbs	162	153	145	137	130	124	117	112	106
Taylor KO Index	5.3	5.1	5.0	4.9	4.7	4.6	4.5	4.4	4.3
Mid-Range Trajectory Height • Inches	0.0	0.5	2.3	5.4	9.8	15.8	23.4	32.8	43.9
Drop • Inches	0.0	-2.3	-9.2	-21.1	-38.2	-60.8	-89.1	-123.5	-164.4

Fiocchi 148-grain Jacketed Hollowpoint (38E)   G1 Ballistic Coefficient = 0.120

Distance • Yards	Muzzle	25	50	75	100	125	150	175	200
Velocity • fps	820	795	772	750	730	710	690	672	654
Energy • Ft-lbs	225	208	196	185	175	165	157	148	140
Taylor KO Index	6.2	6.0	5.8	5.7	5.5	5.4	5.2	5.1	4.9
Mid-Range Trajectory Height • Inches	0.0	0.3	1.7	3.9	7.2	11.6	17.3	24.3	32.7
Drop • Inches	0.0	-1.6	-6.7	-15.4	-28.0	-44.7	-65.7	-91.2	-121.5

Lapua 150-grain SJFN (4319242) (Discontinued in 2004)   G1 Ballistic Coefficient = 0.145

Distance • Yards	Muzzle	25	50	75	100	125	150	175	200
Velocity • fps	1066	1023	987	955	927	902	878	857	836
Energy • Ft-lbs	374	344	320	300	282	271	257	245	233
Taylor KO Index	8.2	7.8	7.6	7.3	7.1	6.9	6.7	6.6	6.4
Mid-Range Trajectory Height • Inches	0.0	0.3	1.3	3.0	4.3	7.1	10.7	15.0	20.1
Drop • Inches	0.0	-1.0	-4.0	-9.3	-17.0	27.2	-40.1	-55.7	-74.4

Aguila 150-grain Lead Round Nose

G1 Ballistic Coefficient = 0.145

Distance • Yards	Muzzle	25	50	75	100	125	150	175	200
Velocity • fps	850	829	810	791	773	756	739	723	707
Energy • Ft-lbs	254	241	230	220	210	200	192	183	176
Taylor KO Index	6.9	6.7	6.5	6.4	6.2	6.1	6.0	5.8	5.7
Mid-Range Trajectory Height • Inches	0.0	0.4	1.6	3.6	6.6	10.6	15.7	21.8	29.1
Drop • Inches	0.0	-1.5	-6.2	-14.2	-25.7	-40.8	-59.7	-82.6	-109.6

Winchester 150-grain Lead (Q4196)

G1 Ballistic Coefficient = 0.175

Distance • Yards	Muzzle	25	50	75	100	125	150	175	200
Velocity • fps	845	828	812	796	781	766	752	738	725
Energy • Ft-lbs	238	228	219	211	203	196	188	182	175
Taylor KO Index	6.5	6.3	6.2	6.1	6.0	5.9	5.8	5.6	5.5
Mid-Range Trajectory Height • Inches	0.0	0.3	1.5	3.6	6.6	10.4	15.4	21.4	28.5
Drop • Inches	0.0	-1.5	-6.2	-14.3	-25.7	-40.7	-59.4	-82.0	-108.5

Sellier & Bellot 158-grain LRN (SBA03802)

G1 Ballistic Coefficient = 0.180

Distance • Yards	Muzzle	25	50	75	100	125	150	175	200
Velocity • fps	997	971	946	924	903	884	865	848	831
Energy • Ft-lbs	349	331	314	299	286	274	263	252	243
Taylor KO Index	8.1	7.8	7.6	7.5	7.3	7.1	7.0	6.9	6.7
Mid-Range Trajectory Height • Inches	0.0	0.3	1.2	2.7	4.9	7.8	11.5	16.0	21.3
Drop • Inches	0.0	-1.1	-4.5	-10.4	-18.8	-29.8	-43.7	-60.4	-80.2

Lapua 158-grain Lead-Round Nose (4319137) (Discontinued in 2004)

G1 Ballistic Coefficient = 0.150

Distance • Yards	Muzzle	25	50	75	100	125	150	175	200
Velocity • fps	837	818	799	781	764	748	732	717	702
Energy • Ft-lbs	246	235	224	214	205	196	188	180	173
Taylor KO Index	6.7	6.6	6.4	6.3	6.2	6.0	5.9	5.8	5.7
Mid-Range Trajectory Height • Inches	0.0	0.4	1.6	3.7	6.8	10.8	16.0	22.3	29.7
Drop • Inches	0.0	-1.6	-6.4	-14.6	-26.4	-41.9	-61.3	-84.7	-112.3

PMC 158-grain Lead Round Nose (38A)

G1 Ballistic Coefficient = 0.147

Distance • Yards	Muzzle	25	50	75	100	125	150	175	200
Velocity • fps	820	801	783	765	749	733	717	701	687
Energy • Ft-lbs	235	225	215	206	197	188	180	173	165
Taylor KO Index	6.6	6.5	6.3	6.2	6.0	5.9	5.8	5.6	5.5
Mid-Range Trajectory Height • Inches	0.0	0.4	1.7	3.9	7.1	11.3	16.6	23.2	31.0
Drop • Inches	0.0	-1.6	-6.7	-15.2	-27.5	-43.6	-63.8	-88.3	-117.1

Magtech 158-grain LFN (38L) (Discontinued in 2005)

G1 Ballistic Coefficient = 0.230

Distance • Yards	Muzzle	25	50	75	100	125	150	175	200
Velocity • fps	800	788	776	764	753	742	731	720	710
Energy • Ft-lbs	225	218	211	205	199	193	187	182	177
Taylor KO Index	6.4	6.3	6.3	6.2	6.1	6.0	5.9	5.8	5.7
Mid-Range Trajectory Height • Inches	0.0	0.3	1.7	3.9	7.2	11.4	16.7	23.1	30.6
Drop • Inches	0.0	-1.7	-6.9	-15.8	-28.3	-44.7	-65.0	-89.4	-118.0

Federal 158-grain Nyclad Round Nose (P38B) (Discontinued in 2004)

G1 Ballistic Coefficient = 0.133

Distance • Yards	Muzzle	25	50	75	100	125	150	175	200
Velocity • fps	760	740	720	710	690	674	659	643	628
Energy • Ft-lbs	200	190	185	175	170	160	152	145	139
Taylor KO Index	6.1	6.0	5.8	5.7	5.6	5.4	5.3	5.2	5.1
Mid-Range Trajectory Height • Inches	0.0	0.5	2.0	4.6	8.3	13.2	19.5	27.3	36.5
Drop • Inches	0.0	-1.9	-77.8	-17.8	-32.1	-51.2	-74.7	-103.4	-137.3

Federal 158-grain Lead Round Nose (C8B) (Discontinued in 2004)

G1 Ballistic Coefficient = 0.133

Distance • Yards	Muzzle	25	50	75	100	125	150	175	200
Velocity • fps	760	740	720	710	690	674	659	643	628
Energy • Ft-lbs	200	190	185	175	170	160	152	145	139
Taylor KO Index	6.1	6.0	5.8	5.7	5.6	5.4	5.3	5.2	5.1
Mid-Range Trajectory Height • Inches	0.0	0.5	2.0	4.6	8.3	13.2	19.5	27.3	36.5
Drop • Inches	0.0	-1.9	-77.8	-17.8	-32.1	-51.2	-74.7	-103.4	-137.3

American Eagle (Federal) 158-grain Lead Round Nose (AE38B)
G1 Ballistic Coefficient = 0.133

Distance • Yards	Muzzle	25	50	75	100	125	150	175	200
Velocity • fps	760	740	720	710	690	674	659	643	628
Energy • Ft-lbs	200	190	185	175	170	160	152	145	139
Taylor KO Index	6.1	6.0	5.8	5.7	5.6	5.4	5.3	5.2	5.1
Mid-Range Trajectory Height • Inches	0.0	0.5	2.0	4.6	8.3	13.2	19.5	27.3	36.5
Drop • Inches	0.0	-1.9	-77.8	-17.8	-32.1	-51.2	-74.7	-103.4	-137.3

CCI 158-grain LRN Blazer (3522)
G1 Ballistic Coefficient = 0.147

Distance • Yards	Muzzle	25	50	75	100	125	150	175	200
Velocity • fps	755	741	728	715	702	690	678	666	655
Energy • Ft-lbs	200	193	186	179	173	167	161	156	150
Taylor KO Index	6.1	6.0	5.9	5.8	5.7	5.6	5.5	5.4	5.3
Mid-Range Trajectory Height • Inches	0.0	0.5	2.0	4.5	8.2	13.0	19.1	26.5	35.3
Drop • Inches	0.0	-1.9	-7.8	-17.8	-32.0	-50.6	-73.8	-101.7	-134.5

Magtech 158-grain LRN (38A)
G1 Ballistic Coefficient = 0.147

Distance • Yards	Muzzle	25	50	75	100	125	150	175	200
Velocity • fps	755	739	723	707	692	678	663	649	636
Energy • Ft-lbs	200	191	183	175	168	161	154	148	142
Taylor KO Index	6.1	6.0	5.8	5.7	5.6	5.5	5.3	5.2	5.1
Mid-Range Trajectory Height • Inches	0.0	0.5	2.0	4.6	8.3	13.2	19.5	27.2	36.3
Drop • Inches	0.0	-1.9	-7.8	-17.8	-32.4	-51.3	-75.0	-103.6	-137.3

Remington 158-grain Lead Round Nose (R38S5)
G1 Ballistic Coefficient = 0.147

Distance • Yards	Muzzle	25	50	75	100	125	150	175	200
Velocity • fps	755	739	723	707	692	678	663	649	636
Energy • Ft-lbs	200	191	183	175	168	161	154	148	142
Taylor KO Index	6.1	6.0	5.8	5.7	5.6	5.5	5.3	5.2	5.1
Mid-Range Trajectory Height • Inches	0.0	0.5	2.0	4.6	8.3	13.2	19.5	27.2	36.3
Drop • Inches	0.0	-1.9	-7.8	-17.8	-32.4	-51.3	-75.0	-103.6	-137.3

UMC (Remington) 158-grain Lead Round Nose (L38S5)
G1 Ballistic Coefficient = 0.146

Distance • Yards	Muzzle	25	50	75	100	125	150	175	200
Velocity • fps	755	739	723	707	692	678	663	649	636
Energy • Ft-lbs	200	191	183	175	168	161	154	148	142
Taylor KO Index	6.1	6.0	5.8	5.7	5.6	5.5	5.3	5.2	5.1
Mid-Range Trajectory Height • Inches	0.0	0.5	2.0	4.6	8.3	13.2	19.5	27.2	36.3
Drop • Inches	0.0	-1.9	-7.8	-17.8	-32.4	-51.3	-75.0	-103.6	-137.3

Winchester 158-grain Lead-Round Nose (X38S1P)
G1 Ballistic Coefficient = 0.147

Distance • Yards	Muzzle	25	50	75	100	125	150	175	200
Velocity • fps	755	739	723	707	692	678	663	649	636
Energy • Ft-lbs	200	191	183	175	168	161	154	148	142
Taylor KO Index	6.1	6.0	5.8	5.7	5.6	5.5	5.3	5.2	5.1
Mid-Range Trajectory Height • Inches	0.0	0.5	2.0	4.6	8.3	13.2	19.5	27.2	36.3
Drop • Inches	0.0	-1.9	-7.8	-17.8	-32.4	-51.3	-75.0	-103.6	-137.3

Federal 158-grain Semi-Wadcutter HP +P (C38G) (Discontinued in 2004)
G1 Ballistic Coefficient = 0.180

Distance • Yards	Muzzle	25	50	75	100	125	150	175	200
Velocity • fps	890	870	860	840	820	805	790	776	761
Energy • Ft-lbs	270	265	260	245	235	227	219	211	203
Taylor KO Index	7.2	7.0	6.9	6.8	6.6	6.5	6.4	6.3	6.1
Mid-Range Trajectory Height • Inches	0.0	0.3	1.4	3.3	5.9	9.4	13.9	19.4	25.8
Drop • Inches	0.0	-1.4	-5.6	-12.9	-23.2	-36.8	-53.7	-74.0	-98.0

Federal 158-grain Lead Semi-Wadcutter +P (C38H) (Discontinued in 2004)
G1 Ballistic Coefficient = 0.180

Distance • Yards	Muzzle	25	50	75	100	125	150	175	200
Velocity • fps	890	870	860	840	820	805	790	776	761
Energy • Ft-lbs	270	265	260	245	235	227	219	211	203
Taylor KO Index	7.2	7.0	6.9	6.8	6.6	6.5	6.4	6.3	6.1
Mid-Range Trajectory Height • Inches	0.0	0.3	1.4	3.3	5.9	9.4	13.9	19.4	25.8
Drop • Inches	0.0	-1.4	-5.6	-12.9	-23.2	-36.8	-53.7	-74.0	-98.0

Federal 158-grain Nyclad SWC-HP +P (P38G) (Discontinued in 2004)
G1 Ballistic Coefficient = 0.180

Distance • Yards	Muzzle	25	50	75	100	125	150	175	200
Velocity • fps	890	870	860	840	820	805	790	776	761
Energy • Ft-lbs	270	265	260	245	235	227	219	211	203
Taylor KO Index	7.2	7.0	6.9	6.8	6.6	6.5	6.4	6.3	6.1
Mid-Range Trajectory Height • Inches	0.0	0.3	11.4	3.3	5.9	9.4	13.9	19.4	25.8
Drop • Inches	0.0	-1.4	-5.6	-12.9	-23.2	-36.8	-53.7	-74.0	-98.0

Remington 158-grain Lead Hollow Point +P (R38S12)
G1 Ballistic Coefficient = 0.188

Distance • Yards	Muzzle	25	50	75	100	125	150	175	200
Velocity • fps	890	872	855	839	823	808	794	780	766
Energy • Ft-lbs	278	267	257	247	238	229	221	213	206
Taylor KO Index	7.2	7.0	6.9	6.8	6.6	6.5	6.4	6.3	6.2
Mid-Range Trajectory Height • Inches	0.0	0.3	1.4	3.3	6.6	9.4	13.8	19.2	25.6
Drop • Inches	0.0	-1.4	-5.6	-12.8	-23.2	-36.8	-53.5	-73.7	-97.6

Remington 158-grain Semi-Wadcutter +P (R38S14)
G1 Ballistic Coefficient = 0.188

Distance • Yards	Muzzle	25	50	75	100	125	150	175	200
Velocity • fps	890	872	855	839	823	808	794	780	766
Energy • Ft-lbs	278	267	257	247	238	229	221	213	206
Taylor KO Index	7.2	7.0	6.9	6.8	6.6	6.5	6.4	6.3	6.2
Mid-Range Trajectory Height • Inches	0.0	0.3	1.4	3.3	6.6	9.4	13.8	19.2	25.6
Drop • Inches	0.0	-1.4	-5.6	-12.8	-23.2	-36.8	-53.5	-73.7	-97.6

Winchester 158-grain Lead-Semi WC HP +P (X38SPD)
G1 Ballistic Coefficient = 0.188

Distance • Yards	Muzzle	25	50	75	100	125	150	175	200
Velocity • fps	890	872	855	839	823	808	794	780	766
Energy • Ft-lbs	278	267	257	247	238	229	221	213	206
Taylor KO Index	7.2	7.0	6.9	6.8	6.6	6.5	6.4	6.3	6.2
Mid-Range Trajectory Height • Inches	0.0	0.3	1.4	3.3	6.6	9.4	13.8	19.2	25.6
Drop • Inches	0.0	-1.4	-5.6	-12.8	-23.2	-36.8	-53.5	-73.7	-97.6

Federal 158-grain Lead Semi-Wadcutter (C38C) (Discontinued in 2004)
G1 Ballistic Coefficient = 0.133

Distance • Yards	Muzzle	25	50	75	100	125	150	175	200
Velocity • fps	760	740	720	710	690	674	659	643	628
Energy • Ft-lbs	200	190	185	175	170	160	152	145	139
Taylor KO Index	6.1	6.0	5.8	5.7	5.6	5.4	5.3	5.2	5.1
Mid-Range Trajectory Height • Inches	0.0	0.5	2.0	4.6	8.3	13.2	19.5	27.3	36.5
Drop • Inches	0.0	-1.9	-77.8	-17.8	-32.1	-51.2	-74.7	-103.4	-137.3

Magtech 158-grain LSWC (38J)
G1 Ballistic Coefficient = 0.140

Distance • Yards	Muzzle	25	50	75	100	125	150	175	200
Velocity • fps	755	738	721	705	689	674	659	645	630
Energy • Ft-lbs	200	191	182	174	167	159	152	146	139
Taylor KO Index	6.1	5.9	5.8	5.7	5.6	5.4	5.3	5.2	5.1
Mid-Range Trajectory Height • Inches	0.0	0.5	2.0	4.6	8.4	13.3	19.6	27.0	36.2
Drop • Inches	0.0	-1.9	-7.9	-18.0	-32.4	-51.5	-75.3	-104.1	-138.2

Remington 158-grain Semi-Wadcutter (R38S6)
G1 Ballistic Coefficient = 0.148

Distance • Yards	Muzzle	25	50	75	100	125	150	175	200
Velocity • fps	755	739	723	707	692	678	663	649	636
Energy • Ft-lbs	200	191	183	175	168	161	154	148	142
Taylor KO Index	6.1	6.0	5.8	5.7	5.6	5.5	5.3	5.2	5.1
Mid-Range Trajectory Height • Inches	0.0	0.5	2.0	4.6	8.3	13.2	19.5	27.2	36.3
Drop • Inches	0.0	-1.9	-7.8	-17.8	-32.4	-51.3	-75.0	-103.6	-137.3

Winchester 158-grain Lead-Semi WC (X38WCPSV)
G1 Ballistic Coefficient = 0.140

Distance • Yards	Muzzle	25	50	75	100	125	150	175	200
Velocity • fps	755	738	721	705	689	674	659	645	630
Energy • Ft-lbs	200	191	182	174	167	159	152	146	139
Taylor KO Index	6.1	5.9	5.8	5.7	5.6	5.4	5.3	5.2	5.1
Mid-Range Trajectory Height • Inches	0.0	0.5	2.0	4.6	8.4	13.3	19.6	27.0	36.2
Drop • Inches	0.0	-1.9	-7.9	-18.0	-32.4	-51.5	-75.3	-104.1	-138.2

Aguila 158-grain Semi Jacketed Soft Point
G1 Ballistic Coefficient = 0.202

Distance • Yards	Muzzle	25	50	75	100	125	150	175	200
Velocity • fps	925	906	889	872	856	841	827	813	799
Energy • Ft-lbs	300	288	277	267	257	248	240	232	224
Taylor KO Index	7.5	7.3	7.2	7.0	6.9	6.8	6.7	6.6	6.5
Mid-Range Trajectory Height • Inches	0.0	0.3	1.3	3.0	5.5	8.8	12.9	17.8	23.7
Drop • Inches	0.0	-1.3	-5.2	-11.9	-21.4	-33.9	-49.5	-68.2	-90.3

Magtech 158-grain SJFP +P (38N)
G1 Ballistic Coefficient = 0.079

Distance • Yards	Muzzle	25	50	75	100	125	150	175	200
Velocity • fps	890	849	812	778	746	717	689	662	636
Energy • Ft-lbs	278	253	231	212	196	180	166	154	142
Taylor KO Index	7.2	6.9	6.6	6.3	6.0	5.8	5.6	5.3	5.1
Mid-Range Trajectory Height • Inches	0.0	0.3	1.5	3.6	6.6	10.8	16.2	23.1	31.4
Drop • Inches	0.0	-1.4	-5.9	-13.6	-24.9	-40.1	-59.6	-83.6	-112.6

Sellier & Bellot 158-grain SP (SBA03803)
G1 Ballistic Coefficient = 0.057

Distance • Yards	Muzzle	25	50	75	100	125	150	175	200
Velocity • fps	889	835	784	741	701	663	628	594	563
Energy • Ft-lbs	278	245	216	193	172	154	138	124	111
Taylor KO Index	7.2	6.7	6.3	6.0	5.7	5.4	5.1	4.8	4.5
Mid-Range Trajectory Height • Inches	0.0	0.4	1.6	3.8	7.1	11.7	17.9	26.0	35.9
Drop • Inches	0.0	-1.4	-6.0	-14.1	-26.2	-42.6	-64.1	-91.0	-124.1

Magtech 158-grain SJSP (38C)
G1 Ballistic Coefficient = 0.192

Distance • Yards	Muzzle	25	50	75	100	125	150	175	200
Velocity • fps	807	793	779	766	753	740	728	716	704
Energy • Ft-lbs	230	221	213	206	199	192	186	180	174
Taylor KO Index	6.5	6.4	6.3	6.2	6.1	6.0	5.9	5.8	5.7
Mid-Range Trajectory Height • Inches	0.0	0.4	1.7	3.9	7.2	11.3	16.6	23.1	30.6
Drop • Inches	0.0	-1.7	-6.8	-15.6	-28.0	-44.2	-64.4	-88.7	-117.3

PMC 158-grain Jacketed Soft Point (38N)
G1 Ballistic Coefficient = 0.127

Distance • Yards	Muzzle	25	50	75	100	125	150	175	200
Velocity • fps	800	780	760	741	722	704	687	670	654
Energy • Ft-lbs	225	213	202	192	183	174	165	157	150
Taylor KO Index	6.5	6.3	6.1	6.0	5.8	5.7	5.6	5.4	5.3
Mid-Range Trajectory Height • Inches	0.0	0.4	1.8	4.1	7.5	12.1	17.9	25.0	33.5
Drop • Inches	0.0	-1.7	-7.0	-16.1	-29.2	-46.4	-68.0	-94.2	-125.2

Magtech 158-grain SJSP Flat (38C)
G1 Ballistic Coefficient = 0.175

Distance • Yards	Muzzle	25	50	75	100	125	150	175	200
Velocity • fps	744	730	723	704	692	679	667	656	644
Energy • Ft-lbs	200	187	183	174	168	162	156	151	146
Taylor KO Index	6.0	5.9	5.8	5.7	5.6	5.5	5.4	5.3	5.2
Mid-Range Trajectory Height • Inches	0.0	0.5	2.0	4.7	8.5	13.4	19.7	27.4	36.4
Drop • Inches	0.0	-2.0	-8.0	-18.3	-33.0	-52.2	-76.1	-104.9	-138.7

Aguila 158-grain Semi Jacketed Hollow Point
G1 Ballistic Coefficient = 0.174

Distance • Yards	Muzzle	25	50	75	100	125	150	175	200
Velocity • fps	900	880	861	844	827	810	795	780	765
Energy • Ft-lbs	284	272	260	250	240	230	222	213	205
Taylor KO Index	7.3	7.1	7.0	6.8	6.7	6.5	6.4	6.3	6.2
Mid-Range Trajectory Height • Inches	0.0	0.3	1.4	3.2	5.9	9.3	13.8	19.1	25.5
Drop • Inches	0.0	-1.4	-5.5	-12.6	-22.8	-36.1	-52.7	-72.8	-96.4

Magtech 158-grain SJHP +P (38H)
G1 Ballistic Coefficient = 0.079

Distance • Yards	Muzzle	25	50	75	100	125	150	175	200
Velocity • fps	890	849	812	778	746	717	689	662	636
Energy • Ft-lbs	278	253	231	212	196	180	166	154	142
Taylor KO Index	7.2	6.9	6.6	6.3	6.0	5.8	5.6	5.3	5.1
Mid-Range Trajectory Height • Inches	0.0	0.3	1.5	3.6	6.6	10.8	16.2	23.1	31.4
Drop • Inches	0.0	-1.4	-5.9	-13.6	-24.9	-40.1	-59.6	-83.6	-112.6

Magtech 158-grain SJHP (38E)

G1 Ballistic Coefficient = 0.192

Distance • Yards	Muzzle	25	50	75	100	125	150	175	200
Velocity • fps	807	793	779	766	753	740	728	716	704
Energy • Ft-lbs	230	221	213	206	199	192	186	180	174
Taylor KO Index	6.5	6.4	6.3	6.2	6.1	6.0	5.9	5.8	5.7
Mid-Range Trajectory Height • Inches	0.0	0.4	1.7	3.9	7.2	11.3	16.6	23.1	30.6
Drop • Inches	0.0	-1.7	-6.8	-15.6	-28.0	-44.2	-64.4	-88.7	-117.3

Hornady 158-grain JHP/XTP (90362)

G1 Ballistic Coefficient = 0.145

Distance • Yards	Muzzle	25	50	75	100	125	150	175	200
Velocity • fps	800	782	765	747	731	715	699	684	670
Energy • Ft-lbs	225	214	205	196	188	179	172	164	157
Taylor KO Index	6.4	6.3	6.2	6.0	5.9	5.8	5.6	5.5	5.4
Mid-Range Trajectory Height • Inches	0.0	0.4	1.8	4.1	7.4	11.8	17.5	24.4	32.5
Drop • Inches	0.0	-1.7	-7.0	-16.0	-28.9	-45.8	-67.0	-92.7	-123.0

Fiocchi 158-grain Full Metal Jacket (38G)

G1 Ballistic Coefficient = 0.160

Distance • Yards	Muzzle	25	50	75	100	125	150	175	200
Velocity • fps	960	934	910	888	867	847	829	811	794
Energy • Ft-lbs	320	306	290	276	264	252	241	231	221
Taylor KO Index	7.7	7.5	7.3	7.2	7.0	6.8	6.7	6.5	6.4
Mid-Range Trajectory Height • Inches	0.0	0.3	1.2	2.9	5.2	8.3	12.4	17.2	23.1
Drop • Inches	0.0	-1.2	-4.9	-11.2	-20.3	-32.2	-47.2	-65.3	-86.7

Aguila 158-grain Full Metal Jacket

G1 Ballistic Coefficient = 0.210

Distance • Yards	Muzzle	25	50	75	100	125	150	175	200
Velocity • fps	950	931	912	895	879	863	848	834	820
Energy • Ft-lbs	317	304	292	281	271	262	253	244	236
Taylor KO Index	7.7	7.5	7.4	7.2	7.1	7.0	6.9	6.7	6.6
Mid-Range Trajectory Height • Inches	0.0	0.3	1.3	2.9	5.2	8.3	12.2	16.9	22.5
Drop • Inches	0.0	-1.2	-5.0	-11.3	-20.3	-32.2	-47.0	-64.8	-85.7

Magtech 158-grain FMJ Flat (38Q)

G1 Ballistic Coefficient = 0.162

Distance • Yards	Muzzle	25	50	75	100	125	150	175	200
Velocity • fps	938	914	891	871	851	833	815	798	782
Energy • Ft-lbs	309	293	279	266	254	243	233	224	214
Taylor KO Index	7.6	7.4	7.2	7.0	6.9	6.7	6.6	6.4	6.3
Mid-Range Trajectory Height • Inches	0.0	0.3	1.3	3.0	5.5	8.7	12.9	18.0	24.0
Drop • Inches	0.0	-1.3	-5.1	-11.7	-21.2	-33.6	-49.2	-68.0	-90.3

Sellier & Bellot 158-grain FMJ (SBA03804)

G1 Ballistic Coefficient = 0.057

Distance • Yards	Muzzle	25	50	75	100	125	150	175	200
Velocity • fps	889	835	784	741	701	663	628	594	563
Energy • Ft-lbs	278	245	216	193	172	154	138	124	111
Taylor KO Index	7.2	6.7	6.3	6.0	5.7	5.4	5.1	4.8	4.5
Mid-Range Trajectory Height • Inches	0.0	0.4	1.6	3.8	7.1	11.7	17.9	26.0	35.9
Drop • Inches	0.0	-1.4	-6.0	-14.1	-26.2	-42.6	-64.1	-91.0	-124.1

CCI 158-grain TMJ +P Blazer (3519)

G1 Ballistic Coefficient = 0.175

Distance • Yards	Muzzle	25	50	75	100	125	150	175	200
Velocity • fps	850	833	816	800	785	771	756	742	729
Energy • Ft-lbs	253	243	234	225	216	208	201	193	186
Taylor KO Index	6.9	6.7	6.6	6.5	6.3	6.2	6.1	6.0	5.9
Mid-Range Trajectory Height • Inches	0.0	0.4	1.6	3.6	6.5	10.3	15.3	21.2	28.2
Drop • Inches	0.0	-1.5	-6.2	-14.1	-25.4	-40.2	-58.7	-81.0	-107.2

CCI 158-grain Clean-Fire—TMJ +P Blazer (3475)

G1 Ballistic Coefficient = 0.175

Distance • Yards	Muzzle	25	50	75	100	125	150	175	200
Velocity • fps	850	833	816	800	785	771	756	742	729
Energy • Ft-lbs	253	243	234	225	216	208	201	193	186
Taylor KO Index	6.9	6.7	6.6	6.5	6.3	6.2	6.1	6.0	5.9
Mid-Range Trajectory Height • Inches	0.0	0.4	1.6	3.6	6.5	10.3	15.3	21.2	28.2
Drop • Inches	0.0	-1.5	-6.2	-14.1	-25.4	-40.2	-58.7	-81.0	-107.2

Speer 158-grain TMJ +P Lawman (53750)

G1 Ballistic Coefficient = 0.175

Distance • Yards	Muzzle	25	50	75	100	125	150	175	200
Velocity • fps	850	833	816	800	785	771	756	742	729
Energy • Ft-lbs	253	243	234	225	216	208	201	193	186
Taylor KO Index	6.9	6.7	6.6	6.5	6.3	6.2	6.1	6.0	5.9
Mid-Range Trajectory Height • Inches	0.0	0.4	1.6	3.6	6.5	10.3	15.3	21.2	28.2
Drop • Inches	0.0	-1.5	-6.2	-14.1	-25.4	-40.2	-58.7	-81.0	-107.2

Speer 158-grain Clean-Fire—TMJ +P Lawman (53833)

G1 Ballistic Coefficient = 0.175

Distance • Yards	Muzzle	25	50	75	100	125	150	175	200
Velocity • fps	850	833	816	800	785	771	756	742	729
Energy • Ft-lbs	253	243	234	225	216	208	201	193	186
Taylor KO Index	6.9	6.7	6.6	6.5	6.3	6.2	6.1	6.0	5.9
Mid-Range Trajectory Height • Inches	0.0	0.4	1.6	3.6	6.5	10.3	15.3	21.2	28.2
Drop • Inches	0.0	-1.5	-6.2	-14.1	-25.4	-40.2	-58.7	-81.0	-107.2

Lapua 158-grain FMJ (4319143) (Discontinued in 2004)

G1 Ballistic Coefficient = 0.160

Distance • Yards	Muzzle	25	50	75	100	125	150	175	200
Velocity • fps	837	819	801	785	769	753	738	723	709
Energy • Ft-lbs	246	235	225	216	207	199	191	184	176
Taylor KO Index	6.7	6.6	6.5	6.3	6.2	6.1	5.9	5.8	5.7
Mid-Range Trajectory Height • Inches	0.0	0.4	1.6	3.7	6.8	10.7	15.8	22.0	29.4
Drop • Inches	0.0	-1.6	-6.4	-14.6	-26.3	-41.7	-60.9	-84.1	-111.5

Norma 158-grain Full jacket semi WC (19114)

G1 Ballistic Coefficient = 0.200

Distance • Yards	Muzzle	25	50	75	100	125	150	175	200
Velocity • fps	804	790	777	765	752	740	729	717	706
Energy • Ft-lbs	226	218	211	205	198	192	186	180	175
Taylor KO Index	6.5	6.4	6.3	6.2	6.1	6.0	5.9	5.8	5.7
Mid-Range Trajectory Height • Inches	0.0	0.4	1.7	4.0	7.2	11.3	16.7	23.1	30.7
Drop • Inches	0.0	-1.7	-6.9	-15.6	-28.1	-44.4	-64.7	-89.1	-117.7

Magtech 158-grain FMJ Flat (38P)

G1 Ballistic Coefficient = 0.148

Distance • Yards	Muzzle	25	50	75	100	125	150	175	200
Velocity • fps	755	739	723	707	692	678	664	650	637
Energy • Ft-lbs	200	191	183	176	168	161	155	148	142
Taylor KO Index	6.1	6.0	5.8	5.7	5.6	5.5	5.4	5.3	5.1
Mid-Range Trajectory Height • Inches	0.0	0.5	2.0	4.6	8.3	13.3	19.6	27.2	36.3
Drop • Inches	0.0	-1.9	-7.9	-17.9	-32.3	-51.3	-74.9	-103.5	-137.3

Magtech 158-grain TMJ (38K) (Discontinued in 2004)

G1 Ballistic Coefficient = 0.146

Distance • Yards	Muzzle	25	50	75	100	125	150	175	200
Velocity • fps	755	739	723	707	692	678	663	649	636
Energy • Ft-lbs	200	191	183	175	168	161	154	148	142
Taylor KO Index	6.1	6.0	5.8	5.7	5.6	5.5	5.3	5.2	5.1
Mid-Range Trajectory Height • Inches	0.0	0.5	2.0	4.6	8.3	13.2	19.5	27.2	36.3
Drop • Inches	0.0	-1.9	-7.8	-17.8	-32.4	-51.3	-75.0	-103.6	-137.3

Cowboy Action Loads

Hornady 140-grain Cowboy (90342)

G1 Ballistic Coefficient = 0.146

Distance • Yards	Muzzle	25	50	75	100	125	150	175	200
Velocity • fps	800	783	767	750	735	720	706	692	678
Energy • Ft-lbs	199	191	183	175	168	161	155	149	143
Taylor KO Index	5.7	5.6	5.5	5.4	5.2	5.1	5.0	4.9	4.8
Mid-Range Trajectory Height • Inches	0.0	0.4	1.7	4.0	7.4	11.7	17.3	24.1	32.2
Drop • Inches	0.0	-1.7	-7.0	-16.0	-28.8	-45.6	-66.7	-92.1	-122.0

Black Hills 158-grain CNL (DCB38N1)

G1 Ballistic Coefficient = 0.140

Distance • Yards	Muzzle	25	50	75	100	125	150	175	200
Velocity • fps	800	781	763	745	728	712	696	681	666
Energy • Ft-lbs	225	214	204	195	186	178	170	163	155
Taylor KO Index	6.4	6.3	6.1	6.0	5.9	5.7	5.6	5.5	5.4
Mid-Range Trajectory Height • Inches	0.0	0.4	1.8	4.1	7.5	11.2	16.9	24.5	37.0
Drop • Inches	0.0	-1.7	-7.0	-16.0	-29.0	-46.0	-67.3	-93.0	-123.5

Magtech 158-grain Lead Flat Nose (38L)

G1 Ballistic Coefficient = 0.140

Distance • Yards	Muzzle	25	50	75	100	125	150	175	200
Velocity • fps	800	788	776	764	753	742	731	720	710
Energy • Ft-lbs	225	218	211	205	199	193	187	182	177
Taylor KO Index	6.4	6.3	6.3	6.2	6.1	6.0	5.9	5.8	5.7
Mid-Range Trajectory Height • Inches	0.0	0.3	1.7	3.9	7.2	11.4	16.7	23.1	30.6
Drop • Inches	0.0	-1.7	-6.9	-15.8	-28.3	-44.7	-65.0	-89.4	-118.0

PMC 158-grain Lead Flat Nose (38CA)

G1 Ballistic Coefficient = 0.133

Distance • Yards	Muzzle	25	50	75	100	125	150	175	200
Velocity • fps	800	780	761	743	725	708	691	675	659
Energy • Ft-lbs	225	214	203	193	185	176	168	160	153
Taylor KO Index	6.4	6.3	6.1	6.0	5.8	5.7	5.6	5.4	5.3
Mid-Range Trajectory Height • Inches	0.0	0.4	1.8	4.1	7.5	11.6	17.7	24.7	33.1
Drop • Inches	0.0	-1.7	-7.0	-16.1	-29.1	-46.2	-67.6	-93.6	-124.3

Winchester 158-grain Cast Lead (CB38SP)

G1 Ballistic Coefficient = 0.133

Distance • Yards	Muzzle	25	50	75	100	125	150	175	200
Velocity • fps	800	780	761	743	725	708	691	675	659
Energy • Ft-lbs	225	214	203	193	185	176	168	160	153
Taylor KO Index	6.4	6.3	6.1	6.0	5.8	5.7	5.6	5.4	5.3
Mid-Range Trajectory Height • Inches	0.0	0.4	1.8	4.1	7.5	11.6	17.7	24.7	33.1
Drop • Inches	0.0	-1.7	-7.0	-16.1	-29.1	-46.2	-67.6	-93.6	-124.3

CCI 158-grain LFN Trailblazer (3516)

G1 Ballistic Coefficient = 0.137

Distance • Yards	Muzzle	25	50	75	100	125	150	175	200
Velocity • fps	750	733	716	699	683	668	653	638	624
Energy • Ft-lbs	197	188	180	172	164	157	150	143	137
Taylor KO Index	6.1	5.9	5.8	5.6	5.5	5.4	5.3	5.2	5.0
Mid-Range Trajectory Height • Inches	0.0	0.5	2.0	4.7	8.5	13.6	20.0	27.9	37.3
Drop • Inches	0.0	-2.0	-8.0	-18.2	-32.9	-52.3	-76.5	-105.8	-140.2

(Left to right) .40 Smith & Wesson, 10mm Auto, .45 Auto.

.40 Smith & Wesson

This cartridge came on the scene in 1990 just after the 10mm Auto was announced. It's easy to guess that some bright lad recognized that if the 10mm cartridge was simply shortened by 0.140 inches, the resulting ammunition would fit in many 9mm pistol frames and still retain enough volume to have plenty of power for the personal defense task. This conversion resulted in an effective round in a more compact pistol than what was needed for the 10mm. The .40 S&W has become the cartridge of choice for many law enforcement groups in the United States.

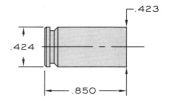

Relative Recoil Factor = 0.74

Specifications

Controlling Agency for Standardization of this Ammunition: SAAMI

Bullet Weight Grains	Velocity fps	Maximum Average Pressure Copper Crusher	Maximum Average Pressure Transducer
155 STHP	1,195	N/S	35,000 psi
155 FMJ	1,115	N/S	35,000 psi
180 JHP	985	N/S	35,000 psi

Standard barrel for velocity testing: 4 inches long—1 turn in 16-inch twist

Availability

CCI 105-grain Shotshell (3970)

Number 9 shot at 1250 fps.

Cor-Bon 115-grain Glaser Safety Slug JHP (03000/03200)

G1 Ballistic Coefficient = 0.110

Distance • Yards	Muzzle	25	50	75	100	125	150	175	200
Velocity • fps	1550	1414	1293	1190	1108	1045	994	952	916
Energy • Ft-lbs	613	510	427	362	314	279	252	232	214
Taylor KO Index	10.2	9.3	8.5	7.8	7.3	6.9	6.5	6.3	6.0
Mid-Range Trajectory Height • Inches	0.0	0.1	0.5	1.4	2.6	4.5	6.9	10.2	14.1
Drop • Inches	0.0	-0.5	-2.1	-4.9	-9.3	-15.5	-23.7	-34.0	-46.8

PMC 115-grain NT/FR (40HRA)

G1 Ballistic Coefficient = 0.120

Distance • Yards	Muzzle	25	50	75	100	125	150	175	200
Velocity • fps	1350	1240	1154	1088	1035	990	952	919	889
Energy • Ft-lbs	466	397	344	304	274	250	231	215	202
Taylor KO Index	8.9	8.2	7.6	7.2	6.8	6.5	6.3	6.0	5.8
Mid-Range Trajectory Height • Inches	0.0	0.2	0.7	1.7	3.2	5.4	8.2	11.8	16.1
Drop • Inches	0.0	-0.6	-2.7	-6.3	-11.8	-19.3	-29.0	-41.1	-55.8

Cor-Bon 135-grain JHP (SD40135/20)

G1 Ballistic Coefficient = 0.125

Distance • Yards	Muzzle	25	50	75	100	125	150	175	200
Velocity • fps	1325	1229	1148	1083	1031	988	951	919	890
Energy • Ft-lbs	526	453	395	352	319	293	271	253	238
Taylor KO Index	10.2	9.5	8.9	8.4	8.0	7.6	7.3	7.1	6.9
Mid-Range Trajectory Height • Inches	0.0	0.1	0.7	1.7	3.2	5.4	8.3	11.9	16.2
Drop • Inches	0.0	-0.7	-2.7	-6.5	-12.1	-19.7	-29.6	-41.8	-56.6

Cor-Bon 135-grain PowRBall

G1 Ballistic Coefficient = 0.125

Distance • Yards	Muzzle	25	50	75	100	125	150	175	200
Velocity • fps	1275	1187	1114	1056	1009	970	936	905	877
Energy • Ft-lbs	487	422	372	334	305	282	263	246	231
Taylor KO Index	9.8	9.2	8.6	8.2	7.8	7.5	7.2	7.0	6.8
Mid-Range Trajectory Height • Inches	0.0	0.2	0.8	1.9	3.5	5.8	8.7	12.5	17.0
Drop • Inches	0.0	-0.7	-3.0	-6.9	-12.9	-21.0	-31.3	-44.2	-59.7

Federal 135-grain Close Quarter Training (BC40NT3) (Discontinued in 2004) G1 Ballistic Coefficient = 0.159

Distance • Yards	Muzzle	25	50	75	100	125	150	175	200
Velocity • fps	1230	1160	1110	1064	1025	992	962	936	911
Energy • Ft-lbs	425	395	370	339	315	295	278	262	249
Taylor KO Index	9.5	8.9	8.6	8.2	7.9	7.7	7.4	7.2	7.0
Mid-Range Trajectory Height • Inches	0.0	0.2	0.8	1.9	3.5	5.6	8.6	12.1	16.4
Drop • Inches	0.0	-0.7	-3.1	-7.2	-13.2	-21.3	-31.5	-44.1	-59.1

Federal 135-grain Hydra-Shok JHP (PD40HS4)   G1 Ballistic Coefficient = 0.109

Distance • Yards	Muzzle	25	50	75	100	125	150	175	200
Velocity • fps	1190	1050	970	900	850	804	762	723	687
Energy • Ft-lbs	420	330	280	245	215	194	174	157	142
Taylor KO Index	9.2	8.1	7.5	6.9	6.6	6.2	5.9	5.6	5.3
Mid-Range Trajectory Height • Inches	0.0	0.2	1.0	2.4	4.5	7.6	11.7	17.0	23.5
Drop • Inches	0.0	-0.8	-3.6	-8.7	-16.3	-26.9	-40.8	-58.2	-79.7

Federal 135-grain EFMJ (PD40CSP2H)   G1 Ballistic Coefficient = 0.109

Distance • Yards	Muzzle	25	50	75	100	125	150	175	200
Velocity • fps	1190	1050	970	900	850	804	762	723	687
Energy • Ft-lbs	420	330	280	245	215	194	174	157	142
Taylor KO Index	9.2	8.1	7.5	6.9	6.6	6.2	5.9	5.6	5.3
Mid-Range Trajectory Height • Inches	0.0	0.2	1.0	2.4	4.5	7.6	11.7	17.0	23.5
Drop • Inches	0.0	-0.8	-3.6	-8.7	-16.3	-26.9	-40.8	-58.2	-79.7

Winchester 140-grain Jacketed Soft Point (SC40NT)   G1 Ballistic Coefficient = 0.130

Distance • Yards	Muzzle	25	50	75	100	125	150	175	200
Velocity • fps	1155	1091	1039	996	960	928	900	873	849
Energy • Ft-lbs	415	370	336	309	286	268	252	237	224
Taylor KO Index	9.2	8.7	8.3	8.0	7.7	7.4	7.2	7.0	6.8
Mid-Range Trajectory Height • Inches	0.0	0.2	0.9	2.1	4.0	6.5	9.7	13.8	18.6
Drop • Inches	0.0	-0.8	-3.5	-8.2	-15.1	-24.2	-35.9	-50.2	-67.4

Cor-Bon 140-grain DPX   G1 Ballistic Coefficient = 0.135

Distance • Yards	Muzzle	25	50	75	100	125	150	175	200
Velocity • fps	1200	1130	1073	1026	987	953	923	896	871
Energy • Ft-lbs	448	397	358	327	303	283	265	250	236
Taylor KO Index	9.6	9.1	8.6	8.2	7.9	7.6	7.4	7.2	7.0
Mid-Range Trajectory Height • Inches	0.0	0.2	0.9	2.0	3.8	6.2	9.3	13.1	17.8
Drop • Inches	0.0	-0.8	-3.3	-7.7	-14.1	-22.7	-33.8	-47.4	-63.7

Remington 141-grain Disintegrator Plated Frangible (LF40SWA) (Discontinued in 2004)

G1 Ballistic Coefficient = 0.190

Distance • Yards	Muzzle	25	50	75	100	125	150	175	200
Velocity • fps	1135	1093	1056	1024	996	970	947	926	906
Energy • Ft-lbs	403	374	349	328	311	295	281	269	257
Taylor KO Index	9.4	9.0	8.7	8.5	8.2	7.8	7.6	7.5	7.3
Mid-Range Trajectory Height • Inches	0.0	0.2	1.0	2.0	3.9	6.2	9.2	13.0	17.4
Drop • Inches	0.0	-0.9	-3.2	-8.2	-14.9	-23.8	-34.9	-48.5	-64.6

Fiocchi 145-grain Jacketed Hollow Point (40SWB) (Discontinued in 2004) G1 Ballistic Coefficient = 0.140

Distance • Yards	Muzzle	25	50	75	100	125	150	175	200
Velocity • fps	1150	1091	1042	1002	967	937	910	884	961
Energy • Ft-lbs	426	383	350	324	302	283	266	252	239
Taylor KO Index	9.5	9.0	8.6	8.3	8.0	7.8	7.5	7.3	7.1
Mid-Range Trajectory Height • Inches	0.0	0.2	0.9	2.1	4.0	6.4	9.6	13.6	18.3
Drop • Inches	0.0	-0.8	-3.5	-8.2	-15.0	-24.1	-35.7	-49.9	-66.8

Cor-Bon 150-grain JHP (SD40150/20)

G1 Ballistic Coefficient = 0.140

Distance • Yards	Muzzle	25	50	75	100	125	150	175	200
Velocity • fps	1200	1132	1076	1030	992	958	929	902	877
Energy • Ft-lbs	480	427	386	354	328	306	287	271	256
Taylor KO Index	10.3	9.7	9.2	8.8	8.5	8.2	8.0	7.7	7.5
Mid-Range Trajectory Height • Inches	0.0	0.2	0.8	2.0	3.7	6.1	9.1	13.0	17.6
Drop • Inches	0.0	-0.8	-3.3	-7.6	-14.0	-22.6	-33.6	-47.1	-63.2

Magtech 155-grain JHP (40D)

G1 Ballistic Coefficient = 0.330

Distance • Yards	Muzzle	25	50	75	100	125	150	175	200
Velocity • fps	1205	1174	1146	1120	1096	1074	1053	1035	1017
Energy • Ft-lbs	500	475	452	432	413	397	382	369	356
Taylor KO Index	10.7	10.4	10.2	9.9	9.7	9.5	9.3	9.2	9.0
Mid-Range Trajectory Height • Inches	0.0	0.1	0.7	1.8	3.3	5.2	7.7	10.8	14.4
Drop • Inches	0.0	-0.7	-3.0	-7.0	-12.7	-20.2	-29.6	-40.9	-54.2

Remington 155-grain Jacketed Hollow Point (R40SW1)

G1 Ballistic Coefficient = 0.165

Distance • Yards	Muzzle	25	50	75	100	125	150	175	200
Velocity • fps	1205	1146	1095	1053	1017	986	956	933	910
Energy • Ft-lbs	499	452	413	382	356	335	316	300	285
Taylor KO Index	10.7	10.2	9.7	9.3	9.0	8.7	8.5	8.3	8.1
Mid-Range Trajectory Height • Inches	0.0	0.2	0.8	1.9	3.6	5.8	8.7	12.3	16.6
Drop • Inches	0.0	-0.8	-3.2	-7.4	-13.6	-21.9	-32.4	-45.2	-60.5

Winchester 155-grain Silvertip Hollow Point (X40SWSTHP)

G1 Ballistic Coefficient = 0.166

Distance • Yards	Muzzle	25	50	75	100	125	150	175	200
Velocity • fps	1205	1146	1096	1054	1018	987	959	934	911
Energy • Ft-lbs	500	452	414	382	357	335	317	300	285
Taylor KO Index	10.7	10.2	9.7	9.3	9.0	8.7	8.5	8.3	8.1
Mid-Range Trajectory Height • Inches	0.0	0.2	0.8	1.9	3.6	5.8	8.7	12.3	16.6
Drop • Inches	0.0	-0.8	-3.2	-7.4	-13.6	-21.9	-32.4	-45.2	-60.4

Speer 155-grain Gold Dot (23961)

G1 Ballistic Coefficient = 0.124

Distance • Yards	Muzzle	25	50	75	100	125	150	175	200
Velocity • fps	1200	1124	1063	1015	974	939	909	880	854
Energy • Ft-lbs	496	435	389	355	326	304	284	266	251
Taylor KO Index	10.6	10.0	9.4	9.0	8.6	8.3	8.1	7.8	7.6
Mid-Range Trajectory Height • Inches	0.0	0.2	0.8	2.0	3.8	6.2	9.4	13.3	18.0
Drop • Inches	0.0	-0.8	-3.3	-7.7	-14.2	-23.0	-34.2	-48.0	-64.6

Hornady 155-grain JHP/XTP (9132)

G1 Ballistic Coefficient = 0.138

Distance • Yards	Muzzle	25	50	75	100	125	150	175	200
Velocity • fps	1180	1115	1061	1017	980	948	919	893	868
Energy • Ft-lbs	479	428	388	356	331	309	291	274	260
Taylor KO Index	10.5	9.9	9.4	9.0	8.7	8.4	8.1	7.9	7.7
Mid-Range Trajectory Height • Inches	0.0	0.2	0.9	2.1	3.8	6.2	9.3	13.2	17.8
Drop • Inches	0.0	-0.8	-3.4	-7.9	-14.4	-23.2	-34.4	-48.2	-64.6

PMC 155-grain Starfire Hollow Point (40SFB)

G1 Ballistic Coefficient = 0.125

Distance • Yards	Muzzle	25	50	75	100	125	150	175	200
Velocity • fps	1160	1092	1039	994	957	924	895	868	843
Energy • Ft-lbs	463	411	371	340	315	294	276	259	245
Taylor KO Index	10.3	9.7	9.2	8.8	8.5	8.2	7.9	7.7	7.5
Mid-Range Trajectory Height • Inches	0.0	0.2	0.9	2.1	4.0	6.5	9.8	13.8	18.7
Drop • Inches	0.0	-0.8	-3.5	-8.2	-15.0	-24.2	-35.9	-50.3	-67.5

Black Hills 155-grain Jacketed Hollow Point—Gold Dot (D40N1)

G1 Ballistic Coefficient = 0.125

Distance • Yards	Muzzle	25	50	75	100	125	150	175	200
Velocity • fps	1150	1085	1032	989	952	920	891	865	840
Energy • Ft-lbs	450	405	367	337	312	292	273	257	243
Taylor KO Index	10.2	9.6	9.1	8.8	8.4	8.1	7.9	7.7	7.4
Mid-Range Trajectory Height • Inches	0.0	0.2	0.9	2.2	4.1	6.6	9.9	14.0	18.9
Drop • Inches	0.0	-0.9	-3.6	-8.3	-15.2	-24.5	-36.4	-50.9	-68.3

Federal 155-grain Hydra-Shok JHP (P40HS2)

G1 Ballistic Coefficient = 0.067

Distance • Yards	Muzzle	25	50	75	100	125	150	175	200
Velocity • fps	1140	1080	1030	990	950	918	890	864	839
Energy • Ft-lbs	445	400	365	335	315	290	273	257	243
Taylor KO Index	10.1	9.6	9.1	8.8	8.4	8.1	7.9	7.7	7.4
Mid-Range Trajectory Height • Inches	0.0	0.2	0.9	2.2	4.1	6.6	9.9	14.1	19.0
Drop • Inches	0.0	-0.9	-3.8	-9.1	-17.1	-24.8	-36.8	-51.4	-68.9

Federal 155-grain Hi-Shok JHP (C40SWB)

G1 Ballistic Coefficient = 0.067

Distance • Yards	Muzzle	25	50	75	100	125	150	175	200
Velocity • fps	1140	1080	1030	990	950	918	890	864	839
Energy • Ft-lbs	445	400	365	335	315	290	273	257	243
Taylor KO Index	10.1	9.6	9.1	8.8	8.4	8.1	7.9	7.7	7.4
Mid-Range Trajectory Height • Inches	0.0	0.2	0.9	2.2	4.1	6.6	9.9	14.1	19.0
Drop • Inches	0.0	-0.9	-3.8	-9.1	-17.1	-24.8	-36.8	-51.4	-68.9

CCI 155-grain TMJ Blazer (3587)

G1 Ballistic Coefficient = 0.125

Distance • Yards	Muzzle	25	50	75	100	125	150	175	200
Velocity • fps	1175	1104	1047	1001	963	929	899	872	846
Energy • Ft-lbs	475	420	377	345	319	297	278	262	246
Taylor KO Index	10.4	9.8	9.3	8.9	8.5	8.2	8.0	7.7	7.5
Mid-Range Trajectory Height • Inches	0.0	0.2	0.9	2.1	4.0	6.4	9.6	13.6	18.4
Drop • Inches	0.0	-0.8	-3.4	-8.0	-14.8	-23.8	-35.3	-49.5	-66.5

CCI 155-grain TMJ Lawman (53957)

G1 Ballistic Coefficient = 0.124

Distance • Yards	Muzzle	25	50	75	100	125	150	175	200
Velocity • fps	1175	1104	1047	1001	963	929	899	872	846
Energy • Ft-lbs	475	420	377	345	319	297	278	262	246
Taylor KO Index	10.4	9.8	9.3	8.9	8.5	8.2	8.0	7.7	7.5
Mid-Range Trajectory Height • Inches	0.0	0.2	0.9	2.1	4.0	6.4	9.6	13.6	18.4
Drop • Inches	0.0	-0.8	-3.4	-8.0	-14.8	-23.8	-35.3	-49.5	-66.5

American Eagle (Federal) 155-grain Full Metal Jacket Ball (AE40R2)

G1 Ballistic Coefficient = 0.150

Distance • Yards	Muzzle	25	50	75	100	125	150	175	200
Velocity • fps	1140	1080	1030	990	960	930	902	877	853
Energy • Ft-lbs	445	400	365	335	315	298	280	265	251
Taylor KO Index	10.1	9.6	9.1	8.8	8.5	8.2	8.0	7.8	7.6
Mid-Range Trajectory Height • Inches	0.0	0.2	0.9	2.2	4.1	6.5	9.8	13.8	18.6
Drop • Inches	0.0	-0.9	-3.6	-8.3	-15.3	-24.6	-36.3	-50.7	-67.9

Magtech 160-grain LSWC (40C)

G1 Ballistic Coefficient = 0.150

Distance • Yards	Muzzle	25	50	75	100	125	150	175	200
Velocity • fps	1165	1107	1059	1018	984	954	927	902	879
Energy • Ft-lbs	484	435	398	369	343	323	305	289	274
Taylor KO Index	10.7	10.1	9.7	9.3	9.0	8.7	8.5	8.2	8.0
Mid-Range Trajectory Height • Inches	0.0	0.2	0.9	2.1	3.9	6.2	9.3	13.1	17.7
Drop • Inches	0.0	-0.8	-3.4	-8.0	-14.6	-23.4	-34.6	-48.4	-64.7

Black Hills 165-grain Extra Power Jacketed Hollow Point (D40N4)

G1 Ballistic Coefficient = 0.140

Distance • Yards	Muzzle	25	50	75	100	125	150	175	200
Velocity • fps	1150	1091	1043	1002	968	937	910	884	861
Energy • Ft-lbs	483	436	398	368	343	322	303	287	272
Taylor KO Index	10.8	10.3	9.8	9.4	9.1	8.8	8.6	8.3	8.1
Mid-Range Trajectory Height • Inches	0.0	0.2	0.9	2.1	3.9	6.4	9.6	13.6	18.3
Drop • Inches	0.0	-0.8	-3.5	-8.2	-15.0	-24.1	-35.7	-49.9	-66.8

Cor-Bon 165-grain JHP (SD40165/20)

G1 Ballistic Coefficient = 0.150

Distance • Yards	Muzzle	25	50	75	100	125	150	175	200
Velocity • fps	1150	1094	1048	1010	976	947	920	896	873
Energy • Ft-lbs	484	439	403	374	349	328	310	294	279
Taylor KO Index	10.8	10.3	9.9	9.5	9.2	8.9	8.7	8.4	8.2
Mid-Range Trajectory Height • Inches	0.0	0.2	0.9	2.1	3.9	6.3	9.5	13.5	18.1
Drop • Inches	0.0	-0.8	-3.5	-8.2	-14.9	-24.0	-35.4	-49.5	-66.2

Remington 165-grain Golden Saber (GS40SWA)
G1 Ballistic Coefficient = 0.136

Distance • Yards	Muzzle	25	50	75	100	125	150	175	200
Velocity • fps	1150	1089	1040	999	964	933	905	879	856
Energy • Ft-lbs	485	435	396	366	340	319	300	283	268
Taylor KO Index	10.8	10.3	9.8	9.4	9.1	8.8	8.5	8.3	8.1
Mid-Range Trajectory Height • Inches	0.0	0.2	0.9	2.1	4.0	6.4	9.7	13.7	18.5
Drop • Inches	0.0	-0.8	-3.5	-8.2	-15.1	-24.2	-35.9	-50.1	-67.2

Winchester 165-grain SXT (S401)
G1 Ballistic Coefficient = 0.165

Distance • Yards	Muzzle	25	50	75	100	125	150	175	200
Velocity • fps	1130	1082	1041	1007	977	950	926	903	832
Energy • Ft-lbs	468	429	397	372	349	331	314	299	285
Taylor KO Index	10.7	10.2	9.8	9.5	9.2	9.0	8.7	8.5	8.3
Mid-Range Trajectory Height • Inches	0.0	0.2	0.9	2.1	4.0	6.4	9.5	13.4	18.0
Drop • Inches	0.0	-0.9	-3.6	-8.3	-15.2	-24.2	-35.8	-49.8	-66.5

Fiocchi 165-grain Jacketed Hollowpoint (40SWC)
G1 Ballistic Coefficient = 0.140

Distance • Yards	Muzzle	25	50	75	100	125	150	175	200
Velocity • fps	1100	1050	1009	973	942	914	889	865	843
Energy • Ft-lbs	450	404	373	347	325	306	289	274	260
Taylor KO Index	10.4	9.9	9.5	9.2	8.9	8.6	8.4	8.2	8.0
Mid-Range Trajectory Height • Inches	0.0	0.2	1.0	2.3	4.3	6.9	10.3	14.5	19.6
Drop • Inches	0.0	-0.9	-3.8	-8.9	-16.2	-25.9	-38.3	-53.4	-71.4

PMC 165-grain JHP (40B)
G1 Ballistic Coefficient = 0.150

Distance • Yards	Muzzle	25	50	75	100	125	150	175	200
Velocity • fps	1040	1002	970	941	915	891	869	848	828
Energy • Ft-lbs	396	368	345	325	307	291	277	265	251
Taylor KO Index	9.8	9.5	9.2	8.9	8.6	8.4	8.2	8.0	7.8
Mid-Range Trajectory Height • Inches	0.0	0.3	1.1	2.5	4.6	7.4	11.0	15.5	20.7
Drop • Inches	0.0	-1.0	-4.2	-9.7	-17.7	-28.2	-41.5	-57.6	-76.8

Federal 165-grain Hydra-Shok JHP (P40HS3)
G1 Ballistic Coefficient = 0.178

Distance • Yards	Muzzle	25	50	75	100	125	150	175	200
Velocity • fps	980	950	930	910	890	871	853	836	820
Energy • Ft-lbs	350	330	315	300	290	278	267	256	246
Taylor KO Index	9.2	9.0	8.8	8.6	8.4	8.2	8.0	7.9	7.7
Mid-Range Trajectory Height • Inches	0.0	0.3	1.2	2.7	5.1	7.9	11.7	16.4	21.9
Drop • Inches	0.0	-1.2	-4.7	-10.7	-19.4	-30.8	-45.0	-62.3	-82.6

Speer 165-grain Gold Dot (23970)
G1 Ballistic Coefficient = 0.138

Distance • Yards	Muzzle	25	50	75	100	125	150	175	200
Velocity • fps	1150	1090	1043	1001	966	935	907	882	858
Energy • Ft-lbs	485	436	399	367	342	320	302	285	270
Taylor KO Index	10.8	10.3	9.8	9.4	9.1	8.8	8.6	8.3	8.1
Mid-Range Trajectory Height • Inches	0.0	0.2	0.9	2.1	3.9	6.4	9.1	13.7	18.4
Drop • Inches	0.0	-0.8	-3.5	-8.2	-15.0	-24.2	-35.8	-50.0	-67.0

CCI 165-grain TMJ Lawman (53955)
G1 Ballistic Coefficient = 0.136

Distance • Yards	Muzzle	25	50	75	100	125	150	175	200
Velocity • fps	1150	1089	1040	999	964	933	905	879	856
Energy • Ft-lbs	484	435	396	366	340	319	300	283	268
Taylor KO Index	10.8	10.2	9.8	9.4	9.1	8.8	8.5	8.3	8.1
Mid-Range Trajectory Height • Inches	0.0	0.2	1.0	2.2	4.1	6.5	9.7	13.7	18.5
Drop • Inches	0.0	-0.8	-3.5	-8.2	-15.1	-24.2	-35.9	-50.1	-67.2

UMC (Remington) 165-grain Metal Case (L40SW4)
G1 Ballistic Coefficient = 0.137

Distance • Yards	Muzzle	25	50	75	100	125	150	175	200
Velocity • fps	1150	1089	1040	999	964	933	905	879	856
Energy • Ft-lbs	484	435	396	366	340	319	300	283	268
Taylor KO Index	10.8	10.2	9.8	9.4	9.1	8.8	8.5	8.3	8.1
Mid-Range Trajectory Height • Inches	0.0	0.2	1.0	2.2	4.1	6.5	9.7	13.7	18.5
Drop • Inches	0.0	-0.8	-3.5	-8.2	-15.1	-24.2	-35.9	-50.1	-67.2

Fiocchi 165-grain Truncated Cone Encapsulated Base (40TCEB)

G1 Ballistic Coefficient = 0.150

Distance • Yards	Muzzle	25	50	75	100	125	150	175	200
Velocity • fps	1140	1086	1042	1004	972	943	916	892	870
Energy • Ft-lbs	476	433	398	370	346	326	308	292	277
Taylor KO Index	10.8	10.3	9.8	9.5	9.2	8.9	8.6	8.4	8.2
Mid-Range Trajectory Height • Inches	0.0	0.2	0.9	2.2	4.0	6.2	9.7	13.7	18.4
Drop • Inches	0.0	-0.9	-3.6	-8.3	-15.1	-24.3	-35.9	-50.1	-67.0

Winchester 165-grain Brass Enclosed Base (WC401)

G1 Ballistic Coefficient = 0.197

Distance • Yards	Muzzle	25	50	75	100	125	150	175	200
Velocity • fps	1130	1089	1054	1024	996	972	950	929	910
Energy • Ft-lbs	468	435	407	384	364	346	331	316	303
Taylor KO Index	10.7	10.3	9.9	9.7	9.4	9.2	9.0	8.8	8.6
Mid-Range Trajectory Height • Inches	0.0	0.2	0.9	2.1	3.9	6.2	9.2	13.0	17.4
Drop • Inches	0.0	-0.9	-3.6	-8.2	-15.0	-23.8	-35.0	-48.6	-64.7

CCI 165-grain TMJ Blazer (3589)

G1 Ballistic Coefficient = 0.140

Distance • Yards	Muzzle	25	50	75	100	125	150	175	200
Velocity • fps	1100	1048	1006	969	938	909	883	859	836
Energy • Ft-lbs	443	403	371	344	321	303	286	270	256
Taylor KO Index	10.4	9.9	9.5	9.1	8.8	8.6	8.3	8.1	7.9
Mid-Range Trajectory Height • Inches	0.0	0.2	0.9	2.3	4.2	6.9	10.3	14.5	19.6
Drop • Inches	0.0	-0.9	-3.9	-8.9	-16.2	-26.0	-38.4	-53.6	-71.7

USA (Winchester) 165-grain Full Metal Jacket—Flat Nose (USA40SW)

G1 Ballistic Coefficient = 0.197

Distance • Yards	Muzzle	25	50	75	100	125	150	175	200
Velocity • fps	1060	1029	1001	976	953	932	913	895	877
Energy • Ft-lbs	412	388	367	349	333	319	305	293	282
Taylor KO Index	10.0	9.7	9.4	9.2	9.0	8.8	8.6	8.4	8.3
Mid-Range Trajectory Height • Inches	0.0	0.2	1.0	2.3	4.3	6.9	10.2	14.2	19.0
Drop • Inches	0.0	-1.0	-4.0	-9.2	-16.7	-26.6	-38.9	-53.9	-71.5

Magtech 165-grain FMJ Flat (40G)

G1 Ballistic Coefficient = 0.092

Distance • Yards	Muzzle	25	50	75	100	125	150	175	200
Velocity • fps	1050	990	941	899	863	830	799	771	744
Energy • Ft-lbs	404	359	325	296	273	252	234	218	203
Taylor KO Index	9.9	9.3	8.9	8.5	8.1	7.8	7.5	7.3	7.0
Mid-Range Trajectory Height • Inches	0.0	0.2	1.1	2.6	4.9	8.0	12.1	17.2	23.4
Drop • Inches	0.0	-1.0	-4.3	-10.0	-18.4	-29.7	-44.1	-62.0	-83.5

PMC 165-grain Full Metal Jacket (40D)

G1 Ballistic Coefficient = 0.160

Distance • Yards	Muzzle	25	50	75	100	125	150	175	200
Velocity • fps	985	957	931	908	885	864	845	826	809
Energy • Ft-lbs	356	335	317	301	287	274	262	250	240
Taylor KO Index	9.3	9.0	8.8	8.6	8.4	8.2	8.0	7.8	7.6
Mid-Range Trajectory Height • Inches	0.0	0.3	1.2	2.8	5.0	8.0	11.9	16.6	22.0
Drop • Inches	0.0	-1.1	-4.7	-10.7	-19.4	-30.8	-45.1	-62.5	-83.1

American Eagle (Federal) 165-grain Full Metal Jacket (AE40R3)

G1 Ballistic Coefficient = 0.158

Distance • Yards	Muzzle	25	50	75	100	125	150	175	200
Velocity • fps	980	950	920	900	880	860	840	822	804
Energy • Ft-lbs	350	330	310	295	280	271	259	247	237
Taylor KO Index	9.2	9.0	8.8	8.5	8.3	8.1	7.9	7.8	7.6
Mid-Range Trajectory Height • Inches	0.0	0.3	1.2	2.8	5.1	8.1	12.0	16.7	22.3
Drop • Inches	0.0	-1.2	-4.7	-10.8	-19.6	-31.1	-45.6	-63.1	-83.9

Fiocchi 170-grain FMJ Truncated Cone (40SWA)

G1 Ballistic Coefficient = 0.150

Distance • Yards	Muzzle	25	50	75	100	125	150	175	200
Velocity • fps	1050	1011	977	948	921	897	874	853	833
Energy • Ft-lbs	416	386	361	339	320	295	280	266	254
Taylor KO Index	10.2	9.8	9.5	9.2	8.9	8.7	8.5	8.3	8.1
Mid-Range Trajectory Height • Inches	0.0	0.2	1.1	2.5	4.5	7.2	10.8	15.2	20.3
Drop • Inches	0.0	-1.0	-4.2	-9.6	-17.4	-27.7	-40.8	-56.7	-75.5

American Eagle (Federal) 180-grain TMJ (AE40N1)
G1 Ballistic Coefficient = 0.164

Distance • Yards	Muzzle	25	50	75	100	125	150	175	200
Velocity • fps	990	960	930	910	890	870	851	832	815
Energy • Ft-lbs	390	365	345	330	315	303	289	277	265
Taylor KO Index	10.2	9.9	9.6	9.4	9.2	8.9	8.8	8.6	8.4
Mid-Range Trajectory Height • Inches	0.0	0.3	1.2	2.8	5.0	7.9	11.7	16.3	21.8
Drop • Inches	0.0	-1.1	-4.6	-10.6	-19.1	-30.4	-44.6	-61.6	-82.0

Speer 180-grain Gold Dot (23962)
G1 Ballistic Coefficient = 0.145

Distance • Yards	Muzzle	25	50	75	100	125	150	175	200
Velocity • fps	1025	989	957	928	902	879	856	835	815
Energy • Ft-lbs	420	391	366	344	325	309	293	279	266
Taylor KO Index	10.5	10.2	9.8	9.5	9.3	9.0	8.8	8.6	8.4
Mid-Range Trajectory Height • Inches	0.0	0.2	1.1	2.5	4.7	7.6	11.3	15.8	21.2
Drop • Inches	0.0	-1.1	-4.5	-10.2	-18.4	-29.4	-43.0	-59.7	-79.4

Remington 180-grain Golden Saber (GS40SWB)
G1 Ballistic Coefficient = 0.178

Distance • Yards	Muzzle	25	50	75	100	125	150	175	200
Velocity • fps	1015	986	960	936	914	894	875	857	840
Energy • Ft-lbs	412	389	368	350	334	320	308	294	282
Taylor KO Index	10.4	10.1	9.9	9.6	9.4	9.2	9.0	8.8	8.6
Mid-Range Trajectory Height • Inches	0.0	0.3	1.3	2.6	4.5	7.5	11.1	15.5	20.7
Drop • Inches	0.0	-1.1	-4.4	-10.0	-18.2	-28.9	-42.4	-58.6	-77.8

Remington 180-grain Jacketed Hollow Point (R40SW2)
G1 Ballistic Coefficient = 0.178

Distance • Yards	Muzzle	25	50	75	100	125	150	175	200
Velocity • fps	1015	986	960	936	914	894	875	857	840
Energy • Ft-lbs	412	389	368	350	334	320	308	294	282
Taylor KO Index	10.4	10.1	9.9	9.6	9.4	9.2	9.0	8.8	8.6
Mid-Range Trajectory Height • Inches	0.0	0.3	1.3	2.6	4.5	7.5	11.1	15.5	20.7
Drop • Inches	0.0	-1.1	-4.4	-10.0	-18.2	-28.9	-42.4	-58.6	-77.8

UMC (Remington) 180-grain JHP (L40SW2)
G1 Ballistic Coefficient = 0.178

Distance • Yards	Muzzle	25	50	75	100	125	150	175	200
Velocity • fps	1015	986	960	936	914	894	875	857	840
Energy • Ft-lbs	412	389	368	350	334	320	308	294	282
Taylor KO Index	10.4	10.1	9.9	9.6	9.4	9.2	9.0	8.8	8.6
Mid-Range Trajectory Height • Inches	0.0	0.3	1.3	2.6	4.5	7.5	11.1	15.5	20.7
Drop • Inches	0.0	-1.1	-4.4	-10.0	-18.2	-28.9	-42.4	-58.6	-77.8

Winchester 180-grain SXT (S40)
G1 Ballistic Coefficient = 0.173

Distance • Yards	Muzzle	25	50	75	100	125	150	175	200
Velocity • fps	1010	981	954	931	909	889	870	851	834
Energy • Ft-lbs	408	385	364	347	330	316	302	290	278
Taylor KO Index	10.4	10.1	9.8	9.6	9.3	9.1	8.9	8.8	8.6
Mid-Range Trajectory Height • Inches	0.0	0.2	1.1	2.6	4.7	7.6	11.2	15.7	20.9
Drop • Inches	0.0	-1.1	-4.4	-10.2	-18.4	-29.2	-42.8	-59.3	-78.7

USA (Winchester) 180-grain SXT (USA40JHP)
G1 Ballistic Coefficient = 0.170

Distance • Yards	Muzzle	25	50	75	100	125	150	175	200
Velocity • fps	1010	980	954	930	907	887	867	848	831
Energy • Ft-lbs	408	384	364	345	329	314	300	288	276
Taylor KO Index	10.4	10.1	9.8	9.6	9.3	9.1	8.9	8.7	8.5
Mid-Range Trajectory Height • Inches	0.0	0.2	1.1	2.6	4.7	7.6	11.2	15.7	21.1
Drop • Inches	0.0	-1.1	-4.4	-10.2	-18.4	-29.2	-42.9	-59.4	-78.9

Black Hills 180-grain Jacketed Hollow Point—Gold Dot (D40N2)
G1 Ballistic Coefficient = 0.175

Distance • Yards	Muzzle	25	50	75	100	125	150	175	200
Velocity • fps	1000	972	947	924	903	883	864	846	829
Energy • Ft-lbs	400	378	359	341	326	312	298	286	275
Taylor KO Index	10.3	10.0	9.7	9.5	9.3	9.1	8.9	8.7	8.5
Mid-Range Trajectory Height • Inches	0.0	0.3	1.2	2.6	4.8	7.7	11.4	15.9	21.2
Drop • Inches	0.0	-1.1	-4.5	-10.3	-18.7	-29.7	-43.5	-60.2	-80.0

Fiocchi 180-grain Jacketed Hollowpoint (40SWE)

G1 Ballistic Coefficient = 0.175

Distance • Yards	Muzzle	25	50	75	100	125	150	175	200
Velocity • fps	1000	972	947	924	903	883	864	846	829
Energy • Ft-lbs	400	378	359	341	326	312	298	286	275
Taylor KO Index	10.3	10.0	9.7	9.5	9.3	9.1	8.9	8.7	8.5
Mid-Range Trajectory Height • Inches	0.0	0.3	1.2	2.6	4.8	7.7	11.4	15.9	21.2
Drop • Inches	0.0	-1.1	-4.5	-10.3	-18.7	-29.7	-43.5	-60.2	-80.0

CCI 180-grain JHP Blazer (3590)

G1 Ballistic Coefficient = 0.144

Distance • Yards	Muzzle	25	50	75	100	125	150	175	200
Velocity • fps	1000	967	937	910	886	863	841	821	802
Energy • Ft-lbs	400	374	351	331	313	298	283	269	257
Taylor KO Index	10.3	10.0	9.6	9.4	9.1	8.9	8.7	8.5	8.3
Mid-Range Trajectory Height • Inches	0.0	0.3	1.2	2.7	5.0	7.9	11.8	16.5	22.2
Drop • Inches	0.0	-1.1	-4.6	-10.5	-19.0	-30.3	-44.5	-61.8	-82.3

Federal 180-grain Hi-Shok JHP (C40SWA)

G1 Ballistic Coefficient = 0.164

Distance • Yards	Muzzle	25	50	75	100	125	150	175	200
Velocity • fps	990	960	930	910	890	870	851	832	815
Energy • Ft-lbs	390	365	345	330	315	303	289	277	265
Taylor KO Index	10.2	9.9	9.6	9.4	9.2	8.9	8.8	8.6	8.4
Mid-Range Trajectory Height • Inches	0.0	0.3	1.2	2.8	5.0	7.9	11.7	16.3	21.8
Drop • Inches	0.0	-1.1	-4.6	-10.6	-19.1	-30.4	-44.6	-61.6	-82.0

Federal 180-grain Hydra-Shok JHP (P40HS1)

G1 Ballistic Coefficient = 0.164

Distance • Yards	Muzzle	25	50	75	100	125	150	175	200
Velocity • fps	990	960	930	910	890	870	851	832	815
Energy • Ft-lbs	390	365	345	330	315	303	289	277	265
Taylor KO Index	10.2	9.9	9.6	9.4	9.2	8.9	8.8	8.6	8.4
Mid-Range Trajectory Height • Inches	0.0	0.3	1.2	2.8	5.0	7.9	11.7	16.3	21.8
Drop • Inches	0.0	-1.1	-4.6	-10.6	-19.1	-30.4	-44.6	-61.6	-82.0

Magtech 180-grain JHP (40A)

G1 Ballistic Coefficient = 0.156

Distance • Yards	Muzzle	25	50	75	100	125	150	175	200
Velocity • fps	990	960	933	909	886	865	845	826	808
Energy • Ft-lbs	390	368	348	330	314	299	285	273	261
Taylor KO Index	10.2	9.9	9.6	9.3	9.1	8.9	8.7	8.5	8.3
Mid-Range Trajectory Height • Inches	0.0	0.3	1.2	2.7	5.0	7.9	11.8	16.5	22.1
Drop • Inches	0.0	-1.1	-4.6	-10.6	-19.2	-30.6	-44.8	-62.1	-82.6

PMC 180-grain Starfire Hollow Point (40SFA)

G1 Ballistic Coefficient = 0.168

Distance • Yards	Muzzle	25	50	75	100	125	150	175	200
Velocity • fps	985	958	933	910	889	869	850	832	815
Energy • Ft-lbs	388	367	348	331	316	302	289	277	266
Taylor KO Index	10.1	9.9	9.6	9.4	9.1	8.9	8.7	8.6	8.4
Mid-Range Trajectory Height • Inches	0.0	0.3	1.2	2.7	5.0	7.9	11.7	16.4	21.9
Drop • Inches	0.0	-1.1	-4.6	-10.7	-19.3	-30.6	-44.9	-62.1	-82.5

Hornady 180-grain JHP/XTP (9136)

G1 Ballistic Coefficient = 0.166

Distance • Yards	Muzzle	25	50	75	100	125	150	175	200
Velocity • fps	950	926	903	882	862	844	826	809	792
Energy • Ft-lbs	361	342	326	311	297	285	273	262	251
Taylor KO Index	9.8	9.5	9.3	9.1	8.9	8.7	8.5	8.3	8.1
Mid-Range Trajectory Height • Inches	0.0	0.3	1.3	2.9	5.3	8.5	12.5	17.5	23.3
Drop • Inches	0.0	-1.2	-5.0	-11.4	-20.6	-32.7	-47.9	-66.3	-87.9

Aguila 180-grain Jacketed

G1 Ballistic Coefficient = 0.097

Distance • Yards	Muzzle	25	50	75	100	125	150	175	200
Velocity • fps	1100	1031	977	933	893	860	829	800	773
Energy • Ft-lbs	484	425	382	348	320	296	275	256	239
Taylor KO Index	11.3	10.6	10.1	9.6	9.2	8.9	8.5	8.2	8.0
Mid-Range Trajectory Height • Inches	0.0	0.2	1.0	2.4	4.5	7.4	11.2	16.0	21.7
Drop • Inches	0.0	-0.9	-3.9	-9.2	-16.9	-27.4	-40.8	-57.4	-77.3

Magtech 180-grain FEB Flat (CR40A)

G1 Ballistic Coefficient = 0.165

Distance • Yards	Muzzle	25	50	75	100	125	150	175	200
Velocity • fps	1040	1002	970	941	915	891	869	848	828
Energy • Ft-lbs	396	368	345	325	307	291	277	265	251
Taylor KO Index	9.8	9.5	9.2	8.9	8.6	8.4	8.2	8.0	7.8
Mid-Range Trajectory Height • Inches	0.0	0.3	1.1	2.5	4.6	7.4	11.0	15.5	20.7
Drop • Inches	0.0	-1.0	-4.2	-9.7	-17.7	-28.2	-41.5	-57.6	-76.8

CCI 180-grain Clean-Fire—TMJ Blazer (3477)

G1 Ballistic Coefficient = 0.144

Distance • Yards	Muzzle	25	50	75	100	125	150	175	200
Velocity • fps	1000	967	937	910	886	863	841	821	802
Energy • Ft-lbs	400	374	351	331	313	298	283	269	257
Taylor KO Index	10.3	10.0	9.6	9.4	9.1	8.9	8.7	8.5	8.3
Mid-Range Trajectory Height • Inches	0.0	0.3	1.2	2.7	5.0	7.9	11.8	16.5	22.2
Drop • Inches	0.0	-1.1	-4.6	-10.5	-19.0	-30.3	-44.5	-61.8	-82.3

Fiocchi 180-grain FMJ Flat Nose (40SWD)

G1 Ballistic Coefficient = 0.175

Distance • Yards	Muzzle	25	50	75	100	125	150	175	200
Velocity • fps	1000	972	947	924	903	883	864	846	829
Energy • Ft-lbs	400	378	359	341	326	312	298	286	275
Taylor KO Index	10.3	10.0	9.7	9.5	9.3	9.1	8.9	8.7	8.5
Mid-Range Trajectory Height • Inches	0.0	0.3	1.2	2.6	4.8	7.7	11.4	15.9	21.2
Drop • Inches	0.0	-1.1	-4.5	-10.3	-18.7	-28.7	-43.5	-60.2	-80.0

CCI 180-grain FMJ Blazer (3591)

G1 Ballistic Coefficient = 0.221

Distance • Yards	Muzzle	25	50	75	100	125	150	175	200
Velocity • fps	1000	967	937	911	886	863	842	822	803
Energy • Ft-lbs	400	374	351	332	323	314	298	283	257
Taylor KO Index	10.3	9.9	9.6	9.4	9.1	8.9	8.7	8.5	8.3
Mid-Range Trajectory Height • Inches	0.0	0.2	1.1	2.6	4.9	7.9	11.7	16.4	22.0
Drop • Inches	0.0	-1.1	-4.5	-10.4	-19.0	-30.2	-44.4	-61.7	-82.1

CCI 180-grain FMJ Lawman (53958)

G1 Ballistic Coefficient = 0.144

Distance • Yards	Muzzle	25	50	75	100	125	150	175	200
Velocity • fps	1000	967	937	910	886	863	841	821	802
Energy • Ft-lbs	400	374	351	331	313	298	283	269	257
Taylor KO Index	10.3	10.0	9.6	9.4	9.1	8.9	8.7	8.5	8.3
Mid-Range Trajectory Height • Inches	0.0	0.3	1.2	2.7	5.0	7.9	11.8	16.5	22.2
Drop • Inches	0.0	-1.1	-4.6	-10.5	-19.0	-30.3	-44.5	-61.8	-82.3

CCI 180-grain Clean-Fire—TMJ Lawman (53880)

G1 Ballistic Coefficient = 0.144

Distance • Yards	Muzzle	25	50	75	100	125	150	175	200
Velocity • fps	1000	967	937	910	886	863	841	821	802
Energy • Ft-lbs	400	374	351	331	313	298	283	269	257
Taylor KO Index	10.3	10.0	9.6	9.4	9.1	8.9	8.7	8.5	8.3
Mid-Range Trajectory Height • Inches	0.0	0.3	1.2	2.7	5.0	7.9	11.8	16.5	22.2
Drop • Inches	0.0	-1.1	-4.6	-10.5	-19.0	-30.3	-44.5	-61.8	-82.3

Magtech 180-grain FMJ Flat (MP40B)

G1 Ballistic Coefficient = 0.156

Distance • Yards	Muzzle	25	50	75	100	125	150	175	200
Velocity • fps	990	960	933	909	886	865	845	826	808
Energy • Ft-lbs	390	368	348	330	314	299	285	273	261
Taylor KO Index	10.2	9.9	9.6	9.3	9.1	8.9	8.7	8.5	8.3
Mid-Range Trajectory Height • Inches	0.0	0.3	1.2	2.7	5.0	7.9	11.8	16.5	22.1
Drop • Inches	0.0	-1.1	-4.6	-10.6	-19.2	-30.6	-44.8	-62.1	-82.6

American Eagle (Federal) 180-grain Full Metal Jacket (AE40R1)

G1 Ballistic Coefficient = 0.164

Distance • Yards	Muzzle	25	50	75	100	125	150	175	200
Velocity • fps	990	960	930	910	890	870	851	832	815
Energy • Ft-lbs	390	365	345	330	315	303	289	277	265
Taylor KO Index	10.2	9.9	9.6	9.4	9.2	8.9	8.8	8.6	8.4
Mid-Range Trajectory Height • Inches	0.0	0.3	1.2	2.8	5.0	7.9	11.7	16.3	21.8
Drop • Inches	0.0	-1.1	-4.6	-10.6	-19.1	-30.4	-44.6	-61.6	-82.0

Winchester 180-grain Brass Enclosed Base (WC402)

G1 Ballistic Coefficient = 0.190

Distance • Yards	Muzzle	25	50	75	100	125	150	175	200
Velocity • fps	990	965	943	922	902	884	866	850	834
Energy • Ft-lbs	392	372	356	340	325	312	330	289	278
Taylor KO Index	10.2	9.9	9.7	9.5	9.3	9.1	8.9	8.7	8.6
Mid-Range Trajectory Height • Inches	0.0	0.3	1.2	2.7	5.0	7.8	11.4	16.0	21.3
Drop • Inches	0.0	-1.1	-4.6	-10.6	-19.2	-30.1	-44.0	-60.7	-80.5

USA (Winchester) 180-grain Full Metal Jacket (Q4238)

G1 Ballistic Coefficient = 0.193

Distance • Yards	Muzzle	25	50	75	100	125	150	175	200
Velocity • fps	990	966	943	923	903	885	868	852	836
Energy • Ft-lbs	391	373	356	340	326	313	301	290	279
Taylor KO Index	10.2	9.9	9.7	9.5	9.3	9.1	8.9	8.8	8.6
Mid-Range Trajectory Height • Inches	0.0	0.3	1.2	2.7	4.9	7.8	11.5	16.0	21.3
Drop • Inches	0.0	-1.1	-4.6	-10.5	-18.9	-30.0	-43.9	-60.7	-80.4

PMC 180-grain FMJ/FP (40E)

G1 Ballistic Coefficient = 0.165

Distance • Yards	Muzzle	25	50	75	100	125	150	175	200
Velocity • fps	985	957	931	908	885	864	845	826	808
Energy • Ft-lbs	388	366	346	329	313	299	285	273	261
Taylor KO Index	10.1	9.8	9.6	9.3	9.1	8.9	8.7	8.5	8.3
Mid-Range Trajectory Height • Inches	0.0	0.2	1.1	2.7	5.0	8.0	11.8	16.5	22.1
Drop • Inches	0.0	-1.1	-4.7	-10.7	-19.3	-30.8	-45.1	-62.5	-83.0

UMC (Remington) 180-grain Metal Case (L40SW3)

G1 Ballistic Coefficient = 0.177

Distance • Yards	Muzzle	25	50	75	100	125	150	175	200
Velocity • fps	985	959	936	913	893	874	8756	839	822
Energy • Ft-lbs	388	368	350	333	319	305	293	281	270
Taylor KO Index	10.1	9.9	9.6	9.4	9.2	9.0	8.8	8.6	8.5
Mid-Range Trajectory Height • Inches	0.0	0.3	1.3	2.9	5.1	7.9	11.7	16.3	21.7
Drop • Inches	0.0	-1.1	-4.6	-10.6	-19.2	-30.5	-44.6	-61.7	-81.9

UMC (Remington) 180-grain FNEB (LL40SW5)

G1 Ballistic Coefficient = 0.177

Distance • Yards	Muzzle	25	50	75	100	125	150	175	200
Velocity • fps	985	959	936	913	893	874	8756	839	822
Energy • Ft-lbs	388	368	350	333	319	305	293	281	270
Taylor KO Index	10.1	9.9	9.6	9.4	9.2	9.0	8.8	8.6	8.5
Mid-Range Trajectory Height • Inches	0.0	0.3	1.3	2.9	5.1	7.9	11.7	16.3	21.7
Drop • Inches	0.0	-1.1	-4.6	-10.6	-19.2	-30.5	-44.6	-61.7	-81.9

Sellier & Bellot 180-grain FMJ (SBA04001)

G1 Ballistic Coefficient = 0.155

Distance • Yards	Muzzle	25	50	75	100	125	150	175	200
Velocity • fps	968	952	915	892	870	850	830	812	794
Energy • Ft-lbs	375	355	335	318	303	289	276	264	252
Taylor KO Index	10.0	9.7	9.4	9.2	9.0	8.8	8.5	8.4	8.2
Mid-Range Trajectory Height • Inches	0.0	0.3	1.2	2.8	5.2	8.3	12.3	17.2	23.0
Drop • Inches	0.0	-1.2	-4.8	-11.1	-20.0	-31.9	-46.7	-64.7	-86.0

10mm Auto

First chambered in the Bren Ten pistol in 1983, the 10mm Auto was a powerful pistol. The first ammo was manufactured by Norma. The Bren Ten went nowhere, and it wasn't until 1989 when the FBI announced the selection of the 10mm Auto as their officially favored sidearm that the 10mm Auto took off. The best performance overall as a pistol round came at velocities near 1,000 fps. The cartridge case has lots more volume than is needed for that kind of performance, leaving room for a considerable jump in performance as a submachine cartridge. The .40 Smith & Wesson Auto is a spinoff design that has taken over the law-enforcement market.

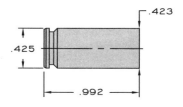

Relative Recoil Factor = 0.96

Specifications

Controlling Agency for Standardization of this Ammunition: SAAMI

Bullet Weight Grains	Velocity fps	Maximum Average Pressure Copper Crusher	Transducer
155 HP/XP	1,410	N/S	37,500 psi
155 FMJ	1,115	N/S	37,500 psi
170 HP/XP	1,320	N/S	37,500 psi
175 STHP	1,275	N/S	37,500 psi
200 FMJ/FP	1,150	N/S	37,500 psi
200 SXT	985	N/S	37,500 psi

Standard barrel for velocity testing: 5 inches long—1 turn in 16-inch twist

Availability

Cor-Bon 115-grain Glaser Safety Slug (03400/03600)
G1 Ballistic Coefficient = 0.110

Distance • Yards	Muzzle	25	50	75	100	125	150	175	200
Velocity • fps	1650	1504	1373	1258	1162	1086	1027	980	940
Energy • Ft-lbs	695	578	481	404	345	301	270	245	226
Taylor KO Index	10.9	9.9	9.0	8.3	7.6	7.1	6.8	6.4	6.2
Mid-Range Trajectory Height • Inches	0.0	0.1	0.5	1.2	2.3	4.0	6.2	9.2	12.9
Drop • Inches	0.0	-0.4	-1.8	-4.4	-8.3	-13.8	-21.2	-30.6	-42.3

PMC 115-grain NT/FR (10HRA)
G1 Ballistic Coefficient = 0.120

Distance • Yards	Muzzle	25	50	75	100	125	150	175	200
Velocity • fps	1350	1240	1154	1088	1035	990	952	919	889
Energy • Ft-lbs	466	397	344	304	274	250	231	215	202
Taylor KO Index	8.9	8.2	7.6	7.2	6.8	6.5	6.3	6.0	5.8
Mid-Range Trajectory Height • Inches	0.0	0.2	0.7	1.7	3.2	5.4	8.2	11.8	16.1
Drop • Inches	0.0	-0.6	-2.7	-6.3	-11.8	-19.3	-29.0	-41.1	-55.8

Cor-Bon 135-grain PowRBall
G1 Ballistic Coefficient = 0.125

Distance • Yards	Muzzle	25	50	75	100	125	150	175	200
Velocity • fps	1400	1294	1202	1127	1066	1017	976	941	910
Energy • Ft-lbs	588	502	434	381	341	310	286	266	248
Taylor KO Index	10.8	10.0	9.3	8.7	8.2	7.8	7.5	7.3	7.0
Mid-Range Trajectory Height • Inches	0.0	0.1	0.6	1.5	3.0	5.0	7.6	11.0	15.1
Drop • Inches	0.0	-0.6	-2.5	-5.8	-11.0	-18.0	-27.1	-38.4	-52.3

Cor-Bon 135-grain JHP (SD10135/20)
G1 Ballistic Coefficient = 0.125

Distance • Yards	Muzzle	25	50	75	100	125	150	175	200
Velocity • fps	1400	1294	1202	1127	1066	1017	976	941	910
Energy • Ft-lbs	588	502	434	381	341	310	286	266	248
Taylor KO Index	10.8	10.0	9.3	8.7	8.2	7.8	7.5	7.3	7.0
Mid-Range Trajectory Height • Inches	0.0	0.1	0.6	1.5	3.0	5.0	7.6	11.0	15.1
Drop • Inches	0.0	-0.6	-2.5	-5.8	-11.0	-18.0	-27.1	-38.4	-52.3

Cor-Bon 150-grain JHP (SD10150/20)

G1 Ballistic Coefficient = 0.130

Distance • Yards	Muzzle	25	50	75	100	125	150	175	200
Velocity • fps	1325	1232	1154	1090	1038	996	959	928	899
Energy • Ft-lbs	585	506	446	396	359	330	307	287	269
Taylor KO Index	11.4	10.6	9.9	9.3	8.9	8.5	8.2	8.0	7.7
Mid-Range Trajectory Height • Inches	0.0	0.1	0.7	1.7	3.2	5.3	8.2	11.7	16.0
Drop • Inches	0.0	-0.6	-2.7	-6.4	-12.0	-19.5	-29.3	-41.4	-56.0

Federal 155-grain Hi-Shok JHP (C10E) (Discontinued in 2004)

G1 Ballistic Coefficient = 0.123

Distance • Yards	Muzzle	25	50	75	100	125	150	175	200
Velocity • fps	1330	1230	1140	1080	1030	987	950	918	888
Energy • Ft-lbs	605	515	450	400	360	335	311	290	272
Taylor KO Index	11.8	10.9	10.1	9.6	9.1	8.7	8.4	8.1	7.9
Mid-Range Trajectory Height • Inches	0.0	0.2	0.7	1.8	3.3	5.4	8.2	11.8	16.0
Drop • Inches	0.0	-0.6	-2.7	-6.4	-12.0	-19.6	-29.4	-41.5	-56.1

Cor-Bon 165-grain JHP (SD10165/20)

G1 Ballistic Coefficient = 0.140

Distance • Yards	Muzzle	25	50	75	100	125	150	175	200
Velocity • fps	1250	1174	1110	1058	1016	976	947	919	893
Energy • Ft-lbs	573	505	452	411	378	351	329	309	292
Taylor KO Index	11.8	11.1	10.5	10.0	9.6	9.2	8.9	8.7	8.4
Mid-Range Trajectory Height • Inches	0.0	0.1	0.7	1.8	3.5	5.7	8.6	12.3	16.7
Drop • Inches	0.0	-0.7	-3.0	-7.1	-13.1	-21.2	-31.6	-44.4	-59.7

Hornady 155-grain JHP/XTP (9122)

G1 Ballistic Coefficient = 0.138

Distance • Yards	Muzzle	25	50	75	100	125	150	175	200
Velocity • fps	1265	1186	1119	1065	1020	983	950	921	895
Energy • Ft-lbs	551	484	431	390	358	333	311	292	276
Taylor KO Index	11.2	10.5	9.9	9.4	9.0	8.7	8.4	8.2	7.9
Mid-Range Trajectory Height • Inches	0.0	0.2	0.8	1.8	3.5	5.6	8.5	12.1	16.4
Drop • Inches	0.0	-0.7	-3.0	-4.0	-12.8	-20.8	-31.0	-43.5	-58.5

PMC 170-grain Jacketed Hollow Point (10B)

G1 Ballistic Coefficient = 0.112

Distance • Yards	Muzzle	25	50	75	100	125	150	175	200
Velocity • fps	1200	1117	1052	1000	958	921	888	858	831
Energy • Ft-lbs	544	471	418	378	347	321	298	278	261
Taylor KO Index	11.7	10.9	10.2	9.7	9.3	8.9	8.6	8.3	8.1
Mid-Range Trajectory Height • Inches	0.0	0.2	0.9	2.1	3.9	6.4	9.6	13.7	18.6
Drop • Inches	0.0	-0.8	-3.3	-7.8	-14.5	-23.5	-35.0	-49.2	-66.3

Winchester 175-grain Silvertip Hollow Point (X10MMSTHP)

G1 Ballistic Coefficient = 0.142

Distance • Yards	Muzzle	25	50	75	100	125	150	175	200
Velocity • fps	1290	1209	1141	1084	1037	998	965	935	908
Energy • Ft-lbs	649	568	506	457	418	387	362	340	320
Taylor KO Index	12.9	12.1	11.4	10.8	10.4	10.0	9.7	9.4	9.1
Mid-Range Trajectory Height • Inches	0.0	0.2	0.7	1.8	3.3	5.4	8.2	11.7	15.9
Drop • Inches	0.0	-0.7	-2.8	-6.7	-12.4	-20.0	-29.9	-42.0	-56.5

Cor-Bon 180-grain Bonded Core SP (HT10180BC/20)

G1 Ballistic Coefficient = 0.165

Distance • Yards	Muzzle	25	50	75	100	125	150	175	200
Velocity • fps	1320	1246	1181	1126	1079	1039	1005	975	945
Energy • Ft-lbs	696	621	558	506	465	431	403	380	359
Taylor KO Index	13.6	12.8	12.1	11.6	11.1	10.7	10.3	10.0	9.8
Mid-Range Trajectory Height • Inches	0.0	0.1	0.7	1.6	3.1	5.0	7.7	10.9	14.8
Drop • Inches	0.0	-0.6	-2.7	-6.3	-11.6	-18.8	-28.0	-39.3	-53.0

American Eagle (Federal) 180-grain FMJ (AE10A)

G1 Ballistic Coefficient = 0.169

Distance • Yards	Muzzle	25	50	75	100	125	150	175	200
Velocity • fps	1030	1000	970	950	920	898	878	859	841
Energy • Ft-lbs	425	400	375	355	340	323	308	295	283
Taylor KO Index	10.6	10.3	10.0	9.8	9.5	9.2	9.0	8.8	8.7
Mid-Range Trajectory Height • Inches	0.0	0.3	1.1	2.5	4.7	7.4	10.9	15.3	20.4
Drop • Inches	0.0	-1.0	-4.3	-9.8	-17.8	-28.3	-41.5	-57.6	-76.5

Hornady 180-grain JHP/XTP (9126)

G1 Ballistic Coefficient = 0.165

Distance • Yards	Muzzle	25	50	75	100	125	150	175	200
Velocity • fps	1180	1124	1077	1038	1004	974	948	923	901
Energy • Ft-lbs	556	505	464	431	403	378	359	341	324
Taylor KO Index	12.1	11.6	11.1	10.7	10.3	10.0	9.8	9.5	9.3
Mid-Range Trajectory Height • Inches	0.0	0.2	0.9	2.0	3.7	6.0	9.0	12.7	17.0
Drop • Inches	0.0	-0.8	-3.3	-7.7	-14.1	-22.7	-33.5	-46.7	-62.4

Federal 180-grain Hydra-Shok JHP (P10HS1)

G1 Ballistic Coefficient = 0.169

Distance • Yards	Muzzle	25	50	75	100	125	150	175	200
Velocity • fps	1030	1000	970	950	920	898	878	859	841
Energy • Ft-lbs	425	400	375	355	340	323	308	295	283
Taylor KO Index	10.6	10.3	10.0	9.8	9.5	9.2	9.0	8.8	8.7
Mid-Range Trajectory Height • Inches	0.0	0.3	1.1	2.5	4.7	7.4	10.9	15.3	20.4
Drop • Inches	0.0	-1.0	-4.3	-9.8	-17.8	-28.3	-41.5	-57.6	-76.5

Federal 180-grain JHP (C10C)

G1 Ballistic Coefficient = 0.169

Distance • Yards	Muzzle	25	50	75	100	125	150	175	200
Velocity • fps	1030	1000	970	950	920	898	878	859	841
Energy • Ft-lbs	425	400	375	355	340	323	308	295	283
Taylor KO Index	10.6	10.3	10.0	9.8	9.5	9.2	9.0	8.8	8.7
Mid-Range Trajectory Height • Inches	0.0	0.3	1.1	2.5	4.7	7.4	10.9	15.3	20.4
Drop • Inches	0.0	-1.0	-4.3	-9.8	-17.8	-28.3	-41.5	-57.6	-76.5

PMC 180-grain Starfire Hollow Point (10SFA)

G1 Ballistic Coefficient = 0.165

Distance • Yards	Muzzle	25	50	75	100	125	150	175	200
Velocity • fps	950	926	903	882	862	843	825	808	792
Energy • Ft-lbs	360	342	326	311	297	284	272	261	251
Taylor KO Index	9.8	9.5	9.3	9.1	8.9	8.7	8.5	8.3	8.1
Mid-Range Trajectory Height • Inches	0.0	0.3	1.3	2.9	5.3	8.5	12.5	17.5	23.3
Drop • Inches	0.0	-1.2	-5.0	-11.4	-20.6	-32.8	-48.0	-66.3	-88.0

UMC (Remington) 180-grain Metal Case (L10MM6)

G1 Ballistic Coefficient = 0.180

Distance • Yards	Muzzle	25	50	75	100	125	150	175	200
Velocity • fps	1150	1103	1063	1023	998	971	947	925	904
Energy • Ft-lbs	529	486	452	423	398	377	359	342	327
Taylor KO Index	11.8	11.3	10.9	10.6	10.3	10.0	9.7	9.5	9.3
Mid-Range Trajectory Height • Inches	0.0	0.2	0.9	2.0	3.7	6.2	9.2	12.9	17.3
Drop • Inches	0.0	-0.8	-3.5	-8.0	-14.6	-23.4	-34.4	-47.9	-63.9

American Eagle (Federal) 180-grain FMJ (AE10A)

G1 Ballistic Coefficient = 0.170

Distance • Yards	Muzzle	25	50	75	100	125	150	175	200
Velocity • fps	1060	1030	1000	970	940	917	896	875	857
Energy • Ft-lbs	450	420	395	375	355	336	321	306	293
Taylor KO Index	10.9	10.6	10.3	10.0	9.7	9.4	9.2	9.0	8.8
Mid-Range Trajectory Height • Inches	0.0	0.2	1.0	2.4	4.4	7.1	10.5	14.7	19.7
Drop • Inches	0.0	-1.0	-4.1	-9.3	-16.9	-27.0	-39.6	-54.9	-73.1

Cor-Bon 200-grain RN PN (HT10200PN/20)

G1 Ballistic Coefficient = 0.200

Distance • Yards	Muzzle	25	50	75	100	125	150	175	200
Velocity • fps	1200	1145	1097	1057	1022	992	965	940	918
Energy • Ft-lbs	640	582	535	496	464	437	413	393	374
Taylor KO Index	13.7	13.1	12.5	12.1	11.7	11.3	11.0	10.7	10.5
Mid-Range Trajectory Height • Inches	0.0	0.2	0.8	1.9	3.6	5.8	8.7	12.3	16.5
Drop • Inches	0.0	-0.8	-3.2	-7.5	-13.6	-21.9	-32.4	-45.2	-60.4

Hornady 200-grain JHP/XTP (9129)

G1 Ballistic Coefficient = 0.200

Distance • Yards	Muzzle	25	50	75	100	125	150	175	200
Velocity • fps	1050	1020	994	970	948	928	909	891	874
Energy • Ft-lbs	490	462	439	418	399	382	367	353	339
Taylor KO Index	12.0	11.7	11.4	11.1	10.8	10.6	10.4	10.2	10.0
Mid-Range Trajectory Height • Inches	0.0	0.2	1.0	2.4	4.4	7.0	10.3	14.4	19.2
Drop • Inches	0.0	-1.0	-4.1	-9.4	-17.0	-27.0	-39.5	-54.6	-72.5

Norma 200-grain Full jacket flat nose (11001) (Discontinued in 2005)

G1 Ballistic Coefficient = 0.182

Distance • Yards	Muzzle	25	50	75	100	125	150	175	200
Velocity • fps	1115	1074	1038	1007	979	955	932	911	891
Energy • Ft-lbs	554	513	480	450	427	405	386	369	353
Taylor KO Index	12.7	12.3	11.9	11.5	11.2	10.9	10.7	10.4	10.2
Mid-Range Trajectory Height • Inches	0.0	0.2	0.9	2.2	4.0	6.4	9.6	13.4	18.0
Drop • Inches	0.0	-0.9	-3.7	-8.5	-15.4	-24.6	-36.1	-50.2	-66.8

CCI 200-grain TMJ Blazer (3597)

G1 Ballistic Coefficient = 0.168

Distance • Yards	Muzzle	25	50	75	100	125	150	175	200
Velocity • fps	1050	1015	985	957	933	910	889	869	850
Energy • Ft-lbs	490	458	431	407	387	368	351	335	321
Taylor KO Index	12.0	11.6	11.3	11.0	10.7	10.4	10.2	9.9	9.7
Mid-Range Trajectory Height • Inches	0.0	0.2	1.1	2.5	4.5	7.2	14.5	14.9	20.0
Drop • Inches	0.0	-1.0	-4.1	-9.5	-17.2	-27.4	-40.3	-55.9	-74.4

PMC 200-grain Truncated Cone—Full Metal Jacket (10A)

G1 Ballistic Coefficient = 0.138

Distance • Yards	Muzzle	25	50	75	100	125	150	175	200
Velocity • fps	1050	1008	972	941	912	887	863	840	819
Energy • Ft-lbs	490	451	420	393	370	349	331	314	298
Taylor KO Index	12.0	11.5	11.1	10.8	10.4	10.1	9.9	9.6	9.4
Mid-Range Trajectory Height • Inches	0.0	0.2	1.1	2.5	4.6	7.4	11.0	15.4	20.7
Drop • Inches	0.0	-1.0	-4.2	-9.6	-17.5	-28.0	-41.2	-57.4	-76.6

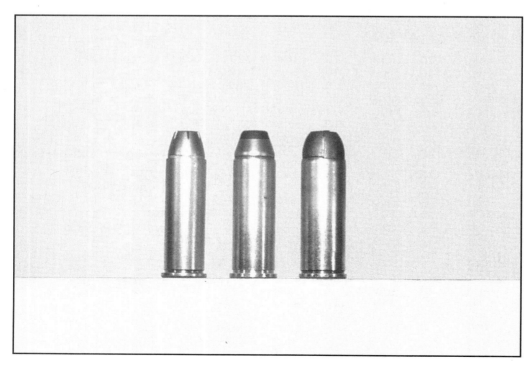

(Left to right) .41 Remington Magnum, .44 Remington Magnum, .45 Colt.)

.41 Remington Magnum

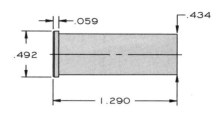

Remington announced the .41 Remington Magnum in 1964 at the same time that Smith & Wesson announced a Model 57 pistol chambered .41 Remington Magnum. The idea in offering the .41 was a simple one. The .357 Magnum wasn't quite enough caliber for some shooters, but the .44 Remington Magnum was too much. The .41 Remington Magnum was supposed to be "just right." While the .41 Remington Magnum does just what it was designed to do, a couple of things happened on the way to the gun shop. The first was that the .41 Remington Magnum was a little too much for many shooters. The second was that the caliber arrived just about the time that semiautomatic pistols were experiencing a big jump in popularity. The .41 Remington Magnum is still a powerful cartridge, one that fills the hunting application very easily.

Relative Recoil Factor = 1.23

Specifications

Controlling Agency for Standardization of this Ammunition: SAAMI

Bullet Weight Grains	Velocity fps	Maximum Average Pressure	
		Copper Crusher	Transducer
170 STHP	1,400	40,000 cup	36,000 psi
175 STHP	1,250	40,000 cup	36,000 psi
210 L	955	40,000 cup	36,000 psi
210 SP-HP	1,280	40,000 cup	36,000 psi

Standard barrel for velocity testing: 4 inches long (vented)—1 turn in 18.75-inch twist.

Alternate one-piece barrel length: 10.135 inches.

Availability

Cor-Bon 170-grain JHP Self Defense (SD41MI170/20)

G1 Ballistic Coefficient = 0.150

Distance • Yards	Muzzle	25	50	75	100	125	150	175	200
Velocity • fps	1275	1200	1136	1083	1039	1001	969	940	914
Energy • Ft-lbs	614	544	487	443	407	379	355	334	316
Taylor KO Index	12.7	11.9	11.3	10.8	10.3	10.0	9.6	9.4	9.1
Mid-Range Trajectory Height • Inches	0.0	0.1	0.7	1.8	3.3	5.5	8.3	11.8	16.0
Drop • Inches	0.0	-0.7	-2.9	-6.8	-12.5	-20.3	-30.2	-42.4	-57.1

Winchester 175-grain Silvertip Hollow Point (X41MSTHP2)

G1 Ballistic Coefficient = 0.153

Distance • Yards	Muzzle	25	50	75	100	125	150	175	200
Velocity • fps	1250	1180	1120	1071	1029	994	963	936	911
Energy • Ft-lbs	607	541	488	446	412	384	361	340	322
Taylor KO Index	12.8	12.1	11.5	11.0	10.5	10.2	9.9	9.6	9.3
Mid-Range Trajectory Height • Inches	0.0	0.2	0.8	1.8	3.4	5.6	8.4	11.9	16.1
Drop • Inches	0.0	-0.7	-3.0	-7.0	-12.9	-20.8	-31.0	-43.4	-58.2

PMC 210-grain Truncated Cone Soft Point (41C)

G1 Ballistic Coefficient = 0.138

Distance • Yards	Muzzle	25	50	75	100	125	150	175	200
Velocity • fps	1300	1210	1141	1065	1038	998	963	933	905
Energy • Ft-lbs	788	689	611	550	502	464	433	406	382
Taylor KO Index	16.0	14.9	14.0	13.1	12.8	12.3	11.8	11.5	11.1
Mid-Range Trajectory Height • Inches	0.0	0.2	0.7	1.8	3.3	5.5	8.3	11.8	16.0
Drop • Inches	0.0	-0.7	-2.8	-6.6	-12.3	-19.9	-29.8	-41.9	-56.6

Remington 210-grain Jacketed Soft Point (R41MG1)

G1 Ballistic Coefficient = 0.160

Distance • Yards	Muzzle	25	50	75	100	125	150	175	200
Velocity • fps	1300	1226	1162	1108	1062	1024	991	962	935
Energy • Ft-lbs	788	702	630	573	526	489	458	431	408
Taylor KO Index	16.0	15.1	14.3	13.6	13.1	12.6	12.2	11.8	11.5
Mid-Range Trajectory Height • Inches	0.0	0.2	0.7	1.7	3.2	5.2	7.9	11.2	15.2
Drop • Inches	0.0	-0.7	-2.8	-6.5	-12.0	-19.4	-28.8	-40.4	-54.4

Cor-Bon 210-grain JHP (HT41210JHP/20)

G1 Ballistic Coefficient = 0.160

Distance • Yards	Muzzle	25	50	75	100	125	150	175	200
Velocity • fps	1350	1271	1201	1141	1090	1047	1011	979	951
Energy • Ft-lbs	850	753	673	607	554	511	476	447	422
Taylor KO Index	16.6	15.6	14.8	14.0	13.4	12.9	12.4	12.0	11.7
Mid-Range Trajectory Height • Inches	0.0	0.1	0.6	1.6	3.0	4.9	7.5	10.7	14.5
Drop • Inches	0.0	-0.6	-2.6	-6.1	-11.2	-18.2	-27.1	-38.2	-51.5

Federal 210-grain Hi-Shok JHP (C41A)

G1 Ballistic Coefficient = 0.133

Distance • Yards	Muzzle	25	50	75	100	125	150	175	200
Velocity • fps	1300	1210	1130	1070	1030	990	956	925	897
Energy • Ft-lbs	790	680	595	540	495	458	426	399	375
Taylor KO Index	16.0	14.9	13.9	13.2	12.7	12.2	11.8	11.4	11.0
Mid-Range Trajectory Height • Inches	0.0	0.2	0.7	1.8	3.3	5.4	8.3	11.8	16.0
Drop • Inches	0.0	-0.7	-2.8	-6.6	-12.3	-20.0	-29.9	-42.1	-56.8

Speer 210-grain Gold Dot Hollow Point (23996)

G1 Ballistic Coefficient = 0.183

Distance • Yards	Muzzle	25	50	75	100	125	150	175	200
Velocity • fps	1280	1217	1162	1114	1073	1038	1007	980	955
Energy • Ft-lbs	764	691	630	579	537	503	473	448	426
Taylor KO Index	15.7	15.0	14.3	13.7	13.2	12.8	12.4	12.1	11.7
Mid-Range Trajectory Height • Inches	0.0	0.2	0.7	1.7	3.2	5.2	7.9	11.1	15.0
Drop • Inches	0.0	-0.7	-2.9	-6.8	-12.4	-19.9	-29.4	-41.0	-54.8

Winchester 240-grain Platinum Tip (S41PTHP)

G1 Ballistic Coefficient = 0.210

Distance • Yards	Muzzle	25	50	75	100	125	150	175	200
Velocity • fps	1250	1198	1151	1111	1075	1044	1016	991	969
Energy • Ft-lbs	833	765	706	658	616	581	551	524	500
Taylor KO Index	17.6	16.8	16.2	15.6	15.1	14.7	14.3	13.9	13.6
Mid-Range Trajectory Height • Inches	0.0	0.2	0.8	1.7	3.3	5.3	7.9	11.1	15.0
Drop • Inches	0.0	-0.7	-2.9	-6.8	-12.4	-19.9	-29.4	-41.0	-54.8

Cor-Bon 250-grain Hard Cast

G1 Ballistic Coefficient = 0.215

Distance • Yards	Muzzle	25	50	75	100	125	150	175	200
Velocity • fps	1325	1267	1215	1167	1125	1088	1056	1028	1002
Energy • Ft-lbs	975	892	819	756	703	658	619	586	558
Taylor KO Index	19.4	18.1	17.8	17.1	16.5	15.9	15.5	15.1	14.7
Mid-Range Trajectory Height • Inches	0.0	0.1	0.6	1.5	2.9	4.7	7.1	10.1	13.6
Drop • Inches	0.0	-0.6	-2.6	-6.1	-11.2	-17.9	-26.5	-37.1	-49.7

Federal 250-grain Cast Core (P41B)

G1 Ballistic Coefficient = 0.218

Distance • Yards	Muzzle	25	50	75	100	125	150	175	200
Velocity • fps	1250	1200	1150	1110	1080	1049	1022	997	975
Energy • Ft-lbs	865	795	735	685	645	611	580	552	528
Taylor KO Index	18.3	17.6	16.8	16.3	15.8	15.4	15.0	14.6	14.3
Mid-Range Trajectory Height • Inches	0.0	0.2	0.8	1.8	3.3	5.2	7.8	11.0	14.8
Drop • Inches	0.0	-0.7	-2.9	-6.8	-12.4	-19.8	-29.3	-40.8	-54.4

.44 Colt

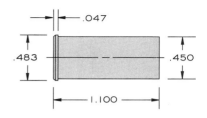

This is really an oldie. The cartridge was introduced in 1870 to be used in centerfire conversions of the percussion .44 Colt. It was also used a few years later in the .44 Remington revolver. When introduced, it was a black-powder number, which resulted in very low pressures. The cartridge dropped out of the factory catalogs in 1940. The popularity of Cowboy Action shooting revived this cartridge. A word of CAUTION here. These cartridges are now loaded with smokeless powder and should NOT be fired in any guns designed or manufactured in the black-powder era. They are suitable only for modern replica guns in good condition.

Relative Recoil Factor = 0.75

Specifications

Controlling Agency for Standardization of this Ammunition: Factory

Cowboy Action Loads
Black Hills 230-grain FPL
G1 Ballistic Coefficient = 0.150

Distance • Yards	Muzzle	25	50	75	100	125	150	175	200
Velocity • fps	730	715	700	685	671	657	641	630	617
Energy • Ft-lbs	272	261	250	240	230	221	212	203	195
Taylor KO Index	10.4	10.1	9.9	9.7	9.5	9.3	9.1	8.9	8.8
Mid-Range Trajectory Height • Inches	0.0	0.5	2.1	4.8	8.8	14.1	20.8	29.0	38.6
Drop • Inches	0.0	-2.1	-8.4	-19.1	-34.5	-54.7	-80.0	-100.4	-146.4

.45 GAP with the .45 Auto loaded and unloaded.

.44 Smith & Wesson Special

The .44 S&W is one of the first generation of pistol cartridges designed to use smokeless powder. At the time of its introduction, the working pressures were kept very low, pretty much a duplication of black-powder pressure levels. As a result, the performance is certainly modest when compared with .44 Remington Magnum performance levels (although very potent compared with calibers like .38 Special). Like the .38 Special in a .357 Magnum revolver, the .44 S&W Special can be fired in modern guns in good condition that are chambered for the .44 Remington Magnum. This provides a way for the non-reloader to get modestly powered ammo for use in the .44 Remington Magnum. Using .44 Remington Magnum ammo in a gun chambered for the .44 S&W Special is definitely NOT recommended.

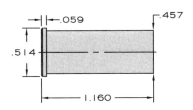

Relative Recoil Factor = 0.81

Specifications

Controlling Agency for Standardization of this Ammunition: SAAMI

Bullet Weight Grains	Velocity fps	Maximum Average Pressure	
		Copper Crusher	Transducer
200 STHP	900	14,000 cup	N/S
200 SWCHP	1,025	14,000 cup	N/S
246 L	800	N/S	15,500 psi

Standard barrel for velocity testing: 4 inches long (vented)—(alternate one-piece barrel is 8.15 inches long)—1 turn in 20-inch twist—Several manufacturers are using 6- or 6.5-inch vented barrels to obtain their velocity data.

Availability

Cor-Bon 135-grain Glaser Safety Slug (03800/04000)

G1 Ballistic Coefficient = 0.125

Distance • Yards	Muzzle	25	50	75	100	125	150	175	200
Velocity • fps	1350	1251	1166	1098	1043	998	961	927	898
Energy • Ft-lbs	546	469	408	361	326	299	277	258	242
Taylor KO Index	11.2	10.4	9.7	9.1	8.7	8.3	8.0	7.7	7.5
Mid-Range Trajectory Height • Inches	0.0	0.2	0.7	1.7	3.2	5.3	8.1	11.6	15.9
Drop • Inches	0.0	-0.6	-2.7	-6.3	-11.7	-19.1	-28.7	-40.6	-55.1

CCI 140-grain Magnum Shotshell (3979)

Shot load using #9 shot—Muzzle Velocity = 1000 fps.

Cor-Bon 165-grain JHP (SD44S165/20)

G1 Ballistic Coefficient = 0.140

Distance • Yards	Muzzle	25	50	75	100	125	150	175	200
Velocity • fps	1500	1396	1301	1218	1147	1089	1041	1001	967
Energy • Ft-lbs	825	714	620	544	482	434	397	367	342
Taylor KO Index	15.3	14.2	13.2	12.4	11.7	11.1	10.6	10.2	9.8
Mid-Range Trajectory Height • Inches	0.0	0.1	0.6	1.4	2.6	4.3	6.6	9.6	13.2
Drop • Inches	0.0	-0.5	-2.1	-5.0	-9.4	-15.4	-23.3	-33.1	-45.2

Hornady 180-grain JHP/XTP (9070)

G1 Ballistic Coefficient = 0.139

Distance • Yards	Muzzle	25	50	75	100	125	150	175	200
Velocity • fps	1000	965	935	907	882	959	837	816	796
Energy • Ft-lbs	400	373	350	329	311	295	280	266	253
Taylor KO Index	11.1	10.7	10.3	10.0	9.8	9.5	9.3	9.1	8.8
Mid-Range Trajectory Height • Inches	0.0	0.3	1.2	2.7	5.0	7.9	11.8	16.6	22.2
Drop • Inches	0.0	-1.1	-4.6	-10.5	-19.0	-30.4	-44.6	-62.0	-82.6

PMC 180-grain Jacketed Hollow Point (44SB)

G1 Ballistic Coefficient = 0.105

Distance • Yards	Muzzle	25	50	75	100	125	150	175	200
Velocity • fps	980	938	902	869	839	812	786	762	739
Energy • Ft-lbs	383	352	325	302	282	264	247	232	218
Taylor KO Index	10.8	10.4	10.0	9.6	9.3	9.0	8.7	8.5	8.2
Mid-Range Trajectory Height • Inches	0.0	0.3	1.2	2.9	5.3	8.6	12.9	18.2	24.6
Drop • Inches	0.0	-1.2	-4.8	-11.1	-20.3	-32.5	-48.0	-67.0	-89.7

Federal 200-grain Semi-Wadcutter HP (C44SA)
G1 Ballistic Coefficient = 0.091

Distance • Yards	Muzzle	25	50	75	100	125	150	175	200
Velocity • fps	900	860	830	800	770	743	717	693	669
Energy • Ft-lbs	360	330	305	285	260	245	228	213	199
Taylor KO Index	11.1	10.6	10.2	9.8	9.5	9.2	8.8	8.6	8.3
Mid-Range Trajectory Height • Inches	0.0	0.3	1.4	3.4	6.3	10.2	15.3	21.7	29.3
Drop • Inches	0.0	-1.4	-5.7	-13.1	-24.0	-38.5	-56.9	-79.6	-106.7

Winchester 200-grain Silvertip Hollow Point (X44STHPS2)
G1 Ballistic Coefficient = 0.162

Distance • Yards	Muzzle	25	50	75	100	125	150	175	200
Velocity • fps	900	879	860	840	822	804	788	772	756
Energy • Ft-lbs	360	343	328	313	300	287	276	265	254
Taylor KO Index	11.1	10.8	10.6	10.3	10.1	9.9	9.7	9.5	9.3
Mid-Range Trajectory Height • Inches	0.0	0.3	1.4	3.2	5.9	9.3	13.8	19.3	25.7
Drop • Inches	0.0	-1.4	-5.5	-12.7	-22.9	-36.3	-53.0	-73.3	-97.2

CCI 200-grain JHP Blazer (3556)
G1 Ballistic Coefficient = 0.145

Distance • Yards	Muzzle	25	50	75	100	125	150	175	200
Velocity • fps	920	895	872	850	829	809	791	773	756
Energy • Ft-lbs	376	356	337	321	305	291	278	265	254
Taylor KO Index	11.4	11.0	10.8	10.5	10.2	10.0	9.8	9.5	9.3
Mid-Range Trajectory Height • Inches	0.0	0.3	1.4	3.1	5.7	9.2	13.6	18.9	25.3
Drop • Inches	0.0	-1.3	-5.3	-12.2	-22.1	-35.1	-51.5	-71.4	-94.8

Speer 200-grain Gold Dot Hollow Point (23980)
G1 Ballistic Coefficient = 0.145

Distance • Yards	Muzzle	25	50	75	100	125	150	175	200
Velocity • fps	920	895	872	850	829	809	791	773	756
Energy • Ft-lbs	376	356	337	321	305	291	278	265	254
Taylor KO Index	11.4	11.0	10.8	10.5	10.2	10.0	9.8	9.5	9.3
Mid-Range Trajectory Height • Inches	0.0	0.3	1.4	3.1	5.7	9.2	13.6	18.9	25.3
Drop • Inches	0.0	-1.3	-5.3	-12.2	-22.1	-35.1	-51.5	-71.4	-94.8

PMC 240-grain SWC W/GC (44SA)
G1 Ballistic Coefficient = 0.102

Distance • Yards	Muzzle	25	50	75	100	125	150	175	200
Velocity • fps	760	737	714	692	670	650	631	612	594
Energy • Ft-lbs	308	289	271	255	240	226	212	200	188
Taylor KO Index	11.3	10.9	10.6	10.2	9.9	9.6	9.3	9.1	8.8
Mid-Range Trajectory Height • Inches	0.0	0.5	2.0	4.7	8.5	13.7	20.5	28.1	38.8
Drop • Inches	0.0	-1.9	-7.9	-18.1	-32.8	-52.4	-77.1	-107.2	-143.2

Remington 246-grain Lead Round Nose (R44SW)
G1 Ballistic Coefficient = 0.154

Distance • Yards	Muzzle	25	50	75	100	125	150	175	200
Velocity • fps	755	739	725	709	695	681	667	654	641
Energy • Ft-lbs	310	299	285	275	265	253	243	233	224
Taylor KO Index	11.4	11.2	11.0	10.7	10.5	10.3	10.1	9.9	9.7
Mid-Range Trajectory Height • Inches	0.0	0.5	2.0	4.6	8.3	13.2	19.4	27.0	36.0
Drop • Inches	0.0	-1.9	-7.8	-17.9	-32.3	-51.1	-74.6	-103.1	-136.6

Winchester 246-grain Lead-Round Nose (X44SP)
G1 Ballistic Coefficient = 0.154

Distance • Yards	Muzzle	25	50	75	100	125	150	175	200
Velocity • fps	755	739	725	709	695	681	667	654	641
Energy • Ft-lbs	310	299	285	275	265	253	243	233	224
Taylor KO Index	11.4	11.2	11.0	10.7	10.5	10.3	10.1	9.9	9.7
Mid-Range Trajectory Height • Inches	0.0	0.5	2.0	4.6	8.3	13.2	19.4	27.0	36.0
Drop • Inches	0.0	-1.9	-7.8	-17.9	-32.3	-51.1	-74.6	-103.1	-136.6

Cowboy Action Loads

Hornady 180-grain Cowboy (9071)

G1 Ballistic Coefficient = 0.114

Distance • Yards	Muzzle	25	50	75	100	125	150	175	200
Velocity • fps	1000	958	923	891	862	835	810	786	764
Energy • Ft-lbs	400	367	340	317	297	279	262	247	233
Taylor KO Index	11.1	10.6	10.3	9.9	9.6	9.3	9.0	8.7	8.5
Mid-Range Trajectory Height • Inches	0.0	0.3	1.2	2.8	5.1	8.3	12.3	17.4	23.5
Drop • Inches	0.0	-1.1	-4.6	-10.6	-19.4	-31.1	-45.9	-64.0	-85.7

CCI 200-grain Cowboy Lead Flat Nose Trailblazer (3558)

G1 Ballistic Coefficient = 0.130

Distance • Yards	Muzzle	25	50	75	100	125	150	175	200
Velocity • fps	750	732	714	697	680	664	648	633	618
Energy • Ft-lbs	250	238	226	216	205	196	187	178	170
Taylor KO Index	9.3	9.0	8.8	8.6	8.4	8.2	8.0	7.8	7.6
Mid-Range Trajectory Height • Inches	0.0	0.5	2.0	4.5	8.5	13.6	20.2	28.2	37.8
Drop • Inches	0.0	-2.0	-8.0	-18.3	-33.0	-52.5	-76.9	-106.4	-141.4

Black Hills 210-grain FPL (DCB44SPLN1)

G1 Ballistic Coefficient = 0.100

Distance • Yards	Muzzle	25	50	75	100	125	150	175	200
Velocity • fps	700	678	657	637	618	599	580	563	545
Energy • Ft-lbs	229	215	202	189	178	167	157	148	139
Taylor KO Index	9.0	8.7	8.5	8.2	8.0	7.8	7.5	7.3	7.1
Mid-Range Trajectory Height • Inches	0.0	0.6	2.4	5.5	10.1	16.1	24.1	33.9	45.7
Drop • Inches	0.0	-2.3	-9.2	-21.3	-38.6	-61.7	-90.8	-126.3	-168.7

PMC 240-grain Lead Flat Point (44CD)

G1 Ballistic Coefficient = 0.153

Distance • Yards	Muzzle	25	50	75	100	125	150	175	200
Velocity • fps	750	734	719	704	690	676	662	649	636
Energy • Ft-lbs	300	287	276	264	254	244	234	224	216
Taylor KO Index	11.0	10.8	10.6	10.4	10.2	10.0	9.8	9.6	9.4
Mid-Range Trajectory Height • Inches	0.0	0.5	2.1	4.8	8.4	13.3	19.7	27.4	36.5
Drop • Inches	0.0	-2.0	-7.9	-18.1	-32.7	-51.8	-75.7	-104.5	-138.5

Winchester 240-grain Cast Lead (CB44SP)

G1 Ballistic Coefficient = 0.153

Distance • Yards	Muzzle	25	50	75	100	125	150	175	200
Velocity • fps	750	734	719	704	690	676	662	649	636
Energy • Ft-lbs	300	287	276	264	254	244	234	224	216
Taylor KO Index	11.0	10.8	10.6	10.4	10.2	10.0	9.8	9.6	9.4
Mid-Range Trajectory Height • Inches	0.0	0.5	2.1	4.8	8.4	13.3	19.7	27.4	36.5
Drop • Inches	0.0	-2.0	-7.9	-18.1	-32.7	-51.8	-75.7	-104.5	-138.5

.44 Remington Magnum (Pistol Data)

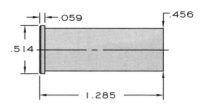

The .44 Remington Magnum cartridge was introduced in 1956. From its inception, it has been the stuff of legends. Many species of the world's dangerous game have been killed at one time or another by a hunter equipped with a .44 Magnum revolver (backed up, usually, by a professional hunter equipped with a suitable large rifle). As a pistol cartridge, the .44 Magnum kills at both ends. Few shooters can get off more than five or six shots without beginning to flinch. Ammunition in .44 S&W Special caliber can be used in revolvers chambered for .44 Remington Magnum, a condition similar to firing .38 Special in a .357 Magnum. See the data in the rifle section for further information. (Ammunition for a .44 S&W Special generally can't be used in tubular magazine rifles designed for the .44 RM because the shorter cartridge promotes feeding problems that aren't present in a revolver.)

Relative Recoil Factor = 1.45

Specifications

Controlling Agency for Standardization of this Ammunition: SAAMI

Bullet Weight Grains	Velocity fps	Maximum Average Pressure Copper Crusher	Transducer
180 JHP	1,400	40,000 cup	36,000 psi
210 STHP	1,250	40,000 cup	36,000 psi
240 L-SWC	995	40,000 cup	36,000 psi
240 L	1,335	40,000 cup	36,000 psi

Standard barrel for velocity testing: 4 inches long (vented)—1 turn in 20-inch twist

Some velocities listed below are taken with "non-standard" barrel lengths

Availability

Cor-Bon 135-grain Glaser Safety Slug (04200/04400)

G1 Ballistic Coefficient = 0.120

Distance • Yards	Muzzle	25	50	75	100	125	150	175	200
Velocity • fps	1850	1703	1506	1438	1323	1224	1142	1076	1023
Energy • Ft-lbs	1026	869	734	620	525	449	391	347	314
Taylor KO Index	15.4	14.2	13.0	12.0	11.0	10.2	9.5	9.0	8.5
Mid-Range Trajectory Height • Inches	0.0	0.1	0.4	0.9	1.8	3.1	4.8	7.2	10.1
Drop • Inches	0.0	-0.3	-1.4	-3.4	-6.4	-10.7	-16.4	-23.8	-33.1

CCI 140-grain Shotshell (3979)

Shotshell load using #9 shot at 1000 fps.

Cor-Bon 165-grain JHP Self Defense (SD44M165/20)

G1 Ballistic Coefficient = 0.140

Distance • Yards	Muzzle	25	50	75	100	125	150	175	200
Velocity • fps	1300	1217	1146	1087	1040	1000	965	935	908
Energy • Ft-lbs	618	542	481	433	396	366	342	320	302
Taylor KO Index	13.2	12.4	11.7	11.1	10.6	10.2	9.8	9.5	9.2
Mid-Range Trajectory Height • Inches	0.0	0.1	0.7	1.7	3.3	5.4	8.2	11.7	15.9
Drop • Inches	0.0	-0.7	-2.8	-6.6	-12.2	-19.9	-29.7	-41.8	-56.5

UMC (Remington) 180-grain Jacketed Soft Point (L44MG7)

G1 Ballistic Coefficient = 0.123

Distance • Yards	Muzzle	25	50	75	100	125	150	175	200
Velocity • fps	1610	1482	1365	1262	1175	1103	1047	1001	962
Energy • Ft-lbs	1036	878	745	637	551	487	438	400	370
Taylor KO Index	17.9	16.5	15.2	14.0	13.1	12.3	11.6	11.1	10.7
Mid-Range Trajectory Height • Inches	0.0	0.1	0.5	1.2	2.3	3.9	6.1	9.0	12.5
Drop • Inches	0.0	-0.4	-1.9	-4.5	-8.4	-14.0	-21.3	-30.6	-41.9

Cor-Bon 180-grain JHP (HT44180JHP/20)

G1 Ballistic Coefficient = 0.125

Distance • Yards	Muzzle	25	50	75	100	125	150	175	200
Velocity • fps	1700	1573	1455	1349	1256	1177	1112	1060	1018
Energy • Ft-lbs	1155	989	847	727	630	553	495	750	414
Taylor KO Index	18.9	17.5	16.2	15.0	14.0	13.1	12.4	11.8	11.3
Mid-Range Trajectory Height • Inches	0.0	0.1	0.4	1.0	2.0	3.5	5.4	7.9	11.0
Drop • Inches	0.0	-0.4	-1.7	-4.0	-7.5	-12.4	-18.8	-27.0	-37.1

Federal 180-grain Hi-Shok JHP (C44B)

G1 Ballistic Coefficient = 0.125

Distance • Yards	Muzzle	25	50	75	100	125	150	175	200
Velocity • fps	1610	1480	1370	1270	1180	1109	1052	1005	966
Energy • Ft-lbs	1035	875	750	640	555	491	442	404	373
Taylor KO Index	17.9	16.4	15.2	14.1	13.1	12.3	11.7	11.2	10.7
Mid-Range Trajectory Height • Inches	0.0	0.1	0.5	1.2	2.3	3.9	6.1	8.9	12.4
Drop • Inches	0.0	-0.4	-1.9	-4.5	-8.4	-13.9	-21.2	-30.4	-41.6

Remington 180-grain Semi-Jacketed Hollow Point (R44MG5)

G1 Ballistic Coefficient = 0.123

Distance • Yards	Muzzle	25	50	75	100	125	150	175	200
Velocity • fps	1610	1482	1365	1262	1175	1103	1047	1001	962
Energy • Ft-lbs	1036	878	745	637	551	487	438	400	370
Taylor KO Index	17.9	16.5	15.2	14.0	13.1	12.3	11.6	11.1	10.7
Mid-Range Trajectory Height • Inches	0.0	0.1	0.5	1.2	2.3	3.9	6.1	9.0	12.5
Drop • Inches	0.0	-0.4	-1.9	-4.5	-8.4	-14.0	-21.3	-30.6	-41.9

UMC (Remington) 180-grain Semi-Jacketed Hollow Point (L44MG5) (Discontinued in 2004)

G1 Ballistic Coefficient = 0.123

Distance • Yards	Muzzle	25	50	75	100	125	150	175	200
Velocity • fps	1610	1482	1365	1262	1175	1103	1047	1001	962
Energy • Ft-lbs	1036	878	745	637	551	487	438	400	370
Taylor KO Index	17.9	16.5	15.2	14.0	13.1	12.3	11.6	11.1	10.7
Mid-Range Trajectory Height • Inches	0.0	0.1	0.5	1.2	2.3	3.9	6.1	9.0	12.5
Drop • Inches	0.0	-0.4	-1.9	-4.5	-8.4	-14.0	-21.3	-30.6	-41.9

Hornady 180-grain JHP/XTP (9081)

G1 Ballistic Coefficient = 0.138

Distance • Yards	Muzzle	25	50	75	100	125	150	175	200
Velocity • fps	1550	1440	1340	1250	1173	1109	1057	1014	977
Energy • Ft-lbs	960	829	717	624	550	492	446	411	382
Taylor KO Index	17.2	16.0	14.9	13.9	13.0	12.3	11.7	11.3	10.9
Mid-Range Trajectory Height • Inches	0.0	0.1	0.5	1.3	2.4	4.0	6.2	9.1	12.5
Drop • Inches	0.0	-0.5	-2.0	-4.7	-8.9	-14.6	-22.0	-31.4	-42.8

PMC 180-grain Jacketed Hollow Point (44B)

G1 Ballistic Coefficient = 0.107

Distance • Yards	Muzzle	25	50	75	100	125	150	175	200
Velocity • fps	1400	1270	1167	1091	1032	983	942	906	874
Energy • Ft-lbs	784	653	553	479	426	387	355	328	305
Taylor KO Index	15.6	14.1	13.0	12.1	11.5	10.9	10.5	10.1	9.7
Mid-Range Trajectory Height • Inches	0.0	0.2	0.7	1.6	3.1	5.3	8.1	11.8	16.2
Drop • Inches	0.0	-0.6	-2.5	-6.0	-11.3	-18.6	-28.2	-40.3	-54.9

Hornady 200-grain JHP/XTP (9080)

G1 Ballistic Coefficient = 0.170

Distance • Yards	Muzzle	25	50	75	100	125	150	175	200
Velocity • fps	1500	1413	1333	1260	1196	1140	1092	1051	1017
Energy • Ft-lbs	999	887	789	706	635	577	530	491	459
Taylor KO Index	18.5	17.4	16.5	15.6	14.8	14.1	13.5	13.0	12.6
Mid-Range Trajectory Height • Inches	0.0	0.1	0.5	1.3	2.5	4.1	6.2	8.9	12.2
Drop • Inches	0.0	-0.5	-2.1	-4.9	-9.1	-14.8	-22.2	-31.4	-42.5

Fiocchi 200-grain Jacketed Hollowpoint (44B)

G1 Ballistic Coefficient = 0.130

Distance • Yards	Muzzle	25	50	75	100	125	150	175	200
Velocity • fps	1475	1365	1267	1183	1113	1058	1012	974	940
Energy • Ft-lbs	966	826	713	622	551	497	455	421	393
Taylor KO Index	18.1	16.8	15.6	14.5	13.7	13.1	12.5	12.0	11.6
Mid-Range Trajectory Height • Inches	0.0	0.1	0.6	1.4	2.7	4.5	6.9	10.0	13.8
Drop • Inches	0.0	-0.5	-2.2	-5.3	-9.9	-16.2	-24.5	-34.8	-47.4

Magtech 200-grain SCHP (44D)

G1 Ballistic Coefficient = 0.166

Distance • Yards	Muzzle	25	50	75	100	125	150	175	200
Velocity • fps	1296	1226	1164	1111	1067	1029	997	968	942
Energy • Ft-lbs	746	667	602	549	506	471	441	416	394
Taylor KO Index	16.0	15.1	14.4	13.7	13.2	12.7	12.3	11.9	11.6
Mid-Range Trajectory Height • Inches	0.0	0.2	0.7	1.7	3.2	5.2	7.9	11.2	15.2
Drop • Inches	0.0	-0.7	-2.8	-6.5	-12.0	-19.4	-28.8	-40.3	-54.4

Speer 210-grain Gold Dot (23972)

G1 Ballistic Coefficient = 0.154

Distance • Yards	Muzzle	25	50	75	100	125	150	175	200
Velocity • fps	1450	1359	1276	1203	1140	1088	1044	1007	975
Energy • Ft-lbs	980	861	759	675	606	552	509	473	443
Taylor KO Index	18.8	17.6	16.5	15.6	14.8	14.1	13.5	13.1	12.6
Mid-Range Trajectory Height • Inches	0.0	0.1	0.6	1.4	2.7	4.4	6.8	9.8	13.4
Drop • Inches	0.0	-0.5	-2.3	-5.3	-9.9	-16.1	-24.1	-34.2	-46.4

Winchester 210-grain Silvertip Hollow Point (X44MS)

G1 Ballistic Coefficient = 0.135

Distance • Yards	Muzzle	25	50	75	100	125	150	175	200
Velocity • fps	1250	1171	1106	1053	1010	973	941	912	886
Energy • Ft-lbs	729	640	570	518	475	442	413	388	366
Taylor KO Index	16.1	15.1	14.3	13.6	13.1	12.6	12.2	11.8	11.5
Mid-Range Trajectory Height • Inches	0.0	0.2	0.8	1.9	3.7	5.7	8.7	12.4	16.7
Drop • Inches	0.0	-0.7	-3.0	-7.1	-13.2	-21.3	-31.7	-44.5	-59.8

Fiocchi 240-grain Jacketed Softpoint (44A)

G1 Ballistic Coefficient = 0.140

Distance • Yards	Muzzle	25	50	75	100	125	150	175	200
Velocity • fps	1375	1283	1202	1133	1077	1031	993	959	930
Energy • Ft-lbs	1008	877	770	685	620	567	525	491	461
Taylor KO Index	20.4	19.0	17.8	16.8	16.0	14.8	14.3	13.8	13.4
Mid-Range Trajectory Height • Inches	0.0	0.2	0.7	1.6	3.0	4.9	7.5	10.8	14.7
Drop • Inches	0.0	-0.6	-2.5	-6.0	-11.1	-18.0	-27.0	-38.2	-51.6

Ultramax 240-grain SWC (44A)

G1 Ballistic Coefficient = 0.125

Distance • Yards	Muzzle	25	50	75	100	125	150	175	200
Velocity • fps	1360	1259	1174	1104	1048	1002	964	930	900
Energy • Ft-lbs	986	845	734	649	585	535	495	461	432
Taylor KO Index	20.1	18.6	17.4	16.4	15.5	14.8	14.3	13.8	13.3
Mid-Range Trajectory Height • Inches	0.0	0.2	0.7	1.7	3.2	5.3	8.0	11.5	15.7
Drop • Inches	0.0	-0.6	-2.6	-6.2	-11.5	-18.9	-28.3	-40.2	-54.5

Sellier & Bellot 240-grain SP (SBA04401)

G1 Ballistic Coefficient = 0.122

Distance • Yards	Muzzle	25	50	75	100	125	150	175	200
Velocity • fps	1181	1114	1050	1003	964	930	899	871	845
Energy • Ft-lbs	743	661	587	536	495	461	431	404	381
Taylor KO Index	17.5	16.5	15.6	14.9	14.3	13.8	13.3	12.9	12.5
Mid-Range Trajectory Height • Inches	0.0	0.2	0.9	2.1	3.9	6.4	9.7	13.7	18.7
Drop • Inches	0.0	-0.8	-3.4	-8.0	-14.7	-23.7	-35.3	-49.5	-66.6

PMC 240-grain Truncated Cone—Soft Point (44D)

G1 Ballistic Coefficient = 0.139

Distance • Yards	Muzzle	25	50	75	100	125	150	175	200
Velocity • fps	1300	1216	1145	1086	1038	999	964	934	906
Energy • Ft-lbs	900	788	699	629	575	532	496	465	438
Taylor KO Index	19.3	18.0	17.0	16.1	15.4	14.8	14.3	13.8	13.4
Mid-Range Trajectory Height • Inches	0.0	0.2	0.7	1.8	3.3	5.4	8.2	11.6	15.8
Drop • Inches	0.0	-0.7	-2.8	-6.6	-12.2	-19.9	-29.6	-41.7	-56.2

Magtech 240-grain SJSP Flat (44A)

G1 Ballistic Coefficient = 0.173

Distance • Yards	Muzzle	25	50	75	100	125	150	175	200
Velocity • fps	1180	1127	1081	1043	1010	981	955	931	909
Energy • Ft-lbs	741	677	624	580	544	513	486	462	440
Taylor KO Index	17.5	16.7	16.0	15.4	15.0	14.5	14.1	13.8	13.5
Mid-Range Trajectory Height • Inches	0.0	0.2	0.9	2.0	3.7	6.0	8.9	12.5	16.8
Drop • Inches	0.0	-0.8	-3.3	-7.7	-14.1	-22.5	-33.2	-46.3	-61.9

Remington 240-grain Soft Point (R44MG2)

G1 Ballistic Coefficient = 0.173

Distance • Yards	Muzzle	25	50	75	100	125	150	175	200
Velocity • fps	1180	1127	1081	1043	1010	981	955	931	909
Energy • Ft-lbs	741	677	624	580	544	513	486	462	440
Taylor KO Index	17.5	16.7	16.0	15.4	15.0	14.5	14.1	13.8	13.5
Mid-Range Trajectory Height • Inches	0.0	0.2	0.9	2.0	3.7	6.0	8.9	12.5	16.8
Drop • Inches	0.0	-0.8	-3.3	-7.7	-14.1	-22.5	-33.2	-46.3	-61.9

USA (Winchester) 240-grain Jacketed Soft Point (Q4240)

G1 Ballistic Coefficient = 0.173

Distance • Yards	Muzzle	25	50	75	100	125	150	175	200
Velocity • fps	1180	1127	1081	1043	1010	981	955	931	909
Energy • Ft-lbs	741	677	624	580	544	513	486	462	440
Taylor KO Index	17.5	16.7	16.0	15.4	15.0	14.5	14.1	13.8	13.5
Mid-Range Trajectory Height • Inches	0.0	0.2	0.9	2.0	3.7	6.0	8.9	12.5	16.8
Drop • Inches	0.0	-0.8	-3.3	-7.7	-14.1	-22.5	-33.2	-46.3	-61.9

PMC 240-grain Lead—Gas Check (44A)

G1 Ballistic Coefficient = 0.133

Distance • Yards	Muzzle	25	50	75	100	125	150	175	200
Velocity • fps	1250	1168	1103	1051	1008	971	939	910	883
Energy • Ft-lbs	833	730	651	590	542	503	470	441	416
Taylor KO Index	18.5	17.3	16.3	15.6	14.9	14.4	13.9	13.5	13.1
Mid-Range Trajectory Height • Inches	0.0	0.2	0.8	1.9	3.6	5.8	8.8	12.6	17.0
Drop • Inches	0.0	-0.7	-3.0	-7.1	-13.2	-21.4	-31.9	-44.8	-60.4

Cor-Bon 240-grain JHP (HT44240JHP/20)

G1 Ballistic Coefficient = 0.150

Distance • Yards	Muzzle	25	50	75	100	125	150	175	200
Velocity • fps	1500	1407	1322	1246	1181	1125	1079	1040	1007
Energy • Ft-lbs	1200	1055	931	828	743	675	621	577	540
Taylor KO Index	22.2	20.8	19.6	18.5	17.5	16.7	16.0	15.4	14.9
Mid-Range Trajectory Height • Inches	0.0	0.1	0.5	1.3	2.4	4.1	6.3	9.0	12.3
Drop • Inches	0.0	-0.5	-2.1	-5.0	-9.2	-15.0	-22.5	-31.8	-43.2

Speer 240-grain Gold Dot HP (23973)

G1 Ballistic Coefficient = 0.177

Distance • Yards	Muzzle	25	50	75	100	125	150	175	200
Velocity • fps	1400	1324	1255	1193	1139	1093	1054	1020	990
Energy • Ft-lbs	1044	934	839	758	691	637	592	554	523
Taylor KO Index	20.7	19.6	18.6	17.7	16.9	16.2	15.6	15.1	14.7
Mid-Range Trajectory Height • Inches	0.0	0.1	0.6	1.4	2.7	4.5	6.8	9.8	13.3
Drop • Inches	0.0	-0.6	-2.3	-5.6	-10.3	-16.7	-24.9	-35.0	-47.2

Ultramax 240-grain JHP (44D)

G1 Ballistic Coefficient = 0.150

Distance • Yards	Muzzle	25	50	75	100	125	150	175	200
Velocity • fps	1360	1275	1200	1137	1084	1040	1002	970	941
Energy • Ft-lbs	986	867	768	689	626	576	535	501	472
Taylor KO Index	20.1	18.9	17.8	16.8	16.1	15.4	14.8	14.4	13.9
Mid-Range Trajectory Height • Inches	0.0	0.2	0.7	1.6	3.0	5.0	7.6	10.8	14.7
Drop • Inches	0.0	-0.6	-2.6	-6.1	-11.2	-18.2	-27.1	-38.3	-51.8

Hornady 240-grain JHP/XTP (9085)

G1 Ballistic Coefficient = 0.205

Distance • Yards	Muzzle	25	50	75	100	125	150	175	200
Velocity • fps	1350	1288	1231	1180	1134	1095	1060	1030	1003
Energy • Ft-lbs	971	884	807	742	685	639	599	566	537
Taylor KO Index	20.0	19.1	18.2	17.5	16.8	16.2	15.7	15.3	14.9
Mid-Range Trajectory Height • Inches	0.0	0.2	0.7	1.6	2.9	4.7	7.0	10.0	13.5
Drop • Inches	0.0	-0.6	-2.5	-5.9	-10.8	-17.4	-25.9	-36.2	-48.6

PMC 240-grain Jacketed Hollow Point (44C)
G1 Ballistic Coefficient = 0.151

Distance • Yards	Muzzle	25	50	75	100	125	150	175	200
Velocity • fps	1300	1217	1151	1098	1053	1014	981	951	924
Energy • Ft-lbs	901	797	712	645	591	548	513	482	455
Taylor KO Index	19.3	18.0	17.0	16.3	15.6	15.0	14.5	14.1	13.7
Mid-Range Trajectory Height • Inches	0.0	0.2	0.7	1.7	3.3	5.3	8.1	11.5	15.6
Drop • Inches	0.0	-0.7	-2.8	-6.5	-12.1	-19.6	-29.2	-41.1	-55.3

PMC 240-grain Starfire Hollow Point (44SFA)
G1 Ballistic Coefficient = 0.133

Distance • Yards	Muzzle	25	50	75	100	125	150	175	200
Velocity • fps	1300	1212	1138	1079	1030	990	956	925	897
Energy • Ft-lbs	900	784	692	621	566	523	487	456	429
Taylor KO Index	19.3	18.0	16.9	16.0	15.3	14.7	14.2	13.7	13.3
Mid-Range Trajectory Height • Inches	0.0	0.2	0.7	1.8	3.3	5.5	8.3	11.8	16.0
Drop • Inches	0.0	-0.7	-2.8	-6.6	-12.3	-20.0	-29.9	-42.1	-56.8

Norma 240-grain "Power Cavity" (11103) (Discontinued in 2005)
G1 Ballistic Coefficient = 0.160

Distance • Yards	Muzzle	25	50	75	100	125	150	175	200
Velocity • fps	1280	1208	1147	1095	1052	1015	983	955	929
Energy • Ft-lbs	875	780	703	640	591	549	515	486	460
Taylor KO Index	19.0	17.9	17.0	16.2	15.6	15.0	14.6	14.1	13.8
Mid-Range Trajectory Height • Inches	0.0	0.2	0.7	1.8	3.3	5.3	8.0	11.4	15.5
Drop • Inches	0.0	-0.7	-2.9	-6.7	-12.3	-19.9	-29.6	-41.4	-55.7

Remington 240-grain JHP Core-Lokt (RH44MGA)
G1 Ballistic Coefficient = 0.217

Distance • Yards	Muzzle	25	50	75	100	125	150	175	200
Velocity • fps	1235	1186	1142	1104	1070	1040	1014	990	968
Energy • Ft-lbs	813	750	695	649	610	577	548	522	500
Taylor KO Index	18.3	17.6	16.9	16.4	15.8	15.4	15.0	14.7	14.3
Mid-Range Trajectory Height • Inches	0.0	0.2	0.8	1.8	3.3	5.3	8.0	11.2	15.0
Drop • Inches	0.0	-0.7	-3.0	-7.0	-12.7	-20.3	-29.9	-41.6	-55.5

Black Hills 240-grain Jacketed Hollow Point (D44MN2)
G1 Ballistic Coefficient = 0.150

Distance • Yards	Muzzle	25	50	75	100	125	150	175	200
Velocity • fps	1260	1187	1125	1074	1031	995	964	936	910
Energy • Ft-lbs	848	751	675	615	567	528	495	467	441
Taylor KO Index	18.7	17.6	16.7	15.9	15.3	14.7	14.3	13.9	13.5
Mid-Range Trajectory Height • Inches	0.0	0.2	0.8	1.8	3.4	5.5	8.4	11.9	16.1
Drop • Inches	0.0	-0.7	-3.0	-6.9	-12.8	-20.6	-30.7	-43.0	-57.8

CCI 240-grain JHP Blazer (3564)
G1 Ballistic Coefficient = 0.165

Distance • Yards	Muzzle	25	50	75	100	125	150	175	200
Velocity • fps	1200	1142	1092	1050	1015	984	956	931	908
Energy • Ft-lbs	767	695	636	588	549	516	487	462	439
Taylor KO Index	17.8	16.9	16.2	15.6	15.0	14.6	14.2	13.8	13.4
Mid-Range Trajectory Height • Inches	0.0	0.2	0.5	1.9	3.3	5.8	8.8	12.4	16.7
Drop • Inches	0.0	-0.8	-3.2	-7.5	-13.7	-22.1	-32.6	-45.5	-60.9

American Eagle (Federal) 240-grain Jacketed Hollow Point (AE44A)
G1 Ballistic Coefficient = 0.173

Distance • Yards	Muzzle	25	50	75	100	125	150	175	200
Velocity • fps	1180	1127	1081	1043	1010	981	955	931	909
Energy • Ft-lbs	741	677	624	580	544	513	486	462	440
Taylor KO Index	17.5	16.7	16.0	15.4	15.0	14.5	14.1	13.8	13.5
Mid-Range Trajectory Height • Inches	0.0	0.2	0.9	2.0	3.7	6.0	8.9	12.5	16.8
Drop • Inches	0.0	-0.8	-3.3	-7.7	-14.1	-22.5	-33.2	-46.3	-61.9

Federal 240-grain Hydra-Shok JHP (P44HS1)
G1 Ballistic Coefficient = 0.173

Distance • Yards	Muzzle	25	50	75	100	125	150	175	200
Velocity • fps	1180	1127	1081	1043	1010	981	955	931	909
Energy • Ft-lbs	741	677	624	580	544	513	486	462	440
Taylor KO Index	17.5	16.7	16.0	15.4	15.0	14.5	14.1	13.8	13.5
Mid-Range Trajectory Height • Inches	0.0	0.2	0.9	2.0	3.7	6.0	8.9	12.5	16.8
Drop • Inches	0.0	-0.8	-3.3	-7.7	-14.1	-22.5	-33.2	-46.3	-61.9

Federal 240-grain JHP (C44A)

G1 Ballistic Coefficient = 0.173

Distance • Yards	Muzzle	25	50	75	100	125	150	175	200
Velocity • fps	1180	1127	1081	1043	1010	981	955	931	909
Energy • Ft-lbs	741	677	624	580	544	513	486	462	440
Taylor KO Index	17.5	16.7	16.0	15.4	15.0	14.5	14.1	13.8	13.5
Mid-Range Trajectory Height • Inches	0.0	0.2	0.9	2.0	3.7	6.0	8.9	12.5	16.8
Drop • Inches	0.0	-0.8	-3.3	-7.7	-14.1	-22.5	-33.2	-46.3	-61.9

Remington 240-grain Semi-Jacketed Hollow Point (R44MG3)

G1 Ballistic Coefficient = 0.173

Distance • Yards	Muzzle	25	50	75	100	125	150	175	200
Velocity • fps	1180	1127	1081	1043	1010	981	955	931	909
Energy • Ft-lbs	741	677	624	580	544	513	486	462	440
Taylor KO Index	17.5	16.7	16.0	15.4	15.0	14.5	14.1	13.8	13.5
Mid-Range Trajectory Height • Inches	0.0	0.2	0.9	2.0	3.7	6.0	8.9	12.5	16.8
Drop • Inches	0.0	-0.8	-3.3	-7.7	-14.1	-22.5	-33.2	-46.3	-61.9

Winchester 240-grain Hollow Soft Point (X44MHSP2)

G1 Ballistic Coefficient = 0.173

Distance • Yards	Muzzle	25	50	75	100	125	150	175	200
Velocity • fps	1180	1127	1081	1043	1010	981	955	931	909
Energy • Ft-lbs	741	677	624	580	544	513	486	462	440
Taylor KO Index	17.5	16.7	16.0	15.4	15.0	14.5	14.1	13.8	13.5
Mid-Range Trajectory Height • Inches	0.0	0.2	0.9	2.0	3.7	6.0	8.9	12.5	16.8
Drop • Inches	0.0	-0.8	-3.3	-7.7	-14.1	-22.5	-33.2	-46.3	-61.9

Magtech 240-grain FMJ Flat (44C)

G1 Ballistic Coefficient = 0.173

Distance • Yards	Muzzle	25	50	75	100	125	150	175	200
Velocity • fps	1180	1127	1081	1043	1010	981	955	931	909
Energy • Ft-lbs	741	677	624	580	544	513	486	462	440
Taylor KO Index	17.5	16.7	16.0	15.4	15.0	14.5	14.1	13.8	13.5
Mid-Range Trajectory Height • Inches	0.0	0.2	0.9	2.0	3.7	6.0	8.9	12.5	16.8
Drop • Inches	0.0	-0.8	-3.3	-7.7	-14.1	-22.5	-33.2	-46.3	-61.9

Winchester 250-grain Partition Gold (S44MP)

G1 Ballistic Coefficient = 0.201

Distance • Yards	Muzzle	25	50	75	100	125	150	175	200
Velocity • fps	1230	1178	1132	1092	1057	1027	1000	975	953
Energy • Ft-lbs	840	770	711	662	620	585	555	528	504
Taylor KO Index	18.9	18.1	17.4	16.8	16.2	15.8	15.4	15.0	14.7
Mid-Range Trajectory Height • Inches	0.0	0.2	0.8	1.8	3.4	5.4	8.1	11.4	15.4
Drop • Inches	0.0	-0.7	-3.0	-7.0	-12.9	-20.6	-30.4	-42.4	-56.6

Winchester 250-grain Platinum Tip (S44PTHP)

G1 Ballistic Coefficient = 0.202

Distance • Yards	Muzzle	25	50	75	100	125	150	175	200
Velocity • fps	1250	1196	1148	1106	1070	1038	1010	985	962
Energy • Ft-lbs	867	794	732	680	635	599	567	539	514
Taylor KO Index	19.3	18.5	17.7	17.1	16.5	16.0	15.6	15.2	14.8
Mid-Range Trajectory Height • Inches	0.0	0.2	0.8	1.8	3.3	5.3	8.0	11.3	15.1
Drop • Inches	0.0	-0.7	-3.0	-6.8	-12.5	-20.0	-29.6	-41.3	-55.2

Cor-Bon 260-grain BondedCore HP (CB44260BHP/20)

G1 Ballistic Coefficient = 0.155

Distance • Yards	Muzzle	25	50	75	100	125	150	175	200
Velocity • fps	1450	1364	1286	1217	1158	1108	1066	1030	998
Energy • Ft-lbs	1214	1074	955	855	774	709	656	612	576
Taylor KO Index	23.3	21.9	20.6	19.5	18.6	17.8	17.1	16.5	16.0
Mid-Range Trajectory Height • Inches	0.0	0.1	0.5	1.4	2.6	4.3	6.6	9.4	12.8
Drop • Inches	0.0	-0.5	-2.2	-5.3	-9.8	-15.9	-23.7	-33.5	-45.2

Speer 270-grain Gold Dot SP (23968) (Discontinued in 2005)

G1 Ballistic Coefficient = 0.189

Distance • Yards	Muzzle	25	50	75	100	125	150	175	200
Velocity • fps	1250	1192	1142	1098	1060	1028	999	973	950
Energy • Ft-lbs	937	853	781	723	674	634	599	568	541
Taylor KO Index	20.7	19.8	18.9	18.2	17.6	17.1	16.6	16.2	15.8
Mid-Range Trajectory Height • Inches	0.0	0.2	0.8	1.8	3.3	5.3	8.0	11.3	15.3
Drop • Inches	0.0	-0.7	-3.0	-6.9	-12.6	-20.2	-29.9	-41.7	-55.8

Cor-Bon 280-grain BondedCore SP (HT44280BC/20)

G1 Ballistic Coefficient = 0.190

Distance • Yards	Muzzle	25	50	75	100	125	150	175	200
Velocity • fps	1400	1333	1271	1216	1167	1124	1087	1055	1027
Energy • Ft-lbs	1219	1105	1005	919	847	786	735	693	656
Taylor KO Index	24.2	23.0	22.0	21.0	20.2	19.4	18.8	18.2	17.7
Mid-Range Trajectory Height • Inches	0.0	0.1	0.6	1.4	2.6	4.3	6.6	9.3	12.7
Drop • Inches	0.0	-0.6	-2.4	-5.5	-10.1	-16.3	-24.2	-34.0	-45.6

Cor-Bon 300-grain JSP (CB44300JSP/20)

G1 Ballistic Coefficient = 0.245

Distance • Yards	Muzzle	25	50	75	100	125	150	175	200
Velocity • fps	1300	1249	1203	1162	1125	1093	1065	1039	1016
Energy • Ft-lbs	1126	1040	965	900	844	796	755	719	687
Taylor KO Index	24.1	23.1	22.3	21.5	20.8	20.2	19.7	19.2	18.8
Mid-Range Trajectory Height • Inches	0.0	0.1	0.7	1.6	3.0	4.4	7.2	10.1	13.6
Drop • Inches	0.0	-0.7	-2.7	-6.3	-11.4	-18.3	-27.0	-37.6	-50.1

Federal 300-grain Cast Core (P44E)

G1 Ballistic Coefficient = 0.219

Distance • Yards	Muzzle	25	50	75	100	125	150	175	200
Velocity • fps	1250	1200	1160	1120	1080	1050	1023	998	976
Energy • Ft-lbs	1040	940	885	825	773	734	697	664	634
Taylor KO Index	23.0	22.1	21.3	20.6	19.9	19.4	18.9	18.5	18.1
Mid-Range Trajectory Height • Inches	0.0	0.2	0.8	1.9	3.4	5.2	7.8	11.0	14.7
Drop • Inches	0.0	-0.7	-2.9	-6.8	-12.4	-19.8	-29.2	-40.7	-54.4

Black Hills 300-grain Jacketed Hollow Point (D44MN3)

G1 Ballistic Coefficient = 0.200

Distance • Yards	Muzzle	25	50	75	100	125	150	175	200
Velocity • fps	1150	1108	1071	1039	1010	985	962	940	921
Energy • Ft-lbs	879	817	764	719	680	646	616	589	565
Taylor KO Index	21.3	20.5	19.8	19.2	18.7	18.2	17.8	17.4	17.1
Mid-Range Trajectory Height • Inches	0.0	0.2	0.9	2.1	3.8	6.1	9.1	12.7	17.0
Drop • Inches	0.0	-0.8	-3.5	-8.0	-14.5	-23.1	-34.0	-47.3	-63.0

Hornady 300-grain JHP/XTP (9088)

G1 Ballistic Coefficient = 0.245

Distance • Yards	Muzzle	25	50	75	100	125	150	175	200
Velocity • fps	1150	1115	1084	1056	1031	1008	987	968	950
Energy • Ft-lbs	881	828	782	743	708	677	649	624	602
Taylor KO Index	21.3	20.6	20.1	19.6	19.1	18.7	18.3	17.9	17.6
Mid-Range Trajectory Height • Inches	0.0	0.2	0.9	2.0	3.7	5.9	8.8	12.2	16.3
Drop • Inches	0.0	-0.8	-3.4	-7.9	-14.2	-22.7	-33.2	-46.0	-61.1

Cor-Bon 305-grain FP Penetrator (HT44305FPPN/20)

G1 Ballistic Coefficient = 0.245

Distance • Yards	Muzzle	25	50	75	100	125	150	175	200
Velocity • fps	1300	1249	1203	1162	1125	1093	1065	1039	1016
Energy • Ft-lbs	1145	1057	981	915	858	810	768	731	699
Taylor KO Index	24.5	23.5	22.6	21.9	21.2	20.6	20.0	19.6	19.1
Mid-Range Trajectory Height • Inches	0.0	0.1	0.7	1.6	3.0	4.4	7.2	10.1	13.6
Drop • Inches	0.0	-0.7	-2.7	-6.3	-11.4	-18.3	-27.0	-37.6	-50.1

Cor-Bon 320-grain Hardcast (HT44320HC/20)

G1 Ballistic Coefficient = 0.225

Distance • Yards	Muzzle	25	50	75	100	125	150	175	200
Velocity • fps	1270	1223	1181	1143	1109	1079	1053	1029	1007
Energy • Ft-lbs	1146	1063	991	928	874	828	788	752	720
Taylor KO Index	25.1	24.2	23.3	22.6	21.9	21.3	20.8	20.3	19.9
Mid-Range Trajectory Height • Inches	0.0	0.1	0.7	1.6	3.1	5.0	7.4	10.4	14.0
Drop • Inches	0.0	-0.7	-2.8	-6.5	-11.9	-19.0	-28.0	-38.9	-51.9

Cowboy Action Loads

Hornady 180-grain Cowboy (9082) (Discontinued in 2004)

G1 Ballistic Coefficient = 0.125

Distance • Yards	Muzzle	25	50	75	100	125	150	175	200
Velocity • fps	725	707	689	672	655	639	624	608	593
Energy • Ft-lbs	210	200	190	181	172	163	155	148	141
Taylor KO Index	8.1	7.9	7.7	7.5	7.3	7.1	6.9	6.8	6.6
Mid-Range Trajectory Height • Inches	0.0	0.5	2.1	5.0	9.1	14.6	21.6	30.3	40.5
Drop • Inches	0.0	-2.1	-8.6	-19.6	-35.4	-56.3	-82.5	-114.3	-151.9

.45 GAP (Glock Automatic Pistol)

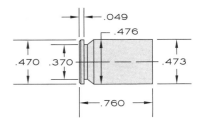

It took much longer than the shrinking of the 10mm Auto into the .40 S&W, but some bright lad finally figured out that the .45 Auto case was just a little larger than it had to be to get the desired performance. Thus the .45 GAP. Now in this sort of situation, it is common for the proponents of the new cartridge to claim, "It'll do everything the .45 Auto will do." Not quite true. But the .45 GAP does do everything its designers wanted it to do, at the price of slightly higher working pressure. Since it is a new caliber, the guns can be given the strength necessary to withstand the higher pressure and there are no old guns to worry about. The result is a very useful cartridge that goes into a gun with a slightly smaller grip. That's a boon to shooters with not-so-large hands. This caliber may not be an exact replacement for the .45 Auto, but it is likely to be with us for a long time.

Relative Recoil Factor = 0.92

Specifications

Controlling Agency for Standardization of this Ammunition: SAAMI

Bullet Weight Grains	Velocity fps	Maximum Average Pressure	
		Copper Crusher	Transducer
185 JHP FMJ	1090	N/S	23,000 psi
200 JHP FMJ	1020	N/S	23,000 psi

Standard barrel for velocity testing: 5 inches long—1 turn in 16-inch twist

Availability

Cor-Bon 145-grain Glaser Safety Slug (04650/04850)
G1 Ballistic Coefficient = 0.125

Distance • Yards	Muzzle	25	50	75	100	125	150	175	200
Velocity • fps	1325	1229	1149	1084	1032	989	952	920	891
Energy • Ft-lbs	565	486	425	378	343	315	292	273	256
Taylor KO Index	12.4	11.5	10.8	10.1	9.7	9.3	8.9	8.6	8.3
Mid-Range Trajectory Height • Inches	0.0	0.2	0.7	1.7	3.3	5.5	8.3	11.9	16.2
Drop • Inches	0.0	-0.7	-2.7	-6.5	-12.1	-19.7	-29.5	-41.8	-56.6

Cor-Bon 165-grain PowRBall
G1 Ballistic Coefficient = 0.145

Distance • Yards	Muzzle	25	50	75	100	125	150	175	200
Velocity • fps	1075	1031	994	961	933	906	882	860	839
Energy • Ft-lbs	424	390	362	339	319	301	285	271	258
Taylor KO Index	11.5	11.0	10.6	10.2	9.9	9.7	9.4	9.2	8.9
Mid-Range Trajectory Height • Inches	0.0	0.2	1.0	2.4	4.4	7.1	10.6	14.9	20.0
Drop • Inches	0.0	-1.0	-4.0	-9.2	-16.8	-26.8	-39.5	-55.0	-73.4

Federal 185-grain Hydra-Shok JHP (PD45G1H)
G1 Ballistic Coefficient = 0.097

Distance • Yards	Muzzle	25	50	75	100	125	150	175	200
Velocity • fps	1090	1020	970	930	890	856	825	796	770
Energy • Ft-lbs	490	430	390	355	325	301	280	261	243
Taylor KO Index	13.0	12.2	11.6	11.1	10.6	10.2	9.9	9.5	9.2
Mid-Range Trajectory Height • Inches	0.0	0.2	1.0	2.5	4.6	7.5	11.4	16.2	22.0
Drop • Inches	0.0	-1.0	-4.0	-9.3	-17.2	-27.8	-41.3	-58.1	-78.3

Speer 185-grain Gold Dot (23977)
G1 Ballistic Coefficient = 0.109

Distance • Yards	Muzzle	25	50	75	100	125	150	175	200
Velocity • fps	1090	1030	982	941	906	874	845	818	793
Energy • Ft-lbs	488	436	396	364	337	314	294	275	243
Taylor KO Index	13.0	12.3	11.7	11.2	10.8	10.4	10.1	9.8	9.5
Mid-Range Trajectory Height • Inches	0.0	0.2	1.0	2.4	4.5	7.3	11.0	15.7	21.2
Drop • Inches	0.0	-1.0	-4.0	-9.2	-16.9	-27.3	-40.4	-56.7	-76.2

Winchester 185-grain Silvertip HP (X45GSHP)

G1 Ballistic Coefficient = 0.146

Distance • Yards	Muzzle	25	50	75	100	125	150	175	200
Velocity • fps	1000	967	938	911	887	864	843	823	804
Energy • Ft-lbs	411	384	361	341	323	307	292	278	265
Taylor KO Index	11.9	11.6	11.2	10.9	10.6	10.3	10.1	9.8	9.6
Mid-Range Trajectory Height • Inches	0.0	0.3	1.2	2.7	4.9	7.9	11.8	16.5	22.1
Drop • Inches	0.0	-1.1	-4.5	-10.5	-19.0	-30.2	-44.4	-61.7	-82.1

Cor-Bon 200-grain JHP (SD45GAP200/20)

G1 Ballistic Coefficient = 0.170

Distance • Yards	Muzzle	25	50	75	100	125	150	175	200
Velocity • fps	950	926	904	884	864	846	828	812	796
Energy • Ft-lbs	401	381	363	347	332	318	305	293	281
Taylor KO Index	12.3	12.0	11.7	11.4	11.2	10.9	10.7	10.5	10.3
Mid-Range Trajectory Height • Inches	0.0	0.3	1.3	2.9	5.3	8.5	12.5	17.5	23.3
Drop • Inches	0.0	-1.2	-5.0	-11.4	-20.6	-32.7	-47.8	-66.1	-87.7

CCI 185-grain TMJ Lawman (53979)

G1 Ballistic Coefficient = 0.095

Distance • Yards	Muzzle	25	50	75	100	125	150	175	200
Velocity • fps	1090	1022	968	925	886	853	821	792	765
Energy • Ft-lbs	488	429	385	352	322	299	277	258	241
Taylor KO Index	13.0	12.2	11.6	11.0	10.6	10.2	9.8	9.5	9.1
Mid-Range Trajectory Height • Inches	0.0	0.2	1.0	2.5	4.6	7.6	11.4	16.3	22.1
Drop • Inches	0.0	-1.0	-4.0	-9.4	-17.2	-27.9	-41.5	-58.4	-78.7

American Eagle (Federal) 185-grain TMJ (AE45GA)

G1 Ballistic Coefficient = 0.097

Distance • Yards	Muzzle	25	50	75	100	125	150	175	200
Velocity • fps	1090	1020	970	930	890	856	825	796	770
Energy • Ft-lbs	490	430	390	355	325	301	280	261	243
Taylor KO Index	13.0	12.2	11.6	11.1	10.6	10.2	9.9	9.5	9.2
Mid-Range Trajectory Height • Inches	0.0	0.2	1.0	2.5	4.6	7.5	11.4	16.2	22.0
Drop • Inches	0.0	-1.0	-4.0	-9.3	-17.2	-27.8	-41.3	-58.1	-78.3

CCI 200-grain TMJ Lawman (53980)

G1 Ballistic Coefficient = 0.103

Distance • Yards	Muzzle	25	50	75	100	125	150	175	200
Velocity • fps	1020	971	930	894	861	832	805	779	754
Energy • Ft-lbs	462	419	384	355	329	307	288	269	253
Taylor KO Index	13.2	12.5	12.0	11.5	11.1	10.7	10.4	10.1	9.7
Mid-Range Trajectory Height • Inches	0.0	0.3	1.2	2.7	5.0	8.2	12.2	17.3	23.4
Drop • Inches	0.0	-1.1	-4.5	-10.4	-19.0	-30.5	-45.2	-63.2	-84.8

Speer 230-grain Gold Dot (23978)

G1 Ballistic Coefficient = 0.139

Distance • Yards	Muzzle	25	50	75	100	125	150	175	200
Velocity • fps	1020	983	950	921	895	871	848	827	806
Energy • Ft-lbs	531	493	461	436	409	387	367	349	332
Taylor KO Index	15.1	14.6	14.1	13.7	13.3	12.9	12.6	12.3	12.0
Mid-Range Trajectory Height • Inches	0.0	0.3	1.1	2.6	4.8	7.7	11.5	16.2	21.7
Drop • Inches	0.0	-1.1	-4.4	-10.1	-18.4	-29.4	-43.2	-60.1	-80.2

Federal 230-grain Hydra-Shok JHP (P45GHS1)

G1 Ballistic Coefficient = 0.207

Distance • Yards	Muzzle	25	50	75	100	125	150	175	200
Velocity • fps	880	870	850	840	820	807	794	781	769
Energy • Ft-lbs	395	380	370	355	345	333	322	312	302
Taylor KO Index	13.1	12.9	12.6	12.5	12.2	12.0	11.8	11.6	11.4
Mid-Range Trajectory Height • Inches	0.0	0.3	1.5	3.3	6.0	9.6	14.0	19.5	25.8
Drop • Inches	0.0	-1.4	-5.8	-13.1	-23.6	-37.2	-54.3	-74.7	-98.8

UMC (Remington) 230-grain Jacketed Hollow Point (L45GAP7)

G1 Ballistic Coefficient = 0.160

Distance • Yards	Muzzle	25	50	75	100	125	150	175	200
Velocity • fps	880	860	841	822	805	788	772	756	741
Energy • Ft-lbs	395	377	361	345	331	317	304	292	280
Taylor KO Index	13.1	12.8	12.5	12.2	12.0	11.7	11.5	11.2	11.0
Mid-Range Trajectory Height • Inches	0.0	0.3	1.5	3.4	6.2	9.8	14.5	20.2	26.9
Drop • Inches	0.0	-1.4	-5.8	-13.2	-23.9	-37.9	-55.4	-76.6	-101.5

USA (Winchester) 230-grain Jacketed Hollow Point (USA45GJHP)

G1 Ballistic Coefficient = 0.165

Distance • Yards	Muzzle	25	50	75	100	125	150	175	200
Velocity • fps	880	860	842	824	807	790	775	759	745
Energy • Ft-lbs	396	378	363	347	332	319	306	294	283
Taylor KO Index	13.1	12.8	12.5	12.2	12.0	11.7	11.5	11.3	11.1
Mid-Range Trajectory Height • Inches	0.0	0.3	1.5	3.4	6.1	9.8	14.4	20.1	26.7
Drop • Inches	0.0	-1.4	-5.8	-13.2	-23.8	-37.8	-55.2	-76.3	-101.1

American Eagle (Federal) 230-grain FMJ (AE45GB)

G1 Ballistic Coefficient = 0.207

Distance • Yards	Muzzle	25	50	75	100	125	150	175	200
Velocity • fps	880	870	850	840	820	807	794	781	769
Energy • Ft-lbs	395	380	370	355	345	333	322	312	302
Taylor KO Index	13.1	12.9	12.6	12.5	12.2	12.0	11.8	11.6	11.4
Mid-Range Trajectory Height • Inches	0.0	0.3	1.5	3.3	6.0	9.6	14.0	19.5	25.8
Drop • Inches	0.0	-1.4	-5.8	-13.1	-23.6	-37.2	-54.3	-74.7	-98.8

Winchester 230-grain Brass Enclosed Base (WC45G)

G1 Ballistic Coefficient = 0.179

Distance • Yards	Muzzle	25	50	75	100	125	150	175	200
Velocity • fps	875	857	840	823	808	793	778	764	750
Energy • Ft-lbs	391	375	360	346	333	321	309	298	287
Taylor KO Index	13.0	12.7	12.5	12.2	12.0	11.8	11.6	11.3	11.1
Mid-Range Trajectory Height • Inches	0.0	0.3	1.5	3.4	6.2	9.8	14.4	20.1	26.7
Drop • Inches	0.0	-1.4	-5.8	-13.3	-24.0	-38.0	-55.5	-76.5	-101.3

UMC (Remington) 230-grain Metal Case (L45GAP4)

G1 Ballistic Coefficient = 0.160

Distance • Yards	Muzzle	25	50	75	100	125	150	175	200
Velocity • fps	880	860	841	822	805	788	772	756	741
Energy • Ft-lbs	395	377	361	345	331	317	304	292	280
Taylor KO Index	13.1	12.8	12.5	12.2	12.0	11.7	11.5	11.2	11.0
Mid-Range Trajectory Height • Inches	0.0	0.3	1.5	3.4	6.2	9.8	14.5	20.2	26.9
Drop • Inches	0.0	-1.4	-5.8	-13.2	-23.9	-37.9	-55.4	-76.6	-101.5

USA (Winchester) 230-grain Full Metal Jacket (USA45G)

G1 Ballistic Coefficient = 0.165

Distance • Yards	Muzzle	25	50	75	100	125	150	175	200
Velocity • fps	850	832	814	798	782	766	751	737	723
Energy • Ft-lbs	369	353	338	325	312	300	288	277	267
Taylor KO Index	12.6	12.4	12.1	11.9	11.6	11.4	11.2	10.9	10.7
Mid-Range Trajectory Height • Inches	0.0	0.3	1.6	3.6	6.6	10.4	15.4	21.4	28.5
Drop • Inches	0.0	-1.5	-6.2	-14.1	-25.5	-40.4	-59.0	-81.5	-107.9

Cor-Bon 230-grain Match (PM45GAP230/20)

G1 Ballistic Coefficient = 0.155

Distance • Yards	Muzzle	25	50	75	100	125	150	175	200
Velocity • fps	750	735	719	705	691	677	663	650	637
Energy • Ft-lbs	287	276	263	254	244	234	225	216	208
Taylor KO Index	11.1	10.9	10.7	10.5	10.3	10.1	9.8	9.7	9.5
Mid-Range Trajectory Height • Inches	0.0	0.5	2.0	4.6	8.4	13.4	19.7	27.4	36.5
Drop • Inches	0.0	-2.0	-7.9	-18.1	32.7	-51.8	-75.6	-104.4	-138.3

.45 Auto (.45 ACP)

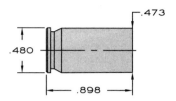

Born in the flurry of gun and cartridge design following the end of the Spanish-American War (1905), the .45 Auto cartridge was designed by John Browning to be fired in his automatic pistol. The first cut at the gun's design didn't do well, so the gun was modified (some might say improved) into what became the M1911 pistol. The original loading for that pistol used a 230-grain bullet at 850 fps. Here we are, nearly 100 years later and the 230-grain bullet at 850 fps is still pretty close to the standard load for the .45. Like most calibers that have been adopted by the US military, the .45 Auto remains a very popular caliber, and certainly a very effective defensive weapon.

Relative Recoil Factor = 0.93

Specifications

Controlling Agency for Standardization of this Ammunition: SAAMI

Bullet Weight Grains	Velocity fps	Maximum Average Pressure	
		Copper Crusher	Transducer
180 JHP	995	18,000 cup	21,000 psi
180 JHP	930	18,000 cup	21,000 psi
230 FMC	830	18,000 cup	21,000 psi
+ P Loads			
185 JHP	1130	N/S	23,000 psi

Standard barrel for velocity testing: 5 inches long—1 turn in 16-inch twist

Availability

CCI 117-grain Shotshell (3567)

Shotshell load using #9 shot at 1,100 fps

Cor-Bon 145-grain Glaser Safety Slug +P (04600/04800)   G1 Ballistic Coefficient = 0.125

Distance • Yards	Muzzle	25	50	75	100	125	150	175	200
Velocity • fps	1350	1251	1166	1098	1043	998	961	927	898
Energy • Ft-lbs	587	504	438	388	350	321	297	277	260
Taylor KO Index	12.6	11.7	10.9	10.3	9.8	9.3	9.0	8.7	8.4
Mid-Range Trajectory Height • Inches	0.0	0.2	0.7	1.7	3.2	5.3	8.1	11.6	15.9
Drop • Inches	0.0	-0.6	-2.7	-6.3	-11.7	-19.1	-28.7	-40.6	-55.1

PMC 150-grain NT/FR (45HRA)   G1 Ballistic Coefficient = 0.095

Distance • Yards	Muzzle	25	50	75	100	125	150	175	200
Velocity • fps	1190	1045	999	961	928	890	855	824	795
Energy • Ft-lbs	472	401	352	316	287	264	244	226	210
Taylor KO Index	11.5	10.1	9.7	9.3	9.0	8.6	8.3	8.0	7.7
Mid-Range Trajectory Height • Inches	0.0	0.2	0.9	2.2	4.1	6.8	10.3	14.8	20.1
Drop • Inches	0.0	-0.8	-3.4	-8.1	-15.1	-25.6	-36.8	-52.0	-70.4

Cor-Bon 165-grain PowRBall +P   G1 Ballistic Coefficient = 0.145

Distance • Yards	Muzzle	25	50	75	100	125	150	175	200
Velocity • fps	1225	1155	1097	1050	1010	975	945	918	893
Energy • Ft-lbs	550	489	441	404	378	349	327	309	292
Taylor KO Index	13.1	12.3	11.7	11.2	10.8	10.4	10.1	9.8	9.5
Mid-Range Trajectory Height • Inches	0.0	0.2	0.8	1.9	3.6	5.9	8.8	12.6	17.0
Drop • Inches	0.0	-0.8	-3.1	-7.3	-13.5	-21.8	-32.3	-45.3	-60.9

Federal 165-grain EFMJ (PD45CSP2H)   G1 Ballistic Coefficient = 0.144

Distance • Yards	Muzzle	25	50	75	100	125	150	175	200
Velocity • fps	1090	1050	1010	970	940	913	888	865	844
Energy • Ft-lbs	435	400	370	345	325	306	289	274	261
Taylor KO Index	11.6	11.2	10.8	10.3	10.0	9.7	9.5	9.2	9.0
Mid-Range Trajectory Height • Inches	0.0	0.2	1.0	2.3	4.3	7.0	10.4	14.6	19.7
Drop • Inches	0.0	-0.9	-3.9	-9.0	-16.4	-26.2	-38.7	-53.9	-72.0

Federal 165-grain Close Quarter Training (BC45NT3) (Discontinued in 2004)   G1 Ballistic Coefficient = 0.184

Distance • Yards	Muzzle	25	50	75	100	125	150	175	200
Velocity • fps	1080	1044	1010	985	960	937	916	896	877
Energy • Ft-lbs	425	399	375	355	335	322	307	294	282
Taylor KO Index	11.5	11.1	10.8	10.5	10.2	10.0	9.8	9.5	9.3
Mid-Range Trajectory Height • Inches	0.0	0.2	1.0	2.3	4.2	6.7	10.0	14.0	18.7
Drop • Inches	0.0	-1.0	-3.9	-9.0	-16.3	-25.9	-38.0	-52.7	-70.1

Cor-Bon 165-grain JHP +P (SD45165/20)   G1 Ballistic Coefficient = 0.140

Distance • Yards	Muzzle	25	50	75	100	125	150	175	200
Velocity • fps	1250	1180	1121	1073	1032	997	967	939	914
Energy • Ft-lbs	573	510	461	422	390	365	342	323	306
Taylor KO Index	13.3	12.6	11.9	11.4	11.0	10.6	10.3	10.0	9.7
Mid-Range Trajectory Height • Inches	0.0	0.1	0.7	1.8	3.4	5.6	8.4	11.9	16.1
Drop • Inches	0.0	-0.7	-3.0	-7.0	-12.9	-20.8	-30.9	-43.2	-58.0

Federal 165-grain Hydra-Shok JHP (PD45HS3)   G1 Ballistic Coefficient = 0.140

Distance • Yards	Muzzle	25	50	75	100	125	150	175	200
Velocity • fps	1060	1020	980	948	920	894	870	847	826
Energy • Ft-lbs	410	375	350	330	310	293	277	263	250
Taylor KO Index	11.3	10.9	10.4	10.1	9.8	9.5	9.3	9.0	8.8
Mid-Range Trajectory Height • Inches	0.0	0.2	1.1	2.5	4.5	7.2	10.8	15.2	20.4
Drop • Inches	0.0	-1.0	-4.1	-9.4	-17.2	-27.5	-40.5	-56.4	-75.3

Winchester 170-grain Jacketed Flat Point—Super Clean (SC45NT)   G1 Ballistic Coefficient = 0.161

Distance • Yards	Muzzle	25	50	75	100	125	150	175	200
Velocity • fps	1050	1013	982	954	928	905	883	863	843
Energy • Ft-lbs	416	388	364	343	325	309	295	281	269
Taylor KO Index	11.5	11.1	10.8	10.5	10.2	9.9	9.7	9.5	9.3
Mid-Range Trajectory Height • Inches	0.0	0.2	0.9	2.4	4.5	7.2	9.7	15.0	20.0
Drop • Inches	0.0	-1.0	-4.1	-9.5	-17.3	-27.5	-40.5	-56.1	-74.7

Remington 175-grain Disintegrator Plated Frangible (LF45APA) (Discontinued in 2004)   G1 Ballistic Coefficient = 0.101

Distance • Yards	Muzzle	25	50	75	100	125	150	175	200
Velocity • fps	1020	967	923	895	851	820	791	764	738
Energy • Ft-lbs	404	364	331	305	281	261	243	227	212
Taylor KO Index	11.5	10.9	10.4	10.1	9.6	9.3	8.9	8.6	8.3
Mid-Range Trajectory Height • Inches	0.0	0.2	1.1	2.7	5.0	8.2	12.4	17.6	23.8
Drop • Inches	0.0	-1.1	-4.5	-10.4	-19.1	-30.8	-45.7	-64.1	-86.1

Cor-Bon 185-grain JHP +P (SD45185/20)   G1 Ballistic Coefficient = 0.150

Distance • Yards	Muzzle	25	50	75	100	125	150	175	200
Velocity • fps	1150	1100	1058	1022	990	962	937	913	891
Energy • Ft-lbs	543	497	460	429	403	381	361	343	326
Taylor KO Index	13.7	13.1	12.6	12.2	11.8	11.5	11.2	10.9	10.6
Mid-Range Trajectory Height • Inches	0.0	0.2	0.9	2.1	3.8	6.2	9.3	13.0	17.5
Drop • Inches	0.0	-0.8	-3.5	-8.1	-14.7	-23.6	-34.8	-48.4	-64.6

Remington 185-grain Golden Saber +P (GS45APC)   G1 Ballistic Coefficient = 0.150

Distance • Yards	Muzzle	25	50	75	100	125	150	175	200
Velocity • fps	1140	1086	1042	1004	971	942	916	892	870
Energy • Ft-lbs	534	485	446	414	388	365	645	327	311
Taylor KO Index	13.6	13.0	12.4	12.0	11.6	11.3	10.9	10.7	10.4
Mid-Range Trajectory Height • Inches	0.0	0.2	1.0	2.2	4.0	6.4	9.6	13.5	18.2
Drop • Inches	0.0	-0.9	-3.6	-8.3	-15.1	-24.3	-35.8	-49.9	-66.8

Cor-Bon 185-grain DPX +P   G1 Ballistic Coefficient = 0.150

Distance • Yards	Muzzle	25	50	75	100	125	150	175	200
Velocity • fps	1075	1032	996	964	936	911	887	865	844
Energy • Ft-lbs	475	438	408	382	360	341	323	307	293
Taylor KO Index	12.8	12.3	11.9	11.5	11.2	10.9	10.6	10.3	10.1
Mid-Range Trajectory Height • Inches	0.0	0.2	1.0	2.4	4.4	7.1	10.5	14.8	19.8
Drop • Inches	0.0	-1.0	-4.0	-9.2	-16.7	-26.7	-39.3	-54.7	-73.0

Speer 185-grain Gold Dot (23964)

G1 Ballistic Coefficient = 0.110

Distance • Yards	Muzzle	25	50	75	100	125	150	175	200
Velocity • fps	1050	998	956	919	886	856	829	803	779
Energy • Ft-lbs	453	409	375	347	322	301	282	265	249
Taylor KO Index	12.5	11.9	11.4	11.0	10.6	10.2	9.9	9.6	9.3
Mid-Range Trajectory Height • Inches	0.0	0.3	1.1	2.6	4.6	7.6	11.5	16.2	22.0
Drop • Inches	0.0	-1.0	-4.2	-9.8	-18.0	-28.8	-42.6	-59.6	-79.9

Remington 185-grain Golden Saber (GS45APA)

G1 Ballistic Coefficient = 0.150

Distance • Yards	Muzzle	25	50	75	100	125	150	175	200
Velocity • fps	1015	981	951	924	899	876	855	835	815
Energy • Ft-lbs	423	395	372	35`	332	316	300	286	273
Taylor KO Index	12.1	11.7	11.4	11.0	10.7	10.5	10.2	10.0	9.7
Mid-Range Trajectory Height • Inches	0.0	0.3	1.1	2.6	4.5	7.6	11.4	16.0	21.4
Drop • Inches	0.0	-1.1	-4.4	-10.2	-18.4	-29.4	-43.2	-59.9	-79.7

Black Hills 185-grain Jacketed Hollow Point (D45N4)

G1 Ballistic Coefficient = 0.130

Distance • Yards	Muzzle	25	50	75	100	125	150	175	200
Velocity • fps	1000	963	931	902	875	851	828	806	785
Energy • Ft-lbs	411	381	356	334	315	298	282	267	254
Taylor KO Index	11.9	11,5	11.1	10.8	10.5	10.2	9.9	9.6	9.4
Mid-Range Trajectory Height • Inches	0.0	0.3	1.2	2.7	5.0	8.0	11.9	16.8	22.6
Drop • Inches	0.0	-1.1	-4.6	-10.5	-19.2	-30.6	-45.0	-62.6	-83.5

Remington 185-grain Jacketed Hollow Point (R45AP2)

G1 Ballistic Coefficient = 0.149

Distance • Yards	Muzzle	25	50	75	100	125	150	175	200
Velocity • fps	1000	968	939	913	889	866	845	826	807
Energy • Ft-lbs	411	385	362	342	324	308	294	280	267
Taylor KO Index	11.9	11.6	11.2	10.9	10.6	10.3	10.1	9.9	9.6
Mid-Range Trajectory Height • Inches	0.0	0.3	1.1	2.7	4.9	7.8	11.7	16.3	21.9
Drop • Inches	0.0	-1.1	-4.5	-10.4	-18.9	-30.2	-44.3	-61.4	-81.8

Winchester 185-grain Silvertip Hollow Point (X45ASHP2)

G1 Ballistic Coefficient = 0.148

Distance • Yards	Muzzle	25	50	75	100	125	150	175	200
Velocity • fps	1000	967	938	912	888	866	845	826	806
Energy • Ft-lbs	411	384	362	342	324	308	293	279	267
Taylor KO Index	11.9	11.6	11.2	10.9	10.6	10.3	10.1	9.9	9.6
Mid-Range Trajectory Height • Inches	0.0	0.3	1.2	2.7	4.9	7.8	11.7	16.3	21.9
Drop • Inches	0.0	-1.1	-4.5	-10.4	-19.0	-30.2	-44.3	-61.5	-81.8

Federal 185-grain JHP (C45C)

G1 Ballistic Coefficient = 0.162

Distance • Yards	Muzzle	25	50	75	100	125	150	175	200
Velocity • fps	950	920	900	880	860	841	823	806	789
Energy • Ft-lbs	370	350	335	320	300	291	278	267	256
Taylor KO Index	11.3	11.0	10.8	10.5	10.3	10.0	9.8	9.6	9.4
Mid-Range Trajectory Height • Inches	0.0	0.4	1.6	3.7	5.4	8.5	12.6	17.5	23.4
Drop • Inches	0.0	-1.2	-5.0	-11.4	-20.7	-32.8	-48.0	-66.4	-88.2

Hornady 185-grain JHP/XTP (9090)

G1 Ballistic Coefficient = 0.140

Distance • Yards	Muzzle	25	50	75	100	125	150	175	200
Velocity • fps	950	921	895	871	848	827	807	788	769
Energy • Ft-lbs	371	349	329	312	295	281	268	255	243
Taylor KO Index	11.3	11.0	10.7	10.4	10.1	9.9	9.6	9.4	9.2
Mid-Range Trajectory Height • Inches	0.0	0.3	1.3	3.0	5.4	8.7	12.9	18.1	24.2
Drop • Inches	0.0	-1.2	-5.0	-11.5	-20.9	-33.3	-48.8	-67.7	-90.1

CCI 185-grain TMJ Lawman (53654)

G1 Ballistic Coefficient = 0.095

Distance • Yards	Muzzle	25	50	75	100	125	150	175	200
Velocity • fps	1050	991	943	903	867	835	805	777	751
Energy • Ft-lbs	453	404	365	335	308	286	266	248	232
Taylor KO Index	12.5	11.8	11.3	10.8	10.4	10.0	9.6	9.3	9.0
Mid-Range Trajectory Height • Inches	0.0	0.3	1.1	2.6	4.9	8.0	12.0	17.1	23.1
Drop • Inches	0.0	-1.0	-4.3	-9.9	-18.3	-29.5	-43.8	-61.5	-82.8

UMC (Remington) 185-grain Metal Case (L45API)

G1 Ballistic Coefficient = 0.162

Distance • Yards	Muzzle	25	50	75	100	125	150	175	200
Velocity • fps	1015	983	955	930	907	885	864	845	827
Energy • Ft-lbs	423	397	375	355	338	322	307	294	281
Taylor KO Index	12.1	11.7	11.4	11.1	10.8	10.6	10.3	10.1	9.9
Mid-Range Trajectory Height • Inches	0.0	0.3	1.1	2.6	4.8	7.6	11.3	15.8	21.1
Drop • Inches	0.0	-1.1	-4.4	-10.1	-18.3	-29.2	-42.8	-59.3	-101.7

Winchester 185-grain Brass Enclosed Base (WC451)

G1 Ballistic Coefficient = 0.087

Distance • Yards	Muzzle	25	50	75	100	125	150	175	200
Velocity • fps	1000	947	902	864	829	796	764	739	712
Energy • Ft-lbs	411	368	334	306	282	261	241	224	208
Taylor KO Index	11.9	11.3	10.8	10.3	9.9	9.5	9.2	8.8	8.5
Mid-Range Trajectory Height • Inches	0.0	0.3	1.2	2.9	5.3	8.7	13.1	18.7	25.4
Drop • Inches	0.0	-1.1	-4.7	-10.9	-20.0	-32.3	-48.0	-67.5	-90.9

PMC 185-grain Jacketed Hollow Point (45B)

G1 Ballistic Coefficient = 0.103

Distance • Yards	Muzzle	25	50	75	100	125	150	175	200
Velocity • fps	900	867	836	805	776	758	735	712	691
Energy • Ft-lbs	339	311	290	270	253	238	223	210	197
Taylor KO Index	10.8	10.4	10.0	9.7	9.4	9.1	8.8	8.5	8.3
Mid-Range Trajectory Height • Inches	0.0	0.3	1.4	3.3	6.2	9.9	14.8	20.9	28.2
Drop • Inches	0.0	-1.4	-5.6	-12.9	-23.9	-37.7	-55.5	-77.4	-103.5

USA (Winchester) 185-grain FMJ—FN (USA45A)

G1 Ballistic Coefficient = 0.140

Distance • Yards	Muzzle	25	50	75	100	125	150	175	200
Velocity • fps	910	885	861	839	818	799	780	762	744
Energy • Ft-lbs	340	322	304	289	275	262	250	238	228
Taylor KO Index	10.9	10.6	10.3	10.0	9.8	9.5	9.3	9.1	8.9
Mid-Range Trajectory Height • Inches	0.0	0.3	1.3	3.2	5.8	9.3	13.8	19.3	25.9
Drop • Inches	0.0	-1.3	-5.5	-12.5	-22.6	-36.0	-52.7	-73.0	-97.1

Federal 185-grain FMJ—SWC Match (GM45B)

G1 Ballistic Coefficient = 0.055

Distance • Yards	Muzzle	25	50	75	100	125	150	175	200
Velocity • fps	780	730	700	660	620	585	553	522	493
Energy • Ft-lbs	245	220	200	175	160	141	126	112	100
Taylor KO Index	9.3	8.7	8.4	7.9	7.4	7.0	6.6	6.2	5.9
Mid-Range Trajectory Height • Inches	0.0	0.5	2.0	4.8	9.0	14.9	22.9	33.2	45.9
Drop • Inches	0.0	-1.9	-7.7	-18.1	-33.6	-54.7	-82.1	116.6	-159.1

Magtech 200-grain LSWC (45C)

G1 Ballistic Coefficient = 0.195

Distance • Yards	Muzzle	25	50	75	100	125	150	175	200
Velocity • fps	950	929	910	891	874	857	842	827	812
Energy • Ft-lbs	401	383	368	353	339	327	315	303	293
Taylor KO Index	12.3	12.0	11.8	11.5	11.3	11.1	10.9	10.7	10.5
Mid-Range Trajectory Height • Inches	0.0	0.3	0.8	2.9	4.8	8.3	12.3	17.1	22.7
Drop • Inches	0.0	-1.2	-5.0	-11.3	-20.4	-32.4	-47.2	-65.2	-86.3

Black Hills 200-grain Match Semi-Wadcutter (D45N1)

G1 Ballistic Coefficient = 0.150

Distance • Yards	Muzzle	25	50	75	100	125	150	175	200
Velocity • fps	875	854	833	814	796	778	762	745	729
Energy • Ft-lbs	340	324	309	294	280	269	258	247	236
Taylor KO Index	11.3	11.0	10.8	10.5	10.3	10.0	9.8	9.6	9.4
Mid-Range Trajectory Height • Inches	0.0	0.4	1.5	3.4	6.2	9.9	14.7	21.8	27.4
Drop • Inches	0.0	-1.4	-5.9	-13.4	-24.2	-38.5	-56.3	-77.9	-103.4

Speer 200-grain Gold Dot +P (23969)

G1 Ballistic Coefficient = 0.139

Distance • Yards	Muzzle	25	50	75	100	125	150	175	200
Velocity • fps	1080	1033	994	960	930	903	878	855	833
Energy • Ft-lbs	518	474	439	410	384	362	343	325	308
Taylor KO Index	13.9	13.3	12.8	12.4	12.0	11.7	11.3	11.0	10.8
Mid-Range Trajectory Height • Inches	0.0	0.2	1.0	2.3	4.3	7.0	10.5	14.8	19.9
Drop • Inches	0.0	-1.0	-4.0	-9.1	-16.7	-26.7	-39.4	-54.9	-73.3

Cor-Bon 200-grain JHP +P (SD45200/20)

G1 Ballistic Coefficient = 0.150

Distance • Yards	Muzzle	25	50	75	100	125	150	175	200
Velocity • fps	1050	1015	984	957	932	909	887	866	847
Energy • Ft-lbs	490	458	430	407	386	367	349	333	319
Taylor KO Index	13.6	13.1	12.7	12.4	12.0	11.7	11.5	11.2	10.9
Mid-Range Trajectory Height • Inches	0.0	0.2	1.0	2.4	4.4	7.1	10.6	14.9	19.9
Drop • Inches	0.0	-1.0	-4.1	-9.5	-17.2	-27.4	-40.2	-55.8	-74.3

Hornady 200-grain JHP/XTP +P (9113)

G1 Ballistic Coefficient = 0.151

Distance • Yards	Muzzle	25	50	75	100	125	150	175	200
Velocity • fps	1055	1015	982	952	925	900	877	856	836
Energy • Ft-lbs	494	458	428	402	380	360	342	326	310
Taylor KO Index	13.6	13.1	12.7	12.3	11.9	11.6	11.3	11.1	10.8
Mid-Range Trajectory Height • Inches	0.0	0.2	1.0	2.4	4.5	7.2	10.7	15.0	20.2
Drop • Inches	0.0	-1.0	-4.1	-9.5	-17.2	-27.5	-40.4	-56.2	-74.9

CCI 200-grain Jacketed Hollow Point (3568)

G1 Ballistic Coefficient = 0.131

Distance • Yards	Muzzle	25	50	75	100	125	150	175	200
Velocity • fps	975	942	917	885	860	836	814	793	773
Energy • Ft-lbs	421	394	372	348	328	311	295	280	266
Taylor KO Index	12.6	12.2	11.8	11.4	11.1	10.8	10.5	10.2	10.0
Mid-Range Trajectory Height • Inches	0.0	0.3	1.4	2.8	5.0	8.3	12.4	17.5	23.4
Drop • Inches	0.0	-1.2	-4.8	-11.0	-20.0	-32.0	-47.0	-65.3	-87.0

Fiocchi 200-grain Jacketed Hollowpoint (45B)

G1 Ballistic Coefficient = 0.150

Distance • Yards	Muzzle	25	50	75	100	125	150	175	200
Velocity • fps	900	877	855	835	816	798	780	763	747
Energy • Ft-lbs	360	342	325	310	296	283	270	259	248
Taylor KO Index	11.6	11.3	11.0	10.8	10.5	10.3	10.1	9.9	9.6
Mid-Range Trajectory Height • Inches	0.0	0.3	1.4	3.2	5.8	9.4	14.0	19.5	26.1
Drop • Inches	0.0	-1.4	-5.6	-12.7	-23.0	-36.5	-53.4	-73.9	-98.1

Hornady 200-grain JHP/XTP (9112)

G1 Ballistic Coefficient = 0.149

Distance • Yards	Muzzle	25	50	75	100	125	150	175	200
Velocity • fps	900	877	855	835	815	797	779	762	746
Energy • Ft-lbs	358	342	325	310	295	282	270	258	247
Taylor KO Index	11.6	11.3	11.0	10.8	10.5	10.3	10.1	9.8	9.6
Mid-Range Trajectory Height • Inches	0.0	0.3	1.4	3.2	5.9	9.4	14.0	19.5	26.1
Drop • Inches	0.0	-1.4	-5.6	-12.7	-23.0	-36.5	-53.5	-74.0	-98.2

PMC 200-grain Full Metal Jacket—Semi-Wadcutter (45C)

G1 Ballistic Coefficient = 0.092

Distance • Yards	Muzzle	25	50	75	100	125	150	175	200
Velocity • fps	850	818	788	761	734	709	685	662	640
Energy • Ft-lbs	321	297	276	257	239	223	209	195	182
Taylor KO Index	11.0	10.6	10.2	9.8	9.5	9.2	8.8	8.5	8.3
Mid-Range Trajectory Height • Inches	0.0	0.4	1.6	3.8	7.0	11.3	16.9	23.9	32.3
Drop • Inches	0.0	-1.5	-6.3	-14.6	-26.7	-42.7	-63.1	-38.1	-118.0

CCI 200-grain TMJ Lawman (53655)

G1 Ballistic Coefficient = 0.137

Distance • Yards	Muzzle	25	50	75	100	125	150	175	200
Velocity • fps	975	943	897	888	864	841	820	800	781
Energy • Ft-lbs	422	395	371	351	332	315	299	284	271
Taylor KO Index	12.6	12.2	11.6	11.5	11.2	10.9	10.6	10.3	10.1
Mid-Range Trajectory Height • Inches	0.0	0.3	1.1	2.6	4.9	8.0	12.0	17.1	23.1
Drop • Inches	0.0	-1.2	-4.8	-11.0	-20.0	-31.8	-46.8	-64.9	-86.5

Black Hills 230-grain Jacketed Hollow Point +P (D45N6)

G1 Ballistic Coefficient = 0.165

Distance • Yards	Muzzle	25	50	75	100	125	150	175	200
Velocity • fps	950	925	903	882	862	843	825	808	792
Energy • Ft-lbs	460	438	418	397	379	363	348	334	320
Taylor KO Index	14.1	13.7	13.4	13.1	12.8	12.5	12.3	12.0	11.8
Mid-Range Trajectory Height • Inches	0.0	0.3	1.2	2.9	5.3	8.5	12.5	17.5	23.3
Drop • Inches	0.0	-1.2	-5.0	-11.4	-20.6	-32.8	-48.0	-66.3	-88.0

Cor-Bon 230-grain JHP +P (SD45230/20)

G1 Ballistic Coefficient = 0.170

Distance • Yards	Muzzle	25	50	75	100	125	150	175	200
Velocity • fps	950	928	908	889	870	853	836	820	805
Energy • Ft-lbs	461	440	421	403	387	372	357	344	331
Taylor KO Index	14.1	13.8	13.5	13.2	12.9	12.7	12.4	12.2	12.0
Mid-Range Trajectory Height • Inches	0.0	0.3	1.2	2.8	5.2	8.3	12.3	17.2	22.9
Drop • Inches	0.0	-1.2	-5.0	-11.3	-20.5	-32.5	-47.4	-65.5	-86.8

Hornady 230-grain JHP/XTP +P (9096)

G1 Ballistic Coefficient = 0.190

Distance • Yards	Muzzle	25	50	75	100	125	150	175	200
Velocity • fps	950	929	908	890	872	855	839	824	809
Energy • Ft-lbs	461	440	422	405	389	374	360	347	334
Taylor KO Index	14.1	13.8	13.5	13.2	13.0	12.7	12.5	12.2	12.0
Mid-Range Trajectory Height • Inches	0.0	0.3	1.3	2.9	5.3	8.4	12.3	17.2	22.9
Drop • Inches	0.0	-1.2	-5.0	-11.3	-20.5	-32.4	-47.4	-65.4	-86.6

Speer 230-grain Gold Dot (23966)

G1 Ballistic Coefficient = 0.192

Distance • Yards	Muzzle	25	50	75	100	125	150	175	200
Velocity • fps	890	867	845	825	805	786	768	751	735
Energy • Ft-lbs	405	384	365	347	331	316	302	288	276
Taylor KO Index	13.2	12.9	12.5	12.3	12.0	11.7	11.4	11.2	10.9
Mid-Range Trajectory Height • Inches	0.0	0.3	1.4	3.3	6.0	9.7	14.3	20.0	26.8
Drop • Inches	0.0	-1.4	-5.7	-13.0	-23.5	-37.4	-54.8	-75.8	-100.7

Winchester 230-grain Jacketed Hollow Point (S45)

G1 Ballistic Coefficient = 0.192

Distance • Yards	Muzzle	25	50	75	100	125	150	175	200
Velocity • fps	880	863	846	831	816	802	788	774	761
Energy • Ft-lbs	396	380	366	353	340	328	317	306	296
Taylor KO Index	13.1	12.8	12.6	12.3	12.1	11.9	11.7	11.5	11.3
Mid-Range Trajectory Height • Inches	0.0	0.3	1.5	3.4	6.1	9.6	14.1	19.6	26.0
Drop • Inches	0.0	-1.4	-5.8	-13.1	-23.6	-37.4	-54.5	-75.2	-99.4

USA (Winchester) 230-grain Jacketed Hollow Point (USA45JHP)

G1 Ballistic Coefficient = 0.168

Distance • Yards	Muzzle	25	50	75	100	125	150	175	200
Velocity • fps	880	861	842	825	808	792	776	761	747
Energy • Ft-lbs	396	378	363	347	334	320	308	296	285
Taylor KO Index	13.1	12.8	12.5	12.3	12.0	11.8	11.5	11.3	11.1
Mid-Range Trajectory Height • Inches	0.0	0.3	1.4	3.4	6.1	9.7	14.3	19.9	26.6
Drop • Inches	0.0	-1.4	-5.8	-13.2	-23.8	-37.7	-55.1	-76.1	-100.9

Fiocchi 230-grain Jacketed Hollowpoint (45T)

G1 Ballistic Coefficient = 0.145

Distance • Yards	Muzzle	25	50	75	100	125	150	175	200
Velocity • fps	875	853	832	812	794	775	758	741	725
Energy • Ft-lbs	390	372	354	337	322	307	294	281	269
Taylor KO Index	13.0	12.7	12.4	12.1	11.8	11.5	11.3	11.0	10.8
Mid-Range Trajectory Height • Inches	0.0	0.3	1.4	3.4	6.2	10.0	14.8	20.6	27.7
Drop • Inches	0.0	-1.4	-5.9	-13.4	-24.3	-38.6	-56.5	-78.2	-103.8

Remington 230-grain Golden Saber (GS45APB)

G1 Ballistic Coefficient = 0.148

Distance • Yards	Muzzle	25	50	75	100	125	150	175	200
Velocity • fps	875	853	833	813	795	777	760	744	728
Energy • Ft-lbs	391	372	355	338	323	309	295	283	271
Taylor KO Index	13.0	12.7	12.4	12.1	11.8	11.5	11.3	11.0	10.8
Mid-Range Trajectory Height • Inches	0.0	0.3	1.5	3.4	6.1	9.9	14.7	20.6	27.5
Drop • Inches	0.0	-1.4	-5.9	-13.4	-24.3	-38.5	-56.4	-78.0	-103.5

Black Hills 230-grain Jacketed Hollow Point (D45N5)

G1 Ballistic Coefficient = 0.165

Distance • Yards	Muzzle	25	50	75	100	125	150	175	200
Velocity • fps	850	832	814	798	782	766	751	737	723
Energy • Ft-lbs	368	353	339	325	312	300	288	277	267
Taylor KO Index	12.6	12.4	12.1	11.9	11.6	11.4	11.2	10.9	10.7
Mid-Range Trajectory Height • Inches	0.0	0.4	1.6	3.6	6.6	10.4	15.4	21.4	28.5
Drop • Inches	0.0	-1.5	-6.2	-14.1	-25.5	-40.4	-59.0	-81.5	-107.9

Federal 230-grain Hi-Shok JHP (C45D)
G1 Ballistic Coefficient = 0.140

Distance • Yards	Muzzle	25	50	75	100	125	150	175	200
Velocity • fps	850	830	810	790	770	753	736	719	703
Energy • Ft-lbs	370	350	335	320	305	289	276	264	252
Taylor KO Index	12.6	12.3	12.0	11.7	11.4	11.2	10.9	10.7	10.4
Mid-Range Trajectory Height • Inches	0.0	0.4	1.6	3.6	6.6	10.6	15.7	21.9	29.3
Drop • Inches	0.0	-1.5	-6.2	-14.2	-25.8	-40.9	-59.9	-82.9	-110.1

Federal 230-grain Hydra-Shok JHP (P45HS1)
G1 Ballistic Coefficient = 0.140

Distance • Yards	Muzzle	25	50	75	100	125	150	175	200
Velocity • fps	850	830	810	790	770	753	736	719	703
Energy • Ft-lbs	370	350	335	320	305	289	276	264	252
Taylor KO Index	12.6	12.3	12.0	11.7	11.4	11.2	10.9	10.7	10.4
Mid-Range Trajectory Height • Inches	0.0	0.4	1.6	3.6	6.6	10.6	15.7	21.9	29.3
Drop • Inches	0.0	-1.5	-6.2	-14.2	-25.8	-40.9	-59.9	-82.9	-110.1

PMC 230-grain Starfire Hollow Point (45SFA)
G1 Ballistic Coefficient = 0.150

Distance • Yards	Muzzle	25	50	75	100	125	150	175	200
Velocity • fps	850	830	810	790	770	753	736	719	703
Energy • Ft-lbs	370	350	335	320	305	289	276	264	252
Taylor KO Index	12.6	12.3	12.0	11.7	11.4	11.2	10.9	10.7	10.4
Mid-Range Trajectory Height • Inches	0.0	0.4	1.6	3.6	6.6	10.6	15.7	21.9	29.3
Drop • Inches	0.0	-1.5	-6.2	-14.2	-25.8	-40.9	-59.9	-82.9	-110.1

Remington 230-grain Jacketed Hollow Point (Subsonic) (R45AP7)
G1 Ballistic Coefficient = 0.160

Distance • Yards	Muzzle	25	50	75	100	125	150	175	200
Velocity • fps	835	817	800	783	767	751	736	722	708
Energy • Ft-lbs	356	341	326	313	300	289	277	266	256
Taylor KO Index	12.4	12.1	11.9	11.6	11.4	11.2	10.9	10.7	10.5
Mid-Range Trajectory Height • Inches	0.0	0.4	1.6	3.7	6.8	10.8	15.9	22.1	29.5
Drop • Inches	0.0	-1.6	-6.4	-14.6	-26.4	-41.9	-61.2	-84.5	-112.0

UMC (Remington) 230-grain Jacketed Hollow Point (L45AP7)
G1 Ballistic Coefficient = 0.160

Distance • Yards	Muzzle	25	50	75	100	125	150	175	200
Velocity • fps	835	817	800	783	767	751	736	722	708
Energy • Ft-lbs	356	341	326	313	300	289	277	266	256
Taylor KO Index	12.4	12.1	11.9	11.6	11.4	11.2	10.9	10.7	10.5
Mid-Range Trajectory Height • Inches	0.0	0.4	1.6	3.7	6.8	10.8	15.9	22.1	29.5
Drop • Inches	0.0	-1.6	-6.4	-14.6	-26.4	-41.9	-61.2	-84.5	-112.0

Fiocchi 230-grain Metal Case (45A)
G1 Ballistic Coefficient = 0.150

Distance • Yards	Muzzle	25	50	75	100	125	150	175	200
Velocity • fps	875	854	833	814	796	778	762	745	729
Energy • Ft-lbs	390	372	355	339	324	310	296	284	272
Taylor KO Index	13.0	12.7	12.4	12.1	11.8	11.6	11.3	11.1	10.8
Mid-Range Trajectory Height • Inches	0.0	0.3	1.5	3.4	6.3	9.9	14.7	20.5	27.4
Drop • Inches	0.0	-1.4	-5.9	-13.4	-24.2	-38.5	-56.3	-77.9	-103.4

Winchester 230-grain Brass Enclosed Base (WC452)
G1 Ballistic Coefficient = 0.180

Distance • Yards	Muzzle	25	50	75	100	125	150	175	200
Velocity • fps	875	857	840	824	808	793	778	765	751
Energy • Ft-lbs	391	375	360	347	334	321	310	298	288
Taylor KO Index	13.0	12.7	12.5	12.2	12.0	11.8	11.6	11.4	11.2
Mid-Range Trajectory Height • Inches	0.0	0.4	1.5	3.4	6.2	9.8	14.4	20.0	26.6
Drop • Inches	0.0	-1.4	-5.8	-13.3	-24.0	-38.0	-55.4	-76.5	-101.2

Federal 230-grain FMJ Match (GM45A)
G1 Ballistic Coefficient = 0.143

Distance • Yards	Muzzle	25	50	75	100	125	150	175	200
Velocity • fps	860	840	820	800	780	763	745	729	713
Energy • Ft-lbs	380	360	340	325	310	297	284	271	260
Taylor KO Index	12.8	12.5	12.2	11.9	11.6	11.3	11.1	10.8	10.6
Mid-Range Trajectory Height • Inches	0.0	0.4	1.5	3.6	6.5	10.4	15.3	21.4	28.6
Drop • Inches	0.0	-1.5	-6.1	-13.9	-25.1	-39.9	-58.5	-80.9	-107.4

Sellier & Bellot 230-grain FMJ (SBA4501)

G1 Ballistic Coefficient = 0.125

Distance • Yards	Muzzle	25	50	75	100	125	150	175	200
Velocity • fps	853	829	806	785	764	745	726	708	690
Energy • Ft-lbs	371	351	331	315	298	283	269	256	243
Taylor KO Index	12.7	12.3	12.0	11.7	11.3	11.1	10.8	10.5	10.2
Mid-Range Trajectory Height • Inches	0.0	0.4	1.5	3.6	6.5	10.4	15.3	21.4	28.6
Drop • Inches	0.0	-1.5	-6.2	-14.2	-25.8	-41.1	-60.2	-83.5	-111.2

American Eagle (Federal) 230-grain Full Metal Jacket (AE45N1)

G1 Ballistic Coefficient = 0.140

Distance • Yards	Muzzle	25	50	75	100	125	150	175	200
Velocity • fps	850	830	810	790	770	753	736	719	703
Energy • Ft-lbs	370	350	335	320	305	289	276	264	252
Taylor KO Index	12.6	12.3	12.0	11.7	11.4	11.2	10.9	10.7	10.4
Mid-Range Trajectory Height • Inches	0.0	0.4	1.6	3.6	6.6	10.6	15.7	21.9	29.3
Drop • Inches	0.0	-1.5	-6.2	-14.2	-25.8	-40.9	-59.9	-82.9	-110.1

American Eagle (Federal) 230-grain TMJ (AE45NT1)

G1 Ballistic Coefficient = 0.140

Distance • Yards	Muzzle	25	50	75	100	125	150	175	200
Velocity • fps	850	830	810	790	770	753	736	719	703
Energy • Ft-lbs	370	350	335	320	305	289	276	264	252
Taylor KO Index	12.6	12.3	12.0	11.7	11.4	11.2	10.9	10.7	10.4
Mid-Range Trajectory Height • Inches	0.0	0.4	1.6	3.6	6.6	10.6	15.7	21.9	29.3
Drop • Inches	0.0	-1.5	-6.2	-14.2	-25.8	-40.9	-59.9	-82.9	-110.1

Black Hills 230-grain Full Metal Jacket (D45N3)

G1 Ballistic Coefficient = 0.150

Distance • Yards	Muzzle	25	50	75	100	125	150	175	200
Velocity • fps	850	830	811	793	775	759	742	727	711
Energy • Ft-lbs	368	352	336	321	307	294	282	270	258
Taylor KO Index	12.6	12.3	12.0	11.8	11.5	11.3	11.0	10.8	10.6
Mid-Range Trajectory Height • Inches	0.0	0.4	1.6	3.6	6.6	10.5	15.5	21.6	28.9
Drop • Inches	0.0	-1.5	-6.2	-14.2	-25.6	-40.7	-59.5	-82.3	-109.1

Federal 230-grain Full Metal Jacket (C45A) (Discontinued in 2004)

G1 Ballistic Coefficient = 0.140

Distance • Yards	Muzzle	25	50	75	100	125	150	175	200
Velocity • fps	850	830	810	790	770	753	736	719	703
Energy • Ft-lbs	370	350	335	320	305	289	276	264	252
Taylor KO Index	12.6	12.3	12.0	11.7	11.4	11.2	10.9	10.7	10.4
Mid-Range Trajectory Height • Inches	0.0	0.4	1.6	3.6	6.6	10.6	15.7	21.9	29.3
Drop • Inches	0.0	-1.5	-6.2	-14.2	-25.8	-40.9	-59.9	-82.9	-110.1

Hornady 230-grain Full Metal Jacket—Flat Point (9098) (Discontinued in 2004)

G1 Ballistic Coefficient = 0.142

Distance • Yards	Muzzle	25	50	75	100	125	150	175	200
Velocity • fps	850	829	809	790	771	754	739	721	705
Energy • Ft-lbs	369	351	334	319	304	290	277	265	254
Taylor KO Index	12.6	12.3	12.0	11.7	11.4	11.2	10.7	10.5	10.1
Mid-Range Trajectory Height • Inches	0.0	0.4	1.6	3.6	6.6	10.6	15.6	21.8	29.2
Drop • Inches	0.0	-1.5	-6.2	-14.2	-25.7	-40.8	-59.8	-82.7	-109.9

Hornady 230-grain FMJ RN ENC (9097)

G1 Ballistic Coefficient = 0.183

Distance • Yards	Muzzle	25	50	75	100	125	150	175	200
Velocity • fps	850	834	818	803	788	774	760	747	734
Energy • Ft-lbs	369	355	342	329	317	306	295	285	275
Taylor KO Index	12.6	12.4	12.1	11.9	11.7	11.5	11.3	11.1	10.9
Mid-Range Trajectory Height • Inches	0.0	0.4	1.6	3.6	6.5	10.3	15.2	21.1	28.0
Drop • Inches	0.0	-1.5	-6.2	-14.1	-25.3	-40.1	-58.5	-80.7	-106.7

CCI 230-grain Full Metal Jacket Blazer (3570)

G1 Ballistic Coefficient = 0.160

Distance • Yards	Muzzle	25	50	75	100	125	150	175	200
Velocity • fps	845	826	804	792	775	760	744	730	715
Energy • Ft-lbs	363	349	329	320	304	295	283	272	261
Taylor KO Index	12.5	12.3	11.9	11.8	11.5	11.3	11.0	10.8	10.6
Mid-Range Trajectory Height • Inches	0.0	0.4	1.6	3.6	6.6	10.5	15.6	21.6	28.9
Drop • Inches	0.0	-1.5	-6.3	-14.3	-25.8	-40.9	-59.8	-82.6	-109.5

CCI 230-grain Clean-Fire—Totally Metal Jacket Blazer (3480)

G1 Ballistic Coefficient = 0.160

Distance • Yards	Muzzle	25	50	75	100	125	150	175	200
Velocity • fps	845	826	804	792	775	760	744	730	715
Energy • Ft-lbs	363	349	329	320	304	295	283	272	261
Taylor KO Index	12.5	12.3	11.9	11.8	11.5	11.3	11.0	10.8	10.6
Mid-Range Trajectory Height • Inches	0.0	0.4	1.6	3.6	6.6	10.5	15.6	21.6	28.9
Drop • Inches	0.0	-1.5	-6.3	-14.3	-25.8	-40.9	-59.8	-82.6	-109.5

Magtech 230-grain FMC (45A)

G1 Ballistic Coefficient = 0.155

Distance • Yards	Muzzle	25	50	75	100	125	150	175	200
Velocity • fps	837	818	800	783	767	751	735	720	706
Energy • Ft-lbs	356	342	326	313	300	288	276	265	254
Taylor KO Index	12.4	12.1	11.9	11.6	11.4	11.2	10.9	10.7	10.5
Mid-Range Trajectory Height • Inches	0.0	0.4	1.6	3.7	6.8	10.8	15.9	22.1	29.5
Drop • Inches	0.0	-1.6	-6.4	-14.6	-26.4	-41.8	-61.1	-84.4	-111.9

Magtech 230-grain FMJ Shootin' Size (MP45A)

G1 Ballistic Coefficient = 0.155

Distance • Yards	Muzzle	25	50	75	100	125	150	175	200
Velocity • fps	837	818	800	783	767	751	735	720	706
Energy • Ft-lbs	356	342	326	313	300	288	276	265	254
Taylor KO Index	12.4	12.1	11.9	11.6	11.4	11.2	10.9	10.7	10.5
Mid-Range Trajectory Height • Inches	0.0	0.4	1.6	3.7	6.8	10.8	15.9	22.1	29.5
Drop • Inches	0.0	-1.6	-6.4	-14.6	-26.4	-41.8	-61.1	-84.4	-111.9

Magtech 230-grain FEB CleanRange (CR45A)

G1 Ballistic Coefficient = 0.155

Distance • Yards	Muzzle	25	50	75	100	125	150	175	200
Velocity • fps	837	818	800	783	767	751	735	720	706
Energy • Ft-lbs	356	342	326	313	300	288	276	265	254
Taylor KO Index	12.4	12.1	11.9	11.6	11.4	11.2	10.9	10.7	10.5
Mid-Range Trajectory Height • Inches	0.0	0.4	1.6	3.7	6.8	10.8	15.9	22.1	29.5
Drop • Inches	0.0	-1.6	-6.4	-14.6	-26.4	-41.8	-61.1	-84.4	-111.9

Remington 230-grain Metal Case (R45AP4)

G1 Ballistic Coefficient = 0.160

Distance • Yards	Muzzle	25	50	75	100	125	150	175	200
Velocity • fps	835	817	800	783	767	751	736	722	708
Energy • Ft-lbs	356	341	326	313	300	289	277	266	256
Taylor KO Index	12.4	12.1	11.9	11.6	11.4	11.2	10.9	10.7	10.5
Mid-Range Trajectory Height • Inches	0.0	0.4	1.6	3.7	6.8	10.8	15.9	22.1	29.5
Drop • Inches	0.0	-1.6	-6.4	-14.6	-26.4	-41.9	-61.2	-84.5	-112.0

UMC (Remington) 230-grain Metal Case (L45AP4)

G1 Ballistic Coefficient = 0.160

Distance • Yards	Muzzle	25	50	75	100	125	150	175	200
Velocity • fps	835	817	800	783	767	751	736	722	708
Energy • Ft-lbs	356	341	326	313	300	289	277	266	256
Taylor KO Index	12.4	12.1	11.9	11.6	11.4	11.2	10.9	10.7	10.5
Mid-Range Trajectory Height • Inches	0.0	0.4	1.6	3.7	6.8	10.8	15.9	22.1	29.5
Drop • Inches	0.0	-1.6	-6.4	-14.6	-26.4	-41.9	-61.2	-84.5	-112.0

UMC (Remington) 230-grain FNEB Leadless (LL45APB)

G1 Ballistic Coefficient = 0.160

Distance • Yards	Muzzle	25	50	75	100	125	150	175	200
Velocity • fps	835	817	800	783	767	751	736	722	708
Energy • Ft-lbs	356	341	326	313	300	289	277	266	256
Taylor KO Index	12.4	12.1	11.9	11.6	11.4	11.2	10.9	10.7	10.5
Mid-Range Trajectory Height • Inches	0.0	0.4	1.6	3.7	6.8	10.8	15.9	22.1	29.5
Drop • Inches	0.0	-1.6	-6.4	-14.6	-26.4	-41.9	-61.2	-84.5	-112.0

USA (Winchester) 230-grain Full Metal Jacket (Q4170)

G1 Ballistic Coefficient = 0.160

Distance • Yards	Muzzle	25	50	75	100	125	150	175	200
Velocity • fps	835	817	800	783	767	751	736	722	708
Energy • Ft-lbs	356	341	326	313	300	289	277	266	256
Taylor KO Index	12.4	12.1	11.9	11.6	11.4	11.2	10.9	10.7	10.5
Mid-Range Trajectory Height • Inches	0.0	0.4	1.6	3.7	6.8	10.8	15.9	22.1	29.5
Drop • Inches	0.0	-1.6	-6.4	-14.6	-26.4	-41.9	-61.2	-84.5	-112.0

Aguila 230-grain Full Metal Jacket

G1 Ballistic Coefficient = 0.130

Distance • Yards	Muzzle	25	50	75	100	125	150	175	200
Velocity • fps	830	809	789	769	749	730	712	695	679
Energy • Ft-lbs	352	334	317	301	286	272	259	247	235
Taylor KO Index	12.3	12.0	11.7	11.4	11.1	10.8	10.6	10.3	10.1
Mid-Range Trajectory Height • Inches	0.0	0.4	1.6	3.8	7.0	11.2	16.6	23.2	31.0
Drop • Inches	0.0	-1.6	-6.5	-15.0	-27.1	-43.1	-63.1	-87.5	-116.3

CCI 230-grain TMJ Lawman (53967)

G1 Ballistic Coefficient = 0.154

Distance • Yards	Muzzle	25	50	75	100	125	150	175	200
Velocity • fps	830	811	794	777	760	744	729	714	700
Energy • Ft-lbs	352	336	322	308	295	283	272	261	250
Taylor KO Index	12.5	12.3	11.9	11.8	11.5	11.3	11.0	10.8	10.6
Mid-Range Trajectory Height • Inches	0.0	0.4	1.7	3.8	6.9	11.0	16.2	22.6	30.1
Drop • Inches	0.0	-1.6	-6.5	-14.9	-26.8	-42.5	-62.1	-85.8	-113.8

CCI 230-grain Clean-Fire—TMJ Lawman (53885)

G1 Ballistic Coefficient = 0.154

Distance • Yards	Muzzle	25	50	75	100	125	150	175	200
Velocity • fps	830	811	794	777	760	744	729	714	700
Energy • Ft-lbs	352	336	322	308	295	283	272	261	250
Taylor KO Index	12.5	12.3	11.9	11.8	11.5	11.3	11.0	10.8	10.6
Mid-Range Trajectory Height • Inches	0.0	0.4	1.7	3.8	6.9	11.0	16.2	22.6	30.1
Drop • Inches	0.0	-1.6	-6.5	-14.9	-26.8	-42.5	-62.1	-85.8	-113.8

PMC 230-grain Full Metal Jacket (45A)

G1 Ballistic Coefficient = 0.130

Distance • Yards	Muzzle	25	50	75	100	125	150	175	200
Velocity • fps	830	809	789	769	749	730	712	695	679
Energy • Ft-lbs	352	334	317	301	286	272	259	247	235
Taylor KO Index	12.3	12.0	11.7	11.4	11.1	10.8	10.6	10.3	10.1
Mid-Range Trajectory Height • Inches	0.0	0.4	1.6	3.8	7.0	11.2	16.6	23.2	31.0
Drop • Inches	0.0	-1.6	-6.5	-15.0	-27.1	-43.1	-63.1	-87.5	-116.3

Magtech 230-grain FMC—SWC (45B)

G1 Ballistic Coefficient = 0.076

Distance • Yards	Muzzle	25	50	75	100	125	150	175	200
Velocity • fps	780	747	720	687	660	633	607	583	560
Energy • Ft-lbs	310	285	265	241	220	205	188	174	160
Taylor KO Index	11.6	11.1	10.7	10.2	9.8	9.4	9.0	8.7	8.3
Mid-Range Trajectory Height • Inches	0.0	0.4	1.8	4.6	7.8	13.7	20.7	29.5	40.2
Drop • Inches	0.0	-1.8	-7.6	-17.5	-32.1	-51.7	-76.6	-107.5	-144.7

.45 Smith & Wesson Schofield

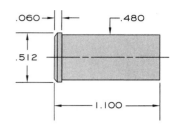

The .45 Schofield is a cartridge that had nearly disappeared into the mists of obsolescence, only to have been given a new life by the introduction of cowboy-action shooting. It was introduced in 1875 as a competitor for the .45 Colt. The Schofield is about 0.2 inches shorter than the .45 Colt and is otherwise very nearly identical in dimensions. For a while in the 1870s, the army had both guns and both calibers of ammunition in the inventory. Can you imagine how many units got the wrong ammunition?

Relative Recoil Factor = 0.76

Specifications

Controlling Agency for Standardization of this Ammunition: Factory
Barrel used for velocity testing: 6 inches long—1 turn in 12-inch twist

Cowboy Action Loads
Black Hills 180-grain Soft Point (DCB45SCHON2)
G1 Ballistic Coefficient = 0.135

Distance • Yards	Muzzle	25	50	75	100	125	150	175	200
Velocity • fps	730	713	696	680	665	650	635	620	606
Energy • Ft-lbs	213	203	195	185	177	169	161	154	147
Taylor KO Index	8.6	8.4	8.2	8.0	7.8	7.6	7.4	7.2	7.0
Mid-Range Trajectory Height • Inches	0.0	0.5	2.1	4.9	9.0	14.2	21.1	29.4	39.4
Drop • Inches	0.0	-2.1	-8.4	-19.2	-34.8	-55.2	-80.7	-111.7	-148.3

Black Hills 230-grain Soft Point (DCB45SCHON1)
G1 Ballistic Coefficient = 0.150

Distance • Yards	Muzzle	25	50	75	100	125	150	175	200
Velocity • fps	730	715	700	685	671	657	644	630	617
Energy • Ft-lbs	272	261	250	240	230	221	212	203	195
Taylor KO Index	10.9	10.7	10.5	10.3	10.1	9.8	9.6	9.4	9.2
Mid-Range Trajectory Height • Inches	0.0	0.5	2.1	4.9	8.9	14.1	20.8	28.9	38.6
Drop • Inches	0.0	-2.1	-8.4	-19.2	-34.5	-54.7	-80.0	-110.4	-146.4

Bill Feldstein shot this buffalo with an 8-bore black-powder rifle. PH Brian Marsh (left) was his guide. (Photo from *A Pioneering Hunter* by Brian Marsh, Safari Press, 2006)

.45 Colt (Often Called .45 Long Colt)

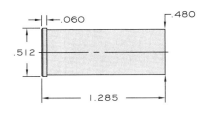

The name of this cartridge is interesting. It is often called .45 Long Colt or .45 Colt Long. Neither name is correct because there never was a .45 Short Colt. The name that gets used today relates to the .45 S&W Schofield. The .45 Colt was adopted by the army in 1873 for the legendary Colt Single Action Army revolver. That made it the first centerfire pistol round in the U.S. inventory. A couple of years later the army adopted the .45 S&W Schofield in a Smith & Wesson revolver as an alternate. That put the army in the position of having two very similar rounds in the inventory at the same time. Guaranteed chaos! The .45 Schofield would fit the Colt revolver, but the Colt ammo wouldn't fit the Smith. Besides, the quartermasters in outfits that used the Colt revolver didn't want any of that shorter ammo (thought of as inferior). They were careful to specify .45 Colt (LONG) when they ordered ammo. While the standard factory ammo is pretty mild by today's standards (because there are still a lot of very old guns in circulation), the advent of cowboy-action shooting is adding new life to this great old cartridge.

Relative Recoil Factor = 0.45

Specifications

Controlling Agency for Standardization of this Ammunition: SAAMI

Bullet Weight Grains	Velocity fps	Maximum Average Pressure	
		Copper Crusher	Transducer
225 STHP	915	14,000 cup	14,000 psi
225 SWC	950	14,000 cup	14,000 psi
250-255 L	900	14,000 cup	14,000 psi

Standard barrel for velocity testing: 4 inches long (vented)—1 turn in 16-inch twist

Availability

CCI 150-grain Magnum Shotshell (3972)
Shot load using #9 shot—Muzzle Velocity = 1000 fps.

Cor-Bon 200-grain JHP (SD45C200/20)   G1 Ballistic Coefficient = 0.150

Distance • Yards	Muzzle	25	50	75	100	125	150	175	200
Velocity • fps	1100	1058	1022	991	962	937	913	891	871
Energy • Ft-lbs	537	497	464	436	412	390	371	353	337
Taylor KO Index	14.3	13.8	13.3	12.9	12.5	12.2	11.9	11.6	11.3
Mid-Range Trajectory Height • Inches	0.0	0.2	0.9	2.2	4.1	6.6	9.9	13.9	18.6
Drop • Inches	0.0	-0.9	-3.8	-8.7	-15.9	-25.4	-37.3	-51.8	-69.1

CCI 200-grain JHP Blazer (3584)   G1 Ballistic Coefficient = 0.150

Distance • Yards	Muzzle	25	50	75	100	125	150	175	200
Velocity • fps	1000	968	938	913	889	867	846	826	808
Energy • Ft-lbs	444	416	391	370	351	334	318	303	290
Taylor KO Index	13.0	12.6	12.2	11.9	11.5	11.2	10.9	10.7	10.4
Mid-Range Trajectory Height • Inches	0.0	0.3	1.3	2.7	4.8	7.8	11.7	16.3	21.9
Drop • Inches	0.0	-1.1	-4.5	-10.4	-18.9	-30.1	-44.2	-61.4	-81.7

Remington 225-grain Semi-Wadcutter (R45C1)   G1 Ballistic Coefficient = 0.110

Distance • Yards	Muzzle	25	50	75	100	125	150	175	200
Velocity • fps	960	923	890	859	832	806	782	759	737
Energy • Ft-lbs	460	425	395	369	346	325	305	288	271
Taylor KO Index	14.1	13.5	13.0	12.6	12.2	11.7	11.4	11.0	10.7
Mid-Range Trajectory Height • Inches	0.0	0.3	1.3	3.0	5.5	8.8	13.2	18.6	25.0
Drop • Inches	0.0	-1.2	-5.0	-11.5	-20.9	-33.5	-49.4	-66.8	-92.0

Winchester 225-grain Silvertip Hollow Point (X45CSHP2)

G1 Ballistic Coefficient = 0.165

Distance • Yards	Muzzle	25	50	75	100	125	150	175	200
Velocity • fps	920	898	877	857	839	821	804	788	772
Energy • Ft-lbs	423	403	384	367	352	337	323	310	298
Taylor KO Index	13.5	13.2	12.9	12.6	12.3	11.9	11.7	11.4	11.2
Mid-Range Trajectory Height • Inches	0.0	0.3	1.4	3.1	5.6	9.0	13.2	18.5	24.6
Drop • Inches	0.0	-1.3	-5.3	-12.1	-21.9	-34.8	-50.8	-70.3	-93.2

Federal 225-grain JHP (C45LCA)

G1 Ballistic Coefficient = 0.159

Distance • Yards	Muzzle	25	50	75	100	125	150	175	200
Velocity • fps	900	880	860	840	820	803	786	770	754
Energy • Ft-lbs	405	385	370	355	340	322	309	296	284
Taylor KO Index	13.2	12.9	12.6	12.3	12.0	11.7	11.4	11.2	11.0
Mid-Range Trajectory Height • Inches	0.0	0.3	1.4	3.2	5.8	9.4	13.9	19.3	25.8
Drop • Inches	0.0	-1.4	-5.5	-12.7	-22.9	-36.3	-53.1	-73.4	-97.4

Speer 250-grain Gold Dot Hollow Point (32984)

G1 Ballistic Coefficient = 0.167

Distance • Yards	Muzzle	25	50	75	100	125	150	175	200
Velocity • fps	875	856	837	820	803	787	772	757	742
Energy • Ft-lbs	425	407	389	373	358	344	331	318	306
Taylor KO Index	14.1	13.8	13.5	13.2	13.0	12.7	12.5	12.2	12.0
Mid-Range Trajectory Height • Inches	0.0	0.4	1.5	3.4	6.2	9.9	14.6	20.0	27.0
Drop • Inches	0.0	-1.4	-5.9	-13.4	-24.1	-38.2	-55.8	-77.0	-102.1

Remington 250-grain Lead Round Nose (R45C)

G1 Ballistic Coefficient = 0.142

Distance • Yards	Muzzle	25	50	75	100	125	150	175	200
Velocity • fps	860	838	820	798	780	762	745	728	712
Energy • Ft-lbs	410	390	375	354	340	322	308	294	281
Taylor KO Index	14.0	13.6	13.4	13.0	12.7	12.3	12.0	11.8	11.5
Mid-Range Trajectory Height • Inches	0.0	0.4	1.6	3.6	6.6	10.3	15.3	21.4	28.6
Drop • Inches	0.0	-1.5	-6.1	-13.9	-25.2	-39.9	-58.5	-80.9	-107.5

PMC 255-grain FMJ-FP (45LB)

G1 Ballistic Coefficient = 0.152

Distance • Yards	Muzzle	25	50	75	100	125	150	175	200
Velocity • fps	800	783	766	750	733	718	704	689	675
Energy • Ft-lbs	355	340	326	312	299	287	275	264	253
Taylor KO Index	12.9	12.6	12.4	12.1	11.8	11.6	11.4	11.1	10.9
Mid-Range Trajectory Height • Inches	0.0	0.4	1.8	4.0	7.4	11.8	17.4	24.2	32.3
Drop • Inches	0.0	-1.7	-7.0	-16.0	-28.8	-45.7	-66.8	-92.2	-122.2

PMC 300-grain JSP +P + (Caution*) (45HA)

G1 Ballistic Coefficient = 0.152

Distance • Yards	Muzzle	25	50	75	100	125	150	175	200
Velocity • fps	1250	1192	1144	1102	1066	1033	1005	980	956
Energy • Ft-lbs	1041	951	874	810	757	712	673	639	609
Taylor KO Index	24.2	23.1	22.2	21.3	20.6	20.0	19.5	19.0	18.5
Mid-Range Trajectory Height • Inches	0.0	0.1	0.7	1.7	3.3	5.3	8.0	11.2	15.1
Drop • Inches	0.0	-0.7	-3.0	-6.8	-12.5	-20.1	-29.7	-41.4	-55.4

*Caution—These are high-pressure rounds and are NOT intended for use in firearms of weaker receiver/frame strength such as the Colt Single Action Army revolver. Please consult your firearms manufacturer for compatibility and use.

Winchester 255-grain Lead-Round Nose (X45CP2)

G1 Ballistic Coefficient = 0.153

Distance • Yards	Muzzle	25	50	75	100	125	150	175	200
Velocity • fps	860	838	820	798	780	762	745	728	712
Energy • Ft-lbs	420	398	380	361	344	329	314	300	237
Taylor KO Index	14.3	13.9	13.6	13.3	13.0	12.5	12.3	12.0	11.7
Mid-Range Trajectory Height • Inches	0.0	0.4	1.5	3.5	6.5	10.3	15.3	21.4	28.4
Drop • Inches	0.0	-1.5	-6.1	-13.9	-25.2	-39.9	-58.5	-80.9	-107.5

Cowboy Action Ammunition

CCI 230-grain LFN Trail Blazer (3586)

G1 Ballistic Coefficient = 0.139

Distance • Yards	Muzzle	25	50	75	100	125	150	175	200
Velocity • fps	750	733	716	700	684	669	654	640	626
Energy • Ft-lbs	287	274	262	250	239	229	219	209	200
Taylor KO Index	11.1	10.9	10.6	10.4	10.2	9.9	9.7	9.5	9.3
Mid-Range Trajectory Height • Inches	0.0	0.4	2.0	4.6	8.4	13.5	19.9	27.8	37.1
Drop • Inches	0.0	-2.0	-8.0	-18.2	-32.9	-52.2	-76.3	-105.6	-140.1

PMC 250-grain LFP (45LA)

G1 Ballistic Coefficient = 0.158

Distance • Yards	Muzzle	25	50	75	100	125	150	175	200
Velocity • fps	800	783	767	751	736	721	707	693	679
Energy • Ft-lbs	355	341	331	313	301	289	277	267	256
Taylor KO Index	13.0	12.8	12.5	12.2	12.0	11.6	11.4	11.2	11.0
Mid-Range Trajectory Height • Inches	0.0	0.4	1.8	4.1	7.4	11.7	17.3	24.1	32.1
Drop • Inches	0.0	-1.7	-7.0	-15.9	-28.8	-45.5	-66.5	-91.8	-121.7

Magtech 250-grain LFN (45D)

G1 Ballistic Coefficient = 0.177

Distance • Yards	Muzzle	25	50	75	100	125	150	175	200
Velocity • fps	761	747	735	720	708	695	683	671	659
Energy • Ft-lbs	313	310	301	288	280	268	259	250	241
Taylor KO Index	12.3	12.1	11.9	11.6	11.4	11.2	11.0	10.8	10.6
Mid-Range Trajectory Height • Inches	0.0	0.5	2.0	4.5	8.1	12.8	18.9	26.1	34.8
Drop • Inches	0.0	-1.9	-7.7	-17.5	-31.5	-49.9	-72.7	-100.2	-132.5

USA (Winchester) 250-grain Cowboy (USA45CB)

G1 Ballistic Coefficient = 0.158

Distance • Yards	Muzzle	25	50	75	100	125	150	175	200
Velocity • fps	750	735	720	706	692	678	665	652	639
Energy • Ft-lbs	312	300	288	277	266	255	245	236	227
Taylor KO Index	12.1	11.9	11.6	11.4	11.2	10.9	10.7	10.5	10.3
Mid-Range Trajectory Height • Inches	0.0	0.4	2.0	4.6	8.4	13.3	19.6	27.2	36.3
Drop • Inches	0.0	-2.0	-7.9	-18.1	-32.6	-51.7	-75.5	-104.2	-138.0

Black Hills 250-grain RNFP (DCB45CLTN1)

G1 Ballistic Coefficient = 0.140

Distance • Yards	Muzzle	25	50	75	100	125	150	175	200
Velocity • fps	725	709	693	677	663	648	634	620	606
Energy • Ft-lbs	292	279	267	255	244	233	223	213	204
Taylor KO Index	11.8	11.5	11.3	11.0	10.8	10.5	10.2	10.0	9.8
Mid-Range Trajectory Height • Inches	0.0	0.5	2.2	5.0	9.1	14.4	21.3	29.7	39.6
Drop • Inches	0.0	-2.1	-8.5	-19.5	-35.2	-55.8	-81.6	-112.8	-149.6

Hornady 255-grain Cowboy (9115)

G1 Ballistic Coefficient = 0.134

Distance • Yards	Muzzle	25	50	75	100	125	150	175	200
Velocity • fps	725	708	692	676	660	645	630	615	601
Energy • Ft-lbs	298	284	271	259	247	235	225	215	205
Taylor KO Index	12.0	11.8	11.5	11.2	11.0	10.6	10.4	10.1	9.9
Mid-Range Trajectory Height • Inches	0.0	0.5	2.2	5.0	9.1	14.5	21.4	29.9	39.9
Drop • Inches	0.0	-2.1	-8.5	-19.5	-35.2	-56.0	-81.9	-113.3	-150.4

.45 Winchester Magnum

In 1979, Winchester introduced their .45 Winchester Magnum cartridge. The round was intended for the gas-operated Wildey pistol. The buying public never took to the Wildey gun, but the cartridge was a real performer. At the time of its introduction, it was the most powerful pistol cartridge in the inventory. While the .45 Casull and the .50 Action Express have pushed it out of first place in the power derby, the .45 Winchester Magnum is still a very potent pistol round. It makes a great hunting cartridge in single-shot, long-barreled pistols.

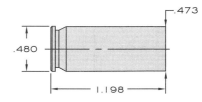

Relative Recoil Factor = 0.1.40

Specifications

Controlling Agency for Standardization of this Ammunition: SAAMI

Bullet Weight Grains	Velocity fps	Maximum Average Pressure	
		Copper Crusher	Transducer
230 MC	1,380	40,000 cup	N/S

Standard barrel for velocity testing: 5 inches long—1 turn in 16-inch twist

Availability

Cor-Bon 200-grain JHP (Discontinued in 2004)
G1 Ballistic Coefficient = 0.150

Distance • Yards	Muzzle	25	50	75	100	125	150	175	200
Velocity • fps	1450	1361	1281	1210	1150	1100	1058	1022	991
Energy • Ft-lbs	934	823	729	651	588	538	497	464	436
Taylor KO Index	18.7	17.6	16.5	15.6	14.9	14.2	13.7	13.2	12.8
Mid-Range Trajectory Height • Inches	0.0	0.1	0.5	1.4	2.6	4.3	6.6	9.5	13.0
Drop • Inches	0.0	-0.5	-2.2	-5.3	-9.8	-16.0	-23.9	-33.8	-45.6

Winchester 260-grain Partition Gold (SPG45WM)
G1 Ballistic Coefficient = 0.190

Distance • Yards	Muzzle	25	50	75	100	125	150	175	200
Velocity • fps	1200	1149	1105	1066	1033	1004	978	954	932
Energy • Ft-lbs	832	762	705	656	617	582	552	525	502
Taylor KO Index	20.1	19.3	18.6	17.9	17.3	16.9	16.4	16.0	15.6
Mid-Range Trajectory Height • Inches	0.0	0.2	0.8	1.9	3.5	5.7	8.5	12.0	16.1
Drop • Inches	0.0	-0.8	-3.2	-7.4	-13.5	-21.6	-31.9	-44.5	-59.4

Winchester 260-grain Jacketed Hollow Point (X45MWA)
G1 Ballistic Coefficient = 0.180

Distance • Yards	Muzzle	25	50	75	100	125	150	175	200
Velocity • fps	1200	1146	1099	1060	1026	996	969	945	923
Energy • Ft-lbs	831	758	698	649	607	573	543	516	492
Taylor KO Index	20.4	19.5	18.7	18.0	17.5	16.7	16.3	15.9	15.5
Mid-Range Trajectory Height • Inches	0.0	0.2	0.8	1.9	3.5	5.7	8.6	12.1	16.3
Drop • Inches	0.0	-0.8	-3.2	-7.4	-13.6	-21.8	-32.2	-44.8	-59.9

Cor-Bon 265-grain BondedCore HP (Discontinued in 2004)
G1 Ballistic Coefficient = 0.180

Distance • Yards	Muzzle	25	50	75	100	125	150	175	200
Velocity • fps	1300	1239	1184	1137	1097	1061	1031	1003	979
Energy • Ft-lbs	995	903	825	761	708	663	625	593	564
Taylor KO Index	22.2	21.2	20.3	19.5	18.8	18.2	17.6	17.2	16.8
Mid-Range Trajectory Height • Inches	0.0	0.2	0.7	1.6	3.0	5.0	7.5	10.6	14.3
Drop • Inches	0.0	-0.7	-2.7	-6.4	-11.7	-18.8	-27.8	-38.8	-52.0

Cor-Bon 320-grain RN Penetrator (HT45WM320PN/20)
G1 Ballistic Coefficient = 0.200

Distance • Yards	Muzzle	25	50	75	100	125	150	175	200
Velocity • fps	1150	1112	1078	1048	1022	998	976	956	937
Energy • Ft-lbs	940	878	826	781	742	708	677	649	624
Taylor KO Index	23.8	23.0	22.3	21.7	21.1	20.6	20.2	19.8	19.4
Mid-Range Trajectory Height • Inches	0.0	0.2	0.8	2.0	3.7	5.9	8.8	12.3	16.5
Drop • Inches	0.0	-0.8	-3.4	-7.9	-14.3	-22.8	-33.5	-46.5	-61.8

.454 Casull

If you look carefully at their dimensions, you'll find that the .454 Casull is really a long version of the .45 Colt (which is often called Long Colt). The Casull is 0.100-inch longer, but the real performance improvement comes from using chamber pressures that approach 50,000 psi. The .454 Casull is one of just a few factory-manufactured cartridges in the USA that have not been standardized by either SAAMI or CIP (the European agency). If a milder loading is desired, .45 Colt ammunition can be fired in .454 Casull chambers. The result is pretty much the same as firing .38 Special in a .357 Magnum.

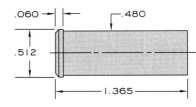

Relative Recoil Factor = 2.20

Specifications

Controlling Agency for Standardization of this Ammunition: Factory
Standard barrel for velocity testing: 7.5 inches long (vented)—1 turn in N/S inch twist*
*Twist not yet defined

Availability

Hornady 240-grain XTP-MAG (9148)
G1 Ballistic Coefficient = 0.162

Distance • Yards	Muzzle	25	50	75	100	125	150	175	200
Velocity • fps	1900	1788	1679	1578	1483	1392	1310	1236	1172
Energy • Ft-lbs	1923	1704	1502	1328	1172	1034	915	815	732
Taylor KO Index	29.4	27.7	26.0	24.5	23.0	21.6	20.3	19.2	18.2
Mid-Range Trajectory Height • Inches	0.0	0.1	0.3	0.8	1.5	2.5	3.9	5.8	8.0
Drop • Inches	0.0	-0.3	-1.3	-3.1	-5.7	-9.3	-14.1	-20.1	-27.6

Cor-Bon 240-grain JHP (HT454240JHP/20)
G1 Ballistic Coefficient = 0.160

Distance • Yards	Muzzle	25	50	75	100	125	150	175	200
Velocity • fps	1450	1362	1282	1210	1148	1096	1053	1016	983
Energy • Ft-lbs	1120	989	876	781	703	641	591	550	516
Taylor KO Index	22.6	21.2	20.2	18.8	17.9	17.1	16.4	15.8	15.3
Mid-Range Trajectory Height • Inches	0.0	0.1	0.5	1.4	2.6	4.3	6.6	9.6	13.1
Drop • Inches	0.0	-0.5	-2.2	-5.3	-9.8	-16.0	-23.9	-33.9	-45.9

Winchester 250-grain Jacketed Flat Point (X454C3)
G1 Ballistic Coefficient = 0.146

Distance • Yards	Muzzle	25	50	75	100	125	150	175	200
Velocity • fps	1300	1220	1151	1094	1047	1008	974	944	917
Energy • Ft-lbs	938	826	735	665	608	564	526	495	467
Taylor KO Index	21.0	19.7	18.6	17.7	16.9	16.3	15.7	15.2	14.8
Mid-Range Trajectory Height • Inches	0.0	0.2	0.8	0.8	3.2	5.3	8.1	11.5	15.6
Drop • Inches	0.0	-0.7	-2.8	-6.6	-12.2	-19.7	-29.4	-41.2	-55.5

Winchester 260-grain Partition Gold (SPG454)
G1 Ballistic Coefficient = 0.175

Distance • Yards	Muzzle	25	50	75	100	125	150	175	200
Velocity • fps	1800	1700	1605	1513	1427	1349	1276	1211	1154
Energy • Ft-lbs	1871	1668	1486	1322	1178	1051	941	847	769
Taylor KO Index	30.4	28.7	27.1	25.5	24.1	22.7	21.5	20.4	19.5
Mid-Range Trajectory Height • Inches	0.0	0.1	0.3	0.9	1.6	2.8	4.3	6.2	8.6
Drop • Inches	0.0	-0.4	-1.4	-3.4	-6.3	-10.2	-15.4	-21.9	-29.9

Winchester 260-grain Platinum Tip (S454PTHP)
G1 Ballistic Coefficient = 0.168

Distance • Yards	Muzzle	25	50	75	100	125	150	175	200
Velocity • fps	1800	1696	1596	1503	1414	1334	1260	1195	1138
Energy • Ft-lbs	1870	1661	1470	1304	1154	1027	917	824	748
Taylor KO Index	30.2	28.5	26.8	25.2	23.7	22.4	21.2	20.1	19.1
Mid-Range Trajectory Height • Inches	0.0	0.1	0.4	0.9	1.7	2.9	4.4	6.4	8.8
Drop • Inches	0.0	-0.4	-1.5	-3.4	-6.3	-10.3	-15.6	-22.2	-30.3

Cor-Bon 265-grain BondedCore HP (HT454265BHP/20)

G1 Ballistic Coefficient = 0.170

Distance • Yards	Muzzle	25	50	75	100	125	150	175	200
Velocity • fps	1800	1697	1599	1506	1418	1338	1264	1199	1142
Energy • Ft-lbs	1907	1695	1504	1334	1184	1053	941	846	768
Taylor KO Index	30.9	29.2	27.5	25.9	24.4	23.0	21.7	20.6	19.6
Mid-Range Trajectory Height • Inches	0.0	0.1	0.3	0.9	1.7	2.8	4.3	6.3	8.7
Drop • Inches	0.0	-0.4	-1.4	-3.4	-6.3	-10.3	-15.5	-22.1	-30.2

Cor-Bon 265-grain BondedCore SP (HT454285BC/20)

G1 Ballistic Coefficient = 0.180

Distance • Yards	Muzzle	25	50	75	100	125	150	175	200
Velocity • fps	1700	1607	1518	1435	1357	1286	1222	1165	1116
Energy • Ft-lbs	1829	1634	1459	1304	1166	1047	945	859	788
Taylor KO Index	31.4	29.7	28.1	26.5	25.1	23.8	22.6	21.5	20.6
Mid-Range Trajectory Height • Inches	0.0	0.1	0.4	1.0	1.8	3.1	4.7	6.9	9.5
Drop • Inches	0.0	-0.4	-1.6	-3.8	-7.0	-11.4	-17.2	-24.3	-33.1

Cor-Bon 300-grain JSP (HT454300JSP/20)

G1 Ballistic Coefficient = 0.185

Distance • Yards	Muzzle	25	50	75	100	125	150	175	200
Velocity • fps	1650	1562	1478	1399	1326	1260	1200	1147	1102
Energy • Ft-lbs	1814	1625	1456	1305	1172	1057	959	877	809
Taylor KO Index	32.1	30.4	28.8	27.2	25.8	24.5	23.3	22.3	21.4
Mid-Range Trajectory Height • Inches	0.0	0.1	0.4	1.0	2.0	3.2	5.0	7.2	9.9
Drop • Inches	0.0	-0.4	-1.7	-4.0	-7.4	-12.1	-18.1	-25.6	-34.8

Hornady 300-grain XTP-MAG (9150)

G1 Ballistic Coefficient = 0.200

Distance • Yards	Muzzle	25	50	75	100	125	150	175	200
Velocity • fps	1650	1568	1490	1417	1348	1285	1227	1175	1089
Energy • Ft-lbs	1813	1639	1480	1338	1210	1100	1003	919	849
Taylor KO Index	32.0	30.4	28.9	27.4	26.1	24.9	23.8	22.8	21.1
Mid-Range Trajectory Height • Inches	0.0	0.1	0.4	1.1	2.0	3.2	4.9	7.1	9.7
Drop • Inches	0.0	-0.4	-1.7	-4.0	-7.3	-11.9	-17.8	-25.1	34.0

Speer 300-grain Gold Dot Hollow Point (23990)

G1 Ballistic Coefficient = 0.233

Distance • Yards	Muzzle	25	50	75	100	125	150	175	200
Velocity • fps	1625	1556	1489	1426	1366	1310	1258	1210	1167
Energy • Ft-lbs	1759	1612	1477	1355	1243	1143	1054	975	907
Taylor KO Index	31.5	30.1	28.8	27.6	26.5	25.4	24.4	23.4	22.6
Mid-Range Trajectory Height • Inches	0.0	0.1	0.4	1.1	2.0	3.2	4.8	6.9	9.4
Drop • Inches	0.0	-0.4	-1.8	-4.1	-7.4	-12.0	-17.8	-24.9	-33.6

Winchester 300-grain Jacketed Flat Point (X454C22)

G1 Ballistic Coefficient = 0.186

Distance • Yards	Muzzle	25	50	75	100	125	150	175	200
Velocity • fps	1625	1538	1451	1380	1308	1244	1186	1136	1092
Energy • Ft-lbs	1759	1577	1413	1268	1141	1031	938	860	795
Taylor KO Index	31.5	29.8	28.1	26.7	25.3	24.1	23.0	22.0	21.2
Mid-Range Trajectory Height • Inches	0.0	0.1	0.5	1.1	2.0	3.3	5.1	7.4	10.2
Drop • Inches	0.0	-0.4	-1.8	-4.1	-7.6	-12.4	-18.6	-26.3	-35.8

Cor-Bon 320-grain FP Penetrator (HT454320FPPN/20)

G1 Ballistic Coefficient = 0.190

Distance • Yards	Muzzle	25	50	75	100	125	150	175	200
Velocity • fps	1600	1516	1437	1364	1295	1233	1178	1129	1087
Energy • Ft-lbs	1816	1634	1469	1321	1192	1081	986	906	841
Taylor KO Index	33.2	31.5	29.8	28.3	26.9	25.6	24.4	23.4	22.6
Mid-Range Trajectory Height • Inches	0.0	0.1	0.4	1.1	2.1	3.4	5.2	7.6	10.4
Drop • Inches	0.0	-0.4	-1.8	-4.3	-7.9	-12.8	-19.1	-27.0	-36.6

Cor-Bon 335-grain HardCast (HT454335HC/20)

G1 Ballistic Coefficient = 0.195

Distance • Yards	Muzzle	25	50	75	100	125	150	175	200
Velocity • fps	1600	1519	1441	1369	1302	1241	1186	1137	1096
Energy • Ft-lbs	1905	1716	1546	1395	1261	1145	1046	963	893
Taylor KO Index	34.8	33.0	31.3	29.7	28.3	27.0	25.8	24.7	23.8
Mid-Range Trajectory Height • Inches	0.0	0.1	0.4	1.1	2.1	3.4	5.2	7.5	10.3
Drop • Inches	0.0	-0.4	-1.8	-4.2	-7.8	-12.7	-19.0	-26.8	-36.3

.475 Linebaugh

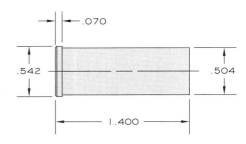

This cartridge is very similar in both size and performance to the .480 Ruger. Both cartridges use .475-diameter bullets. The Linebaugh case is a bit longer (0.115 inch), but both use the same dies for reloading. Judging by the factory numbers, the Linebaugh is loaded to slightly higher pressures. This suggests you might be able to shoot the .480 Ruger ammo in the .475 Linebaugh chamber, although the only reason I can see for doing that would be for the sake of availability.

Relative Recoil Factor = 2.30

Specifications

Controlling Agency for Standardization of this Ammunition: SAAMI
Standard barrel for velocity testing: 7.5 inches long [Vented]—1 turn in 18-inch twist

Availability

Hornady 400-grain XTP-MAG (9140)

G1 Ballistic Coefficient = 0.182

Distance • Yards	Muzzle	25	50	75	100	125	150	175	200
Velocity • fps	1300	1235	1177	1127	1084	1047	1015	987	961
Energy • Ft-lbs	1501	1355	1231	1129	1043	974	915	865	821
Taylor KO Index	35.3	33.5	31.9	30.6	29.4	28.4	27.6	26.8	26.1
Mid-Range Trajectory Height • Inches	0.0	0.2	0.7	1.7	3.1	5.1	7.7	10.9	14.7
Drop • Inches	0.0	-0.7	-2.8	-6.4	-11.8	-19.0	-28.2	-39.5	-53.0

Austrian hunter Carl Pisec and his son pose next to the lion Carl shot in the Zambezi Valley. (Photo from *A Pioneering Hunter* by Brian Marsh, Safari Press, 2006)

.480 Ruger

Here's another entrant in the powerful pistol category. Hornady and Ruger cooperated to produce a totally new round. Everything about this cartridge is big. It has slightly less relative recoil than either the .454 Cassul or the .50 Action Express, but it is far from wimpy. This cartridge will find some immediate favor with pistol hunters, but it has no application to any of the current competition games. This cartridge should be an excellent performer in lever-action, carbine-style rifles.

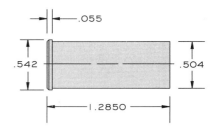

Relative Recoil Factor = 1.95

Specifications

Controlling Agency for Standardization of this Ammunition: Factory
Standard barrel for velocity testing: 7.5 inches long (vented)—1 turn in N/S-inch twist*
*Twist not yet defined

Availability

Hornady 325-grain XTP-MAG (9138)

G1 Ballistic Coefficient = 0.149

Distance • Yards	Muzzle	25	50	75	100	125	150	175	200
Velocity • fps	1350	1265	1191	1129	1076	1033	997	965	936
Energy • Ft-lbs	1315	1156	1023	919	835	771	717	672	633
Taylor KO Index	30.1	28.2	26.5	25.2	24.0	23.0	22.2	21.5	20.9
Mid-Range Trajectory Height • Inches	0.0	0.1	0.6	1.6	3.0	5.0	7.6	10.9	14.7
Drop • Inches	0.0	-0.6	-2.6	-6.1	-11.3	-18.4	-27.5	-38.7	-52.2

Hornady 400-grain XTP-MAG (9144)

G1 Ballistic Coefficient = 0.182

Distance • Yards	Muzzle	25	50	75	100	125	150	175	200
Velocity • fps	1100	1061	1027	997	971	947	925	904	885
Energy • Ft-lbs	1075	1000	937	884	838	797	760	726	696
Taylor KO Index	29.9	28.8	27.9	27.1	26.4	25.7	25.1	24.5	24.0
Mid-Range Trajectory Height • Inches	0.0	0.2	1.0	2.3	4.1	6.6	9.8	13.8	18.4
Drop • Inches	0.0	-0.9	-3.8	-8.7	-15.8	-25.2	-37.0	-51.3	-68.4

.500 Smith & Wesson Special Magnum and .500 Smith & Wesson Magnum.

.50 Action Express

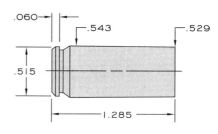

This is no longer the "big boomer" of the pistol rounds, having been replaced by the .500 S&W. It remains the king of the auto pistol hill. The .50 Action Express, which was introduced in 1991, packs about the same muzzle energy as a .30-30 with much higher Taylor KO Index values. This is because the .50 AE pushes a very much heavier bullet but at a lower velocity. This is one of those calibers for the macho pistol shooter. As with the .44 Remington Magnum and the .454 Casull, there are few shooters who can shoot the .50 AE really well. The .50 AE cartridge chambered into a carbine-style gun would make an interesting deer rifle for brushy hunting conditions where long shots aren't normally encountered.

Relative Recoil Factor = 2.05

Specifications

Controlling Agency for Standardization of this Ammunition: SAAMI

Bullet Weight Grains	Velocity fps	Maximum Average Pressure	
		Copper Crusher	Transducer
300 PHP	1,400	N/S	35,000 psi

Standard barrel for velocity testing: 6 inches long—1 turn in 20-inch twist

Availability

Speer 300-grain Gold Dot Hollow Point (23995)

G1 Ballistic Coefficient = 0.155

Distance • Yards	Muzzle	25	50	75	100	125	150	175	200
Velocity • fps	1550	1452	1361	1278	1205	1143	1090	1047	1009
Energy • Ft-lbs	1600	1404	1233	1089	968	870	792	730	679
Taylor KO Index	33.2	31.1	29.2	27.4	25.8	24.5	23.4	22.4	21.6
Mid-Range Trajectory Height • Inches	0.0	0.1	0.5	1.3	2.4	3.9	6.0	8.7	12.0
Drop • Inches	0.0	-0.5	-2.0	-4.7	-8.7	-14.2	-21.3	-30.3	-41.3

Speer 325-grain UCHP (3977)

G1 Ballistic Coefficient = 0.169

Distance • Yards	Muzzle	25	50	75	100	125	150	175	200
Velocity • fps	1400	1321	1249	1185	1130	1084	1044	1010	980
Energy • Ft-lbs	1414	1259	1125	1014	921	848	787	737	694
Taylor KO Index	32.5	30.7	29.0	27.5	26.2	25.2	24.2	23.4	22.8
Mid-Range Trajectory Height • Inches	0.0	0.1	0.6	1.5	2.8	4.6	7.0	10.0	13.6
Drop • Inches	0.0	-0.6	-2.4	-5.6	-10.4	-16.8	-25.2	-35.5	-47.9

.500 Smith & Wesson Special

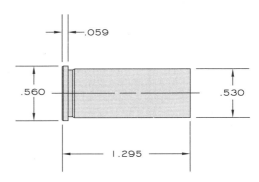

In 2005, Cor-Bon reversed a page out of an old book. Recognizing that the .500 Smith & Wesson Magnum cartridge was not going to be a lot of fun to shoot, they came up with the .500 Smith & Wesson Special. The dimensions are such that just as with the .38 Special and the .357 Magnum or the .45 Colt in the .454 Casull, this cartridge can be fired in S&W Magnum guns. With the milder impulse of this smaller cartridge, the recoil will be down about 20 percent. This is still a pretty potent round and it may well be that reloaders will be making up some even milder loads in the cowboy action class, even though the gun wouldn't qualify for Single Action events.

Relative Recoil Factor = 2.36

Specifications

Controlling Agency for Standardization of this Ammunition: Factory
Standard barrel for velocity testing: 10 inches long—1 turn in 18.75-inch twist

Availability

Cor-Bon 275-grain Barnes-X (HT500S275/12)

G1 Ballistic Coefficient = 0.120

Distance • Yards	Muzzle	25	50	75	100	125	150	175	200
Velocity • fps	1350	1247	1160	1090	1035	990	952	919	889
Energy • Ft-lbs	1113	949	822	726	654	599	554	515	482
Taylor KO Index	26.5	24.5	22.8	21.4	20.4	19.4	18.7	18.1	17.5
Mid-Range Trajectory Height • Inches	0.0	0.2	0.4	1.4	2.9	5.1	7.8	11.5	15.8
Drop • Inches	0.0	-0.6	-2.7	-6.3	-11.8	-19.3	-29.0	-41.1	-55.8

Cor-Bon 275-grain JHP (HT500S275/12)

G1 Ballistic Coefficient = 0.154

Distance • Yards	Muzzle	25	50	75	100	125	150	175	200
Velocity • fps	1350	1268	1196	1135	1083	1040	1004	972	944
Energy • Ft-lbs	1417	1250	1112	1001	912	841	783	734	692
Taylor KO Index	33.8	31.7	29.9	28.4	27.1	26.0	25.1	24.3	23.6
Mid-Range Trajectory Height • Inches	0.0	0.2	0.4	1.6	2.7	5.0	7.2	10.8	14.4
Drop • Inches	0.0	-0.6	-2.6	-6.1	-11.3	-18.3	-27.3	-38.5	-52.0

Cor-Bon 350-grain FMJ (HT500S275/12)

G1 Ballistic Coefficient = 0.154

Distance • Yards	Muzzle	25	50	75	100	125	150	175	200
Velocity • fps	1200	1138	1086	1042	1006	974	945	919	896
Energy • Ft-lbs	1119	1006	917	845	786	737	695	657	624
Taylor KO Index	30.0	28.5	27.2	26.1	25.2	24.4	23.6	23.0	22.4
Mid-Range Trajectory Height • Inches	0.0	0.1	0.8	1.9	3.6	5.9	8.9	12.6	17.1
Drop • Inches	0.0	-0.8	-3.2	-7.5	-13.8	-22.3	-33.0	-46.2	-61.9

.500 Smith & Wesson Special Magnum

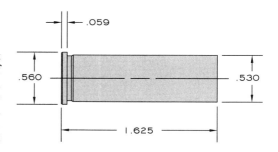

This cartridge was introduced in 2004. For now, this is the most potent handgun in the commercial inventory. By all accounts it is a beast to shoot, but if the idea of a hugely powerful handgun turns you on, this is the gun for you. A glance at the energy and Taylor numbers shows some loadings of this round to be more potent than the .308 Winchester. But the numbers don't matter a bit if you can't shoot the gun accurately and I wonder how many shooters can. Like several other large, rimmed, pistol cartridges, the .500 S&W would make an excellent cartridge for lever-action carbines.

Relative Recoil Factor = 2.95

Specifications

Controlling Agency for Standardization of this Ammunition: SAAMI

Bullet Weight Grains	Velocity fps	Maximum Average Pressure	
		Copper Crusher	Transducer
N/A	1400	N/S	N/A

Standard barrel for velocity testing: 10 inches long—1 turn in 18.75-inch twist

Availability

Cor-Bon 275-grain (HT500SW275/12)
G1 Ballistic Coefficient = 0.120

Distance • Yards	Muzzle	25	50	75	100	125	150	175	200
Velocity • fps	1600	1470	1352	1249	1162	1092	1036	991	953
Energy • Ft-lbs	1564	1320	1117	952	824	728	656	600	554
Taylor KO Index	31.4	28.9	26.6	24.5	22.8	21.5	20.4	19.6	18.7
Mid-Range Trajectory Height • Inches	0.0	0.1	0.5	1.3	2.4	4.1	6.3	9.3	12.8
Drop • Inches	0.0	-0.4	-1.9	-4.6	-8.6	-14.2	-21.7	-31.2	-42.9

Magtech 275-grain SCHP (500C)
G1 Ballistic Coefficient = 0.120

Distance • Yards	Muzzle	25	50	75	100	125	150	175	200
Velocity • fps	1667	1555	1443	1354	1267	1192	1128	1075	1032
Energy • Ft-lbs	1696	1477	1272	1120	964	868	778	706	650
Taylor KO Index	32.7	30.5	28.3	26.6	24.9	23.4	22.2	21.1	20.3
Mid-Range Trajectory Height • Inches	0.0	0.1	0.5	1.1	2.1	3.5	5.4	7.9	10.9
Drop • Inches	0.0	-0.4	-1.7	-4.1	-7.6	-12.5	-18.9	-27.0	-37.0

Magtech 325-grain SCSP—Flat (500A)
G1 Ballistic Coefficient = 0.154

Distance • Yards	Muzzle	25	50	75	100	125	150	175	200
Velocity • fps	1801	1655	1520	1396	1286	1192	1115	1054	1005
Energy • Ft-lbs	2341	1978	1667	1407	1194	1025	897	802	730
Taylor KO Index	41.8	38.4	35.3	32.4	29.9	27.7	25.9	24.5	23.3
Mid-Range Trajectory Height • Inches	0.0	0.1	0.4	1.0	1.9	3.3	5.1	7.6	10.7
Drop • Inches	0.0	-0.4	-1.5	-3.6	-6.8	-11.3	-17.4	-25.2	-34.9

Cor-Bon 325-grain XPB (HT500SW325/12)
G1 Ballistic Coefficient = 0.130

Distance • Yards	Muzzle	25	50	75	100	125	150	175	200
Velocity • fps	1800	1666	1541	1425	1321	1229	1151	1088	1037
Energy • Ft-lbs	2338	2004	1714	1467	1259	1090	957	855	776
Taylor KO Index	41.8	38.7	35.8	33.1	30.7	28.5	26.7	25.3	24.1
Mid-Range Trajectory Height • Inches	0.0	0.1	0.4	1.0	1.8	3.2	4.9	9.2	10.1
Drop • Inches	0.0	-0.4	-1.5	-3.5	-6.7	-11.0	-16.8	-24.3	-33.6

Hornady 350-grain XTP—MAG (9250)

G1 Ballistic Coefficient = 0.145

Distance • Yards	Muzzle	25	50	75	100	125	150	175	200
Velocity • fps	1900	1775	1656	1544	1439	1344	1258	1183	1069
Energy • Ft-lbs	2805	2449	2131	1853	1610	1404	1230	1089	979
Taylor KO Index	47.5	44.4	41.4	38.6	36.0	33.6	31.5	29.6	26.7
Mid-Range Trajectory Height • Inches	0.0	0.1	0.4	0.9	1.6	2.7	4.2	6.1	8.6
Drop • Inches	0.0	-0.3	-1.3	-3.1	-5.8	-9.6	-14.6	-20.9	-28.8

Cor-Bon 350-grain JHP (HT500SW350/12)

G1 Ballistic Coefficient = 0.145

Distance • Yards	Muzzle	25	50	75	100	125	150	175	200
Velocity • fps	1600	1492	1391	1300	1220	1151	1094	1047	1007
Energy • Ft-lbs	1990	1730	1505	1314	1157	1030	930	852	788
Taylor KO Index	40.0	37.3	34.8	32.5	30.5	28.8	27.4	26.2	25.2
Mid-Range Trajectory Height • Inches	0.0	0.1	0.5	1.2	2.3	3.8	5.8	8.5	11.7
Drop • Inches	0.0	-0.4	-1.9	-4.4	-8.2	-13.5	-20.5	-29.2	-39.9

Cor-Bon 385-grain BC (HT500SW385/12)

G1 Ballistic Coefficient = 0.150

Distance • Yards	Muzzle	25	50	75	100	125	150	175	200
Velocity • fps	1725	1613	1507	1409	1319	1239	1169	1110	1062
Energy • Ft-lbs	2554	2240	1942	1697	1487	1312	1168	1054	964
Taylor KO Index	47.4	44.4	41.4	38.7	36.3	34.1	32.1	30.5	29.2
Mid-Range Trajectory Height • Inches	0.0	0.1	0.4	1.0	2.0	3.2	5.0	7.3	10.1
Drop • Inches	0.0	-0.4	-1.6	-3.8	-7.0	-11.6	-17.5	-25.0	-34.3

Magtech 400-grain SJSP—Flat (500A)

G1 Ballistic Coefficient = 0.154

Distance • Yards	Muzzle	25	50	75	100	125	150	175	200
Velocity • fps	1608	1505	1408	1322	1242	1175	1117	1068	1028
Energy • Ft-lbs	2297	2013	1762	1552	1370	1226	1108	1014	938
Taylor KO Index	45.9	43.0	40.2	37.8	35.5	33.6	31.9	30.5	29.4
Mid-Range Trajectory Height • Inches	0.0	0.1	0.5	1.2	2.2	3.7	5.6	8.2	11.3
Drop • Inches	0.0	-0.4	-1.8	-4.3	-8.1	-13.2	-19.9	-28.4	-38.8

Cor-Bon 400-grain SP (HT500SW400SP/12)

G1 Ballistic Coefficient = 0.154

Distance • Yards	Muzzle	25	50	75	100	125	150	175	200
Velocity • fps	1625	1521	1424	1335	1255	1185	1125	1075	1034
Energy • Ft-lbs	2346	2056	1802	1584	1400	1247	1125	1027	949
Taylor KO Index	46.4	43.5	40.7	38.1	35.9	33.9	32.1	30.7	29.5
Mid-Range Trajectory Height • Inches	0.0	0.1	0.5	1.1	2.2	3.6	5.5	8.1	11.1
Drop • Inches	0.0	-0.4	-1.8	-4.2	-7.9	-12.9	-19.5	-27.8	-38.0

Cor-Bon 440-grain HC (HT500SW440HC/12)

G1 Ballistic Coefficient = 0.160

Distance • Yards	Muzzle	25	50	75	100	125	150	175	200
Velocity • fps	1625	1525	1431	1345	1267	1197	1138	1087	1045
Energy • Ft-lbs	2580	2272	2002	1767	1568	1401	1265	1156	1068
Taylor KO Index	51.1	47.9	45.0	42.3	39.8	37.5	35.8	34.2	32.8
Mid-Range Trajectory Height • Inches	0.0	0.1	0.5	1.1	2.1	3.5	5.4	7.9	10.9
Drop • Inches	0.0	-0.4	-1.8	-4.2	-7.8	-12.8	-19.3	-27.5	-37.5

Hornady 500-grain FP—XTP (9252)

G1 Ballistic Coefficient = 0.176

Distance • Yards	Muzzle	25	50	75	100	125	150	175	200
Velocity • fps	1425	1347	1281	1211	1154	1106	1065	1029	998
Energy • Ft-lbs	2254	2014	1823	1627	1505	1358	1258	1176	1107
Taylor KO Index	50.9	48.1	45.8	43.3	41.2	39.5	38.0	36.8	35.6
Mid-Range Trajectory Height • Inches	0.0	0.1	0.6	1.4	2.7	4.4	6.7	9.6	13.0
Drop • Inches	0.0	-0.6	-2.3	-5.4	-10.0	-16.2	-24.2	-34.0	-46.0

A Tale of Two Rimfires

James E. House

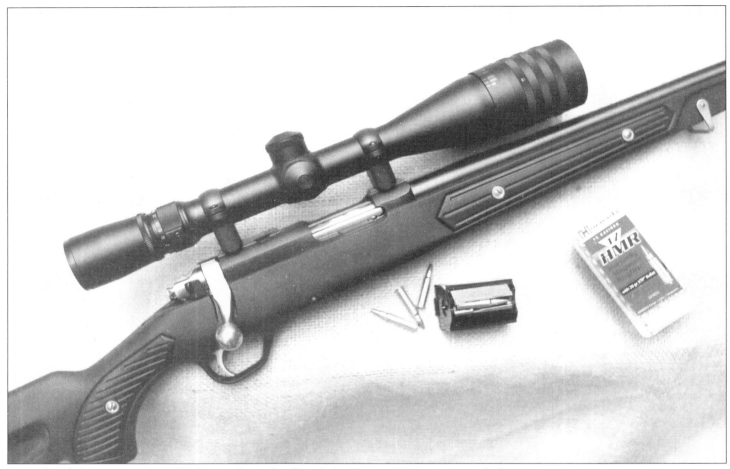

Ruger's 77/17 is an accurate rifle that performed well with the Weaver V-16 scope attached.

A century ago, there were many rimfire cartridges with diameters larger than .22. The .25 Stevens was one of the most useful because it let shooters use a rimfire rifle on larger animals, such as foxes and coyotes. However, the .25, .32, .38, and .44 rimfires—some in both short and long versions—are gone. The .22 WMR was introduced in 1959, and it has been very successful.

But a couple of years ago, a new kid hit the scene: the .17 Hornady Magnum Rimfire (HMR). The rimfire shooting sports will never be the same.

Comparisons, Contrasts

Advances in propellants made it possible to produce an efficient, bottlenecked, small-caliber rimfire cartridge. But although it has received lots of press, the .17 HMR is not the first such venture.

In 1970, the 5mm Remington hit the scene. It used a case with a base diameter slightly larger than that of the .22 WMR, but it was necked down to hold a .20-caliber bullet. The 5mm was supposed to drive a 38-grain bullet at 2,100 feet per second. Given the propellants available at that time, pressures apparently were higher than those produced by the .22 WMR, and problems arose. As a result, few 5mm rifles were produced, and the ammunition now sells as a collectible for around 50 to 75 dollars per box.

The .17 HMR is a .22 WMR case necked to hold a 0.172-inch-diameter bullet. The first ammunition used a 17-grain spitzer bullet with a polycarbonate tip and a boattail configuration. Soon afterward, the 17-grain TNT hollowpoint was introduced by CCI. Federal and Remington joined the marketing frenzy with cartridges featuring polymer-tipped 17-grain bullets. (Incidentally,

CCI loads both cartridges, and they have advertised muzzle velocities of 2,550 fps.)

Soon, folks formed varying opinions about using the .17 HMR on varmints. At short ranges, the tiny bullet traveling at high velocity produces dramatic effects. However, at ranges of 150 yards or farther, the bullets lose enough velocity that they sometimes have little or no expansion. Also, they sometimes don't penetrate adequately with varmints such as foxes, coyotes, or large groundhogs because the bullet expands violently. It soon became evident that a heavier bullet was needed, so Hornady introduced the 20-grain XTP hollowpoint, and CCI introduced the 20-grain Game Point, another hollowpoint. Both loads have advertised muzzle velocities of 2,375 fps. These bullets have heavier jackets and are intended to make the .17 HMR more reliable on larger varmints.

The initial idea behind the .17 HMR was to produce a rimfire cartridge that provided greater accuracy, a flatter trajectory, and less noise than the .22 WMR. To some extent, the cartridge met those goals. However, the .17 HMR is different from the .22 WMR. First, .17 HMR ammo is produced with what are essentially premium bullets. That's not true with the .22 WMR, for which some of the rounds use ordinary jacketed or plated bullets. So, the accuracy of the cartridges should only be compared using premium .22 WMR ammo. The .17 HMR produces 245 foot-pounds of muzzle energy, and the .22 WMR produces about 320 foot-pounds. At 50 yards, the remaining energies are 185 and 220 foot-

The Ruger 77/22M is a beautiful rifle that will handle many types of varmints.

pounds, respectively. At 100 yards, they are 135 and 155 foot-pounds, respectively, depending on the load.

A friend who uses both cartridges for coyotes said it's not uncommon to see a coyote go down but then get up and run for 40 to 50 yards when shot with a .17 HMR. He said coyotes that are hit similarly with a .22 WMR usually stay down. Greater energy and deeper penetration make the .22 WMR better for larger varmints. Actually, the .17 HMR was never intended as a cartridge for coyote hunting. However, part of the performance disparity will disappear if you use newer .17 HMR ammunition with 20-grain bullets.

Accuracy Assessment

To compare the accuracy of the .17 HMR and .22 WMR, I used two Ruger bolt-action rifles: a 77/17 with a synthetic stock, and a 77/22M with a walnut stock. The 77/17 had a Weaver Classic V-16 scope, and the 77/22M

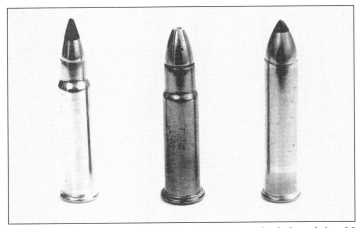

The magnum rimfires include the .17 HMR on the left and the .22 WMR on the right. In the middle is the 5mm Remington which had a short life in the 1970s.

This lineup of .22 WMR cartridges includes (left to right) the Remington Premier, Winchester Supreme, CCI Maxi Mag TMJ, Winchester Super-X HP, CCI Maxi Mag HP, and the 50-grain Federal HP. More types of ammunition are available in .22 WMR than are in .17 HMR.

had an older Weaver V-12 scope. The 16X scope gave the 77/17 a slight advantage. I fired five five-shot groups with each rifle at 50 yards. I determined group size by measuring the distance between the centers of the two widest shots.

With the .22 WMR, I fired Winchester Super-X, CCI Maxi Mag, CCI TNT, Remington Premier, and Federal Premium. Three of the four types of .17 HMR ammo tested had 17-grain polymer-tip bullets; the CCI TNT is a hollowpoint.

I've reported the results, in inches, in the accompanying tables.

.17 HMR Groups

Ammunition	Smallest	Largest	Average
CCI TNT	0.38	0.73	0.67
Federal V Shok	0.33	0.75	0.57
Hornady V-Max	0.52	0.63	0.53
Remington Premier	0.50	0.84	0.63
Overall average			0.60

.22 WMR Groups

Ammunition	Smallest	Largest	Average
CCI Maxi Mag 40-grain HP	0.57	0.72	0.65
CCI TNT 30-grain HP	0.63	1.01	0.77
Federal Premium 30-grain HP	0.48	1.03	0.72
Remington Premier 33-grain V-Max	0.62	0.81	0.73
Winchester Super-X 40-grain HP	0.57	0.89	0.78
Overall average			0.73

Though my tests are far from exhaustive, they indicate that—at least in my Rugers—the .17 HMR has a slight accuracy advantage. Of course, part of that might stem from the higher power and very fine cross hairs of the Weaver V-16 scope on the .17.

Many people believe the .17 HMR is inherently more accurate. However, if the barrels in a .22 WMR and in a .17 HMR have the same outside contour—which is usually the case—the .17 HMR barrel has thicker walls because of the smaller bore. Almost any .17 HMR barrel should perform like a heavy barrel would in .22 caliber.

I believe there's little difference in accuracy if you use bullets of equivalent quality. Because accuracy is a strong point with the .17 HMR, tolerances are likely tighter than with most .22 WRM ammo. In my rifles, there's no significant difference when shooting varmints at 100 to 125 yards.

Head to Head

The .17 HMR and the .22 WMR let you do some serious varmint hunting out to 150 yards. With smaller

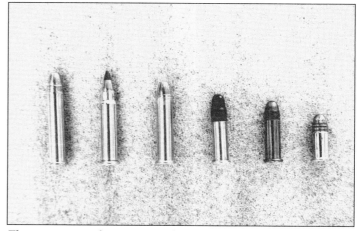

The spectrum of current rimfire ammunition includes (left to right) the .22 WMR, .17 HMR, .22 WRF, .22 Long Rifle, .22 Long, and .22 Short.

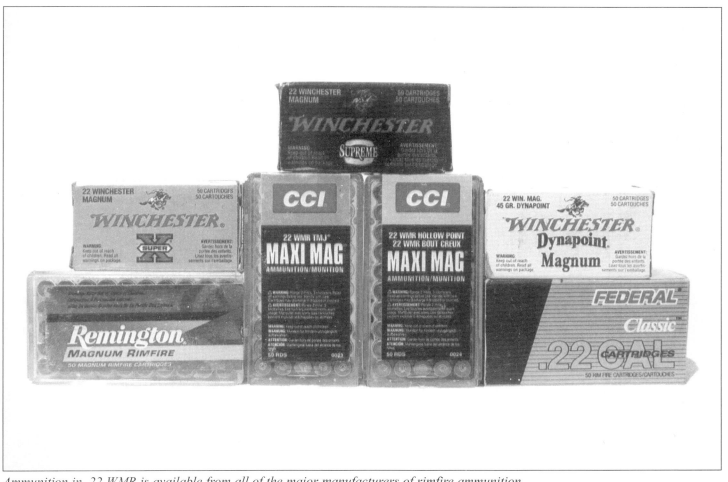

Ammunition in .22 WMR is available from all of the major manufacturers of rimfire ammunition.

varmints, the .17 HMR has the edge, but the .22 WMR works better on larger animals.

The major advantage of the .17 HMR over the .22 WMR is in trajectory. Because the velocity of the .17 HMR is considerably higher than that of the .22 WMR, you can hit varmints at longer distances. However, for the .17 HMR the remaining energy at 150 yards is only 100 foot-pounds, which is comparable to a .22 LR at 50 yards. That is adequate for small varmints, but with groundhogs or prairie dogs, you must place your shots accurately for quick kills.

I've measured velocities produced by all .17 HMR loads and most .22 WMR loads, and usually they are close to the advertised velocities. The Remington Premier .22 WMR load, which has a 33-grain Hornady V-Max bullet with a polymer tip, is an exception. I measured the average velocity from my Ruger 77/22M at 2,253 fps, which is about 200 fps faster than the published value. That load would produce a muzzle energy of about 370 foot-pounds, which is much higher than that of any .17

HMR load. It also gives a trajectory that's not much different from that of the .17 HMR.

Remember, you have much more .22 WMR ammo from which to choose, including 30- to 50-grain bullets with full metal jackets, and in soft- and hollowpoint. With the .17 HMR, only 17-grain polymer-tip and hollowpoint, and 20-grain hollowpoint bullets, are available.

Two Capable Performers

The .22 WMR and .17 HMR are powerful, accurate cartridges that perform well in many situations. Either works fine if you place the bullets properly, but you shouldn't expect them to equal the performance of a centerfire rifle.

Now, if someone would just resurrect the 5mm Remington, varmint hunters would have a range of rimfire calibers that would fulfill almost any need.

It's an exciting time for rimfire shooters.

Data for Rimfire Ammunition

This section covers rimfire ammunition in its various forms. While some of this ammunition is used primarily in pistols, the SAAMI specifications for all .22 rimfire variations call for testing in 24-inch barrels. Some manufacturers also report performance in pistol-length barrels, but because these data are somewhat unstandardized in terms of barrel lengths used, the results can't always be used for detailed comparison. In the final analysis, if knowing the exact velocity is really critical to your shooting application, you have to chronograph a sample of the ammunition in question in your own gun.

There's an interesting situation regarding some brands of match and training ammunition. These manufacturers make their match and training ammo on the same production line, using identical components, the same everything. In fact, they don't know which grade they are making until it is tested, then the best becomes the match grade. Quite often the ammo coming off the production line is so good that there's more match quality ammo than can be sold, so the excess supply simply becomes the training grade. It could be just as good as the match-quality grade, but of course there's no guarantee. There is at least one manufacturer that makes three grades on the same production line.

.17 PMC–.17 Aguila

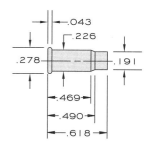

Small calibers have always held a special fascination for shooters. It was pretty much a sure thing that when the .17 HMR took hold, a .17-caliber rimfire based on the .22 Long Rifle case was not going to be far behind. Early in 2005 there were actually two slightly different new .17s introduced. This version was initially developed by Aguila. It is based on the standard length .22 LR case. With a 20-grain jacketed bullet at or in excess of 1800 fps, it provides a flat-shooting, light-varmint capability out to at least 100 yards. This round can be adapted to conversions of Ruger's 10-22 semi-auto with nothing more than a switch of barrel (a 5-minute job.)

Relative Recoil Factor = 0.16

Specifications

Controlling Agency for Standardization of this Ammunition: SAAMI (Pending)

Bullet Weight Grains	Velocity fps	Maximum Average Pressure	
		Copper Crusher	Transducer

Standard barrel for velocity testing: 24 inches long—1 turn in 16-inch twist

Availability

Aguila 20-grain Jacketed Soft Point
G1 Ballistic Coefficient = 0.105

Distance • Yards	Muzzle	25	50	75	100	125	150	175	200
Velocity • fps	1850	1682	1527	1387	1267	1163	1084	1023	975
Energy • Ft-lbs	152	126	104	86	71	60	52	46	42
Path • Inches	-1.5	+0.2	+1.1	+1.1	0.0	-2.5	-6.6	-12.5	-20.6
Wind Drift • Inches	0.0	0.4	1.5	3.4	6.2	10.0	14.6	20.0	26.1

PMC 20-grain JSP (.17PMC)
G1 Ballistic Coefficient = 0.134

Distance • Yards	Muzzle	25	50	75	100	125	150	175	200
Velocity • fps	1800	1672	1552	1439	1332	1242	1164	1100	1048
Energy • Ft-lbs	144	124	106	92	79	68	60	54	49
Path • Inches	-1.5	+0.2	+1.1	+1.1	0.0	-2.3	-6.0	-11.3	-18.4
Wind Drift • Inches	0.0	0.3	1.2	2.7	4.9	7.8	11.1	15.8	20.8

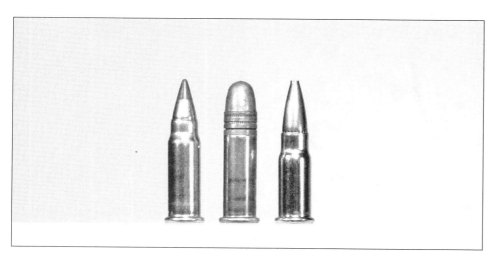

(Left to right) .17 Mach 2, .22 Long Rifle, and .17 PMC/Aguila.

.17 Mach 2

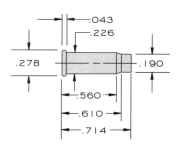

In 2005, Hornady followed their .17 HMR with the .17 Mach 2. This is another .17 rimfire based on the .22 Long Rifle case (well sort of). This particular round seems to be based on the Stinger case, which is slightly longer than the regular .22 LR. Overall length is the same as for .22 LR ammo so gun conversion problems are somewhat minimized. Not all blowback-style .22 semi-auto rifles can be converted to this cartridge without altering the bolt or mainspring along with a new barrel. That's not surprising since this round is somewhat more energetic than the .17 PMC.

Relative Recoil Factor = 0.17

Specifications

Controlling Agency for Standardization of this Ammunition: SAAMI (Pending)

Bullet Weight Grains	Velocity fps	Maximum Average Pressure Copper Crusher	Transducer

Standard barrel for velocity testing: 24 inches long—1 turn in 16-inch twist

Availability

Hornady 17-grain V-Max (83177)
G1 Ballistic Coefficient = 0.125

Distance • Yards	Muzzle	25	50	75	100	125	150	175	200
Velocity • fps	2100	1946	1799	1660	1530	1411	1304	1212	1134
Energy • Ft-lbs	166	143	122	104	88	75	64	55	49
Path • Inches	-1.5	-0.2	+0.7	+0.7	0.0	-1.6	-4.4	-8.3	-13.8
Wind Drift • Inches	0.0	0.2	1.0	2.4	4.4	7.1	10.3	14.7	19.7

Remington 17-grain AccuTip-V (PR17LR)
G1 Ballistic Coefficient = 0.125

Distance • Yards	Muzzle	25	50	75	100	125	150	175	200
Velocity • fps	2100	1946	1799	1660	1530	1411	1304	1212	1134
Energy • Ft-lbs	166	143	122	104	88	75	64	55	49
Path • Inches	-1.5	-0.2	+0.7	+0.7	0.0	-1.6	-4.4	-8.3	-13.8
Wind Drift • Inches	0.0	0.2	1.0	2.4	4.4	7.1	10.3	14.7	19.7

CCI 17-grain V-Max (0048)
G1 Ballistic Coefficient = 0.148

Distance • Yards	Muzzle	25	50	75	100	125	150	175	200
Velocity • fps	2010	1883	1759	1645	1535	1434	1341	1257	1184
Energy • Ft-lbs	153	134	117	102	89	78	68	60	53
Path • Inches	-1.5	-0.1	+0.7	+0.7	0.0	-1.6	-4.4	-8.3	-13.6
Wind Drift • Inches	0.0	0.2	0.9	2.1	3.8	6.2	9.1	12.7	17.0

Federal 17-grain Hornady V-Max (P780)
G1 Ballistic Coefficient = 0.125

Distance • Yards	Muzzle	25	50	75	100	125	150	175	200
Velocity • fps	2010	1860	1720	1584	1460	1348	1250	1165	1097
Energy • Ft-lbs	152	131	111	95	80	69	59	51	45
Path • Inches	-1.5	-0.1	+0.7	+0.8	0.0	-1.8	-4.8	-9.2	-15.3
Wind Drift • Inches	0.0	0.3	1.1	2.5	4.6	7.5	11.1	15.5	20.6

.17 Hornady Magnum Rimfire (HMR)

Hornady introduced their first entry into the rimfire field in 2002 with a .17 caliber that fires a jacketed ballistic tip bullet. Performance is not unlike the wildcat centerfires based on the .22 Hornet case. The ballistic performance is good. The fact that there are so many loadings available today illustrates the growing popularity of this little screamer.

Relative Recoil Factor = 0.19

Specifications

Controlling Agency for Standardization of this Ammunition: SAAMI (Pending)

Bullet Weight Grains	Velocity fps	Maximum Average Pressure	
		Copper Crusher	Transducer

Standard barrel for velocity testing: 24 inches long—1 turn in 16-inch twist

Availability

CCI 17-grain V-Max Bullet (83170)
G1 Ballistic Coefficient = 0.123

Distance • Yards	Muzzle	25	50	75	100	125	150	175	200
Velocity • fps	2550	2375	2199	2046	1892	1745	1608	1480	1364
Energy • Ft-lbs	246	213	184	158	135	115	98	83	70
Path • Inches	-1.5	-0.5	+0.2	+0.3	0.0	-0.9	-2.6	-5.1	-9.9
Wind Drift • Inches	0.0	0.2	0.8	1.8	3.4	5.4	8.1	11.5	15.6

CCI 17-grain V-Max (0049)
G1 Ballistic Coefficient = 0.139

Distance • Yards	Muzzle	25	50	75	100	125	150	175	200
Velocity • fps	2550	2395	2239	2101	1962	1828	1702	1582	1470
Energy • Ft-lbs	246	217	190	167	145	126	109	95	82
Path • Inches	-1.5	-0.5	+0.1	+0.3	0.0	-0.9	-2.4	-4.7	-7.8
Wind Drift • Inches	0.0	0.2	0.7	1.6	2.9	4.7	7.0	9.9	13.4

Federal 17-grain Hornady V-Max (P771)
G1 Ballistic Coefficient = 0.125

Distance • Yards	Muzzle	25	50	75	100	125	150	175	200
Velocity • fps	2550	2378	2210	2053	1900	1757	1620	1494	1378
Energy • Ft-lbs	245	213	185	159	135	117	100	84	72
Path • Inches	-1.5	-0.5	+0.2	+0.3	0.0	-0.9	-2.6	-5.0	-8.5
Wind Drift • Inches	0.0	0.2	0.8	1.8	3.3	5.3	8.0	11.3	15.3

Federal 17-grain Speer TNT JHP (P770)
G1 Ballistic Coefficient = 0.110

Distance • Yards	Muzzle	25	50	75	100	125	150	175	200
Velocity • fps	2550	2355	2170	1990	1820	1663	1520	1383	1267
Energy • Ft-lbs	245	209	175	150	125	104	85	72	61
Path • Inches	-1.5	-0.5	+0.2	+0.4	0.0	-1.0	-2.8	-5.6	-9.5
Wind Drift • Inches	0.0	0.2	0.9	2.0	3.8	6.2	9.4	13.3	18.1

Hornady 17-grain V-Max Bullet (83170)
G1 Ballistic Coefficient = 0.125

Distance • Yards	Muzzle	25	50	75	100	125	150	175	200
Velocity • fps	2550	2378	2212	2053	1902	1757	1621	1494	1380
Energy • Ft-lbs	245	213	185	159	136	116	99	84	72
Path • Inches	-1.5	-0.5	+0.2	+0.3	0.0	-0.9	-2.6	-5.0	-8.5
Wind Drift • Inches	0.0	0.2	0.8	1.8	3.3	5.3	8.0	11.3	15.3

Remington 17-grain AccuTip-V (PR17HM1)
G1 Ballistic Coefficient = 0.125

Distance • Yards	Muzzle	25	50	75	100	125	150	175	200
Velocity • fps	2550	2378	2212	2053	19012	1757	1620	1494	1378
Energy • Ft-lbs	245	213	185	159	136	117	99	84	72
Path • Inches	-1.5	-0.5	+0.1	+0.3	0.0	-0.9	-2.6	-5.0	-8.5
Wind Drift • Inches	0.0	0.2	0.8	1.8	3.3	5.3	8.0	11.3	15.3

CCI 20-grain GamePoint (0052)

G1 Ballistic Coefficient = 0.142

Distance • Yards	Muzzle	25	50	75	100	125	150	175	200
Velocity • fps	2375	2229	2083	1953	1824	1699	1582	1472	1372
Energy • Ft-lbs	251	221	194	169	148	128	111	96	84
Path • Inches	-1.5	-0.4	+0.2	+0.4	0.0	-1.1	-2.9	-5.6	-9.3
Wind Drift • Inches	0.0	0.2	0.7	1.7	3.2	5.1	7.6	10.7	14.4

Hornady 20-grain XTP (833172)

G1 Ballistic Coefficient = 0.130

Distance • Yards	Muzzle	25	50	75	100	125	150	175	200
Velocity • fps	2375	2216	2063	1916	1776	1644	1520	1406	1304
Energy • Ft-lbs	250	218	189	163	140	120	103	88	75
Path • Inches	-1.5	-0.4	+0.3	+0.4	0.0	-1.1	-3.1	-5.9	-9.9
Wind Drift • Inches	0.0	0.2	0.8	1.9	3.5	5.7	8.5	11.9	16.1

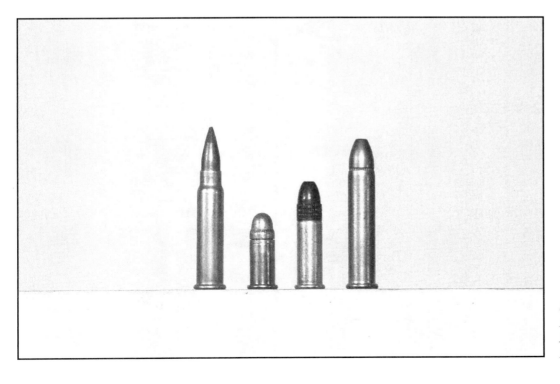

(Left to right) .17 Hornady Magnum Rimfire, .22 Short, .22 Long Rifle, .22 Winchester Magnum Rimfire.

.22 Short

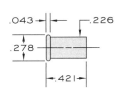

The .22 Short has the distinction of being the cartridge that has been in continuous production for longer than any other. Introduced in 1857 (loaded with black powder, of course), the short today has been relegated, for the most part, to specialized applications.

Relative Recoil Factor = 0.13

Specifications

Controlling Agency for Standardization of this Ammunition: SAAMI

Bullet Weight Grains	Velocity fps	Maximum Average Pressure Copper Crusher	Transducer
29 CB	710	N/S	21,000 psi
29 SV	1,035	N/S	21,000 psi
27 HP	1,105	N/S	21,000 psi
29 HV	1,080	N/S	21,000 psi

Standard barrel for velocity testing: 24 inches long—1 turn in 16-inch twist

Availability

PMC 20-grain Lead Solid Super Subsonic (22SCAT)
G1 Ballistic Coefficient = 0.050

Distance • Yards	Muzzle	25	50	75	100	125	150	175	200
Velocity • fps	500	469	440	412	386	361	338	316	295
Energy • Ft-lbs	11	10	9	8	7	6	5	4	4
Path • Inches	-1.5	+15.1	+21.8	+17.3	0.0	-32.0	-80.6	-148.5	-238.2
Wind Drift • Inches	0.0	0.9	3.5	8.2	14.9	23.9	35.4	49.5	66.5

CCI 27-grain GLHP (0028)
G1 Ballistic Coefficient = 0.086

Distance • Yards	Muzzle	25	50	75	100	125	150	175	200
Velocity • fps	1105	1027	975	920	879	842	808	777	748
Energy • Ft-lbs	73	63	57	51	46	42	39	36	34
Path • Inches	-1.5	+2.2	+3.9	+3.2	0.0	-6.0	-15.1	-27.6	-43.6
Wind Drift • Inches	0.0	0.5	1.8	3.8	6.6	10.0	14.0	18.8	24.1

Sellier & Bellot 28-grain Short (SBA02204)
G1 Ballistic Coefficient = 0.065

Distance • Yards	Muzzle	25	50	75	100	125	150	175	200
Velocity • fps	932	876	829	786	747	711	678	646	616
Energy • Ft-lbs	54	48	43	38	35	31	29	26	24
Path • Inches	-1.5	+3.4	+5.6	+4.5	0.0	-8.4	-21.1	-38.4	-123.6
Wind Drift • Inches	0.0	0.4	1.8	4.0	7.0	11.0	15.8	21.6	45.1

RWS 28-grain Short R25 (213 4276)
G1 Ballistic Coefficient = 0.047

Distance • Yards	Muzzle	25	50	75	100	125	150	175	200
Velocity • fps	560	524	490	457	427	398	371	345	321
Energy • Ft-lbs	20	17	15	13	11	10	9	7	6
Path • Inches	-1.5	+12.0	+17.5	+13.9	0.0	-25.7	-65.4	-120.8	-194.6
Wind Drift • Inches	0.0	0.8	3.3	7.6	13.9	22.4	33.2	46.5	62.6

Aguila 29-grain Short High Velocity
G1 Ballistic Coefficient = 0.105

Distance • Yards	Muzzle	25	50	75	100	125	150	175	200
Velocity • fps	1095	1032	981	939	903	870	841	813	787
Energy • Ft-lbs	77	69	62	57	52	49	46	43	40
Path • Inches	-1.5	+2.2	+3.8	+3.1	0.0	-5.7	-14.3	-25.9	-40.8
Wind Drift • Inches	0.0	0.4	1.4	3.2	5.4	8.3	11.7	15.6	20.0

Remington 29-grain Plated Lead Round Nose (1022)

G1 Ballistic Coefficient = 0.105

Distance • Yards	Muzzle	25	50	75	100	125	150	175	200
Velocity • fps	1095	1032	981	939	903	870	841	813	787
Energy • Ft-lbs	77	69	62	57	52	49	46	43	40
Path • Inches	-1.5	+2.2	+3.8	+3.1	0.0	-5.7	-14.3	-25.9	-40.8
Wind Drift • Inches	0.0	0.4	1.4	3.2	5.4	8.3	11.7	15.6	20.0

Winchester 29-grain Short Standard Velocity Solid (X22S)

G1 Ballistic Coefficient = 0.105

Distance • Yards	Muzzle	25	50	75	100	125	150	175	200
Velocity • fps	1095	1032	981	939	903	870	841	813	787
Energy • Ft-lbs	77	69	62	57	52	49	46	43	40
Path • Inches	-1.5	+2.2	+3.8	+3.1	0.0	-5.7	-14.3	-25.9	-40.8
Wind Drift • Inches	0.0	0.4	1.4	3.2	5.4	8.3	11.7	15.6	20.0

CCI 29-grain GLRN (0027)

G1 Ballistic Coefficient = 0.104

Distance • Yards	Muzzle	25	50	75	100	125	150	175	200
Velocity • fps	1080	1020	959	930	895	863	833	806	780
Energy • Ft-lbs	75	67	59	56	52	48	45	42	39
Path • Inches	-1.5	+2.2	+3.8	+3.2	0.0	-5.9	-14.7	-26.6	-41.9
Wind Drift • Inches	0.0	0.4	1.4	3.1	5.4	8.2	11.5	15.4	19.8

PMC 29-grain Lead Solid (22SH)

G1 Ballistic Coefficient = 0.054

Distance • Yards	Muzzle	25	50	75	100	125	150	175	200
Velocity • fps	1030	975	900	835	775	731	689	650	614
Energy • Ft-lbs	71	59	50	44	39	34	31	27	24
Path • Inches	-1.5	+2.8	+4.8	+4.0	0.0	-7.6	-19.3	-35.5	-56.9
Wind Drift • Inches	0.0	0.6	2.5	5.4	9.3	14.2	20.3	27.4	35.8

Aguila 29-grain Short Match

G1 Ballistic Coefficient = 0.100

Distance • Yards	Muzzle	25	50	75	100	125	150	175	200
Velocity • fps	850	820	793	767	742	719	697	675	655
Energy • Ft-lbs	47	43	40	38	36	33	31	29	28
Path • Inches	-1.5	+4.0	+6.2	+4.9	0.0	-8.9	-21.9	-39.5	-61.8
Wind Drift • Inches	0.0	0.3	1.1	2.5	4.5	7.0	10.2	13.9	18.2

CCI 29-grain Short Target Solid (0037)

G1 Ballistic Coefficient = 0.065

Distance • Yards	Muzzle	25	50	75	100	125	150	175	200
Velocity • fps	830	787	731	713	679	647	617	588	561
Energy • Ft-lbs	44	40	36	33	30	27	24	22	20
Path • Inches	-1.5	+4.5	+7.0	+5.6	0.0	-10.4	-25.9	-47.2	-74.8
Wind Drift • Inches	0.0	0.4	1.7	3.9	7.0	11.0	16.0	22.0	29.1

Eley 29-grain Short Rapid Fire Match

G1 Ballistic Coefficient = 0.050

Distance • Yards	Muzzle	25	50	75	100	125	150	175	200
Velocity • fps	750	703	661	621	583	548	515	483	453
Energy • Ft-lbs	36	32	28	25	22	19	17	15	13
Path • Inches	-1.5	+6.1	+9.2	+7.4	0.0	-13.8	-34.8	-64.1	-102.6
Wind Drift • Inches	0.0	0.6	2.3	5.4	9.7	15.4	22.7	31.6	42.2

CCI 29-grain Short CB (0026)

G1 Ballistic Coefficient = 0.063

Distance • Yards	Muzzle	25	50	75	100	125	150	175	200
Velocity • fps	710	675	642	612	581	554	527	502	477
Energy • Ft-lbs	32	29	27	24	22	20	18	16	15
Path • Inches	-1.5	+6.5	+9.8	+7.8	0.0	-14.2	-35.5	-64.6	-102.4
Wind Drift • Inches	0.0	0.5	1.9	4.4	7.9	12.6	18.4	25.5	33.9

Fiocchi 29-grain Short Round Nose Compensated Solid (22SM200)

G1 Ballistic Coefficient = 0.110

Distance • Yards	Muzzle	25	50	75	100	125	150	175	200
Velocity • fps	650	632	614	597	580	564	548	533	518
Energy • Ft-lbs	27	26	24	23	22	21	19	18	17
Path • Inches	-1.5	+7.4	+10.8	+8.4	0.0	-14.9	-36.6	-65.5	-102.1
Wind Drift • Inches	0.0	0.3	1.2	2.7	4.8	7.5	11.0	15.1	20.9

.22 Long

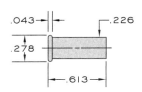

The .22 Long has just about dropped from the inventory. There was a time when not all the .22-caliber rifles were chambered for .22 Long Rifle. Since today's .22 Long Rifle ammunition will do everything the .22 Long cartridges will do, and most of it a lot better, the .22 Long is sliding quickly down the chute to the scrap pile of history.

Relative Recoil Factor = 0.14

Specifications

Controlling Agency for Standardization of this Ammunition: SAAMI

Bullet Weight Grains	Velocity fps	Maximum Average Pressure	
		Copper Crusher	Transducer
29 HV	1,215	N/S	24,000 psi

Standard barrel for velocity testing: 24 inches long—1 turn in 16-inch twist

Availability

CCI 29-grain GLRN (0029)

G1 Ballistic Coefficient = 0.133

Distance • Yards	Muzzle	25	50	75	100	125	150	175	200
Velocity • fps	1215	1141	1081	1033	992	957	926	898	873
Energy • Ft-lbs	95	84	75	69	63	59	55	52	49
Path • Inches	-1.5	+1.6	+3.0	+2.5	0.0	-4.7	-11.8	-21.4	-33.7
Wind Drift • Inches	0.0	0.4	1.4	3.0	5.2	7.9	11.0	14.6	18.7

CCI 29-grain CB (0038)

G1 Ballistic Coefficient = 0.062

Distance • Yards	Muzzle	25	50	75	100	125	150	175	200
Velocity • fps	710	675	642	610	581	552	525	499	474
Energy • Ft-lbs	32	29	27	24	22	20	18	16	14
Path • Inches	-1.5	+6.6	+9.8	+7.8	0.0	-14.3	-35.7	-65.0	-103.1
Wind Drift • Inches	0.0	0.5	2.0	4.5	8.0	12.8	18.7	25.9	34.5

Sable antelope are sometimes still referred to as Harris buck after the European discoverer of this species, William Cornwallis Harris. (Photo from *Hunting for Trouble* by Geoff Wainwright, Safari Press, 2006)

.22 Standard Velocity and Match Ammunition

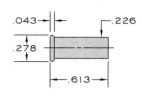

This is what the .22 rimfire does best. Even the most expensive .22 Long Rifle match ammunition is inexpensive when compared to centerfire ammo. It's not reloadable, but that's not a factor since the .22 rimfire case is so inexpensive that there just isn't anything worth saving. On an accuracy basis, it is sometimes very difficult to tell the difference in performance between "regular" standard velocity ammo and match ammo, especially since match ammo comes in at least three grades: club or practice, match grade, and the super-match grade. That's a good class of problem. Unless you have a pretty high-quality target rifle, you probably won't notice any improvement if you buy better than the standard velocity or the practice grade. In competition, you should use whatever you think works best for you. Mental attitude is an essential part of competition.

Relative Recoil Factor = 0.19

Specifications

Controlling Agency for Standardization of this Ammunition: SAAMI

Bullet Weight Grains	Velocity fps	Maximum Average Pressure	
		Copper Crusher	Transducer
40 SV	1,135	N/S	24,000 psi

Standard barrel for velocity testing: 24 inches long—1 turn in 16-inch twist

Availability

Lapua 36-grain Long Rifle Subsonic Hollow Point (4312246)
G1 Ballistic Coefficient = 0.109

Distance • Yards	Muzzle	25	50	75	100	125	150	175	200
Velocity • fps	1034	985	945	908	876	847	820	795	771
Energy • Ft-lbs	86	78	71	66	61	57	54	51	48
Path • Inches	-1.5	+2.4	+4.1	+3.4	0.0	-6.2	-15.4	-27.9	-43.8
Wind Drift • Inches	0.0	0.3	1.2	2.7	4.8	7.3	10.4	14.0	18.1

Remington 38-grain Long Rifle Subsonic Hollow Point (SUB22HP)
G1 Ballistic Coefficient = 0.125

Distance • Yards	Muzzle	25	50	75	100	125	150	175	200
Velocity • fps	1050	1004	965	932	901	874	849	825	802
Energy • Ft-lbs	93	85	79	73	69	64	61	57	54
Path • Inches	-1.5	+2.3	+3.9	+3.2	0.0	-5.9	-14.5	-26.2	-41.0
Wind Drift • Inches	0.0	0.3	1.1	2.5	4.3	6.6	9.4	12.6	16.2

Aguila 38-grain LR Subsonic Hollow Point
G1 Ballistic Coefficient = 0.111

Distance • Yards	Muzzle	25	50	75	100	125	150	175	200
Velocity • fps	1025	978	939	904	873	845	818	794	770
Energy • Ft-lbs	88	81	74	69	64	60	57	53	50
Path • Inches	-1.5	+2.5	+4.2	+3.4	0.0	-6.2	-15.5	-28.0	-43.9
Wind Drift • Inches	0.0	0.3	1.2	2.7	4.6	7.1	10.1	13.6	17.6

PMC 38-grain LR Moderator Subsonic Vel. (22SS)
G1 Ballistic Coefficient = 0.107

Distance • Yards	Muzzle	25	50	75	100	125	150	175	200
Velocity • fps	1000	957	921	886	854	826	800	775	752
Energy • Ft-lbs	84	77	71	66	62	58	54	51	48
Path • Inches	-1.5	+2.6	+4.4	+3.6	0.0	-6.6	-16.3	-29.3	-46.0
Wind Drift • Inches	0.0	0.3	1.2	2.7	4.6	7.2	10.2	13.8	17.8

RWS 40-grain R100 (213 4195)
G1 Ballistic Coefficient = 0.130

Distance • Yards	Muzzle	25	50	75	100	125	150	175	200
Velocity • fps	1175	1107	1065	1007	970	937	907	880	855
Energy • Ft-lbs	123	109	98	90	84	78	73	69	65
Path • Inches	-1.5	+1.7	+3.2	+2.6	0.0	-4.9	-12.3	-22.3	-35.0
Wind Drift • Inches	0.0	0.4	1.4	2.0	5.1	7.7	10.8	14.3	18.3

Remington 40-grain Long Rifle Target Solid (6122) (6100)   G1 Ballistic Coefficient = 0.149

Distance • Yards	Muzzle	25	50	75	100	125	150	175	200
Velocity • fps	1150	1094	1048	1009	976	946	919	895	872
Energy • Ft-lbs	117	106	98	90	85	80	75	71	68
Path • Inches	-1.5	+1.8	+3.2	+2.7	0.0	-4.9	-12.3	-22.1	-34.7
Wind Drift • Inches	0.0	0.3	1.2	2.5	4.4	6.6	9.3	12.4	15.8

Winchester 40-grain T22 Long Rifle Standard Velocity Solid (XT22LR)   G1 Ballistic Coefficient = 0.149

Distance • Yards	Muzzle	25	50	75	100	125	150	175	200
Velocity • fps	1150	1094	1048	1009	976	946	919	895	872
Energy • Ft-lbs	117	106	98	90	85	80	75	71	68
Path • Inches	-1.5	+1.8	+3.2	+2.7	0.0	-4.9	-12.3	-22.1	-34.7
Wind Drift • Inches	0.0	0.3	1.2	2.5	4.4	6.6	9.3	12.4	15.8

Fiocchi 40-grain Training (22MAXAC)   G1 Ballistic Coefficient = 0.150

Distance • Yards	Muzzle	25	50	75	100	125	150	175	200
Velocity • fps	1148	1089	1042	1001	967	937	909	884	861
Energy • Ft-lbs	117	105	96	89	83	78	73	69	66
Path • Inches	-1.5	+1.8	+3.2	+2.7	0.0	-5.0	-12.5	-22.7	-35.6
Wind Drift • Inches	0.0	0.3	1.2	2.6	4.6	6.9	9.8	13.0	16.6

Federal 40-grain Long Rifle Ultramatch Solid (UM1) (Discontinued in 2004)   G1 Ballistic Coefficient = 0.149

Distance • Yards	Muzzle	25	50	75	100	125	150	175	200
Velocity • fps	1140	1090	1040	1000	970	941	915	891	868
Energy • Ft-lbs	115	105	95	90	80	79	74	71	67
Path • Inches	-1.5	+1.8	+3.2	+2.7	0.0	-5.0	-12.4	-22.4	-35.1
Wind Drift • Inches	0.0	0.3	1.1	2.5	4.3	6.5	9.2	12.2	15.6

Federal 40-grain Long Rifle Match Solid (900) (Discontinued in 2004)   G1 Ballistic Coefficient = 0.149

Distance • Yards	Muzzle	25	50	75	100	125	150	175	200
Velocity • fps	1140	1090	1040	1000	970	941	915	891	868
Energy • Ft-lbs	115	105	95	90	80	79	74	71	67
Path • Inches	-1.5	+1.8	+3.2	+2.7	0.0	-5.0	-12.4	-22.4	-35.1
Wind Drift • Inches	0.0	0.3	1.1	2.5	4.3	6.5	9.2	12.2	15.6

PMC 40-grain Scoremaster Long Rifle Standard Velocity Solid (22SM)   G1 Ballistic Coefficient = 0.111

Distance • Yards	Muzzle	25	50	75	100	125	150	175	200
Velocity • fps	1135	1066	1012	967	929	896	865	838	812
Energy • Ft-lbs	114	101	91	83	77	71	67	62	59
Path • Inches	-1.5	+1.9	+3.4	+3.4	0.0	-5.4	-13.4	-24.4	-38.3
Wind Drift • Inches	0.0	0.4	1.5	3.2	5.5	8.4	11.7	15.6	20.0

Fiocchi 40-grain Long Rifle Biathlon Match Solid (22SM340)   G1 Ballistic Coefficient = 0.140 (Est.)

Distance • Yards	Muzzle	25	50	75	100	125	150	175	200
Velocity • fps	1120	1066	1022	985	953	924	897	873	850
Energy • Ft-lbs	111	101	93	86	81	76	72	68	64
Path • Inches	-1.5	+1.9	+3.4	+2.8	0.0	-5.2	-12.9	-23.3	-36.5
Wind Drift • Inches	0.0	0.3	1.2	2.5	4.4	6.7	9.4	12.5	16.1

Aguila 40-grain Long Rifle Match Golden Eagle (Discontinued in 2005)   G1 Ballistic Coefficient = 0.109

Distance • Yards	Muzzle	25	50	75	100	125	150	175	200
Velocity • fps	1100	1038	988	946	910	878	849	822	796
Energy • Ft-lbs	110	96	87	80	73	69	64	60	56
Path • Inches	-1.5	+2.1	+3.7	+3.0	0.0	-5.6	-14.1	-25.5	-40.1
Wind Drift • Inches	0.0	0.4	1.4	3.1	5.3	8.1	11.4	15.2	19.5

Lapua 40-grain Long Rifle Polar Biathlon Solid (4317023)   G1 Ballistic Coefficient = 0.100

Distance • Yards	Muzzle	25	50	75	100	125	150	175	200
Velocity • fps	1100	1033	981	937	899	865	834	806	779
Energy • Ft-lbs	107	95	86	78	72	66	62	58	54
Path • Inches	-1.5	+2.2	+3.8	+3.1	0.0	-5.8	-14.5	-26.4	-41.5
Wind Drift • Inches	0.0	0.4	1.5	3.3	5.7	8.7	12.2	16.3	21.0

Eley 40-grain Tenex Ultimate EPS

G1 Ballistic Coefficient = 0.150

Distance • Yards	Muzzle	25	50	75	100	125	150	175	200
Velocity • fps	1085	1041	1003	971	941	915	891	869	848
Energy • Ft-lbs	105	96	89	84	79	74	71	67	64
Path • Inches	-1.5	+2.0	+3.6	+2.9	0.0	-5.4	-13.3	-24.0	-37.5
Wind Drift • Inches	0.0	0.3	1.0	2.2	3.9	5.9	8.4	11.2	14.4

Eley 40-grain Match EPS

G1 Ballistic Coefficient = 0.150

Distance • Yards	Muzzle	25	50	75	100	125	150	175	200
Velocity • fps	1085	1041	1003	971	941	915	891	869	848
Energy • Ft-lbs	105	96	89	84	79	74	71	67	64
Path • Inches	-1.5	+2.0	+3.6	+2.9	0.0	-5.4	-13.3	-24.0	-37.5
Wind Drift • Inches	0.0	0.3	1.0	2.2	3.9	5.9	8.4	11.2	14.4

Eley 40-grain Club

G1 Ballistic Coefficient = 0.150

Distance • Yards	Muzzle	25	50	75	100	125	150	175	200
Velocity • fps	1085	1041	1003	971	941	915	891	869	848
Energy • Ft-lbs	105	96	89	84	79	74	71	67	64
Path • Inches	-1.5	+2.0	+3.6	+2.9	0.0	-5.4	-13.3	-24.0	-37.5
Wind Drift • Inches	0.0	0.3	1.0	2.2	3.9	5.9	8.4	11.2	14.4

Eley 40-grain Target

G1 Ballistic Coefficient = 0.150

Distance • Yards	Muzzle	25	50	75	100	125	150	175	200
Velocity • fps	1085	1041	1003	971	941	915	891	869	848
Energy • Ft-lbs	105	96	89	84	79	74	71	67	64
Path • Inches	-1.5	+2.0	+3.6	+2.9	0.0	-5.4	-13.3	-24.0	-37.5
Wind Drift • Inches	0.0	0.3	1.0	2.2	3.9	5.9	8.4	11.2	14.4

Eley 40-grain Practice

G1 Ballistic Coefficient = 0.150

Distance • Yards	Muzzle	25	50	75	100	125	150	175	200
Velocity • fps	1085	1041	1003	971	941	915	891	869	848
Energy • Ft-lbs	105	96	89	84	79	74	71	67	64
Path • Inches	-1.5	+2.0	+3.6	+2.9	0.0	-5.4	-13.3	-24.0	-37.5
Wind Drift • Inches	0.0	0.3	1.0	2.2	3.9	5.9	8.4	11.2	14.4

Eley 40-grain Standard

G1 Ballistic Coefficient = 0.150

Distance • Yards	Muzzle	25	50	75	100	125	150	175	200
Velocity • fps	1085	1041	1003	971	941	915	891	869	848
Energy • Ft-lbs	105	96	89	84	79	74	71	67	64
Path • Inches	-1.5	+2.0	+3.6	+2.9	0.0	-5.4	-13.3	-24.0	-37.5
Wind Drift • Inches	0.0	0.3	1.0	2.2	3.9	5.9	8.4	11.2	14.4

Eley 40-grain Biathlon Match

G1 Ballistic Coefficient = 0.150

Distance • Yards	Muzzle	25	50	75	100	125	150	175	200
Velocity • fps	1085	1041	1003	971	941	915	891	869	848
Energy • Ft-lbs	105	96	89	84	79	74	71	67	64
Path • Inches	-1.5	+2.0	+3.6	+2.9	0.0	-5.4	-13.3	-24.0	-37.5
Wind Drift • Inches	0.0	0.3	1.0	2.2	3.9	5.9	8.4	11.2	14.4

Eley 40-grain LR Silhouex

G1 Ballistic Coefficient = 0.150

Distance • Yards	Muzzle	25	50	75	100	125	150	175	200
Velocity • fps	1085	1041	1003	971	941	915	891	869	848
Energy • Ft-lbs	105	96	89	84	79	74	71	67	64
Path • Inches	-1.5	+2.0	+3.6	+2.9	0.0	-5.4	-13.3	-24.0	-37.5
Wind Drift • Inches	0.0	0.3	1.0	2.2	3.9	5.9	8.4	11.2	14.4

Remington/Eley 40-grain Match EPS (RE22EPS)

G1 Ballistic Coefficient = 0.149

Distance • Yards	Muzzle	25	50	75	100	125	150	175	200
Velocity • fps	1085	1040	1006	970	941	915	891	868	847
Energy • Ft-lbs	105	96	90	84	79	74	70	67	64
Path • Inches	-1.5	+2.0	+3.6	+2.9	0.0	-5.4	-13.3	-24.0	-37.5
Wind Drift • Inches	0.0	0.3	1.0	2.2	3.9	6.0	8.4	11.3	14.5

Remington/Eley 40-grain Club Extra (RE22CX)
G1 Ballistic Coefficient = 0.149

Distance • Yards	Muzzle	25	50	75	100	125	150	175	200
Velocity • fps	1085	1040	1006	970	941	915	891	868	847
Energy • Ft-lbs	105	96	90	84	79	74	70	67	64
Path • Inches	-1.5	+2.0	+3.6	+2.9	0.0	-5.4	-13.3	-24.0	-37.5
Wind Drift • Inches	0.0	0.3	1.0	2.2	3.9	6.0	8.4	11.3	14.5

Remington/Eley 40-grain Target Rifle (RE22T)
G1 Ballistic Coefficient = 0.149

Distance • Yards	Muzzle	25	50	75	100	125	150	175	200
Velocity • fps	1085	1040	1006	970	941	915	891	868	847
Energy • Ft-lbs	105	96	90	84	79	74	70	67	64
Path • Inches	-1.5	+2.0	+3.6	+2.9	0.0	-5.4	-13.3	-24.0	-37.5
Wind Drift • Inches	0.0	0.3	1.0	2.2	3.9	6.0	8.4	11.3	14.5

Aguila 40-grain Match Rifle
G1 Ballistic Coefficient = 0.117

Distance • Yards	Muzzle	25	50	75	100	125	150	175	200
Velocity • fps	1080	1026	981	943	910	880	853	827	803
Energy • Ft-lbs	104	93	86	79	74	69	65	61	57
Path • Inches	-1.5	+2.2	+3.8	+3.1	0.0	-5.7	-14.2	-25.8	-40.4
Wind Drift • Inches	0.0	0.3	1.3	2.8	4.8	7.3	10.4	13.9	17.8

Aguila 40-grain Target
G1 Ballistic Coefficient = 0.117

Distance • Yards	Muzzle	25	50	75	100	125	150	175	200
Velocity • fps	1080	1026	981	943	910	880	853	827	803
Energy • Ft-lbs	104	93	86	79	74	69	65	61	57
Path • Inches	-1.5	+2.2	+3.8	+3.1	0.0	-5.7	-14.2	-25.8	-40.4
Wind Drift • Inches	0.0	0.3	1.3	2.8	4.8	7.3	10.4	13.9	17.8

Aguila 40-grain Long Rifle Standard Velocity
G1 Ballistic Coefficient = 0.097

Distance • Yards	Muzzle	25	50	75	100	125	150	175	200
Velocity • fps	1080	1016	965	922	885	852	821	793	766
Energy • Ft-lbs	104	92	83	76	70	64	60	56	52
Path • Inches	-1.5	+2.3	+3.9	+3.2	0.0	-6.0	-15.0	-27.2	-42.9
Wind Drift • Inches	0.0	0.4	1.5	3.3	5.7	8.7	12.2	16.4	21.1

Sellier & Bellot 40-grain LR SB Standard (SBA02201)
G1 Ballistic Coefficient = 0.131

Distance • Yards	Muzzle	25	50	75	100	125	150	175	200
Velocity • fps	1084	1034	994	957	926	897	871	847	825
Energy • Ft-lbs	104	95	88	81	76	72	67	64	60
Path • Inches	-1.5	+2.1	+3.6	+3.0	0.0	-5.5	-13.7	-24.8	-38.8
Wind Drift • Inches	0.0	0.3	1.2	2.5	4.4	6.7	9.4	12.6	16.2

Sellier & Bellot 40-grain LR SB Club (SBA02202)
G1 Ballistic Coefficient = 0.131

Distance • Yards	Muzzle	25	50	75	100	125	150	175	200
Velocity • fps	1084	1034	994	957	926	897	871	847	825
Energy • Ft-lbs	104	95	88	81	76	72	67	64	60
Path • Inches	-1.5	+2.1	+3.6	+3.0	0.0	-5.5	-13.7	-24.8	-38.8
Wind Drift • Inches	0.0	0.3	1.2	2.5	4.4	6.7	9.4	12.6	16.2

Federal 40-grain Long Rifle Ultramatch Solid (UM1B) (Discontinued in 2004)
G1 Ballistic Coefficient = 0.139

Distance • Yards	Muzzle	25	50	75	100	125	150	175	200
Velocity • fps	1080	1030	1000	960	930	903	878	855	833
Energy • Ft-lbs	105	95	90	80	75	72	69	65	62
Path • Inches	-1.5	+2.1	+3.6	+3.0	0.0	-5.5	-13.6	-24.6	-38.4
Wind Drift • Inches	0.0	0.3	1.1	2.4	4.1	6.3	8.9	11.9	15.3

Federal 40-grain Long Rifle Target Solid (711B) (Discontinued in 2004)
G1 Ballistic Coefficient = 0.138

Distance • Yards	Muzzle	25	50	75	100	125	150	175	200
Velocity • fps	1080	1030	1000	960	930	902	877	854	832
Energy • Ft-lbs	105	95	90	80	75	72	68	65	62
Path • Inches	-1.5	+2.1	+3.6	+3.0	0.0	-5.5	-13.6	-24.6	-38.5
Wind Drift • Inches	0.0	0.3	1.0	2.2	3.9	6.4	9.0	12.0	23.5

Aguila 40-grain Match Rifle
G1 Ballistic Coefficient = 0.117

Distance • Yards	Muzzle	25	50	75	100	125	150	175	200
Velocity • fps	1080	1026	981	943	910	880	853	827	803
Energy • Ft-lbs	104	93	86	79	74	69	65	61	57
Path • Inches	-1.5	+2.2	+3.8	+3.1	0.0	-5.7	-14.2	-25.8	-40.4
Wind Drift • Inches	0.0	0.3	1.3	2.8	4.8	7.3	10.4	13.9	17.8

Federal 40-grain Long Rifle Match Solid (900B) (Discontinued in 2004)
G1 Ballistic Coefficient = 0.139

Distance • Yards	Muzzle	25	50	75	100	125	150	175	200
Velocity • fps	1080	1030	1000	960	930	903	878	855	833
Energy • Ft-lbs	105	95	90	80	75	72	69	65	62
Path • Inches	-1.5	+2.1	+3.6	+3.0	0.0	-5.5	-13.6	-24.6	-38.4
Wind Drift • Inches	0.0	0.3	1.1	2.4	4.1	6.3	8.9	11.9	15.3

RWS 40-grain L.R. Target Rifle (213 2478)
G1 Ballistic Coefficient = 0.109

Distance • Yards	Muzzle	25	50	75	100	125	150	175	200
Velocity • fps	1080	1022	990	935	900	869	841	814	789
Energy • Ft-lbs	100	93	85	78	70	67	63	59	55
Path • Inches	-1.5	+2.2	+3.8	+3.1	0.0	-5.8	-14.4	-26.1	-41.0
Wind Drift • Inches	0.0	0.4	1.4	3.0	5.1	7.8	11.1	14.8	19.0

CCI 40-grain Long Rifle Standard Velocity Solid (0032)
G1 Ballistic Coefficient = 0.168

Distance • Yards	Muzzle	25	50	75	100	125	150	175	200
Velocity • fps	1070	1032	1001	971	945	921	899	879	860
Energy • Ft-lbs	102	95	89	84	79	75	72	69	66
Path • Inches	-1.5	+2.1	+3.6	+3.0	0.0	-5.4	-13.3	-24.0	-37.4
Wind Drift • Inches	0.0	0.2	0.9	2.0	3.4	5.2	7.4	9.9	12.8

CCI 40-grain Long Rifle Green Tag Comp. Solid (0033)
G1 Ballistic Coefficient = 0.168

Distance • Yards	Muzzle	25	50	75	100	125	150	175	200
Velocity • fps	1070	1032	1001	971	945	921	899	879	860
Energy • Ft-lbs	102	95	89	84	79	75	72	69	66
Path • Inches	-1.5	+2.1	+3.6	+3.0	0.0	-5.4	-13.3	-24.0	-37.4
Wind Drift • Inches	0.0	0.2	0.9	2.0	3.4	5.2	7.4	9.9	12.8

CCI 40-grain Long Rifle Pistol Match Solid (0051)
G1 Ballistic Coefficient = 0.168

Distance • Yards	Muzzle	25	50	75	100	125	150	175	200
Velocity • fps	1070	1032	1001	971	945	921	899	879	860
Energy • Ft-lbs	102	95	89	84	79	75	72	69	66
Path • Inches	-1.5	+2.1	+3.6	+3.0	0.0	-5.4	-13.3	-24.0	-37.4
Wind Drift • Inches	0.0	0.2	0.9	2.0	3.4	5.2	7.4	9.9	12.8

RWS 40-grain LR R50 (21304187)
G1 Ballistic Coefficient = 0.105

Distance • Yards	Muzzle	25	50	75	100	125	150	175	200
Velocity • fps	1070	1012	970	926	890	859	830	803	778
Energy • Ft-lbs	100	91	80	76	70	66	61	57	54
Path • Inches	-1.5	+2.3	+3.9	+3.2	0.0	-5.9	-14.8	-26.7	-42.0
Wind Drift • Inches	0.0	0.4	1.4	3.0	5.2	8.0	11.3	15.1	19.5

Lapua 40-grain Long Rifle Master M (4317033)
G1 Ballistic Coefficient = 0.132

Distance • Yards	Muzzle	25	50	75	100	125	150	175	200
Velocity • fps	1066	1020	981	947	917	889	864	841	819
Energy • Ft-lbs	101	92	85	80	75	70	66	63	60
Path • Inches	-1.5	+2.2	+3.8	+3.1	0.0	-5.7	-14.0	-25.3	-39.6
Wind Drift • Inches	0.0	0.3	1.1	2.4	4.3	6.5	9.1	12.2	15.8

Lapua 40-grain Long Rifle Master L (4317020)
G1 Ballistic Coefficient = 0.132

Distance • Yards	Muzzle	25	50	75	100	125	150	175	200
Velocity • fps	1066	1020	981	947	917	889	864	841	819
Energy • Ft-lbs	101	92	85	80	75	70	66	63	60
Path • Inches	-1.5	+2.2	+3.8	+3.1	0.0	-5.7	-14.0	-25.3	-39.6
Wind Drift • Inches	0.0	0.3	1.1	2.4	4.3	6.5	9.1	12.2	15.8

Lapua 40-grain Signum (4317040)

G1 Ballistic Coefficient = 0.132

Distance • Yards	Muzzle	25	50	75	100	125	150	175	200
Velocity • fps	1066	1020	981	947	917	889	864	841	819
Energy • Ft-lbs	101	92	85	80	75	70	66	63	60
Path • Inches	-1.5	+2.2	+3.8	+3.1	0.0	-5.7	-14.0	-25.3	-39.6
Wind Drift • Inches	0.0	0.3	1.1	2.4	4.3	6.5	9.1	12.2	15.8

Lapua 40-grain Long Rifle Midas L Solid (4317022)

G1 Ballistic Coefficient = 0.132

Distance • Yards	Muzzle	25	50	75	100	125	150	175	200
Velocity • fps	1066	1020	981	947	917	889	864	841	819
Energy • Ft-lbs	101	92	85	80	75	70	66	63	60
Path • Inches	-1.5	+2.2	+3.8	+3.1	0.0	-5.7	-14.0	-25.3	-39.6
Wind Drift • Inches	0.0	0.3	1.1	2.4	4.3	6.5	9.1	12.2	15.8

Lapua 40-grain Long Rifle Midas M Solid (4317021)

G1 Ballistic Coefficient = 0.132

Distance • Yards	Muzzle	25	50	75	100	125	150	175	200
Velocity • fps	1066	1020	981	947	917	889	864	841	819
Energy • Ft-lbs	101	92	85	80	75	70	66	63	60
Path • Inches	-1.5	+2.2	+3.8	+3.1	0.0	-5.7	-14.0	-25.3	-39.6
Wind Drift • Inches	0.0	0.3	1.1	2.4	4.3	6.5	9.1	12.2	15.8

Norma 1 40-grain Lead Round Nose (15613) (Discontinued in 2004)

G1 Ballistic Coefficient = 0.132

Distance • Yards	Muzzle	25	50	75	100	125	150	175	200
Velocity • fps	1066	1020	981	947	917	889	864	841	819
Energy • Ft-lbs	101	92	85	80	75	70	66	63	60
Path • Inches	-1.5	+2.2	+3.8	+3.1	0.0	-5.7	-14.0	-25.3	-39.6
Wind Drift • Inches	0.0	0.3	1.1	2.4	4.3	6.5	9.1	12.2	15.8

Norma 2 40-grain Lead Round Nose (15614) (Discontinued in 2004)

G1 Ballistic Coefficient = 0.132

Distance • Yards	Muzzle	25	50	75	100	125	150	175	200
Velocity • fps	1066	1020	981	947	917	889	864	841	819
Energy • Ft-lbs	101	92	85	80	75	70	66	63	60
Path • Inches	-1.5	+2.2	+3.8	+3.1	0.0	-5.7	-14.0	-25.3	-39.6
Wind Drift • Inches	0.0	0.3	1.1	2.4	4.3	6.5	9.1	12.2	15.8

Norma 3 40-grain Lead Round Nose (15615) (Discontinued in 2004)

G1 Ballistic Coefficient = 0.132

Distance • Yards	Muzzle	25	50	75	100	125	150	175	200
Velocity • fps	1066	1020	981	947	917	889	864	841	819
Energy • Ft-lbs	101	92	85	80	75	70	66	63	60
Path • Inches	-1.5	+2.2	+3.8	+3.1	0.0	-5.7	-14.0	-25.3	-39.6
Wind Drift • Inches	0.0	0.3	1.1	2.4	4.3	6.5	9.1	12.2	15.8

CCI 40-grain Sub-sonic (0058)

G1 Ballistic Coefficient = 0.152

Distance • Yards	Muzzle	25	50	75	100	125	150	175	200
Velocity • fps	1050	1012	981	949	923	899	876	855	835
Energy • Ft-lbs	98	91	85	80	76	72	68	65	62
Path • Inches	-1.5	+2.2	+3.8	+3.1	0.0	-5.6	-14.0	-25.2	-39.3
Wind Drift • Inches	0.0	0.2	0.9	2.1	3.6	5.5	7.8	10.5	13.6

Fiocchi 40-grain Long Rifle—Rifle Match Solid (22SM320)

G1 Ballistic Coefficient = 0.140

Distance • Yards	Muzzle	25	50	75	100	125	150	175	200
Velocity • fps	1050	1008	973	942	914	888	865	843	822
Energy • Ft-lbs	98	90	84	79	74	70	66	63	60
Path • Inches	-1.5	+2.2	+3.8	+3.1	0.0	-5.7	-14.2	-25.5	-39.9
Wind Drift • Inches	0.0	0.3	1.0	2.2	3.9	6.0	8.5	11.4	14.7

Fiocchi 40-grain Long Rifle Match Training Solid (22M320)

G1 Ballistic Coefficient = 0.130

Distance • Yards	Muzzle	25	50	75	100	125	150	175	200
Velocity • fps	1050	1006	968	935	906	879	854	831	809
Energy • Ft-lbs	98	90	83	78	73	69	65	61	58
Path • Inches	-1.5	+2.3	+3.9	+3.2	0.0	-5.8	-14.4	-26.0	-40.6
Wind Drift • Inches	0.0	0.3	1.1	2.4	4.2	6.4	9.1	12.2	15.7

Lapua 40-grain Long Rifle Super Club Solid (4317066)

G1 Ballistic Coefficient = 0.114

Distance • Yards	Muzzle	25	50	75	100	125	150	175	200
Velocity • fps	1050	1000	958	922	891	861	835	809	786
Energy • Ft-lbs	98	89	82	76	70	66	62	58	55
Path • Inches	-1.5	+2.3	+4.0	+3.3	0.0	-6.0	-14.9	-26.8	-42.1
Wind Drift • Inches	0.0	0.3	1.2	2.7	4.7	7.2	10.2	13.7	17.7

Lapua 40-grain Long Rifle Standard Club (4312242)

G1 Ballistic Coefficient = 0.114

Distance • Yards	Muzzle	25	50	75	100	125	150	175	200
Velocity • fps	1050	1000	958	922	891	861	835	809	786
Energy • Ft-lbs	98	89	82	76	70	66	62	58	55
Path • Inches	-1.5	+2.3	+4.0	+3.3	0.0	-6.0	-14.9	-26.8	-42.1
Wind Drift • Inches	0.0	0.3	1.2	2.7	4.7	7.2	10.2	13.7	17.7

PMC 40-grain Match Rifle (22MR)

G1 Ballistic Coefficient = 0.110

Distance • Yards	Muzzle	25	50	75	100	125	150	175	200
Velocity • fps	1050	1000	956	919	885	856	829	803	779
Energy • Ft-lbs	98	89	81	75	70	65	61	57	54
Path • Inches	-1.5	+2.3	+4.0	+3.3	0.0	-6.0	-15.0	-27.1	-42.5
Wind Drift • Inches	0.0	0.3	1.3	2.8	4.9	7.4	10.5	14.2	18.3

RWS 40-grain LR Rifle Match (213 4225)

G1 Ballistic Coefficient = 0.096

Distance • Yards	Muzzle	25	50	75	100	125	150	175	200
Velocity • fps	1035	980	945	895	860	829	800	772	747
Energy • Ft-lbs	95	85	80	71	65	61	57	53	50
Path • Inches	-1.5	+2.5	+4.2	+3.4	0.0	-6.4	-15.9	-28.7	-45.2
Wind Drift • Inches	0.0	0.4	1.4	3.1	5.4	8.3	11.7	15.8	20.4

Eley 40-grain Tenex Ultimate EPS Pistol

G1 Ballistic Coefficient = 0.109

Distance • Yards	Muzzle	25	50	75	100	125	150	175	200
Velocity • fps	1030	993	960	932	906	881	859	838	818
Energy • Ft-lbs	94	88	82	77	73	69	66	62	59
Path • Inches	-1.5	+2.3	+4.0	+3.2	0.0	-5.9	-14.5	-26.1	-40.7
Wind Drift • Inches	0.0	0.2	1.0	2.1	3.6	5.6	8.0	10.7	13.8

Eley 40-grain Pistol Xtra

G1 Ballistic Coefficient = 0.109

Distance • Yards	Muzzle	25	50	75	100	125	150	175	200
Velocity • fps	1030	993	960	932	906	881	859	838	818
Energy • Ft-lbs	94	88	82	77	73	69	66	62	59
Path • Inches	-1.5	+2.3	+4.0	+3.2	0.0	-5.9	-14.5	-26.1	-40.7
Wind Drift • Inches	0.0	0.2	1.0	2.1	3.6	5.6	8.0	10.7	13.8

Eley 40-grain Target Pistol

G1 Ballistic Coefficient = 0.109

Distance • Yards	Muzzle	25	50	75	100	125	150	175	200
Velocity • fps	1030	993	960	932	906	881	859	838	818
Energy • Ft-lbs	94	88	82	77	73	69	66	62	59
Path • Inches	-1.5	+2.3	+4.0	+3.2	0.0	-5.9	-14.5	-26.1	-40.7
Wind Drift • Inches	0.0	0.2	1.0	2.1	3.6	5.6	8.0	10.7	13.8

Lapua 40-grain Long Rifle Pistol Trainer Solid (4312260)

G1 Ballistic Coefficient = 0.130

Distance • Yards	Muzzle	25	50	75	100	125	150	175	200
Velocity • fps	1033	991	956	924	896	870	846	823	801
Energy • Ft-lbs	95	87	81	76	71	67	64	60	57
Path • Inches	-1.5	+2.4	+4.0	+3.3	0.0	-6.0	-14.8	-26.6	-41.6
Wind Drift • Inches	0.0	0.3	1.1	2.3	4.1	6.2	8.8	11.9	15.4

Aguila 40-grain Subsonic Solid Point

G1 Ballistic Coefficient = 0.110

Distance • Yards	Muzzle	25	50	75	100	125	150	175	200
Velocity • fps	1025	978	938	904	873	844	817	792	769
Energy • Ft-lbs	93	85	78	73	68	63	59	56	52
Path • Inches	-1.5	+2.5	+4.2	+3.4	0.0	-6.3	-15.6	-28.2	-44.2
Wind Drift • Inches	0.0	0.3	1.2	2.7	4.7	7.2	10.2	13.7	17.8

Eley 40-grain Pistol Match

G1 Ballistic Coefficient = 0.140

Distance • Yards	Muzzle	25	50	75	100	125	150	175	200
Velocity • fps	1000	966	935	908	883	859	838	817	797
Energy • Ft-lbs	89	83	78	73	69	66	62	59	56
Path • Inches	-1.5	+2.5	+4.2	+3.4	0.0	-6.2	-15.3	-27.5	-43.0
Wind Drift • Inches	0.0	0.2	0.9	2.1	3.6	5.6	7.9	10.7	13.8

Fiocchi 40-grain Long Rifle—Pistol Match Solid (22SM300)

G1 Ballistic Coefficient = 0.130

Distance • Yards	Muzzle	25	50	75	100	125	150	175	200
Velocity • fps	984	949	918	891	865	841	819	797	777
Energy • Ft-lbs	86	80	75	70	66	63	60	56	54
Path • Inches	-1.5	+2.6	+4.4	+3.6	0.0	-6.5	-16.0	-28.7	-44.9
Wind Drift • Inches	0.0	0.3	1.0	2.2	3.8	5.8	8.3	11.3	14.6

Fiocchi 40-grain Long Rifle Match Training Solid (22M300)

G1 Ballistic Coefficient = 0.125

Distance • Yards	Muzzle	25	50	75	100	125	150	175	200
Velocity • fps	984	948	916	887	861	837	813	792	771
Energy • Ft-lbs	86	80	75	70	66	62	59	56	53
Path • Inches	-1.5	+2.7	+4.4	+3.6	0.0	-6.5	-16.1	-29.0	-45.3
Wind Drift • Inches	0.0	0.3	1.0	2.2	3.9	6.1	8.6	11.7	15.2

Lapua 40-grain Long Rifle Pistol King Solid (4317031)

G1 Ballistic Coefficient = 0.118

Distance • Yards	Muzzle	25	50	75	100	125	150	175	200
Velocity • fps	952	918	890	860	834	810	787	765	744
Energy • Ft-lbs	81	75	71	66	62	58	55	52	49
Path • Inches	-1.5	+2.9	+4.8	+3.8	0.0	-7.0	-17.3	-31.1	-48.6
Wind Drift • Inches	0.0	0.3	1.0	2.3	4.0	6.2	8.9	12.0	15.6

Aguila 40-grain Pistol Match

G1 Ballistic Coefficient = 0.124

Distance • Yards	Muzzle	25	50	75	100	125	150	175	200
Velocity • fps	925	895	868	843	819	797	776	756	736
Energy • Ft-lbs	76	71	67	63	59	56	54	51	48
Path • Inches	-1.5	+3.1	+5.0	+4.0	0.0	-7.3	-18.0	-32.3	-50.4
Wind Drift • Inches	0.0	0.2	0.9	2.1	3.7	5.8	8.3	11.3	14.7

PMC 40-grain Match Pistol (22MP)

G1 Ballistic Coefficient = 0.095

Distance • Yards	Muzzle	25	50	75	100	125	150	175	200
Velocity • fps	900	867	835	804	774	748	723	700	677
Energy • Ft-lbs	72	66	62	57	53	50	46	43	41
Path • Inches	-1.5	+3.5	+5.5	+4.4	0.0	-8.1	-20.0	-36.0	-56.5
Wind Drift • Inches	0.0	0.3	1.2	2.7	4.8	7.4	10.7	14.6	19.1

Winchester 40-grain Long Rifle Lead Hollow Point (W22LRB)

G1 Ballistic Coefficient = 0.150

Distance • Yards	Muzzle	25	50	75	100	125	150	175	200
Velocity • fps	1150	1094	1048	1010	976	947	920	896	873
Energy • Ft-lbs	117	106	98	91	85	80	75	71	68
Path • Inches	-1.5	+1.8	+3.2	+2.7	0.0	-4.9	-12.2	-22.1	-34.6
Wind Drift • Inches	0.0	0.3	1.2	2.5	4.3	6.6	9.2	12.3	15.7

Eley 40-grain LR Subsonic Xtra Plus

G1 Ballistic Coefficient = 0.115

Distance • Yards	Muzzle	25	50	75	100	125	150	175	200
Velocity • fps	1065	1013	970	932	900	870	843	817	794
Energy • Ft-lbs	100	91	83	77	72	67	63	59	56
Path • Inches	-1.5	+2.2	+3.9	+3.2	0.0	-5.8	-14.5	-26.2	-41.2
Wind Drift • Inches	0.0	0.3	1.3	2.8	4.8	7.3	10.3	13.8	17.8

Aguila 40-grain Subsonic Hollow Point

G1 Ballistic Coefficient = 0.110

Distance • Yards	Muzzle	25	50	75	100	125	150	175	200
Velocity • fps	1025	978	938	904	873	844	817	792	769
Energy • Ft-lbs	93	85	78	73	68	63	59	56	52
Path • Inches	-1.5	+2.5	+4.2	+3.4	0.0	-6.3	-15.6	-28.2	-44.2
Wind Drift • Inches	0.0	0.3	1.2	2.7	4.7	7.2	10.2	13.7	17.8

RWS 40-grain LR Subsonic HP (213 2494)

G1 Ballistic Coefficient = 0.092

Distance • Yards	Muzzle	25	50	75	100	125	150	175	200
Velocity • fps	1000	949	915	869	835	805	776	749	723
Energy • Ft-lbs	90	80	75	67	60	58	53	50	46
Path • Inches	-1.5	+2.7	+4.5	+3.7	0.0	-6.8	-16.9	-30.6	-48.1
Wind Drift • Inches	0.0	0.4	1.4	3.1	5.4	8.2	11.8	15.9	20.6

Lapua 48-grain Long Rifle Scoremax Solid (4317030)

G1 Ballistic Coefficient = 0.144

Distance • Yards	Muzzle	25	50	75	100	125	150	175	200
Velocity • fps	1033	995	962	933	907	882	860	838	818
Energy • Ft-lbs	114	106	99	93	88	83	79	75	71
Path • Inches	-1.5	+2.3	+3.9	+3.2	0.0	-5.8	-14.5	-26.0	-40.6
Wind Drift • Inches	0.0	0.2	1.0	2.1	3.7	5.7	8.0	10.8	14.0

Lapua 48-grain Scoremax (4317030)

G1 Ballistic Coefficient = 0.133

Distance • Yards	Muzzle	25	50	75	100	125	150	175	200
Velocity • fps	1034	993	959	927	899	874	850	827	806
Energy • Ft-lbs	114	105	98	92	86	81	77	73	69
Path • Inches	-1.5	+2.3	+4.0	+3.2	0.0	-5.9	-14.7	-26.5	-41.5
Wind Drift • Inches	0.0	0.3	1.0	2.3	4.0	6.1	8.7	11.6	15.0

Aguila 60-grain SSS Sniper Subsonic

G1 Ballistic Coefficient = 0.090

Distance • Yards	Muzzle	25	50	75	100	125	150	175	200
Velocity • fps	950	906	868	834	802	773	746	719	695
Energy • Ft-lbs	120	109	100	93	86	80	74	69	64
Path • Inches	-1.5	+3.1	+5.0	+4.1	0.0	-7.4	-18.5	-33.4	-52.5
Wind Drift • Inches	0.0	0.3	1.3	3.0	5.2	8.1	11.6	15.7	20.5

This buffalo charged the Land Rover before being killed. (Photo from *A Pioneering Hunter* by Brian Marsh, Safari Press, 2006)

.22 Long Rifle High Velocity and Hyper Velocity

This ammunition is the generic form of the .22 Long Rifle caliber. There is more of this ammo made than any other basic performance category. The bullets are available in a variety of forms and weights. In general, the high-speed ammunition is not quite as accurate as the standard-velocity form, but from time to time you will run across a gun and ammo combination that shoots extremely well with high-velocity ammunition.

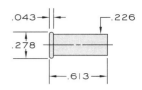

Relative Recoil Factor = 0.22

Specifications

Controlling Agency for Standardization of this Ammunition: SAAMI

Bullet Weight Grains	Velocity fps	Maximum Average Pressure	
		Copper Crusher	Transducer
36 HVHP	1,260	N/S	24,000 psi
37 HVHP	1,260	N/S	24,000 psi
40 HV	1,235	N/S	24,000 psi
33 Hyper HP	1,465	N/S	24,000 psi
36 Hyper	1,385	N/S	24,000 psi

Standard barrel for velocity testing: 24 inches long—1 turn in 16-inch twist

Availability

Aguila 30-grain Super Maximum Solid Point
G1 Ballistic Coefficient = 0.110

Distance • Yards	Muzzle	25	50	75	100	125	150	175	200
Velocity • fps	1700	1550	1414	1293	1191	1109	1045	994	952
Energy • Ft-lbs	193	160	133	111	95	82	73	66	60
Path • Inches	-1.5	+0.4	+1.4	+1.4	0.0	-2.9	-7.6	-14.2	-23.1
Wind Drift • Inches	0.0	0.4	1.5	3.5	6.4	10.2	14.7	19.9	25.7

Aguila 30-grain Super Maximum Hollow Point
G1 Ballistic Coefficient = 0.110

Distance • Yards	Muzzle	25	50	75	100	125	150	175	200
Velocity • fps	1700	1550	1414	1293	1191	1109	1045	994	952
Energy • Ft-lbs	193	160	133	111	95	82	73	66	60
Path • Inches	-1.5	+0.4	+1.4	+1.4	0.0	-2.9	-7.6	-14.2	-23.1
Wind Drift • Inches	0.0	0.4	1.5	3.5	6.4	10.2	14.7	19.9	25.7

Federal 31-grain Long Rifle Hyper Velocity Hollow Point Copper Plated (724)
G1 Ballistic Coefficient = 0.107

Distance • Yards	Muzzle	25	50	75	100	125	150	175	200
Velocity • fps	1550	1410	1280	1182	1100	1036	986	944	908
Energy • Ft-lbs	165	137	115	96	83	74	67	61	57
Path • Inches	-1.5	+0.7	+1.9	+1.7	0.0	-3.5	-9.0	-16.6	-26.6
Wind Drift • Inches	0.0	0.4	1.7	3.9	7.0	10.8	15.4	20.6	26.3

CCI 32-grain Long Rifle Stinger Hollow Point (0050)
G1 Ballistic Coefficient = 0.103

Distance • Yards	Muzzle	25	50	75	100	125	150	175	200
Velocity • fps	1640	1486	1348	1229	1132	1060	1003	957	918
Energy • Ft-lbs	191	157	129	107	91	80	72	65	60
Path • Inches	-1.5	+0.6	+1.9	+1.6	0.0	-3.2	-8.4	-15.6	-25.1
Wind Drift • Inches	0.0	0.4	1.7	3.9	7.1	11.1	15.8	21.3	27.3

CCI 32-grain Quik-Shok (0064)
G1 Ballistic Coefficient = 0.103

Distance • Yards	Muzzle	25	50	75	100	125	150	175	200
Velocity • fps	1640	1486	1348	1229	1132	1060	1003	957	918
Energy • Ft-lbs	191	157	129	107	91	80	72	65	60
Path • Inches	-1.5	+0.6	+1.7	+1.6	0.0	-3.2	-8.4	-15.6	-25.1
Wind Drift • Inches	0.0	0.4	1.7	3.9	7.1	11.1	15.8	21.3	27.3

Remington 33-grain Long Rifle Yellow Jacket Hollow Point (1722) G1 Ballistic Coefficient = 0.107

Distance • Yards	Muzzle	25	50	75	100	125	150	175	200
Velocity • fps	1500	1365	1247	1151	1075	1018	971	931	896
Energy • Ft-lbs	165	137	114	97	85	76	69	64	59
Path • Inches	-1.5	+0.9	+2.0	+1.8	0.0	-3.7	-9.4	-17.4	-27.8
Wind Drift • Inches	0.0	0.4	1.8	4.0	7.0	10.9	15.4	20.4	26.1

Remington 36-grain Long Rifle Viper Solid (1922) G1 Ballistic Coefficient = 0.117

Distance • Yards	Muzzle	25	50	75	100	125	150	175	200
Velocity • fps	1410	1296	1198	1119	1056	1006	965	926	897
Energy • Ft-lbs	159	134	115	100	89	81	74	69	64
Path • Inches	-1.5	+1.0	+2.3	+2.0	0.0	-3.9	-10.0	-18.2	-29.0
Wind Drift • Inches	0.0	0.4	1.6	3.7	6.5	9.9	14.0	18.6	23.7

Sellier & Bellot 36-grain LR HV (SBA02206) G1 Ballistic Coefficient = 0.196

Distance • Yards	Muzzle	25	50	75	100	125	150	175	200
Velocity • fps	1330	1267	1209	1158	1114	1075	1042	1013	986
Energy • Ft-lbs	141	128	117	107	99	92	87	82	78
Path • Inches	-1.5	+1.0	+2.2	+1.9	0.0	-3.7	-9.2	-16.7	-26.3
Wind Drift • Inches	0.0	0.2	1.0	2.2	3.9	6.1	8.6	11.6	14.8

Lapua 36-grain Long Rifle Hollow Point (4312245) G1 Ballistic Coefficient = 0.110

Distance • Yards	Muzzle	25	50	75	100	125	150	175	200
Velocity • fps	1280	1180	1100	1038	988	948	912	880	851
Energy • Ft-lbs	132	111	98	86	79	72	66	62	58
Path • Inches	-1.5	+1.4	+2.8	+2.4	0.0	-4.6	-11.7	-21.4	-33.8
Wind Drift • Inches	0.0	0.4	1.7	3.8	6.5	9.8	13.7	18.1	23.1

Remington 36-grain Long Rifle Cyclone Hollow Point (CY22HP) (GL22HP) G1 Ballistic Coefficient = 0.124

Distance • Yards	Muzzle	25	50	75	100	125	150	175	200
Velocity • fps	1280	1190	1117	1057	1010	970	935	905	877
Energy • Ft-lbs	131	113	100	89	82	75	70	65	61
Path • Inches	-1.5	+1.4	+2.7	+2.3	0.0	-4.4	-11.1	-20.3	-32.0
Wind Drift • Inches	0.0	0.4	1.5	3.4	5.9	8.9	12.4	16.5	21.0

Remington 36-grain Long Rifle Hollow Point (1622/1600+) G1 Ballistic Coefficient = 0.124

Distance • Yards	Muzzle	25	50	75	100	125	150	175	200
Velocity • fps	1280	1190	1117	1057	1010	970	935	905	877
Energy • Ft-lbs	131	113	100	89	82	75	70	65	61
Path • Inches	-1.5	+1.4	+2.7	+2.3	0.0	-4.4	-11.1	-20.3	-32.0
Wind Drift • Inches	0.0	0.4	1.5	3.4	5.9	8.9	12.4	16.5	21.0

CCI 36-grain Long Rifle Mini-Mag Hollow Point (0031) G1 Ballistic Coefficient = 0.153

Distance • Yards	Muzzle	25	50	75	100	125	150	175	200
Velocity • fps	1260	1189	1118	1077	1035	999	968	940	914
Energy • Ft-lbs	127	113	100	93	86	80	75	71	67
Path • Inches	-1.5	+1.4	+2.7	+2.3	0.0	-4.3	-10.8	-19.6	-30.8
Wind Drift • Inches	0.0	0.3	1.2	2.8	4.8	7.3	10.2	13.6	17.4

Federal 36-grain Long Rifle (745) G1 Ballistic Coefficient = 0.139

Distance • Yards	Muzzle	25	50	75	100	125	150	175	200
Velocity • fps	1260	1182	1100	1064	1020	983	940	922	895
Energy • Ft-lbs	140	118	110	96	90	82	80	72	68
Path • Inches	-1.5	+1.4	+2.7	+2.3	0.0	-4.4	-11.1	-20.1	-31.8
Wind Drift • Inches	0.0	0.4	1.4	3.0	5.2	7.9	11.1	14.8	18.8

Federal 36-grain Long Rifle Hollow Point (730) (Discontinued in 2004) G1 Ballistic Coefficient = 0.125

Distance • Yards	Muzzle	25	50	75	100	125	150	175	200
Velocity • fps	1255	1170	1100	1045	1000	962	930	899	871
Energy • Ft-lbs	125	109	95	87	80	74	70	65	61
Path • Inches	-1.5	+1.4	+2.8	+2.4	0.0	-4.6	-11.4	-20.7	-32.7
Wind Drift • Inches	0.0	0.4	1.5	3.3	5.7	8.7	12.1	16.1	20.5

Winchester 36-grain Long Rifle Hollow Point (XPERT22)

G1 Ballistic Coefficient = 0.105

Distance • Yards	Muzzle	25	50	75	100	125	150	175	200
Velocity • fps	1220	1128	1057	1002	956	918	884	853	825
Energy • Ft-lbs	122	102	89	80	75	67	62	58	54
Path • Inches	-1.5	+1.7	+3.1	+2.6	0.0	-5.0	-12.5	-22.7	-35.8
Wind Drift • Inches	0.0	0.4	1.7	3.8	6.4	9.7	13.6	17.9	22.9

Winchester 37-grain Long Rifle Hollow Point (X22LRH)

G1 Ballistic Coefficient = 0.128

Distance • Yards	Muzzle	25	50	75	100	125	150	175	200
Velocity • fps	1280	1193	1120	1062	1015	976	941	911	883
Energy • Ft-lbs	135	117	103	93	85	78	73	68	64
Path • Inches	-1.5	+1.4	+2.7	+2.3	0.0	-4.4	-11.0	-20.1	-31.6
Wind Drift • Inches	0.0	0.4	1.5	3.3	5.7	8.7	12.1	16.1	20.5

Eley 37.5-grain LR HV Hollow

G1 Ballistic Coefficient = 0.193

Distance • Yards	Muzzle	25	50	75	100	125	150	175	200
Velocity • fps	1312	1249	1200	1143	1100	1063	1031	1002	977
Energy • Ft-lbs	143	130	121	109	100	94	88	84	79
Path • Inches	-1.5	+1.1	+2.3	+2.0	0.0	-3.8	-9.4	-17.2	-27.0
Wind Drift • Inches	0.0	0.2	1.0	2.3	4.0	6.1	8.7	11.6	14.9

Sellier & Bellot 38-grain HV HP (SBA02203)

G1 Ballistic Coefficient = 0.243

Distance • Yards	Muzzle	25	50	75	100	125	150	175	200
Velocity • fps	1281	1233	1190	1150	1115	1083	1055	1030	1007
Energy • Ft-lbs	138	128	119	112	105	99	94	90	86
Path • Inches	-1.5	+1.1	+2.3	+2.0	0.0	-3.7	-9.3	-16.8	-26.4
Wind Drift • Inches	0.0	0.2	0.8	1.8	3.1	4.8	6.9	9.2	11.9

Aguila 38-grain LR High Velocity Hollow Point

G1 Ballistic Coefficient = 0.124

Distance • Yards	Muzzle	25	50	75	100	125	150	175	200
Velocity • fps	1280	1190	1116	1057	1010	970	935	905	877
Energy • Ft-lbs	138	120	105	94	86	79	74	69	65
Path • Inches	-1.5	+1.4	+2.7	+2.3	0.0	-4.4	-11.1	-20.3	-21.0
Wind Drift • Inches	0.0	0.4	1.5	3.4	5.9	8.9	12.4	16.5	21.0

Federal 38-grain Long Rifle Hollow Point Copper-Plated (712)

G1 Ballistic Coefficient = 0.132

Distance • Yards	Muzzle	25	50	75	100	125	150	175	200
Velocity • fps	1280	1195	1120	1067	1020	981	947	917	890
Energy • Ft-lbs	140	121	105	96	88	81	76	71	67
Path • Inches	-1.5	+1.4	+2.7	+2.3	0.0	-4.4	-10.9	-19.9	-31.3
Wind Drift • Inches	0.0	0.4	1.4	3.2	5.6	8.4	11.8	15.7	20.0

PMC 38-grain Zapper LR High Vel. HP CC (22D)

G1 Ballistic Coefficient = 0.109

Distance • Yards	Muzzle	25	50	75	100	125	150	175	200
Velocity • fps	1280	1174	1097	1036	987	946	910	878	848
Energy • Ft-lbs	138	117	102	91	82	75	70	65	61
Path • Inches	-1.5	+1.4	+2.8	+2.4	0.0	-4.6	11.6	21.2	33.4
Wind Drift • Inches	0.0	0.4	1.8	3.8	6.6	9.9	13.8	18.3	23.3

American Eagle (Federal) 38-grain Long Rifle Hollow Point, Copper Plated (AE22)

G1 Ballistic Coefficient = 0.139

Distance • Yards	Muzzle	25	50	75	100	125	150	175	200
Velocity • fps	1260	1182	1100	1064	1020	983	940	922	895
Energy • Ft-lbs	140	118	110	96	90	82	80	72	68
Path • Inches	-1.5	+1.4	+2.7	+2.3	0.0	-4.4	-11.1	-20.1	-31.8
Wind Drift • Inches	0.0	0.4	1.4	3.0	5.2	7.9	11.1	14.8	18.8

CCI 40-grain Velocitor HP (0047)

G1 Ballistic Coefficient = 0.141

Distance • Yards	Muzzle	25	50	75	100	125	150	175	200
Velocity • fps	1435	1337	1249	1174	1112	1060	1017	981	949
Energy • Ft-lbs	183	159	139	123	110	100	92	86	80
Path • Inches	-1.5	+0.9	+2.0	+1.8	0.0	-3.6	-9.1	-16.6	-26.5
Wind Drift • Inches	0.0	0.3	1.4	3.1	5.4	8.4	11.9	15.9	20.4

Eley 40-grain LR HV Solid

G1 Ballistic Coefficient = 0.193

Distance • Yards	Muzzle	25	50	75	100	125	150	175	200
Velocity • fps	1312	1249	1200	1143	1100	1063	1031	1002	977
Energy • Ft-lbs	153	139	126	116	107	100	94	89	85
Path • Inches	-1.5	+1.1	+2.3	+2.0	0.0	-3.8	-9.4	-17.2	-27.0
Wind Drift • Inches	0.0	0.2	1.0	2.3	4.0	6.1	8.7	11.6	14.9

Lapua 40-grain Long Rifle Speed Ace Solid (4312243)

G1 Ballistic Coefficient = 0.110

Distance • Yards	Muzzle	25	50	75	100	125	150	175	200
Velocity • fps	1280	1180	1100	1038	988	948	912	880	851
Energy • Ft-lbs	132	111	98	86	79	72	66	62	58
Path • Inches	-1.5	+1.4	+2.8	+2.4	0.0	-4.6	-11.7	-21.4	-33.8
Wind Drift • Inches	0.0	0.4	1.7	3.8	6.5	9.8	13.7	18.1	23.1

American Eagle (Federal) 40-grain Long Rifle Solid (AE5022)

G1 Ballistic Coefficient = 0.138

Distance • Yards	Muzzle	25	50	75	100	125	150	175	200
Velocity • fps	1260	1182	1100	1064	1020	981	949	920	893
Energy • Ft-lbs	140	124	110	101	90	86	80	75	71
Path • Inches	-1.5	+1.4	+2.7	+2.3	0.0	-4.4	-11.0	-20.0	-31.5
Wind Drift • Inches	0.0	0.4	1.4	3.0	5.2	8.0	11.2	14.9	19.0

Federal 40-grain Long Rifle Solid, Copper Plated (710)

G1 Ballistic Coefficient = 0.138

Distance • Yards	Muzzle	25	50	75	100	125	150	175	200
Velocity • fps	1260	1182	1100	1064	1020	981	949	920	893
Energy • Ft-lbs	140	124	110	101	90	86	80	75	71
Path • Inches	-1.5	+1.4	+2.7	+2.3	0.0	-4.4	-11.0	-20.0	-31.5
Wind Drift • Inches	0.0	0.4	1.4	3.0	5.2	8.0	11.2	14.9	19.0

Federal 40-grain Long Rifle Solid (510)

G1 Ballistic Coefficient = 0.138

Distance • Yards	Muzzle	25	50	75	100	125	150	175	200
Velocity • fps	1260	1182	1100	1064	1020	981	949	920	893
Energy • Ft-lbs	140	124	110	101	90	86	80	75	71
Path • Inches	-1.5	+1.4	+2.7	+2.3	0.0	-4.4	-11.0	-20.0	-31.5
Wind Drift • Inches	0.0	0.4	1.4	3.0	5.2	8.0	11.2	14.9	19.0

Aguila 40-grain Long Rifle High Velocity

G1 Ballistic Coefficient = 0.139

Distance • Yards	Muzzle	25	50	75	100	125	150	175	200
Velocity • fps	1255	1178	1113	1061	1017	981	949	920	894
Energy • Ft-lbs	139	123	110	100	92	86	80	75	71
Path • Inches	-1.5	+1.4	+2.8	+2.3	0.0	-4.4	-11.1	-20.2	-31.9
Wind Drift • Inches	0.0	0.4	1.4	3.0	5.2	7.9	11.1	14.7	18.7

PMC 40-grain Zapper LR High Velocity Solid CC (22CC)

G1 Ballistic Coefficient = 0.121

Distance • Yards	Muzzle	25	50	75	100	125	150	175	200
Velocity • fps	1255	1156	1083	1025	978	939	904	873	844
Energy • Ft-lbs	140	119	104	93	85	78	73	68	63
Path • Inches	-1.5	+1.5	+2.9	+2.5	0.0	-4.7	-11.9	-21.6	-34.1
Wind Drift • Inches	0.0	0.4	1.7	3.7	6.4	9.6	13.5	17.8	22.7

Remington 40-grain Long Rifle Solid (1522)

G1 Ballistic Coefficient = 0.138

Distance • Yards	Muzzle	25	50	75	100	125	150	175	200
Velocity • fps	1255	1167	1113	1061	1017	979	947	918	892
Energy • Ft-lbs	140	123	110	100	92	85	80	75	71
Path • Inches	-1.5	+1.4	+2.8	+2.3	0.0	-4.4	-11.1	-20.1	-31.7
Wind Drift • Inches	0.0	0.4	1.4	3.0	5.2	8.0	11.2	14.8	18.9

Remington 40-grain Long Rifle Thunderbolt Solid (TB22A)

G1 Ballistic Coefficient = 0.138

Distance • Yards	Muzzle	25	50	75	100	125	150	175	200
Velocity • fps	1255	1177	1110	1060	1017	979	949	920	892
Energy • Ft-lbs	140	123	109	100	92	85	80	75	71
Path • Inches	-1.5	+1.4	+2.8	+2.3	0.0	-4.4	-11.1	-20.1	-31.7
Wind Drift • Inches	0.0	0.4	1.4	3.0	5.2	8.0	11.2	14.8	18.9

Winchester 40-grain Long Rifle Wildcat Solid (WW22LR)

G1 Ballistic Coefficient = 0.139

Distance • Yards	Muzzle	25	50	75	100	125	150	175	200
Velocity • fps	1255	1177	1110	1060	1017	979	949	920	892
Energy • Ft-lbs	140	123	109	100	92	85	80	75	71
Path • Inches	-1.5	+1.4	+2.8	+2.3	0.0	-4.4	-11.1	-20.1	-31.7
Wind Drift • Inches	0.0	0.4	1.4	3.0	5.2	8.0	11.2	14.8	18.9

Winchester 40-grain Long Rifle Solid (X22LR)

G1 Ballistic Coefficient = 0.139

Distance • Yards	Muzzle	25	50	75	100	125	150	175	200
Velocity • fps	1255	1177	1110	1060	1017	979	949	920	892
Energy • Ft-lbs	140	123	109	100	92	85	80	75	71
Path • Inches	-1.5	+1.4	+2.8	+2.3	0.0	-4.4	-11.1	-20.1	-31.7
Wind Drift • Inches	0.0	0.4	1.4	3.0	5.2	8.0	11.2	14.8	18.9

PMC 40-grain Sidewinder LR High Velocity Solid (22SC)

G1 Ballistic Coefficient = 0.121

Distance • Yards	Muzzle	25	50	75	100	125	150	175	200
Velocity • fps	1250	1153	1080	1023	976	937	902	871	843
Energy • Ft-lbs	139	119	104	93	85	78	72	67	63
Path • Inches	-1.5	+1.5	+3.0	+2.5	0.0	-4.8	-11.9	-21.7	-34.2
Wind Drift • Inches	0.0	0.4	1.7	3.7	6.4	9.6	13.4	17.7	22.6

CCI 40-grain Long Rifle HS Mini-Mag Solid (0030)

G1 Ballistic Coefficient = 0.157

Distance • Yards	Muzzle	25	50	75	100	125	150	175	200
Velocity • fps	1235	1169	1104	1066	1026	992	962	936	911
Energy • Ft-lbs	135	121	108	101	93	88	82	78	74
Path • Inches	-1.5	+1.4	+2.8	+2.3	0.0	-4.4	-11.0	-19.9	-31.4
Wind Drift • Inches	0.0	0.3	1.2	2.6	4.6	7.0	9.8	13.0	16.6

CCI 40-grain Long Rifle Silhouette (0065)

G1 Ballistic Coefficient = 0.157

Distance • Yards	Muzzle	25	50	75	100	125	150	175	200
Velocity • fps	1235	1169	1104	1066	1026	992	962	936	911
Energy • Ft-lbs	135	121	108	101	93	88	82	78	74
Path • Inches	-1.5	+1.4	+2.8	+2.3	0.0	-4.4	-11.0	-19.9	-31.4
Wind Drift • Inches	0.0	0.3	1.2	2.6	4.6	7.0	9.8	13.0	16.6

CCI 40-grain LFP (0058)

G1 Ballistic Coefficient = 0.146

Distance • Yards	Muzzle	25	50	75	100	125	150	175	200
Velocity • fps	1235	1164	1096	1056	1015	981	950	922	897
Energy • Ft-lbs	135	120	107	99	91	85	80	76	72
Path • Inches	-1.5	+1.4	+2.8	+2.4	0.0	-4.5	-11.2	-20.4	-32.1
Wind Drift • Inches	0.0	0.3	1.3	2.8	4.9	7.4	10.4	13.8	17.7

RWS 40-grain High Velocity Hollow Point (213 2494)

G1 Ballistic Coefficient = 0.104

Distance • Yards	Muzzle	25	50	75	100	125	150	175	200
Velocity • fps	1310	1199	1120	1043	990	947	909	875	845
Energy • Ft-lbs	150	128	110	97	85	80	73	68	63
Path • Inches	-1.5	+1.4	+2.8	+2.4	0.0	-4.5	-11.4	-20.9	-33.1
Wind Drift • Inches	0.0	0.5	1.8	4.0	7.0	10.5	14.7	19.4	24.7

Winchester 40-grain Long Rifle Power-Point Hollow Point (X22LRPP)

G1 Ballistic Coefficient = 0.118

Distance • Yards	Muzzle	25	50	75	100	125	150	175	200
Velocity • fps	1280	1186	1110	1049	1001	961	926	894	866
Energy • Ft-lbs	146	125	109	98	89	82	76	71	67
Path • Inches	-1.5	+1.4	+2.8	+2.4	0.0	-4.5	-11.3	-20.6	-32.5
Wind Drift • Inches	0.0	0.4	1.6	3.6	6.1	9.3	13.0	17.2	21.9

.22 Winchester Magnum Rimfire (WMR)

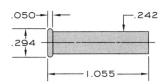

The .22 WMR cartridge can be thought of as a .22 Long Rifle on steroids. The bad news is that the .22 WMR is a significantly larger cartridge and will NOT fit into standard .22 guns chambered for .22 Long Rifle (nor for that matter can the .22 Long Rifle cartridge be fired in a .22 WMR chamber). The good news is that in the fastest loadings the .22 WMR begins to approach the performance of the .22 Hornet. That's a lot of performance from a rimfire cartridge.

Relative Recoil Factor = 0.34

Specifications

Controlling Agency for Standardization of this Ammunition: SAAMI

Bullet Weight Grains	Velocity fps	Maximum Average Pressure	
		Copper Crusher	Transducer
40	1,875	N/S	24,000 psi

Standard barrel for velocity testing: 24 inches long—1 turn in 16-inch twist

Availability

CCI 30-grain WMR Maxi-Mag + V Hollow Point (0059)
G1 Ballistic Coefficient = 0.090

Distance • Yards	Muzzle	25	50	75	100	125	150	175	200
Velocity • fps	2200	1982	1777	1589	1419	1273	1155	1067	1002
Energy • Ft-lbs	322	262	210	168	134	108	89	76	67
Path • Inches	-1.5	-0.2	+0.6	+0.7	0.0	-1.8	-5.0	-9.8	-16.5
Wind Drift • Inches	0.0	0.3	1.4	3.2	6.0	9.8	14.7	20.6	27.4

CCI 30-grain WMR TNT Hollow Point (0063)
G1 Ballistic Coefficient = 0.090

Distance • Yards	Muzzle	25	50	75	100	125	150	175	200
Velocity • fps	2200	1982	1777	1589	1419	1273	1155	1067	1002
Energy • Ft-lbs	322	262	210	168	134	108	89	76	67
Path • Inches	-1.5	-0.2	+0.6	+0.7	0.0	-1.8	-5.0	-9.8	-16.5
Wind Drift • Inches	0.0	0.3	1.4	3.2	6.0	9.8	14.7	20.6	27.4

Federal 30-grain WMR Speer TNT HP (P765)
G1 Ballistic Coefficient = 0.091

Distance • Yards	Muzzle	25	50	75	100	125	150	175	200
Velocity • fps	2200	1984	1780	1595	1420	1281	1160	1073	1007
Energy • Ft-lbs	320	262	210	169	135	109	90	77	68
Path • Inches	-1.5	-0.2	+0.6	+0.8	0.0	-1.8	-5.0	-9.7	-16.4
Wind Drift • Inches	0.0	0.3	1.3	3.2	5.9	9.7	14.6	20.4	27.1

Federal 30-grain WMR Jacketed Hollow Point (767)
G1 Ballistic Coefficient = 0.087

Distance • Yards	Muzzle	25	50	75	100	125	150	175	200
Velocity • fps	2200	1974	1760	1570	1400	1251	1135	1050	986
Energy • Ft-lbs	325	260	205	164	130	104	85	73	65
Path • Inches	-1.5	-0.1	+0.7	+0.8	0.0	-1.9	-5.2	-10.2	-17.1
Wind Drift • Inches	0.0	0.3	1.4	3.3	6.3	10.2	15.4	21.5	28.5

Remington 33-grain WMR Premier AccuTip-V (PR22M1)
G1 Ballistic Coefficient = 0.137

Distance • Yards	Muzzle	25	50	75	100	125	150	175	200
Velocity • fps	2000	1836	1730	1609	1495	1388	1292	1208	1138
Energy • Ft-lbs	293	254	219	190	164	141	122	107	95
Path • Inches	-1.5	-0.1	+0.7	+0.8	0.0	-1.8	-4.6	-8.8	-14.5
Wind Drift • Inches	0.0	0.2	1.0	2.3	4.2	6.8	10.0	14.0	18.7

Winchester 34-grain WMR Jacketed Hollow Point (S22WM)

G1 Ballistic Coefficient = 0.102

Distance • Yards	Muzzle	25	50	75	100	125	150	175	200
Velocity • fps	2120	1931	1753	1537	1435	1304	1192	1104	1037
Energy • Ft-lbs	338	282	232	190	155	132	113	100	90
Path • Inches	-1.5	-0.1	+0.7	+0.8	0.0	-1.8	-5.0	-9.6	-16.1
Wind Drift • Inches	0.0	0.3	1.2	2.9	5.5	8.9	13.3	18.6	24.7

CCI 40-grain WMR Maxi-Mag Solid (0023)

G1 Ballistic Coefficient = 0.130

Distance • Yards	Muzzle	25	50	75	100	125	150	175	200
Velocity • fps	1875	1737	1607	1486	1375	1277	1191	1120	1063
Energy • Ft-lbs	312	268	229	196	168	145	126	112	100
Path • Inches	-1.5	+0.1	+1.0	+1.0	0.0	-2.1	-5.6	-10.5	-17.2
Wind Drift • Inches	0.0	0.3	1.1	2.6	4.8	7.8	11.4	15.8	20.9

PMC 40-grain WMR Predator Magnum Jacketed Soft Point (22WMA)

G1 Ballistic Coefficient = 0.183

Distance • Yards	Muzzle	25	50	75	100	125	150	175	200
Velocity • fps	1910	1808	1711	1619	1533	1451	1373	1302	1237
Energy • Ft-lbs	324	291	261	234	209	187	168	151	136
Path • Inches	-1.5	0.0	+0.7	+0.8	0.0	-1.7	-4.4	-8.3	-13.5
Wind Drift • Inches	0.0	0.2	0.8	1.8	3.2	5.2	7.6	10.6	14.1

Remington 40-grain WMR Pointed Soft Point Solid (R22M2)

G1 Ballistic Coefficient = 0.114

Distance • Yards	Muzzle	25	50	75	100	125	150	175	200
Velocity • fps	1910	1751	1600	1466	1340	1235	1147	1076	1021
Energy • Ft-lbs	324	272	227	191	159	136	117	103	93
Path • Inches	-1.5	+0.1	+1.0	+1.0	0.0	-2.2	-5.8	-11.1	-18.2
Wind Drift • Inches	0.0	0.3	1.3	3.0	5.5	8.8	13.0	18.0	23.7

RWS 40-grain WMR Hollow Point

G1 Ballistic Coefficient = 0.116

Distance • Yards	Muzzle	25	50	75	100	125	150	175	200
Velocity • fps	2020	1858	1710	1563	1430	1314	1213	1130	1065
Energy • Ft-lbs	360	307	260	217	180	153	131	114	101
Path • Inches	-1.5	0.0	+0.8	+0.8	0.0	-1.9	-5.0	-9.7	-16.0
Wind Drift • Inches	0.0	0.3	1.2	2.7	5.0	8.1	12.0	16.8	22.3

PMC 40-grain WMR Predator Magnum Jacketed Hollow Point (22WMB)

G1 Ballistic Coefficient = 0.183

Distance • Yards	Muzzle	25	50	75	100	125	150	175	200
Velocity • fps	1910	1808	1711	1619	1533	1451	1373	1302	1237
Energy • Ft-lbs	324	291	261	234	209	187	168	151	136
Path • Inches	-1.5	0.0	+0.7	+0.8	0.0	-1.7	-4.4	-8.3	-13.5
Wind Drift • Inches	0.0	0.2	0.8	1.8	3.2	5.2	7.6	10.6	14.1

Remington 40-grain WMR Jacketed Hollow Point (R22M2)

G1 Ballistic Coefficient = 0.116

Distance • Yards	Muzzle	25	50	75	100	125	150	175	200
Velocity • fps	1910	1754	1610	1472	1350	1244	1155	1084	1028
Energy • Ft-lbs	324	273	230	193	162	137	118	104	94
Path • Inches	-1.5	+0.1	+1.0	+1.0	0.0	-2.2	-5.8	-11.0	-18.0
Wind Drift • Inches	0.0	0.3	1.2	2.9	5.4	8.7	12.8	17.7	23.3

Winchester 40-grain WMR Jacketed Hollow Point (X22MH)

G1 Ballistic Coefficient = 0.110

Distance • Yards	Muzzle	25	50	75	100	125	150	175	200
Velocity • fps	1910	1746	1592	1452	1326	1218	1130	1061	1007
Energy • Ft-lbs	324	271	225	187	156	132	113	100	90
Path • Inches	-1.5	+0.1	+1.0	+1.0	0.0	-2.2	-6.0	-11.4	-18.7
Wind Drift • Inches	0.0	0.3	1.3	3.1	5.7	9.2	13.6	18.7	24.6

CCI 40-grain WMR Maxi-Mag Hollow Point (0024)

G1 Ballistic Coefficient = 0.130

Distance • Yards	Muzzle	25	50	75	100	125	150	175	200
Velocity • fps	1875	1737	1607	1486	1375	1277	1191	1120	1063
Energy • Ft-lbs	312	268	229	196	168	145	126	112	100
Path • Inches	-1.5	+0.1	+1.0	+1.0	0.0	-2.1	-5.6	-10.5	-17.2
Wind Drift • Inches	0.0	0.3	1.1	2.6	4.8	7.8	11.4	15.8	20.9

Federal 40-grain WMR Full Metal Jacket Solid (737)

G1 Ballistic Coefficient = 0.111

Distance • Yards	Muzzle	25	50	75	100	125	150	175	200
Velocity • fps	1910	1747	1600	1455	1330	1222	1134	1065	1011
Energy • Ft-lbs	325	271	225	188	155	133	114	101	91
Path • Inches	-1.5	+0.1	+1.0	+1.0	0.0	-2.2	-5.9	-11.3	-18.6
Wind Drift • Inches	0.0	0.3	1.3	3.1	5.6	9.1	13.4	18.5	24.4

Winchester 40-grain WMR Full Metal Jacket Solid (X22M)

G1 Ballistic Coefficient = 0.110

Distance • Yards	Muzzle	25	50	75	100	125	150	175	200
Velocity • fps	1910	1746	1592	1452	1326	1218	1130	1061	1007
Energy • Ft-lbs	324	271	225	187	156	132	113	100	90
Path • Inches	-1.5	+0.1	+1.0	+1.0	0.0	-2.2	-6.0	-11.4	-18.7
Wind Drift • Inches	0.0	0.3	1.3	3.1	5.7	9.2	13.6	18.7	24.6

PMC 40-grain WMR FMJ (22WMC)

G1 Ballistic Coefficient = 0.183

Distance • Yards	Muzzle	25	50	75	100	125	150	175	200
Velocity • fps	1910	1808	1711	1619	1533	1451	1373	1302	1237
Energy • Ft-lbs	324	291	261	234	209	187	168	151	136
Path • Inches	-1.5	0.0	+0.7	+0.8	0.0	-1.7	-4.4	-8.3	-13.5
Wind Drift • Inches	0.0	0.2	0.8	1.8	3.2	5.2	7.6	10.6	14.1

Winchester 45-grain Dynapoint (USA22M)

G1 Ballistic Coefficient = 0.126

Distance • Yards	Muzzle	25	50	75	100	125	150	175	200
Velocity • fps	1550	1430	1322	1227	1147	1083	1032	989	953
Energy • Ft-lbs	240	204	175	150	131	117	106	98	91
Path • Inches	-1.5	+0.7	+1.8	+1.6	0.0	-3.2	-8.3	-15.5	-24.8
Wind Drift • Inches	0.0	0.4	1.4	3.3	5.9	9.2	13.2	17.8	22.9

Federal 50-grain WMR Jacketed Hollow Point (757)

G1 Ballistic Coefficient = 0.158

Distance • Yards	Muzzle	25	50	75	100	125	150	175	200
Velocity • fps	1650	1547	1450	1361	1280	1208	1146	1094	1050
Energy • Ft-lbs	302	266	234	206	182	162	146	133	122
Path • Inches	-1.5	+0.4	+1.3	+1.2	0.0	-2.6	-6.6	-12.4	-19.9
Wind Drift • Inches	0.0	0.3	1.1	2.5	4.5	7.1	10.3	14.1	18.4

North American bears remain a focal point of fascination for hunters worldwide. (Photo from *The Dangerous Game* by Walt Prothero, Safari Press, 2006)

.22 Rimfire Shotshells

In the 1940s my father took me to some outdoor shows. One of the booths that got my interest was a trap-shooting game that used .22 rimfire shotshells and miniature clay targets. The backstop was nothing more than a sheet of heavy canvas hung from the ceiling of the hall. That was enough to stop the very fine shot. It's hard to imagine anyone getting away with that today, but I never heard of any accident resulting from those shows. The .22 rimfire shotshells also make a fine load for a snake gun.

Relative Recoil Factor = 0.14

Specifications

Controlling Agency for Standardization of this Ammunition: SAAMI

Bullet Weight Grains	Velocity fps	Maximum Average Pressure	
		Copper Crusher	Transducer
25 #12 Shot	1,000	N/S	24,000 psi

Standard barrel for velocity testing: 24 inches long—1 turn in 16-inch twist

Availability

Federal 25-grain Long Rifle Bird Shot (716)

This load uses #10 shot. No performance data are given.

Remington 25-grain Long Rifle Bird Shot (9322)

This load uses #10 shot. No performance data is given.

CCI 31-grain Long Rifle Shotshell 0039)

This load uses #12 shot.
Muzzle Velocity is listed at 950 fps.

Winchester Long Rifle Shot (X22LRS)

This load uses #12 shot. No performance data are given.

CCI 52-grain WMR Shotshell (0025)

This load uses #11 shot.
Muzzle velocity is listed at 1,000 fps.

454

Interesting Facts and Figures
from Ammo & Ballistics 3

- Total number of calibers listed: 167.

- Most factory loads listed for one caliber: 131 for the .30-06.

- Most factory loads listed for a dangerous-game caliber: 14 for the .458 Winchester.

- Most factory loads listed for a handgun caliber: 109 for the .38 Special.

- Highest muzzle velocity listed: 4,250 feet per second for the .17 Remington and also the .220 Swift. The .17 Remington velocity is attained with a Remington load using the 20-grain Accutip VT bullet. The .220 Swift's highest velocity load is Federal's 40-grain Nosler Ballistic Tip combination.

- Lightest bullet listed: 17 grains, loaded in various .17 Mach 2 and .17 Hornady Magnum Rimfire loads.

- Lightest centerfire bullet listed: 20 grains, loaded by the Remington Company with an AccuTip bullet in their .17 Remington caliber.

- Heaviest bullet listed: 1,000 grains for the .700 Nitro Express. Both the Kynoch and the A-Square Company have a 1,000-grain load.

- Highest muzzle energy listed: 10,077 foot pounds for the A-Square 750-grain loads (3 loads) in .577 Tyrannosaur.

- Lowest muzzle energy listed: 11 foot pounds for the PMC 20-grain Lead Solid Super Subsonic in .22 Short.